TENTH EDITION

CURRENT ISSUES and ENDURING QUESTIONS

A Guide to Critical Thinking and Argument, with Readings

SYLVAN BARNET
Professor of English, Tufts University

HUGO BEDAU
Professor of Philosophy, Tufts University

Bedford/St. Martin's   BOSTON ◆ NEW YORK

For Bedford / St. Martin's
Senior Developmental Editor: Adam Whitehurst
Senior Production Editor: Harold Chester
Senior Production Supervisor: Jennifer Peterson
Marketing Manager: Emily Rowin
Copy Editor: Virginia Perrin
Indexer: Melanie Belkin
Photo Researcher: Connie Gardner
Art Director: Lucy Krikorian
Text Design: Linda M. Robertson
Cover Design: Donna Dennison
Cover Photo: Igloo with Electricity © Thomas Roepke/Corbis
Composition: Cenveo
Printing and Binding: RR Donnelley-Crawfordsville

President, Bedford/St. Martin's: Denise B. Wydra
Editor in Chief: Karen S. Henry
Director of Development: Erica T. Appel
Director of Marketing: Karen R. Soeltz
Production Director: Susan W. Brown
Director of Rights and Permissions: Hilary Newman

8 7 6 5 4 3
f e d c b a

For information, write: Bedford/St. Martin's, 75 Arlington Street, Boston, MA 02116 (617-399-4000)

ISBN: 978-1-4576-2260-1

Preface

This book is a text—a book about reading other people's arguments and writing your own arguments—and it is also an anthology—a collection of more than a hundred selections, ranging from Plato to the present, with a strong emphasis on contemporary arguments and, in this edition, new modes of argument, from documentary film trailers to political speeches to infographics. Before we describe these selections further, we'd like to describe our chief assumptions about the aims of a course that might use *Current Issues and Enduring Questions: A Guide to Critical Thinking and Argument, with Readings.*

Probably most students and instructors would agree that, as *critical readers,* students should be able to

- Summarize accurately an argument they have read;
- Locate the thesis (the claim) of an argument;
- Locate the assumptions, stated and unstated, of an argument;
- Analyze and evaluate the strength of the evidence and the soundness of the reasoning offered in support of the thesis; and
- Analyze, evaluate, and account for discrepancies among various readings on a topic (for example, explain why certain facts are used, why probable consequences of a proposed action are examined or are ignored, or why two sources might interpret the same facts differently).

Probably, too, students and instructors would agree that, as *thoughtful writers,* students should be able to

- Imagine an audience and write effectively for it (for instance, by using the appropriate tone and providing the appropriate amount of detail);

- Present information in an orderly and coherent way;
- Be aware of their own assumptions;
- Locate sources and incorporate them into their own writing, not simply by quoting extensively or by paraphrasing but also by having digested material so that they can present it in their own words;
- Properly document all borrowings—not merely quotations and paraphrases but also borrowed ideas; and
- Do all these things in the course of developing a thoughtful argument of their own.

In the first edition of this book we quoted Edmund Burke and John Stuart Mill. Burke said,

> He that wrestles with us strengthens our nerves, and sharpens our skill. Our antagonist is our helper.

Mill said,

> He who knows only his own side of the cause knows little.

These two quotations continue to reflect the view of argument that underlies this text: In writing an essay one is engaging in a serious effort to know what one's own ideas are and, having found them, to contribute to a multisided conversation. One is not setting out to trounce an opponent, and that is partly why such expressions as "marshaling evidence," "attacking an opponent," and "defending a thesis" are misleading. True, on television talk shows we see right-wingers and left-wingers who have made up their minds and who are concerned only with pushing their own views and brushing aside all others. But in an academic community, and indeed in our daily lives, we learn by listening to others and also by listening to ourselves.

We draft a response to something we have read, and in the very act of drafting we may find—if we think critically about the words we are putting down on paper—we are changing (perhaps slightly, perhaps radically) our own position. In short, one reason that we write is so that we can improve our ideas. And even if we do not drastically change our views, we and our readers at least come to a better understanding of why we hold the views we do.

FEATURES

The Text

Parts One and Two   Critical Thinking and Reading (Chapters 1–4) and Critical Writing (Chapters 5–7), together offer a short course in methods of thinking about and writing arguments. By "thinking" we mean serious analytic thought, including analysis of one's own assumptions (Chapter 1); by "writing" we mean the use of effective, respectable techniques, not gimmicks (such as the notorious note a politician scribbled in the margin of the text of his speech: "Argument weak; shout here"). For a delightfully wry account of the use of gimmicks, we recommend that you consult "The Art of Controversy" in *The Will to Live* by the nineteenth-century German philosopher Arthur Schopenhauer. Schopenhauer reminds readers that a Greek or Latin quotation (however irrelevant) can be impressive to the uninformed and that one can knock down almost any proposition by loftily saying, "That's all very well in theory, but it won't do in practice."

We offer lots of advice about how to set forth an argument, but we do not offer instruction in one-upmanship. Rather, we discuss responsible ways of arguing persuasively. We know, however, that before one can write a persuasive argument, one must clarify one's own ideas—a process that includes arguing with oneself—to find out what one really thinks about a problem. Therefore, we devote Chapter 1 to critical thinking, Chapters 2, 3, and 4 to critical reading (Chapter 4 is about reading images), and Chapters 5, 6, and 7 to critical writing.

Parts One and Two together contain thirty-four readings (six are student papers) for analysis and discussion. Some of these essays originated as op-ed newspaper pieces, and we reprint some of the letters to the editor that they generated, so students can easily see several sides to a given issue. In this way students can, in their own responses, join the conversation, so to speak. (We have found, by the way, that using the format of a letter helps students to frame their ideas, and therefore in later chapters we occasionally suggest writing assignments in the form of a letter to the editor. In an e-Pages section on ethical arguments, we reprint three letters written by Randy Cohen of the *New York Times Magazine,* and we invite students to write their own responses.)

All of the essays in the book are accompanied by a list of Topics for Critical Thinking and Writing.[1] This is not surprising, given the emphasis we place on asking questions in order to come up with ideas for writing. Among the chief questions that writers should ask, we suggest, are "What is *X*?" and "What is the value of *X*?" (pp. 232–33). By asking such questions—for instance (to look only at these two types of questions), "Is the fetus a person?" or "Is Arthur Miller a better playwright than Tennessee Williams?"—a writer probably will find ideas coming, at least after a few moments of head scratching. The device of developing an argument by identifying issues is, of course, nothing new. Indeed, it goes back to an ancient method of argument used by classical rhetoricians, who identified a stasis (an issue) and then asked questions about

---

[1]With a few exceptions, the paragraphs in the essays are, for ease of reference, numbered in increments of five (5, 10, 15, and so on). The exceptions involve essays in which paragraphs are uncommonly long; in such cases, every paragraph is numbered.

it: Did *X* do such and such? If so, was the action bad? If bad, how bad? (Finding an issue or stasis—a position where one stands—by asking questions is discussed in Chapter 6.)

In keeping with our emphasis on writing as well as reading, we raise issues not only of what can roughly be called the "content" of the essays but also of what can (equally roughly) be called the "style"—that is, the *ways* in which the arguments are set forth. Content and style, of course, cannot finally be kept apart. As Cardinal Newman said, "Thought and meaning are inseparable from each other. . . . *Style is thinking out into language.*" In our Topics for Critical Thinking and Writing we sometimes ask the student

- To evaluate the effectiveness of an essay's opening paragraph,
- To explain a shift in tone from one paragraph to the next, or
- To characterize the persona of the author as revealed in the whole essay.

In short, the book is not designed as an introduction to some powerful ideas (though in fact it is that, too); it is designed as an aid to *writing* thoughtful, effective arguments on important political, social, scientific, ethical, legal, and religious issues.

The essays reprinted in this book also illustrate different styles of argument that arise, at least in part, from the different disciplinary backgrounds of the various authors. Essays by journalists, lawyers, judges, social scientists, policy analysts, philosophers, critics, activists, and other writers—including first-year undergraduates—will be found in these pages. The authors develop and present their views in arguments that have distinctive features reflecting their special training and concerns. The differences in argumentative styles found in these essays foreshadow the differences students will encounter in the readings assigned in many of their other courses.

Parts One and Two, then, offer a preliminary (but we hope substantial) discussion of such topics as

- Identifying assumptions;
- Getting ideas by means of invention strategies;
- Finding, evaluating, and citing printed and electronic sources;
- Interpreting visual sources;
- Evaluating kinds of evidence; and
- Organizing material

as well as an introduction to some ways of thinking.

Part Three Further Views on Argument consists of Chapters 8 through 13.

- Chapter 8, A Philosopher's View: The Toulmin Model, is a summary of the philosopher Stephen Toulmin's method for analyzing arguments. This summary will assist those who wish to apply Toulmin's methods to the readings in our book.

- Chapter 9, A Logician's View: Deduction, Induction, Fallacies, offers a more rigorous analysis of these topics than is usually found in composition courses and reexamines from a logician's point of view material already treated briefly in Chapter 3.

- Chapter 10, A Psychologist's View: Rogerian Argument, with an essay by psychotherapist Carl R. Rogers and an essay by a student, complements the discussion of audience, organization, and tone in Chapter 6.

- Chapter 11, A Rhetorician's View: Rhetorical Analysis of Nontraditional Texts, offers students strategies for analyzing and writing about artifacts of popular culture, from public service announcements to reality television.

- Chapter 12, A Literary Critic's View: Arguing about Literature, should help students to see the things literary critics argue about and *how* they argue. Students can apply what they learn not only to the literary readings that appear in the chapter (poems by Robert Frost and Andrew Marvell and a story by Kate Chopin) but also to the readings that appear in Part Six, Enduring Questions: Essays, a Story, Poems, and a Play. Finally, Part Three concludes with

- Chapter 13, A Debater's View: Individual Oral Presentations and Debate, which introduces students to standard presentation strategies and debate format.

- In e-Pages, A Moralist's View: Ways of Thinking Ethically, consists of a discussion of amoral, immoral, and moral reasoning; A Checklist for Moral Reasoning; two challenging essays; and three short responses to highly specific moral questions.

- Also in e-Pages, A Lawyer's View: Steps toward Civic Literacy, introduces students to some basic legal concepts, such as the distinction between civil and criminal cases, and then gives majority and minority opinions in two cases: searching students for drugs and establishing the right to an abortion. We accompany these judicial opinions with questions that invite the student to participate in these exercises in democracy.

The Anthology

Part Four Current Issues: Occasions for Debate (Chapters 14–18) begins with some comments on binary, or pro-con, thinking. It then gives a Checklist for Analyzing a Debate and reprints five pairs of arguments—on student loan debt (should it be forgiven?), using integrated instead of handheld devices while driving (is it safer?), the local food movement (is it a better way to eat?), the death penalty, and genetic modification of human beings. Here, as elsewhere in the book, many of the selections (drawn from popular journals and newspapers) are very short—scarcely longer than the 500-word essays that students are often asked to write. Thus, students can easily study the *methods* the writers use, as well as the issues themselves.

Part Five   Current Issues: Casebooks (Chapters 19–25) presents seven chapters on issues discussed by several writers. For example, the first casebook concerns the nature and purpose of a college education: Is college a place where students learn citizenship, a place for vocational training, or some combination of these?

Part Six   Enduring Questions: Essays, a Story, Poems, and a Play (Chapters 26–28) extends the arguments to three topics: Chapter 26, What Is the Ideal Society? (the nine voices here range from Thomas More, Thomas Jefferson, and Martin Luther King Jr. to literary figures W. H. Auden, Langston Hughes, and Ursula K. Le Guin); Chapter 27, How Free Is the Will of the Individual within Society? (among the authors are Plato, Susan Glaspell, and George Orwell); and Chapter 28, What Is Happiness? (among the nine selections in this chapter are writings by Epictetus, C. S. Lewis, and the Dalai Lama).

WHAT'S NEW IN THE TENTH EDITION

We have made some significant changes in the tenth edition that we believe enrich the book and make the content more accessible.

Fresh and timely new readings. Thirty-eight of the essays (about one-third of the total) are new, as are a dozen topics such as student loan debt, government regulation of large sodas, social media dependency, women in combat, the regulation of firearms, and hydraulic fracturing. (In fact, the number of new readings is more than thirty-eight because some of these new essays were editorials and op-ed pieces that generated letters, some of which we have reprinted.)

New debates and casebook topics. New debates include Student Loans: Should Some Indebtedness Be Forgiven?, Are Integrated Devices Safer Than Using Handheld Devices While Driving?, The Local Food Movement: Is It a Better Way to Eat?, and The Death Penalty: Is It Ever Justified? New casebooks include Junk Food: Should the Government Regulate Our Intake?, Hydraulic Fracturing: Is Fracking Worth the Environmental Cost?, and Facebook: How Has Social Networking Changed How We Relate to Others?

A new chapter on rhetorical analysis of popular culture (Chapter 11) gives students a framework for making arguments about popular culture, from public service announcements to *Here Comes Honey Boo Boo.*

More help for research. This edition includes a new MLA research paper on corporate social responsibility and additional material about working with sources, including a heavily revised section on summary, paraphrase, and patchwriting (the practice of copying and pasting material from sources without appropriate integration or attribution).

More help with writing strategies. Three new Idea Prompts, or templates, offer strategies for establishing *ethos,* varying tone, and constructing Toulmin arguments. Three new checklists break down strategies for considering audience and conducting sound rhetorical analysis.

e-Pages for *Current Issues and Enduring Questions* take advantage of what the Web can do with coverage of ethical and legal arguments as well as additional multimodal readings, from speeches to documentary film trailers. For example, students can watch a speech by President Obama on the death of Osama bin Laden and then answer questions about how such a speech seeks to connect with both Americans and a broader world audience. For a complete list of e-Pages, see the book's table of contents. Instructors can also use the free tools accompanying the e-Pages to upload a syllabus, readings, and assignments to share with the class.

You and your students can access the e-Pages at **bedfordstmartins .com/barnetbedau**, the media page for *Current Issues and Enduring Questions.* Students receive access automatically with the purchase of a new book. If the activation code printed on the inside back cover of the student edition doesn't work, it might have expired. Students can purchase access at **bedfordstmartins.com/barnetbedau**. To get instructor access, register as an instructor at this site.

ACKNOWLEDGMENTS

Finally, it is our pleasant duty to thank those who have strengthened this book by their comments and advice on the ninth edition: Anton Agafonov, Jamestown Community College; Liana Andreasen, South Texas College; Joseph Bizup, Boston University; Jennifer Chunn, Harrisburg Area Community College; Patrick Clauss, University of Notre Dame; Mary Grace Collier-Kisler, Jamestown Community College–Cattarugus County; Denise Diamond, College of the Desert; Helen Doss, Wilbur Wright College; Jessica Enoch, University of Maryland; Paul Gagliardi, Carroll University; Karen Gardiner, University of Alabama; Michael George, Millikin University; Steven Harless, Wake Technical Community College; Doris Jellig, Tidewater Community College; John McKinnis, Buffalo State College; Kay Mizell, Collin College; Gary Montano, Tarrant County College; Michael Moreau, Glendale Community College; Matthew Newcomb, SUNY New Paltz; Christina Nunez, Allan Hancock College; Karla Odenwald, Mass College of Art & Design; Martin Orzeck, Community College of Philadelphia; Jenni Runte, Metropolitan State

University; Judy Schmidt, Harrisburg Area Community College; Jerry Scott, Cardinal Stritch University; Sarah Sims, Campbellsville University; Renee Shea, Bowie State University; Jason Tougaw, Queens College; Paul Walker, Murray State University; and Sabine Winter, Eastfield College.

We would also like to thank Anthony Atkins, who graciously provided his feedback on the text and contributed a new chapter on rhetorical analysis and popular culture, and Martha Friedman, Connie Gardner, Linda Winters, and Margaret Gorenstein, who adeptly managed art research and text permissions.

We are also deeply indebted to the people at Bedford/St. Martin's, especially to our editor, Adam Whitehurst, who is wise, patient, supportive, and unfailingly helpful. Steve Scipione, Maura Shea, and John Sullivan, our editors for all of the preceding editions, have left a lasting impression on us and on the book; without their work on the first nine editions, there probably would not be a tenth. Others at Bedford/St. Martin's to whom we are deeply indebted include Charles H. Christensen, Joan E. Feinberg, Denise Wydra, Shuli Traub, and Harold Chester, all of whom have offered countless valuable (and invaluable) suggestions. Intelligent, informed, firm yet courteous, persuasive—all of these folks know how to think and how to argue.

YOU GET MORE DIGITAL CHOICES FOR *CURRENT ISSUES AND ENDURING QUESTIONS*

Current Issues and Enduring Questions doesn't stop with a book. Online, you'll find both free and affordable premium resources to help students get even more out of the book and your course. You'll also find convenient instructor resources, such as downloadable sample syllabi, classroom activities, and even a nationwide community of teachers. To learn more about or order any of the products below, contact your Bedford/St. Martin's sales representative, e-mail sales support (sales_support@bedfordstmartins.com), or visit the Web site at **bedfordstmartins.com**.

Student Resources

ReWriting **3.0, bedfordstmartins.com/rewriting.** The best collection of open writing resources on the Web, *Re:Writing* 3.0 gives you and your students even more ways to think, watch, practice, and learn about writing concepts. Listen to Nancy Sommers on using a teacher's comments to revise. Try a logic puzzle. Consult our resources for writing centers. Send your students to free and open resources, choose flexible premium resources to supplement your print text, or upgrade to an expanding collection of innovative digital content.

Bedford e-Book to Go for *Current Issues and Enduring Questions.* Let students choose their format. Students can purchase *Current*

Issues and Enduring Questions in downloadable e-book formats for computers, tablets, and e-readers. For more details, visit **bedfordstmartins .com/cieq/formats**.

VideoCentral is a growing collection of videos for the writing class that captures real-world, academic, and student writers talking about how and why they write. VideoCentral can be packaged for free with *Current Issues and Enduring Questions*. An activation code is required. To order VideoCentral packaged with the print book, use **ISBN 978-1-4576-7682-6**.

i-series

Add more value to your text by choosing one of the following tutorial series, free when packaged with *Current Issues and Enduring Questions*. This popular series presents multimedia tutorials in a flexible format—because there are things you can't do in a book. To learn more about package options or any of the products below, contact your Bedford/St. Martin's sales representative or visit **bedfordstmartins.com**.

i-claim: visualizing argument 2.0. (available online) shows students how to analyze and compose arguments in words, images, and sounds with six tutorials, an illustrated glossary, and over seventy multimedia arguments. To order *i-claim: visualizing argument* packaged with the print book, use **ISBN 978-1-4576-7680-2**.

ix visualizing composition 2.0. (available online) helps students put into practice key rhetorical and visual concepts. To order *ix visualizing composition* packaged with the print book, use **ISBN 978-1-4576-7681-9**.

Instructor Resources

You have a lot to do in your course. Bedford/St. Martin's wants to make it easy for you to find the support you need—and to get it quickly.

Resources for Teaching Current Issues and Enduring Questions is available in a PDF file that can be downloaded from **bedfordstmartins .com/barnetbedau/catalog**. In addition to chapter overviews and discussion prompts, *Resources for Teaching* includes suggested answers to the questions in the text.

TeachingCentral (**bedfordstmartins.com/teachingcentral**) offers the entire list of Bedford/St. Martin's print and online professional resources in one place. You'll find landmark reference works, sourcebooks on pedagogical issues, award-winning collections, and practical advice for the classroom—all free for instructors.

Bits (**bedfordbits.com**) collects creative ideas for teaching a range of composition topics in an easily searchable blog. A community of teachers—leading scholars, authors, and editors—discusses revision, research, grammar and style, technology, peer review, and much more. Take, use, adapt, and pass the ideas around. Then, come back to the site to comment or share your own suggestions.

Brief Contents

Contents

 For readings that go beyond the printed page,
see **bedfordstmartins.com/barnetbedau.**

bedfordstmartins.com/barnetbedau

e bedfordstmartins.com/barnetbedau

bedfordstmartins.com/barnetbedau

6 Developing an Argument of Your Own 228

Planning, Drafting, and Revising an Argument 228

[e] bedfordstmartins.com/barnetbedau

e   **bedfordstmartins.com/barnetbedau**

🄴 bedfordstmartins.com/barnetbedau

16 The Local Food Movement: Is It a Better Way to Eat?   476

17 The Death Penalty: Is It Ever Justified?   483

18 Genetic Modification of Human Beings: Is It Acceptable?   495

PART FIVE   CURRENT ISSUES: CASEBOOKS   503

19 A College Education: What Is Its Purpose?   505

e bedfordstmartins.com/barnetbedau

28 What Is Happiness?   774

Thoughts about Happiness, Ancient and Modern   774

PART ONE

CRITICAL THINKING
and READING

Critical Thinking

What is the hardest task in the world? To think.

—RALPH WALDO EMERSON

I write entirely to find out what I'm thinking, what I'm looking at, what I see and what it means. What I want and what I fear.

—JOAN DIDION

In all affairs it's a healthy thing now and then to hang a question mark on the things you have long taken for granted.

—BERTRAND RUSSELL

Although Emerson said simply "to think," he clearly was using the word *think* in the sense of *critical thinking*. By itself, *thinking* can mean almost any sort of mental activity, from idle daydreaming ("During the chemistry lecture I kept thinking about how I'd like to go camping") to careful analysis ("I'm thinking about whether I can afford more than one week—say two weeks—of camping in the Rockies," or even "I'm thinking about whether Emerson's comment is true").

In short, when we add the adjective *critical* to the noun *thinking*, we eliminate reveries, just as we also eliminate snap judgments. We are talking about searching for hidden assumptions, noticing various facets, unraveling different strands, and evaluating what is most significant. The word *critical* comes from a Greek word, *krinein*, meaning "to separate," "to choose"; it implies conscious, deliberate inquiry, and especially it implies adopting a skeptical state of mind. To say that it implies a skeptical state of mind is by no means to say that it implies a self-satisfied faultfinding state of mind. Quite the reverse: Because critical thinkers seek to draw intelligent conclusions, they are sufficiently open-minded that they can adopt a skeptical attitude

- Toward *their own* ideas,
- Toward *their own* assumptions, and
- Toward the evidence *they themselves* tentatively offer,

"He saves all his critical thinking for my behavior."

as well as toward the assumptions and evidence offered by others. When they reread a draft they have written, they read it with a skeptical frame of mind, seeking to improve the thinking that has gone into it.

THINKING ABOUT DRIVERS' LICENSES AND PHOTOGRAPHIC IDENTIFICATION

By way of illustration, let's think about a case that was in the news in 2003. When Sultaana Freeman, an American Muslim woman in Florida, first applied for a driver's license, she refused on religious grounds to unveil her face for the photograph that Florida requires. She was allowed to remain veiled for the photo, with only her eyes showing. Probably in a response to the terrorist attacks of September 11, 2001, she was informed in 2002 that her license would be revoked if she refused to allow the Department of Motor Vehicles to photograph her face. She sued the state of Florida, saying that unveiling would violate her Islamic beliefs. "I'm fighting for the principle and the religious freedom of all people in the country," she said. "It's not about me."

Well, let's think about this—let's think critically, and, to do this, we will use a simple aid that is equal to the best word processor, a pencil. Your own experience has already taught you that thinking is largely a matter of association; one thought leads to another, as when you jot down "peanut butter" on a shopping list and then add "bread," and "bread" somehow reminds you—you don't know why—that you also need paper napkins. As the humorist Finley Peter Dunne observed, philosophers and cows have the gift of meditation, but "others don't begin to think till they begin to talk or write." So what are some thoughts that come to mind when we begin to talk or write about this Florida case?

Critical thinking means questioning not only the assumptions of others but also questioning *your own* assumptions. We will discuss this point at some length later in this chapter, but here we want to say only that when you write an argument, you ought to be *thinking*, evaluating evidence and assumptions, not merely collecting evidence to support a preestablished conclusion.

Back to the Florida case: Here is what we came up with in a few minutes, using a process called *clustering*. (We illustrate clustering again on page 230.)

In the center of a sheet of paper, we jotted down a phrase summarizing the basic issue, and then we began jotting down what must be the most obvious justification for demanding the picture—national

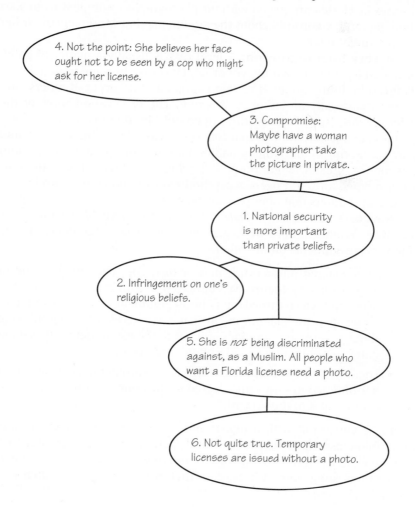

safety. (We might equally well have begun with the most obvious justifications for refusing to be photographed—religious belief and perhaps privacy, to think of arguments that Sultaana Freeman—or, more likely, her lawyer—might set forth.) Then we let our minds work, and one thought led to another. Sometimes almost as soon as we jotted down an idea we saw that it wasn't very good, but we made considerable progress.

In the illustration, we have added numbers to the ideas, simply so that you can see how our minds worked, which is to say how we jumped around. Notice, for instance, that our fifth point—our fifth idea— is connected to our first point. When we were rereading our first four jottings, the fifth idea—that she is not being discriminated against as a Muslim—came to mind, and we saw that it should be linked with the first point. Our sixth point—a modification of our fifth, occurred to us even before we finished writing the fifth. The sixth point, that temporary licenses in Florida are issued without photographs, prompted us to start thinking more vigorously about the arguments that Ms. Freeman, or her lawyer, might offer.

A very brief digression: A legal case is usually a matter of guilty or not guilty, right or wrong, yes or no. Of course in some trials a defendant can be found guilty of certain charges and innocent of others, but, again, it is usually an either/or situation: The prosecution wins, or the defense wins. But in many other aspects of life, there is room for compromise, and it may well be that *both* sides win—by seeing what ground they share and by developing additional common ground. We go into this topic at greater length on p. 392, where we discuss Rogerian argument (named for Carl Rogers, a psychotherapist) and in our introduction to several chapters that offer pairs of debates.

Now back to *Freeman v. State of Florida, Department of Highway Safety and Motor Vehicles*, where we began by trying to list arguments on one side versus arguments on the other.

- After making our seventh note, which goes back to the issue of religious liberty (hence we connected it with a line to the central issue) and which turned out to be an argument that the government rather than the plaintiff might make, we decided to keep thinking about government positions and wrote the eighth note—that some states do not require pictures on drivers' licenses.

- The ninth note—that the government is prohibiting a belief, not a harmful action—in some degree refutes our seventh note, so we connected it to the seventh.

Again, if you think with a pencil and a sheet of paper and let your mind make associations, you will find, perhaps to your surprise, that you have plenty of interesting ideas. Doubtless you will also have some not-so-interesting ones. We confess that we have slightly edited our

notes; originally they included two points that we are ashamed we thought of:

- "What is she complaining about? In some strict Islamic countries they don't even let women drive, period."
- "Being deprived of a license isn't a big deal. She can take the bus."

It will take only a moment of reflection to decide that these thoughts can scarcely be offered as serious arguments: What people do in strict Islamic countries has nothing to do with what we should do in ours, and that bus service is available is utterly irrelevant to the issue of whether this woman's rights are being infringed. Still, if a fear of making fools of ourselves had prevented us from jotting down ideas, we would not have jotted down any decent ideas, and the page would not have gotten written.

Plaintiff in *Freeman v. State of Florida, Department of Highway Safety and Motor Vehicles.* (Peter Cosgrove/© AP/Worldwide Photos.)

The outcome of the driver's license photo case? Judge Janet C. Thorpe ruled against the plaintiff, explaining that "the State has always had a compelling interest in promoting public safety. That interest is served by having the means to accurately and swiftly determine identities in given circumstances." (You can read Judge Thorpe's entire decision online—sixteen highly readable double-spaced pages—by going to Google and typing in "Sultaana Lakiana.")

> **A RULE FOR WRITERS:** One good way to start writing an essay is to start generating ideas—and at this point don't worry that some of them may be nonsense. Just get ideas down on paper, and evaluate them later.

TOPICS FOR CRITICAL THINKING AND WRITING

1. Think about Judge Thorpe's comment, quoted in the preceding paragraph. Even if we agree that a photograph establishes identity—itself a debatable point—one might raise a question: Given the fact that Florida has not passed a law requiring a photo ID, why should it say that the driver of a vehicle must provide a photo ID? Isn't a driver's license a mere certification of permission to drive?

2. Judge Thorpe wrote the following as part of her explanation for her decision:

> Although the Court acknowledges that Plaintiff herself most likely poses no threat to national security, there likely are people who would be willing to use a ruling permitting the wearing of fullface cloaks in driver's license photos by pretending to ascribe to religious beliefs in order to carry out activities that would threaten lives.

Is the judge in effect saying that we should infringe on Sultaana Freeman's religious beliefs because someone else might do something wicked?

3. In England in 2006 a Muslim woman—a British citizen—was removed from her job as a schoolteacher because she wore a veil. The stated reason was that the veil prevented her from effectively communicating with children. What do you think of the view that a woman has a right to wear a veil, but when she enters the marketplace she may rightly be denied certain jobs? What are your reasons?

THINKING ABOUT ANOTHER ISSUE CONCERNING DRIVERS' LICENSES: ANALYZING AND EVALUATING MULTIPLE PERSPECTIVES

Let's think critically about a law passed in West Virginia in 1989. The law provides that although students may drop out of school at the age of sixteen, no dropout younger than eighteen can hold a driver's license. (Several states now have comparable laws.)

What ought we to think of such a law?

- Is it fair?
- What is its purpose?
- Is it likely to accomplish its purpose?
- Might it unintentionally cause some harm?
- If so, can we weigh the potential harm against the potential good? Who gains something and who loses something?

Suppose you had been a member of the West Virginia state legislature in 1989: How would you have voted? Why?

In thinking critically about a topic, we try to see it from all sides before we come to our conclusion. We conduct an argument with ourselves, advancing and then questioning opinions:

- What can be said *for* the proposition, and
- What can be said *against* it?

Our first reaction may be quite uncritical, quite unthinking: "What a good idea!" or "That's outrageous!" But critical thinking requires us to reflect further, trying to support our position *and also* trying to see the other side. One can almost say that the heart of critical thinking is a *willingness to face objections to one's own beliefs,* a willingness to adopt a skeptical attitude not only toward authority and toward views opposed to our own but also toward common sense—that is, toward the views that seem obviously right to us. If we assume we have a monopoly on the truth and we dismiss as bigots those who oppose us, or if we say our opponents are acting merely out of self-interest and we do not in fact analyze their views, we are being critical but we are not engaged in critical thinking.

> **A RULE FOR WRITERS:** Early in the process of jotting down your ideas on a topic, stop to ask yourself, "What might reasonably be offered as an *objection* to my view?"

In short, as we will say several times (because we think the point is basic, *argument is an instrument of learning* as well as of persuasion.

Critical thinking requires us to see things from perspectives other than our own and to envision the likely consequences of our positions. (This sort of imaginative thinking—grasping a perspective other than our own and considering the possible consequences of positions—is imperative if we want others to take our positions seriously.)

Thinking critically involves a twofold activity:

analysis, finding the parts of the problem and then separating them, trying to see how things fit together; and

evaluation, judging the merit of our claims and assumptions and the weight of the evidence in their favor.

If we engage in imaginative, analytic, and evaluative thought, we will have second and third ideas; almost to our surprise we may find ourselves adopting a position that we initially couldn't imagine we would hold. As we think about the West Virginia law, we might find ourselves coming up with a fairly wide variety of ideas, each triggered by the preceding idea but not necessarily carrying it a step further. For instance, we may think X and then immediately think, "No, that's not quite right. In fact, come to think of it, the opposite of X is probably true." We haven't carried X further, but we have progressed in our thinking.

Critical Thinking at Work: From Jottings to a Short Essay

We have already seen examples of **clustering** or **mapping** on pages 5 and 7, which is to say we have seen examples of *thinking* or, more specifically, generating ideas by imagining responses—counterthoughts—to first thoughts. Here is another example, this time showing a student's thoughts about the issue of whether homeschooled students should be permitted to participate in extracurricular activities, especially varsity sports, in public schools.

A first reaction might be, "Yes, of course. Their parents pay taxes, so the schools should be available, even if the parents have chosen not to make full use of them," or, on the other hand, a first reaction might be, "Certainly not. The parents have opted out of the system. School is not a cafeteria where one chooses the things one likes, and rejects the rest."

One of our students, Steve Jeffries, began by jotting down his first thoughts—and also the counterresponses that he himself generated. He numbered his notes so that we could easily see their sequence.

IDEA PROMPT 1.1 MAPPING PROS AND CONS

Should homeschooled students be allowed to play on public school sports teams?

Yes	No
1. Parents of homeschoolers pay taxes that support public schools.	2. But so what? They have chosen homeschooling. They have rejected the ideas of the public school.
3. Homeschooling is <u>officially</u> approved. These aren't truant students. It's just that they or their parents think they can do a better job on <u>some</u> things—not all things—than the public schools.	4. But it is unfair to deprive a public school student of the shot to play on the high school football team because an outside kid gets the spot.
5. Speaking of unfairness, is it fair to deprive a talented homeschooler of the possibility of an athletic scholarship? Or of participating in a National Academy of Science project?	6. Yes, it <u>is</u> fair. The public school students get the opportunity because they have competed under conditions that are monitored. They have their coursework standardized and their grades are monitored according to the same criteria as other students.
	7. By the way, I have learned that some homeschool proponents <u>oppose</u> the idea of kids participating in public school activities. They say it <u>weakens</u> the homeschool program.

A STUDENT'S ESSAY, DEVELOPED FROM
A CLUSTER AND A LIST

Steve Jeffries, the student who submitted the cluster or preliminary map of ideas concerning homeschooling, transformed the material into a list and ultimately wrote a short essay (the assigned essay was to be "250–500 words") on the topic. Notice that in the essay—the product of several revised drafts—the student introduced points he had *not* thought of when he was mapping, notably the material about the football player Tim Tebow. The cluster, in short, was a *first* step, not a road map of the final essay.

Play Ball! Why Homeschoolers Should Be Allowed to Play on Public School Teams

Perhaps the most famous homeschooler is Tim Tebow, now a star quarterback with the New York Jets, but how can a homeschooler have much chance to play high school football? How can a young person, however talented in a sport that is a team sport, further develop this talent if there is no team on which he or she can play? Fortunately for Tebow—and for football fans throughout the country—Tebow was raised in Florida, a state that allows homeschoolers to play on teams in their school districts. Most states are not so enlightened.

The chief arguments against homeschoolers playing on public school teams seem to be three: First, they (or their parents) have chosen *not* to participate in the public school system; second, if they do get on the team, they may deprive a public school student of his or her place on the team; and, third, public school students are eligible to play on a team only if they meet certain standards concerning grades and the number of courses they are taking, but homeschoolers sometimes are not evaluated in this way. A fourth argument comes, surprisingly, from some homeschool parents themselves: Some of these parents say they do *not* want their children to participate in the extracurricular activities of the public school because such participation undermines the very idea of homeschooling. We do not need to consider this last objection, since if the parents don't want their children to participate in any of the activities, there is no problem for the public school, no question about whether the students are eligible.

The first argument is correct in saying that the parents have chosen to homeschool the children, but this does not mean, or should not mean, that the parents have also chosen to prevent the children from participating in extracurricular activities. It merely means that for various reasons the parents think they can do a better job of *teaching* their children than the public school system does—and the plan of the parents has been officially approved by the local school board. The plan concerns reading, writing, and 'rithmetic, not sports, or, for that matter, the chess team or the band. The second argument, about depriving a public school student of a place on the team, perhaps has some merit, but surely all members of a team want—for their *own* sake—all of the players to be the best available players, and if a home-schooler is (say) a better quarterback than any present student in the public school, almost surely the members of the team want the home-schooler. Chess players and musicians similarly want to play with the best players, knowing that their own skills are improved when they are teamed with superior players. Third, although homeschoolers are not always evaluated in terms of numbers of courses they are taking, everyone knows that homeschoolers (or at least their parents!) are very serious, and that homeschooled children are being well-educated.

Not every homeschooler is a Tim Tebow, who brought fame to his Florida high school, but every talented homeschooler ought to be given the opportunity to participate in extracurricular affairs in the local school if their parents are willing to let them. It's good for *all* of the people concerned and, what's more, it is fair, and fairness is part of what American education is about.

Tim Tebow

The Essay Analyzed

The title, by its first two words, immediately engages a reader's attention, and the subtitle states the thesis. This introductory material—a paper begins with its title, not with its first paragraph—lets the readers know where they will be going.

The first paragraph mentions a name familiar to many—probably to most—readers, and reminds them that Tebow was a homeschooler who was allowed to play on the team of a public high school. The writer's implication presumably is this: If Tebow, an American hero, did it, it must be OK.

The second paragraph draws heavily on the student's preliminary map. It sets forth pretty much all of the objections, and, at the end of this paragraph, the writer explains to the readers why only three of the four points will be discussed. Again, the writer is keeping the readers informed of where they are going. And presumably the readers are interested in hearing more from this thoughtful writer.

The third paragraph fulfills the expectations that the second paragraph set up. Ordinarily a writer would not attempt to cover three objections in one paragraph—probably each objection would get a paragraph to itself—but the assignment limited the student to 250–500 words. The second and third paragraphs are in effect the central body of this essay. By the end of the third paragraph the author has argued his case—offered his evidence in support of his thesis—and now the writer merely has to wrap things up, to make an effective exit.

The fourth paragraph employs a time-tested formula for ending: It returns to a point made at the beginning—Tebow—and thus the wheel comes full circle. This paragraph, in addition to providing a sense of completeness or finality, also appeals to the reader's sense of fairness—normally an effective gesture, though in this instance a reader may wonder if the writer has convincingly demonstrated that fairness requires public schools to admit homeschoolers to extracurricular activities. Are *you* convinced that it is *unfair* to deny homeschoolers access to a public school's extracurricular activities? Why, or why not?

WRITING AS A WAY OF THINKING

We have already seen, in the clusters that students have written, concise examples of how the act of writing helps thinkers to think. "To learn to write," Robert Frost said, "is to learn to have ideas." But how do you "learn to have ideas"? Often we discover ideas while we are in the process of talking with others. A friend says *X* about some issue, and we—who have never really thought much about the matter—say,

- "Well, yes, I see what you are saying, but, come to think of it, I'm not of your opinion. I see it differently—*not* X *but* Y." Or maybe we say,

- "*Yes,* X, *sure, and also* a bit of *Y,* too."

Mere chance—the comment of a friend—has led us to an idea that we didn't know we had. This sort of discovery may at first seem something like the discovery we make when we reach under the couch to retrieve a ball that the dog has pushed and we find a ten-dollar bill instead. "How it got there, I'll never know, but I'm glad I found it."

In fact, learning to have ideas is not largely a matter of chance. Or if chance *is* involved, well, as Louis Pasteur put it, "Chance favors the prepared mind." What does this mean? It means that somehow, lurking in the mind, are some bits of information or hints or maybe hunches that in the unexpected circumstance—when talking, or when listening to a lecture or a classroom discussion, or especially when reading—are triggered and result in useful thoughts. A sort of seat-of-the-pants knowledge that, when brought to the surface, when worked on, when thought about, produces good results.

Consider the famous episode of Archimedes, the ancient Greek mathematician, who discovered a method to determine the volume of an irregularly shaped object. The problem: A king gave a goldsmith a specific weight of gold with which to make a crown in the shape of laurel leaves. When the job was finished the king weighed the crown, found that it was the weight of the gold he had provided, but he nevertheless suspected that the goldsmith might have substituted some silver for the gold. How could Archimedes find out (without melting or in any other way damaging the crown) if the crown was pure gold? Meditating produced no ideas, but when he entered a bathtub Archimedes noticed that the level of water rose as he immersed his body. He suddenly realized that he could thus determine the volume of the crown—by measuring the amount of displaced water. Since silver is less dense than gold, it takes a greater volume of silver to equal a given weight of gold. That is, a given weight of gold will displace less water than the same weight of silver. Archimedes then immersed the given weight of gold, measured the water it displaced, and found that indeed the crown displaced more water than the gold did. In his excitement at hitting upon his idea, Archimedes is said to have leaped out of the tub and run naked through the street, shouting "Eureka" (Greek for "I have found [it]").

Getting Ideas

Why do we tell this story? Partly because we like it, but chiefly because the word *eureka* comes from the same Greek word that has given our language the word **heuristic** (pronounced hyooRIStik), a method or process of discovering ideas, in short, of thinking. In this method, one thing triggers another. (Note: In computer science *heuristic* has a more special-ized meaning.) Now, one of the best ways of getting ideas is to hear what is going on around you—and what is going on around you is talk, in and out of the classroom, and talk in the world of books. You will find, as we said at the beginning of this discussion, that your response may be, "Well, yes, I see what you are saying, but, come to think of it, I don't see it quite that way. I see it differently—not *X* but *Y*." As we said earlier, argument is an instrument of learning as well as of persuasion. For instance,

> *Yes*, solar power is a way of conserving energy, *but* do we need to de-spoil the Mojave Desert and endanger desert life with—literally—fifty thousand solar mirrors, so that folks in Los Angeles can heat their pools? Doesn't it make sense to reduce our use of energy, rather than merely to develop sources of renewable energy that violate the environ-ment? Some sites should be off-limits.

Or maybe your response to the proposal (now at least ten years old) that wind turbines be placed in Cape Cod, Massachusetts, is,

> *Given our need* for wind power, *how can a reasonable person object* to the proposal that we put 130 wind turbines in Cape Cod, Massachusetts? *Yes*, the view will be changed, *but* in fact the turbines are quite attrac-tive. No one thinks that windmills in Holland spoil the landscape. So the view will be changed, but not spoiled, *and furthermore* wind turbines do not endanger birds or aquatic life.

When you are asked to write about something you have read in this book, if your first response is that you have no ideas, remember the re-sponses that we have mentioned—"No, I don't see it that way," or "Yes, but," or "Yes, and moreover"—and see if one of them helps you to re-spond to the work—helps you, in short, to get ideas.

A related way of getting ideas practiced by the ancient Greeks and Romans and still regarded as among the best ways, is to consider what the ancients called **topics,** from the Greek word *topos*, meaning "place," as in our word *topography* (a description or representation of a place). For the ancients, certain topics, put into the form of questions, were in ef-fect places where one went to find ideas. Among the classical topics were definition, comparison, relationship, and testimony. By prompting one-self with questions about these topics, one finds oneself moving toward answers (see Idea Prompt 1.2).

If you think you are at a loss for ideas when confronted with an issue (and when confronted with an assignment to write about it), you probably will find ideas coming to you if you turn to the relevant classical topics and begin jotting down your responses. (In classical terminology, you are en-gaged in the process of invention, from the Latin *invenire*, "to come upon," "to find.") Seeing your ideas on paper—even in the briefest form—will help bring other ideas to mind and will also help you to evaluate them. For instance, after jotting down ideas as they come and responses to them,

IDEA PROMPT 1.2 UNDERSTANDING CLASSICAL TOPICS

Definition	*What is it?*	"The West Virginia law defines a high school dropout as . . ."
Comparison	*What is it like or unlike?*	"Compared with the national rate of teenagers involved in fatal accidents, teenagers from West Virginia . . ."
Relationship	*What caused it, and what will it cause?*	"The chief cause of teenage fatal driving accidents is alcohol. Admittedly, there are no statistics on whether high school dropouts have a higher rate of alcoholism than teenagers who remain in school, but nevertheless . . ."
Testimony	*What is said about it, for instance, by experts?*	"Judge Smith, in sentencing the youth, said that in all of his long experience . . ."

1. You might go on to organize them into two lists, pro and con;
2. Next, you might delete ideas that, when you come to think about them, strike you as simply wrong or irrelevant; and
3. Then you might develop those ideas that strike you as pretty good.

You probably won't know where you stand until you have gone through some such process. It would be nice if we could make a quick decision, immediately justify it with three excellent reasons, and then give three further reasons showing why the opposing view is inadequate. In fact, however, we almost never can come to a reasoned decision without a good deal of preliminary thinking.

Consider again the West Virginia law we discussed earlier in this chapter. Here is a kind of inner dialogue that you might engage in as you think critically about it:

The purpose is to give students an incentive to stay in school by making them pay a price if they choose to drop out.

Adolescents will get the message that education really is important.

But come to think of it, *will* they? Maybe they will see this as just another example of adults bullying young people.

According to a newspaper article, the dropout rate in West Virginia decreased by 30 percent in the year after the bill was passed.

Well, that sounds good, but is there any reason to think that kids who are pressured into staying really learn anything? The *assumption* behind the bill is that if would-be dropouts stay in school, they—and society—will gain. But is the assumption sound? Maybe such students will become resentful, will not learn anything, and may even be so disruptive that they will interfere with the learning of other students.

Notice how part of the job is *analytic,* recognizing the elements or complexities of the whole, and part is *evaluative,* judging the adequacy of all of these ideas, one by one. Both tasks require critical thinking in the form of analyzing and evaluating, and those processes themselves require a disciplined *imagination.*

So far we have jotted down a few thoughts and then immediately given some second thoughts contrary to the first. Of course, the counterthoughts might not immediately come to mind. For instance, they might not occur until we reread our notes or try to explain the law to a friend, or until we sit down and begin drafting an essay aimed at supporting or undermining the law. Most likely, in fact, some good ideas won't occur until a second or third or fourth draft.

Here are some further thoughts on the West Virginia law. We list them more or less as they arose and as we typed them into a computer—not sorted out neatly into two groups, pro and con, or evaluated as you would want to do in further critical thinking of your own. And, of course, a later step would be to organize the material into some useful pattern. As you read, you might write your own responses in the margin.

Education is *not* optional, something left for the individual to take or not to take—like going to a concert, jogging, getting annual health checkups, or getting eight hours of sleep each night. Society has determined that it is *for the public good* that citizens have a substantial education, so we require education up to a certain age.

Come to think about it, maybe the criterion of age doesn't make much sense. If we want an educated citizenry, it would make more sense to require people to attend school until they demonstrated competence in certain matters rather than until they reached a certain age. Exceptions, of course, would be made for mentally challenged persons and perhaps for certain other groups with special needs.

What is needed is not legal pressure to keep teenagers in school but schools that hold the interest of teenagers.

A sixteen-year-old usually is not mature enough to make a decision of this importance.

Still, a sixteen-year-old who finds school unsatisfying and who therefore drops out may become a perfectly useful citizen.

Denying a sixteen-year-old a driver's license may work in West Virginia, but it would scarcely work in a state with great urban areas, where most high school students rely on public transportation.

We earn a driver's license by demonstrating certain skills. The state has no right to take away such a license unless we have demonstrated that we are unsafe drivers.

To prevent a person of sixteen from having a driver's license prevents that person from holding certain kinds of jobs, and that's unfair.

A law of this sort deceives adults into thinking that they have really done something constructive for teenage education, but it may work *against* improving the schools. It may be *counterproductive:* If we are really serious about educating youngsters, we have to examine the curriculum and the quality of our teachers.

Doubtless there is much that we haven't said, on both sides, but we hope you will agree that the issue deserves thought. In fact, several states now revoke the driver's license of a teenager who drops out of school, and four of these states go even further and revoke the licenses of students whose academic work does not reach a given standard. On the other hand, Louisiana, which for a while had a law like West Virginia's, dropped it in 1997.

If you were a member of a state legislature voting on this proposal, you would *have* to think about the issue. But just as a thought experiment, try to put into writing your tentative views.

✔ A CHECKLIST FOR CRITICAL THINKING

Attitudes

☐ Does my thinking show imaginative open-mindedness and intellectual curiosity?

  ☐ Am I willing to examine my assumptions?

  ☐ Am I willing to entertain new ideas—both those that I encounter while reading and those that come to mind while writing?

  ☐ Am I willing to exert myself—for instance, to do research—to acquire information and to evaluate evidence?

Skills

☐ Can I summarize an argument accurately?

☐ Can I evaluate assumptions, evidence, and inferences?

☐ Can I present my ideas effectively—for instance, by organizing and by writing in a manner appropriate to my imagined audience?

One other point about this issue. If you had to think about the matter *today*, you might also want to know whether the West Virginia legislation of 1989 is considered a success and on what basis. That is, you would want to get answers to such questions as the following:

- What sort of evidence tends to support the law or tends to suggest that the law is a poor idea?
- Did the reduction in the dropout rate continue, or did the reduction occur only in the first year following the passage of the law?
- If indeed students who wanted to drop out did not, was their presence in school a good thing, both for them and for their classmates?
- Have some people emerged as authorities on this topic? What makes them authorities, and what do they have to say?
- Has the constitutionality of the bill been tested? With what results?

Some of these questions require you to do **research** on the topic. The questions raise issues of fact, and some relevant evidence probably is available. If you are to arrive at a conclusion in which you can have confidence, you will have to do some research to find out what the facts—the objective data—are. Merely explaining your position, without giving the evidence, will not be very convincing.

Even without doing any research, however, you might want to look over the ideas, pro and con, perhaps adding some totally new thoughts or perhaps modifying or even rejecting (for reasons that you can specify) some of those already given. If you do think a bit further about this issue, and we hope that you will, notice an interesting point about *your own* thinking: It probably is not *linear* (moving in a straight line from A to B to C) but *recursive*, moving from A to C and back to B or starting over at C and then back to A and B. By zigging and zagging almost despite yourself, you'll get to a conclusion that may finally seem correct. In retrospect it seems obvious; *now* you can chart a nice line from A to B to C—but that was not at all evident to you at the start.

A SHORT ESSAY ILLUSTRATING CRITICAL THINKING

When we read an essay, we expect the writer to have thought things through, at least to a considerable degree. We do not want to read every false start, every fuzzy thought, every ill-organized paragraph that the writer knocked off. Yes, writers make false starts, put down fuzzy thoughts, write ill-organized paragraphs, but then they revise and revise yet again, and they end by giving us a readable essay that seems effortlessly written. Still—and here we get to our real point—in argumentative essays, writers need to show their readers that they have made some effort; they need to show us *how* they got to their final (for the moment) views. It is not enough for the writer to say, "I believe *X*"; rather, the writer must in effect say, "I believe X—and I hope you will believe it also—because Y and Z, though attractive, just don't stand up to inquiry as well as X does. Y is superficially plausible, but..., and Z, which is an attractive alternative to Y, nevertheless fails because..."

Notice in the following short essay—on parents putting spyware into the computers of their children—that Harlan Coben frequently brings up objections to his own position; that is, he shows his awareness of other views and then tries to show why he thinks his position is preferable. Presumably he thus communicates to his readers a sense that he is thoughtful, well-informed, and fair-minded.

Harlan Coben

Harlan Coben (b. 1962) is the author of Hold Tight *(2009). Reprinted here is an essay published in the* New York Times *on March 16, 2008. Following is a letter that was written in response and was later published in the* Times.

The Undercover Parent

Not long ago, friends of mine confessed over dinner that they had put spyware on their fifteen-year-old son's computer so they could monitor all he did online. At first I was repelled at this invasion of privacy. Now, after doing a fair amount of research, I get it.

Make no mistake: If you put spyware on your computer, you have the ability to log every keystroke your child makes and thus a good portion of his or her private world. That's what spyware is—at least the parental monitoring kind. You don't have to be an expert to put it on your computer. You just download the software from a vendor and you will receive reports—weekly, daily, whatever—showing you everything your child is doing on the machine.

Scary. But a good idea. Most parents won't even consider it.

Maybe it's the word: spyware. It brings up associations of Dick Cheney sitting in a dark room, rubbing his hands together and reading your most private thoughts. But this isn't the government we are talking about—this is your family. It's a mistake to confuse the two. Loving parents are doing the surveillance here, not faceless bureaucrats. And most parents already monitor their children, watching over their home environment, their school.

Today's overprotective parents fight their kids' battles on the playground, berate coaches about playing time and fill out college applications— yet when it comes to chatting with pedophiles or watching beheadings or gambling away their entire life savings, then ... then their children deserve independence? 5

Some will say that you should simply trust your child, that if he is old enough to go on the Internet he is old enough to know the dangers. Trust is one thing, but surrendering parental responsibility to a machine that allows the entire world access to your home borders on negligence.

Some will say that it's better just to use parental blocks that deny access to risky sites. I have found that they don't work. Children know how to get around them. But more than that—and this is where it gets tough—I want to know what's being said in e-mail and instant messages and in chat rooms.

There are two reasons for this. First, we've all read about the young boy unknowingly conversing with a pedophile or the girl who was cyber-bullied to the point where she committed suicide. Would a watchful eye have helped? We rely in the real world on teachers and parents to guard against bullies—do we just dismiss bullying on the Internet and all it entails because we are entering difficult ethical ground?

Second, everything your child types can already be seen by the world—teachers, potential employers, friends, neighbors, future dates. Shouldn't he learn now that the Internet is not a haven of privacy?

One of the most popular arguments against spyware is the claim that   10 you are reading your teenager's every thought, that in today's world, a computer is the little key-locked diary of the past. But posting thoughts on the Internet isn't the same thing as hiding them under your mattress. Maybe you should buy your children one of those little key-locked diaries so that they too can understand the difference.

Am I suggesting eavesdropping on every conversation? No. With new technology comes new responsibility. That works both ways. There is a fine line between being responsibly protective and irresponsibly nosy. You shouldn't monitor to find out if your daughter's friend has a crush on Kevin next door or that Mrs. Peterson gives too much homework or what schoolmate snubbed your son. You are there to start conversations and to be a safety net. To borrow from the national intelligence lexicon—and yes, that's uncomfortable—you're listening for dangerous chatter.

Will your teenagers find other ways of communicating to their friends when they realize you may be watching? Yes. But text messages and cell phones don't offer the anonymity and danger of the Internet. They are usually one-on-one with someone you know. It is far easier for a predator to troll chat rooms and MySpace and Facebook.

There will be tough calls. If your sixteen-year-old son, for example, is visiting hardcore pornography sites, what do you do? When I was sixteen, we looked at *Playboy* centerfolds and read *Penthouse Forum*. You may argue that's not the same thing, that Internet pornography makes that stuff seem about as harmful as "SpongeBob."

And you're probably right. But in my day, that's all you could get. If something more graphic had been out there, we probably would have gone for it. Interest in those, um, topics is natural. So start a dialogue based on that knowledge. You should have that talk anyway, but now you can have it with some kind of context.

Parenting has never been for the faint of heart. One friend of mine,   15 using spyware to monitor his college-bound, straight-A daughter, found out that not only was she using drugs but she was sleeping with her dealer. He wisely took a deep breath before confronting her. Then he decided to come clean, to let her know how he had found out, to speak with her about the dangers inherent in her behavior. He'd had these conversations before, of course, but this time he had context. She listened. There was no anger. Things seem better now.

Our knee-jerk reaction as freedom-loving Americans is to be suspicious of anything that hints at invasion of privacy. That's a good and noble thing. But it's not an absolute, particularly in the face of the new and evolving challenges presented by the Internet. And particularly when it comes to our children.

Do you tell your children that the spyware is on the computer? I side with yes, but it might be enough to show them this article, have a discussion about your concerns and let them know the possibility is there.

Overall View of the Essay

Before we comment in some detail on Coben's essay, we need to say that in terms of the length of its paragraphs, this essay is not a model for you to imitate. Material in newspapers customarily is given in very short paragraphs, partly because readers are reading it while eating breakfast or while commuting to work, and partly because the columns are narrow; a paragraph of only two or three sentences may still be an inch or two deep.

The title, "The Undercover Parent" is provocative, attention-getting.

Paragraph 1 contains cues that telegraph the reader that there will be a change ("Not long ago," "At first," and "Now"). These cues set up expectations, and then Coben to some degree fulfills the expectations. We say "to some degree" because the essay still has a number of paragraphs to go.

Paragraph 2 presses the point, almost aggressively ("Make no mistake").

Paragraph 3 pretty much does the same. The writer is clearly reassuring the readers that he knows how most of them feel. The idea is "scary," yes—and then comes a crucial word, "but," signaling to the reader that Coben takes a different view. We then expect him to tell us why. And—who knows?—he may even convince us.

Paragraph 4 reassures us that Coben does have some idea of why the idea is "scary," and it goes on—with another "but"—to clarify the point. We may not agree with Coben, but it is evident that he is *thinking*, inching along from one idea to the next, frequently to an opposing idea.

Paragraph 5 shows that again Coben has a sense of what is going on in the world ("Today's overprotective parents"), or, rather, he has two senses, because he adds "yet," equivalent to "but." In effect he says, "Yes A, but also B."

Paragraph 6 begins "Some will say," another indication that the writer knows what is going on. And we can expect that "some will say" will, sooner or later, lead into another "but" (or other comparable word), indicating that although some say *X*, he says *Y*.

Paragraph 7 again begins "Some will say." *We* will say that again the reader knows Coben's report of what "some" say will lead to a report that what *Coben* says (i.e., thought) is different.

Paragraph 8 begins, "There are two reasons." OK, we as readers know where we will be going: We will hear two reasons. Now, when Coben drafted this paragraph he may—who knows?—have first written "There are three reasons," or "There is one reason." Whatever he wrote as a prompt, it got him moving, got him thinking, and then, in the course of writing, of finding ideas, he revised when he found out exactly how many reasons he could offer. In any case, in the paragraph as we have it, he promises to give two reasons, and in this paragraph he gives the first, nicely labeled "First." Notice too, that he provides *evidence*, and he draws in the reader: "we've all read." In short, he establishes a cozy relationship with his reader.

Paragraph 9 begins, helpfully, "Second." Fine, we know exactly where Coben is taking us: He is giving us the second of the two reasons that he discovered, and that he implicitly promised to give when in the previous paragraph he said, "There are two reasons."

Paragraph 10 begins, "One of the most popular arguments against spying is," and so we know, again, where Coben will be taking us: He will, in effect, be telling us what some folks—but not Coben—say. Very simple, very obvious—Coben will be summarizing one of the most popular arguments against spying—and we are grateful to him for letting us know at the beginning of the paragraph what his intentions are.

Paragraph 11 continues his intimate relation with the reader ("Am I suggesting eavesdropping . . . ?") He thus lets us know that he has a good sense of how the reader probably is responding. As we will say several times in this book, good writers are able to put themselves into their readers' shoes. Because they have a sense of how the reader is responding, they offer whatever the reader needs at the moment, for instance a definition, or an example.

Paragraph 12 begins with a question ("Will your teenagers find other ways of communicating . . . ?"), and this question again indicates that Coben is walking in the shoes of his readers; he knows that this question is on their minds. His answer is twofold, "Yes," and "But." Again the "but" is a sign of critical thinking, a sign that Coben has a clear sense of position *A* but wants to move his reader from *A* to *B*.

Paragraph 13, beginning "There will be tough calls," is yet another example of Coben's demonstration to his readers that he is aware of their doubts, aware that they may be thinking Coben has simplified things.

Paragraph 14 (beginning "And you're probably right") continues his demonstration that he is aware of how his readers may respond—but it is immediately followed with a "But." Again, he is nudging us from position *A* to his position, position *B*.

Paragraph 15, like several of the earlier paragraphs, shows Coben is sympathetic to the real-world problems of his readers ("Parenting has never been for the faint of heart"), and it also shows that he is a person of experience. In this paragraph, where he refers to the problem of a friend, he tells us of the happy solution. In short, he tells us that life is tough, but experience shows that there is hope. (The letter-writer, Carol Weston, strongly implies that this bit of experience Coben offers in this paragraph is *not* at all typical.)

Paragraph 16 again indicates the writer's sense of the reader ("Our knee-jerk reaction"), and it again evokes a "But."

Paragraph 17, the final paragraph, pretty directly addresses the reader ("Do you tell your children that the spyware is on the computer?"), and it offers a mixed answer: "I side with yes, but . . . ." Again Coben is showing not only his awareness of the reader but also his awareness that the problem is complicated: There is something to be said for *A* but also something to be said for *B*. He ends by suggesting that indeed this article might be discussed by parents with their children, thereby conveying to his readers the suggestion that he is a fair-minded guy, willing to have his ideas put up for discussion.

Since this essay was published, smartphones have become increasingly popular, complicating Coben's point that "text messages and cell phones don't offer the anonymity and danger of the Internet." Many students' phones are now their primary means of accessing the Internet. How does this trend invite you to reconsider Coben's argument?

Following is Carol Weston's response to Coben's essay that the *Times* later published (March 23, 2008).

Letter of Response by Carol Weston

To the Editor:

In "The Undercover Parent" (Op-Ed, March 16), the novelist Harlan Coben writes that putting spyware on a child's computer is a "good idea."

As a mother and advice columnist for girls, I disagree. For most families, spyware is not only unnecessary, but it also sends the unfortunate message, "I don't trust you."

Mr. Coben said a friend of his "using spyware to monitor his college-bound, straight-A daughter, found out that not only was she using drugs but she was sleeping with her dealer." He confronted her about her behavior. "She listened. There was no anger. Things seem better now."

Huh?! No anger? No tears or shouting or slammed doors? C'mon. If only raising teenagers were that simple.

Parenting is both a job and a joy. It does not require spyware, but it does require love, respect, time, trust, money, and being as available as possible 24/7. Luck helps, too.

CAROL WESTON
New York, March 16, 2008

The writer is an advice columnist for Girls' Life *magazine.*

Topics for Critical Thinking and Writing

1. How important is the distinction (para. 4) between government invasion of privacy and parental invasion of privacy?

2. Complete the following sentence: An invasion of privacy is permissible if and only if . . .

3. Identify the constructive steps a normal parent might consider taking before going so far as to install spyware.

4. Do you agree with Weston's statement that installing spyware translates to "I don't trust you"? Would you feel differently (or not) if you were a parent?

5. How does Weston effectively use her audience when responding to Coben?

6. Write your own letter to the editor, indicating your reasons for supporting or rejecting Coben's argument.

> ✓ A CHECKLIST FOR EVALUATING LETTERS OF RESPONSE
>
> After reading the letters responding to an editorial or to a previous letter, go back and read each letter. Have you asked yourself the following questions?
>
> ☐ What assumption(s) does the letter-writer make? Do you share the assumption(s)?
>
> ☐ What is the writer's claim?
>
> ☐ In what ways does the writer consider the audience?
>
> ☐ What evidence, if any, does the writer offer to support the claim?
>
> ☐ Is there anything about the style of the letter—the distinctive use of language, the tone—that makes the letter especially engaging or especially annoying?

EXAMINING ASSUMPTIONS

In Chapter 3 we will discuss **assumptions** in some detail, but here we want to introduce the topic by emphasizing the importance of *identifying* and *examining* assumptions—the assumptions you will encounter in the writings of others and the assumptions you will rely on in your own essays.

With this in mind, let's return again to considering the West Virginia driver's license law. What assumptions did the legislature make in enacting this statute? We mentioned earlier one such assumption: If the law helped to keep teenagers from dropping out of school, then that was a good thing for them and for society in general. For all we know, the advocates of this legislation may have made this assumption *explicit* in the course of their argument in favor of the statute. Perhaps they left this assumption *tacit*, believing that the point was obvious and that everyone shared this assumption. The assumption may be obvious, but it was not universally shared; the many teenagers who wanted to drop out of school at sixteen and keep their drivers' licenses did not share it.

Another assumption that the advocates of this legislation may have made is this:

> The provisions of this statute are the most efficient way to keep teenagers in high school.

Defending such an assumption is no easy task because it requires identifying other possible legislative strategies and evaluating their merits against those of the proposed legislation.

✓ A CHECKLIST FOR EXAMINING ASSUMPTIONS

☐ What assumptions does the writer's argument presuppose?

☐ Are these assumptions explicit or implicit?

☐ Are these assumptions important to the author's argument or only incidental?

☐ Does the author give any evidence of being aware of the hidden assumptions in her or his argument?

☐ Would a critic be likely to share these assumptions, or are they exactly what a critic would challenge?

☐ What sort of evidence would be relevant to supporting or rejecting these assumptions?

☐ Am I willing to grant the author's assumptions? Would most readers grant them?

  ☐ If not, why not?

Consider now two of the assumptions involved in the Sultaana Freeman case. Thanks to the "clustering" exercise (pp. 4–8), these and other assumptions are already on display. Perhaps the most important and fundamental assumption Ms. Freeman made is this:

> Where private religious beliefs conflict with duly enacted laws, the former should prevail.

This assumption is widely shared in our society and is by no means unique to Muslim women seeking drivers' licenses in Florida after September 11, 2001. Freeman's opponents, however, probably assumed a very different but equally fundamental proposition:

> Private religious practices and beliefs must yield to the demands of national security.

Obviously these two assumptions were on a collision course and neither side could hope to prevail so long as the key assumptions of the other side were ignored.

Jena McGregor

Jena McGregor, a graduate of the University of Georgia, writes a daily blog for the Washington Post. *We reprint a piece that she published on May 25, 2012, when women in the military forces were still prohibited from serving in combat positions. On January 24, 2013, Defense Secretary Leon Panetta, acting on a recommendation from the Joint Chiefs of Staff, lifted the ban on women in combat roles, but opposition remains. For example, a group called Concerned Women for America immediately protested that "our military cannot continue to choose social experimentation and political correctness over combat readiness." Other topics for discussion are printed below, after the essay.*

Military Women in Combat: Why Making It Official Matters

It's been a big couple of weeks for women in the military.

Last week, female soldiers began formally moving into jobs in previously all-male battalions, a program that will later go Army-wide. The move is a result of rule changes following a February report that opened some 14,000 new positions to women in critical jobs much closer to the front lines. However, some 250,000 combat jobs still remain officially closed to them.

The same week, Rep. Loretta Sanchez (D, Calif.) and Sen. Kirsten Gillibrand (D, N.Y.) introduced legislation in both houses of Congress that would encourage the "repeal of the Ground Combat Exclusion policy" for women in the armed forces. Then this Wednesday, two female U.S. Army reservists filed a lawsuit that seeks to overturn the remaining restrictions on women in combat, saying they limit "their current and future earnings, their potential for promotion and advancement, and their future retirement benefits." (A Pentagon spokesperson told Bloomberg News that Defense Secretary Leon Panetta "is strongly committed to examining the expansion of roles for women in the U.S. military, as evidenced by the recent step of opening up thousands of more assignments to women.")

One of the arguments behind both the lawsuit and the new legislation is that the remaining restrictions hurt women's opportunities for advancement. Advocates for women in the military say that even if women like Gen. Ann Dunwoody have reached four-star general status, she and women like her without official frontline combat experience apparently haven't been considered for the military's very highest posts. "If women remain restricted to combat service and combat service support specialties, we will not see a woman as Commandant of the Marine Corps, or CENTCOM commander, or Chairman of the Joint Chiefs of Staff," writes Greg Jacob, policy director for the Service Women's Action Network. "Thus women in the military are being held back simply because they are women. Such an idea is not only completely at odds with military ethics, but is distinctly un-American."

Women have been temporarily "attached" to battalions for the last 5 decade; still, allowing women to formally serve in combat operations could help to break down the so-called brass ceiling.

Another way to break down the ceiling would be to consider talented women for top military leadership positions, whether or not they've officially held certain combat posts. Presidents have chosen less-senior officers for Joint Chiefs roles, which are technically staff jobs, wrote Laura Conley and Lawrence Korb, a former assistant defense secretary in the Reagan administration and a senior fellow at the Center for American Progress, in the *Armed Forces Journal* last year. They argue that putting a woman on the Joint Chiefs would help the military grapple with rising sexual harassment issues, bring nontraditional expertise (which women have developed because of some of their role exclusions) at a time when that's increasingly critical, and send the signal that the military is not only open to women, but puts no barriers in their way.

Yes, putting women in combat roles beyond those that have been recently formalized would require many adjustments, both logistical and psychological, for the military and for its male troops. There are plenty of women who may not be interested in these jobs, or who do not meet the physical demands required of them. And gradual change may be prudent. The recent openings are a start; Army Chief of Staff Ray Odierno's acknowledgment last week that if women are allowed into infantry, they will at some point probably go through Ranger School, is encouraging.

But at a time when experience like the infantry is reportedly crucial for getting top posts, it's easy to see how official and sizable policy changes are needed in order to create a system that lets talented women advance to the military's highest echelons. In any field where there are real or perceived limitations for women's advancement, it's that much harder to attract the best and brightest. Indeed, the Military Leadership Diversity Commission recommended last March that the services end combat exclusion policies for women, along with other "barriers and inconsistencies, to create a level playing field for all qualified service members." As the commission chairman, Retired Air Force Gen. Lester L. Lyles, told the American Forces Press Service at the time, "we know that [the exclusion] hinders women from promotion."

For the military to achieve the diverse workforce it seeks, interested and capable women should either not face exclusions, or the culture of the armed forces needs to change so that women without that particular experience can still reach the very top. Both changes may be difficult, but the latter is extraordinarily so. Ending the restrictions is the shortest route to giving the military the best pool of talent possible and the most diverse viewpoints for leading it.

TOPICS FOR CRITICAL THINKING AND WRITING

1. How would you characterize McGregor's tone (her manner)? Thoughtful? Pushy? Point to passages that support your view.

2. Explain the term *brass ceiling* (para. 5).

3. One argument *against* sending women onto an actual battlefield, as infantry or as members of a tank crew, is that if they are captured they might be gang-raped. In your view, how significant is this as an argument?

4. Here is a second argument that has been made against sending women into direct combat: Speaking generally, women do not have the upper-body strength that men have, and a female soldier (again, we are speaking generally, not about a particular individual) would thus be less able to pull a wounded companion out of a burning tank or off a battlefield. To put the matter strongly: Male soldiers might feel that they could not count on their female comrades in a time of need. What is your reply?

5. In her final paragraph, McGregor suggests that if the armed forces changed their policy and did not in effect require battlefield experience for the very highest jobs, the military thus would achieve diversity at the top and women would have an opportunity for top pay. What are your thoughts? For instance, is the idea that the top officers should have experienced hand-to-hand combat out of date, romantic, hopelessly *macho*, or irrelevant to modern warfare? Explain.

6. What do you make of the following argument? If women in the military should be treated exactly the way men are, why, if there is a national draft, should the draft be limited to males? If a national emergency requires conscription, why shouldn't women be drafted, just like men?

Five Exercises in Critical Thinking

As you are drafting your essays for one or more of the assignments, consider typing your notes in a Google document and writing your essay in a blog so that you can easily share your thoughts on your topic. As always, submit and complete assignments the way that your teacher directs. However, free online venues can serve as good places for you to maintain copies of your notes and essays for later consultation.

1. Think further about the 1989 West Virginia law that prohibits high school dropouts younger than eighteen from holding a driver's license. Jot down pros and cons, and then write a balanced dialogue between two imagined speakers who hold opposing views on the merits of the law. You'll doubtless have to revise your dialogue several times, and in revising your drafts you will find that further ideas come to you. Present *both* sides as strongly as possible. (You may want to give the two speakers distinct characters; for instance, one may be a student who has dropped out and the other a concerned teacher, or one a parent—who perhaps argues that he or she needs the youngster to work full-time driving a delivery truck—and one a legislator. But do not write as if the speakers must present the arguments they might be expected to hold. A student might argue *for* the law, and a teacher *against* it.)

2. Take one of the following topics and write down all the pro and con arguments you can think of in, say, ten minutes. Then, at least an hour

or two later, return to your notes and see whether you can add to them. Finally, as in Exercise 1, write a balanced dialogue, presenting each idea as strongly as possible. (If none of these topics interests you, talk with your instructor about the possibility of choosing a topic of your own.) Suggested topics:

   a. Colleges should not award athletic scholarships.
   b. Bicyclists and motorcyclists should be required by law to wear helmets.
   c. High school teachers should have the right to search students for drugs on school grounds.
   d. Smoking should be prohibited in all parts of all college buildings.
   e. College administrators should take no punitive action against students who use racist language or language that offends any minority.
   f. Students should have the right to drop out of school at any age.
   g. In rape trials, the names of the alleged victims should not be released to the public.
   h. The United States ought to require a national identity card.

3. On the evening of July 31, 2001, after court employees had left the Alabama Judicial Building in Montgomery, Chief Justice Roy S. Moore of the Alabama Supreme Court and his supporters installed in the lobby of the courthouse a four-foot-high, 5,200-pound granite block bearing the text of the Ten Commandments. Moore had not discussed his plan with other justices. Civil liberties groups complained that the monument was an unconstitutional attempt to endorse a specific religion (the First Amendment to the U.S. Constitution says, "Congress shall make no law respecting an establishment of religion"), and in 2002 a federal judge ordered Moore to remove the monument. He refused, saying that the monument is a symbol of the roots of American law. He also said, "To do my duty, I must obey God." His supporters have offered several arguments on his behalf, notably that (a) the Founding Fathers often spoke of God; (b) every courtroom has a Bible to swear in witnesses and jurors; (c) the U.S. Supreme Court has a frieze of lawgivers, including Moses with the Ten Commandments, Hammurabi, Confucius, and Muhammad. In August 2003, Moore was suspended from his position on the court, and the monument was removed from view. Your views?

4. Since 1937, when San Francisco's Golden Gate Bridge opened, some 1,200 people have leaped from it to their deaths. The board of the Golden Gate Bridge, Highway and Transportation District periodically contemplates plans to make it suicide-proof. It discusses the kinds of devices proposed (railings, nets, or a combination), the cost (an estimated $15.25 million, which could be used for other civic purposes), the aesthetic factor (the devices may spoil the appearance of this renowned art deco work), and the engineering uncertainties (some engineers express reservations about the aerodynamic drag the barrier may create). And now consider these additional arguments against altering the bridge: (a) the government has no business paternalistically interfering with the free will of persons who wish to commit suicide; (b) if the Golden Gate Bridge is made suicide-proof, persons who wish to commit suicide will easily find some other site, such as the nearby Bay Bridge; (c) only 3 percent

of the persons who commit suicide in the Bay Area do so by leaping from the bridge.

The assignment: You are on the board of the Golden Gate Bridge. Suicides on the bridge are now averaging two a month, and a proposal to make the bridge suicide-proof has come up. Taking account of the arguments just mentioned, and any others—pro and con—that you can think of, what is your well-reasoned 500-word response?

5. In September 2004, the year of a presidential election, the Bush-Cheney campaign approached Allegheny College (in northwest Pennsylvania), asking to rent for October 13 the college's gymnasium, the largest en-closed space in the area. Because the electoral votes of Pennsylvania were uncertain, Vice President Cheney's appearance at Allegheny was likely to get national attention, at least briefly. The college did *not* have in place a policy against renting space to a political organization, so re-fusal to rent the gymnasium might seem like discrimination against the Republican Party. Further, the college faculty and administrators involved in making the decision concluded that the event would strengthen town–gown relationships and energize the students to participate in the political process. The gymnasium was therefore rented to the Bush-Cheney campaign, so that the vice president could appear.

The event was a sort of town-hall-style presentation, but tickets were limited: The campaign personnel distributed most of the six hun-dred tickets to local Republican activists; forty tickets were given to a group called College Republicans, who could distribute the tickets as they saw fit. Obviously the idea was to keep out hecklers and demon-strators, an entirely reasonable plan from the Republican point of view. Why should Republicans rent a hall and stage an event that might get national coverage if the opposing party could use it to get TV attention?

The issue: Should a college—supposedly a site where inquiry is open, where ideas are exchanged freely in robust debate—allow its facilities to be used by those who would stifle debate? Professor Dan-iel M. Shea, who initially favored the decision to rent the gymnasium, ultimately concluded that he was mistaken. In an essay in the *Chronicle of Higher Education* (August 4, 2006), Shea discusses the affair, and he suggests that colleges and universities ought to band together to "form an open-event alliance." Candidates might have at their disposal half of the available seats, but the other half would be for the college to distrib-ute through some sort of open procedure, perhaps a lottery.

The assignment: Assume that a political party wanted to rent your institution's gymnasium or a large lecture hall. What would your posi-tion be? Why? In a letter of about 500 words addressed to the college paper, set forth your views.

 For additional arguments online, visit the e-Pages at **bedfordstmartins.com/barnetbedau**.

2

Critical Reading: Getting Started

Some books are to be tasted, others to be swallowed, and some few to be chewed and digested.

—FRANCIS BACON

ACTIVE READING

In the passage that we quote at the top of this page, Bacon makes at least two good points. One is that books are of varying worth; the second is that a taste of some books may be enough.

But even a book (or an essay) that you will chew and digest is one that you first may want to taste. How can you get a taste—that is, how can you get some sense of a piece of writing *before* you sit down to read it carefully?

Previewing

Even before you read a work, you may have some ideas about it, perhaps because you already know something about the **author.** You know, for example, that a work by Martin Luther King Jr. will probably deal with civil rights. You know, too, that it will be serious and eloquent. On the other hand, if you pick up an essay by Woody Allen, you will probably expect it to be amusing. It may be serious—Allen has written earnestly about many topics, especially those concerned with the media—but it's your hunch that the essay will be at least somewhat entertaining and probably will not be terribly difficult to understand. In short, a reader who has some knowledge of the author probably has some idea of what the writing will be like, and so the reader reads it in a certain mood. Admittedly, most of the authors represented in this book are not widely known, but we give biographical notes that may provide you with some sense of what to expect.

The **place of publication** may also tell you something about the essay. For instance, the *National Review* is a conservative journal. If you notice that an essay on affirmative action was published in the *National Review,* you are probably safe in tentatively assuming that the essay will not endorse affirmative action. On the other hand, *Ms. Magazine* is a liberal publication, and an essay on affirmative action published in *Ms.* will probably be an endorsement. You often can learn a good deal about a journal or magazine simply by flipping through it and looking at the kinds of advertisements in it.

The **title** of an essay, too, may give you an idea of what to expect. Of course, a title may announce only the subject and not the author's thesis or point of view ("On Gun Control," "Should Drugs Be Legal?"), but fairly often it will indicate the thesis too, as in "Give Children the Vote" and "Gay Marriages: Make Them Legal." Knowing more or less what to expect, you can probably take in some of the major points even on a quick reading.

Skimming: Finding the Thesis

Although most of the material in this book is too closely argued to be fully understood by merely skimming, still, skimming can tell you a good deal. Read the first paragraph of an essay carefully because it may announce the author's **thesis** (chief point, major claim), and it may give you some sense of how the argument for that thesis will be conducted. (What we call the *thesis* can also be called the *main idea*, the *point*, or even the *argument*, but in this book we use *argument* to refer not only to the thesis statement but also to the entire development of the thesis in the essay.) Run your eye over the rest, looking for key expressions that indicate the author's conclusions, such as "It follows, then, that . . ." Passages of this sort often occur as the first or last sentence in a paragraph. And of course, pay attention to any headings within the text. Finally, pay special attention to the last paragraph because it probably will offer a summary and a brief restatement of the writer's thesis.

Having skimmed the work, you probably know the author's thesis, and you may detect the author's methods—for instance, whether the author supports the thesis chiefly by personal experience, by statistics, or by ridiculing the opposition. You also have a clear idea of the length and some idea of the difficulty of the piece. You know, then, whether you can read it carefully now before dinner or whether you had better put off a careful reading until you have more time.

Reading with a Careful Eye: Underlining, Highlighting, Annotating

Once you have a general idea of the work—not only an idea of its topic and thesis but also a sense of the way in which the thesis is argued—you can then go back and start reading it carefully.

As you read, **underline** or **highlight** key passages, and make **annotations** in the margins. Because you are reading actively, or interacting with the text, you will not simply let your eye rove across the page.

- You will highlight what seem to be the chief points, so that later when you review the essay you can easily locate the main passages.

- But don't overdo a good thing. If you find yourself highlighting most of a page, you are probably not thinking carefully enough about what the key points are.

- Similarly, your marginal annotations should be brief and selective. They will probably consist of hints or clues, things like "really?" "doesn't follow," "good," "compare with Jones," and "check this."

- In short, in a paragraph you might highlight a key definition, and in the margin you might write "good," or "on the other hand," or "?" if you think the definition is fuzzy or wrong.

- With many electronic formats you can use tools to highlight or annotate. Also consider copying and pasting passages you would normally highlight in a Google document. Include a link to the piece and create an RSS feed to the journal's Web site. Having your notes in an electronic format makes it easy to access and use them later.

You are interacting with the text and laying the groundwork for eventually writing your own essay on what you have read.

What you annotate will depend largely on your **purpose.** If you are reading an essay in order to see the ways in which the writer organizes an argument, you will annotate one sort of thing. If you are reading in order to challenge the thesis, you will annotate other things. Here is a passage from an essay entitled "On Racist Speech," with a student's rather skeptical, even aggressive annotations. But notice that at least one of the annotations—"Definition of 'fighting words'"—apparently was made chiefly in order to remind the reader of where an important term appears in the essay. The essay, printed in full on page 64, is by Charles R. Lawrence III, a professor of law at Georgetown University. It originally appeared in the *Chronicle of Higher Education* (October 25, 1989), a publication read chiefly by college and university faculty members and administrators.

Example of such a policy?

University officials who have formulated <u>policies</u> to respond to incidents of racial harassment have been characterized in the press as "thought police," but such policies generally do nothing more than **?** impose (sanctions) against intentional face-to-face insults. When *What about* racist speech takes the form of <u>face-to-face insults</u>, catcalls, or other *sexist speech?* assaultive speech aimed at <u>an individual or small group of persons</u>, *Example?* it falls directly within the "fighting words" exception to First *Definition of* Amendment protection. The Supreme Court has held that <u>words</u> *"fighting* <u>which "by their very utterance inflict</u> injury or tend to <u>incite</u> *words"* an immediate breach of the peace" are not protected by the First Amendment.

If the purpose of the First Amendment is to foster the greatest amount of speech, racial insults disserve that purpose. Assaultive racist speech functions as a preemptive strike. The <u>invective is</u> *Really? Probably depends* <u>experienced as a blow, not as a proffered idea</u>, and once the blow *on the individual.*

is struck, it is unlikely that a dialogue will follow. Racial insults are particularly undeserving of First Amendment protection because the perpetrator's intention is not to discover truth or initiate dialogue but to injure the victim. In most situations, members of minority groups realize that they are likely to lose if they respond to epithets by fighting and are forced to remain silent and submissive.

Why must speech always seek "to discover truth"?

How does he know?

"This; Therefore, That"

To arrive at a coherent thought or a coherent series of thoughts that will lead to a reasonable conclusion, a writer has to go through a good deal of preliminary effort. On page 14 we talked about patterns of thought that stimulate the generation of specific ideas. The path to sound conclusions involves similar thought patterns that carry forward the arguments presented in the essay:

- While these arguments are convincing, they fail to consider . . .
- While these arguments are convincing, they must also consider . . .
- These arguments, rather than being convincing, instead prove . . .
- While these authors agree, in my opinion . . .
- Although it is often true that . . .

And consider also

- What sort of audience would agree with such an argument?
- What sort of audience would be opposed?
- What are the differences in values between these two kinds of audiences?

All of these patterns can serve as heuristics or prompts—that is, they can stimulate the creation of ideas.

And if the writer is to convince the reader that the conclusion is sound, the reasoning that led to the conclusion must be set forth in detail, with a good deal of "This; therefore, that"; "If this, then that"; and "It might be objected at this point that . . ." The arguments in this book require more comment than President Calvin Coolidge provided when his wife, who hadn't been able to go to church on a Sunday, asked him what the preacher's sermon was about. "Sin," he said. His wife persisted: "What did the preacher say about it?" Coolidge's response: "He was against it."

But, again, when we say that most of the arguments in this book are presented at length and require careful reading, we do not mean that they are obscure; we mean, rather, that the reader has to take the sentences thoughtfully, one by one. And speaking of one by one, we are reminded of an episode in Lewis Carroll's *Through the Looking-Glass:*

> "Can you do Addition?" the White Queen asked. "What's one and one and one and one and one and one and one and one and one and one?"
>
> "I don't know," said Alice. "I lost count."
>
> "She can't do Addition," the Red Queen said.

It's easy enough to add one and one and one and so on, and Alice can, of course, do addition, but not at the pace that the White Queen sets. Fortunately, you can set your own pace in reading the cumulative thinking set forth in the essays we reprint. Skimming won't work, but slow reading—and thinking about what you are reading—will.

When you first pick up an essay, you may indeed want to skim it, for some of the reasons mentioned on page 35, but sooner or later you have to settle down to read it and to think about it. The effort will be worthwhile. John Locke, the seventeenth-century English philosopher, said,

> *Reading* furnishes the mind with materials of knowledge; it is *thinking* [that] makes what we read ours. We are of the ruminating kind, and it is not enough to cram ourselves with a great load of collections; unless we chew them over again they will not give us strength and nourishment.

First, Second, and Third Thoughts

Suppose you are reading an argument about pornographic pictures. For the present purpose, it doesn't matter whether the argument favors or opposes censorship. As you read the argument, ask yourself whether *pornography* has been adequately defined. Has the writer taken the trouble to make sure that the reader and the writer are thinking about the same thing? If not, the very topic under discussion has not been adequately fixed; and therefore further debate over the issue may well be so unclear as to be futile. How, then, ought a topic such as this be defined for effective critical thinking?

It goes without saying that pornography can't be defined simply as pictures of nude figures or even of nude figures copulating, for such a definition would include not only photographs taken for medical, sociological, and scientific purposes but also some of the world's great art. Nobody seriously thinks that such images should be called pornography.

Is it enough, then, to say that pornography "stirs lustful thoughts" or "appeals to prurient interests"? No, because pictures of shoes probably stir lustful thoughts in shoe fetishists, and pictures of children in ads for underwear probably stir lustful thoughts in pedophiles. Perhaps, then, the definition must be amended to "material that stirs lustful thoughts in the average person." But will this restatement do? First, it may be hard to agree on the characteristics of "the average person." In other matters, the law often does assume that there is such a creature as "the reasonable person," and most people would agree that in a given situation there might be a reasonable response—for almost everyone. But we cannot be so sure that the same is true about the emotional responses of this "average person." In any case, far from stimulating sexual impulses, sadomasochistic pictures of booted men wielding whips on naked women probably turn off "the average person," yet this is the sort of material that most people would agree is pornographic.

Something must be wrong, then, with the definition that pornography is material that "stirs lustful thoughts in the average person." We began with a definition that was too broad ("pictures of nude figures"), but now we have a definition that is too narrow. We must go back to the drawing board. This is not nitpicking. The label "average person" was found to be inadequate in a pornography case argued before the Supreme Court; because the materials in question were aimed at a homosexual audience, it was agreed that the average person would not find them sexually stimulating.

One difficulty has been that pornography is often defined according to its effect on the viewer ("genital commotion," Father Harold Gardiner, S.J., called it, in *Catholic Viewpoint on Censorship*), but different people, we know, may respond differently. In the first half of the twentieth century, in an effort to distinguish between pornography and art—after all, most people don't want to regard Botticelli's *Venus* or Michelangelo's *David* as "dirty"—it was commonly said that a true work of art does not stimulate in the spectator ideas or desires that the real object might stimulate. But in 1956, Kenneth Clark, probably the most influential English-speaking art critic of the twentieth century, changed all that; in a book called *The Nude* he announced that "no nude, however abstract, should fail to arouse in the spectator some vestige of erotic feeling."

SUMMARIZING AND PARAPHRASING

Perhaps the best approach to a fairly difficult essay is, after first reading, to reread it and simultaneously to take notes on a sheet of paper, perhaps summarizing each paragraph in a sentence or two. Writing a summary will help you to

- understand the contents and
- see the strengths and weaknesses of the piece.

Don't confuse a summary with a paraphrase. A paraphrase is a word-by-word or phrase-by-phrase rewording of a text, a sort of translation of the author's language into your own. A paraphrase is therefore as long as the original or even longer; a summary is much shorter. A book may be summarized in a page, or even in a paragraph or a sentence. Obviously the summary will leave out all detail, but—if the summary is a true summary—it accurately states the gist, the essential thesis or claim or point of the original.

Why would anyone ever summarize, and why would anyone ever paraphrase? Because, as we have already said, these two activities—in different ways—help readers follow the original author's ideas. But, again, summarizing and paraphrasing are not the same.

- **When you summarize,** you are standing back, saying very briefly what the whole adds up to; you are seeing the forest, not the individual trees.

- **When you paraphrase,** you are inching through the forest, scrutinizing each tree—that is, finding a synonym for almost every word in the original, in an effort to make sure that you know exactly what you are dealing with. (*Caution:* Do not incorporate a summary or a paraphrase into your own essay without acknowledging your source and stating that you are summarizing or paraphrasing.)

Let's examine the distinction between summary and paraphrase in connection with the first two paragraphs of Paul Goodman's essay, "A Proposal to Abolish Grading," which is excerpted from Goodman's book, *Compulsory Miseducation and the Community of Scholars* (1966). The two paragraphs run thus:

> Let half a dozen of the prestigious universities—Chicago, Stanford, the Ivy League—abolish grading, and use testing only and entirely for pedagogic purposes as teachers see fit.
>   Anyone who knows the frantic temper of the present schools will understand the transvaluation of values that would be effected by this modest innovation. For most of the students, the competitive grade has come to be the essence. The naive teacher points to the beauty of the subject and the ingenuity of the research; the shrewd student asks if he is responsible for that on the final exam.

A **summary** of these two paragraphs might run thus:

> If some top universities used tests only to help students to learn, students would stop worrying about grades and might share the teacher's interest in the beauty of the subject.

We hope we have accurately summarized Goodman's point, though we know we have lost his flavor, his style—for instance, the wry tone in his pointed contrast between "the naive teacher" and "the shrewd student."

Now for a **paraphrase.** Suppose you are not quite sure what Goodman is getting at, maybe because you are uncertain about the meanings of some words (perhaps *pedagogic* and *transvaluation*?), or maybe just because the whole passage is making such a startling point that you want to make sure that you have understood it. In such a case, you may want to move slowly through the sentences, translating them (so to speak) into your own English. For instance, you might turn Goodman's "pedagogic purposes" into "goals in teaching" or "attempts to help students to learn" or something else. Here is a paraphrase—not a summary but an extensive rewording—of Goodman's paragraphs:

Suppose some of the top universities—such as Chicago, Stanford, Harvard, and Yale, and whatever other schools are in the Ivy League—stopped using grades and used tests only in order to help students to learn.

Everyone who is aware of the hysterical mood in schools today will understand the enormous change in views of what is good and bad that would come about by this small change. At present, instructors, unworldly folk, talk about how beautiful their subjects are, but smart students know that grades are what count, so they listen to instructors only if they know that the material the instructor is talking about will be on the exam.

In short, you may want to paraphrase an important text that your imagined reader may find obscure because it is written in specialized, technical language, for instance, the language of psychiatry or of sociology. You want the reader to see the passage itself—you don't want to give just the gist, just a summary—but you know that the full passage will puzzle the reader, so you offer help, giving a paraphrase before going on to make your own point about the author's point.

A second good reason to offer a paraphrase is if there is substantial disagreement about what the text says. The Second Amendment to the U.S. Constitution is a good example of this sort of text:

> A well regulated Militia being necessary to the security of a free State, the right of the people to keep and bear Arms shall not be infringed.

Exactly what, one might ask, is a "Militia"? And what does it mean for a militia to be "well regulated"? And does "the people" mean each individual, or does it mean—something very different—the citizenry as some sort of unified group? After all, elsewhere in the document, when the Constitution speaks of individuals, it speaks of a "man" or a "person," not "the people." To speak of "the people" is to use a term (some argue) that sounds like a reference to a unified group—perhaps the citizens of each of the thirteen states?—rather than a reference to individuals. On the other hand, if Congress did mean a unified group rather than individuals, why didn't it say "Congress shall not prohibit the states from organizing militias"?

In fact, thousands of pages have been written about this sentence, and if you are going to talk about it, you certainly have to let your reader know exactly what you make out of each word. In short, you almost surely will paraphrase it, going word by word, giving your reader your sense of what each word or phrase says. Here is one paraphrase:

> Because an independent society needs the protection of an armed force if it is to remain free, the government may not limit the right of the individuals (who may some day form the militia needed to keep the society free) to possess weapons.

In this interpretation, the Constitution grants individuals the right to possess weapons, and that is that. Other students of the Constitution, however, offer very different paraphrases, usually along these lines:

> Because each state that is now part of the United States may need to protect its freedom [from the new national government], the national government may not infringe on the right of each state to form its own disciplined militia.

This second paraphrase says that the federal government may not prevent each state from having a militia; it says nothing about every individual person having a right to possess weapons. The first of these two paraphrases, or something like it, is one that might be offered by the National Rifle Association or any other group that interprets the Constitution as guaranteeing individuals the right to own guns. The second paraphrase, or something like it, might be offered by groups that seek to limit the ownership of guns.

Why paraphrase? Here are two reasons (perhaps the *only* two reasons) why you might paraphrase a passage:

- To help yourself to understand it. In this case, the paraphrase does not appear in your essay.

- To help your reader to understand a passage that is especially important but that for one reason or another is not immediately clear. In this case, you paraphrase the passage to let the reader know exactly what it means. This paraphrase, of course, does appear in your essay.

PARAPHRASE, PATCHWRITING, AND PLAGIARISM

We have indicated that only on rare occasions will you have a reason to introduce a paraphrase into your essays, but in your preliminary work, when you take notes, you may find yourself sometimes copying word for word, sometime paraphrasing (usually in an effort to get the author's idea clearly into your mind), sometimes summarizing, and—here we get to patchwriting—sometimes producing a medley of borrowed words and original words that, if submitted in the final essay, opens you to the charge of **plagiarism** *even if you have rearranged the phrases and clauses, and even if you have cited your source.*

Here is an example. First, we give the source, a paragraph from Jena McGregor's essay on whether women serving in the armed forces should be allowed to participate directly in combat. (The entire essay is printed on pages 28–30.)

> Last week, female soldiers began formally moving into jobs in previously all-male battalions, a program that later will go Army-wide. The move

is a result of rule changes following a February report that opened some 14,000 new positions to women in critical jobs much closer to the front lines. However, some 250,000 jobs still remain officially closed to them.

Now for a student's patchwriting version:

> Women in the army recently began to formally move into jobs in battalions that previously were all-male. This program later will go throughout the Army. According to author Jena McGregor, the move comes from changes in the rules following a February report that opened about 14,000 new jobs to women in critical jobs that are much closer to the front lines. About 250,000 jobs, however — as McGregor points out — continue to be officially closed to women.

As you can see, the writer has followed the source, pretty much phrase by phrase — certainly sentence by sentence — making small verbal changes, such as substituting

> Women in the army recently

for McGregor's

> Last week, female soldiers

and substituting

> the move comes from changes in the rules

for McGregor's

> The move is a result of rule changes. . . .

What the student should have done is either (a) *quote the passage exactly,* setting it off to indicate that it is a quotation and indicating the source, or (b) *summarize it briefly* and give credit to the source — maybe in a sentence such as

> Jena McGregor points out that although a recent change in army rules has resulted in new jobs being opened for women in the military, some 250,000 jobs "continue to be officially closed."

We think you will agree that patchwriting — as opposed to this example of a sentence frankly summarizing a source — is *not* essentially the student's writing but, rather, is the source material thinly disguised: In a given paragraph of patchwriting, usually some of the words are copied from the source, and all or almost all of the rest consists of synonyms substituted for the words of the source, sometimes with minor rearrangement of phrases and clauses. That is, the sequence of ideas and their arrangement, as well as most of the language, are entirely or almost entirely derived from the source, even if some of the words are different. **The fact that you may cite a source is not enough to protect you from the charge of plagiarism.** The citation of a source tells a reader that some fact or some idea—or some groups of words enclosed within quotation marks or set off by indentation—is derived from the named source; it does *not* tell the reader that almost everything in the paragraph is, in effect, the writing of someone else with a few words changed, a few words added, and a few phrases moved around.

The best way to prevent yourself from introducing patchwriting into your final essay is to make certain that when you take notes you indicate, *in the notes themselves,* what sorts of notes they are. For example:

- When you are quoting word for word, put the passage within quotation marks, and cite the page number(s) of the source.
- When you are paraphrasing—perhaps in an effort to make certain that you understand the writer's idea, or perhaps because the original uses highly technical language and you know that your reader will not understand the idea unless you put it into somewhat simpler nontechnical language—use some sign, perhaps *(par),* to remind yourself later that this passage is a paraphrase and thus is not really *your* writing.
- When you are summarizing, again use some key, such as *(sum),* and cite the page(s) of the source.

Make certain that in your notes you indicate the degree of indebtedness to your source, and, again, do *not* think that in a paraphrase if you name a source you are not plagiarizing. The reader assumes the name indicates the source of a fact or an idea—not that it indicates that the paragraph is essentially a rewriting of the original with perhaps an occasional original phrase inserted here and there.

If you have taken notes properly, with indications of the sort we have mentioned, when you write your paper you can say things like

> *X*'s first reason is simple. He says, " . . ." (and here you quote *X*'s words, putting them within quotation marks).

or

> *X*'s point can be summarized thus . . . . (and here too you will cite the page).

or

> *X*, writing for lawyers, not surprisingly uses some technical language, but we can paraphrase her conclusion thus: . . . . (here you give the citation).

In short,

- Avoid patchwriting; it is *not* acceptable.
- Enclose direct quotations within quotation marks, or, if the quotations are long, set them off.
- If you offer a paraphrase, tell your readers that you are paraphrasing and tell them *why* you are paraphrasing rather than quoting directly or summarizing.

For additional information about plagiarism, see page 283.

✓ A CHECKLIST FOR A PARAPHRASE

☐ Do I have a good reason offering a paraphrase rather than a summary?

☐ Is the paraphrase entirely in my own words—a sort of word-by-word translation—rather than a patchwork of the source's words and my own words with some of my own rearrangement of phrases and clauses?

☐ Do I not only cite the source but also explicitly say that the entire passage is a paraphrase?

A RULE FOR WRITERS: Your essay is *likely to include brief summaries* of points of view that you are agreeing or disagreeing with, but it will *rarely include a paraphrase* unless the original is obscure and you think you need to present a passage at length but in words that are clearer than those of the original. If you do paraphrase, explicitly identify the material as a paraphrase. Never submit patchwriting.

Last Words (Almost) about Summarizing

Summarizing each paragraph or each group of closely related paragraphs will help you to follow the thread of the discourse and, when you are finished, will provide you with a useful map of the essay. Then, when you reread the essay yet again, you may want to underline passages that you now understand are the author's key ideas—for instance, definitions, generalizations, summaries—and you may want to jot notes in the margins, questioning the logic, expressing your uncertainty, or calling attention to other writers who see the matter differently. Here is a paragraph from a 1973 decision of the U.S. Supreme Court, written by Chief Justice Warren Burger, setting forth reasons that the government may censor obscene material. We follow it with a sample summary.

If we accept the unprovable assumption that a complete education requires the reading of certain books, and the well-nigh universal belief that good books, plays, and art lift the spirit, improve the mind, enrich the human personality, and develop character, can we then say that a state legislature may not act on the corollary assumption that commerce in obscene books, or public exhibitions focused on obscene conduct, have a tendency to exert a corrupting and debasing impact leading to antisocial behavior? The sum of experience, including that of the past two decades, affords an ample basis for legislatures to conclude that a sensitive, key relationship of human existence, central to family life, community welfare, and the development of human personality, can be debased and distorted by crass commercial exploitation of sex. Nothing in the Constitution prohibits a State from reaching such a conclusion and acting on it legislatively simply because there is no conclusive empirical data.

Now for a student's summary. Notice that the summary does not include the reader's evaluation or any other sort of comment on the original; it is simply an attempt to condense the original. Notice too that, because its purpose is merely to assist the reader to grasp the ideas of the original by focusing on them, it is written in a sort of shorthand (not every sentence is a complete sentence), though, of course, if this summary were being presented in an essay, it would have to be grammatical.

> Unprovable but acceptable assumption that good books etc. shape character, so that legislature can assume obscene works debase character. Experience lets one conclude that exploitation of sex debases the individual, family, and community. Though "there is no conclusive empirical data" for this view, the Constitution lets states act on it legislatively.

Notice that

- A few words (in the last sentence of the summary) are quoted exactly as in the original. They are enclosed within quotation marks.
- For the most part, the original material is drastically reduced. The first sentence of the original, some eighty words, is reduced in the summary to nineteen words.

Of course, the summary loses much of the detail and flavor of the original: "Good books etc." is not the same as "good books, plays, and art"; and "shape character" is not the same as "lift the spirit, improve the mind, enrich the human personality, and develop character." But the statement in the summary will do as a rough approximation, useful for a quick review. More important, the act of writing a summary forces the reader to go slowly and to think about each sentence of the original. Such thinking may help the reader–writer to see the complexity—or the hollowness—of the original.

The sample summary in the preceding paragraph was just that, a summary; but when writing your own summaries, you will often find it useful to inject your own thoughts ("seems far-fetched," "strong point," "I don't get it"), enclosing them within square brackets or in some other way to keep these responses distinct from your summary of the writer's argument.

Review: If your instructor asks you to hand in a summary,

- It should not contain ideas other than those found in the original piece.
- You can rearrange these, add transitions as needed, and so forth, but the summary should give the reader nothing but a sense of the original piece.
- If the summary includes any of the original wording, these words should be enclosed within quotation marks.
- In your notes, keep a clear distinction between *your* writing and the writing of your *source.* For the most part you will summarize, but if you paraphrase, indicate that the words are a paraphrase, and if you quote directly, indicate that you are quoting.

We don't want to nag you, but we do want to emphasize the need to read with a close eye, taking notes as you go along using a pen or pencil or highlighter or a computer program, blog, or Google document. If you read slowly and take notes, you will find that what you read will give you the "strength and nourishment" that John Locke spoke of.

> **A RULE FOR WRITERS:** Remember that when you write a summary, you are putting yourself into the author's shoes.

Having insisted that the essays in this book need to be read slowly because the writers build one reason on another, we will now seem to contradict ourselves by presenting an essay that can almost be skimmed. Susan Jacoby's essay originally appeared in the *New York Times*, a thoroughly respectable newspaper but not one that requires its readers to linger over every sentence. Still, compared with most of the news accounts, Jacoby's essay requires close reading. When you read the essay, you will notice that it zigs and zags, not because Jacoby is careless or wants to befuddle her readers but because she wants to build a strong case to support her point of view and must therefore look at some widely held views that she does *not* accept; she must set these forth and then give her reasons for rejecting them.

Susan Jacoby

Susan Jacoby (b. 1946), a journalist since the age of seventeen, is well known for her feminist writings. "A First Amendment Junkie" (our title) appeared in the Hers column in the New York Times *in 1978.*

A First Amendment Junkie

It is no news that many women are defecting from the ranks of civil libertarians on the issue of obscenity. The conviction of Larry Flynt, publisher of *Hustler* magazine—before his metamorphosis into a born-again Christian—was greeted with unabashed feminist approval. Harry Reems, the unknown actor who was convicted by a Memphis jury for conspiring to distribute the movie *Deep Throat,* has carried on his legal battles with almost no support from women who ordinarily regard themselves as supporters of the First Amendment. Feminist writers and scholars have even discussed the possibility of making common cause against pornography with adversaries of the women's movement—including opponents of the equal rights amendment and "right-to-life" forces.

All of this is deeply disturbing to a woman writer who believes, as I always have and still do, in an absolute interpretation of the First Amendment. Nothing in Larry Flynt's garbage convinces me that the late Justice Hugo L. Black was wrong in his opinion that "the Federal Government is without any power whatsoever under the Constitution to put any type of burden on free speech and expression of ideas of any kind (as distinguished from conduct)." Many women I like and respect tell me I am wrong; I cannot remember having become involved in so many heated discussions of a public issue since the end of the Vietnam War. A feminist writer described my views as those of a "First Amendment junkie."

Many feminist arguments for controls on pornography carry the implicit conviction that porn books, magazines, and movies pose a greater threat to women than similarly repulsive exercises of free speech pose to other offended groups. This conviction has, of course, been shared by everyone—regardless of race, creed, or sex—who has ever argued in favor of abridging the First Amendment. It is the argument used by some Jews who have withdrawn their support from the American Civil Liberties Union because it has defended the right of American Nazis to march through a community inhabited by survivors of Hitler's concentration camps.

If feminists want to argue that the protection of the Constitution should not be extended to *any* particularly odious or threatening form of speech, they have a reasonable argument (although I don't agree with it). But it is ridiculous to suggest that the porn shops on 42nd Street are more disgusting to women than a march of neo-Nazis is to survivors of the extermination camps.

The arguments over pornography also blur the vital distinction be- 5 tween expression of ideas and conduct. When I say I believe unreservedly in the First Amendment, someone always comes back at me with the issue of "kiddie porn." But kiddie porn is not a First Amendment issue. It is an issue of the abuse of power—the power adults have over children—and not of obscenity. Parents and promoters have no more right to use their children to make porn movies than they do to send them to work in coal mines. The responsible adults should be prosecuted, just as adults who use children for back-breaking farm labor should be prosecuted.

Susan Brownmiller, in *Against Our Will: Men, Women, and Rape,* has described pornography as "the undiluted essence of antifemale propaganda." I think this is a fair description of some types of pornography, especially of the brutish subspecies that equates sex with death and portrays women primarily as objects of violence.

The equation of sex and violence, personified by some glossy rock record album covers as well as by *Hustler,* has fed the illusion that censorship of pornography can be conducted on a more rational basis than other types of censorship. Are all pictures of naked women obscene? Clearly not, says a friend. A Renoir nude is art, she says, and *Hustler* is trash. "Any reasonable person" knows that.

But what about something between art and trash—something, say, along the lines of *Playboy* or *Penthouse* magazines? I asked five women for their reactions to one picture in *Penthouse* and got responses that ranged from "lovely" and "sensuous" to "revolting" and "demeaning." Feminists, like everyone else, seldom have rational reasons for their preferences in erotica. Like members of juries, they tend to disagree when confronted with something that falls short of 100 percent vulgarity.

In any case, feminists will not be the arbiters of good taste if it becomes easier to harass, prosecute, and convict people on obscenity charges. Most of the people who want to censor girlie magazines are equally opposed to open discussion of issues that are of vital concern to women: rape, abortion, menstruation, contraception, lesbianism—in fact, the entire range of sexual experience from a women's viewpoint.

Feminist writers and editors and filmmakers have limited financial resources: Confronted by a determined prosecutor, Hugh Hefner[1] will fare better than Susan Brownmiller. Would the Memphis jurors who convicted Harry Reems for his role in *Deep Throat* be inclined to take a more positive view of paintings of the female genitalia done by sensitive feminist artists? *Ms.* magazine has printed color reproductions of some of those art works; *Ms.* is already banned from a number of high school libraries because someone considers it threatening and/or obscene.   10

Feminists who want to censor what they regard as harmful pornography have essentially the same motivation as other would-be censors: They want to use the power of the state to accomplish what they have been unable to achieve in the marketplace of ideas and images. The impulse to censor places no faith in the possibilities of democratic persuasion.

It isn't easy to persuade certain men that they have better uses for $1.95 each month than to spend it on a copy of *Hustler*? Well, then, give the men no choice in the matter.

---

[1]**Hugh Hefner** Founder and longtime publisher of *Playboy* magazine. [Editors' note.]

I believe there is also a connection between the impulse toward censorship on the part of people who used to consider themselves civil libertarians and a more general desire to shift responsibility from individuals to institutions. When I saw the movie *Looking for Mr. Goodbar,* I was stunned by its series of visual images equating sex and violence, coupled with what seems to me the mindless message (a distortion of the fine Judith Rossner novel) that casual sex equals death. When I came out of the movie, I was even more shocked to see parents standing in line with children between the ages of ten and fourteen.

I simply don't know why a parent would take a child to see such a movie, any more than I understand why people feel they can't turn off a television set their child is watching. Whenever I say that, my friends tell me I don't know how it is because I don't have children. True, but I do have parents. When I was a child, they did turn off the TV. They didn't expect the Federal Communications Commission to do their job for them.

I am a First Amendment junkie. You can't OD on the First Amend-   15
ment, because free speech is its own best antidote.

Summarizing Jacoby, Paragraph by Paragraph

Suppose we want to make a rough summary, more or less paragraph by paragraph, of Jacoby's essay. Such a summary might look something like this (the numbers refer to Jacoby's paragraphs):

1. Although feminists usually support the First Amendment, when it comes to pornography, many feminists take pretty much the position of those who oppose ERA and abortion and other causes of the women's movement.
2. Larry Flynt produces garbage, but I think his conviction represents an unconstitutional limitation of freedom of speech.
3, 4. Feminists who want to control (censor) pornography argue that it poses a greater threat to women than similar repulsive speech poses to other groups. If feminists want to say that all offensive speech should be restricted, they can make a case, but it is absurd to say that pornography is a "greater threat" to women than a march of neo-Nazis is to survivors of concentration camps.
5. Trust in the First Amendment is not refuted by kiddie porn; kiddie porn is not a First Amendment issue but an issue of child abuse.
6, 7, 8. Some feminists think censorship of pornography can be more "rational" than other kinds of censorship, but a picture of a nude woman strikes some women as base and others as "lovely." There is no unanimity.
9, 10. If feminists censor girlie magazines, they will find that they are unwittingly helping opponents of the women's movement to censor discussions of rape, abortion, and so on. Some of the art in the feminist magazine *Ms.* would doubtless be censored.

11, 12. Like other would-be censors, feminists want to use the power of the state to achieve what they have not achieved in "the marketplace of ideas." They display a lack of faith in "democratic persuasion."

13, 14. This attempt at censorship reveals a desire to "shift responsibility from individuals to institutions." The responsibility—for instance, to keep young people from equating sex with violence—is properly the parents'.

15. We can't have too much of the First Amendment.

Jacoby's **thesis**, or major claim, or chief proposition—that any form of censorship of pornography is wrong—is clear enough, even as early as the end of her first paragraph, but it gets its life or its force from the **reasons** offered throughout the essay. If we want to reduce our summary even further, we might say that Jacoby supports her thesis by arguing several subsidiary points. We will merely assert them briefly, but Jacoby **argues** them—that is, she gives reasons:

a. Pornography can scarcely be thought of as more offensive than Nazism.

b. Women disagree about which pictures are pornographic.

c. Feminists who want to censor pornography will find that they help antifeminists to censor discussions of issues advocated by the women's movement.

d. Feminists who favor censorship are in effect turning to the government to achieve what they haven't achieved in the free marketplace.

e. One sees this abdication of responsibility in the fact that parents allow their children to watch unsuitable movies and television programs.

If we want to present a brief summary in the form of one coherent paragraph—perhaps as part of our own essay to show the view we are arguing in behalf of or against—we might write something like this summary. (The summary would, of course, be prefaced by a **lead-in** along these lines: "Susan Jacoby, writing in the *New York Times,* offers a forceful argument against censorship of pornography. Jacoby's view, briefly, is . . .".)

When it comes to censorship of pornography, some feminists take a position shared by opponents of the feminist movement. They argue that pornography poses a greater threat to women than other forms of offensive speech offer to other groups, but this interpretation is simply a mistake. Pointing to kiddie porn is also a mistake, for kiddie porn is an issue involving not the First Amendment but child abuse. Feminists who support censorship of pornography will inadvertently aid those who wish to censor discussions of abortion and rape or censor art that is published in magazines such as *Ms.* The solution is not for individuals to turn to

institutions (that is, for the government to limit the First Amendment)
but for individuals to accept the responsibility for teaching young people
not to equate sex with violence.

Whether we agree or disagree with Jacoby's thesis, we must admit
that the reasons she sets forth to support it are worth thinking about. Only
a reader who closely follows the reasoning with which Jacoby buttresses
her thesis is in a position to accept or reject it. Indeed, one might want to
do research on some of her points to see if her interpretation is satisfactory.

Topics for Critical Thinking and Writing

1. What does Jacoby mean when she says she is a "First Amendment junkie"
   (para. 15)?

2. The essay is primarily an argument against the desire of some feminists
   to try to censor pornography of the sort that appeals to some heterosexual adult males, but the next-to-last paragraph is about television and
   children. Is the paragraph connected to Jacoby's overall argument? If so,
   how?

3. Evaluate the final paragraph as a final paragraph. (Effective final paragraphs are not, of course, all of one sort. Some, for example, round off
   the essay by echoing something from the opening; others suggest that
   the reader, having now seen the problem, should think further about
   it or even act on it. But a good final paragraph, whatever else it does,
   should make the reader feel that the essay has come to an end, not just
   broken off.)

4. This essay originally appeared in the *New York Times*. If you are unfamiliar with this newspaper, consult an issue or two in your library. Next,
   in a paragraph, try to characterize the readers of the paper—that is,
   Jacoby's audience.

5. Jacoby claims in paragraph 2 that she "believes . . . in an absolute interpretation of the First Amendment." What does such an interpretation involve? Would it permit shouting "Fire!" in a crowded theater
   even though the shouter knows there is no fire? Would it permit shouting racist insults at blacks or immigrant Vietnamese? Spreading un-
   truths about someone's past? If the "absolutist" interpretation of the
   First Amendment does permit these statements, does that argument
   show that nothing is morally wrong with uttering them? (*Does* the First
   Amendment, as actually interpreted by the Supreme Court today, permit any or all of these claims? Consult your reference librarian for help
   in answering this question.)

6. Jacoby implies that permitting prosecution of persons on obscenity charges
   will lead eventually to censorship of "open discussion" of important issues such as "rape, abortion, menstruation, contraception, lesbianism"
   (para. 9). Do you find her fears convincing? Does she give any evidence
   to support her claim?

✓ A CHECKLIST FOR GETTING STARTED

☐ Have I adequately previewed the work?

☐ Can I state the thesis?

☐ If I have written a summary,

   ☐ Is the summary accurate?

   ☐ Does the summary mention all the chief points?

   ☐ If there are inconsistencies, are they in the summary or the original selection?

   ☐ Will the summary be clear and helpful?

   ☐ Have I considered the audience for whom the author is writing?

ESSAYS FOR ANALYSIS

Zachary Shemtob and David Lat

Zachary Shemtob teaches criminal justice at Central Connecticut State University; David Lat is a former federal prosecutor. We reprint an essay that originally appeared in the New York Times *in 2011.*

Executions Should Be Televised

Earlier this month, Georgia conducted its third execution this year. This would have passed relatively unnoticed if not for a controversy surrounding its videotaping. Lawyers for the condemned inmate, Andrew Grant DeYoung, had persuaded a judge to allow the recording of his last moments as part of an effort to obtain evidence on whether lethal injection caused unnecessary suffering.

Though he argued for videotaping, one of Mr. DeYoung's defense lawyers, Brian Kammer, spoke out against releasing the footage to the public. "It's a horrible thing that Andrew DeYoung had to go through," Mr. Kammer said, "and it's not for the public to see that."

We respectfully disagree. Executions in the United States ought to be made public.

Right now, executions are generally open only to the press and a few select witnesses. For the rest of us, the vague contours are provided in the morning paper. Yet a functioning democracy demands maximum accountability and transparency. As long as executions remain behind closed doors, those are impossible. The people should have the right to see what is being done in their name and with their tax dollars.

This is particularly relevant given the current debate on whether ₅
specific methods of lethal injection constitute cruel and unusual punishment and therefore violate the Constitution.

There is a dramatic difference between reading or hearing of such an event and observing it through image and sound. (This is obvious to those who saw the footage of Saddam Hussein's hanging in 2006 or the death of Neda Agha-Soltan during the protests in Iran in 2009.) We are not calling for opening executions completely to the public—conducting them before a live crowd—but rather for broadcasting them live or recording them for future release, on the Web or TV.

When another Georgia inmate, Roy Blankenship, was executed in June, the prisoner jerked his head, grimaced, gasped, and lurched, according to a medical expert's affidavit. The *Atlanta Journal-Constitution* reported that Mr. DeYoung, executed in the same manner, "showed no violent signs in death." Voters should not have to rely on media accounts to understand what takes place when a man is put to death.

Cameras record legislative sessions and presidential debates, and courtrooms are allowing greater television access. When he was an Illinois state senator, President Obama successfully pressed for the videotaping of homicide interrogations and confessions. The most serious penalty of all surely demands equal if not greater scrutiny.

Opponents of our proposal offer many objections. State lawyers argued that making Mr. DeYoung's execution public raised safety concerns. While rioting and pickpocketing occasionally marred executions in the public square in the eighteenth and nineteenth centuries, modern security and technology obviate this concern. Little would change in the death chamber; the faces of witnesses and executioners could be edited out, for privacy reasons, before a video was released.

Of greater concern is the possibility that broadcasting executions ₁₀ could have a numbing effect. Douglas A. Berman, a law professor, fears that people might come to equate human executions with putting pets to sleep. Yet this seems overstated. While public indifference might result over time, the initial broadcasts would undoubtedly get attention and stir debate.

Still others say that broadcasting an execution would offer an unbalanced picture—making the condemned seem helpless and sympathetic, while keeping the victims of the crime out of the picture. But this is beside the point: the defendant is being executed precisely because a jury found that his crimes were so heinous that he deserved to die.

Ultimately the main opposition to our idea seems to flow from an unthinking disgust—a sense that public executions are archaic, noxious, even barbarous. Albert Camus related in his essay "Reflections on the Guillotine" that viewing executions turned him against capital punishment. The legal scholar John D. Bessler suggests that public executions might have the same effect on the public today; Sister Helen Prejean, the death penalty abolitionist, has urged just such a strategy.

That is not our view. We leave open the possibility that making executions public could strengthen support for them; undecided viewers might find them less disturbing than anticipated.

Like many of our fellow citizens, we are deeply conflicted about the death penalty and how it has been administered. Our focus is on accountability and openness. As Justice John Paul Stevens wrote in *Baze v. Rees*, a 2008 case involving a challenge to lethal injection, capital punishment is too often "the product of habit and inattention rather than an acceptable deliberative process that weighs the costs and risks of administering that penalty against its identifiable benefits."

A democracy demands a citizenry as informed as possible about the   15
costs and benefits of society's ultimate punishment.

Topics for Critical Thinking and Writing

1. In paragraphs 9–13 the authors discuss objections to their position. Are you satisfied with their responses to the objections, or do you think the authors do not satisfactorily dispose of one or more of the objections. Explain.

2. In paragraph 4 the authors say that "the people should have the right to see what is being done in their name and with their tax dollars." But while we are on the subject of *rights*, might the person who is being executed not have a right to die in privacy? Articulate your view.

"And now let's welcome, for the first and last time . . ."

3. In their concluding paragraph the authors imply that their proposal, if enacted, will help to inform citizens "about the costs and benefits of society's ultimate punishment." Do you agree? What reasons do they offer to support their proposal?

4. In your view, what is the strongest argument the authors give on behalf of their proposal? What is the weakest? Explain why you made these choices.

Gwen Wilde

This essay was written for a composition course at Tufts University.

Why the Pledge of Allegiance Should Be Revised

(Student Essay)

All Americans are familiar with the Pledge of Allegiance, even if they cannot always recite it perfectly, but probably relatively few know that the *original* Pledge did *not* include the words "under God." The original Pledge of Allegiance, published in the September 8, 1892, issue of the *Youth's Companion*, ran thus:

> I pledge allegiance to my flag, and to the Republic for which it stands:
> one Nation indivisible, with Liberty and justice for all. (Djupe 329)

In 1923, at the first National Flag Conference in Washington, D.C., it was argued that immigrants might be confused by the words "my Flag," and it was proposed that the words be changed to "the Flag of the United States." The following year it was changed again, to "the Flag of the United States of America," and this wording became the official—or, rather, unofficial—wording, unofficial because no wording had ever been nationally adopted (Djupe 329).

In 1942, the United States Congress included the Pledge in the United States Flag Code (4 USC 4, 2006), thus for the first time officially sanctioning the Pledge. In 1954, President Dwight D. Eisenhower approved adding the words "under God." Thus, since 1954 the Pledge reads:

> I pledge allegiance to the flag of the United States of America, and to
> the Republic for which it stands: one nation under God, indivisible,with
> Liberty and Justice for all. (Djupe 329)

In my view, the addition of the words "under God" is inappropriate, and they are needlessly divisive—an odd addition indeed to a Nation that is said to be "indivisible."

Very simply put, the Pledge in its latest form requires all Americans to say something that some Americans do not believe. I say "requires" because although the courts have ruled that students may not be compelled to recite the Pledge, in effect peer pressure does compel all but the bravest to join in the recitation. When President Eisenhower authorized the change, he said,

> In this way we are reaffirming the transcendence of religious faith in America's heritage and future; in this way we shall constantly strengthen those spiritual weapons which forever will be our country's most powerful resource in peace and war. (Sterner)

Exactly what did Eisenhower mean when he spoke of "the transcendence of faith in America's heritage," and when he spoke of "spiritual weapons"? I am not sure what "the transcendence of faith in America's heritage" means. Of course many Americans have been and are deeply religious—no one doubts it—but the phrase certainly goes far beyond saying that many Americans have been devout. In any case, many Americans have *not* been devout, and many Americans have *not* believed in "spiritual weapons," but they have nevertheless been patriotic Americans. Some of them have fought and died to keep America free.

In short, the words "under God" cannot be uttered in good faith by many Americans. True, something like 70 or even 80% of Americans say they are affiliated with some form of Christianity, and approximately another 3% say they are Jewish. I don't have the figures for persons of other faiths, but in any case we can surely all agree that although a majority of Americans say they have a religious affiliation, nevertheless several million Americans do *not* believe in God.

If one remains silent while others are reciting the Pledge, or even if ₅ one remains silent only while others are speaking the words "under God," one is open to the charge that one is unpatriotic, is "unwilling to recite the Pledge of Allegiance." In the Pledge, patriotism is connected with religious belief, and it is this connection that makes it divisive and (to be blunt) un-American. Admittedly the belief is not very specific: one is not required to say that one believes in the divinity of Jesus, or in the power of Jehovah, but the fact remains, one is required to express belief in a divine power, and if one doesn't express this belief one is—according to the Pledge—somehow not fully an American, maybe even un-American.

Please notice that I am not arguing that the Pledge is unconstitutional. I understand that the First Amendment to the Constitution says that "Congress shall make no law respecting an establishment of religion, or prohibiting the free exercise thereof." I am not arguing that the words "under God" in the Pledge add up to the "establishment of religion," but they certainly do assert a religious doctrine. Like the words "In God we trust," found on all American money, the words "under God" express an idea that many Americans do not hold, and there is no reason why these Americans—loyal people who may be called upon to defend the country with their lives—should be required to say that America is a nation "under God."

It has been argued, even by members of the Supreme Court, that the words "under God" are not to be taken terribly seriously, not to be taken to say what they seem to say. For instance, Chief Justice Rehnquist wrote,

> To give the parent of such a child a sort of "heckler's veto" over a patriotic ceremony willingly participated in by other students, simply because the Pledge of Allegiance contains the descriptive phrase "under God," is an unwarranted extension of the establishment clause, an extension which would have the unfortunate effect of prohibiting a commendable patriotic observance. (qtd. in Mears)

Chief Justice Rehnquist here calls "under God" a "descriptive phrase," but descriptive of *what*? If a phrase is a "descriptive phrase," it describes something, real or imagined. For many Americans, this phrase does *not* describe a reality. These Americans may perhaps be mistaken—if so, they may learn of their error at Judgment Day—but the fact is, millions of intelligent Americans do not believe in God.

Notice, too, that Chief Justice Rehnquist goes on to say that reciting the Pledge is "a commendable patriotic observance." Exactly. That is my point. It is a *patriotic* observance, and it should not be connected with religion. When we announce that we respect the flag—that we are loyal Americans—we should not also have to announce that we hold a particular religious belief, in this case a belief in monotheism, a belief that there is a God and that God rules.

One other argument defending the words "under God" is often heard: The words "In God We Trust" appear on our money. It is claimed that these words on American money are analogous to the words "under God" in the Pledge. But the situation really is very different. When we hand some coins over, or some paper money, we are concentrating on the business transaction, and we are not making any affirmation about God or our country. But when we recite the Pledge—even if we remain silent at the point when we are supposed to say "under God"—we are very conscious that we are supposed to make this affirmation, an affirmation that many Americans cannot in good faith make, even though they certainly can unthinkingly hand over (or accept) money with the words "In God We Trust."

Because I believe that *reciting* the Pledge is to be taken seriously, 10 with a full awareness of the words that is quite different from when we hand over some money, I cannot understand the recent comment of Supreme Court Justice Souter, who in a case said that the phrase "under God" is "so tepid, so diluted, so far from compulsory prayer, that it should, in effect, be beneath the constitutional radar" (qtd. in "Guide"). I don't follow his reasoning that the phrase should be "beneath the constitutional radar," but in any case I am willing to put aside the issue of constitutionality. I am willing to grant that this phrase does not in any significant sense signify the "establishment of religion" (prohibited by the First Amendment) in the United States. I insist, nevertheless, that the phrase is neither "tepid" nor "diluted." It means what it says—it *must* and *should* mean what it says, to everyone who utters it—and, since millions of loyal Americans cannot say it, it should not be included in a statement in which Americans affirm their loyalty to our great country.

In short, the Pledge, which ought to unite all of us, is divisive; it includes a phrase that many patriotic Americans cannot bring themselves to utter. Yes, they can remain silent when others recite these two words, but, again, why should they have to remain silent? The Pledge of Allegiance should be something that *everyone* can say, say out loud, and say with pride. We hear much talk of returning to the ideas of the Founding Fathers. The Founding Fathers did not create the Pledge of Allegiance, but we do know that they never mentioned God in the Constitution. Indeed the only reference to religion, in the so-called establishment clause of the First Amendment, says, again, that "Congress shall make no law respecting an establishment of religion, or prohibiting the free exercise thereof." Those who wish to exercise religion are indeed free to do so, but the place to do so is not in a pledge that is required of all schoolchildren and of all new citizens.

WORKS CITED

Djupe, Paul A. "Pledge of Allegiance." *Encyclopedia of American Religion and Politics.* Ed. Paul A. Djupe and Laura R. Olson. New York: Facts on File, 2003. Print.
"Guide to Covering 'Under God' Pledge Decision." *ReligionLink.* Religion Newswriters Foundation, 17 Sept. 2005. Web. 9 Feb. 2007.
Mears, Bill. "Court Dismisses Pledge Case." *CNN.com* Cable News Network 15 June 2004. Web. 9 Feb. 2007.
Sterner, Doug. "The Pledge of Allegiance." *Home of Heroes.* N.p., n.d. Web. 9 Feb. 2007.

TOPICS FOR CRITICAL THINKING AND WRITING

1. Summarize the essay in a paragraph.

2. Does the background material about the history of the pledge serve a useful purpose? Should it be deleted? Why, or why not?

3. Does the writer give enough weight to the fact that no one is compelled to recite the pledge? Explain your answer.

4. What arguments does the writer offer in support of her position?

5. Does the writer show an adequate awareness of other counterarguments?

6. Which is the writer's strongest argument? Is any argument notably weak, and, if so, how could it be strengthened?

7. What assumptions—tacit or explicit—does the author make? Do you agree or disagree with them? Please explain.

8. What do you take the words "under God" to mean? Do they mean "under God's special protection"? Or "acting in accordance with God's rules"? Or "accountable to God"?

9. Chief Justice Rehnquist wrote that the words "under God" are a "descriptive phrase." What do you think he meant by this?

10. What is the purpose of the Pledge of Allegiance? Does the phrase "under God" promote or defeat that purpose? Explain your answer.

11. What do you think about substituting "with religious freedom" for "under God"? Set forth your response, supported by reasons, in about 250 words.

12. Wilde makes a distinction between the reference to God on U.S. money and the reference to God in the Pledge. Do you agree with her that the two cases are not analogous? Explain.

13. What readers might *not* agree with Wilde's arguments? What values do they hold? How might you try to persuade an audience who disagrees with her to consider her proposal?

14. Putting aside your own views on the issue, what grade would you give this essay as a work of argumentative writing? Support your evaluation with reasons.

A CASEBOOK FOR CRITICAL READING:
Should Some Kinds of Speech Be Censored?

Now we present a series of essays that we think are somewhat more difficult than Jacoby's, Shemtob and Lat's, and Wilde's but that address in more detail some of the issues of free speech that they raise. We suggest you read each one through to get its gist and then read it a second time, writing down after each paragraph a sentence or two summarizing the paragraph. Keep in mind the First Amendment to the Constitution, which reads, in its entirety,

> Congress shall make no law respecting an establishment of religion, or prohibiting the free exercise thereof; or abridging the freedom of speech, or of the press; or the right of the people peaceably to assemble, and to petition the government for a redress of grievances.

> For links related to free speech, see the companion Web site
> **bedfordstmartins.com/barnetbedau.**

Susan Brownmiller

Susan Brownmiller (b. 1935), a graduate of Cornell University, is the founder of Women against Pornography *and the author of several books, including* Against Our Will: Men, Women, and Rape *(1975). The essay reprinted here is from* Take Back the Night *(1980), a collection of essays edited by Laura Lederer. The book has been called "the manifesto of antipornography feminism."*

Let's Put Pornography Back in the Closet

Free speech is one of the great foundations on which our democracy rests. I am old enough to remember the Hollywood Ten, the screenwriters who went to jail in the late 1940s because they refused to testify before a congressional committee about their political affiliations. They tried to use the First Amendment as a defense, but they went to jail because in those days there were few civil liberties lawyers around who cared to champion the First Amendment right to free speech, when the speech concerned the Communist party.

The Hollywood Ten were correct in claiming the First Amendment. Its high purpose is the protection of unpopular ideas and political dissent. In the dark, cold days of the 1950s, few civil libertarians were willing to declare themselves First Amendment absolutists. But in the brighter, though frantic, days of the 1960s, the principle of protecting unpopular political speech was gradually strengthened.

It is fair to say now that the battle has largely been won. Even the American Nazi party has found itself the beneficiary of the dedicated, tireless work of the American Civil Liberties Union. But—and please notice the quotation marks coming up—"To equate the free and robust exchange of ideas and political debate with commercial exploitation of obscene material demeans the grand conception of the First Amendment and its high purposes in the historic struggle for freedom. It is a misuse of the great guarantees of free speech and free press."

I didn't say that, although I wish I had, for I think the words are thrilling. Chief Justice Warren Burger said it in 1973, in the United States Supreme Court's majority opinion in *Miller v. California.* During the same decades that the right to political free speech was being strengthened in the courts, the nation's obscenity laws also were undergoing extensive revision.

It's amazing to recall that in 1934 the question of whether James 5 Joyce's *Ulysses* should be banned as pornographic actually went before the Court. The battle to protect *Ulysses* as a work of literature with redeeming social value was won. In later decades, Henry Miller's *Tropic* books, *Lady Chatterley's Lover,* and the *Memoirs of Fanny Hill* also were adjudged not obscene. These decisions have been important to me. As the author of *Against Our Will,* a study of the history of rape that does contain explicit sexual material, I shudder to think how my book would have fared if James Joyce, D. H. Lawrence, and Henry Miller hadn't gone before me.

I am not a fan of *Chatterley* or the *Tropic* books, I should quickly mention. They are not to my literary taste, nor do I think they represent female sexuality with any degree of accuracy. But I would hardly suggest that we ban them. Such a suggestion wouldn't get very far anyway. The battle to protect these books is ancient history. Time does march on, quite methodically. What, then, is unlawfully obscene, and what does the First Amendment have to do with it?

In the *Miller* case of 1973 (not Henry Miller, by the way, but a porn distributor who sent unsolicited stuff through the mails), the Court came up with new guidelines that it hoped would strengthen obscenity laws by giving more power to the states. What it did in actuality was throw everything into confusion. It set up a three-part test by which materials can be adjudged obscene. The materials are obscene if they depict patently offensive, hard-core sexual conduct; lack serious scientific, literary, artistic, or political value; and appeal to the prurient interest of an average person—as measured by contemporary community standards.

"Patently offensive," "prurient interest," and "hard-core" are indeed words to conjure with. "Contemporary community standards" are what we're trying to redefine. The feminist objection to pornography is not based on prurience, which the dictionary defines as lustful, itching desire. We are not opposed to sex and desire, with or without the itch, and we certainly believe that explicit sexual material has its place in literature, art, science, and education. Here we part company rather swiftly with old-line conservatives who don't want sex education in the high schools, for example.

No, the feminist objection to pornography is based on our belief that pornography represents hatred of women, that pornography's intent is to humiliate, degrade, and dehumanize the female body for the purpose of erotic stimulation and pleasure. We are unalterably opposed to the presentation of the female body being stripped, bound, raped, tortured, mutilated, and murdered in the name of commercial entertainment and free speech.

These images, which are standard pornographic fare, have nothing 10 to do with the hallowed right of political dissent. They have everything to do with the creation of a cultural climate in which a rapist feels he is merely giving in to a normal urge and a woman is encouraged to believe that sexual masochism is healthy, liberated fun. Justice Potter Stewart once said about hard-core pornography, "You know it when you see it," and that certainly used to be true. In the good old days, pornography looked awful. It was cheap and sleazy, and there was no mistaking it for art.

Nowadays, since the porn industry has become a multimillion dollar business, visual technology has been employed in its service. Pornographic movies are skillfully filmed and edited, pornographic still shots using the newest tenets of good design artfully grace the covers of *Hustler, Penthouse,* and *Playboy,* and the public—and the courts—are sadly confused.

The Supreme Court neglected to define "hard-core" in the *Miller* decision. This was a mistake. If "hard-core" refers only to explicit sexual intercourse, then that isn't good enough. When women or children or men—no matter how artfully—are shown tortured or terrorized in the service of sex, that's obscene. And "patently offensive," I would hope, to our "contemporary community standards."

Justice William O. Douglas wrote in his dissent to the *Miller* case that no one is "compelled to look." This is hardly true. To buy a paper at the corner newsstand is to subject oneself to a forcible immersion in pornography, to be demeaned by an array of dehumanized, chopped-up parts of the female anatomy, packaged like cuts of meat at the supermarket. I happen to like my body and I work hard at the gym to keep it in good shape, but I am embarrassed for my body and for the bodies of all women when I see the fragmented parts of us so frivolously, and so flagrantly, displayed.

Some constitutional theorists (Justice Douglas was one) have maintained that any obscenity law is a serious abridgement of free speech. Others (and Justice Earl Warren was one) have maintained that the First Amendment was never intended to protect obscenity. We live quite compatibly with a host of free-speech abridgements. There are restraints against false and misleading advertising or statements—shouting "fire" without cause in a crowded movie theater, etc.—that do not threaten, but strengthen, our societal values. Restrictions on the public display of pornography belong in this category.

The distinction between permission to publish and permission 15 to display publicly is an essential one and one which I think consonant with First Amendment principles. Justice Burger's words which I quoted above support this without question. We are not saying "Smash the presses" or "Ban the bad ones," but simply "Get the stuff out of our sight." Let the legislatures decide—using realistic and humane contemporary community standards—what can be displayed and what cannot. The courts, after all, will be the final arbiters.

TOPICS FOR CRITICAL THINKING AND WRITING

1. Objecting to Justice Douglas's remark that no one is "'compelled to look'" (para. 13), Brownmiller says, "This is hardly true. To buy a paper at the corner newsstand is to subject oneself to a forcible immersion in pornography, to be demeaned by an array of dehumanized, chopped-up parts of the female anatomy, packaged like cuts of meat at the supermarket." Is this true at your local newsstand, or are the sex magazines kept in one place, relatively remote from the newspapers?

2. Who is Brownmiller talking to—that is, who is her audience? Do you think she holds the attention of her intended audience?

3. When Brownmiller attempts to restate the "three-part test" for obscenity established by the Supreme Court in *Miller v. California*, she writes (para. 7): "The materials are obscene if they depict . . ." and so on. She should have written: "The materials are obscene if and only if they depict . . ." and so on. Explain what is wrong here with her "if," and why "if and only if" is needed.

4. In her next-to-last paragraph, Brownmiller reminds us that we already live quite comfortably with some "free-speech abridgements." The examples she gives are that we may not falsely shout "fire" in a crowded theater and may not issue misleading advertisements. Do you think that these widely accepted restrictions are valid evidence in arguing on behalf of limiting the display of what Brownmiller considers pornography? Why, or why not?

5. Brownmiller insists that defenders of the First Amendment, who will surely oppose laws that interfere with the freedom to publish, need not go on to condemn laws that regulate the freedom to publicly display pornographic publications. Do you agree? Suppose a publisher insists that he cannot sell his product at a profit unless he is permitted to display it to advantage and that restriction on the latter amounts to interference with his freedom to publish. How might Brownmiller reply?

6. In her last paragraph Brownmiller says that "contemporary community standards" should be decisive. Can it be argued that because standards vary from one community to another and from time to time even in the same place, her recommendation subjects the rights of a minority to the whims of a majority? (The Bill of Rights, after all, was supposed to safeguard the constitutional rights of the minority from the possible tyranny of the majority.) How is "contemporary community standards" defined in the essay? How do you define the term?

7. When Brownmiller accuses "the public . . . and the courts" of being "sadly confused" (para. 11), what does she think they are confused about? The definition of *pornography* or *obscenity*? The effects of such literature on men and women? Or is it something else?

Charles R. Lawrence III

Charles R. Lawrence III (b. 1943), author of numerous articles in law journals and coauthor of We Won't Go Back: Making the Case for Affirmative Action *(1997), teaches law at Georgetown University. This essay originally appeared in the* Chronicle of Higher Education *(October 25, 1989), a publication read chiefly by faculty and administrators at colleges and universities. An amplified version of the essay appeared in* Duke Law Journal *(February 1990).*

On Racist Speech

I have spent the better part of my life as a dissenter. As a high school student, I was threatened with suspension for my refusal to participate in a civil defense drill, and I have been a conspicuous consumer of my First Amendment liberties ever since. There are very strong reasons for protecting even racist speech. Perhaps the most important of these is that such protection reinforces our society's commitment to tolerance as a value, and that by protecting bad speech from government regulation, we will be forced to combat it as a community.

But I also have a deeply felt apprehension about the resurgence of racial violence and the corresponding rise in the incidence of verbal and symbolic assault and harassment to which blacks and other traditionally subjugated and excluded groups are subjected. I am troubled by the way the debate has been framed in response to the recent surge of racist incidents on college and university campuses and in response to some universities' attempts to regulate harassing speech. The problem has been framed as one in which the liberty of free speech is in conflict with the elimination of racism. I believe this has placed the bigot on the moral high ground and fanned the rising flames of racism.

Above all, I am troubled that we have not listened to the real victims, that we have shown so little understanding of their injury, and that we have abandoned those whose race, gender, or sexual preference continues to make them second-class citizens. It seems to me a very sad irony that the first instinct of civil libertarians has been to challenge even the smallest, most narrowly framed efforts by universities to provide black and other minority students with the protection the Constitution guarantees them.

The landmark case of *Brown v. Board of Education* is not a case that we normally think of as a case about speech. But *Brown* can be broadly read as articulating the principle of equal citizenship. *Brown* held that segregated schools were inherently unequal because of the *message* that segregation conveyed—that black children were an untouchable caste, unfit to go to school with white children. If we understand the necessity of eliminating the system of signs and symbols that signal the inferiority of blacks, then we should hesitate before proclaiming that all racist speech that stops short of physical violence must be defended.

University officials who have formulated policies to respond to incidents of racial harassment have been characterized in the press as "thought police," but such policies generally do nothing more than impose sanctions against intentional face-to-face insults. When racist speech takes the form of face-to-face insults, catcalls, or other assaultive speech aimed at an individual or small group of persons, it falls directly within the "fighting words" exception to First Amendment protection. The Supreme Court has held that words which "by their very utterance inflict injury or tend to incite an immediate breach of the peace" are not protected by the First Amendment.

If the purpose of the First Amendment is to foster the greatest amount of speech, racial insults disserve that purpose. Assaultive racist speech functions as a preemptive strike. The invective is experienced as a blow, not as a proffered idea, and once the blow is struck, it is unlikely that a dialogue will follow. Racial insults are particularly undeserving of First Amendment protection because the perpetrator's intention is not to discover truth or initiate dialogue but to injure the victim. In most situations, members of minority groups realize that they are likely to lose if they respond to epithets by fighting and are forced to remain silent and submissive.

Courts have held that offensive speech may not be regulated in public forums such as streets where the listener may avoid the speech by moving on, but the regulation of otherwise protected speech has been permitted when the speech invades the privacy of the unwilling listener's home or when the unwilling listener cannot avoid the speech. Racist posters, fliers, and graffiti in dormitories, bathrooms, and other common living spaces would seem to clearly fall within the reasoning of these cases. Minority students should not be required to remain in their rooms in order to avoid racial assault. Minimally, they should find a safe haven in their dorms and in all other common rooms that are a part of their daily routine.

I would also argue that the university's responsibility for ensuring that these students receive an equal educational opportunity provides a compelling justification for regulations that ensure them safe passage in all common areas. A minority student should not have to risk becoming the target of racially assaulting speech every time he or she chooses to walk across campus. Regulating vilifying speech that cannot be anticipated or avoided would not preclude announced speeches and rallies—situations that would give minority-group members and their allies the chance to organize counterdemonstrations or avoid the speech altogether.

The most commonly advanced argument against the regulation of racist speech proceeds something like this: We recognize that minority groups suffer pain and injury as the result of racist speech, but we must allow this hate mongering for the benefit of society as a whole. Freedom of speech is the lifeblood of our democratic system. It is especially important for minorities because often it is their only vehicle for rallying support for the redress of their grievances. It will be impossible to formulate a prohibition so precise that it will prevent the racist speech you want to suppress without catching in the same net all kinds of speech that it would be unconscionable for a democratic society to suppress.

Whenever we make such arguments, we are striking a balance on 10 the one hand between our concern for the continued free flow of ideas and the democratic process dependent on that flow, and, on the other, our desire to further the cause of equality. There can be no meaningful discussion of how we should reconcile our commitment to equality and our commitment to free speech until it is acknowledged that there is real harm inflicted by racist speech and that this harm is far from trivial.

To engage in a debate about the First Amendment and racist speech without a full understanding of the nature and extent of that harm is to risk making the First Amendment an instrument of domination rather than a vehicle of liberation. We have not known the experience of victimization by racist, misogynist, and homophobic speech, nor do we equally share the burden of the societal harm it inflicts. We are often quick to say that we have heard the cry of the victims when we have not.

The *Brown* case is again instructive because it speaks directly to the psychic injury inflicted by racist speech by noting that the symbolic message of segregation affected "the hearts and minds" of Negro children "in a way unlikely ever to be undone." Racial epithets and harassment often cause deep emotional scarring and feelings of anxiety and fear that pervade every aspect of a victim's life.

Brown also recognized that black children did not have an equal opportunity to learn and participate in the school community if they bore the additional burden of being subjected to the humiliation and psychic assault contained in the message of segregation. University students bear an analogous burden when they are forced to live and work in an environment where at any moment they may be subjected to denigrating verbal harassment and assault. The same injury was addressed by the Supreme Court when it held that sexual harassment that creates a hostile or abusive work environment violates the ban on sex discrimination in employment of Title VII of the Civil Rights Act of 1964.

Carefully drafted university regulations would bar the use of words as assault weapons and leave unregulated even the most heinous of ideas when those ideas are presented at times and places and in manners that provide an opportunity for reasoned rebuttal or escape from immediate injury. The history of the development of the right to free speech has been one of carefully evaluating the importance of free expression and its effects on other important societal interests. We have drawn the line between protected and unprotected speech before without dire results. (Courts have, for example, exempted from the protection of the First Amendment obscene speech and speech that disseminates official secrets, that defames or libels another person, or that is used to form a conspiracy or monopoly.)

Blacks and other people of color are skeptical about the argument 15 that even the most injurious speech must remain unregulated because, in an unregulated marketplace of ideas, the best ones will rise to the top and gain acceptance. Our experience tells us quite the opposite. We have seen too many good liberal politicians shy away from the issues that might brand them as being too closely allied with us.

Whenever we decide that racist speech must be tolerated because of the importance of maintaining societal tolerance for all unpopular speech, we are asking blacks and other subordinated groups to bear the burden for the good of all. We must be careful that the ease with which we strike the balance against the regulation of racist speech is in no way influenced by the fact that the cost will be borne by others. We must be certain that those who will pay that price are fairly represented in our deliberations and that they are heard.

At the core of the argument that we should resist all government regulation of speech is the ideal that the best cure for bad speech is good, that ideas that affirm equality and the worth of all individuals will ultimately prevail. This is an empty ideal unless those of us who would fight racism are vigilant and unequivocal in that fight. We must look for ways to offer assistance and support to students whose speech and political participation are chilled in a climate of racial harassment.

Civil rights lawyers might consider suing on behalf of blacks whose right to an equal education is denied by a university's failure to ensure a nondiscriminatory educational climate or conditions of employment. We must embark upon the development of a First Amendment jurisprudence grounded in the reality of our history and our contemporary experience. We must think hard about how best to launch legal attacks against the most indefensible forms of hate speech. Good lawyers can create exceptions and narrow interpretations that limit the harm of hate speech without opening the floodgates of censorship.

Everyone concerned with these issues must find ways to engage actively in actions that resist and counter the racist ideas that we would have the First Amendment protect. If we fail in this, the victims of hate speech must rightly assume that we are on the oppressors' side.

TOPICS FOR CRITICAL THINKING AND WRITING

1. Summarize Lawrence's essay in a paragraph. (You may find it useful first to summarize each paragraph in a sentence and then to revise these summary sentences into a paragraph.)

2. In a sentence state Lawrence's thesis (his main point).

3. Why do you suppose Lawrence included his first paragraph? What does it contribute to his argument?

4. In paragraph 8 Lawrence speaks of "racially assaulting speech" and of "vilifying speech." It is easy to think of words that fit these descriptions, but what about other words? Is *Uncle Tom,* used by an African American about another African American who is eager to please whites, an example of "racially assaulting speech"? Or take the word *gay.* Surely this word is acceptable because it is widely used by homosexuals, but what about *queer* (used by some homosexuals but usually derogatory when used by heterosexuals)? What might makes these words seem "assaulting" or "vilifying"?

5. Think about those provisions in the Code of Conduct of Shippensburg University in Pennsylvania: The code says that each student has a "primary" right to be free from harassment, intimidation, physical harm, and emotional abuse, and has a "secondary" right to express personal beliefs in a manner that does not "provoke, harass, demean, intimidate,

or harm" another. The code prohibits conduct that "annoys, threatens, or alarms a person or group," such as sexual harassment, "innuendo," "comments, insults," "propositions," "humor/jokes about sex or gender-specific traits," and "suggestive or insulting sounds, leering, whistling, [and] obscene gestures." The president of the university has said (according to the *New York Times,* April 24, 2003, p. A23) that the university encourages free speech as a means to examine ideas and that the university is "committed to the principle that this discussion be conducted appropriately. We do have expectations that our students will conduct themselves in a civil manner that allows them to express their opinions without interfering with the rights of others." Use this material to help you generate your own thoughts about speech on college campuses.

6. Find out if your college or university has a code — perhaps online — governing hate speech. If it does, evaluate it. If your college has no such code, make a case for why such a policy should be readily available to students and faculty. Compose a blog entry evaluating your current code, or draft your own code.

Derek Bok

Derek Bok was born in 1930 in Bryn Mawr, Pennsylvania, and educated at Stanford University and Harvard University, where he received a law degree. From 1971 to 1991 he served as president of Harvard University. The following essay, first published in the Boston Globe *in 1991, was prompted by the display of Confederate flags hung from a window of a Harvard dormitory.*

Protecting Freedom of Expression on the Campus

For several years, universities have been struggling with the problem of trying to reconcile the rights of free speech with the desire to avoid racial tension. In recent weeks, such a controversy has sprung up at Harvard. Two students hung Confederate flags in public view, upsetting students who equate the Confederacy with slavery. A third student tried to protest the flags by displaying a swastika.

These incidents have provoked much discussion and disagreement. Some students have urged that Harvard require the removal of symbols that offend many members of the community. Others reply that such symbols are a form of free speech and should be protected.

Different universities have resolved similar conflicts in different ways. Some have enacted codes to protect their communities from forms of speech that are deemed to be insensitive to the feelings of other groups. Some have refused to impose such restrictions.

It is important to distinguish between the appropriateness of such communications and their status under the First Amendment. The fact that speech is protected by the First Amendment does not necessarily mean that it is right, proper, or civil. I am sure that the vast majority of Harvard students believe that hanging a Confederate flag in public view—or displaying a swastika in response—is insensitive and unwise because any satisfaction it gives to the students who display these symbols is far outweighed by the discomfort it causes to many others.

I share this view and regret that the students involved saw fit to 5 behave in this fashion. Whether or not they merely wished to manifest their pride in the South—or to demonstrate the insensitivity of hanging Confederate flags, by mounting another offensive symbol in return—they must have known that they would upset many fellow students and ignore the decent regard for the feelings of others so essential to building and preserving a strong and harmonious community.

To disapprove of a particular form of communication, however, is not enough to justify prohibiting it. We are faced with a clear example of the conflict between our commitment to free speech and our desire to foster a community founded on mutual respect. Our society has wrestled with this problem for many years. Interpreting the First Amendment, the Supreme Court has clearly struck the balance in favor of free speech.

While communities do have the right to regulate speech in order to uphold aesthetic standards (avoiding defacement of buildings) or to protect the public from disturbing noise, rules of this kind must be applied across the board and cannot be enforced selectively to prohibit certain kinds of messages but not others.

Under the Supreme Court's rulings, as I read them, the display of swastikas or Confederate flags clearly falls within the protection of the free-speech clause of the First Amendment and cannot be forbidden simply because it offends the feelings of many members of the community. These rulings apply to all agencies of government, including public universities.

Although it is unclear to what extent the First Amendment is enforceable against private institutions, I have difficulty understanding why a university such as Harvard should have less free speech than the surrounding society—or than a public university.

One reason why the power of censorship is so dangerous is that it is 10 extremely difficult to decide when a particular communication is offensive enough to warrant prohibition or to weigh the degree of offensiveness against the potential value of the communication. If we begin to forbid flags, it is only a short step to prohibiting offensive speakers.

I suspect that no community will become humane and caring by restricting what its members can say. The worst offenders will simply find other ways to irritate and insult.

In addition, once we start to declare certain things "offensive," with all the excitement and attention that will follow, I fear that much ingenuity will be exerted trying to test the limits, much time will be expended trying to draw tenuous distinctions, and the resulting publicity will eventually attract more attention to the offensive material than would ever have occurred otherwise.

Rather than prohibit such communications, with all the resulting risks, it would be better to ignore them, since students would then have little reason to create such displays and would soon abandon them. If this response is not possible—and one can understand why—the wisest course is to speak with those who perform insensitive acts and try to help them understand the effects of their actions on others.

Appropriate officials and faculty members should take the lead, as the Harvard House Masters have already done in this case. In talking with students, they should seek to educate and persuade, rather than resort to ridicule or intimidation, recognizing that only persuasion is likely to produce a lasting, beneficial effect. Through such effects, I believe that we act in the manner most consistent with our ideals as an educational institution and most calculated to help us create a truly understanding, supportive community.

Topics for Critical Thinking and Writing

1. Bok sketches the following argument (paras. 8 and 9): The First Amendment protects free speech in public universities and colleges; Harvard is not a public university; therefore, Harvard does not enjoy the protection of the First Amendment. Bok finds this argument plainly invalid. He clearly rejects the conclusion. "I have difficulty understanding why . . . Harvard should have less free speech . . . than a public university." What would need to be revised in the premises to make the argument valid? Do you think Bok would accept or reject such a revision?

2. Bok objects to censorship that simply prevents students from being "offended." He would not object to the campus police preventing students from being harmed. In an essay of 100 words, explain the difference between conduct that is *harmful* and conduct that is (merely?) *offensive.* (If you think that such a distinction cannot be made, explain why.)

3. Bok advises campus officials (and students) simply to "ignore" offensive words, flags, and so forth (para. 13). Do you agree with this advice? Or do you favor a different kind of response? Write a 250-word essay on the theme "How We Ought to Respond to the Offensive Misconduct of Others."

Thinking Further about Freedom of Expression and Facebook

On February 8, 2009, the *New York Times* reported that a high school senior, Katherine Evans, believed that her English teacher, Sarah Phelps, behaved offensively in two ways: Evans said that the teacher ignored her requests for help with assignments and, further, that Phelps brusquely reproached her when Evans missed a class because she attended a blood drive. Evans, an honor student, logged into Facebook and wrote about her teacher:

> To those select students who have had the displeasure of having Ms. Sarah Phelps, or simply knowing her and her insane antics: Here is the place to express your feelings of hatred.

The posting drew several responses, including some that criticized the student and supported the teacher. Here is one, written by a former student of Ms. Phelps, quoted by the *Times*:

> Whatever your reasons for hating her are, they're probably very immature.

Ms. Evans removed the posting a few days later but subsequently she was nevertheless reprimanded by the principal and was given a three-day suspension for "cyberbullying." Ms. Evans sued the principal of the high school. She was not asking for money other than legal fees: She wanted the suspension removed from her record. (She eventually settled the suit, and the suspension was wiped from her record.)

The issue to think about: Was the suspension an attack on Ms. Evans's right to free speech? Or did her comment and her invitation to "express feelings of hatred" constitute a verbal assault that crossed the line of freedom of expression? Howard Simon, executive director of the American Civil Liberties Union of Florida, takes the first position. The *Times* quotes him as saying, "Since when did criticism of a teacher morph into assault? If Katie Evans said what she said over burgers with her friends at the mall, there is no question it would be protected by free speech."

Two Writing Assignments

1. Construct a definition (perhaps two or three sentences) of *cyberbullying*. (If you draw on any sources be sure to cite them.)

2. Given the admittedly scanty information that we have on the Evans case, do you think a suspension was reasonable? If you think it was reasonable, explain why. If you think it was unreasonable, explain why, and indicate whether you think some other (lesser) punishment might have been appropriate. Your essay should be about 250 to 300 words long.

Exercise: Letter to the Editor

Your college newspaper has published a letter that links a hateful attribute to a group and that clearly displays hate for the entire group. (For instance, the letter charges that interracial marriages should be made illegal because "African Americans contain a criminal gene," or that "Jews should not be elected to office because their loyalty is to Israel, not the United States," or that "Muslims should not be allowed to enter the country because they are intent on destroying America.") The letter generates many letters of response; some responses, supporting the editor's decision to publish the letter, make these points:

- The writer of the offending letter is a student in the college, and she has a right to express her views.
- The point of view expressed is probably held only by a few persons, but conceivably it expresses a view held by a significant number of students.
- Editors should not act as censors.
- The First Amendment guarantees freedom of speech.
- Freedom of expression is healthy, i.e., society gains.

On the other hand, among the letters opposing the editor's decision to publish, some make points along these lines:

- Not every view of every nutty student can be printed; editors must make responsible choices.
- The First Amendment, which prohibits the government from controlling the press, has nothing to do with a college newspaper.
- Letters of this sort do not foster healthy discussion; they merely heat things up.

Write a 250- to 500-word letter to the editor, expressing your view of the editor's decision to publish the first letter. (If you wish, you can assume that the letter was on one of the topics we specify in the second sentence of this exercise. But in any case, address the general issue of the editor's decision, not only the specific issue of the charge or charges made in the first letter.)

3

Critical Reading: Getting Deeper into Arguments

He that wrestles with us strengthens our nerves, and sharpens our skill. Our antagonist is our helper.

—EDMUND BURKE

PERSUASION, ARGUMENT, DISPUTE

When we think seriously about an argument (not name calling or mere rationalization), not only do we hear ideas that may be unfamiliar, but we are also forced to examine closely our own cherished opinions, and perhaps for the first time really come to see the strengths and weaknesses of what we believe. As John Stuart Mill put it, "He who knows only his own side of the case knows little."

It is customary, and useful, to distinguish between **persuasion** and **argument**. Persuasion has the broader meaning. To **persuade** is to win over—whether

- by giving reasons (that is, by argument, by logic),
- by appealing to the emotions, or, for that matter,
- by using torture.

Argument, one form of persuasion, relies on reason; *it offers statements as reasons for other statements*. Rhetoricians often use the Greek word *logos*, which merely means "word" or "reason," to denote this aspect of persuasive writing—the appeal to reason. An appeal to reason may by supported by

- physical evidence;
- the testimony of experts;
- common sense; and
- probability.

We can put it this way: The goal of *argument* is to convince by demonstrating the truth (or probable truth) of an assertion, whereas the goal of *persuasion* is to conquer, by one means or another.

The appeal to the emotions is known as **pathos.** Strictly speaking, *pathos* is Greek for "feeling," and especially for "suffering," but it now covers all sorts of emotional appeals—for instance, to one's sense of pity or sympathy (Greek for "feeling with") or one's sense of patriotism.

Notice that an argument, in the sense of statements that are offered as reasons for other statements, does not require two speakers or writers who represent opposed positions. The Declaration of Independence is an argument, setting forth the colonists' reasons for declaring their independence. In practice, of course, someone's argument usually advances reasons for a claim in opposition to someone else's position or belief. But even if one is writing only for oneself, trying to clarify one's thinking by setting forth reasons, the result is an argument. **Dispute,** however, is a special kind of argument in which two or more people express views that are at odds.

Most of this book is about argument in the sense of the presentation of reasons in support of claims, but of course, reason is not the whole story. If an argument is to be effective, it must be presented persuasively. For instance, the writer's **tone** (attitude toward self, topic, and audience) must be appropriate if the discourse is to persuade the reader. The careful presentation of the self is not something disreputable, nor is it something that publicity agents or advertising agencies invented. Aristotle (384–322 B.C.) emphasized the importance of impressing on the audience that the speaker is a person of good sense and high moral character. (He called this aspect of persuasion *ethos,* the Greek word for "character," a basis of persuasion different from *logos,* which we have noted is the word for persuasion by appealing to reason.)

Writers convey their trustworthiness by

- using language appropriate to the setting, avoiding vulgar language;
- showing an awareness of the complexity of the issue (for instance, by granting the goodwill of those offering other points of view and by recognizing that there may be some merit to contrary points of view); and
- showing attention to detail (for instance, by citing relevant statistics).

In short, writers who are concerned with *ethos*—and all writers should be—employ devices that persuade readers that the writers are trustworthy, are fair-minded, intelligent persons in whom the reader can have confidence.

We talk at length about tone, along with other matters such as the organization of an argument, in Chapter 5, Writing an Analysis of an Argument, but here we deal with some of the chief devices used in reasoning, and we glance at emotional appeals.

We should note at once, however, that an argument presupposes a fixed **topic**. Suppose we are arguing about Thomas Jefferson's assertion, in the Declaration of Independence, that "all men are created equal." Jones subscribes to this statement, but Smith says it is nonsense and argues that one has only to look around to see that some people are brighter than others, or healthier, or better coordinated, or whatever. Jones and Smith, if they intend to argue the point, will do well to examine what Jefferson actually wrote:

> We hold these truths to be self-evident, that all men are created equal: that they are endowed by their Creator with certain unalienable rights; and that among these are life, liberty, and the pursuit of happiness.

There is room for debate over what Jefferson really meant and about whether he is right, but clearly he was talking about *equality of rights*. If Smith and Jones wish to argue about Jefferson's view of equality—that is, if they wish to offer their reasons for accepting, rejecting, or modifying it—they will do well first to agree on what Jefferson said or what he probably meant to say. Jones and Smith may still hold different views; they may continue to disagree on whether Jefferson was right and proceed to offer arguments and counterarguments to settle the point. But only if they can agree on *what* they disagree about will their dispute get somewhere.

IDEA PROMPT 3.1 ESTABLISHING TRUSTWORTHINESS AND CREDIBILITY

Acknowledge weaknesses, exceptions, and complexities.	"Although the unemployment rate continues to decline, further investigation into underemployment and the loss of jobless benefits is necessary in order to truly understand the unemployment crisis in the United States."
Use personal experience when appropriate.	"As a student who works and attends school full time, I can speak firsthand about the importance of increased availability of financial aid."
Use a tone that respects your audience.	When appropriate, use humor to connect to your readers. Avoid vulgarity or incendiary language that might alienate an audience.
Mention the qualifications of any sources as a way to boost your own credibility.	"According to Deborah Tannen, author and noted professor of linguistics at Georgetown University . . ."

REASON VERSUS RATIONALIZATION

Reason may not be our only way of finding the truth, but it is a way we often rely on. The subway ran yesterday at 6:00 A.M. and the day before at 6:00 A.M. and the day before, and so I infer from this evidence that it will also run today at 6:00 A.M. (a form of reasoning known as **induction**). Bus drivers require would-be passengers to present the exact change; I do not have the exact change; therefore, I infer I cannot ride on the bus (**deduction**). (The terms *deduction* and *induction* are discussed in more detail on pages 55–86 and 90–91.)

We also know that, if we set our minds to a problem, we can often find reasons (not necessarily sound ones but reasons nevertheless) for almost anything we want to justify. Here is an entertaining example from Benjamin Franklin's *Autobiography:*

> I believe I have omitted mentioning that in my first voyage from Boston, being becalmed off Block Island, our people set about catching cod and hauled up a great many. Hitherto I had stuck to my resolution of not eating animal food, and on this occasion, I considered with my master Tryon the taking of every fish as a kind of unprovoked murder, since none of them had or ever could do us any injury that might justify the slaughter. All this seemed very reasonable. But I had formerly been a great lover of fish, and when this came hot out of the frying pan, it smelt admirably well. I balanced some time between principle and inclination, till I recollected that when the fish were opened I saw smaller fish taken out of their stomachs. Then thought I, if you eat one another, I don't see why we mayn't eat you. So I dined upon cod very heartily and continued to eat with other people, returning only now and then occasionally to a vegetable diet. So convenient a thing it is to be a *reasonable creature,* since it enables one to find or make a reason for everything one has a mind to do.

Franklin is being playful; he is *not* engaging in critical thinking. He tells us that he loved fish, that this fish "smelt admirably well," and so we are prepared for him to find a reason (here one as weak as "Fish eat fish, therefore people may eat fish") to abandon his vegetarianism. (But think: Fish also eat their own young. May we therefore eat ours?)

Still, Franklin touches on a truth: If necessary, we can find reasons to justify whatever we want. That is, instead of reasoning we may *rationalize* (devise a self-serving but dishonest reason), like the fox in Aesop's fables who, finding the grapes he desired were out of his reach, consoled himself with the thought that they were probably sour.

Perhaps we can never be certain that we are not rationalizing, except when, like Franklin, we are being playful—but we can seek to think critically about our own beliefs, scrutinizing our assumptions, looking for counterevidence, and wondering if different conclusions can reasonably be drawn.

SOME PROCEDURES IN ARGUMENT

Definition

Definition, we mentioned in our first chapter, is one of the classical topics, a "place" to which one goes with questions; in answering the questions, one finds ideas. When we define, we are answering the question "What is it?" and in answering this question as precisely as we can, we will find, clarify, and develop ideas.

We have already glanced at an argument over the proposition that "all men are created equal," and we saw that the words needed clarification. *Equal* meant, in the context, not physically or mentally equal but something like "equal in rights," equal politically and legally. (And of course, *men* meant "white men and women.") Words do not always mean exactly what they seem to: There is no lead in a lead pencil, and a standard 2-by-4 is currently $1^5/_8$ inches in thickness and $3^3/_8$ inches in width.

Definition by Synonym   Let's return, for a moment, to *pornography,* a word that, we saw, is not easily defined. One way to define a word is to offer a **synonym.** Thus, pornography can be defined, at least roughly, as "obscenity" (something indecent). But definition by synonym is usually only a start because we find that we will have to define the synonym and, besides, that very few words have exact synonyms. (In fact, *pornography* and *obscenity* are not exact synonyms.)

"It all depends on how you define 'chop.'"

Definition by Example   A second way to define something is to point to an example (this is often called **ostensive definition,** from the Latin *ostendere,* "to show"). This method can be very helpful, ensuring that both writer and reader are talking about the same thing, but it also has its limitations. A few decades ago many people pointed to James Joyce's *Ulysses* and D. H. Lawrence's *Lady Chatterley's Lover* as examples of obscene novels, but today these books are regarded as literary masterpieces. Possibly they can be obscene and also be literary masterpieces. (Joyce's wife is reported to have said of her husband, "He may have been a great writer, but . . . he had a very dirty mind.")

One of the difficulties of using an example, however, is that the example is richer and more complex than the term it is being used to define, and this richness and complexity get in the way of achieving a clear definition. Thus, if one cites Lawrence's *Lady Chatterley's Lover* as an example of pornography, a reader may erroneously think that pornography has something to do with British novels or with heterosexual relationships outside of marriage. Yet neither of these ideas is part of the concept of pornography.

We are not trying here to formulate a satisfactory definition of *pornography.* Our object is to show that:

- An argument will be most fruitful if the participants first agree on what they are talking about.
- One way to secure such agreement is to define the topic ostensively.
- Choosing the right example, one that has all the central or typical characteristics, can make a topic not only clear but also vivid.

Definition by Stipulation   Arguments frequently involve matters of definition: In a discussion of gun control, for instance, you probably will hear one side speak of *assault weapons* and the other side reject the term and speak of *so-called assault weapons.* In arguing, you can hope to get agreement—at least on what the topic of argument is—by offering a **stipulative definition** (from a Latin verb, "to bargain"). You and a representative of the other side can agree, for instance, that by *assault weapon* you both mean (and this was the meaning of the term in the ban approved by Congress in 1994, which expired in 2004, and which President Obama in 2013 asked Congress to renew) a semiautomatic firearm (the spent cartridge case is automatically extracted and a new round is automatically reloaded into the chamber but is not fired until the trigger is pulled again) with a detachable magazine *and at least two of the following five characteristics:*

- collapsible or folding stock
- pistol grip (thus allowing the weapon to be fired from the hip)

- bayonet mount
- grenade launcher
- flash suppressor (to keep the shooter from being blinded by muzzle flashes).

Again, this is an agreed-upon definition. Congress put *fully* automatic weapons into an entirely different category, and the legislatures of California and of New York each agreed on a stipulation different from that of Congress: In these two states, an assault weapon is a semiautomatic firearm with a detachable magazine and with any *one* (not two) of the five bulleted items.

Let's now look at stipulative definitions in other contexts. Who is a *Native American*? In discussing this issue, you might stipulate that by *Native American* you mean any person with any Native American blood; or you might say, "For the purpose of the present discussion, I mean by a *Native American* any person who has at least one grandparent of pure Native American blood." A stipulative definition is appropriate where

- no fixed or standard definition is available, and
- some arbitrary specification is necessary to fix the meaning of a key term in the argument.

Not everyone may be willing to accept your stipulative definition, and alternatives can probably be defended. In any case, when you stipulate a definition, your audience knows what *you* mean by the term thus defined.

It would *not* be reasonable, of course, to stipulate that by *Native American* you mean anyone with a deep interest in North American aborigines. That's just too idiosyncratic to be useful. Similarly, an essay on Jews in America will have to rely on some definition of the key idea. Perhaps the writer will stipulate the definition used in Israel: A Jew is a person who has a Jewish mother or, if not born of a Jewish mother, a person who has formally adopted the Jewish faith. Or perhaps the writer will stipulate another meaning: Jews are people who consider themselves to be Jews. Some sort of reasonable definition must be offered.

To stipulate, however, that by *Jews* you mean "persons who believe that the area formerly called Palestine rightfully belongs to the Jews" would hopelessly confuse matters. Remember the old riddle and the answer: If you call a dog's tail a leg, how many legs does a dog have? Answer: Four. Calling a tail a leg doesn't make it a leg.

Later in this chapter you will see, in an essay called "When 'Identity' Politics Is Rational," Stanley Fish begin by stipulating a definition. His first paragraph begins thus:

> If there's anything everyone is against in these election times, it's "identity politics,"a phrase that covers a multitude of sins. Let me start with a definition. (It may not be yours, but it will at least allow the discussion

to be framed.) You're practicing identity politics when you vote for or against someone because of his or her skin color, ethnicity, religion, gender, sexual orientation, or any other marker that leads you to say yes or no independently of a candidates' ideas or policies.

Fish will go on to argue, in later paragraphs, that sometimes identity politics makes very good sense, that it is *not* irrational, is *not* logically indefensible, but here we simply want to make two points—one about how a definition helps the writer, the second about how it helps the reader:

- A definition is a good way to get yourself started when you are drafting an essay, a useful stimulus (idea prompt, pattern, template, heuristic) that will help *you* to think about the issue, a device that will stimulate your further thinking.

- A definition lets readers be certain that they are clear about what the author means by a crucial word.

Readers may disagree with Fish, but at least they know what he means when he speaks of identity politics.

A stipulation may be helpful and legitimate. Here is the opening paragraph of an essay by Richard B. Brandt titled "The Morality and Rationality of Suicide" (from *A Handbook for the Study of Suicide*, edited by Seymour Perlin). Notice that

- the author first stipulates a definition, and

- then, aware that the definition may strike some readers as too broad and therefore unreasonable or odd, he offers a reason on behalf of his definition.

"Suicide" is conveniently defined, for our purposes, as doing something which results in one's death, either from the intention of ending one's life or the intention to bring about some other state of affairs (such as relief from pain) which one thinks it certain or highly probable can be achieved only by means of death or will produce death. It may seem odd to classify an act of heroic self-sacrifice on the part of a soldier as suicide. It is simpler, however, not to try to define "suicide" so that an act of suicide is always irrational or immoral in some way; if we adopt a neutral definition like the above we can still proceed to ask when an act of suicide in that sense is rational, morally justifiable, and so on, so that all evaluations anyone might wish to make can still be made.

Sometimes a definition that at first seems extremely odd can be made acceptable, if strong reasons are offered in its support. Sometimes, in fact, an odd definition marks a great intellectual step forward. For instance, in 1990 the U.S. Supreme Court recognized that *speech* includes symbolic nonverbal expression such as protesting against a war by wearing armbands or by flying the American flag upside down. Such actions, because they express ideas or emotions, are now protected by the First

Amendment. Few people today would disagree that *speech* should include symbolic gestures. (We include an example of controversy over precisely this issue, in Derek Bok's "Protecting Freedom of Expression on the Campus," in Chapter 2, Critical Reading: Getting Started.)

A definition that seems notably eccentric to many readers and thus far has not gained much support is from page 94 of Peter Singer's *Practical Ethics*, in which the author suggests that a nonhuman being can be a *person*. He admits that "it sounds odd to call an animal a person" but says that it seems so only because of our bad habit of sharply separating ourselves from other species. For Singer, *persons* are "rational and self-conscious beings, aware of themselves as distinct entities with a past and a future." Thus, although a newborn infant is a human being, it is not a person; on the other hand, an adult chimpanzee is not a human being but probably is a person. You don't have to agree with Singer to know exactly what he means and where he stands. Moreover, if you read his essay, you may even find that his reasons are plausible and that by means of his unusual definition he has enlarged your thinking.

The Importance of Definitions   Trying to decide on the best way to define a key idea or a central concept is often difficult as well as controversial. *Death*, for example, has been redefined in recent years. Traditionally, a person was dead when there was no longer any heartbeat. But with advancing medical technology, the medical profession has persuaded legislatures to redefine death as cessation of cerebral and cortical functions—so-called brain death.

Some scholars have hoped to bring clarity into the abortion debate by redefining *life*. Traditionally, human life begins at birth or perhaps at viability (the capacity of a fetus to live independently of the uterine environment). However, some have proposed a *brain birth* definition, in the hope of resolving the abortion controversy. Some thinkers want abortion to be prohibited by law at the point where "integrated brain functioning begins to emerge," allegedly about seventy days after conception. Whatever the merits of such a redefinition, the debate is convincing evidence of just how important the definition of certain terms can be.

Last Words about Definition   Since Plato's time, in the fourth century B.C., it has often been argued that the best way to give a definition is to state the *essence* of the thing being defined. Thus, the classic example defines *man* as "a rational animal." (Today, to avoid sexist implications, instead of *man* we would say *human being* or *person*.) That is, the property of *rational animality* is taken to be the essence of every human creature, and so it must be mentioned in the definition of *man*. This statement guarantees that the definition is neither too broad nor too narrow. But philosophers have long criticized this alleged ideal type of definition, on several grounds, one of which is that no one can propose such definitions without assuming that the thing being defined has an essence in the first place—an assumption that is not necessary. Thus, we may want to define *causality,* or *explanation,* or even *definition* itself, but it is doubtful whether it is sound to assume that any of these things has an essence.

A much better way to provide a definition is to offer a set of **sufficient and necessary conditions.** Suppose we want to define the word *circle* and are conscious of the need to keep circles distinct from other geometrical figures such as rectangles and spheres. We might express our definition by citing sufficient and necessary conditions as follows: "Anything is a circle *if and only if* it is a closed plane figure and all points on the circumference are equidistant from the center." Using the connective "if and only if" (called the *biconditional*) between the definition and what is being defined helps to force into our consciousness the need to make the definition neither too exclusive (too narrow) nor too inclusive (too broad). Of course, for most ordinary purposes we don't require such a formally precise and explicit definition. Nevertheless, perhaps the best criterion to keep in mind when assessing a proposed definition is whether it can be stated in the "if and only if" form, and whether, if it is so stated, it is true; that is, if it truly specifies *all and only* the things covered by the word being defined. Idea Prompt 3.2 provides examples.

We are not saying that the four sentences in the table are incontestable. They are arguable. We offer them merely to show ways of defining, and the act of defining is one way of helping you to get your own thoughts going. Notice, too, that the fourth of these examples, a "statement of necessary and sufficient conditions" (indicated by "if and only if") is a bit stiff for ordinary writing. An informal prompt along this line might begin, "Essentially, something can be called *pornography* if it presents. . . ."

IDEA PROMPT 3.2 WAYS TO GIVE DEFINITIONS

Synonym	"Pornography, simply stated, is obscenity."
Example	"Pornography is easily seen in D. H. Lawrence's *Lady Chatterley's Lover* in the scene where . . ."
Stipulation	"For the purposes of this essay, *pornography* refers to . . ."
Statement of necessary and sufficient conditions	"Something can be called pornography if and only if it presents sexually stimulating material without offering anything of redeeming social value."

Assumptions

In Chapter 1, Critical Thinking, we discussed the **assumptions** made by the authors of two essays on campus discipline. But we have more to say about assumptions. We have already said that in the form of discourse known as argument certain statements are offered as reasons for other statements. But even the longest and most complex chain of reasoning or proof is fastened to assumptions—one or more *unexamined beliefs*. (Even if such a belief is shared by writer and reader, it is no less an assumption.) Benjamin Franklin argued against paying salaries to the holders of executive offices in the federal government on the grounds that men are moved by ambition (love of power) and by avarice (love of money) and that powerful positions conferring wealth incite men to do their worst. These assumptions he stated, though he felt no need to argue them at length because he assumed that his readers shared them.

An assumption may be unstated. A writer, painstakingly arguing specific points, may choose to keep one or more of the argument's assumptions tacit. Or the writer may be as unaware of some underlying assumption as of the surrounding air. For example, Franklin didn't even bother to state another assumption. He must have assumed that persons of wealth who accept an unpaying job (after all, only persons of wealth could afford to hold unpaid government jobs) will have at heart the interests of all classes of people, not only the interests of their own class. Probably Franklin did not state this assumption because he thought it was perfectly obvious, but if you think critically about the assumption, you may find reasons to doubt it. Surely one reason we pay our legislators is to make certain that the legislature does not consist only of people whose incomes may give them an inadequate view of the needs of others.

An Example: Assumptions in the Argument Permitting Abortion

1. Ours is a pluralistic society, in which we believe that the religious beliefs of one group should not be imposed on others.
2. Personal privacy is a right, and a woman's body is hers, not to be violated by laws that tell her she may not do certain things to her body.

But these (and other) arguments *assume* that a fetus is not—or not yet—a person and therefore is not entitled to the same protection against assaults that we are. Virtually all of us assume that it is usually wrong to kill a human being. Granted, we may find instances in which we believe it is acceptable to take a human life, such as self-defense against a would-be murderer. But even here we find a shared assumption that persons are ordinarily entitled not to be killed.

The argument about abortion, then, usually depends on opposed assumptions: For one group, the fetus is a human being and a potential person—and this potentiality is decisive. But for the other group it is not. Persons arguing one side or the other of the abortion issue ought to be aware that opponents may not share their assumptions.

Premises and Syllogisms

Premises are stated assumptions used as reasons in an argument. (The word comes from a Latin word meaning "to send before" or "to set in front.") A premise thus is a statement set down—assumed—before the argument is begun. The joining of two premises—two statements taken to be true—to produce a conclusion, a third statement, is called a **syllogism** (Greek for "a reckoning together"). The classic example is this:

Major premise: All human beings are mortal.
Minor premise: Socrates is a human being.
Conclusion: Socrates is mortal.

Deduction

The mental process of moving from one statement ("All human beings are mortal") through another ("Socrates is a human being") to yet a further statement ("Socrates is mortal") is called **deduction,** from Latin for "lead down from." In this sense, deductive reasoning does not give us any new knowledge, although it is easy to construct examples that have so many premises, or premises that are so complex, that the conclusion really does come as news to most who examine the argument. Thus, the great detective Sherlock Holmes was credited by his admiring colleague, Dr. Watson, with unusual powers of deduction. Watson meant in part that Holmes could see the logical consequences of apparently disconnected reasons, the number and complexity of which left others at a loss. What is common in all cases of deduction is that the reasons or premises offered are supposed to contain within themselves, so to speak, the conclusion extracted from them.

Often a syllogism is abbreviated. Martin Luther King Jr., defending a protest march, wrote in "Letter from Birmingham Jail":

You assert that our actions, even though peaceful, must be condemned because they precipitate violence.

Fully expressed, the argument that King attributes to his critics would be stated thus:

Society must condemn actions (even if peaceful) that precipitate violence.

This action (though peaceful) will precipitate violence.

Therefore, society must condemn this action.

An incomplete or abbreviated syllogism in which one of the premises is left unstated, of the sort found in King's original quotation, is called an **enthymeme** (Greek for "in the mind").

Here is another, more whimsical example of an enthymeme, in which both a premise and the conclusion are left implicit. Henry David Thoreau remarked that "circumstantial evidence can be very strong, as when you find a trout in the milk." The joke, perhaps intelligible only to people born before 1930 or so, depends on the fact that milk used to be sold "in bulk"—that is, ladled out of a big can directly to the customer by the farmer or grocer. This practice was finally prohibited in the 1930s because for centuries the sellers, in order to increase their profit, were diluting the milk with water. Thoreau's enthymeme can be fully expressed thus:

Trout live only in water.

This milk has a trout in it.

Therefore, this milk has water in it.

These enthymemes have three important properties: Their premises are *true*, the form of their argument is *valid*, and they leave *implicit* either the conclusion or one of the premises.

Sound Arguments

The purpose of a syllogism is to present reasons that establish its conclusion. This is done by making sure that the argument satisfies both of two independent criteria:

- First, all of the premises must be *true.*
- Second, the syllogism must be *valid.*

Once these criteria are satisfied, the conclusion of the syllogism is guaranteed. Any such argument is said to establish or to prove its conclusion, or to use another term, it is said to be **sound.** Here's an example of a sound argument, a syllogism that proves its conclusion:

Extracting oil from the Arctic Wildlife Refuge would adversely affect the local ecology.

Adversely affecting the local ecology is undesirable, unless there is no better alternative fuel source.

Therefore, extracting oil from the Arctic Wildlife Refuge is undesirable, unless there is no better alternative fuel source.

Each premise is **true,** and the syllogism is **valid,** so it establishes its conclusion.

But how do we tell in any given case that an argument is sound? We perform two different tests, one for the truth of each of the premises and another for the validity of the argument.

The basic test for the **truth** of a premise is to determine whether what it asserts corresponds with reality; if it does, then it is true, and if it doesn't, then it is false. Everything depends on the content of the premise—what it asserts—and the evidence for it. (In the preceding syllogism, the truth of the premises can be tested by checking the views of experts and interested parties, such as policymakers, environmental groups, and experts on energy.)

The test for **validity** is quite different. We define a valid argument as one in which the conclusion follows from the premises, so that if all the premises are true then the conclusion *must* be true, too. The general test for validity, then, is this: If one grants the premises, one must also grant the conclusion. Or to put it another way, if one grants the premises but denies the conclusion, is one caught in a self-contradiction? If so, the argument is valid; if not, the argument is invalid.

The preceding syllogism passes this test. If you grant the information given in the premises but deny the conclusion, you have contradicted yourself. Even if the information were in error, the conclusion in this syllogism would still follow from the premises—the hallmark of a valid argument! The conclusion follows because the validity of an argument is a purely formal matter concerning the *relation* between premises and conclusion based on what they mean.

This relationship can be seen more clearly by examining an argument that is valid but that, because one or both of the premises are false, does *not* establish its conclusion. Here is an example of such a syllogism:

The whale is a large fish.

All large fish have scales.

Therefore, whales have scales.

We know that the premises and the conclusion are false: Whales are mammals, not fish, and not all large fish have scales (sharks have no scales, for instance). But when the validity of the argument is being determined, the truth of the premises and the conclusion is beside the point. Just a little reflection assures us that *if* both of these premises were true, then the conclusion would have to be true as well. That is, anyone who grants the premises of this syllogism and yet denies the conclusion has contradicted herself. So the validity of an argument does not in any way depend on the truth of the premises or the conclusion.

A sound argument, as we said, is an argument that passes both the test of true premises and the test of valid inference. To put it another way, a sound argument

- passes the test of content (the premises are true, as a matter of fact) and it
- passes the test of form (its premises and conclusion, by virtue of their very meanings, are so related that it is impossible for the premises to be true and the conclusion false).

Accordingly, an unsound argument, an argument that fails to prove its conclusion, suffers from one or both of two defects.

- First, not all of the premises are true.
- Second, the argument is invalid.

Usually, we have in mind one or both of these defects when we object to someone's argument as "illogical." In evaluating someone's deductive argument, therefore, you must always ask: Is it vulnerable to criticism on the ground that one (or more) of its premises is false? Or is the inference itself vulnerable because even if all the premises are all true, the conclusion still wouldn't follow?

A deductive argument *proves* its conclusion if and only if *two conditions* are satisfied: (1) All the premises are *true*, and (2) it would be *inconsistent to assert the premises and deny the conclusions.*

A Word about False Premises   Suppose that one or more of the premises of a syllogism are false but the syllogism itself is valid. What does that tell us about the truth of the conclusion? Consider this example:

All Americans prefer vanilla ice cream to other flavors.

Tiger Woods is an American.

Therefore, Tiger Woods prefers vanilla ice cream to other flavors.

The first (or major) premise in this syllogism is false. Yet the argument passes our formal test for validity; it is clear that if one grants both premises, then one must accept the conclusion. So we can say that the conclusion *follows from* its premises, even though the premises *do not prove* the conclusion. This is not as paradoxical as it may sound. For all we know, the conclusion of this argument may in fact be true; Tiger Woods may indeed prefer vanilla ice cream, and the odds are that he does because consumption statistics show that a majority of Americans prefer vanilla. Nevertheless, if the conclusion in this syllogism is true, it is not because this argument proved it.

A Word about Invalid Syllogisms   Usually, one can detect a false premise in an argument, especially when the suspect premise appears in someone else's argument. A trickier business is the invalid syllogism. Consider this argument:

All terrorists seek publicity for their violent acts.

John Doe seeks publicity for his violent acts.

Therefore, John Doe is a terrorist.

In the preceding syllogism, let us grant that the first (major) premise is true. Let us also grant that the conclusion may well be true. Finally, the person mentioned in the second (minor) premise could indeed be a terrorist. But it is also possible that the conclusion is false; terrorists are not the only ones who seek publicity for their violent acts; think, for example, of the violence committed against doctors, clinic workers, and patients at clinics where abortions are performed. In short, the truth of the two premises is no guarantee that the conclusion is also true. It is possible to assert both premises and deny the conclusion without self-contradiction.

How do we tell, in general and in particular cases, whether a syllogism is valid? Chemists use litmus paper to enable them to tell instantly whether the liquid in a test tube is an acid or a base. Unfortunately, logic has no litmus test to tell us instantly whether an argument is valid or invalid. Logicians beginning with Aristotle have developed techniques that enable them to test any given argument, no matter how complex or subtle, to determine its validity. But the results of their labors cannot be expressed in a paragraph or even a few pages; not for nothing are semester-long courses devoted to teaching formal deductive logic. Apart from advising you to consult Chapter 9, A Logician's View: Deduction, Induction, Fallacies, all we can do here is repeat two basic points.

First, validity of deductive arguments is a matter of their *form* or *structure.* Even syllogisms like the one on the Arctic Wildlife Refuge on page 87 come in a large variety of forms (256 different ones, to be precise), and only some of these forms are valid. Second, all valid deductive arguments (and only such arguments) pass this test: If one accepts all the premises, then one must accept the conclusion as well. Hence, if it is possible to accept the premises but reject the conclusion (without self-contradiction, of course), then the argument is invalid.

Let us exit from further discussion of this important but difficult subject on a lighter note. Many illogical arguments masquerade as logical. Consider this example: If it takes a horse and carriage four hours to go from Pinsk to Chelm, does it follow that a carriage with two horses will get there in two hours?

Note: In Chapter 9, we discuss at some length other kinds of deductive arguments, as well as **fallacies,** which are kinds of invalid reasoning.

Induction

Whereas deduction takes our beliefs and assumptions and extracts their hidden consequences, **induction** uses information about observed cases to reach a conclusion about unobserved cases. (The word comes from the Latin *in ducere,* "to lead into" or "to lead up to.") If we observe that the bite of a certain snake is poisonous, we may conclude on this evidence that another snake of the same general type is also poisonous. Our inference might be even broader. If we observe that snake after snake of a certain type has a poisonous bite and that these snakes are all rattlesnakes, we are tempted to **generalize** that all rattlesnakes are poisonous.

By far the most common way to test the adequacy of a generalization is to confront it with one or more **counterexamples.** If the counterexamples are genuine and reliable, then the generalization must be false. For example, Ronald Takaki's essay on the "myth" of Asian racial superiority (p. 123) is full of examples that contradict the alleged superiority of Asians; they are counterexamples to that thesis, and they help to expose it as a "myth." What is true of Takaki's reasoning is true generally in argumentative writing. We are constantly testing our generalizations against actual or possible counterexamples, or by doing research on the issue.

Unlike deduction, induction gives us conclusions that go beyond the information contained in the premises used in their support. Not surprisingly, the conclusions of inductive reasoning are not always true, even when all the premises are true. On page 77, we gave as an example our observation that on previous days a subway has run at 6:00 A.M. and that therefore we believe that it runs at 6:00 A.M. every day. Suppose, following this reasoning, we arrive at the subway platform just before 6:00 A.M. on a given day and wait an hour without a train. What inference should we draw to explain this? Possibly today is Sunday, and the subway doesn't run before 7:00 A.M. Or possibly there was a breakdown earlier this morning. Whatever the explanation, we relied on a sample that was not large enough (a larger sample might have included some early morning breakdowns) or not representative enough (a more representative sample would have included the later starts on holidays).

A Word about Samples   When we reason inductively, much depends on the size and the quality of the sample—"sample" because a writer probably cannot examine every instance. If, for example, we are offering an argument concerning the politics of members of sororities and fraternities, we probably cannot interview *every* member. Rather, we select a sample. But is the sample a fair sample? Is it representative of the larger group? We may interview five members of Alpha Tau Omega and find that all five are Republicans, yet we cannot legitimately conclude that all members of ATO are Republicans. The problem is not always one of failing to interview large numbers. A poll of ten thousand college students tells us very little about "college students" if all ten thousand are white males at the University of Texas. Such a sample, because it leaves out women and minority males, obviously is not sufficiently *representative* of "college students" as a group. Further, though not all of the students at the University of Texas are from Texas or even from the Southwest, it is quite likely that the student body is not fully representative (for instance, in race and in income) of American college students. If this conjecture is correct, even a truly representative sample of University of Texas students would not allow one to draw firm conclusions about American college students.

In short: An argument that uses samples ought to tell the reader how the samples were chosen. If it does not provide this information, the argument may rightly be treated with suspicion.

Evidence: Experimentation, Examples, Authoritative Testimony, Statistics

Different disciplines use different kinds of evidence:

- In literary studies, the texts are usually the chief evidence.
- In the social sciences, field research (interviews, surveys) usually provides evidence.

In the sciences, reports of experiments are the usual evidence; if an assertion cannot be tested—if an assertion is not capable of being shown to be false—it is a *belief*, an *opinion*, not a scientific hypothesis.

Experimentation   Induction is obviously useful in arguing. If, for example, one is arguing that handguns should be controlled, one will point to specific cases in which handguns caused accidents or were used to commit crimes. If one is arguing that abortion has a traumatic effect on women, one will point to women who testify to that effect. Each instance constitutes **evidence** for the relevant generalization.

In a courtroom, evidence bearing on the guilt of the accused is introduced by the prosecution, and evidence to the contrary is introduced by the defense. Not all evidence is admissible (hearsay, for example, is not, even if it is true), and the law of evidence is a highly developed subject in jurisprudence. In the forum of daily life, the sources of evidence are less disciplined. Daily experience, a particularly memorable observation, an unusual event we witnessed—any or all of these may be used as evidence for (or against) some belief, theory, hypothesis, or explanation. The systematic study of what experience can yield is what science does, and one of the most distinctive features of the evidence that scientists can marshal on behalf of their claims is that it is the result of **experimentation.** Experiments are deliberately contrived situations that are often complex in their technology and designed to yield particular observations. What the ordinary person does with unaided eye and ear, the scientist does, much more carefully and thoroughly, with the help of laboratory instruments.

The variety, extent, and reliability of the evidence obtained in daily life and in the laboratory are quite different. It is hardly a surprise that in our civilization much more weight is attached to the "findings" of scientists than to the corroborative (much less the contrary) experiences of the ordinary person. No one today would seriously argue that the sun really does go around the earth just because it looks that way; nor would we argue that because viruses are invisible to the naked eye they cannot cause symptoms such as swellings and fevers, which are quite plainly visible.

Examples   One form of evidence is the **example.** Suppose that we argue that a candidate is untrustworthy and should not be elected to public office. We point to episodes in his career—his misuse of funds in 1998 and the false charges he made against an opponent in 2002—as examples of his untrustworthiness. Or if we are arguing that President Truman ordered the atom bomb dropped to save American (and, for that matter, Japanese) lives that otherwise would have been lost in a hard-fought invasion of Japan, we point to the stubbornness of the Japanese defenders in battles on the islands of Saipan, Iwo Jima, and Okinawa, where Japanese soldiers fought to the death rather than surrender.

These examples, we say, show us that the Japanese defenders of the main islands would have fought to their deaths without surrendering, even though they knew they would be defeated. Or if we argue that the war was nearly won when Truman dropped the bomb, we can cite secret peace feelers as examples of the Japanese willingness to end the war.

An example is a sample; these two words come from the same Old French word, *essample,* from the Latin *exemplum,* which means "something taken out"—that is, a selection from the group. A Yiddish proverb shrewdly says that "'For example' is no proof," but the evidence of well-chosen examples can go a long way toward helping a writer to convince an audience.

In arguments, three sorts of examples are especially common:

- real events,
- invented instances (artificial or hypothetical cases), and
- analogies.

We will treat each of these briefly.

REAL EVENTS   In referring to Truman's decision to drop the atom bomb, we have already touched on examples drawn from real events—the battles at Saipan and elsewhere. And we have also seen Ben Franklin pointing to an allegedly real happening, a fish that had consumed a smaller fish. The advantage of an example drawn from real life, whether a great historical event or a local incident, is that its reality gives it weight. It can't simply be brushed off.

On the other hand, an example drawn from reality may not provide as clear-cut an instance as could be wished for. Suppose, for instance, that someone cites the Japanese army's behavior on Saipan and on Iwo Jima as evidence that the Japanese later would have fought to the death in an American invasion of Japan and would therefore have inflicted terrible losses on themselves and on the Americans. This example is open to the response that in June and July 1945, Japanese diplomats sent out secret peace feelers, so that in August 1945, when Truman authorized dropping the bomb, the situation was very different.

Similarly, in support of the argument that nations will no longer resort to atomic weapons, some people have offered as evidence the fact that since World War I the great powers have not used poison gas. But the argument needs more support than this fact provides. Poison gas was not decisive or even highly effective in World War I. Moreover, the invention of gas masks made it obsolete.

In short, any *real* event is so entangled in its historical circumstances that it might not be adequate or even relevant evidence in the case being argued. In using a real event as an example (and real events certainly can be used), the writer ordinarily must demonstrate that the event can be taken out of its historical context and be used in the new context of argument. Thus, in an argument against using atomic weapons in warfare, the many deaths and horrible injuries inflicted on the Japanese at Hiroshima and Nagasaki can be cited as effects of nuclear weapons that would invariably occur and did not depend on any special circumstances of their use in Japan in 1945.

INVENTED INSTANCES   **Artificial** or **hypothetical cases—invented instances**—have the great advantage of being protected from objections of the sort just given. Recall Thoreau's trout in the milk; that was a colorful hypothetical case that nicely illustrated his point. An invented instance ("Let's assume that a burglar promises not to shoot a householder if the householder swears not to identify him. Is the householder bound by the oath?") is something like a drawing of a flower in a botany textbook or a diagram of the folds of a mountain in a geology textbook. It is admittedly false, but by virtue of its simplifications it sets forth the relevant details very clearly. Thus, in a discussion of rights, the philosopher Charles Frankel says,

> Strictly speaking, when we assert a right for *X*, we assert that *Y* has
> a duty. Strictly speaking, that *Y* has such a duty presupposes that *Y*
> has the capacity to perform this duty. It would be nonsense to say, for
> example, that a nonswimmer has a moral duty to swim to the help of a
> drowning man.

This invented example is admirably clear, and it is immune to charges that might muddy the issue if Frankel, instead of referring to a wholly abstract person, *Y*, talked about some real person, Jones, who did not rescue a drowning man. For then he would get bogged down over arguing about whether Jones *really* couldn't swim well enough to help, and so on.

Yet invented cases have their drawbacks. First and foremost, they cannot be used as evidence. A purely hypothetical example can illustrate a point or provoke reconsideration of a generalization, but it cannot substitute for actual events as evidence supporting an inductive inference. Sometimes such examples are so fanciful, so remote from life that they fail to carry conviction with the reader. Thus the philosopher Judith Jarvis Thomson, in the course of her argument entitled "A Defense of Abortion," asks you to imagine that you wake up one day and find that against your will a celebrated violinist whose body is not adequately functioning has been hooked up into your body for life support. Do you have the right to unplug the violinist? Readers of the essays in this book will have to decide for themselves whether the invented cases proposed by various authors are helpful or whether they are so remote that they hinder thought. Readers will have to decide, too, about when they can use invented cases to advance their own arguments.

But we add one point: Even a highly fanciful invented case can have the valuable effect of forcing us to see where we stand. We may say that we are, in all circumstances, against vivisection—the practice of performing operations on live animals for the purpose of research. But what would we say if we thought that an experiment on one mouse would save the life of someone we love? Or conversely, if one approves of vivisection, would one also approve of sacrificing the last giant panda to save the life of a senile stranger, a person who in any case probably would not live longer than another year? Artificial cases of this sort can help us to see that, well, no, we didn't really mean to say such-and-such when we said so-and-so.

ANALOGIES   The third sort of example, **analogy,** is a kind of comparison. An analogy asserts that things that are alike in some ways are alike in yet another way. Example: "Before the Roman Empire declined as a world power, it exhibited a decline in morals and in physical stamina; our culture today shows a decline in morals (look at the high divorce rate, and look at the crime rate) and we also show a decline in physical culture (just read about obesity in children). America, like Rome, will decline as a world power."

Strictly, an analogy is an extended comparison in which different things are shown to be similar in several ways. Thus, if one wants to argue that a head of state should have extraordinary power during wartime, one can argue that the state at such a time is like a ship in a storm: The crew is needed to lend its help, but the decisions are best left to the captain. (Notice that an analogy compares things that are relatively *un*like. Comparing the plight of one ship to another or of one government to another is not an analogy; it is an inductive inference from one case of the same sort to another such case.)

Or take another analogy: We have already glanced at Judith Thomson's hypothetical case in which the reader wakes up to find himself or herself hooked up to a violinist. Thomson uses this situation as an analogy in an argument about abortion. The reader stands for the mother, the violinist for the unwanted fetus. Whether this analogy is close enough to pregnancy to help illuminate our thinking about abortion is something that you may want to think about.

The problem with argument by analogy is this: Two admittedly different things are agreed to be similar in several ways, and the arguer goes on to assert or imply that they are also similar in another way—the point that is being argued. (That is why Thomson argues that if something is true of the reader-hooked-up-to-a-violinist, it is also true of the pregnant mother-hooked-up-to-a-fetus.) But the two things that are said to be analogous and that are indeed similar in characteristics A, B, and C are also different—let's say in characteristics D and E. As Bishop Butler is said to have remarked in the early eighteenth century, "Everything is what it is, and not another thing."

Analogies can be convincing, especially because they can make complex issues simple. "Don't change horses in midstream," of course, is not a statement about riding horses across a river but about choosing leaders in critical times. Still, in the end, analogies do not necessarily prove anything. What may be true about riding horses across a stream may not be true about choosing leaders in troubled times or about deciding on a given change of leadership. Riding horses across a stream and choosing leaders are, at bottom, different things, and however much these activities may be said to resemble one another, they remain different, and what is true for one need not be true for the other.

Analogies can be helpful in developing our thoughts and in helping listeners or readers to understand a point we are trying to make. It is sometimes argued, for instance—on the analogy of the doctor–patient or the lawyer–client or the priest–penitent relationship—that newspaper and television reporters should not be required to reveal their confidential sources. That is worth thinking about: Do the similarities run deep enough, or are there fundamental differences? Or take another example: Some writers who support abortion argue that the fetus is not a person any more than the acorn is an oak. That is also worth thinking about. But one should also think about this response: A fetus is not a person, just as an acorn is not an oak, but an acorn is a potential oak, and a fetus is a potential person, a potential adult human being. Children, even newborn infants, have rights, and one way to explain this claim is to call attention to their potentiality to become mature adults. And so some people argue that the fetus, by analogy, has the rights of an infant, for the fetus, like the infant, is a potential adult.

Three analogies for consideration: First, let's examine a brief comparison made by Jill Knight, a member of the British Parliament, speaking about abortion:

Babies are not like bad teeth, to be jerked out because they cause suffering.

Her point is effectively put; it remains for the reader to decide whether or not fetuses are *babies* and if a fetus is not a baby, *why* it can or can't be treated like a bad tooth.

Now, a second bit of analogical reasoning, again about abortion: Thomas Sowell, an economist at the Hoover Institute, grants that women have a legal right to abortion, but he objects to a requirement that the government pay for abortions:

Because the courts have ruled that women have a legal right to an abortion, some people have jumped to the conclusion that the government has to pay for it. You have a constitutional right to privacy, but the government has no obligation to pay for your window shades. (*Pink and Brown People*, 1981, p. 57)

We leave it to the reader to decide whether the analogy is compelling—that is, if the points of resemblance are sufficiently significant to allow one to conclude that what is true of people wanting window shades should be true of people wanting abortions.

And one more: A common argument on behalf of legalizing gay marriage draws an analogy between gay marriage and interracial marriage, a practice that was banned in sixteen states until 1967, when the Supreme Court declared miscegenation statutes unconstitutional. The gist of the analogy is this: Racism and discrimination against gay and lesbian people are the same. If marriage is a fundamental right—as the Supreme Court held in its 1967 decision when it struck down bans on miscegenation—then it is a fundamental right for gay people as well as heterosexual people.

Authoritative Testimony   Another form of evidence is **testimony,** the citation or quotation of authorities. In daily life we rely heavily on authorities of all sorts: We get a doctor's opinion about our health, we read a book because an intelligent friend recommends it, we see a movie because a critic gave it a good review, and we pay at least a little attention to the weather forecaster.

In setting forth an argument, one often tries to show that one's view is supported by notable figures, perhaps Jefferson, Lincoln, Martin Luther King Jr., or scientists who won the Nobel Prize. You may recall that in the second chapter, in talking about definitions of pornography, we referred to Kenneth Clark. To make certain that you were impressed by his testimony even if you had never heard of him, we described him as "probably the most influential English-speaking art critic of the twentieth century." But heed some words of caution:

- Be sure that the authority, however notable, is an authority on the topic in question (a well-known biologist might be an authority on vitamins but not on the justice of a war).

- Be sure that the authority is not biased. A chemist employed by the tobacco industry isn't likely to admit that smoking may be harmful, and a "director of publications" (that means a press agent) for a hockey team isn't likely to admit that watching or even playing ice hockey stimulates violence.

- Beware of nameless authorities: "a thousand doctors," "leading educators," "researchers at a major medical school."

- Be careful when using authorities who indeed were great authorities in their day but who now may be out of date (Adam Smith on economics, Julius Caesar on the art of war, Louis Pasteur on medicine).

- Cite authorities whose opinions your readers will value. William F. Buckley Jr.'s conservative/libertarian opinions mean a good deal to readers of the magazine that he founded, the *National Review*, but probably not to most liberal thinkers. Gloria Steinem's liberal/ feminist opinions carry weight with the readers of the magazines that she cofounded, *New York* and *Ms.* magazine, but probably not to most conservative thinkers. If you are writing for the general reader, your usual audience, cite authorities who are likely to be accepted by the general reader.

One other point: *You* may be an authority. You probably aren't nationally known, but on some topics you perhaps can speak with the authority of personal experience. You may have been injured on a motorcycle while riding without wearing a helmet, or you may have escaped injury because you wore a helmet; you may have dropped out of school and then returned; you may have tutored a student whose native language is not English, or you may be such a student and you may have received tutoring. You may have attended a school with a bilingual education program. In short, your personal testimony on topics relating to these issues may be invaluable, and a reader will probably consider it seriously.

Statistics   The last sort of evidence we discuss here is quantitative or statistical. The maxim "More is better" captures a basic idea of quantitative evidence. Because we know that 90 percent is greater than 75 percent, we are usually ready to grant that any claim supported by experience in 90 percent of the cases is more likely to be true than an alternative claim supported by experience only 75 percent of the time. The greater the difference, the greater our confidence. Consider an example. Honors at graduation from college are often computed on a student's cumulative grade-point average (GPA). The undisputed assumption is that the nearer a student's GPA is to a perfect record (4.0), the better scholar he or she is and therefore the more deserving of highest honors. Consequently, a student with a GPA of 3.9 at the end of her senior year is a stronger candidate for graduating summa cum laude than another student with a GPA of 3.6. When faculty members on the honors committee argue over the relative academic merits of graduating seniors, we know that these quantitative, statistical differences in student GPAs will be the basic (even if not the only) kind of evidence under discussion.

GRAPHS, TABLES, NUMBERS   Statistical information can be marshaled and presented in many forms, but it tends to fall into two main types: the graphic and the numerical. Graphs, tables, and pie charts are familiar ways of presenting quantitative data in an eye-catching manner. (See pages 163–65.) To prepare the graphics, however, one first has to get the numbers themselves under control, and for some purposes it may be acceptable simply to stick with the numbers themselves.

But should the numbers be presented in percentages or in fractions? Should one report, say, that the federal budget underwent a two-fold increase over the decade, that it increased by 100 percent, that it doubled, or that the budget at the beginning of the decade was one-half what it was at the end? Taken strictly, these are equivalent ways of saying the same thing. Choice among them, therefore, in an example like this perhaps will rest on whether one's aim is to dramatize the increase (a 100 percent increase looks larger than a doubling) or to play down the size of the increase.

THINKING ABOUT STATISTICAL EVIDENCE   Statistics often get a bad name because it is so easy to misuse them, unintentionally or not, and so difficult to be sure that they have been correctly gathered in the first place. (We remind you of the old saw "There are lies, damned lies, and statistics.") Every branch of social science and natural science needs statistical information, and countless decisions in public and private life are based on quantitative data in statistical form. It is important, therefore, to be sensitive to the sources and reliability of the statistics and to develop a healthy skepticism when confronted with statistics whose parentage is not fully explained.

Consider, for instance, statistics that kept popping up during the baseball strike of 1994. The owners of the clubs said that the average salary of a major-league player was $1.2 million. (The **average** in this case—technically the **mean**—is the result of dividing the total number of salary dollars by the number of players.) The players' union, however, did not talk about the average; rather, the union talked about the **median,** which was less than half of the average, a mere $500,000. (The *median* is the middle value in a distribution. Thus, of the 746 players, 363 earned less than $500,000, 361 earned more, and 22 earned exactly $500,000.) The union said, correctly, that *most* players earned a good deal less than the $1.2 million figure that the owners kept citing; but the $1.2 million average sounded more impressive to the general public, and that is the figure that the guy in the street mentioned when asked for an opinion about the strike.

Consider this statistic: In Smithville in 2011, 1 percent of the victims in fatal automobile accidents were bicyclists. In 2012 the percentage of bicyclists killed in automobile accidents was 2 percent. Was the increase 1 percent (not an alarming figure), or was it 100 percent (a staggering figure)? The answer is both, depending on whether we are comparing (a) bicycle deaths in automobile accidents with *all* deaths in automobile accidents (that's an increase of 1 percent), or (b) bicycle deaths in automobile accidents *only with other bicycle deaths* in automobile accidents (an increase of 100 percent). An honest statement would say that bicycle deaths due to automobile accidents doubled in 2012, increasing from 1 to 2 percent. But here's another point: Although every such death is lamentable, if there was one such death in 2009 and two in 2010, the increase from one death to two (an increase of 100 percent!) hardly suggests that there is a growing problem that needs attention. No one would be surprised to learn that in the next year there were no deaths, or only one or even two.

If it is sometimes difficult to interpret statistics, it is often at least equally difficult to establish accurate statistics. Consider this example:

> Advertisements are the most prevalent and toxic of the mental pollutants. From the moment your radio alarm sounds in the morning to the

wee hours of late-night TV, microjolts of commercial pollution flood into your brain at the rate of about three thousand marketing messages per day. (Kalle Lasn, *Culture Jam*, 1999, pp. 18–19)

Lasn's book includes endnotes as documentation, so, curious about the statistics, we turn to the appropriate page and we find this information concerning the source of his data:

> "three thousand marketing messages per day." Mark Landler, Walecia Konrad, Zachary Schiller, and Lois Therrien, "What Happened to Advertising?" *BusinessWeek*, September 23, 1991, page 66. Leslie Savan in *The Sponsored Life* (Temple University Press, 1994), page 1, estimated that "16,000 ads flicker across an individual's consciousness daily." I did an informal survey in March 1995 and found the number to be closer to 1,500 (this included all marketing messages, corporate images, logos, ads, brand names, on TV, radio, billboards, buildings, signs, clothing, appliances, in cyberspace, etc., over a typical twenty-four hour period in my life). (219)

Well, this endnote is odd. In the earlier passage, you will recall, the author asserted that "about three thousand marketing messages per day" flood into a person's brain. Now, in the documentation, he helpfully cites a source for that statistic, from *BusinessWeek*—though we have not the faintest idea of how the authors of the article in *BusinessWeek* came up with that figure. Oddly, he goes on to offer a very different figure (16,000 ads), and then, to our utter confusion, he offers yet a third figure, 1,500, based on his own "informal survey."

Probably the one thing we can safely say about all three figures is that none of them means very much. Even if the compilers of the statistics told us exactly how they counted—let's say that among countless other criteria they assumed that the average person reads one magazine per day and that the average magazine contains 124 advertisements—it would be hard to take them seriously. After all, in leafing through a magazine, some people may read many ads, some may read none. Some people may read some ads carefully—but perhaps to enjoy their absurdity. Our point: Although the author in his text said, without implying any uncertainty, that "about three thousand marketing messages per day" reach an individual, it is evident (if one checks the endnote) that even he is confused about the figure he gives.

Some last words about the unreliability of some statistical information, stuff that looks impressive but that is, in fact, insubstantial. Marilyn Jager Adams studied the number of hours that families read to their children in the five or so years before the children go to school. In her book on the topic, *Beginning to Read: Thinking and Learning about Print*, she pointed out that in all those preschool years, poor families read to their children only twenty-five hours, whereas in the same period middle-income families read 1,000 to 1,700 hours. The figures were much

---

✔ A CHECKLIST FOR EVALUATING STATISTICAL EVIDENCE

Regard statistical evidence (like all other evidence) cautiously, and don't accept it until you have thought about these questions:

☐ Was it compiled by a disinterested (impartial) source? Of course, the name of the source does not always reveal its particular angle (for example, People for the American Way), but sometimes the name lets you know what to expect (National Rifle Association, American Civil Liberties Union).

☐ Is it based on an adequate sample? (A study pointed out that criminals have an average IQ of 91 to 93, whereas the general population has an IQ of 100. The conclusion drawn was that criminals have a lower IQ than the general population. This reading may be accurate, but some doubts have been expressed. For instance, because the entire sample of criminals consisted only of convicted criminals, this sample may be biased; possibly the criminals with higher IQs have enough intelligence not to get caught. Or if they are caught, perhaps they are smart enough to hire better lawyers.)

☐ Is the statistical evidence recent enough to be relevant?

☐ How many of the factors likely to be relevant were identified and measured?

☐ Are the figures open to a different and equally plausible interpretation?

☐ If a percentage is cited, is it the average (or *mean*), or is it the median?

---

quoted in newspapers and by children's advocacy groups. Dr. Adams could not, of course, interview every family in these two groups; she had to rely on samples. What were her samples? For poor families, she selected twenty-four children in twenty families, all in Southern California. One might wonder if families from only one geographic area can provide an adequate sample, but let's think about Dr. Adams's sample of middle-class families. How many families constituted the sample? Exactly one, her own. We leave it to you to decide how much value her findings—again, they were much cited—have.

We are not suggesting that everyone who uses statistics is trying to deceive or even that many who use statistics are unconsciously deceived by them. We mean to suggest only that statistics are open to widely different interpretations and that often those columns of numbers, so precise with their decimal points, are in fact imprecise and possibly even worthless because they may be based on insufficient or biased samples.

QUIZ

What is wrong with the following statistical proof that children do not have time for school?

One-third of the time they are sleeping (about 122 days);

One-eighth of the time they are eating (three hours a day, totaling 45 days);

One-fourth of the time is taken up by summer and other vacations (91 days);

Two-sevenths of the year is weekends (104 days).

Total: 362 days—so how can a kid have time for school?

NONRATIONAL APPEALS

Satire, Irony, Sarcasm, Humor

In talking about definition, deduction, and evidence, we have been talking about means of rational persuasion. But as mentioned earlier, there are also other means of persuasion. Take force, for example. If X kicks Y, threatens to destroy Y's means of livelihood, or threatens Y's life, X may persuade Y to cooperate. One form of irrational but sometimes highly effective persuasion is **satire**—that is, witty ridicule. A cartoonist may persuade viewers that a politician's views are unsound by caricaturing (and thus ridiculing) the politician's appearance or by presenting a grotesquely distorted (funny, but unfair) picture of the issue.

Satiric artists often use caricature; satiric writers, also seeking to persuade by means of ridicule, often use **verbal irony.** Irony of this sort contrasts what is said and what is meant. For instance, words of praise may be meant to imply blame (when Shakespeare's Cassius says, "Brutus is an honorable man," he means his hearers to think that Brutus is dishonorable), and words of modesty may be meant to imply superiority ("Of course, I'm too dumb to understand this problem"). Such language, when heavy-handed, is called **sarcasm** ("You're a great guy," said to someone who will not lend the speaker ten dollars). If it is witty—if the jeering is in some degree clever—it is called irony rather than sarcasm.

Although ridicule is not a form of argument (because it is not a form of reasoning), passages of ridicule, especially verbal irony, sometimes appear in essays that are arguments. These passages, like reasons, or for that matter like appeals to the emotions, are efforts to persuade the hearer to accept the speaker's point of view. The great trick in using humor in an argument is, on the one hand, to avoid mere wisecracking, which makes the writer seem like a smart aleck, and, on the other hand, to avoid mere clownishness, which makes the writer seem like a fool. Later in this chapter (p. 107) we print an essay by George F. Will that is (or seeks to be?) humorous in places. You be the judge.

Emotional Appeals

It is sometimes said that good argumentative writing appeals only to reason, never to emotion, and that any sort of emotional appeal is illegitimate, irrelevant. "Tears are not arguments," the Brazilian writer Machado de Assis said. Logic textbooks may even stigmatize with Latin labels the various sorts of emotional appeal—for instance, *argumentum ad populam* (appeal to the prejudices of the mob, as in "Come on, we all know that schools don't teach anything anymore") and *argumentum ad misericordiam* (appeal to pity, as in "No one ought to blame this poor kid for stabbing a classmate because his mother was often institutionalized for alcoholism and his father beat him").

True, appeals to emotion may get in the way of the facts of the case; they may blind the audience by, in effect, throwing dust in its eyes or by stimulating tears.

Learning from Shakespeare   A classic example is found in Shakespeare's *Julius Caesar,* when Marc Antony addresses the Roman populace after Brutus, Cassius, and others have assassinated Caesar. The real issue is whether Caesar was becoming tyrannical (as the assassins claim) and would therefore curtail the freedom of the people. Antony turns from the evidence and stirs the mob against the assassins by appealing to its emotions. In the ancient Roman biographical writing that Shakespeare drew on, Sir Thomas North's translation of Plutarch's *Lives of the Noble Grecians and Romans,* Plutarch says that Antony,

> perceiving that his words moved the common people to compassion, . . . framed his eloquence to make their hearts yearn [that is, grieve] the more, and, taking Caesar's gown all bloody in his hand, he laid it open to the sight of them all, showing what a number of cuts and holes it had upon it. Therewithal the people fell presently into such a rage and mutiny that there was no more order kept.

Here are a few extracts from Antony's speeches in Shakespeare's play. Antony begins by asserting that he will speak only briefly:

> Friends, Romans, countrymen, lend me your ears;
> I come to bury Caesar, not to praise him.

After briefly offering some rather insubstantial evidence that Caesar gave no signs of behaving tyrannically (for example, "When that the poor have cried, Caesar hath wept"), Antony begins to play directly on the emotions of his hearers. Descending from the platform so that he may be in closer contact with his audience (like a modern politician, he wants to work the crowd), he calls attention to Caesar's bloody toga:

> If you have tears, prepare to shed them now.
> You all do know this mantle; I remember

> The first time ever Caesar put it on:
> 'Twas on a summer's evening, in his tent,
> That day he overcame the Nervii.
> Look, in this place ran Cassius' dagger through;
> See what a rent the envious Casca made;
> Through this, the well-belovèd Brutus stabbed. . . .

In these few lines Antony

- first prepares the audience by suggesting to them how they should respond ("If you have tears, prepare to shed them now"),

- then flatters them by implying that they, like Antony, were intimates of Caesar (he credits them with being familiar with Caesar's garment),

- then evokes a personal memory of a specific time ("a summer's evening")—not just any old specific time but a very important one, the day that Caesar won a battle against the Nervii (a particularly fierce tribe in what is now France).

In fact, Antony was not at the battle, and he did not join Caesar until three years later.

Antony does not mind being free with the facts; his point here is not to set the record straight but to stir the mob against the assassins. He goes on, daringly but successfully, to identify one particular slit in the garment with Cassius's dagger, another with Casca's, and a third with Brutus's. Antony cannot know which slit was made by which dagger, but his rhetorical trick works.

Notice, too, that Antony arranges the three assassins in climactic order, since Brutus (Antony claims) was especially beloved by Caesar:

> Judge, O you gods, how dearly Caesar loved him!
> This was the most unkindest cut of all;
> For when the noble Caesar saw him stab,
> Ingratitude, more strong than traitor's arms,
> Quite vanquished him. Then burst his mighty heart. . . .

Nice. According to Antony, the noble-minded Caesar—Antony's words have erased all thought of the tyrannical Caesar—died not from the wounds inflicted by daggers but from the heartbreaking perception of Brutus's ingratitude. Doubtless there was not a dry eye in the house. We can all hope that if we are ever put on trial, we have a lawyer as skilled in evoking sympathy as Antony.

Are Emotional Appeals Fallacious?   The oration is obviously successful in the play and apparently was successful in real life, but it is the sort of speech that prompts logicians to write disapprovingly of attempts to stir feeling in an audience. (As mentioned earlier in this chapter, the evocation of emotion in an audience is called *pathos,* from the Greek word for "emotion" or "suffering.") There is nothing inherently wrong in stimulating our audience's emotions when attempting to establish a claim, but when an emotional appeal confuses the issue that is being argued about or shifts the attention away from the facts of the issue, we can reasonably speak of the fallacy of emotional appeal.

No fallacy is involved, however, when an emotional appeal heightens the facts, bringing them home to the audience rather than masking them. If we are talking about legislation that would govern police actions, it is legitimate to show a photograph of the battered, bloodied face of an alleged victim of police brutality. True, such a photograph cannot tell the whole truth; it cannot tell us if the subject threatened the officer with a gun or repeatedly resisted an order to surrender. But it can tell us that the victim was severely beaten and (like a comparable description in words) evoke in us emotions that may properly enter into our decision about the permissible use of police evidence. Similarly, an animal rights activist who is arguing that calves are cruelly confined might reasonably tell us about the size of the pen in which the beast—unable to turn around or even to lie down—is kept. Others may argue that calves don't much care about turning around or have no right to turn around, but the verbal description, which unquestionably makes an emotional appeal, can hardly be called fallacious or irrelevant.

In appealing to emotions then, the important things are

- not to falsify (especially by oversimplifying) the issue,
- not to distract attention from the facts of the case,
- to think ethically about how emotions may affect the audience.

Focus on the facts and concentrate on offering reasons (essentially, statements linked with "because"), but you may also legitimately bring the facts home to your readers by seeking to induce in them the appropriate emotions. Your words will be fallacious only if you stimulate emotions that are not rightly connected with the facts of the case.

DOES ALL WRITING CONTAIN ARGUMENTS?

Our answer to the question we have just posed is no—but probably *most* writing *does* contain an argument of sorts. Or put it this way: The writer wants to persuade the reader to see things the way the writer sees them—at least until the end of the essay. After all, even a recipe for a cherry pie in a food magazine—a piece of writing that is primarily expository (how to do it) rather than argumentative (how a reasonable person ought to think about this topic)—probably includes, near the beginning, a sentence with a hint of an argument in it, such as *"Because* [a sign that a *reason* will be offered] this pie can be made quickly and with ingredients (canned cherries) that are always available, give it a try, and it will surely become one of your favorites." Clearly, such a statement cannot stand as a formal argument—a discussion that takes account of possible counterarguments, that relies chiefly on logic and little if at all on emotional appeal, and that draws a conclusion that seems irrefutable.

Still, the statement is something of an argument on behalf of making a pie with canned cherries. In this case, a claim is made (the pie will become a favorite), and two *reasons* are offered in support of this claim:

- It can be made quickly, and
- the chief ingredient—because it is canned—can always be at hand.

The underlying *assumptions* are

- You don't have a great deal of time to waste in the kitchen.
- Canned cherries are just as tasty as fresh cherries—and even if they aren't, well, you wouldn't know the difference.

✓ A CHECKLIST FOR ANALYZING AN ARGUMENT

NOTE: See also Chapter 11, A Rhetorician's View, pages 404–19.

☐ What is the writer's claim or thesis? Ask yourself:
  ☐ What claim is being asserted?
  ☐ What evidence is imagined?
  ☐ What assumptions are being made—and are they acceptable?
  ☐ Are important terms satisfactorily defined?
☐ What support (evidence) is offered on behalf of the claim? Ask yourself:
  ☐ Are the examples relevant, and are they convincing?
  ☐ Are the statistics (if any) relevant, accurate, and complete? Do they allow only the interpretation that is offered in the argument?
  ☐ If authorities are cited, are they indeed authorities on this topic, and can they be regarded as impartial?
  ☐ Is the logic—deductive and inductive—valid?
  ☐ If there is an appeal to emotion—for instance, if satire is used to ridicule the opposing view—is this appeal acceptable?
☐ Does the writer seem to you to be fair? Ask yourself:
  ☐ Are counterarguments adequately considered?
  ☐ Is there any evidence of dishonesty or of a discreditable attempt to manipulate the reader?
  ☐ How does the writer establish the image of himself or herself that we sense in the essay? What is the writer's tone, and is it appropriate?

When we read a lead-in to a recipe, then, we won't find a formal argument, but we probably will get a few words that seek to persuade us to keep reading. And most writing does contain such material—sentences that give us a reason to keep reading, that engage our interests, and that make us want to stay with the writer for at least a little longer. If the recipe happens to be difficult and time-consuming, the lead-in may say,

> Although this recipe for a cherry pie, using fresh cherries that you will have to pit, is a bit more time-consuming than the usual recipe that calls for canned cherries, once you have tasted it you will never go back to canned cherries.

Again, although the logic is scarcely compelling, the persuasive element is evident. The assumption here is that you have a discriminating palate; once you have tasted a pie made with fresh cherries, you will never again enjoy the canned stuff. The writer is not giving us a formal argument, with abundant evidence and with a detailed refutation of counterarguments, but we do know where the writer stands and how the writer wishes us to respond.

In short, almost all writers are trying to persuade readers to see things *their* way.

AN EXAMPLE: AN ARGUMENT AND A LOOK AT THE WRITER'S STRATEGIES

This essay concerns President George W. Bush's proposal that drilling be allowed in part of the Arctic National Wildlife Refuge (ANWR, pronounced "An-war"). The section of the ANWR that is proposed for drilling is called the "1002 area," as defined by Section 1002 of the Alaska National Interest Lands Conservation Act of 1980. In March 2003, the Senate rejected the Bush proposal, but the issue remains alive.

We follow George F. Will's essay with some comments about the ways in which he constructs his argument.

George F. Will

George F. Will (b. 1941), a syndicated columnist whose writing appears in 460 newspapers, was born in Champaign, Illinois, and educated at Trinity College (Hartford), Oxford University, and Princeton University. Will has served as the Washington, D.C., editor of the National Review *and now writes a regular column for* Newsweek. *His essays have been collected in several books.*

This essay was originally published in 2002, and therefore it is in some respects dated—for instance in its reference to the price of gasoline—but we think you can still learn from it a great deal about certain ways to argue.

Being Green at Ben and Jerry's

Some Environmental Policies Are Feel-Good Indulgences for an Era of Energy Abundance

If you have an average-size dinner table, four feet by six feet, put a dime on the edge of it. Think of the surface of the table as the Arctic National Wildlife Refuge in Alaska. The dime is larger than the piece of the coastal plain that would have been opened to drilling for oil and natural gas. The House of Representatives voted for drilling, but the Senate voted against access to what Sen. John Kerry, Massachusetts Democrat and presidential aspirant, calls "a few drops of oil." ANWR could produce, for twenty-five years, at least as much oil as America currently imports from Saudi Arabia.

Six weeks of desultory Senate debate about the energy bill reached an almost comic culmination in . . . yet another agriculture subsidy. The subsidy is a requirement that will triple the amount of ethanol, which is made from corn, that must be put in gasoline, ostensibly to clean America's air, actually to buy farmers' votes.

Over the last three decades, energy use has risen about 30 percent. But so has population, which means per capita energy use is unchanged. And per capita GDP has risen substantially, so we are using 40 percent less energy per dollar output. Which is one reason there is no energy crisis, at least none as most Americans understand such things—a shortage of, and therefore high prices of, gasoline for cars, heating oil for furnaces and electricity for air conditioners.

In the absence of a crisis to concentrate the attention of the inattentive American majority, an intense faction—full-time environmentalists—goes to work. Spencer Abraham, the secretary of Energy, says "the previous administration . . . simply drew up a list of fuels it *didn't* like— nuclear energy, coal, hydropower, and oil—which together account for 73 percent of America's energy supply." Well, there are always windmills.

Sometimes lofty environmentalism is a cover for crude politics. The 5 United States has the world's largest proven reserves of coal. But Mike Oliver, a retired physicist and engineer, and John Hospers, professor emeritus of philosophy at USC, note that in 1996 President Clinton put 68 billion tons of America's cleanest-burning coal, located in Utah, off-limits for mining, ostensibly for environmental reasons. If every existing U.S. electric power plant burned coal, the 68 billion tons could fuel them for forty-five years at the current rate of consumption. Now power companies must import clean-burning coal, some from mines owned by Indonesia's Lippo Group, the heavy contributor to Clinton, whose decision about Utah's coal vastly increased the value of Lippo's coal.

The United States has just 2.14 percent of the world's proven reserves of oil, so some people say it is pointless to drill in places like ANWR because "energy independence" is a chimera. Indeed it is. But domestic supplies can provide important insurance against uncertain foreign supplies. And domestic supplies can mean exporting hundreds of billions of dollars less to oil-producing nations, such as Iraq.

Besides, when considering proven reserves, note the adjective. In 1930 the United States had proven reserves of 13 billion barrels. We then fought the Second World War and fueled the most fabulous economic expansion in human history, including the electricity-driven "New Economy." (Manufacturing and running computers consume 15 percent of U.S. electricity. Internet use alone accounts for half of the growth in demand for electricity.) So by 1990 proven reserves were . . . 17 billion barrels, not counting any in Alaska or Hawaii.

In 1975 proven reserves in the Persian Gulf were 74 billion barrels. In 1993 they were 663 billion, a ninefold increase. At the current rate of consumption, today's proven reserves would last 150 years. New discoveries will be made, some by vastly improved techniques of deep-water drilling. But environmental policies will define opportunities. The government estimates that beneath the U.S. outer continental shelf, which the government owns, there are at least 46 billion barrels of oil. But only 2 percent of the shelf has been leased for energy development.

Opponents of increased energy production usually argue for decreased consumption. But they flinch from conservation measures. A new $1 gasoline tax would dampen demand for gasoline, but it would stimulate demands for the heads of the tax increasers. After all, Americans get irritable when impersonal market forces add 25 cents to the cost of a gallon. Tougher fuel-efficiency requirements for vehicles would save a lot of energy. But who would save the legislators who passed those requirements? Beware the wrath of Americans who like to drive, and autoworkers who like to make cars that are large, heavy, and safer than the gasoline-sippers that environmentalists prefer.

Some environmentalism is a feel-good indulgence for an era of 10
energy abundance, which means an era of avoided choices. Or ignored choices—ignored because if acknowledged, they would not make the choosers feel good. Karl Zinsmeister, editor in chief of the *American Enterprise* magazine, imagines an oh-so-green environmentalist enjoying the most politically correct product on the planet—Ben & Jerry's ice cream. Made in a factory that depends on electricity-guzzling refrigeration, a gallon of ice cream requires four gallons of milk. While making that much milk, a cow produces eight gallons of manure, and flatulence with another eight gallons of methane, a potent "greenhouse" gas. And the cow consumes lots of water plus three pounds of grain and hay, which is produced with tractor fuel, chemical fertilizers, herbicides and insecticides, and is transported with truck or train fuel:

"So every time he digs into his Cherry Garcia, the conscientious environmentalist should visualize (in addition to world peace) a pile of grain, water, farm chemicals, and energy inputs much bigger than his ice cream bowl on one side of the table, and, on the other side of the table, a mound of manure eight times the size of his bowl, plus a balloon of methane that would barely fit under the dining room table."

Cherry Garcia. It's a choice. *Bon appétit.*

George F. Will's Strategies

Now let's look at Will's essay, to see some of the techniques that he uses, techniques that enable him to engage a reader's interest and perhaps enable him to convince the reader, or at least make the reader think, that Will probably is on to something.

We need hardly add that if you think some or all of his techniques—his methods, his strategies—are effective, you will consider adapting them for use in your own essays.

The title, "Being Green at Ben and Jerry's," does not at all prepare the reader for an argument about drilling in the National Arctic Wildlife Refuge, but if you have read any of Will's other columns in *Newsweek*, you probably know that he is conservative and that he will be poking some fun at the green folk—the environmentalists. Will can get away with using a title that is not focused because he has a body of loyal readers—people who will read him because they want to read him, whatever the topic is—but the rest of us writers have to give our readers some idea of what we will be talking about. In short, let your readers know early, perhaps in the title, where you will be taking them.

The subtitle, "Some Environmental Policies Are Feel-Good Indulgences for an Era of Energy Abundance," perhaps added by an editor of the magazine, does suggest that the piece will concern energy, and the words "feel-good indulgence" pretty clearly tell readers that Will believes the environmentalists are indulging themselves.

Paragraph 1 offers a striking comparison. Will wants us to believe that the area proposed for drilling is tiny, so he says that if we imagine the entire Arctic National Wildlife Refuge as a dinner table, the area proposed for drilling is the size of a dime. We think you will agree that this opening seizes a reader's attention. Assuming the truth of the figure—but there seems to be some dispute, since opponents have said that the area would be more like the size of a dinner plate—the image is highly effective. A dime is so small! And is worth so little! Still, one might ask (but probably one doesn't, because Will's figure is so striking) if the tininess of the area really is decisive. One might easily, and apparently with reason, dismiss as absurd the idea that a minuscule tsetse fly could kill a human being, or that the plague is spread by fleas that have bitten rats, because these proposals sound ridiculous—but they are true.

One other point about the first paragraph: Will's voice sounds like a voice you might hear in your living room: "If you have an average-size dinner table," "the dime is larger," "at least as much oil." Don't think that in your own essays you need to adopt a highly formal style. Your reader should think of you as serious but not solemn.

Will goes on to say that Senator John Kerry, an opponent of drilling and therefore on the side that Will opposes, dismisses the oil in the refuge as "a few drops." Will replies that it "could produce, for twenty-five years, at least as much oil as America currently imports from Saudi Arabia." Kerry's "a few drops" is, of course, not to be taken literally; he means, in effect, that the oil is a drop in the bucket. But when one looks into the issue, one finds that estimates by responsible sources vary considerably, from 3.2 billion barrels to 11.5 billion barrels.

Paragraph 2 dismisses the Senate's debate ("almost comic . . . actually to buy farmers' votes").

Paragraph 3 offers statistics to make the point that "there is no energy crisis." Here, as in the first paragraph (where he showed his awareness of Kerry's view), Will indicates that he is familiar with views other than his own. In arguing a case, it is important for the writer to let readers know that indeed there are other views—which the writer then goes on to show are less substantial than the writer's. Will is correct in saying that "per capita energy use is unchanged," but those on the other side might say, "Yes, per capita consumption has not increased, but given the population increase, the annual amount has vastly increased, which means that resources are being depleted and that pollution is increasing."

Paragraph 4 asserts again that there is no energy crisis, pokes fun at "fulltime environmentalists" (perhaps there is a suggestion that such people really ought to get a respectable job), and ends with a bit of whimsy: These folks probably think we should go back to using windmills.

Paragraph 5, in support of the assertion that "Sometimes lofty environmentalism is a cover for crude politics," cites an authority (often an effective technique), and, since readers are not likely to recognize the name, it also identifies him ("professor emeritus of philosophy at USC"), and it then offers further statistics (again effective). The paragraph begins by talking about "crude politics" and ends with the assertion that "Now power companies must import clean-burning coal, some from mines owned by Indonesia's Lippo Group, the heavy contributor to Clinton." In short, Will does what he can to suggest that the views of at least some environmentalists are rooted in money and politics.

Paragraph 6 offers another statistic ("The United States has just 2.14 percent of the world's proven reserves of oil"), and he turns it against those who argue that therefore it is pointless for us to drill in Alaska. In effect, Will is replying to people like Senator Kerry who say that the Arctic refuge provides only "a few drops of oil." The point, Will suggests, is not that we can't achieve independence; the point is that "domestic supplies can provide important insurance against uncertain foreign supplies."

Paragraph 7 begins nicely with a transition, "Besides," and then offers additional statistics concerning the large amount of oil that we have. It was, for instance, enough to fuel "the most fabulous economic expansion in human history."

Paragraph 8 offers additional statistics, first about "proven reserves" in the Persian Gulf and then about an estimate—but it is only an estimate—of oil "beneath the U.S. outer continental shelf." We are not certain of Will's point, but in any case the statistics suggest to a reader that the author has done his homework.

Paragraph 9 summarizes the chief position (as Will sees it) of those on the other side: They usually argue for decreased consumption, but they are afraid to argue for the sort of tax on gasoline that might indeed decrease consumption because they know that many Americans want to drive large, heavy cars. Further, the larger, heavier cars that the environmentalists object to are in fact "safer than the gasoline-sippers that environmentalists prefer."

Paragraph 10 uses the term "feel-good indulgence," which is also found in the subtitle of the essay, and now, in the third sentence of the paragraph, we hear again of Ben and Jerry, who have not been in our minds since the title of the essay, "Being Green at Ben and Jerry's." Perhaps we have been wondering all this while why Ben and Jerry are in the title. Almost surely the reader knows that Ben and Jerry are associated with ice cream and therefore with cows and meadows, and probably many readers know, at least vaguely, that Ben and Jerry are somehow associated with environmentalism and with other causes often thought to be on the left. Will (drawing on an article by Karl Zinsmeister, editor of the *American Enterprise*) writes what we consider an extremely amusing paragraph in which he points out that the process of making ice cream "depends on electricity-guzzling refrigeration" and that the cows are, so to speak, supported by fuel that transports fertilizers, herbicides, and insecticides. Further, in the course of producing the four gallons of milk that are required for one gallon of ice cream, the cows themselves—those darlings of environmentalists—contribute "eight gallons of manure, and flatulence with another eight gallons of methane, a potent 'greenhouse' gas." As we see when we read Will's next paragraph, the present paragraph is in large measure a lead-in for the following quotation. Will knows it is is not enough to give a quotation; a writer has to make use of the quotation—has to lead in to it or, after quoting, has to comment on it, or do both.

Paragraph 11 is entirely devoted to quoting Zinsmeister, who imagines an environmentalist digging into a dish of one of Ben and Jerry's most popular flavors, Cherry Garcia. We are invited to see the bowl of ice cream on one side of the table—here Will effectively evokes the table of his first paragraph—and a pile of manure on the other side, "plus a balloon of methane that would barely fit under the dining room table." Vulgar, no doubt, but funny too. George Will knows that humor as well as logic (and statistics and other kinds of evidence) can be among the tools a writer uses in getting an audience to accept or at least to consider an argument.

Paragraph 12 consists of three short sentences, adding up to less than a single line of type: "Cherry Garcia. It's a choice. *Bon appêtit.*" None of the sentences mentions oil or the Arctic Refuge or statistics, and therefore this ending might seem utterly irrelevant to the topic, but we think Will is very effectively saying, "Sure, you have a choice about drilling in the Arctic Refuge; any sensible person will choose the ice cream (drilling) rather than the manure and the gas (not drilling).

TOPICS FOR CRITICAL THINKING AND WRITING

1. What, if anything, makes Will's essay interesting? What, if anything, makes it highly persuasive? How might it be made more persuasive?

2. In paragraph 10, Will clowns a bit about the gas that cows emit, but apparently this gas, which contributes to global warming, is no laughing matter. The government of New Zealand, in an effort to reduce livestock emissions of methane and nitrous oxide, proposed a tax that would subsidize future research on the emissions. The tax would cost the average farmer $300 a year. Imagine that you are a New Zealand farmer. Write a letter to your representative, arguing for or against the tax.

3. Senator Barbara Boxer, campaigning against the proposal to drill in ANWR, spoke of the refuge as "God's gift to us" (*New York Times*, March 20, 2002). How strong an argument is she offering? Some opponents of drilling have said that drilling in ANWR is as unthinkable as drilling in Yosemite or the Grand Canyon. Again, how strong is this argument? Can you imagine circumstances in which you would support drilling in these places? Do we have a moral duty to preserve certain unspoiled areas?

4. The Inupiat (Eskimo) who live in and near ANWR by a large majority favor drilling, seeing it as a source of jobs and a source of funding for schools, hospitals, and police. But the Ketchikan Indians, who speak of themselves as the "Caribou People," see drilling as a threat to the herds that they depend on for food and hides. How does one balance the conflicting needs of these two groups?

5. Opponents of drilling in ANWR argue that over its lifetime of fifty years, the area would produce less than 1 percent of the fuel we need during the period and that therefore we should not risk disturbing the area. Further, they argue that drilling in ANWR is an attempt at a quick fix to U.S. energy needs, whereas what is needed are sustainable solutions, such as the development of renewable energy sources (e.g., wind and sun) and fuel-efficient automobiles. How convincing do you find these arguments?

6. Proponents of drilling include a large majority — something like 75 percent — of the people of Alaska, including its governor and its two senators. How much attention should be paid to their voices?

7. Analyze the essay in terms of its use of *ethos, pathos,* and *logos.*

8. What sort of audience do you think Will is addressing? What values do his readers probably share? What makes you think so?

ARGUMENTS FOR ANALYSIS

Stanley Fish

Stanley Fish (b. 1938) established his reputation as a student of English litera-ture—he has taught literature at the University of California, Berkeley, Johns Hopkins University, and Duke University—but he has also published on legal issues. He now teaches at Florida International University's College of Law. This essay was published in 2008, when Hillary Clinton and Barack Obama were candidates for the Democratic Party's nomination for president, and inevitably there was much talk about the candidacy of a woman and an African American.

When "Identity Politics" Is Rational

If there's anything everyone is against in these election times, it's "identity politics," a phrase that covers a multitude of sins. Let me start with a definition. (It may not be yours, but it will at least allow the dis-cussion to be framed.) You're practicing identity politics when you vote for or against someone because of his or her skin color, ethnicity, religion, gender, sexual orientation, or any other marker that leads you to say yes or no independently of a candidate's ideas or policies. In essence identity politics is an affirmation of the tribe against the claims of ideology, and by ideology I do not mean something bad (a mistake frequently made), but any agenda informed by a vision of what the world should be like.

An identity politics voter says, in effect, I don't care what views he holds, or even what bad things he may have done, or what lack of ability he may display; he's my brother, or he's my kinsman, or he's my lands-man, or he comes from the neighborhood, or he's a Southerner, or (and here the tribe is really big) my country right or wrong. "My country right or wrong" is particularly useful in making clear how identity politics dif-fers from politics as many Americans would prefer to see it practiced. Rather than saying she's right on immigration or he's wrong on the war, the identity-politics voter says he looks like me or she and I belong to the same church.

Identity politics is illiberal. That is, it is particularist whereas liberalism is universalist. The history of liberalism is a history of extending the fran-chise to those who were once excluded from it by their race, gender, or national origin. Although these marks of identification were retained (by the census and other forms of governmental classification) and could still be celebrated in private associations like the church and the social club, they were not supposed to be the basis of decisions one might make "as a citizen," decisions about who might best lead the country or what laws should be enacted or voted down. Deciding as a citizen means deciding not as a man or a woman or a Jew or an African American or a Caucasian or a heterosexual, but as a human being.

Stanley Crouch believes that the project of liberal universalizing is now pretty much complete and that "elements of distinction"—his phrase for the thinking that was fashionable in "the era of 'identity politics'"—"have become secondary to the power of human qualities with which anyone can identify or reject" (*Daily News*, Feb. 11). But his judgment is belied by almost everything that is going on in this campaign. As I write this I am watching the returns from the "Potomac Primary" and the news is being presented entirely in racial, ethnic, and gender terms. Every newspaper or magazine article I read does the same thing. The Obama and Clinton campaigns accuse each other of playing the race card or the gender card. An Hispanic superdelegate warns that by replacing her Latino campaign manager with a black one, Senator Clinton risks losing his vote and the vote of other Hispanic delegates he is in the process of contacting.

Christopher Hitchens looks at the scene and is disgusted by behavior   5
that, in his view, "keeps us anchored in the past" (*Wall Street Journal*, Jan. 18). He will not, he tells us, vote for Clinton just so that we can have the "'first woman president'" (I don't remember that one from the past); and he won't vote for Obama who, he says, "wants us to transcend something at the same time he implicitly asks us to give that same something as a reason to vote for him." It would seem that we are far from realizing Ken Connor's dream that we might judge "all of the presidential hopefuls on the basis of the content of their character and their qualifications to serve" (Townhall.com, Jan. 20).

But is it as bad as all that? Is it so irrational and retrograde to base one's vote on the gender or race or religion or ethnicity of a candidate? Not necessarily. If the vote is given (or withheld) only because the candidate looks like you or has the same religion, it does seem a shallow and meretricious act, for it is an act unsupported by reasons. "Because she is a woman as I am" is of course a reason, but it is not a reason of the relevant kind, a reason that cites goals and programs, and argues for them. But suppose what was said was something like this: "As a woman I find government sponsored research skewed in the direction of diseases that afflict men and inattentive to the medical problems faced by women, and it is my belief that a woman president will devote resources to the solution of those problems." That's an identity politics argument which is thick, not thin; the she's-like-me point is not invoked as sufficient unto itself, but as it relates to a matter of policy. The calculation may or may not pan out (successful candidates both disappoint and surprise), but it is a calculation of the right kind.

One objection to identity politics (Crouch makes it in the same column) is that groups and populations are not monolithic, but display a diversity of attitudes and positions. Yes they do, but members of a group who might disagree with each other on any number of things could nevertheless come together on a matter of shared concern. American Jews, for example, have widely varying views on many important issues—tax cuts, tort reform, gay marriage, the Iraq war. Still, the vast majority believes that it is important to defend the security of Israel. This is a belief shared even by those American Jews who are strongly critical of Israel's treatment of the Palestinians. They may deplore Israel's actions and agree with Jimmy Carter when he likens them to apartheid, but if the choice is between a politician who pledges to support Israel and a politician who would withdraw support and leave the Jewish state to fend for itself, most of them would vote for the first candidate every time.

African Americans are no less heterogeneous in their views than Jewish Americans. Yet every African American—conservative or liberal, rich or poor, barely educated or highly educated—meets with obstacles to his or her success and mobility that are all the more frustrating because they are structural (built into the culture's ways of perceiving) rather than official. To the non–African American these obstacles will be more or less invisible, especially in a country where access to opportunity is guaranteed by law. It makes sense, therefore, that an African American voter could come to the conclusion that an African American candidate would be likely to fight for changes that could remove barriers a white candidate might not even see. A vote given for that reason would be a vote based on identity, but it would be more than a mere affirmation of fellowship (he's one of mine and I have to support him); it would be a considered political judgment as to which candidate will move the country in a preferred direction. Identity might be the trigger of the vote, but it would not be the whole of its content.

We should distinguish, I think, between two forms of identity politics. The first I have already named "tribal"; it is the politics based on who a candidate is rather than on what he or she believes or argues for. And that, I agree, is usually a bad idea. (I say "usually" because it is possible to argue that the election of a black or female president, no matter what his or positions happen to be, will be more than a symbolic correction of the errors that have marred the country's history, and an important international statement as well.) The second form of identity politics is what I call "interest" identity politics. It is based on the assumption (itself resting on history and observation) that because of his or her race or ethnicity or gender a candidate might pursue an agenda that would advance the interests a voter is committed to. Not only is there nothing wrong with such a calculation—it is both rational and considered—I don't see that there is an alternative to voting on the basis of interest.

The alternative usually put forward is Crouch's: Vote "for human 10 qualities" rather than sectarian qualities. That is, vote on the basis of reasons everyone, no matter what his or her identity, will acknowledge as worthy. But there are no such reasons and no such human qualities. To be sure, there are words often attached to this chimera—integrity, dedication, honesty, intellect, to name a few. But these qualities, even when they are found, will always be in the service of some set of policies you either favor or reject. It is those policies, not the probity of their proposer, that you will be voting for. (If your candidate is also a good person, that's a nice bonus, but it isn't the essential thing.) You will be voting, in short, for interests, and those who do not have an investment in those interests will be voting for someone else.

What this means is that the ritual deprecation of "special interests" makes no sense. All interests are special interests—proceed from some contestable point of view—and none is "generally human." And that is why identity interests, as long as they are ideological and not merely tribal, constitute a perfectly respectable reason for awarding your vote.

TOPICS FOR CRITICAL THINKING AND WRITING

1. Fish starts out his essay with a formal and explicit definition of "identity politics." What do you think of that definition? Is it too broad? Too narrow? Too vague? Can you think of any ways to improve it?

2. What is the origin of the epigram, "My country right or wrong"? Does Fish endorse it? Do you? Why is it offered as an example of identity politics? Explain your views.

3. Suppose someone said that it is naïve to advocate deciding issues of public concern by appeal to one's status as "a human being" (para. 3). How would you reply? Do so in an essay of 300 words.

4. Fish speaks of two different practices under the rubric of "identity politics." What are they? Which, if either, does Fish prefer, and why? Is either of these related to what Fish in the title of his essay refers to as "rational" politics?

5. Is the appeal at Fish's essay all *logos* and *ethos*, or do you also find some humor and some *pathos*? If so, cite passages.

Gloria Jiménez

Gloria Jiménez married immediately after she graduated from high school, worked briefly, had two children, and then, after her younger child started school, continued her own formal education. This essay, written for a composition course at Tufts University in 2003, is her first publication.

Against the Odds, and against the Common Good

(Student Essay)

State-run lotteries are now so common—thirty-nine states and Washington, D.C., operate lotteries—that the states probably will never get out of the lottery business. Still, when all is said and done about lotteries bringing a bit of excitement into the lives of many people and bringing a vast amount of money into the lives of a few, the states should not be in the business of urging people to gamble.

And they *do* urge people. Consider a slogan used in Maryland, "Play Today. Cash Tomorrow." If the statement were, "Get a job today and you will have cash tomorrow," it would be true; it would make sense, however small the earnings might be. But "Play Today. Cash Tomorrow" falsely suggests that the way to have money tomorrow is to buy a ticket today. In fact, buying a ticket is an almost sure-fire way of getting nothing for something.

Maryland is not the only state that uses a clever slogan to get its citizens to part with hard-earned money. New York's ads say, "You Can't Win If You Don't Play," and Oregon's ads say, "There Is No Such Thing as a Losing Ticket." This last slogan—which at first glance seems to say that every ticket will benefit the purchaser—is built on the idea that the state's share of the money goes to a worthy cause, usually education or some social service. But no matter how you look at it, this slogan, like the others, urges people to buy a product—a jackpot—that they have almost no chance of receiving.

The chief arguments *in favor* of state-run lotteries seem to be these: (1) people freely choose to participate; (2) funds are used for education or for other important services; (3) if this source of funding disappears, the states will have to compensate by imposing taxes of one sort or another; (4) operation by the government ensures that the lotteries are run honestly; and (5) lotteries create jobs. We can respond briefly to the last two points, and then concentrate on the first three.

It probably is true that the lotteries are run honestly (though I 5 seem to recall reading in the newspaper about one state in which corruption was found in administering the lottery), but that is not the point. If it is wrong to encourage people to gamble, it is hardly relevant to say that the game is run honestly. The other point that can be dismissed briefly is that lotteries create jobs. This argument is usually advanced in connection with the creation of casinos, which surely do create jobs, not only in the casinos but also in nearby restaurants, parking lots, movie theaters, and so forth. But lottery tickets are sold in places where the clerks are already employed. Presumably the only new jobs created by the lottery are the relatively few jobs of the people who dream up the slogans or who are in charge of collecting and processing the receipts.

The three other claims require more attention. The first, that people freely choose to participate, probably is largely true. Although some buyers are compulsive gamblers, people who are addicted and therefore cannot really be said to choose freely, I grant that most people do have a free choice—although, as I have already said, I think that some of the slogans that states use are deceptive, and if this is the case, purchasers who are misled by the ads are not entirely free. Consider a slogan that Illinois used on billboards, especially in poor neighborhoods: "This Could Be Your Ticket Out." Yes, a person might hit the jackpot and get out of poverty, but the chances are one in several million, and to imply that the lottery is a reasonable option to get out of present poverty is to be deceptive. Further, the message is essentially unwholesome. It implies that the way out is luck, rather than education and hard work. Of course, luck plays a part in life, but 99.99 percent of the people who rely on the ticket as the "ticket out" of poverty are going to be terribly disappointed. But again, we can grant that except for gambling addicts, people who buy lottery tickets are freely doing so.

Probably the strongest claim is that the funds are used for important purposes, usually education. This claim apparently is true: The legislators are smart enough to package the lottery bills this way. And the revenue gained seems enormous—$20 billion in 2002, according to the *New York Times* (May 18, 2003, sec. 4, p. 1). On the other hand, this amount is only about 4 percent of the total revenue of the states. That is, this amount *could* be raised by other means, specifically by taxation, but legislators understandably do not want to be associated with increasing taxes. And so, again, advocates of state lotteries emphasize the voluntary nature of the lottery: By buying lottery tickets, they say, people are in effect volunteering to give money to the states, in exchange for the chance (however remote) of getting a ticket out. Buying a ticket, in this view, is paying an optional tax; if you don't want to pay the tax, don't buy the ticket.

I now get to the point in my argument where I may sound condescending, where I may offend decent people. The point is this: Studies show that most of the tickets are bought by people who don't have much money, people who are near the bottom of the economic scale. According to one study, adults whose income was under $10,000 spent nearly three times as much buying lottery tickets as did adults who earned $50,000 or more.[1] I say that this argument is delicate because anyone who advances it is liable to be accused of being snobbish and paternalistic, of saying, in effect, "Poor people don't know how to manage their money, so we ought to remove temptation from their eyes." But such a reply does not get to the central issues: The central issues are (1) that the state should not tempt people, rich or poor, with dreams of an easy buck

---

[1] Verna V. Gehring, "The American State Lottery: Sale or Swindle?" *Report from the Institute for Philosophy and Public Policy* 20 (Winter/Spring 2000): 15.

and (2) that education and social services are immensely important to the whole of society, so they should not be disproportionately financed by the poor and the addicted.

Let me end a bit indirectly. Surely everyone will grant that tobacco is a harmful product. Yes, it is legal, but everyone knows it is harmful. The state puts very heavy taxes on it, presumably not to raise revenue but to discourage the use of tobacco. We agree, surely, that it would be almost criminal if, in an effort to increase its revenues, the state *enticed* people to smoke—for example, by posting billboards showing attractive people smoking or cartoon characters that appealed to children. Would we say, "Oh, well, we need the revenue (from the taxes) to provide services, so let's make smoking as attractive as we can to get people to buy cigarettes"? No, we would say, "People should not smoke, but if they will, well, let's use the revenue from the taxes for two chief purposes: *to dissuade* people from smoking and *to treat* people who have become ill from smoking."

State legislators who genuinely have the interests of their constitu- 10 ents at heart will not pass bills that put the state into the lottery business and that cause the state to engage in an activity that is close to pickpocketing. Rather, they will recognize that, however unpopular taxes are, taxes may have to be raised to support education and social services that the people rightly expect the state to provide. It's against the odds to expect politicians to act this way, but let's hope that some politicians will do the right thing and will vote for the common good.

Topics for Critical Thinking and Writing

1. Jiménez omits at least one important argument that advocates of state-run lotteries sometimes offer: If our state doesn't run a lottery, residents will simply go to nearby states to buy tickets, so we will just be losing revenue that other states pick up; poor people will still be spending money that they can't afford, and our state will in no way benefit. What do you suppose Jiménez might say in reply? And what is your own view of this argument?

2. A bit of humor appears at the end of Jiménez's second paragraph. Is it appropriate? Or is the essay too solemn, too preachy? If you think it is too preachy, cite some sentences, and then revise them to make them more acceptable.

3. What would you say are the strengths and the weaknesses of this essay? What grade would you give it, and why? If you were the instructor in this first-year composition course, what comment (three or four sentences) would you write at the end of the essay?

4. The essay was written in a composition course. If you were the editor of your college's newspaper, might you run it as an op-ed piece? Why or why not?

Anna Lisa Raya

Daughter of a second-generation Mexican American father and a Puerto Rican mother, Anna Lisa Raya grew up in Los Angeles. While an undergraduate at Columbia University in New York, she wrote and published this essay on identity.

It's Hard Enough Being Me

(Student Essay)

When I entered college, I *discovered* I was Latina. Until then, I had never questioned who I was or where I was from: My father is a second-generation Mexican American, born and raised in Los Angeles, and my mother was born in Puerto Rico and raised in Compton, California. My home is El Sereno, a predominantly Mexican neighborhood in L.A. Every close friend I have back home is Mexican. So I was always just Mexican. Though sometimes I was just Puerto Rican—like when we would visit Mamo (my grandma) or hang out with my Aunt Titi.

Upon arriving in New York as a first-year student, 3,000 miles from home, I not only experienced extreme culture shock, but for the first time I had to define myself according to the broad term "Latina." Although culture shock and identity crisis are common for the newly minted collegian who goes away to school, my experience as a newly minted Latina was, and still is, even more complicating. In El Sereno, I felt like I was part of a majority, whereas at the College I am a minority.

I've discovered that many Latinos like myself have undergone similar experiences. We face discrimination for being a minority in this country while also facing criticism for being "whitewashed" or "sellouts" in the countries of our heritage. But as an ethnic group in college, we are forced to define ourselves according to some vague, generalized Latino experience. This requires us to know our history, our language, our music, and our religion. I can't even be a content "Puerto Mexican" because I have to be a politically-and-socially-aware-Latina-with-a-chip-on-my-shoulder-because-of-how-repressed-I-am-in-this-country.

I am none of the above. I am the quintessential imperfect Latina. I can't dance salsa to save my life, I learned about Montezuma and the Aztecs in sixth grade, and I haven't prayed to the *Virgen de Guadalupe* in years.

Apparently I don't even look Latina. I can't count how many times ⁵ people have just assumed that I'm white or asked me if I'm Asian. True, my friends back home call me *güera* ("whitey") because I have green eyes and pale skin, but that was as bad as it got. I never thought I would wish my skin were a darker shade or my hair a curlier texture, but since I've been in college, I have—many times.

Another thing: My Spanish is terrible. Every time I call home, I berate my mama for not teaching me Spanish when I was a child. In fact, not knowing how to speak the language of my home countries is the biggest problem that I have encountered, as have many Latinos. In Mexico there is a term, *pocha,* which is used by native Mexicans to ridicule Mexican Americans. It expresses a deep-rooted antagonism and dislike for those of us who were raised on the other side of the border. Our failed attempts to speak pure, Mexican Spanish are largely responsible for the dislike. Other Latin American natives have this same attitude. No matter how well a Latino speaks Spanish, it can never be good enough.

Yet Latinos can't even speak Spanish in the U.S. without running the risk of being called "spic" or "wetback." That is precisely why my mother refused to teach me Spanish when I was a child. The fact that she spoke Spanish was constantly used against her: It prevented her from getting good jobs, and it would have placed me in bilingual education—a construct of the Los Angeles public school system that has proved to be more of a hindrance to intellectual development than a help.

To be fully Latina in college, however, I *must* know Spanish. I must satisfy the equation: Latina [equals] Spanish-speaking.

So I'm stuck in this black hole of an identity crisis, and college isn't making my life any easier, as I thought it would. In high school, I was being prepared for an adulthood in which I would be an individual, in which I wouldn't have to wear a Catholic school uniform anymore. But though I led an anonymous adolescence, I knew who I was. I knew I was different from white, black, or Asian people. I knew there was a language other than English that I could call my own if I only knew how to speak it better. I knew there were historical reasons why I was in this country, distinct reasons that make my existence here easier or more difficult than other people's existence. Ultimately, I was content.

Now I feel pushed into a corner, always defining, defending, and 10 proving myself to classmates, professors, or employers. Trying to understand who and why I am, while understanding Plato or Homer, is a lot to ask of myself.

A month ago, I heard three Nuyorican (Puerto Ricans born and raised in New York) writers discuss how New York City has influenced their writing. One problem I have faced as a young writer is finding a voice that is true to my community. I was surprised and reassured to discover that as Latinos, these writers had faced similar pressures and conflicts as myself; some weren't even taught Spanish in childhood. I will never forget the advice that one of them gave me that evening: She said that I need to be true to myself. "Because people will always complain about what you are doing—you're a 'gringa' or a 'spic' no matter what," she explained. "So you might as well do things for yourself and not for them."

I don't know why it has taken 20 years to hear this advice, but I'm going to give it a try. *Soy yo* and no one else. *Punto.*[1]

---

[1]**Soy yo . . . Punto.** I'm me . . . Period (Spanish). [Editors' note.]

Topics for Critical Thinking and Writing

1. When Raya says she "discovered" she was Latina (para. 1), to what kind of event is she referring? Was she coerced or persuaded to declare herself as Latina, or did it come about in some other way?

2. Is Raya on balance glad or sorry that she did not learn Spanish as a child? What evidence can you point to in her essay one way or the other?

3. What is an "identity crisis" (para. 9)? Does everyone go through such a crisis about the time one enters college? Did you? Or is this an experience that only racial minorities in predominantly white American colleges undergo?

Ronald Takaki

Ronald Takaki (1939–2009), the grandson of agricultural laborers who had come from Japan, was a professor of ethnic studies at the University of California at Berkeley. He edited From Different Shores: Perspectives on Race and Ethnicity in America *(1987) and wrote (among other writings)* Strangers from a Different Shore: A History of Asian-Americans *(1989). The essay that we reprint appeared originally in the* New York Times *on June 16, 1990.*

The Harmful Myth of Asian Superiority

Asian Americans have increasingly come to be viewed as a "model minority." But are they as successful as claimed? And for whom are they supposed to be a model?

Asian Americans have been described in the media as "excessively, even provocatively" successful in gaining admission to universities. Asian American shopkeepers have been congratulated, as well as criticized, for their ubiquity and entrepreneurial effectiveness.

If Asian Americans can make it, many politicians and pundits ask, why can't African Americans? Such comparisons pit minorities against each other and generate African American resentment toward Asian Americans. The victims are blamed for their plight, rather than racism and an economy that has made many young African American workers superfluous.

The celebration of Asian Americans has obscured reality. For example, figures on the high earnings of Asian Americans relative to Caucasians are misleading. Most Asian Americans live in California, Hawaii, and New York—states with higher incomes and higher costs of living than the national average.

Even Japanese Americans, often touted for their upward mobility, 5 have not reached equality. While Japanese American men in California earned an average income comparable to Caucasian men in 1980, they did so only by acquiring more education and working more hours.

Comparing family incomes is even more deceptive. Some Asian American groups do have higher family incomes than Caucasians. But they have more workers per family.

The "model minority" image homogenizes Asian Americans and hides their differences. For example, while thousands of Vietnamese American young people attend universities, others are on the streets. They live in motels and hang out in pool halls in places like East Los Angeles; some join gangs.

Twenty-five percent of the people in New York City's Chinatown lived below the poverty level in 1980, compared with 17 percent of the city's population. Some 60 percent of the workers in the Chinatowns of Los Angeles and San Francisco are crowded into low-paying jobs in garment factories and restaurants.

"Most immigrants coming into Chinatown with a language barrier cannot go outside this confined area into the mainstream of American industry," a Chinese immigrant said. "Before, I was a painter in Hong Kong, but I can't do it here. I got no license, no education. I want a living; so it's dishwasher, janitor, or cook."

Hmong and Mien refugees from Laos have unemployment rates that 10 reach as high as 80 percent. A 1987 California study showed that three out of ten Southeast Asian refugee families had been on welfare for four to ten years.

Although college-educated Asian Americans are entering the professions and earning good salaries, many hit the "glass ceiling"—the barrier through which high management positions can be seen but not reached. In 1988, only 8 percent of Asian Americans were "officials" and "managers," compared with 12 percent for all groups.

Finally, the triumph of Korean immigrants has been exaggerated. In 1988, Koreans in the New York metropolitan area earned only 68 percent of the median income of non-Asians. More than three-quarters of Korean greengrocers, those so-called paragons of bootstrap entrepreneurialism, came to America with a college education. Engineers, teachers, or administrators while in Korea, they became shopkeepers after their arrival. For many of them, the greengrocery represents dashed dreams, a step downward in status.

For all their hard work and long hours, most Korean shopkeepers do not actually earn very much: $17,000 to $35,000 a year, usually representing the income from the labor of an entire family.

But most Korean immigrants do not become shopkeepers. Instead, many find themselves trapped as clerks in grocery stores, service workers in restaurants, seamstresses in garment factories, and janitors in hotels.

Most Asian Americans know their "success" is largely a myth. They 15 also see how the celebration of Asian Americans as a "model minority" perpetuates their inequality and exacerbates relations between them and African Americans.

TOPICS FOR CRITICAL THINKING AND WRITING

1. What is the thesis of Takaki's essay? What is the evidence he offers for its truth? Do you find his argument convincing? Explain your answers to these questions in an essay of 500 words. Alternatively, write a 500-word blog post that responds to this essay.

2. Takaki several times uses statistics to make a point. What effect do the statistics have on the reader? Do some of the statistics seem more convincing than others? Explain.

3. Consider Takaki's title. To what group(s) is the myth of Asian superiority harmful?

4. Suppose you believed that Asian Americans are economically more successful in America today, relative to white Americans, than African Americans are. Does Takaki agree or disagree with you? What evidence, if any, does he cite to support or reject the belief?

5. Takaki attacks the "myth" of Asian American success and thus rejects the idea that they are a "model minority" (recall the opening and closing paragraphs). What do you think a genuine model minority would be like? Can you think of any racial or ethnic minority in the United States that can serve as a model? Explain why or why not in an essay of 500 words.

James Q. Wilson

James Q. Wilson (1931–2012) was Collins Professor of Management and Public Policy at the University of California at Los Angeles. Among his books are Thinking about Crime *(1975),* Bureaucracy *(1989),* The Moral Sense *(1993), and* Moral Judgment *(1997). The essay that we reprint appeared originally in the* New York Times Magazine *on March 20, 1994.*

Just Take Away Their Guns

The president wants still tougher gun control legislation and thinks it will work. The public supports more gun control laws but suspects they won't work. The public is right.

Legal restraints on the lawful purchase of guns will have little effect on the illegal use of guns. There are some 200 million guns in private ownership, about one-third of them handguns. Only about 2 percent of the latter are employed to commit crimes. It would take a Draconian, and politically impossible, confiscation of legally purchased guns to make much of a difference in the number used by criminals. Moreover, only about one-sixth of the handguns used by serious criminals are purchased from a gun shop or pawnshop. Most of these handguns are stolen, borrowed, or obtained through private purchases that wouldn't be affected by gun laws.

What is worse, any successful effort to shrink the stock of legally purchased guns (or of ammunition) would reduce the capacity of law-abiding people to defend themselves. Gun control advocates scoff at the importance of self-defense, but they are wrong to do so. Based on a household survey, Gary Kleck, a criminologist at Florida State University, has estimated that every year, guns are used—that is, displayed or fired—for defensive purposes more than a million times, not counting their use by the police. If his estimate is correct, this means that the number of people who defend themselves with a gun exceeds the number of arrests for violent crimes and burglaries.

Our goal should not be the disarming of law-abiding citizens. It should be to reduce the number of people who carry guns unlawfully, especially in places—on streets, in taverns—where the mere presence of a gun can increase the hazards we all face. The most effective way to reduce illegal gun-carrying is to encourage the police to take guns away from people who carry them without a permit. This means encouraging the police to make street frisks.

The Fourth Amendment to the Constitution bans "unreasonable 5 searches and seizures." In 1968 the Supreme Court decided (*Terry v. Ohio*) that a frisk—patting down a person's outer clothing—is proper if the officer has a "reasonable suspicion" that the person is armed and dangerous. If a pat-down reveals an object that might be a gun, the officer can enter the suspect's pocket to remove it. If the gun is being carried illegally, the suspect can be arrested.

The reasonable-suspicion test is much less stringent than the probable-cause standard the police must meet in order to make an arrest. A reasonable suspicion, however, is more than just a hunch; it must be supported by specific facts. The courts have held, not always consistently, that these facts include someone acting in a way that leads an experienced officer to conclude criminal activity may be afoot; someone fleeing at the approach of an officer; a person who fits a drug courier profile; a motorist stopped for a traffic violation who has a suspicious bulge in his pocket; a suspect identified by a reliable informant as carrying a gun. The Supreme Court has also upheld frisking people on probation or parole.

Some police departments frisk a lot of people, but usually the police frisk rather few, at least for the purpose of detecting illegal guns. In 1992 the police arrested about 240,000 people for illegally possessing or carrying a weapon. This is only about one-fourth as many as were arrested for public drunkenness. The average police officer will make *no* weapons arrests and confiscate *no* guns during any given year. Mark Moore, a professor of public policy at Harvard University, found that most weapons arrests were made because a citizen complained, not because the police were out looking for guns.

It is easy to see why. Many cities suffer from a shortage of officers, and even those with ample law-enforcement personnel worry about having their cases thrown out for constitutional reasons or being accused of police harassment. But the risk of violating the Constitution or engaging in actual, as opposed to perceived, harassment can be substantially reduced.

Each patrol officer can be given a list of people on probation or parole who live on that officer's beat and be rewarded for making frequent stops to insure that they are not carrying guns. Officers can be trained to recognize the kinds of actions that the Court will accept as providing the "reasonable suspicion" necessary for a stop and frisk. Membership in a gang known for assaults and drug dealing could be made the basis, by statute or Court precedent, for gun frisks.

The available evidence supports the claim that self-defense is a 10 legitimate form of deterrence. People who report to the National Crime Survey that they defended themselves with a weapon were less likely to lose property in a robbery or be injured in an assault than those who did not defend themselves. Statistics have shown that would-be burglars are threatened by gun-wielding victims about as many times a year as they are arrested (and much more often than they are sent to prison) and that the chances of a burglar being shot are about the same as his chances of going to jail. Criminals know these facts even if gun control advocates do not and so are less likely to burgle occupied homes in America than occupied ones in Europe, where the residents rarely have guns.

Some gun control advocates may concede these points but rejoin that the cost of self-defense is self-injury: Handgun owners are more likely to shoot themselves or their loved ones than a criminal. Not quite. Most gun accidents involve rifles and shotguns, not handguns. Moreover, the rate of fatal gun accidents has been declining while the level of gun ownership has been rising. There are fatal gun accidents just as there are fatal car accidents, but in fewer than 2 percent of the gun fatalities was the victim someone mistaken for an intruder.

Those who urge us to forbid or severely restrict the sale of guns ignore these facts. Worse, they adopt a position that is politically absurd. In effect, they say, "Your government, having failed to protect your person and your property from criminal assault, now intends to deprive you of the opportunity to protect yourself."

Opponents of gun control make a different mistake. The National Rifle Association and its allies tell us that "guns don't kill, people kill" and urge the Government to punish more severely people who use guns to commit crimes. Locking up criminals does protect society from future crimes, and the prospect of being locked up may deter criminals. But our experience with meting out tougher sentences is mixed. The tougher the prospective sentence the less likely it is to be imposed, or at least to be imposed swiftly. If the Legislature adds on time for crimes committed with a gun, prosecutors often bargain away the add-ons; even when they do not, the judges in many states are reluctant to impose add-ons.

Worse, the presence of a gun can contribute to the magnitude of the crime even on the part of those who worry about serving a long prison sentence. Many criminals carry guns not to rob stores but to protect themselves from other armed criminals. Gang violence has become more threatening to bystanders as gang members have begun to arm themselves. People may commit crimes, but guns make some crimes worse. Guns often convert spontaneous outbursts of anger into fatal encounters. When some people carry them on the streets, others will want to carry them to protect themselves, and an urban arms race will be underway.

And modern science can be enlisted to help. Metal detectors at airports have reduced the number of airplane bombings and skyjackings to nearly zero. But these detectors only work at very close range. What is needed is a device that will enable the police to detect the presence of a large lump of metal in someone's pocket from a distance of ten or fifteen feet. Receiving such a signal could supply the officer with reasonable grounds for a pat-down. Underemployed nuclear physicists and electronics engineers in the post-cold-war era surely have the talents for designing a better gun detector.

Even if we do all these things, there will still be complaints. Innocent people will be stopped. Young black and Hispanic men will probably be stopped more often than older white Anglo males or women of any race. But if we are serious about reducing drive-by shootings, fatal gang wars and lethal quarrels in public places, we must get illegal guns off the street. We cannot do this by multiplying the forms one fills out at gun shops or by pretending that guns are not a problem until a criminal uses one.

TOPICS FOR CRITICAL THINKING AND WRITING

1. If you had to single out one sentence in Wilson's essay as coming close to stating his thesis, what sentence would that be? Why do you think it states, better than any other sentence, the thesis of the essay?

2. In his third paragraph Wilson reviews some research by a criminologist purporting to show that guns are important for self-defense in American households. Does the research as reported show that displaying or firing guns in self-defense actually prevented crimes? Or wounded aggressors? Suppose you were also told that in households where guns may be used defensively, thousands of innocent people are injured, and hundreds are killed—for instance, children who find a loaded gun and play with it. Would you regard these injuries and deaths as a fair trade-off? Explain. What does the research presented by Wilson really show?

3. In paragraph 12 Wilson says that people who want to severely restrict the ownership of guns are in effect saying, "'Your government, having failed to protect your person and your property from criminal assault,

now intends to deprive you of the opportunity to protect yourself.'" What reply might an advocate of severe restrictions make? (Even if you strongly believe Wilson's summary is accurate, try to put yourself in the shoes of an advocate of gun control, and come up with the best reply that you can.)

4. Wilson reports in paragraph 7 that the police arrest four times as many drunks on the streets as they do people carrying unlicensed firearms. Does this strike you as absurd, reasonable, or mysterious? Does Wilson explain it to your satisfaction?

5. In his final paragraph Wilson grants that his proposal entails a difficulty: "Innocent people will be stopped. Young black and Hispanic men will probably be stopped more often than older white Anglo males or women of any race." Assuming that his predictions are accurate, is Wilson's proposal therefore fatally flawed and worth no further thought, or (to take the other extreme view) do you think that innocent people who fall into certain classifications will just have to put up with frisking for the public good?

6. In an essay of no more than 100 words, explain the difference between the "reasonable-suspicion" test (para. 5) and the "probable-cause standard" (para. 6) that the courts use in deciding whether a street frisk is lawful. (You may want to organize your essay into two paragraphs, one on each topic, or perhaps into three if you want to use a brief introductory paragraph.)

7. Wilson criticizes both gun control advocates and the National Rifle Association for their ill-advised views. In an essay of 500 words, state his criticisms of each side, and explain whether and to what extent you agree.

Kayla Webley

Kayla Webley, the education correspondent for Time *magazine, did her undergraduate work at the University of Washington, concentrating on journalism and political science, and her graduate work at Northwestern University, specializing in new media. The essay that we reprint originally appeared in* Time *magazine on April 20, 2012.*

Is Forgiving Student Loan Debt a Good Idea?

Every few weeks now a petition pops up in my Facebook newsfeed urging the government to forgive all student debt. The comment from the person posting the petition usually goes something like this, "Guessing this will never happen, but can't hurt to sign on!"

The petition now has nearly 670,000 signatures. Scrolling through the stories posted on the petition (and similar stories told on the related

Occupy Student Debt site) can be a heart-wrenching experience. Former students tell stories of unemployment, worthless majors, low-paying jobs and resulting six-figure debt, insurmountable interest, forbearance and default. From a human standpoint, it's easy to see why forgiving student debt holds some appeal. But many have questioned not only the enormous and economically unfeasible cost, but the purported benefits and fairness of a one-time student loan bailout.

Feeling shackled by an estimated $88,000 in student loan debt, Robert Applebaum started the petition in 2009 and has seen its popularity skyrocket since last fall as some members of the Occupy Wall Street movement adopted the battle cry. His proposal is simple: Provide a one-time bailout of student loan debt—currently valued at $1 trillion—as a way to stimulate the still-limping economy. After all, college graduates are the type of people society needs to do things like start businesses, buy homes and cars, invent things, and make babies—and people burdened with debt are less likely to make those kinds of decisions. Unburden them and the housing market might improve, along with the overall economy. "With the stroke of the President's pen, millions of Americans would suddenly have hundreds, or in some cases, thousands of extra dollars in their pockets each and every month with which to spend on ailing sectors of the economy," Applebaum writes in the petition.

That sounds like a very expensive proposition, of course. But so were the bank and auto bailouts—and, the thinking goes, if "fat cat" bankers and auto makers got a bailout, why not college graduates?

Well, as Justin Wolfers writes on the Freakonomics blog, one rea- 5
son why not is that such a scheme wouldn't be a particularly efficient fiscal stimulus. Someone who has $50,000 in debt forgiven isn't likely to pump all those dollars back into the economy in a short amount of time. A much more effective stimulus, Wolfers says, would be to give fifty poor people $1,000 each because that money would almost immediately be spent.

Another problem with such a plan is that most borrowers actually can afford to pay off their student loan debt. There are some borrowers who desperately need relief, but there are many others who would just rather not have to fork over a certain percentage of their income each month to pay for the education they received years ago. But if forgiveness was offered, who wouldn't take the handout?

As it turns out, the six-figure debts that we keep hearing about in the media are actually pretty unusual. By most estimates, only a tiny minority of student loan borrowers—as little as 1 percent—graduate with more than $100,000 in debt. Mark Kantrowitz of FinAid.org and FastWeb.com says that only a few thousand students out of the several million who finish college each year graduate with that much debt. The average debt total at graduation is a much more reasonable—yet still significant—$27,500.

What's more, even borrowers who can't afford the standard repayment plan have existing alternatives if the loan is from the government. There are already programs in place that offer forgiveness, not to mention the government's effective and underutilized Income Based Repayment program. What might be a more politically viable approach to student debt—although it would provide less fiscal stimulus—would be for the government and loan providers to have a better way of distinguishing between those borrowers who really need help and those who don't. But of course that's no easy task.

Many of the concerns surrounding Applebaum's plan involve the idea of fairness. Why should current debt holders be forgiven when for years people have paid their debts? Why should taxpayers—especially those who never attended college in the first place—foot the bill for the borrowers' education? What about future generations? Will they just take out loads of money in college and cross their fingers for a bailout? There are no easy answers to these questions other than to say, life isn't fair.

But perhaps the biggest roadblock to Applebaum's plan is that a one-time bailout is a temporary fix to an ongoing problem. What's really needed is a long look at how higher education in the United States is financed. Many would argue the current model is fundamentally broken. Virtually everyone who applies is approved for almost unlimited student loans, regardless of how likely they are to be able to pay them back. But lenders aren't really concerned about that because student loans cannot be discharged in bankruptcy. They know they'll get their money back one way or another.

As a result, lenders have no incentive to work with students toward a reasonable repayment plan. And further, colleges have no incentive to keep tuition low—tuition is increasing at a rate double that of inflation—because whether they can afford it or not, students will find a way to pay the bill.

Applebaum's proposal offers a radical and wildly unfeasible solution, both politically and economically, but it's an idea nonetheless. "I'm not saying my solution to the student debt crisis is the very best," he says. "If you disagree with me, what's your solution?"

Topics for Critical Thinking and Writing

1. Why do you suppose Webley prefaces her argument by telling us in paragraph 2 that some of the stories on the Occupy Student Debt site are "heart-wrenching"?

2. What do you think of Webley's final paragraph as a way of ending her essay?

3. Do you have any ideas about forgiving student debts that are not touched on in Webley's essay? If so, what are they? How would you work them into the essay?

"I'm looking for a career that won't be obsolete before my student loan is paid off."

Alfred Edmond Jr.

Alfred Edmond Jr. is senior vice president/multimedia editor-at-large of Black Enterprise, a media organization that publishes Black Enterprise *magazine. He appears often on television and on nationally syndicated radio programs.*

Why Asking for a Job Applicant's Facebook Password Is Fair Game

"Should business owners be allowed to ask job applicants for their Facebook passwords?" Many people who watched me on MSNBC's *Your Business* on Sunday were surprised to hear that my answer is "Yes," including the show's host, J. J. Ramberg. This question became a hot news topic last week, especially in business and social media circles, when Congress failed to pass legislation that would have banned the practice of employers asking employees to reveal their Facebook passwords.

Now, if I was asked the same question as a guest on a show called *Your Career*, I would have been hard-pressed to think of a situation where I would share my Facebook password with a potential employer. For me to consider it, I would have to want the job pretty badly, with the amount and type of compensation (including benefits, perks, and even an equity stake in the company) being major considerations. But before doing so, I would see if there were other ways I could address the potential employer's concerns without revealing my password, such as changing my privacy settings to give them the ability to view all of my Facebook content. If they persisted with their request for my password, I would try to negotiate terms to strictly limit both their use of the password and the length of time the potential employer would have access to it before I could change it. I might even consider getting an employment attorney to negotiate an agreement, including terms of confidentiality, to be signed by both me and the potential employer before sharing my password.

Of course, for the vast majority of positions, neither I nor a company looking to hire would deem it worth the time and expense to jump through all of these hoops. Most companies would not care to have password access to an applicant's social media accounts. (For what it's worth, Facebook's terms of rights and responsibilities forbids users from sharing their passwords.) In probably 99 percent of such cases, if a potential employer made such a request, my answer would be, "No, I will not share my password. Are there alternatives you are willing to consider to satisfy your concerns?" I'd accept that I'd risk not being hired as a result. On the other hand, if that was all it took for me not to be hired, I'd question how badly they really wanted me in the first place, as well as whether that was the kind of place I would have been happy working for. But for certain companies and positions, especially if I wanted the job badly enough, I'd consider a request for my Facebook password at least up for negotiation.

That said, my response on *Your Business* was from the perspective of the business owner. And if I'm the owner of certain types of businesses, or trying to fill certain types of positions, I believe I should be able to ask job applicants for access to their Facebook accounts. The applicant may choose not to answer, but I should be able to ask. Depending on the position, knowing everything I possibly can about an applicant is critical to not only making the best hire, but to protecting the interests of my current employees, customers, and partners as well as the financial interests of the company.

On *Your Business*, I pointed to an example where I believe a request 5 for a Facebook password as part of the hiring process is entirely reasonable: the child care industry. If I am running a school or a day care center, the time to find out that a teacher or other worker has a record of inappropriate social media communication with minors, or worse, a history of or predilection for sexual relationships with students, is during the hiring process—as New York City is finding out the hard way, with an epidemic of public school employees being revealed to have had such relationships with students. To me, such a request falls into the same category of checking the backgrounds of potential employees as the common (also still debated) practice of asking job applicants to agree to a credit check, especially for jobs that will require them to handle money, keep the books, or carry out other fiscal duties on behalf of a company. In these and other cases, safety and security issues, and the legal liability that they create for business owners if they are not adequately addressed during the hiring process, outweigh the job applicant's expectation of privacy when it comes to their social media activities.

Speaking of which, I can still hear people screaming (actually tweeting and retweeting) that an employer asking for your Facebook password is a horrible invasion of privacy. Well, for those of you who still believe in Santa Claus, I strongly recommend that you read *The Filter Bubble: What the Internet Is Hiding from You* by Eli Pariser (Penguin Press). Or you can just take my advice and let go of the illusion of privacy on social media. The courts are conflicted, at best, on whether we as social media users have a right to an expectation of privacy, with many cases being decided against such expectations. The last place you want to share anything that is truly private is on your Facebook page or any other social media platform. Better to think of social media as the ultimate "Front Street." No matter what Facebook's privacy policies are (which they can change at will without your permission) and what privacy tools and settings they offer (which they also change whenever it suits their business models), always assume that posting on Facebook is just the ticking time bomb version of you shouting your private business from the middle of Times Square—on steroids.

To paraphrase a quote shared in *The Filter Bubble*, if you're getting something for free, you're not the customer, you're the product. Social media is designed for the information shared on it to be searched and shared—and mined for profit. The business model is the very antithesis of the expectation of privacy. To ignore that reality is to have blind faith in Facebook, Google, Twitter, etc., operating in your best interests above all else, at all times. (I don't.)

Whether you agree with me or not about whether a potential employer asking you for your Facebook password is fair game, I hope you'll take my advice: When considering what to share via social media, don't think business vs. personal. Think public vs. private. And if something is truly private, do not share it on social media out of a misplaced faith in the expectation of privacy.

This debate is far from over, and efforts to update existing, but woefully outdated, privacy laws—not to mention the hiring practices of companies—to catch up with the realities of social media will definitely continue. I'd like to know where you stand, both as entrepreneurs and business owners, as well as potential job applicants. And I'd especially like to hear from human resources and recruiting experts. How far is too far when it comes to a potential employer investigating the social media activity of a job applicant?

Topics for Critical Thinking and Writing

1. Employers *do* (at least at the time we are writing) have the right to require drug tests and personality tests. Do you think they should also legally be allowed to ask for a password to Facebook, or should Congress pass legislation outlawing the practice? If employers are legally allowed to ask, would you provide the password? Why, or why not?

2. Would Edmond's case be strengthened if he gave one or two additional examples—beyond the "child care industry" that he mentions in paragraph 5—of jobs that, a reader might agree, require a thorough background check? What examples can you think of? Would you say that applicants for these jobs should be willing to reveal their Facebook password to a potential employer?

3. In paragraph 7 Edmond paraphrases: "If you're getting something for free, you're not the customer, you're the product." Paraphrase this passage yourself (on paraphrase, see page 39) so that it would be clear to a reader who tells you that he or she finds it puzzling.

Sherry Turkle

Sherry Turkle, born in Brooklyn, New York, in 1948, is Professor of the Social Studies of Science and Technology at the Massachusetts Institute of Technology. Turkle, the author of numerous books, including Alone Together *(2011), often appears on television as a commentator on media. We reprint an essay that originally appeared in the* New York Times, *April 22, 2012.*

The Flight from Conversation

We live in a technological universe in which we are always communicating. And yet we have sacrificed conversation for mere connection.

At home, families sit together, texting and reading e-mail. At work executives text during board meetings. We text (and shop and go on Facebook) during classes and when we're on dates. My students tell me about an important new skill: It involves maintaining eye contact with someone while you text someone else; it's hard, but it can be done.

Over the past fifteen years, I've studied technologies of mobile connection and talked to hundreds of people of all ages and circumstances about their plugged-in lives. I've learned that the little devices most of us carry around are so powerful that they change not only what we do, but also who we are.

We've become accustomed to a new way of being "alone together." Technology-enabled, we are able to be with one another, and also elsewhere, connected to wherever we want to be. We want to customize our lives. We want to move in and out of where we are because the thing we value most is control over where we focus our attention. We have gotten used to the idea of being in a tribe of one, loyal to our own party.

Our colleagues want to go to that board meeting but pay attention 5 only to what interests them. To some this seems like a good idea, but we can end up hiding from one another, even as we are constantly connected to one another.

A businessman laments that he no longer has colleagues at work. He doesn't stop by to talk; he doesn't call. He says that he doesn't want to interrupt them. He says they're "too busy on their e-mail." But then he pauses and corrects himself. "I'm not telling the truth. I'm the one who doesn't want to be interrupted. I think I should. But I'd rather just do things on my BlackBerry."

A sixteen-year-old boy who relies on texting for almost everything says almost wistfully, "Someday, someday, but certainly not now, I'd like to learn how to have a conversation."

In today's workplace, young people who have grown up fearing conversation show up on the job wearing earphones. Walking through a college library or the campus of a high-tech start-up, one sees the same thing: We are together, but each of us is in our own bubble, furiously connected to keyboards and tiny touch screens. A senior partner at a Boston law firm describes a scene in his office. Young associates lay out their suite of technologies: laptops, iPods, and multiple phones. And then they put their earphones on. "Big ones. Like pilots. They turn their desks into cockpits." With the young lawyers in their cockpits, the office is quiet, a quiet that does not ask to be broken.

In the silence of connection, people are comforted by being in touch with a lot of people—carefully kept at bay. We can't get enough of one another if we can use technology to keep one another at distances we can control: not too close, not too far, just right. I think of it as a Goldilocks effect.

Texting and e-mail and posting let us present the self we want to be.   10
This means we can edit. And if we wish to, we can delete. Or retouch: the voice, the flesh, the face, the body. Not too much, not too little—just right.

Human relationships are rich; they're messy and demanding. We have learned the habit of cleaning them up with technology. And the move from conversation to connection is part of this. But it's a process in which we shortchange ourselves. Worse, it seems that over time we stop caring, we forget that there is a difference.

We are tempted to think that our little "sips" of online connection add up to a big gulp of real conversation. But they don't. E-mail, Twitter, Facebook, all of these have their places—in politics, commerce, romance, and friendship. But no matter how valuable, they do not substitute for conversation.

Connecting in sips may work for gathering discrete bits of information or for saying, "I am thinking about you." Or even for saying, "I love you." But connecting in sips doesn't work as well when it comes to understanding and knowing one another. In conversation we tend to one another. (The word itself is kinetic; it's derived from words that mean to move, together.) We can attend to tone and nuance. In conversation, we are called upon to see things from another's point of view.

Face-to-face conversation unfolds slowly. It teaches patience. When we communicate on our digital devices, we learn different habits. As we ramp up the volume and velocity of online connections, we start to expect faster answers. To get these, we ask one another simpler questions; we dumb down our communications, even on the most important matters. It is as though we have all put ourselves on cable news. Shakespeare might have said, "We are consum'd with that which we were nourish'd by."

And we use conversation with others to learn to converse with our-   15
selves. So our flight from conversation can mean diminished chances to learn skills of self-reflection. These days, social media continually asks us what's "on our mind," but we have little motivation to say something truly self-reflective. Self-reflection in conversation requires trust. It's hard to do anything with 3,000 Facebook friends except connect.

As we get used to being shortchanged on conversation and to getting by with less, we seem almost willing to dispense with people altogether. Serious people muse about the future of computer programs as psychiatrists. A high school sophomore confides to me that he wishes he could talk to an artificial intelligence program instead of his dad about dating; he says the A.I. would have so much more in its database. Indeed, many people tell me they hope that as Siri, the digital assistant on Apple's iPhone, becomes more advanced, "she" will be more and more like a best friend—one who will listen when others won't.

During the years I have spent researching people and their relationships with technology, I have often heard the sentiment "No one is listening to me." I believe this feeling helps explain why it is so appealing to have a Facebook page or a Twitter feed—each provides so many automatic listeners. And it helps explain why—against all reason—so many of us are willing to talk to machines that seem to care about us. Researchers around the world are busy inventing sociable robots, designed to be companions to the elderly, to children, to all of us.

One of the most haunting experiences during my research came when I brought one of these robots, designed in the shape of a baby seal, to an elder-care facility, and an older woman began to talk to it about the loss of her child. The robot seemed to be looking into her eyes. It seemed to be following the conversation. The woman was comforted.

And so many people found this amazing. Like the sophomore who wants advice about dating from artificial intelligence and those who look forward to computer psychiatry, this enthusiasm speaks to how much we have confused conversation with connection and collectively seem to have embraced a new kind of delusion that accepts the simulation of compassion as sufficient unto the day. And why would we want to talk about love and loss with a machine that has no experience of the arc of human life? Have we so lost confidence that we will be there for one another?

We expect more from technology and less from one another and 20 seem increasingly drawn to technologies that provide the illusion of companionship without the demands of relationship. Always-on/always-on-you devices provide three powerful fantasies: that we will always be heard; that we can put our attention wherever we want it to be; and that we never have to be alone. Indeed our new devices have turned being alone into a problem that can be solved.

When people are alone, even for a few moments, they fidget and reach for a device. Here connection works like a symptom, not a cure, and our constant, reflexive impulse to connect shapes a new way of being.

Think of it as "I share, therefore I am." We use technology to define ourselves by sharing our thoughts and feelings as we're having them. We used to think, "I have a feeling; I want to make a call." Now our impulse is, "I want to have a feeling; I need to send a text."

So, in order to feel more, and to feel more like ourselves, we connect. But in our rush to connect, we flee from solitude, our ability to be separate and gather ourselves. Lacking the capacity for solitude, we turn to other people but don't experience them as they are. It is as though we use them, need them as spare parts to support our increasingly fragile selves.

We think constant connection will make us feel less lonely. The opposite is true. If we are unable to be alone, we are far more likely to be lonely. If we don't teach our children to be alone, they will know only how to be lonely.

I am a partisan for conversation. To make room for it, I see some   25 first, deliberate steps. At home, we can create sacred spaces: the kitchen, the dining room. We can make our cars "device-free zones." We can demonstrate the value of conversation to our children. And we can do the same thing at work. There we are so busy communicating that we often don't have time to talk to one another about what really matters. Employees asked for casual Fridays; perhaps managers should introduce conversational Thursdays. Most of all, we need to remember—in between texts and e-mails and Facebook posts—to listen to one another, even to the boring bits, because it is often in unedited moments, moments in which we hesitate and stutter and go silent, that we reveal ourselves to one another.

I spend the summers at a cottage on Cape Cod, and for decades I walked the same dunes that Thoreau once walked. Not too long ago, people walked with their heads up, looking at the water, the sky, the sand, and at one another, talking. Now they often walk with their heads down, typing. Even when they are with friends, partners, children, everyone is on their own devices.

So I say, look up, look at one another, and let's start the conversation.

Topics for Critical Thinking and Writing

1. Imagine a period when the book—or even the handwritten manuscript—was not yet invented. Now look at Turkle's first paragraph. Think of someone saying what Turkle says, but saying it about the invention of writing, and of the manuscript or book.

2. In paragraph 3 Turkle says that the little devices that we carry "change not only what we we do, but also who we are." We might reply that, yes, of course, almost everything that touches us changes what we are. The invention of the movie theater changed us: Instead of conversing with family or friends, and generating our own entertainment, we sat isolated in the dark for several hours. The possession of an automobile changes us, the move to a new address brings us into contact with new people who may change us—we may even marry one of them—and certainly the engendering of children changes us (or it ought to). But

do you agree with Turkle that the recent electronic devices produce changes of an unexpected sort?

3. In paragraph 14 Turkle suggests that when we communicate electronically, as opposed to when we communicate face-to-face or with pen and paper, "we dumb down our communications, even on the most important matters." Is she describing your behavior? Explain.

4. In paragraph 23 Turkle says, "we flee from solitude, our ability to be separate and gather ourselves." Is this passage true for you? Explain. Might a case be made that, far from being lonely, people who use Facebook and comparable sites are often stimulated to participate in civic and political activities? Does your own experience offer any evidence, one way or the other? Explain.

5. Do you think Turkle's final two paragraphs make an effective ending? Explain.

 For additional arguments online, visit the e-Pages at **bedfordstmartins.com/barnetbedau**.

4

Visual Rhetoric: Images as Arguments

A picture is worth a thousand words.

——PROVERB

"What is the use of a book," thought Alice, "without pictures or conversations?"

——LEWIS CARROLL

SOME USES OF IMAGES

Most visual materials that accompany written arguments serve one of two functions—they appeal to the emotions (e.g., a photograph of a calf in a pen so narrow that the calf cannot turn, in an essay on animal liberation) or they clarify numerical data (e.g., a graph showing five decades of male and female law school enrollments). There are of course additional uses for pictures, for example, cartoons may add a welcome touch of humor or satire, but in this chapter we concentrate on appeals to emotion and briefly on graphs and related images.

APPEALS TO THE EYE

We began the preceding chapter by distinguishing between *argument,* which we said relies on reason (*logos*), and *persuasion,* which we said is a broad term that can include appeals to the emotions (*pathos*)—for example, an appeal to pity. Threats, too, can be persuasive. As Al Capone famously said, "You can get a lot more done with a kind word and a gun than with a kind word alone." Indeed, most of the remarks that we can think of link persuasion not with the power of reason but with the power of emotional appeals, of flattery, of threats, and of appeals to self-interest. We have in mind passages spoken not only by the likes of the racketeer

Al Capone, but by more significant figures. Consider these two remarks, which both use the word *interest* in the sense of "self-interest":

> Would you persuade, speak of Interest, not Reason.
> —Ben Franklin

> There are two levers for moving men—interest and fear.
> —Napoleon Bonaparte

An appeal to self-interest is obviously at the heart of most advertisements: "Buy *X* automobile, and members of the opposite sex will find you irresistible," "Use *Y* instant soup, and your family will love you more," "Try *Z* cereal and enjoy regularity." We will look at advertisements later in this chapter, but first let's talk a bit more about the use and abuse of visual material in persuasion.

When we discussed the appeal to emotion (p. 103), we quoted from Mark Antony's speech to the Roman populace in Shakespeare's *Julius Caesar*. You will recall that Antony stirred the mob by displaying Caesar's blood-stained mantle, that is, by supplementing his words with visual material:

> Look, in this place ran Cassius' dagger through;
> See what a rent the envious Casca made;
> Through this, the well-belovèd Brutus stabbed. . . .

In courtrooms today, trial lawyers and prosecutors still do this sort of thing when

- they exhibit photos of a bloody corpse, or
- they introduce as witnesses small children who sob as they describe the murder of their parents.

The appeal clearly is not to reason but to the jurors' emotions—and yet, can we confidently say that this sort of visual evidence—this attempt to stir anger at the alleged perpetrator of the crime and pity for the victims—is irrelevant? Why shouldn't jurors vicariously experience the assault?

When we think about it—and it takes only a moment of thinking—the appeal in the courtroom to the eye and then to the heart or mind is evident even in smaller things, such as the clothing that the lawyers wear and the clothing that they advise their clients to wear. To take the most obvious, classic example: The mugger who normally wears jeans, a T-shirt, and a leather jacket appears in court in a three-piece suit, dress shirt, and necktie. Lawyers know that in arguing a case, visuals make statements—perhaps not logical arguments but nevertheless meaningful statements that will attract or repel jurors.

Another sort of visual appeal connected with some arguments should be mentioned briefly—the visual appeal of the specific setting in which the argument occurs. Martin Luther King Jr.'s great speech of August 28, 1963, "I Have a Dream," still reads very well on the page, but part of its

Martin Luther King Jr. delivering his "I Have a Dream" speech on August 28, 1963, from the steps of the Lincoln Memorial. The visual aspects—the setting (the Lincoln Memorial with the Washington Monument and the Capitol in the distance) and King's gestures—are part of the persuasive rhetoric of the speech.

immense appeal when it was first given was due to its setting: King spoke to some 200,000 people in Washington, D.C., as he stood on the steps of the Lincoln Memorial. That setting, rich with associations of slavery and of freedom, was part of King's argument.

Pictures—and here we get to our chief subject—are also sometimes used as parts of arguments because pictures make statements. Some pictures, like Edvard Munch's *The Scream* (below), make obvious statements: The swiftly receding diagonal lines of the fence and the walkway, the wavy sky, and the vibrating vertical lines to the right of the figure all convey the great agitation experienced by the figure in the woodcut.

Some pictures, like the photographs shown to members of Congress during the debate over whether permission should be given to drill in the Arctic National Wildlife Refuge are a bit less obvious:

- *Opponents* of drilling showed beautiful pictures of polar bears frolicking, wildflowers in bloom, and caribou on the move.
- *Proponents* of drilling showed bleak pictures of what they called "barren land" and "a frozen wasteland."

Both sides knew very well that images are powerful persuaders, and they did not hesitate to use images as supplements to words.

We again invite you to think about the appropriateness of using images in arguments. Should argument be entirely a matter of reason, of logic (*logos*), without appeals to the emotions (*pathos*)? Or can images

(Edvard Munch, *The Scream.* © 2007 The Munch Museum/ The Munch-Ellingsen Group/Artists Rights Society [ARS], NY. Digital Image ©/The Museum of Modern Art, NY. Licensed by SCALA/Art Resource. Reproduction, including downloading, of Munch works is prohibited by copyright laws and international conventions without the express written permission of Artists Rights Society [ARS], New York.)

of the sort that we have already mentioned provide visual (and emotional) support for reasons that are offered? The statement that "the Arctic National Wildlife Refuge is a home for abundant wildlife, notably polar bears, caribou, and wildflowers" may not mean much until it is reinforced with breathtaking images. (And, similarly, the statement that "most of the ANWR land is barren" may not mean much until it is corroborated by images of the vast bleakness.)

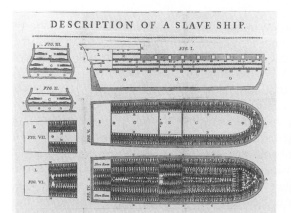

Images played an important role in the activities of the antislavery movement in the nineteenth century. On the top left is a diagram that shows how human cargo was packed into a slave ship; it was distributed with Thomas Clarkson's *Essay on the Slavery and Commerce of the Human Species* (1804). On the top right is Frederick W. Mercer's photograph (April 2, 1863) of Gordon, a "badly lacerated" runaway slave. Images such as the slave ship and Gordon were used against the claims of slaveowners that slavery was a humane institution—claims that also were supported by illustrations, such as the woodcut at the bottom, titled *Attention Paid to a Poor Sick Negro*, from Josiah Priest's *In Defense of Slavery* (1843).

A RULE FOR WRITERS: If you think that pictures will help you to make the point you are arguing, include them with captions explaining sources and relevance.

ARE SOME IMAGES NOT FIT TO BE SHOWN?

Images of suffering—human or, as animal rights activists have made us see, animal—can be immensely persuasive. In the nineteenth century, for instance, the antislavery movement made extremely effective use of images in its campaign. We reproduce two antislavery images here, as well as a counterimage that sought to assure viewers that slavery is a beneficent system (p. 145). But are there some images not fit to print?

Until recently, many newspapers did not print pictures of lynched African Americans, hanged and burned and maimed. The reasons for not printing such images probably differed in the South and North: Southern papers may have considered the images to be discreditable to whites, while Northern papers may have deemed the images too revolting. Even today, when it is commonplace to see in newspapers and on television

Huynh Cong (Nick) Ut, *The Terror of War: Children on Route 1 near Trang Bang*

Eddie Adams, *Execution of Viet Cong prisoner, Saigon,* 1968

screens pictures of dead victims of war, or famine, or traffic accidents, one rarely sees bodies that are horribly maimed. (For traffic accidents, the body is usually covered, and we see only the smashed car.) The U.S. government has refused to release photographs showing the bodies of American soldiers killed in the war in Iraq, and it has been most reluctant to show pictures of dead Iraqi soldiers and civilians. Only after many Iraqis refused to believe that Saddam Hussein's two sons had been killed did the U.S. government reluctantly release pictures showing the blood-spattered faces of the two men—and some American newspapers and television programs refused to use the images.

There have been notable exceptions to this practice, such as Huynh Cong (Nick) Ut's 1972 photograph of children fleeing a napalm attack in Vietnam (p. 146), which was widely reproduced in the United States and won the photographer a Pulitzer Prize in 1973. The influence of this particular photograph cannot be measured, but it is widely felt to have played a substantial role in increasing public pressure to end the Vietnam War. Another widely reproduced picture of horrifying violence is Eddie Adams's picture (1968, above) of a South Vietnamese chief of police firing a pistol into the head of a Viet Cong prisoner.

The issue remains: Are some images unacceptable? For instance, although capital punishment is legal in parts of the United States—by methods including lethal injection, hanging, shooting, and electrocution—every state in the Union prohibits the publication of pictures showing a criminal being executed. (On this topic, see Wendy Lesser, *Pictures at an Execution* [1993].)

The most famous recent example of an image widely thought to be unprintable concerns the murder of Daniel Pearl, a Jewish reporter for the *Wall Street Journal*. Pearl was captured and murdered in June 2002 by Islamic terrorists in Pakistan. His killers videotaped Pearl reading a statement denouncing American policy and being decapitated. The video also shows a man's arm holding Pearl's head. The video ends with the killers making several demands (such as the release of the Muslim prisoners being held by the United States in Guantánamo Bay, Cuba) and asserting that "if our demands are not met, this scene will be repeated again and again."

The chief arguments against reproducing in newspapers material from this video were that

- the video and even still images from it are unbearably gruesome;
- showing the video would traumatize the Pearl family; and
- the video is propaganda by an enemy.

Those who favored broadcasting the video on television and printing still images from it in newspapers tended to argue that

- the photo will show the world what sort of enemy the United States is fighting;
- newspapers have published pictures of other terrifying sights (notably, people leaping out of windows of New York's twin towers and endless pictures of the space shuttle *Challenger* exploding); and
- no one was worried about protecting the families of these other victims from seeing painful images.

But ask yourself if the comparison of the Daniel Pearl video to the photos of the twin towers and of the *Challenger* is valid. You may respond that the individuals in the twin towers pictures are not specifically identifiable and that the images of the *Challenger*, though horrifying, are not as visually revolting as the picture of a severed head held up for view.

The *Boston Phoenix*, a weekly newspaper, published some images from the Daniel Pearl video and also put a link to the video (with a warning that the footage is "extremely graphic") on its Web site. The editor of the *Phoenix* justified publication on the three grounds we list. Pearl's wife, Mariane Pearl, was quoted in various newspapers as condemning the "heartless decision to air this despicable video," and a spokeswoman for the Pearl family, when asked for comment, referred reporters to a statement issued earlier, which said that broadcasters who show the video

fall without shame into the terrorists' plan. . . . Danny believed that journalism was a tool to report the truth and foster understanding—not perpetuate propaganda and sensationalize tragedy. We had hoped that no part of this tape would ever see the light of day. . . . We urge all networks and news outlets to exercise responsibility and not aid the terrorists in spreading their message of hate and murder.[1]

Although some journalists expressed regret that Pearl's family was distressed, they insisted that journalists have a right to reproduce such material and that the images can serve the valuable purpose of shocking viewers into awareness.

Politics and Pictures

Consider, too, the controversy that erupted in 1991, during the Persian Gulf War, when the U.S. government decided that newspapers would not be allowed to photograph coffins returning with the bodies of military personnel killed during the war. In later years the policy was sometimes ignored, but in 2003 the George W. Bush administration decreed that there would be "no arrival ceremony for, or media coverage of, deceased military personnel returning [from Iraq or Afghanistan] . . . to the Dover (Delaware) base." The government enforced the policy strictly.

Members of the news media strongly protested, as did many others, chiefly arguing that

- The administration was trying to sanitize the war, i.e., was depriving the public of important information—images—that showed the real cost of the war.
- Grief for the deaths of military personnel is not a matter only for the families of the deceased. The sacrifices were made for the nation, and the nation should be allowed to grieve. Canada and Britain have no such ban, and when the coffins are transported the public lines the streets to pay honor to the fallen warriors. In fact, in Canada a portion of the highway near the Canadian base has been renamed, "Highway of Heroes."
- The coffins at Dover Air Force base are not identified by name, so there is no issue about intruding on the privacy of grieving families.

The chief arguments in defense of the ban were

- Photographs violate the privacy of the families.
- If the arrival of the coffins at Dover is given publicity, some grieving families will think they should go to Dover to be present when the bodies arrive, and this may cause a financial hardship on the families.
- If the families give their consent, the press is *not* barred from individual graveside ceremonies at hometown burials. The ban extends only to the arrival of the coffins at Dover Air Force Base.

---

[1]Quoted in the *Hartford Courant*, June 5, 2002, and reproduced on the Internet by the Freedom of Information Center, under the heading "Boston Paper Creates Controversy."

Coffins at Dover Air Force Base, Delaware

In February 2009, President Obama changed the policy and permitted coverage of the transfer of bodily remains. In his Address to the Joint
Session of Congress, February 24, 2009, he said, "For seven years we
have been a nation at war. No longer will we hide its price." On February 27, Defense Secretary Robert M. Gates announced that the government ban was lifted and that families will decide whether to allow
photographs and videos of the "dignified transfer process at Dover."

EXERCISE

In an argumentative essay of about 250 words—perhaps two or three
paragraphs—give your view of the issue of permitting photos of military

Alexander Gardner, *Home of a Rebel Sharpshooter*

coffins. In an opening paragraph you may want to explain the issue, and in this same paragraph you may want to summarize the arguments that you reject. The second (and perhaps final) paragraph of a two-paragraph essay may give the reasons you reject those arguments. Additionally, you may want to devote a third paragraph to a more general reflection.

TOPIC FOR CRITICAL THINKING AND WRITING

Marvin Kalb, a distinguished journalist, was quoted as saying that the public has a right to see the tape of Daniel Pearl's murder but that "common sense, decency, [and] humanity would encourage editors . . . to say 'no, it is not necessary to put this out.' There is no urgent demand on the part of the American people to see Daniel Pearl's death." What is your view?

Query   In June 2006 two American soldiers were captured in Iraq. Later their bodies were found, dismembered and beheaded. Should newspapers have shown photographs of the mutilated bodies? Why, or why not? (In July 2006, insurgents in Iraq posted images on the Internet, showing a soldier's severed head beside his body.)

Another issue concerning the appropriateness or inappropriateness of showing images occurred early in 2006. In September 2005 a Danish newspaper, accused of being afraid to show political cartoons that were hostile to Muslim terrorists, responded by publishing twelve cartoons. One cartoon, for instance, showed the Prophet Muhammad wearing a turban that looked like a bomb. The images at first did not arouse much attention, but when in January 2006 they were reprinted in Norway, they attracted worldwide attention and outraged Muslims, most of whom regard any depiction of the Prophet as blasphemous. The upshot is that some Muslims in various Islamic nations burned Danish embassies and engaged in other acts of violence. Most non-Muslims agreed that the images were in bad taste, and apparently in deference to Islamic sensibilities (but possibly also out of fear of reprisals) very few Western newspapers reprinted the cartoons when they covered the news events. Most newspapers (including the *New York Times*) were content merely to describe the images. These papers believed that readers had to be told the news but because the drawings were so offensive to some persons they should be described rather than reprinted. A controversy then arose: Do readers of a newspaper deserve to *see* the evidence for themselves, or can a newspaper adequately fulfill its function by offering only a verbal description?

Persons who argued that the images should be reproduced generally made these points:

- Newspapers should yield neither to the delicate sensibilities of some readers nor to threats of violence.

- Jews for the most part do not believe that God should be depicted (the prohibition against "graven images" is found in Exodus 20.3), but they raise no objections to such Christian images as Michelangelo's painting of God awakening Adam, depicted on the ceiling of the Sistine Chapel. Further, when Andres Serrano (a Christian) in 1989 exhibited a photograph of a small plastic crucifix submerged in urine, it outraged a wider public—several U.S. senators condemned it because the artist had received federal funds—but virtually all newspapers showed the image, and many even printed its title, *Piss Christ*. That is, the subject was judged to be newsworthy, and the fact that some viewers would regard the image as blasphemous was not considered highly relevant.

- We value freedom of speech, and newspapers should not be intimidated. When certain pictures are a matter of news, the pictures should be shown to readers.

On the other hand, opposing voices were heard:

- Newspapers should—must—recognize deep-seated religious beliefs. They should indeed report the news, but there is no reason to *show* images that some people regard as blasphemous. The images can be adequately *described* in words.

- The Jewish response to Christian images of God and even the tolerant Christian's response to Serrano's image of Christ immersed in urine are simply irrelevant to the issue of whether images of the Prophet Muhammad should be represented in a Western newspaper. Virtually all Muslims regard depictions of the Prophet as blasphemous, and that is what counts.

- Despite all the Western talk about freedom of the press, the press does *not* reproduce all images that become matters of news. For instance, news items about the sale of child pornography do not include images of the pornographic photos.

EXERCISES: THINKING ABOUT IMAGES

1. Does the display of the cartoons constitute an argument? If so, what is the conclusion, and what are the premises? If not, then what sort of statement, if any, does publishing these cartoons constitute?

2. Hugh Hewitt, an evangelical Christian, offered a comparison to the cartoon of Muhammad with a bomblike turban. Suppose, he asked, an abortion clinic had been bombed by someone who said he was an Evangelical Christian. Would newspapers publish "a cartoon of Christ's crown of thorns transformed into sticks of TNT?" Do you think they would? If you were the editor of a paper, would you? Why, or why not?

3. One American newspaper, the *Boston Phoenix*, did not publish any of the cartoons "out of fear of retaliation from the international brotherhood of radical and bloodthirsty Islamists who seek to impose their will on those who do not believe as they do. . . . We could not in good conscience place the men and women who work at the *Phoenix* and its related companies in physical jeopardy." Evaluate this position.

READING ADVERTISEMENTS

Advertising is one of the most common forms of visual persuasion we encounter in everyday life. None of us is so unsophisticated these days as to believe everything we see in an ad, yet the influence of advertising in our culture is pervasive and subtle. Consider, for example, a much-reproduced poster sponsored by Gatorade and featuring Michael Jordan. Such an image costs an enormous amount to produce and disseminate, and nothing in it is left to chance. The photograph of Jordan is typical, his attitude simultaneously strained and graceful, his face exultant, as he performs the feat for which he is so well known and about which most of us could only dream. We are aware of a crowd watching him, but the people in this crowd appear tiny, blurred, and indistinct compared to the huge image in the foreground; the photograph, like the crowd, focuses solely on Jordan. He is a legend, an icon of American culture. He is dressed not in his Chicago Bulls uniform but in a USA jersey, connecting his act of gravity-defying athleticism with the entire nation and with our sense of patriotism. The red, white, and blue of the uniform strengthens this impression in the original color photograph of the advertisement.

What do we make of the verbal message boldly written along the left-hand margin of the poster, "Be like Mike"? We are certainly not foolish enough to believe that drinking Gatorade will enable us to perform like Michael Jordan on the basketball court. But who among us wouldn't like to "Be like Mike" in some small way, to enjoy even a glancing association with his athletic grace and power—to say nothing of his fame, wealth, and sex appeal? Though the makers of Gatorade surely know we will not all rush out to buy their drink to improve our game, they are banking on the expectation that the association of their name with Jordan, and our memory of their logo in association with Jordan's picture, will create a positive impression of their product. If Mike drinks Gatorade—well, why shouldn't I give it a try? The good feelings and impressions created by the ad will, the advertisers hope, travel with us the next time we consider buying a sports drink.

As we discuss the power of advertising, it is appropriate to say a few words about the corporate logos that appear everywhere these days—on billboards, in newspapers and magazines, on television, on Web sites, and on T-shirts. It is useful to think of a logo as a sort of advertisement in shorthand. It is a single, usually simple, image that carries with it a world of associations and impressions. (The makers of Gatorade would certainly hope that we will be reminded of Michael Jordan and his slam dunk when we see their product name superimposed over the orange lightning bolt.)

Let's look at two additional advertisements, each of which relies almost entirely on an image rather than on words. The first, an ad for a TV comedy that made its debut in 2009, boldly gives the title of the show and the name of the network, but the most interesting words are in tiny print:

Funny. On so many levels.

These words flatter the readers, thus making the readers highly susceptible to the implicit message, "Look at this program." Why do we say the words are flattering? For three reasons:

- The small size of the type implies that the reader is not someone whose attention can be caught only by headlines.
- The pun on "levels" (physical levels, and levels of humor) is a witty way of telling us that the show offers not only the low comedy of physical actions but also the high comedy of witty talk—talk that, for instance, may involve puns.

- The two terse incomplete sentences assume that the sophisticated reader does not need to have things explained at length.

The picture itself is attractive, showing what seems to be a wide variety of people (though of course we are not shown any faces or bodies that in real life might cause us some uneasiness) posed in the style of a family portrait. Indeed, these wholesome figures, standing in affectionate poses, are all dressed in white (without any ketchup stains) and are neatly framed (except for the patriarch, at the extreme right) by a pair of seated youngsters whose legs dangle down from the levels. The modern family, we are told, is large and varied (this one includes a gay son and his partner, and their adopted Vietnamese baby), smart and warm. And best of all, it is "Funny. On so many levels."

The second ad features two lines of text that are also short and sweet: "Set yourself free" and "When you're ready to quit smoking, we're here to help." The first of these lines—with "free" in large letters—is reinforced by the image of free-floating balloons, which in this context almost seem to be giant lungs. The implication is that once the viewer decides to quit smoking, the air will be purer, lungs will fully distend, and there will be a great sense of freedom; one will no longer be tied down in the way that an addiction to tobacco ties one down or restrains one's freedom. The second sentence, beneath the picture—on ground level, so to speak—assures the reader that when the addict is "ready to quit smoking, we're here to help." Who, after all, wouldn't want to be "set . . . free" (especially into the wonderful world of the floating balloons that soar in

---

✓ A CHECKLIST FOR ANALYZING IMAGES
(ESPECIALLY ADVERTISEMENTS)

☐ What is the overall effect of the design? Colorful and busy (suggesting activity)? Quiet and understated (for instance, chiefly white and grays, with lots of empty space)? Old-fashioned or cutting edge?

☐ What about the image immediately gets your attention? Size? Position on the page? Beauty of the image? Grotesqueness of the image? Humor?

☐ Who is the audience for the image? Affluent young men? Housewives? Retired persons?

☐ What is the argument?

☐ Does the text make a rational appeal (*logos*) ("Tests at a leading university prove that . . . ," "If you believe X, you should vote 'No' on this referendum")?

☐ Does the image appeal to the emotions, to dearly held values (*pathos*)? Examples: Images of starving children or maltreated animals appeal to our sense of pity; images of military valor may appeal to our patriotism; images of luxury may appeal to our envy; images of sexually attractive people may appeal to our desire to be like them; images of violence or of extraordinary ugliness (as, for instance, in some ads showing a human fetus being destroyed) may seek to shock us.

☐ Does the image make an ethical appeal — that is, does it appeal to our character as a good human being (*ethos*)? Ads by charitable organizations often appeal to our sense of decency, fairness, and pity, but ads that appeal to our sense of prudence (ads for insurance companies or for investment houses) also essentially are making an ethical appeal.

☐ What is the relation of print to image? Does the image do most of the work, or does it serve to attract us and to lead us on to read the text?

---

the tobacco-free air), and who wouldn't want the assurance that, if the experience is a bit risky, someone is there to help?

Topics for Critical Thinking and Writing

1. Imagine that you work for a business that advertises in a publication such as *Time* or *Newsweek,* for instance, a vacation resort, a manufacturer of clothes, or an automaker. Design an advertisement: Describe the picture and write the text, and then, in an essay of 500 words, explain who

your target audience is (college students? young couples about to buy their first home? retired persons?) and explain why you use the sorts of appeals (for instance, to reason, to the emotions, to a sense of humor) that you do.

2. It is often said that colleges, like businesses, are selling a product. Examine a brochure or catalog that is sent to prospective applicants to a college, and analyze the kinds of appeals that some of the images make.

WRITING ABOUT A POLITICAL CARTOON

Most editorial pages print political cartoons as well as editorials. Like the writers of editorials, cartoonists seek to persuade, but they rarely use words to *argue* a point. True, they may use a few words in speech balloons or in captions, but generally the drawing does most of the work. Because their aim usually is to convince the viewer that some person's action or proposal is ridiculous, cartoonists almost always **caricature** their subjects:

- They exaggerate the subject's distinctive features to the point where
- The subject becomes grotesque and ridiculous—absurd, laughable, contemptible.

True, it is scarcely fair to suggest that because, say, the politician who proposes such-and-such is short, fat, and bald his proposal is ridiculous, but that is the way cartoonists work. Further, cartoonists are concerned with producing a striking image, not with exploring an issue, so they almost always oversimplify, implying that there really is no other sane view.

In the course of saying that (a) the figures in the cartoon are ridiculous and *therefore* their ideas are contemptible, and (b) there is only one side to the issue, cartoonists often use **symbolism**, for instance:

- symbolic figures (Uncle Sam),
- animals (the Democratic donkey and the Republican elephant),
- buildings (the White House stands symbolically for the president of the United States),
- things (a bag with a dollar sign on it usually symbolizes a bribe).

For anyone brought up in our culture, these symbols (like the human figures who are represented) are obvious, and cartoonists assume that viewers will instantly recognize the symbols and figures, will get the joke, and will see the absurdity of whatever it is that the cartoonist is seeking to demolish.

In writing about the argument presented in a cartoon, normally you will discuss the ways in which the cartoon makes its point. Caricature, we have said, usually implies, "This is ridiculous, as you can plainly see by the absurdity of the figures depicted" or "What *X*'s proposal adds up to, despite

---

✓ **A CHECKLIST FOR EVALUATING AN ANALYSIS OF POLITICAL CARTOONS**

☐ Is a lead-in provided?

☐ Is a brief but accurate description of the drawing provided?

☐ Is the source of the cartoon cited (and perhaps commented on)?

☐ Is a brief report of the event or issue that the cartoon is dealing with and an explanation of all of the symbols included?

☐ Is there a statement of the cartoonist's claim (point, thesis)?

☐ Is there an analysis of the evidence, if any, that the image offers in support of the claim?

☐ Is there an analysis of the ways in which the content and style of the drawing help to convey the message?

☐ Is there adequate evaluation of the effectiveness of the drawing?

☐ Is there adequate evaluation of the effectiveness of the text (caption or speech balloons) and of the fairness of the cartoon?

---

its apparent complexity, is nothing more than . . ." As we have already said, this sort of persuasion, chiefly by ridicule, probably is unfair: A funny-looking person *can offer* a thoughtful political proposal, and almost certainly the issue is more complicated than the cartoonist indicates. But this is largely the way cartoons work, by ridicule and by omitting counter-arguments, and we should not reject the possibility that the cartoonist has indeed put his or her finger on the absurdity of the issue.

Probably your essay will include an *evaluation* of the cartoon; indeed, the *thesis* underlying your analytic/argumentative essay may be (for instance) that the cartoon is effective (persuasive) for such-and-such reasons, but it is also unfair for such-and-such reasons.

In analyzing the cartoon—in grasping the attitude of the cartoonist—consider such things as

- the relative size of the figures in the image;
- the quality of the lines—thin and spidery, or thick and seemingly aggressive;
- the amount of empty space in comparison with the amount of heavily inked space (a drawing with lots of inky areas will convey a more oppressive sense than a drawing that is largely open);
- the degree to which text is important, and what the text says—is it witty? Heavy-handed?

Caution: If your instructor lets you choose a cartoon, be sure to choose one with sufficient complexity to make the exercise worthwhile. (See also Idea Prompt 4.1.)

IDEA PROMPT 4.1 ANALYSIS OF A POLITICAL CARTOON

Context	*Who is the artist? Where and when was it published?*	"This cartoon by Walt Handelsman was originally published in *Newsday* on September 12, 2009. Handelsman, a Pulitzer Prize–winning cartoonist, drew this cartoon in response to recent breaches of political decorum."
Description	*What does the cartoon look like?*	"It depicts a group of Washington, D.C., tourists being driven past what the guide calls 'The Museum of Modern American Political Discourse,' a building in the shape of a giant toilet."
Analysis	*How does the cartoon make its point? Is it effective?*	"The toilet as a symbol of the level of political discussion dominates the cartoon, effectively driving home the point that as Americans we are watching our leaders sink to new lows as they debate the future of our nation. Seen on a scale similar to familiar monuments in Washington, Handelsman may be in fact pointing out that today's politicians, rather than being remembered for great achievements like those of George Washington or Abraham Lincoln, will instead be remembered for their rudeness and aggression."

Let's look at an example. Jackson Smith wrote this essay in a composition course at Tufts University.

Jackson Smith

Pledging Nothing?

(Student Essay)

Gary Markstein's cartoon about the Pledge of Allegiance is one of dozens that can be retrieved by a search engine. It happens that every one of the cartoons that I retrieved mocked the courts for ruling that schools cannot require students to recite the Pledge of Allegiance in its present form, which includes the words "under God." I personally object to these words, so the cartoons certainly do not speak for me, but I'll try as impartially as possible to analyze the strength of Markstein's cartoon.

Markstein shows us, in the cartoon, four school children reciting the Pledge. Coming out of all four mouths is a speech balloon with the words, "One nation under nothing in particular." The children are facing a furled American flag, and to the right of the flag is a middle-aged female teacher, whose speech balloon is in the form of a cloud, indicating that she is *thinking* rather than saying the words, "God help us."

Certainly the image grabs us: Little kids lined up reciting the Pledge of Allegiance, an American flag, a maternal-looking teacher, and, in fact, if one examines the cartoon closely, one sees an apple on the teacher's desk. It's almost a Norman Rockwell scene, except, of course, it is a cartoon, so the figures are all a bit grotesque—but, still, they are nice folks. What is *not* nice, Markstein says, is what these kids must recite, "One nation under nothing in particular." In fact the cartoon is far from telling the truth. Children who recite the Pledge without the words "under God" will still be saying that they are pledging allegiance to something quite specific—the United States:

> I pledge allegiance to the flag of the United States of America, and to the Republic for which it stands: one nation indivisible, with Liberty and Justice for all.

That's really quite a lot, very far from Markstein's "under nothing in particular." But no one, I suppose, expects fairness in a political cartoon—and of course this cartoon *is* political, because the issue of the Pledge has become a political football, with liberals on the whole wanting the words "under God" removed and conservatives on the whole wanting the words retained.

Let's now look at some of the subtleties of the cartoon. First, although, as I have said, cartoons present grotesque caricatures, the figures here

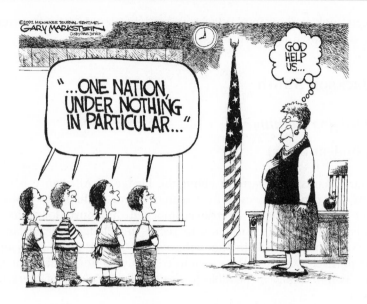

are all affectionately presented. None of these figures is menacing. The teacher, with her spectacles and her rather dumpy figure, is clearly a benevolent figure, someone who in the eyes of the cartoonist rightly is disturbed about the fate of these little kids who are not allowed to say the words "under God." (Nothing, of course, prevents the children from speaking about God when they are not in the classroom. Those who believe in God can say grace at mealtime, can go to Sunday School, can go to church regularly, can pray before they go to bed, etc.) Markstein suggests that the absence of these words makes the entire Pledge meaningless ("under nothing in particular"), and in a master stroke he has conveyed this idea of impoverishment by showing a tightly furled flag, a flag that is presented as minimally as possible. After all, the flag could have been shown more fully, perhaps hanging from a pole that extended from a wall into the classroom, or the flag could have been displayed extended against a wall. Instead we get the narrowest of flags, something that is not much more than a furled umbrella, identifiable as the American flag by its stripes and a few stars in the upper third. Markstein thus cleverly suggests that with the loss of the words "under God," the flag itself is reduced to almost nothing.

Fair? No. Effective? Yes, and that's the job of a cartoonist. Readers 5 probably give cartoons no more than three or four seconds, and Markstein has made the most of those few seconds. The reader gets his point, and if the reader already holds this view, he or she probably says, "Hey, here's a great cartoon." I don't hold that view, but I am willing to grant that it is a pretty good cartoon, effectively making a point that I think is wrong-headed.

VISUALS AS AIDS TO CLARITY: MAPS, GRAPHS, TABLES, AND PIE CHARTS

Maps were obviously part of the argument in the debate over drilling in the Arctic National Wildlife Refuge.

- Advocates of drilling argued that drilling would take place only in a tiny area. Their map showed Alaska, with an indication (in gray) of the much smaller part of Alaska that was the Refuge, and a further indication (cross-hatched) of what these advocates of drilling emphasized was a minuscule part of the Refuge.

- Opponents, however, showed maps indicating the path of migrating caribou and the roads that would have to be constructed across the refuge to get to the area where the drilling would take place.

Graphs, tables, and pie charts usually present quantitative data in visual form, helping writers clarify mind-numbing statistical assertions. For instance, a line graph may tell us how many immigrants came to the United States in each decade of the last century.

A bar graph (the bars can run either horizontally or vertically) offers similar information; we can see at a glance that, say, the second bar is almost double the length of the first, indicating that the number is almost double.

A pie chart is a circle divided into wedges so that we can see—literally—how a whole is divided into its parts. We can see, for instance, that of the entire pie—which may represent registered voters in a certain state—one-fourth are registered Democrats, one-fifth are registered Republicans, and the remainder do not give a party affiliation.

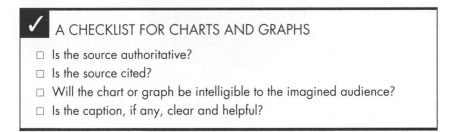

✓ A CHECKLIST FOR CHARTS AND GRAPHS

☐ Is the source authoritative?
☐ Is the source cited?
☐ Will the chart or graph be intelligible to the imagined audience?
☐ Is the caption, if any, clear and helpful?

A NOTE ON USING VISUALS IN YOUR OWN PAPER

Every paper uses some degree of visual persuasion, merely in its appearance: perhaps a title page, certainly margins (ample—but not so wide that they tell the reader that the writer is unable to write a paper of the assigned length), double-spacing for the convenience of the reader, paragraphing

COMING TO AMERICA . . .

Both the percentage and number of foreign-born people in the United States dropped during much of the twentieth century, but after 1970, the tide was turning again.

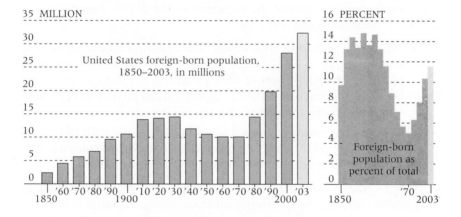

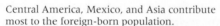

. . . FROM NEAR AND FAR

Central America, Mexico, and Asia contribute most to the foreign-born population.

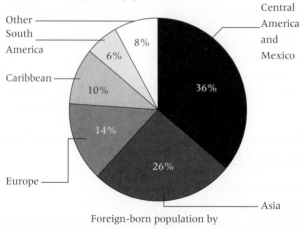

Foreign-born population by
region of birth, 2002

*Most recent estimate
Source: United States Census Bureau

(again for the convenience of the reader), and so on. But you may also want to use images—for example, pictures, graphs, or pie charts. Keep a few guidelines in mind as you begin to work with images, "writing" visuals into your own argument with at least as much care as you would read them in others':

- Consider the needs and attitudes of your audience, and select the type of visuals—graphs, drawings, photographs—likely to be most persuasive to that audience.

(DILBERT © Scott Adams. Distributed by permission of United Features Syndicate, Inc.)

- Consider the effect of color, composition, and placement within your document. Because images are most effective when they appear near the text that supplements them, do not group all of your images at the end of the paper.

Remember especially that images are almost never self-supporting or self-explanatory. They may be evidence for your argument (Ut's photograph of napalm victims is *very* compelling evidence of suffering), but they are not arguments themselves.

- Be sure to explain each image that you use, integrating it into the verbal text that provides the logic and principal support of your thesis.
- Be sure to cite the source of any image, for instance, a graph or a pie chart, that you paste into your argument.

A NOTE ON FORMATTING YOUR PAPER: DOCUMENT DESIGN

Even if you do not use pictures or graphs or charts, the format you use—the margins, the font, the headings and subheadings, if any, will still give your paper a visual aspect. NoonewantstoreadapaperthatlookslikethisOR LIKETHIS*ORLIKETHIS*ANDCERTAINLYNOT**LIKETHIS**ORLIKETHIS. For academic papers, margins (one inch on each side), spacing (double-spaced), and font and size (Times New Roman, 12 point) are pretty well standardized, and it is usually agreed that the text should be justified at the left rather than centered (to avoid rivers of white down the page), but you are still in charge of some things, notably headings and bulleted or numbered lists—as well as, of course, the lengths of your paragraphs.

Headings in a long paper (more than five pages) are functional, helping to guide the reader from unit to unit, but the extra white space—a decorative element—is also functional, giving the reader's eye a moment of rest. Longish academic papers often use one, two, or even three levels of headings, normally distinguished by type size, position, and highlighting

("highlighting" includes the use of CAPITALS, **boldface**, and *italic*). Here are examples of three levels:

FIRST-LEVEL HEADING

Second-Level Heading

Third-Level Heading

If you use headings, you must be consistent in the form. For instance, if you use a noun phrase such as "the present system" printed in CAPITAL LETTERS for the first of your first-level headings, you must use noun phrases and caps for the rest of your first-level headings, thus:

THE PRESENT SYSTEM
THE NEED TO CHANGE

But you need not use noun phases and you need not use capitals. You may use, for instance, *-ing* headings (gerund phrases), and you may decide to capitalize only the first letter of each word other than prepositions and articles, thus:

Thinking about Immigration

Reviewing the Past

Thinking about the Future

Reconsidering Legislation

And here are headings that use a single word:

Problems

Answers

Strengths

Weaknesses

Finally, headings that consist of questions can be effective:

What Are We Now Doing?

Why Should We Change?

Caution: Although headings can be useful in a paper of moderate or considerable length, they almost never are useful in a paper of five or fewer pages.

ADDITIONAL IMAGES FOR ANALYSIS

In 1936, photographer Dorothea Lange (1895–1965) took a series of pictures, including the two below, of a migrant mother and her children. Widely reprinted in the nation's newspapers, these photographs helped to dramatize for the American public the poverty of displaced workers during the Great Depression.

TOPICS FOR CRITICAL THINKING AND WRITING

1. Lange drew increasingly near to her subject as she took a series of pictures. Make a list of details gained and lost by framing the mother and children more closely. The final shot in the series (above) became the most famous and most widely reprinted. Do you find it more effective than the other? Why, or why not?

2. Note the expression on the mother's face, the position of her body, and the way she interacts with her children. What sorts of relationships are implied? Why is it significant that she does not look at her children or at the camera? How is the effect of the photographs altered based on how much we can see of the children's faces?

3. As we mentioned earlier in this chapter, these photographs constitute a sort of persuasive "speech." Of what, exactly, might the photographer be trying to persuade her viewers? Try to state the purpose of Lange's photographs by completing this sentence, "Lange would like the viewers of her photographs to . . ." Write a brief essay (250 words) making the same case. Compare your written argument to Lange's visual one. Which form of persuasion do you find more effective? Why?

4. Whom do you think Lange had in mind as her original audience? What assumptions does she make about that audience? What sorts of evidence does she use to reach them?

During World War II, the U.S. government produced a series of posters bearing the legend "This is the enemy." These posters depicted racially stereotyped images of both German and Japanese soldiers, generally engaged in acts of savage violence.

TOPICS FOR CRITICAL THINKING AND WRITING

1. It has been claimed that one role of propaganda is to dehumanize the enemy so that (a) soldiers will feel less remorse about killing opposing soldiers and (b) civilians will continue to support the war effort. What specific features of this poster contribute to this propaganda function?

2. Some would claim that such a racially provocative image of a Japanese soldier should never have been used because of the potential harm to all Asians, including patriotic Asian Americans. (Consisting solely of Japanese American volunteers, the 442nd Regimental Combat Team was by war's end the most decorated unit in U.S. military history for its size and length of service.) Others believe that the ordinary rules do not apply in times of national crisis and that, as the old saying has it, "All's fair in love and war." In an essay of 500 words, argue for one or the other of these propositions. Refer to this poster as one piece of your evidence.

From ancient times until the eighteenth century, when newspapers began to be read widely, public posting was about the only way to reach a large audience. The invention of movable type in the fifteenth century made the dissemination of posted bills and handbills inexpensive, and such bills (along with newspaper

advertisements) were the most common forms of advertising until well into the twentieth century. (Commercial radio broadcasting began only in 1920, and television was not an important medium before 1945.) I Want You *is by James Montgomery Flagg.*

TOPICS FOR CRITICAL THINKING AND WRITING

1. Imagine that this figure of Uncle Sam was in profile, pointing either to the right or left. Would the effect be the same? Why? Imagine the figure as a three-quarter view. Again, would the effect be different? Why? Which of the three versions do you think would be the most effective? Explain your reasons.

2. Approximately what is the date of this poster? What makes you give it this date?

ADDITIONAL TOPICS FOR CRITICAL THINKING AND WRITING

Gather some of the graphic materials used to promote and reflect your college or university—including a screen shot of its Web site, the college catalog, and the brochures and other materials sent to prospective students.

1. What is the dominant image that your college or university administration seems to be putting forth? Are there different, maybe even competing, images of your school at work? How accurate a story do these materials tell about your campus? Write an essay (250 words) in which you explain to prospective students the ways in which the promotional materials capture, or fail to capture, the true spirit of your campus.

2. Compare the Web site of your institution to one or two from very different institutions—perhaps a community college, a large state university, or an elite private college. How do you account for the similarities and differences among the sites?

Nora Ephron

Nora Ephron, (1941–2012) attended Wellesley College. She worked as a reporter for the New York Post *and as a columnist and senior editor for* Esquire. *Ephron wrote screenplays and directed films, including* Sleepless in Seattle *(1993), and continued to write essays on a wide variety of topics. "The Boston Photographs" is from her collection* Scribble, Scribble: Notes on the Media *(1978).*

The Boston Photographs

"I made all kinds of pictures because I thought it would be a good rescue shot over the ladder . . . never dreamed it would be anything

else. . . . I kept having to move around because of the light set. The sky was bright and they were in deep shadow. I was making pictures with a motor drive and he, the fire fighter, was reaching up and, I don't know, everything started falling. I followed the girl down taking pictures. . . . I made three or four frames. I realized what was going on and I completely turned around, because I didn't want to see her hit."

You probably saw the photographs. In most newspapers, there were three of them. The first showed some people on a fire escape — a fireman, a woman, and a child. The fireman had a nice strong jaw and looked very brave. The woman was holding the child. Smoke was pouring from the building behind them. A rescue ladder was approaching, just a few feet away, and the fireman had one arm around the woman and one arm reaching out toward the ladder. The second picture showed the fire escape slipping off the building. The child had fallen on the escape and seemed about to slide off the edge. The woman was grasping desperately at the legs of the fireman, who had managed to grab the ladder. The third picture showed the woman and child in midair, falling to the ground. Their arms and legs were outstretched, horribly distended. A potted plant was falling too. The caption said that the woman, Diana Bryant, nineteen, died in the fall. The child landed on the woman's body and lived.

The pictures were taken by Stanley Forman, thirty, of the *Boston Herald American*. He used a motor-driven Nikon F set at 1/250, f5.6-S. Because of the motor, the camera can click off three frames a second. More than four hundred newspapers in the United States alone carried the photographs: The tear sheets from overseas are still coming in. The

New York Times ran them on the first page of its second section; a paper in south Georgia gave them nineteen columns; the *Chicago Tribune,* the *Washington Post,* and the *Washington Star* filled almost half their front pages, the *Star* under a somewhat redundant headline that read: SENSA-TIONAL PHOTOS OF RESCUE ATTEMPT THAT FAILED.

The photographs are indeed sensational. They are pictures of death in action, of that split second when luck runs out, and it is impossible to look at them without feeling their extraordinary impact and remember-ing, in an almost subconscious way, the morbid fantasy of falling, falling off a building, falling to one's death. Beyond that, the pictures are clas-sics, old-fashioned but perfect examples of photojournalism at its most spectacular. They're throwbacks, really, fire pictures, 1930s tabloid shots; at the same time they're technically superb and thoroughly modern— the sequence could not have been taken at all until the development of the motor-driven camera some sixteen years ago.

Most newspaper editors anticipate some reader reaction to pho-   5
tographs like Forman's; even so, the response around the country was enormous, and almost all of it was negative. I have read hundreds of the letters that were printed in letters-to-the-editor sections, and they repeat the same points. "Invading the privacy of death." "Cheap sensa-tionalism." "I thought I was reading the *National Enquirer.*" "Assigning the agony of a human being in terror of imminent death to the status of a side-show act." "A tawdry way to sell newspapers." The *Seattle Times* received sixty letters and calls; its managing editor even got a couple of them at home. A reader wrote the *Philadelphia Inquirer: "Jaws* and *Tower-ing Inferno* are playing downtown; don't take business away from people who pay good money to advertise in your own paper." Another reader wrote the *Chicago Sun-Times:* "I shall try to hide my disappointment that Miss Bryant wasn't wearing a skirt when she fell to her death. You could have had some award-winning photographs of her underpants as her skirt billowed over her head, you voyeurs." Several newspaper editors wrote columns defending the pictures: Thomas Keevil of the *Costa Mesa* (California) *Daily Pilot* printed a ballot for readers to vote on whether they would have printed the pictures; Marshall L. Stone of Maine's *Ban-gor Daily News,* which refused to print the famous assassination picture of the Vietcong prisoner in Saigon, claimed that the Boston pictures showed the dangers of fire escapes and raised questions about slumlords. (The burning building was a five-story brick apartment house on Marlbor-ough Street in the Back Bay section of Boston.)

For the last five years, the *Washington Post* has employed various journalists as ombudsmen, whose job is to monitor the paper on be-half of the public. The *Post*'s current ombudsman is Charles Seib, former managing editor of the *Washington Star;* the day the Boston photographs appeared, the paper received over seventy calls in protest. As Seib later wrote in a column about the pictures, it was "the largest reaction to a published item that I have experienced in eight months as the *Post*'s ombudsman. . . .

"In the *Post*'s newsroom, on the other hand, I found no doubts, no second thoughts . . . the question was not whether they should be printed but how they should be displayed. When I talked to editors . . . they used words like 'interesting' and 'riveting' and 'gripping' to describe them. The pictures told of something about life in the ghetto, they said (although the neighborhood where the tragedy occurred is not a ghetto, I am told). They dramatized the need to check on the safety of fire es-capes. They dramatically conveyed something that had happened, and that is the business we're in. They were news. . . .

"Was publication of that [third] picture a bow to the same taste for the morbidly sensational that makes gold mines of disaster movies? Most papers will not print the picture of a dead body except in the most un-usual circumstances. Does the fact that the final picture was taken a mil-lisecond before the young woman died make a difference? Most papers will not print a picture of a bare female breast. Is that a more inappropri-ate subject for display than the picture of a human being's last agonized instant of life?" Seib offered no answers to the questions he raised, but he went on to say that although as an editor he would probably have run the pictures, as a reader he was revolted by them.

In conclusion, Seib wrote: "Any editor who decided to print those pictures without giving at least a moment's thought to what purpose they served and what their effect was likely to be on the reader should ask another question: Have I become so preoccupied with manufactur-ing a product according to professional traditions and standards that I have forgotten about the consumer, the reader?"

It should be clear that the phone calls and letters and Seib's own 10 reaction were occasioned by one factor alone: the death of the woman. Obviously, had she survived the fall, no one would have protested; the pictures would have had a completely different impact. Equally obvi-ously, had the child died as well—or instead—Seib would undoubtedly have received ten times the phone calls he did. In each case, the pictures would have been exactly the same—only the captions, and thus the re-sponses, would have been different.

But the questions Seib raises are worth discussing—though not exactly for the reasons he mentions. For it may be that the real lesson of the Boston photographs is not the danger that editors will be forget-ful of reader reaction, but that they will continue to censor pictures of death precisely because of that reaction. The protests Seib fielded were really a variation on an old theme—and we saw plenty of it during the Nixon-Agnew years—the "Why doesn't the press print the good news?" argument. In this case, of course, the objections were all dressed up and cleverly disguised as righteous indignation about the privacy of death. This is a form of puritanism that is often justifiable; just as often it is merely puritanical.

Seib takes it for granted that the widespread though fairly recent newspaper policy against printing pictures of dead bodies is a sound one; I don't know that it makes any sense at all. I recognize that printing pictures of corpses raises all sorts of problems about taste and titillation and sensationalism; the fact is, however, that people die. Death happens to be one of life's main events. And it is irresponsible—and more than that, inaccurate—for newspapers to fail to show it, or to show it only when an astonishing set of photos comes in over the Associated Press wire. Most papers covering fatal automobile accidents will print pictures of mangled cars. But the significance of fatal automobile accidents is not that a great deal of steel is twisted but that people die. Why not show it? That's what accidents are about. Throughout the Vietnam war, editors were reluctant to print atrocity pictures. Why *not* print them? That's what that was about. Murder victims are almost never photographed; they are granted their privacy. But their relatives are relentlessly pictured on their way in and out of hospitals and morgues and funerals.

I'm not advocating that newspapers print these things in order to teach their readers a lesson. The *Post* editors justified their printing of the Boston pictures with several arguments in that direction; every one of them is irrelevant. The pictures don't show anything about slum life; the incident could have happened anywhere, and it did. It is extremely unlikely that anyone who saw them rushed out and had his fire escape strengthened. And the pictures were not news—at least they were not national news. It is not news in Washington, or New York, or Los Angeles that a woman was killed in a Boston fire. The only newsworthy thing about the pictures is that they were taken. They deserve to be printed because they are great pictures, breathtaking pictures of something that happened. That they disturb readers is exactly as it should be: that's why photojournalism is often more powerful than written journalism.

TOPICS FOR CRITICAL THINKING AND WRITING

1. In paragraph 5 Ephron refers to "the famous assassination picture of the Vietcong prisoner in Saigon" (see p. 147). The photo shows the face of a prisoner who is about to be shot in the head at close range. Jot down the reasons why you would or would not approve of printing this photo in a newspaper. Think, too, about this: If the photo on page 146 were not about a war—if it did not include the soldiers and the burning village in the rear but instead showed children fleeing from an abusive parent or from an abusive sibling—would you approve of printing it in a newspaper?

2. In paragraph 9 Ephron quotes a newspaperman as saying that before printing Forman's pictures of the woman and the child falling from the fire escape, editors should have asked themselves "what purpose they served and what their effect was likely to be on the reader." If you were

an editor, what would your answers be? By the way, the pictures were *not* taken in a poor neighborhood, and they did *not* expose slum conditions.

3. In 50 words or so, write a precise description of what you see in the third of the Boston photographs. Do you think readers of your description would be "revolted" by the picture (para. 8), as were many viewers, the *Washington Post*'s ombudsman among them? Why, or why not?

4. Ephron thinks it would be a good thing if more photographs of death and dying were published by newspapers (paras. 11–13). In an essay of 500 words, state her reasons and your evaluation of them.

 For additional arguments online, visit the e-Pages at
bedfordstmartins.com/barnetbedau.

PART TWO

CRITICAL WRITING

5

Writing an Analysis of an Argument

This is what we can all do to nourish and strengthen one another: listen to one another very hard, ask questions, too, send one another away to work again, and laugh in all the right places.

—NANCY MAIRS

I don't wait for moods. You accomplish nothing if you do that. Your mind must know it has got to get down to work.

—PEARL S. BUCK

Fear not those who argue but those who dodge.

—MARIE VON EBNER-ESCHENBACH

ANALYZING AN ARGUMENT

Examining the Author's Thesis

Most of your writing in other courses will require you to write an analysis of someone else's writing. In a course in political science you may have to analyze, say, an essay first published in *Foreign Affairs,* perhaps reprinted in your textbook, that argues against raising tariff barriers to foreign trade. Or a course in sociology may require you to analyze a report on the correlation between fatal accidents and drunk drivers under the age of twenty-one. Much of your writing, in short, will set forth reasoned responses to your reading as preparation for making an argument of your own.

Obviously you must understand an essay before you can analyze it thoughtfully. You must read it several times—not just skim it—and (the hard part) you must think critically about it. Again, you'll find that your thinking is stimulated if you take notes and if you ask yourself questions about the material. Are there any Web sites or organizations dedicated to the material you are analyzing? If there are, visit some to see what others are saying about the material you are reviewing. Notes will help you to keep track of the writer's thoughts and also of your own responses to the writer's thesis. The writer probably *does* have a thesis, a claim, a point, and if so, you must try to locate it. Perhaps the thesis is explicitly stated in the title or in a sentence or two near the beginning of the essay or in a concluding paragraph, but perhaps you will have to infer it from the essay as a whole.

Notice that we said the writer *probably* has a thesis. Much of what you read will indeed be primarily an argument; the writer explicitly or implicitly is trying to support some thesis and to convince you to agree with it. But some of what you read will be relatively neutral, with the argument just faintly discernible—or even with no argument at all. A work may, for instance, chiefly be a report: Here are the data, or here is what *X, Y,* and *Z* said; make of it what you will. A report might simply state how various ethnic groups voted in an election. In a report of this sort, of course, the writer hopes to persuade readers that the facts are correct, but no thesis is advanced, at least not explicitly or perhaps even consciously; the writer is not evidently arguing a point and trying to change our minds. Such a document differs greatly from an essay by a political analyst who presents similar findings to persuade a candidate to sacrifice the votes of this ethnic bloc and thereby get more votes from other blocs.

Examining the Author's Purpose

While reading an argument, try to form a clear idea of the author's **purpose.** Judging from the essay or the book, was the purpose to persuade, or was it to report? An analysis of a pure report (a work apparently without a thesis or argumentative angle) on ethnic voting will deal chiefly with the accuracy of the report. It will, for example, consider whether the sample poll was representative.

Much material that poses as a report really has a thesis built into it, consciously or unconsciously. The best evidence that the prose you are reading is argumentative is the presence of two kinds of key terms: transitions that imply the drawing of a conclusion and verbs that imply proof (see Idea Prompt 5.1). Keep your eye out for such terms, and scrutinize

IDEA PROMPT 5.1 DRAWING CONCLUSIONS
AND IMPLYING PROOF

Transitions that imply the drawing of a conclusion	*therefore, because, for the reason that, consequently*
Verbs that imply proof	*confirms, verifies, accounts for, implies, proves, disproves, is (in)consistent with, refutes, it follows that*

their precise role whenever they appear. If the essay does not advance a thesis, think of one that it might support or some conventional belief that it might undermine.

Examining the Author's Methods

If the essay advances a thesis, you will want to analyze the strategies or methods of argument that allegedly support the thesis.

- Does the writer quote authorities? Are these authorities competent in this field? Are equally competent authorities who take a different view considered?

- Does the writer use statistics? If so, who compiled them, and are they appropriate to the point being argued? Can they be interpreted differently?

- Does the writer build the argument by using examples or analogies? Are they satisfactory?

- Are the writer's assumptions acceptable?

- Does the writer consider all relevant factors? Has he or she omitted some points that you think should be discussed? For instance, should the author recognize certain opposing positions and perhaps concede something to them?

- Does the writer seek to persuade by means of ridicule? If so, is the ridicule fair: Is it supported also by rational argument?

- Is the argument aimed at a particular audience?

In writing your analysis, you will want to tell your reader something about the author's purpose and something about the author's **methods.** It is usually a good idea at the start of your analysis—if not in the first paragraph, then in the second or third—to let the reader know the purpose (and thesis, if there is one) of the work you are analyzing and then to summarize the work briefly.

Next you will probably find it useful (your reader will certainly find it helpful) to write out *your* thesis (your evaluation or judgment). You might say, for instance, that the essay is impressive but not conclusive, or is undermined by convincing contrary evidence, or relies too much on unsupported generalizations, or is wholly admirable. Remember, because your paper is itself an argument, it needs its own thesis.

And then, of course, comes the job of setting forth your analysis and the support for your thesis. There is no one way of going about this work. If, say, your author gives four arguments (for example, an appeal to common sense, the testimony of authorities, the evidence of comparisons, and an appeal to self-interest), you might want to do one of the following:

- Take up these four arguments in sequence.

- Discuss the simplest of the four and then go on to the more difficult ones.

- Discuss the author's two arguments that you think are sound and then turn to the two that you think are not sound (or perhaps the reverse).
- Take one of these approaches and then clinch your case by constructing a fifth argument that is absent from the work under scrutiny but in your view highly important.

In short, the organization of your analysis may or may not follow the organization of the work you are analyzing.

Examining the Author's Persona

You will probably also want to analyze something a bit more elusive than the author's explicit arguments: the author's self-presentation. Does the author seek to persuade readers partly by presenting himself or herself as conscientious, friendly, self-effacing, authoritative, tentative, or in some other light? Most writers do two things:

- They present evidence.
- They present themselves (or, more precisely, they present the image of themselves that they wish us to behold).

In some persuasive writing this **persona** or **voice** or presentation of the self may be no less important than the presentation of evidence. In other cases, the persona may not much matter, but our point is that you should spend a little time looking at the author's self-presentation to consider if it's significant.

In establishing a persona, writers adopt various rhetorical strategies, ranging from the use of characteristic words to the use of a particular form of organization. For instance,

- The writer who speaks of an opponent's "gimmicks" instead of "strategy" probably is trying to downgrade the opponent and also to convey the self-image of a streetwise person.
- On a larger scale, consider the way in which evidence is presented and the kind of evidence offered. One writer may first bombard the reader with facts and then spend relatively little time drawing conclusions. Another may rely chiefly on generalizations, waiting until the end of the essay to bring the thesis home with a few details. Another may begin with a few facts and spend most of the space reflecting on these. One writer may seem professorial or pedantic, offering examples of an academic sort; another, whose examples are drawn from ordinary life, may seem like a regular guy.

All such devices deserve comment in your analysis.

The writer's persona, then, may color the thesis and help it develop in a distinctive way. If we accept the thesis, it is partly because the writer has won our goodwill by persuading us of his or her good character (*ethos,* in Aristotle's terms). Later we talk more about the appeal to the character of the speaker—the so-called *ethical appeal,* but here we may say that good writers present themselves not as wise-guys, bullies, or pompous asses but as decent people whom the reader would like to invite to dinner.

The author of an essay may, for example, seem fair-minded and open-minded, treating the opposition with great courtesy and expressing interest in hearing other views. Such a tactic is itself a persuasive device. Or take an author who appears to rely on hard evidence such as statistics. This reliance on seemingly objective truths is itself a way of seeking to persuade—a rational way, to be sure, but a mode of persuasion nonetheless.

Especially in analyzing a work in which the author's persona and ideas are blended, you will want to spend some time commenting on the persona. Whether you discuss it near the beginning of your analysis or near the end will depend on your own sense of how you want to construct your essay, and this decision will partly depend on the work you are analyzing. For example, if the author's persona is kept in the background and is thus relatively invisible, you may want to make that point fairly early to get it out of the way and then concentrate on more interesting matters. If, however, the persona is interesting—and perhaps seductive, whether because it seems so scrupulously objective or so engagingly subjective—you may want to hint at this quality early in your essay and then develop the point while you consider the arguments.

In short, the author's self-presentation usually matters. Reorganize its effect, whether positive or negative.

Examining Persona and Intended Audience

A key element in understanding an argument lies in thinking about the intended audience—how the author perceives the audience and what strategies the author uses to connect to it. We have already said something about the creation of the author's persona. An author with a loyal following is, almost by definition, someone who in earlier writings has presented an engaging persona, a persona with a trustworthy *ethos.* A trusted author can sometimes cut corners and can perhaps adopt a colloquial tone that would be unacceptable in the writing of an unknown author.

Authors who want to win the assent of their audiences need to think about how they present information and how they present *themselves.* Think about how you prefer people to talk to you or address you. What sorts of language do you find engaging? Much of course depends on the circumstances, notably the topic, the audience, and the place. A joke may be useful in an argument about whether the government should regulate junk food, but almost surely a joke will be inappropriate—will backfire, will alienate the audience—in an argument about abortion. The *way* an author addresses the reader (through an invented persona) can have a significant impact on the reader's perception of the author, which is to say perception of the author's *views,* the author's *argument.* A slip in tone or an error of fact, however small, may be enough for the audience to dismiss the author's argument. Understanding audience means thinking about all of the possible audiences that may come into contact with your writing or your message, and thinking about the consequences of what you write and where it is published.

You may recall a tweet by Lebron James, who formerly played basketball for the Cleveland Cavaliers but who now plays for the Miami Heat. After James left the Cavaliers (and his home state of Ohio), the Los Angeles Lakers beat the Cavaliers by fifty-five points, and James tweeted: "Crazy. Karma is a b****. Gets you every time. It's not good to wish bad on anybody. God sees everything!" Cleveland fans not surprisingly perceived his tweet as a slap in the face. The broader audience, too, outside of Cleveland, perceived it as uncalled for. Lebron James clearly did not think about his audience(s). To put it in rhetorical terms, Lebron James vastly diminished his *ethos.* Doubtless he wishes he could retract the tweet, but, as the ancient Roman poet Horace said, *"Nescit vox missa reverti"* ("The word once spoken can never be recalled"), or, in plain proverbial English, "Think twice before you speak."

Consider Facebook status updates. Have you ever posted a status update and wished you could take it back only to find out it was too late? People you did not want to see it saw it before you could remove it. Have you ever

---

✓ A CHECKLIST FOR ANALYZING AN AUTHOR'S INTENDED AUDIENCE

- ☐ Where did the piece appear? Who published it? Why, in your view, might someone have found it worth publishing?

- ☐ In what technological format does this piece appear? Print journal? Online magazine? Blog? What does the technological format say about the piece or the author?

- ☐ Is the writing relatively informal, for instance, a tweet or a Facebook status update? Who is the intended audience? Are there other audiences who may also have an interest but whom the author has failed to consider? Why is this medium good or bad for the message?

- ☐ If *you* are the intended audience, what shared values do you have with the author?

- ☐ What strategies does the writer use to create a connection with the audience?

tweeted or even texted something you wished you hadn't? When reading and writing more formal essays, it is equally important to think about who wrote what you are reading, and who will read what you are writing.

Summary

In the last few pages we have tried to persuade you that, in writing an analysis of your reading, you must do the following:

- Read and reread thoughtfully. Composing and keeping notes will help you to think about what you are reading.
- Be aware of the purpose of the material to which you are responding.

We have also tried to point out these facts:

- Most of the nonliterary material that you will read is designed to argue, to report, or to do both.
- Most of this material also presents the writer's personality, or voice, and this voice usually merits attention in an analysis. An essay on, say, nuclear war, in a journal devoted to political science may include a voice that moves from an objective tone to a mildly ironic tone to a hortatory tone, and this voice is worth commenting on.

Possibly all this explanation is obvious. There is yet another point, equally obvious but often neglected by students who begin by writing an analysis and end up by writing only a summary, a shortened version of the work they have read: Although your essay is an analysis of someone else's writing, and you may have to include a summary of the work you are writing about, your essay is *your* essay, your analysis, not a mere summary. The thesis, the organization, and the tone are yours.

- Your thesis, for example, may be that, although the author is convinced she has presented a strong case, her case is far from proved because, . . .
- Your organization may be deeply indebted to the work you are analyzing, but it need not be. The author may have begun with specific examples and then gone on to make generalizations and to draw conclusions, but you may begin with the conclusions.
- Your tone, similarly, may resemble your subject's (let's say the voice is courteous academic), but it will nevertheless have its own ring, its own tone of, say, urgency, caution, or coolness.

Most of the essays that we have included thus far are more or less in an academic style, and indeed several are by students and by professors. But argumentative writing is not limited to academicians—if it were, your college would not be requiring you to take a course in the subject. The following essay, in a breezy style, comes from a columnist who writes for the *New York Times*.

✓ A CHECKLIST FOR ANALYZING A TEXT

Have I considered all of the following matters?

☐ Who is the author? What stake might he or she have in writing this piece?

☐ Is the piece aimed at a particular audience? A neutral audience? What is your evidence? Persons who are already sympathetic to the author's point of view? A hostile audience?

☐ What is the author's thesis (argument, main point, claim)?

☐ What assumptions does the author make? Do I share them? If not, why not?

☐ Does the author ever confuse facts with beliefs or opinions?

☐ What appeals does the author make? To reason (*logos*), for instance, with statistics, the testimony of authorities, and personal experience? To the emotions (*pathos*), for instance, by an appeal to "our better nature," or to widely shared values? To our sense that the speaker is trustworthy (*ethos*)?

☐ How convincing is the evidence? Why do you think so?

☐ Are significant objections and counterevidence adequately discussed?

☐ How is the text organized, and is the organization effective? Are the title, the opening paragraphs, and the concluding paragraphs effective? In what ways?

☐ If visual materials such as graphs, pie charts, or pictures are used, how persuasive are they? Do they make a logical appeal? (Charts and graphs presumably make a logical appeal.) Do they make an emotional appeal? An ethical appeal?

☐ What is the author's tone? Is it appropriate?

☐ To what extent has the author convinced me? Why?

AN ARGUMENT, ITS ELEMENTS,
AND A STUDENT'S ANALYSIS
OF THE ARGUMENT

Nicholas D. Kristof

Nicholas D. Kristof (b. 1959) grew up on a farm in Oregon. After graduating from Harvard, he was awarded a Rhodes scholarship to Oxford, where he studied law. In 1984 he joined the New York Times *as a correspondent, and since 2001 he has written as a columnist. He has won two Pulitzer Prizes.*

For Environmental Balance, Pick Up a Rifle

Here's a quick quiz: Which large American mammal kills the most humans each year?

It's not the bear, which kills about two people a year in North America. Nor is it the wolf, which in modern times hasn't killed anyone in this country. It's not the cougar, which kills one person every year or two.

Rather, it's the deer. Unchecked by predators, deer populations are exploding in a way that is profoundly unnatural and that is destroying the ecosystem in many parts of the country. In a wilderness, there might be ten deer per square mile; in parts of New Jersey, there are up to 200 per square mile.

One result is ticks and Lyme disease, but deer also kill people more directly. A study for the insurance industry estimated that deer kill about 150 people a year in car crashes nationwide and cause $1 billion in damage. Granted, deer aren't stalking us, and they come out worse in these collisions—but it's still true that in a typical year, an American is less likely to be killed by Osama bin Laden than by Bambi.

If the symbol of the environment's being out of whack in the 1960s 5 was the Cuyahoga River in Cleveland catching fire, one such symbol today is deer congregating around what they think of as salad bars and what we think of as suburbs.

So what do we do? Let's bring back hunting.

Now, you've probably just spilled your coffee. These days, among the university-educated crowd in the cities, hunting is viewed as barbaric.

The upshot is that towns in New York and New Jersey are talking about using birth control to keep deer populations down. (Liberals presumably support free condoms, while conservatives back abstinence education.) Deer contraception hasn't been very successful, though.

Meanwhile, the same population bomb has spread to bears. A bear hunt has been scheduled for this week in New Jersey—prompting outrage from some animal rights groups (there's also talk of bear contraception: make love, not cubs).

As for deer, partly because hunting is perceived as brutal and vaguely 10 psychopathic, towns are taking out contracts on deer through discreet private companies. Greenwich, Connecticut, budgeted $47,000 this year to pay a company to shoot eighty deer from raised platforms over four nights—as well as $8,000 for deer birth control.

Look, this is ridiculous.

We have an environmental imbalance caused in part by the decline of hunting. Humans first wiped out certain predators—like wolves and cougars—but then expanded their own role as predators to sustain a rough ecological balance. These days, though, hunters are on the decline.

According to "Families Afield: An Initiative for the Future of Hunting," a report by an alliance of shooting organizations, for every hundred hunters who die or stop hunting, only sixty-nine hunters take their place.

I was raised on *Bambi*—but also, as an Oregon farm boy, on venison and elk meat. But deer are not pets, and dead deer are as natural as live deer. To wring one's hands over them, perhaps after polishing off a hamburger, is soggy sentimentality.

What's the alternative to hunting? Is it preferable that deer die of   15
disease and hunger? Or, as the editor of *Adirondack Explorer* magazine suggested, do we introduce wolves into the burbs?

To their credit, many environmentalists agree that hunting can be green. The New Jersey Audubon Society this year advocated deer hunting as an ecological necessity.

There's another reason to encourage hunting: it connects people with the outdoors and creates a broader constituency for wilderness preservation. At a time when America's wilderness is being gobbled away for logging, mining, or oil drilling, that's a huge boon.

Granted, hunting isn't advisable in suburban backyards, and I don't expect many soccer moms to install gun racks in their minivans. But it's an abdication of environmental responsibility to eliminate other predators and then refuse to assume the job ourselves. In that case, the collisions with humans will simply get worse.

In October, for example, Wayne Goldsberry was sitting in a home in northwestern Arkansas when he heard glass breaking in the next room. It was a home invasion—by a buck.

Mr. Goldsberry, who is six feet one inch and weighs two hundred   20
pounds, wrestled with the intruder for forty minutes. Blood spattered the walls before he managed to break the buck's neck.

So it's time to reestablish a balance in the natural world—by accepting the idea that hunting is as natural as bird-watching.

TOPICS FOR CRITICAL THINKING AND WRITING

1. What is Kristof's chief thesis? (State it in one sentence.)

2. Does Kristof make any assumptions—tacit or explicit—with which you disagree? With which you agree? Write them down.

3. Is the slightly humorous tone of Kristof's essay inappropriate for a discussion of deliberately killing wild animals? Why, or why not?

4. If you are familiar with *Bambi*, does the story make any *argument* against killing deer, or does the story appeal only to our emotions?

5. Do you agree that "hunting is as natural as bird-watching" (para. 21)? In any case, do you think that an appeal to what is "natural" is a good argument for expanding the use of hunting?

6. To whom is Kristof talking? How do you know?

The Essay Analyzed

OK, time's up. Let's examine Kristof's essay with an eye to identifying those elements we mentioned earlier in this chapter (pp. 179–86) that deserve notice when examining *any* argument: the author's *thesis, purpose, methods, persona,* and *audience.* And while we're at it, let's also notice some other features of Kristof's essay that will help us appreciate its effects and evaluate it. We will thus be in a good position to write an evaluation or an argument that confirms, extends, or even rebuts Kristof's argument.

But first, a caution: Kristof's essay appeared in a newspaper where paragraphs are customarily very short, partly to allow for easy reading and partly because the columns are narrow and even short paragraphs may extend for an inch or two. If his essay were to appear in a book, doubtless the author would join many of the paragraphs, making longer units. In analyzing a work, think about where it originally appeared. A blog, a print journal, an online magazine? Does the format in some measure influence the piece?

Title   By combining "Environmental Balance" with "Rifle"—terms that don't seem to go together—Kristof starts off with a bang. He gives a hint of his *topic* (something about the environment) and of his thesis (some sort of way of introducing ecological balance). He also conveys something of his persona by introducing a rifle into the environment. He is, the title suggests, a no-nonsense, hard-hitting guy.

Opening Paragraphs   Kristof immediately grabs hold of us ("Here's a quick quiz") and asks a simple question, but one that we probably have not thought much about: "Which large American mammal kills the most humans each year?" In his second paragraph he tells us it is *not* the bear—the answer most readers probably come up with—nor is it the cougar. Not until the third paragraph does Kristof give us the answer, the deer. But remember, Kristof is writing in a newspaper, where paragraphs customarily are very short. It takes us only a few seconds to get to the third paragraph and the answer.

Thesis   What is the basic thesis Kristof is arguing? Somewhat unusually, Kristof does *not* announce it in its full form until his sixth paragraph ("Let's bring back hunting"), but, again, his paragraphs are very short, and if the essay were published in a book, Kristof's first two paragraphs probably would be combined, as would the third and fourth.

Purpose   Kristof's purpose is clear: He wants to *persuade* readers to adopt his view. This amounts to trying to persuade us that his thesis (stated above) is *true.* Kristof, however, does not show that his essay is argumentative or persuasive by using many of the key terms that normally mark argumentative prose. He doesn't call anything his *conclusion,* none of his statements is labeled *my premises,* and he doesn't connect clauses or sentences with *therefore* or *because.* Almost the only traces of the language of argument are "Granted" (para. 18) and "So" (that is, *therefore*) in his final paragraph.

Despite the lack of argumentative language, the argumentative nature of his essay is clear. He has a thesis—one that will strike many readers as highly unusual—and he wants readers to accept it, so he must go on to *support* it; accordingly, after his introductory paragraphs, in which he calls attention to a problem and offers a solution (his thesis), he must offer evidence, and that is what much of the rest of the essay seeks to do.

Methods   Although Kristof will have to offer evidence, he begins by recognizing the folks on the other side, "the university-educated crowd in the cities, [for whom] hunting is viewed as barbaric" (para. 7). He goes on to spoof this "crowd" when, speaking of methods of keeping the deer population down, he says in paragraph 8, "Liberals presumably support free condoms, while conservatives back abstinence education." Ordinarily it is a bad idea to make fun of persons who hold views other than your own—after all, they just may be on to something, they just might know something you don't know, and, in any case, impartial readers rarely want to align themselves with someone who mocks others. In the essay we are looking at, however, Kristof gets away with this smart-guy tone because he (a) has loyal readers and (b) has written the entire essay in a highly informal or playful manner. Think again about the first paragraph, which begins "Here's a quick quiz." The informality is not only in the contraction (*Here's* versus *Here is*), but in the very idea of beginning by grabbing the readers and thrusting a quiz at them. The playfulness is evident throughout: For instance, immediately after Kristof announces his thesis, "Let's bring back hunting," he begins a new paragraph (7) with, "Now, you've probably just spilled your coffee."

Kristof's methods of presenting evidence include providing **statistics** (paras. 3, 4, 10, and 13), giving **examples** (paras. 10, 19–20), and citing **authorities** (paras. 13 and 16).

Persona   Kristof presents himself as a confident, no-nonsense fellow, a persona that not many writers can get away with, but that probably is acceptable in a journalist who regularly writes a newspaper column. His readers know what to expect, and they read him with pleasure. But it probably would be inadvisable for an unknown writer to adopt this persona, unless perhaps he or she were writing for an audience that could be counted on to be friendly (in this instance, an audience of hunters). If this essay appeared in a hunting magazine, doubtless it would please and entertain its audience. It would not convert anybody, but conversion would not be its point if it were published in a magazine read by hunters. In the *New York Times*, where the essay originally appeared, Kristof could count on a moderately sympathetic audience because he has a large number of faithful readers, but one can guess that many of these readers—chiefly city dwellers—read him for entertainment rather than for information about how they should actually behave.

By the way, when we speak of "faithful readers" we are in effect saying that the author has established good *ethos*, has convinced those readers that he or she is *worth* reading.

Closing Paragraphs   The first two of the last three paragraphs report an episode (the 200-pound buck inside the house) that Kristof presumably thinks is pretty conclusive evidence. The final paragraph begins with "So," strongly implying a logical conclusion to the essay.

Let's now turn to a student's analysis of Kristof's essay and then to our analysis of the student's analysis. (We should say that the analysis of Kristof's essay that you have just read is partly indebted to the student's essay that you are about to read.)

Betsy Swinton

Professor Knowles

English 101B

March 12, 2013

Tracking Kristof

Nicholas D. Kristof's "For Environmental Balance, Pick Up a Rifle" is an engaging piece of writing, but whether it is convincing is something I am not sure about. And I am not sure about it for two reasons: (1) I don't know much about the deer problem, and that's my fault; (2) I don't know much about the deer problem, and that's Kristof's fault. The first point needs no explanation, but let me explain the second.

Kristof is making an argument, offering a thesis: Deer are causing destruction, and the best way to reduce the destruction is to hunt deer. For all that I know, he may be correct both in his comment about what deer are doing and also in his comment about what must be done about deer. My ignorance of the situation is regrettable, but I don't think that I am the only reader from Chicago who doesn't know much about the deer problems in New Jersey, Connecticut, and Arkansas, the states that Kristof specifically mentions in connection with the deer problem. He announces his thesis early enough, in his sixth paragraph, and he is entertaining throughout his essay, but does he make a convincing case? To ask "Does he make a convincing case?" is to ask "Does he offer adequate evidence?" and "Does he show that his solution is better than other possible solutions?"

To take the first question: In a short essay Kristof can hardly give overwhelming evidence, but he does convince me that there is a problem. The most convincing evidence he gives appears in paragraph 16, where he says that the New Jersey Audubon Society "advocated deer hunting as an ecological necessity." I don't really know anything about the New Jersey Audubon Society, but I suppose that they are people with a deep interest in nature and in conservation, and if even such a group advocates deer hunting, there must be something to this solution.

I am even willing to accept his argument that, in this nation of meat-eaters, "to wring one's hands over them [dead deer], perhaps after polishing off a hamburger, is soggy sentimentality" (para. 14). According to Kristof, the present alternative to hunting deer is that we leave the deer to "die of disease and hunger" (para. 15). But what I am not convinced of is that there is no way to reduce the deer population other than by hunting. I don't think Kristof adequately explains why some sort of birth control is inadequate. In his eighth paragraph he makes a joke about controlling the birth of deer ("Liberals presumably support free condoms, while conservatives back abstinence education"), and the joke is funny, but it isn't an argument, it's just a joke. Why can't food containing some sort of sterilizing medicine be put out for the starving deer, food that will nourish them and yet make them unreproductive? In short, I don't think he has fairly informed his readers of alternatives to his own positions, and because he fails to look at counterproposals, he weakens his own proposal.

Although Kristof occasionally uses a word or phrase that suggests argument, such as "Granted" (para. 18), "So" (final paragraph), and "There's another reason" (para. 17), he relies chiefly on forceful writing rather than on reasoning. And the second of his two reasons for hunting seems utterly unconvincing to me. His first, as we have seen, is that the deer population (and apparently the bear population) is out of control. His second (para. 17) is that hunting "connects people with the outdoors and creates a broader constituency for wilderness preservation." I am not a hunter and I have never been one. Perhaps that's my misfortune, but I don't think I am missing anything. And when I hear Kristof say, in his final sentence—the climactic place in his essay—that "hunting is as

Swinton 3

natural as bird-watching," I rub my eyes in disbelief. If he had me at least half-convinced by his statistics and his citation of the Audubon Society, he now loses me when he argues that hunting is "natural." One might as well say that war is natural, rape is natural, bribery is natural—all these terrible things occur, but we ought to deplore them and we ought to make every effort to see that they disappear.

In short, I think that Kristof has written an engaging essay, and he may well have an important idea, but I think that in his glib final paragraph, where he tells us that "hunting is as natural as bird-watching," he utterly loses the reader's confidence.

AN ANALYSIS OF THE STUDENT'S ANALYSIS

Swinton's essay seems to us to be excellent, doubtless the product of a good deal of thoughtful revision. She does not cover every possible aspect of Kristof's essay—she concentrates on his reasoning and she says very little about his style—but we think that, given the limits of space (about 500 words), she does a good job. What makes this student's essay effective?

- The essay has a title ("Tracking Kristof") that is of at least a little interest; it picks up Kristof's point about hunting, and it gives a hint of what is to come.

✓ A CHECKLIST FOR WRITING AN ANALYSIS OF AN ARGUMENT

Have I asked myself the following questions?

☐ Early in my essay have I accurately stated the writer's thesis (claim) and summarized his or her supporting reasons? Have I explained to my reader any disagreement about definitions of important terms?

☐ Have I, again fairly early in my essay, indicated where I will be taking my reader, i.e., have I indicated my general response to the essay I am analyzing?

☐ Have I called attention to the strengths, if any, and the weaknesses, if any, of the essay?

☐ Have I commented not only on the *logos* (logic, reasoning) but also on the *ethos* (character of the writer, as presented in the essay)? For instance, has the author convinced me that he or she is well-informed and is a person of goodwill? Or, on the other hand, does the writer seem to be chiefly concerned with ridiculing those who hold a different view?

☐ If there is an appeal to *pathos* (emotion, originally meaning "pity for suffering," but now interpreted more broadly to include appeals to patriotism, humor, or loyalty to family, for example), is it acceptable? If not, why not?

☐ Have I used occasional brief quotations to let my reader hear the author's tone and to ensure fairness and accuracy?

☐ Is my analysis effectively organized?

☐ Have I taken account of the author's audience(s)?

☐ Does my essay, perhaps in the concluding paragraphs, indicate my agreement or disagreement with the writer but also my view of the essay as a piece of argumentative writing?

☐ Is my tone appropriate?

- The author promptly identifies her subject (she names the writer and the title of his essay) early.

- Early in the essay she gives us a hint of where she will be going (in her first paragraph she tells us that Kristof's essay is "engaging . . . but . . .").

- She recognizes Kristof's audience at the start, and she suggests that he may not have given thought to this matter of the audience.

- She uses a few brief quotations, to give us a feel for Kristof's essay and to let us hear the evidence for itself, but she does not pad her essay with long quotations.

- She takes up all of Kristof's main points.

- She gives her essay a reasonable organization, letting us hear Kristof's thesis, letting us know the degree to which she accepts it, and finally letting us know her specific reservations about the essay.

- She concludes without the formality of "in conclusion"; "in short" nicely does the trick.

- Notice, finally, that she sticks closely to Kristof's essay. She does not go off on a tangent about the virtues of vegetarianism or the dreadful politics of the *New York Times,* the newspaper that published Kristof's essay. She was asked to analyze the essay, and she has done so.

EXERCISE

Take one of the essays not yet discussed in class or an essay assigned now by your instructor, and in an essay of 500 words analyze and evaluate it, guided by the checklists and examples we have provided.

ARGUMENTS FOR ANALYSIS

Jeff Jacoby

Jeff Jacoby is a columnist for the Boston Globe, *where this essay was originally published on the op-ed page on February 20, 1997.*

Bring Back Flogging

Boston's Puritan forefathers did not indulge miscreants lightly.

For selling arms and gunpowder to Indians in 1632, Richard Hopkins was sentenced to be "whipt, & branded with a hott iron on one of his cheekes." Joseph Gatchell, convicted of blasphemy in 1684, was ordered "to stand in pillory, have his head and hand put in & have his toung drawne forth out of his mouth, & peirct through with a hott iron." When Hannah Newell pleaded guilty to adultery in 1694, the court ordered "fifteen stripes Severally to be laid on upon her naked back at the Common Whipping post." Her consort, the aptly named Lambert Despair, fared worse: He was sentenced to twenty-five lashes "and that on the next Thursday Immediately after Lecture he stand upon the Pillory for . . . a full hower with Adultery in Capitall letters written upon his brest."

Corporal punishment for criminals did not vanish with the Puritans—Delaware didn't get around to repealing it until 1972—but for all relevant purposes, it has been out of fashion for at least 150 years. The day is long past when the stocks had an honored place on the Boston Common, or when offenders were publicly flogged. Now we practice a more enlightened, more humane way of disciplining wrongdoers: We lock them up in cages.

Imprisonment has become our penalty of choice for almost every offense in the criminal code. Commit murder; go to prison. Sell cocaine; go to prison. Kite checks; go to prison. It is an all-purpose punishment, suitable—or so it would seem—for crimes violent and nonviolent, motivated by hate or by greed, plotted coldly or committed in a fit of passion. If anything, our preference for incarceration is deepening—behold the slew of mandatory minimum sentences for drug crimes and "three-strikes-you're-out" life terms for recidivists. Some 1.6 million Americans are behind bars today. That represents a 250 percent increase since 1980, and the number is climbing.

We cage criminals at a rate unsurpassed in the free world, yet few 5 of us believe that the criminal justice system is a success. Crime is out of control, despite the deluded happy talk by some politicians about how "safe" cities have become. For most wrongdoers, the odds of being arrested, prosecuted, convicted, and incarcerated are reassuringly long. Fifty-eight percent of all murders do *not* result in a prison term. Likewise 98 percent of all burglaries.

Many states have gone on prison-building sprees, yet the penal system is choked to bursting. To ease the pressure, nearly all convicted felons are released early—or not locked up at all. "About three of every four convicted criminals," says John DiIulio, a noted Princeton criminologist, "are on the streets without meaningful probation or parole supervision." And while everyone knows that amateur thugs should be deterred before they become career criminals, it is almost unheard of for judges to send first- or second-time offenders to prison.

Meanwhile, the price of keeping criminals in cages is appalling—a common estimate is $30,000 per inmate per year. (To be sure, the cost to society of turning many inmates loose would be even higher.) For tens of thousands of convicts, prison is a graduate school of criminal studies: They emerge more ruthless and savvy than when they entered. And for many offenders, there is even a certain cachet to doing time—a stint in prison becomes a sign of manhood, a status symbol.

But there would be no cachet in chaining a criminal to an outdoor post and flogging him. If young punks were horsewhipped in public after their first conviction, fewer of them would harden into lifelong felons. A humiliating and painful paddling can be applied to the rear end of a crook for a lot less than $30,000—and prove a lot more educational than ten years' worth of prison meals and lockdowns.

Are we quite certain the Puritans have nothing to teach us about dealing with criminals?

Of course, their crimes are not our crimes: We do not arrest blas-   10 phemers or adulterers, and only gun control fanatics would criminal- ize the sale of weapons to Indians. (They would criminalize the sale of weapons to anybody.) Nor would the ordeal suffered by poor Joseph Gatchell—the tongue "peirct through" with a hot poker—be regarded today as anything less than torture.

But what is the objection to corporal punishment that doesn't maim or mutilate? Instead of a prison term, why not sentence at least some criminals—say, thieves and drunk drivers—to a public whipping?

"Too degrading," some will say. "Too brutal." But where is it written that being whipped is more degrading than being caged? Why is it more brutal to flog a wrongdoer than to throw him in prison—where the risk of being beaten, raped, or murdered is terrifyingly high?

The *Globe* reported in 1994 that more than two hundred thousand prison inmates are raped each year, usually to the indifference of the guards. "The horrors experienced by many young inmates, particularly those who . . . are convicted of nonviolent offenses," former Supreme Court Justice Harry Blackmun has written, "border on the unimagina- ble." Are those horrors preferable to the short, sharp shame of corporal punishment?

Perhaps the Puritans were more enlightened than we think, at least on the subject of punishment. Their sanctions were humiliating and painful, but quick and cheap. Maybe we should readopt a few.

TOPICS FOR CRITICAL THINKING AND WRITING

1. When Jacoby says (para. 3) that today we are more "enlightened" than our Puritan forefathers because where they used flogging, "We lock them up in cages," is he being ironic? Explain.

2. Suppose you agree with Jacoby. Explain precisely (a) what you mean by *flogging* (does Jacoby explain what he means?) and (b) how much flogging is appropriate for the crimes of housebreaking, rape, robbery, and murder.

3. In an essay of 250 words, explain why you think that flogging would be more (or less) degrading and brutal than imprisonment.

4. At the end of his essay Jacoby draws to our attention the terrible risk of being raped in prison as an argument in favor of replacing imprisonment

with flogging. Do you think he mentions this point at the end because he believes it is the strongest or most persuasive of all those he mentions? Why, or why not?

5. It is often said that corporal punishment does not have any effect or, if it does, that the effect is the negative one of telling the recipient that violence is an acceptable form of behavior. But suppose it were demonstrated that the infliction of physical pain reduced at least certain kinds of crimes, perhaps shoplifting or unarmed robbery. Should we adopt the practice?

6. Jacoby draws the line (para. 11) at punishment that would "maim or mutilate." Why draw the line here? Some societies punish thieves by amputating a hand. Suppose we knew that this practice really did seriously reduce theft. Should we adopt it? How about adopting castration (surgical or chemical) for rapists? For child molesters?

Gerard Jones

Gerard Jones (b. 1957), author of several works of fiction and nonfiction, has written many comic books for Marvel Comics and other publishers.

Violent Media Is Good for Kids

At thirteen I was alone and afraid. Taught by my well-meaning, progressive, English-teacher parents that violence was wrong, that rage was something to be overcome and cooperation was always better than conflict, I suffocated my deepest fears and desires under a nice-boy persona. Placed in a small, experimental school that was wrong for me, afraid to join my peers in their bumptious rush into adolescent boyhood, I withdrew into passivity and loneliness. My parents, not trusting the violent world of the late 1960s, built a wall between me and the crudest elements of American pop culture.

Then the Incredible Hulk smashed through it.

One of my mother's students convinced her that Marvel Comics, despite their apparent juvenility and violence, were in fact devoted to lofty messages of pacifism and tolerance. My mother borrowed some, thinking they'd be good for me. And so they were. But not because they preached lofty messages of benevolence. They were good for me because they were juvenile. And violent.

The character who caught me, and freed me, was the Hulk: overgendered and undersocialized, half-naked and half-witted, raging against a frightened world that misunderstood and persecuted him. Suddenly I had a fantasy self to carry my stifled rage and buried desire for power. I had a fantasy self who was a self: unafraid of his desires and the world's disapproval, unhesitating and effective in action. "Puny boy follow Hulk!" roared my fantasy self, and I followed.

I followed him to new friends—other sensitive geeks chasing their own inner brutes—and I followed him to the arrogant, self-exposing, self-assertive, superheroic decision to become a writer. Eventually, I left him behind, followed more sophisticated heroes, and finally my own lead along a twisting path to a career and an identity. In my thirties, I found myself writing action movies and comic books. I wrote some Hulk stories, and met the geek-geniuses who created him. I saw my own creations turned into action figures, cartoons, and computer games. I talked to the kids who read my stories. Across generations, genders, and ethnicities I kept seeing the same story: people pulling themselves out of emotional traps by immersing themselves in violent stories. People integrating the scariest, most fervently denied fragments of their psyches into fuller senses of selfhood through fantasies of superhuman combat and destruction.

A scene from Gerard Jones and Gene Ha's comic book "Oktane"

I have watched my son living the same story — transforming himself into a blood-thirsty dinosaur to embolden himself for the plunge into preschool, a Power Ranger to muscle through a social competition in kindergarten. In the first grade, his friends started climbing a tree at school. But he was afraid: of falling, of the centipedes crawling on the trunk, of sharp branches, of his friends' derision. I took my cue from his own fantasies and read him old Tarzan comics, rich in combat and bright with flashing knives. For two weeks he lived in them. Then he put them aside. And he climbed the tree.

But all the while, especially in the wake of the recent burst of school shootings, I heard pop psychologists insisting that violent stories are harmful to kids, heard teachers begging parents to keep their kids away from "junk culture," heard a guilt-stricken friend with a son who loved Pokémon lament, "I've turned into the bad mom who lets her kid eat sugary cereal and watch cartoons!"

That's when I started the research.

"Fear, greed, power-hunger, rage: these are aspects of our selves that we try not to experience in our lives but often want, even need, to experience vicariously through stories of others," writes Melanie Moore, Ph.D., a psychologist who works with urban teens. "Children need violent entertainment in order to explore the inescapable feelings that they've been taught to deny, and to reintegrate those feelings into a more whole, more complex, more resilient selfhood."

Moore consults to public schools and local governments, and is also 10 raising a daughter. For the past three years she and I have been studying the ways in which children use violent stories to meet their emotional and developmental needs—and the ways in which adults can help them use those stories healthily. With her help I developed Power Play, a program for helping young people improve their self-knowledge and sense of potency through heroic, combative storytelling.

We've found that every aspect of even the trashiest pop-culture story can have its own developmental function. Pretending to have superhuman powers helps children conquer the feelings of powerlessness that inevitably come with being so young and small. The dual-identity concept at the heart of many superhero stories helps kids negotiate the conflicts between the inner self and the public self as they work through the early stages of socialization. Identification with a rebellious, even destructive, hero helps children learn to push back against a modern culture that cultivates fear and teaches dependency.

At its most fundamental level, what we call "creative violence"—head-bonking cartoons, bloody videogames, playground karate, toy guns—gives children a tool to master their rage. Children will feel rage. Even the sweetest and most civilized of them, even those whose parents read the better class of literary magazines, will feel rage. The world is uncontrollable and incomprehensible; mastering it is a terrifying, enraging task. Rage can be an energizing emotion, a shot of courage to push us to resist greater threats, take more control, than we ever thought we could. But rage is also the emotion our culture distrusts the most. Most of us are taught early on to fear our own. Through immersion in imaginary combat and identification with a violent protagonist, children engage the rage they've stifled, come to fear it less, and become more capable of utilizing it against life's challenges.

I knew one little girl who went around exploding with fantasies so violent that other moms would draw her mother aside to whisper, "I think you should know something about Emily. . . ." Her parents were separating, and she was small, an only child, a tomboy at an age when her classmates were dividing sharply along gender lines. On the

The title character of "Oktane" gets nasty.

playground she acted out *Sailor Moon* fights, and in the classroom she wrote stories about people being stabbed with knives. The more adults tried to control her stories, the more she acted out the roles of her angry heroes: breaking rules, testing limits, roaring threats.

Then her mother and I started helping her tell her stories. She wrote them, performed them, drew them like comics: sometimes bloody, sometimes tender, always blending the images of pop culture with her own most private fantasies. She came out of it just as fiery and strong, but more self-controlled and socially competent: a leader among her peers, the one student in her class who could truly pull boys and girls together.

I worked with an older girl, a middle-class "nice girl," who held 15
herself together through a chaotic family situation and a tumultuous adolescence with gangsta rap. In the mythologized street violence of Ice T, the rage and strutting of his music and lyrics, she found a theater of the mind in which she could be powerful, ruthless, invulnerable. She avoided the heavy drug use that sank many of her peers, and flowered in college as a writer and political activist.

I'm not going to argue that violent entertainment is harmless. I think it has helped inspire some people to real-life violence. I am going to argue that it's helped hundreds of people for every one it's hurt, and that it can help far more if we learn to use it well. I am going to argue that our fear of "youth violence" isn't well-founded on reality, and that the fear can do more harm than the reality. We act as though our highest priority is to prevent our children from growing up into murderous thugs—but modern kids are far more likely to grow up too passive, too distrustful of themselves, too easily manipulated.

We send the message to our children in a hundred ways that their craving for imaginary gun battles and symbolic killings is wrong, or at least dangerous. Even when we don't call for censorship or forbid *Mortal Kombat*, we moan to other parents within our kids' earshot about the "awful violence" in the entertainment they love. We tell our kids that it isn't nice to play-fight, or we steer them from some monstrous action figure to a prosocial doll. Even in the most progressive households, where we make such a point of letting children feel what they feel, we rush to substitute an enlightened discussion for the raw material of rageful fantasy. In the process, we risk confusing them about their natural aggression in the same way the Victorians confused their children about their sexuality. When we try to protect our children from their own feelings and fantasies, we shelter them not against violence but against power and selfhood.

TOPICS FOR CRITICAL THINKING AND WRITING

1. In his final paragraph Jones mentions the Victorian treatment of sexuality. Why does he bring this in? Does his use of this point make for an effective ending? Explain.

2. In an essay of 300 words, explain whether you think Jones has made the case for violence in an effective and persuasive way. If so, what is it about his article that makes it effective and persuasive? If it is not, where do the problems lie?

3. What kinds of violence does Jones advocate?

4. Does violence play as large a part in the life of teenage girls as it does in the life of teenage boys? Why, or why not?

5. How would you characterize the audience Jones is addressing? What is your evidence?

Justin Cronin

Justin Cronin is an award-winning novelist who teaches at Rice University, in Houston, Texas.

Confessions of a Liberal Gun Owner

I am a New England liberal, born and bred. I have lived most of my life in the Northeast—Boston, New York, and Philadelphia—and my politics are devoutly Democratic. In three decades, I have voted for a Republican exactly once, holding my nose, in a mayoral election in which the Democratic candidate seemed mentally unbalanced.

I am also a Texas resident and a gun owner. I have half a dozen pistols in my safe, all semiautomatics, the largest capable of holding twenty rounds. I go to the range at least once a week, have applied for a concealed carry license, and am planning to take a tactical training course in the spring. I'm currently shopping for a shotgun, either a Remington 870 Express Tactical or a Mossberg 500 Flex with a pistol grip and adjustable stock.

Except for shotguns (firing one feels like being punched by a prizefighter), I enjoy shooting. At the range where I practice, most of the staff knows me by sight if not by name. I'm the guy in the metrosexual eyeglasses and Ralph Lauren polo, and I ask a lot of questions: What's the best way to maintain my sight picture with both eyes open? How do I clear a stove-piped round?

There is pleasure to be had in exercising one's rights, learning something new in midlife, and mastering the operation of a complex tool, which is one thing a gun is. But I won't deny the seductive psychological power that firearms possess. I grew up playing shooting games, pretending to be Starsky or Hutch or one of the patrolmen on *Adam-12*, the two most boring TV cops in history.

A prevailing theory holds that boys are simultaneously aware of 5 their own physical powerlessness and society's mandate that they serve as protectors of the innocent. Pretending to shoot a bad guy assuages this anxiety, which never goes away completely. This explanation makes sense to me. Another word for it is catharsis, and you could say that, as a novelist, I've made my living from it.

There are a lot of reasons that a gun feels right in my hand, but I also own firearms to protect my family. I hope I never have to use one for this purpose, and I doubt I ever will. But I am my family's last line of defense. I have chosen to meet this responsibility, in part, by being armed. It wasn't a choice I made lightly. I am aware that, statistically speaking, a gun in the home represents a far greater danger to its inhabitants than to an intruder. But not every choice we make is data-driven. A lot comes from the gut.

Apart from the ones in policemen's holsters, I don't think I saw a working firearm until the year after college, when a friend's girlfriend, after four cosmopolitans, decided to show off the .38 revolver she kept in her purse. (Half the party guests dived for cover, including me.)

It wasn't until my mid-forties that my education in guns began, in the course of writing a novel in which pistols, shotguns, and rifles, but also heavy weaponry like the AR-15 and its military analogue, the M-16, were widely used. I suspected that much of the gunplay I'd witnessed in movies and television was completely wrong (it is) and hired an instructor for a daylong private lesson "to shoot everything in the store." The gentleman who met me at the range was someone whom I would have called "a gun nut." A former New Yorker, he had relocated to Texas because of its lax gun laws and claimed to keep a pistol within arm's reach even when he showered. He was perfect, in other words, for my purpose.

My relationship to firearms might have ended there, if not for a coincidence of weather. Everybody remembers Hurricane Katrina; fewer recall Hurricane Rita, an even more intense storm that headed straight for Houston less than a month later. My wife and I arranged to stay at a friend's house in Austin, packed up the kids and dog, and headed out of town — or tried to. As many as 3.7 million people had the same idea, making Rita one of the largest evacuations in history, with predictable results.

By two in the morning, after six hours on the road, we had made   10
it all of fifty miles. The scene was like a snapshot from the Apocalypse: crowds milling restlessly, gas stations and mini-marts picked clean and heaped with trash, families sleeping by the side of the road. The situation had the hopped-up feel of barely bottled chaos. After Katrina, nobody had any illusions that help was on its way. It also occurred to me that there were probably a lot of guns out there—this was Texas, after all. Here I was with two tiny children, a couple of thousand dollars in cash, a late-model S.U.V. with half a tank of gas and not so much as a heavy book to throw. When my wife wouldn't let me get out of the car so the dog could do his business, that was it for me. We jumped the median, turned around, and were home in under an hour.

As it happened, Rita made a last-minute turn away from Houston. But what if it hadn't? I believe people are basically good, but not all of them and not all the time. Like most citizens of our modern, technological world, I am wholly reliant upon a fragile web of services to meet my most basic needs. What would happen if those services collapsed? Chaos, that's what.

It didn't happen overnight, but before too long my Northeastern liberal sensibilities, while intact on other issues, had shifted on the question of gun ownership. For my first pistol I selected a little Walther .380. I shot it enough to decide it was junk, upgraded to a full-size Springfield 9-millimeter, liked it but wanted something with a thumb safety, found a nice Smith & Wesson subcompact that fit the bill, but along the way got a little bit of a gun-crush on the Beretta M-9—and so on.

Lots of people on both sides of the aisle own firearms, or don't, for reasons that supersede their broader political and cultural affiliations. Let me be clear: my personal armory notwithstanding. I think guns are woefully under-regulated. It's far too easy to buy a gun—I once bought one in a parking lot—and I loathe the National Rifle Association. Some of the Obama administration's proposals strike me as more symbolic than effective, with some 300 million firearms on the loose. But the White House's recommendations seem like a good starting point and nothing that would prevent me from protecting my family in a crisis. The AR-15 is a fascinating weapon, and, frankly, a gas to shoot. So is a tank, and I don't need to own a tank.

Alas, the days of à la carte politics like mine seem over, if they ever even existed. The bigger culprit is the far right and the lunatic pronouncements of those like Rush Limbaugh. But in the weeks since

Newtown, I've watched my Facebook feed, which is dominated by my coastal friends, fill up with antigun dispatches that seemed divorced from reality. I agree it would be nice if the world had exactly zero guns in it. But I don't see that happening, and calling gun owners "a bunch of inbred rednecks" doesn't do much to advance rational discussion.

Thus, my secret life—though I guess it's not such a secret anymore. 15 My wife is afraid of my guns (though she also says she's glad I have them). My sixteen-year-old daughter is a different story. The week before her fall semester exams, we allowed her to skip school for a day, a tradition in our house. The rule is, she gets to do whatever she wants. This time, she asked to take a pistol lesson. She's an NPR listener like me, but she's also grown up in Texas, and the fact that one in five American women is a victim of sexual assault is not lost on her. In the windowless classroom off the range, the instructor ran her through the basics, demonstrating with a Glock 9-millimeter: how to hold it, load it, pull back the slide.

"You'll probably have trouble with that part," he said. "A lot of the women do."

"Oh really?" my daughter replied, and with a cagey smile proceeded to rack her weapon with such authority you could have heard it in the parking lot.

A proud-papa moment? I confess it was.

Topics for Critical Thinking and Writing

1. This essay could with equal accuracy be called "Confessions of a Texas Gun Owner." Why do you suppose Cronin chose the title he did, rather than our imagined title? That is, why is his title better—better for his purposes—than our invented title?

2. Why does Cronin devote so many sentences to autobiographical matters, since, in fact, none of the autobiography actually involves using a gun to protect himself or his family against an intruder?

3. How would you characterize Cronin's persona as he presents it in this essay? Does he try to speak with authority, connect with his audience on a personal level, or employ another strategy to gain his reader's trust? Do you feel that his persona effectively connects with you as a reader? Why, or why not?

4. What *arguments* does Cronin offer on behalf of gun ownership? Do you think his case—his thesis, his point, his Big Idea—might have been strengthened if he had cited statistics or authorities, or do you think that such evidence probably would have been inappropriate in what is essentially a highly personal essay?

5. In paragraph 12 Cronin writes, "It didn't happen overnight, but before too long my Northeastern liberal sensibilities ... had shifted on the question of gun ownership." Suppose a reader said to you, "I don't

really understand exactly why his attitude shifted. What *happened* that made him shift? I don't get it." What would you say to this questioner?

6. In paragraph 13 Cronin says that he believes "guns are woefully under-regulated," and that he "loathe[s] the National Rifle Association," but he doesn't go into any detail about what sorts of regulations he favors. Do you think his essay might have been more convincing if he had given us details along these lines? Explain.

7. Each of Cronin's last three paragraphs is very short. We have discussed how, in general, a short paragraph is usually an underdeveloped paragraph. Do you think these paragraphs are underdeveloped—or do you think Cronin knows exactly what he is doing? Explain.

Peter Singer

Peter Singer (b. 1946) is the Ira W. DeCamp Professor of Bioethics at Princeton University. A native of Australia, he is a graduate of the University of Melbourne and Oxford University and the author or editor of more than two dozen books, including Animal Liberation *(1975),* Practical Ethics *(1979),* Rethinking Life and Death *(1995), and* One World: The Ethics of Globalization *(2002). He has written on a variety of ethical issues, but he is especially known for caring about the welfare of animals.*

This essay originally appeared in the New York Review of Books *(April 5, 1973), as a review of* Animals, Men and Morals, *edited by Stanley and Roslind Godlovitch and John Harris.*

Animal Liberation

I

We are familiar with Black Liberation, Gay Liberation, and a variety of other movements. With Women's Liberation some thought we had come to the end of the road. Discrimination on the basis of sex, it has been said, is the last form of discrimination that is universally accepted and practiced without pretense, even in those liberal circles which have long prided themselves on their freedom from racial discrimination. But one should always be wary of talking of "the last remaining form of discrimination." If we have learned anything from the liberation movements, we should have learned how difficult it is to be aware of the ways in which we discriminate until they are forcefully pointed out to us. A liberation movement demands an expansion of our moral horizons, so that practices that were previously regarded as natural and inevitable are now seen as intolerable.

Animals, Men and Morals is a manifesto for an Animal Liberation movement. The contributors to the book may not all see the issue this way. They are a varied group. Philosophers, ranging from professors to graduate students, make up the largest contingent. There are five of them, including the three editors, and there is also an extract from the unjustly neglected German philosopher with an English name, Leonard Nelson, who died in 1927. There are essays by two novelist/critics, Brigid Brophy and Maureen Duffy, and another by Muriel the Lady Dowding, widow of Dowding of Battle of Britain fame and the founder of "Beauty without Cruelty," a movement that campaigns against the use of animals for furs and cosmetics. The other pieces are by a psychologist, a botanist, a sociologist, and Ruth Harrison, who is probably best described as a professional campaigner for animal welfare.

Whether or not these people, as individuals, would all agree that they are launching a liberation movement for animals, the book as a whole amounts to no less. It is a demand for a complete change in our attitudes to nonhumans. It is a demand that we cease to regard the exploitation of other species as natural and inevitable, and that, instead, we see it as a continuing moral outrage. Patrick Corbett, Professor of Philosophy at Sussex University, captures the spirit of the book in his closing words:

> We require now to extend the great principles of liberty, equality, and fraternity over the lives of animals. Let animal slavery join human slavery in the graveyard of the past.

The reader is likely to be skeptical. "Animal Liberation" sounds more like a parody of liberation movements than a serious objective. The reader may think: We support the claims of blacks and women for equality because blacks and women really are equal to whites and males—equal in intelligence and in abilities, capacity for leadership, rationality, and so on. Humans and nonhumans obviously are not equal in these respects. Since justice demands only that we treat equals equally, unequal treatment of humans and nonhumans cannot be an injustice.

This is a tempting reply, but a dangerous one. It commits the non- 5 racist and nonsexist to a dogmatic belief that blacks and women really are just as intelligent, able, etc., as whites and males—and no more. Quite possibly this happens to be the case. Certainly attempts to prove that racial or sexual differences in these respects have a genetic origin have not been conclusive. But do we really want to stake our demand for equality on the assumption that there are no genetic differences of this kind between the different races or sexes? Surely the appropriate response to those who claim to have found evidence for such genetic differences is not to stick to the belief that there are no differences, whatever the evidence to the contrary; rather one should be clear that the claim to equality does not depend on IQ. Moral equality is distinct from factual equality. Otherwise it would be nonsense to talk to the equality of human beings, since humans, as individuals, obviously differ in intelligence and almost any ability one cares to name. If possessing greater intelligence does not entitle one human to exploit another, why should it entitle humans to exploit nonhumans?

Jeremy Bentham expressed the essential basis of equality in his famous formula: "Each to count for one and none for more than one."

In other words, the interests of every being that has interests are to be taken into account and treated equally with the like interests of any other being. Other moral philosophers, before and after Bentham, have made the same point in different ways. Our concern for others must not depend on whether they possess certain characteristics, though just what that concern involves may, of course, vary according to such characteristics.

Bentham, incidentally, was well aware that the logic of the demand for racial equality did not stop at the equality of humans. He wrote:

> The day *may* come when the rest of the animal creation may acquire those rights which never could have been withholden from them but by the hand of tyranny. The French have already discovered that the blackness of the skin is no reason why a human being should be abandoned without redress to the caprice of a tormentor. It may one day come to be recognized that the number of the legs, the villosity of the skin, or the termination of the *os sacrum*, are reasons equally insufficient for abandoning a sensitive being to the same fate. What else is it that should trace the insuperable line? Is it the faculty of reason, or perhaps the faculty of discourse? But a full-grown horse or dog is beyond comparison a more rational, as well as a more conversable animal, than an infant of a day, or a week, or even a month, old. But suppose they were otherwise, what would it avail? The question is not, Can they *reason*? nor Can they *talk*? but, Can they *suffer*?[1]

Surely Bentham was right. If a being suffers, there can be no moral justification for refusing to take that suffering into consideration, and, indeed, to count it equally with the like suffering (if rough comparisons can be made) of any other being.

So the only question is: Do animals other than man suffer? Most people agree unhesitatingly that animals like cats and dogs can and do suffer, and this seems also to be assumed by those laws that prohibit wanton cruelty to such animals. Personally, I have no doubt at all about this and find it hard to take seriously the doubts that a few people apparently do have. The editors and contributors of *Animals, Men and Morals* seem to feel the same way, for although the question is raised more than once, doubts are quickly dismissed each time. Nevertheless, because this is such a fundamental point, it is worth asking what grounds we have for attributing suffering to other animals.

It is best to begin by asking what grounds any individual human has for supposing that other humans feel pain. Since pain is a state of consciousness, a "mental event," it can never be directly observed. No observations, whether behavioral signs such as writhing or screaming or physiological or neurological recordings, are observations of pain itself. Pain is something one feels, and one can only infer that others are feeling it from various external indications. The fact that only philosophers

---

[1] *The Principles of Morals and Legislation,* ch. XVII, sec. 1, footnote to paragraph 4. [All notes are the author's unless otherwise specified.]

are ever skeptical about whether other humans feel pain shows that we regard such inference as justifiable in the case of humans.

Is there any reason why the same inference should be unjustifiable 10 for other animals? Nearly all the external signs which lead us to infer pain in other humans can be seen in other species, especially "higher" animals such as mammals and birds. Behavioral signs—writhing, yelping, or other forms of calling, attempts to avoid the source of pain, and many others—are present. We know, too, that these animals are biologically similar in the relevant respects, having nervous systems like ours which can be observed to function as ours do.

So the grounds for inferring that these animals can feel pain are nearly as good as the grounds for inferring other humans do. Only nearly, for there is one behavioral sign that humans have but nonhumans, with the exception of one or two specially raised chimpanzees, do not have. This, of course, is a developed language. As the quotation from Bentham indicates, this has long been regarded as an important distinction between man and other animals. Other animals may communicate with each other, but not in the way we do. Following Chomsky,[2] many people now mark this distinction by saying that only humans communicate in a form that is governed by rules of syntax. (For the purposes of this argument, linguists allow those chimpanzees who have learned a syntactic sign language to rank as honorary humans.) Nevertheless, as Bentham pointed out, this distinction is not relevant to the question of how animals ought to be treated, unless it can be linked to the issue of whether animals suffer.

This link may be attempted in two ways. First, there is a hazy line of philosophical thought, stemming perhaps from some doctrines associated with Wittgenstein, which maintains that we cannot meaningfully attribute states of consciousness to beings without language. I have not seen this argument made explicit in print, though I have come across it in conversation. This position seems to me very implausible, and I doubt that it would be held at all if it were not thought to be a consequence of a broader view of the significance of language. It may be that the use of a public, rule-governed language is a precondition of conceptual thought. It may even be, although personally I doubt it, that we cannot meaningfully speak of a creature having an intention unless that creature can use a language. But states like pain, surely, are more primitive than either of these, and seem to have nothing to do with language.

Indeed, as Jane Goodall points out in her study of chimpanzees, when it comes to the expression of feelings and emotions, humans tend to fall back on nonlinguistic modes of communication which are often found among apes, such as a cheering pat on the back, an exuberant embrace, a clasp of hands, and so on.[3] Michael Peters makes a similar

---

[2]**Chomsky** Noam Chomsky (b. 1928), a professor of linguistics and the author of (among other books) *Language and Mind* (1972). [Editors' note.]

[3]Jane van Lawick-Goodall, *In the Shadow of Man* (Houghton Mifflin, 1971), p. 225.

point in his contribution to *Animals, Men and Morals* when he notes that the basic signals we use to convey pain, fear, sexual arousal, and so on are not specific to our species. So there seems to be no reason at all to believe that a creature without language cannot suffer.

The second, and more easily appreciated way of linking language and the existence of pain is to say that the best evidence that we can have that another creature is in pain is when he tells us that he is. This is a distinct line of argument, for it is not being denied that a non-language-user conceivably could suffer, but only that we could know that he is suffering. Still, this line of argument seems to me to fail, and for reasons similar to those just given. "I am in pain" is not the best possible evidence that the speaker is in pain (he might be lying) and it is certainly not the only possible evidence. Behavioral signs and knowledge of the animal's biological similarity to ourselves together provide adequate evidence that animals do suffer. After all, we would not accept linguistic evidence if it contradicted the rest of the evidence. If a man was severely burned, and behaved as if he were in pain, writhing, groaning, being very careful not to let his burned skin touch anything, and so on, but later said he had not been in pain at all, we would be more likely to conclude that he was lying or suffering from amnesia than that he had not been in pain.

Even if there were stronger grounds for refusing to attribute pain to   15
those who do not have a language, the consequences of this refusal might lead us to examine these grounds unusually critically. Human infants, as well as some adults, are unable to use language. Are we to deny that a year-old infant can suffer? If not, how can language be crucial? Of course, most parents can understand the responses of even very young infants better than they understand the responses of other animals, and sometimes infant responses can be understood in the light of later development.

This, however, is just a fact about the relative knowledge we have of our own species and other species, and most of this knowledge is simply derived from closer contact. Those who have studied the behavior of other animals soon learn to understand their responses at least as well as we understand those of an infant. (I am not referring to Jane Goodall's and other well-known studies of apes. Consider, for example, the degree of understanding achieved by Tinbergen from watching herring gulls.[4]) Just as we can understand infant human behavior in the light of adult human behavior, so we can understand the behavior of other species in the light of our own behavior (and sometimes we can understand our own behavior better in the light of the behavior of other species).

The grounds we have for believing that other mammals and birds suffer are, then, closely analogous to the grounds we have for believing that other humans suffer. It remains to consider how far down the evolutionary scale this analogy holds. Obviously it becomes poorer when we get further away from man. To be more precise would require a detailed

[4]N. Tinbergen, *The Herring Gull's World* (Basic Books, 1961).

examination of all that we know about other forms of life. With fish, reptiles, and other vertebrates the analogy still seems strong, with molluscs like oysters it is much weaker. Insects are more difficult, and it may be that in our present state of knowledge we must be agnostic about whether they are capable of suffering.

If there is no moral justification for ignoring suffering when it occurs, and it does occur in other species, what are we to say of our attitudes toward these other species? Richard Ryder, one of the contributors to *Animals, Men and Morals,* uses the term "speciesism" to describe the belief that we are entitled to treat members of other species in a way in which it would be wrong to treat members of our own species. The term is not euphonious, but it neatly makes the analogy with racism. The nonracist would do well to bear the analogy in mind when he is inclined to defend human behavior toward nonhumans. "Shouldn't we worry about improving the lot of our own species before we concern ourselves with other species?" he may ask. If we substitute "race" for "species" we shall see that the question is better not asked. "Is a vegetarian diet nutritionally adequate?" resembles the slaveowner's claim that he and the whole economy of the South would be ruined without slave labor. There is even a parallel with skeptical doubts about whether animals suffer, for some defenders of slavery professed to doubt whether blacks really suffer in the way whites do.

I do not want to give the impression, however, that the case for Animal Liberation is based on the analogy with racism and no more. On the contrary, *Animals, Men and Morals* describes the various ways in which humans exploit nonhumans, and several contributors consider the defenses that have been offered, including the defense of meat-eating mentioned in the last paragraph. Sometimes the rebuttals are scornfully dismissive, rather than carefully designed to convince the detached critic. This may be a fault, but it is a fault that is inevitable, given the kind of book this is. The issue is not one on which one can remain detached. As the editors state in their Introduction:

> Once the full force of moral assessment has been made explicit there can be no rational excuse left for killing animals, be they killed for food, science, or sheer personal indulgence. We have not assembled this book to provide the reader with yet another manual on how to make brutalities less brutal. Compromise, in the traditional sense of the term, is simple unthinking weakness when one considers the actual reasons for our crude relationships with the other animals.

The point is that on this issue there are few critics who are genuinely 20 detached. People who eat pieces of slaughtered nonhumans every day find it hard to believe that they are doing wrong; and they also find it hard to imagine what else they could eat. So for those who do not place nonhumans beyond the pale of morality, there comes a stage when further argument seems pointless, a stage at which one can only accuse one's opponent of hypocrisy and reach for the sort of sociological account of our practices and the way we defend them that is attempted by David Wood in his contribution to his book. On the other hand, to those unconvinced by the arguments, and unable to accept that they are merely rationalizing their dietary preferences and their fear of being thought peculiar, such sociological explanations can only seem insultingly arrogant.

II

The logic of speciesism is most apparent in the practice of experimenting on nonhumans in order to benefit humans. This is because the issue is rarely obscured by allegations that nonhumans are so different from humans that we cannot know anything about whether they suffer. The defender of vivisection cannot use this argument because he needs to stress the similarities between man and other animals in order to justify the usefulness to the former of experiments on the latter. The researcher who makes rats choose between starvation and electric shocks to see if they develop ulcers (they do) does so because he knows that the rat has a nervous system very similar to man's, and presumably feels an electric shock in a similar way.

Richard Ryder's restrained account of experiments on animals made me angrier with my fellow men than anything else in this book. Ryder, a clinical psychologist by profession, himself experimented on animals before he came to hold the view he puts forward in his essay. Experimenting on animals is now a large industry, both academic and commercial. In 1969, more than 5 million experiments were performed in Britain, the vast majority without anesthetic (though how many of these involved pain is not known). There are no accurate U.S. figures, since there is no federal law on the subject, and in many cases no state law either. Estimates vary from 20 million to 200 million. Ryder suggests that 80 million may be the best guess. We tend to think that this is all for vital medical research, but of course it is not. Huge numbers of animals are used in university departments from Forestry to Psychology, and even more are used for commercial purposes, to test whether cosmetics can cause skin damage, or shampoos eye damage, or to test food additives or laxatives or sleeping pills or anything else.

A standard test for foodstuffs is the "LD50." The object of this test is to find the dosage level at which 50 percent of the test animals will die. This means that nearly all of them will become very sick before finally succumbing or surviving. When the substance is a harmless one, it may be necessary to force huge doses down the animals, until in some cases sheer volume or concentration causes death.

Ryder gives a selection of experiments, taken from recent scientific journals. I will quote two, not for the sake of indulging in gory details, but in order to give an idea of what normal researchers think they may legitimately do to other species. The point is not that the individual researchers are cruel men, but that they are behaving in a way that is allowed by our speciesist attitudes. As Ryder points out, even if only 1 percent of the experiments involve severe pain, that is 50,000 experiments in Britain each year, or nearly 150 every day (and about fifteen times as many in the United States, if Ryder's guess is right). Here then are two experiments:

> O. S. Ray and R. J. Barrett of Pittsburgh gave electric shocks to the feet of 1,042 mice. They then caused convulsions by giving more intense shocks through cup-shaped electrodes applied to the animals' eyes or through pressure spring clips attached to their ears. Unfortunately some of the mice who "successfully completed Day One training were found sick or dead prior to testing on Day Two." [*Journal of Comparative and Physiological Psychology*, 1969, vol. 67, pp. 110–116]
>
> At the National Institute for Medical Research, Mill Hill, London, W. Feldberg and S. L. Sherwood injected chemicals into the brains of cats—"with a number of widely different substances, recurrent patterns of reaction were obtained. Retching, vomiting, defecation, increased salivation and greatly accelerated respiration leading to panting were common features." . . .
>
> The injection into the brain of a large dose of Tubocuraine caused the cat to jump "from the table to the floor and then straight into its cage, where it started calling more and more noisily whilst moving about restlessly and jerkily . . . finally the cat fell with legs and neck flexed, jerking in rapid clonic movements, the condition being that of a major [epileptic] convulsion . . . within a few seconds the cat got up, ran for a few yards at high speed, and fell in another fit. The whole process was repeated several times within the next ten minutes, during which the cat lost faeces and foamed at the mouth."
>
> This animal finally died thirty-five minutes after the brain injection. [*Journal of Physiology*, 1954, vol. 123, pp. 148–167]

There is nothing secret about these experiments. One has only to open any recent volume of a learned journal, such as the *Journal of Comparative and Physiological Psychology*, to find full descriptions of experiments of this sort, together with the results obtained—results that are frequently trivial and obvious. The experiments are often supported by public funds.

It is a significant indication of the level of acceptability of these practices that, although these experiments are taking place at this moment on university campuses throughout the country, there has, so far as I know, not been the slightest protest from the student movement. Students have been rightly concerned that their universities should not discriminate on grounds of race or sex, and that they should not serve the purposes of the military or big business. Speciesism continues undisturbed, and many students participate in it. There may be a few qualms at first, but since everyone regards it as normal, and it may even be a required part of a course, the student soon becomes hardened and, dismissing his earlier feelings as "mere sentiment," comes to regard animals as statistics rather than sentient beings with interests that warrant consideration.

Argument about vivisection has often missed the point because it has been put in absolutist terms: Would the abolitionist be prepared to let thousands die if they could be saved by experimenting on a single animal? The way to reply to this purely hypothetical question is to pose another: Would the experimenter be prepared to experiment on a human orphan under six months old, if it were the only way to save many lives? (I say "orphan" to avoid the complication of parental feelings, although in doing so I am being overfair to the experimenter, since the nonhuman subjects of experiments are not orphans.) A negative answer to this question indicates that the experimenter's readiness to use nonhumans is simple discrimination, for adult apes, cats, mice, and other mammals are more conscious of what is happening to them, more self-directing, and, so far as we can tell, just as sensitive to pain as a human infant. There is no characteristic that human infants possess that adult mammals do not have to the same or a higher degree.

(It might be possible to hold that what makes it wrong to experiment on a human infant is that the infant will in time develop into more than the nonhuman, but one would then, to be consistent, have to oppose abortion, and perhaps contraception, too, for the fetus and the egg and sperm have the same potential as the infant. Moreover, one would still have no reason for experimenting on a nonhuman rather than a human with brain damage severe enough to make it impossible for him to rise above infant level.)

The experimenter, then, shows a bias for his own species whenever he carries out an experiment on a nonhuman for a purpose that he would not think justified him in using a human being at an equal or lower level of sentience, awareness, ability to be self-directing, etc. No one familiar with the kind of results yielded by these experiments can have the slightest doubt that if this bias were eliminated the number of experiments performed would be zero or very close to it.

III

If it is vivisection that shows the logic of speciesism most clearly, it is 30 the use of other species for food that is at the heart of our attitudes toward them. Most of *Animals, Men and Morals* is an attack on meat eating—an attack which is based solely on concern for nonhumans, without reference to arguments derived from consideration of ecology, macrobiotics, health, or religion.

The idea that nonhumans are utilities, means to our ends, pervades our thought. Even conservationists who are concerned about the slaughter of wildfowl but not about the vastly greater slaughter of chickens for our tables are thinking in this way—they are worried about what we would lose if there were less wildlife. Stanley Godlovitch, pursuing the Marxist idea that our thinking is formed by the activities we undertake in satisfying our needs, suggests that man's first classification of his environment was into Edibles and Inedibles. Most animals came into the first category, and there they have remained.

Man may always have killed other species for food, but he has never exploited them so ruthlessly as he does today. Farming has succumbed to business methods, the objective being to get the highest possible ratio of output (meat, eggs, milk) to input (fodder, labor costs, etc.). Ruth Harrison's essay "On Factory Farming" gives an account of some aspects of modern methods, and of the unsuccessful British campaigns for effective controls, a campaign which was sparked off by her *Animal Machines* (London: Stuart, 1964).

Her article is in no way a substitute for her earlier book. This is a pity since, as she says, "Farm produce is still associated with mental pictures of animals browsing in the fields . . . of hens having a last forage before going to roost. . . ." Yet neither in her article nor elsewhere in *Animals, Men and Morals* is this false image replaced by a clear idea of the nature and extent of factory farming. We learn of this only indirectly, when we hear of the code of reform proposed by an advisory committee set up by the British government.

Among the proposals, which the government refused to implement on the grounds that they were too idealistic, were: *"Any animal should at least have room to turn around freely."*

Factory farm animals need liberation in the most literal sense. Veal calves are kept in stalls 5 feet by 2 feet. They are usually slaughtered when about four months old, and have been too big to turn in their stalls for at least a month. Intensive beef herds, kept in stalls only proportionately larger for much longer periods, account for a growing percentage of beef production. Sows are often similarly confined when pregnant, which, because of artificial methods of increasing fertility, can be most of the time. Animals confined in this way do not waste food by exercising, nor do they develop unpalatable muscle. 35

"A dry bedded area should be provided for all stock." Intensively kept animals usually have to stand and sleep in slatted floors without straw, because this makes cleaning easier.

"Palatable roughage must be readily available to all calves after one week of age." In order to produce the pale veal housewives are said to prefer, calves are fed on an all-liquid diet until slaughter, even though they are long past the age at which they would normally eat grass. They develop a craving for roughage, evidenced by attempts to gnaw wood from their stalls. (For the same reason, their diet is deficient in iron.)

"Battery cages for poultry should be large enough for a bird to be able to stretch one wing at a time." Under current British practice, a cage for four or five laying hens has a floor area of 20 inches by 18 inches, scarcely larger than a double page of the *New York Review of Books*. In this space,

on a sloping wire floor (sloping so the eggs roll down, wire so the dung drips through) the birds live for a year or eighteen months while artificial lighting and temperature conditions combine with drugs in their food to squeeze the maximum number of eggs out of them. Table birds are also sometimes kept in cages. More often they are reared in sheds, no less crowded. Under these conditions all the birds' natural activities are frustrated, and they develop "vices" such as pecking each other to death. To prevent this, beaks are often cut off, and the sheds kept dark.

How many of those who support factory farming by buying its produce know anything about the way it is produced? How many have heard something about it, but are reluctant to check up for fear that it will make them uncomfortable? To nonspeciesists, the typical consumer's mixture of ignorance, reluctance to find out the truth, and vague belief that nothing really bad could be allowed seems analogous to the attitudes of "decent Germans" to the death camps.

There are, of course, some defenders of factory farming. Their arguments are considered, though again rather sketchily, by John Harris. Among the most common: "Since they have never known anything else, they don't suffer." This argument will not be put by anyone who knows anything about animal behavior, since he will know that not all behavior has to be learned. Chickens attempt to stretch wings, walk around, scratch, and even dustbathe or build a nest, even though they have never lived under conditions that allowed these activities. Calves can suffer from maternal deprivation no matter at what age they were taken from their mothers. "We need these intensive methods to provide protein for a growing population." As ecologists and famine relief organizations know, we can produce far more protein per acre if we grow the right vegetable crop, soy beans for instance, than if we use the land to grow crops to be converted into protein by animals who use nearly 90 percent of the protein themselves, even when unable to exercise.

There will be many readers of this book who will agree that factory farming involves an unjustifiable degree of exploitation of sentient creatures, and yet will want to say that there is nothing wrong with rearing animals for food, provided it is done "humanely." These people are saying, in effect, that although we should not cause animals to suffer, there is nothing wrong with killing them.

There are two possible replies to this view. One is to attempt to show that this combination of attitudes is absurd. Roslind Godlovitch takes this course in her essay, which is an examination of some common attitudes to animals. She argues that from the combination of "animal suffering is to be avoided" and "there is nothing wrong with killing animals" it follows that all animal life ought to be exterminated (since all sentient creatures will suffer to some degree at some point in their lives). Euthanasia is a contentious issue only because we place some value on living. If we did not, the least amount of suffering would justify it. Accordingly, if we

deny that we have a duty to exterminate all animal life, we must concede that we are placing some value on animal life.

This argument seems to me valid, although one could still reply that
the value of animal life is to be derived from the pleasures that life can
have for them, so that, provided their lives have a balance of pleasure
over pain, we are justified in rearing them. But this would imply that
we ought to produce animals and let them live as pleasantly as possible,
without suffering.

At this point, one can make the second of the two possible replies to
the view that rearing and killing animals for food is all right so long as
it is done humanely. This second reply is that so long as we think that a
nonhuman may be killed simply so that a human can satisfy his taste for
meat, we are still thinking of nonhumans as means rather than as ends
in themselves. The factory farm is nothing more than the application of
technology to this concept. Even traditional methods involve castration,
the separation of mothers and their young, the breaking up of herds,
branding or earpunching, and of course transportation to the abattoirs
and the final moments of terror when the animal smells blood and
senses danger. If we were to try rearing animals so that they lived and
died without suffering, we should find that to do so on anything like
the scale of today's meat industry would be a sheer impossibility. Meat
would become the prerogative of the rich.

I have been able to discuss only some of the contributions to this   45
book, saying nothing about, for instance, the essays on killing for furs
and for sport. Nor have I considered all the detailed questions that need
to be asked once we start thinking about other species in the radically different way presented by this book. What, for instance, are we to do about
genuine conflicts of interest like rats biting slum children? I am not sure
of the answer, but the essential point is just that we *do* see this as a conflict of interests, that we recognize that rats have interests too. Then we
may begin to think about other ways of resolving the conflict—perhaps
by leaving out rat baits that sterilize the rats instead of killing them.

I have not discussed such problems because they are side issues compared with the exploitation of other species for food and for experimental purposes. On these central matters, I hope that I have said enough
to show that this book, despite its flaws, is a challenge to every human
to recognize his attitudes to nonhumans as a form of prejudice no less
objectionable than racism or sexism. It is a challenge that demands not
just a change of attitudes, but a change in our way of life, for it requires
us to become vegetarians.

Can a purely moral demand of this kind succeed? The odds are certainly against it. The book holds out no inducements. It does not tell us
that we will become healthier, or enjoy life more, if we cease exploiting animals. Animal Liberation will require greater altruism on the
part of mankind than any other liberation movement, since animals
are incapable of demanding it for themselves, or of protesting against

their exploitation by votes, demonstrations, or bombs. Is man capable of such genuine altruism? Who knows? If this book does have a significant effect, however, it will be a vindication of all those who have believed that man has within himself the potential for more than cruelty and selfishness.

Topics for Critical Thinking and Writing

1. In his fourth paragraph Singer formulates an argument on behalf of the skeptical reader. Examine that argument closely, restate it in your own words, and evaluate it. Which of its premises is most vulnerable to criticism? Why?

2. Singer quotes with approval (para. 7) Bentham's comment, "The question is not, Can they *reason*? nor Can they *talk*? but, Can they *suffer*?" Do you find this argument persuasive? Can you think of any effective challenge to it?

3. Singer allows that, although developed linguistic capacity is not necessary for a creature to have pain, perhaps such a capacity is necessary for "having an intention" (para. 12). Do you think this concession is correct? Have you ever seen animal behavior that you would be willing to describe or explain as evidence that the animal has an intention to do something, despite knowing that the animal cannot talk?

4. Singer thinks that the readiness to experiment on animals argues against believing that animals don't suffer pain (see para. 21). Do you agree with this reasoning?

5. Singer confesses (para. 22) to being made especially angry "with my fellow men" after reading the accounts of animal experimentation. What is it that aroused his anger? Do such feelings, and the acknowledgment that one has them, have any place in a sober discussion about the merits of animal experimentation? Why, or why not?

6. What is "factory farming" (paras. 32–40)? Why is Singer opposed to it?

7. To the claim that there is nothing wrong with "rearing animals for food," provided it is done "humanely" (para. 41), Singer offers two replies (paras. 42–44). In an essay of 250 words summarize them briefly, and then indicate whether either persuades you and why or why not.

8. Suppose someone were to say to Singer: "You claim that capacity to suffer is the relevant factor in deciding whether a creature deserves to be treated as my moral equal. But you're wrong. The relevant factor is whether the creature is *alive*. Being alive is what matters, not being capable of feeling pain." In one or two paragraphs declare what you think would be Singer's reply.

9. Do you think it is worse to kill an animal for its fur than to kill, cook, and eat an animal? Is it worse to kill an animal for sport than to kill it for medical experimentation? What is Singer's view? Explain your view, making use of Singer's if you wish, in an essay of 500 words.

10. Are there any arguments, in your opinion, that show the immorality of eating human flesh (cannibalism) but that do not show a similar objection to eating animal flesh? Write a 500-word essay in which you discuss the issue.

Jonathan Swift

Jonathan Swift (1667–1745) was born in Ireland of English stock. An Anglican clergyman, he became Dean of St. Patrick's in Dublin in 1723, but the post he really wanted, one of high office in England, was never given to him. A prolific pamphleteer on religious and political issues, Swift today is known not as a churchman but as a satirist. His best-known works are Gulliver's Travels *(1726, a serious satire but now popularly thought of as a children's book) and "A Modest Proposal" (1729). In "A Modest Proposal," which was published anonymously, Swift addresses the great suffering that the Irish endured under the British.*

A Modest Proposal

For Preventing the Children of Poor People in Ireland from Being a Burden to Their Parents or Country, and for Making Them Beneficial to the Public

It is a melancholy object to those who walk through this great town or travel in the country, when they see the streets, the roads, and cabin doors, crowded with beggars of the female sex, followed by three, four, or six children, all in rags and importuning every passenger for an alms. These mothers, instead of being able to work for their honest livelihood, are forced to employ all their time in strolling to beg sustenance for their helpless infants: who as they grow up either turn thieves for want of work, or leave their dear native country to fight for the Pretender in Spain, or sell themselves to the Barbadoes.

I think it is agreed by all parties that this prodigious number of children in the arms, or on the backs, or at the heels of their mothers, and frequently of their fathers, is in the present deplorable state of the kingdom a very great additional grievance; and, therefore, whoever could find out a fair, cheap, and easy method of making these children sound, useful members of the commonwealth, would deserve so well of the public as to have his statue set up for a preserver of the nation.

But my intention is very far from being confined to provide only for the children of professed beggars; it is of a much greater extent, and shall take in the whole number of infants at a certain age who are born of parents in effect as little able to support them as those who demand our charity in the streets.

As to my own part, having turned my thoughts for many years upon this important subject, and maturely weighed the several schemes of our

projectors,[1] I have always found them grossly mistaken in their compu-
tation. It is true, a child just dropped from its dam may be supported
by her milk for a solar year, with little other nourishment; at most not
above the value of 2s.,[2] which the mother may certainly get, or the value
in scraps, by her lawful occupation of begging; and it is exactly at one
year old that I propose to provide for them in such a manner as instead
of being a charge upon their parents or the parish, or wanting food and
raiment for the rest of their lives, they shall on the contrary contribute to
the feeding, and partly to the clothing, of many thousands.

There is likewise another great advantage in my scheme, that it will
prevent those voluntary abortions, and that horrid practice of women
murdering their bastard children, alas! too frequent among us! sacrificing the poor innocent babes I doubt more to avoid the expense than the
shame, which would move tears and pity in the most savage and inhuman breast.

The number of souls in this kingdom being usually reckoned one
million and a half, of these I calculate there may be about 200,000 couple
whose wives are breeders; from which number I subtract 30,000 couple who are able to maintain their own children (although I apprehend
there cannot be so many, under the present distress of the kingdom); but
this being granted, there will remain 170,000 breeders. I again subtract
50,000 for those women who miscarry, or whose children die by accident or disease within the year. There only remain 120,000 children of
poor parents annually born. The question therefore is, how this number
shall be reared and provided for? which, as I have already said, under
the present situation of affairs, is utterly impossible by all the methods
hitherto proposed. For we can neither employ them in handicraft or
agriculture; we neither build houses (I mean in the country) nor cultivate land; they can very seldom pick up a livelihood by stealing, till they
arrive at six years old, except where they are of towardly parts; although
I confess they learn the rudiments much earlier; during which time they
can, however, be properly looked upon only as probationers; as I have
been informed by a principal gentleman in the county of Cavan, who
protested to me that he never knew above one or two instances under
the age of six, even in a part of the kingdom so renowned for the quick-
est proficiency in that art.

I am assured by our merchants, that a boy or a girl before twelve
years old is no salable commodity; and even when they come to this age
they will not yield above 3£. or 3£. 2s. 6d.[3] at most on the exchange;
which cannot turn to account either to the parents or kingdom, the
charge of nutriment and rags having been at least four times that value.

[1] **projectors** Persons who devise plans. [All notes are the editors'.]
[2] **2s** Two shillings.
[3] **£. . . . d** £ is an abbreviation for "pound sterling" and *d.*, for "pence."

I shall now therefore humbly propose my own thoughts, which I hope will not be liable to the least objection.

I have been assured by a very knowing American of my acquaintance in London, that a young healthy child well nursed is at a year old a most delicious, nourishing, and wholesome food, whether stewed, roasted, baked, or broiled; and I make no doubt that it will equally serve in a fricassee or a ragout.

I do therefore humbly offer it to public consideration that of the 120,000 children already computed, 20,000 may be reserved for breed, whereof only one-fourth part to be males; which is more than we allow to sheep, black cattle, or swine; and my reason is, that these children are seldom the fruits of marriage, a circumstance not much regarded by our savages; therefore one male will be sufficient to serve four females. That the remaining 100,000 may, at a year old, be offered in sale to the persons of quality and fortune through the kingdom; always advising the mother to let them suck plentifully in the last month, so as to render them plump and fat for a good table. A child will make two dishes at an entertainment for friends; and when the family dines alone, the fore or hind quarter will make a reasonable dish, and seasoned with a little pepper or salt will be very good boiled on the fourth day, especially in winter.

I have reckoned upon a medium that a child just born will weigh twelve pounds, and in a solar year, if tolerably nursed, will increase to twenty-eight pounds.

I grant this food will be somewhat dear, and therefore very proper for landlords, who, as they have already devoured most of the parents, seem to have the best title to the children.

Infant's flesh will be in season throughout the year, but more plentiful in March, and a little before and after: for we are told by a grave author, an eminent French physician, that fish being a prolific diet, there are more children born in Roman Catholic countries about nine months after Lent than at any other season; therefore, reckoning a year after Lent, the markets will be more glutted than usual, because the number of popish infants is at least three to one in this kingdom: and therefore it will have one other collateral advantage, by lessening the number of papists among us.

I have already computed the charge of nursing a beggar's child (in which list I reckon all cottagers, laborers, and four-fifths of the farmers) to be about 2s. per annum, rags included; and I believe no gentleman would repine to give 10s. for the carcass of a good fat child, which, as I have said, will make four dishes of excellent nutritive meat, when he has only some particular friend or his own family to dine with him. Thus the squire will learn to be a good landlord, and grow popular among the tenants; the mother will have 8s. net profit, and be fit for work till she produces another child.

Those who are more thrifty (as I must confess the times require) may flay the carcass; the skin of which artificially dressed will make admirable gloves for ladies, and summer boots for fine gentlemen.

As to our city of Dublin, shambles[4] may be appointed for this purpose in the most convenient parts of it, and butchers we may be assured will not be wanting: although I rather recommend buying the children alive, and dressing them hot from the knife as we do roasting pigs.

A very worthy person, a true lover of his country, and whose virtues I highly esteem, was lately pleased in discoursing on this matter to offer a refinement upon my scheme. He said that many gentlemen of this kingdom, having of late destroyed their deer, he conceived that the want of venison might be well supplied by the bodies of young lads and maidens, not exceeding fourteen years of age nor under twelve; so great a number of both sexes in every country being now ready to starve for want of work and service; and these to be disposed of by their parents, if alive, or otherwise by their nearest relations. But with due deference to so excellent a friend and so deserving a patriot, I cannot be altogether in his sentiments; for as to the males, my American acquaintance assured me from frequent experience that their flesh was generally tough and lean, like that of our schoolboys by continual exercise, and their taste disagreeable; and to fatten them would not answer the charge. Then as to the females, it would, I think, with humble submission be a loss to the public, because they soon would become breeders themselves: and besides, it is not improbable that some scrupulous people might be apt to censure such a practice (although indeed very unjustly), as a little bordering upon cruelty; which, I confess, has always been with me the strongest objection against any project, how well soever intended.

But in order to justify my friend, he confessed that this expedient was put into his head by the famous Psalmanazar[5] a native of the island Formosa, who came from thence to London about twenty years ago: and in conversation told my friend, that in his country when any young person happened to be put to death, the executioner sold the carcass to persons of quality as a prime dainty; and that in his time the body of a plump girl of fifteen, who was crucified for an attempt to poison the emperor, was sold to his imperial majesty's prime minister of state, and other great mandarins of the court, in joints from the gibbet, at 400 crowns. Neither indeed can I deny, that if the same use were made of several plump young girls in this town, who without one single groat to their fortunes cannot stir abroad without a chair, and appear at the playhouse and assemblies in foreign fineries which they never will pay for, the kingdom would not be the worse.

Some persons of a depending spirit are in great concern about the vast number of poor people, who are aged, diseased, or maimed, and I have been desired to employ my thoughts what course may be taken to

---

[4]**shambles** Slaughterhouses.
[5]**Psalmanazar** George Psalmanazar (c. 1679–1763), a Frenchman who claimed to be from Formosa (now Taiwan); he wrote *An Historical and Geographical Description of Formosa* (1704). The hoax was exposed soon after publication.

ease the nation of so grievous an encumbrance. But I am not in the least pain upon that matter, because it is very well known that they are every day dying and rotting by cold and famine, and filth and vermin, as fast as can be reasonably expected. And as to the young laborers, they are now in as hopeful a condition: They cannot get work, and consequently pine away for want of nourishment, to a degree that if at any time they are accidentally hired to common labor, they have not strength to perform it; and thus the country and themselves are happily delivered from the evils to come.

I have too long digressed, and therefore shall return to my subject. 20 I think the advantages by the proposal which I have made are obvious and many, as well as of the highest importance.

For first, as I have already observed, It would greatly lessen the number of papists, with whom we are yearly overrun, being the principal breeders of the nation as well as our most dangerous enemies; and who stay at home on purpose to deliver the kingdom to the Pretender, hoping to take their advantage by the absence of so many good Protestants, who have chosen rather to leave their country than stay at home and pay tithes against their conscience to an Episcopal curate.

Secondly, The poor tenants will have something valuable of their own, which by law may be made liable to distress and help to pay their landlord's rent, their corn and cattle being already seized, and money a thing unknown.

Thirdly, Whereas the maintenance of 100,000 children from two years old and upward, cannot be computed at less than 10s. apiece per annum, the nation's stock will be thereby increased £50,000 per annum, beside the profit of a new dish introduced to the tables of all gentlemen of fortune in the kingdom who have any refinement in taste. And the money will circulate among ourselves, the goods being entirely of our own growth and manufacture.

Fourthly, The constant breeders beside the gain of 8s. sterling per annum by the sale of their children, will be rid of the charge of maintaining them after the first year.

Fifthly, This food would likewise bring great custom to taverns, 25 where the vintners will certainly be so prudent as to procure the best receipts for dressing it to perfection, and consequently have their houses frequented by all the fine gentlemen, who justly value themselves upon their knowledge in good eating; and a skillful cook who understands how to oblige his guests will contrive to make it as expensive as they please.

Sixthly, This would be a great inducement to marriage, which all wise nations have either encouraged by rewards or enforced by laws and penalties. It would increase the care and tenderness of mothers toward their children, when they were sure of a settlement for life to the poor babes, provided in some sort by the public, to their annual profit instead of expense. We should see an honest emulation among the married women, which of them would bring the fattest child to the market. Men would become as fond of their wives during the time of their pregnancy as they are now of their mares in foal, their cows in calf, their sows when they are ready to farrow; nor offer to beat or kick them (as is too frequent a practice) for fear of a miscarriage.

Many other advantages might be enumerated. For instance, the addition of some thousand carcasses in our exportation of barreled beef, the propagation of swine's flesh, and improvement in the art of making good bacon, so much wanted among us by the great destruction of pigs, too frequent at our table; which are no way comparable in taste or magnificence to a well-grown, fat, yearling child, which roasted whole will make a considerable figure at a lord mayor's feast or any other public entertainment. But this and many others I omit, being studious of brevity.

Supposing that 1,000 families in this city would be constant customers for infants' flesh, besides others who might have it at merry-meetings, particularly at weddings and christenings, I compute that Dublin would take off annually about 20,000 carcasses; and the rest of the kingdom (where probably they will be sold somewhat cheaper) the remaining 80,000.

I can think of no one objection that will possibly be raised against this proposal, unless it should be urged that the number of people will be thereby much lessened in the kingdom. This I freely own, and it was indeed one principal design in offering it to the world. I desire the reader will observe, that I calculate my remedy for this one individual kingdom of Ireland and for no other that ever was, is, or I think ever can be upon earth. Therefore let no man talk to me of other expedients: of taxing our absentees at 5s. a pound; of using neither clothes nor household furniture except what is of our own growth and manufacture; of utterly rejecting the materials and instruments that promote foreign luxury; of curing the expensiveness of pride, vanity, idleness, and gaming in our women; of introducing a vein of parsimony, prudence, and temperance; of learning to love our country, in the want of which we differ even from Laplanders and the inhabitants of Topinamboo; of quitting our animosities and factions, nor acting any longer like the Jews, who were murdering one another at the very moment their city was taken; of being a little cautious not to sell our country and conscience for nothing; of teaching landlords to have at least one degree of mercy toward their tenants; lastly, of putting a spirit of honesty, industry, and skill into our shopkeepers; who, if a resolution could now be taken to buy only our native goods, would immediately unite to cheat and exact upon us in the price the measure, and the goodness, nor could ever yet be brought to make one fair proposal of just dealing, though often and earnestly invited to it.

Therefore I repeat, let no man talk to me of these and the like expedients, till he has at least some glimpse of hope that there will be ever some hearty and sincere attempt to put them in practice. ³⁰

But as to myself, having been wearied out for many years with offering vain, idle, visionary thoughts, and at length utterly despairing of success, I fortunately fell upon this proposal; which, as it is wholly new, so it has something solid and real, of no expense and little trouble, full in our own power, and whereby we can incur no danger in disobliging England. For this kind of commodity will not bear exportation, the flesh being of too tender a consistence to admit a long continuance in salt, although perhaps I could name a country which would be glad to eat up our whole nation without it.

After all, I am not so violently bent upon my own opinion as to reject any offer proposed by wise men, which shall be found equally innocent, cheap, easy, and effectual. But before something of that kind shall be advanced in contradiction to my scheme, and offering a better, I desire the author or authors will be pleased maturely to consider two points. First, as things now stand, how they will be able to find food and raiment for 100,000 useless mouths and backs. And secondly, there being a round million of creatures in human figure throughout this kingdom, whose subsistence put into a common stock would leave them in debt 2,000,000£. sterling, adding those who are beggars by profession to the bulk of farmers, cottagers, and laborers, with the wives and children who are beggars in effect; I desire those politicians who dislike my overture, and may perhaps be so bold as to attempt an answer, that they will first ask the parents of these mortals, whether they would not at this day think it a great happiness to have been sold for food at a year old in the manner I prescribe, and thereby have avoided such a perpetual scene of misfortunes as they have since gone through by the oppression of landlords, the impossibility of paying rent without money or trade, the want of common sustenance, with neither house nor clothes to cover them from the inclemencies of the weather, and the most inevitable prospect of entailing the like or greater miseries upon their breed for ever.

I profess, in the sincerity of my heart, that I have not the least personal interest in endeavoring to promote this necessary work, having no other motive than the public good of my country, by advancing our trade, providing for infants, relieving the poor, and giving some pleasure to the rich. I have no children by which I can propose to get a single penny; the youngest being nine years old, and my wife past childbearing.

TOPICS FOR CRITICAL THINKING AND WRITING

1. In paragraph 4 the speaker of the essay mentions proposals set forth by "projectors"—that is, by advocates of other proposals or projects. On the basis of the first two paragraphs of "A Modest Proposal," how would you characterize *this* projector, the speaker of the essay? Write your characterization in one paragraph. Then, in a second paragraph, characterize the projector as you understand him, having read the entire essay. In your second paragraph, indicate what *he thinks he is* and also what the reader sees he really is.

2. The speaker or persona of "A Modest Proposal" is confident that selling children "for a good table" (para. 10) is a better idea than any of

the then current methods of disposing of unwanted children, including abortion and infanticide. Can you think of any argument that might favor abortion or infanticide for parents in dire straits, rather than the projector's scheme?

3. In paragraph 29 the speaker considers, but dismisses out of hand, several other solutions to the wretched plight of the Irish poor. Write a 500-word essay in which you explain each of these ideas and their combined merits as an alternative to the solution he favors.

4. What does the projector imply are the causes of the Irish poverty he deplores? Are there possible causes he has omitted? If so, what are they?

5. Imagine yourself as one of the poor parents to whom Swift refers, and write a 250-word essay explaining why you prefer not to sell your infant to the local butcher.

6. The modern version of the problem to which the proposal is addressed is called "population policy." How would you describe our nation's current population policy? Do we have a population policy, in fact? If not, what would you propose? If we do have one, would you propose any changes in it? Why, or why not?

7. It is sometimes suggested that just as persons need to get a license to drive a car, to hunt with a gun, or to marry, a husband and wife ought to be required to get a license to have a child. Would you favor this idea, assuming that it applied to you as a possible parent? Would Swift? Explain your answers in an essay of 500 words.

8. Consider the six arguments advanced in paragraphs 21 to 26, and write a 1,000-word essay criticizing all of them. Or if you find that one or more of the arguments are really unanswerable, explain why you find it so compelling.

9. By means of research online or at the library, find out what audience Swift was addressing. How do you think the audience responded?

10. Write your own "modest proposal," ironically suggesting a solution to a problem. Possible topics: health care or schooling for the children of illegal immigrants, overcrowded jails, children who have committed a serious crime, homeless people.

 For additional arguments online, visit the e-Pages at
bedfordstmartins.com/barnetbedau.

6

Developing an Argument of Your Own

The difficult part in an argument is not to defend one's opinion but to know what it is.

—ANDRÉ MAUROIS

Imagine that you enter a parlor. You come late. When you arrive, others have long preceded you, and they are engaged in a heated discussion, a discussion too heated for them to pause and tell you exactly what it is about. In fact, the discussion had already begun long before any of them got there, so that no one present is qualified to retrace for you all the steps that had gone before. You listen for a while, until you decide that you have caught the tenor of the argument; then you put in your oar. Someone answers; you answer him; another comes to your defense; another aligns himself against you, to either the embarrassment or gratification of your opponent, depending upon the quality of your ally's assistance. However, the discussion is interminable. The hour grows late, you must depart. And you do depart, with the discussion still vigorously in progress.

—KENNETH BURKE

No greater misfortune could happen to anyone than that of developing a dislike for argument.

—PLATO

PLANNING, DRAFTING, AND REVISING AN ARGUMENT

First, hear the wisdom of Mark Twain: "When the Lord finished the world, He pronounced it good. That is what I said about my first work, too. But Time, I tell you, Time takes the confidence out of these incautious early opinions."

All of us, teachers and students, have our moments of confidence, but for the most part we know that it takes considerable effort to write clear, thoughtful, seemingly effortless prose. In a conversation we can cover ourselves with such expressions as "Well, I don't know, but I sort of think . . . ," and we can always revise our position ("Oh, well, I didn't mean it that way"), but once we have handed in the final version of our writing, we are helpless. We are (putting it strongly) naked to our enemies.

Getting Ideas: Argument as an Instrument of Inquiry

In Chapter 1 we quoted Robert Frost, "To learn to write is to learn to have ideas," and we offered suggestions about getting ideas, a process traditionally called **invention**. A moment ago we said that we often improve our ideas when we try to explain them to someone else. Partly, of course, we are responding to questions or objections raised by our companion in the conversation. But partly we are responding to ourselves: Almost as soon as we hear what we have to say, we may find that it won't do, and, if we are lucky, we may find a better idea surfacing. One of the best ways of getting ideas is to talk things over.

The process of talking things over usually begins with the text that you are reading: Your notes, your summary, and your queries parenthetically incorporated within your summary are a kind of dialogue between you and the author you are reading. More obviously, when you talk with friends about your topic, you are trying out and developing ideas. You are arguing, but not chiefly to persuade; rather, you are using argument in order to find the truth. Finally, after reading, taking notes, and talking, you may feel that you now have clear ideas and need only put them into writing. And so you take a sheet of blank paper, and perhaps a paralyzing thought suddenly strikes: "I have ideas but just can't put them into words."

Despite what many people believe,

- Writing is not only a matter of putting one's ideas into words.
- Just as talking with others is a way of getting ideas, *writing is a way of getting and developing ideas.* Or, as we have already said, *argument* is an instrument of inquiry as well as of persuasion.

Writing, in short, can be an important part of critical thinking. One big reason we have trouble writing is our fear of putting ourselves on record, but another big reason is our fear that we have no ideas worth putting down. But by writing notes—or even free associations—and by writing a draft, however weak, we can help ourselves to think our way toward good ideas.

Freewriting   Writing for five or six minutes, nonstop, without censoring what you produce is one way of improving your thoughts. Some people who write on a computer find it useful to dim the screen so they won't be tempted to look up and fiddle too soon with what they have just written. Later they illuminate the screen, scroll back, and notice some keywords or passages that can be used later in drafting a paper. If you've kept notes on your blog or in a Google Doc, now is a good time to access them and to copy and paste some of your ideas.

Listing   Writing down keywords, just as you do when you make a shopping list, is another way of getting ideas. When you make a shopping list, you write *ketchup,* and the act of writing it reminds you that you also need hamburger rolls—and *that* in turn reminds you (who knows how or why?) that you also need a can of tuna fish. Similarly, when you prepare a list of ideas for a paper, just writing down one item will often generate another. Of course, when you look over the list, you will probably drop some of these ideas—the dinner menu will change—but you are making progress. If you have a smartphone, use it to write down thoughts. You can even e-mail these notes to yourself so you can access them later.

Diagramming   Sketching some sort of visual representation of an essay is a kind of listing. Three methods of diagramming are especially common:

- **Clustering**   Write, in the middle of a sheet of paper, a word or phrase summarizing your topic (for instance, *health care;* see diagram, below), circle it, and then write down and circle a related word (for example, *gov't-provided*). Perhaps this leads you to write *higher taxes,* and you then circle this phrase and connect it to *gov't-provided.* The next thing that occurs to you is *employer-provided*—and so you write this down and circle it. You will not connect this to *higher taxes,* but you will connect it to *health care* because it is a sort of parallel to *gov't-provided.* The next thing that occurs to you is *unemployed people.* This category does not connect easily with *employer-provided,* so you won't connect these two terms with a line, but you probably will connect *unemployed people* with *health care* and maybe also with *gov't-provided.* Keep going, jotting down ideas and making connections where possible, indicating relationships.

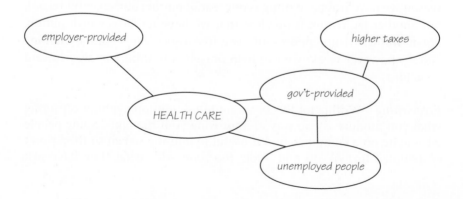

- **Branching**   Some writers find it useful to build a tree, moving from the central topic to the main branches (chief ideas) and then to the twigs (aspects of the chief ideas).

- **Comparing in columns**   Draw a line down the middle of the page, and then set up two columns showing oppositions. For instance, if you are concerned with health care, you might head one column *gov't-provided* and the other *employer-provided.* Under the first column, you might write *covers unemployed,* and under the second column, you might write *omits unemployed.* You might go on to write, under the first column, *higher taxes,* and under the second, *higher prices*—or whatever else relevant comes to mind.

All of these methods can, of course, be executed with pen and paper, but you may also be able to use them on your computer depending on the capabilities of your software.

Whether you are using a computer or a pen, you put down some words and almost immediately see that they need improvement, not simply a little polishing but a substantial overhaul. You write, "Race should be counted in college admissions for two reasons," and as soon as you write these words, a third reason comes to mind. Or perhaps one of those "two reasons" no longer seems very good. As E. M. Forster said, "How can I know what I think till I see what I say?" We have to see what we say, we have to get something down on paper, before we realize that we need to make it better.

Writing, then, is really **rewriting**—that is, **revising**—and a revision is a *re-vision,* a second look. The essay that you submit—whether a hard copy or on Blackboard—should be clear and may even seem effortless to the reader, but in all likelihood the clarity and apparent ease are the result of a struggle with yourself, a struggle during which you greatly improved your first thoughts. You begin by putting down your ideas, such as they are, perhaps even in the random order in which they occurred, but sooner or later comes the job of looking at them critically, developing what is useful in them and removing what is not. If you follow this procedure you will be in the company of Picasso, who said that he "advanced by means of destruction." Those passages that you cut or destroy can be kept in another file in case you want to revisit what you have removed. Sometimes, you end up restoring them.

Whether you advance bit by bit (writing a sentence, revising it, writing the next, and so on) or whether you write an entire first draft and then revise it and revise it again and again is chiefly a matter of temperament. Probably most people combine both approaches, backing up occasionally but trying to get to the end fairly soon so that they can see rather quickly what they know, or think they know, and can then start the real work of thinking, of converting their initial ideas into something substantial.

Asking Questions   Getting ideas, we said when we talked about **topics** and **invention** strategies in Chapter 1 (p. 16) is mostly a matter of asking (and then thinking about) questions. We append questions to the end of each argumentative essay in this book, not to torment you but to help you to think about the arguments—for instance, to turn your attention to especially important matters. If your instructor asks you to write an answer to one of these questions, you are lucky: Examining the question will stimulate your mind to work in a definite direction.

If a topic is not assigned, and you are asked to write an argumentative essay, you will find that some ideas (possibly poor ones, at this stage, but that doesn't matter because you will soon revise) will come to mind if you ask yourself questions. You can begin finding where you stand on an issue (**stasis**) by asking the following five basic questions:

1. What is X?
2. What is the value of X?
3. What are the causes (or the consequences) of X?
4. What should (or ought or must) we do about X?
5. What is the evidence for my claims about X?

Let's spend a moment looking at each of these questions.

1. **What is X?** We can hardly argue about the number of people sentenced to death in the United States in 2000—a glance at the appropriate government report will give the answer—but we can argue about whether capital punishment as administered in the United States is discriminatory. Does the evidence, we can ask, support the view that in the United States the death penalty is unfair? Similarly, we can ask whether a human fetus is a human being (in saying what something is, must we take account of its potentiality?), and, even if we agree that a fetus is a human being, we can further ask about whether it is a person. In *Roe v. Wade* the U.S. Supreme Court ruled that even the "viable" unborn human fetus is not a "person" as that term is used in the Fifth and Fourteenth Amendments. Here the question is this: Is the essential fact about the fetus that it is a person?

An argument of this sort makes a claim—that is, it takes a stand, but notice that it does not also have to argue for an action. Thus, it may argue that the death penalty is administered unfairly—that's a big enough issue—but it need not go on to argue that the death penalty should be abolished. After all, another possibility is that the death penalty should be administered fairly. The writer of the essay may be doing enough if he or she establishes the truth of the claim and leaves to others the possible responses.

2. **What is the value of X?** College courses often call for literary judgments. No one can argue with you if you say you prefer the plays of Tennessee Williams to those of Arthur Miller. But academic papers are not mere declarations of preferences. As soon as you say that Williams is a better playwright than Miller, you have based your preference on implicit standards, and it is incumbent on you to support your preference by giving

evidence about the relative skill, insight, and accomplishments of Williams and of Miller. Your argument is an evaluation. The question now at issue is the merits of the two authors and the standards appropriate for such an appraisal.

In short, an essay offering an evaluation normally has two purposes:

- to set forth an assessment, and
- to convince the reader that the assessment is reasonable.

In writing an evaluation, you will have to rely on criteria, and these will vary depending on your topic. For instance, if you are comparing the artistic merit of the plays by Williams and by Miller, you may want to talk about the quality of the characterization, the importance of the theme, and so on. But if the topic is "Which playwright is more suitable to be taught in high school?" other criteria may be appropriate, such as

- the difficulty of the author's language,
- the sexual content of some scenes, and
- the presence of obscene words.

Or consider a nonliterary issue: On balance, are college fraternities and sororities good or bad? If good, how good? If bad, how bad? What criteria can we use in making our evaluation? Probably some or all of the following:

- testimony of authorities (for instance, persons who can offer first-hand testimony about the good or bad effects),
- inductive evidence (we can collect examples of good or bad effects),
- appeals to logic ("it follows, therefore, that . . ."), and
- appeals to emotion (for instance, an appeal to our sense of fairness).

3. **What are the causes (or the consequences) of *X*?** Why did the rate of auto theft increase during a specific period? If we abolish the death penalty, will that cause the rate of murder to increase? Notice, by the way, that such problems may be complex. The phenomena that people usually argue about—say, such things as inflation, war, suicide, crime—have many causes, and it is therefore often a mistake to speak of *the* cause of *X*. A writer in *Time* mentioned that the life expectancy of an average American male is about sixty-seven years, a figure that compares unfavorably with the life expectancy of males in Japan and Israel. The *Time* writer suggested that an important cause of the relatively short life span is "the pressure to perform well in business." Perhaps. But the life expectancy of plumbers is no greater than that of managers and executives. Nutrition authority Jean Mayer, in an article in *Life*, attributed the relatively poor longevity of American males to a diet that is "rich in fat and poor in nutrients." Doubtless other authorities propose other causes, and in all likelihood no one cause accounts for the phenomenon.

Or take a second example of discussions of causality, this one concerning the academic performance of girls in single-sex schools, middle schools, and high schools. It is pretty much agreed (based on statistical evidence) that the graduates of these schools do better, as a group, than girls who graduate from co-educational schools. *Why* do girls in single-sex schools tend, as a group, to do better? What is the *cause*? The administrators of girls' schools usually attribute the success to the fact (we are admittedly putting the matter bluntly) that young women flourish better in an atmosphere free from male intimidation: They allegedly gain confidence and become more expressive when they are not threatened by males. And this may be the answer, but skeptics have attributed the success to two other causes:

- Most single-sex schools require parents to pay tuition and it is a documented fact that the children of well-to-do parents do better, academically, than the children of poor parents.

- Further, most single-sex schools are private schools, and they select their students from a pool of candidates. Admissions officers naturally select those candidates who seem to be academically promising—that is, they select students who have *already done well academically*.[1]

In short, the girls who graduate from single-sex schools may owe their later academic success not to the atmosphere inside the schools but to the fact that even at the time they were admitted to these schools they were academically stronger—we are, again, speaking of a cohort, not of individuals—than the girls who attend co-ed schools.

The lesson? Be cautious in attributing a cause. There may be several causes.

The kinds of support that usually accompany claims of cause include:

- factual data, especially statistics;

- analogies ("The Roman Empire declined because of X and Y," "Our society exhibits X and Y, and therefore . . ."); and

- inductive evidence.

4. **What should (or ought or must) we do about X?** Must we always obey the law? Should the law allow eighteen-year-olds to drink alcohol? Should eighteen-year-olds be drafted to do one year of social service? Should pornography be censored? Should steroid use by athletes be banned? Ought there to be Good Samaritan laws, making it a

---

[1]Until 2004 federal regulations discouraged public schools from separating boys from girls. As of the time of this comment [2009] there are only ninety-five single-sex public schools, twelve of which are in New York City. An article in the *New York Times*, 11 March 2009, page A20, suggests that there is little evidence that girls do better than boys in these schools. Indeed, in California a much-touted program in which six public middle schools and high schools were turned into single-sex academies has been abandoned.

legal duty for a stranger to intervene to save a person from death or great bodily harm, when one might do so with little or no risk to oneself? These questions involve conduct and policy; how we answer them will reveal our values and principles.

An essay answering questions of this sort usually

- begins by explaining what the issue (the problem) is, then
- states why the reader should care about it, then
- offers the proposed solution, then
- considers alternative solutions, and finally
- reaffirms the merit of the proposed solution, especially in the light of the audience's interests and needs.

You will recall that throughout this book we have spoken about devices that help a writer to get ideas. If in drafting an essay concerned with policy you begin by writing down your thoughts on the five bulleted items we have just given, you will almost surely uncover ideas that you didn't know you had.

Support for claims of policy usually include

- statistics,
- appeals to common sense and to the reader's moral sense, and
- testimony of authorities.

5. **What is the evidence for my claims about X?** In commenting on the four previous topics, we have talked about the kinds of support that are commonly offered, but a few additional points can be made.

Critical reading, writing, and thinking depend essentially on identifying and evaluating the evidence for and against the claims one makes and encounters in the writings of others. It is not enough to have an *opinion* or belief one way or the other; you need to be able to support your opinions—the bare fact of your sincere belief in what you say or write is not itself any *evidence* that what you believe is true.

So what are good reasons for opinions, adequate evidence for one's beliefs? The answer, of course, depends on what kind of belief or opinion, assertion or hypothesis, claim or principle you want to assert. For example, there is good evidence that President John F. Kennedy was assassinated on November 22, 1963, because this is the date for his death reported in standard almanacs. You could further substantiate the date by checking the back issues of the *New York Times*. But a different kind of evidence is needed to support the proposition that the chemical composition of water is H_2O. And you will need still other kinds of evidence to support your beliefs about the likelihood of rain tomorrow, the probability that the Red Sox will win the pennant this year, the twelfth digit in the decimal expansion of pi, the average cumulative grades of the graduating seniors over the past three years in your college, the relative merits of *Hamlet* and *Death of a Salesman,* and the moral dimensions of sexual harassment. None of these issues is merely a matter of opinion; yet about some of them, educated and informed people may disagree over the reasons and the evidence and what they show. Your job as a critical thinker is to be alert to the relevant reasons and evidence and to make the most of them as you present your views.

Again, an argument may answer two or more of these five basic questions. Someone who argues that pornography should (or should not) be censored

- will have to mark out the territory of the discussion by defining pornography (our first question: What is *X*?). The argument probably
- will also need to examine the consequences of adopting the preferred policy (our third question) and
- may even have to argue about its value (our second question). Some people maintain that pornography produces crime, but others maintain that it provides a harmless outlet for impulses that otherwise might vent themselves in criminal behavior.
- Further, someone arguing about the wisdom of censoring pornography might have to face the objection that censorship, however desirable on account of some of its consequences, may be unconstitutional and that, even if censorship were constitutional, it would (or might) have undesirable side effects, such as repressing freedom of political opinion.
- And one will always have to keep asking oneself our fifth question, What is the evidence for my claims?

Thinking about one or more of these questions may get you going. For instance, thinking about the first question, What is *X*?, will require you to produce a definition, and as you work at producing a satisfactory definition, you may find new ideas arising. If a question seems relevant, start writing, even if you write only a fragmentary sentence. You'll probably find that one word leads to another and that ideas begin to appear. Even if these ideas seem weak as you write them, don't be discouraged; you have put something on paper, and returning to these words, perhaps in five minutes or perhaps the next day, you will probably find that some are not at all bad and that others will stimulate you to better ones.

It may be useful to record your ideas in a special notebook or in a private blog or a Google Doc reserved for the purpose. Such a **journal** can be a valuable resource when it comes time to write your paper. Many students find it easier to focus their thoughts on writing if during the period of gestation they have been jotting down relevant ideas on something more substantial than slips of paper or loose sheets. The very act of designating a notebook or blog as your journal for a course can be the first step in focusing your attention on the eventual need to write a paper.

Take advantage of the free tools at your disposal. Use the Internet and free Web tools, including RSS feeds, Google (Drive, sites, and others), Yahoo!, blogs, and wikis to help you organize your initial ideas and to solicit feedback. Talking with others can help, but sometimes we do not have time to chat about our ideas. By using an RSS feed on a Web site that you think will provide good information on your topic (or a topic you are thinking about), you can notify yourself via e-mail if the site has uploaded new material such as news links or op-eds. Posting a blog entry in a public space about your topic can also foster conversations about your topic and help you discover other opinions. Using the Internet to uncover and refine your topic is common, especially in the beginning of the research process.

If what we have just said does not sound convincing, and you know from experience that you often have trouble getting started with your writing, don't despair; first aid is at hand in a sure-fire method that we will now explain.

The Thesis or Main Point

Let's assume that you are writing an argumentative essay—perhaps an evaluation of an argument in this book—and you have what seems to be a pretty good draft or at least a bunch of notes that are the result of hard thinking. You really do have ideas now, and you want to present them effectively. How will you organize your essay? No one formula works best for every essayist and for every essay, but it is usually advisable to formulate a basic **thesis** (a claim, a central point, a chief position) and to state it early. Every essay that is any good, even a book-length one, has a thesis (a main point), which can be stated briefly, usually in a sentence. Remember Coolidge's remark on the preacher's sermon on sin: "He was against it." Don't confuse the **topic** (sin) with the thesis (sin is bad). The thesis is the argumentative theme, the author's primary claim or contention, the proposition that the rest of the essay will explain and defend. Of course, the thesis may sound commonplace, but the book or essay or sermon ought to develop it interestingly and convincingly.

 A CHECKLIST FOR A THESIS STATEMENT

Consider the following questions:

- ☐ Does the statement make an arguable assertion rather than (a) merely assert an unarguable fact, (b) merely announce a topic, or (c) declare an unarguable opinion or belief?
- ☐ Is the statement broad enough to cover the entire argument that I will be presenting, and is it narrow enough for me to be able to cover the topic in the space allotted?

Here are some sample theses:

- Smoking should be prohibited in all enclosed public places.
- Smoking should be limited to specific parts of enclosed public places and entirely prohibited in small spaces, such as elevators.
- Proprietors of public places such as restaurants and sports arenas should be free to determine whether they wish to prohibit, limit, or impose no limitations on smokers.

Imagining an Audience

Of course, the questions that you ask yourself to stimulate your thoughts will depend primarily on what you are writing about, but additional questions are always relevant:

- Who are my readers?
- What do they believe?
- What common ground do we share?
- What do I want my readers to believe?
- What do they need to know?
- Why should they care?

These questions require a little comment. The literal answer to the first probably is "my teacher," but (unless you are given instructions to the contrary) you should not write specifically for your teacher. Instead, you should write for an audience that is, generally speaking, like your classmates. In short, your imagined audience is literate, intelligent, and moderately well-informed, but it does not know everything that you know, and it does not know your response to the problem that you are addressing. It needs more information to make an intelligent decision.

The essays in this book are from many different sources, each with its own audience. An essay from the *New York Times* is addressed to the educated general reader; an essay from *Ms.* magazine is addressed to readers sympathetic to feminism. An essay from *Commonweal,* a Roman Catholic publication addressed to the nonspecialist, is likely to differ in point of view or tone from one in *Time,* even though both articles may advance approximately the same position. The writer of the article in *Commonweal* may, for example, effectively cite church fathers and distinguished Roman Catholic writers as authorities, whereas the writer of the *Time* article would probably cite few or even none of these figures because a non-Catholic audience might be unfamiliar with them or, even if familiar, might be unimpressed by their views.

The tone as well as the gist of the argument is in some degree shaped by the audience. For instance, popular journals, such as the *National Review* and *Ms.* magazine, are more likely to use ridicule than are journals chiefly addressed to, say, an academic audience.

The Audience as Collaborator

If you imagine an audience and keep asking yourself what this audience needs to be told and what it doesn't need to be told, you will find that material comes to mind, just as it comes to mind when a friend asks you what a film you saw was about, who was in it, and how you liked it.

Your readers do not have to be told that Thomas Jefferson was an American statesman in the early years of this country's history, but they do have to be told that Elizabeth Cady Stanton was a late-nineteenth-century American feminist. Why? You need to identify Stanton because it's your hunch that your classmates never heard of her, or even if they may have heard the name, they can't quite identify it. But what if your class has been assigned an essay by Stanton? In that case your imagined reader knows Stanton's name and knows at least a little about her, so you don't have to identify Stanton as an American of the nineteenth century. But you do still have to remind your reader about relevant aspects of her essay, and you do have to tell your reader about your responses to them.

After all, even if the instructor has assigned an essay by Stanton, you cannot assume that your classmates know the essay inside out. Obviously, you can't say, "Stanton's third reason is also unconvincing," without reminding the reader, by means of a brief summary, of her third reason. Again,

- Think of your classmates—people like you—as your imagined readers; and
- Be sure that your essay does not make unreasonable demands.

If you ask yourself,

- "What do my readers need to know?" and
- "What do I want them to believe?"

you will find some answers arising, and you will start writing.

We have said that you should imagine your audience as your classmates. But this is not the whole truth. In a sense, your argument is addressed not simply to your classmates but to the world interested in ideas. Even if you can reasonably assume that your classmates have read only one work by Stanton, you will not begin your essay by writing "Stanton's essay is deceptively easy." You will have to name the work; it is possible that a reader has read some other work by Stanton. And by precisely identifying your subject, you help to ease the reader into your essay.

Similarly, you won't begin by writing,

The majority opinion in *Walker v. City of Birmingham* held that . . .

Rather, you'll write something like this:

In *Walker v. City of Birmingham*, the U.S. Supreme Court ruled in 1966 that city authorities acted lawfully when they jailed Martin Luther King

Jr. and other clergymen in 1963 for marching in Birmingham without a permit. Justice Potter Stewart delivered the majority opinion, which held that . . .

By the way, if you think you suffer from a writing block, the mere act of writing out such readily available facts will help you to get started. You will find that writing a few words, perhaps merely copying the essay's title or an interesting quotation from the essay, will stimulate you to write down thoughts that you didn't know you had in you.

Here, again, are the questions about audience. If you write on a computer, consider putting these questions into a file. For each assignment, copy the questions into the file you are currently working on, and then, as a way of generating ideas, *enter your responses, indented, under each question.*

1. Who are my readers?
2. What do they believe?
3. What common ground do we share?
4. What do I want my readers to believe?
5. What do they need to know?
6. Why should they care?

Thinking about your audience can help you to get started; even more important, it can help you to get ideas. Our second and third questions about the audience ("What do they believe?" and "How much common ground do we share?") will usually help you get ideas flowing.

- Presumably your imagined audience does not share your views, or at least does not fully share them. But why?
- How can these readers hold a position that to you seems unreasonable?

If you try to put yourself into your readers' shoes—and in your essay you will almost surely summarize the views that you are going to speak against—and if you think about what your audience knows or thinks it knows, you will find yourself getting ideas. Spend time online reviewing Web sites that are dedicated to your topic. What do they have to say, and why do the authors hold these views?

You do not believe (let's assume) that people should be allowed to smoke in enclosed public places, but you know that some people hold a different view. Why do they hold it? Try to state their view *in a way that would be satisfactory to them.* Having done so, you may come to perceive that your conclusions and theirs differ because they are based on different premises, perhaps different ideas about human rights. Examine the opposition's premises carefully, and explain, first to yourself and ultimately to your readers, why you find some premises unacceptable.

Possibly some facts are in dispute, such as whether nonsmokers may be harmed by exposure to tobacco. The thing to do, then, is to check the facts. If you find that harm to nonsmokers has not been proved, but you nevertheless believe that smoking should be prohibited in enclosed public places, of course you can't premise your argument on the wrongfulness of harming the innocent (in this case, the nonsmokers). You will have to develop arguments that take account of the facts, whatever they are.

Among the relevant facts there surely are some that your audience or your opponent will not dispute. The same is true of the values relevant to the discussion; the two of you are very likely to agree, if you stop to think about it, that you share belief in some of the same values (such as the principle mentioned above, that it is wrong to harm the innocent). These areas of shared agreement are crucial to effective persuasion in argument.

> **A RULE FOR WRITERS:** If you wish to persuade, you'll have to begin by finding premises you can share with your audience.

There are two good reasons why you should identify and isolate the areas of agreement:

- There is no point in disputing facts or values on which you and your readers really agree.
- It usually helps to establish goodwill between you and your opponent when you can point to beliefs, assumptions, facts, and values that the two of you share.

In a few moments we will return to the need to share some of the opposition's ideas.

Recall that in composing college papers it is usually best to write for a general audience, an audience rather like your classmates but without the specific knowledge that they all share as students enrolled in one course. If the topic is smoking in public places, the audience presumably consists of smokers and nonsmokers. Thinking about our fifth question on page 240 — "What do [readers] need to know?" — may prompt you to give statistics about the harmful effects of smoking. Or if you are arguing on behalf of smokers, it may prompt you to cite studies claiming that no evidence conclusively demonstrates that cigarette smoking is harmful to nonsmokers. If indeed you are writing for a general audience and you are not advancing a highly unfamiliar view, our second question ("What does the audience believe?") is less important here, but if the audience is specialized, such as an antismoking group, a group of restaurant owners who fear that antismoking regulations will interfere with their business, or a group of civil libertarians, an effective essay will have to address their special beliefs.

In addressing their beliefs (let's assume that you do not share them or do not share them fully), you must try to establish some common

---

✓ A CHECKLIST FOR IMAGINING AN AUDIENCE

Have I asked myself the following questions?

☐ Who are my readers? How do I know?

☐ How much about the topic do they know?

☐ Have I provided necessary background (including definitions of special terms) if the imagined readers probably are not especially familiar with the topic?

☐ Are these imagined readers likely to be neutral? Sympathetic? Hostile? Have I done enough online research to have something to offer to a hostile audience?

☐ If they are neutral, have I offered good reasons to persuade them? If they are sympathetic, have I done more than merely reaffirm their present beliefs? That is, have I perhaps enriched their views or encouraged them to act? If they are hostile, have I taken account of their positions, recognized their strengths but also called attention to their limitations, and offered a position that may persuade these hostile readers to modify their position?

---

ground. If you advocate requiring restaurants to provide nonsmoking areas, you should at least recognize the possibility that this arrangement will result in inconvenience for the proprietor. But perhaps (the good news) the restaurant will regain some lost customers or will attract some new customers. This thought should prompt you to think of kinds of evidence, perhaps testimony or statistics.

When you formulate a thesis and ask questions about it, such as who the readers are, what do they believe, what do they know, and what do they need to know, you begin to get ideas about how to organize the material or at least to see that some sort of organization will have to be worked out. The thesis may be clear and simple, but the reasons (the argument) may take many pages. The thesis is the point; the argument sets forth the evidence that is offered to support the thesis.

The Title

It's not a bad idea to announce your thesis in your **title.** If you scan the table of contents of this book, you will notice that a fair number of essayists use the title to let the readers know, at least in a very general way, what position will be advocated. Here are a few examples of titles that take a position:

Gay Marriages: Make Them Legal

"Diversity" Is a Smoke Screen for Discrimination

Why Handguns Must Be Outlawed

CALVIN AND HOBBES. © 1993 Bill Watterson. Reprinted with permission of Universal Press Syndicate. All rights reserved.

True, these titles are not especially engaging, but the reader welcomes them because they give some information about the writer's thesis.

Some titles do not announce the thesis, but they at least announce the topic:

Is All Discrimination Unfair?

On Racist Speech

Why Make Divorce Easy?

Although not clever or witty, these titles are informative.

Some titles seek to attract attention or to stimulate the imagination:

A First Amendment Junkie

A Crime of Compassion

Addicted to Health

All of these are effective, but a word of caution is appropriate here. In your effort to engage your reader's attention, be careful not to sound like a wise guy. You want to engage your readers, not turn them off.

Finally, be prepared to rethink your title *after* you have finished the last draft of your paper. A title somewhat different from your working title may be an improvement because the emphasis of your finished paper may have turned out to be rather different from what you expected when you first thought of a title.

The Opening Paragraphs

Opening paragraphs are difficult to write, so don't worry about writing an effective opening when you are drafting. Just get some words down on paper, and keep going. But when you revise your first draft—really a zero draft—you probably should begin to think seriously about the effect of your opening.

A good introduction arouses the reader's interest and helps prepare the reader for the rest of the paper. How? Opening paragraphs usually do at least one (and often all) of the following:

- attract the reader's interest (often with a bold statement of the thesis or with an interesting relevant statistic, quotation, or anecdote),
- prepare the reader's mind by giving some idea of the topic and often of the thesis,
- give the reader an idea of how the essay is organized, and
- define a key term.

You may not wish to announce your thesis in your title, but if you don't announce it there, you should set it forth early in the argument, in your introductory paragraph or paragraphs. In an essay called "Human Rights and Foreign Policy," Jeanne J. Kirkpatrick merely announces her topic (subject) as opposed to her thesis (point), but she begins to hint at the thesis in her first paragraph, by deprecating President Jimmy Carter's policy:

> In this paper I deal with three broad subjects: first, the content and consequences of the Carter administration's human rights policy; second, the prerequisites of a more adequate theory of human rights; and third, some characteristics of a more successful human rights policy.

Or consider this opening paragraph from Peter Singer's "Animal Liberation" (p. 207):

> We are familiar with Black Liberation, Gay Liberation, and a variety of other movements. With Women's Liberation some thought we had come to the end of the road. Discrimination on the basis of sex, it has been said, is the last form of discrimination that is universally accepted and practiced without pretense, even in those liberal circles which have long prided themselves on their freedom from racial discrimination. But one should always be wary of talking of "the last remaining form of discrimination." If we have learned anything from the liberation movements, we should have learned how difficult it is to be aware of the ways in which we discriminate until they are forcefully pointed out to us. A liberation movement demands an expansion of our moral horizons, so that practices that were previously regarded as natural and inevitable are now seen as intolerable.

Although Singer's introductory paragraph nowhere mentions animal liberation, in conjunction with the essay's title it gives us a good idea of what Singer is up to and where he is going. Singer knows that his audience will be skeptical, so he reminds them that in previous years many were skeptical of reforms now taken for granted. He adopts a strategy used fairly often by writers who advance unconventional theses: Rather than beginning with a bold announcement of a thesis that may turn off some of his readers because it sounds offensive or absurd, Singer warms up his audience, gaining their interest by cautioning them politely that although they may at first be skeptical of animal liberation, if they stay with his essay they may come to feel that they have expanded their horizons.

Notice, too, that Singer begins by establishing common ground with his readers; he assumes, probably correctly, that they share his view that other forms of discrimination (now seen to be unjust) were once widely practiced and were assumed to be acceptable and natural. In this paragraph, then, Singer is not only showing himself to be fair-minded but is also letting readers know that he will advance a daring idea. His opening wins their attention and goodwill. A writer can hardly hope to do more. (In a few pages we will talk a little more about winning the audience.)

In your introductory paragraphs:

- You may have to give some background information that your readers will need to keep in mind if they are to follow your essay.
- You may wish to define some terms that are unfamiliar or that you use in an unusual sense.
- If you are writing for an online publication (where your teacher or audience will encounter your argument on the Web), you might establish a context for your argument by linking to a news video that outlines your topic, or you might offer your thesis and then link to a news story that supports your claim. (Remember that using any videos, images, or links also requires a citation of some kind.) The beauty of publishing the piece in an online environment is that you can often link directly to your sources and use sources more easily than if you were submitting a hard copy.

After announcing the topic, giving the necessary background, and stating your position (and perhaps the opposition's) in as engaging a manner as possible, it is usually a good idea to give the reader an idea of *how* you will proceed—that is, what the organization will be. In other words, use the introduction to set up the organization of your essay. Your teachers may assign four- to six-page mini-research papers or they may assign ten- to fifteen-page research papers; if they assign an online venue, ask them about the approximate word count. Whatever the length, every paper needs to have a clear organization. The introduction is where you can

- hook your reader
- reveal your thesis and topic, and
- explain how you will organize your discussion of the topic—what you will do first, second, third, etc.

Look at Kirkpatrick's opening paragraph (page 244) for an obvious illustration. She tells us she will deal with three subjects, and she names them. Her approach in the paragraph is concise, obvious, and effective.

> **A RULE FOR WRITERS:** In writing or at least in revising these paragraphs, keep in mind this question: What do my readers need to know? Remember, your aim throughout is to write *reader-friendly* prose, and keeping the needs and interests of your audience constantly in mind will help you achieve this goal.

Similarly, you may, for instance, want to announce fairly early that there are four common objections to your thesis and that you will take them up one by one, beginning with the weakest (or most widely held, or whatever) and moving to the strongest (or least familiar), after which you will advance your own view in greater detail. Not every argument begins with refuting the other side, though many arguments do. The point to remember is that you usually ought to tell your readers where you will be taking them and by what route. In effect, you are giving them an outline.

Organizing and Revising the Body of the Essay

We begin with a wise remark by a newspaper columnist, Robert Cromier: "The beautiful part of writing is that you don't have to get it right the first time—unlike, say, a brain surgeon."

In drafting your essay you will of course begin with an organization that seems to you to make sense, but you may well find, in rereading the draft, that some other organization is better. Here, for a start, is an organization that is common in argumentative essays.

1. Statement of the problem or issue
2. Statement of the structure of the essay (its organization)
3. Statement of alternative solutions
4. Arguments in support of the proposed solution
5. Arguments answering possible objections
6. A summary, resolution, or conclusion

Let's look at each of these six steps.

1. **Statement of the problem or issue** Whether the problem is stated briefly or at length depends on the nature of the problem and the writer's audience. If you haven't already defined unfamiliar terms or terms you use in a special way, probably now is the time to do so. In any case, it is advisable here to state the problem objectively (thereby gaining the trust of the reader) and to indicate why the reader should care about the issue.

2. **Statement of the structure of the essay** After stating the problem at the appropriate length, the writer often briefly indicates the structure of the rest of the essay. The commonest structure is suggested below, in points 3 and 4.

3. **Statement of alternative (but less adequate) solutions** In addition to stating the alternatives fairly—let the readers know that you

have done your homework—the writer probably conveys willingness to recognize not only the integrity of the proposals but also the (partial) merit of at least some of the alternative solutions.

The point made in the previous sentence is important and worth amplifying. Because it is important to convey your goodwill—your sense of fairness—to the reader, it is advisable to let your reader see that you are familiar with the opposition and that you recognize the integrity of those who hold that view. This you do by granting its merits as far as you can. (For more about this approach, see the essay by Carl R. Rogers on p. 394.)

The next stage, which constitutes most of the body of the essay, usually is this:

4. **Arguments in support of the proposed solution**   The evidence offered will, of course, depend on the nature of the problem. Relevant statistics, authorities, examples, or analogies may come to mind or be available. This is usually the longest part of the essay.

5. **Arguments answering possible objections**   These arguments may suggest that

    a. The proposal won't work (perhaps it is alleged to be too expensive, to make unrealistic demands on human nature, or to fail to get to the heart of the problem).

    b. The proposed solution will create problems greater than the difficulty to be resolved. (A good example of a proposal that produced dreadful unexpected results is the law mandating a prison term for anyone over eighteen in possession of an illegal drug. Heroin dealers then began to use children as runners, and cocaine importers followed the practice.)

6. **A summary, resolution, or conclusion**   Here the writer may seek to accommodate the views of the opposition as far as possible but clearly suggest that the writer's own position makes good sense. A conclusion—the word comes from the Latin *claudere*, "to shut"—ought to provide a sense of closure, but it can be much more than a restatement of the writer's thesis. It can, for instance, make a quiet emotional appeal by suggesting that the issue is important and that the ball is now in the reader's court.

Of course not every essay will follow this six-step pattern, but let's assume that in the introductory paragraphs you have sketched the topic (and have shown or nicely said, or implied, that the reader doubtless is interested in it) and have fairly and courteously set forth the opposition's view, recognizing its merits ("I grant that," "admittedly," "it is true that") and indicating the degree to which you can share part of that view. You now want to set forth your arguments explaining why you differ on some essentials.

In setting forth your own position, you can begin either with your strongest reasons or your weakest. Each method of organization has advantages and disadvantages.

- If you begin with your strongest reason, the essay may seem to peter out.
- If you begin with your weakest reason, you build to a climax, but your readers may not still be with you because they may have felt at the start that the essay was frivolous.

The solution to this last possibility is to make sure that even your weakest argument is an argument of some strength. You can, moreover, assure your readers that stronger points will soon be offered and you offer this point first only because you want to show that you are aware of it and that, slight though it is, it deserves some attention. The body of the essay, then, is devoted to arguing a position, which means offering not only supporting reasons but also refutations of possible objections to these reasons.

Doubtless you will sometimes be uncertain, as you draft your essay, whether to present a given point before or after another point. When you write, and certainly when you revise, try to put yourself into your reader's shoes: Which point do you think the reader needs to know first? Which point *leads to* which further point? Your argument should not be a mere list of points, of course; rather, it should clearly integrate one point with another in order to develop an idea. But in all likelihood you won't have a strong sense of the best organization until you have written a draft and have reread it.

> **A RULE FOR WRITERS:** When you revise, make sure that your organization is clear to your readers.

Checking Paragraphs   When you revise your draft, watch out also for short paragraphs. Although a paragraph of only two or three sentences (like some in this chapter) may occasionally be helpful as a transition between complicated points, most short paragraphs are undeveloped paragraphs. Newspaper editors favor very short paragraphs because they can be read rapidly when printed in the narrow columns typical of newspapers. Many of the essays reprinted in this book originally were published in newspapers, hence they consist of very short paragraphs, but they should *not* be regarded as models for your own writing. A second note about paragraphs: Writers for online venues often "chunk" (that is, they provide extra space for paragraph breaks) rather than write a continuous flow. These writers chunk their text for several reasons, but chiefly because breaking up paragraphs and adding space between them makes some types of writing "scannable": The screen is easier to navigate because it is not packed with text in a 12-pt font. The breaks in paragraphs also allow the reader to see a complete paragraph without having to scroll.

Checking Transitions   Make sure, too, in revising, that the reader can move easily from the beginning of a paragraph to the end and from one

paragraph to the next. Transitions help the reader to perceive the connections between the units of the argument. For example ("For example" is a transition, of course, indicating that an illustration will follow),
they may illustrate, establish a sequence, connect logically, amplify,
compare, contrast, summarize, or concede (see Idea Prompt 6.1). Transitions serve as guideposts that enable your reader to move easily through
your essay.

When writers revise an early draft, they chiefly

- **unify** the essay by eliminating irrelevancies;
- **organize** the essay by keeping in mind an imagined audience;
- **clarify** the essay by fleshing out thin paragraphs, by making certain that the transitions are adequate and by making certain that
  generalizations are adequately supported by concrete details and
  examples.

We are not talking about polish or elegance; we are talking about
fundamental matters. Be especially careful not to abuse the logical connectives (*thus, as a result,* and so on). If you write several sentences followed by *therefore* or a similar word or phrase, be sure that what you
write after the *therefore* really *does follow* from what has gone before.
Logical connectives are not mere transitional devices used to link disconnected bits of prose. They are supposed to mark a real movement of
thought—the essence of an argument.

The Ending

What about concluding paragraphs, in which you try to summarize the
main points and reaffirm your position?

If you can look back over your essay and add something that
enriches it and at the same time wraps it up, fine, but don't feel compelled
to say, "Thus, in conclusion, I have argued *X, Y,* and *Z,* and I have refuted
Jones." After all, *conclusion* can have two meanings: (1) ending, or finish,
as the ending of a joke or a novel; or (2) judgment or decision reached
after deliberation. Your essay should finish effectively (the first sense),
but it need not announce a judgment (the second).

If the essay is fairly short, so that a reader can more or less keep the
whole thing in mind, you may not need to restate your view. Just make
sure that you have covered the ground and that your last sentence is
a good one. Notice that the student essay printed later in this chapter
(p. 264) does not end with a formal conclusion, though it ends conclusively, with a note of finality.

By a note of finality we do *not* mean a triumphant crowing. It's usually far better to end with the suggestion that you hope you have by
now indicated why those who hold a different view may want to modify
it and accept yours.

IDEA PROMPT 6.1 USING TRANSITIONS IN ARGUMENT

Illustrate	*for example, for instance, consider this case*	"Many television crime dramas contain scenes of graphic violence. For example, in the episode of *Law and Order* titled..."
Establish a sequence	*a more important objection, a stronger example, the best reason*	"A stronger example of the ways that TV violence is susceptible to being mimicked is..."
Connect logically	*thus, as a result, therefore, so, it follows*	"Therefore, the Federal Communications Commission ought to consider more carefully regulating what types of violence they allow on the air."
Amplify	*further, in addition to, moreover*	"Further, fines for networks that violate these regulations should be steeper because..."
Compare	*similarly, in a like manner, just as, analogously*	"Just as the FCC regulates language and sexuality on broadcast TV..."
Contrast	*on the other hand, in contrast, however, but*	"On the other hand, studies have shown that violent television..."
Summarize	*in short, briefly*	"In short, the basic premise of his argument is..."
Concede	*admittedly, granted, to be sure*	"Admittedly, there are many points on which the author is correct."

If you study the essays in this book, or, for that matter, the editorials and op-ed pieces in a newspaper, you will notice that writers often provide a sense of closure by using one of the following devices:

- a return to something in the introduction,
- a glance at the wider implications of the issue (for example, if smoking is restricted, other liberties are threatened),
- an anecdote that engagingly illustrates the thesis,
- a suggestion that the reader can take some specific action, i.e., that the ball is now in the reader's court, or

- a brief summary (but this sort of ending may seem unnecessary and even tedious, especially if the paper is short and if the summary merely repeats what has already been said).

> **A RULE FOR WRITERS:** Emulate John Kenneth Galbraith, a distinguished writer on economics. Galbraith said that in his fifth draft he introduced the note of spontaneity for which his writing was famous.

Two Uses of an Outline

The Outline as a Preliminary Guide   Some writers find it useful to sketch an **outline** as soon as they think they know what they want to say, even before they write a first draft. This procedure can be helpful in planning a tentative organization, but remember that in revising a draft new ideas will arise, and the outline may have to be modified. A preliminary outline is chiefly useful as a means of getting going, not as a guide to the final essay.

The Outline as a Way of Checking a Draft   Whether or not you use a preliminary outline, we strongly suggest that after you have written what you hope is your last draft, you make an outline of it; there is no better way of finding out whether the essay is well organized.

Go through the draft and write down the chief points in the order in which you make them. That is, prepare a table of contents—perhaps a phrase for each paragraph. Next, examine your notes to see what kind of sequence they reveal in your paper:

- Is the sequence reasonable? Can it be improved?
- Are any passages irrelevant?
- Does something important seem to be missing?

If no coherent structure or reasonable sequence clearly appears in the outline, then the full prose version of your argument probably doesn't have any either. Therefore, produce another draft, moving things around, adding or subtracting paragraphs—cutting and pasting into a new sequence, with transitions as needed—and then make another outline to see if the sequence now is satisfactory.

You are probably familiar with the structure known as a **formal outline.** Major points are indicated by I, II, III; points within major points are indicated by A, B, C; divisions within A, B, C are indicated by 1, 2, 3; and so on. Thus,

I. Arguments for opening all Olympic sports to professionals
   A. Fairness
      1. Some Olympic sports are already open to professionals.
      2. Some athletes who really are not professionals are classified as professionals.
   B. Quality (achievements would be higher)

You may want to outline your draft according to this principle, or it may be enough if you simply write a phrase for each paragraph and indent the subdivisions. But keep these points in mind:

- It is not enough for the parts to be ordered reasonably.
- The order must be made clear to the reader, probably by means of transitions such as *for instance, on the other hand, we can now turn to an opposing view,* and so on.

Here is another way of thinking about an outline. For each paragraph, write

- what the paragraph *says,* and
- what the paragraph *does.*

An opening paragraph might be outlined thus:

- What the paragraph *says* is that the words "under God" in the Pledge of Allegiance should be omitted.
- What the paragraph *does* is, first, it informs the reader of the thesis, and second, it *provides some necessary background,* for instance, that the words were not in the original wording of the Pledge.

A dual outline of this sort will help you to see whether you have a final draft or a draft that needs refinement.

A Last Word about Outlines

Outlines may seem rigid to many writers, especially to writers who customarily compose online, where we are accustomed to cutting, copying, moving, and deleting as we draft. However, as we said earlier, an outline—whether you write it before you draft a single word or use it to evaluate the organization of something you have already written—is meant to be a guide rather than a straitjacket that confines you. Many writers who compose electronically find that the ability to keep banging out words—typing is so much easier than pushing a pen or pencil—and to cut and paste without actually reaching for scissors makes it easy to produce an essay that readers may find difficult to follow. (There is much truth in the proverb, "Easy writing makes hard reading.") If you compose electronically, and especially if you find yourself continually adding, deleting, and moving text around without a clear organizational goal in mind, be sure to read and outline your draft, and then examine the outline to see if indeed there is a reasonable organization.

Outlines are especially helpful for long essays, but even short ones benefit from a bit of advanced planning, a list of a few topics (drawn from notes already taken) that help to keep the writer moving in an orderly way. A longer work such as an honors or a master's thesis typically requires careful planning. An outline will be a great help in assuring that you will produce something that a reader can easily follow—but of course you may find, as you write, that the outline needs to be altered.

✓   A CHECKLIST FOR ORGANIZING AN ARGUMENT

☐ Does the introduction let the readers know where the author is taking them?

☐ Does the introduction state the problem or issue?

  ☐ Does it state the claim (the thesis)?

  ☐ Does it suggest the organization of the essay, thereby helping the reader to follow the argument?

☐ Do subsequent paragraphs support the claim?

  ☐ Do they offer evidence?

  ☐ Do they face objections to the claim and offer reasonable responses?

  ☐ Do they indicate why the author's claim is preferable?

  ☐ Do transitions (signposts such as "Furthermore," "On the other hand,"and "Consider as an example") guide the reader through the argument?

☐ Does the essay end effectively, with a paragraph (or at most two paragraphs) bringing a note of closure, for instance, by indicating that the proposed solution is relatively simple? By admitting that, although the proposed solution will be difficult to implement, it is certainly feasible? By reminding the reader of the urgency of the problem?

When readers finish reading, they should feel that the writer has brought them to a decisive point and now is not just abruptly and unexpectedly stopping.

Tone and the Writer's Persona

Although this book is chiefly about argument in the sense of rational discourse—the presentation of reasons in support of a thesis or conclusion—the appeal to reason is only one form of persuasion. Another form is the appeal to emotion—to pity, for example. Aristotle saw, in addition to the appeal to reason and the appeal to emotion, a third form of persuasion, the appeal to the character of the speaker. He called it the **ethical appeal** (the Greek word for this kind of appeal is **ethos,** "character"). The idea is that effective speakers convey the suggestion that they are

- informed,
- intelligent,
- fair-minded (persons of goodwill), and
- honest.

Because they are perceived as trustworthy, their words inspire confidence in their listeners. It is, of course, a fact that when we read an argument we are often aware of the *person* or *voice* behind the words, and our assent to the argument depends partly on the extent to which we can share the speaker's assumptions, look at the matter from the speaker's point of view—in short, *identify* with this speaker.

How can a writer inspire the confidence that lets readers identify themselves with him or her? To begin with, the writer should possess the virtues Aristotle specified: intelligence or good sense, honesty, and benevolence or goodwill. As the Roman proverb puts it, "No one gives what he does not have." Still, possession of these qualities is not a guarantee that you will convey them in your writing. Like all other writers, you will have to revise your drafts so that these qualities become apparent, or, stated more moderately, you will have to revise so that nothing in the essay causes a reader to doubt your intelligence, honesty, and goodwill. A blunder in logic, a misleading quotation, a snide remark, even an error in spelling—all such slips can cause readers to withdraw their sympathy from the writer.

But of course all good argumentative essays do not sound exactly alike; they do not all reveal the same speaker. Each writer develops his or her own voice or (as literary critics and teachers call it) **persona.** In fact, one writer will have several voices or personae, depending on the topic and the audience. The president of the United States delivering an address on the State of the Union has one persona; chatting with a reporter at his summer home he has another. This change is not a matter of hypocrisy. Different circumstances call for different language. As a French writer put it, there is a time to speak of "Paris" and a time to speak of "the capital of the nation." When Lincoln spoke at Gettysburg, he didn't say "Eighty-seven years ago," but "Four score and seven years ago." We might say that just as some occasions required him to be the folksy Honest Abe, the occasion of the dedication of hallowed ground required him to be formal and solemn, and so the president of the United States appropriately used biblical language. The election campaigns called for one persona, and the dedication of a military cemetery—a different rhetorical situation—called for a different persona. For examples on how to vary tone, see Idea Prompt 6.2.

> **A RULE FOR WRITERS:** Present yourself so that your readers see you as knowledgeable, honest, open-minded, and interested in helping them to think about an issue of significance.

When we talk about a writer's persona, we mean the way in which the writer presents his or her attitudes

IDEA PROMPT 6.2 VARYING TONE

Abraham Lincoln	*Four score and seven years ago our fathers brought forth on this continent a new nation, conceived in liberty, and dedicated to the proposition that all men are created equal.*	Invokes Biblical rhetoric ("Four score and seven years ago") in an appeal to national unity
More academic tone	*In 1776, America's Founding Fathers drafted and signed the Declaration of Independence, at the heart of which were the Enlightenment ideals of equality and individual liberty.*	Incorporates specific factual information and connects to overarching ideas
More informal tone	*Nearly a hundred years ago, the United States was founded in order to provide greater freedom and equality to its citizens.*	Is accurate but simplified, forgoing much detail
Too informal for most academic writing	*The US was created way back then so that everyone would be free.*	Mischaracterizes or oversimplifies the thought process

- toward *the self,*
- toward *the audience,* and
- toward *the subject.*

Thus, if a writer says,

> I have thought long and hard about this subject, and I can say with assurance that . . .

we may feel that we are listening to a self-satisfied ass who probably is simply mouthing other people's opinions. Certainly he is mouthing clichés: "long and hard," "say with assurance."

Let's look at a slightly subtler example of an utterance that reveals an attitude. When we read that

> President Nixon was hounded out of office by journalists,

we hear a respectful attitude toward Nixon ("President Nixon") and a hostile attitude toward the press (they are beasts, curs who "hounded" our elected leader). If the writer's attitudes were reversed, she might have said something like this:

> The press turned the searchlight on Tricky Dick's criminal shenanigans.

"Tricky Dick" and "criminal" are obvious enough, but notice that "shenanigans" also implies the writer's contempt for Nixon, and of course, "turned the searchlight" suggests that the press is a source of illumination, a source of truth. The original version and the opposite version both say that the press was responsible for Nixon's resignation, but the original version ("President Nixon was hounded") conveys indignation toward journalists, whereas the revision conveys contempt for Nixon.

These two versions suggest two speakers who differ not only in their view of Nixon but also in their manner, including the seriousness with which they take themselves. Although the passage is very short, it seems to us that the first speaker conveys righteous indignation ("hounded"), whereas the second conveys amused contempt ("shenanigans"). To our ears the tone, as well as the point, differs in the two versions.

We are talking about **loaded words,** words that convey the writer's attitude and that by their connotations are meant to win the reader to the writer's side. Compare the words in the left-hand column with those in the right:

freedom fighter	terrorist
pro-choice	pro-abortion
pro-life	antichoice
economic refugee	illegal alien
terrorist surveillance	domestic spying

The words in the left-hand column sound like good things; speakers who use these words are seeking to establish themselves as virtuous people who are supporting worthy causes. The **connotations** (associations, overtones) of these pairs of words differ, even though the **denotations** (explicit meanings, dictionary definitions) are the same, just as the connotations of *mother* and *female parent* differ, although the denotations are the same. Similarly, although Lincoln's "four score and seven" and "eighty-seven" both denote "thirteen less than one hundred," they differ in connotation.

Tone is not only a matter of connotations (*hounded out of office* versus, let's say, *compelled to resign,* or *pro-choice* versus *pro-abortion*); it is also a matter of such things as the selection and type of examples. A writer who offers many examples, especially ones drawn from ordinary life, conveys a persona different from that of a writer who offers no examples or only an occasional invented instance. The first of these probably is, one might say, friendlier, more down-to-earth.

Last Words on Tone   On the whole, when writing an argument, it is advisable to be courteous and respectful of your topic, of your audience, and of people who hold views you are arguing against. It is rarely good for one's own intellectual development to regard as villains or fools persons who hold views different from one's own, especially if some of them are in the audience. Keep in mind the story of the two strangers on a train who, striking up a conversation, found that both were clergymen, though of different faiths. Then one said to the other, "Well, why shouldn't we be friends? After all, we both serve God, you in your way and I in His."

Complacency is all right when telling a joke but not when offering an argument:

- Recognize opposing views.
- Assume they are held in good faith.
- State them fairly (if you don't, you do a disservice not only to the opposition but also to your own position because the perceptive reader will not take you seriously).
- Be temperate in arguing your own position: "If I understand their view correctly . . ."; "It seems reasonable to conclude that . . ."; "Perhaps, then, we can agree that . . ."
- Write calmly: If you become overly emotional your readers may interpret you as biased or unreasonable—even a bit nutty—and they may lose their confidence in you.

One way to practice thinking about tone and persona is in your professional e-mails. As a student you probably send many e-mails to your classmates and to your instructors or other offices on campus (the financial aid office, the parking/traffic office, your instructors, your advisor, etc.). As teachers, we are often surprised at how flippant and inattentive students are when e-mailing.

We, One, or I?

The use of *we* in the last sentence brings us to another point: May the first-person pronouns *I* and *we* be used? In this book, because two of us are writing, we often use *we* to mean the two authors. And we sometimes use *we* to mean the authors and the readers. This shifting use of one word can be troublesome, but we hope (clearly the *we* here refers only to the authors) that we have avoided any ambiguity. But can, or should, or must an individual use *we* instead of *I*? The short answer is no.

If you are simply speaking for yourself, use *I*. Attempts to avoid the first-person singular by saying things like "This writer thinks . . . ," and "It is thought that . . . ," and "One thinks that . . . ," are far more irritating (and wordy) than the use of *I*. The so-called editorial *we* is as odd-sounding in a student's argument as is the royal *we*. Mark Twain said that the only ones who can appropriately say *we* are kings, editors, and people with a tapeworm. And because one *one* leads to another, making the sentence sound (James Thurber's words) "like a trombone solo," it's best to admit that you are the author, and to use *I*. But there is no need to preface every sentence with "I think." The reader knows that the essay is yours; just write it, using *I* when you must, but not needlessly.

Often you will see *I* in journalistic writing and of course in autobiographical writing—and you will see it in some argumentative writing, too—but in most argumentative writing it is best to state the facts and (when drawing reasonable conclusions from them) to keep yourself in the background. Why? The more you use *I* in an essay, the more your readers will attach *you* directly to the argument and may regard your position as personal rather than as relevant to themselves.

✓ A CHECKLIST FOR ATTENDING TO THE NEEDS OF THE AUDIENCE

☐ Do I have a sense of what the audience probably knows about the issue?

☐ Do I have a sense of what the audience probably thinks about the issue?

☐ Have I stated the thesis clearly and sufficiently early in the essay?

☐ How much common ground do we probably share?

☐ Have I, in the paper, tried to establish common ground and then moved on to advance my position?

☐ Have I supported my arguments with sufficient details?

☐ Have I used the appropriate language (for instance, defined terms that are likely to be unfamiliar)?

☐ Have I indicated why my readers should care about the issue and should accept or at least take seriously my views?

☐ Is the organization clear?

☐ Have I used transitions where they are needed?

☐ If visual material (charts, graphs, pictures) will enhance my arguments, have I used them?

☐ Have I presented myself as a person who is (a) fair, (b) informed, and (c) worth listening to? In short, have I conveyed a strong *ethos*?

Avoiding Sexist Language

Courtesy as well as common sense requires that you respect the feelings of your readers. Many people today find offensive the implicit sexism in the use of male pronouns to denote not only men but also women ("As the reader follows the argument, he will find . . ."). And sometimes the use of the male pronoun to denote all people is ridiculous: "An individual, no matter what his sex, . . ."

In most contexts there is no need to use gender-specific nouns or pronouns. One way to avoid using *he* when you mean any person is to use *he or she* (or *she or he*) instead of *he*, but the result is sometimes a bit cumbersome—although it is superior to the overly conspicuous *he/she* and to *s/he*.

Here are two simple ways to solve the problem:

- *Use the plural* ("As readers follow the argument, they will find . . ."), or

- *Recast the sentence* so that no pronoun is required ("Readers following the argument will find . . .").

Because *man* and *mankind* strike many readers as sexist when used in such expressions as "Man is a rational animal" and "Mankind has not yet solved this problem," consider using such words as *human being, person, people, humanity*, and *we*. (*Examples:* "Human beings are rational animals"; "We have not yet solved this problem.")

PEER REVIEW

Your instructor may suggest—or may even require—that you submit an early draft of your essay to a fellow student or small group of students for comment. Such a procedure benefits both author and readers: You get the responses of a reader and the student-reader gets experience in thinking about the problems of developing an argument, especially in thinking about such matters as the degree of detail that a writer needs to offer to a reader and the importance of keeping the organization evident to a reader.

Oral peer reviews allow for the give and take of discussion, but probably most students and most instructors find written peer reviews more helpful because reviewers think more carefully about their responses to the draft, and they help essayists to get beyond a knee-jerk response to criticism. Online reviews on a class Web site or through e-mail are especially helpful precisely because they are not face to face; the peer reviewer gets practice *writing*, and the essayist is not directly challenged. Sharing documents via Google Doc works well for peer review. You can copy and paste your essay into a Google Doc (if you did not compose it there) and then share it with a classmate who is sitting next to you.

✓ A PEER REVIEW CHECKLIST FOR A DRAFT
OF AN ARGUMENT

Read the draft through quickly. Then read it again, with the following questions in mind. Remember: You are reading a draft, a work in progress. You are expected to offer suggestions, and it is also expected that you will offer them courteously.

☐ In a sentence, indicate the degree to which the draft shows promise of fulfilling the assignment.

☐ Is the writer's tone appropriate? Who is the audience?

☐ Looking at the essay as a whole, what thesis (main idea) is advanced?

☐ Are the needs of the audience kept in mind? For instance, do some words need to be defined? Is the evidence (for instance, the examples and the testimony of authorities) clear and effective?

☐ Can I accept the assumptions? If not, why not?

☐ Is any obvious evidence (or counterevidence) overlooked?

☐ Is the writer proposing a solution? If so,

  ☐ Are other equally attractive solutions adequately examined?

  ☐ Has the writer overlooked some unattractive effects of the proposed solution?

☐ Looking at each paragraph separately,

  ☐ What is the basic point?

  ☐ How does each paragraph relate to the essay's main idea or to the previous paragraph?

  ☐ Should some paragraphs be deleted? Be divided into two or more paragraphs? Be combined? Be put elsewhere? (If you outline the essay by writing down the gist of each paragraph, you will get help in answering these questions.)

  ☐ Is each sentence clearly related to the sentence that precedes and to the sentence that follows? If not, in a sentence or two indicate examples of good and bad transitions.

  ☐ Is each paragraph adequately developed? Are there sufficient details, perhaps brief supporting quotations from the text?

  ☐ Are the introductory and concluding paragraphs effective?

☐ What are the paper's chief strengths?

☐ Make at least two specific suggestions that you think will assist the author to improve the paper.

A STUDENT'S ESSAY, FROM ROUGH NOTES TO FINAL VERSION

While we were revising this textbook, we asked the students in one of our classes to write a short essay (500–750 words) on some ethical problem that concerned them. Because this assignment was the first writing assignment in the course, we explained that a good way to get ideas is to ask oneself some questions, write down responses, question those responses, and write freely for ten minutes or so, not worrying about contradictions. We invited our students to hand in their initial notes along with the finished essay, so that we could get a sense of how they proceeded as writers. Not all of them chose to hand in their notes, but we were greatly encouraged by those who did. What was encouraging was the confirmation of an old belief, the belief—we call it a fact—that students will hand in a thoughtful essay if before they prepare a final version they nag themselves, ask themselves *why* they think this or that, write down their responses, and are not afraid to change their minds as they proceed.

Here are the first notes of a student, Emily Andrews, who elected to write about whether to give money to street beggars. She simply put down ideas, one after the other.

Help the poor? Why do I (sometimes) do it?

I feel guilty, and think I should help them: poor, cold, hungry (but also some of them are thirsty for liquor, and will spend the money on liquor, not on food).

I also feel annoyed by them—most of them.

Where does the expression "the deserving poor" come from?

And "poor but honest"? Actually, that sounds a bit odd. Wouldn't "rich but honest" make more sense?

Why don't they work? Fellow with red beard, always by bus stop in front of florist's shop, always wants a handout. He is a regular, there all day every day, so I guess he is in a way "reliable," so why doesn't he put the same time in on a job?

Or why don't they get help? Don't they know they need it? They *must* know they need it.

Maybe that guy with the beard is just a con artist. Maybe he makes more money by panhandling than he would by working, and it's a lot easier!

Kinds of poor — how to classify??

    drunks, druggies, etc.

    mentally ill (maybe drunks belong here, too)

    decent people who have had terrible luck

Why private charity?

Doesn't it make sense to say we (fortunate individuals) should give something — an occasional handout — to people who have had terrible luck? (I suppose some people might say that there is no need for any of us to give anything — the government takes care of the truly needy — but I *do* believe in giving charity. A month ago a friend of the family passed away, and the woman's children suggested that people might want to make a donation in her name, to a shelter for battered women. I know my parents made a donation.)

BUT how can I tell who is who, which are which? Which of these people asking for "spare change" really need (deserve???) help, and which are phonies? Impossible to tell.

Possibilities:

    Give to no one

    Give to no one but make an annual donation, maybe to United Way

    Give a dollar to each person who asks. This would probably not cost me even a dollar a day

    Occasionally do without something — maybe a CD — or a meal in a restaurant — and give the money I save to people who seem worthy.

WORTHY? What am I saying? How can I, or anyone, tell? The neat-looking guy who says he just lost his job may be a phony, and the dirty bum — probably a drunk — may desperately need food. (OK, so what if he spends the money on liquor instead of food? At least he'll get a little pleasure in life. No! It's not all right if he spends it on drink.)

Other possibilities:

    Do some volunteer work?

    To tell the truth, I don't want to put in the time. I don't feel *that* guilty.

So what's the problem?

Is it, How I can help the very poor (handouts, or through an organization)? or

How I can feel less guilty about being lucky enough to be able to go to college, and to have a supportive family?

I can't quite bring myself to believe I should help every beggar who approaches, but I also can't bring myself to believe that I should do nothing, on the grounds that:
   a. it's probably their fault
   b. if they are deserving, they can get gov't help. No, I just can't believe that. Maybe some are too proud to look for government help, or don't know that they are entitled to it.

What to do?

On balance, it seems best to
   a. give to United Way
   b. maybe also give to an occasional individual, if I happen to be moved, without worrying about whether he or she is "deserving" (since it's probably impossible to know).

A day after making these notes Emily reviewed them, added a few points, and then made a very brief selection from them to serve as an outline for her first draft:

Opening para.: "poor but honest"? Deserve "spare change"?

Charity: private or through organizations?
      pros and cons
      guy at bus
      it wouldn't cost me much, but . . . better to give through organizations

Concluding para.: still feel guilty?
      maybe mention guy at bus again?

After writing and revising a draft, Emily Andrews submitted her essay to a fellow student for peer review. She then revised her work in light of the suggestions she received and in light of her own further thinking.

On the next page we give the final essay. If after reading the final version you reread the early notes, you will notice that some of the notes never made it into the final version. But without the notes, the essay probably could not have been as interesting as it is. When the writer made the notes, she was not so much putting down her ideas as *finding* ideas by the process of writing.

Andrews 1

Emily Andrews

Professor Barnet

English 102

January 15, 2010

Why I Don't Spare "Spare Change"

"Poor but honest." "The deserving poor." I don't know the origin of these quotations, but they always come to mind when I think of "the poor." But I also think of people who, perhaps through alcohol or drugs, have ruined not only their own lives but also the lives of others in order to indulge in their own pleasure. Perhaps alcoholism and drug addiction really are "diseases," as many people say, but my own feeling — based, of course, not on any serious study — is that most alcoholics and drug addicts can be classified with the "undeserving poor." And that is largely why I don't distribute spare change to panhandlers.

But surely among the street people there are also some who can rightly be called "deserving." Deserving what? My spare change? Or simply the government's assistance? It happens that I have been brought up to believe that it is appropriate to make contributions to charity — let's say a shelter for battered women — but if I give some change to a panhandler, am I making a contribution to charity and thereby helping someone, or, on the contrary, am I perhaps simply encouraging someone not to get help? Or maybe even worse, am I supporting a con artist?

If one believes in the value of private charity, one can give either to needy individuals or to charitable organizations. In giving to a panhandler one may indeed be helping a person who badly needs help, but one cannot be certain that one is giving to a needy individual. In giving to an organization such as the United Way, on the other hand, one can feel that one's money is likely to be used wisely. True, confronted by a beggar one may feel that *this* particular unfortunate individual needs help at *this* moment — a cup of coffee or a sandwich — and the need will not be met unless I put my hand in my pocket right now. But I have come to think that the beggars whom I encounter can get along without my spare change, and indeed perhaps they are actually better off for not having money to buy liquor or drugs.

It happens that in my neighborhood I encounter few panhandlers. There is one fellow who is always by the bus stop where I catch the bus to the college, and I never give him anything precisely because he is always there. He is such a regular that, I think, he ought to be able to hold a regular job. Putting him aside, I probably don't encounter more than three or four beggars in a week. (I'm not counting street musicians. These people seem quite able to work for a living. If they see their "work" as playing or singing, let persons who enjoy their performances pay them. I do not consider myself among their audience.) The truth of the matter is that, since I meet so few beggars, I could give each one a dollar and hardly feel the loss. At most, I might go without seeing a movie some week. But I know nothing about these people, and it's my impression — admittedly based on almost no evidence — that they simply prefer begging to working. I am not generalizing about street people, and certainly I am not talking about street people in the big urban centers. I am talking only about the people whom I actually encounter.

That's why I usually do not give "spare change," and I don't think I will in the future. These people will get along without me. Someone else will come up with money for their coffee or their liquor, or, at worst, they will just have to do without. I will continue to contribute occasionally to a charitable organization, not simply (I hope) to salve my conscience but because I believe that these organizations actually do good work. But I will not attempt to be a mini-charitable organization, distributing (probably to the unworthy) spare change.

THE ESSAY ANALYZED

Finally, here are a few comments about the essay:

The title is informative, alerting the reader to the topic and the author's position. (By the way, the student told us that in her next-to-last draft the title was "Is It Right to Spare 'Spare Change'?" This title, like the revision, introduces the topic but not the author's position.)

The opening paragraph holds a reader's interest, partly by alluding to the familiar phrase "the deserving poor" and partly by introducing the *un*familiar phrase "the *un*deserving poor." Notice, too, that this opening paragraph ends by clearly asserting the author's thesis. Writers need not always announce their thesis early, but it is usually advisable to do so.

Paragraph two begins by voicing what probably is the reader's somewhat uneasy—perhaps even negative—response to the first paragraph. That is, *the writer has a sense of her audience;* she knows how her reader feels, and she takes account of the feeling.

Paragraph three clearly sets forth the alternatives. A reader may disagree with the writer's attitude, but the alternatives seem to be stated fairly.

Paragraphs four and five are more personal than the earlier paragraphs. The writer, more or less having stated what she takes to be the facts, now is entitled to offer a highly personal response to them.

The final paragraph nicely wraps things up by means of the words "spare change," which go back to the title and to the end of the first paragraph. The reader thus experiences a sensation of completeness. The essayist, of course, has not solved the problem for all of us for all time, but she presents a thoughtful argument and ends the essay effectively.

EXERCISE

In a brief essay, state a claim and support it with evidence. Choose an issue in which you are genuinely interested and about which you already know something. You may want to interview a few experts and do some reading, but don't try to write a highly researched paper. Sample topics:

1. Students in laboratory courses should not be required to participate in the dissection of animals.
2. Washington, D.C., should be granted statehood.
3. Women should, in wartime, be exempted from serving in combat.
4. The annual Miss America contest is an insult to women.
5. The government should not offer financial support to the arts.
6. The chief fault of the curriculum in high school was . . .
7. No specific courses should be required in colleges or universities.

 For additional arguments online, visit the e-Pages at **bedfordstmartins.com/barnetbedau**.

Using Sources

Research is formalized curiosity. It is poking and prying with a purpose.
————ZORA NEALE HURSTON

There is no way of exchanging information that does not involve an act of judgment.
————JACOB BRONOWSKI

For God's sake, stop researching for a while and begin to think.
————WALTER HAMILTON MOBERLY

A problem adequately stated is a problem on its way to being solved.
————R. BUCKMINSTER FULLER

I have yet to see any problem, however complicated, which, when you looked at it in the right way, did not become still more complicated.
————POUL ANDERSON

WHY USE SOURCES?

We have pointed out that one gets ideas by writing. In the exercise of writing a draft, ideas begin to form, and these ideas stimulate further ideas, especially when one questions—when one *thinks* about—what one has written. But of course in writing about complex, serious questions, nobody is expected to invent all the answers. On the contrary, a writer is expected to be familiar with the chief answers already produced by others and to make use of them through selective incorporation and criticism. In short, writers are not expected to reinvent the wheel; rather, they are expected to make good use of it and perhaps round it off a bit or replace a defective spoke. In order to think out your own views in writing, you are expected do some preliminary research into the views of others.

When you are trying to understand an issue, high-quality sources will inform you of the various approaches others have taken and will help you establish what the facts are. Once you are informed enough to take a position, the sources you present to your readers will inform and persuade them, just as expert witnesses are sometimes brought in to inform and persuade a jury.

Research isn't limited to the world of professors and scientists. In one way or another, everyone does research at some point. If you want to persuade your city council to increase the number of bicycle lanes on city streets, you could bolster your argument with statistics on how much money the city could save if more people rode their bikes to work. If you decide to open your own business, you would do plenty of market research to persuade your bank that you could repay a loan. Sources (whether published information or data you gather yourself through interviews, surveys, or observation) are not only useful for background information; well-chosen and carefully analyzed sources are evidence for your readers that you know what you're talking about and that your interpretation is sound.

In Chapters 5 and 6 we discussed *ethos* as an appeal that establishes credibility with readers. When you do competent research and thereby let your audience see that you have done your homework, it increases your *ethos*; your audience will trust you because they see that you are well-informed, offering them not just your opinions but also an awareness of other opinions and of the relevant facts. Conducting thorough research not only helps you to develop your argument but it also shows respect for your audience.

Research is often misconstrued as the practice of transcribing information. In fact, it's a process of asking questions and gathering information that helps you come to conclusions about an issue. By using the information you find as evidence, you can develop an effective argument. But don't spend too much time searching and then waiting until the last minute to start writing. As you begin your search, write down observations and questions. When you find a useful source, take notes on what you think it means in your own words. This way, you won't find yourself with a pile of printouts and books and no idea what to say about them. What you have to say will flow naturally out of the prewriting you've already done—and that prewriting will help guide your search.

The process of research isn't always straightforward and neat. It involves scanning what other people have said about a topic and seeing what kinds of questions have been raised. As you poke and pry, you will learn more about the issue, and that, in turn, will help you develop a question to focus your efforts. Once you have a central idea—a thesis—you can sharpen your search to seek out the evidence that will make your readers sit up and take notice.

Consider arguments about whether athletes should be permitted to take anabolic steroids, drugs that supposedly build up muscle, restore energy, and enhance aggressiveness. A thoughtful argument on this subject will have to take account of information that the writer can gather only by doing some research.

- Do steroids really have the effects commonly attributed to them?
- Are they dangerous?
- If they are dangerous, how dangerous are they?

After all, competitive sports are inherently dangerous, some of them highly so. Many boxers, mixed martial arts fighters, jockeys, and football players have suffered severe injury, even death, from competing. Does anyone believe that anabolic steroids are more dangerous than the contests themselves? Obviously, again, a respectable argument about steroids will have to show awareness of what is known about them.

Or take this question:

Why did President Truman order that atomic bombs be dropped on Hiroshima and Nagasaki?

The most obvious answer is to end the war, but some historians believe he had a very different purpose. In their view, Japan's defeat was ensured before the bombs were dropped, and the Japanese were ready to surrender; the bombs were dropped not to save American (or Japanese) lives but to show Russia that the United States would not be pushed around. Scholars who hold this view, such as Gar Alperovitz in *Atomic Diplomacy* (1965), argue that Japanese civilians in Hiroshima and Nagasaki were incinerated not to save the lives of American soldiers who otherwise would have died in an invasion of Japan but to teach Stalin a lesson. Dropping the bombs, it is argued, marked not the end of the Pacific War but the beginning of the cold war.

One must ask: What evidence supports this argument or claim or thesis, which assumes that Truman could not have thought the bomb was needed to defeat the Japanese because the Japanese knew they were defeated and would soon surrender without a hard-fought defense that would cost hundreds of thousands of lives? What about the momentum that had built up to use the bomb? After all, years of effort and $2 billion had been expended to produce a weapon with the intention of using it to end the war against Germany. But Germany had been defeated without the use of the bomb. Meanwhile, the war in the Pacific continued unabated. If the argument we are considering is correct, all this background counted for little or nothing in Truman's decision, a decision purely diplomatic and coolly indifferent to human life. The task for the writer is to evaluate the evidence available and then to argue for or against the view that Truman's purpose in dropping the bomb was to impress the Soviet government.

A student writing on the topic will certainly want to consult the chief books on the subject (Alperovitz's, cited above, Martin Sherwin's *A World Destroyed* [1975], and John Toland's *The Rising Sun* [1970]) and perhaps reviews of them, especially the reviews in journals devoted to political science. (Reading a searching review of a serious scholarly book is a good way to identify quickly some of the book's main contributions and controversial claims.) Truman's letters and statements and books and articles about Truman are also clearly relevant, and doubtless important articles are to be found in recent issues of scholarly journals and electronic sources. In fact, even an essay on such a topic as whether Truman was morally justified in using the atomic bomb for *any* purpose will be a stronger essay if it is well-informed about such matters as the estimated loss of life that an invasion would have cost, the international rules governing weapons, and Truman's own statements about the issue.

How does one go about finding the material needed to write a well-informed argument? We will provide help, but first we want to offer a few words about choosing a topic.

CHOOSING A TOPIC

We will be brief. If a topic is not assigned, choose one that

- interests you and
- can be researched with reasonable thoroughness in the allotted time.

Topics such as censorship, the environment, and sexual harassment obviously impinge on our lives, and it may well be that one such topic is of especial interest to you. But the scope of these topics makes researching them potentially overwhelming. Type the word *censorship* into an **Internet** search engine, and you will be referred to millions of information sources.

This brings us to our second point—a manageable topic. Any of the previous topics would need to be narrowed substantially before you could begin searching in earnest. Similarly, a topic such as the causes of World War II can hardly be mastered in a few weeks or argued in a ten-page paper. It is simply too big.

You can, however, write a solid paper analyzing, evaluating, and arguing for or against General Eisenhower's views on atomic warfare. What were they, and when did he hold them? (In his books of 1948 and 1963 Eisenhower says that he opposed the use of the bomb before Hiroshima and that he argued with Secretary of War Henry Stimson against dropping it, but what evidence supports these claims? Was Eisenhower attempting to rewrite history in his books?) Eisenhower's own writings and books and other information sources on Eisenhower will, of course, be the major sources for a paper on this topic, but you will also want to look at books and articles about Stimson and at publications that contain information about the views of other generals, so that, for instance, you can compare Eisenhower's view with Marshall's or MacArthur's.

Spend a little time exploring a topic to see if it will be interesting and manageable by taking one or more of these approaches.

- Do a Web search on the topic. Though you may not use any of the sites that turn up, you can quickly put your finger on the pulse of popular approaches to the issue by scanning the first page or two of results to see what issues are getting the most attention.

- Plug the topic into one of the library's article databases. Again, just by scanning titles you can get a sense of what questions are being raised.

- Browse the library shelves where books on the topic are kept. A quick check of the tables of contents of recently published books may give you ideas of how to narrow the topic.

- Ask a librarian to show you where specialized reference books on your topic are found. Instead of general encyclopedias, try sources like these:
  CQ Researcher
  Encyclopedia of Applied Ethics
  Encyclopedia of Bioethics
  Encyclopedia of Crime and Justice
  Encyclopedia of Science, Technology, and Ethics

- Talk to an expert. Members of the faculty who specialize in the area of your topic might be able to spell out some of the most significant controversies around a topic and may point you toward key sources.

FINDING MATERIAL

What strategy you use for finding good sources will depend on your topic. Researching a current issue in politics or popular culture may involve reading recent newspaper articles, scanning information on government Web sites, and locating current statistics. Other topics may be best tackled by seeking out books and scholarly journal articles that are less timely but more in-depth and analytical. You may want to supplement library and Web sources with your own fieldwork by conducting surveys or interviews.

Critical thinking is crucial to every step of the research process. Whatever strategy you use, remember that you will want to find material that is authoritative, represents a balanced approach to the issues, and is persuasive. As you choose your sources, bear in mind they will be serving as your "expert witnesses" as you make a case to your audience. Their quality and credibility are crucial to your argument.

If you find what seems to be an excellent source, look at some of the sources that this author repeatedly cites.

Finding Quality Information on the Web

The Web is a valuable source of information for many topics and less helpful for others. In general, if you're looking for information on public policy, popular culture, current events, legal affairs, or for any subject of interest to agencies of the federal or state government, the Web is likely to have useful material. If you're looking for literary criticism or scholarly analysis of historical or social issues, you will be better off using library databases, described later in this chapter.

To make good use of the Web, try these strategies.

- Use the most specific terms possible when using a general search engine; put phrases in quotes.

- Use the advanced search option to limit a search to a domain (e.g., *.gov* for government sites) or by date (such as Web sites updated in the past week or month).

- If you're not sure which sites might be good ones for research, try starting with one of the selective directories listed below instead of a general search engine.

- Consider which government agencies and organizations might be interested in your topic and go directly to their Web sites.

- Follow "about" links to see who is behind a Web site and why they put the information on the Web. If there is no "about" link, delete everything after the first slash in the URL to go to the parent site to see if it provides information.

- Use clues in URLs to see where sites originate. For example, URLs containing *.k12* are hosted at elementary and secondary schools, so may be intended for a young audience; those ending in *.gov* are government agencies, so they tend to provide official information.

- Always bear in mind that the sources you choose must be persuasive to your audience. Avoid sites that may be dismissed as unreliable or biased.

Some useful Web sites include the following:

Selective Web Site Directories
  Infomine <http://infomine.ucr.edu/>
  ipl2 <http://www.ipl.org>
  Open Directory Project <http://www.dmoz.org>

Current News Sources
  Google News <http://news.google.com>
  Kidon Media-Link <http://www.kidon.com/media-link/index.php>

Digital Primary Sources
  American Memory <http://memory.loc.gov>
  American Rhetoric <http://www.americanrhetoric.com>
  Avalon Project <http://avalon.law.yale.edu/default.asp>

Government Information
  GPO Access <http://www.gpoaccess.gov>
  Thomas (federal legislation) <http://thomas.loc.gov>
  University of Michigan Documents Center <http://www.lib.umich.edu/
    govdocs/>

Scholarly or Scientific Information
  Google Scholar <http://scholar.google.com>
  Scirus <http://www.scirus.com/>

Statistical Information
  American FactFinder <http://factfinder2.census.gov>
  Fedstats <http://www.fedstats.gov>
  Pew Global Attitudes Project <http://pewglobal.org>
  U.S. Census Bureau <http://www.census.gov>

A WORD ABOUT WIKIPEDIA

Links to Wikipedia (http://www.wikipedia.org) often rise to the top of Web search results. This vast and decentralized site provides over a million articles on a wide variety of topics. However, anyone can contribute to the online encyclopedia, so the accuracy of articles varies, and in some cases, the coverage of a controversial issue is one-sided or disputed. Even when the articles are accurate, they provide only basic information. Wikipedia's founder, Jimmy Wales, cautions students against using it as a source, except for obtaining general background knowledge: "You're in college; don't cite the encyclopedia."[1] Still, Wikipedia often provides valuable bibliographies that will help you to get going.

Finding Articles Using Library Databases

Your library has a wide range of general and specialized databases available through its Web site. Some databases provide references to articles (and perhaps abstracts or summaries) or may provide direct links to the entire text of articles. General and interdisciplinary databases include Academic Search Premier (produced by the EBSCOhost company) and Expanded Academic Index (from InfoTrac).

More specialized databases include PsycINFO (for psychology research) and ERIC (focused on topics in education). Others, such as JSTOR, are full-text digital archives of scholarly journals. You will likely have access to newspaper articles through LexisNexis or Proquest Newsstand, particularly useful for articles that are not available for free on the Web. Look at your library's Web site to see what your options are, or stop by the reference desk for a quick personalized tutorial.

[1]"Wikipedia Founder Discourages Academic Use of His Creation," *Chronicle of Higher Education: The Wired Campus,* 12 June 2006, 16 Nov. 2006. http://chronicle.com/wiredcampus/ article/ 1328/wikipedia-founder-discourages-academic-use-of-his-creation

FIGURE 7.1   AN ADVANCED WEB SEARCH

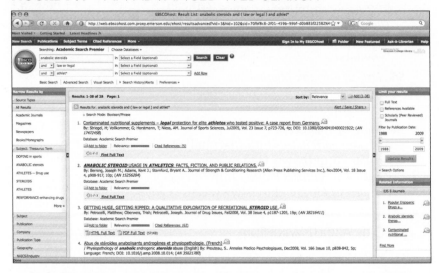

When using databases, first think through your topic using the listing and diagramming techniques described on pages 230–31. List synonyms for your key search terms. As you search, look at words used in titles and descriptors for alternative ideas and make use of the "advanced search" option so that you can easily combine multiple terms. Rarely will you find exactly what you're looking for right away. Try different search terms and different ways to narrow your topic.

Most databases have an advanced search option that offers forms for combining multiple terms. In Figure 7.1, a search on "anabolic steroids" retrieved far too many articles. In this advanced search, three concepts are being combined in a search: anabolic steroids, legal aspects of their use, and use of them by athletes. Related terms are combined with the word "or": *law* or *legal*. The last letters of a word have been replaced with an asterisk so that any ending will be included in the search. *Athlet** will search for *athlete, athletes,* or *athletics.* Options on both sides of the list of articles retrieved offer opportunities to refine a search by date of publication or to restrict the results to only academic journals, magazines, or newspapers.

As with a Web search, you'll need to make critical choices about which articles are worth pursuing. In this example, the first article may not be useful because it concerns German law. The second and third look fairly current and potentially useful. Only the third has a full text link, but the others may be available in another database. Many libraries have a program that will check other databases for you at the push of a button; in this case it's indicated by the "Find full text" button.

As you choose sources, keep track of them by selecting them. Then you can print off, save, or e-mail yourself the references you have selected. You may also have an option to export references to a citation management program such as RefWorks or EndNote. These programs allow you to create your own personal database of sources in which you can store your references and take notes. Later, when you're ready to create a bibliography, these programs will automatically format your references in MLA, APA, or another style. Ask a librarian if one of these programs is available to students on your campus.

Locating Books

The books that your library owns can be found through its online catalog. Typically, you can search by author or title or, if you don't have a specific book in mind, by keyword or subject. As with databases, think about different search terms to use, keeping an eye out for subject headings used for books that appear relevant. Take advantage of an "advanced search" option. You may, for example, be able to limit a search to books on a particular topic in English published within recent years. In addition to books, the catalog will also list DVDs, sound recordings, and other formats.

Unlike articles, books tend to cover broad topics, so be prepared to broaden your search terms. It may be that a book has a chapter or ten pages that are precisely what you need, but the catalog typically doesn't index the contents of books in detail. Think instead of what kind of book might contain the information you need.

Once you've found some promising books in the catalog, note down the call numbers, find them on the shelves, and then browse. Since books on the same topic are shelved together, you can quickly see what additional books are available by scanning the shelves. As you browse, be sure to look for books that have been published recently enough for your purposes. You do not have to read a book cover-to-cover to use it in your research. Instead, skim the introduction to see if it will be useful, then use its table of contents and index to pinpoint the sections of the book that are the most relevant.

If you have a very specific name or phrase you are searching for, you might try typing it into Google Book Search (http://books.google.com), which searches the contents of over 7 million scanned books. Though it tends to retrieve too many results for most topics, and you may only be able to see a snippet of context, it can help you locate a particular quote or identify which books might include an unusual name or phrase. There is a "find in a library" link that will help you determine whether the books are available in your library.

INTERVIEWING PEERS AND LOCAL AUTHORITIES

You ought to try to consult experts—for instance, members of the faculty or other local authorities on art, business, law, and so forth. You can also consult interested laypersons. Remember, however, that experts have their biases and that "ordinary" people may have knowledge that experts lack. When interviewing experts, keep in mind Picasso's comment: "You mustn't always believe what I say. Questions tempt you to tell lies, particularly when there is no answer."

If you are interviewing your peers, you will probably want to make an effort to get a representative sample. Of course, even within a group not all members share a single view—many African Americans favor affirmative action but not all do, and many gays favor legalizing gay marriage but, again, some don't. Make an effort to talk to a range of people who might be expected to offer varied opinions. You may learn some unexpected things.

Here we will concentrate, however, on interviews with experts.

1. **Finding subjects for interviews**   If you are looking for expert opinions, you may want to start with a faculty member on your campus. You may already know the instructor, or you may have to scan the catalog to see who teaches courses relevant to your topic. Department secretaries and college Web sites are good sources of information about the special interests of the faculty and also about lecturers who will be visiting the campus.

2. **Doing preliminary homework**   (a) In requesting the interview, make evident your interest in the topic and in the person. (If you know something about the person, you will be able to indicate why you are asking him or her.) (b) Request the interview, preferably in writing, a week in advance, and ask for ample time—probably half an hour to an hour. Indicate whether the material will be confidential, and (if you want to use a recorder) ask if you may record the interview. (c) If the person accepts the invitation, ask if he or she recommends any preliminary reading, and establish a time and a suitable place, preferably not the cafeteria during lunchtime.

3. **Preparing thoroughly**   (a) If your interviewee recommended any reading or has written on the topic, read the material. (b) Tentatively formulate some questions, keeping in mind that (unless you are simply gathering material for a survey of opinions) you want more than yes or no answers. Questions beginning with *Why* and *How* will usually require the interviewee to go beyond yes and no.

Even if your subject has consented to let you bring a recorder, be prepared to take notes on points that strike you as especially significant; without written notes, you will have nothing if the recorder has malfunctioned. Further, by taking occasional notes you will give the interviewee some time to think and perhaps to rephrase or to amplify a remark.

4. **Conducting the interview**   (a) Begin by engaging in brief conversation, without taking notes. If the interviewee has agreed to let you use a recorder, settle on the place where you will put it. (b) Come prepared with an opening question or two, but as the interview proceeds,

don't hesitate to ask questions that you had not anticipated asking. (c) Near the end (you and your subject have probably agreed on the length of the interview) ask the subject if he or she wishes to add anything, perhaps by way of clarifying some earlier comment. (d) Conclude by thanking the interviewee and by offering to provide a copy of the final version of your paper.

5. **Writing up the interview**   (a) As soon as possible—certainly within twenty-four hours after the interview—review your notes and clarify them. At this stage, you can still remember the meaning of your abbreviated notes and shorthand devices (maybe you have been using *n* to stand for *nurses* in clinics where abortions are performed), but if you wait even a whole day you may be puzzled by your own notes. If you have recorded the interview, you may want to transcribe all of it—the laboriousness of this task is one good reason why many interviewers do not use recorders—and you may then want to scan the whole and mark the parts that now strike you as especially significant. If you have taken notes by hand, type them up, along with your own observations, for example, "Jones was very tentative on this matter, but she said she was inclined to believe that. . . ." (b) Be especially careful to indicate which words are direct quotations. If in doubt, check with the interviewee.

EVALUATING YOUR SOURCES

Each step of the way, you will be making choices about your sources. As your research proceeds, from selecting promising items in a database search to browsing the book collection, you will want to use the techniques for previewing and skimming detailed on pages 34–35 in order to make your first selection. Ask yourself some basic questions.

- Is this source relevant?
- Is it current enough?
- Does the title and/or abstract suggest it will address an important aspect of my topic?
- Am I choosing sources that represent a range of ideas, not simply ones that support my opinion?
- Do I have a reason to believe that these sources are trustworthy?

Once you have collected a number of likely sources, you will want to do further filtering. Examine each one with these questions in mind.

- *Is this source credible? Does it include information about the author and his or her credentials that can help me decide whether to rely on it?* In the case of books, you might check a database for book reviews for a second opinion. In the case of Web sites, find out where the site came from and why it has been posted on the Web. Don't use a Web source if you can't determine its authorship or purpose.

- *Will my audience find this source credible and persuasive?* Some publishers are more selective about which books they publish than others. University presses, for instance, have several experts read and comment on manuscripts before they decide which to publish. A story about U.S. politics from the *Washington Post,* whose writers conduct firsthand reporting in the nation's capital, carries more clout than a story from a small-circulation newspaper that is drawing its information from a wire service. A scholarly source may be more impressive than a magazine article.

- *Am I using the best evidence available?* Quoting directly from a government report may be more effective than quoting a news story that summarizes the report. Finding evidence that supports your claims in a president's speeches or letters is more persuasive than drawing your conclusions from a page or two of a history textbook.

- *Am I being fair to all sides?* Make sure you are prepared to address alternate perspectives, even if you ultimately take a position. Avoid sources that clearly promote an agenda in favor of ones that your audience will consider balanced and reliable.

- *Can I corroborate my key claims in more than one source?* Compare your sources to ensure that you aren't relying on facts that can't be confirmed. If you're having trouble confirming a source, check with a librarian.

- *Do I really need this source?* It's tempting to use all the books and articles you have found, but if two sources say essentially the same thing, choose the one that is likely to carry the most weight with your audience.

The information you will look for as you evaluate a Web source is often the same as what you need to record in a citation. You can streamline the process of creating a list of works cited by identifying these elements as you evaluate a source.

In Figure 7.2, the URL includes the ending *.gov*—meaning it is a government Web site, an official document that has been vetted. There is an "about" link that will explain the government agency's mission. The date is found at the bottom of the page: "revised 2006." This appears to be a high-quality source of basic information on the issue.

The information you need to cite this report is also on the page; make sure you keep track of where you found the source and when, since Web sites can change. One way to do this is by creating an account

FIGURE 7.2   A HOMEPAGE FROM A GOVERNMENT WEB SITE

1 URL—Site has a .gov domain.

2 Sponsor

3 Author

4 Link will explain that this institute is a government agency.

5 Corporate author

6 Web site name

7 Title of page

8 Table of contents

9 Scanning list will give an idea of whether source is reliable and useful.

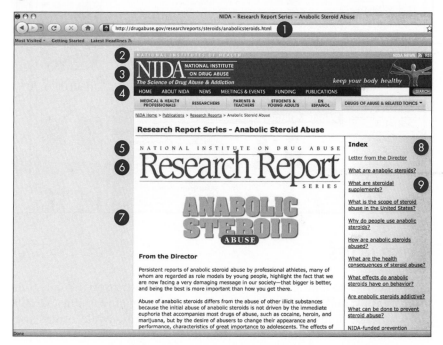

at a social bookmarking site such as Delicious (http://delicious.com) or Diigo (http://diigo.com) where you can store and annotate Web sites.

Figure 7.3 shows how the information on a Web page might lead you to reject it as a source. Clearly, though this site purports to provide educational information, its primary purpose is to sell products. The graphics emphasize the supposed benefits of these performance-enhancing drugs, a visual incentive to promote their use. The disclaimers about legal liability and age requirements send up a red flag.

FIGURE 7.3   A HOMEPAGE FROM A COMMERCIAL WEB SITE

This is a .com (commercial) site.

Table of contents looks useful, but . . .   Images seem to promote steriod use.

Disclaimers seem defensive.   Steroids are for sale.

TAKING NOTES

When it comes to taking notes, all researchers have their own habits that they swear by, and they can't imagine any other way of working. We still prefer to take notes on four-by-six-inch index cards, while others use a notebook or a computer for note taking. If you use a citation management program, such as RefWorks or EndNote, you can store your personal notes and commentary with the citations you have saved. Using the program's search function, you can easily pull together related notes and citations, or you can create project folders for your references so that you can easily review what you've collected.

Whatever method you use, the following techniques should help you maintain consistency and keep organized during the research process:

1. If you use a notebook or cards, write in ink (pencil gets smudgy), and write on only one side of the card or paper. (Notes on the backs of cards tend to get lost, and writing on the back of paper will prevent you from later cutting up and rearranging your notes.) Con-

✓ A CHECKLIST FOR EVALUATING PRINT SOURCES

For Books:

☐ Is the book recent? If not, is the information I will be using from it likely or unlikely to change over time?

☐ What are the author's credentials?

☐ Is the book titled toward entertainment, or is it in-depth and even-handed?

☐ Is the book broad enough in its focus and written in a style I can understand?

☐ Does the book relate directly to my tentative thesis, or is it of only tangential interest?

☐ Do the arguments in the book seem sound, based on what I have learned about skillful critical reading and writing?

For Articles from Periodicals:

☐ Is the periodical recent?

☐ Is the author's name given? Does he or she seem a credible source?

☐ Does the article treat the topic superficially or in-depth? Does it take sides, or does it offer enough context so that you can make up your own mind?

☐ How directly does the article speak to my topic and tentative thesis?

☐ If the article is from a scholarly journal, am I sure I understand it?

sider using an online tool to keep up with your notes and ideas, for instance, a Google Doc, private blog, or wiki.

2. Summarize, for the most part, rather than quote at length.

3. Quote only passages in which the writing is especially effective or passages that are in some way crucial. These will be easy to access and use if kept in an online venue.

4. Make sure that all quotations are exact. Enclose quoted words within quotation marks, indicate omissions by ellipses (three spaced periods: . . .), and enclose within square brackets ([]) any insertions or other additions you make.

5. *Never* copy a passage, changing an occasional word. *Either* copy it word for word, with punctuation intact, and enclose it within quotation marks, *or* summarize it drastically. If you copy a passage but change a word here and there, you may later make the mistake of using your note verbatim in your essay, and you will be guilty of plagiarism.

6. Give the page number of your source, whether you summarize or quote. If a quotation you have copied runs in the original from the bottom of page 210 to the top of page 211, in your notes put

✓ A CHECKLIST FOR EVALUATING ELECTRONIC SOURCES

An enormous amount of valuable material is available on the World Wide Web—but so is an enormous amount of junk. True, there is also plenty of junk in books and journals, but most printed material has been subjected to a review process: Book publishers and editors of journals send manuscripts to specialized readers who evaluate them and recommend whether the material should or should not be published. Publishing on the Web is quite different. Anyone can publish on the Web with no review process: All that is needed is sufficient access to the Internet. Ask yourself:

☐ What person or organization produced the site (a commercial entity, a nonprofit entity, a student, an expert)? Check the electronic address to get a clue about the authorship. If there is a link to the author's homepage, check it out to learn about the author. Does the author have an affiliation with a respectable institution?

☐ What is the purpose of the site? Is the site in effect an infomercial, or is it an attempt to contribute to a thoughtful discussion?

☐ Are the sources of information indicated and verifiable? If possible, check the sources.

☐ Is the site authoritative enough to use? (If it seems to contain review materials or class handouts, you probably don't want to take it too seriously.)

☐ When was the page made available? Is it out of date?

a diagonal line (/) after the last word on page 210, so that later, if in your paper you quote only the material from page 210, you will know that you must cite 210 and not 210–11.

7. Indicate the source. The author's last name is enough if you have consulted only one work by the author; but if you consult more than one work by an author, you need further identification, such as both the author's name and a short title.

8. Add your own comments about the substance of what you are recording. Such comments as "but contrast with Sherwin" or "seems illogical" or "evidence?" will ensure that you are thinking as well as writing and will be of value when you come to transform your notes into a draft. Be sure, however, to enclose such notes within double diagonals (//), or to mark them in some other way, so that later you will know they are yours and not your source's. If you use a computer for note taking, you may wish to write your comments in italics or in a different font.

9. In a separate computer file or notebook page or on separate index cards, write a bibliographic entry for each source. The information in each entry will vary, depending on whether the source is a book,

a periodical, an electronic document, and so forth. The kind of information (for example, author and title) needed for each type of source can be found in the sections on MLA Format: The List of Works Cited (p. 301) or APA Format: The List of References (p. 314).

A NOTE ON PLAGIARIZING, PARAPHRASING, AND USING COMMON KNOWLEDGE

Plagiarism is the unacknowledged use of someone else's work. The word comes from a Latin word for "kidnapping," and plagiarism is indeed the stealing of something engendered by someone else. We won't deliver a sermon on the dishonesty (and folly) of plagiarism; we intend only to help you understand exactly what plagiarism is. The first thing to say is that plagiarism is not limited to the unacknowledged quotation of words.

A *paraphrase* is a sort of word-by-word or phrase-by-phrase translation of the author's language into your own language. Unlike a summary, then, a paraphrase is approximately as long as the original. Why would anyone paraphrase something? There are two good reasons:

- You may, as a reader, want to paraphrase a passage in order to make certain that you are thinking carefully about each word in the original;
- You may, as a writer, want to paraphrase a difficult passage in order to help your reader.

Paraphrase thus has its uses, but it is often unnecessarily used, and students who overuse it may find themselves crossing the border into plagiarism. True, if you paraphrase you are using your own words, but

- you are also using someone else's ideas, and, equally important,
- you are using this other person's sequence of thoughts.

Even if you change every third word in your source, you are plagiarizing. Here is an example of this sort of plagiarism, based on the previous sentence:

> Even if you alter every second or third word that your source gives, you still are plagiarizing.

Further, even if the writer of this paraphrase had cited a source after the paraphrase, he or she would still have been guilty of plagiarism. How, you may ask, can a writer who cites a source be guilty of plagiarism? Easy. Readers assume that only the gist of the idea is the source's and that the development of the idea—the way it is set forth—is the present writer's work. A paraphrase that runs to several sentences is in no significant way the writer's work: The writer is borrowing not only the idea but the shape of the presentation, the sentence structure. What the writer needs to do is to write something like this:

> Changing an occasional word does not free the writer from the obligation to cite a source.

And the source would still need to be cited, if the central idea were not a commonplace one.

The point that even if you cite a source for your paraphrase you are nevertheless plagiarizing—unless you clearly indicate that the entire passage is a paraphrase of the source—cannot be overemphasized.

You are plagiarizing if, without giving credit, you use someone else's ideas—even if you put these ideas entirely into your own words. When you use another's ideas, you must indicate your indebtedness by saying something like "Alperovitz points out that . . ." or "Secretary of War Stimson, as Martin Sherwin notes, never expressed himself on this point." Alperovitz and Sherwin pointed out something that you had not thought of, and so you must give them credit if you want to use their findings.

Again, even if after a paraphrase you cite your source, you are plagiarizing. How, you may wonder, can you be guilty of plagiarism if you cite a source? Easy. A reader assumes that the citation refers to information or an opinion, *not* to the presentation or development of the idea; and of course, in a paraphrase you are not presenting or developing the material in your own way.

Now consider this question: *Why* paraphrase? Often there is no good answer. Since a paraphrase is as long as the original, you may as well quote the original, if you think that a passage of that length is worth quoting. Probably it is *not* worth quoting in full; probably you should *not* paraphrase but rather should drastically *summarize* most of it, and perhaps quote a particularly effective phrase or two. As we explained on pages 39–45, the chief reason to paraphrase a passage is to clarify it—that is, to make certain that you and your readers understand a passage that—perhaps because it is badly written—is obscure.

Generally, what you should do is

- Take the idea and put it entirely into your own words, perhaps reducing a paragraph of a hundred words to a sentence of ten words, but you must still give credit for the idea.

- If you believe that the original hundred words are so perfectly put that they cannot be transformed without great loss, you'll have to quote them in full and cite your source. You may in this case want to tell the reader *why* you are quoting at such great length.

In short, chiefly you will quote or you will summarize, and only rarely will you paraphrase, but in all cases you will cite your source. There is no point in paraphrasing an author's hundred words into a hundred of your own. Either quote or summarize, but cite the source.

✓ A CHECKLIST FOR AVOIDING PLAGIARISM

☐ In my notes did I *always* put quoted material within quotation marks?

☐ In my notes did I summarize *in my own words* and give credit to the source for the idea?

☐ In my notes did I avoid paraphrasing, that is, did I avoid copying, keeping the structure of the source's sentences but using some of my own words? (Paraphrases of this sort, even with a footnote citing the source, are *not* acceptable, since the reader incorrectly assumes that the writing is essentially yours.)

☐ If in my paper I set forth a borrowed idea, do I give credit, even though the words and the shape of the sentences are entirely my own?

☐ If in my paper I quote directly, do I put the words within quotation marks and cite the source?

☐ Do I *not* cite material that can be considered common knowledge (material that can be found in numerous reference works, such as the date of a public figure's birth or the population of San Francisco or the fact that *Hamlet* is regarded as a great tragedy)?

☐ If I have the slightest doubt about whether I should or should not cite a source, have I taken the safe course and cited the source?

Keep in mind, too, that almost all generalizations about human nature, no matter how common and familiar (for instance, "males are innately more aggressive than females") are not indisputable facts; they are at best hypotheses on which people differ and therefore should either not be asserted at all or should be supported by some cited source or authority. Similarly, because nearly all statistics (whether on the intelligence of criminals or the accuracy of lie detectors) are the result of some particular research and may well have been superseded or challenged by other investigators, it is advisable to cite a source for any statistics you use unless you are convinced they are indisputable, such as the number of registered voters in Memphis in 1988.

On the other hand, there is something called **common knowledge,** and the sources for such information need not be cited. The term does not, however, mean exactly what it seems to. It is common knowledge, of course, that Ronald Reagan was an American president (so you don't cite a source when you make that statement), and under the conventional interpretation of this doctrine, it is also common knowledge that he was born in 1911. In fact, of course, few people other than Reagan's wife and children know this date. Still, information that can be found in many places and that is indisputable belongs to all of us; therefore, a writer need not cite her source when she says that Reagan was born in 1911. Probably she checked a dictionary or an encyclopedia for the date, but the source doesn't matter. Dozens of sources will give exactly the same information, and in fact, no reader wants to be bothered with a citation on such a point.

Some students have a little trouble developing a sense of what is and what is not common knowledge. Although, as we have just said, readers don't want to hear about the sources for information that is indisputable and can be documented in many places, if you are in doubt about whether to cite a source, cite it. Better risk boring the reader a bit than risk being accused of plagiarism.

Your college probably has issued a statement concerning plagiarism. If there is such a statement, be sure to read it carefully.

COMPILING AN ANNOTATED BIBLIOGRAPHY

When several sources have been identified and gathered, many researchers prepare an annotated bibliography. This is a list providing all relevant bibliographic information (just as it will appear in your Works Cited list or References list) as well as a brief descriptive and evaluative summary of each source—perhaps one to three sentences. Your instructor may ask you to provide an annotated bibliography for your research project.

An annotated bibliography serves four main purposes:

- First, constructing such a document helps you to master the material contained in any given source. To find the heart of the argument presented in an article or book, phrase it briefly, and comment on it, you must understand it fully.

- Second, creating an annotated bibliography helps you to think about how each portion of your research fits into the whole of your project, how you will use it, and how it relates to your topic and thesis.

- Third, an annotated bibliography helps your readers: They can quickly see which items may be especially helpful in their own research.

- Fourth, in constructing an annotated bibliography at this early stage, you will get some hands-on practice at bibliographic format, thereby easing the job of creating your final bibliography (the Works Cited list or References list for your paper).

Following are two examples of entries for an annotated bibliography in MLA (Modern Language Association) format for a project on the effect of violence in the media. The first is for a book, the second for an article from a periodical. Notice that each

- begins with a bibliographic entry—author (last name first), title, and so forth—and then

- provides information about the content of the work under consideration, suggesting how each may be of use to the final research paper.

Clover, Carol J. *Men, Women, and Chain Saws: Gender in the Modern Horror Film*. Princeton: Princeton UP, 1992. The author focuses on Hollywood horror movies of the 1970s and 1980s. She studies representations of women and girls in these movies and the responses of male viewers to female characters, suggesting that this relationship is more complex and less exploitative than the common wisdom claims.

Winerip, Michael. "Looking for an Eleven O'Clock Fix." *New York Times Magazine* 11 Jan. 1998: 30-40. The article focuses on the rising levels of violence on local television news and highlights a station in Orlando, Florida, that tried to reduce its depictions of violence and lost viewers as a result. Winerip suggests that people only claim to be against media violence, while their actions prove otherwise.

As you construct your annotated bibliography, consider posting your Word document in Google Drive for easy access and sharing.

A Rule for Writers: Citation Generators

There are many citation generators available online. These generators allow you to enter the information about your source, and, with a click, they will create Works Cited entries in APA or MLA format. But just as you cannot trust spell- and grammar-checkers in Microsoft Word, you cannot trust these generators. You can use them to cite works, but if you do, be sure to double-check what they produce before submitting your essay. Always remember that responsible writers take care to cite their sources properly and that failure to do so puts you at risk for accusations of plagiarism.

WRITING THE PAPER

Organizing Your Notes

If you have read thoughtfully, taken careful (and, again, thoughtful) notes on your reading, and then (yet again) thought about these notes, you are well on the way to writing a good paper. You have, in fact, already written some of it, in your notes. By now you should clearly have in mind the thesis you intend to argue. But you still have to organize the material, and, doubtless, even as you set about organizing it, you will find points that will require you to do some additional research and much additional thinking.

Divide your notes into clusters, each devoted to one theme or point (for instance, one cluster on the extent of use of steroids, another on evidence that steroids are harmful, yet another on arguments that even if harmful they should be permitted). If your notes are in a computer file, rearrange the notes into appropriate clusters. If you use index cards, simply sort them into packets. If you take notes in a notebook, either mark each note with a number or name indicating the cluster to which it belongs, or cut the notes apart and arrange them as you would cards. Put aside all notes that—however interesting—you now see are irrelevant to your paper.

Next, arrange the clusters or packets into a tentative sequence. In effect, you are preparing a **working outline.** At its simplest, say, you will give three arguments on behalf of X and then three counterarguments. (Or you might decide that it is better to alternate material from the two sets of three clusters each, following each argument with an objection. At this stage, you can't be sure of the organization you will finally use, but you can make a tentative decision.)

The First Draft

Draft the essay, without worrying much about an elegant opening paragraph. Just write some sort of adequate opening that states the topic and your thesis. When you revise the whole later, you can put some effort into developing an effective opening. (Most experienced writers find that the opening paragraph in the final version is almost the last thing they write.)

If your notes are on cards or notebook paper, carefully copy into the draft all quotations that you plan to use. If your notes are in a computer, you may simply cut and paste them from one file to another. Do keep in mind, however, that rewriting or retyping quotations will make you think carefully about them and may result in a more focused and thoughtful paper. (In the next section of this chapter we will talk briefly about leading into quotations and about the form of quotations.) Be sure to include citations in your drafts so that if you must check a reference later it will be easy to do so.

Later Drafts

Give the draft, and yourself, a rest—perhaps for a day or two—and then go back to it. Read it over, make necessary revisions, and then **outline** it. That is, on a sheet of paper chart the organization and development, perhaps by jotting down a sentence summarizing each paragraph or each group of closely related paragraphs. Your outline or map may now show you that the paper obviously suffers from poor organization. For instance, it may reveal that you neglected to respond to one argument or that one point is needlessly treated in two places. It may also help you to see that if you gave three arguments and then three counterarguments, you probably should instead have followed each argument with its rebuttal. On the other hand, if you alternated arguments and objections, it may now seem better to use two main groups, all the arguments and then all the criticisms.

No one formula is always right. Much will depend on the complexity of the material. If the arguments are highly complex, it is better to respond to them one by one than to expect a reader to hold three complex arguments in mind before you get around to responding. If, however, the arguments can be stated briefly and clearly, it is effective to state all three and then to go on to the responses. If you write on a computer, you will find it easy, even fun, to move passages of text around. Even so, you will probably want to print out a hard copy from time to time to review the structure of your paper. Allow enough time to produce several drafts.

A Few More Words about Organization

There is a difference between

- a paper that *has* an organization and
- a paper that helpfully lets the reader know what the organization is.

Write papers of the second sort, but (there is always a "but") take care not to belabor the obvious. Inexperienced writers sometimes either hide the organization so thoroughly that a reader cannot find it or they so ploddingly lay out the structure ("Eighth, I will show...") that the reader becomes impatient. Yet it is better to be overly explicit than to be obscure.

The ideal, of course, is the middle route. Make the overall strategy of your organization evident by occasional explicit signs at the beginning of a paragraph ("We have seen...," "It is time to consider the objections...," "By far the most important..."); elsewhere make certain that the implicit structure is evident to the reader. When you reread your draft, if you try to imagine that you are one of your classmates, you will probably be able to sense exactly where explicit signs are needed and where they are not needed. Better still, exchange drafts with a classmate in order to exchange (tactful) advice.

Choosing a Tentative Title

By now a couple of tentative titles for your essay should have crossed your mind. If possible, choose a title that is both interesting and informative. Consider these three titles:

Are Steroids Harmful?

The Fuss over Steroids

Steroids: A Dangerous Game

"Are Steroids Harmful?" is faintly interesting, and it lets the reader know the gist of the subject, but it gives no clue about the writer's thesis, the writer's contention or argument. "The Fuss over Steroids" is somewhat better, for it gives information about the writer's position. "Steroids: A Dangerous Game" is still better; it announces the subject ("steroids") and the thesis ("dangerous"), and it also displays a touch of wit because "game" glances at the world of athletics.

Don't try too hard, however; better a simple, direct, informative title than a strained, puzzling, or overly cute one. And remember to make sure that everything in your essay is relevant to your title. In fact, your title should help you to organize the essay and to delete irrelevant material.

The Final Draft

When at last you have a draft that is for the most part satisfactory, check to make sure that **transitions** from sentence to sentence and from paragraph to paragraph are clear ("Further evidence," "On the other hand," "A weakness, however, is apparent"), and then worry about your opening and your closing paragraphs. Your **opening paragraph** should be clear, interesting, and focused; if neither the title nor the first paragraph announces your thesis, the second paragraph probably should do so.

The **final paragraph** need not say, "In conclusion, I have shown that. . . ." It should effectively end the essay, but it need not summarize your conclusions. We have already offered a few words about final paragraphs (p. 249), but the best way to learn how to write such paragraphs is to study the endings of some of the essays in this book and to adopt the strategies that appeal to you.

Be sure that all indebtedness is properly acknowledged. We have talked about plagiarism; now we will turn to the business of introducing quotations effectively.

QUOTING FROM SOURCES

Incorporating Your Reading into Your Thinking: The Art and Science of Synthesis

At the beginning of Chapter 6 we quoted a passage by Kenneth Burke (1887–1993), a college dropout who became one of America's most important twentieth-century students of rhetoric. It is worth repeating:

> Imagine that you enter a parlor. You come late. When you arrive, others have long preceded you, and they are engaged in a heated discussion, a discussion too heated for them to pause and tell you exactly what it is about. In fact, the discussion had already begun long before any of them got there, so that no one present is qualified to retrace for you all the steps that had gone before. You listen for a while, until you decide that you have caught the tenor of the argument; then you put in your oar. Someone answers; you answer him; another comes to your defense; another aligns himself against you, to either the embarrassment

or gratification of your opponent, depending upon the quality of your ally's assistance. However, the discussion is interminable. The hour grows late, you must depart. And you do depart, with the discussion still vigorously in progress.

> — *The Philosophy of Literary Form* (Baton Rouge: Louisiana State University Press, 1941), 110–11.

Why do we quote this passage? Because it is your turn to join the unending conversation.

During the process of reading, and afterward, you will want to listen, think, say to yourself something like

- "No, no, I see things very differently; it seems to me that . . . " or
- "Yes, of course, but on one large issue I think I differ," or
- "Yes, sure, I agree, but I would go further and add . . ." or
- "Yes, I agree with your conclusion, but I hold this conclusion for reasons very different from the ones that you offer."

During your composition courses, at least (and we think during your entire life), you will be reading or listening and will sometimes want to put in your oar—you will sometimes want to respond in writing, for example in the form of a Letter to the Editor or in a memo at your place of employment. In the course of your response you almost surely will have to summarize very briefly the idea or ideas you are responding to, so that your readers will understand the context of your remarks. These ideas may not come from a single source; you may be responding to several sources. For instance, you may be responding to a report and also to some comments that the report evoked. In any case, you will state these ideas briefly and fairly and will then set forth your thoughtful responses, thereby giving the reader a statement that you hope represents an advance in the argument, even if only a tiny one. That is, you will **synthesize** sources, combining existing material into something new, drawing nourishment from what has already been said (giving credit, of course), and converting it into something new—a view that you think is worth considering.

Let's pause for a moment and consider this word **synthesis.** You probably are familiar with *photosynthesis*, the chemical process in green plants that produces carbohydrates from carbon dioxide and hydrogen. Synthesis, again, combines pre-existing elements and produces something new. In our use of the word *synthesis*, even a view that you utterly reject becomes a part of your new creation *because it helped to stimulate you to formulate your view*; without the idea that you reject, you might not have developed the view that you now hold. Consider the words of Francis Bacon, Shakespeare's contemporary:

> Some books are to be tasted, others to be swallowed, and some few to be chewed and digested.

Your instructor will expect you to digest your sources—this does not mean you need to accept them but only that you need to read them thoughtfully—and that, so to speak, you make them your own thoughts by refining them. Your readers will expect you to tell them *what you make out of your sources*, which means that you will go beyond writing a summary and will synthesize the material into your own contribution. *Your* view is what is wanted, and readers expect this view to be thoughtful—not mere summary and not mere tweeting.

A RULE FOR WRITERS: In your final draft *you must give credit to all of your sources.* Let your reader know whether you are quoting (in this case, you will use quotation marks around all material directly quoted), or whether you are summarizing (you will explicitly say so), or whether you are paraphrasing (again, you will explicitly say so).

The Use and Abuse of Quotations

When is it necessary, or appropriate, to quote? Sometimes the reader must see the exact words of your source; the gist won't do. If you are arguing that Z's definition of *rights* is too inclusive, your readers have to know exactly how Z defined *rights*. Your brief summary of the definition may be unfair to Z; in fact, you want to convince your readers that you are being fair, and so you quote Z's definition, word for word. Moreover, if the passage is only a sentence or two long, or even if it runs to a paragraph, it may be so compactly stated that it defies summary. And to attempt to paraphrase it—substituting *natural* for *inalienable*, and so forth—saves no space and only introduces imprecision. There is nothing to do but to quote it, word for word.

Second, you may want to quote a passage that could be summarized but that is so effectively stated that you want your readers to have the pleasure of reading the original. Of course, readers will not give you credit for writing these words, but they will give you credit for your taste and for your effort to make especially pleasant the business of reading your paper.

In short, use (but don't overuse) quotations. Speaking roughly, quotations

- should occupy no more than 10 to 15 percent of your paper, and
- they may occupy much less.

Most of your paper should set forth your ideas, not other people's ideas.

How to Quote

Long and Short Quotations   **Long quotations** (more than four lines of typed prose or three or more lines of poetry) are set off from your text. To set off material, start on a new line, indent one inch from the left margin, and type the quotation double-spaced. Do not enclose quotations within quotation marks if you are setting them off.

Short quotations are treated differently. They are embedded within the text; they are enclosed within quotation marks, but otherwise they do not stand out.

All quotations, whether set off or embedded, must be exact. If you omit any words, you must indicate the ellipsis by substituting three spaced periods for the omission; if you insert any words or punctuation, you must indicate the addition by enclosing it within square brackets, not to be confused with parentheses.

Leading into a Quotation   Now for a less mechanical matter, the way in which a quotation is introduced. To say that it is "introduced" implies that one leads into it, though on rare occasions a quotation appears without an introduction, perhaps immediately after the title. Normally one leads into a quotation by giving

- the *name of the author* and (no less important)
- *clues signaling the content of the quotation and the purpose* it serves in the present essay. For example:

William James provides a clear answer to Huxley when he says that ". . ."

The writer has been writing about Huxley and now is signaling readers that they will be getting James's reply. The writer is also signaling (in "a clear answer") that the reply is satisfactory. If the writer believed that James's answer was not really acceptable, the lead-in might have run thus:

William James attempts to answer Huxley, but his response does not really
meet the difficulty Huxley calls attention to. James writes, ". . ."

or thus:

William James provided what he took to be an answer to Huxley when he
said that ". . ."

In this last example, clearly the words "what he took to be an answer" imply that the essayist will show, after the quotation from James, that the answer is in some degree inadequate. Or the essayist may wish to suggest the inadequacy even more strongly:

William James provided what he took to be an answer to Huxley, but
he used the word *religion* in a way that Huxley would not have allowed.
James argues that ". . ."

IDEA PROMPT 7.1 SIGNAL PHRASES

Think of your writing as a conversation between you and your sources. As in conversation, you want to be able to move smoothly between different, sometimes contrary, points of view. You also want to be able to set your thoughts apart from those of your sources. Signal phrases make it easy for your readers to know where your information came from and why it's trustworthy by including key facts about the source.

> According to psychologist Stephen Ceci . . .

> A report published by the U.S. Bureau of Justice Statistics concludes . . .

> Feminist philosopher Sandra Harding argues . . .

To avoid repetitiveness, vary your sentence structure.

> . . . claims Stephen Ceci.

> . . . according to a report published by the U.S. Bureau of Statistics.

Useful verbs to introduce sources:

acknowledges	contends	points out
argues	denies	recommends
believes	disputes	reports
claims	observes	suggests

Note that papers written using MLA style refer to sources in the present tense. Papers written in APA style use the past tense (acknowledged, argued, believed).

 A CHECKLIST FOR USING QUOTATIONS
RATHER THAN SUMMARIES

Ask yourself the following questions. If you cannot answer yes to at least one of the questions, consider *summarizing* the material rather than quoting it in full.

☐ Is the quotation given because it is necessary for the reader to see the exact wording of the original?

☐ Is the quotation given because the language is especially engaging?

☐ Is the quotation given because the author is a respected authority and the passage lends weight to my argument?

If after reading something by Huxley the writer had merely given us "William James says . . . ," we wouldn't know whether we were getting confirmation, refutation, or something else. The essayist would have put a needless burden on the readers. Generally speaking, the more difficult the quotation, the more important is the introductory or explanatory lead-in, but even the simplest quotation profits from some sort of brief lead-in, such as "James reaffirms this point when he says . . ."

> **A RULE FOR WRITERS:** In introducing a quotation, it is usually advisable to signal the reader *why* you are using the quotation by means of a lead-in consisting of a verb or a verb and adverb, such as *claims*, or *convincingly shows*, or *admits*.

DOCUMENTATION

In the course of your essay, you will probably quote or summarize material derived from a source. You must give credit, and although there is no one form of documentation to which all scholarly fields subscribe, you will probably be asked to use one of two. One, established by the Modern Language Association (MLA), is used chiefly in the humanities; the other, established by the American Psychological Association (APA), is used chiefly in the social sciences.

We include two papers that use sources. "An Argument for Corporate Responsibility" (p. 319) uses the MLA format. "The Role of Spirituality and Religion in Mental Health" (p. 327) follows the APA format. (You may notice that various styles are illustrated in other selections we have included.)

In some online venues you can link directly to your sources. If your assignment is to write a blog or other online text, linking helps the reader to look at a note or citation or the direct source quickly and easily. For example, if you are describing or referencing a scene in a movie, you can link to reviews of the movie, or to a YouTube of the trailer, or to the exact scene that you are writing about. These kinds of links can help your audience get a clearer sense of your point. When formatting such a link in your text, make sure the link opens in a new window so that readers will not lose their place in the text they are reading. In a blog, linking to your sources usually is easy and helpful.

A Note on Footnotes (and Endnotes)

Before we discuss these two formats, a few words about footnotes are in order. Before the MLA and the APA developed their rules of style, citations commonly were given in footnotes. Although today footnotes are not so frequently used to give citations, they still may be useful for another purpose. (The MLA suggests endnotes rather than footnotes, but most readers seem to think that, in fact, footnotes are preferable to endnotes. After all, who wants to keep shifting from a page of text to a page of notes at the rear?) If you want to include some material that may seem intrusive in the body of the paper, you may relegate it to a footnote. For example, in a footnote you might translate a quotation given in a foreign language, or you might demote from text to footnote a paragraph explaining why you are not taking account of such-and-such a point. By putting the matter in a footnote you are signaling the reader that it is dispensable; it is something relevant but not essential, something extra that you are, so to speak, tossing in. Don't make a habit of writing this sort of note, but there are times when it is appropriate.

MLA Format: Citations within the Text

Brief citations within the body of the essay give credit, in a highly abbreviated way, to the sources for material you quote, summarize, or make use of in any other way. These *in-text citations* are made clear by a list of sources, titled Works Cited, appended to the essay. Thus, in your essay you may say something like this:

> Commenting on the relative costs of capital punishment and life imprisonment, Ernest van den Haag says that he doubts "that capital punishment really is more expensive" (33).

The **citation,** the number 33 in parentheses, means that the quoted words come from page 33 of a source (listed in the Works Cited) written by van den Haag. Without a Works Cited, a reader would have no way of knowing that you are quoting from page 33 of an article that appeared in the February 8, 1985, issue of the *National Review.*

Usually the parenthetic citation appears at the end of a sentence, as in the example just given, but it can appear elsewhere; its position will depend chiefly on your ear, your eye, and the context. You might, for example, write the sentence thus:

> Ernest van den Haag doubts that "capital punishment really is more expensive" than life imprisonment (33), but other writers have presented figures that contradict him.

Five points must be made about these examples:

1. **Quotation marks** The closing quotation mark appears after the last word of the quotation, *not* after the parenthetic citation. Since the citation is not part of the quotation, the citation is not included within the quotation marks.

2. **Omission of words (ellipsis)**   If you are quoting a complete sentence or only a phrase, as in the examples given, you do not need to indicate (by three spaced periods) that you are omitting material before or after the quotation. But if for some reason you want to omit an interior part of the quotation, you must indicate the omission by inserting an *ellipsis,* the three spaced dots. To take a simple example, if you omit the word "really" from van den Haag's phrase, you must alert the reader to the omission:

> Ernest van den Haag doubts that "capital punishment . . . is more expensive" than life imprisonment (33).

Suppose you are quoting a sentence but wish to omit material from the end of the sentence. Suppose, also, that the quotation forms the end of your sentence. Write a lead-in phrase, quote what you need from your source, then type the bracketed ellipses for the omission, close the quotation, give the parenthetic citation, and finally type a fourth period to indicate the end of your sentence.

Here's an example. Suppose you want to quote the first part of a sentence that runs, "We could insist that the cost of capital punishment be reduced so as to diminish the differences." Your sentence would incorporate the desired extract as follows:

> Van den Haag says, "We could insist that the cost of capital punishment be reduced . . ." (33).

3. **Punctuation with parenthetic citations**   In the preceding examples, the punctuation (a period or a comma in the examples) *follows* the citation. If, however, the quotation ends with a question mark, include the question mark *within* the quotation, since it is part of the quotation, and put a period *after* the citation:

> Van den Haag asks, "Isn't it better — more just and more useful — that criminals, if they do not have the certainty of punishment, at least run the risk of suffering it?" (33).

But if the question mark is your own and not in the source, put it after the citation, thus:

> What answer can be given to van den Haag's doubt that "capital punishment really is more expensive" (33)?

4. **Two or more works by an author**   If your list of Works Cited includes two or more works by an author, you cannot, in your essay, simply cite a page number because the reader will not know which of

the works you are referring to. You must give additional information. You can give it in your lead-in, thus:

> In "New Arguments against Capital Punishment," van den Haag expresses doubt "that capital punishment really is more expensive" than life imprisonment (33).

Or you can give the title, in a shortened form, within the citation:

> Van den Haag expresses doubt that "capital punishment really is more expensive" than life imprisonment ("New Arguments" 33).

5. Citing even when you do not quote   Even if you don't quote a source directly, but use its point in a paraphrase or a summary, you will give a citation:

> Van den Haag thinks that life imprisonment costs more than capital punishment (33).

Note that in all of the previous examples, the author's name is given in the text (rather than within the parenthetic citation). But there are several other ways of giving the citation, and we shall look at them now. (We have already seen, in the example given under paragraph 4, that the title and the page number can be given within the citation.)

AUTHOR AND PAGE NUMBER IN PARENTHESES

> It has been argued that life imprisonment is more costly than capital punishment (van den Haag 33).

AUTHOR, TITLE, AND PAGE NUMBER IN PARENTHESES

We have seen that if the Works Cited list includes two or more works by an author, you will have to give the title of the work on which you are drawing, either in your lead-in phrase or within the parenthetic citation. Similarly, if you are citing someone who is listed more than once in the Works Cited, and for some reason you do not mention the name of the author or the work in your lead-in, you must add the information in your citation:

> Doubt has been expressed that capital punishment is as costly as life imprisonment (van den Haag, "New Arguments" 33).

A GOVERNMENT DOCUMENT OR A WORK
OF CORPORATE AUTHORSHIP

Treat the issuing body as the author. Thus, you will write something like this:

The Commission on Food Control, in *Food Resources Today*, concludes that
there is no danger (37-38).

A WORK BY TWO OR MORE AUTHORS

If a work is by *two or three authors,* give the names of all authors,
either in the parenthetic citation (the first example below) or in a lead-in
(the second example below):

There is not a single example of the phenomenon (Smith, Dale, and Jones
182-83).

Smith, Dale, and Jones insist there is not a single example of the phenomenon (182-83).

If there are *more than three authors,* give the last name of the first author,
followed by *et al.* (an abbreviation for *et alii,* Latin for "and others"),
thus:

Gittleman et al. argue (43) that . . .

or

On average, the cost is even higher (Gittleman et al. 43).

PARENTHETIC CITATION OF AN INDIRECT SOURCE
(CITATION OF MATERIAL THAT ITSELF WAS QUOTED
OR SUMMARIZED IN YOUR SOURCE)

Suppose you are reading a book by Jones in which she quotes
Smith and you wish to use Smith's material. Your citation must refer
the reader to Jones—the source you are using—but of course, you
cannot attribute the words to Jones. You will have to make it clear that
you are quoting Smith, and so after a lead-in phrase like "Smith says,"
followed by the quotation, you will give a parenthetic citation along
these lines:

(qtd. in Jones 324-25).

PARENTHETIC CITATION OF TWO OR MORE WORKS

The costs are simply too high (Smith 301; Jones 28).

Notice that a semicolon, followed by a space, separates the two sources.

A WORK IN MORE THAN ONE VOLUME

This is a bit tricky. If you have used only one volume, in the Works
Cited you will specify the volume, and so in the parenthetic in-text

citation you will not need to specify the volume. All that you need to include in the citation is a page number, as illustrated by most of the examples that we have given.

If you have used more than one volume, your parenthetic citation will have to specify the volume as well as the page, thus:

> Jackson points out that fewer than one hundred fifty people fit this description (2: 351).

The reference is to page 351 in volume 2 of a work by Jackson.

If, however, you are citing not a page but an entire volume—let's say volume 2—your parenthetic citation will look like this:

> Jackson exhaustively studies this problem (vol. 2).

or

> Jackson (vol. 2) exhaustively studies this problem.

Notice the following points:

- In citing a volume and page, the volume number, like the page number, is given in arabic (not roman) numerals, even if the original used roman numerals to indicate the volume number.
- The volume number is followed by a colon, then a space, then the page number.
- If you cite a volume number without a page number, as in the last example quoted, the abbreviation is *vol.* Otherwise do *not* use such abbreviations as *vol.* and *p.* and *pg.*

AN ANONYMOUS WORK

For an anonymous work, give the title in your lead-in, or give it in a shortened form in your parenthetic citation:

> *A Prisoner's View of Killing* includes a poll taken of the inmates on death row (32).

or

> A poll is available (*Prisoner's View* 32).

AN INTERVIEW

Probably you won't need a parenthetic citation because you'll say something like

> Vivian Berger, in an interview, said . . .

or

> According to Vivian Berger, in an interview . . .

and when your reader turns to the Works Cited, he or she will see that Berger is listed, along with the date of the interview. But if you do not mention the source's name in the lead-in, you will have to give it in the parentheses, thus:

> Contrary to popular belief, the death penalty is not reserved for serial
> killers and depraved murderers (Berger).

AN ELECTRONIC SOURCE

Electronic sources, such as those found on the Internet, are generally not divided into pages. Therefore, the in-text citation for such sources cites only the author's name (or, if a work is anonymous, the title):

> According to the World Wide Web site for the American Civil Liberties
> Union . . .

If the source does use pages or breaks down further into paragraphs or screens, insert the appropriate identifier or abbreviation (*p.* or *pp.* for page or pages; *par.* or *pars.* for paragraph or paragraphs; *screen* or *screens*) before the relevant number:

> The growth of day care has been called "a crime against posterity" by a
> spokesman for the Institute for the American Family (Terwilliger, screens 1-2).

MLA Format: The List of Works Cited

As the previous pages explain, parenthetic documentation consists of references that become clear when the reader consults the list titled Works Cited given at the end of an essay.

The list of Works Cited continues the pagination of the essay; if the last page of text is 10, then the Works Cited begins on its own page, in this case page 11. Type the page number in the upper right corner, a half inch from the top of the sheet and flush with the right margin. Next, type the heading Works Cited (*not* enclosed within quotation marks and not italic), centered, one inch from the top, and then double-space and type the first entry.

An Overview   Here are some general guidelines.

FORM ON THE PAGE

- Begin each entry flush with the left margin, but if an entry runs to more than one line, indent a half inch for each succeeding line of the entry. This is known as a hanging indent, and most word processing programs can achieve this effect easily.

- Double-space each entry, and double-space between entries.
- Italicize titles of works published independently—for instance, books, pamphlets, and journals. Enclose within quotation marks a work not published independently—for instance, an article in a journal or a short story.
- If you are citing a book that includes the title of another book, italicize the main title, but do *not* italicize the title mentioned. Example:

  A Study of Mill's On Liberty

- In the sample entries below, pay attention to the use of commas, colons, and the space after punctuation.

ALPHABETICAL ORDER

- Arrange the list alphabetically by author, with the author's last name first.
- For information about anonymous works, works with more than one author, and two or more works by one author, see below.

A Closer Look   Here is more detailed advice.

THE AUTHOR'S NAME

Notice that the last name is given first, but otherwise the name is given as on the title page. Do not substitute initials for names written out on the title page.

If your list includes two or more works by an author, do not repeat the author's name for the second title but represent it by three hyphens followed by a period. The sequence of the works is determined by the alphabetical order of the titles. Thus, Smith's book titled *Poverty* would be listed ahead of her book *Welfare*. See the example on page 303, listing two works by Roger Brown.

Anonymous works are listed under the first word of the title or the second word if the first is *A, An,* or *The* or a foreign equivalent. We discuss books by more than one author, government documents, and works of corporate authorship on pages 304 and 304–305.

THE TITLE

After the period following the author's name, allow one space and then give the title. Take the title from the title page, not from the cover or the spine, but disregard any unusual typography such as the use of all capital letters or the use of the ampersand (&) for *and*. Italicize the title and subtitle (separate them by a colon), but do not italicize the period that concludes this part of the entry.

- Capitalize the first word and the last word.
- Capitalize all nouns, pronouns, verbs, adjectives, adverbs, and sub-ordinating conjunctions (for example, *although, if, because*).
- Do not capitalize (unless it's the first or last word of the title or the first word of the subtitle) articles (*a, an, the*), prepositions (for instance, *in, on, toward, under*), coordinating conjunctions (for instance, *and, but, or, for*), or the *to* in infinitives.

Examples:

The Death Penalty: A New View

On the Death Penalty: Toward a New View

On the Penalty of Death in a Democracy

PLACE OF PUBLICATION, PUBLISHER, DATE, AND MEDIUM OF PUBLICATION

For the place of publication, provide the name of the city; you can usually find it either on the title page or on the reverse of the title page. If a number of cities are listed, provide only the first. If the city is not likely to be known, or if it may be confused with another city of the same name (as is Oxford, Mississippi, with Oxford, England), add the name of the state, abbreviated using the two-letter postal code.

The name of the publisher is abbreviated. Usually the first word is enough (*Random House* becomes *Random*), but if the first word is a first name, such as in *Alfred A. Knopf*, the surname (*Knopf*) is used instead. University presses are abbreviated thus: *Yale UP, U of Chicago P, State U of New York P.*

The date of publication of a book is given when known; if no date appears on the book, write *n.d.* to indicate "no date."

Because you may find your sources in any number of places, each entry should end by indicating the medium of publication for each source ("Print" for books or periodicals, "Web," for sources found on the Internet, and so on).

SAMPLE ENTRIES   Here are some examples illustrating the points we have covered thus far:

Brown, Roger. *Social Psychology*. New York: Free, 1965. Print.

- - - . *Words and Things*. Glencoe, IL: Free, 1958. Print.

Douglas, Ann. *The Feminization of American Culture*. New York: Knopf, 1977. Print.

Hartman, Chester. *The Transformation of San Francisco*. Totowa, NJ: Rowman, 1984. Print.

> Kellerman, Barbara. *The Political Presidency: Practice of Leadership from Kennedy through Reagan*. New York: Oxford UP, 1984. Print.

Notice that a period follows the author's name and another period follows the title. If a subtitle is given, as it is for Kellerman's book, it is separated from the title by a colon and a space. A colon follows the place of publication, a comma follows the publisher, and a period follows the date.

A BOOK BY MORE THAN ONE AUTHOR

The book is alphabetized under the last name of the first author named on the title page. If there are *two or three authors,* the names of these are given (after the first author's name) in the normal order, *first name first:*

> Gilbert, Sandra M., and Susan Gubar. *The Madwoman in the Attic: The Woman Writer and the Nineteenth-Century Literary Imagination*. New Haven: Yale UP, 1979. Print.

Notice, again, that although the first author's name is given *last name first,* the second author's name is given in the normal order, first name first. Notice, too, that a comma is put after the first name of the first author, separating the authors.

If there are *more than three authors,* give the name only of the first and then add (but *not* enclosed within quotation marks and not italic) *et al.* (Latin for "and others").

> Altshuler, Alan, et al. *The Future of the Automobile*. Cambridge: MIT P, 1984. Print.

GOVERNMENT DOCUMENTS

If the writer is not known, treat the government and the agency as the author. Most federal documents are issued by the Government Printing Office (abbreviated to *GPO*) in Washington, D.C.

> United States. Office of Technology Assessment. *Computerized Manufacturing Automation: Employment, Education, and the Workplace*. Washington: GPO, 1984. Print.

WORKS OF CORPORATE AUTHORSHIP

Begin the citation with the corporate author, even if the same body is also the publisher, as in the first example:

> American Psychiatric Association. *Psychiatric Glossary*. Washington: American Psychiatric Association, 1984. Print.

Carnegie Council on Policy Studies in Higher Education. *Giving Youth a Better Chance: Options for Education, Work, and Service*. San Francisco: Jossey, 1980. Print.

A REPRINT (FOR INSTANCE, A PAPERBACK VERSION OF AN OLDER CLOTHBOUND BOOK)

After the title, give the date of original publication (it can usually be found on the reverse of the title page of the reprint you are using), then a period, and then the place, publisher, and date of the edition you are using. The example indicates that Gray's book was originally published in 1970 and that the student is using the Vintage reprint of 1971.

Gray, Francine du Plessix. *Divine Disobedience: Profiles in Catholic Radicalism*. 1970. New York: Vintage, 1971. Print.

A BOOK IN SEVERAL VOLUMES

If you have used more than one volume, in a citation within your essay you will (as explained on p. 299) indicate a reference to, say, page 250 of volume 3 thus: (3: 250).

If, however, you have used only one volume of the set—let's say volume 3—in your entry in the Works Cited, specify which volume you used, as in the next example:

Friedel, Frank. *Franklin D. Roosevelt*. Vol. 3. Boston: Little, 1973. Print. 4 vols.

With such an entry in the Works Cited, the parenthetic citation within your essay would be to the page only, not to the volume and page, because a reader who consults the Works Cited will understand that you used only volume 3. In the Works Cited, you may specify volume 3 and not give the total number of volumes, or you may add the total number of volumes, as in the preceding example.

ONE BOOK WITH A SEPARATE TITLE IN A SET OF VOLUMES

Sometimes a set with a title makes use also of a separate title for each book in the set. If you are listing such a book, use the following form:

Churchill, Winston. *The Age of Revolution*. New York: Dodd, 1957. Vol. 3 of *History of the English-Speaking Peoples*. Print. 4 vols. 1956-58.

A BOOK WITH AN AUTHOR AND AN EDITOR

Churchill, Winston, and Franklin D. Roosevelt. *The Complete Correspondence*. Ed. Warren F. Kimball. 3 vols. Princeton: Princeton UP, 1985. Print.

Kant, Immanuel. *The Philosophy of Kant: Immanuel Kant's Moral and Political Writings*. Ed. Carl J. Friedrich. New York: Modern, 1949. Print.

If you are making use of the editor's introduction or other editorial material rather than of the author's work, list the book under the name of the editor rather than of the author, as shown below under An Introduction, Foreword, or Afterword.

A REVISED EDITION OF A BOOK

Arendt, Hannah. *Eichmann in Jerusalem*. Rev. and enlarged ed. New York: Viking, 1965. Print.

Honour, Hugh, and John Fleming. *The Visual Arts: A History*. 5th ed. Englewood Cliffs, NJ: Prentice, 1999. Print.

A TRANSLATED BOOK

Franqui, Carlos. *Family Portrait with Fidel: A Memoir*. Trans. Alfred MacAdam. New York: Random, 1984. Print.

AN INTRODUCTION, FOREWORD, OR AFTERWORD

Goldberg, Arthur J. Foreword. *An Eye for an Eye? The Morality of Punishing by Death*. By Stephen Nathanson. Totowa, NJ: Rowman, 1987. v-vi. Print.

Usually an introduction or comparable material is listed under the name of the author of the book (here Nathanson) rather than under the name of the writer of the foreword (here Goldberg), but if you are referring to the apparatus rather than to the book itself, use the form just given. The words *Introduction, Preface, Foreword,* and *Afterword* are neither enclosed within quotation marks nor italicized.

A BOOK WITH AN EDITOR BUT NO AUTHOR

Let's assume that you have used a book of essays written by various people but collected by an editor (or editors), whose name(s) appears on the collection.

LaValley, Albert J., ed. *Focus on Hitchcock*. Englewood Cliffs, NJ: Prentice, 1972. Print.

If the book has one editor, the abbreviation is *ed.;* if two or more editors, *eds.*

A WORK WITHIN A VOLUME OF WORKS BY ONE AUTHOR

The following entry indicates that a short work by Susan Sontag, an essay called "The Aesthetics of Silence," appears in a book by Sontag titled *Styles of Radical Will*. Notice that the inclusive page numbers of the short work are cited, not merely page numbers that you may happen to refer to but the page numbers of the entire piece.

Sontag, Susan. "The Aesthetics of Silence." *Styles of Radical Will*. New
    York: Farrar, 1969. 3-34. Print.

A BOOK REVIEW

Here is an example, citing Gerstein's review of Walker's book. Gerstein's
review was published in a journal called *Ethics*.

Gerstein, Robert S. Rev. of *Punishment, Danger and Stigma: The Morality
    of Criminal Justice*, by Nigel Walker. *Ethics* 93 (1983): 408-10. Print.

If the review has a title, give the title between the period following the
reviewer's name and *Rev.*

If a review is anonymous, list it under the first word of the title,
or under the second word if the first is *A, An,* or *The*. If an anonymous
review has no title, begin the entry with *Rev. of*, and then give the title
of the work reviewed; alphabetize the entry under the title of the work
reviewed.

AN ARTICLE OR ESSAY (NOT A REPRINT) IN A COLLECTION

A book may consist of a collection (edited by one or more persons)
of new essays by several authors. Here is a reference to one essay in such
a book. (The essay by Balmforth occupies pages 19 to 35 in a collection
edited by Bevan.)

Balmforth, Henry. "Science and Religion." *Steps to Christian Understanding*.
    Ed. R. J. W. Bevan. London: Oxford UP, 1958. 19-35. Print.

AN ARTICLE OR ESSAY REPRINTED IN A COLLECTION

The previous example (Balmforth's essay in Bevan's collection) was
for an essay written for a collection. But some collections reprint earlier material, such as essays from journals or chapters from books. The
following example cites an essay that was originally printed in a book
called *The Cinema of Alfred Hitchcock*. This essay has been reprinted in a
later collection of essays on Hitchcock, edited by Albert J. LaValley, and it
was LaValley's collection that the student used.

Bogdanovich, Peter. "Interviews with Alfred Hitchcock." *The Cinema of Al-
    fred Hitchcock*. New York: Museum of Modern Art, 1963. 15-18. Rpt.
    in *Focus on Hitchcock*. Ed. Albert J. LaValley. Englewood Cliffs, NJ:
    Prentice, 1972. 28-31. Print.

The student has read Bogdanovich's essay or chapter, but not in
Bogdanovich's book, where it occupied pages 15 to 18. The material was
actually read on pages 28 to 31 in a collection of writings on Hitchcock

edited by LaValley. Details of the original publication—title, date, page numbers, and so forth—were found in LaValley's collection. Almost all editors will include this information, either on the copyright page or at the foot of the reprinted essay, but sometimes they do not give the original page numbers. In such a case, you need not include the original numbers in your entry.

Notice that the entry begins with the author and the title of the work you are citing (here, Bogdanovich's interviews), not with the name of the editor of the collection or the title of the collection.

AN ENCYCLOPEDIA OR OTHER ALPHABETICALLY ARRANGED REFERENCE WORK

The publisher, place of publication, volume number, and page number do *not* have to be given. For such works, list only the edition (if it is given) and the date.

For a *signed* article, begin with the author's last name. (If the article is signed with initials, check elsewhere in the volume for a list of abbreviations, which will inform you who the initials stand for, and use the following form.)

> Williams, Donald C. "Free Will and Determinism." *Encyclopedia Americana*.
>   1987 ed. Print.

For an *unsigned article,* begin with the title of the article:

> "Automation." *The Business Reference Book*. 1977 ed. Print.

> "Tobacco." *Encyclopaedia Britannica: Macropaedia*. 1988 ed. Print.

A TELEVISION OR RADIO PROGRAM

Be sure to include the title of the episode or segment (in quotation marks), the title of the show (italicized), the network, the call letters and city of the station, and the date of broadcast. Other information, such as performers, narrator, and so forth, may be included if pertinent.

> "Back to My Lai." *60 Minutes*. Narr. Mike Wallace. CBS. 29 Mar. 1998.
>   Television.

> "Juvenile Justice." *Talk of the Nation*. Narr. Ray Suarez. Natl. Public Radio.
>   WBUR, Boston. 15 Apr. 1998. Radio.

AN ARTICLE IN A SCHOLARLY JOURNAL   The title of the article is enclosed within quotation marks, and the title of the journal is italicized.

Some journals are paginated consecutively; the pagination of the second issue begins where the first issue leaves off. Other journals begin each issue with page 1.

A JOURNAL THAT IS PAGINATED CONSECUTIVELY

Vilas, Carlos M. "Popular Insurgency and Social Revolution in Central
America." *Latin American Perspectives* 15.1 (1988): 55-77. Print.

Vilas's article occupies pages 55 to 77 in volume 15, which was published in 1988. (Notice that the volume number is followed by a space, then by the year in parentheses, and then by a colon, a space, and the page numbers of the entire article.) When available, give the issue number.

A JOURNAL THAT BEGINS EACH ISSUE WITH PAGE 1

If the journal is, for instance, a quarterly, there will be four page 1's each year, so the issue number must be given. After the volume number, type a period and (without hitting the space bar) the issue number, as in the next example:

Greenberg, Jack. "Civil Rights Enforcement Activity of the Department of
Justice." *Black Law Journal* 8.1 (1983): 60-67. Print.

Greenberg's article appeared in the first issue of volume 8 of the *Black Law Journal.*

AN ARTICLE IN A WEEKLY, BIWEEKLY, MONTHLY, OR BIMONTHLY PUBLICATION

Do not include volume or issue numbers, even if given.

Lamar, Jacob V. "The Immigration Mess." *Time* 27 Feb. 1989: 14-15. Print.

Markowitz, Laura. "A Different Kind of Queer Marriage." *Utne Reader*
Sept.-Oct. 2000: 24-26. Print.

AN ARTICLE IN A NEWSPAPER

Because a newspaper usually consists of several sections, a section number or a capital letter may precede the page number. The example indicates that an article begins on page 1 of section 2 and is continued on a later page.

Chu, Harry. "Art Thief Defends Action." *New York Times* 8 Feb. 1989, sec.
2: 1+. Print.

AN UNSIGNED EDITORIAL

"The Religious Tyranny Amendment." Editorial. *New York Times* 15 Mar.
1998, sec. 4: 16. Print.

A LETTER TO THE EDITOR

Lasken, Douglas. Letter. *New York Times* 15 Mar. 1998, sec. 4: 16. Print.

A PUBLISHED OR BROADCAST INTERVIEW

Give the name of the interview subject and the interviewer, followed by
the relevant publication or broadcast information, in the following format:

Green, Al. Interview with Terry Gross. *Fresh Air*. Natl. Public Radio. WFCR,
Amherst, MA. 16 Oct. 2000. Radio.

AN INTERVIEW YOU CONDUCT

Jevgrafovs, Alexandre L. Personal [or Telephone] interview. 14 Dec. 2003.

PERSONAL CORRESPONDENCE

Add "TS" for a typed letter, "MS" for a handwritten letter, or "E-mail"
to the end of the citation.

Paso, Robert. Letter [or Message, in the case of E-mail] to the author.
6 Jan. 2004. TS.

CD-ROM

Books on CD-ROMs are cited very much like their printed counterparts. Add the medium (*CD-ROM*) after the publication information. For
articles, to the usual print citation information, add (1) the title of the
database, italicized; (2) the medium (*CD-ROM*); (3) the vendor's name;
and (4) the date of electronic publication.

Louisberg, Margaret. *Charlie Brown Meets Godzilla: What Are Our Children
Watching?* Urbana: ERIC Clearinghouse on Elementary and Early
Childhood Education, 1990. CD-ROM.

"Pornography." *The Oxford English Dictionary*. 2nd ed. CD-ROM. Oxford:
Oxford UP, 1992.

A PERSONAL OR PROFESSIONAL WEB SITE

Include the following elements, separated by periods: the name of
the person who created the site (omit if not given, as in Figure 7.4), site

FIGURE 7.4 CITING A BLOG

1 Include the URL only if your Instructor requires it.

2 Sponsor of Web site

3 No author given; start citation with the title

4 Title of Web page

5 Publication date

6 Include the medium (Web) and the date you retrieved it.

title (italicized), name of any sponsoring institution or organization; date of electronic publication or of the latest update (if given), the medium (*Web*), and the date of access.

> *Legal Guide for Bloggers.* Electronic Frontier Foundation. 11 Feb. 2009.
>
> > Web. 30 May 2009.

AN ARTICLE IN AN ONLINE PERIODICAL

Give the same information as you would for a print article, plus the medium (*Web*) and the date of access. (See Figure 7.5.)

FIGURE 7.5   CITING AN ONLINE MAGAZINE

1. Include the URL only if your Instructor requires it.
2. Title of periodical
3. Title of article
4. Subtitle of article
5. Author
6. Publication date
7. Include the medium (Web) and the date you retrieved it.

Acocella, Joan. "In the Blood: Why Do Vampires Still Thrill?" *New Yorker*.
    16 March 2009. Web. 30 May 2009.

AN ONLINE POSTING

The citation includes the author's name, subject line of posting, description *Online posting* if the posting has no title, name of the forum, date material was posted, the medium (*Web*), and date of access.

Ricci, Paul. "Global Warming." Global Electronic Science Conference, 10
    June. 1996. Web. 22 Sept. 1997.

A DATABASE SOURCE

Treat material obtained from a computer service, such as Biblio-graphic Retrieval Service (BRS), like other printed material, but at the end of the entry add (if available) the title of the database (italicized), publication medium (*Web*), name of the computer service if known, and date of access.

> Jackson, Morton. "A Look at Profits." *Harvard Business Review* 40 (1962): 106-13. *BRS*. Web. 23 Dec. 2006.

Caution: Although we have covered the most usual kinds of sources, it is entirely possible that you will come across a source that does not fit any of the categories that we have discussed. For approximately two hundred pages of explanations of these matters, covering the proper way to cite all sorts of troublesome and unbelievable (but real) sources, see *MLA Handbook for Writers of Research Papers,* Seventh Edition (New York: Modern Language Association of America, 2009).

APA Format: Citations within the Text

Your paper will conclude with a separate page headed References, on which you list all of your sources. If the last page of your essay is numbered 10, number the first page of the References 11.

The APA style emphasizes the date of publication; the date appears not only in the list of references at the end of the paper but also in the paper itself, when you give a brief parenthetic citation of a source that you have quoted or summarized or in any other way used. Here is an example:

> Statistics are readily available (Smith, 1989, p. 20).

The title of Smith's book or article will be given at the end of your paper in the list titled References. We discuss the form of the material listed in the References after we look at some typical citations within the text of a student's essay.

A SUMMARY OF AN ENTIRE WORK

> Smith (1988) holds the same view.

or

> Similar views are held widely (Smith, 1988; Jones & Metz, 1990).

A REFERENCE TO A PAGE OR TO PAGES

> Smith (1988) argues that "the death penalty is a lottery, and blacks usually are the losers" (p. 17).

**A REFERENCE TO AN AUTHOR WHO HAS MORE THAN
ONE WORK IN THE LIST OF REFERENCES**

If in the References you list two or more works that an author published in the same year, the works are listed in alphabetical order, by the first letter of the title. The first work is labeled *a,* the second *b,* and so on. Here is a reference to the second work that Smith published in 1989:

> Florida presents "a fair example" of how the death penalty is administered (Smith, 1989b, p. 18).

APA Format: The List of References

Your brief parenthetic citations are made clear when the reader consults the list you give in the References. Type this list on a separate page, continuing the pagination of your essay.

An Overview   Here are some general guidelines.

FORM ON THE PAGE

- Begin each entry flush with the left margin, but if an entry runs to more than one line, indent five spaces for each succeeding line of the entry.
- Double-space each entry, and double-space between entries.

ALPHABETICAL ORDER

- Arrange the list alphabetically by author.
- Give the author's last name first and then the initial of the first name and of the middle name (if any).
- If there is more than one author, name all of the authors up to seven, again inverting the name (last name first) and giving only initials for first and middle names. (But do not invert the editor's name when the entry begins with the name of an author who has written an article in an edited book.) When there are two or more authors, use an ampersand (&) before the name of the last author. Example (here, of an article in the tenth volume of a journal called *Developmental Psychology*):

> Drabman, R. S., & Thomas, M. H. (1974). Does media violence increase children's tolerance of real-life aggression? *Developmental Psychology,* *10,* 418-421.

- For eight or more authors, list the first six followed by three ellipses dots and then the last author. If you list more than one work by an author, do so in the order of publication, the earliest first. If two works by an author were published in the same year, give them in alphabetical order by the first letter of the title, disregarding *A, An,* or *The,* and their foreign equivalent. Designate the first work as *a,* the second as *b.* Repeat the author's name at the start of each entry.

Donnerstein, E. (1980a). Aggressive erotica and violence against women. *Journal of Personality and Social Psychology, 39,* 269-277.

Donnerstein, E. (1980b). Pornography and violence against women. *Annals of the New York Academy of Sciences, 347,* 227-288.

Donnerstein, E. (1983). Erotica and human aggression. In R. Green & E. Donnerstein (Eds.), *Aggression: Theoretical and empirical reviews* (pp. 87-103). New York, NY: Academic Press.

FORM OF TITLE

- In references to books, capitalize only the first letter of the first word of the title (and of the subtitle, if any) and capitalize proper nouns. Italicize the complete title (but not the period at the end).

- In references to articles in periodicals or in edited books, capitalize only the first letter of the first word of the article's title (and subtitle, if any) and all proper nouns. Do not put the title within quotation marks or italicize it. Type a period after the title of the article. For the title of the journal and the volume and page numbers, see the next instruction.

- In references to periodicals, give the volume number in arabic numerals, and italicize it. Do *not* use *vol.* before the number, and do not use *p.* or *pg.* before the page numbers.

Sample References   Here are some samples to follow.

A BOOK BY ONE AUTHOR

Pavlov, I. P. (1927). *Conditioned reflexes* (G. V. Anrep, Trans.). London, England: Oxford University Press.

A BOOK BY MORE THAN ONE AUTHOR

Belenky, M. F., Clinchy, B. M., Goldberger, N. R., & Torule, J. M. (1986). *Women's ways of knowing: The development of self, voice, and mind.* New York, NY: Basic Books.

A COLLECTION OF ESSAYS

Christ, C. P., & Plaskow, J. (Eds.). (1979). *Woman-spirit rising: A feminist reader in religion*. New York, NY: Harper & Row.

A WORK IN A COLLECTION OF ESSAYS

Fiorenza, E. (1979). Women in the early Christian movement. In C. P. Christ & J. Plaskow (Eds.), *Woman-spirit rising: A feminist reader in religion* (pp. 84-92). New York, NY: Harper & Row.

GOVERNMENT DOCUMENTS

If the writer is not known, treat the government and the agency as the author. Most federal documents are issued by the U.S. Government Printing Office in Washington, D.C. If a document number has been assigned, insert that number in parentheses between the title and the following period.

United States Congress. Office of Technology Assessment. (1984). *Computerized manufacturing automation: Employment, education, and the workplace*. Washington, DC: U.S. Government Printing Office.

AN ARTICLE IN A JOURNAL WITH CONTINUOUS PAGINATION

Tversky, A., & Kahneman, D. (1981). The framing of decisions and the psychology of choice. *Science, 211*, 453-458.

AN ARTICLE IN A JOURNAL THAT PAGINATES EACH ISSUE SEPARATELY

Foot, R. J. (1988-89). Nuclear coercion and the ending of the Korean conflict. *International Security, 13*(4), 92-112.

The reference informs us that the article appeared in issue number 4 of volume 13.

AN ARTICLE FROM A MONTHLY OR WEEKLY MAGAZINE

Greenwald, J. (1989, February 27). Gimme shelter. *Time, 133,* 50-51.

Maran, S. P. (1988, April). In our backyard, a star explodes. *Smithsonian, 19,* 46-57.

AN ARTICLE IN A NEWSPAPER

Connell, R. (1989, February 6). Career concerns at heart of 1980s campus protests. *Los Angeles Times*, pp. 1, 3.

✓ A CHECKLIST FOR PAPERS USING SOURCES

Ask yourself the following questions:

☐ Are all borrowed words and ideas credited, including those from Internet sources?

☐ Are all summaries and paraphrases acknowledged as such?

☐ Are quotations and summaries not too long?

☐ Are quotations accurate? Are omissions of words indicated by three spaced periods? Are additions of words enclosed within square brackets?

☐ Are quotations provided with helpful lead-ins?

☐ Is documentation in proper form?

And of course, you will also ask yourself the questions that you would ask of a paper that did not use sources, such as:

☐ Is the topic sufficiently narrowed?

☐ Is the thesis (to be advanced or refuted) stated early and clearly, perhaps even in the title?

☐ Is the audience kept in mind? Are opposing views stated fairly and as sympathetically as possible? Are controversial terms defined?

☐ Are assumptions likely to be shared by readers? If not, are they argued rather than merely asserted?

☐ Is the focus clear (evaluation, recommendation of policy)?

☐ Is evidence (examples, testimony, statistics) adequate and sound?

☐ Are inferences valid?

☐ Is the organization clear (effective opening, coherent sequence of arguments, unpretentious ending)?

☐ Is all worthy opposition faced?

☐ Is the tone appropriate?

☐ Has the paper been carefully proofread?

☐ Is the title effective?

☐ Is the introduction effective?

☐ Is the structure reader-friendly?

☐ Is the ending effective?

(*Note:* If no author is given, simply begin with the title followed by the date in parentheses.)

A BOOK REVIEW

Daniels, N. (1984). Understanding physician power [Review of the book *The social transformation of American medicine*]. *Philosophy and Public Affairs, 13,* 347-356.

Daniels is the reviewer, not the author of the book. The book under review is called *The Social Transformation of American Medicine*, but the review, published in volume 13 of *Philosophy and Public Affairs*, had its own title, "Understanding Physician Power."

If the review does not have a title, retain the square brackets, and use the material within as the title. Proceed as in the example just given.

A WEB SITE

American Psychological Association. (1995). Lesbian and gay parenting.
    Retrieved June 12, 2000, from http://www.apa.org/pi/parent.html

AN ARTICLE IN AN ONLINE PERIODICAL

Carpenter, S. (2000, October). Biology and social environments jointly in-
    fluence gender development. *Monitor on Psychology 31*(9). Retrieved
    from http://www.apa.org/monitor/

For a full account of the APA method of dealing with all sorts of unusual citations, see the sixth edition (2010) of the APA manual, *Publication Manual of the American Psychological Association.*

AN ANNOTATED STUDENT RESEARCH PAPER IN MLA FORMAT

The following argument makes good use of sources. Early in the semester the students were asked to choose one topic from a list of ten and to write a documented argument of 750 to 1,250 words (three to five pages of double-spaced typing). The completed paper was due two weeks after the topics were distributed. The assignment, a prelude to working on a research paper of 2,500 to 3,000 words, was in part designed to give students practice in finding and in using sources. Citations are given in the MLA form.

Lesley Timmerman

Professor Jennifer Wilson

English 102

15 August 2012

An Argument for Corporate Responsibility

Opponents of corporate social responsibility (CSR) argue that a company's sole duty is to generate profits. According to them, by acting for the public good, corporations are neglecting their primary obligation to make money. However, as people are becoming more and more conscious of corporate impacts on society and the environment, separating profits from company practices and ethics does not make sense. Employees want to work for institutions that share their values, and consumers want to buy products from companies that are making an impact and improving people's lives. Furthermore, businesses exist in an interdependent world where the health of the environment and the well-being of society really do matter. For these reasons, corporations have to take responsibility for their actions, beyond making money for shareholders. For their own benefit as well as the public's, companies must strive to be socially responsible.

In his article "The Case against Corporate Responsibility," *Wall Street Journal* writer Aneel Karnani argues that CSR will never be able to solve the world's problems. Thinking it can, Karnani says, is a dangerous illusion. He recommends that instead of expecting corporate managers to act in the public interest, we should rely on philanthropy and government regulation. Karnani maintains that "Managers who sacrifice profit for the common good [. . .] are in effect imposing a tax on their shareholders and arbitrarily deciding how that money should be spent." In other words, according to Karnani, corporations should not be determining what constitutes

---

Title is focused and announces the thesis.

Double-space between the title and first paragraph—and throughout the essay.

Brief statement of one side of the issue.

Summary of the opposing view.

Lead-in to quotation.

1″ margin on each side and at bottom.

Timmerman 2

Essayist's
response to
the quota-
tion.

Author
concisely
states her
position.

Transitions
("For exam-
ple," "also")
alert readers
to where the
writer is tak-
ing them.

socially responsible behavior; individual donors and the government should. Certainly, individuals should continue to make charitable gifts, and governments should maintain laws and regulations to protect the public interest. However, Karnani's reasoning for why corporations should be exempt from social responsibility is flawed. With very few exceptions, corporations' socially responsible actions are not arbitrary and do not sacrifice long-term profits.

In fact, corporations have already proven that they can contribute profitably and meaningfully to solving significant global problems by integrating CSR into their standard practices and long-term visions. Rather than focusing on shareholders' short-term profits, many companies have begun measuring their success by "profit, planet and people" — what is known as the "triple bottom line." Businesses operating under this principle consider their environmental and social impacts, as well as their financial impacts, and make responsible and compassionate decisions. For example, such businesses use resources efficiently, create healthy products, choose suppliers who share their ethics, and improve economic opportunities for people in the communities they serve. By doing so, companies often save money. They also contribute to the sustainability of life on earth and ensure the sustainability of their own businesses. In their book *The Triple Bottom Line: How Today's Best-Run Companies Are Achieving Economic, Social, and Environmental Success*, coauthors Savitz and Weber demonstrate that corporations need to become sustainable, in all ways. They argue that "the only way to succeed in today's interdependent world is to embrace sustainability" (xi). The authors go on to show that, for the vast majority of companies, a broad commitment to sustainability enhances profitability (Savitz and Weber 39).

For example, PepsiCo has been able to meet the financial expectations of its shareholders while demonstrating its commitment to the triple bottom line. In addition to donating over $16 million to help victims of natural disasters, Pepsi has woven concerns for people and for the planet into its company practices and culture (Bejou 4). For instance, because of a recent water shortage in an area of India where Pepsi runs a plant, the company began a project to build community wells (Savitz and Weber 160). Though Pepsi did not cause the water shortage nor was its manufacturing threatened by it, "Pepsi realizes that the well-being of the community is part of the company's responsibility" (Savitz and Weber 161). Ultimately, Pepsi chose to look beyond the goal of maximizing short-term profits. By doing so, the company improved its relationship with this Indian community, improved people's daily lives and opportunities, and improved its own reputation. In other words, Pepsi embraced CSR and ensured a more sustainable future for everyone involved.

Another example of a wide-reaching company that is working toward greater sustainability on all fronts is Walmart. The corporation has issued a CSR policy that includes three ambitious goals: "to be fully supplied by renewable energy, to create zero waste and to sell products that sustain people and the environment" ("From Fringe to Mainstream"). As Dr. Doug Guthrie, dean of George Washington University's School of Business, noted in a recent lecture, if a company as powerful as Walmart were to succeed in these goals, the impact would be huge. To illustrate Walmart's potential influence, Dr. Guthrie pointed out that the corporation's exports from China to the United States are equal to Mexico's total exports to the United States. In committing to CSR, the company's leaders are acknowledging how much their power depends on the earth's natural resources, as well as the communities who produce, distribute, sell, and purchase Walmart's products. The company is also well aware that achieving its goals will "ultimately save the company a great deal of money" ("From Fringe to Mainstream"). For good reason, Walmart, like other

Timmerman 4

companies around the world, is choosing to act in *everyone's* best interest.

Author now introduces statistical evidence that, if introduced earlier, might have turned the reader off.

Recent research on employees' and consumers' social consciousness offers companies further reason to take corporate responsibility seriously. For example, studies show that workers care about making a difference (Meister). In many cases, workers would even take a pay cut to work for a more responsible, sustainable company. In fact, 45 percent of workers said they would take a 15 percent reduction in pay "for a job that makes a social or environmental impact" (Meister). Even more said they would take a 15 percent cut in pay to work for a company with values that match their own (Meister). The numbers are most significant amongst Millennials (those born between, approximately, 1980 and the early 2000s). Eighty percent of Millennials said they "wanted to work for a company that cares about how it impacts and contributes to society," and over half said they would not work for an "irresponsible company" (Meister). Given this more socially conscious generation, companies are going to find it harder and harder to ignore CSR. To recruit and retain employees, employers will need to earn the admiration, respect, and loyalty of their workers by becoming "good corporate citizen[s]" (qtd. in "From Fringe to Mainstream").

Similarly, studies clearly show that CSR matters to today's consumers. According to an independent report, 80 percent of Americans say they would switch brands to support a social cause (Cone Communications 6). Eighty-eight percent say they approve of companies' using social or environmental issues in their marketing (Cone Communications 5). And 83 percent say they "wish more of the products, services and retailers would support causes" (Cone Communications 5). Other independent surveys corroborate these results, confirming that today's customers, especially Millennials, care about more than just price ("From Fringe to Mainstream").

Furthermore, plenty of companies have seen what happens when they assume that consumers do not care about CSR. For example, in 1997, when Nike customers discovered that their shoes were manufactured by child laborers in Indonesia, the company took a huge financial hit (Guthrie). Today, Information-Age customers are even more likely to educate themselves about companies' labor practices and environmental records. Smart corporations will listen to consumer preferences, provide transparency, and commit to integrating CSR into their long-term business plans.

Author argues that it is to the *companies'* interest to be socially responsible.

In this increasingly interdependent world, the case against CSR is becoming more and more difficult to defend. Exempting corporations and relying on government to be the world's conscience does not make good social, environmental, or economic sense. Contributors to a recent article in the online journal *Knowledge@ Wharton,* published by the Wharton School of Business, agree. Professor Eric Orts maintains that "it is an outmoded view to say that one must rely only on the government and regulation to police business responsibilities. What we need is re-conception of what the purpose of business is" (qtd. in "From Fringe to Mainstream"). The question is, what should the purpose of a business be in today's world? Professor of Business Administration David Bejou of Elizabeth City State University has a thoughtful and sensible answer to that question. He writes,

Author's lead-in to the quotation guides the reader's response to the quotation.

> . . . it is clear that the sole purpose of a business is not merely
> that of generating profits for its owners. Instead, because
> compassion provides the necessary equilibrium between
> a company's purpose and the needs of its communities, it
> should be the new philosophy of business. (Bejou 1)

As Bejou implies, the days of allowing corporations to act in their own financial self-interest with little or no regard for their effects on

Timmerman 6

others are over. None of us can afford such a narrow view of business. The world is far too interconnected. A seemingly small corporate decision — to buy coffee beans directly from local growers or to install solar panels — can affect the lives and livelihoods of many people and determine the environmental health of whole regions. A business, just like a government or an individual, therefore has an ethical responsibility to act with compassion for the public good.

Upbeat
ending.

Fortunately, corporations have many incentives to act responsibly. Customer loyalty, employee satisfaction, overall cost-saving, and long-term viability are just some of the advantages businesses can expect to gain by embracing comprehensive CSR policies. Meanwhile, companies have very little to lose by embracing a socially conscious view. These days, compassion is profitable. Corporations would be wise to recognize the enormous power, opportunity, and responsibility they have to effect positive change.

Works Cited

Bejou, David. "Compassion as the New Philosophy of Business." *Journal of Relationship Marketing* 10.1 (2011): 1-6. *Business Source Complete*. Web. 15 Aug. 2012.

Cone Communications. *2010 Cone Cause Evolution Study*. Cone, Inc., 2010. Web. 15 Aug. 2012.

"From Fringe to Mainstream: Companies Integrate CSR Initiatives into Everyday Business." *Knowledge@Wharton*. The Wharton School of the University of Pennsylvania, 23 May 2012. Web. 14 Aug. 2012.

Guthrie, Doug. Keynote address. *Promoting a Comprehensive Approach to Corporate Social Responsibility (CSR)*. *YouTube*. YouTube, 22 May 2012. Web. 11 Aug. 2012.

Karnani, Aneel. "The Case against Corporate Social Responsibility." *The Wall Street Journal*. Dow Jones & Co., Inc., 14 June 2012. Web. 12 Aug. 2012.

Meister, Jeanne. "Corporate Social Responsibility: A Lever for Employee Attraction & Engagement." *Forbes*. Forbes.com, 7 June 2012. Web. 12 Aug. 2012.

Savitz, Andrew W., with Karl Weber. *The Triple Bottom Line: How Today's Best-Run Companies Are Achieving Economic, Social, and Environmental Success*. San Francisco: Jossey-Bass, 2006. Print.

Alphabetical by author's last name.

Hanging indent ½".

An article on a blog without a known author.

A clip from YouTube.

AN ANNOTATED STUDENT RESEARCH PAPER IN APA FORMAT

The following paper is an example of a student paper that uses APA format.

Running Head: RELIGION IN MENTAL HEALTH 1

The Role of Spirituality and Religion
in Mental Health

Laura DeVeau
English 102
Professor Gardner
April 12, 2010

The APA-style cover page gives title, author, and course information.

Short form of
title and page
number as
running head.

The Role of Spirituality and Religion

in Mental Health

It has been called "a vestige of the childhood of mankind,"
"the feeling of something true, total and absolute," "an otherworldly
answer as regards the meaning of life" (Jones, 1991, p. 1; Amaro,
1998; Kristeva, 1987, p. 27). It has been compared to medicine,

Citation of
multiple
works from
references.

described as a psychological cure for mental illness, and also
referred to as the cause of a dangerous fanaticism. With so many
differing opinions on the impact of religion in people's lives, where
would one begin a search for the truth? Who has the answer:
Christians, humanists, objectivists, atheists, psychoanalysts,
Buddhists, philosophers, cults? This was my dilemma at the advent
of my research into how religion and spirituality affect the mental
health of society as a whole.

In this paper, I explore the claims, widely accepted by professionals in the field of psychology, that religious and spiritual practices
have a negative impact on mental health. In addition, though, I
cannot help but reflect on how this exploration has changed my

Acknowledg-
ment of
opposing
viewpoints.

beliefs as well. Religion is such a personal experience that one cannot
be dispassionate in reporting it. One can, however, subject the
evidence provided by those who have studied the issue to critical
scrutiny. Having done so, I find myself in disagreement with those
who claim religious feelings are incompatible with sound mental
health. There is a nearly limitless number of beliefs regarding
spirituality. Some are organized and involve rituals like mass or
worship. Many are centered around the existence of a higher being,
while others focus on the self. I have attempted to uncover the perfect
set of values that lead to a better lifestyle, but my research has
pointed me in an entirely different direction, where no single belief

Thesis
explicitly
introduced.

seems to be adequate but where spiritual belief in general should be
valued more highly than it is currently in mental health circles.

I grew up in a moderately devout Catholic family. Like many young people raised in a household where one religion is practiced by both parents, it never occurred to me to question those beliefs. I went through a spiritual cycle, which I believe much of Western society also experiences. I attended religious services because I had to. I possessed a blind, unquestioning acceptance of what I was being taught because the adults I trusted said it was so. Like many adolescents and young adults, though, I stopped going to church when I was old enough to decide because I thought I had better things to do. At this stage, we reach a point when we begin searching for a meaning to our existence. For some, this search is brought on by a major crisis or a feeling of emptiness in their daily lives, while for others it is simply a part of growing up. This is where we begin to make personal choices, but with the barrage of options, where do we turn?

Beginning with the holistic health movement in the eighties, there has been a mass shift from traditional religions to less structured spiritual practices such as meditation, yoga, the Cabala, and mysticism (Beyerman, 1989). They venture beyond the realm of conventional dogmatism and into the new wave of spirituality. Many of these practices are based on the notion that health of the mind and spirit equals health of the body. Associated with this movement is a proliferation of retreats offering a chance to get in touch with the beauty and silence of nature and seminars where we can take "a break from our everyday environment where our brains are bustling and our bodies are exhausting themselves" ("Psychological benefits," 1999). A major concept of the spiritual new wave is that it focuses inward toward the individual psyche, rather than outward toward another being like a god. Practitioners do not deny the existence of this being, but they believe that to fully love another, we must first understand ourselves. Many find this a preferable alternative to

> Author and date cited for summary or paraphrase.

> Anonymous source cited by title and date.

RELIGION IN MENTAL HEALTH   4

religions where the individual is seen as a walking dispenser of sin who is very fortunate to have a forgiving creator. It is also a relief from the scare tactics like damnation used by traditional religions to make people behave. Many, therefore, praise the potential psychological benefits of such spirituality.

While I believe strongly in the benefits of the new wave, I am not willing to do away with structured religion, for I find that it also has its benefits. Without the existence of churches and temples, it would be harder to expose the public to values beneficial to mental stability. It is much more difficult to hand a child a copy of the Cabala and say "Read this, and then get back to me on it" than it is to bring a child to a service where the ideas are represented with concrete examples. My religious upbringing presented me with a set of useful morals and values, and it does the same for millions of others who are brought up in this manner. Many people, including some followers of the new wave, are bitter toward Christianity because of events in history like the Crusades, the Inquisition, the Salem witch trials, and countless other horrific acts supposedly committed in the name of God. But these events were based not on biblical teachings but on pure human greed and lust for power. We should not reject the benevolent possibilities of organized religion on the basis of historical atrocities any more than we should abandon public education because a few teachers are known to mistreat children.

Another factor contributing to the reluctance concerning religion is the existence of cults that seduce people into following their extreme teachings. The victims are often at vulnerable times in their lives, and the leaders are usually very charming, charismatic, and sometimes also psychotic or otherwise mentally unstable. Many argue that if we acknowledge these groups as dangerous cults, then we must do the same for traditional religions such as Christianity and Islam, which are likewise founded on the teachings of charismatic leaders.

Clear transition refers to previous paragraph.

Again, though, critics are too quick to conflate all religious and spiritual practice; we must distinguish between those who pray and attend services and those who commit group suicide because they think that aliens are coming to take over the world. Cults have provided many psychologists, who are eager to discount religion as a factor in improving mental health, with an easy target. Ellis (1993), the founder of rational-emotive therapy, cites many extreme examples of religious commitment, such as cults and antiabortion killings, to show that commitment is hazardous to one's sanity. Anomalies like these should not be used to speak of religion as a whole, though. Religion is clearly the least of these people's mental problems.

When the author's name appears in text, only the date is cited in parentheses.

Besides Ellis, there are many others in the field of psychology who do not recognize religion as a potential aid for improving the condition of the psyche. Actually, fewer than 45 percent of the members of the American Psychiatric Association even believe in God. The general American public has more than twice that percentage of religious devotees (Larson, 1998). Going back to the days of Freud, many psychologists have held atheist views. The father of psychoanalysis himself called religion a "universal obsessional neurosis." Psychologists have long rejected research that demonstrates the benefits of spirituality by saying that this research is biased. They claim that such studies are out to prove that religion helps because the conductors are religious people who need to justify their beliefs.

While this may be true in some instances, there is also some quite empirical research available to support the claims of those who promote religion and spirituality. The *Journal for the Scientific Study of Religion* has conducted many studies examining the effects of religion on individuals and groups. In one example, the relationship between religious coping methods and positive recovery after major stressful events was observed. The results indicated not only that spirituality was not harmful to the mind but that "the positive religious coping

RELIGION IN MENTAL HEALTH   6

Bracketed word in
quotation not in
original source.

pattern was tied to benevolent outcomes, including fewer symptoms
of psychological distress, [and] reports of psychological and spiritual
growth as a result of the stressor" (Pargament et al., 1998, p. 721).

Author, date, and
page number are
cited for a direct
quotation.

Clearly, the benefits of piety can, in fact, be examined empirically,
and in some cases the results point to a positive correlation between
religion and mental health.

But let us get away from statistics and studies. If religion is
both useless and dangerous, as so many psychologists claim, we must
ask why has it remained so vital a part of humanity for so long. Even
if it can be reduced to a mere coping method that humans use to justify their existence and explain incomprehensible events, is it futile?
I would suggest that this alone represents a clear benefit to society.
Should religion, if it cannot be proven as "true," be eliminated and
life based on scientific fact alone? Surely many would find this a
pointless existence. With all the conflicting knowledge I have gained
about spirituality during my personal journey and my research, one
idea is clear. It is not the depth of devotion, the time of life when
one turns to religion, or even the particular combination of beliefs

Conclusion
restates and
strengthens
thesis.

one chooses to adopt that will improve the quality of life. There is no
right or wrong answer when it comes to self-fulfillment. It is whatever
works for the individual, even if that means holding no religious or
spiritual beliefs at all. But clearly there *are* benefits to be gained, at
least for some individuals, and mental health professionals need to
begin acknowledging this fact in their daily practice.

References

Amaro, J. (1998). Psychology, psychoanalysis and religious faith.
    Nielsen's psychology of religion pages. Retrieved from http://
    www.psywww.com/psyrelig/amaro.html

Beyerman A. K. (1989). *The holistic health movement*. Tuscaloosa, AL:
    Alabama University Press.

Ellis, A. (1993). Dogmatic devotion doesn't help, it hurts. In B. Slife
    (Ed.), *Taking sides: Clashing views on controversial psychological
    issues* (pp. 297-301). New York, NY: Scribner.

Jones, J. W. (1991). *Contemporary psychoanalysis and religion:
    Transference and transcendence*. New Haven, CT: Yale University
    Press.

Kristeva, J. (1987). *In the beginning was love: Psychoanalysis and
    faith*. New York, NY: Columbia University Press.

Larson, D. (1998). Does religious commitment improve mental health?
    In B. Slife (Ed.), *Taking sides: Clashing views on controversial
    psychological issues* (pp. 292-296). New York, NY: Scribner.

Pargament, K. I., Smith, B. W., Koening, H. G., & Perez, L. (1998).
    Patterns of positive and negative religious coping with major
    life stressors. *Journal for the Scientific Study of Religion, 37*,
    710-724.

"Psychological benefits." (1999). *Walking the labyrinth*. Retrieved April
    3, 2000, from http://www.labyrinthway.com/html/benefits.html

References begin on a new page.

An online source.

A book.

An article or a chapter in a book.

An article in a journal.

Anonymous source alphabetized by title.

PART THREE

FURTHER VIEWS
on ARGUMENT

8

A Philosopher's View: The Toulmin Model

All my ideas hold together, but I cannot elaborate them all at once.

—JEAN-JACQUES ROUSSEAU

Clarity has been said to be not enough. But perhaps it will be time to go into that when we are within measurable distance of achieving clarity on some matter.

—J. L. AUSTIN

[Philosophy is] a peculiarly stubborn effort to think clearly.

—WILLIAM JAMES

Philosophy is like trying to open a safe with a combination lock: Each little adjustment of the dials seems to achieve nothing, only when everything is in place does the door open.

—LUDWIG WITTGENSTEIN

In Chapter 3, we explained the contrast between making *deductive* and *inductive* arguments, the two main methods people use to reason. Either:

- we make explicit something concealed in what we already accept (**deduction**), or
- we use what we have observed as a basis for asserting or proposing something new (**induction**).

These two types of reasoning share some structural features, as we also noticed. Both deductive and inductive reasoning seek to establish a **thesis** (or conclusion) by offering **reasons** for accepting the conclusion. Thus every argument contains both a thesis and one or more supportive reasons.

After a little scrutiny, we can in fact point to several features shared by all arguments, whether deductive or inductive, good or bad. We use the vocabulary popularized by Stephen Toulmin, Richard Rieke, and

Allan Janik in their book *An Introduction to Reasoning* (1979; second edition 1984) to explore the various elements of argument. Once these elements are understood, it is possible to analyze an argument using their approach and their vocabulary in what has come to be known as "The Toulmin Method."

THE CLAIM

Every argument has a purpose, goal, or aim—namely, to establish a **claim** (*conclusion* or *thesis*). Suppose you are arguing in favor of equal rights for women. You might state your thesis or claim as follows:

Men and women ought to have equal rights.

A more precise formulation of the claim might be

Men and women ought to have equal legal rights.

A still more precise formulation might be

Equal legal rights for men and women ought to be protected by our Constitution.

The third version of this claim states what the controversy in the 1970s over the Equal Rights Amendment was all about. (Both houses of Congress passed it in 1972, but the number of state legislatures that needed to ratify it before the Amendment could be added to the Constitution failed to do so before Congress's mandated deadline of June 30, 1982.)

In other words, the *claim* being made in an argument is the whole point of making the argument in the first place. Consequently, when you read or analyze someone else's argument, the first questions you should ask are these:

- What is the argument intended to prove or establish?
- *What claim is it making?*
- Has this claim been clearly and precisely formulated, so that it unambiguously asserts what its advocate wants it to assert?

GROUNDS

Once we have the argument's purpose or point clearly in mind and thus know what the arguer is aiming to establish, then we can look for the evidence, reasons, support—in short, for the **grounds**—on which that claim is based. In a *deductive* argument, these grounds are the premises from which the claim is deduced; in an *inductive* argument, the grounds are the evidence—which could be based on a sample, an observation, or an experiment—that makes the claim plausible or probable.

Not every kind of claim can be supported by every kind of ground, and, conversely, not every kind of ground gives equally good support for every kind of claim. Suppose, for instance, that I claim half the students in the classroom are women. I can establish the *ground* for this claim in any of several ways. For example:

1. I can count all the women and all the men. Suppose the total equals fifty. If the number of women is twenty-five and the number of men is twenty-five, I have vindicated my claim.
2. I can count a sample of ten students—perhaps the first ten to walk into the classroom—and find that in the sample five of the students are women. I thus have inductive—plausible but not conclusive—grounds for my claim.
3. I can point out that the students in the college divide equally into men and women and then claim that this class is a representative sample of the whole college.

Clearly, ground 1 is stronger than ground 2, and 2 is much stronger than 3.

Up to this point, we have merely restated points about premises and conclusions that were covered in Chapter 3. We want now to consider four additional features of arguments.

WARRANTS

Once we have the claim or the point of an argument fixed in mind and have isolated the evidence or reasons offered in its support, the next question you need to ask is this:

> Exactly how do the reasons offered in support of the conclusion work? In other words, what kind of guarantee—**warrant**—is provided to demonstrate that the reasons proffered actually do support the claim or lead to the conclusion? (A *warrant* in this context is like the *warranty* you get when you buy something.)

In ordinary and straightforward *deductive* arguments, warrants take different forms. In the simplest cases, we can point to the way in which the *meanings* of the key terms are really equivalent. Thus, if John is taller than Bill, then Bill must be shorter than John. We know this because we know what "is shorter than" and "is taller than" mean. If *A* is taller than *B*, it must be the case that *B* is shorter than *A*; those are the meanings of the phrases being used here. Of course everyone involved does have to know the language well enough to understand the relationship between "is taller than" and "is shorter than." The *warrant* in this case is the common understanding of what those two phrases mean.

In other cases, we may need to be more resourceful. A reliable tactic is to think up a simple *parallel argument,* an argument exactly parallel in form and structure to the argument we are trying to defend. If the two arguments really do have the same form and structure, and we are ready to accept the simpler one, then we can point out that the more complex argument must be accepted—because the two arguments have exactly the same structure. For example, if we want to argue that it is reasonable for FedEx to charge more for their delivery services than the U.S. Postal Service (USPS) does, we could point out that, since it seems entirely reasonable to pay higher costs for special services from the USPS such as overnight delivery promised by a certain time (depending on factors such as location), then it is reasonable to pay even higher fees for similar overnight delivery by FedEx because that service includes sending someone to pick up what you want delivered.

In simple *inductive* arguments, we are likely to point to the way in which observations or sets of data constitute a *representative sample* of a whole population, even if not every member of the sample is strictly in evidence. For instance, when scattered information is plotted on a graph, the trend line does not have to touch each (or even any) of the data points as long as they are scattered above and below the line in roughly equal numbers in pairs that are roughly equidistant from the trend line. We can defend this projection on the grounds that it takes all of the points into account in the least complicated way. In such a case, the warrant is this combination of *inclusiveness* and *simplicity.*

Establishing the warrants for our reasoning—that is, explaining why our grounds really do support our claims—can quickly become a highly technical and exacting procedure that goes far beyond the aims of this book. Even so, developing a "feel" for why reasons or grounds are or are not relevant to what they are alleged to support is important. "That's just my view" is *not* a convincing warrant for any argument. Even without formal training, however, one can sense that something is wrong with many bad arguments. Here is one example: British professor C. E. M. Joad found himself standing on a station platform, annoyed because he had just missed his train. Then another train, making an unscheduled stop, pulled up to the platform in front of him. Joad decided to jump aboard, only to hear the conductor say, "I'm afraid you'll have to get off, Sir. This train doesn't stop here." "In that case," replied the professor, "don't worry. I'm not on it."

BACKING

A really solid argument may need even further support, especially if what is being argued is complicated. *Warrants,* remember, explain the way our *grounds* support our *claims.* The next task, however, is to be able to show that we can back up what we have claimed by showing that the reasons we have given for a claim are good reasons. To establish that kind of further support for an argument is to provide **backing.**

What is appropriate backing for one kind of argument might be quite inappropriate for another kind of argument. For example, the kinds of reasons relevant to support an amendment to the Constitution are completely different from the kinds appropriate to settle the question of what caused the defeat of Napoleon's invasion of Russia. Arguments for the amendment might be rooted in an appeal to fairness, whereas arguments about the military defeat might be rooted in letters and other documents in French and Russian archives. The *canons* (established conventions) of good argument in two such dramatically different cases have to do with the means that scholarly communities in law and history, respectively, have developed over the years to support, defend, challenge, and undermine a given kind of argument.

Another way of stating this point is to recognize that once you have given reasons for a claim, you are then likely to be challenged to explain why your reasons are good reasons—why, that is, anyone should believe your reasons rather than regard them skeptically. They have to be the right kinds of reasons, given the field you are arguing about. Why (to give a simple example) should we accept the testimony of Dr. *X* when Dr. *Y*, equally renowned, supports the opposite side? What more do we need to know before "expert testimony" is appropriately invoked? For a different kind of case: When and why is it safe to rest a prediction on a small though admittedly carefully selected sample? And still another: Why is it legitimate to argue that (1) if I dream I am the King of France, then I must exist, whereas it is illegitimate to argue that (2) if I dream I am the King of France, then the King of France must exist?

To answer challenges of these sorts is to back up one's reasons, to give them legitimate *backing*. No argument is any better than its backing.

MODAL QUALIFIERS

As we have seen, all arguments are made up of assertions or propositions that can be sorted into four categories:

- the *claim* (conclusion, thesis to be established),
- the *grounds* (explicit reasons advanced),
- the *warrant* (guarantee, evidence, or principle that legitimates the ground by connecting it to the claim), and
- the *backing* (relevant support, implicit assumptions).

All of the kinds of propositions that emerge when we assert something in an argument have what philosophers call a **modality**. This means that propositions generally indicate—explicitly or tacitly—the *character* and *scope* of what is believed to be their likely truth.

Character has to do with the nature of the claim being made, the extent of an argument's presumed reach. Both making and evaluating arguments require being clear about whether they are *necessary, probable, plausible,* or *possible.* Consider, for example, a claim that it is to the advantage of a college to have a racially diverse student body. Is that *necessarily* or only *probably* true? What about an argument that a runner who easily wins a 100-meter race should also be able to win at 200 meters? Is this *plausible*—or only *possible?* Indicating the *character* with which an assertion is advanced is crucial to any argument for or against it. Furthermore, if there is more than one reason for making a claim, and all of those reasons are *good,* it is still possible that one of those good reasons may be *better* than the others. If so, the better reason should be stressed.

Indicating the *scope* of an assertion is equally crucial to how an argument plays out. *Scope* entails such considerations as whether the proposition is thought to be true *always* or just *sometimes.* Further, is the claim being made supposed to apply in *all* instances or just in *some?* Assertions are usually clearer, as well as more likely to be true, if they are explicitly *quantified* and *qualified.* Suppose, for example, that you are arguing against smoking, and the ground for your claim is this:

Heavy smokers cut short their life span.

In this case, there are three obvious alternative quantifications to choose among: *all* smokers cut short their life span, *most* do, or only *some* do. Until the assertion is quantified in one of these ways, we really do not know what is being asserted—and so we do not know what degree and kind of evidence or counterevidence is relevant. Other quantifiers include *few, rarely, often, sometimes, perhaps, usually, more or less, regularly, occasionally.*

Scope also has to do with the fact that empirical generalizations are typically *contingent* on various factors. Indicating such contingencies clearly is an important way to protect a generalization against obvious counterexamples. Thus, consider this empirical generalization:

Students do best on final examinations if they study hard for them.

Are we really to believe that students who cram ("study hard" in that concentrated sense) for an exam will do better than those who do the work diligently throughout the whole course ("study hard" in that broader sense) and therefore do not need to cram for the final? Probably not; what is really meant is that *all other things being equal* (in Latin, *ceteris paribus*), concentrated study just before an exam will yield good results. Alluding in this way to the contingencies—the things that might derail the argument—shows that the writer is aware of possible exceptions and is conceding them from the start.

In sum, sensitivity to both character and (especially) scope—paying attention to the role played by quantifiers, qualifiers, and contingencies and making sure you use appropriate ones for each of your assertions — will strengthen your arguments enormously. Not least of the benefits is that you will reduce the peculiar vulnerabilities of an argument that is undermined by exaggeration and other misguided generalizations.

REBUTTALS

Very few arguments of any interest are beyond dispute, conclusively knockdown affairs. Only very rarely is the claim of an argument so rigidly tied to its grounds, warrants, and backing — and with its quantifiers and qualifiers argued in so precise a manner — that it proves its conclusion beyond any possibility of doubt. On the contrary, most arguments have many counterarguments, and sometimes one of these counterarguments is more convincing than the original argument.

Suppose someone has taken a sample that appears to be random: An interviewer on your campus accosts the first ten students she encounters, and seven of them are fraternity or sorority members. She is now ready to argue that seven-tenths of enrolled students belong to Greek organizations.

You believe, however, that the Greeks are in the minority and point out that she happens to have conducted her interview around the corner from the Panhellenic Society's office just off Sorority Row. Her random sample is anything but. The ball is now back in her court as you await her response to your rebuttal.

As this example illustrates, it is safe to say that we do not understand our own arguments very well until we have tried to get a grip on the places in which they are vulnerable to criticism, counterattack, or refutation. We have already, in Chapter 3, quoted Edmund Burke — but the passage is worth repeating: "He that wrestles with us strengthens our nerves, and sharpens our skill. Our antagonist is our helper."

To be sure, in everyday conversation we may not enjoy being in the company of people who interrupt to ask what are our grounds, warrants, backing, and so forth. The poet T. S. Eliot amusingly characterized himself as such a person:

How Unpleasant to Meet Mr. Eliot!

How unpleasant to meet Mr. Eliot!
With his features of clerical cut.
And his brow so grim
And his mouth so prim
And his conversation, so nicely
Restricted to What Precisely

And If and Perhaps and But . . .
How unpleasant to meet Mr. Eliot!
(Whether his mouth be open or shut.)

Still, if we wish to make serious progress in thinking and arguing about significant issues, cultivating alertness to possible weak spots in arguments—our own arguments as well as the arguments of others— and incorporating thoughtful responses to anticipated criticisms will always be helpful.

IDEA PROMPT 8.1 CONSTRUCTING A TOULMIN ARGUMENT

Claim	What is your argument?	"Driving while texting should be made illegal."
Grounds	What is your evidence?	"A 2011 study shows an increase in accidents due to drivers who drive and text."
Warrant	What reasoning connects your evidence to your argument?	"We should pass laws that promote safer roads."
Backing	Why should the reader agree with your grounds?	"We all use the roads, and we have a duty to make our shared roads as safe as possible."
Rebuttal	What are the objections to this argument?	"Many people would ignore this law just as they ignore laws about seatbelts, thereby making it ineffective, so why pass it in the first place?"
Qualifier	What are the limits of your argument?	"A ban on texting and driving might save some lives, even if it doesn't fix the whole problem."
One possible Toulmin argument	"In light of a 2011 study that shows that texting while driving has contributed to an increase in deadly automobile accidents, texting while driving should be banned. As a community, we have a responsibility to address such serious threats to our safety. Although many people would continue to text while driving, creating penalties for texting while driving may deter some drivers from engaging in such unsafe behavior."	

PUTTING THE TOULMIN METHOD TO WORK:
Responding to an Argument

Let's take a look at another argument—it happens to be on why buying directly from farmers near you won't save the planet—and see how the Toulmin method can be applied. The checklist on page 346 can help you focus your thoughts as you read.

James E. McWilliams

James E. McWilliams, the author of Just Food, *is an associate professor of history at Texas State University. This piece first appeared in* Forbes Magazine *on August 3, 2009.*

The Locavore Myth: Why Buying from Nearby Farmers Won't Save the Planet

Buy local, shrink the distance food travels, save the planet. The locavore movement has captured a lot of fans. To their credit, they are highlighting the problems with industrialized food. But a lot of them are making a big mistake. By focusing on transportation, they overlook other energy-hogging factors in food production.

Take lamb. A 2006 academic study (funded by the New Zealand government) discovered that it made more environmental sense for a Londoner to buy lamb shipped from New Zealand than to buy lamb raised in the U.K. This finding is counterintuitive—if you're only counting food miles. But New Zealand lamb is raised on pastures with a small carbon footprint, whereas most English lamb is produced under intensive factory-like conditions with a big carbon footprint. This disparity overwhelms domestic lamb's advantage in transportation energy.

New Zealand lamb is not exceptional. Take a close look at water usage, fertilizer types, processing methods, and packaging techniques and you discover that factors other than shipping far outweigh the energy it takes to transport food. One analysis, by Rich Pirog of the Leopold Center for Sustainable Agriculture, showed that transportation accounts for only 11 percent of food's carbon footprint. A fourth of the energy required to produce food is expended in the consumer's kitchen. Still more energy is consumed per meal in a restaurant, since restaurants throw away most of their leftovers.

Locavores argue that buying local food supports an area's farmers and, in turn, strengthens the community. Fair enough. Left unacknowledged, however, is the fact that it also hurts farmers in other parts of the world. The U.K. buys most of its green beans from Kenya. While it's true that the beans almost always arrive in airplanes—the form of transportation that consumes the most energy—it's also true that a campaign to shame English consumers with small airplane stickers affixed to flown-in produce threatens the livelihood of 1.5 million sub-Saharan farmers.

Another chink in the locavores' armor involves the way food miles are calculated. To choose a locally grown apple over an apple trucked in from across the country might seem easy. But this decision ignores economies of scale. To take an extreme example, a shipper sending a truck with 2,000 apples over 2,000 miles would consume the same amount of fuel per apple as a local farmer who takes a pickup 50 miles to sell 50 apples at his stall at the green market. The critical measure here is not food miles but apples per gallon.

The one big problem with thinking beyond food miles is that it's hard to get the information you need. Ethically concerned consumers know very little about processing practices, water availability, packaging waste, and fertilizer application. This is an opportunity for watchdog groups. They should make life-cycle carbon counts available to shoppers.

Until our food system becomes more transparent, there is one thing you can do to shrink the carbon footprint of your dinner: Take the meat off your plate. No matter how you slice it, it takes more energy to bring meat, as opposed to plants, to the table. It takes 6 pounds of grain to make a pound of chicken and 10 to 16 pounds to make a pound of beef. That difference translates into big differences in inputs. It requires 2,400 liters of water to make a burger and only 13 liters to grow a tomato. A majority of the water in the American West goes toward the production of pigs, chickens, and cattle.

The average American eats 273 pounds of meat a year. Give up red meat once a week and you'll save as much energy as if the only food miles in your diet were the distance to the nearest truck farmer.

If you want to make a statement, ride your bike to the farmer's market. If you want to reduce greenhouse gases, become a vegetarian.

✓ A CHECKLIST FOR USING THE TOULMIN METHOD

Have I asked the following questions?
- ☐ What claim does the argument make?
- ☐ What grounds are offered for the claim?
- ☐ What warrants the inferences from the grounds to the claim?
- ☐ What backing supports the claim?
- ☐ With what modalities are the claim and grounds asserted?
- ☐ To what rebuttals are the claim, grounds, and backing vulnerable?

See the companion Web site
bedfordstmartins.com/barnetbedau
for links related to the Toulmin model.

THINKING WITH TOULMIN'S METHOD

Remember to make use of the checklist above as you work to find the claim(s), grounds, and warrant(s) that McWilliams puts forward in this short essay.

- First and foremost, what is the **claim** being made by the author? Is it in his title? The opening sentence? Or is it buried in the first paragraph?

McWilliams really gives away his game in his title, even though he opens the essay itself in a way that might make the reader think he is about to launch into a defense of the locavore movement. He even goes out of his way to praise its members ("To their credit . . ."). The signal that his claim really appears already in the title and that he is *not* going to defend the locavore movement is the way he begins the fourth sentence. Notice that, although you may have been told that starting a sentence with *But* is not the best way to write, McWilliams here does so to good effect. Not only does he dramatically counter what he said just prior to that; he also sets up the final sentence of the paragraph, which turns out to be crucial. In this way, he draws sharp attention to his *claim*. How would you state his claim?

- Second, what are the **grounds,** the evidence or reasons, that the author advances in support of his claim?

As it turns out, McWilliams spells out only one example as evidence for his claim. What is it? Is it convincing? Should he have provided more evidence or reasons at this point? It turns out that he does have other grounds to offer—but he mentions them only later. What are those other pieces of evidence?

- Third, what **warrants** does McWilliams offer to show why we should accept his grounds? What authority does he cite? How effective and convincing is this way of trying to get us to accept the grounds he offered in support of his claim?

The essence of the Toulmin method lies in these three elements: the claim(s), the grounds, and the warrant(s). If you have extracted these from McWilliams's essay, you are well on the way to being able to identify the argument he is putting forward. So far, so good. Further probing, however—looking for the other three elements of the Toulmin method (the backing, the modal qualifiers and quantifiers, and the rebuttal)—is essential before you are in a position to actually evaluate the argument. So let's go on.

- Fourth, what **backing** does McWilliams provide? What reasons does he give that might persuade us to accept his argument? Look for what he claimed came out of the analysis that was his basic warrant. He certainly seems to be using factual information—but what if you challenged him? Has he provided adequate reasons for us to believe him? What could he (or would he have to) be able to tell us if we challenged him with questions like "How do you know . . . ?" or "Why do you believe . . . ?" In other words, has he provided adequate backing? Or does he want us to just accept his statement of the facts?

- Fifth, does McWilliams use **modal qualifiers**? Can you find phrases like "in most cases" or "generally it is true that . . . "? Or does he write so boldly—with little in the way of qualifiers or quantifiers—that one is left uncertain about whether to accept his position? Where might he have effectively used qualifiers?

- Finally, does McWilliams use **rebuttals**, the reasons given in anticipation of someone rejecting the author's claim, or conceding the claim but rejecting the grounds? Does McWilliams anticipate rejections and prepare rebuttals? Does he offer anything to forestall criticisms? If so, what is it that he does? If not, what could or should he have done?

Just how good an argument has McWilliams made? Is he convincing? If you identified weak points in his argument, what are they? Can you help strengthen the argument?

9

A Logician's View: Deduction, Induction, Fallacies

Logic is the anatomy of thought.

— JOHN LOCKE

Logic takes care of itself; all we have to do is to look and see how it does it.

— LUDWIG WITTGENSTEIN

In Chapter 3 we introduced the terms *deduction, induction,* and *fallacy.* Here we discuss them in greater detail.

DEDUCTION

The basic aim of deductive reasoning is to start with some assumption or premise and extract from it a conclusion—a logical consequence—that is concealed but implicit in it. Thus, taking the simplest case, if I assert as a premise

  1a. Nuclear power poses more risks of harm to the environment than fossil fuels.

then it is a matter of simple deduction to infer the conclusion that

  1b. Fossil fuels pose fewer risks of harm to the environment than nuclear power.

Anyone who understands English would grant that 1b follows 1a—or equivalently, that 1b can be validly deduced from 1a—because whatever two objects, *A* and *B,* you choose, if *A* does *more things than B,* then *B* must do *fewer things than A.*

  Thus, in this and all other cases of valid deductive reasoning, we can say not only that we are entitled to *infer* the conclusion from the premise—in this case, infer 1b from 1a—but that the premise *implies* the conclusion. Remember, too, the conclusion (1b) that fossil fuels pose fewer risks than nuclear power—inferred or deduced from the statement (1a) that nuclear power poses more risks—does not depend on the truth of the statement that nuclear power poses more risks. If the speaker (falsely) asserts that nuclear power poses more risks, then the hearer validly (that is to say, logically) concludes that fossil fuels pose fewer risks. Thus, 1b follows from 1a whether or not 1a is true; consequently, if 1a is true, then so is 1b; but if 1a is false, then 1b must be false also.

Let's take another example—more interesting but comparably simple:

2a. President Truman was underrated by his critics.

Given 2a, a claim amply verified by events of the 1950s, one is entitled to infer

2b. His critics underrated President Truman.

On what basis can we argue that 2a implies 2b? The two propositions are equivalent because a rule of English grammar assures us that we can convert the position of subject and predicate phrases in a sentence by shifting from the passive to the active voice (or vice versa) without any change in the conditions that make the proposition true (or false).

Both pairs of examples illustrate that in deductive reasoning, our aim is to transform, reformulate, or restate in our conclusion some (or, as in the two examples above, all) of the information contained in our premises.

Remember, even though a proposition or statement follows from a previous proposition or statement, the statements need not be true. We can see why if we consider another example. Suppose someone asserts or claims that

3a. The Gettysburg Address is longer than the Declaration of Independence.

As every student of American history knows, 3a is false. But false or not, we can validly deduce from it that

3b. The Declaration of Independence is shorter than the Gettysburg Address.

This inference is valid (even though the conclusion is untrue) because the conclusion follows logically (more precisely, deductively) from 3a: In English, as we know, the meaning of "*A* is shorter than *B*," which appears in 3b, is simply the converse of "*B* is longer than *A*," which appears in 3a.

The deductive relation between 3a and 3b reminds us again that the idea of validity, which is so crucial to deduction, is not the same as the idea of truth. False propositions have implications—logical consequences—too, just as true propositions do.

In the three pairs of examples so far, what can we point to as the warrant for our claims? Well, look at the reasoning in each case; the arguments rely on rules of ordinary English, on the accepted meanings of words like *on*, *under*, and *underrated*.

In many cases, of course, the deductive inference or pattern of reasoning is much more complex than that which we have seen in the examples so far. When we introduced the idea of deduction in Chapter 3, we gave as our primary example the *syllogism*. Here is another example:

> 4. Texas is larger than California; California is larger than Arizona; therefore, Texas is larger than Arizona.

The conclusion in this syllogism is derivable from the two premises; that is, anyone who asserts the two premises is committed to accepting the conclusion as well, whether or not one thinks of it.

Notice again that the *truth* of the conclusion is not established merely by validity of the inference. The conclusion in this syllogism happens to be true. And the premises of this syllogism imply the conclusion. But the argument establishes the conclusion only because both of the premises on which the conclusion depends are true. Even a Californian admits that Texas is larger than California, which in turn is larger than Arizona. In other words, argument 4 is a *sound* argument because (as we explained in Chapter 3) it is valid and all its premises are true. All—and only—arguments that *prove* their conclusions have these two traits.

How might we present the warrant for the argument in 4? Short of a crash course in formal logic, either of two strategies might suffice. One is to argue from the fact that the validity of the inference depends on the meaning of a key concept, *being larger than*. This concept has the property of *transitivity*, a property that many concepts share (for example, *is equal to, is to the right of, is smarter than*—all are transitive concepts). Consequently, whatever *A*, *B*, and *C* are, if *A* is larger than *B*, and *B* is larger than *C*, then *A* will be larger than *C*. The final step is to substitute "Texas," "California," and "Arizona" for *A*, *B*, and *C*, respectively.

A second strategy, less abstract and more graphic, is to think of representing Texas, California, and Arizona by nested circles. Thus, the first premise in argument 4 would look like this:

The second premise would look like this:

The conclusion would look like this:

We can see that this conclusion follows from the premises because it amounts to nothing more than what one gets by superimposing the two premises on each other. Thus, the whole argument can be represented like this:

The so-called middle term in the argument—California—disappears from the conclusion; its role is confined to be the link between the other two terms, Texas and Arizona, in the premises. (This is an adaptation of the technique used in elementary formal logic known as Venn diagrams.) In this manner one can give graphic display to the important fact that the conclusion follows from the premises because one can literally *see* the conclusion represented by nothing more than a representation of the premises.

Both of these strategies bring out the fact that validity of deductive inference is a purely *formal* property of argument. Each strategy abstracts the form from the content of the propositions involved to show how the concepts in the premises are related to the concepts in the conclusion.

For the sake of illustration, here is another syllogistic argument with the same logical features as argument 4. (A nice exercise is to restate argument 5 using diagrams in the manner of argument 4.)

> 5. African American slaves were treated worse than white indentured servants. Indentured white servants were treated worse than free white labor. Therefore, African American slaves were treated worse than free white labor.

Not all deductive reasoning occurs in syllogisms, however, or at least not in syllogisms like the ones in 4 and 5. (The term *syllogism* is sometimes used to refer to any deductive argument of whatever form, provided only that it has two premises.) In fact, syllogisms such as 4 are not the commonest form of our deductive reasoning at all. Nor are they the simplest (and of course, not the most complex). For an argument that is even simpler, consider this:

> 6. If a youth is an African American slave, he is probably treated worse than a youth in indentured service. This youth is an African American slave. Therefore, he is probably treated worse than if he had been an indentured servant.

Here the pattern of reasoning has the form: If *A*, then *B*; *A*; there-fore, *B*. Notice that the content of the assertions represented by *A* and *B* do not matter; any set of expressions having the same form or structure will do equally well, including assertions built out of meaningless terms, as in this example:

7. If the slithy toves, then the gyres gimble. The slithy toves. There-fore, the gyres gimble.

Argument 7 has the form: If *A*, then *B*; *A*; therefore *B*. As a piece of deduc-tive inference it is every bit as good as argument 6. Unlike 6, however, 7 is of no interest to us because none of its assertions make any sense (unless you are a reader of Lewis Carroll's "Jabberwocky," and even then the sense of 7 is doubtful). You cannot, in short, use a valid deductive argument to prove anything unless the premises and the conclusion are *true,* but they can't be true unless they *mean* something in the first place.

This parallel between arguments 6 and 7 shows once again that deductive validity in an argument rests on the *form* or structure of the argument, and not on its content or meaning. If all one can say about an argument is that it is valid—that is, its conclusion follows from the premises—one has not given a sufficient reason for accepting the argu-ment's conclusion. It has been said that the Devil can quote Scripture; similarly, an argument can be deductively valid and of no further interest or value whatever because valid (but false) conclusions can be drawn from false or even meaningless assumptions. For example,

8. New York's Metropolitan Museum of Art has the finest collection of abstract impressionist painting in the world. The finest collec-tion of abstract impressionist paintings includes dozens of can-vases by Winslow Homer. Therefore, the Metropolitan Museum of Art has dozens of paintings by Winslow Homer.

Here, the conclusion follows validly from the premises, even though all three propositions are false. Nevertheless, although validity by itself is not enough, it is a necessary condition of any deductive argument that purports to establish its conclusion.

Now let us consider another argument with the same form as 8, only more interesting.

9. If President Truman knew the Japanese were about to surrender, then it was immoral of him to order that atom bombs be dropped on Hiroshima and Nagasaki. Truman knew the Japanese were about to surrender. Therefore, it was immoral of him to order dropping those bombs.

As in the two previous examples, anyone who assents to the premises in argument 9 must assent to the conclusion; the form of arguments 8 and 9 is identical. But do the premises of argument 9 *prove* the conclu-sion? That depends on whether both premises are true. Well, are they?

This turns on a number of considerations, and it is worthwhile pausing to examine this argument closely to illustrate the kinds of things that are involved in answering this question.

Let us begin by examining the second (minor) premise. Its truth is controversial even to this day. Autobiography, memoranda, other documentary evidence—all are needed to assemble the evidence to back up the grounds for the thesis or claim made in the conclusion of this valid argument. Evaluating this material effectively will probably involve not only further deductions but inductive reasoning as well.

Now consider the first (major) premise in argument 9. Its truth doesn't depend on what history shows but on the moral principles one accepts. The major premise has the form of a hypothetical proposition ("if . . . then . . .") and asserts a connection between two very different kinds of things. The antecedent of the hypothetical (the clause following "if") mentions facts about Truman's *knowledge,* and the consequent of the hypothetical (the clause following "then") mentions facts about the *morality* of his conduct in light of such knowledge. The major premise as a whole can thus be seen as expressing *a principle of moral responsibility.*

Such principles can, of course, be controversial. In this case, for instance, is the principle peculiarly relevant to the knowledge and conduct of a president of the United States? Probably not; it is far more likely that this principle is merely a special case of a more general proposition about anyone's moral responsibility. (After all, we know a great deal more about the conditions of our own moral responsibility than we do about those of high government officials.) We might express this more general principle in this way: If we have knowledge that would make our violent conduct unnecessary, then we are immoral if we deliberately act violently anyway. Thus, accepting this general principle can serve as a basis for defending the major premise of argument 9.

We have examined this argument in some detail because it illustrates the kinds of considerations needed to test whether a given argument is not only valid but whether its premises are true—that is, whether its premises really prove the conclusion.

The great value of the form of argument known as hypothetical syllogism, exemplified by arguments 6 and 7, is that the structure of the argument is so simple and so universally applicable in reasoning that it is often both easy and worthwhile to formulate one's claims so that they can be grounded by an argument of this sort.

Before leaving the subject of deductive inference, consider three other forms of argument, each of which can be found in actual use elsewhere in the readings in this volume. The simplest of these is **disjunctive syllogism,** so called because its major premise is a **disjunction.** For example,

> 10. Either censorship of television shows is overdue, or our society
>   is indifferent to the education of its youth. Our society is not

indifferent to the education of its youth. Therefore, censorship of television is overdue.

Notice, by the way, that the validity of an argument, as in this case, does not turn on pedantic repetition of every word or phrase as the argument moves along; nonessential elements can be dropped, or equivalent expressions substituted for variety without adverse effect on the reasoning. Thus, in conversation or in writing, the argument in 10 might actually be presented like this:

11. Either censorship of television is overdue, or our society is indifferent to the education of its youth. But, of course, we aren't indifferent; it's censorship that's overdue.

The key feature of disjunctive syllogism, as example 11 suggests, is that the conclusion is whichever of the disjuncts is left over after the others have been negated in the minor premise. Thus, we could easily have a very complex disjunctive syllogism, with a dozen disjuncts in the major premise, and seven of them denied in the minor premise, leaving a conclusion of the remaining five. Usually, however, a disjunctive argument is formulated in this manner: Assert a disjunction with two or more disjuncts in the major premise; then *deny all but one* in the minor premise; and infer validly the remaining disjunct as the conclusion. That was the form of argument 11.

Another type of argument, especially favored by orators and rhetoricians, is the **dilemma.** Ordinarily we use the term *dilemma* in the sense of an awkward predicament, as when we say, "His dilemma was that he didn't have enough money to pay the waiter." But when logicians refer to a dilemma, they mean a forced choice between two or more equally unattractive alternatives. For example, the predicament of the U.S. government during the mid-1980s as it faced the crisis brought on by terrorist attacks on American civilian targets, which were believed, during that time, to be inspired and supported by the Libyan government, can be formulated in a dilemma:

12. If the United States bombs targets in Libya, innocent people will be killed, and the Arab world will be angered. If the United States doesn't bomb Libyan targets, then terrorists will go unpunished, and the United States will lose respect among other governments. Either the United States bombs Libyan targets, or it doesn't. Therefore, in either case unattractive consequences will follow: The innocent will be killed, or terrorists will go unpunished.

Notice first the structure of the argument: two conditional propositions asserted as premises, followed by another premise that states a **necessary truth.** (The premise, "Either we bomb the Libyans, or we don't," is a disjunction; since its two alternatives are exhaustive, one of the two alternatives must be true. Such a statement is often called analytically true, or a *tautology*.) No doubt the conclusion of this dilemma follows from its premises.

But does the argument prove, as it purports to do, that whatever the U.S. government does, it will suffer "unattractive consequences"? It is customary to speak of "the horns of the dilemma," as though the challenge posed by the dilemma were like a bull ready to gore you whichever direction you turn. But if the two conditional premises failed to exhaust the possibilities, then one can escape from the dilemma by going "between the horns," that is, by finding a third alternative. If (as in this case) that is not possible, one can still ask whether both of the main premises are true. (In this argument, it should be clear that neither of these main premises spells out all or even most of the consequences that could be foreseen.) Even so, in cases where both these conditional premises are true, it may be that the consequences of one alternative are nowhere nearly so bad as those of the other. If that is true, but our reasoning stops before evaluating that fact, we may be guilty of failing to distinguish between the greater and the lesser of two admitted evils. The logic of the dilemma itself cannot decide this choice for us. Instead, we must bring to bear empirical inquiry and imagination to the evaluation of the grounds of the dilemma itself.

Writers commonly use the term *dilemma* without explicitly formulating the dilemma to which they refer, leaving it for the readers to do. And sometimes, what is called a dilemma really isn't one. (Remember the dog's tail? Calling it a leg doesn't make it a leg.) As an example, consider the plight of Sophie in William Styron's novel, *Sophie's Choice*. The scene is Birkenau, the main Nazi extermination camp during World War II. Among the thousands arriving at the prison gates are Sophie and her two children, Jan and Eva. On the train platform they are confronted by a Nazi SS medical officer. He will decide which are the lucky ones; they will live to work in the camp. The rest will go to their death in the gas chambers. When Sophie insists she is Polish but not Jewish, the officer says she may choose one of her children to be saved. Which of the two ought to be saved? On what basis ought Sophie resolve her dilemma? It looks as if she has only two alternatives, each of which presents her with an agonizing outcome. Or is there a third way out?

Finally, one of the most powerful and dramatic forms of argument is **reductio ad absurdum** (from the Latin, meaning "reduction to absurdity"). The idea of a reductio argument is to disprove a proposition by showing the absurdity of its inevitable conclusion. It is used, of course, to refute your opponent's position and prove your own. For example, in Plato's *Republic,* Socrates asks an old gentleman, Cephalus, to define what right conduct is. Cephalus says that it consists of paying your debts and keeping your word. Socrates rejects this answer by showing that it leads to a contradiction. He argues that Cephalus cannot have given the correct answer because if we believe that he did, we will be quickly led into contradictions; in some cases when you keep your word you will nonetheless be doing the wrong thing. For suppose, says Socrates, that you borrowed a weapon from a man, promising to return it when he asks for it. One day he comes to your door, demanding his weapon and swearing angrily that he intends to murder a neighbor. Keeping your word under those circumstances is absurd, Socrates implies, and the reader of the dialogue is left to infer that Cephalus's definition, which led to this result, is refuted.

Let's take a closer look at another example. Suppose you are opposed to any form of gun control, whereas I am in favor of gun control. I might try to refute your position by attacking it with a reductio argument. To do that, I start out by assuming the very opposite of what I believe or favor and try to establish a contradiction that results from following out the consequences of this initial assumption. My argument might look like this:

13. Let's assume your position—namely, that there ought to be no legal restrictions whatever on the sale and ownership of guns. That means that you'd permit having every neighborhood hardware store sell pistols and rifles to whoever walks in the door. But that's not all. You apparently also would permit selling machine guns to children, antitank weapons to lunatics, small-bore cannons to the nearsighted, as well as guns and the ammunition to go with them to anyone with a criminal record. But this is utterly preposterous. No one could favor such a dangerous policy. So the only question worth debating is what kind of gun control is necessary.

Now in this example, my reductio of your position on gun control is not based on claiming to show that you have strictly contradicted yourself, for there is no purely logical contradiction in opposing all forms of gun control. Instead, what I have tried to do is to show that there is a contradiction between what you profess—no gun controls whatever—and what you probably really believe, if only you will stop to think about it—no lunatic should be allowed to buy a loaded machine gun.

My refutation of your position rests on whether I succeed in establishing an inconsistency among your own beliefs. If it turns out that you really believe lunatics should be free to purchase guns and ammunition, then my attempted refutation fails.

In explaining reductio ad absurdum, we have had to rely on another idea fundamental to logic, that of **contradiction,** or inconsistency. (We used this idea, remember, to define validity in Chapter 3. A deductive argument is valid if and only if affirming the premises and denying the conclusion results in a contradiction.) The opposite of contradiction is **consistency,** a notion of hardly less importance to good reasoning than validity. These concepts deserve a few words of further explanation and illustration. Consider this pair of assertions:

14. Abortion is homicide.

15. Racism is unfair.

No one would plausibly claim that we can infer or deduce 15 from 14, or, for that matter, 14 from 15. This almost goes without saying because there is no evident connection between these two assertions. They are unrelated assertions; logically speaking, they are *independent* of each other. In such cases the two assertions are mutually *consistent;* that is, both could be true—or both could be false. But now consider another proposition:

16. Euthanasia is not murder.

Could a person assert 14 (*Abortion is homicide*) and also assert 16 (*Euthanasia is not murder*) and be consistent? This question is equivalent to asking whether one could assert the **conjunction** of these two propositions—namely,

17. Abortion is homicide, and euthanasia is not murder.

It is not so easy to say whether 17 is consistent or inconsistent. The kinds of moral scruples that might lead a person to assert one of these conjuncts (that is, one of the two initial propositions, *Abortion is homicide* and *Euthanasia is not murder*) might lead to the belief that the other one must be false and thus to the conclusion that 17 is inconsistent. (Notice that if 14 were the assertion that *Abortion is murder,* instead of *Abortion is homicide,* the problem of asserting consistently both 14 and 16 would be more acute.) Yet if we think again, we might imagine someone being convinced that there is no inconsistency in asserting that *Abortion is homicide,* say, and that *Euthanasia is not murder,* or even the reverse. (For instance, suppose you believed that the unborn deserve a chance to live and that putting elderly persons to death in a painless manner and with their consent confers a benefit on them.)

Let us generalize: We can say of any set of propositions that they are *consistent* if and only if *all could be true together.* (Notice that it follows from this definition that propositions mutually imply each other, as do *Seabiscuit was America's fastest racehorse* and *America's fastest racehorse was Seabiscuit.*) Remember that, once again, the truth of the assertions in question does not matter. Two propositions can be consistent or not, quite apart from whether they are true. Not so with falsehood: It follows from our definition of consistency that an *inconsistent* proposition must be *false.* (We have relied on this idea in explaining how a reductio ad absurdum works.)

Assertions or claims that are not consistent can take either of two forms. Suppose you assert proposition 14, that abortion is homicide, early in an essay you are writing, but later you assert that

18. Abortion is harmless.

You have now asserted a position on abortion that is strictly contrary to the one with which you began; contrary in the sense that both assertions 14 and 18 cannot be true. It is simply not true that, if an abortion involves killing a human being (which is what *homicide* strictly means), then it causes no one any harm (killing a person always causes harm—even if it is excusable, justifiable, not wrong, the best thing to do in the circumstances, and so on). Notice that although 14 and 18 cannot both be true, they can both be false. In fact, many people who are perplexed about the morality of abortion believe precisely this. They concede that abortion does harm the fetus, so 18 must be false; but they also believe that abortion doesn't kill a person, so 14 must also be false.

Or consider another, simpler case. If you describe the glass as half empty and I describe it as half full, both of us can be right; the two assertions are consistent, even though they sound vaguely incompatible. (This is the reason that disputing over whether the glass is half full or half empty has become the popular paradigm of a futile, purely *verbal disagreement*.) But if I describe the glass as half empty whereas you insist that it is two-thirds empty, then we have a real disagreement; your description and mine are strictly contrary, in that both cannot be true—although both can be false. (Both are false if the glass is only one-quarter full.)

This, by the way, enables us to define the difference between a pair of **contradictory** propositions and a pair of **contrary** propositions. Two propositions are contrary if and only if both cannot be true (though both can be false); two propositions are contradictory if and only if they are such that if one is true the other must be false, and vice versa. Thus, if Jack says that Alice Walker's *The Color Purple* is a better novel than Mark Twain's *Huckleberry Finn*, and Jill says, "No, *Huckleberry Finn* is better than *The Color Purple*," she is contradicting Jack. If what either one of them says is true, then what the other says must be false.

A more subtle case of contradiction arises when two or more of one's own beliefs implicitly contradict each other. We may find ourselves saying "Travel is broadening," and saying an hour later, "People don't really change." Just beneath the surface of these two beliefs lies a self-contradiction: How can travel broaden us unless it influences—and changes—our beliefs, values, and outlook? But if we can't really change ourselves, then traveling to new places won't change us, either. (Indeed, there is a Roman saying to the effect that travelers change the skies above them, not their hearts.) "Travel is broadening" and "People don't change" collide with each other; something has to give.

Our point, of course, is not that you must never say today something that contradicts something you said yesterday. Far from it; if you think you were mistaken yesterday, of course you will take a different position today. But what you want to avoid is what George Orwell called *doublethink* in his novel *1984*: "*Doublethink* means the power of holding two contradictory beliefs in one's mind simultaneously, and accepting them both."

Genuine contradiction, and not merely contrary assertion, is the situation we should expect to find in some disputes. Someone advances a thesis—such as the assertion in 14, *Abortion is homicide*—and someone else flatly contradicts it by the simple expedient of negating it, thus:

19. Abortion is not homicide.

If we can trust public opinion polls, many of us are not sure whether to agree with 14 or with 19. But we should agree that whichever is true, *both* cannot be true, and *both* cannot be false. The two assertions, between them, exclude all other possibilities; they pose a forced choice for our belief. (Again, we have met this idea, too, in a reductio ad absurdum.)

Now it is one thing for Jack and Jill in a dispute or argument to contradict each other. It is quite another matter for Jack to contradict himself. One wants (or should want) to avoid self-contradiction because of the embarrassing position in which one then finds oneself. Once I have contradicted myself, what are others to believe I really believe? What, indeed, *do* I believe, for that matter?

It may be, as Emerson observed, that a "foolish consistency is the hobgoblin of little minds"—that is, it may be shortsighted to purchase a consistency in one's beliefs at the expense of flying in the face of common sense. But making an effort to avoid a foolish inconsistency is the hallmark of serious thinking.

While we are speaking of inconsistency, we should spend a moment on **paradox.** The word refers to two different things:

- an assertion that is essentially self-contradictory and therefore cannot be true and

- a seemingly contradictory assertion that nevertheless may be true.

An example of the first might be, "Evaluations concerning quality in literature are all a matter of personal judgment, but Shakespeare is the world's greatest writer." It is hard to make any sense out of this assertion. Contrast it with a paradox of the second sort, a *seeming* contradiction that may make sense, such as "The longest way round is the shortest way home," or "Work is more fun than fun," or "The best way to find happiness is not to look for it." Here we have assertions that are striking because as soon as we hear them we realize that, although they seem inconsistent and self-defeating, they contain (or may contain) profound truths. Paradoxes of this second sort are especially common in religious texts, where they may imply a mysterious reality concealed by a world of contradictory appearances. Examples are "Some who are last shall be first, and some who are first shall be last" (Jesus, quoted in Luke 13:30), and "Death, thou shalt die" (the poet John Donne, alluding to the idea that the person who has faith in Jesus dies to this world but lives eternally). If you use the word *paradox* in your own writing—for instance, to characterize an argument that you are reading—be sure that your reader will understand in which sense you are using the word. (And, of course, you will not want to write paradoxes of the first, self-contradictory sort.)

INDUCTION

Deduction involves logical thinking that applies to any assertion or claim whatever—because every possible statement, true or false, has its deductive logical consequences. Induction is relevant to one kind of assertion only; namely, to **empirical** or *factual* claims. Other kinds of assertions (such as definitions, mathematical equations, and moral or legal norms) simply are not the product of inductive reasoning and cannot serve as a basis for further inductive thinking.

And so, in studying the methods of induction, we are exploring tactics and strategies useful in gathering and then using **evidence**—empirical, observational, experimental—in support of a belief as its ground. Modern scientific knowledge is the product of these methods, and they differ somewhat from one science to another because they depend on the theories and technology appropriate to each of the sciences. Here, all we can do is discuss generally the more abstract features common to inductive inquiry generally. For fuller details, you must eventually consult your local physicist, chemist, geologist, or their colleagues and counterparts in other scientific fields.

Observation and Inference

Let us begin with a simple example. Suppose we have evidence (actually we don't, but that will not matter for our purposes) in support of the claim that

1. In a sample of 500 smokers, 230 persons observed have cardiovascular disease.

The basis for asserting 1—the evidence or ground—would be, presumably, straightforward physical examination of the 500 persons in the sample, one by one.

With this claim in hand, we can think of the purpose and methods of induction as being pointed in both of two opposite directions: toward establishing the basis or ground of the very empirical proposition with which we start (in this example, the observation stated in 1) or toward understanding what that observation indicates or suggests as a more general, inclusive, or fundamental fact of nature.

In each case, we start from something we *do* know (or take for granted and treat as a sound starting point)—some fact of nature, perhaps a striking or commonplace event that we have observed and recorded—and then go on to something we do *not* fully know and perhaps cannot directly observe. In example 1, only the second of these two orientations is of any interest, and so let us concentrate exclusively on it. Let us also generously treat as a *method* of induction any regular pattern or style of nondeductive reasoning that we could use to support a claim such as that in 1.

Anyone truly interested in the observed fact that *230 of 500 smokers have cardiovascular disease* is likely to start speculating about, and thus be interested in finding out, whether any or all of several other propositions are also true. For example, one might wonder whether

> 2. *All* smokers have cardiovascular disease or will develop it during their lifetimes.

This claim is a straightforward generalization of the original observation as reported in claim 1. When we think inductively about the linkage between 1 and 2, we are reasoning from an observed sample (some smokers—that is, 230 of the 500 *observed*) to the entire membership of a more inclusive class (*all* smokers, whether observed or not). The fundamental question raised by reasoning from the narrower claim 1 to the broader claim 2 is whether we have any ground for believing that what is true of *some* members of a class is true of them *all*. So the difference between 1 and 2 is that of *quantity* or scope.

We can also think inductively about the *relation* between the factors mentioned in 1. Having observed data as reported in 1, we may be tempted to assert a different and profounder kind of claim:

> 3. Smoking *causes* cardiovascular disease.

Here our interest is not merely in generalizing from a sample to a whole class; it is the far more important one of *explaining* the observation with which we began in claim 1. Certainly the preferred, even if not the only, mode of explanation for a natural phenomenon is a *causal* explanation. In proposition 3, we propose to explain the presence of one phenomenon (cardiovascular disease) by the prior occurrence of an independent phenomenon (smoking). The observation reported in 1 is now being used as evidence or support for this new conjecture stated in 3.

Our original claim in 1 asserted no causal relation between anything and anything else; whatever the cause of cardiovascular disease may be, that cause is not observed, mentioned, or assumed in assertion 1. Similarly, the observation asserted in claim 1 is consistent with many explanations. For example, the explanation of 1 might not be 3, but some other, undetected, carcinogenic factor unrelated to smoking—for instance, exposure to high levels of radon. The question one now faces is what can be added to 1, or teased out of it, to produce an adequate ground for claiming 3. (We shall return to this example for closer scrutiny.)

But there is a third way to go beyond 1. Instead of a straightforward generalization, as we had in 2, or a pronouncement on the cause of a phenomenon, as in 3, we might have a somewhat more complex and cautious further claim in mind, such as this:

4. Smoking is a factor in the causation of cardiovascular disease in some persons.

This proposition, like 3, advances a claim about causation. But 4 is obviously a weaker claim than 3. That is, other observations, theories, or evidence that would require us to reject 3 might be consistent with 4; evidence that would support 4 could easily fail to be enough to support 3. Consequently, it is even possible that 4 is true although 3 is false, because 4 allows for other (unmentioned) factors in the causation of cardiovascular disease (genetic or dietary factors, for example) that may not be found in all smokers.

Propositions 2, 3, and 4 differ from proposition 1 in an important respect. We began by assuming that 1 states an empirical fact based on direct observation, whereas these others do not. Instead, they state empirical *hypotheses* or conjectures—tentative generalizations not fully confirmed—each of which goes beyond the observed facts asserted in 1. Each of 2, 3, and 4 can be regarded as an *inductive inference* from 1. We can also say that 2, 3, and 4 are hypotheses relative to 1, even if relative to some other starting point (such as all the information that scientists today really have about smoking and cardiovascular disease) they are not.

Probability

Another way of formulating the last point is to say that whereas proposition 1, a statement of observed fact (*230 out of 500 smokers have cardiovascular disease*), has a **probability** of 1.0—that is, it is absolutely certain—the probability of each of the hypotheses stated in 2, 3, and 4, *relative* to 1 is smaller than 1.0. (We need not worry here about how much smaller than 1.0 the probabilities are, nor about how to calculate these probabilities precisely.) Relative to some starting point other than 1, however, the probability of these same three hypotheses might be quite different. Of course, it still would not be 1.0, absolute certainty. But it takes only a moment's reflection to realize that, whatever may be the probability of 2 or 3 or 4 relative to 1, those probabilities in each case will be quite different relative to different information, such as this:

5. Ten persons observed in a sample of 500 smokers have cardiovascular disease.

The idea that a *given proposition can have different probabilities* relative to different bases is fundamental to all inductive reasoning. It can be convincingly illustrated by the following example. Suppose we want to consider the probability of this proposition being true:

6. Susanne Smith will live to be eighty.

Taken as an abstract question of fact, we cannot even guess what the probability is with any assurance. But we can do better than guess; we can in fact even calculate the answer, if we are given some further information. Thus, suppose we are told that

    7. Susanne Smith is seventy-nine.

Our original question then becomes one of determining the probability that 6 is true given 7; that is, relative to the evidence contained in proposition 7. No doubt, if Susanne Smith really is seventy-nine, then the probability that she will live to be eighty is greater than if we know only that

    8. Susanne Smith is more than nine years old.

Obviously, a lot can happen to Susanne in the seventy years between nine and seventy-nine that is not very likely to happen to her in the one year between seventy-nine and eighty. And so, proposition 6 is more probable relative to proposition 7 than it is relative to proposition 8.

    Let us suppose for the sake of the argument that the following is true:

    9. Ninety percent of the women alive at seventy-nine live to be eighty.

Given this additional information, and the information that Susanne is seventy-nine, we now have a basis for answering our original question about proposition 6 with some precision. But suppose, in addition to 8, we are also told that

    10. Susanne Smith is suffering from inoperable cancer.

and also that

    11. The survival rate for women suffering from inoperable cancer is 0.6 years (that is, the average life span for women after a diagnosis of inoperable cancer is about seven months).

With this new information, the probability that 6 will be true has dropped significantly, all because we can now estimate the probability in relation to a new body of evidence.

    The probability of an event, thus, is not a fixed number but one that varies because it is always relative to some evidence—and given different evidence, one and the same event can have different probabilities. In other words, the probability of any event is always relative to how much is known (assumed, believed), and because different persons may know different things about a given event, or the same person may know different things at different times, one and the same event can have two or more probabilities. This conclusion is not a paradox but a logical consequence of the concept of what it is for an event to have (that is, to be assigned) a probability.

    If we shift to the *calculation* of probabilities, we find that generally we have two ways to calculate them. One way to proceed is by the method of **a priori** or **equal probabilities**—that is, by reference to the relevant possibilities taken abstractly and apart from any other information. Thus, in an election contest with only two candidates, Smith and Jones, each of the candidates has a fifty-fifty chance of winning (whereas in a three-candidate race, each candidate would have one chance in three of winning). Therefore, the probability that Smith will win is 0.5, and the probability that Jones will win is also 0.5. (The sum of the probabilities of all possible independent outcomes must always equal 1.0, which is obvious enough if you think about it.)

But in politics the probabilities are not reasonably calculated so abstractly. We know that many empirical factors affect the outcome of an election and that a calculation of probabilities in ignorance of those factors is likely to be drastically misleading. In our example of the two-candidate election, suppose Smith has strong party support and is the incumbent, whereas Jones represents a party long out of power and is further handicapped by being relatively unknown. No one who knows anything about electoral politics would give Jones the same chance of winning as Smith. The two events are not equiprobable in relation to all the information available.

Not only that, a given event can have more than one probability. This happens whenever we calculate a probability by relying on different bodies of data that report how often the event in question has been observed to happen. Probabilities calculated in this way are **relative frequencies.** Our earlier hypothetical example of Susanne Smith provides an illustration. If she is a smoker and we have observed that 100 out of a random set of 500 smokers are observed to have cardiovascular disease, we have a basis for claiming that she has a probability of 100 in 500, or 0.2 (one-fifth), of having this disease. However, if we had other data showing that 250 out of 500 women smokers ages eighty or older have cardiovascular disease, we have a basis for believing that there is a probability of 250 in 500, or 0.5 (one-half), that she has this disease. Notice, of course, that in both calculations we assume that Susanne Smith is not among the persons we have examined. In both cases we infer the probability with which she has this disease from observing its frequency in populations that exclude her.

Both methods of calculating probabilities are legitimate; in each case the calculation is relative to observed circumstances. But as the examples show, it is most reasonable to have recourse to the method of equiprobabilities only when few or no other factors affecting possible outcomes are known.

Mill's Methods

Let us return to our earlier discussion of smoking and cardiovascular disease and consider in greater detail the question of a causal connection between the two phenomena. We began thus:

1. In a sample of 500 smokers, 230 persons observed have cardiovascular disease.

We regarded 1 as an observed fact, though in truth, of course, it is mere supposition. Our question now is, how might we augment this information so as to strengthen our confidence that

    3. Smoking *causes* cardiovascular disease.

or at least

    4. Smoking is a factor in the causation of cardiovascular disease in some persons.

Suppose further examination showed that

    12. In the sample of 230 smokers with cardiovascular disease, no other suspected factor (such as genetic predisposition, lack of physical exercise, age over fifty) was also observed.

Such an observation would encourage us to believe 3 or 4 is true. Why? We are encouraged to believe it because we are inclined to believe also that whatever the cause of a phenomenon is, it must *always* be present when its effect is present. Thus, the inference from 1 to 3 or 4 is supported by 12, using **Mill's Method of Agreement,** named after the British philosopher, John Stuart Mill (1806–1873), who first formulated it. It is called a method of agreement because of the way in which the inference relies on *agreement* among the observed phenomena where a presumed cause is thought to be *present.*

    Let us now suppose that in our search for evidence to support 3 or 4 we conduct additional research and discover that

    13. In a sample of 500 nonsmokers, selected to be representative of both sexes, different ages, dietary habits, exercise patterns, and so on, none is observed to have cardiovascular disease.

This observation would further encourage us to believe that we had obtained significant additional confirmation of 3 or 4. Why? Because we now know that factors present (such as male sex, lack of exercise, family history of cardiovascular disease) in cases where the effect is absent (no cardiovascular disease observed) cannot be the cause. This is an example of **Mill's Method of Difference,** so called because the cause or causal factor of an effect must be *different* from whatever the factors are that are present when the effect is *absent.*

    Suppose now that, increasingly confident we have found the cause of cardiovascular disease, we study our first sample of 230 smokers ill with the disease, and discover this:

    14. Those who smoke two or more packs of cigarettes daily for ten or more years have cardiovascular disease either much younger or much more severely than those who smoke less.

This is an application of **Mill's Method of Concomitant Variation,** perhaps the most convincing of the three methods. Here we deal not merely with the presence of the conjectured cause (smoking) or the absence of the effect we are studying (cardiovascular disease), as we were previously, but with the more interesting and subtler matter of the *degree and regularity of the correlation* of the supposed cause and effect. According to the observations reported in 14, it strongly appears that the more we have of the "cause" (smoking), the sooner or the more intense the onset of the "effect" (cardiovascular disease).

Notice, however, what happens to our confirmation of 3 and 4 if, instead of the observation reported in 14, we had observed

15. In a representative sample of 500 nonsmokers, cardiovascular disease was observed in 34 cases.

(Let us not pause here to explain what makes a sample more or less representative of a population, although the representativeness of samples is vital to all statistical reasoning.) Such an observation would lead us almost immediately to suspect some other or additional causal factor: Smoking might indeed be *a* factor in causing cardiovascular disease, but it can hardly be *the* cause because (using Mill's Method of Difference) we cannot have the effect, as we do in the observed sample reported in 15, unless we also have the cause.

An observation such as the one in 15, however, is likely to lead us to think our hypothesis that *smoking causes cardiovascular disease* has been disconfirmed. But we have a fallback position ready; we can still defend a weaker hypothesis, namely 4, *Smoking is a factor in the causation of cardiovascular disease in some persons.* Even if 3 stumbles over the evidence in 15, 4 does not. It is still quite possible that smoking is a factor in causing this disease, even if it is not the *only* factor—and if it is, then 4 is true.

Confirmation, Mechanism, and Theory

Notice that in the discussion so far, we have spoken of the *confirmation* of a hypothesis, such as our causal claim in 4, but not of its *verification*. (Similarly, we have imagined very different evidence, such as that stated in 15, leading us to speak of the *dis*confirmation of 3, though not of its *falsi*fication.) Confirmation (getting some evidence for) is weaker than verification (getting sufficient evidence to regard as true), and our (imaginary) evidence so far in favor of 4 falls well short of conclusive support. Further research—the study of more representative or much larger samples, for example—might yield very different observations. It might lead us to conclude that although initial research had confirmed our hypothesis about smoking as the cause of cardiovascular disease, the additional information obtained subsequently disconfirmed the hypothesis. For most interesting hypotheses, both in detective stories and in modern science, there is both confirming and disconfirming evidence simultaneously. The challenge is to evaluate the hypothesis by considering such conflicting evidence.

As long as we confine our observations to *correlations* of the sort reported in our several (imaginary) observations, such as proposition 1, *230 smokers in a group of 500 have cardiovascular disease,* or 12, *230 smokers with the disease share no other suspected factors,* such as lack of exercise, any defense of a *causal* hypothesis such as claim 3, *Smoking causes cardiovascular disease,* or claim 4, *Smoking is a factor in causing the disease,* is not likely to convince the skeptic or lead those with beliefs alternative to 3 and 4 to abandon them and agree with us. Why is that? It is because a causal hypothesis without any account of the *underlying mechanism* by means of which the (alleged) cause produces the effect will seem superficial. Only when we can specify in detail *how* the (alleged) cause produces the effect will the causal hypothesis be convincing.

In other cases, in which no mechanism can be found, we seek instead to embed the causal hypothesis in a larger *theory,* one that rules out as incompatible any causal hypothesis except the favored one. (That is, we appeal to the test of consistency and thereby bring deductive reasoning to bear on our problem.) Thus, perhaps we cannot specify any mechanism — any underlying structure that generates a regular sequence of events, one of which is the effect we are studying — to explain why, for example, the gravitational mass of a body causes it to attract other bodies. But we can embed this claim in a larger body of physical theory that rules out as inconsistent any alternative causal explanation. To do that convincingly in regard to any given causal hypothesis, as this example suggests, requires detailed knowledge of the current state of the relevant body of scientific theory, something far beyond our aim or need to consider in further detail here.

FALLACIES

The straight road on which sound reasoning proceeds gives little latitude for cruising about. Irrationality, carelessness, passionate attachment to one's unexamined beliefs, and the sheer complexity of some issues occasionally spoil the reasoning of even the best of us. Although in this book we reprint many varied voices and arguments, we hope we have reprinted no readings that exhibit the most flagrant errors or commit the graver abuses against the canons of good reasoning. Nevertheless, an inventory of those abuses and their close examination can be an instructive (as well as an amusing) exercise — instructive because the diagnosis and repair of error helps to fix more clearly the principles of sound reasoning on which such remedial labors depend; amusing because we are so constituted that our perception of the nonsense of others can stimulate our mind, warm our heart, and give us comforting feelings of superiority.

The discussion that follows, then, is a quick tour through the twisting lanes, mudflats, forests, and quicksands of the faults that one sometimes encounters in reading arguments that stray from the highway of clear thinking.

Fallacies of Ambiguity

Ambiguity Near the center of the town of Concord, Massachusetts, is an empty field with a sign reading "Old Calf Pasture." Hmm. A pasture in former times in which calves grazed? A pasture now in use for old calves? An erstwhile pasture for old calves? These alternative readings arise because of **ambiguity;** brevity in the sign has produced a group of words that give rise to more than one possible interpretation, confusing the reader and (presumably) frustrating the sign writer's intentions.

Consider a more complex example. Suppose someone asserts *People have equal rights* and also *Everyone has a right to property.* Many people believe both these claims, but their combination involves an ambiguity. According to one interpretation, the two claims entail that everyone has an *equal right* to property. (That is, you and I each have an equal right to whatever property we have.) But the two claims can also be interpreted to mean that everyone has a *right to equal property.* (That is, whatever property you have a right to, I have a right to the same, or at least equivalent, property.) The latter interpretation is revolutionary, whereas the former is not. Arguments over equal rights often involve this ambiguity.

Division In the Bible, we are told that the apostles of Jesus were twelve and that Matthew was an apostle. Does it follow that Matthew was twelve? No. To argue in this way from a property of a group to a property of a member of that group is to commit the **fallacy of division.** The example of the apostles may not be a very tempting instance of this error; here is a classic version that is a bit more interesting. If it is true that the average American family has 1.8 children, does it follow that your brother and sister-in-law are likely to have 1.8 children? If you think it does, you have committed the fallacy of division.

Composition Could an all-star team of professional basketball players beat the Boston Celtics in their heyday—say, the team of 1985 to 1986? Perhaps in one game or two, but probably not in seven out of a dozen games in a row. As students of the game know, teamwork is an indispensable part of outstanding performance, and the 1985 to 1986 Celtics were famous for their self-sacrificing style of play.

The **fallacy of composition** can be convincingly illustrated, therefore, in this argument: *A team of five NBA all-stars is the best team in basketball if each of the five players is the best at his position.* The fallacy is called composition because the reasoning commits the error of arguing from the true premise that each member of a group has a certain property to the not necessarily true conclusion that the group (the composition) itself has the property. (That is, because *A* is the best player at forward, *B* is the best center, and so on, therefore, the team of *A, B,* . . . is the best team.)

Equivocation   In a delightful passage in Lewis Carroll's *Through the Looking-Glass*, the king asks his messenger, "Who did you pass on the road?" and the messenger replies, "Nobody." This prompts the king to observe, "Of course, Nobody walks slower than you," provoking the messenger's sullen response: "I do my best. I'm sure nobody walks much faster than I do." At this the king remarks with surprise, "He can't do that or else he'd have been here first!" (This, by the way, is the classic predecessor of the famous comic dialogue "Who's on First?" between the comedians Bud Abbott and Lou Costello.) The king and the messenger are equivocating on the term *nobody*. The messenger uses it in the normal way as an indefinite pronoun equivalent to "not anyone." But the king uses the word as though it were a proper noun, *Nobody,* the rather odd name of some person. No wonder the king and the messenger talk right past each other.

Equivocation (from the Latin for "equal voice" — that is, giving utterance to two meanings at the same time in one word or phrase) can ruin otherwise good reasoning, as in this example: *Euthanasia is a good death; one dies a good death when one dies peacefully in old age; therefore, euthanasia is dying peacefully in old age.* The etymology of *euthanasia* is literally "a good death," and so the first premise is true. And the second premise is certainly plausible. But the conclusion of this syllogism is false. Euthanasia cannot be defined as a peaceful death in one's old age, for two reasons. First, euthanasia requires the intervention of another person who kills someone (or lets the person die); second, even a very young person can be euthanized. The problem arises because "a good death" is used in the second premise in a manner that does not apply to euthanasia. Both meanings of "a good death" are legitimate, but when used together, they constitute an equivocation that spoils the argument.

The fallacy of equivocation takes us from the discussion of confusions in individual claims or grounds to the more troublesome fallacies that infect the linkages between the claims we make and the grounds (or reasons) for them. These are the fallacies that occur in statements that, following the vocabulary of the Toulmin method, are called the *warrant* of reasoning. Each fallacy is an example of reasoning that involves a **non sequitur** (Latin for "It does not follow"). That is, the *claim* (the conclusion) does not follow from the *grounds* (the premises).

For a start, here is an obvious non sequitur: "He went to the movies on three consecutive nights, so he must love movies." Why doesn't the claim ("He must love movies") follow from the grounds ("He went to the movies on three consecutive nights")? Perhaps the person was just fulfilling an assignment in a film course (maybe he even hated movies so much that he had postponed three assignments to see films and now had to see them all in quick succession), or maybe he went with a girlfriend who was a movie buff, or maybe . . .—well, one can think of any number of other possible reasons.

Fallacies of Presumption

Distorting the Facts   Facts can be distorted either intentionally (to deceive or mislead) or unintentionally, and in either case usually (but not invariably) to the benefit of whoever is doing the distortion. Consider this not entirely hypothetical case. A pharmaceutical company spends millions of dollars to develop a new drug that will help pregnant women avoid spontaneous abortion. The company reports its findings, but it does not also report that it has learned from its researchers of a serious downside for this drug in many cases, resulting in deformed limbs in the neonate. Had the company informed the public of this fact, the drug would not have been certified for use.

Here is another case. Half a century ago the surgeon general reported that smoking cigarettes increased the likelihood that smokers would eventually suffer from lung cancer. The cigarette manufacturers vigorously protested that the surgeon general relied on inconclusive research and was badly misleading the public about the health risks of smoking. It later turned out that the tobacco companies knew that smoking increased the risk of lung cancer—a fact established by the company's own laboratories but concealed from the public. Today, thanks to public access to all the facts, it is commonplace knowledge that inhaled smoke—including secondhand smoke—is a risk factor for many illnesses.

Post Hoc, Ergo Propter Hoc   One of the most tempting errors in reasoning is to ground a claim about causation on an observed temporal sequence; that is, to argue "after this, therefore because of this" (which is what the phrase ***post hoc, ergo propter hoc*** means in Latin). Nearly forty years ago, when the medical community first announced that smoking tobacco caused lung cancer, advocates for the tobacco industry replied that doctors were guilty of this fallacy.

These industry advocates argued that medical researchers had merely noticed that in some people, lung cancer developed *after* considerable smoking, indeed, years after; but (they insisted) this correlation was not at all the same as a causal relation between smoking and lung cancer. True enough. The claim that *A causes B* is not the same as the claim that *B* comes after *A*. After all, it was possible that smokers as a group had some other common trait and that this factor was the true cause of their cancer.

As the long controversy over the truth about the causation of lung cancer shows, to avoid the appearance of fallacious *post hoc* reasoning one needs to find some way to link the observed phenomena (the correlation of smoking and the onset of lung cancer). This step requires some further theory and preferably some experimental evidence for the exact sequence or physical mechanism, in full detail, of how ingestion of tobacco smoke is a crucial factor—and is not merely an accidental or happenstance prior event—in the subsequent development of the cancer.

Many Questions   The old saw, "When did you stop beating your wife?" illustrates the **fallacy of many questions.** This question, as one can readily see, is unanswerable unless all three of its implicit presuppositions are true. The questioner presupposes that (1) the addressee has or had a wife, (2) he has beaten her, and (3) he has stopped beating her. If any of these presuppositions is false, then the question is pointless; it cannot be answered strictly and simply with a date.

Hasty Generalization   From a logical point of view, **hasty generalization** is the precipitous move from true assertions about *one* or a *few* instances to dubious or even false assertions about *all*. For example, while it may be true, based on your personal experience, that the only native Hungarians you personally know do not speak English very well, that is no basis for asserting that all Hungarians do not speak English very well. Or if the clothes you recently ordered online turn out not to fit very well, it doesn't follow that *all* online clothes turn out to be too large or too small. A hasty generalization usually lies behind a **stereotype**—that is, a person or event treated as typical of a whole class. Thus, in 1914, after the German invasion of Belgium, during which some atrocities were committed by the invaders, the German troops were quickly stereotyped by the Allies as brutal savages who skewered helpless babies on their bayonets.

The Slippery Slope   One of the most familiar arguments against any type of government regulation is that if it is allowed, then it will be just the first step down the path that leads to ruinous interference, overregulation, and totalitarian control. Fairly often we encounter this mode of argument in the public debates over handgun control, the censorship of pornography, and physician-assisted suicide. The argument is called the **slippery slope argument** (or the **wedge argument,** from the way we use the thin end of a wedge to split solid things apart; it is also called, rather colorfully, "letting the camel's nose under the tent"). The fallacy here is in implying that the first step necessarily leads to the second, and so on down the slope to disaster, when in fact there is no necessary slide from the first step to the second. (Would handgun registration lead to a police state? Well, it hasn't in Switzerland.) Sometimes the argument takes the form of claiming that a seemingly innocent or even attractive principle that is being applied in a given case (censorship of pornography, to avoid promoting sexual violence) requires one for the sake of consistency to apply the same principle in other cases, only with absurd and catastrophic results (censorship of everything in print, to avoid hurting anyone's feelings).

Here's an extreme example of this fallacy in action:

Automobiles cause more deaths than handguns do. If you oppose
handguns on the ground that doing so would save lives of the innocent,
you'll soon find yourself wanting to outlaw the automobile.

Does opposition to handguns have this consequence? Not necessarily. Most people accept without dispute the right of society to regulate the operation of motor vehicles by requiring drivers to have a license, a greater restriction than many states impose on gun ownership. Besides, a gun is a lethal weapon designed to kill, whereas an automobile or truck is a vehicle designed for transportation. Private ownership and use in both cases entail risks of death to the innocent. But there is no inconsistency in a society's refusal to tolerate this risk in the case of guns and its willingness to do so in the case of automobiles.

Closely related to the slippery slope is what lawyers call a **parade of horrors,** an array of examples of terrible consequences that will or might follow if we travel down a certain path. A good example appears in Justice William Brennan's opinion for the Supreme Court in *Texas v. Johnson* (1989), concerned with a Texas law against burning the American flag in political protest. If this law is allowed to stand, Brennan suggests, we may next find laws against burning the presidential seal, state flags, and the Constitution.

False Analogy   Argument by analogy, as we point out in Chapter 3 and as many of the selections in this book show, is a familiar and even indispensable mode of argument. But it can be treacherous because it runs the risk of the **fallacy of false analogy.** Unfortunately, we have no simple or foolproof way of distinguishing between the useful, legitimate analogies and the others. The key question to ask yourself is this: Do the two things put into analogy differ in any essential and relevant respect, or are they different only in unimportant and irrelevant aspects?

In a famous example from his discussion in support of suicide, philosopher David Hume rhetorically asked: "It would be no crime in me to divert the Nile or Danube from its course, were I able to effect such purposes. Where then is the crime of turning a few ounces of blood from their natural channel?" This is a striking analogy, except that it rests on a false assumption. No one has the right to divert the Nile or the Danube or any other major international watercourse; it would be a catastrophic crime to do so without the full consent of people living in the region, their government, and so forth. Therefore, arguing by analogy, one might well say that no one has the right to take his or her own life, either. Thus, Hume's own analogy can be used to argue against his thesis that suicide is no crime. But let us ignore the way in which his example can be turned against him. The analogy is a terrible one in any case. Isn't it obvious that the Nile, whatever its exact course, would continue to nourish Egypt and the Sudan, whereas the blood flowing out of someone's veins will soon leave that person dead? The fact that the blood is the same blood, whether in one's body or in a pool on the floor (just as the water of the Nile is the same body of water whatever path it follows to the sea) is, of course, irrelevant to the question of whether one has the right to commit suicide.

Let us look at a more complex example. During the 1960s, when the United States was convulsed over the purpose and scope of its military involvement in Southeast Asia, advocates of more vigorous U.S. military participation appealed to the so-called domino effect, supposedly inspired by a passing remark from President Eisenhower in the 1950s. The analogy refers to the way in which a row of standing dominoes will collapse, one after the other, if the first one is pushed. If Vietnam turns Communist, according to this analogy, so too will its neighbors, Laos and Cambodia, followed by Thailand and then Burma, until the whole region is as communist as China to the north. The domino analogy (or metaphor) provided, no doubt, a vivid illustration and effectively portrayed the worry of many anti-Communists. But did it really shed any light on the likely pattern of political and military developments in the region? The history of events there during the 1970s and 1980s did not bear out the domino analogy.

Straw Man   It is often tempting to reframe or report your opponent's thesis to make it easier to attack and perhaps refute it. If you do this in the course of an argument, you are creating a straw man, a thing of no substance and easily blown away. The straw man you've constructed is usually a radically conservative or extremely liberal thesis, which few if any would want to defend. That is why it is easier to refute than the view your opponent actually holds. "So you defend the death penalty—and all the horrible things done in its name. No one in his right mind would hold such a view." It's highly unlikely that your friend supports *everything* that has been done in the name of capital punishment—crucifixion and beheading, for example, or execution of the children of the guilty offender.

Special Pleading   We all have our favorites—relatives, friends, and neighbors—and we are all too likely to show that favoritism in unacceptable ways. How about this: "Yes, I know Billy hit Sally first, but he's my son. He's a good boy, and I know he must have had a good reason." Or this: "True, she's late for work again—the third time this week!—but her uncle's my friend, and it will be embarrassing to me if she is fired, so we'll just ignore it." Special pleading inevitably leads to unmerited advantages, as illustrated above.

Begging the Question   The argument over whether the death penalty is a deterrent illustrates another fallacy. From the fact that you live in a death-penalty state and were not murdered yesterday, we cannot infer that the death penalty was a deterrent. Yet it is tempting to make this inference, perhaps because—all unawares—we are relying on the **fallacy of begging the question.** If someone tacitly assumes from the start that the death penalty is an effective deterrent, then the fact that you weren't murdered yesterday certainly looks like evidence for the truth of that assumption. But it isn't, so long as there are competing but unexamined alternative explanations, as in this case. (The fallacy is called "begging the question," *petitio principii* in Latin, because the conclusion of the argument is hidden among its assumptions—and so the conclusion, not surprisingly, follows from the premises.)

Of course, the fact that you weren't murdered is *consistent* with the claim that the death penalty is an effective deterrent, just as someone else's being murdered is also consistent with that claim (for an effective deterrent need not be a *perfect* deterrent). In general, from the fact that two propositions are consistent with each other, we cannot infer that either is evidence for the other.

Note: The term "begging the question" is often wrongly used to mean "raises the question," as in "His action of burning the flag begs the question, What drove him to do such a thing?"

False Dichotomy Sometimes oversimplification takes a more complex form, in which contrary possibilities are wrongly presented as though they were exhaustive and exclusive. "Either we get tough with drug users, or we must surrender and legalize all drugs." Really? What about doing neither and instead offering education and counseling, detoxification programs, and incentives to "Say no"? A favorite of debaters, **either/or** reasoning always runs the risk of ignoring a third (or fourth) possibility. Some disjunctions are indeed exhaustive: "Either we get tough with drug users, or we do not." This proposition, though vague (what does "get tough" really mean?), is a tautology; it cannot be false, and there is no third alternative. But most disjunctions do not express a pair of *contradictory* alternatives: They offer only a pair of *contrary* alternatives, and mere contraries do not exhaust the possibilities (recall our discussion of contraries versus contradictories on p. 359).

An example of **false dichotomy** can be found in the essay by Jeff Jacoby on flogging (p. 196). His entire discussion is built on the relative superiority of whipping over imprisonment, as though there was no alternative punishment worth considering. But of course, there is, notably community service (especially for white-collar offenders, juveniles, and many first offenders).

Oversimplification "Poverty causes crime," "Taxation is unfair," "Truth is stranger than fiction"—these are examples of generalizations that exaggerate and therefore oversimplify the truth. Poverty as such can't be the sole cause of crime because many poor people do not break the law.

Some taxes may be unfairly high, others unfairly low—but there is no reason to believe that *every* tax is unfair to all those who have to pay it. Some true stories do amaze us as much or more than some fictional stories, but the reverse is true, too. (In the language of the Toulmin method, **oversimplification** is the result of a failure to use suitable modal qualifiers in formulating one's claims or grounds or backing.)

Red Herring   The fallacy of **red herring,** less colorfully named irrelevant thesis, occurs when one tries to distract one's audience by invoking a consideration that is irrelevant to the topic under discussion. (This fallacy probably gets its name from the fact that a rotten herring, or a cured herring, which is reddish, will throw pursuing hounds off the right track.) Consider this case. Some critics, seeking to defend our government's refusal to sign the Kyoto accords to reduce global warming, argue that signing is supported mainly by left-leaning scientists. This argument supposedly shows that global warming—if there is such a thing—is not a serious, urgent issue. But claiming that the supporters of these accords are left-inclined is a red herring, an irrelevant thesis. By raising doubts about the political views of the advocates of signing, it distracts attention from the scientific question (Is there global warming?) and also from the separate political question (Ought the United States sign these accords?). The refusal of a government to sign these accords does not show there is no such thing as global warming. And even if all of the advocates of signing were left-leaning (they aren't), this fact (if it were a fact, but it isn't) would not show that worries about global warming are exaggerated.

Fallacies of Relevance

Tu Quoque   The Romans had a word for it: *Tu quoque* means "you, too." Consider this: "You're a fine one, trying to persuade me to give up smoking when you indulge yourself with a pipe and a cigar from time to time. Maybe I should quit, but then so should you. As things stand now, however, it's hypocritical of you to complain about my smoking when you persist in the same habit." The fallacy is this: The merit of a person's argument has nothing to do with the person's character or behavior. Here, the assertion that smoking is bad for one's health is *not* weakened by the fact that a smoker offers the argument.

The Genetic Fallacy   A member of the family of fallacies that includes poisoning the well and ad hominem is the **genetic fallacy.** Here the error takes the form of arguing against some claim by pointing out that its origin (genesis) is tainted or that it was invented by someone deserving our contempt. Thus, one might attack the ideas of the Declaration of Independence by pointing out that its principal author, Thomas Jefferson, was a slaveholder. Assuming that it is not anachronistic and inappropriate to criticize a public figure of two centuries ago for practicing slavery, and conceding that slavery is morally outrageous, it is nonetheless fallacious to attack the ideas or even the sincerity of the Declaration by attempting to impeach the credentials of its author. Jefferson's moral faults do not by themselves falsify, make improbable, or constitute counterevidence to the truth or other merits of the claims made in his writings. At most, one's faults cast doubt on one's integrity or sincerity if one makes claims at odds with one's practice.

The genetic fallacy can take other forms less closely allied to ad hominem argument. For example, an opponent of the death penalty might argue,

> Capital punishment arose in barbarous times; but we claim to be civilized; therefore, we should discard this relic of the past.

Such reasoning shouldn't be persuasive because the question of the death penalty for our society must be decided by the degree to which it serves our purposes—justice and defense against crime, presumably—to which its historic origins are irrelevant. The practices of beer- and winemaking are as old as human civilization, but their origin in antiquity is no reason to outlaw them in our time. The curious circumstances in which something originates usually play no role whatever in its validity. Anyone who would argue that nothing good could possibly come from molds and fungi is refuted by Sir Alexander Fleming's discovery of penicillin in 1928.

Poisoning the Well   During the 1970s some critics of the Equal Rights Amendment (ERA) argued against it by pointing out that Marx and Engels, in their *Communist Manifesto,* favored equality of women and men—and therefore the ERA was immoral, undesirable, and perhaps even a Communist plot. This kind of reasoning is an attempt to **poison the well;** that is, an attempt to shift attention from the merits of the argument—the validity of the reasoning, the truth of the claims—to the source or origin of the argument. Such criticism deflects attention from the real issue; namely, whether the view in question is true and what the quality of evidence is in its support. The mere fact that Marx (or Hitler, for that matter) believed something does not show that the belief is false or immoral; just because some scoundrel believes the world is round, that is no reason for you to believe it is flat.

Appeal to Ignorance   In the controversy over the death penalty, the issues of deterrence and executing the innocent are bound to be raised. Because no one knows how many innocent persons have been convicted for murder and wrongfully executed, it is tempting for abolitionists to argue that the death penalty is too risky. It is equally tempting for the proponent of the death penalty to argue that since no one knows how many people have been deterred from murder by the threat of execution, we abolish it at our peril.

Each of these arguments suffers from the same flaw: the **fallacy of appeal to ignorance.** Each argument invites the audience to draw an inference from a premise that is unquestionably true—but what is that premise? It asserts that there is something "we don't know." But what we *don't* know cannot be *evidence* for (or against) anything. Our ignorance is no reason for believing anything, except perhaps that we ought to try to undertake an appropriate investigation in order to reduce our ignorance and replace it with reliable information.

Ad Hominem   Closely allied to poisoning the well is another fallacy, **ad hominem** argument (from the Latin for "against the person"). A critic can easily yield to the temptation to attack an argument or theory by trying to impeach or undercut the credentials of its advocates.

Example: Jones is arguing that prayer should not be permitted in public schools, and Smith responds by pointing out that Jones has twice been convicted of assaulting members of the clergy. Jones's behavior doubtless is reprehensible, but the issue is not Jones, it is prayer in school, and what must be scrutinized is Jones's argument, not his police record or his character.

Appeal to Authority   The example of Jefferson given to illustrate the genetic fallacy can be turned around to illustrate another fallacy. One might easily imagine someone from the South in 1860 defending the slave-owning society of that day by appealing to the fact that no less a person than Jefferson—a brilliant public figure, thinker, and leader by any measure—owned slaves. Or today one might defend capital punishment on the ground that Abraham Lincoln, surely one of the nation's greatest presidents, signed many death warrants during the Civil War, authorizing the execution of Union soldiers. No doubt the esteem in which such figures as Jefferson and Lincoln are deservedly held amounts to impressive endorsement for whatever acts and practices, policies and institutions, they supported. But the **authority** of these figures in itself is not evidence for the truth of their views, and so their authority cannot be a reason for anyone to agree with them. Obviously, Jefferson and Lincoln themselves could not support their beliefs by pointing to the fact that they held them. Because their own authority is no reason for them to believe what they believe, it is no reason for anyone else, either.

Sometimes the appeal to authority is fallacious because the authoritative person is not an expert on the issue in dispute. The fact that a high-energy physicist has won the Nobel Prize is no reason for attaching any special weight to her views on the causes of cancer, the reduction of traffic accidents, or the legalization of marijuana. On the other hand, one would be well advised to attend to her views on the advisability of ballistic missile-defense systems, for there may be a connection between the kind of research for which she received the prize and the defense research projects.

All of us depend heavily on the knowledge of various experts and authorities, and so we tend not to ignore their views. Conversely, we should resist the temptation to accord their views on diverse subjects the same respect that we grant them in the area of their expertise.

Appeal to Fear   The Romans called this fallacy *ad baculum*, "resorting to violence" (*baculum* means "stick," or "club"). Trying to persuade people to agree with you by threatening them with painful consequences is obviously an appeal that no rational person would contemplate. The violence need not be physical; if you threaten someone with the loss of a job, for instance, you are still using a stick. Violence or the threat of harmful consequences in the course of an argument is beyond reason and always shows the haste or impatience of those who appeal to it. It is also an indication that the argument on its merits would be unpersuasive, inconclusive, or worse. President Teddy Roosevelt's epigrammatic doctrine for the kind of foreign policy he favored—"Speak softly but carry a big stick"—illustrates an attempt to have it both ways, an appeal to reason for starters but a recourse to coercion, or the threat of coercion, as a backup if needed.

Finally, we add two fallacies, not easily embraced by Engel's three categories that have served us well thus far (ambiguity, erroneous presumption, and irrelevance): death by a thousand qualifications and protecting the hypothesis.

Death by a Thousand Qualifications   In a letter of recommendation sent in support of an applicant for a job on your newspaper, you find this sentence: "Young Smith was the best student I've ever taught in an English course." Pretty strong endorsement, you think, except that you do not know, because you have not been told, the letter writer is a very junior faculty member, has been teaching for only two years, is an instructor in the history department, taught a section of freshman English as a courtesy for a sick colleague, and had only eight students enrolled in the course. Thanks to these implicit qualifications, the letter writer did not lie or exaggerate in his praise; but the effect of his sentence on you, the unwitting reader, is quite misleading. The explicit claim in the letter, and its impact on you, is quite different from the tacitly qualified claim in the mind of the writer.

Death by a thousand qualifications gets its name from the ancient torture of death by a thousand small cuts. Thus, a bold assertion can be virtually killed, its true content reduced to nothing, bit by bit, as all the appropriate or necessary qualifications are added to it. Consider another example. Suppose you hear a politician describing another country (let's call it Ruritania so as not to offend anyone) as a "democracy"—except it turns out that Ruritania doesn't have regular elections, lacks a written constitution, has no independent judiciary, prohibits religious worship except of the state-designated deity, and so forth. So what is left of the

original claim that Ruritania is a democracy is little or nothing. The qualifications have taken all the content out of the original description.

Protecting the Hypothesis   In Chapter 3, we contrasted *reasoning* and *rationalization* (or the finding of bad reasons for what one intends to believe anyway). Rationalization can take subtle forms, as the following
example indicates. Suppose you're standing with a friend on the shore
or on a pier, and you watch as a ship heads out to sea. As it reaches the
horizon, it slowly disappears—first the hull, then the upper decks, and
finally the tip of the mast. Because the ship (you both assume) isn't sinking, it occurs to you that you have in this sequence of observations convincing evidence that the earth's surface is curved. Nonsense, says your
companion. Light waves sag, or bend down, over distances of a few miles,
and so a flat surface (such as the ocean) can intercept them. Hence the
ship, which appears to be going "over" the horizon, really isn't: It's just
moving steadily farther and farther away in a straight line. Your friend,
you discover to your amazement, is a card-carrying member of the Flat
Earth Society (yes, there really is such an organization). Now most of us
would regard the idea that light rays bend down in the manner required
by the Flat Earther's argument as a rationalization whose sole purpose is
to protect the flat-earth doctrine against counterevidence. We would be
convinced it was a rationalization, and not a very good one at that, if the
Flat Earther held to it despite a patient and thorough explanation from
a physicist that showed modern optical theory to be quite incompatible
with the view that light waves sag.

✓ **A CHECKLIST FOR EVALUATING AN ARGUMENT FROM A LOGICAL POINT OF VIEW**

☐ Is the argument purely deductive, purely inductive, or a mixture of the two?

☐ If it is deductive, is it valid?

☐ If it is valid, are all its premises and assumptions true?

☐ If it is not valid, what fallacy does it commit?

☐ If it is not valid, are the claims at least consistent with each other?

☐ If it is not valid, can you think of additional plausible assumptions that would make it valid?

☐ If the argument is inductive, on what observations is it based?

☐ If the argument is deductive, how probable are its premises and its conclusion?

☐ In any case, can you think of evidence that would further confirm the conclusion? Disconfirm the conclusion?

This example illustrates two important points about the *backing* of arguments. First, it is always possible to protect a hypothesis by abandoning adjacent or connected hypotheses; this is the tactic our Flat Earth friend has used. This maneuver is possible, however, only because—and this is the second point—whenever we test a hypothesis, we do so by taking for granted (usually quite unconsciously) many other hypotheses as well. So the evidence for the hypothesis we think we are confirming is impossible to separate entirely from the adequacy of the connected hypotheses. As long as we have no reason to doubt that light rays travel in straight lines (at least over distances of a few miles), our Flat Earth friend's argument is unconvincing. But once that hypothesis is itself put in doubt, the idea that looked at first to be a pathetic rationalization takes on an even more troublesome character.

There are, then, not one but two fallacies exposed by this example. The first and perhaps graver is in rigging your hypothesis so that *no matter what* observations are brought against it, you will count nothing as falsifying it. The second and subtler is in thinking that as you test one hypothesis, all of your other background beliefs are left safely to one side, immaculate and uninvolved. On the contrary, our beliefs form a corporate structure, intertwined and connected to each other with great complexity, and no one of them can ever be singled out for unique and isolated application, confirmation, or disconfirmation, to the world around us.

EXERCISE: FALLACIES—OR NOT?

Here, for diversion and practice, are some fallacies in action. Some of these statements, however, are not fallacies. Can you tell which is which? Can you detect *what* has gone wrong in the cases where something has gone wrong? Please explain your reasoning.

1. Abortion is murder—and it doesn't matter whether we're talking about killing a human embryo or a human fetus.
2. Euthanasia is not a good thing, it's murder—and it doesn't matter how painful one's dying may be.
3. Never loan a tool to a friend. I did once and never got it back.
4. If the neighbors don't like our loud music, that's just too bad. After all, we have a right to listen to the music we like when and where we want to play it.
5. The Good Samaritan in the Bible was pretty foolish; he was taking grave risks with no benefits for him in sight.
6. "Shoot first and ask questions afterward" is a good epigram for the kind of foreign policy we need.
7. "You can fool some of the people all of the time, and you can fool all the people some of the time, but you can't fool all the people all of the time." That's what Abraham Lincoln said, and he was right.
8. It doesn't matter whether Shakespeare wrote the plays attributed to him. What matters is whether the plays are any good.

9. The Golden Gate Bridge in San Francisco ought to be closed down. After all, just look at all the suicides that have occurred there.

10. Reparations for African Americans are way overdue; it's just another version of the reparations eventually paid to the Japanese Americans who were wrongly interned in 1942 during World War II.

11. Animals don't have rights any more than do trees or stones. They don't have desires, either. What they have are feelings and needs.

12. The average American family is said to have 2.1 children. This is absurd—did you ever meet 2.1 children?

13. My marriage was a failure, which just proves my point: Don't ever get married in the first place.

14. The Red Queen in *Alice in Wonderland* was right: Verdict first, evidence later.

15. Not until astronauts sailed through space around the moon and could see its back side for themselves did we have adequate reason to believe that the moon even had a back side.

16. If you start out with a bottle of beer a day and then go on to a glass or two of wine on the weekends, you're well on your way to becoming a hopeless drunk.

17. Two Indians are sitting on a fence. The small Indian is the son of the big Indian, but the big Indian is not the small Indian's father. How is that possible?

18. If you toss a coin five times and each time it come up heads, is it more likely than not that on the sixth throw you'll come up heads again—or is it more likely that you'll come up tails? Or is neither more likely?

19. Going to church on a regular basis is bad for your health. Instead of sitting in a pew for an hour each Sunday you'd be better off taking an hour's brisk walk.

20. You can't trust anything he says. When he was young he was an avid Communist.

21. Since 9/11 we've tried and convicted few terrorists, so our defense systems must be working.

22. We can trust the White House in its press releases because it's a reliable source of information.

23. Intelligent design must be true because the theory of evolution can't explain how life began.

24. Andreas Serrano's notorious photograph called *Piss Christ* (1989), showing a small plastic crucifix submerged in a glass of urine, never should have been put on public display, let alone financed by public funds.

25. Doubting Thomas was right—you need more than somebody's say-so to support a claim of resurrection.

26. You are a professional baseball player and you have a good-luck charm. When you wear it the team wins. When you don't wear it the team loses. What do you infer?

27. Resolve the following dilemma: When it rains you can't fix the hole in the roof. When it's not raining there is no need to mend the roof. Conclusion: Leave the roof as it is.

28. You are at the beach and you watch a ship steaming toward the horizon. Bit by bit it disappears from view—first the masts, then the upper deck, then the main deck, then the stern, and then it's gone. Why would it be wrong to infer that the ship is sinking?

29. How can it be true that "it's the exception that proves the rule"? If anything, isn't it the exception that *dis*proves the rule?
30. How come herbivores don't eat herbs?
31. In the 1930s it was commonplace to see ads announcing "More Doctors Smoke Camels." What do you make of such an ad?
32. Suppose the only way you could save five innocent people was by killing one of them. Would you do it? Suppose the only way you could save one innocent person was by killing five others. Would you do it?

Max Shulman

Having read about proper and improper arguments, you are now well equipped to read a short story on the topic.

Max Shulman (1919–1988) began his career as a writer when he was a journalism student at the University of Minnesota. Later he wrote humorous novels, stories, and plays. One of his novels, Barefoot Boy with Cheek *(1943), was made into a musical, and another,* Rally Round the Flag, Boys! *(1957), was made into a film starring Paul Newman and Joanne Woodward.* The Tender Trap *(1954), a play he wrote with Robert Paul Smith, still retains its popularity with theater groups.*

"Love Is a Fallacy" was first published in 1951, when demeaning stereotypes about women and minorities were widely accepted in the marketplace as well as the home. Thus, jokes about domineering mothers-in-law or about dumb blondes routinely met with no objection.

Love Is a Fallacy

Cool was I and logical. Keen, calculating, perspicacious, acute, and astute—I was all of these. My brain was as powerful as a dynamo, as precise as a chemist's scales, as penetrating as a scalpel. And—think of it!—I was only eighteen.

It is not often that one so young has such a giant intellect. Take, for example, Petey Bellows, my roommate at the university. Same age, same background, but dumb as an ox. A nice enough fellow, you understand, but nothing upstairs. Emotional type. Unstable. Impressionable. Worst of all, a faddist. Fads, I submit, are the very negation of reason. To be swept up in every new craze that comes along, to surrender yourself to idiocy just because everybody else is doing it—this, to me, is the acme of mindlessness. Not, however, to Petey.

One afternoon I found Petey lying on his bed with an expression of such distress on his face that I immediately diagnosed appendicitis. "Don't move," I said. "Don't take a laxative. I'll call a doctor."

"Raccoon," he mumbled thickly.

"Raccoon?" I said, pausing in my flight.

"I want a raccoon coat," he wailed.

I perceived that his trouble was not physical, but mental. "Why do you want a raccoon coat?"

5

"I should have known it," he cried, pounding his temples. "I should have known they'd come back when the Charleston came back. Like a fool I spent all my money for textbooks, and now I can't get a raccoon coat."

"Can you mean," I said incredulously, "that people are actually wearing raccoon coats again?"

"All the Big Men on Campus are wearing them. Where've you been?"   10

"In the library," I said, naming a place not frequented by Big Men on Campus.

He leaped from the bed and paced the room. "I've got to have a raccoon coat," he said passionately. "I've got to!"

"Petey, why? Look at it rationally. Raccoon coats are unsanitary. They shed. They smell bad. They weigh too much. They're unsightly. They——"

"You don't understand," he interrupted impatiently. "It's the thing to do. Don't you want to be in the swim?"

"No," I said truthfully.   15

"Well, I do," he declared. "I'd give anything for a raccoon coat. Anything!"

My brain, that precision instrument, slipped into high gear. "Anything?" I asked, looking at him narrowly.

"Anything," he affirmed in ringing tones.

I stroked my chin thoughtfully. It so happened that I knew where to get my hands on a raccoon coat. My father had had one in his undergraduate days; it lay now in a trunk in the attic back home. It also happened that Petey had something I wanted. He didn't *have* it exactly, but at least he had first rights on it. I refer to his girl, Polly Espy.

I had long coveted Polly Espy. Let me emphasize that my desire for   20 this young woman was not emotional in nature. She was, to be sure, a girl who excited the emotions, but I was not one to let my heart rule my head. I wanted Polly for a shrewdly calculated, entirely cerebral reason.

I was a freshman in law school. In a few years I would be out in practice. I was well aware of the importance of the right kind of wife in furthering a lawyer's career. The successful lawyers I had observed were, almost without exception, married to beautiful, gracious, intelligent women. With one omission, Polly fitted these specifications perfectly.

Beautiful she was. She was not yet of pin-up proportions, but I felt sure that time would supply the lack. She already had the makings.

Gracious she was. By gracious I mean full of graces. She had an erectness of carriage, an ease of bearing, a poise that clearly indicated the best of breeding. At table her manners were exquisite. I had seen her at the Kozy Kampus Korner eating the specialty of the house—a sandwich that contained scraps of pot roast, gravy, chopped nuts, and a dipper of sauerkraut—without even getting her fingers moist.

Intelligent she was not. In fact, she veered in the opposite direction. But I believed that under my guidance she would smarten up. At any rate, it was worth a try. It is, after all, easier to make a beautiful dumb girl smart than to make an ugly smart girl beautiful.

"Petey," I said, "are you in love with Polly Espy?"

"I think she's a keen kid," he replied, "but I don't know if you'd call it love. Why?"

"Do you," I asked, "have any kind of formal arrangement with her? I mean are you going steady or anything like that?"

"No. We see each other quite a bit, but we both have other dates. Why?"

"Is there," I asked, "any other man for whom she has a particular fondness?"

"Not that I know of. Why?"

I nodded with satisfaction. "In other words, if you were out of the picture, the field would be open. Is that right?"

"I guess so. What are you getting at?"

"Nothing, nothing," I said innocently, and took my suitcase out of the closet.

"Where you going?" asked Petey.

"Home for the week end." I threw a few things into the bag.

"Listen," he said, clutching my arm eagerly, "while you're home, you couldn't get some money from your old man, could you, and lend it to me so I can buy a raccoon coat?"

"I may do better than that," I said with a mysterious wink and closed my bag and left.

"Look," I said to Petey when I got back Monday morning. I threw open the suitcase and revealed the huge, hairy, gamy object that my father had worn in his Stutz Bearcat in 1925.

"Holy Toledo!" said Petey reverently. He plunged his hands into the raccoon coat and then his face. "Holy Toledo!" he repeated fifteen or twenty times.

"Would you like it?" I asked.

"Oh yes!" he cried, clutching the greasy pelt to him. Then a canny look came into his eyes. "What do you want for it?"

"Your girl," I said, mincing no words.

"Polly?" he said in a horrified whisper. "You want Polly?"

"That's right."

He flung the coat from him. "Never," he said stoutly.

I shrugged. "Okay. If you don't want to be in the swim, I guess it's your business."

I sat down in a chair and pretended to read a book, but out of the corner of my eye I kept watching Petey. He was a torn man. First he looked at the coat with the expression of a waif at a bakery window. Then he turned away and set his jaw resolutely. Then he looked back at the coat, with even more longing in his face. Then he turned away, but with not so much resolution this time. Back and forth his head swiveled, desire waxing, resolution waning. Finally he didn't turn away at all; he just stood and stared with mad lust at the coat.

"It isn't as though I was in love with Polly," he said thickly. "Or going steady or anything like that."

"That's right," I murmured.

"What's Polly to me, or me to Polly?"   50

"Not a thing," said I.

"It's just been a casual kick—just a few laughs, that's all."

"Try on the coat," said I.

He complied. The coat bunched high over his ears and dropped all the way down to his shoe tops. He looked like a mound of dead raccoons. "Fits fine," he said happily.

I rose from my chair. "Is it a deal?" I asked, extending my hand.   55

He swallowed. "It's a deal," he said and shook my hand.

I had my first date with Polly the following evening. This was in the nature of a survey; I wanted to find out just how much work I had to do to get her mind up to the standard I required. I took her first to dinner. "Gee, that was a delish dinner," she said as we left the restaurant. Then I took her to a movie. "Gee, that was a marvy movie," she said as we left the theater. And then I took her home. "Gee, I had a sensaysh time," she said as she bade me good night.

I went back to my room with a heavy heart. I had gravely underestimated the size of my task. This girl's lack of information was terrifying. Nor would it be enough merely to supply her with information. First she had to be taught to *think*. This loomed as a project of no small dimensions, and at first I was tempted to give her back to Petey. But then I got to thinking about her abundant physical charms and about the way she entered a room and the way she handled a knife and fork, and I decided to make an effort.

I went about it, as in all things, systematically. I gave her a course in logic. It happened that I, as a law student, was taking a course in logic myself, so I had all the facts at my fingertips. "Polly," I said to her when I picked her up on our next date, "tonight we are going over to the Knoll and talk."

"Oo, terrif," she replied. One thing I will say for this girl: You would   60
go far to find another so agreeable.

We went to the Knoll, the campus trysting place, and we sat down under an old oak, and she looked at me expectantly: "What are we going to talk about?" she asked.

"Logic."

She thought this over for a minute and decided she liked it. "Magnif," she said.

"Logic," I said, clearing my throat, "is the science of thinking. Before we can think correctly, we must first learn to recognize the common fallacies of logic. These we will take up tonight."

"Wow-dow!" she cried, clapping her hands delightedly.   65

I winced, but went bravely on. "First let us examine the fallacy called Dicto Simpliciter."

"By all means," she urged, batting her lashes eagerly.

"Dicto Simpliciter means an argument based on an unqualified generalization. For example: Exercise is good. Therefore everybody should exercise."

"I agree," said Polly earnestly. "I mean exercise is wonderful. I mean it builds the body and everything."

"Polly," I said gently, "the argument is a fallacy. *Exercise is good* is an 70 unqualified generalization. For instance, if you have heart disease, exercise is bad, not good. Many people are ordered by their doctors *not* to exercise. You must *qualify* the generalization. You must say exercise is *usually* good, or exercise is good *for most people.* Otherwise you have committed a Dicto Simpliciter. Do you see?"

"No," she confessed. "But this is marvy. Do more! Do more!"

"It will be better if you stop tugging at my sleeve," I told her, and when she desisted, I continued. "Next we take up a fallacy called Hasty Generalization. Listen carefully: You can't speak French. I can't speak French. Petey Bellows can't speak French. I must therefore conclude that nobody at the University of Minnesota can speak French."

"Really?" said Polly, amazed. "*Nobody?*"

I hid my exasperation. "Polly, it's a fallacy. The generalization is reached too hastily. There are too few instances to support such a conclusion."

"Know any more fallacies?" she asked breathlessly. "This is more fun 75 than dancing even."

I fought off a wave of despair. I was getting nowhere with this girl, absolutely nowhere. Still, I am nothing if not persistent. I continued. "Next comes Post Hoc. Listen to this: Let's not take Bill on our picnic. Every time we take him out with us, it rains."

"I know somebody just like that," she exclaimed. "A girl back home — Eula Becker, her name is. It never fails. Every single time we take her on a picnic ——"

"Polly," I said sharply, "it's a fallacy. Eula Becker doesn't *cause* the rain. She has no connection with the rain. You are guilty of Post Hoc if you blame Eula Becker."

"I'll never do it again," she promised contritely. "Are you mad at me?"

I sighed. "No, Polly, I'm not mad." 80

"Then tell me some more fallacies."

"All right. Let's try Contradictory Premises."

"Yes, let's," she chirped, blinking her eyes happily.

I frowned, but plunged ahead. "Here's an example of Contradictory Premises: If God can do anything, can He make a stone so heavy that He won't be able to lift it?"

"Of course," she replied promptly. 85

"But if He can do anything, He can lift the stone," I pointed out.

"Yeah," she said thoughtfully. "Well, then I guess He can't make the stone."

"But He can do anything," I reminded her.

She scratched her pretty, empty head. "I'm all confused," she admitted.

"Of course you are. Because when the premises of an argument con-   90
tradict each other, there can be no argument. If there is an irresistible
force, there can be no immovable object. If there is an immovable object,
there can be no irresistible force. Get it?"

"Tell me some more of this keen stuff," she said eagerly.

I consulted my watch. "I think we'd better call it a night. I'll take you
home now, and you go over all the things you've learned. We'll have another session tomorrow night."

I deposited her at the girls' dormitory, where she assured me that
she had had a perfectly terrif evening, and I went glumly home to my
room. Petey lay snoring in his bed, the raccoon coat huddled like a great
hairy beast at his feet. For a moment I considered waking him and telling
him that he could have his girl back. It seemed clear that my project was
doomed to failure. The girl simply had a logic-proof head.

But then I reconsidered. I had wasted one evening; I might as well
waste another. Who knew? Maybe somewhere in the extinct crater of
her mind a few embers still smoldered. Maybe somehow I could fan them
into flame. Admittedly it was not a prospect fraught with hope, but I decided to give it one more try.

Seated under the oak the next evening I said, "Our first fallacy to-   95
night is called Ad Misericordiam."

She quivered with delight.

"Listen closely," I said. "A man applies for a job. When the boss asks
him what his qualifications are, he replies that he has a wife and six children at home, the wife is a helpless cripple, the children have nothing to
eat, no clothes to wear, no shoes on their feet, there are no beds in the
house, no coal in the cellar, and winter is coming."

A tear rolled down each of Polly's pink cheeks. "Oh, this is awful,
awful," she sobbed.

"Yes, it's awful," I agreed, "but it's no argument. The man never answered the boss's question about his qualifications. Instead he appealed to
the boss's sympathy. He committed the fallacy of Ad Misericordiam. Do
you understand?"

"Have you got a handkerchief?" she blubbered.   100

I handed her a handkerchief and tried to keep from screaming while
she wiped her eyes. "Next," I said in a carefully controlled tone, "we will
discuss False Analogy. Here is an example: Students should be allowed
to look at their textbooks during examinations. After all, surgeons have
X rays to guide them during an operation, lawyers have briefs to guide
them during a trial, carpenters have blueprints to guide them when they
are building a house. Why, then, shouldn't students be allowed to look at
their textbooks during an examination?"

"There now," she said enthusiastically, "is the most marvy idea I've
heard in years."

"Polly," I said testily, "the argument is all wrong. Doctors, lawyers,
and carpenters aren't taking a test to see how much they have learned,

but students are. The situations are altogether different, and you can't make an analogy between them."

"I still think it's a good idea," said Polly.

"Nuts," I muttered. Doggedly I pressed on. "Next we'll try Hypothesis 105 Contrary to Fact."

"Sounds yummy," was Polly's reaction.

"Listen: If Madame Curie had not happened to leave a photographic plate in a drawer with a chunk of pitchblende, the world today would not know about radium."

"True, true," said Polly, nodding her head. "Did you see the movie? Oh, it just knocked me out. That Walter Pidgeon is so dreamy. I mean he fractures me."

"If you can forget Mr. Pidgeon for a moment," I said coldly, "I would like to point out that the statement is a fallacy. Maybe Madame Curie would have discovered radium at some later date. Maybe somebody else would have discovered it. Maybe any number of things would have happened. You can't start with a hypothesis that is not true and then draw any supportable conclusions from it."

"They ought to put Walter Pidgeon in more pictures," said Polly. "I 110 hardly ever see him any more."

One more chance, I decided. But just one more. There is a limit to what flesh and blood can bear. "The next fallacy is called Poisoning the Well."

"How cute!" she gurgled.

"Two men are having a debate. The first one gets up and says, 'My opponent is a notorious liar. You can't believe a word that he is going to say.' . . . Now, Polly, think. Think hard. What's wrong?"

I watched her closely as she knit her creamy brow in concentration. Suddenly a glimmer of intelligence—the first I had seen—came into her eyes. "It's not fair," she said with indignation. "It's not a bit fair. What chance has the second man got if the first man calls him a liar before he even begins talking?"

"Right!" I cried exultantly. "One hundred percent right. It's not fair. 115 The first man has *poisoned the well* before anybody could drink from it. He has hamstrung his opponent before he could even start. . . . Polly, I'm proud of you."

"Pshaw," she murmured, blushing with pleasure.

"You see, my dear, these things aren't so hard. All you have to do is concentrate. Think—examine—evaluate. Come now, let's review everything we have learned."

"Fire away," she said with an airy wave of her hand.

Heartened by the knowledge that Polly was not altogether a cretin, I began a long, patient review of all I had told her. Over and over and over again I cited instances, pointed out flaws, kept hammering away without letup. It was like digging a tunnel. At first everything was work, sweat, and darkness. I had no idea when I would reach the light, or even *if* I would. But I persisted. I pounded and clawed and scraped, and finally I was rewarded. I saw a chink of light. And then the chink got bigger and the sun came pouring in and all was bright.

Five grueling nights this took, but it was worth it. I had made a logi- 120 cian out of Polly; I had taught her to think. My job was done. She was worthy of me at last. She was a fit wife for me, a proper hostess for my many mansions, a suitable mother for my well-heeled children.

It must not be thought that I was without love for this girl. Quite the contrary. Just as Pygmalion loved the perfect woman he had fashioned, so I loved mine. I decided to acquaint her with my feelings at our very next meeting. The time had come to change our relationship from academic to romantic.

"Polly," I said when next we sat beneath our oak, "tonight we will not discuss fallacies."

"Aw, gee," she said, disappointed.

"My dear," I said, favoring her with a smile, "we have now spent five evenings together. We have gotten along splendidly. It is clear that we are well matched."

"Hasty Generalization," said Polly brightly.   125

"I beg your pardon," said I.

"Hasty Generalization," she repeated. "How can you say that we are well matched on the basis of only five dates?"

I chuckled with amusement. The dear child had learned her lessons well. "My dear," I said, patting her hand in a tolerant manner, "five dates is plenty. After all, you don't have to eat a whole cake to know that it's good."

"False Analogy," said Polly promptly. "I'm not a cake. I'm a girl."

I chuckled with somewhat less amusement. The dear child had 130 learned her lesson perhaps too well. I decided to change tactics. Obviously the best approach was a simple, strong, direct declaration of love. I paused for a moment while my massive brain chose the proper words. Then I began:

"Polly, I love you. You are the whole world to me, and the moon and the stars and the constellations of outer space. Please, my darling, say that you will go steady with me, for if you will not, life will be meaningless. I will languish. I will refuse my meals. I will wander the face of the earth, a shambling, hollow-eyed hulk."

There, I thought, folding my arms, that ought to do it.

"Ad Misericordiam," said Polly.

I ground my teeth. I was not Pygmalion; I was Frankenstein, and my monster had me by the throat. Frantically I fought back the tide of panic surging through me. At all costs I had to keep cool.

"Well, Polly," I said, forcing a smile, "you certainly have learned your 135 fallacies."

"You're darn right," she said with a vigorous nod.

"And who taught them to you, Polly?"

"You did."

"That's right. So you do owe me something, don't you, my dear? If I hadn't come along you never would have learned about fallacies."

"Hypothesis Contrary to Fact," she said instantly.   140

I dashed perspiration from my brow. "Polly," I croaked, "you mustn't take all these things so literally. I mean this is just classroom stuff. You know that the things you learn in school don't have anything to do with life."

"Dicto Simpliciter," she said, wagging her finger at me playfully.

That did it. I leaped to my feet, bellowing like a bull. "Will you or will you not go steady with me?"

"I will not," she replied.

"Why not?" I demanded.   145

"Because this afternoon I promised Petey Bellows that I would go steady with him."

I reeled back, overcome with the infamy of it. After he promised, after he made a deal, after he shook my hand! "That rat!" I shrieked, kicking up great chunks of turf. "You can't go with him, Polly. He's a liar. He's a cheat. He's a rat."

"Poisoning the Well," said Polly, "and stop shouting. I think shouting must be a fallacy too."

With an immense effort of will, I modulated my voice. "All right," I said. "You're a logician. Let's look at this thing logically. How could you choose Petey Bellows over me? Look at me—a brilliant student, a tremendous intellectual, a man with an assured future. Look at Petey—a knothead, a jitterbug, a guy who'll never know where his next meal is coming from. Can you give me one logical reason why you should go steady with Petey Bellows?"

"I certainly can," declared Polly. "He's got a raccoon coat."   150

TOPIC FOR CRITICAL THINKING AND WRITING

After you have finished reading "Love Is a Fallacy," you may want to write an argumentative essay of 500 to 750 words on one of the following topics: (1) the story, rightly understood, is not antiwoman; (2) if the story is anti-woman, it is equally antiman; (3) the story is antiwoman but nevertheless belongs in this book; or (4) the story is antiwoman and does not belong in the book.

See the companion Web site
bedfordstmartins.com/barnetbedau
for a series of brain teasers and links related to
the logical point of view in argument.

A Psychologist's View: Rogerian Argument

Real communication occurs . . . when we listen with understanding.
— CARL ROGERS

The first duty of a wise advocate is to convince his opponents that he understands their arguments, and sympathizes with their just feelings.
— SAMUEL TAYLOR COLERIDGE

ROGERIAN ARGUMENT: AN INTRODUCTION

Carl R. Rogers (1902–1987), perhaps best known for his book entitled *On Becoming a Person* (1961), was a psychotherapist, not a teacher of writing. This short essay by Rogers has, however, exerted much influence on instructors who teach argument. Written in the 1950s, this essay reflects the political climate of the cold war between the United States and the Soviet Union, which dominated headlines for more than forty years (1947–1989). Several of Rogers's examples of bias and frustrated communication allude to the tensions of that era.

On the surface, many arguments seem to show *A* arguing with *B*, presumably seeking to change *B*'s mind; but *A*'s argument is really directed not to *B* but to *C*. This attempt to persuade a nonparticipant is evident in the courtroom, where neither the prosecutor (*A*) nor the defense lawyer (*B*) is really trying to convince the opponent. Rather, both are trying to convince a third party, the jury (*C*). Prosecutors do not care whether they convince defense lawyers; they don't even mind infuriating defense lawyers because their only real goal is to convince the jury. Similarly, the writer of a letter to a newspaper, taking issue with an editorial, does not expect to change the paper's policy. Rather, the writer hopes to convince a third party, the reader of the newspaper.

But suppose *A* really does want to bring *B* around to *A*'s point of view. Suppose Mary really wants to persuade the teacher to allow her little lamb to stay in the classroom. Rogers points out that when we engage in an argument, if we feel our integrity or our identity is threatened, we will stiffen our position. (The teacher may feel that his or her dignity is compromised by the presence of the lamb and will scarcely attend to Mary's argument.) The sense of threat may be so great that we are unable to consider the alternative views being offered, and we therefore remain unpersuaded. Threatened, we may defend ourselves rather than our argument, and little communication takes place. Of course, a third party might say that we or our opponent presented the more convincing case, but we, and perhaps the opponent, have scarcely listened to each other, and so the two of us remain apart.

Rogers suggests, therefore, that a writer who wishes to communicate with someone (as opposed to convincing a third party) needs to reduce the threat. In a sense, the participants in the argument need to become partners rather than adversaries. Rogers writes, "Mutual communication tends to be pointed toward solving a problem rather than toward attacking a person or group." Thus, an essay on whether schools should test students for use of drugs, need not—and probably should not—see the issue as black or white, *either/or*. Such an essay might indicate that testing is undesirable because it may have bad effects, *but in some circumstances* it may be acceptable. This qualification does not mean that one must compromise. Thus, the essayist might argue that the potential danger to liberty is so great that no circumstances justify testing students for drugs. But even such an essayist should recognize the merit (however limited) of the opposition and should grant that the position being advanced itself entails great difficulties and dangers.

A writer who wishes to reduce the psychological threat to the opposition and thus facilitate the partnership in the study of some issue can do several things:

- one can show sympathetic understanding of the opposing argument,
- one can recognize what is valid in it, and
- one can recognize and demonstrate that those who take the other side are nonetheless persons of goodwill.

Advocates of Rogerian argument are likely to contrast it with Aristotelian argument, saying that the style of argument associated with Aristotle (384–322 B.C., Greek philosopher and rhetorician)

- is adversarial, seeking to refute other views; and
- sees the listener as wrong, someone who now must be overwhelmed by evidence.

In contrast to the confrontational Aristotelian style, which allegedly seeks to present an airtight case that compels belief, Rogerian argument (it is said)

- is nonconfrontational, collegial, and friendly;
- respects other views and allows for plural truths; and
- seeks to achieve some degree of assent rather than convince utterly.

Thus a writer who takes Rogers seriously will, usually, in the first part of an argumentative essay

1. state the problem,
2. give the opponent's position, and
3. grant whatever validity the writer finds in that position—for instance, will recognize the circumstances in which the position would indeed be acceptable.

Next, the writer will, if possible,

4. attempt to show how the opposing position will be improved if the writer's own position is accepted.

Sometimes, of course, the differing positions may be so far apart that no reconciliation can be proposed, in which case the writer will probably seek to show how the problem can best be solved by adopting the writer's own position. We have discussed these matters in Chapter 6, but not from the point of view of a psychotherapist, and so we reprint Rogers's essay here.

Carl R. Rogers

Communication: Its Blocking and Its Facilitation

It may seem curious that a person whose whole professional effort is devoted to psychotherapy should be interested in problems of communication. What relationship is there between providing therapeutic help to individuals with emotional maladjustments and the concern of this conference with obstacles to communication? Actually the relationship is very close indeed. The whole task of psychotherapy is the task of dealing with a failure in communication. The emotionally maladjusted person, the "neurotic," is in difficulty first because communication within himself has broken down, and second because as a result of this his communication with others has been damaged. If this sounds somewhat strange, then let me put it in other terms. In the "neurotic" individual, parts of himself which have been termed unconscious, or repressed, or denied to awareness, become blocked off so that they no longer communicate themselves to the conscious or managing part of himself. As long as this is true, there are distortions in the way he communicates himself to others, and so he suffers both within himself, and in his interpersonal relations. The task of psychotherapy is to help the person achieve, through a special relationship with a therapist, good communication within himself. Once this is achieved he can communicate more freely and more effectively with others. We may say then that psychotherapy is good communication, within and between men. We may also turn that statement around and it will still be true. Good communication, free communication, within or between men, is always therapeutic.

It is, then, from a background of experience with communication in counseling and psychotherapy that I want to present here two ideas. I wish to state what I believe is one of the major factors in blocking or impeding communication, and then I wish to present what in our experience has proven to be a very important way to improving or facilitating communication.

I would like to propose, as an hypothesis for consideration, that the major barrier to mutual interpersonal communication is our very natural tendency to judge, to evaluate, to approve or disapprove, the statement of the person, or the other group. Let me illustrate my meaning with some very simple examples. As you leave the meeting tonight, one of the statements you are likely to hear is, "I didn't like that man's talk." Now what do you respond? Almost invariably your reply will be either approval or disapproval of the attitude expressed. Either you respond, "I didn't either. I thought it was terrible," or else you tend to reply, "Oh, I thought it was really good." In other words, your primary reaction is to evaluate what has just been said to you, to evaluate it from *your* point of view, your own frame of reference.

Or take another example. Suppose I say with some feeling, "I think the Republicans are behaving in ways that show a lot of good sound sense these days," what is the response that arises in your mind as you listen? The overwhelming likelihood is that it will be evaluative. You will find yourself agreeing, or disagreeing, or making some judgment about me such as "He must be a conservative," or "He seems solid in his thinking." Or let us take an illustration from the international scene. Russia says vehemently, "The treaty with Japan is a war plot on the part of the United States." We rise as one person to say "That's a lie!"

This last illustration brings in another element connected with my 5 hypothesis. Although the tendency to make evaluations is common in almost all interchange of language, it is very much heightened in those situations where feelings and emotions are deeply involved. So the stronger our feelings, the more likely it is that there will be no mutual element in the communication. There will be just two ideas, two feelings, two judgments, missing each other in psychological space. I'm sure you recognize this from your own experience. When you have not been emotionally involved yourself, and have listened to a heated discussion, you often go away thinking, "Well, they actually weren't talking about the same thing." And they were not. Each was making a judgment, an evaluation, from his own frame of reference. There was really nothing which could be called communication in any genuine sense. This tendency to react to any emotionally meaningful statement by forming an evaluation of it from our own point of view, is, I repeat, the major barrier to interpersonal communication.

But is there any way of solving this problem, of avoiding this barrier? I feel that we are making exciting progress toward this goal and I would like to present it as simply as I can. Real communication occurs, and this evaluative tendency is avoided, when we listen with understanding. What does that mean? It means *to see the expressed idea and attitude from the other person's point of view, to sense how it feels to him, to achieve his frame of reference in regard to the thing he is talking about.*

Stated so briefly, this may sound absurdly simple, but it is not. It is an approach which we have found extremely potent in the field of psychotherapy. It is the most effective agent we know for altering the basic personality structure of an individual, and improving his relationships and his communications with others. If I can listen to what he can tell me, if I can understand how it seems to him, if I can see its personal meaning for him, if I can sense the emotional flavor which it has for him, then I will be releasing potent forces of change in him. If I can really understand how he hates his father, or hates the university, or hates communists—if I can catch the flavor of his fear of insanity, or his fear of atom bombs, or of Russia—it will be of the greatest help to him in altering those very hatreds and fears, and in establishing realistic and harmonious relationships with the very people and situations toward which he has felt hatred and fear. We know from our research that such empathic understanding—understanding *with* a person, not *about* him—is such an effective approach that it can bring about major changes in personality.

Some of you may be feeling that you listen well to people, and that you have never seen such results. The chances are very great indeed that your listening has not been of the type I have described. Fortunately I can suggest a little laboratory experiment which you can try to test the quality of your understanding. The next time you get into an argument with your wife, or your friend, or with a small group of friends, just stop the discussion for a moment and for an experiment, institute this rule. "Each person can speak up for himself only *after* he has first restated the ideas and feelings of the previous speaker accurately, and to that speaker's satisfaction." You see what this would mean. It would simply mean that before presenting your own point of view, it would be necessary for you to really achieve the other speaker's frame of reference—to understand his thoughts and feelings so well that you could summarize them for him. Sounds simple, doesn't it? But if you try it you will discover it one of the most difficult things you have ever tried to do. However, once you have been able to see the other's point of view, your own comments will have to be drastically revised. You will also find the emotion going out of the discussion, the differences being reduced, and those differences which remain being of a rational and understandable sort.

Can you imagine what this kind of an approach would mean if it were projected into larger areas? What would happen to a labor-management dispute if it was conducted in such a way that labor, without necessarily agreeing, could accurately state management's point of view in a way that management could accept; and management, without approving labor's stand, could state labor's case in a way that labor agreed was accurate? It would mean that real communication was established, and one could practically guarantee that some reasonable solution would be reached.

If then this way of approach is an effective avenue to good commu-   10
nication and good relationships, as I am quite sure you will agree if you try the experiment I have mentioned, why is it not more widely tried and used? I will try to list the difficulties which keep it from being utilized.

In the first place it takes courage, a quality which is not too widespread. I am indebted to Dr. S. I. Hayakawa, the semanticist, for pointing out that to carry on psychotherapy in this fashion is to take a very real risk, and that courage is required. If you really understand another person in this way, if you are willing to enter his private world and see the way life appears to him, without any attempt to make evaluative judgments, you run the risk of being changed yourself. You might see it his way, you might find yourself influenced in your attitudes or your personality. This risk of being changed is one of the most frightening prospects most of us can face. If I enter, as fully as I am able, into the private world of a neurotic or psychotic individual, isn't there a risk that I might become lost in that world? Most of us are afraid to take that risk. Or if we had a Russian communist speaker here tonight, or Senator Joe McCarthy, how many of us would dare to try to see the world from each of these points of view? The great majority of us could not *listen;* we would find ourselves compelled to *evaluate,* because listening would seem too dangerous. So the first requirement is courage, and we do not always have it.

But there is a second obstacle. It is just when emotions are strongest that it is most difficult to achieve the frame of reference of the other person or group. Yet it is the time the attitude is most needed, if communication is to be established. We have not found this to be an insuperable obstacle in our experience in psychotherapy. A third party, who is able to lay aside his own feelings and evaluations, can assist greatly by listening with understanding to each person or group and clarifying the views and attitudes each holds. We have found this very effective in small groups in which contradictory or antagonistic attitudes exist. When the parties to a dispute realize that they are being understood, that someone sees how the situation seems to them, the statements grow less exaggerated and less defensive, and it is no longer necessary to maintain the attitude, "I am 100 percent right and you are 100 percent wrong." The influence of such an understanding catalyst in the group permits the members to come closer and closer to the objective truth involved in the relationship. In this way mutual communication is established and some type of agreement becomes much more possible. So we may say that though heightened emotions make it much more difficult to understand *with* an opponent, our experience makes it clear that a neutral, understanding, catalyst type of leader or therapist can overcome this obstacle in a small group.

This last phrase, however, suggests another obstacle to utilizing the approach I have described. Thus far all our experience has been with small face-to-face groups—groups exhibiting industrial tensions, religious tensions, racial tensions, and therapy groups in which many personal tensions are present. In these small groups our experience, confirmed by a limited amount of research, shows that this basic approach leads to improved communication, to greater acceptance of others and by others, and to attitudes which are more positive and more problem-solving in nature. There is a decrease in defensiveness, in exaggerated statements, in evaluative and critical behavior. But these findings are from small groups. What about trying to achieve understanding between larger groups that are geographically remote? Or between face-to-face groups who are not speaking for themselves, but simply as representatives of others, like the delegates at Kaesong?[1] Frankly we do not know the answers to these questions. I believe the situation might be put this way. As social scientists we have a tentative test-tube solution of the problem of breakdown in communication. But to confirm the validity of this test-tube solution, and to adapt it to the enormous problems of communication breakdown between classes, groups, and nations, would involve additional funds, much more research, and creative thinking of a high order.

Even with our present limited knowledge we can see some steps which might be taken, even in large groups, to increase the amount of listening *with*, and to decrease the amount of evaluation *about*. To be imaginative for a moment, let us suppose that a therapeutically oriented international group went to the Russian leaders and said, "We want to achieve a genuine understanding of your views and even more important, of your attitudes and feelings, toward the United States. We will summarize and resummarize the views and feelings if necessary, until you agree that our description represents the situation as it seems to you." Then suppose they did the same thing with the leaders in our own country. If they then gave the widest possible distribution to these two views, with the feelings clearly described but not expressed in name-calling, might not the effect be very great? It would not guarantee the type of understanding I have been describing, but it would make it much more possible. We can understand the feelings of a person who hates us much more readily when his attitudes are accurately described to us by a neutral third party, than we can when he is shaking his fist at us.

But even to describe such a first step is to suggest another obstacle to   15
this approach of understanding. Our civilization does not yet have enough faith in the social sciences to utilize their findings. The opposite is true of the physical sciences. During the war[2] when a test-tube solution was

---

[1]**the delegates at Kaesong** Representatives of North and South Korea met at the border town of Kaesong to arrange terms for an armistice to hostilities during the Korean War (1950–1953). [All notes are the editors'.]
[2]**the war** World War II.

found to the problem of synthetic rubber, millions of dollars and an army of talent was turned loose on the problem of using that finding. If synthetic rubber could be made in milligrams, it could and would be made in the thousands of tons. And it was. But in the social science realm, if a way is found of facilitating communication and mutual understanding in small groups, there is no guarantee that the finding will be utilized. It may be a generation or more before the money and the brains will be turned loose to exploit that finding.

In closing, I would like to summarize this small-scale solution to the problem of barriers in communication, and to point out certain of its characteristics.

I have said that our research and experience to date would make it appear that breakdowns in communication, and the evaluative tendency which is the major barrier to communication, can be avoided. The solution is provided by creating a situation in which each of the different parties come to understand the other from the *other's* point of view. This has been achieved, in practice, even when feelings run high, by the influence of a person who is willing to understand each point of view empathically, and who thus acts as a catalyst to precipitate further understanding.

This procedure has important characteristics. It can be initiated by one party, without waiting for the other to be ready. It can even be initiated by a neutral third person, providing he can gain a minimum of cooperation from one of the parties.

This procedure can deal with the insincerities, the defensive exaggerations, the lies, the "false fronts" which characterize almost every failure in communication. These defensive distortions drop away with astonishing speed as people find that the only intent is to understand, not judge.

This approach leads steadily and rapidly toward the discovery of the 20 truth, toward a realistic appraisal of the objective barriers to communication. The dropping of some defensiveness by one party leads to further dropping of defensiveness by the other party, and truth is thus approached.

This procedure gradually achieves mutual communication. Mutual communication tends to be pointed toward solving a problem rather than toward attacking a person or group. It leads to a situation in which I see how the problem appears to you, as well as to me, and you see how it appears to me, as well as to you. Thus accurately and realistically defined, the problem is almost certain to yield to intelligent attack, or if it is in part insoluble, it will be comfortably accepted as such.

This then appears to be a test-tube solution to the breakdown of communication as it occurs in small groups. Can we take this small-scale answer, investigate it further, refine it; develop it and apply it to the tragic and well-nigh fatal failures of communication which threaten the very existence of our modern world? It seems to me that this is a possibility and a challenge which we should explore.

✓ A CHECKLIST FOR ANALYZING ROGERIAN ARGUMENT

☐ Have I stated the problem and indicated that a dialogue is possible?

☐ Have I stated at least one other point of view in a way that would satisfy its proponents?

☐ Have I been courteous to those who hold views other than mine?

☐ Have I enlarged my own understanding to the extent that I can grant validity, at least in some circumstances, to at least some aspects of other positions?

☐ Have I stated my position and indicated the contexts in which I believe it is valid?

☐ Have I pointed out the ground that we share?

☐ Have I shown how other positions will be strengthened by accepting some aspects of my position?

See the companion Web site **bedfordstmartins.com /barnetbedau** for links related to Rogerian argument.

Edward O. Wilson

Edward O. Wilson, born in in Birmingham, Alabama, in 1929, is an emeritus professor of evolutionary biology at Harvard University. A distinguished writer as well as a researcher and teacher, Wilson has twice won the Pulitzer Prize for General Non-Fiction. We reprint a piece first published in 2006.

Letter to a Southern Baptist Minister

Dear Pastor:

We have not met, yet I feel I know you well enough to call you friend. First of all, we grew up in the same faith. As a boy I too answered the altar call; I went under the water. Although I no longer belong to that faith, I am confident that if we met and spoke privately of our deepest beliefs, it would be in a spirit of mutual respect and good will. I know we share many precepts of moral behavior. Perhaps it also matters that we are both Americans and, insofar as it might still affect civility and good manners, we are both Southerners.

I write to you now for your counsel and help. Of course, in doing so, I see no way to avoid the fundamental differences in our respective worldviews. You are a literalist interpreter of Christian Holy Scripture. You reject the conclusion of science that mankind evolved from lower forms. You believe that each person's soul is immortal, making this planet a way station to a second, eternal life. Salvation is assured those who are redeemed in Christ.

I am a secular humanist. I think existence is what we make of it as individuals. There is no guarantee of life after death, and heaven and hell are what we create for ourselves, on this planet. There is no other home. Humanity originated here by evolution from lower forms over millions of years. And yes, I will speak plain, our ancestors were apelike animals. The human species has adapted physically and mentally to life on Earth and no place else. Ethics is the code of behavior we share on the basis of reason, law, honor, and an inborn sense of decency, even as some ascribe it to God's will.

For you, the glory of an unseen divinity; for me, the glory of the universe revealed at last. For you, the belief in God made flesh to save mankind; for me, the belief in Promethean fire seized to set men free. You have found your final truth; I am still searching. I may be wrong, you may be wrong. We may both be partly right.

Does this difference in worldview separate us in all things? It does not. 5 You and I and every other human being strive for the same imperatives of security, freedom of choice, personal dignity, and a cause to believe in that is larger than ourselves.

Let us see, then, if we can, and you are willing, to meet on the near side of metaphysics in order to deal with the real world we share. I put it this way because you have the power to help solve a great problem about which I care deeply. I hope you have the same concern. I suggest that we set aside our differences in order to save the Creation. The defense of living Nature is a universal value. It doesn't rise from, nor does it promote, any religious or ideological dogma. Rather, it serves without discrimination the interests of all humanity.

Pastor, we need your help. The Creation—living Nature—is in deep trouble. Scientists estimate that if habitat conversion and other destructive human activities continue at their present rates, half the species of plants and animals on Earth could be either gone or at least fated for early extinction by the end of the century. A full quarter will drop to this level during the next half century as a result of climate change alone. The ongoing extinction rate is calculated in the most conservative estimates to be about a hundred times above that prevailing before humans appeared on Earth, and it is expected to rise to at least a thousand times greater or more in the next few decades. If this rise continues unabated, the cost to humanity, in wealth, environmental security, and quality of life, will be catastrophic.

Surely we can agree that each species, however inconspicuous and humble it may seem to us at this moment, is a masterpiece of biology, and well worth saving. Each species possesses a unique combination of genetic traits that fits it more or less precisely to a particular part of the environment. Prudence alone dictates that we act quickly to prevent the extinction of species and, with it, the pauperization of Earth's ecosystems—hence of the Creation.

You may well ask at this point, Why me? Because religion and science are the two most powerful forces in the world today, including especially the United States. If religion and science could be united on the common ground of biological conservation, the problem would soon be solved. If there is any moral precept shared by people of all beliefs, it is that we owe ourselves and future generations a beautiful, rich, and healthful environment.

I am puzzled that so many religious leaders, who spiritually repre- 10 sent a large majority of people around the world, have hesitated to make protection of the Creation an important part of their magisterium. Do they believe that human-centered ethics and preparation for the afterlife are the only things that matter? Even more perplexing is the widespread conviction among Christians that the Second Coming is imminent, and that therefore the condition of the planet is of little consequence. Sixty percent of Americans, according to a 2004 poll, believe that the prophecies of the book of Revelation are accurate. Many of these, numbering in the millions, think the End of Time will occur within the life span of those now living. Jesus will return to Earth, and those redeemed by Christian faith will be transported bodily to heaven, while those left behind will struggle through severe hard times and, when they die, suffer eternal damnation. The condemned will remain in hell, like those already consigned in the generations before them, for a trillion trillion years, enough for the universe to expand to its own, entropic death, time enough for countless universes like it afterward to be born, expand, and likewise die away. And that is just the beginning of how long condemned souls will suffer in hell—all for a mistake they made in choice of religion during the infinitesimally small time they inhabited Earth.

For those who believe this form of Christianity, the fate of 10 million other life forms indeed does not matter. This and other similar doctrines are not gospels of hope and compassion. They are gospels of cruelty and despair. They were not born of the heart of Christianity. Pastor, tell me I am wrong!

However you will respond, let me here venture an alternative ethic. The great challenge of the twenty-first century is to raise people everywhere to a decent standard of living while preserving as much of the rest of life as possible. Science has provided this part of the argument for the ethic: the more we learn about the biosphere, the more complex and beautiful it turns out to be. Knowledge of it is a magic well: the more you draw from it, the more there is to draw. Earth, and especially the razor-thin film of life enveloping it, is our home, our wellspring, our physical and much of our spiritual sustenance.

I know that science and environmentalism are linked in the minds of many with evolution, Darwin, and secularism. Let me postpone disentangling all this (I will come back to it later) and stress again: to protect the beauty of Earth and of its prodigious variety of life forms should be a common goal, regardless of differences in our metaphysical beliefs.

To make the point in good Gospel manner, let me tell the story of a young man, newly trained for the ministry, and so fixed in his Christian faith that he referred all questions of morality to readings from the Bible. When he visited the cathedral-like Atlantic rainforest of Brazil, he saw the manifest hand of God and in his notebook wrote, "It is not possible to give an adequate idea of the higher feelings of wonder, admiration, and devotion which fill and elevate the mind."

That was Charles Darwin in 1832, early into the voyage of HMS *Bea-*   15 *gle*, before he had given any thought to evolution.

And here is Darwin, concluding *On the Origin of Species* in 1859, having first abandoned Christian dogma and then, with his newfound intellectual freedom, formulated the theory of evolution by natural selection: "There is grandeur in this view of life, with its several powers, having been originally breathed into a few forms or into one; and that, whilst this planet has gone cycling on according to the fixed law of gravity, from so simple a beginning endless forms most beautiful and most wonderful have been, and are being, evolved."

Darwin's reverence for life remained the same as he crossed the seismic divide that divided his spiritual life. And so it can be for the divide that today separates scientific humanism from mainstream religion. And separates you and me.

You are well prepared to present the theological and moral arguments for saving the Creation. I am heartened by the movement growing within Christian denominations to support global conservation. The stream of thought has arisen from many sources, from evangelical to unitarian. Today it is but a rivulet. Tomorrow it will be a flood.

I already know much of the religious argument on behalf of the Creation, and would like to learn more. I will now lay before you and others who may wish to hear it the scientific argument. You will not agree with all that I say about the origins of life—science and religion do not easily mix in such matters—but I like to think that in this one life-and-death issue we have a common purpose.

Topics for Critical Thinking and Writing

1. Wilson claims to be a "secular humanist" (para. 3). How would you define that term? Are you a secular humanist? Why, or why not?

2. What does Wilson mean by "metaphysics" (para. 6)? Which if any of his views qualify as metaphysical?

3. Wilson obviously seeks to present his views in a fashion that makes them as palatable as possible. Do you think he succeeds in this endeavor? Write an essay of 500 words arguing for or against his achievement in this regard.

A Rhetorician's View: Rhetorical Analysis of Nontraditional Texts[1]

The media work us over completely. They are so pervasive in their personal, political, economic, aesthetic, psychological, moral, ethical, and social consequences that they leave no part of us untouched, unaffected, unaltered. The medium is the massage.

— MARSHALL MCLUHAN

We not only interpret the character of events . . . we may also interpret our interpretations.

— KENNETH BURKE

A twenty-first-century rhetorician must now consider not only print and traditional texts but also the kinds and types of technologies used to compose and design those texts. Chapters 4, 5, and 6 discussed both reading and analyzing arguments as well as making them, partly in the light of Aristotle's ideas of *ethos* (the character of the speaker or writer), *pathos* (appeals to the emotions), and *logos* (appeals to reason, notably the use of induction and deduction, but also the testimony of authorities and the display of evidence). Aristotle (384–322 B.C.E.), writing almost two thousand years before Gutenberg's invention of movable type and the printing press, was talking chiefly about *oral* arguments, though the Greeks did have written arguments also, in the form of words handwritten on scrolls. Relatively soon after the introduction of movable type and the printing press in the mid-fifteenth century, *written* arguments—books—largely displaced oral arguments, though oral arguments of course remain important even today, notably in courts and classrooms. Nor should we forget political oratory, in Congress and other

[1]This section was contributed by Anthony Atkins, associate professor of English and composition coordinator at the University of North Carolina Wilmington.

political arenas, including televised debates between the candidates for the presidency of the United States.

Compared with Aristotle's chiefly oral world, or even compared with the print world of our parents, today we work with a much more diverse range of texts—for instance, Web sites, Twitter, Facebook, and memes. Nevertheless, we can engage rhetorically with these new texts just as we would with oral texts and with traditional print texts. Furthermore, we engage with these technologic texts for the same reasons that the ancients engaged with their texts. In the world of classical Greece, teachers of rhetoric (at least the best of them) hoped that their teaching would create ethical citizens—effective speakers promoting good causes. Today, rhetoric is an established discipline of study that seeks both to record how people communicate and to teach students how to clearly and responsibly connect their messages with society at large.

> **A RULE FOR WRITERS:** Although the word *rhetoric* today is frequently used with unfavorable connotations, as in *empty rhetoric* and *mere rhetoric*, the traditional meaning of rhetoric (and the meaning in this essay) is the study of language in use, language in real-life situations.

While we still use the Aristotelian strategies of traditional rhetoric, we must acknowledge that even Aristotle, wise though he was, did not envision the rise of the Internet and social and mass media, and the impact those modes of communication would have on our day-to-day communications. Instead of witnessing live speeches in the town square, today we witness and experience Tweets, status updates, online journals and magazines, blogs, and interactive news and sports and entertainment Web sites. Today's town squares exist online, and they are highly interactive; we can instantly respond in detail to most of what we encounter on the Internet, whereas persons listening in the actual physical presence of the speaker cannot do much more than mutter, or, at most boo, hiss, or applaud. The new ways in which we communicate, share ideas, and conduct our private and work lives depend on using digital technologies. Because digital technologies are becoming the backbone of information exchange, rhetoricians have to develop new modes of studying writing and receiving (i.e., interpreting) arguments in a digital age. The New London Group, an association of ten scholars in media, rhetoric, and communication, says:

> [P]rivate lives are being made more public as everything becomes a potential subject of media discussion, resulting in what we refer to as a "conversationalization" of public language. Discourses that were once the domain of the private—the intricacies of the sexual lives of public

figures, discussion of repressed memories of child abuse—are now made unashamedly public.

About the ways in which our work lives are changing, the group says:

> With a new worklife comes a new language. A good deal of this change is the result of new technologies, such as the iconographic, text, and screen-based modes of interacting with automated machinery; "user-friendly" interfaces operate with more subtle levels of cultural embed-dedness than interfaces based on abstract commands. But much of the change is also the result of the new social relationships of work.

Along with these massive but sometimes subtle changes, rhetoric shifts its focus from the traditional concern with writer, message, and audience to a concern with the context surrounding publication or distri-bution, which requires us to ask three additional questions:

- Who is publishing the message?
- In what medium (e.g., print, blog, television) is it published?
- How has the message been adapted to suit the medium in which it is published?

You may be familiar with the sentence, "The medium is the mes-sage," coined by Marshall McLuhan in 1964. McLuhan's point was that the *medium*—a book versus television, for instance—itself is a message. The idea that each medium is in itself a unique kind of stimulus under-lies a pun McLuhan also made, "The medium is the massage."

For a simple example of how technology shapes the message, con-sider a presidential debate. Ordinarily the candidates stand at podiums several yards apart; viewers in the auditorium look chiefly at which-ever person is speaking and pay little attention to the silent candidate. But television directors now commonly use a split screen, bringing the two figures next to each other, and viewers inevitably see not only the speaker but also the immediate reactions of the silent opponent—the raised eyebrows, the frowns, the rolling eyes. In short, the viewers at home, watching the debate on television, experience—because of the medium—a debate that is somewhat different from the debate witnessed by persons in the auditorium, and the home viewer also experiences a debate that is very different from the printed text of the debate a reader encounters in a newspaper.

The three bulleted questions ("Who," "In what medium," "How") influence not only how we read and analyze arguments, but also how we create them. Suppose, for example, you want to make an argument about an aspect of reality TV (as Michelle Dean does on page 415). You may feel that print is not sufficient for your argument; you may decide that you can make a stronger argument by using a blog that allows you to embed clips from the show or links to additional reading.

HOW RHETORICIANS ANALYZE ARGUMENTS

When we interact with texts, we automatically make judgments about them. We come out of a movie theater grumbling that the movie wasn't worth the cost of the ticket, or, on the other hand, perhaps we tell our companion that we are going to recommend this film to our parents. Or we see an ad on TV, and we admire or hate it. Such responses are often the root of rhetorical analysis. When we begin by considering *why* we dislike or like something, we are then in a position to go on—first explaining to ourselves and then to others what the *reasons* are for our judgments. The most important thing for you to do in your role as a rhetorician is to use evidence from your text—whatever the medium—to support your judgments. Nontraditional texts—that is, nonprint texts—can be slightly more difficult to analyze, but you can get a good start by thinking about what evidence from the text you can use to support your opinion. Exactly which aspects of the movie make it not worth the cost of the ticket? What aspect of that television show makes it "the best show on TV"? Why does that commercial make you feel as if you can't live another day without the product it is promoting? When you review the text for evidence, you are clarifying your own initial thoughts; you are searching for truth, and when you think you have found it, you will then try to communicate it to your audience.

You are familiar with analyzing an argument on the basis of its authorship, content, purpose, and audience, and you are familiar with applying the principles of *ethos, pathos,* and *logos.* Although you almost surely will consider these traditional principles when analyzing arguments put forward in emerging media, digital texts may call for additional points of analysis. New technologies require that we continue to rethink what counts as an argument. For example, would you consider a Twitter post an argument? Suppose a politician running for office has used Twitter to criticize an opponent's stance on taxing the wealthy. You could analyze the substance of the tweet and decide that this candidate is arguing that we should raise taxes on people who make above a certain amount each year, and you may be correct. But your analysis shouldn't stop there, because you haven't yet considered how the politician has adapted his argument so that it is uniquely suitable to Twitter, which takes advantage of social media tools that traditional texts cannot. Suppose the politician had tagged the tweet with the hashtag #payyourshare. Adding a hashtag would share that tweet with anyone following that tag rather than sharing the tweet only with people who follow the politician. Your analysis would require you to consider how the politician chose a tag that might connect with a new, perhaps sympathetic, audience because a hashtag, while it may seem like a simple tool, is also a critical part of the text.

Blogs, text messages, tweets, and Facebook status updates are significant texts and may well contain genuine arguments. They deserve the same close analysis that we give to traditional print essays, images, and videos. The increasing presence of visual communication in our lives also forces us to contend with and consider just what effect the visual can have on the meaning of a message. For better, or worse, we live in a world where technology increasingly blurs the line between what counts as print and what counts as visual.

Facebook, for example, requires that we post and share our private lives with the public. Facebook users connect, share, and interact with each other by posting, forwarding, liking, and commenting. Facebook contains elements common to print and to visual media, but it is also interactive in a way traditional print and visual media are not. If you have a Facebook account, but you aren't posting or sharing, are you really using Facebook? One way we might think about rhetoric in the twenty-first century, then, is to think about Facebook, Twitter, and most other free Web applications as new categories of media. The application is carrying information to you or from you, and it therefore becomes the vehicle with which you interact with others, with which you convey and receive information.

PRODUCTION, DISTRIBUTION, AND CONSUMPTION: PERFORMING A RHETORICAL ANALYSIS

When you analyze a traditional print argument, you focus much of your analysis on the author's words. Nontraditional texts, however, have proven that arguments do not necessarily rely on words. On a daily basis, you probably interact with complex texts that mix written, visual, and aural elements far more frequently than you do with traditional print. These texts require more than an analysis of their words. If you want to analyze a music video, for example, and you focus your analysis on only the song's lyrics, your analysis is notably incomplete; you have ignored the music and the visuals.

One way to analyze a text, whether print or other, involves thinking about it not as a solitary piece but as part of a social process, that is, considering its function in society and how it incorporates social rules as part of its argument. You might at first think, for example, that a music video is not an argument, but if you consider that a music video is likely to communicate a point of view about what good music is or what it means to be young, then you begin to see a music video in a new light. In order to analyze a cultural artifact, you must consider who produces the text, where it is distributed, and who consumes that text (and how). Put it this way: You want to

- investigate who is making/developing/creating/producing the text you are analyzing;
- explore where that text is displayed/shown/viewed/distributed; and
- think critically about how you/we consume/think about that text.

In the scheme that we describe below, we explain the key words and concepts needed to perform the analysis; we also explain production, distribution, and consumption.

When you analyze the **producer** of a text, consider what cultural values are present in the text, whether they are stated explicitly or implicitly. These values can be examined in the form of **cultural codes,** that is, as statements of an ideal, such as "The ideal X should (be/do/ have) Y." Cultural codes are perhaps easiest to see in advertisements. For example, when you watch a commercial for running shoes, the producer of the commercial may seek to entice you to buy these shoes by including footage of athletic people. In this case, the text is telling you, "The ideal healthy body should be sculpted and lean."

When you have decided what text you will be analyzing, brainstorm as many cultural codes (i.e., intended effects) as you can from it. Remember to phrase them in the form of codes: "The ideal X should (be/ do/have) Y." The more codes you can generate, the easier it will be to find the most important ones and critique them on the basis of your own experience. Here are some examples of cultural codes:

Gender: Women should be glamorous. (*Sex in the City*)

Gender: Men should be rugged. (an ad for Eddie Bauer)

Ethnicity: Beautiful people have exotic features. (*Elle*)

Economic class: The American dream is to be famous and live a raucous lifestyle. (*US Weekly*)

Age: The elderly are active and vital. (*Betty White's Off Their Rockers*)

As you can see, cultural codes construct *ideal* images (the ideal X should be/do/have Y), and they are adapted to particular media/ideologies.

In the preceding examples, cultural codes are arranged according to cultural categories (gender, ethnicity, class, political and national identity, age, etc.) as represented in assorted media/ideologies. When you analyze a text, ask yourself whether it endorses one or more of these cultural codes. What evidence from the text can you point to that illustrates the ideal?

Distribution is where (the location) the audience encounters the produced effects (the cultural codes). For example, you are likely to encounter codes related to ideals of beauty in magazines such as *Vogue*. Thus distribution refers to the point of intersection between those who produce cultural artifacts (and the cultural codes associated with them) and those who consume and interact with these artifacts and codes.

Today, the spread of technology has assured that points of distribution are more diverse than ever. Cultural codes are conveyed in different ways through different media. Every medium of distribution—from TV shows like *Snapped* and *TMZ* to magazines like *Sports Illustrated* to radio shock jocks like Howard Stern to Web sites like the *Huffington Post*—has a different feel to it, a different *technology* and a different *ideology*. The twenty-first-century rhetorician has to pay careful attention to the particular medium of distribution. Is the artifact distributed via a blog or some other online tool or application? What impact will its distribution have on how the message is promoted and on how it is consumed? Consider, for example, that the *New York Times* is published both in print and in an iPad edition. You may read the print edition from front to back, or skim each page, but if you are an iPad subscriber, the app may recommend stories to you based on what topics have interested you in the past, or those stories may include videos or interactive graphics that change the way you interact with an article. The method of distribution matters, then, in how the *New York Times* reaches different consumers and attracts different audiences.

When we think about **consumption**, we consider the impact cultural codes have on us as *consumers*, people who come into contact with the cultural codes produced by certain artifacts and texts through the media that distribute these artifacts. As consumers (whether readers, viewers, or hearers), we often *accommodate* (passively accept) the cultural codes promoted in the media. For example, in our earlier example concerning the commercial for running shoes, you might accept the producer's communicated ideal that "The ideal healthy body is sculpted and lean." When we accommodate cultural codes without understanding them critically, we allow the media that perpetuate these codes to interpret our worlds for us. That is, we accept their interpretations without questioning the social and cultural values implicit in their assumptions, many of which may run counter to our own social and cultural values.

Suppose, for instance, you have just watched a viral video that promotes environmentalism by showing someone driving a Hummer that is spewing toxic fumes into the air. You could say that this argument relies on the code, "The ideal environmentalist does not drive a Hummer." You could react to this code in one of three ways:

- If you agree that Hummers are terrible for the environment, you are **accommodating** the idea of the video.
- If you deny that global warming is an established scientific fact, or even if you grant that it is a scientific fact but you deny that science has proven that global warming results from combustion of carbon-based fuels, and you further deny that decreased use of these fuels will stop global warming—and therefore you see nothing wrong with buying a Hummer (except maybe the high price)—you are **resisting** the video.

- If you think there is indeed something sound in the anti-Hummer advertisement but you have a wife and four children and two dogs, and, further, you spend a lot of time working "off-road," you might carefully analyze the fuel-consumption of competing vehicles before you make your purchase, in which case you are **negotiating** the anti-Hummer video.

Negotiation, the most useful mode of consumption, involves a process of revision, a process of changing the conditions that give rise to negative aspects of cultural codes. Negotiation also necessitates practical intervention into the processes that construct oppressive social formations, for without intervention, there can be no revision, no positive social or cultural change. We *negotiate* cultural codes when

- we understand their underlying messages and accept the general cultural implications of these codes
- but we acknowledge that there are specific circumstances to which the general codes do not apply.

Using this scheme will help you analyze diverse kinds of texts as well as develop more nuanced arguments about the messages these texts send. In the next section, we'll walk through the analysis of a public service announcement about bullying.

A SAMPLE ANALYSIS: PUBLIC SERVICE ANNOUNCEMENT

Consider the following public service announcement (PSA) on bullying. Public service announcements are usually intended to advise or warn the general public or to facilitate proper civic engagement or participation within a community.

Production

Let's begin our analysis by thinking about the intended audience and cultural codes the PSA produces. We immediately know who the ideal audience is: parents. How do we know this? The evidence is in the artifact/text: "Teach your kids how to be more than a bystander." This is a PSA from StopBullying.gov, a government Web site. What codes can we generate from this simple message?

Class: Ideal parents have access to technologies that distribute PSA announcements.

Class: Ideal parents regardless of class should "teach" their kids how to handle bullying.

Age: Ideal parents are out of high school.

Everybody hates you.

You don't see bullying like this every day.

Your kids do.

Teach your kids how to **be more than a bystander.**

Learn how at
StopBullying.gov

Political Orientation: Ideal parents should have jobs and occupations.
> *Ideal parents should recognize the government as a resource for parenting help.*
> *Ideal parents should trust the government.*
> *Ideal parents believe that bullying can be controlled or stopped.*
> *Ideal parents should be involved with their kids' school.*

Along with the cultural codes that we have generated, we want to think about what else we know about the text's production, distribution, and consumption. We also know that this text can be found both online and in print. There is a link on the text, so if we take this piece seriously we ought to visit the site to get more information.

This text is produced by the federal government. Evidence from the text tells us that this announcement is from StopBullying.gov. The fact that we know this helps us understand the context and the nature of the text. When we visit this site, we find out very quickly that October is Bullying Prevention Month. Furthermore, we learn that calling October "Bullying Prevention Month" is not new. In fact, it started in 2006, when it was initiated by PACER's (Parent Advocacy Coalition for Education Rights) National Bullying Prevention Center. Every October, this site presents activities and resources on bullying. We also learn something by looking at who is partnering with StopBullying.gov: The National Education Association, National PTA, American Federation for Teachers, and the National Coalition for Parent Involvement. We also find out that October 10 is designated as Unity Day, a day when people across the country are encouraged to wear orange as a show of support for students who have been bullied. The goal at StopBullying.gov is to help prevent bullying. It aims to send a message around the world to prevent the bullying of students. Given the partners involved, we can infer that much of the interest in this cause comes from parents and teachers.

At this point, you may be wondering why you are being told all this stuff about the background. Well, now that we have done a little research on this text and what it stands for, we are in a better position to think about two of the arguments the text might be making:

- what role the government should play in not only helping to stop bullying but in providing parents and teachers with resources to work to that end and
- what the producers of the text consider to be an ideal family.

For example, the Web site and the PSA are directly targeted to parents who are out of high school. Together, the PSA and the Web site also tell us that parents should trust the government, be involved with their kids' school, and have jobs or occupations. When the text says, "You don't see bullying like this every day. Your kids do," this assertion rests on an assumption that parents do not see bullying because they are not in school or not at school. Presumably, parents have jobs and other grown-up things to do, so would not notice, witness, or see the kinds of bullying that their kids do. Based on the number and kinds of organizations that partner with StopBullying.gov, we also know that the main source of concern is from parents and teachers and presupposes that most bullying occurs at school.

Distribution

This PSA, designed to appear in a magazine, is a *print text*, but PSAs are typically distributed as widely as possible. We may see them on television, hear them on the radio, or read them on billboards at the side of the road; nowadays, we also see them online as we surf various Web sites. Thinking about the distribution for PSAs matters: particular consumers may not come into contact with billboards (lack of car), may not hear radio announcements (no radio), may not see ads on television (no television), or may not find banners online (no Internet access). In thinking about the distribution of this PSA, we have to acknowledge that economic class plays a significant role in the distribution and accessibility of information in multiple venues. And, in fact, if you visit StopBullying.gov, you will see that this PSA is accompanied by additional ones designed for distribution to different media. How do those vary from this one?

Consumption

As we think more about the PSA on bullying, our minds are bound to turn to the question of how we consume the message. If we *accommodate* it, we could focus our argument on what a good job the government is doing to help protect kids from bullying. We might say, for example, that the government is helping parents, schools, teachers, and students have a better educational experience, free from bullying. The large headline "Everybody hates you" grabs the attention of anyone who sees the announcement. We could also argue that it is a good use of tax dollars because the PSA is an effort on the part of the government to protect its citizens—in particular, America's children.

If we *resist* this PSA, we could argue that the government is not responsible for helping parents raise their kids or even that government help of this sort is another example of the government meddling in the lives of citizens. We might also argue that bullying cannot be stopped because the psychological makeup of some students makes bullying inevitable. Some kids just are more aggressive than others, and they always have been. The PSA does not consider what medical or psychological issues might cause bullying. We might continue by arguing that the government should focus its energies and finances on other more serious causes where there was more reason to expect success.

If we decide to *negotiate* the PSA, we might argue that, yes, the PSA does consider a number of reasons for why someone bullies another but the announcement also serves as a reminder that grown-ups, parents, and teachers should pay closer attention to behaviors in the classroom, that we should do a better job of helping kids and students get along and become productive citizens of the community. The PSA, targeted at parents and teachers, also speaks to those without children when it pleads for the reader or viewer of the announcement not to be a "bystander." Although we may not think the government is the best resource for helping to raise our children, we recognize the efforts being made to

---

✓ A CHECKLIST FOR CULTURAL ANALYSIS

☐ What sort of text are you analyzing? A Web site (what kind of Web site?), a printed text, an image, an advertisement, a song or an album, an artifact (for instance a toy, a grocery item, a magazine), a Twitter feed? The kind of text you are analyzing will determine your approach.

☐ Have you thought about the cultural codes of your text: The ideal X should be/do/have Y?

☐ Have you described the codes and—*using evidence from the text*—have you explained how you reached your conclusion?

☐ Have you thought about where your text is distributed and where people come into contact with your text? Is it online, on television, in a newspaper, a film, etc.?

☐ Have you thought about whether you accommodate, resist, or negotiate the cultural codes illustrated by the text? Do you explain *why* you feel the way you do?

☐ Who is the main audience for the text you are analyzing? How can you tell? Who might be the main audience for the essay or project that you are composing?

☐ What should readers or viewers of your essay or project take away about the text you have analyzed, and what value can others get from it?

---

keep kids as safe and protected as possible. In short, we would recognize in our argument the ways that the PSA is productive and helpful to its audience, but we would also point out its weaknesses.

A SAMPLE CULTURAL ANALYSIS

Michelle Dean

The following essay, a rhetorical analysis of the reality TV phenomenon Here Comes Honey Boo Boo, *was originally published online at* Slate *on August 24, 2012. It was written by Michelle Dean, a lawyer who now writes about class, gender, and television. As you read the essay, think about how Dean constructs an analysis that considers audience, production, distribution, and consumption.*

Here Comes the Hillbilly, Again

Somehow America always goes a little off the rails in the allegedly slow month of August, and this year's party is as wild as any. Republicans can't figure out how babies are made; cutting-and-pasting an article from *The New Yorker* into your *Time* column is no longer a fireable offense; and all the way down in McIntyre, Ga., there is a mother who feeds her child a Mountain Dew-and-Red Bull concoction before the six-year-old gets onstage at beauty pageants. June Shannon, who stars with her daughter Alana "Honey Boo Boo Child" Thompson in TLC's controversial hit *Here Comes Honey Boo Boo*, would have provoked a firestorm even if what she calls "go-go juice" were the only sin she was broadcasting all over Christendom. All that caffeine, pop-culture commentators everywhere clucked, and all that sugar.

Lost in the outrage is just how squarely "go-go juice" fits into America's long tradition of "white trash" entertainment, which for decades has elevated characters like Honey Boo Boo into the nation's objects of fun. The Pepsi Co. borrowed the Mountain Dew brand-name from slang for moonshine; in the 1960s, it was explicitly advertised as a "hillbilly" drink. The campaign's entertaining TV ads, which you can watch on YouTube, were scored by twangy banjos and errant buckshot and plotted around a "stone-hearted gal" who will open her heart to you if you only take a swig. Watching these old videos after an episode or two of *Honey Boo Boo* makes at least one thing clear: The hillbilly has regained the spotlight in American culture.

As Anthony Harkins observes in *Hillbilly: A Cultural History of an American Icon*, one of the hillbilly's signature moves is to peak, popularity-wise, just when Americans sense that things in general are headed south. Its first true zenith came in the depressed 1930s, a handmaiden to the birth of commercial country music. Another arrived in the turbulent 1960s, when *The Beverly Hillbillies* and *Green Acres* and *Hee Haw* were in their prime. (Those are hardly the only examples, of course: It also popped up in the Ma and Pa Kettle films of the 1940s and 1950s and Paul Webb's 1930s *Esquire* cartoons about "The Mountain Boys," among other places.)

Though the term first referred to mountaineers in the Appalachians and the Ozarks, the hillbilly trope spread to cover pretty much all non-urban territory in America, joined by its cousins in cultural iconography, the "redneck" and "white trash." Today, people even apply that last term to residents of certain New Jersey beachfronts, for instance. Yet, as Harkins points out, no matter where an alleged country bumpkin comes from, he will be derided for his crass behavior. And such ridicule has always been politically coded: The hillbilly figure allows middle-class white people to offload the venality and sin of the nation onto some other constituency, people who live somewhere — anywhere — else. The hillbilly's backwardness highlights the progress more upstanding

Americans in the cities or the suburbs have made. These fools haven't crawled out of the muck, the story goes, because they don't want to.

This idea that the hillbilly's poverty is a choice allows more upscale 5 Americans to feel comfortable while laughing at the antics before them. It also pushes some people to embrace the stereotype as a badge of honor. "Guitars, Cadillacs, hillbilly music / It's the only thing that keeps me hangin' on," Dwight Yoakam once sang. For more contemporary examples of reappropriation, you can attend any number of Tea Party rallies. The classist term "redneck," originally coined to indicate those who worked so hard and so long in the sun that they sported sunburns in the designated anatomical location, likewise has been adopted in the name of all that's good and holy. What's more American than a hard day's work?

June Shannon is a reappropriator par excellence. One of her signature phrases on *Here Comes Honey Boo Boo* is a call to, as she puts it, "redneck-ognize." And yet all the cultural chatter that's attended *Honey Boo Boo* has been less than affectionate. The word of the day across the media is "apocalypse"—that is, the show is a sign of it. It's not just the caffeine highs, either. It's a family of six chopping up a roadkill deer for dinner, belly-flopping in the mud, and—those with delicate constitutions may want to avert their eyes for this next part—farting in public. Even critics who enjoy the show do so from a crouched, defensive posture. People seem to think this has all gone a little too far. Even the *Today Show* is starting to wonder if reality television just might be "exploitative."

I'm not a *Toddlers & Tiaras* fan, so I missed out on Alana's big splash on that show earlier this year. Beauty pageants in general are foreign and noxious to me: I can barely muster the energy to put on lip gloss and mascara. But I watched *Honey Boo Boo* out of curiosity about the fuss, and found myself, somewhat surprisingly, relating to Alana and her milieu. I have fond memories of that Dwight Yoakam song playing softly on my parents' radio as we drove home through the dark from a visit to my grandparents' house in rural Quebec. My family isn't from the South—we're not even from the United States—but I know enough of the land Honey Boo Boo lives in to be dubious of simple accusations of bad parenting and worse morals.

The practices are different, of course, and no, I'm not wild about the caffeine and sugar thing, either. Alana's little-girl grandiosity must become exhausting when experienced in more than thirty-minute increments. But the people raising her are clearly aware of your disdain. Shannon can be delightfully funny when she self-consciously plays with her hillbilly image, warning the audience that she's about to "scratch her bugs," or speaking of her beauty routine: "Granted, I ain't the most beautimous out the box, but a little paint on this barn, shine it back to its original condition. 'Cause it shines up like it's brand new."

That's not to say the humor is always comfortable or even funny. Alana's trademark phrases and mannerisms—"a dollar makes me holler," a particular head swivel she does—are informed by racist stereotypes of black women. This ambiguous borrowing from black culture has always been part of the hillbilly trope as well. Early commercial country music borrowed liberally from black folk music. (Hank Williams learned to play guitar, he said, from a black street performer.) And this borrowing often turned into racist mimicry: The Grand Ole Opry included minstrelsy shows in the 1920s and 1930s. Interestingly, the term "white trash" may have been coined by black slaves in the early nineteenth century to describe poor white people in the South; American attitudes toward poor white people have long been tangled up with "the race problem."

And hillbilly stereotypes have always made it easier for middle-class   10 whites to presume that racism is the exclusive province of "that kind" of person. As Ta-Nehisi Coates has written, "It is comforting to think of racism as species of misanthropy, or akin to child molestation, thus exonerating all those who bear no real hatred in their heart. It's much more troubling to think of it as it's always been—a means of political organization and power distribution."

As that distribution of power becomes more and more unequal, it's no surprise to see the hillbilly here again—on *Here Comes Honey Boo Boo*, on Jersey Shore, on MTV's *16 & Pregnant* and *Teen Mom* franchises. These shows reassure us that our struggle is worth it, all economic evidence to the contrary—if only because we would never belly-flop into the mud on cable television. *Here Comes Honey Boo Boo* casts this socioeconomic divide in especially sharp relief, since the show is rooted partly in beauty pageant culture, which, in its own idiosyncratic way, indulges the American belief that you can work and spend your way to greatness. If you can afford the entry fees, the glitter, the makeup, the coach, and the stylists, you will be the Ultimate Supreme, as they say in the business. You'll have the sash to prove it.

But tiny, six-year-old Alana is too crass and happy to get it. She is a terrible pageant queen. Her wigs are always askew, her daisy-dukes ill-fitting, and sometimes she grinds her fake teeth. Those rhinestone-studded bootstraps simply can't pull her up the way she needs them to.

Topics for Critical Thinking and Writing

1. What would you say was Dean's main argument? Support your reasoning with examples.

2. What cultural codes does Dean see as present both in *Here Comes Honey Boo Boo* and in the ensuing criticism of it?

3. *Here Comes Honey Boo Boo* is a reality TV show. How does Dean characterize this medium of distribution?

4. Visit slate.com, where Dean's essay was originally published. With respect to distribution, how would you characterize the technology and

ideology of *Slate*? Is it the kind of site where you would expect to find an essay defending *Here Comes Honey Boo Boo*? Why, or why not?

5. Would you say that Dean's essay accommodates, resists, or negotiates the codes imposed by *Here Comes Honey Boo Boo*?

6. Write an essay (about 500 words) in which you analyze a nontraditional text—perhaps a popular cultural artifact (such as a magazine, toy, or product), a Web site, a smartphone application, a commercial, television show, or anything else, preferably a text with which you have regular contact and to which you have easy access. Get a copy of the text you plan to analyze (you will submit a copy of it when you turn in your final critical essay). Your essay should follow the general structure discussed in this chapter (production, distribution, consumption); you may wish to use Dean's essay as a model. Your essay should have a strong introduction, in which you introduce your text and lay out your basic points of analysis, and a strong conclusion. Within the body of your analysis, make sure you do the following: Discuss who the audience for your text is, what codes the text produces, how the codes are distributed and whether this distribution is effective, and how this text targets you as a consumer, including whether you accommodate, resist, or negotiate the cultural codes you have found within the text. Make certain to use evidence from the text to support your claims.

12

A Literary Critic's View: Arguing about Literature

Literary criticism [is] a reasoned account of the feeling produced upon the critic by the book he is reading.

— D. H. LAWRENCE

A writer is someone for whom writing is more difficult than it is for other people.

— THOMAS MANN

You can never draw the line between aesthetic criticism and social criticism. . . . You start with literary criticism, and however rigorous an aesthete you may be, you are over the frontier into something else sooner or later. The best you can do is to accept these conditions and know what you are doing when you are doing it.

— T. S. ELIOT

Nothing is as easy as it looks.

— MURPHY'S LAW #23

Everything is what it is and not another thing.

— BISHOP JOSEPH BUTLER

You might think that literature—fiction, poetry (including songs), drama— is meant only to be enjoyed, not to be argued about. Yet literature is constantly the subject of argumentative writing—not all of it by teachers of English. For instance, if you glance at the current issue of *Time* or the *New Yorker*, you probably will find a review of a play suggesting that the play is worth seeing or is not worth seeing. Or in the same magazine you may find an article reporting that a senator or member of Congress argued that the National Endowment for the Humanities wasted its grant money by funding research on such-and-such an author or that the National Endowment for the Arts insulted taxpayers by making an award to a writer who defamed the American family.

Probably most writing about literature, whether done by college students, their professors, journalists, members of Congress, or whomever, is devoted to interpreting, judging (evaluating), and theorizing. Let's look at each of these, drawing our examples chiefly from comments about Shakespeare's *Macbeth*.

INTERPRETING

Interpreting is a matter of setting forth the *meaning* or the meanings of a work. For some readers, a work has *a* meaning, the one intended by the writer, which we may or may not perceive. For most critics today, however, a work has *many* meanings—for instance, the meaning it had for the writer, the meanings it has accumulated over time, and the meanings it has for each of today's readers. Take *Macbeth*, a play about a Scottish king, written soon after a Scot—James VI of Scotland—had been installed as James I, King of England. The play must have meant something special to the king—we know that it was presented at court—and something a little different to the ordinary English citizen. And surely it means something different to us. For instance, few if any people today believe in the divine right of kings, although James I certainly did; and few if any people today believe in malignant witches, although witches play an important role in the tragedy. What *we* see in the play must be rather different from what Shakespeare's audience saw in it.

Many interpretations of *Macbeth* have been offered. Let's take two fairly simple and clearly opposed views:

1. Macbeth is a villain who, by murdering his lawful king, offends God's rule, so he is overthrown by God's earthly instruments, Malcolm and Macduff. Macbeth is justly punished; the reader or spectator rejoices in his defeat.

One can offer a good deal of evidence—and if one is taking this position in an essay, of course one must *argue* it—by giving supporting reasons rather than merely asserting the position.

2. Macbeth is a hero-villain, a man who commits terrible crimes but who never completely loses the reader's sympathy; although he is justly punished, the reader believes that with the death of Macbeth the world has become a smaller place.

Again, one *must* offer evidence in an essay that presents this thesis or indeed presents any interpretation. For instance, one might offer as evidence the fact that the survivors, especially Macduff and Malcolm, have not interested us nearly as much as Macbeth has. One might argue, too, that although Macbeth's villainy is undeniable, his conscience never deserts him—here one would point to specific passages and would offer some brief quotations. Macbeth's pained awareness of what he has done, it can be argued, enables the reader to sympathize with him continually.

Or consider an interpretation of Lady Macbeth. Is she simply evil through and through, or are there mitigating reasons for her actions? Might one argue, perhaps in a feminist interpretation, that despite her intelligence and courage she had no outlet for expression except through her husband? To make this argument, the writer might want to go beyond the text of the play, offering as evidence Elizabethan comments about the proper role of women.

JUDGING (OR EVALUATING)

Literary criticism is also concerned with such questions as these: Is *Macbeth* a great tragedy? Is *Macbeth* a greater tragedy than *Romeo and Juliet*? The writer offers an opinion about the worth of the literary work, but the opinion must be supported by an argument, expressed in sentences that offer supporting evidence.

Let's pause for a moment to think about evaluation in general. When we say "This is a great play," are we in effect saying only "I like this play"? That is, are we merely *expressing* our taste rather than *asserting* anything about something out there—something independent of our tastes and feelings? (The next few paragraphs will not answer this question, but they may start you thinking about your own answer.) Consider these three sentences:

1. It's raining outside.
2. I like vanilla.
3. This is a really good book.

If you are indoors and you say that it is raining outside, a hearer may ask for verification. Why do you say what you say? "Because," you reply, "I'm looking out the window." Or "Because Jane just came in, and she is drenched." Or "Because I just heard a weather report." If, on the other hand, you say that you like vanilla, it's almost unthinkable that anyone would ask you why. No one expects you to justify—to support, to give a reason for—an expression of taste.

Now consider the third statement, "This is a really good book." It is entirely reasonable, we think, for someone to ask you *why* you say that. And you reply, "Well, the characters are realistic, and the plot held my interest," or "It really gave me an insight into what life among the rich [or the poor] must be like," or some such thing.

That is, statement 3 at least seems to be stating a fact, and it seems to be something we can discuss, even argue about, in a way that we cannot argue about a personal preference for vanilla. Almost everyone would agree that when we offer an aesthetic judgment we ought to be able to give reasons for it. At the very least, we might say, we hope to show *why* we evaluate the work as we do and to suggest that if our readers try to see it from our point of view they may then accept our evaluation.

Evaluations are always based on assumptions, although these assumptions may be unstated, and in fact the writer may even be unaware of them. Some of these assumptions play the role of criteria; they control the sort of evidence the writer believes is relevant to the evaluation. What sorts of assumptions may underlie value judgments? We will mention a few, merely as examples. Other assumptions are possible, and all of these assumptions can themselves become topics of dispute:

1. A good work of art, although fictional, says something about real life.
2. A good work of art is complex yet unified.
3. A good work of art sets forth a wholesome view of life.
4. A good work of art is original.
5. A good work of art deals with an important subject.

Let's look briefly at these views, one by one.

1. *A good work of art, although fictional, says something about real life.* If you hold the view that literature is connected to life and believe that human beings behave in fairly consistent ways—that is, that each of us has an enduring "character"—you probably will judge as inferior a work in which the figures behave inconsistently or seem not to be adequately motivated. (The point must be made, however, that different literary forms or genres are governed by different rules. For instance, consistency of character is usually expected in tragedy but not in melodrama or in comedy, where last-minute reformations may be welcome and greeted with applause. The novelist Henry James said, "You will not write a good novel unless you possess the sense of reality." He is probably right—but does his view hold for the writer of farces?) In the case of *Macbeth* you might well find that the characters are consistent: Although the play begins by showing Macbeth as a loyal defender of King Duncan, Macbeth's later treachery is understandable, given the temptation and the pressure. Similarly, Lady Macbeth's descent into madness, although it may come as a surprise, may strike you as entirely plausible: At the beginning of the play she is confident that she can become an accomplice to a murder, but she has overestimated herself (or, we might say, she has underestimated her own humanity, the power of her guilty conscience, which drives her to insanity).

2. *A good work of art is complex yet unified.* If Macbeth is only a "tyrant" (Macduff's word) or a "butcher" (Malcolm's word), he is a unified character but he may be too simple and too uninteresting a character to be the subject of a great play. But, one argument holds, Macbeth in fact is a complex character, not simply a villain but a hero-villain, and the play as a whole is complex. *Macbeth* is a good work of art, one might argue, partly because it shows us so many aspects of life (courage, fear, loyalty, treachery, for a start) through a richly varied language (the diction

ranges from a grand passage in which Macbeth says that his bloody hands will "incarnadine," or make red, "the multitudinous seas" to colloquial passages such as the drunken porter's "Knock, knock"). The play shows us the heroic Macbeth tragically destroying his own life, and it shows us the comic porter making coarse jokes about deceit and damnation, jokes that (although the porter doesn't know it) connect with Macbeth's crimes.

3. *A good work of art sets forth a wholesome view of life.* The idea that a work should be judged partly or largely on the moral view that it contains is widely held by the general public. (It has also been held by esteemed philosophers, notably Plato.) Thus, a story that demeans women—perhaps one that takes a casual view of rape—would be given a low rating and so would a play that treats a mass murderer as a hero.

Implicit in this approach is what is called an *instrumentalist* view—the idea that a work of art is an instrument, a means, to some higher value. Thus, many people hold that reading great works of literature makes us better—or at least does not make us worse. In this view, a work that is pornographic or in some other way thought to be immoral will be given a low value. At the time we are writing this chapter, a law requires the National Endowment for the Arts to take into account standards of decency when making awards.

Moral judgments, it should be noted, do not come only from the conservative right; the liberal left has been quick to detect political incorrectness. In fact, except for those people who subscribe to the now unfashionable view that a work of art is an independent aesthetic object with little or no connection to the real world—something like a pretty floral arrangement or a wordless melody—most people judge works of literature largely by their content, by what the works seem to say about life.

- Marxist critics, for instance, have customarily held that literature should make the reader aware of the political realities of life.

- Feminist critics are likely to hold that literature should make us aware of gender relationships—for example, aware of patriarchal power and of female accomplishments.

4. *A good work of art is original.* This assumption puts special value on new techniques and new subject matter. Thus, the *first* playwright who introduces a new subject (say, AIDS) gets extra credit, so to speak. Or to return to Shakespeare, one sign of his genius, it is held, is that he was so highly varied; none of his tragedies seems merely to duplicate another, each is a world of its own, a new kind of achievement. Compare, for instance, *Romeo and Juliet*, with its two youthful and innocent heroes, with *Macbeth*, with its deeply guilty hero. Both plays are tragedies, but we can hardly imagine two more different plays—even if a reader perversely argues that the young lovers are guilty of impetuosity and of disobeying appropriate authorities.

5. *A good work of art deals with an important subject.* Here we are concerned with theme: Great works, in this view, must deal with great themes. Love, death, patriotism, and God, say, are great themes; a work that deals with these may achieve a height, an excellence, that, say, a work describing a dog scratching for fleas may not achieve. (Of course, if the reader feels that the dog is a symbol of humanity plagued by invisible enemies, then the poem about the dog may reach the heights, but then, too, it is *not* a poem about a dog and fleas: It is really a poem about humanity and the invisible.)

The point: In writing an evaluation you must let your reader know *why* you value the work as you do. Obviously, it is not enough just to keep saying that *this* work is great whereas *that* work is not so great; the reader wants to know *why* you offer the judgments that you do, which means that you

- must set forth your criteria and then
- offer evidence that is in accord with them.

THEORIZING

Some literary criticism is concerned with such theoretical questions as these:

What is tragedy? Can the hero be a villain? How does tragedy differ from melodrama?

✓ A CHECKLIST FOR AN ARGUMENT ABOUT LITERATURE

☐ Is my imagined reader like a typical classmate of mine, someone who is not a specialist in literature but who is open-minded and interested in hearing my point of view about a work?

☐ Is the essay supported with evidence, usually from the text itself but conceivably from other sources (such as a statement by the author, a statement by a person regarded as an authority, or perhaps the evidence of comparable works)?

☐ Is the essay inclusive? Does it take into account all relevant details (which is not to say that it includes everything the writer knows about the work—for instance, that it was made into a film or that the author died poor)?

☐ Is the essay focused? Does the thesis stay steadily before the reader?

☐ Does the essay use quotations, but as evidence, not as padding? Whenever possible, does it abridge or summarize long quotations?

☐ Are all sources fully acknowledged? (For the form of documentation, see Chapter 7.)

Why do tragedies—works showing good or at least interesting people destroyed—give us pleasure?

Does a work of art—a play or a novel, say, a made-up world with imagined characters—offer anything that can be called "truth"? Does an experience of a work of art affect our character?

Does a work of art have meaning in itself, or is the meaning simply whatever anyone wishes to say it is? Does *Macbeth* tell us anything about life, or is it just an invented story?

And, yet again, one hopes that anyone asserting a thesis concerned with any of these topics will offer evidence—will, indeed, *argue* rather than merely assert.

EXAMPLES:

Two Students Interpret Robert Frost's "Mending Wall"

Let's consider two competing interpretations of a poem, Robert Frost's "Mending Wall." We say "competing" because these interpretations clash head-on. Differing interpretations need not be incompatible, of course. For instance, a historical interpretation of *Macbeth*, arguing that an understanding of the context of English-Scottish politics around 1605 helps us to appreciate the play, need not be incompatible with a psychoanalytic interpretation that tells us that Macbeth's murder of King Duncan is rooted in an Oedipus complex, the king being a father figure. Different approaches thus can illuminate different aspects of the work, just as they can emphasize or subordinate different elements in the plot or characters portrayed. But, again, in the next few pages we will deal with mutually incompatible interpretations of the meaning of Frost's poem—of what Frost's poem is about.

After reading the poem and the two interpretations written by students, spend a few minutes thinking about the questions that we raise after the second interpretation.

Robert Frost

Robert Frost (1874–1963) studied for part of one term at Dartmouth College in New Hampshire, then did odd jobs (including teaching), and from 1897 to 1899 was enrolled as a special student at Harvard. He then farmed in New Hampshire, published a few poems in newspapers, did some more teaching, and in 1912 left for England, where he hoped to achieve success as a writer. By 1915 he was known in England, and he returned to the United States. By the time of his death he was the nation's unofficial poet laureate. "Mending Wall" was first published in 1914.

Mending Wall

Something there is that doesn't love a wall,
That sends the frozen-ground-swell under it,
And spills the upper boulders in the sun;
And makes gaps even two can pass abreast.
The work of hunters is another thing: 5
I have come after them and made repair
Where they have left not one stone on a stone,
But they would have the rabbit out of hiding,
To please the yelping dogs. The gaps I mean,
No one has seen them made or heard them made,   10
But at spring mending-time we find them there.
I let my neighbor know beyond the hill;
And on a day we meet to walk the line
And set the wall between us once again.
We keep the wall between us as we go.   15
To each the boulders that have fallen to each.
And some are loaves and some so nearly balls
We have to use a spell to make them balance:
"Stay where you are until our backs are turned!"
We wear our fingers rough with handling them.   20
Oh, just another kind of outdoor game,
One on a side. It comes to little more:
There where it is we do not need the wall:
He is all pine and I am apple orchard.
My apple trees will never get across   25
And eat the cones under his pines, I tell him.
He only says, "Good fences make good neighbors."
Spring is the mischief in me, and I wonder
If I could put a notion in his head:
"*Why* do they make good neighbors? Isn't it   30
Where there are cows? But here there are no cows.
Before I built a wall I'd ask to know
What I was walling in or walling out,
And to whom I was like to give offense.
Something there is that doesn't love a wall,   35
That wants it down." I could say "Elves" to him,
But it's not elves exactly, and I'd rather
He said it for himself. I see him there

Bringing a stone grasped firmly by the top
In each hand, like an old-stone savage armed.   40
He moves in darkness as it seems to me,
Not of woods only and the shade of trees.
He will not go behind his father's saying,
And he likes having thought of it so well
He says again, "Good fences make good neighbors."   45

Deutsch 1

Jonathan Deutsch

Professor Walton

English 102

5 March 2009

The Deluded Speaker in Frost's "Mending Wall"

Our discussions of "Mending Wall" in high school showed that most people think Frost is saying that walls between people are a bad thing and that we should not try to separate ourselves from each other unnecessarily. Perhaps the wall, in this view, is a symbol for race prejudice or religious differences, and Frost is suggesting that these differences are minor and that they should not keep us apart. In this common view, the neighbor's words, "Good fences make good neighbors" (lines 27 and 45) show that the neighbor is shortsighted. I disagree with this view, but first I want to present the evidence that might be offered for it, so that we can then see whether it really is substantial.

First of all, someone might claim that in lines 23 to 26 Frost offers a good argument against walls:

There where it is we do not need the wall:

He is all pine and I am apple orchard.

My apple trees will never get across

And eat the cones under his pines, I tell him.

The neighbor does not offer a valid reply to this argument; in fact, he doesn't offer any argument at all but simply says, "Good fences make good neighbors."

Another piece of evidence supposedly showing that the neighbor is wrong, it is said, is found in Frost's description of him as "an old-stone savage" and someone who "moves in darkness" (40, 41). And a third piece of evidence is said to be that the neighbor "will not go behind his father's saying" (43), but he merely repeats the saying.

There is, however, another way of looking at the poem. As I see it, the speaker is a very snide and condescending person. He is confident that he knows it all and that his neighbor is an ignorant savage; he is even willing to tease his supposedly ignorant neighbor. For instance, the speaker admits to "the mischief in me" (28), and he is confident that he could tell the truth to the neighbor but arrogantly thinks that it would be a more effective form of teaching if the neighbor "said it for himself" (38).

The speaker is not only unpleasantly mischievous and condescending toward his neighbor, but he is also shallow, for he does not see the great wisdom that there is in proverbs. The *American Heritage Dictionary of the English Language*, Third Edition, defines a proverb as "A short, pithy saying in frequent and widespread use that expresses a basic truth." Frost, or at least the man who speaks this poem, does not seem to realize that proverbs express truths. He just dismisses them, and he thinks the neighbor is wrong not to "go behind his father's saying" (43). But there is a great deal of wisdom in the sayings of our fathers. For instance, in the Bible (in the Old Testament) there is a whole book of proverbs, filled with wise sayings such as "Reprove not a scorner, lest he hate thee: rebuke a wise man, and he will love thee" (9:8); "He that trusteth in his riches shall fall" (11:28); "The way of a fool is right in his own eyes" (12:15; this might be said of the speaker of "Mending Wall"); "A soft answer turneth away wrath" (15:1); and (to cut short what could be a list many pages long), "Whoso diggeth a pit shall fall therein" (26:27).

The speaker is confident that walls are unnecessary and probably bad, but he doesn't realize that even where there are no cattle, walls serve the valuable purpose of clearly marking out our territory. They help us to preserve our independence and our individuality. Walls — man-made structures — are a sign of civilization. A wall more or less says, "*This* is mine, but I respect *that* as yours."

Frost's speaker is so confident of his shallow view that he makes fun
of his neighbor for repeating that "Good fences make good neighbors"
(27, 45). But he himself repeats his own saying, "Something there
is that doesn't love a wall" (1, 35). And at least the neighbor has age-
old tradition on his side, since the proverb is the saying of his father.
On the other hand, the speaker has only his own opinion, and he can't
even say what the "something" is.

It may be that Frost meant for us to laugh at the neighbor and
to take the side of the speaker, but I think it is much more likely that
he meant for us to see that the speaker is mean-spirited (or at least
given to unpleasant teasing), too self-confident, foolishly dismissing
the wisdom of the old times, and entirely unaware that he has these
unpleasant characteristics.

Felicia Alonso

Professor Walton

English 102

5 March 2009

The Debate in Robert Frost's "Mending Wall"

I think the first thing to say about Frost's "Mending Wall" is this: The poem is not about a debate over whether good fences do or do not make good neighbors. It is about two debaters: One of the debaters is on the side of vitality, and the other is on the side of an unchanging, fixed — dead, we might say — tradition.

How can we characterize the speaker? For one thing, he is neighborly. Interestingly, it is *he*, and not the neighbor, who initiates the repairing of the wall: "I let my neighbor know beyond the hill" (line 12). This seems strange, since the speaker doesn't see any point in this wall, whereas the neighbor is all in favor of walls. Can we explain this apparent contradiction? Yes; the speaker is a good neighbor, willing to do his share of the work and willing (perhaps in order not to upset his neighbor) to maintain an old tradition even though he doesn't see its importance. It may not be important, he thinks, but it is really rather pleasant, "another kind of outdoor game" (21). In fact, sometimes he even repairs fences on his own, after hunters have destroyed them.

Second, we can say that the speaker is on the side of nature. "Something there is that doesn't love a wall," he says (1, 35), and of course, the "something" is nature itself. Nature "sends the frozen-ground-swell" under the wall and "spills the upper boulders in the sun; / And makes gaps even two can pass abreast" (2–4). Notice that nature itself makes the gaps and that "two can pass abreast" — that is, people can walk together in a companionable way. It is hard to imagine the neighbor walking side by side with anyone.

Alonso 2

Third, we can say that the speaker has a sense of humor. When he thinks of trying to get his neighbor interested in the issue, he admits that "the mischief" is in him (28), and he amusingly attributes his playfulness to a natural force, the spring. He playfully toys with the obviously preposterous idea of suggesting to his neighbor that elves caused the stones to fall, but he stops short of making this amusing suggestion to his very serious neighbor. Still, the mere thought assures us that he has a playful, genial nature, and the idea also again implies that not only the speaker but also some sort of mysterious natural force dislikes walls.

Finally, though, of course, he thinks he is right and that his neighbor is mistaken, he at least is cautious in his view. He does not call his neighbor "an old-stone savage" (40); rather, he uses a simile ("like") and then adds that this is only his opinion, so the opinion is softened quite a bit. Here is the description of the neighbor, with italics added to clarify my point. The neighbor is . . .

> *like* an old-stone savage armed. / He moves
>
> in darkness *as it seems to me* . . . (40–41)

Of course, the only things we know about the neighbor are those things that the speaker chooses to tell us, so it is not surprising that the speaker comes out ahead. He comes out ahead not because he is right about walls (real or symbolic) and his neighbor is wrong—that's an issue that is not settled in the poem. He comes out ahead because he is a more interesting figure, someone who is neighborly, thoughtful, playful. Yes, maybe he seems to us to feel superior to his neighbor, but we can be certain that he doesn't cause his neighbor any embarrassment. Take the very end of the poem. The speaker tells us that the neighbor

> . . . will not go behind his father's saying,
>
> And he likes having thought of it so well
>
> He says again, "Good fences make good neighbors."

The speaker is telling *us* that the neighbor is utterly unoriginal and that the neighbor confuses *remembering* something with *thinking*. But the speaker doesn't get into an argument; he doesn't rudely challenge his neighbor and demand reasons, which might force the neighbor to see that he can't think for himself. And in fact we probably like the neighbor just as he is, and we don't want him to change his mind. The words that ring in our ears are not the speaker's but the neighbor's: "Good fences make good neighbors." The speaker of the poem is a good neighbor. After all, one can hardly be more neighborly than to let the neighbor have the last word.

Topics for Critical Thinking and Writing

1. State the thesis of each essay. Do you believe the theses are sufficiently clear and appear sufficiently early in the essays?

2. Consider the evidence that each essay offers by way of supporting its thesis. Do you find some of the evidence unconvincing? Explain.

3. Putting aside the question of which interpretation you prefer, comment on the organization of each essay. Is the organization clear? Do you want to propose some other pattern that you think might be more effective?

4. Consult the Checklist for Peer Review on page 260, and offer comments on one of the two essays. Or: If you were the instructor in the course in which these two essays were submitted, what might be your final comments on each of them? Or: Write an analysis (250–500 words) of the strengths and weaknesses of either essay.

EXERCISES: READING A POEM AND A STORY

Andrew Marvell

Andrew Marvell (1621–1678), born in Hull, England, and educated at Trinity College, Cambridge, was traveling in Europe when the civil war between the Royalists and the Puritans broke out in England in 1642. The Puritans were victorious and established the Commonwealth (the monarchy was restored later, in 1660), and Marvell became a tutor to the daughter of the victorious Lord-General. In 1657 he became an assistant to the blind poet John Milton, who held the title of Latin Secretary (Latin was the language of international diplomacy). In 1659 Marvell was elected to represent Hull in Parliament. As a man of letters, during his lifetime he was known chiefly for some satiric prose and poetry; most of the writings for which he is now esteemed were published posthumously. The following poem was first published in 1681.

To His Coy Mistress°

    Had we but world enough, and time,
This coyness,° Lady, were no crime.
We would sit down, and think which way
To walk, and pass our long love's day.
Thou by the Indian Ganges' side   5
Shouldst rubies find; I by the tide
Of Humber° would complain. I would
Love you ten years before the Flood,
And you should, if you please, refuse

Mistress Beloved woman.
coyness Reluctance.
Humber An estuary at Hull, Marvell's birthplace.

Till the Conversion of the Jews.°   10
My vegetable° love should grow
Vaster than empires and more slow;
An hundred years should go to praise
Thine eyes, and on thy forehead gaze;
Two hundred to adore each breast,   15
But thirty thousand to the rest;
An age at least to every part,
And the last age should show your heart.
For, Lady, you deserve this state,°
Nor would I love at lower rate.   20
  But at my back I always hear
Time's wingèd chariot hurrying near;
And yonder all before us lie
Deserts of vast eternity.
Thy beauty shall no more be found,   25
Nor, in thy marble vault, shall sound
My echoing song; then worms shall try°
That long-preserved virginity,
And your quaint° honour turn to dust,
And into ashes all my lust: 30
The grave's a fine and private place,
But none, I think, do there embrace.
  Now therefore, while the youthful hue
Sits on thy skin like morning dew,
And while thy willing soul transpires   35
At every pore with instant fires,
Now let us sport us while we may,
And now, like amorous birds of prey,
Rather at once our time devour
Than languish in his slow-chapt° power.   40
Let us roll all our strength and all
Our sweetness up into one ball,
And tear our pleasures with rough strife
Thorough° the iron gates of life:
Thus, though we cannot make our sun   45
Stand still,° yet we will make him run.

Conversion of the Jews Something that would take place in the remote future, at the
end of history.
vegetable Vegetative or growing.
state Ceremonious treatment.
try Test.
quaint Fastidious or finicky, with a pun on a coarse word defined in an Elizabethan dictionary as "a woman's privities."
slow-chapt Slow-jawed.
Thorough Through.
make our sun stand still An allusion to Joshua, the ancient Hebrew who, according to
the Book of Joshua (10.12–13), made the sun stand still.

TOPICS FOR CRITICAL THINKING AND WRITING

1. The motif that life is short and that we should seize the day (Latin: *Vita brevis carpe diem*) is old. Marvell's poem, in fact, probably has its ultimate source in a classical text called *The Greek Anthology*, a collection of about six thousand short Greek poems composed between the first century B.C. and the tenth century A.D. One poem goes thus, in a fairly literal translation:

   > You spare your maidenhead, and to what profit? For when you come to Hades you will not find your lover, girl. Among the living are the delights of Venus, but, maiden, we shall lie in the underworld mere bones and dust.

   If you find Marvell's poem more impressive, offer reasons for your belief.

2. A student, working from the translation just given, produced this rhyming version:

   > You keep your virginity, but to what end?
   > Below, in Hades, you won't find your friend.
   > On earth we enjoy Venus' sighs and moans;
   > Buried below, we are senseless bones.

   What do you think of this version? Why? Prepare your own version — your instructor may divide the class into groups of four, and each group can come up with a collaborative version — and then compare it with other versions, giving reasons for your preferences.

3. Marvell's poem takes the form of a syllogism (see pp. 85–90). It can be divided into three parts:

   a. "Had we" (that is, "If we had") (line 1), a supposition, or suppositional premise;
   b. "But at my back" (line 21), a refutation;
   c. "Now therefore" (line 33), a deduction.

   Look closely at the poem and develop the argument using these three parts, devoting a few sentences to each part.

4. A student wrote of this poem:

   > As a Christian I can't accept the lover's statement that "yonder all before us lie / Deserts of vast eternity" (lines 23–24). The poem may contain beautiful lines, and it may offer clever reasoning, but the reasoning is based on what my religion tells me is wrong. I not only cannot accept the idea of the poem, but I also cannot enjoy the poem, since it presents a false view of reality.

   What assumptions is this student making about a reader's response to a work of literature? Do you agree or disagree? Why?

5. Here are three additional comments by students. For each, list the writer's assumptions, and then evaluate each comment. You may agree or disagree, in whole or in part, with any comment, but give your reasons.

   a. The poem is definitely clever, and that is part of what is wrong with it. It is a blatant attempt at seduction. The man seems to think he is smarter than the woman he is speaking to, and he "proves" that she should go to bed with him. Since we don't hear her side of the argument, Marvell implies that she has nothing to say and that his argument is sound. What the poet doesn't seem to understand is that there is such a thing as virtue, and a woman need not sacrifice virtue just because death is inevitable.

b. On the surface, "To His Coy Mistress" is an attempt to persuade a woman to go to bed with the speaker, but the poem is really less about sex than it is about the terrifying shortness of life.

c. This is not a love poem. The speaker admits that his impulse is "lust" (line 30), and he makes fun of the girl's conception of honor and virginity. If we enjoy this poem at all, our enjoyment must be in the hope that this would-be date-rapist is unsuccessful.

6. Read the poem several times slowly, perhaps even aloud. Do certain lines seem especially moving, especially memorable? If so, which ones? Give reasons for your belief.

7. In *On Deconstruction* (1982), a study of contemporary literary theory, Jonathan Culler remarks that feminist criticism has often stressed "reading as a woman." This concept, Culler says, affirms the "continuity between women's experience of social and familial structures and their experiences as readers." Do you agree with his suggestion that men and women often interpret literary works differently? Consider Marvell's poem in particular: Identify and discuss phrases and images in it to which men and women readers might (or might not) respond very differently.

8. A small point, but perhaps one of some interest. In the original text, line 34 ends with *glew*, not with *dew*. Most editors assume that the printer made an error, and—looking for a word to rhyme with *hue*—they replace *glew* with *dew*. Another possible emendation is *lew*, an archaic word meaning "warmth." But the original reading has been defended, as a variant of the word *glow*. Your preference? Your reasons?

Kate Chopin

Kate Chopin (1851–1904) was born in St. Louis and named Katherine O'Flaherty. At the age of nineteen she married a cotton broker in New Orleans, Oscar Chopin (the name is pronounced something like "show pan"), who was descended from the early French settlers in Louisiana. After her husband's death in 1883, Kate Chopin turned to writing fiction. The following story was first published in 1894.

The Story of an Hour

Knowing that Mrs. Mallard was afflicted with a heart trouble, great care was taken to break to her as gently as possible the news of her husband's death.

It was her sister Josephine who told her, in broken sentences, veiled hints that revealed in half concealing. Her husband's friend Richards was there, too, near her. It was he who had been in the newspaper office when intelligence of the railroad disaster was received, with

Brently Mallard's name leading the list of "killed." He had only taken the time to assure himself of its truth by a second telegram, and had hastened to forestall any less careful, less tender friend in bearing the sad message.

She did not hear the story as many women have heard the same, with a paralyzed inability to accept its significance. She wept at once, with sudden, wild abandonment, in her sister's arms. When the storm of grief had spent itself she went away to her room alone. She would have no one follow her.

There stood, facing the open window, a comfortable, roomy armchair. Into this she sank, pressed down by a physical exhaustion that haunted her body and seemed to reach into her soul.

She could see in the open square before her house the tops of trees 5 that were all aquiver with the new spring life. The delicious breath of rain was in the air. In the street below a peddler was crying his wares. The notes of a distant song which some one was singing reached her faintly, and countless sparrows were twittering in the eaves.

There were patches of blue sky showing here and there through the clouds that had met and piled one above the other in the west facing her window.

She sat with her head thrown back upon the cushion of the chair, quite motionless, except when a sob came up into her throat and shook her, as a child who has cried itself to sleep continues to sob in its dreams.

She was young, with a fair, calm face, whose lines bespoke repression and even a certain strength. But now there was a dull stare in her eyes, whose gaze was fixed away off yonder on one of those patches of blue sky. It was not a glance of reflection, but rather indicated a suspension of intelligent thought.

There was something coming to her and she was waiting for it, fearfully. What was it? She did not know; it was too subtle and elusive to name. But she felt it, creeping out of the sky, reaching toward her through the sounds, the scents, the color that filled the air.

Now her bosom rose and fell tumultuously. She was beginning to rec- 10 ognize this thing that was approaching to possess her, and she was striving to beat it back with her will—as powerless as her two white slender hands would have been.

When she abandoned herself a little whispered word escaped her slightly parted lips. She said it over and over under her breath: "Free, free, free!" The vacant stare and the look of terror that had followed it went from her eyes. They stayed keen and bright. Her pulses beat fast, and the coursing blood warmed and relaxed every inch of her body.

She did not stop to ask if it were not a monstrous joy that held her. A clear and exalted perception enabled her to dismiss the suggestion as trivial.

She knew that she would weep again when she saw the kind, tender hands folded in death; the face that had never looked save with love upon her, fixed and gray and dead. But she saw beyond that bitter moment a long procession of years to come that would belong to her absolutely. And she opened and spread her arms out to them in welcome.

There would be no one to live for her during those coming years; she would live for herself. There would be no powerful will bending her in that blind persistence with which men and women believe they have a right to impose a private will upon a fellow creature. A kind intention or a cruel intention made the act seem no less a crime as she looked upon it in that brief moment of illumination.

And yet she had loved him—sometimes. Often she had not. What 15 did it matter! What could love, the unsolved mystery, count for in face of this possession of self-assertion which she suddenly recognized as the strongest impulse of her being.

"Free! Body and soul free!" she kept whispering.

Josephine was kneeling before the closed door with her lips to the keyhole, imploring for admission. "Louise, open the door! I beg; open the door—you will make yourself ill. What are you doing, Louise? For heaven's sake open the door."

"Go away. I am not making myself ill." No; she was drinking in a very elixir of life through that open window.

Her fancy was running riot along those days ahead of her. Spring days, and summer days, and all sorts of days that would be her own. She breathed a quick prayer that life might be long. It was only yesterday she had thought with a shudder that life might be long.

She arose at length and opened the door to her sister's importuni- 20 ties. There was a feverish triumph in her eyes, and she carried herself unwittingly like a goddess of Victory. She clasped her sister's waist, and together they descended the stairs. Richards stood waiting for them at the bottom.

Some one was opening the front door with a latchkey. It was Brently Mallard who entered, a little travel-stained, composedly carrying his grip-sack and umbrella. He had been far from the scene of accident, and did not even know there had been one. He stood amazed at Josephine's piercing cry; at Richards' quick motion to screen him from the view of his wife.

But Richards was too late.

When the doctors came they said she had died of heart disease—of joy that kills.

TOPICS FOR CRITICAL THINKING AND WRITING

Read the following assertions, and consider whether you agree or disagree, and why. For each assertion, draft a paragraph with your arguments.

1. The railroad accident is a symbol of the destructiveness of the industrial revolution.

2. The story claims that women rejoice in the deaths of their husbands.

3. Mrs. Mallard's death at the end is a just punishment for the joy she takes in her husband's death.

4. The story is rich in irony. Some examples: (1) The other characters think she is grieving, but she is rejoicing; (2) she prays for a long life, but she dies almost immediately; (3) the doctors say she died of "the joy that kills," but they think her joy was seeing her husband alive.

5. The story is excellent because it has a surprise ending.

THINKING ABOUT THE EFFECTS OF LITERATURE

Works of art are artifacts—things constructed, made up, fashioned, just like chairs and houses and automobiles. In analyzing works of literature it is therefore customary to keep one's eye on the complex, constructed object and not simply tell the reader how one feels about it. Instead of reporting their feelings, critics usually analyze the relationships between the parts and the relationship of the parts to the whole.

For instance, in talking about literature we can examine the relationship of plot to character, of one character to another, or of one stanza in a poem to the next. Still, although we may try to engage in this sort of analysis as dispassionately as possible, we all know that inevitably

- we are not only examining something out there,
- but are also examining our own responses.

Why? Because literature has an effect on us. Indeed, it probably has several kinds of effects, ranging from short-range emotional responses ("I really enjoyed this," "I burst out laughing," "It revolted me") to long-range effects ("I have always tried to live up to a line in *Hamlet*, 'This above all, to thine own self be true'"). Let's first look at, very briefly, immediate emotional responses.

Analysis usually begins with a response: "This is marvelous," or "What a bore," and we then go on to try to account for our response. A friend mentions a book or a film to us, and we say, "I couldn't stay with it for five minutes." The friend expresses surprise, and we then go on to explain, giving reasons (to the friend and also to ourselves) why we couldn't stay with it. Perhaps the book seemed too remote from life, or perhaps, on the other hand, it seemed to be nothing more than a transcript of the boring talk that we can overhear on a bus or in an elevator.

In such discussions, when we draw on our responses, as we must, the work may disappear; we find ourselves talking about ourselves. Let's take two extreme examples: "I can't abide *Huckleberry Finn*. How am I expected to enjoy a so-called masterpiece that has a character in it called 'Nigger Jim?'" Or: "T. S. Eliot's anti-Semitism is too much for me to take. Don't talk to me about Eliot's skill with meter, when he has such lines as 'Rachel, *née* Rabinovitch / Tears at the grapes with murderous paws.'"

Although everyone agrees that literature can evoke this sort of strong emotional response, not everyone agrees on how much value we should put on our personal experience. Several of the Topics for Critical Thinking and Writing below invite you to reflect on this issue.

What about the *consequences of the effects* of literature? Does literature shape our character and therefore influence our behavior? It is generally believed that it does have an effect. One hears, for example, that literature (like travel) is broadening, that it makes us aware of, and tolerant of, kinds of behavior that differ from our own and from what we see around us. One of the chief arguments against pornography, for instance, is that it desensitizes us, makes us too tolerant of abusive relationships, relationships in which people (usually men) use other people (usually women) as mere things or instruments for pleasure. (A contrary view should be mentioned: Some people argue that pornography provides a relatively harmless outlet for fantasies that otherwise might be given release in the real world. In this view, pornography acts as a sort of safety valve.)

Discussions of the effects of literature that get into the popular press almost always involve pornography, but other topics are also the subjects of controversy. For instance, in recent decades parents and educators have been much concerned with fairy tales. Does the violence in some fairy tales ("Little Red Riding Hood," "The Three Little Pigs") have a bad effect on children? Do some of the stories teach the wrong lessons, implying that women should be passive, men active ("Sleeping Beauty," for instance, in which the sleeping woman is brought to life by the action of the handsome prince)? The Greek philosopher Plato (427–347 B.C.) strongly believed that the literature we hear or read shapes our later behavior, and since most of the ancient Greek traditional stories (notably Homer's *Odyssey* and *Iliad*) celebrate acts of love and war rather than of justice, he prohibited the reading of such material in his ideal society. (We reprint a relevant passage from Plato on page 443.)

Topics for Critical Thinking and Writing

1. If you have responded strongly (favorably or unfavorably) to some aspect of the social content of a literary work—for instance, its depiction of women or of a particular minority group—in an essay of 250 to 500 words analyze the response, and try to determine whether you are talking chiefly about yourself or the work. (Two works widely regarded as literary masterpieces but nonetheless often banned from classrooms are Shakespeare's *The Merchant of Venice* and Mark Twain's *Huckleberry Finn.* If you have read either of these, you may want to write about it and your response.) Can we really see literary value—*really* see it—in a work that deeply offends us?

2. Most people believe that literature influences life—that in some perhaps mysterious way it helps to shape character. Certainly anyone who believes that some works should be censored, or at least should be made unavailable to minors, assumes that they can have a bad influence, so why not assume that other works can have a good influence?

Read the following brief claims about literature; then choose one and write a 250-word essay offering support or taking issue with it.

The pen is mightier than the sword. —EDWARD BULWER LYTTON

The writer isn't made in a vacuum. Writers are witnesses. The reason we need writers is because we need witnesses to this terrifying century. —E. L. DOCTOROW

When we read of human beings behaving in certain ways, with the approval of the author, who gives his benedictions to this behavior by his attitude towards the result of the behavior arranged by himself, we can be influenced towards behaving in the same way. —T. S. ELIOT

Poetry makes nothing happen. —W. H. AUDEN

Literature is *without proofs*. By which it must be understood that it cannot prove, not only *what* it says, but even that it is worth the trouble of saying it. —ROLAND BARTHES

Of course the illusion of art is to make one believe that great literature is very close to life, but exactly the opposite is true. Life is amorphous, literature is formal. —FRANÇOISE SAGAN

3. At least since the time of Plato (see the piece directly following) some thoughtful people have wanted to ban certain works of literature because they allegedly stimulate the wrong sorts of pleasure or cause us to take pleasure in the wrong sorts of things. Consider, by way of comparison, bullfighting and cockfighting. Of course, they cause pain to the animals, but branding animals also causes pain and is not banned. Bullfighting and cockfighting probably are banned in the United States largely because most of us believe that people should not take pleasure in these activities. Now to return to literature: Should some kinds of writing be prohibited because they offer the wrong sorts of pleasure?

Plato

Plato (427–347 B.C.), an Athenian aristocrat by birth, was the student of one great philosopher (Socrates) and the teacher of another (Aristotle). His legacy of more than two dozen dialogues—imaginary discussions between Socrates and one or more other speakers, usually young Athenians—has been of such influence that the whole of Western philosophy can be characterized, A. N. Whitehead wrote, as "a series of footnotes to Plato." Plato's interests encompassed the full range of topics in philosophy: ethics, politics, logic, metaphysics, epistemology, aesthetics, psychology, and education.

This selection from Plato's Republic, *one of his best-known and longest dialogues, is about the education suitable for the rulers of an ideal society.*

The Republic *begins, typically, with an investigation into the nature of justice. Socrates (who speaks for Plato) convincingly explains to Glaucon that we cannot reasonably expect to achieve a just society unless we devote careful attention to the moral education of the young men who are scheduled in later life to become the rulers. (Here as elsewhere, Plato's elitism and aristocratic bias shows itself; as readers of* The Republic *soon learn, Plato is no admirer of democracy or of a classless society.) Plato cares as much about what the educational curriculum should exclude as what it should include. His special target was the common practice in his day of using for pedagogy the Homeric tales and other stories about the gods. He readily embraces the principle of censorship, as the excerpt explains, because he thinks it is a necessary means to achieve the ideal society.*

"The Greater Part of the Stories Current Today We Shall Have to Reject"

"What kind of education shall we give them then? We shall find it difficult to improve on the time-honored distinction between the physical training we give to the body and the education we give to the mind and character."

"True."

"And we shall begin by educating mind and character, shall we not?"

"Of course."

"In this education you would include stories, would you not?"   5

"Yes."

"These are of two kinds, true stories and fiction.[1] Our education must use both, and start with fiction."

"I don't know what you mean."

"But you know that we begin by telling children stories. These are, in general, fiction, though they contain some truth. And we tell children stories before we start them on physical training."

"That is so."   10

"That is what I meant by saying that we must start to educate the mind before training the body."

"You are right," he said.

"And the first step, as you know, is always what matters most, particularly when we are dealing with those who are young and tender. That is the time when they are easily molded and when any impression we choose to make leaves a permanent mark."

"That is certainly true."

---

[1]The Greek word *pseudos* and its corresponding verb meant not only "fiction" — stories, tales — but also "what is not true" and so, in suitable contexts, "lies": and this ambiguity should be borne in mind. [Editors' note: All footnotes are by the translator, but some have been omitted.]

"Shall we therefore readily allow our children to listen to any sto- 15
ries made up by anyone, and to form opinions that are for the most
part the opposite of those we think they should have when they
grow up?"

"We certainly shall not."

"Then it seems that our first business is to supervise the production of
stories, and choose only those we think suitable, and reject the rest. We
shall persuade mothers and nurses to tell our chosen stories to their children, and by means of them to mold their minds and characters which are
more important than their bodies. The greater part of the stories current
today we shall have to reject."

"Which are you thinking of?"

"We can take some of the major legends as typical. For all, whether
major or minor, should be cast in the same mold and have the same
effect. Do you agree?"

"Yes: but I'm not sure which you refer to as major." 20

"The stories in Homer and Hesiod and the poets. For it is the poets
who have always made up fictions and stories to tell to men."

"What sort of stories do you mean and what fault do you find in
them?"

"The worst fault possible," I replied, "especially if the fiction is an ugly
one."

"And what is that?"

"Misrepresenting the nature of gods and heroes, like a portrait painter 25
whose portraits bear no resemblance to their originals."

"That is a fault which certainly deserves censure. But give me more
details."

"Well, on the most important of subjects, there is first and foremost the foul story about Ouranos[2] and the things Hesiod says he did, and
the revenge Cronos took on him. While the story of what Cronos did,
and what he suffered at the hands of his son, is not fit as it is to be lightly
repeated to the young and foolish, even if it were true; it would be best to
say nothing about it, or if it must be told, tell it to a select few under oath
of secrecy, at a rite which required, to restrict it still further, the sacrifice
not of a mere pig but of something large and difficult to get."

"These certainly are awkward stories."

"And they shall not be repeated in our state, Adeimantus," I said. "Nor
shall any young audience be told that anyone who commits horrible crimes,
or punishes his father unmercifully, is doing nothing out of the ordinary
but merely what the first and greatest of the gods have done before."

"I entirely agree," said Adeimantus, "that these stories are unsuitable." 30

---

[2]**Ouranos** The sky, the original supreme god. Ouranos was castrated by his son Cronos to
separate him from Gaia (mother earth). Cronos was in turn deposed by Zeus in a struggle
in which Zeus was helped by the Titans.

"Nor can we permit stories of wars and plots and battles among the gods; they are quite untrue, and if we want our prospective guardians to believe that quarrelsomeness is one of the worst of evils, we must certainly not let them be told the story of the Battle of the Giants or embroider it on robes, or tell them other tales about many and various quarrels between gods and heroes and their friends and relations. On the contrary, if we are to persuade them that no citizen has ever quarreled with any other, because it is sinful, our old men and women must tell children stories with this end in view from the first, and we must compel our poets to tell them similar stories when they grow up. But we can admit to our state no stories about Hera being tied up by her son, or Hephaestus being flung out of Heaven by his father for trying to help his mother when she was getting a beating, nor any of Homer's Battles of the Gods, whether their intention is allegorical or not. Children cannot distinguish between what is allegory and what isn't, and opinions formed at that age are usually difficult to eradicate or change; we should therefore surely regard it as of the utmost importance that the first stories they hear shall aim at encouraging the highest excellence of character."

"Your case is a good one," he agreed, "but if someone wanted details, and asked what stories we were thinking of, what should we say?"

To which I replied, "My dear Adeimantus, you and I are not engaged on writing stories but on founding a state. And the founders of a state, though they must know the type of story the poet must produce, and reject any that do not conform to that type, need not write them themselves."

"True: but what are the lines on which our poets must work when they deal with the gods?"

"Roughly as follows," I said. "God must surely always be represented as he really is, whether the poet is writing epic, lyric, or tragedy." 35

"He must."

"And in reality of course god is good, and he must be so described."

"Certainly."

"But nothing good is harmful, is it?"[3]

"I think not." 40

"Then can anything that is not harmful do harm?"

"No."

"And can what does no harm do evil?"

"No again."

"And can what does no evil be the cause of any evil?" 45

---

[3]The reader of the following passage should bear the following ambiguities in mind: (1) the Greek word for good (*agathos*) can mean (a) morally good, (b) beneficial or advantageous; (2) the Greek word for evil (*kakos*) can also mean harm or injury; (3) the adverb of *agathos* (*eu*—the well) can imply either morally right or prosperous. The word translated "cause of" could equally well be rendered "responsible for."

"How could it?"

"Well then; is the good beneficial?"

"Yes."

"So it must be the cause of well-being."

"Yes."

"So the good is not the cause of everything, but only of states of well-being and not of evil."

"Most certainly," he agreed.

"Then god, being good, cannot be responsible for everything, as is commonly said, but only for a small part of human life, for the greater part of which he has no responsibility. For we have a far smaller share of good than of evil, and while god must be held to be the sole cause of good, we must look for some factors other than god as cause of the evil."

"I think that's very true," he said.

"So we cannot allow Homer or any other poet to make such a stupid mistake about the gods, as when he says that

> Zeus has two jars standing on the floor of his palace, full of fates, good in one and evil in the other

and that the man to whom Zeus allots a mixture of both has 'varying fortunes sometimes good and sometimes bad,' while the man to whom he allots unmixed evil is 'chased by ravening despair over the face of the earth.'[4] Nor can we allow references to Zeus as 'dispenser of good and evil.' And we cannot approve if it is said that Athene and Zeus prompted the breach of solemn treaty and oath by Pandarus, or that the strife and contentions of the gods were due to Themis and Zeus. Nor again can we let our children hear from Aeschylus that

> God implants a fault in man, when he wishes to destroy a house utterly.

No: We must forbid anyone who writes a play about the sufferings of Niobe (the subject of the play from which these last lines are quoted), or the house of Pelops, or the Trojan war, or any similar topic, to say they are acts of god; or if he does he must produce the sort of interpretation we are now demanding, and say that god's acts were good and just, and that the sufferers were benefited by being punished. What the poet must not be allowed to say is that those who were punished were made wretched through god's action. He may refer to the wicked as wretched because they needed punishment, provided he makes it clear that in punishing them god did them good. But if a state is to be run on the right lines, every possible step must be taken to prevent anyone, young or old, either saying or being told, whether in poetry or prose, that god,

---

[4]Quotations from Homer are generally taken from the translations by Dr. Rieu in the Penguin series. At times (as here) the version quoted by Plato differs slightly from the accepted text.

being good, can cause harm or evil to any man. To say so would be sinful, inexpedient, and inconsistent."

"I should approve of a law for this purpose and you have my vote for it," he said.

"Then of our laws laying down the principles which those who write or speak about the gods must follow, one would be this: *God is the cause, not of all things, but only of good.*"

"I am quite content with that," he said.

TOPICS FOR CRITICAL THINKING AND WRITING

1. In the beginning of the dialogue Plato says that adults recite fictions to very young children and that these fictions help to mold character. Think of some stories that you heard or read when young, such as "Snow White and the Seven Dwarfs" or "Ali Baba and the Forty Thieves." Try to think of a story that, in the final analysis, is not in accord with what you consider to be proper morality, such as a story in which a person triumphs through trickery or a story in which evil actions—perhaps murders—are set forth without unfavorable comment. (Was it naughty of Jack to kill the giant?) On reflection, do you think children should not be told such stories? Why, or why not? Or think of the early film westerns, in which, on the whole, the Indians (except for an occasional Uncle Tonto) are depicted as bad guys and the whites (except for an occasional coward or rustler) are depicted as good guys. Many people who now have gray hair enjoyed such films in their childhood. Are you prepared to say that such films are not damaging? Or on the other hand, are you prepared to say they are damaging and should be prohibited?

2. It is often objected that censorship of reading matter and of television programs available to children underrates their ability to think for themselves and to discount the dangerous, obscene, and tawdry. Do you agree with this objection? Does Plato?

3. Plato says that allowing poets to say what they please about the gods in his ideal state would be "inconsistent." Explain what he means by this criticism, and then explain why you agree or disagree with it.

4. Do you believe that parents should censor the "fiction" their children encounter (literature, films, pictures, music) but that the community should not censor the "fiction" of adults? Write an essay of 500 words on one of these topics: "Censorship and Rock Lyrics"; "X-Rated Films"; "Ethnic Jokes." (These topics are broadly worded; you can narrow one and offer whatever thesis you wish.)

5. Were you taught that any of the founding fathers ever acted disreputably or that any American hero had any serious moral flaw? Or that America ever acted immorally in its dealings with other nations? Do you think it appropriate for children to hear such things?

THINKING ABOUT GOVERNMENT FUNDING FOR THE ARTS

Our government supports the arts, including writers, by giving grants to numerous institutions. On the other hand, the amount that the government contributes is extremely small when compared to the amounts given to the arts by most European governments. Consider the following questions.

1. Should taxpayers' dollars be used to support the arts? Why, or why not?
2. What possible public benefit can come from supporting the arts? Can one argue that we should support the arts for the same reasons that we support the public schools, that is, to have a civilized society?
3. If dollars are given to the arts, should the political content of the works be taken into account, or only the aesthetic merit? Can we separate content from aesthetic merit? (The best way to approach this issue probably is to begin by thinking of a strongly political work.)
4. Is it censorship not to award public funds to writers whose work is not approved of, or is it simply a matter of refusing to reward them with taxpayers' dollars?
5. Should decisions about grants to writers be made chiefly by government officials or chiefly by experts in the field? Why?

13

A Debater's View: Individual Oral Presentations and Debate

He who knows only his own side of the case knows little of that.

—JOHN STUART MILL

A philosopher who is not taking part in discussions is like a boxer who never goes into the ring.

—LUDWIG WITTGENSTEIN

Freedom is hammered out on the anvil of dissension, dissent, and debate.

—HUBERT HUMPHREY

INDIVIDUAL ORAL PRESENTATIONS

Forensic comes from a Latin word *foris,* meaning "out of doors," which also produced the word *forum,* an open space in front of a public building. In the language of rhetoricians, the place where one delivers a speech to an audience is the forum—whether it is a classroom, a court of law, or the steps of the Lincoln Memorial.

Your instructor may ask you to make an oral presentation (in this case the forum is the classroom), and if your instructor doesn't make such a demand, later life almost certainly will: You will find that at a job interview you will be expected to talk persuasively about what good qualities or experience you can bring to the place of employment. When you have a job you will sometimes have to summarize a report orally or orally argue a case—for instance, that your colleagues should do something they may be hesitant to do.

The goal of your classroom talk is to persuade the audience to share your view, or, if you can't get them to agree completely, to get them to see that at least there is something to be said for this view—that it is a position a reasonable person can hold.

Elsewhere in this book we have said that the subjects of persuasive writing are usually

- matters of fact (for instance, statistics show that the death penalty does—or does not—deter crime), or
- matters of value (abortion is—or is not—immoral), or
- matters of policy (government should—or should not—give money to faith-based institutions).

TWO RULES FOR SPEAKERS:
- *In preparing your oral presentation, keep your thesis in mind.* You may be giving counterarguments, examples, definitions, and so forth, but make sure that your thesis is always evident to your audience.
- *Keep your audience in mind.* Inevitably you will have to make assumptions about what the audience does and does not know about your topic. Do not overestimate their knowledge, and do not underestimate their intelligence.

Whatever your subject, when you draft and revise your talk, make certain that a thesis statement underlies the whole (for instance, "Proposition 2 is a bad idea because. . . .")

The text of an oral presentation ought not to be identical with the text of a written presentation. Both must have a clear **organization,** but oral presentations usually require that the organization be made a bit more obvious, with abundant **signposts** such as "Before I talk about *X*," "When I discussed *Y*, I didn't mention such-and-such because I wanted to concentrate on a single instance, but now is the time to consider *Y*," and so on. You will also have to repeat a bit more than you would in a written presentation. After all, a reader can turn back to check a sentence or a statistic but an auditor cannot, so rather than saying (as one might in a printed text), "When we think further about Smith's comment, we realize. . . ," you will repeat what Smith said before you go on to analyze the statement.

You will want to think carefully about the organization of your talk. We've already stressed the need to develop essays with clear thesis statements and logical supporting points. Oral presentations are no different, but remember that when you are speaking in public, a clear organization will always help alleviate anxiety and reassure you. Thus, you can deliver a powerful message without getting tripped up yourself. We suggest you try the following:

- Outline your draft in advance in order to make sure that it has clear organization.

- Inform your audience at the start what the organization of your presentation will be. Early in the talk you probably should say something along these lines, though not in so abbreviated a form:

  "In talking about *A*, I'll have to define a few terms, *B* and *C*, and I will also have to talk about two positions that differ from mine, *D* and *E*. I'll then try to show why *A* is the best policy to pursue, clearly better than *D* and *E*."

- So that your listeners can easily follow you, be sure to use transitions such as "Furthermore," "Therefore," "Although it is often said," and "It may be objected that," so that your listeners can easily follow your train of thought. Sometimes you may even remind the listeners what the previous stages were, with such a comment as "We have now seen three approaches to the problem of. . . ."

Methods of Delivery

After thinking about helping your audience to follow your speech, you might want to consider how much help you'll need delivering it. Depending on your comfort level with the topic and your argument, you might decide to

- deliver a memorized talk without notes,
- read the talk from a text, or
- speak from an outline, perhaps with quotations and statistics written down.

Each of these methods has its strengths and its weaknesses. A memorized talk allows for plenty of eye contact with the audience but unless you are a superb actor it is almost surely going to seem a bit mechanical. A talk that you read from a text will indeed let you say to an audience exactly what you want to say (with the best possible wording), but reading a text inevitably establishes some distance between you and the audience, even if you occasionally glance up from your pages. If you talk from a mere outline, almost surely some of your sentences will turn out to be a bit awkward—though a tiny bit of awkwardness may help to convey sincerity and may therefore be a plus.

Whatever the form of delivery, try to convey the impression that you are conversing with your audience, not talking down to them—even though if you are on a platform you will be literally talking down.

You may want to use **audiovisual aids** in your presentation. These can range from such low-tech materials as handouts, blackboards, and whiteboards to high-tech PowerPoint presentations. Each has its advantages and its disadvantages. For instance, if you distribute handouts when the talk begins, the audience may start thumbing through them even while you are making your opening comments. And although PowerPoint can be a highly useful aid, some speakers make too much use of it simply because it is available. It happens that the day before writing this discussion the author witnessed a PowerPoint presentation, which began with the speaker projecting on the screen the date, the speaker's name, and the name of the university at which the talk was being delivered. Well, most of us knew the date, and we all knew the speaker's name and the name of the university where we were. It seemed like overkill. The truth is, the talk simply did not need any images at all, and we ended up wondering why the speaker bothered with PowerPoint.

For a delightful parody of this sort of talk, consider "The Gettysburg Powerpoint Presentation" (http://norvig.com/Gettysburg/). It begins thus:

> **And now please welcome President Abraham Lincoln.**
> Good morning. Just a second while I get this connection to work. Do I press this button here? Function-F7? No, that's not right. Hmmm. Maybe I'll have to reboot. Hold on a minute. Um, my name is Abe Lincoln and I'm your president. While we're waiting, I want to thank Judge David Wills, chairman of the committee supervising the dedication of the Gettysburg cemetery. It's great to be here, Dave, and you and the committee are doing a great job. Gee, sometimes this new **technology** does have glitches, but **we couldn't live without it, could we?** Oh—is it ready? OK, here we go.

The lesson? Yes, use audiovisual material if it will help you to present your material, but do not use it if it adds nothing or if you have not mastered the technology.

✓ A CHECKLIST FOR AN ORAL PRESENTATION

Keep the following in mind, whether you are evaluating someone else's talk or preparing your own.

Delivery

☐ Voice loud enough but not too loud.

☐ Appropriate degree of speed — neither hurried nor drawn out.

☐ Dress and attitude toward audience appropriate.

☐ Gestures and eye contact appropriate.

☐ Language clear, e.g., technical words adequately explained.

☐ Visual aids, if any, appropriate and effectively used.

Content

☐ Thesis clear, and kept in view.

☐ Argument steadily advanced, with helpful transitions.

☐ Thesis supported by evidence.

☐ Lightweight material, e.g., bits of humor, relevant and genuinely engaging.

One final point: If you do use visual material, *make certain that any words on the images are large enough to be legible to your audience:* A graph with tiny words will not impress your audience, even if you read the words aloud.

THE AUDIENCE

It is not merely because topics are complicated that we cannot agree that one side is reasonable and right and the other side irrational and wrong. The truth is, we are swayed not only by reason (*logos*) but also by appeals to the emotions (*pathos*) and by the character of the speaker (*ethos*). We can combine these last two things and put it this way: Sometimes we are inclined to agree with X rather than with Y because X strikes us as a more appealing person (perhaps more open-minded, more intelligent, better informed, more humane, and less cold). X is the sort of person we want to have as a friend. We disagree with Y—or at least we are unwilling to associate ourselves with Y—because Y is, well, Y just isn't the sort of person we want to agree with. Y's statistics don't sound right, or Y seems like a bully; for some reason, we just don't have confidence in Y. Confidence is easily lost: Alas, even a mispronunciation will diminish the audience's confidence in Y. As Peter de Vries said, "You can't be happy with someone who pronounces both *d*'s in Wednesday."

Earlier in the book we talked about the importance of **tone** and of the writer's **persona.** And we have made the point that the writer's tone will depend partly on the audience. A person who is writing for a conservative journal whose readership is almost entirely conservatives can adopt a highly satiric manner in talking about liberals and will meet with much approval. But if this conservative writer is writing in a liberal journal and hopes to get at least a sympathetic hearing, he or she will have to avoid satire and wisecracks and will have to present himself or herself as a person of goodwill who is open-minded and eager to address the issue seriously.

The **language** that you use—the degree to which it is formal as opposed to colloquial, and the degree to which it is technical as opposed to general—will also depend on the audience. Speaking a bit broadly, in oral argument speak politely but not formally. You do *not* want to be one of those people who "talk like a book." But you also don't want to be overly colloquial. Choose a middle course, probably a notch below the style you would use if you were handing in a written paper. For instance, in an oral presentation you might say, "We'll consider this point in a minute or two," whereas in a written paper you probably will write "We will consider this point shortly."

Technical language is entirely appropriate *if* your audience is familiar with it. If you are arguing before members of Amnesty International about the use of torture, you can assume certain kinds of specialized knowledge. You can, for instance, breezily speak of the DRC and of KPCS, and your listeners will know what you are talking about because Amnesty International has been active with issues concerning the Democratic Republic of Congo and the Kimberley Process Certification Scheme. On the other hand, if you are arguing the same case before a general public, you will have to explain these abbreviations, and you may even have to explain what Amnesty International is.

If you are arguing before your classmates, you probably have a pretty good idea of what you can assume they know and what you can assume they do not know.

DELIVERY

Your audience will in some measure determine not only your tone but also the way you appear when you give the speech. Part of the delivery is the speaker's **appearance.** The medium is part of the message. The president can appear in jeans when he chats about his reelection plans, but he wears a suit and a tie when he delivers the State of the Union address. Just as we wear one kind of **clothing** when we play tennis, another when we attend classes, and yet another when we go for a job interview, an effective speaker dresses appropriately. A lawyer arguing before the Supreme Court wears a dark suit or dress, and if the lawyer is male he wears a necktie. The same lawyer, arguing at a local meeting, speaking as a community resident who objects to a proposal to allow a porno store to open near a school, may well dress informally, maybe in jeans, to show that he or she is not at all stuffy but still feels that a porno store goes too far.

Your appearance when you speak is not merely a matter of your clothing; it includes your **facial expressions,** your **posture,** your **gestures,** your general demeanor. All that we can say here is that you should avoid those bodily motions—swaying, thumping the table, putting on and taking off eyeglasses, craning your neck, smirking—that are so distracting that they cause the audience to concentrate on the distraction rather than on the argument. ("That's the third time he straightened his necktie. I wonder how many more times he will—oops, that's the fourth!"). Most of us are not aware of our annoying habits; if you are lucky, a friend, when urged, will tell you about them. You may lose a friend, but you will gain some good advice.

You probably can't do much about your **voice**—it may be high-pitched, or it may be gravelly—but you can make sure that you speak loudly enough for the audience to hear you, slowly enough for it to understand you, and clearly enough for it to understand you.

We have some advice about **quotations.** First, if possible, use an effective quotation or two, partly because—we will be frank—the quotations probably are more impressively worded than anything you can come up with on your own. A quotation may be the chief thing that your audience comes away with: "Hey, yes, I liked that: 'War is too important to be left to the generals'" or "When it comes down to it, I agree with that Frenchman who said 'If we are to abolish the death penalty, I should like to see the first step taken by the murderers'" or "You know, I think it was all summed up in that line by Margaret Mead, something like, 'No one would remember the Good Samaritan if he'd had only good intentions. He had money as well.' Yes, that's pretty convincing. Morality isn't enough. You need money." You didn't invent the words that you quote, but you did bring them to the attention of your listeners, and your listeners will be grateful to you.

A second bit of advice about quotations: When you quote, do *not* begin by saying "quote," and do not end by saying "end quote" (or as we once heard a speaker endlessly say, quotation after quotation, "unquote") and do not hook the air with your fingers. How do you make it clear that you are quoting, and how do you make it clear that you have finished quoting? Begin with a clear lead-in ("In *Major Barbara* George Bernard Shaw touches on this issue, when Barbara says, . . ."), slightly pause, and then slightly change (for instance, elevate) your voice. When you have finished quoting—again a slight pause and a return to your normal voice—be sure to use words that clearly indicate the quotation is finished, such as "Shaw here says what everyone thinks," or "Shaw's comment is witty but short-sighted," or "Barbara's point, then, is. . . ."

Our third and last piece of advice concerning quotations is this: If the quotation is only a phrase or a brief sentence, you can memorize it and be confident that you will remember it, but if it is longer than a sentence, write it on a sheet in your notes or on a four-by-six-inch card in print large enough for you to read easily. You have chosen these words because they are effectively put, so you don't want to misquote them or even hesitate in delivering them.

THE TALK

As for the talk itself, well, we have been touching on it in our discussion of such matters as the speaker's relation to the audience, the speaker's need to provide signposts, and the use of quotations. All of our comments in earlier chapters about developing a written argument are relevant also to oral arguments, but here we should merely emphasize that because the talk is oral and the audience cannot look back to an earlier page to remind itself of some point, the speaker may have to repeat and summarize a bit more than is usual in a written essay.

Remember, too, that a reader can *see* when the essay ends—there is blank space at the end of the page—but a listener depends on aural cues. Nothing is more embarrassing—and less effective as argument—than a speaker who seems (to the audience) to suddenly stop and sit down. In short, give your hearers ample clues that you are ending (post such signs as "Finally" or "Last" or "Let me end by saying"), and be sure to end with a strong sentence. It probably won't be as good as the end of the Gettysburg address ("government of the people, by the people, for the people, shall not perish from the earth"), nor will it be as good as the end of Martin Luther King's "I Have a Dream" speech ("Free at last! Free at last! Thank God Almighty, we are free at last!"), but those are the models to emulate.

FORMAL DEBATES

It would be nice if all arguments ended with everyone, participants and spectators, agreeing that the facts are clear, that one presentation is more reasonable than the other, and therefore that one side is right and the other side is wrong. But in life, most issues are complicated. High school students may earnestly debate—this is a real topic in a national debate—

Resolved: That education has failed its mission in the United States,

but it takes only a moment of reflection to see that neither the affirmative nor the negative can be true. Yes, education has failed its mission in many ways, but, No, it has succeeded in many ways. Its job now is (in the words of Samuel Beckett) to try again: "Fail. Fail again. Fail better."

Debates of this sort, conducted before a judge and guided by strict rules concerning "Constructive Speeches," "Rebuttal Speeches," and "Cross-Examinations" are not attempts to get at the truth; like lawsuits, they are attempts to win a case. Each speaker seeks not to persuade the opponent but only to convince the judge. Although most of this section is devoted not to forensics in the strictest sense but more generally to the presentation of oral arguments, we begin with the standard format.

Standard Debate Format

Formal debates occur within a structure that governs the number of speeches, the order of the speeches, and the maximum time for each speech. The format may vary from place to place, but there is always a structure. In most debates, a formal resolution states the reason for the debate ("Resolved: That capital punishment be abolished in juvenile cases"). The affirmative team supports the resolution; the negative team denies its legitimacy. The basic structure has three parts:

- *The constructive phase,* in which the debaters construct their cases and develop their arguments (usually for ten minutes);
- *The rebuttal,* in which debaters present their responses and also present their final summary (usually for five minutes); and
- *The preparation,* in which the debater prepares for presenting the next speech. (During the preparation—a sort of time-out—the

debater is not addressing the opponent or audience. The total time allotted to a team is usually six or eight minutes, which the individual debaters divide as they wish.)

We give, very briefly, the usual structure of each part, though it should be mentioned that another common format calls for a cross-examination of the First Affirmative Construction by the Second Negative, a cross-examination of the First Negative Construction by the First Affirmative, a cross-examination of the Second Affirmative by the First Negative, and a cross-examination of the Second Negative by the Second Affirmative:

First Affirmative Constructive Speech: Serves as introduction, giving summary overview, definitions, criteria for resolution, major claims and evidence, statement, and intention to support the resolution.

First Negative Constructive Speech: Responds by introducing the basic position, challenges the definitions and criteria, suggests the line of attack, emphasizes that the burden of proof lies with the affirmative, rejects the resolution as unnecessary or dangerous, and supports the status quo.

Second Affirmative Constructive: Rebuilds the affirmative case; refutes chief attacks, especially concerning definitions, criteria, and rationale (philosophic framework); and further develops the affirmative case.

Second Negative Constructive: Completes the negative case, if possible advances it by rebuilding portions of the first negative construction, and contrasts the entire negative case with the entire affirmative case.

✓ A CHECKLIST FOR PREPARING FOR A DEBATE

☐ Have I done adequate preparation in research?

☐ Are my notes legible, with accurate quotations and impressive sources?

☐ Am I prepared to take good notes during the debate?

☐ Is my proposition clearly stated?

☐ Do I have adequate evidence to support the thesis (main point)?

☐ Do I have backup points in mind?

☐ Have I given thought to issues opponents may raise?

☐ Does the opening properly address the instructor, the audience, the opponents? (Remember, you are addressing an audience, not merely the opponents.)

☐ Are my visual aids focused on major points?

☐ Is my demeanor professional, and is my dress appropriate?

First Negative Rebuttal: Attacks the opponents' arguments and defends the negative constructive arguments (but a rebuttal may *not* introduce new constructive arguments).

First Affirmative Rebuttal: Usually responds first to the second negative construction and then to the first negative rebuttal.

Second Negative Rebuttal: Constitutes final speech for the negative, summarizing the case and explaining to the judge why the negative should be declared the winner.

Second Affirmative Rebuttal: Summarizes the debate, responds to issues pressed by the second negative rebuttal, and suggests to the judge that the affirmative team should win.

PART FOUR

CURRENT ISSUES:
OCCASIONS for DEBATE

DEBATES AS AN AID TO THINKING

Throughout this book we emphasize critical thinking, which—to put the matter briefly—means thinking analytically not only about the ideas of others but also about one's *own* ideas. As we often say in these pages, *you* are your first reader, and you should be a demanding one. You have ideas, but you want to think further about them, to improve them—partly so that you can share them with others but also so that you will live a thoughtful, useful, satisfying life.

This means, as we say elsewhere in the book, that you have (or at least try to have) an open mind, a mind that welcomes comments on your own ideas. You are, we hope, ready to grant that someone whose views differ from yours may indeed have something to teach you. When you have heard other views, of course you will not always embrace them, but sometimes you may find merit in some aspects of them, and you will to some degree reshape your own views. (We discuss the importance of trying to find shared ground and trying to move onward and upward from there in Chapter 10, A Psychologist's View: Rogerian Argument.)

Much of the difficulty in improving our ideas lies in our tendency to think in an either/or pattern. To put the point in academic terms, we incline toward *binary* (Latin, "two by two") or *dichotomous* (Greek, "divided into two") thinking. We often think in terms of contrasts: life and death, good and evil, right and left, up and down, on and off, white and black, boys and girls, men and women (men are from Mars; women from Venus), yes and no, freedom and tyranny. We understand what something is partly by thinking of what it is not: "He is liberal; she is conservative." In Gilbert and Sullivan's *Iolanthe*, one of the characters sees things this way:

> I am an intellectual chap,
> And think of things that would astonish you.
> I often think it is comical
> How nature always does contrive
> That every boy and every gal,
> That's born into the world alive,
> Is either a little Liberal,
> Or else a little Conservative.

We have our liberals and conservatives too, our Democrats and Republicans, and we talk about fate and free will, day and night, and so on. But we also know that there are imperceptible gradations. We know that there are conservative Democrats and liberal Republicans, and we know that although day differs from night, we cannot say at any given moment, "We have just now gone from day to night." True, there are times when gradations are irrelevant: In the polling booth, when we vote for a political candidate or for a particular bill, we must decide between

X and *Y*. At that stage it is either/or, not both/and or "Well, let's think further about this." But in much of life we are finding our way, acting provisionally—decisively at the moment, yes, but later we may modify our ideas in the light of further thinking, thinking that often is stimulated by the spoken or written thoughts of someone who holds a different view. Elsewhere we quote Virginia Woolf on the topic of writing about complex issues, but the comment is worth repeating:

> When a subject is highly controversial . . . one cannot hope to tell the truth. One can only show how one came to hold whatever opinion one does hold. One can only give one's audience the chance of drawing their own conclusions as they observe the limitations, the prejudices, the idiosyncrasies of the speaker.

What we are getting at is this: The debates in the next five chapters present sharply opposed views, usually of an either/or, day/night sort. Each essay sets forth a point of view, often with the implication that on this particular issue there are only two points of view—the writer's view and the wrong view. Some of the writers in these debates, convinced that only one view makes sense, evidently are not interested in hearing other opinions; they are out to convince, indeed to conquer.

The very word *debate* (from Latin *battere*, "to fight," "to battle") implies a combative atmosphere, a contest in which there will be a winner and a loser. And indeed the language used to describe a debate is often militant. Debaters *aim* their arguments, *destroy* the arguments of their *opponents* by *rebutting* (from Old French, *boter*, "to butt") and *refuting* (from Latin *futare*, "to beat") them.

We urge you, however, to read these arguments not in order to decide who is right and who is wrong but in order to think about the issues. In short, although the debates may be reductive, stating only two sides and supporting only one, think critically about both sides of any given argument, and allow the essays to enrich your own ideas about the topics. Above all, use the cut and thrust of debate as a device to explore the controversy, not as a weapon to force the other side into submission.

See, too, what you can learn about *writing* from these essays—about ways of organizing thoughts, about ways of presenting evidence, and especially about ways of establishing a voice, a *tone* that the reader takes as a representation of the sort of person you are. Remember, as E. B. White said, "No author long remains incognito." Authors reveal their personalities—belligerent, witty, thoughtful, courteous, whatever. If an author here turns you off, let's say by using heavy sarcasm or by an obvious unwillingness to face contrary evidence, well, there is a lesson for you as a writer.

In reading essays debating a given issue, keep in mind the questions given on page 106, "A Checklist for Analyzing an Argument." They are listed again below, with a few additional points of special relevance to debates.

✓ A CHECKLIST FOR ANALYZING A DEBATE

Have I asked myself the following questions?
☐ What is the writer's thesis?
  ☐ What claim is asserted?
  ☐ What assumptions are made?
  ☐ Are key terms defined satisfactorily?
☐ What support is offered on behalf of the claim?
  ☐ Are examples relevant and convincing?
  ☐ Are statistics relevant, accurate, and convincing?
  ☐ Are the authorities appropriate?
  ☐ Is the logic — deductive and inductive — valid?
  ☐ If there is an appeal to emotion, is this appeal acceptable?
☐ Does the writer seem fair?
  ☐ Are counterarguments considered?
  ☐ Is there any evidence of dishonesty?
Have I asked myself the following additional questions?
☐ Do the disputants differ in
  ☐ assumptions?
  ☐ interpretations of relevant facts?
  ☐ selection of and emphasis on these facts?
  ☐ definitions of key terms?
  ☐ values and norms?
  ☐ goals?
☐ What common ground do the disputants share?
☐ Which disputant seems to me to have the better overall argument?
  Why?

14

Student Loans: Should Some Indebtedness Be Forgiven?

Robert Applebaum

Congressman Hansen Clarke (D-MI) in 2012 introduced (with seventeen cosponsors) The Student Loan Forgiveness Act of 2012 (HR 4170). This proposal included the 10/10 Loan Repayment Plan, which (a) would for ten years automatically withdraw 10 percent of the debtor's income and then (b) would forgive loan debt up to $45,000. Robert Applebaum a graduate of Fordham University School of Law, initiated a petition—now signed by well over a million people—supporting Congressman Clarke's proposal. The petition claimed that forgiving debt would stimulate the economy by in effect giving the former students more money to spend. In the petition Applebaum wrote:

> Student loan debt has become the latest financial crisis in America and, if we do absolutely nothing, the entire economy will eventually come crashing down again, just as it did when the housing bubble popped. . . . [T]hose buried under the weight of their student loan debt are not buying homes or cars, not starting businesses or families, and they're not investing, inventing, innovating, or otherwise engaged in any of the economically stimulative activities that we need all Americans to be engaged in if we're ever to dig ourselves out of the giant hole created by the greed of those at the very top.

We reprint here a short essay Applebaum later published, in 2012, in the Hill, *a Washington, D.C., publication.*

Debate on Student Loan Debt Doesn't Go Far Enough

As Congress debates the extremely narrow issue of whether to extend the current 3.4 percent interest rate on Federal Student Loans, or to let that rate expire and, thus, double to its previous level of 6.8 percent, both sides of the aisle are missing an opportunity to do something unique, decisive, and bold: adopt legislation that forgives excessive student loan debt after a reasonable repayment period.

Representative Hansen Clarke (D-MI) introduced an unprecedented piece of legislation in March—HR 4170, The Student Loan Forgiveness Act of 2012, in response to over 660,000 people who signed a petition I started in favor of student loan forgiveness. Yet, despite the public outcry, only one member initially stepped up to put his name and reputation on the line in order to draw attention to the ever-growing crisis of student loan debt. Rep. Clarke has taken on the role of Champion for the educated poor—the 36 million Americans who are drowning under the weight of their student loan debts. A new petition I started in favor of HR 4170 currently has over 939,000 signatures.

The Student Loan Forgiveness Act of 2012 is not a free ride, nor is it a bailout. It's a recognition that millions of Americans have grossly overpaid for their educations, due in part to governmental interference in the marketplace. With the availability of so much seemingly "free money" available to anyone with a pulse who wants to take out a student loan, colleges and universities have had no incentive to keep costs down—and they haven't. The outrageous costs of obtaining a college education or beyond today have very little to do with the inherent value of the degrees sought; rather, it has much more to do with brand new stadiums and six-figure administrative salaries. After all, if the degrees obtained today were worth the increased cost to obtain them, compared with thirty to forty years ago, then shouldn't those degrees also yield greater salaries upon graduation?

Tuition rates continue to soar and students are required to go further and further into debt each year, merely to obtain an education. Every other country in the industrialized world has figured out how to pay for higher education for its citizens, but here in America, we continue to treat education as a commodity that benefits only the individual obtaining the education, rather than what it truly is: a public good and an investment in our collective future as a country.

Education should be a right, not a commodity reserved only for the rich or those willing to hock their futures for the chance (not a guarantee) to get a job. Gone are the days when tuition rates had any kind of rational connection to the salaries one could expect upon graduating. With each passing year, students are left with no choice but to borrow more and more through both Federal and private student loans to finance their educations, as if the degrees obtained today are worth any more than they were a generation or two ago. In fact, they're worth far, far less than in years past, precisely because of the high cost of tuition combined with the decimated job market where middle-class wages have gone down, not up, over the last decade. 5

We've long ago passed the point where we have become what my friend, Aaron Calafato, writer, director, and star of the play *For Profit*, would call a "borrow to work" society. Far worse than "pay to play," borrow to work is a modern form of indentured servitude, where millions of Americans are told since birth that, in order to get ahead, they must obtain a higher education.

What they aren't being told, however, is that, in order to obtain that education, students must necessarily mortgage their futures and spend the rest of their lives paying back the loans that gave them the "privilege" of working at jobs they hate for salaries that simply do not allow them to make ends meet.

How do we ever expect the housing market to improve when the very people we rely upon to purchase homes—college grads and professionals—are graduating with mortgage-sized debts that they can neither live in, nor use as intended in today's job market?

Are we content to live in a society where only the privileged few are able to obtain an education without sacrificing their future? Do we really want to price the middle and working classes out of public service? And who's going to be buying cars, starting businesses, and making investments in our future if not the middle class? We're not yet an oligarchy, but we're fast on our way toward becoming one if we knowingly fail to address this ever-growing crisis, before it's too late.

Unfortunately, the $1 trillion in student loan debt outstanding in 10 America is not a ceiling, merely a disturbing milestone along the national path to poverty. If Congress does nothing, it'll only get worse.

Topics for Critical Thinking and Writing

1. In his first paragraph Applebaum speaks of "excessive" student debt. Whom does he blame for this debt—students, colleges, lenders, or someone else? And in this context, is he committing the fallacy of begging the question (on this fallacy, see page 374)?

2. In the fifth paragraph Applebaum says that education—meaning higher education—should be a right. In the United States, education through high school is of course free—is a right—though one can argue that there really is no such thing as "free"education (or "free" medical care, etc.); somebody pays for it. Should all citizens have a right to (presumably *free*) post–high school education? Does this include programs in vocational training? Explain.

3. By the end of the sixth paragraph, if not earlier, it is evident that Applebaum is furious with the present system. Do you think his essay would be more persuasive if he were less evidently angry? Explain.

ANALYZING A VISUAL: STUDENT LOAN DEBT

Student loan debt impacts millions

The New York Federal Reserve estimates 37 million Americans have student loan debt, totaling $870 billion.

Outstanding student
loan debt, by loan holders

Private loans: 15%

Federal government
loans: 85%

Delinquent student loan
borrowers in repayment cycle,
Q3 2011 (20 million borrowers)

Past balance due: 27%

No past balance due;
balance decreasing: 73%

Breakdown of loan balance
by age, Q3 2011 ($870 billion total)

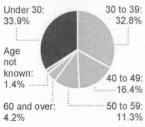

Under 30:
33.9%

30 to 39:
32.8%

Age
not
known:
1.4%

40 to 49:
16.4%

60 and over:
4.2%

50 to 59:
11.3%

Past due student loan balance
by age, Q3 2011 ($85 billion total)

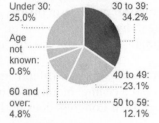

Under 30:
25.0%

30 to 39:
34.2%

Age
not
known:
0.8%

40 to 49:
23.1%

60 and
over:
4.8%

50 to 59:
12.1%

Average student debt for 2010 college graduates, in thousands

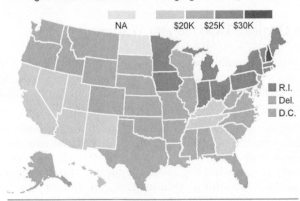

NA $20K $25K $30K

R.I.
Del.
D.C.

SOURCE: Institute for College Access & Success, Project on Student   AP
Debt; Federal Reserve Bank of New York

Topic for Critical Thinking and Writing

Briefly, what argument do you think this infographic makes? What particular aspects of college education and the career market might it be critical of, and why?

Justin Wolfers

Justin Wolfers, an economist at the Wharton School, University of Pennsylvania, was invited by Freakonomics *to comment on Robert Applebaum's idea in his petition* Signon.org *that forgiving student loan indebtedness would stimulate the nation's economy: Freed from debt, Applebaum argued, consumers would spend thousands of additional dollars, which would then encourage businesses to hire more workers to meet the increased demand for goods. (The argument that forgiveness of loans will stimulate job growth is offered also in Congressman Clarke's The Student Loan Forgiveness Act of 2012 [HR 4170]).*

We reprint Wolfers's contribution to Freakonomics, *September 19, 2011. When he wrote this short piece, in 2011, Applebaum's petition had 300,000 signatures. It now has well over a million signatures.*

Forgive Student Loans? Worst Idea Ever

Let's look at this through five separate lenses:

Distribution: If we are going to give money away, why on earth would we give it to college grads? This is the one group who we know typically have high incomes, and who have enjoyed income growth over the past four decades. The group who has been hurt over the past few decades is high school dropouts.

Macroeconomics: This is the worst macro policy I've ever heard of. If you want stimulus, you get more bang-for-your-buck if you give extra dollars to folks who are most likely to spend each dollar. Imagine what would happen if you forgave $50,000 in debt. How much of that would get spent in the next month or year? Probably just a couple of grand (if that). Much of it would go into the bank. But give $1,000 to each of fifty poor people, and nearly all of it will get spent, yielding a larger stimulus. Moreover, it's not likely that college grads are the ones who are liquidity-constrained. Most of 'em could spend more if they wanted to; after all, they are the folks who could get a credit card or a car loan fairly easily. It's the hand-to-mouth consumers—those who can't get easy access to credit—who are most likely to raise their spending if they get the extra dollars.

Education Policy: Perhaps folks think that forgiving educational loans will lead more people to get an education. No, it won't. This is a proposal to forgive the debt of folks who already have an education. Want to increase access to education? Make loans more widely available, or subsidize those who are yet to choose whether to go to school. But this proposal is just a lump-sum transfer that won't increase education attainment. So why transfer to these folks?

Political Economy: This is a bunch of kids who don't want to pay 5 their loans back. And worse: Do this once, and what will happen in the next recession? More lobbying for free money, rather than doing something socially constructive. Moreover, if these guys succeed, others will try, too. And we'll just get more spending in the least socially productive part of our economy — the lobbying industry.

Politics: Notice the political rhetoric? Give free money to us, rather than "corporations, millionaires, and billionaires." Opportunity cost is one of the key principles of economics. And that principle says to compare your choice with the next best alternative. Instead, they're comparing it with the worst alternative. So my question for the proponents: Why give money to college grads rather than the 15 percent of the population in poverty?

Conclusion: Worst. Idea. Ever.

And I bet that the proponents can't find a single economist to support this idiotic idea.

Topics for Critical Thinking and Writing

1. What do you think of Wolfers's suggestion that if we want individuals to put money into circulation, it makes more sense to give $1,000 to each of fifty poor people than to forgive $50,000 of a college graduate's debt?

2. Would Wolfers's essay be more effective if he omitted his final paragraph? Or if he reversed the sequence of the last two paragraphs? Explain.

3. Imagine that you are Applebaum. Write a response to Wolfers.

15

Are Integrated Devices Safer Than Using Handheld Devices While Driving?

Mitch Bainwol

Mitch Bainwol has served as a congressional staff intern and as staff chief to Senator Connie Mack. He is now the president and CEO of the Alliance of Automobile Manufacturers. We reprint a piece that he wrote for CQ Researcher *in May 2012.*

Pro

There is no debate about whether distracted driving is a concern. It is. The salient question is how best to ameliorate it in the real world where drivers demand connectivity—and with the prevalence of portable smartphones, they have it.

Technology has transformed our society forever. According to CTIA, The Wireless Association, at the end of 2011 there were 331.6 million wireless subscriber connections—more than the entire U.S. population.

We share Transportation Secretary Ray LaHood's conviction that drivers should not use handheld devices to communicate when driving. Looking away from the road to dial, surf, text, or navigate is dangerous. Research confirms that 80 percent of crashes involve the driver looking away from the roadway just prior to the crash.

We can put our heads in the sand and demand a behavioral shift—as some policymakers advocate—or we can find ways to make communication in the car safe.

Automakers are relying on integrated systems to operate as a "safety 5 filter" to channel driver behavior in a way that mitigates accident risk and saves lives.

Consumers are going to communicate; the only viable path to make that activity safe is to provide a technological answer that addresses the

471

visual distraction. Built-in communications systems are that answer. They rely on the cell phone passively and only for connectivity—so with the integrated system, you can lock that phone up in the glove box as you depart.

Whether it's for communicating or listening to music or getting travel information, the objective of policymakers should be to encourage drivers to utilize the vehicle's hard-wired system rather than looking away from the road to concentrate on a handheld's small display screen—a screen never designed for use while driving.

In contrast—and by definition—auto displays, and other in-vehicle technologies, are designed from the very beginning to facilitate safe travel. They're easier to read and less distracting—much like tuning a car radio.

All this is covered in the Alliance's guidelines on in-vehicle technologies. They've been in place for a full decade now, serving as the base for the National Traffic Highway Safety Administration's recently proposed guidelines.

We know drivers are going to insist on staying connected behind the   10 wheel. Our shared challenge is to construct policy and rely on technology that enables drivers to keep their eyes on the road and hands on the wheel.

Topics for Critical Thinking and Writing

1. What are Bainwol's basic assumptions? Do you accept these assumptions? Why, or why not?

2. Suppose someone—possibly someone who was not a native speaker of English—said that he or she did not understand paragraph 4, partly because of its comment about putting one's head in the sand but also because the entire sentence seemed unclear. Paraphrase the sentence (on paraphrase, see page 39), and then answer this question: Do you agree that (as Bainwol seems to suggest) the issue is an either/or situation: We can do X or we can do Y, and that's it?

ANALYZING A VISUAL: TEXTING WHILE DRIVING

GET THE MESSAGE.
TEXTING WHILE DRIVING IS A DEADLY DISTRACTION.

Join the conversation.
Visit DecideToDrive.org.

AUTO ALLIANCE
DRIVING INNOVATION®

ORTHOPAEDIC
—TRAUMA—
ASSOCIATION

AAOS
AMERICAN ACADEMY OF
ORTHOPAEDIC SURGEONS

TOPICS FOR CRITICAL THINKING AND WRITING

1. This public service announcement portrays in a very stark and shocking manner the dangers of texting and driving. What are the elements of the advertisement, and how does each function to reinforce this argument?

2. How does the ad's caption "Get the Message" have a double meaning? Do you find the caption effective? Why or why not?

3. Briefly argue how a visual argument about texting and driving (like this one) might be more or less effective than an essay on the same subject.

Rob Reynolds

Rob Reynolds is the executive director of FocusDriven, an organization whose mission is to "prevent injuries and save lives by eliminating cell phone use while driving." We reprint a piece from CQ Researcher, where it was paired with the previous piece.

Con

The growing use of electronic devices built into car dashboards mostly grows out of studies that have found a greater risk from holding a cell phone and conversing over talking "hands free." Automakers use some of these studies to explain how adding hands-free texting, e-mailing, Web surfing, social networking, and talking apps into their infotainment systems make you "safer."

However, these so-called naturalistic studies have inherent characteristics that make relying on their results as the basis for these assumptions problematic, at best.

The studies themselves rely on observation and measurement of physical data using vehicles rigged with expensive cameras and monitoring equipment in the hopes that "events" (crashes) and "near events" can be recorded and later examined in detail.

But several points should be raised about their results:

- Participants know they are driving rigged vehicles, so it's questionable whether they are driving "naturally."

- The cost of the equipment and the fact that crashes/near crashes are infrequent events in most drivers' experience make both the sample size and the target for the study (crash causation) too small to draw widespread conclusions from.

- None of the monitoring equipment measures so-called "cognitive distractions of the brain caused by the cell phone and other applications."

The majority of research on distractions with cell phones and smart- 5 phones has been done with epidemiological and lab research. In fact, at least thirty studies put the increased risk of conversing on a cell phone while driving (handheld or hands-free) at four times the risk of driving alone. All of this is being ignored by automakers in lieu of a select few studies that create a favorable argument for these applications.

In addition, automakers have said that "drivers will use these apps anyway; we just want to make it safer." I recall cigarette makers using similar arguments for adding filters to cigarettes (that doesn't work either— the behavior is unsafe regardless).

Think if we had used naturalistic studies to address intoxicated driving. Would we really rig cars with cameras and just wait and see or would/did we rely upon actual crash data and blood alcohol concentration (BAC) levels?

Impairment is impairment, whether it's temporary or constant. Four times increased crash risk is equal to the crash risk of driving at .08 BAC, the legal limit in most states. We can only reduce distracted-driving crash rates by banning the activity — not by trying to enhance the experience.

TOPICS FOR CRITICAL THINKING AND WRITING

1. In paragraph 2 Reynolds speaks of "so-called naturalistic studies," and in paragraph 7 he indicates that the studies were not "naturalistic." What does he mean by "naturalistic studies"?

2. In paragraph 3, why does Reynolds speak of vehicles "rigged with expensive cameras" rather than of vehicles "equipped with cameras"? (He uses "rigged" again in the next paragraph.) And why does he put the word *events* within quotation marks?

3. In paragraph 6 Reynolds introduces the behavior of cigarette makers decades ago. Do you find the comparison relevant and therefore helpful, or not? Why?

16

The Local Food Movement: Is It a Better Way to Eat?

Stephen Budiansky

Stephen Budiansky, a former editor of U.S. News & World Report *and of* Nature *and the recipient of a Guggenheim Award, writes chiefly about history and science. We reprint a piece that was originally published in the* New York Times *in 2010, and we follow it with a response.*

Math Lessons for Locavores

It's forty-two steps from *my* back door to the garden that keeps my family supplied nine months of the year with a modest cornucopia of lettuce, beets, spinach, beans, tomatoes, basil, corn, squash, brussels sprouts, the occasional celeriac and, once when I was feeling particularly energetic, a couple of small but undeniable artichokes. You'll get no argument from me about the pleasures and advantages to the palate and the spirit of eating what's local, fresh and in season.

But the local food movement now threatens to devolve into another one of those self-indulgent—and self-defeating—do-gooder dogmas. Arbitrary rules, without any real scientific basis, are repeated as gospel by "locavores," celebrity chefs, and mainstream environmental organizations. Words like "sustainability" and "food-miles" are thrown around without any clear understanding of the larger picture of energy and land use.

The result has been all kinds of absurdities. For instance, it is sinful in New York City to buy a tomato grown in a California field because of the energy spent to truck it across the country; it is virtuous to buy one grown in a lavishly heated greenhouse in, say, the Hudson Valley.

The statistics brandished by local-food advocates to support such doctrinaire assertions are always selective, usually misleading, and often bogus. This is particularly the case with respect to the energy costs of transporting food. One popular and oft-repeated statistic is that it takes thirty-six (sometimes it's ninety-seven) calories of fossil fuel energy to bring one calorie of iceberg lettuce from California to the East Coast. That's an apples and oranges (or maybe apples and rocks) comparison to begin with, because you can't eat petroleum or burn iceberg lettuce.

It is also an almost complete misrepresentation of reality, as those numbers reflect the entire energy cost of producing lettuce from seed to dinner table, not just transportation. Studies have shown that whether it's grown in California or Maine, or whether it's organic or conventional, about 5,000 calories of energy go into one pound of lettuce. Given how efficient trains and tractor-trailers are, shipping a head of lettuce across the country actually adds next to nothing to the total energy bill.

It takes about a tablespoon of diesel fuel to move one pound of freight 3,000 miles by rail; that works out to about 100 calories of energy. If it goes by truck, it's about 300 calories, still a negligible amount in the overall picture. (For those checking the calculations at home, these are "large calories," or kilocalories, the units used for food value.) Overall, transportation accounts for about 14 percent of the total energy consumed by the American food system.

Other favorite targets of sustainability advocates include the fertilizers and chemicals used in modern farming. But their share of the food system's energy use is even lower, about 8 percent.

The real energy hog, it turns out, is not industrial agriculture at all, but you and me. Home preparation and storage account for 32 percent of all energy use in our food system, the largest component by far.

A single ten-mile round trip by car to the grocery store or the farmers' market will easily eat up about 14,000 calories of fossil fuel energy. Just running your refrigerator for a week consumes 9,000 calories of energy. That assumes it's one of the latest high-efficiency models; otherwise, you can double that figure. Cooking and running dishwashers, freezers, and second or third refrigerators (more than 25 percent of American households have more than one) all add major hits. Indeed, households make up for 22 percent of all the energy expenditures in the United States.

Agriculture, on the other hand, accounts for just 2 percent of our nation's energy usage; that energy is mainly devoted to running farm machinery and manufacturing fertilizer. In return for that quite modest energy investment, we have fed hundreds of millions of people, liberated tens of millions from backbreaking manual labor, and spared hundreds of millions of acres for nature preserves, forests, and parks that otherwise would have come under the plow.

Don't forget the astonishing fact that the total land area of American farms remains almost unchanged from a century ago, at a little under a billion acres, even though those farms now feed three times as many Americans and export more than ten times as much as they did in 1910.

The best way to make the most of these truly precious resources of land, favorable climates, and human labor is to grow lettuce, oranges, wheat, peppers, bananas, whatever, in the places where they grow best and with the most efficient technologies—and then pay the relatively tiny energy cost to get them to market, as we do with every other commodity in the economy. Sometimes that means growing vegetables in your backyard. Sometimes that means buying vegetables grown in California or Costa Rica.

Eating locally grown produce is a fine thing in many ways. But it is not an end in itself, nor is it a virtue in itself. The relative pittance of our energy budget that we spend on modern farming is one of the wisest energy investments we can make, when we honestly look at what it returns to our land, our economy, our environment, and our well-being.

Topics for Critical Thinking and Writing

1. What does Budiansky's opening paragraph do, in terms of building his argument?

2. Budiansky's second paragraph begins "But." Did this word come as a surprise or did you sense, even in reading the first paragraph, that he was soon going to sing a different song?

3. How would you characterize the overall tone of this essay? Genial? No-nonsense? Aggressive? If tomorrow you came across another example of Budiansky's writing, would you pick it up eagerly, or would you pass it by? Why?

ANALYZING A VISUAL: LOCAL FARMING

Topics for Critical Thinking and Writing

1. Why should a consumer care whether a farm is "locally owned" and whether food is "locally grown"?

2. How would you define *local*? A common definition is "within 100 miles, or, if further, still within the state where the product is sold." Does this make sense to you? Why or why not?

3. Why do you suppose the farmer chose to put the message on the side of a horse-drawn wagon rather than on a pickup truck or a billboard?

Kerry Trueman

Kerry Trueman is a cofounder of EatingLiberally.org, a netroots Web site that, in her words, "advocates sustainable agriculture, progressive politics, and a less consumption-driven way of life." We reprint her response, published in the Huffington Post, *to the preceding essay. In her final paragraph, Trueman refers to "the Old Grey Lady," an allusion to the* New York Times, *which had published the essay she is commenting on.*

The Myth of the Rabid Locavore

Stephen Budiansky, self-proclaimed "liberal curmudgeon," has stuffed together another flimsy, flammable straw man out of boilerplate antilocavore rhetoric on the *New York Times* op-ed page, with the patronizing title "Math Lessons for Locavores."

It's a familiar formula: start by establishing yourself as the voice of reason by professing your own deep appreciation of the merits of locally grown food as evidenced by the bounty of your own backyard. Then, launch into a diatribe against a mythical army of dour, sour food nazis, including "celebrity chefs and mainstream environmental organizations," whose support for local farmers is based on wildly misguided and naïve notions about curbing one's carbon "foodprint."

Throw in a bunch of dubious and/or irrelevant statistics that appear to be truly locally sourced—i.e., pulled out of your own behind. Add a few disingenuous claims about the environmental benefits of industrial agriculture. Wrap things up with a statement so ludicrous that you have to publish it on your own Web site because hey, the *New York Times* is only willing to go so far:

> . . . eating food from a long way off is often the single best thing you can do for the environment, as counterintuitive as that sounds.

Budiansky's argument tars all eat-local proponents with the same broad brush, warning us that we're turning into a bunch of joyless, sanctimonious schmucks who are flimflamming an unsuspecting public:

For instance, it is sinful in New York City to buy a tomato grown in a California field because of the energy spent to truck it across the country; it is virtuous to buy one grown in a lavishly heated greenhouse in, say, the Hudson Valley.

Sinful according to whom? As I wrote on page 27 of Rodale's *Whole*   5
Green Catalog:

> Bear in mind that buying local is often the most low-impact choice — but not always: an out-of-season local tomato grown in a fossil fuel-heated greenhouse could consume more energy than one that's been field grown and shipped from Mexico.

But hey, what do I know? I'm just one of those local-food advocates who brandishes statistics that are "always selective, usually misleading and often bogus" to back up our "doctrinaire assertions."

That describes Budiansky's own modus operandi in a nutshell. His op-ed focuses almost exclusively on the question of how much fossil fuel is used to grow and ship food, and concludes that the amount of energy used is negligible in the grand scheme of things.

Sure, and because eggs weigh less than the grain it costs to feed the factory farm hens that produce them, it was presumably quite energy efficient to ship those 380 million factory farmed eggs that have since been recalled for possible salmonella contamination from Iowa to fourteen other states.

But energy efficiency is only one small part of the equation when you add up the reasons to buy local. Other factors include: flavor and nutrition; support for more ecological farming practices; reduction of excess packaging; avoidance of pesticides and other toxins; more humane treatment of livestock and workers; preservation of local farmland; spending one's dollars closer to home; the farmers' market as community center, and so on.

Budiansky totally ignores these issues, except to challenge the as-   10
sumption that sustainable agriculture is better for the environment than industrial agriculture. After establishing the folly of food miles, he goes on to note:

> Other favorite targets of sustainability advocates include the fertilizers and chemicals used in modern farming. But their share of the food system's energy use is even lower, about 8 percent.

Again with the energy usage! Geez. As if that were our big beef with fertilizers and chemicals. What about soil erosion, pollution, loss of biodiversity, the rise of superweeds and antibiotic-resistant infections, the dead zones in our oceans and rivers, exposure to contaminants, and all the other environmentally disastrous consequences of "conventional" farming?

According to Budiansky, the real culprit, when it comes to squandering energy, is us:

> Home preparation and storage account for 32 percent of all energy use in our food system, the largest component by far.

He cites the miles we drive to do our grocery shopping and the energy it takes to run our fridges, dishwashers, stoves, etc. But what do any of these things have to do with whether you choose to buy food locally? Your fridge uses the same amount of energy regardless of where the food you put in it came from.

If Budiansky sincerely cares to examine what constitutes a truly low-impact diet, why does he ignore one of the biggest sources of food-related wasted energy in the average American household? As *New Scientist* recently noted:

> More energy is wasted in the perfectly edible food discarded by people in the US each year than is extracted annually from the oil and gas reserves off the nation's coastlines.

What's so maddening about sloppy op-eds like this is that they give 15 fodder to folks who hate the very notion that their food choices have any consequences beyond their own waistlines and bank balances. At a time when global warming is surely fueling fires, floods, and drought all over the world, we need to have an honest conversation about how the way we eat contributes to climate change.

What we don't need is dishonest misrepresentations and tiresome stereotypes about the eat local movement. If you actually read what us good food folks have to say about eating ecologically, you'll see that the emphasis is on adopting a predominantly plant-based diet, eating foods when they're in season, limiting your consumption of animal products and processed convenience foods, and avoiding the chemicals and pesticides that are used in conventional farming.

Buying local produce is obviously a part of the equation. But to portray it as the sole consideration of sustainable food advocates is to adopt a lazy contrarian position that is guaranteed to generate controversy, and just as sure to do absolutely nothing to engender a meaningful discussion about these issues. Budiansky needs to be taken out to the foodshed and pummeled with his own lousy logic.

At the end of his blog post elaborating on his op-ed, he writes: "More seriously: environmentalism ought to be about pragmatism, not dogmatism."

Seriously? Such a deeply unserious piece such as his doesn't deserve to take up valuable real estate like the *Times* op-ed page. Though, like most real estate, it's worth less than it once was. Publishing stuff like this doesn't do much for the Old Grey Lady's property values.

TOPICS FOR CRITICAL THINKING AND WRITING

1. Do you think Trueman's opening paragraph is effective, or do you think it is too aggressive? Explain.

2. Has Trueman's essay helped you to think about Budiansky's essay and perhaps caused you to seriously modify your earlier view of his essay? Explain.

3. Now that you have read the two essays, do you think that either essay may cause you to change your eating habits in any way? Explain.

17

The Death Penalty: Is It Ever Justified?

Edward I. Koch

Edward I. Koch (1924–2013), long active in Democratic politics, was mayor of New York from 1978 to 1989. This essay first appeared in the New Republic *on April 15, 1985.*

Death and Justice: How Capital Punishment Affirms Life

Last December a man named Robert Lee Willie, who had been con-victed of raping and murdering an eighteen-year-old woman, was exe-cuted in the Louisiana state prison. In a statement issued several minutes before his death, Mr. Willie said: "Killing people is wrong. . . . It makes no difference whether it's citizens, countries, or governments. Killing is wrong." Two weeks later in South Carolina, an admitted killer named Joseph Carl Shaw was put to death for murdering two teenagers. In an appeal to the governor for clemency, Mr. Shaw wrote: "Killing was wrong when I did it. Killing is wrong when you do it. I hope you have the courage and moral strength to stop the killing."

It is a curiosity of modern life that we find ourselves being lectured on morality by cold-blooded killers. Mr. Willie previously had been convicted of aggravated rape, aggravated kidnapping, and the murders of a Louisiana deputy and a man from Missouri. Mr. Shaw committed another murder a week before the two for which he was executed, and admitted mutilating the body of the fourteen-year-old girl he killed. I can't help wondering what prompted these murderers to speak out against killing as they entered the deathhouse door. Did their newfound reverence for life stem from the realization that they were about to lose their own?

Life is indeed precious, and I believe the death penalty helps to affirm this fact. Had the death penalty been a real possibility in the minds of these murderers, they might well have stayed their hand. They might have shown moral awareness before their victims died, and not after. Consider the tragic death of Rosa Velez, who happened to be home when a man named Luis Vera burglarized her apartment in Brooklyn. "Yeah, I shot her," Vera admitted. "She knew me, and I knew I wouldn't go to the chair."

During my twenty-two years in public service, I have heard the pros and cons of capital punishment expressed with special intensity. As a district leader, councilman, congressman, and mayor, I have represented constituencies generally thought of as liberal. Because I support the death penalty for heinous crimes of murder, I have sometimes been the subject of emotional and outraged attacks by voters who find my position reprehensible or worse. I have listened to their ideas. I have weighed their objections carefully. I still support the death penalty. The reasons I maintain my position can be best understood by examining the arguments most frequently heard in opposition.

1. The death penalty is "barbaric." Sometimes opponents of 5 capital punishment horrify with tales of lingering death on the gallows, of faulty electric chairs, or of agony in the gas chamber. Partly in response to such protests, several states such as North Carolina and Texas switched to execution by lethal injection. The condemned person is put to death painlessly, without ropes, voltage, bullets, or gas. Did this answer the objections of death penalty opponents? Of course not. On June 22, 1984, the *New York Times* published an editorial that sarcastically attacked the new "hygienic" method of death by injection, and stated that "execution can never be made humane through science." So it's not the method that really troubles opponents. It's the death itself they consider barbaric.

Admittedly, capital punishment is not a pleasant topic. However, one does not have to like the death penalty in order to support it any more than one must like radical surgery, radiation, or chemotherapy in order to find necessary these attempts at curing cancer. Ultimately we may learn how to cure cancer with a simple pill. Unfortunately, that day has not yet arrived. Today we are faced with the choice of letting the cancer spread or trying to cure it with the methods available, methods that one day will almost certainly be considered barbaric. But to give up and do nothing would be far more barbaric and would certainly delay the discovery of an eventual cure. The analogy between cancer and murder is imperfect, because murder is not the "disease" we are trying to cure. The disease is injustice. We may not like the death penalty, but it must be available to punish crimes of cold-blooded murder, cases in which any other form of punishment would be inadequate and, therefore, unjust. If we create a society in which injustice is not tolerated, incidents of murder — the most flagrant form of injustice — will diminish.

2. No other major democracy uses the death penalty. No other major democracy—in fact, few other countries of any description—are plagued by a murder rate such as that in the United States. Fewer and fewer Americans can remember the days when unlocked doors were the norm and murder was a rare and terrible offense. In America the murder rate climbed 122 percent between 1963 and 1980. During that same period, the murder rate in New York City increased by almost 400 percent, and the statistics are even worse in many other cities. A study at M.I.T. showed that based on 1970 homicide rates a person who lived in a large American city ran a greater risk of being murdered than an American soldier in World War II ran of being killed in combat. It is not surprising that the laws of each country differ according to differing conditions and traditions. If other countries had our murder problem, the cry for capital punishment would be just as loud as it is here. And I dare say that any other major democracy where 75 percent of the people supported the death penalty would soon enact it into law.

3. An innocent person might be executed by mistake. Consider the work of Hugo Adam Bedau, one of the most implacable foes of capital punishment in this country. According to Mr. Bedau, it is "false sentimentality to argue that the death penalty should be abolished because of the abstract possibility that an innocent person might be executed." He cites a study of the seven thousand executions in this country from 1892 to 1971, and concludes that the record fails to show that such cases occur. The main point, however, is this. If government functioned only when the possibility of error didn't exist, government wouldn't function at all. Human life deserves special protection, and one of the best ways to guarantee that protection is to assure that convicted murderers do not kill again. Only the death penalty can accomplish this end. In a recent case in New Jersey, a man named Richard Biegenwald was freed from prison after serving eighteen years for murder; since his release he has been convicted of committing four murders. A prisoner named Lemuel Smith, who, while serving four life sentences for murder (plus two life sentences for kidnapping and robbery) in New York's Green Haven Prison, lured a woman corrections officer into the chaplain's office and strangled her. He then mutilated and dismembered her body. An additional life sentence for Smith is meaningless. Because New York has no death penalty statute, Smith has effectively been given a license to kill.

But the problem of multiple murder is not confined to the nation's penitentiaries. In 1981, ninety-one police officers were killed in the line of duty in this country. Seven percent of those arrested in the cases that have been solved had a previous arrest for murder. In New York City in 1976 and 1977, eighty-five persons arrested for homicide had a previous arrest for murder. Six of these individuals had two previous arrests for murder, and one had four previous murder arrests. During those two years the New York police were arresting for murder persons with a previous arrest for murder on the average of one every eight and a half days. This is not surprising when we learn that in 1975, for example, the median time served in Massachusetts for homicide was less than two and a half years. In 1976 a study sponsored by the Twentieth Century Fund found that the average time served in the United States for first-degree murder is ten years. The median time served may be considerably lower.

4. Capital punishment cheapens the value of human life. 10 On the contrary, it can be easily demonstrated that the death penalty strengthens the value of human life. If the penalty for rape were lowered, clearly it would signal a lessened regard for the victim's suffering, humiliation, and personal integrity. It would cheapen their horrible experience, and expose them to an increased danger of recurrence. When we lower the penalty for murder, it signals a lessened regard for the value of the victim's life. Some critics of capital punishment, such as columnist Jimmy Breslin, have suggested that a life sentence is actually a harsher penalty for murder than death. This is sophistic nonsense. A few killers may decide not to appeal a death sentence, but the overwhelming majority make every effort to stay alive. It is by exacting the highest penalty for the taking of human life that we affirm the highest value of human life.

5. The death penalty is applied in a discriminatory manner. This factor no longer seems to be the problem it once was. The appeals process for a condemned prisoner is lengthy and painstaking. Every effort is made to see that the verdict and sentence were fairly arrived at. However, assertions of discrimination are not an argument for ending the death penalty but for extending it. It is not justice to exclude everyone from the penalty of the law if a few are found to be so favored. Justice requires that the law be applied equally to all.

6. Thou Shalt Not Kill. The Bible is our greatest source of moral inspiration. Opponents of the death penalty frequently cite the sixth of the Ten Commandments in an attempt to prove that capital punishment is divinely proscribed. In the original Hebrew, however, the Sixth Commandment reads "Thou Shalt Not Commit Murder," and the Torah specifies capital punishment for a variety of offenses. The biblical viewpoint has been upheld by philosophers throughout history. The greatest thinkers of the nineteenth century—Kant, Locke, Hobbes, Rousseau, Montesquieu, and Mill—agreed that natural law properly authorizes the sovereign to take life in order to vindicate justice. Only

Jeremy Bentham was ambivalent. Washington, Jefferson, and Franklin endorsed it. Abraham Lincoln authorized executions for deserters in wartime. Alexis de Tocqueville, who expressed profound respect for American institutions, believed that the death penalty was indispensable to the support of social order. The United States Constitution, widely admired as one of the seminal achievements in the history of humanity, condemns cruel and inhuman punishment, but does not condemn capital punishment.

7. The death penalty is state-sanctioned murder. This is the defense with which Messrs. Willie and Shaw hoped to soften the resolve of those who sentenced them to death. By saying in effect, "You're no better than I am," the murderer seeks to bring his accusers down to his own level. It is also a popular argument among opponents of capital punishment, but a transparently false one. Simply put, the state has rights that the private individual does not. In a democracy, those rights are given to the state by the electorate. The execution of a lawfully condemned killer is no more an act of murder than is legal imprisonment an act of kidnapping. If an individual forces a neighbor to pay him money under threat of punishment, it's called extortion. If the state does it, it's called taxation. Rights and responsibilities surrendered by the individual are what give the state its power to govern. This contract is the foundation of civilization itself.

Everyone wants his or her rights, and will defend them jealously. Not everyone, however, wants responsibilities, especially the painful responsibilities that come with law enforcement. Twenty-one years ago a woman named Kitty Genovese was assaulted and murdered on a street in New York. Dozens of neighbors heard her cries for help but did nothing to assist her. They didn't even call the police. In such a climate the criminal understandably grows bolder. In the presence of moral cowardice, he lectures us on our supposed failings and tries to equate his crimes with our quest for justice.

The death of anyone—even a convicted killer—diminishes us all. 15 But we are diminished even more by a justice system that fails to function. It is an illusion to let ourselves believe that doing away with capital punishment removes the murderer's deed from our conscience. The rights of society are paramount. When we protect guilty lives, we give up innocent lives in exchange. When opponents of capital punishment say to the state, "I will not let you kill in my name," they are also saying to murderers: "You can kill in your *own* name as long as I have an excuse for not getting involved."

It is hard to imagine anything worse than being murdered while neighbors do nothing. But something worse exists. When those same neighbors shrink back from justly punishing the murderer, the victim dies twice.

Topics for Critical Thinking and Writing

1. In paragraph 6 Koch draws an analogy between cancer and murder and observes that imperfect as today's cures for cancer are, "to give up and do nothing would be far more barbaric." What is the relevance of this comment in the context of the analogy and the dispute over the death penalty?

2. In paragraph 8 Koch describes a convicted but unexecuted recidivist murderer as someone who "has effectively been given a license to kill." But a license to kill, as in a deer-hunter's license, entitles the holder to engage in lawful killing. (Think of the fictional hero James Bond—Agent 007—who, we are told, had a "license to kill.") What is the difference between having a license and "effectively" having one? How might the opponent of the death penalty reply to Koch's position here?

3. Koch distinguishes between the "median time" served by persons convicted of murder but not sentenced to death and the "average time" they serve, and he adds that the former "may be considerably lower" than the latter (para. 9). Explain the difference between a "median" and an "average" (review the section on statistics, p. 98). Is knowing one of these statistics more important for certain purposes than the other? Why?

4. Koch identifies seven arguments against the death penalty, and he rejects them all. Which of the seven arguments seems to you to be the strongest objection to the death penalty? Which the weakest? Why? Does Koch effectively refute the strongest argument? Can you think of any argument(s) against the death penalty that he neglects?

5. Koch says he supports the death penalty "for heinous crimes of murder" (para. 4). Does he imply that all murders are heinous crimes or only some? If the latter, what criteria seem to you to be the appropriate ones to distinguish the heinous murders from the rest? Why these criteria?

6. Koch asserts that the death penalty "strengthens the value of human life" (para. 10). Yet opponents of the death penalty often claim the reverse, arguing that capital punishment undermines the idea that human life is precious. Write an essay of 500 words in which you explain what it means to assert that life is precious and why one of the two positions—support for or opposition to the death penalty—best supports (or is consistent with) this principle.

ANALYZING A VISUAL: THE DEATH PENALTY

California's Death Penalty by the Numbers

84 INMATES DIED OF OLD AGE OR OTHER CAUSES BEFORE THEY COULD BE EXECUTED, WHILE ONLY **13** WERE ACTUALLY EXECUTED SINCE 1978.

COST OF ADMINISTERING THE DEATH PENALTY SINCE 1978: **$4 BILLION**

THE CHANCES OF YOUR BEING KILLED BY LIGHTNING ARE **NEARLY THE SAME** AS A MURDERER BEING KILLED BY LETHAL INJECTION IN CALIFORNIA.

AVERAGE LENGTH OF THE DEATH PENALTY APPEALS PROCESS: **25 YEARS**

PROJECTED ANNUAL SAVINGS IF THE DEATH PENALTY WAS ENDED: **$130 MILLION**

34 THE PROPOSITION THAT WILL END ALL THIS INSANITY.

steve@greenberg-art.com GREENBERG

TOPICS FOR CRITICAL THINKING AND WRITING

1. The title of this cartoon is witty, or at least is intended to be witty. Explain the intended joke in the title to someone who doesn't get it. (By the way, "34" in the final box refers to Proposition 34, an attempt in California, in 2012, to outlaw the death penalty and to replace it with life imprisonment. Voters did *not* pass the proposition.)

2. Do you think it is inappropriate to joke—verbally, or with drawings—about the death penalty? Explain.

3. Putting aside your own position on the issue of whether or not the death penalty should be abolished, do you think this cartoon is at least moderately effective? Explain. By the way, suppose someone told you that the cartoon could be taken as arguing that the appeals lodged by persons sentenced to death take so long, and cost so much, that something must be done about speeding up the cases and/or limiting the appeals. What would you say to the person who offered this interpretation of the cartoon?

David Bruck

David Bruck (b. 1949) graduated from Harvard College and received his law degree from the University of South Carolina. Since 2004, Bruck has been Clinical Professor of Law and director to the Virginia Capital Case Cleaning

House (a death penalty defense clinic) at Washington and Lee University School at Law. The essay reprinted here originally appeared on May 20, 1985, in the New Republic *as a response to the preceding essay by Edward I. Koch.*

The Death Penalty

Mayor Ed Koch contends that the death penalty "affirms life." By failing to execute murderers, he says, we "signal a lessened regard for the value of the victim's life." Koch suggests that people who oppose the death penalty are like Kitty Genovese's neighbors, who heard her cries for help but did nothing while an attacker stabbed her to death.

This is the standard "moral" defense of death as punishment: Even if executions don't deter violent crime any more effectively than imprisonment, they are still required as the only means we have of doing justice in response to the worst of crimes.

Until recently, this "moral" argument had to be considered in the abstract, since no one was being executed in the United States. But the death penalty is back now, at least in the southern states, where every one of the more than thirty executions carried out over the last two years has taken place. Those of us who live in those states are getting to see the difference between the death penalty in theory, and what happens when you actually try to use it.

South Carolina resumed executing prisoners in January with the electrocution of Joseph Carl Shaw. Shaw was condemned to death for helping to murder two teenagers while he was serving as a military policeman at Fort Jackson, South Carolina. His crime, propelled by mental illness and PCP, was one of terrible brutality. It is Shaw's last words ("Killing was wrong when I did it. It is wrong when you do it. . . .") that so outraged Mayor Koch: He finds it "a curiosity of modern life that we are being lectured on morality by cold-blooded killers." And so it is.

But it was not "modern life" that brought this curiosity into being.   5 It was capital punishment. The electric chair was J. C. Shaw's platform. (The mayor mistakenly writes that Shaw's statement came in the form of a plea to the governor for clemency: Actually Shaw made it only seconds before his death, as he waited, shaved and strapped into the chair, for the switch to be thrown.) It was the chair that provided Shaw with celebrity and an opportunity to lecture us on right and wrong. What made this weird moral reversal even worse is that J. C. Shaw faced his own death with undeniable dignity and courage. And while Shaw died, the TV crews recorded another "curiosity" of the death penalty—the crowd gathered outside the death-house to cheer on the executioner. Whoops of elation greeted the announcement of Shaw's death. Waiting at the penitentiary gates for the appearance of the hearse bearing Shaw's remains, one demonstrator started yelling, "Where's the beef?"

For those who had to see the execution of J. C. Shaw, it wasn't easy to keep in mind that the purpose of the whole spectacle was to affirm life. It will be harder still when Florida executes a cop-killer named Alvin Ford. Ford has lost his mind during his years of death-row confinement, and now spends his days trembling, rocking back and forth, and muttering unintelligible prayers. This has led to litigation over whether Ford meets a centuries-old legal standard for mental competency. Since the Middle Ages, the Anglo-American legal system has generally prohibited the execution of anyone who is too mentally ill to understand what is about to be done to him and why. If Florida wins its case, it will have earned the right to electrocute Ford in his present condition. If it loses, he will not be executed until the state has first nursed him back to some semblance of mental health.[1]

We can at least be thankful that this demoralizing spectacle involves a prisoner who is actually guilty of murder. But this may not always be so. The ordeal of Lenell Jeter—the young black engineer who recently served more than a year of a life sentence for a Texas armed robbery that he didn't commit—should remind us that the system is quite capable of making the very worst sort of mistake. That Jeter was eventually cleared is a fluke. If the robbery had occurred at 7 P.M. rather than 3 P.M., he'd have had no alibi, and would still be in prison today. And if someone had been killed in that robbery, Jeter probably would have been sentenced to death. We'd have seen the usual execution-day interviews with state officials and the victim's relatives, all complaining that Jeter's appeals took too long. And Jeter's last words from the gurney would have taken their place among the growing literature of death-house oration that so irritates the mayor.

Koch quotes Hugo Adam Bedau, a prominent abolitionist, to the effect that the record fails to establish that innocent defendants have been executed in the past. But this doesn't mean, as Koch implies, that it hasn't happened. All Bedau was saying was that doubts concerning executed prisoners' guilt are almost never resolved. Bedau is at work now on an effort to determine how many wrongful death sentences may have been imposed: His list of murder convictions since 1900 in which the state eventually *admitted* error is some four hundred cases long. Of course, very few of these cases involved actual executions: The mistakes that Bedau documents were uncovered precisely because the prisoner was alive and able to fight for his vindication. The cases where someone is executed are the very cases in which we're least likely to learn that we got the wrong man.

---

[1]Florida lost its case to execute Ford. On June 26, 1986, the U.S. Supreme Court ruled that the execution of an insane person violates the Eighth Amendment, which forbids cruel and unusual punishments. Therefore, convicted murderers cannot be executed if they have become so insane that they do not know that they are about to be executed and do not understand the reason for their sentence. If Ford regains his sanity, however, he can be executed. [Editors' note.]

I don't claim that executions of entirely innocent people will occur very often. But they will occur. And other sorts of mistakes already have. Roosevelt Green was executed in Georgia two days before J. C. Shaw. Green and an accomplice kidnapped a young woman. Green swore that his companion shot her to death after Green had left, and that he knew nothing about the murder. Green's claim was supported by a statement that his accomplice made to a witness after the crime. The jury never resolved whether Green was telling the truth, and when he tried to take a polygraph examination a few days before his scheduled execution, the state of Georgia refused to allow the examiner into the prison. As the pressure for symbolic retribution mounts, the courts, like the public, are losing patience with such details. Green was electrocuted on January 9, while members of the Ku Klux Klan rallied outside the prison.

Then there is another sort of arbitrariness that happens all the 10 time. Last October, Louisiana executed a man named Ernest Knighton. Knighton had killed a gas station owner during a robbery. Like any murder, this was a terrible crime. But it was not premeditated, and is the sort of crime that very rarely results in a death sentence. Why was Knighton electrocuted when almost everyone else who committed the same offense was not? Was it because he was black? Was it because his victim and all twelve members of the jury that sentenced him were white? Was it because Knighton's court-appointed lawyer presented no evidence on his behalf at his sentencing hearing? Or maybe there's no reason except bad luck. One thing is clear: Ernest Knighton was picked out to die the way a fisherman takes a cricket out of a bait jar. No one cares which cricket gets impaled on the hook.

Not every prisoner executed recently was chosen that randomly. But many were. And having selected these men so casually, so blindly, the death penalty system asks us to accept that the purpose of killing each of them is to affirm the sanctity of human life.

The death penalty states are also learning that the death penalty is easier to advocate than it is to administer. In Florida, where executions have become almost routine, the governor reports that nearly a third of his time is spent reviewing the clemency requests of condemned prisoners. The Florida Supreme Court is hopelessly backlogged with death cases. Some have taken five years to decide, and the rest of the Court's work waits in line behind the death appeals. Florida's death row currently holds more than 230 prisoners. State officials are reportedly considering building a special "death prison" devoted entirely to the isolation and electrocution of the condemned. The state is also considering the creation of a special public defender unit that will do nothing else but handle death penalty appeals. The death penalty, in short, is spawning death agencies.

And what is Florida getting for all of this? The state went through almost all of 1983 without executing anyone: Its rate of intentional homicide declined by 17 percent. Last year Florida executed eight people—

the most of any state, and the sixth highest total for any year since Florida started electrocuting people back in 1924. Elsewhere in the United States last year, the homicide rate continued to decline. But in Florida, it actually rose by 5.1 percent.

But these are just the tiresome facts. The electric chair has been a centerpiece of each of Koch's recent political campaigns, and he knows better than anyone how little the facts have to do with the public's support for capital punishment. What really fuels the death penalty is the justifiable frustration and rage of people who see that the government is not coping with violent crime. So what if the death penalty doesn't work? At least it gives us the satisfaction of knowing that we got one or two of the sons of bitches.

Perhaps we want retribution on the flesh and bone of a handful of 15 convicted murderers so badly that we're willing to close our eyes to all of the demoralization and danger that come with it. A lot of politicians think so, and they may be right. But if they are, then let's at least look honestly at what we're doing. This lottery of death both comes from and encourages an attitude toward human life that is not reverent, but reckless.

And that is why the mayor is dead wrong when he confuses such fury with justice. He suggests that we trivialize murder unless we kill murderers. By that logic, we also trivialize rape unless we sodomize rapists. The sin of Kitty Genovese's neighbors wasn't that they failed to stab her attacker to death. Justice does demand that murderers be punished. And common sense demands that society be protected from them. But neither justice nor self-preservation demands that we kill men whom we have already imprisoned.

The electric chair in which J. C. Shaw died earlier this year was built in 1912 at the suggestion of South Carolina's governor at the time, Cole Blease. Governor Blease's other criminal justice initiative was an impassioned crusade in favor of lynch law. Any lesser response, the governor insisted, trivialized the loathsome crimes of interracial rape and murder. In 1912, a lot of people agreed with Governor Blease that a proper regard for justice required both lynching and the electric chair. Eventually we are going to learn that justice requires neither.

Topics for Critical Thinking and Writing

1. After three introductory paragraphs, Bruck devotes two paragraphs to Shaw's execution. In a sentence or two, state the point he is making in his discussion of this execution. Then in another sentence or two (or three), indicate the degree to which this point refutes Edward I. Koch's argument (p. 483).

2. In paragraph 7, Bruck refers to the case of Lenell Jeter, an innocent man who was condemned to a life sentence. Evaluate this point as a piece of evidence used to support an argument against the death penalty.

3. In paragraph 8, Bruck says that "the state eventually *admitted* error" in some four hundred cases. He goes on: "Of course, very few of these cases involved actual executions." How few is "very few"? Why do you suppose Bruck doesn't specify the number? If it is only, say, two, in your opinion does that affect Bruck's point?

4. Discussing the case of Roosevelt Green (para. 9), Bruck points out that Green offered to take a polygraph test but "the state of Georgia refused to allow the examiner into the prison." In a paragraph evaluate the state's position on this matter.

5. In paragraph 13 Bruck points out that although "last year" (1984) the state executed eight people, the homicide rate in Florida rose 5.1 percent, whereas elsewhere in the United States the homicide rate declined. What do you make of these figures? What do you think Koch would make of them?

6. In his next-to-last paragraph Bruck says that Koch "suggests that we trivialize murder unless we kill murderers. By that logic, we also trivialize rape unless we sodomize rapists." Do you agree that this statement brings out the absurdity of Koch's thinking?

7. Evaluate Bruck's final paragraph (a) as a concluding paragraph and (b) as a piece of argumentation.

8. Bruck, writing early in 1985, stresses that all the "more than thirty" executions in the nation "over the last two years" have taken place in the South (para. 3). Why does he think this figure points to a vulnerability in Koch's argument? Would Bruck's argument here be spoiled if some executions were to occur outside of the South? (By the way, where exactly have most of the recent executions in the nation occurred?)

9. Bruck argues that the present death-penalty system—in practice even if not in theory—utterly fails to "affirm the sanctity of human life" (para. 11). Do you think Bruck would, or should, concede that at least in theory it is possible for a death-penalty system to be no more offensive to the value of human life than, say, a system of imprisonment is offensive to the value of human liberty or a system of fines is offensive to the value of human property?

10. Can Bruck be criticized for implying that cases like those he cites—Shaw, Ford, Green, and Knightson, in particular—are the rule rather than the exception? Does either Bruck or Koch cite any evidence to help settle this question?

11. Write a paragraph explaining which of these events seems to you to be the more unseemly: a condemned prisoner, on the threshold of execution, lecturing the rest of us on the immorality of killing; or the crowd that bursts into cheers outside a prison when it learns that a scheduled execution has been carried out.

Genetic Modification of Human Beings: Is It Acceptable?

Ronald M. Green

Ronald M. Green teaches in the Religion Department at Dartmouth College, where he is the director of the Ethics Institute. He is the author of several books, including Babies by Design: The Ethics of Genetic Choice *(2007). This article was posted online at washingtonpost.com on April 1, 2008.*

Building Baby from the Genes Up

The two British couples no doubt thought that their appeal for medical help in conceiving a child was entirely reasonable. Over several generations, many female members of their families had died of breast cancer. One or both spouses in each couple had probably inherited the genetic mutations for the disease, and they wanted to use in-vitro fertilization and preimplantation genetic diagnosis (PGD) to select only the healthy embryos for implantation. Their goal was to eradicate breast cancer from their family lines once and for all.

In the United States, this combination of reproductive and genetic medicine—what one scientist has dubbed "reprogenetics"—remains largely unregulated, but Britain has a formal agency, the Human Fertilization and Embryology Authority (HFEA), that must approve all requests for PGD. In July 2007, after considerable deliberation, the HFEA approved the procedure for both families. The concern was not about the use of PGD to avoid genetic disease, since embryo screening for serious disorders is commonplace now on both sides of the Atlantic. What troubled the HFEA was the fact that an embryo carrying the cancer mutation could go on to live for forty or fifty years before ever developing cancer, and there was a chance it might never develop. Did this warrant selecting and discarding embryos? To its critics, the HFEA, in approving this request, crossed a bright line separating legitimate medical genetics from the quest for "the perfect baby."

495

Like it or not, that decision is a sign of things to come—and not necessarily a bad sign. Since the completion of the Human Genome Project in 2003, our understanding of the genetic bases of human disease and non-disease traits has been growing almost exponentially. The National Institutes of Health has initiated a quest for the "$1,000 genome," a ten-year program to develop machines that could identify all the genetic letters in anyone's genome at low cost (it took more than $3 billion to sequence the first human genome). With this technology, which some believe may be just four or five years away, we could not only scan an individual's—or embryo's—genome, we could also rapidly compare thousands of people and pinpoint those DNA sequences or combinations that underlie the variations that contribute to our biological differences.

With knowledge comes power. If we understand the genetic causes of obesity, for example, we can intervene by means of embryo selection to produce a child with a reduced genetic likelihood of getting fat. Eventually, without discarding embryos at all, we could use gene-targeting techniques to tweak fetal DNA sequences. No child would have to face a lifetime of dieting or experience the health and cosmetic problems associated with obesity. The same is true for cognitive problems such as dyslexia. Geneticists have already identified some of the mutations that contribute to this disorder. Why should a child struggle with reading difficulties when we could alter the genes responsible for the problem?

Many people are horrified at the thought of such uses of genetics, seeing echoes of the 1997 science-fiction film *Gattaca*, which depicted a world where parents choose their children's traits. Human weakness has been eliminated through genetic engineering, and the few parents who opt for a "natural" conception run the risk of producing offspring—"invalids" or "degenerates"—who become members of a despised under-class. Gattaca's world is clean and efficient, but its eugenic obsessions have all but extinguished human love and compassion. 5

These fears aren't limited to fiction. Over the past few years, many bioethicists have spoken out against genetic manipulations. The critics tend to voice at least four major concerns. First, they worry about the effect of genetic selection on parenting. Will our ability to choose our children's biological inheritance lead parents to replace unconditional love with a consumerist mentality that seeks perfection?

Second, they ask whether gene manipulations will diminish our freedom by making us creatures of our genes or our parents' whims. In his book *Enough*, the techno-critic Bill McKibben asks: If I am a world-class runner, but my parents inserted the "Sweatworks2010 GenePack" in my genome, can I really feel pride in my accomplishments? Worse, if I refuse to use my costly genetic endowments, will I face relentless pressure to live up to my parents' expectations?

Third, many critics fear that reproductive genetics will widen our social divisions as the affluent "buy" more competitive abilities for their offspring. Will we eventually see "speciation," the emergence of two or more human populations so different that they no longer even breed with one another? Will we re-create the horrors of eugenics that led, in Europe, Asia, and the United States, to the sterilization of tens of thousands of people declared to be "unfit" and that in Nazi Germany paved the way for the Holocaust?

Finally, some worry about the religious implications of this technology. Does it amount to a forbidden and prideful "playing God"?

To many, the answers to these questions are clear. Not long ago, when I asked a large class at Dartmouth Medical School whether they thought that we should move in the direction of human genetic engineering, more than 80 percent said no. This squares with public opinion polls that show a similar degree of opposition. Nevertheless, "babies by design" are probably in our future—but I think that the critics' concerns may be less troublesome than they first appear.

Will critical scrutiny replace parental love? Not likely. Even today, parents who hope for a healthy child but have one born with disabilities tend to love that child ferociously. The very intensity of parental love is the best protection against its erosion by genetic technologies. Will a child somehow feel less free because parents have helped select his or her traits? The fact is that a child is already remarkably influenced by the genes she inherits. The difference is that we haven't taken control of the process. Yet.

Knowing more about our genes may actually increase our freedom by helping us understand the biological obstacles—and opportunities—we have to work with. Take the case of Tiger Woods. His father, Earl, is said to have handed him a golf club when he was still in the playpen. Earl probably also gave Tiger the genes for some of the traits that help make him a champion golfer. Genes and upbringing worked together to inspire excellence. Does Tiger feel less free because of his inherited abilities? Did he feel pressured by his parents? I doubt it. Of course, his story could have gone the other way, with overbearing parents forcing a child into their mold. But the problem in that case wouldn't be genetics, but bad parenting.

Granted, the social effects of reproductive genetics are worrisome. The risks of producing a "genobility," genetic overlords ruling a vast genetic underclass, are real. But genetics could also become a tool for reducing the class divide. Will we see the day when perhaps all youngsters are genetically vaccinated against dyslexia? And how might this contribute to everyone's social betterment?

As for the question of intruding on God's domain, the answer is less clear than the critics believe. The use of genetic medicine to cure or prevent disease is widely accepted by religious traditions, even those that oppose discarding embryos. Speaking in 1982 at the Pontifical Academy of Sciences, Pope John Paul II observed that modern biological research "can ameliorate the condition of those who are affected by chromosomic diseases," and he lauded this as helping to cure "the smallest and weakest of human beings . . . during their intrauterine life or in the period immediately after birth." For Catholicism and some other traditions, it is one thing to cure disease, but another to create children who are faster runners, longer-lived, or smarter.

But why should we think that the human genome is a once-and-for-   15 all-finished, untamperable product? All of the biblically derived faiths permit human beings to improve on nature using technology, from agriculture to aviation. Why not improve our genome? I have no doubt that most people considering these questions for the first time are certain that human genetic improvement is a bad idea, but I'd like to shake up that certainty.

Genomic science is racing toward a future in which foreseeable improvements include reduced susceptibility to a host of diseases, increased life span, better cognitive functioning, and maybe even cosmetic enhancements such as whiter, straighter teeth. Yes, genetic orthodontics may be in our future. The challenge is to see that we don't also unleash the demons of discrimination and oppression. Although I acknowledge the risks, I believe that we can and will incorporate gene technology into the ongoing human adventure.

TOPICS FOR CRITICAL THINKING AND WRITING

1. By the end of the second paragraph did you think that the British are probably right to be cautious, to require approval for all requests for PGD? Explain your position.

2. The fourth paragraph talks, by way of example, about avoiding obesity and "cognitive problems." At this stage in your reading of the essay, did you find yourself saying "Great, let's go for it," or were you thinking, "Wait a minute"? Why?

3. Do the fifth and sixth paragraphs pretty much set forth your response? If not, what *is* your response?

4. Does Bill McKibben's view, mentioned in the seventh paragraph, represent your view? If not, what would you say to McKibben?

5. If you are a believer in any of "the biblically derived faiths," does the comment in paragraph 15 allay whatever doubts you may have had about the acceptability of human genetic improvement? Explain.

6. In his final paragraph Green says, "I acknowledge the risks." Are you satisfied that he does acknowledge them adequately? Explain.

ANALYZING A VISUAL: GENETIC MODIFICATION OF HUMAN BEINGS

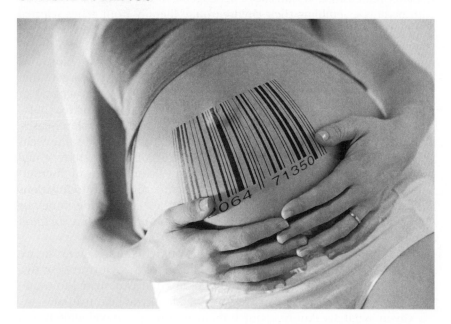

TOPICS FOR CRITICAL THINKING AND WRITING

1. What does this photograph seem to say about human genetic modification? Why do you think the photographer included a bar code in
   this image? In a couple of paragraphs, please evaluate this photo's
   effectiveness.

2. Do you agree with this photograph's point of view? In 250 words, write
   up a description of a photograph that might work as a rebuttal to this one.

Richard Hayes

*Born in 1945, Richard Hayes is executive director of the Center for Genetics and
Society, an organization that describes itself as "working to encourage responsible
uses and effective society governance of the new human genetic and reproductive technologies. . . . The Center supports benign and beneficent medical applications of the
new human genetic and reproductive technologies, and opposes those applications
that objectify and commodify human life and threaten to divide human society."*

This reprinted essay originally appeared in the Washington Post *on April
15, 2008.*

Genetically Modified Humans? No Thanks

In an essay in Sunday's Outlook section, Dartmouth ethics professor Ronald Green asks us to consider a neoeugenic future of "designer babies," with parents assembling their children quite literally from genes selected from a catalogue. Distancing himself from the compulsory, state-sponsored eugenics that darkened the first half of the last century, Green instead celebrates the advent of a libertarian, consumer-driven eugenics motivated by the free play of human desire, technology, and markets. He argues that this vision of the human future is desirable and very likely inevitable.

To put it mildly: I disagree. Granted, new human genetic technologies have real potential to help prevent or cure many terrible diseases, and I support research directed towards that end. But these same technologies also have the potential for real harm. If misapplied, they would exacerbate existing inequalities and reinforce existing modes of discrimination. If more widely abused, they could undermine the foundations of civil and human rights. In the worst case, they could undermine our experience of being part of a single human community with a common human future.

Once we begin genetically modifying our children, where do we stop? If it's acceptable to modify one gene, why not two, or twenty or two hundred? At what point do children become artifacts designed to someone's specifications rather than members of a family to be nurtured?

Given what we know about human nature, the development and commercial marketing of human genetic modification would likely spark a techno-eugenic rat-race. Even parents opposed to manipulating their children's genes would feel compelled to participate in this race, lest their offspring be left behind.

Green proposes that eugenic technologies could be used to reduce 5 "the class divide." But nowhere in his essay does he suggest how such a proposal might ever be made practicable in the real world.

The danger of genetic misuse is equally threatening at the international level. What happens when some rogue country announces an ambitious program to "improve the genetic stock" of its citizens? In a world still barely able to contain the forces of nationalism, ethnocentrism, and militarism, the last thing we need to worry about is a high-tech eugenic arms race.

In his essay, Green doesn't distinguish clearly between different uses of genetic technology—and the distinctions are critical. It's one thing to enable a couple to avoid passing on a devastating genetic condition, such as Tay-Sachs. But it's a different thing altogether to create children with a host of "enhanced" athletic, cosmetic, and cognitive traits that could be passed to their own children, who in turn could further genetically modify their children, who in turn . . . you get the picture. It's this second use of gene technology (the technical term is "heritable genetic enhancement") that Green most fervently wants us to embrace.

In this position, Green is well outside the growing national and international consensus on the proper use of human genetic science and technology. To his credit, he acknowledges that 80 percent of the medical school students he surveyed said they were against such forms of human genetic engineering, and that public opinion polls show equally dramatic opposition. He could have noted, as well, that nearly forty countries—including Brazil, Canada, France, Germany, India, Japan, and South Africa—have adopted socially responsible policies regulating the new human genetic technologies. They allow genetic research (including stem cell research) for medical applications, but prohibit its use for heritable genetic modification and reproductive human cloning.

In the face of this consensus, Green blithely announces his confidence that humanity "can and will" incorporate heritable genetic enhancement into the "ongoing human adventure."

Well, it's certainly possible. Our desires for good looks, good brains, 10 wealth and long lives, for ourselves and for our children, are strong and enduring. If the gene-tech entrepreneurs are able to convince us that we can satisfy these desires by buying into genetic modification, perhaps we'll bite. Green certainly seems eager to encourage us to do so.

But he would be wise to listen to what medical students, the great majority of Americans, and the international community appear to be saying: We want all these things, yes, and genetic technology might help us attain them, but we don't want to run the huge risks to the human community and the human future that would come with altering the genetic basis of our common human nature.

TOPICS FOR CRITICAL THINKING AND WRITING

1. Do you believe that in his first paragraph Hayes fairly summarizes Green's essay? If your answer is no, what are your objections?

2. Does the prospect raised in paragraph 6 frighten you? Why, or why not?

3. In his final paragraph Hayes speaks of "huge risks." What are these risks? Are you willing to take them? Why, or why not?

PART FIVE

CURRENT ISSUES:
CASEBOOKS

19

A College Education: What Is Its Purpose?

Andrew Delbanco

Andrew Delbanco, born in 1952, teaches at Columbia University, where he is director of American Studies. We reprint an essay that first appeared in Parade, *a magazine-like supplement that is part of the Sunday edition of many news-papers, and then was published in Delbanco's book* College: What It Was, Is, and Should Be *(2012).*

3 Reasons College Still Matters

The American college is going through a period of wrenching change, buffeted by forces—globalization, economic instability, the information technology revolution, the increasingly evident inadequacy of K–12 education, and, perhaps most important, the collapse of consensus about what students should know—that make its task more difficult and contentious than ever before.

For a relatively few students, college remains the sort of place that Anthony Kronman, former dean of Yale Law School, recalls from his days at Williams, where his favorite class took place at the home of a philosophy professor whose two golden retrievers slept on either side of the fireplace "like bookends beside the hearth" while the sunset lit the Berkshire Hills "in scarlet and gold." For many more students, college means the anxious pursuit of marketable skills in overcrowded, under-resourced institutions. For still others, it means traveling by night to a fluorescent office building or to a "virtual classroom" that only exists in cyberspace.

It is a pipe dream to imagine that every student can have the sort of experience that our richest colleges, at their best, provide. But it is a nightmare society that affords the chance to learn and grow only to the wealthy, brilliant, or lucky few. Many remarkable teachers in America's community colleges, unsung private colleges, and underfunded public colleges live this truth every day, working to keep the ideal of democratic education alive. And so it is my unabashed aim to articulate in my forthcoming book, *College: What It Was, Is, and Should Be*, what a college—any college—should seek to do for its students.

What, then, are today's prevailing answers to the question, what is college for? The most common answer is an economic one. It's clear that a college degree long ago supplanted the high school diploma as the minimum qualification for entry into the skilled labor market, and there is abundant evidence that people with a college degree earn more money over the course of their lives than people without one. Some estimates put the worth of a bachelor of arts degree at about a million dollars in incremental lifetime earnings.

For such economic reasons alone, it is alarming that for the first time   5 in history, we face the prospect that the coming generation of Americans will be less educated than its elders.

Within this gloomy general picture are some especially disturbing particulars. For one thing, flat or declining college attainment rates (relative to other nations) apply disproportionately to minorities, who are a growing portion of the American population. And financial means have a shockingly large bearing on educational opportunity, which, according to one authority, looks like this in today's America: If you are the child of a family making more than $90,000 per year, your odds of getting a BA by age twenty-four are roughly one in two; if your parents make less than $35,000, your odds are one in seventy.

Moreover, among those who do get to college, high-achieving students from affluent families are four times more likely to attend a selective college than students from poor families with comparable grades and test scores. Since prestigious colleges serve as funnels into leadership positions in business, law, and government, this means that our "best" colleges are doing more to foster than to retard the growth of inequality in our society. Yet colleges are still looked to as engines of social mobility in American life, and it would be shameful if they became, even more than they already are, a system for replicating inherited wealth.

Not surprisingly, as in any discussion of economic matters, one finds dissenters from the predominant view. Some on the right say that pouring more public investment into higher education, in the form of enhanced subsidies for individuals or institutions, is a bad idea. They argue against the goal of universal college education as a fond fantasy and, instead, for a sorting system such as one finds in European countries: vocational training for the low scorers, who will be the semiskilled laborers and functionaries; advanced education for the high scorers, who will be the diplomats and doctors.

Other thinkers, on the left, question whether the aspiration to go to college really makes sense for "low-income students who can least afford to spend money and years" on such a risky venture, given their low graduation rates and high debt. From this point of view, the "education gospel" seems a cruel distraction from "what really provides security to families and children: good jobs at fair wages, robust unions, affordable access to health care and transportation."

One can be on either side of these questions, or somewhere in the middle, and still believe in the goal of achieving universal college education. Consider an analogy from another sphere of public debate: health care. One sometimes hears that eliminating smoking would save untold billions because of the immense cost of caring for patients who develop lung cancer, emphysema, heart disease, or diabetes. It turns out, however, that reducing the incidence of disease by curtailing smoking may actually end up costing us more, since people who don't smoke live longer and eventually require expensive therapies for chronic diseases and the inevitable infirmities of old age.

In other words, measuring the benefit as a social cost or gain does not quite get the point—or at least not the whole point. The best reason to end smoking is that people who don't smoke have a better chance to lead better lives. The best reason to care about college—who goes, and what happens to them when they get there—is not what it does for society in economic terms but what it can do for individuals, in both calculable and incalculable ways.

The second argument for the importance of college is a political one, though one rarely hears it from politicians. This is the argument on behalf of democracy. "The basis of our government," as Thomas Jefferson put the matter near the end of the eighteenth century, is "the opinion of the people." If the new republic was to flourish and endure, it required, above all, an educated citizenry.

This is more true than ever. All of us are bombarded every day with pleadings and persuasions—advertisements, political appeals, punditry of all sorts—designed to capture our loyalty, money, or, more narrowly, our vote. Some say health care reform will bankrupt the country, others that it is an overdue act of justice; some believe that abortion is the work of Satan, others think that to deny a woman the right to terminate an unwanted pregnancy is a form of abuse. The best chance we have to maintain a functioning democracy is a citizenry that can tell the difference between demagoguery and responsible arguments.

Education for democracy also implies something about what kind of education democratic citizens need. A very good case for college in this sense has been made recently by Kronman, the former Yale dean who now teaches in a Great Books program for Yale undergraduates. In his book *Education's End*, Kronman argues for a course of study that introduces students to the constitutive ideas of Western culture, including, among many others, "the ideals of individual freedom and toleration," "a reliance on markets as a mechanism for the organization of economic life," and "an acceptance of the truths of modern science."

Anyone who earns a BA from a reputable college ought to understand something about the genealogy of these ideas and practices, about the historical processes from which they have emerged, the tragic cost when societies fail to defend them, and about alternative ideas both within the Western tradition and outside it. That's a tall order for anyone to satisfy on his or her own—and one of the marks of an educated person is the recognition that it can never be adequately done and is therefore all the more worth doing.

There is a third case for college, seldom heard, perhaps because it is harder to articulate without sounding platitudinous and vague. I first heard it stated in a plain and passionate way after I had spoken to an alumni group from Columbia, where I teach. The emphasis in my talk was on the Jeffersonian argument—education for citizenship. When I had finished, an elderly alumnus stood up and said more or less the following: "That's all very nice, professor, but you've missed the main point." With some trepidation, I asked him what that point might be. "Columbia," he said, "taught me how to enjoy life."

What he meant was that college had opened his senses as well as his mind to experiences that would otherwise be foreclosed to him. Not only had it enriched his capacity to read demanding works of literature and to grasp fundamental political ideas, it had also heightened and deepened his alertness to color and form, melody and harmony. And now, in the late years of his life, he was grateful. Such an education is a hedge against utilitarian values. It slakes the human craving for contact with works of art that somehow register one's own longings and yet exceed what one has been able to articulate by and for oneself.

If all that seems too pious, I think of a comparably personal comment I once heard my colleague Judith Shapiro, former provost of Bryn Mawr and then president of Barnard, make to a group of young people about what they should expect from college: "You want the inside of your head to be an interesting place to spend the rest of your life."

What both Shapiro and the Columbia alum were talking about is sometimes called "liberal education"—a hazardous term today, since it has nothing necessarily to do with liberal politics in the modern sense of the word. The phrase "liberal education" derives from the classical tradition of *artes liberales*, which was reserved in Greece and Rome—where women were considered inferior and slavery was an accepted feature of civilized society—for "those free men or gentlemen possessed of the requisite leisure for study." The tradition of liberal learning survived and thrived throughout European history but remained largely the possession of ruling elites. The distinctive American contribution has been the attempt to democratize it, to deploy it on behalf of the cardinal American principle that all persons, regardless of origin, have the right to pursue happiness—and that "getting to know," in poet and critic Matthew Arnold's much-quoted phrase, "the best which has been thought and said in the world" is helpful to that pursuit.

This view of what it means to be educated is often caricatured as 20 snobbish and narrow, beholden to the old and wary of the new; but in fact it is neither, as Arnold makes clear by the (seldom quoted) phrase with which he completes his point: "and through this knowledge, turning a stream of fresh and free thought upon our stock notions and habits."

In today's America, at every kind of institution—from underfunded community colleges to the wealthiest Ivies—this kind of education is at risk. Students are pressured and programmed, trained to live from task to task, relentlessly rehearsed and tested until winners are culled from the rest. Too many colleges do too little to save them from the debilitating frenzy that makes liberal education marginal—if it is offered at all.

In this respect, notwithstanding the bigotries and prejudices of earlier generations, we might not be so quick to say that today's colleges mark an advance over those of the past.

Consider a once-popular college novel written a hundred years ago, *Stover at Yale*, in which a young Yalie declares, "I'm going to do the best thing a fellow can do at our age, I'm going to loaf." The character speaks from the immemorial past, and what he says is likely to sound to us today like a sneering boast from the idle rich. But there is a more dignified sense in which "loaf " is the colloquial equivalent of contemplation and has always been part of the promise of American life. "I loaf and invite my soul," says Walt Whitman in that great democratic poem "Song of Myself."

Surely, every American college ought to defend this waning possibility, whatever we call it. And an American college is only true to itself when it opens its doors to all—the rich, the middle, and the poor—who have the capacity to embrace the precious chance to think and reflect before life engulfs them. If we are serious about democracy, that means everyone.

TOPICS FOR CRITICAL THINKING AND WRITING

1. In a sentence or two, state the author's thesis.

2. In your view, does the author offer adequate *support* for the thesis?

3. Do you think the final paragraph makes an effective ending? Why, or why not?

4. In his third paragraph Delbanco speaks of "a pipe dream" and of "a nightmare." Explain his use of these terms to a student who doesn't quite grasp Delbanco's meaning.

5. In his sixth paragraph Delbanco says that "if your parents make less than $35,000, your odds [of getting a BA by age 24] are one in seventy." Does this assertion disturb you? Why, or why not? (Before you respond, read Delbanco's next three paragraphs.)

6. In paragraph 10 Delbanco introduces, as an analogy—though he goes on to reject this comparison—the cost of lung cancer. Do you think his use of this analogy is effective? Why, or why not?

7. Delbanco gives three reasons that college matters. Why do you think he puts the three in the sequence that he does? If you were advising him, might you have recommended a different sequence? If so, why?

8. What sort of personality does the author convey? If he were teaching at your college, would you consider taking a course with him? Why, or why not?

Patrick Allitt

Patrick Allitt, a professor of American history at Emory University, is the author of I'm a Teacher, You're a Student: A Semester in the University Classroom *(2005). We reprint an essay that first appeared in 2006 in the* Chronicle of Higher Education, *a weekly publication read chiefly by college teachers and administrators. Letters of response to this article follow.*

Should Undergraduates Specialize?

I was a college freshman thirty-two years ago, in 1974. My daughter, Frances, is about to become a college freshman this fall. I went to the University of Oxford in England. She's going to Emory University in America, and her experience is going to be completely different. There are some obvious outward contrasts. I was a shabby pseudo-hippie with a tangle of crazy hair and no decent clothes. She's well dressed, groomed, and presentable. I had a fountain pen and a record player. She has a computer and an iPod.

The ideas and justifications surrounding these two college adventures differ sharply. I was a product of the British meritocratic system which, after World War II, had nationalized higher education. The governing idea was that intelligent people were a national asset and that the nation was investing wisely by educating them, no matter their social origins.

Every student's tuition was paid in full, and every student was given, in addition, a grant to cover living expenses, board, and lodging. Only very wealthy Britons had to pay more than a token sum toward their children's college education. My three years at Oxford cost my parents a total of about $400. In those days, however, only a very small minority of British kids went to any kind of college. Most dropped out of school on the day of their sixteenth birthday, breathed a great sigh of relief, and never thought about education again.

The only criterion for British university admission then was academic. Oxford and Cambridge held their own entrance exams, interviewed students who wrote good answers, and chose the best of the interviewees. My class at Hertford College, Oxford, consisted of ninety students, all of them academic achievers.

Resources for Teaching

Tenth Edition

Current Issues
and Enduring Questions

A Guide to Critical Thinking and Argument, with Readings

Sylvan Barnet
Hugo Bedau

Current Issues
and
Enduring Questions

A Guide to Critical Thinking
and Argument,
with Readings

Current Issues and Enduring Questions

A Guide to Critical Thinking and Argument, with Readings

Tenth Edition

SYLVAN BARNET
Professor of English, Tufts University

HUGO BEDAU
Professor of Philosophy, Tufts University

Bedford/St. Martin's   Boston • New York

Manufactured in the United States of America.

8   7   6   5   4   3
f   e   d   c   b   a

For information, write: Bedford/St. Martin's, 75 Arlington Street, Boston, MA 02116 (617-399-4000)

ISBN 978-1-4576-6153-2

Preface

These notes, like the book they accompany, are the work of two people—one a teacher of literature and composition, the other a teacher of philosophy. No single set of notes can fully satisfy all instructors or even be of much use to all instructors, but we hope that our alliance enables us to produce material that has something of interest for almost everyone.

THE SCOPE OF THESE NOTES

If the two of us succeed in being of some use, it is partly because we have different approaches and partly because we do not methodically treat every anthologized essay the same way. We treat all of the essays and literary works, but we treat some briefly, some extensively, some chiefly from a rhetorician's point of view, and some chiefly from a philosopher's point of view. We consistently keep in mind, however, the fact that because teachers of composition courses devote many hours to reading students' papers, they have correspondingly fewer hours to devote to working up the background for unfamiliar essays. We therefore provide fairly extensive background on some topics, notably animal rights and immigration, so that an instructor who happens to be relatively unfamiliar with a topic nevertheless can teach with ease the essays we reprint.

Beyond providing background on specialized topics, in these notes we simply touch on various matters we discuss in our classes. We realize that something is artificial here: What you do in class depends heavily on your students and also on the stage in the course at which you are discussing an essay. Further, what you do in class depends even more heavily on your ideas of what teaching is. Still, we hope you will scan these comments and find at least some of them useful; if the comments seem utterly wrongheaded, they may nevertheless be useful in providing material to react against.

THE SYLLABUS

All instructors have their own ideas about how to use the text in a composition course. Which essays are assigned, and in what sequence and at what pace, depends partly on whether you require a short research paper, several short research papers, or a long research paper. Still, our suggestion (for what it is worth) is to teach the first six chapters (Parts One and Two) in sequence.

Part One: In Chapter 1 we would glance fairly briefly at Jena McGregor's essay and would spend more time on Harlan Coben's "The Undercover Parent." We say we would spend more time on Coben's essay not because it is better written or is more interesting or more important, but simply because Coben's essay is followed by letters of response, and we would ask students to write their own letters, imagining as an audience the readers of Coben's essay. Coben's topic is one that allows students to offer opinions based on experience.

In Chapter 2 we would deal briefly with Susan Jacoby's essay (it is examined at some length in the text) and would spend considerably more time on the three essays that constitute the casebook on free speech. We certainly would discuss, in Chapter 2, the student's essay on the Pledge of Allegiance, and again, we would ask students to evaluate it and to explain why they would give it the grades they do. Such discussion, obviously, will help you to understand what students' ideas are concerning good and bad writing. In Chapter 3, we probably would teach two or three of the eight essays. Notice that Chapter 3 includes an essay on student indebtedness (Webley's) and two essays on Facebook—topics later addressed by a pair of essays on indebtedness (Chapter 14) and a casebook (Chapter 23) on Facebook. You may want to introduce these topics now and return to them later, or you may want to teach these essays later if you teach the debate or the casebook.

To cover Part One (Chapters 1–4) will take about four meetings if, at the beginning of the course, you give only brief writing assignments, or five or six meetings if you require substantial writing to accompany the reading assignments. In our discussions of these chapters in this manual, we offer a few suggestions about essays printed later in the book that go well with the early chapters, but we don't think it is necessary to supplement these first three chapters.

If in teaching Chapter 3—on syllogisms, evidence, and so on—you wish to inform students about the Toulmin model, you will want to supplement Chapter 3 with Chapter 8, which is devoted to that topic. Also relevant to Chapter 3 is Chapter 9, A Logician's View: Deduction, Induction, Fallacies, a fuller and somewhat more difficult discussion of topics set forth in Chapter 3. Our suggestion is this: If you have strong students and you wish to emphasize the role of logic in persuasive writing, assign Chapter 9. Otherwise, skip Chapter 9.

We also would spend part of a class hour discussing the images in Chapter 4, in particular Dorothea Lange's Migrant Mother and the anonymous poster entitled "Our Homes Are in Danger Now!" partly because students enjoy discussing them and partly because later in the term, we may ask our students to analyze images in the casebooks.

Part Two: Although Part One includes a discussion of writing (especially concerning annotating and summarizing), our chief discussion of writing is in Part Two (Chapters 5–7): writing an analysis of an argument, writing an argument, and using sources to write a research paper. Each chapter in Part Two can be covered in a meeting, but you probably will want to give two meetings to Chapter 5, Writing an Analysis of an Argument—one to discuss Nicholas Kristof's editorial and the student's analysis of it, and another to discuss the arguments in at least one of the other essays included in the chapter. In connection with these chapters on writing an argument—especially in connection with Chapter 6, where we talk about the audience as a collaborator—you may also want to assign Chapter 10 in Part Three, A Psychologist's View: Rogerian Argument.

Part Three, Further Views on Argument, contains three chapters already mentioned, A Philosopher's View: The Toulmin Model (8), A Logician's View: Deduction, Induction, Fallacies (9), A Psychologist's View: Rogerian Argument (10), it also contains three additional chapters, A Rhetorician's View (11), A Literary Critic's View (12), and A Debater's View (13). The chapter on literary criticism can stand alone, but it is especially useful as preparation for some of the readings in Part Six, Enduring Questions: Essays, a Story, Poems, and a Play.

Part Four, each chapter of which contains a pair of sharply opposed arguments, lets students examine strong, for the most part unnuanced, statements. If Rogerian argument interests you (it is the subject of Chapter 10), you may want to examine one or more of these debates in Rogerian tems, inviting students to search for common ground, in effect asking them to act as mediators or facilitators.

Part Five offers seven casebooks on current issues (for example, the purposes of a college education, the possible value and the possible danger of hydraulic fracturing, the pros and cons of governmental regulation of junk food). Each issue is represented by several voices, in no case fewer than four arguments, and in one case by as many as nine, including an advertisement with an illustration.

Part Six offers three enduring questions (What Is the Ideal Society?, How Free Is the Will of the Individual within Society?, and What Is Happiness?). These chapters include some literary material: poems by W. H. Auden, T. S. Eliot, Thomas Hardy, Langston Hughes, and Mitsuye Yamada; a short story by Ursula Le Guin; and a one-act play by Susan Glaspell. If you teach some of this literary material, you may also want to assign by way of preparation Chapter 12, A Literary Critic's View.

Although any essay in the book can be taken by itself, we hope that you will assign most or even all of the essays within at least one thematic chapter (Chapters 19–28), But of course good arguments can be made for being highly selective, and again, much depends on the abilities of the students and on your overall aims.

EXERCISES

All of the essays and literary selections in the text are followed by exercises, but in these notes, we include some additional topics for discussion and writing.

Contents

xiii

Part One

CRITICAL THINKING AND READING

1
Critical Thinking (p. 3)

Although the ideas in this introductory chapter are pretty straightforward, many of them will be new to some students, and we have therefore tried to illustrate them with a fairly extended discussion of just one example—the West Virginia law in 1989 that restricts a driver's license to those over eighteen, unless they are still in school, in which case they are eligible for a license at sixteen.

It's extremely instructive to see that sometimes a great deal can be extracted from very little—in this instance, from one statute on a perfectly ordinary matter. We've tried to present in the manageable scope of this humdrum example many of the considerations discussed in greater detail elsewhere in the book. This example gives the student a real taste of what critical thinking, reading, and writing involve, as well as of what lies ahead in the rest of the book.

Bruce Eric Kaplan

He Saves All His Critical Thinking for My Behavior (p. 4)

We reproduce this cartoon because we think it is amusing, and of course what makes it amusing is largely the fact that it sets forth a concept of "critical thinking" that is exactly the opposite of the kind of critical thinking we recommend in the text. The text empha-sizes the importance of questioning *one's own* assumptions, but the man in the cartoon clearly does *not* question his assumptions; rather, according to the caption, he questions the behavior (and presumably the assumptions beneath the behavior) of his wife. His stance and his facial expression—especially his down-turned mouth—clearly indicate his self-confidence and his disapproval of the world around him.

The Florida Case (p. 4)

First of all, it may be helpful to remind students that the First Amendment to the U.S. Constitution says, "Congress shall make no law respecting an establishment of religion, or prohibiting the free exercise thereof."

Now for the veil case in Florida. We confess that we don't understand the judge's deci-sion. In our view, it is unreasonable to require a photograph on the license on the grounds that the state has a compelling need for persons to carry an ID. Neither the state nor the federal government requires an ID of all citizens and aliens resident in the United States, and indeed tens of thousands of people in Florida do not carry a photo ID. These people include not only those who do not drive but also those who do legally drive on the basis of a driver's license issued by one of the fourteen states that do not require a photograph on the license.

As our second question (in Topics for Critical Thinking and Writing) implies, we are also uneasy about the logic of saying that although this plantiff is *un*likely to cause harm, she must remove the veil because *other* veiled persons might cause harm.

1

In our draft of the text manuscript, we had a third question along these lines: "Some strict Islamic countries prohibit women from driving. Can it therefore be argued that if Ms. Freeman is a sincere Muslim, she should not seek a driver's license?" We dropped this question because it seemed to us that the rules of certain Islamic countries are not necessarily relevant to the beliefs and actions of a Muslim in this country, but conceivably the question might be raised in class.

According to newspaper reports, American Muslims were divided about the case, and indeed it took the Council on American-Islamic Relations several months before it reached a consensus supporting Freeman, agreement that the state was violating her religious freedom. Among the opinions offered by Muslims were these:

- Islamic law does not oblige women to cover their faces in all circumstances.

- She could have her photo taken by a woman, and if stopped by a male police officer, she could explain the issue and request that he call a female police officer, to whom she would then show the license.

- She could unveil for the picture because she tried her best to follow God's will.

- She could unveil for the picture because Muslims need to support the U.S. national security efforts.

- She is drawing bad publicity for Muslims, and this episode is getting in the way of more important civil liberties where Muslim rights are being attacked.

- She is right to refuse; the court is infringing on religious liberty.

A very different but, in a way, faintly related matter: While we were working on this material, we happened, by sheer chance, to be reading a collection of essays, *The Visual Culture of American Religions* (2001), edited by David Morgan and Sally M. Promey. This book contains an essay by Promey in which she mentions (p. 40) that in 1997, a coalition of Muslim groups wrote a letter to the justices of the U.S. Supreme Court asking them to remove from Adolph Weinman's frieze in the North Courtroom (1931–1932) the face on an image of Muhammad. The image appears with those of other lawgivers, such as Moses, Confucius, and Napoleon. The relevant part of the relief is reproduced on page 41 of Promey's essay.

Islamic art, within a religious context, rarely represents living forms—such representation is thought to be a sacrilegious imitation of the work of Allah—and even more rarely does it represent holy figures. On the rare occasions when Muhammad is shown, his face is veiled, and sometimes his body is represented by a halo of light. One can easily grasp, then, the distress experienced by most Muslims who may see the relatively realistic image in the frieze. Nihad Awad, for instance, director of the Council on American-Islamic Relations, had told the Court that he viewed the image as "sacrilege." At the risk of seeming facetious or blasphemous or both—we are neither; we are in earnest—we might compare the response of a Muslim to the unveiled Muhammad with the response of a devout Christian who might somehow encounter a frontal representation of a nude adult Jesus. The Court replied with a letter from Chief Justice Rehnquist, dated March 11, 1997, saying that the image of Muhammad would not be changed because "it was intended only to recognize him, among many other lawgivers, as an important figure on the history of law . . . [and not] as a form of idol worship." The Court did, however, order a change in the brochure distributed to visitors to the Court. Promey quotes part of the description, but by means of Google we summoned up the whole brochure. (Just type "courtroom friezes north and south walls," and you will get it.) The revised description of Muhammad runs thus:

Muhammad (c. 570–632) The Prophet of Islam. He is depicted holding the Qur'an. The Qur'an provides the primary source of Islamic Law. Prophet Muhammad's teachings explain and implement Qur'anic principles. The figure above is a well-intentioned attempt by the sculptor, Adolph Weinman, to honor Muhammad and it bears no resemblance to Muhammad. Muslims generally have a strong aversion to sculptured or pictured representations of their Prophet.

2

Again, the issue of veiled women is different from the issue of representing the Prophet, but conceivably it may come up in class. You may want to ask your students to write letters representing their views of what the Court's letter should have said.

Speaking of courts and religion, for a comment on question 3 in the text concerning a monument of the Ten Commandments in a courtroom, see p. 6 in this manual.

Drivers' Licenses and Dropouts (p. 9)

An update on the issue of preventing dropouts from holding drivers' licenses before they are eighteen: We have been told that several states have found that confiscating the licenses of dropouts does *not* keep youngsters in school and taking away the licenses of failing or disruptive youngsters does not spur them to better work or to better behavior. In fact, some teachers say it is counterproductive because it turns the teacher (in the view of these students) into even more of an enemy than is usual.

Steve Jeffries

Play Ball! (student essay) (p. 12)

We briefly discuss this essay in the text, so we need not spend much time here, though we want to add a few points.

First, although our own view about the issue of homeschoolers participating in public school extracurricular activities differs from Jeffries's view, we think this is a very good essay—thoughtful, clear, effectively written. We do, however, have a mixed response to the title. When we first saw the essay, we liked the title—and we continue to think it has merit—but on reflection, we wonder if "Play Ball!" (a term associated with baseball) goes well with an opening paragraph that is devoted to a football player. Does it set up the expectation that we will hear something about baseball and thus disappoint the reader?

To our brief discussion of the opening paragraph, we would add that in our view, the sentences are shapely and interestingly balanced. Notice, for instance, that the longish penultimate sentence (twenty-eight words) in this paragraph is effectively followed by a short decisive sentence (six words).

The second paragraph is devoted to setting forth the opposing views. We cannot think of any significant objection that it ignores, and, given the imposed limitations of space, we believe it does a good job of stating the objections.

Our chief objection to the essay, perhaps oddly, is that Jeffries pretty much limits his discussion to extracurricular sports. We think he might have strengthened it—been more appealing to academic folks like us—if he talked about letting homeschoolers participate in those kinds of activities, *including academic subjects,* that public schools offer but home-schooling usually cannot. For instance, if his argument had said that, yes, homeschool-ers in effect opt out of certain things because their families believe they can cover those things better than the public school can. But there are of course certain kinds of things that homeschooling cannot do as well. For instance, chemistry probably cannot be taught effectively at home, and, similarly, Chinese probably cannot be learned at home unless a parent reads and speaks Chinese or is willing to hire a tutor. That is, we think the essay might have been stronger—might have been more appealing to *us*—if the argument covered academic work as well as extracurricular activities. The overall angle would be that it is in the interest of *society* to let homeschoolers participate in public school activities when homeschooling cannot offer the appropriate facilities. We probably would be more likely to go along with the idea of letting homeschoolers play on the baseball team if we thought they might also take the public school chemistry or Chinese course.

Harlan Coben

The Undercover Parent (p. 21)

In the text itself, we offer our own paragraph-by-paragraph discussion of the rhetoric of Coben's essay, and rhetoric—the art of using language persuasively—is what we think should be the primary subject of the discussion in a composition course rather than the issue that Coben addresses. But yes, we also recognize that the rhetoric is *about* something that it is used in the service of arguing a particular cause. The cause Coben advocates is probably unpopular with adults, as his first paragraph indicates. We have never taught this essay: It will be interesting to hear how students respond. Our guess is that many students will think that Coben is making a good point.

You or your students may find that our analysis in the text is defective in one way or another. If so, the class can have a good time pointing out its inadequacies and can thereby learn that not everything they read in print is true. But if you think our analysis is a satisfactory interpretation of the ways in which Coben makes his point, you may want to turn directly to the topics that we offer, or to issues that students raise in class. (Our own favorite pedagogical practice when we teach an op-ed piece is is to ask students to write a response.)

Jena McGregor

Military Women in Combat: Why Making It Official Matters (p. 28)

We address, in sequence, the topics that we set forth in the book.

1. McGregor's tone: We think readers will agree that McGregor appears to be unpretentious, reasonable, fair-minded, a person of goodwill, not a one-sided bullying advocate. Indeed, at least at the beginning, one almost thinks one is reading a news report, a narrative ("Last week, female soldiers began formally moving into jobs in previously all-male battalions") rather than an argument. But of course the piece *is* an argument, and this is indicated at the very outset, in the subtitle: "Why Making It Official Matters."

   The tone throughout is thoughtful and courteous (e.g., "Another way to break down the ceiling would be," "But . . . it's easy to see," "Both changes may be difficult"), and we believe that even readers who ultimately are unconvinced will nevertheless agree that McGregor is, as we have just said, reasonable and fair-minded.

2. The term *brass ceiling* by means of a rhyme, of course, plays on the term *glass ceiling*, the transparent barrier that lets women (in the business world) see the higher echelons but keeps women from reaching them. The barrier in the military is here called *brass* because the insignia of commissioned officers (the admiral's gold stripes, the general's stars) are colloquially called *brass,* as in "the top brass will never approve of this."

3. McGregor does *not* mention one argument that is sometimes offered against putting women into direct combat: A captured female soldier might be raped. You may want to invite your students to discuss the strengths and weaknesses of this argument. When we raised the issue, the general response was that the argument had no weight at all: (a) Captured men, too, can be raped, and (b) captured men and women can be tortured and killed. So given the circumstances, the issue of possible rape is hardly decisive. Still, even if your students raise these responses, we think it is worth discussing whether McGregor should have introduced the argument and then briefly rebutted it.

4. The argument concerning body strength is almost always present in discussions of the issue of women in combat. In comparing such matters as upper-body strength

4

or bone density of men and of women, one of course is speaking in generalities, not about particular individuals. But the gist is (as we say in our fourth topic in the text), some people argue that in some circumstances, women—again, we are speaking in general—are less competent than men are. Usually, in discussions about women in combat, upper-body strength is cited, and the standard examples concern pulling a wounded comrade out of a tank or off a battlefield. The idea is females are OK as, say, tank mechanics behind the lines, but not as members of a tank crew. We assume everyone would agree about the difference in upper-body strength, but we have also encountered the statement that when males enter competition, their testosterone level rises, increasing their hemoglobin and hence (this is getting complicated) their blood's capacity to carry oxygen, thus heightening the brain's sense of confidence and appetite for risk (the so-called *winner effect*). In short, heightened testosterone supposedly heightens courage. We have no idea if any of this business about testosterone = courage = a better fighter on the battlefield is true.

In any case, putting aside the issue of whether women should be allowed on the frontlines, we see the force of McGregor's argument that battlefield experience should not be a requirement for top command. Surely the requirement is a vestige of antiquated macho thoughts about what war is.

5. Presumably, the change in policy—women are now allowed to be in combat—makes women eligible for the top posts; so presumably, (a) the possibility of a military career is more attractive to the best and brightest women and (b) as McGregor points out, there may indeed be more diversity of thought at the top (the assumption here is that diversity of thought is a good thing because it may lead to wiser decisions).

6. As for whether—if there is a national draft—women should be drafted, well, discuss. (Please notice that we devote a casebook, Chapter 25, to the issue of whether young people should be required to perform public service.)

EXERCISE 3 *(p. 32)*

As we mention earlier in this manual in connection with the case of the Muslim woman vs. Florida, a frieze in the Supreme Court depicts Muhammad, along with Moses and other lawgivers, so there is some sort of precedent for introducing religion into the courthouse.

In the wee hours of the morning on July 31, 2001, Chief Justice Roy Moore of the Alabama Supreme Court had a 5,280-pound granite monument that was engraved with the Ten Commandments placed in the lobby of the Alabama Supreme Court. Civil liberties groups sued, arguing that the monument violated the First Amendment, which prohibits the government from supporting religion. Judge Moore insisted that the Ten Commandments are the basis of the secular law of our country. In November 2002, Federal District Court Judge Myron H. Thompson ordered Moore to remove the monument. Thompson noted that the excerpts from Exodus 20:1–17 (and also with slight differences in Deuteronomy 5:6–21) are a Protestant version of the commandments (the translation Moore used is the King James Version). Jewish, Roman Catholic, Lutheran, and Eastern Orthodox scriptures use slightly different versions of the Ten Commandments; so the version in the courthouse seems to endorse one particular faith, though (as we say in the text) the judge and his supporters say that the monument is a symbol of the roots of American law, not an endorsement of one religion.

A very few words about the differences may be useful. The Roman Catholic and Lutheran churches combine (take as one commandment) the passage forbidding the worship of other gods and the passage forbidding the making of images, and they treat as two commandments the prohibition in Exodus 20:17 against coveting a neighbor's wife (the ninth commandment) and house (the tenth). Most Protestants and Eastern Orthodox

Christians take the first commandment to be "You shall have no other gods before me" and the second commandment to be the injunction against the making of images. Modern Jewish usage counts verse 2 as the first commandment and verses 3–6 as the second.

When the federal judge ruled that the monument must be removed, there was considerable public protest. Rev. Patrick Mahoney of the Christian Defense Coalition and Rev. Rob Schenck, president of the National Clergy Council, led supporters to Montgomery, where they kneeled en masse in front of the monument. A round-the-clock operation was begun, with people unfurling bedrolls on the courthouse steps.

Moore is no stranger to controversy. When he was a circuit court judge in Gadsden, he hung a wooden plaque with the commandments in his courtroom. It generated controversy—enough controversy to encourage him to run as "the Ten Commandments judge" in 2000 in his successful campaign for chief justice. When the associate justices unanimously overruled the chief justice, he was temporarily removed from presiding over the court, pending a trial by the Alabama Court of the Judiciary.

The last time that the U.S. Supreme Court ruled on a case concerning government display of the Ten Commandments was in 1980, in *Stone v. Graham*. Stone was one of a group of parents who challenged a Kentucky law that required all public schools to post the Ten Commandments in every classroom. The money for the printed commandments was provided by private sources, and each copy said, at the bottom, "Secular application of the Ten Commandments is clearly seen in its adoption as the fundamental legal code of Western civilization and the Common Law of the United States." The Court, however, rejected (five to four) this argument, holding that just because Kentucky said that its law had a secular purpose did not make it so. And it rejected as irrelevant the fact that private funds were used.

Justice Rehnquist, in a dissenting opinion, wrote:

> The Supreme Court should defer to the State in determining the secular purpose of postings. The State Legislature and State Courts both believe that the postings have a secular purpose, and the Court should respect this; especially given that the secular purpose, the "Ten Commandments have had a significant impact on the development of the legal codes of the Western world," is acknowledged to be true.

Back to Judge Moore: On August 21, 2003, the eight associated justices of the Alabama Supreme Court overruled Moore, their chief justice, and unanimously ordered that the monument be removed from the lobby. Starting the next day, a fine of $5,000 a day was to be imposed if the monument remained in public view. Moore had been told by the federal judge that he could display the monument in his private chambers, if he wished.

Here are two interesting complications concerning the display of the Ten Commandments in or on a courthouse. (1) As we mention in our discussion of the Florida veil case, the image of Muhammad appears on a frieze in the U.S. Supreme Court. The image of Moses also appears there, holding the Ten Commandments as part of a display of lawgivers, including Hammurabi and Confucius. The courts have ruled that this sort of display of the Ten Commandments within a court is acceptable because it is part of a larger historical display. (2) On August 13, 2003, a federal appeals court in Pennsylvania refused to reconsider a ruling that allowed a 1920 plaque with the Ten Commandments to remain on the façade of a courthouse in suburban Philadelphia. The three-judge panel of the Third U.S. Circuit Court of Appeals had ruled in June that the plaque did *not* constitute an official endorsement of religion because the county commissioners who wanted to keep it were moved by an interest in historic preservation, not religion.

It is probably true—at least Gallup Polls suggest this—that most Americans consider the Ten Commandments as valid rules for a good secular life, but few can give a moderately accurate rendition of even half of the commandments. And in any case, the argument that the commandments are a symbol of the roots of American law, not an endorsement of one religion, seems odd when one remembers that the very first commandment concerns monotheism, the second prohibits the making of "graven images" (by the way, how many Americans adhere to this commandment?), the third prohibits taking the Lord's name in vain, and the fourth concerns observing the sabbath. True, the remaining commandments (concerning respect for parents, killing, adultery, stealing, perjury, and covetousness) are more evidently secular, but even these are ultimately rooted in a particular theology.

We will let Judge Moore have the next-to-last word. According to a report in the *Boston Globe,* August 21, 2003, on CBS's *The Early Show* he said:

> This case is not about politics or religion. It's about the acknowledgement of God. . . . We must acknowledge God because our Constitution says our Judicial system is established upon God.

The last word: A special ethics panel (appointed by various legal organizations, the Alabama governor, and the lieutenant governor) on November 13, 2003, unanimously voted to remove Chief Justice Roy Moore from the Alabama Supreme Court. (The panel's vote was binding only if unanimous.) A topic for argument: Should an *un*elected panel have the power to remove an elected judge?

EXERCISE 4 *(p. 32)*

In addition to arguments concerning aesthetics and cost, the chief argument seems to be that a barrier is not effective: People who want to commit suicide will find other sites where they can kill themselves. That is, according to persons who hold this view, the bridge does not cause suicide, it does not tempt people who otherwise would not commit suicide. Further, it has been argued that barriers might actually increase the number of people who jump to their deaths because barriers would drive such people to other locations—let's say a cliff or a tall building—where there is no possibility that they would be talked out of their acts. Apparently, a considerable number—but we don't have the statistics—of potential bridge-jumpers are persuaded not to jump.

2
Critical Reading: Getting Started (p. 34)

The major points made in this chapter—that one should read carefully and that making a summary helps one to grasp an argument—are obvious, and perhaps that's why students often ignore them. Our experience suggests that students often fail to grasp the main points of an argument not because it is especially difficult but merely because they do not read it carefully. But if they do read it carefully (aided by writing a summary), they are likely to find ideas arising—differences with the author. Therefore, the process of writing a summary of someone else's ideas can be a way of generating ideas of one's own. Drawing on the assumptions in Chapter 1, it may be useful to ask students to underline any explicit assumptions that the writer makes (these will probably appear in the summary) and then to think about, and to jot down, any assumptions present but *not* stated.

Susan Jacoby

A First Amendment Junkie (p. 47)

With Susan Jacoby's essay, we hope to show that even where the language is informal, the topic is familiar, and the argument is fairly easy, a second or third reading may reveal things not perceived in a quick scanning.

At this stage in the course, we are less intent on exploring the pros and cons of the issue than on teaching how to read, how to summarize, and how to become aware of explicit and implicit assumptions. "How to read" includes developing awareness of persona and tone, and it is worth discussing the title (even though it is the editors', because the original title was simply "Hers," the unvarying title of a weekly column in the *New York Times*), and worth discussing the ways in which Jacoby establishes a persona.

Although in the text we do not discuss the role of a persona until Chapter 5, preliminary discussion in class can help to pave the way for the students' later encounter with the topic. Because a writer's choice of a persona depends partly on the audience, it is appropriate to discuss this essay *as an argument for readers of a specific newspaper*. It's not a bad idea to ask students to read a couple of issues of the *Times*. Students who have been taught to write in a somewhat stiff, impersonal manner may be surprised to learn from Jacoby (and other columnists in the paper) that they can use "I" and that they can even use colloquial diction ("junkie") in some contexts.

Our second question in the text, on Jacoby's next-to-last paragraph, is prompted by our thought that although the essay is always clear, she makes some leaps. The women who favor censorship in paragraph 1 are, on the whole, women who see pornography as one kind of violence against women. Paragraph 5 gets into kiddie porn—a related issue, but not the same issue. Jacoby probably introduces it to dissociate herself from the extreme position of some opponents of censorship. (It is usually a good idea to distance oneself from extremists who share one's views.) But the issue of young people surfaces again in paragraphs 13 and 14. There is, of course, a connection between Jacoby's arguments that parents should protect the young and her argument that adult-oriented pornography, however objectionable, should not be censored. The connection is that it is the job of adults to fulfill their responsibilities, and not to "shift responsibility from individuals to institutions" (para. 13).

Question 3, on the final paragraph, aims at getting students to see that a final paragraph need not begin "Thus we see" and need not summarize all the points argued earlier.

Question 5, about what is or is not permitted under the "absolute interpretation of the First Amendment," is meant to provoke some thought about whether anyone does or should want the free-speech clause to include protection of offensive and possibly harmful acts — when the acts are wholly verbal (as seems tolerated by Justice Black's remark quoted in Jacoby's para. 2). Falsely shouting "Fire!" in a crowded theater may be no more than a speech act, but it was Justice Holmes's famous example of speech *not* protected by the First Amendment because in a context of utterance such as his example provides, these words would cause "a clear and present danger" of *harm* (and not merely annoyance, offense, or other hostile feelings) to the innocent.

For a discussion of constitutional law on the First Amendment, see Archibald Cox, *Freedom of Expression* (1981). An older book, still of great value, is Thomas I. Emerson's *The System of Freedom of Expression* (1970). A somewhat more recent book on the subject is by Anthony Lewis, *Make No Law* (1991).

Note: We discuss in the text, on page 50, Jacoby's essay from the point of view of the Toulmin method.

Zachary Shemtob and David Lat

Executions Should Be Televised (p. 53)

In stating the objections to their view that (to quote the title of the essay) "Executions Should Be Televised," the authors insist (para. 13) that they do not assume (with Sister Helen Prejean and other foes of capital punishment) that visibility would engender revulsion against the practice and thus would stimulate support for opposition to capital punishment. The authors, claiming to be open-minded, say that they advocate making executions public simply because (to quote their final paragraph), "A democracy demands a citizenry as informed as possible about the costs and benefits of society's ultimate punishment."

To our ears, this statement does not quite ring true. We can't understand how seeing a televised image of an execution — whether the criminal dies with a smile or a grimace on his or her face, whether his or her body is contorted or apparently relaxed — gives us much information "about the costs and benefits of society's ultimate punishment." We somehow cannot escape thinking that Shemtob and Lat oppose capital punishment and think (like Prejean and others whom they name) that if the public could see it put into practice, the public would be so repelled that it would oppose the punishment. That is, we think there is an underlying irony here: The authors argue, with a straight face, that executions should be televised so that the public can be better informed, but the reader — well, the writer of this page in this instructor's handbook — believes that their proposal is so monstrous that its real purpose is to engender opposition to capital punishment. (Yes, we use the word *proposal* because we we wish to evoke thoughts of Swift's "A Modest *Proposal*," which similarly offers a monstrous argument with a straight face.)

Maybe. Or maybe some folks would take pleasure in witnessing a painful death. Here's something to think about. Thomas Macaulay (1800–1859) famously said, "The Puritans hated bear-baiting, not because it gave pain to the bear, but because it gave pleasure to the spectators." Macaulay was being witty, taking a poke at what he assumed were pleasure-hating Puritans. But can't a good case be made that indeed we ought not to take pleasure in certain kinds of things (in Macaulay's comment, setting dogs upon a chained bear)? If this is true, and if we think that some viewers will relish the spectacle offered by executions, well, then, shouldn't such spectacles be banned? Discuss. (We return to this point in our discussion [p. 26 in this manual] of Nora Ephron's essay of photographs of a woman falling to her death.)

Gwen Wilde (student essay)

Why the Pledge of Allegiance Should Be Revised (p. 56)

We begin by saying that we would give this essay an A. We think it is clear, thoughtful, and courteous—on a subject that has engendered plenty of intemperate writing. Admittedly, the title is not especially engaging, but it has the merit of clearly announcing both the topic and the thesis, and for those reasons we think it is not bad.

The first paragraph is informative, probably telling most readers something they did not know (that the original version of the Pledge did not include the words "under God"). The next paragraph advances the necessary information—that the phrase was added in 1954—and the paragraph ends with an explicit statement of the thesis:

> In my view, the addition of the words "under God" is inappropriate, and they are needlessly divisive—an odd revision for a Nation that is said to be "indivisible."

If we had written the sentence, we probably would have used *because* instead of *and* ("because they are needlessly divisive" rather than "and they are needlessly divisive"), but that's a small point. What we like about the student's sentence is the wordplay involved with *divisive* and *indivisible.*

Wilde goes on to question the meaning of President Eisenhower's words—we our- selves find them a bit fuzzy—and she then points out (para. 5) that "in the Pledge patrio- tism is connected with religious belief." She goes on to give a reason for suggesting that even though a large percentage of Americans believe in God, the words "under God" do not belong in the Pledge ("several million Americans do *not* believe in God").

We find especially interesting her brief discussion (para. 9) of the use of the motto "In God We Trust" on American coinage. Given Wilde's position on the words "under God" in the Pledge, we would have guessed that she would also object to the motto on coins. Presumably, she introduces this issue—effectively, we believe—to show that she is *not* a fanatic who objects to every tiny hint of religion in American public life.

The quotation from Associate Justice David Souter lets the reader know that Wilde has done some homework, and her comment on the quotation shows that she is thinking care- fully about the quotation. In her final paragraph, she reiterates her thesis, but she manages not to be merely repetitive. For instance, in this paragraph she introduces the information that "the Founding Fathers . . . never mentioned God in the Constitution." But perhaps what especially animates this final paragraph, in which there is little new information, is the note of urgency, for instance, when Wilde says, "Yes, they [students] can remain silent when others recite these two words, but, again, why should they have to remain silent?"

A week or two after we drafted the material that you have just read, we came across some comments by Ronald Dworkin on this topic (as well as on intelligent design and on gay marriage) in the *New York Review of Books* (September 21, 2006). Dworkin finds the Pledge "coercive," but he adds, "That coercive impact, however, is in fact not very strong and so though the official Pledge is a violation of liberty it is not a practically serious one." Dworkin goes on (as in fact the student did) to introduce a comparison with the pious words on our coinage, but unlike the student, Dworkin thinks the words in the Pledge are as innocuous as the words on money. Dworkin says:

> Just as an atheist can fish in his pocket for a coin that bears a message of trust in God or stand at the opening ceremony of prayer in congressional or court sessions without any sense of self-betrayal, so he can mouth the words of the Pledge, or skip the words he finds objectionable, without loss of integrity. (p. 28)

Our own view, for what it is worth, is that Wilde is right in thinking that a child recit- ing the Pledge is *not at all* like (to quote Dworkin) "an atheist fish[ing] in his pocket for a coin that bears a message of trust in God." The atheist—unless he or she is dedicated to removing every vestige of religion—probably hardly thinks of the words when fishing for a coin, but a child reciting the Pledge must be thinking of the words, whether he or she recites them or remains silent.

Discuss.

A Note on Hate Speech

The argument about whether hate speech (for example, racial epithets) should be permitted on the campus is not likely to go away, nor is it likely to be answered definitively. Here are the chief arguments that we have encountered.

Arguments in favor of restricting speech on the campus:

1. Speech demeaning a person's color, creed, sex, sexual orientation, or other personal attributes creates a hostile learning environment—a workplace in which work cannot be done—and thus such speech infringes on the rights of others. Sometimes this argument is supported by being compared with sexual harassment: The courts have upheld regulations against sexual harassment in the workplace. Thus, if women have a right to work in a nonthreatening environment, then students have a right to study in an atmosphere free of racial (or other) harassment. But how exact is the comparison?

2. Limitation of such speech is allowable under the "fighting-words" doctrine. A face-to-face insult using four-letter words or other epithets addressed to an individual or a small group is not intended to discover truth or initiate dialogue; rather, it is an attempt to injure and inflame. Such language is not protected by the First Amendment, according to the Supreme Court in *Chaplinsky v. New Hampshire* (1942). (In this case, a man shouted into the face of a police officer that he was a "Goddamned racketeer and a damned fascist.")

3. A college or university fosters unlimited inquiry, *not* unlimited speech. Hate speech does not lead to advances in knowledge.

4. Outlawing hate speech would not mean that there would be limitations on discussions even of heinous ideas in situations that allow for rebuttal or for persons to choose not to attend.

Arguments against restricting speech on campus:

1. Restrictions against remarks about race, creed, and so forth, violate the rights of free speech under the First Amendment. Such remarks do not come under the fighting-words doctrine because it is not clear that they will produce violence, especially if they are comments about groups rather than specific individuals.

2. By tolerating (rather than suppressing) such speech, we are in a better position to diagnose the real problems that give rise to racist speech and can try to face them directly, not indirectly through regulation and prohibition.

3. We all need to develop a thicker skin to merely verbal utterances that offend. If we don't, then either we will foolishly attempt to protect *everyone* from whatever speech offends them, or we will yield the platform and rostrum to whoever is nastiest among us. Either way threatens disaster; the best remedy for bad speech is still better speech, not silence.

4. Exactly which words are to be prohibited? When three students at the University of Wisconsin complained that they had been called *rednecks,* the administration told them that *redneck* is "not a demeaning term." Or consider the word *Negro,* once considered a polite term, used by African Americans both privately and publicly, but now regarded by many as demeaning. Another example: *Queer* used to be, and for many people still is, a demeaning term for a homosexual, but in the last few years, many homosexuals have used the term, as in the group called Queer Nation.

11

The Supreme Court decided (June 1992) that an ordinance against hate speech enacted by the city of St. Paul was unconstitutional. The ordinance banned any action "which one knows . . . arouses anger, alarm, or resentment in others on the basis of race, color, creed, religion or gender." The case did not concern speech on the campus, but it did concern expression of racial hate—the burning of a cross on the lawn of a black family that had recently moved into a white neighborhood. In *R.A.V. v. St. Paul*, Justice Scalia, writing for the majority of five (Kennedy, Rehnquist, Scalia, Souter, Thomas) held that government may not opt for "silencing speech on the basis of its content."

The majority opinion, holding that the St. Paul ordinance was impermissibly narrow, acknowledged that hate speech directed at race or religion was hurtful but did not concede that there was any difference in kind between a racial epithet and, for instance, an insult directed at union membership or political affiliation. The court made the point that burning a cross on someone's lawn is "reprehensible," but it insisted that "St. Paul has sufficient means [such as trespassing laws] to prevent such behavior without adding the First Amendment to the fire."

The other four justices agreed that the St. Paul ordinance was unconstitutional, but they would have struck it down on the less-sweeping ground that it was written in too broad a manner. The justices who did not sign the majority opinion (Blackmun, O'Connor, Stevens, White) were troubled by the refusal of the majority to see that certain kinds of hate speech are especially evil. Justice White, for instance, said that the city's

> selective regulation reflects the city's judgment that harms based on race, color, creed, religion, or gender are more pressing public concerns than the harms caused by other fighting words. . . . In light of our nation's long and painful experience with discrimination, this determination is plainly reasonable.

Justice Stevens, in a footnote, glancing at the Los Angeles riots earlier in the year, wrote:

> One need look no further than the recent social unrest in the nation's cities to see that race-based threats may cause more harm to society and to individuals than other threats. . . . Until the nation matures beyond that condition, laws such as St. Paul's ordinance will remain reasonable and justifiable.

In short, the justices who refrained from joining the majority valued free speech not as something good in itself but as something instrumental. That is, they valued speech on the ground, that it serves a constructive purpose by helping to create a better informed electorate and therefore a better country. In this view, speech that is harmful need not be protected.

According to a report in the *New York Times* (June 24, 1992), a spokesperson for the American Council on Education said that the consequences of the decision for colleges and universities were unclear. Private institutions faced fewer constitutional restraints, the report said, than did public institutions, but it was thought that those educational institutions with codes would probably modify them. For instance, after a federal court in 1989 declared unconstitutional the code of the University of Michigan in Ann Arbor, the university adopted a provisional code prohibiting

> physical acts or threats or verbal slurs, invectives or epithets referring to an individual's race, ethnicity, religion, sex, sexual orientation, creed, national origin, ancestry, age, or handicap made with the purpose of injuring the person to whom the words or actions are directed and that are not made as part of a discussion or exchange of an idea, ideology, or philosophy.

You might want to ask your students to evaluate the Michigan provisional code.

A CASEBOOK FOR CRITICAL READING: SHOULD SOME KINDS OF SPEECH BE CENSORED? (p. 60)

Preliminary Note: Free Speech in the Age of YouTube

Our heading, "Free Speech in the Age of YouTube," is the title of an article in the *New York Times* by Somini Sengupta (September 23, 2012). We summarize Sengupta's piece here.

Companies are usually accountable only to shareholders, but Internet companies—because they deal in speech—must make decisions about what kind of expression is allowed. In September 2012, a video mocking Mohammad circulated on YouTube (owned by Google) and provoked a storm of protest in the Islamic world. An attack on the American Embassy in Libya resulted in the death of the ambassador and three other Americans.

The question: Should Google allow access to the video in Libya (or in other Muslim countries)? Google in fact then restricted the piece in Libya and in six other countries where it is unlawful to show disrespect for the Prophet.

Two additional points:

- Apple and Google ordinarily obey the laws of countries in which they do business.

- International law does *not* protect speech designed to cause violence.

A CASEBOOK FOR CRITICAL READING: SHOULD SOME KINDS OF SPEECH BE CENSORED? (p. 60)

Susan Brownmiller

Let's Put Pornography Back in the Closet (p. 61)

First, a point made by Wendy Kaminer in an essay in *Take Back the Night*, edited by Laura Lederer (the book in which Susan Brownmiller's essay also appears): In recent years, feminists such as Brownmiller have been arguing that pornography is not merely dirty (obscene) but is, by virtue of images of violence against women, a threat to society. The distinction, Kaminer explains, is important. "Obscenity" is not constitutionally protected, but it is very narrowly defined. According to the Supreme Court ruling in *Miller v. California* (1973), obscene material is material "that the average person, applying community standards . . . would find . . . as a whole, appeals to the prurient interest" and "taken as a whole, lacks serious artistic, political, or scientific value." It is extremely difficult to prove in court that a work is obscene. Moreover, although almost any piece of hard-core pornography probably fits this description, enforcement of obscenity laws is difficult because the government may not prohibit publication of any material before the courts decide it is obscene. Each book or magazine must individually be judged obscene before it may be enjoined. Kaminer points out that a store with one thousand books cannot be closed because of fifty or even five hundred obscenity convictions. The stock that has not been judged obscene can be sold.

The newer view of pornography, developed especially by Catharine MacKinnon and Andrea Dworkin, sees it not merely as obscenity but as material that depicts the subjugation of women. Pornography is said to represent violence against women, thereby impeding their chances of achieving equal opportunity. It should be mentioned, by the way, that although some feminists oppose pornography on the grounds that it is humiliating to women, other feminists argue that (1) modern feminism is itself linked to sexual liberation, and (2) feminists who fear pornography unwittingly reinforce the notion that women are sexually passive.

Brownmiller, claiming that the battle for free speech has on the whole been won, asserts that pornography is not chiefly a matter of free speech; but she, like MacKinnon and Dworkin, politicizes the issue and thereby tends to legitimize pornography. That is, by seeing it as political speech, these writers bring it into a constitutionally protected area. Of course if they can demonstrate that pornography is a threat to society—a "clear and present danger"—then they will have put it in an area not constitutionally protected, but it is very difficult to prove that something is a "clear and present danger" (cf. question 3).

A February 1986 ruling of the Supreme Court is relevant. The Court ruled *un*constitutional an Indianapolis ordinance that forbade pornography on the ground that it is a form of discrimination against women. The ordinance, drafted with the help of MacKinnon and Dworkin, defined pornography as "the graphic sexually explicit subordination of women, whether in pictures or in words," if it showed them enjoying "pain or humiliation" or if they were in "positions of servility or submission or display." Brownmiller is especially concerned about images of these sorts. Although the Supreme Court did not explain why it declared the ordinance unconstitutional, perhaps we can guess the rationale by considering the explanation of Judge Frank Easterbrook, for the court of appeals, when he ruled against the city ordinance. Easterbrook said that the Indianapolis law "discriminates on the grounds of the content of speech" by establishing "an 'approved' view of women." "This is thought control," he said, for this law attempted to silence explicit speech that did not conform to a particular view of women. He also pointed out that the law could be applied to Homer's epics and to Joyce's *Ulysses*.

Now to look, briefly, a little more closely at Brownmiller's essay. She begins by calling free speech "one of the great foundations on which our democracy rests," thus putting herself on the side of virtue, a good strategy when arguing. Brownmiller then goes on to indicate that she would not burn *Ulysses, Lady Chatterley's Lover,* and the *Tropic* books. Again she is on the side of virtue, or at least of classic liberal thought. In short, Brownmiller devotes her first seven paragraphs to showing that she is for democracy and the arts. In paragraph 8 she says she is "not opposed to sex and desire," again establishing her credentials as a liberal. In paragraph 9 she briefly explains why feminists *do* object to pornography (it degrades women), and the remainder of the essay (less than half of the total) amplifies the point. In paragraph 14 she raises an important point that we mentioned earlier in this commentary—not all speech is protected. But as we suggested, although the Constitution does not protect a person who falsely shouts "Fire!" in a crowded theater (a "clear and present danger"), there is some question about whether pornography represents such a danger. Still, by mentioning false advertising and the cry of "Fire," paragraph 14 effectively suggests that pornography is not necessarily protected.

Charles R. Lawrence III

On Racist Speech (p. 64)

In recent year, so-called hate speech on campus has provoked anger and dismay among students, faculty, staff, and the public at large. Any attempt to control such speech by official regulation seems likely to be on a collision course with the First Amendment. Or so most academic administrators concluded, after *Doe v. University of Michigan* (1989). In that case, regulations restricting free speech on the Michigan campus, arising out of a desire to resist "a rising tide of racial intolerance and harassment on campus," were permanently enjoined by Judge Avern Cohn. Judge Cohn had no difficulty permitting regulations as to time, place, and manner of speech. His concern was about the way the university's regulations governed *content*. He held that any regulations against the content of "speech" on no stronger ground than that it was "offensive"—even "gravely so [to] large numbers of people"—was unconstitutionally vague and overbroad.

14

Charles R. Lawrence is himself African American (see his para. 15) (by the way, he's the brother of Sara Lawrence Lightfoot, author of the widely acclaimed *Balm in Gilead: Journey of a Healer* [1988]), and he presents a measured defense of narrowly drawn regulations against hate speech. No enemy of the First Amendment (see paras. 1 and 14–19), he nonetheless doubts whether its defenders really will act on the proposition, touted by the American Civil Liberties Union in its perennial defense of the First Amendment, that the best remedy for bad speech is more and better speech (para. 17).

Lawrence's position (question 2) is clear from the opening sentence of paragraph 8: If regulations of conduct on campus are needed to protect minority students from harassment and personal vilification, then "equal educational opportunity" is the "compelling justification" for them. We would agree; a few students have no right to make campus life intolerable for others by language, gesture, or symbol that interferes with their rightful access to all the campus has to offer.

But we would also urge that before any such regulations are adopted, one needs to reflect carefully on several basic facts. Everyone finds some words or pictures offensive, but what offends one does not always offend others. Not everything that is offensive is seriously harmful (or counts as harassment). Finally, not everything offensive can be prevented. We all need to develop a thick skin to the merely offensive, lest we find ourselves provoked into violent response or timidly cowering before verbal bullies. We all also need to cultivate a civil environment, free of insulting, degrading, and offensive behavior, verbal or otherwise, especially on a college campus.

Part of what makes the whole hate speech issue so controversial and difficult are the uncertainties that surround the key words "assaultive speech," "verbal vilification," and the like (question 4). Lawrence does not attempt to define these terms explicitly, nor does he provide illustrative and convincing examples of verbal conduct that is "assaultive" or "vilifying." (Students could be usefully asked to give such examples—genuine or hypothetical—and then see whether they can give sensible definitions of these terms.) Nor does Lawrence draft a model set of regulations for hate speech that would prevent (or make liable to punishment for) the harm such speech causes and still pass constitutional muster.

We suspect that Lawrence would deny that straight white males are as vulnerable to insulting posters and the like as are certain other classes of students (blacks, women, gays). The reason is that political power and social status have traditionally been the preserve of white males so that as a class they are relatively immune to the power of offensive language to degrade and intimidate. Of course, Lawrence might still argue (as we would) that straight white males ought not to have to endure insults because of their race or sexual orientation and that regulations protecting women or blacks or homosexuals from vilification ought to be extended equally to all classes of students.

Derek Bok

Protecting Freedom of Expression on the Campus (p. 69)

Like Charles R. Lawrence III (see the previous essay in the chapter), Derek Bok is trained as a lawyer, avows his personal allegiance to the First Amendment, and speaks from a position of concern about racially provocative speech and symbols on a private university campus. (This last point is important because the courts seem to agree that *private* colleges and universities are not bound by the First Amendment, as are public institutions. Notice that in paragraph 9, Bok rightly refuses to use this reason for favoring regulations of free speech on the Harvard campus.) But where Lawrence speaks in measured tones on behalf of the victims of "hate speech," Bok seems to speak for the vast majority of bystanders, those who are neither victims nor offenders where hate speech is concerned.

Bok offers three very different reasons for opposing attempts to curtail hate speech. First, unlike Lawrence, he is doubtful whether the class of harmful verbal and graphic symbols can be suitably defined so that they can be regulated without infringing on full freedom of expression (para. 10). Second, even if such regulations could be drafted and enforced, they would not change racist attitudes or bring greater mutual respect and decency to campus life (para. 11). Finally, irrepressible adolescents will gleefully "test the limits" of these regulations, thereby aggravating the nuisance and trying the patience of deans and disciplinary committees (para. 12). From our own experience, we are strongly inclined to agree with Bok on all these points, even if they do not constitute the last word on the subject.

What constructive measures against hate speech does Bok recommend? First, prospective victims ought to learn to "ignore" nasty and hateful speech; second, the rest of the campus community ought to counsel and persuade would-be vilifiers to mend their ways, lest they do grave harm to some of their fellow students (para. 13). Sensible advice, indeed—but perhaps too easily issued by one who himself is neither black, female, gay, or (it would appear) in any other way a member of a group specially vulnerable to verbal assault. Indeed, we can understand how some will judge Bok's counsels to be unimaginative and deeply disappointing.

Notice, too, that although Bok cites several grounds for restricting speech (para. 7), they do not include the ground Lawrence mentioned in the previous essay—namely, ensuring equal educational opportunity to minority students.

Pedagogical Note: One case study that students have enjoyed exploring in relation to Bok's essay is the topic of flag burning.

If some students do see the American flag as sacred, as something that is desecrated when it is burned by angry protestors, do they also see the Confederate flag as sacred, as something that deserves special protection? You might remind them (or inform them) that the Confederate flag (or a variation) has flown over the capitol buildings of some southern states and has evoked strong protests. In the early months of 2000, for instance, the National Association for the Advancement of Colored People (NAACP) organized a boycott of South Carolina because the Confederate battle flag was displayed over the state's capitol. For some citizens, the flag celebrated the "southern heritage"—for instance, the gallantry of Confederate soldiers. For others, most obviously the NAACP, the flag offensively celebrated slavery. Incidentally, a compromise was reached that satisfied almost no one: The flag was removed from the capitol building and was flown elsewhere on the capitol grounds.

3
Critical Reading: Getting Deeper into Arguments (p. 74)

This chapter may seem to hold our major discussion of arguing, for in it we talk about definitions, assumptions, induction, deduction, and evidence (and we do think it is essential reading for students), but we think that the upcoming three chapters — Writing an Analysis of an Argument, Developing an Argument of Your Own, and Using Sources — are equally important. Moreover, for especially strong students, Part Three will be valuable. It includes a summary of the Toulmin method for analyzing arguments and then offers further discussion of deduction and induction from a philosophic point of view. It also includes a survey of fallacies (Chapter 9), Carl R. Rogers's "Communication: Its Blocking and Its Facilitation" (Chapter 10), and Max Shulman's entertaining and informative "Love Is a Fallacy" (Chapter 9).

Nothing is particularly difficult in the chapter; most students should have no trouble with it.

Note: In our discussion of *analogy* we give Judith Thomson's example in which (during the course of an argument on abortion) she invites the reader to imagine that he or she wakes up and finds that a violinist whose body has not been functioning adequately has been hooked up to the reader's body. Thomson's essay originally appeared in *Philosophy and Public Affairs* 1.1 (Fall 1971): 47–66, and is reprinted in her book *Rights, Restitution, and Risk* (1986).

George F. Will

Being Green at Ben and Jerry's (p. 107)

We discuss this essay at length in the text, so there is no need for much additional comment here. We do want to say, however, that you may find it useful to discuss not only Will's essay but also our comments on it: We will not be surprised if students (and some instructors) markedly disagree with our observations. We think the piece is engaging, largely because it is so entertaining. In our view, what makes it at least moderately persuasive is not so much the statistics (though these do have some power) but the wit that pervades the essay and (we confess sheepishly) the hint of scatology in those sentences about the mound of manure and the bag of flatulence. As we say in the text, Will's final paragraph says nothing about oil or the Arctic National Wildlife Refuge, and thus it might seem ("'seem?' nay, '*is!*'") irrelevant, but it is entertaining and, alas, a bit of humor may outweigh a good deal of earnest logic. Having said this — and we continue to believe that much of Will's effectiveness here is in his wit — we want to say again that he does have other arrows in his quiver, such as statistics.

Apparently the problem of bovine burps and flatulence continues to be serious and will get worse because the production of beef and milk is expected to double in the next thirty years. It turns out that the most damaging aspect of the milk industry (from an environmental point of view) is not the burning of fossil fuels for transportation or packaging, but the emissions of cows — 200–400 pounds of methane a year per cow. (Methane is second only to carbon dioxide as a heat-trapping emission associated with global warming.) The *New York Times* ran an article ("Greening the Herds," June 5, 2009, p. A12) about some dairy farmers who are making an effort to reduce the methane output of cows. These farmers have adjusted the diet of the herds, diminishing the amount of corn and soy and increasing the amount of alfalfa and flaxseed. The results are said to be very encouraging, but the feed now costs more, so there is some uncertainty about whether this practice will be widely imitated.

Stanley Fish

When "Identity Politics" Is Rational (p. 114)

Consider the definition of "identity politics" that Fish offers in his first paragraph. If we follow the guidance we offer in *Current Issues* on the best way to write a definition, we get something slightly at variance with what he offers. Thus, we would say that one engages in identity politics if and only if one votes for or against someone or something because of his or her skin color, ethnicity, religion, gender, sexual orientation, or any other marker that leads one to affirm or deny what someone says independently of that person's reasons, ideas, or politics. A bit of a mouthful, to be sure, but it captures the essential idea of a good definition, namely, that it be neither too broad nor too narrow.

Fish identifies two different forms of identity politics in paragraph 9: The tribal version and the interest version. He argues that the tribal version has little to recommend it (there are, he admits, rare exceptions to this generalization). As for the interest version, he sees no alternative to it. If you can't rely on your considered judgments, on what can you rely? Fish devotes paragraph 10 to a good account of his answer to this implicit rhetorical question.

Gloria Jiménez (student essay)

Against the Odds, and against the Common Good (p. 118)

We think this is a first-rate essay—thoughtful and effectively written. The title has a nice parallel: The first sentence is informative and sensible, and the second sentence, though long, is shapely and easily readable. We think this long sentence is readable partly because it begins with a strong signal at the start (the transitional word *Still*), because it contains a parallel ("bringing a bit of excitement . . . bringing a vast amount of money"), and because it ends with an independent clause ("the states should not be in the business of urging people to gamble"). The second paragraph amplifies the point, again with a clear transition (*and*, plus a word—*urge*—picked up from the previous sentence). The organization of the entire essay also, in our view, contributes to its clarity: The opening states the thesis clearly; arguments in favor of lotteries are then presented lucidly (in fact, they are numbered); and we are told which are the less important arguments (discussed first and relatively briefly) and which are more important (discussed last and relatively fully).

Jiménez's idea of putting some emphasis on the slogans strikes us as especially interesting. Anyone can talk, rather generally, about the pros and cons of the issue, but she has shrewdly presented some highly engaging sentences ("There Is No Such Thing as a Losing Ticket") and then discusses their implications. She has also done a little research so that she can offer effective details rather than mere opinions.

In our first question in the text, we do raise what we think is a significant point. Jiménez neglects to discuss a common argument: If our state doesn't run a lottery, our citizens will just gamble in the lottery of some other state, so we will lose revenue and gain nothing. We don't know what Jiménez's response would be, and we are not sure even of our own, but we are inclined to think along these lines: (1) Although some people—those who live near the border of the state—will gamble in the lottery of another state, many will not; (2) if gambling is wrong, especially because the majority of people who gamble are the ones who can least afford it, the state should not sponsor it in any case, even if adjoining states do sponsor it.

Our second question in the text asks if readers find the essay a bit "too preachy." (This was the response of one of our students when we showed her the essay.) We don't see it that way. Admittedly, the essay is highly schematic and takes the high moral ground, but we think the tone is engaging ("an almost sure-fire way of getting nothing for something," "dreams of an easy buck," "It's against the odds," "an activity that is close to pickpocketing"). Our chief uneasiness—and we want to say again that we think this is a first-rate essay—is with the somewhat solemn introduction of the first person: "I now get to the point in my argument." "I say that this argument is delicate," "Let me end a bit indirectly." On the other hand, we do tell students that there is nothing wrong with using the first person and that obvious evasions ("It has been argued in this paper") usually are not the way to go. Perhaps Jiménez might have reduced the use of the first person slightly—for instance, by saying "This argument is delicate" rather than "I say that this argument is delicate"—but we want to reiterate that we think the essay is excellent.

Anna Lisa Raya (student essay)

It's Hard Enough Being Me (p. 121)

As we weigh in our headnote in the text, Anna Lisa Raya published this essay while she was an undergraduate. Your students may very well find that they can do just as well.

If you have looked at the questions that we pose in the text, you have probably guessed that we think Raya is a bit unclear about *why* she "had to define [herself] according to the broad term 'Latina'" (para. 2). The closest she comes, we think, to offering an explanation is when she says that in "El Sereno, I felt like I was part of a majority, whereas at the College I am a minority" (para. 2).

But even this sentence, we think, doesn't say *why* she "had" to define herself. Pressure from the majority? From the minority? Again, she says (para. 8), "To be fully Latina in college . . . I *must* know Spanish." But (again) *who* demands that she be "fully Latina"? As we read the essay, we are inclined to guess that the demand comes from Latinos and Latinas who emphasize their heritage and want Raya to celebrate it, but we don't think she is explicit on the point. She ends by asserting—briefly, in Spanish and in English—that she will be herself. We think this ending is rhetorically effective since it uses both languages.

There is, however, a further difficulty. Exactly what does it mean to be true to oneself? Of course, we can say that we don't steal (we are not that sort of person) or that we don't cheat (again, we are not that sort of person). But isn't "the self" really constructed out of relationships to others? We are loving (or neglectful) parents or children, we are serious (or frivolous) students, we are serious (or casual) about advancing in a career, and so on. We have many selves (parent, child, student, worker), and it is not always easy to know *which* self we must be true to.

Ronald Takaki

The Harmful Myth of Asian Superiority (p. 123)

In his first paragraph, Ronald Takaki introduces the term *model minority,* a term our fifth question asks students to consider. Takaki couples this term with being financially *successful,* and it's our impression that when Asian Americans are said to be a *model minority,* the term does usually imply financial success, conjuring up images of prosperous merchants, engineers, lawyers, and so on. But it's our impression, too, that the term also implies three other things: academic success (strong undergraduate work and graduate or professional work), family stability, and a low crime rate. Takaki is scarcely concerned with these matters, though in paragraph 7 he mentions "gangs" of Asian Americans (an indirect glance at crime), and in paragraphs 8–10 he touches on Asian American laborers—though it turns out, in paragraph 12, that some Korean greengrocers are highly educated.

19

Chiefly, Takaki is concerned with disproving the myth of financial success, and he wants to do this for two reasons: The myth is harmful to Asian Americans (because the rest of America mistakenly thinks this minority is doing very well), and it is harmful to African Americans (because the rest of America uses the Asian Americans as a stick to beat the African Americans). To demonstrate that the financial success of the Asian Americans is a myth, Takaki introduces statistics—and indeed it is partly because of his statistics and because of his comments on the possible deceptiveness of some figures that we include Takaki's essay in this chapter. As early as his fourth paragraph, he points out that statistics may be misleading. He doesn't cite specific figures, but he says (convincingly, we think) that it's not enough to point to "figures on the high earnings of Asian Americans relative to Caucasians." Why not? Because, he says, Asian Americans tend to be concentrated in places with a high cost of living (Hawaii, California, New York). This is a telling point. Again, even without giving specific figures, he sets the reader thinking, giving the reader cause to be skeptical about the figures.

The bulk of the essay (paras. 4–14) is devoted to the finances of Asian Americans, but surely Takaki's purpose in demythologizing Asian Americans is twofold: to say something that will help Asian Americans and to say something that will help African Americans. Although African Americans are mentioned in only paragraphs 3 and 15, their appearance is significant, especially because one of the two appearances is in the final paragraph.

This essay makes use of statistics and also calls attention to the misuse of statistics. You may want to invite students to examine Takaki's statistics. We wonder, for instance, exactly how significant it is that "twenty-five percent of the people in New York City's Chinatown lived below the poverty level in 1980" (para. 8). For the figure to be meaningful, one would probably have to know what percentage of the rest of America lived below the poverty level in 1980. And in any case, why cite a figure from 1980 in an essay written in 1990? That's a long time ago; surely there must be a more recent figure.

You may want to invite the class to bring in some statistics on this or another issue, perhaps gathered from an article in *Time* or *Newsweek* or from a textbook, and to discuss their possible limitations.

James Q. Wilson

Just Take Away Their Guns (p. 125)

Our question 1 goes to the heart of this essay: What sentence in James Wilson's essay best expresses his thesis? We suggest the answer is in this sentence in paragraph 4, when Wilson writes: "The most effective way to reduce illegal gun-carrying is to encourage the police to take guns away from people who carry them without a permit." Why do we focus on this sentence? First, it echoes the title of the essay ("Just Take Away Their Guns"). As we suggest elsewhere in the text, a good title will often signal the writer's main thesis. Second, the quoted sentence implies that the *goal* of gun control is to get guns out of the hands of those most likely to use them illegally, and that the *best means to this end* is authorizing the police to stop and frisk. Any careful reader of Wilson's essay will see that it is this second point and its ramifications that get most of Wilson's attention in the rest of the article.

Our second question is intended to get the student to look carefully at the research Wilson cites and to evaluate just what that research implies. One cannot infer that displaying or firing guns in self-defense actually prevented victimization in all, most, or even many of the million cases where guns were used for this purpose. Nor are we told in how many of these million cases the gun user was under a misapprehension (no robbery or other crime was in the offing) or in how many other cases children or others in the household caused accidental deaths or injuries by firearms. So on balance, we do not know anything from this research about the extent to which safety in the home was increased (or decreased) by the availability and use of firearms by ordinary citizens to prevent crimes. The only legitimate use of the statistics Wilson reports here is the very limited use he himself makes of them in the final sentence of his paragraph.

How might a defender of gun control respond to Wilson's barb quoted in our question 3? In his twelfth paragraph, Wilson thinks it is "politically absurd" for a citizen in crime-infested America to seek laws that "forbid or severely restrict the sale of guns." This is the preface to his remark we quote in the question.

Before proceeding with a reply, as the question asks, we draw the reader's attention to the extreme and perhaps misleading generalization in his remark quoted above. Are the restrictions and prohibitions to which he refers here confined only to handguns? Or does he think all restrictions on firearms of whatever sort are "politically absurd"? We do not think it is "politically absurd" for the government to forbid outright all sales of automatic weapons, dumdum bullets, antitank weapons, and the like except to authorized purchasers. Perhaps Wilson would agree. If so, he might have easily made that clear.

More to the point, we think the gun-control advocate might reply to Wilson's challenge along these lines:

First, no government can hope to shield its citizens against all criminal harms, even if by deterrence and incapacitation, not to mention moral education, government does keep crime from overwhelming us. (Ask the class: How many of you were the victims of crime earlier today? Earlier this week? This month? How many of you were *not* victims only because you used a weapon to frighten off a would-be assailant?) So it is unfair to describe our "government" as "having failed to protect" our persons and property. Its successes vastly outnumber its failures.

Second, society has to weigh *all* the consequences of our current virtually uncontrolled gun ownership practices against the alternative of varying degrees of restriction and prohibition. It is not enough just to look at the ways in which guns in the hands of the citizenry have deterred crime. Those successes have to be measured against the many costs that Wilson nowhere mentions (notably, suicides and other killings and accidents that would not have occurred except for the availability at all hours of loaded handguns).

In our question 5, we ask the reader to confront the racial impact of Wilson's proposal, which he candidly mentions. We agree with his prediction: Widespread use of stop-and-frisk practices aimed at removing guns from those without permits to possess them will in practice do exactly what he says. Is this a fatal objection to his proposal? Yes, if you think that young black males have enough problems already without the added burden of heightened attention from the police, or that stop-and-frisk practices will lead mainly to more shoot-outs with police on the mean streets of urban America. No, if you think that black neighborhoods are far more likely to be victimized by black offenders than are white neighborhoods, that the best way to protect the bulk of the black population is to get illegal guns out of the hands of would-be black offenders, and that the best way to do this is to encourage adoption of Wilson's stop-and-frisk proposal.

Kayla Webley

Is Forgiving Student Loan Debt a Good Idea? (p. 129)

Our first question in the book asks why, in her second paragraph, Webley makes the point that reading some of the stories retold on the Student Debt site is a heartrending experience. The answer, of course—at least from the point of view of someone writing an argument—is that (to get directly to the point) this author will soon reject the views expressed by the authors of those stories; so at the outset, she wants to express her sympathy, to establish an engaging *ethos* lest she later seem coldhearted. And indeed, at the end of her essay, she again expresses sympathy with Robert Applebaum's idea, though she characterizes it as "wildly unfeasible."

In short, she begins and ends by indicating that her heart is in the right place—but the body of the essay severely criticizes Applebaum's idea. First, she quotes Justin Wolfers's devastating critique (we print it on p. 469). Then she goes on to assert that, in fact, most indebted students *can* repay the loans (paras. 6–7), and in paragraph 8 she talks about alternatives for those who cannot repay the loans. In 9 she raises the issue of fairness: Why should taxpayers foot the bill for college graduates?

In short, she sees no merit in Applebaum's idea—except (and here we get to Webley's final paragraph) that it *is* an idea, and ideas are what is wanted. Thus, although she shreds Applebaum in the body of the essay, she expresses sympathy for debtors at the beginning, and at the end she gives credit to Applebaum for at least offering an idea, even if it is "wildly unfeasible."

The essay ends in a time-tested way by putting the ball in the reader's court: "[W]hat's your solution?" We have often heard our colleagues grumpily say that they do not want their students to use formulas, but in fact real writers—Webley writes for *Time* magazine— often *do* use formulas, time-tested patterns and devices. The important point is that within the formulaic structure, they write carefully, thoughtfully, engagingly.

Later in the book, in Chapter 14, we offer two additional essays on student indebtedness.

Alfred Edmond Jr.

Why Asking for a Job Applicant's Facebook Password Is Fair Game (p. 132)

We were astounded to learn that some employers ask job candidates for their passwords to Facebook, and that this request is legal. But, well, lots of things astound us today. (Reminder: It is *not* legal for a potential employer to inquire about age, race or ethnicity, sex [gender], marital status, pregnancy, religion, or disability.)

Given the fact that (in our view) Edmond is taking an outrageous position, we think he does a pretty good job of defending it. First of all, in his second paragraph he indicates that in other circumstances he would take a different position. Then, with a clear transition at the beginning of his fourth paragraph ("That said, my response"), he begins a defense of his earlier position, and we think he gives a good example, in the fifth paragraph, when he cites "the child care industry." The trouble, from our point of view, is that we cannot think of any other example that is equally forceful. Working in a facility with mentally impaired persons might come close.

The problem, as we see it, is that some (many?) people think they are performing a helpful social service when they reveal highly personal information. Thus, they may think they are helping to break down harmful stereotypes, helping to reduce prejudices, when they reveal to certain persons that, for instance, they are gay or deeply depressed or addicted to certain medicines. In our view, Edmond gives sound advice when he says, "Don't think business vs. personal. Think public vs. private. And if something is truly private, do not share it on social media out of a misplaced faith in the expectation of privacy."

These words of Edmond make sense to us, but we continue to doubt that sense can be made out of his title, beyond perhaps the child care industry.

Addendum: Should Colleges Monitor the Posts and Tweets of Athletes?

The issue is different, of course, but a discussion of Edmond's essay can easily get into related issues of what is and what is not acceptable in posts and tweets. Here we want to summarize a discussion that we came across in *Time*, October 22, 2012, pages 56–57.

North Carolina (UNC) defensive tackle Marvin Austin in 2011 posted something about partying that led the National Collegiate Athletic Association (NCAA) to investigate, and it found that he had received cash gifts. Other athletes on the team also had broken rules, and the NCAA ultimately banned UNC's football team from the 2012 postseason and reduced its allotment of football scholarships for the next three years.

Because some colleges receive a great deal of money from their football program, they of course worry that athletes may inflict damage on the program. Therefore some of these colleges prohibit the athletes from using Twitter. Some colleges permit the use of Twitter but require the athletes (in the words of Utah State University) to "grant full remission for the university and other third-party monitors to gain access to the 'friends only,' 'private,' and similarly designated areas." Such a policy even requires a student athlete to sign a waiver: "To the extent that any federal, state, or local law prohibits the Athletic Department from accessing my social networking accounts, I hereby waive any and all such rights and protections." As *Time* puts it, the university thus requires the student to license the university to ignore the law. On the other hand, some states have offered protection to the students. *Time* reports that California has a law forbidding colleges to "require or request" that a student or prospective student "divulge any personal social media information."

Sherry Turkle

The Flight from Conversation (p. 136)

Turkle's essay is one of many essays we have encountered that express alarm at the alleged harmful effects of social media. There are, of course, counterviews, and we want to begin this brief discussion by mentioning Adam Gopnik's entertaining survey of books on the topic, "How the Internet Gets Inside Us," *New Yorker,* February 14, 2011. Gopnik divides the commentaries into three groups:

> Call them the Never-Betters, the Better-Nevers, and the Ever-Wasers. The Never-Betters believe that we're on the brink of a new utopia, where information will be free and democratic, news will be made from the bottom up, love will reign, and cookies will bake themselves. The Better-Nevers think that we would have been better off if the whole thing had never happened, that the world that is coming to an end is superior to the one that is taking its place, and that, at a minimum, books and magazines create private space for minds in ways that twenty-second bursts of information don't. The Ever-Wasers insist that at any moment in modernity something like this is going on, and that a new way of organizing data and connecting users is always thrilling to some and chilling to others—that something like this is going on is exactly what makes it a modern moment.

Gopnik amusingly illustrates his categories thus:

> When the electric toaster was invented, there were, no doubt, books that said that the toaster would open up horizons for breakfast undreamed of in the days of burning bread over an open flame; books that told you that the toaster would bring an end to the days of creative breakfast, since our children, growing up with uniformly sliced bread, made to fit a single opening, would never know what a loaf of their own was like; and books that told you that sometimes the toaster would make breakfast better and sometimes it would make breakfast worse, and that the cost for finding this out would be the price of the book you'd just bought.

Probably most of us sometimes feel one way, sometimes another way, and sometimes a third way—in Gopknik's terms, Never-Better, Better-Never, and Ever-Waser—which is to say that we think there is something important here, and yet . . . . Take Turkle's eighth paragraph, in which she comments on today's young people in a library, together but each in his or her own bubble. Yes, thinks the Ever-Waser, just like when people in olden decades sat in a library reading books, together but each in his or her own bubble.

One other point: When we first read Turkle's essay, we were briefly puzzled by her reference in paragraph 13 to "the word," and we had to reread a few sentences. She is in fact talking about the word *conversation,* ultimately derived from the Latin verb *convertere,* "to turn around." You may want to ask students to offer conjectures about other words with *vers* in them, for instance, *averse, adversary, diverse, obverse, reverse.*

Note: Chapter 23 offers a casebook (five essays) on Facebook.

4
Visual Rhetoric: Images as Arguments (p. 141)

Dorothea Lange

Migrant Mother (photographs) (p. 167)

We think most students will agree that the more tightly framed image is more moving. The other is interesting, but the lamp in the lower left, the lean-to, the landscape at the right, and the faces of the two children—especially the appealing face of the child resting her chin on the mother's shoulder—provide distractions. In the famous image, which is more symmetrical than the other and almost surely puts us in mind of traditional paintings of the Madonna and child, the two faceless children have turned to the mother for comfort. Further, the mother's hand touches her chin, somewhat suggesting the pose of Rodin's *The Thinker;* but whereas Rodin's muscular man is an image of strength—mental as well as physical—Lange's migrant mother is an image of powerlessness. We can admire her courage, and we know that her children love her because they turn to her for comfort, but we also know that however hard she thinks, she is not going to solve her problem.

A few further points about the image: In 1958, one Florence Thompson (1903–1983), a woman of Cherokee heritage, revealed that she was the subject of the photograph. In 1936, when the photograph was taken, Thompson was the mother of eight childen, two of whom were illegitimate. (She later had three children by a man to whom she was not married.) Question: What might the effect of the photo be if it showed eight children rather than three? Our own view—purely a conjecture, of course, since Lange did not take such a photograph—is that an image showing an impoverished woman with eight children might provoke some thoughts that she was irresponsible. In any case, we find it hard to imagine that a photograph showing Thompson with eight children could have the dignity and the power that the famous image does have.

Among the useful books on Lange are Linda Gordon's *Dorothea Lange: A Life Beyond Limits* (2009) and Anne Whiston Spirn's *Daring to Look: Dorothea Lange's Photographs and Reports from the Field* (2009).

Anonymous

Our Homes Are in Danger Now! (poster) (p. 168)

We think it is interesting that although Hitler is shown, a specific Japanese person (Emperor Hirohito or General and later Prime Minister Tojo) is not shown. Apparently during World War II, no single Japanese face was sufficiently familiar to American viewers to stand for Japanese aggression. Perhaps behind this failure to identify an individual Japanese is the common Western stereotype that "they all look alike."

Why does Hitler have a gun and the Japanese a knife? There is no need to comment on the gun, but probably the knife suggests the racist idea that Asians are more primitive than Caucasians.

The globe that Hitler and the Japanese are grabbing shows the United States, and the text ("OUR HOMES ARE IN DANGER <u>NOW</u>!") is given visual form by little houses on the map. Speaking of little houses, why is the image of the American response—a bomber and a tank, encircled by the words "*OUR JOB* KEEP 'EM FIRING"—so small? Presumably to emphasize our vulnerability. We Americans are the little kids on the block, menaced by hulking bullies.

James Montgomery Flagg

I Want YOU (poster) (p. 169)

We are concerned here less with the medium than with the message. Our concern with the medium is with body language initiated on Flagg's poster. The assertive pointing scarcely needs explanation, but most students will be less aware of the implication of the full-face view, versus, say, a three-quarter view, or a profile. Facial expression is more conspicuous in a front view than in a profile. A profile tends to be expressionless, immutable (that is why it is commonly used on coins and medals), but a front view can more obviously catch the emotion of a moment. Moreover, a front view confronts the spectator, looks into the spectator's space, and suggests an all-seeing and inescapable presence. Flagg's Uncle Sam unreservedly reveals his emotions, dominates us, stares us down. Although the written message ("I want YOU for U.S. Army") is, when you think about it, directed only to poten-tial recruits, Uncle Sam's assertive finger and his penetrating eyes are directed to every viewer; the effect is to make *all* passersby feel guilty, so that they will make additional efforts on behalf of their country.

Two notes: (1) The origin of Uncle Sam is obscure, but he seems to have come into being during the War of 1812. It is said that the name derives from "Uncle" Sam Wilson, an inspector of army supplies. The initials "U.S." (to indicate government property) were stamped on army barrels and crates, but they apparently were taken to stand for "Uncle Sam." The iconography was fixed by the latter part of the nineteenth century; Uncle Sam was tall and lean with white hair and chin whiskers, tall hat with stars and stripes, swallowtail coat, vest, and striped pants. He can be kindly in a gruff way, but for the most part, despite the clownish costume, he is stern and energetic. (2) Flagg eliminated the usual stripes from the hat, and by eliminating the lower half of the body, with its striped pants, he made the figure less extravagant. He modeled the face on his own but took the composition from a British poster by Alfred Leete, which showed the head of Lord Kitchener, the Recruiting General, and a foreshortened hand emerging from a cuff, above the legend "Your Country Needs YOU." Leete's poster is reproduced in John Barnicoat's *A Concise History of Posters* (1969, p. 226), and in Harold F. Henderson's *The Poster* (1968, p. 75). For German and Italian versions of similarly gesturing figures, see Max Gallo's *The Poster in History* (1974, pp. 166–67). See also Robert Phillipe's *Political Graphics* (1982), not only for the illustrations but also for the valuable text. For anony-mous parodies of Flagg's poster, produced to oppose the Vietnam War, as well as for a large, color reproduction of Flagg's poster itself, see *Arms and the Artist* (1977), selected by Denis Thomas: No. 94 shows a bandaged Uncle Sam, not pointing vigorously, but weakly extending a hand as if in need of support, with the legend, in Flagg's lettering, "I Want OUT"; no. 96 reproduces Flagg's format, but with Uncle Sam as a skeleton. We have heard of (but not seen) a more affectionate parody, suitable for hanging in a child's room: Uncle Sam, pointing the usual accusatory finger, stares out above the legend, "I Want YOU to Clean Up Your Room."

A comment toward a suggestion for writing: There is yet another aspect to Flagg's message. How do we know the approximate date? That is, what in the *style* lets us know that this poster is from World War I? After all, the hairstyle and the costume of the figure are not a giveaway, as they would be in most old posters and advertisements, and as they are in Leete's picture of Kitchener. It might be interesting to ask a class what approximate date they would give to Flagg's poster, and why. (The poster was created in 1917. It was used again in World War II, but that is irrelevant.) Perhaps the resulting discussion (or essays) will help students understand something of what instructors mean by "style." Our own feeling is that the lettering, indebted to hand-painted signs of the late nineteenth century, clearly belongs to the early part of the twentieth century, and the realistic drawing is characteristic of posters for World War I rather than for World War II. The posters of World War II tended to show, in a very simple way, the influence of cubism and of abstract art; figures, if they were not photographs or close copies of photographs, tended to be flat and even geometric. A face might be a mere plane with no shading, or it might have a strongly demarked shadow, giving it at most only two planes. Often the designs give the effect of a collage or montage, thus further moving away from the tradition of illusionistic drawing.

Nora Ephron

The Boston Photographs (p. 170)

Many people get agitated when images that they take to be pornographic are published in magazines or are hung on museum walls. Your students know this, but they may not know that until quite recently, many people thought that images of violence should not be shown. Respectable newspapers did not show the blood-spattered corpses of gangland killings. That sort of image was left to the tabloids. The chief exceptions were photographs of persons killed in war, but even these were acceptable only if the dead seemed intact and asleep. Severed limbs, decapitated bodies, and agonized faces were not tolerated. But exactly why were they not tolerated?

"All the news that's fit to print" was and still is the slogan of the *New York Times*. And just as some news stories were judged unprintable—let's say stories about prostitution and abortion—so were some images. Probably the idea behind this informal code was that such stories and images pander to a taste that ought not to be nourished. We are reminded of Thomas Babington Macaulay's comment on bearbaiting: "The Puritan hated bear-baiting not because it gave pain to the bear, but because it gave pleasure to the spectators." An astute remark, not merely a wisecrack at the expense of Puritans. Why, indeed, do we in the United States prohibit cockfighting in all but two states? Surely not merely because a few birds suffer for relatively brief periods—a tiny number, when compared with the enormous numbers of birds that suffer for months until they have grown large enough to be slaughtered for food. Presumably forty-eight states prohibit cockfighting because their citizens think—rightly—that spectators ought not to take pleasure in the sight of birds maiming each other. The idea is as old as Plato: Our base appetites ought not to be nourished.

To get back to certain kinds of pictures of violence, the idea behind censoring them was that these images appeal to impulses that ought to be suppressed, not nourished. It is pretty hard for anyone today to favor censorship, but when you look at the pictures in James Allen et al., *Without Sanctuary: Lynching Photography in America* (2000), and you learn that some of these horrifying images of burned and castrated bodies were printed as picture postcards and inscribed with playful comments (e.g., "This is the barbecue we had last night"), well, one understands what Plato and the Puritans were getting at.

In our text, the most horrifying image is not reproduced in Ephron's essay but is Huynh Cong (Nick) Ut's photograph on page 146, "The Terror of War" (1972). This picture, which was widely printed in newspapers, is said to have played an enormous role in turning American public opinion against the war in Vietnam. (For details, see Denise Chong's *The Girl in the Picture: The Story of Kim Phuc, the Photograph, and the Vietnam War* [2000].) Conceivably, some people take pleasure in the horror it depicts, but surely its publication was justified by its message: "What is going on over there is unbelievably horrifying." On June 8, 1972, American-backed South Vietnamese pilots trying to kill Viet Cong troops dropped napalm canisters near a pagoda where villagers had taken refuge. The girl in the center of the picture had torn off her clothing in an effort to free herself from the searing napalm jelly. A viewer looks with horror at the picture, but—and we say this with much unease—part of our interest in the photograph probably is aesthetic. In its terrifying way, it is a beautiful photograph, admirably composed, the sort of composition that

Henri Cartier-Bresson called "the decisive moment," the moment when the flux of the world suddenly takes shape and seems to say something. The four figures nearest to the camera run forward, but they take us back relentlessly. The boy at the extreme left shows his agony in his wide-open mouth and his slightly contorted posture; the naked girl in the center, vulnerable in her nudity, is by virtue of her outstretched arms in a posture that reminds a viewer of the crucified Jesus; the small boy toward the right (like the smaller boy who is the second figure from the left) is apparently too young to understand the horror, but the girl who holds his hand reveals her terror in her face. And behind them, apparently walking rather than running, apparently a relentless and unemotional force (we can see no expression on their faces) pushing these victims forward, are four soldiers (one is almost totally hidden by the girl at the right). And still further back, behind the soldiers, is a flat backdrop of the smoking village.

Is this photo merely an image of a most regrettable incident—like, say, a fire in Boston that kills a woman who falls from an unstable fire escape? Or does it have meaning? And, if so, what is its meaning? Ephron doesn't talk about this image, but she does make a relevant point in her next-to-last photograph, when she talks about car wrecks and says that newspapers will print images of wrecked cars but not of dead bodies: "But the significance of fatal automobile accidents is not that a great deal of steel is twisted but that people die. Why not show it?" And in her final paragraph she introduces an aesthetic element when she says, of the Boston photographs, "They deserve to be printed because they are great pictures, breathtaking pictures of something that happened. That they disturb readers is exactly as it should be: that's why photojournalism is often more powerful than written journalism."

In short, although doubtless there are some people who enjoy the violence depicted in some images, images of the sort that Ephron is talking about (photos by Stanley Forman) and images like Ut's rivet our attention because—one can hardly dare to say it—the horror is transformed by the artistry. This is *not* to say that the horror is diminished. Far from it; the horror is made memorable, enduring, and perhaps even eternal.

Part Two

CRITICAL WRITING

5
Writing an Analysis of an Argument (p. 179)

Although we offer incidental comments about *writing* in Chapters 2 and 3—with comments on audience, tone, organization, and so on—this chapter and Chapter 6 contain our primary discussions of writing.

In Chapter 10, we reprint Carl R. Rogers's "Communication: Its Blocking and Its Facilitation," an essay that has interested many teachers of rhetoric because of its emphasis on psychological aspects of persuasion. The essay is fairly short and easy, and because it is mainly about a writer's interaction with an audience, it may well be assigned in conjunction with this chapter.

If you want to give a writing assignment *not* based on a reading assignment, this suggestion may be useful:

Write a letter (150–300 words) to the editor of a newspaper, responding to an editorial or to a published letter. Hand in the material you are responding to, along with your essay.

Nicholas D. Kristof

For Environmental Balance, Pick Up a Rifle (p. 186)

The student essay by Betsy Swinton, "Tracking Kristof," provides what we think is a thorough discussion of Kristof's essay. We in turn discuss Swinton's analysis, so we won't rehash the issue any further here.

Jeff Jacoby

Bring Back Flogging (p. 196)

Our society takes pretty much for granted that punishment for crimes will take the form of imprisonment, except for juveniles and first offenders, who may be offered probation instead. But the prison (as distinct from the jail, traditionally used only to detain accused persons prior to trial) is a relatively new invention in England and the United States, dating only from the end of the eighteenth century (see Michel Foucault, *Discipline and Punish: The Birth of the Prison* [1977], and Michael Ignatieff, *A Just Measure of Pain: The Penitentiary in the Industrial Revolution, 1750–1850* [1978]). Corporal punishments—the stocks, flogging, branding, mutilation, and hanging—are as old as recorded history, and some of these modes of punishment remain in use today, for example, in Saudi Arabia. Except for the death penalty, all such practices have been abandoned in the United States, and probably few would survive constitutional challenge were a legislature foolish enough to reintroduce them.

The case of flogging (or whipping) is different. Whipping survived in Delaware until 1952; in 1989, a bill was filed in the Delaware legislature to bring back the whipping post (see *New York Times*, January 29, 1989), but it failed to pass. It may come as a surprise to learn that the U.S. Supreme Court has yet to rule on the constitutionality of this classic mode of punishment. And for reasons Jeff Jacoby offers in his essay—inexpensiveness, brevity of duration, humiliation of offenders, and above all, physical pain—it retains a certain attractiveness in some quarters. Not until 1983, however, in the book *Just and Painful: A Case for the Corporal Punishment of Criminals* by criminologist Graeme Newman, did anyone in recent years seriously defend flogging. (Newman proposed electric shocks, carefully calibrated to suit the crime of the offender, followed by whipping if the offender recidivates, and incarceration only after repeated convictions for violent crimes.)

Our question 3 goes to the heart of the issue, as Jacoby realizes: Is it true that flogging (in whatever form and degree) is more degrading or brutal than imprisonment, and on that ground—entirely apart from any other consideration—ought to be abolished? Jacoby raises the issue and disposes of it with a rhetorical question ("where is it written, . . .?" para. 12). Flogging always brings to mind scenes of merciless beating; but such brutality is not necessary. It also often has overtones of sadistic pleasure aroused by the sight of naked flesh being turned to a bloody pulp; but, again, that is not necessary. Some opponents of flogging as punishment (including the authors of this manual) are repelled by the whole idea and cannot imagine ourselves inflicting such punishment on anyone, no matter what the crime, or of encouraging others to do it for us. But is this mere sentimentality, or is detesting such a practice a good enough reason for opposing it? Perhaps one can argue that when the abuses of imprisonment that Jacoby rightly reminds us of are compared with the abuses of flogging that Jacoby ignores, it is far from clear whether a reasonable and humane person ought to join him in preferring flogging.

Gerard Jones

Violent Media Is Good for Kids (p. 199)

First, we must confess that Jones's title irritates us: Pedants that we are, we wince when we see or hear *media* (from the Latin plural of *medium*) used as a singular noun. Still, we do understand that this usage is widely accepted, so we will grit our teeth and say only that we think "media is" sounds dreadful.

Jones's essay is not at all the sort of thing that most instructors want their students to write—it is essentially a personal essay—but it is devoted to a topic that has received a good deal of academic attention: the effect of imaginary violence on human beings. Probably the earliest extant major treatment of the issue in Western writing is Plato's denunciation of the poets in *The Republic*. The argument comes down to the idea that tragic and epic poets nourish the passions of their auditors, in other words stimulate human passions and therefore diminish human rationality. An almost comic version of this position appears in Boswell's *Life of Johnson*, where Boswell reports (September 23, 1777) a conversation with Johnson on the topic of the effect of music. Johnson told Boswell that music had little effect on him, and Boswell then reports his own responses to the power of music:

> I told him that [music] affected me to such a degree as often to agitate my nerves painfully, producing in my mind alternate sensations of pathetic dejection so that I was ready to shed tears, and of daring resolution, so that I was inclined to rush into the thickest part of the battle. "Sir," said he, "I should never hear it, if it made me such a fool."

Plenty of people agree that the arts stimulate passion, and that this is a Bad Thing. A common argument against pornography is that it stimulates unwholesome passions, and indeed plenty of sex offenders have said that they got their ideas (e.g., for bizarre forms of assault and murder) from films or books. On the other hand, one of the arguments offered in defense of pornography is that it may serve as a harmless release: The man who might otherwise rape a woman allegedly finds a release in a pornographic DVD.

The most famous defense of the depiction of antisocial emotions in literature is Aristotle's reply to Plato in the *Poetics*. Aristotle is talking about tragic drama in verse, but if what he says is true, it probably applies equally well to prose fiction. He says that when

29

we perceive the artistic presentation of violence, we experience a *catharsis*. The trouble is, there is much argument about the exact meaning of *catharsis*. The basic Greek sense of the term is "purgation," in the medical sense—a laxative that purges the bowels. If something close to this is Aristotle's meaning, the idea is that we get rid of our emotions by experiencing them and discharging them harmlessly in the theater. It apparently is sort of like smashing a dish when one is angry; but do people really do this sort of thing, and if they do, does it work? That is, do the arts offer a sort of laxative for the emotions? We are back to the idea that porno allows the reader/viewer to get rid of unwholesome passions in a harmless way. But many scholars say that "purification" (or "cleansing") rather than "purgation" (or "discharge") is what Aristotle meant. Things get complicated here, but one version of this interpretation holds that by purification, Aristotle means that we see the *proper* objects of such emotions as pity and terror. For instance, when we witness a production of *King Lear*, we see an action that indeed evokes pity and terror, and we thus learn which kinds of actions should be pitied, and which kinds of actions are terrifying.

Some decades ago, Bruno Bettelheim, in *The Uses of Enchantment* (1976), argued that fairy tales that are filled with violence serve a wholesome purpose. In the story of "Hansel and Gretel," for example, there is a wicked witch, and the story ends with the children pushing the witch into an oven. Plenty of violence there. But, Bettelheim said, that's not bad. For one thing, he argued, such stories let children know that there are monstrous people in the world. Not everyone is a loving mother or father. Second, Bettelheim claimed, these stories serve to assure children that *their own* savage impulses are not unique, not aberrations, but are part of what all people have. That is, these stories serve the useful purpose of introducing children to the dark side of life. According to Bettelheim, children need to see that there are such impulses and need to learn how to handle them so that they may act maturely.

If you reread Jones's essay, you will hear plenty of Bettelheim. In the first paragraph Jones tells us that his parents insulated him from the real world of violence and that he "suffocated [his] deepest fears and desires under a nice-boy persona." In the fourth paragraph he tells us that he was "freed" by the image of the Hulk, who was an image of his own "stifled rage and buried desire for power." Jones claims to have seen something of his own history repeated in the life of his son. In the eleventh paragraph Jones says:

> Pretending to have superhuman powers helps children conquer the feelings of powerlessness that inevitably come with being so young and small.

We have not taught this essay, but we think that one good way to handle it is to ask students if parts or all of it rings true to their experience. They might then be asked to write an analysis of violence in media (or in one medium), drawing on their own experience but using a rather more academic style than Jones uses.

Justin Cronin

Confessions of a Liberal Gun Owner (p. 203)

We address, in sequence, the topics that we set forth in the book.

1. Cronin's title—rather than our imagined title of "Confessions of a Texas Gun Owner"—offers an engaging surprise. Gun owners in Texas presumably are not a rare species, but liberal gun owners are. In short, Cronin's title contains a hook, something that snares the reader's attention, whereas our invented alternative invites the response of "Ho hum, so what's new?"

2. Why so much autobiography? Because Cronin, in effect, is offering an essay based chiefly on one big—indeed, life-changing—experience, rather than an essay based largely on thinking analytically while sitting at desk, the sort of argumentative essay that would include statements such as "The three principle arguments in

favor of. . . ," and "On the other hand, we can counter the first of these arguments by offering two objections. . . ," and so forth.

3. Our view (based exclusively on our reading of the essay) is that Cronin is a very engaging guy, a good teacher, and a good colleague. He is earnest, clear, respectful of other ideas, and so on.

4. What *arguments* does he offer? Here, alas, we get uneasy. He does a good job of telling us how he came to feel the way he feels—but does he convince his readers that his position is sound? Because he does not much concern himself with setting forth and refuting opposing views, or offering anything in the way of statistics, we think that the skeptical reader probably remains skeptical. And there is a further problem: The life-changing experience that he reports (his decision to arm himself) is based on something that did *not* happen: He assures us (para. 11) that "chaos" would have occurred if the storm had hit Houston. But the storm did not hit Houston, and Cronin therefore cannot point to chaos—and the consequent need for a gun. Doubtless he could have called attention to other cities that have experienced looting, and these instances might have provided support for the argument that law-abiding folks need guns to protect their families—but he does not provide such evidence (e.g., statistics about looting after the flood in New Orleans), and we think this omission weakens his essay.

5. To this question (What would you say to a reader who told you that he or she didn't quite get Cronin's essay?) we offer no response—because, as we have just indicated, we are puzzled by Cronin's strategy of building an argument largely on something that did not happen. We will be interested in the responses of students.

6. Cronin in paragraph 13 sets forth his credentials as a liberal (he favors gun regulation, and he "loathes" the NRA), in effect reaffirming the strategy of his title and of his first paragraph. Still, it would have been interesting (and we think it would have been more convincing) if he had indicated exactly what sort of regulation he favors.

7. The comment that a short paragraph is usually an *underdeveloped* paragraph is true for analytic paragraphs (i.e., for most paragraphs in most argumentative essays) but of course is not true for some other kinds of paragraphs, and certainly not for all paragraphs in an essay that is largely biographical, as here, where Cronin reports the responses of a gun instructor and of his sixteen-year-old daughter. The paragraphs are especially effective partly *because* they are so short; they are packed with dynamite.

Peter Singer

Animal Liberation (p. 207)

This essay is an earlier version of text that became the opening chapter of Peter Singer's remarkably influential *Animal Liberation: A New Ethics for Our Treatment of Animals* (1975). In his book, Singer elaborates all his basic ideas, and especially "speciesism" (para. 18), to which he devotes a whole chapter.

Speciesism is the arbitrary favorable preference for members of our own species, and its logical consequence is an equally arbitrary but indifferent or hostile attitude toward lower species. Whether the analogy to racism, sexism, and other *-isms* is as instructive as Singer implies is another matter. In any case, he argues (para. 19) that the "case for Animal Liberation" does not depend on the analogy.

What, then, is animal liberation? Singer never says in so many words (see para. 3), but it amounts to, or at least can be stated as, a series of dos and don'ts: Don't kill animals to eat their flesh or to clothe your body, don't experiment on animals to save human lives or to reduce human misery, don't remove animals from their natural habitat. In short, don't treat animals as you would not like to be treated yourself.

Singer's opening paragraph is a model for the use of analogy to gain the high ground right from the start. Each of his readers will be able to identify with one or another of the groups he mentions that has been discriminated against in the past and so is immediately but unwittingly vulnerable to the "expansion of our moral horizons" about to unfold.

Singer worries (para. 12; our question 3) whether having intentions is necessarily, albeit mysteriously, connected with having the capacity to use language. We doubt that it is, and he does, too. Surely anyone who spends time with dogs and cats readily ascribes intentions to them ("He's trying to catch the stick when you throw it," "She's waiting to pounce on the mouse as soon as it moves"), and this use of intentional thinking is no more anthropomorphic than is ascribing intentions to other people. To insist that the latter is intelligible but the former isn't, because other people can speak a language whereas animals can't, pretty obviously begs the question. To insist that no creature can have an intention unless it can state what its intentions are is far too broad a thesis to defend; it would entail insisting that many human creatures do not have intentions, or act intentionally, when we believe they do. And so even if animals can't use language, because they lack the capacity, they may yet have minds enough to warrant a concern about how we intentionally treat them.

On what grounds does Singer base drawing the line where he does to demark the creatures that deserve our concern from those that don't? Why not draw the line elsewhere, particularly at the point that divides the living from the nonliving (not dead but inorganic or inert)? It wouldn't be at all satisfactory for Singer to answer: "Because I talk about creatures that can feel, and I don't about those that can't," although this reading seems to be true. But this can't be his answer because he does not want his argument to turn on who cares about what; he knows that most of us simply do not and will not easily come to care about animal welfare. A better line for him to take would be to refer to the *interests* of creatures and to the *equality* of their interests (para. 6), on the ground that only creatures with a capacity to suffer have interests, the first and foremost of which is to diminish their own suffering, pain, and discomfort. But on closer inspection, is it not still true that *all living* things have interests? Surely, a dogwood tree in the front yard has an interest in air, water, sunlight, and space to grow, even if it feels no pain when it is denied these things or when its leaves are plucked or—heaven forfend!—its branches slashed. To reason in this manner is to tie the concept of having an interest in something to the concept of something being good for a thing (water is surely good for a plant). But this is not what Singer does; rather, he ties a creature's interests to what it can feel. (See how he handles the case of the year-old infant in para. 15.)

When one goes in the other direction, as some have (for example, Christopher Stone, in *Should Trees Have Standing?* [1988]), a whole environmental ethic begins to unfold, but with alarming consequences, for even all but the most scrupulous vegetarian will neglect and even ruthlessly violate the interests of other living entities.

If we enlarge our moral community to include plants as well as animals—because all living entities have interests and because one interest is as good as another "from the point of view of the universe" (the criterion proposed by the utilitarian Henry Sidgwick, which Singer invokes in his *Animal Liberation*)—what will our moral principles permit us to eat? Not much, perhaps only unfruitful food, such as some of the surfeit of seeds and nuts produced by plants, and dead flesh, perhaps including even human flesh (our question 10). Killing to eat may be entirely ruled out, but eating what is dead isn't unless one appeals to some other moral principles besides the utilitarian notions Singer relies on.

This discussion can be put into an argument of this form: Because we have to eat to live, either we eat things that have interests or we don't. If we do, then we violate the equal interests of other creatures and thus act immorally. If we don't, then we can't kill living plants to eat them, any more than we can kill living animals to eat them. Instead, our survival depends on eating dropped fruit and seeds and carrion. Some readers will regard this argument as a reductio ad absurdum of Singer's position. Others will argue that it shows how difficult it is to formulate moral principles that we can really live by consistently and self-consciously.

Although persons who in journals debate with Singer often say that he subscribes to "animal rights," Singer has repeatedly denied that he believes that animals have "rights." Setting forth his disagreement with Tom Regan's *The Case for Animal Rights* (1983), Singer discusses the point at some length in the *New York Review of Books* (January 17, 1985, pp. 46–52). In a letter in the issue of April 25, 1985 (p. 57), he reaffirms his point. Singer explains that his view is utilitarian; he grants that conceivably there would be circumstances in which an experiment on an animal stands to reduce human suffering so much that it would be permissible to carry it out even if it involved some harm to the animal. (This would be true, he says in his letter of April 25, 1985, even if the animal were a human being.) In this letter he explains that, as a utilitarian, he advocates stopping animal experiments because

1. The suffering of an immense number of animals would be spared,

2. "The benefits lost would be uncertain," and

3. "The incentive thus provided for the speedy development of alternative methods of conducting research [would be] the most powerful imaginable."

Singer's essay, as we say in our headnote in the text, was first published in 1973 in the *New York Review of Books*. In the issue of May 15, 2003, Singer published, again in the *New York Review of Books*, "Animal Liberation at Thirty," a review of the state of the argument. His new essay makes special mention of the following books: Roger Scruton, *Animal Rights and Wrongs* (London: Metro, 1998); Paola Cavalieri, *The Animal Question: Why Non-human Animals Deserve Human Rights* (Oxford: Oxford University Press, 2001); David DeGrazia, *Taking Animals Seriously: Mental Life and Moral Status* (Cambridge: Cambridge University Press, 1996); Matthew Scully, *Dominion: The Power of Man, Suffering of Animals, and the Call to Mercy* (New York: St. Martin's, 2002).

We considered using the new piece instead of the first piece, but we finally decided that the first piece is much better for our use (the basic argument is set forward with few distractions), whereas in the recent piece Singer tries to take account of numerous questions and developments. But anyone — teacher or student — doing further work on this topic will want to consult the new essay.

Jonathan Swift

A Modest Proposal (p. 220)

Our discussion (p. 129) in these notes of Judy Brady's "I Want a Wife" offers a few general comments on satire, some of which are relevant to Jonathan Swift.

Unlike Brady's essay, where the title in conjunction with the author's name immediately alerts the reader that the essay cannot be taken straight, Swift's essay does not provide an obvious clue right away. In fact, some students don't perceive the irony until it is pointed out to them. Such imperceptiveness is entirely understandable. Swift's language is somewhat remote from twenty-first-century language, and in any case students don't expect satire in a collection of arguments. Moreover, it's hard today to know when a projector (the eighteenth-century name for someone with a bright idea) is kidding. A student who has not understood that "A Modest Proposal" is a satire may be extremely embarrassed upon learning the truth in public. To avoid this possibility, we usually begin the discussion by talking about Swift as a satirist who is known chiefly through *Gulliver's Travels,* and so on.

Most commentators on "A Modest Proposal" have concentrated on the persona of the speaker—his cool use of statistics, his way of regarding human beings as beasts ("a child just dropped from its dam" in para. 4, for example, or his reference to wives as "breeders" in para. 6), and, in short, his unawareness of the monstrosity of his plan to turn the children into "sound, useful members of the commonwealth" (para. 2), a plan that, by destroying children, will supposedly make the proposer "a preserver of the nation" (para. 2). Much of this complacent insensitivity and even craziness is apparent—on rereading—fairly early, as in the odd reference (para. 1) to "three, four, or six children" (what happened to five?), or, for that matter, in the phrases already quoted from paragraph 2. And of course it is true that one object of Swift's attack is the persona, a figure who, despite his profession that he is rational, practical, and compassionate, perhaps can be taken as an emblem of English indifference to Irish humanity. (But the speaker is an Irishman, not an Englishman.) More specifically, the leading object of attack can be said to be political reformers, especially those who heartlessly bring statistics ("I calculate," "I have reckoned," "I have already computed") where humane feelings should rule.

It is less often perceived, however, that the satire is also directed against the Irish themselves, with whom Swift was, by this time, fed up. *Satire* is almost too mild a word for the vehemence of "savage indignation" (Swift's own epitaph refers to his *saeva indignatio*) with which Swift denounces the Irish. Yes, he in effect says, the English treat the Irish abominably, but the Irish take no reasonable steps to help themselves. Even in so small a detail as the proposer's observation that his plan would cause husbands to stop beating pregnant wives (para. 26), we hear criticism not of the English but of the Irish. The chief denunciation of the Irish is evident, however, in the passage beginning with paragraph 29, in which Swift lists the "other expedients" that indeed the Irish themselves could (but do not) undertake to alleviate their plight.

In short, commentators who see Swift's essay simply as a scathing indictment of English hardheartedness are missing much of the point. One can almost go so far as to say that Swift's satire against the projector is directed not only against his impracticality and his unconscious cruelty but also against his folly in trying to help a nation that, out of stupidity and vanity, obstinately refuses to help itself. The projector sees the Irish as mere flesh; Swift at this time apparently saw them as something more exasperating, flesh that is stupid and vain. Swift was, we think, more than half in earnest when he had his crazy projector say, "I desire the reader will observe, that I calculate my remedy for this one individual kingdom of Ireland and for no other that was, is, or, I think ever can be upon earth."

If you wish students to do some research, you can ask them to look at Swift's "Irish Tracts" (*Prose Works*, ed. Herbert Davis, 12: 1–90, especially *Intelligencer* 19: 54–61), where they will find Swift arguing for the "other expedients" that his projector dismisses.

Related points:

1. This essay has ample material to demonstrate the use of the method that Aristotle calls "the ethical proof," that is, the pleader's use of his or her ethical character to persuade an audience. (Of course, here it backfires: We soon see a monster, not a benevolist.) Thus, in paragraph 1, the author shows his moral sensibility in using such expressions as "melancholy object" and "helpless infants." Also relevant is the projector's willingness to listen to other views—which he then of course always complacently rejects. (One might ask students to examine this issue through the eyes of Carl Rogers, who in his essay in Chapter 10 of the text urges writers to regard the views of the opposition sympathetically, not merely as points to be dismissed.)

2. A scattering of anti–Roman Catholic material (for example, references to "papists") indicates that the speaker, for all his insistence on his objectivity, is making a prejudiced appeal to emotions.

3. Instructors interested in satiric techniques will probably want to call attention to Swift's abundant use of diminution, such as people reduced to animals and to statistics.

1. Drawing only on the first three paragraphs, write a brief characterization (probably three or four sentences) of the speaker—that is, of the persona whom Swift invents. Do not talk about Swift the author; talk only about the anonymous speaker of these three paragraphs. Support your assertions by quoting words or phrases from the paragraphs.

2. In an essay of 150–250 words, characterize the speaker of "A Modest Proposal," and explain how Swift creates this character. You may want to make use of your answer to the previous question, pointing out that at first we think such-and-such, but later, picking up clues that Swift provides, we begin to think thus-and-so. You may wish, also, to devote a few sentences to the last paragraph of Swift's essay.

3. What is the speaker arguing for? What is Swift arguing for?

4. Write a modest proposal of your own, suggesting a solution to some great social problem. Obvious topics include war, crime, and racism, but choose any topic that almost all people agree is a great evil. Do not choose a relatively controversial topic such as gay rights, vivisection, gun control, or right-to-work laws. Your proposed solution should be, like Swift's, outrageous, but your essay should not be silly. In the essay, you should satirize some identifiable way of thinking.

5. Following the same basic assignment as the previous one, this time write an essay on a topic that is controversial and about which you have strong feelings.

6
Developing an Argument of Your Own (p. 228)

In this chapter we try to help students get and develop ideas, chiefly by urging them (1) to ask themselves questions, (2) to write and rewrite, (3) to think of their audience as their collaborator, and (4) to submit drafts to peers for review. We think instructors will agree with us on the value of these practices. The trick is to convince students that even those who are pretty good writers will profit by working along these lines and, similarly, that even those who have difficulty writing *can* write interesting and effective papers if they make use of these suggestions.

All writers have their own methods of writing. Some can write only with a pen, whereas others can write only with a word processor; Balzac believed he needed the smell of rotten apples to stimulate his pen. Still, allowing for individual needs, we think it is honest to tell students that, in general, the sooner they begin an assignment, and the more they think about it and put their thoughts into notes and drafts, the better their essay will be. In an effort to make this point, we give in the text Emily Andrews's preliminary notes and second thoughts, as well as the final version of her essay.

Emily Andrews (student essay)

Why I Don't Spare "Spare Change" (p. 264)

As our comments in the text indicate, we think the essay is an effective piece of writing, but you may disagree, and you may want students to discuss its strengths and weaknesses and perhaps even to write a critical analysis or a response.

7
Using Sources (p. 267)

In our teaching, we try to inculcate the idea that the "research paper" is not a genre found only in the land of Freshman English or even in the larger realm of College Writing but is something that flourishes (under different descriptions, of course) wherever writing is required. That is, we try to help students to see that when, say, one writes a letter to a school newspaper, complaining that a coach has been fired, one first does (or ought to do) a little homework, finding out the won-lost record to strengthen the letter. And of course almost all reports written for businesses require research.

Students are more likely to work enthusiastically on their papers if they understand that using sources is an activity in which all literate people sometimes engage. In fact, students engage in research all the time, for instance, when they consult a book of baseball statistics or a catalog of recordings or when they talk with friends to find out what courses they should take next semester.

To give students some practice in finding materials (and in learning something), you might ask them to produce a bibliography of recent writings on, say, pornography, racist speech, or euthanasia, with summaries of two or three articles.

Part Three

FURTHER VIEWS ON ARGUMENT

8
A Philosopher's View:
The Toulmin Model (p. 337)

Of the many attempts by philosophers in recent decades to explain the logic of ordinary argumentation—and to do so in a manner that the general reader (especially undergraduates and faculty not trained in formal logic) can grasp—none has been as well received as the work of Stephen Toulmin. Toulmin began his career at Cambridge at the end of Ludwig Wittgenstein's tenure there as a professor and for many years was on the philosophy faculty of the University of Southern California.

Why Toulmin's model of argumentation should have proved so popular where others have failed is not entirely clear to us. No doubt his reputation as a philosopher among philosophers has helped; but that is hardly the whole story because few philosophers teach informal logic and fewer still use his book *The Uses of Argument* (1958, 1969) to do it. Surely his desire to avoid forcing every kind of argument into some version of an Aristotelian syllogism is attractive. Perhaps it is mostly that the six-step model he offers with its untechnical nomenclature ("claim," "ground," and so on) is relatively more user-friendly than what the competition has to offer. Whatever the explanation, we think instructors using this book, especially those making their first acquaintance with Toulmin's method here, will find it rewarding to study (if not also to teach).

James E. McWilliams

The Locavore Myth: Why Buying from Nearby Farmers Won't Save the Planet (p. 345)

If you assign this essay, you may want your students also to read the paired essays that constitute a debate in Chapter 16, The Local Food Movement: Is It a Better Way to Eat? They are Stephen Budiansky, "Math Lessons for Locavores," and Kerry Trueman, "The Myth of the Rabid Locavore."

9
A Logician's View:
Deduction, Induction, Fallacies (p. 349)

The purpose of this chapter is to develop at somewhat greater length the tools of reasoning introduced in Chapter 3. Here, in a few dozen pages, we divide the subject into three natural and familiar parts: deductive reasoning, inductive reasoning, and fallacious reasoning.

To take them in reverse order, we identify and illustrate eighteen fallacies. The list can be extended; for example, in the latest edition of his standard textbook, *With Good Reason,* 6th ed. (2004), S. Morris Engel identifies and discusses a dozen more. Few instructors will want to introduce their students to all the fallacies that we discuss; but we would hope that instructors would find it useful to dwell on a few from time to time. Here, we want to mention a popular fallacy (of the sort that logicians call "formal") that does not appear in our text or in Engel's textbook: the fallacy of *denying the antecedent.*

Consider this argument:

1. If it's raining, then the streets will be wet.

2. It isn't raining.

3. Therefore, the streets aren't wet.

This argument has the obvious form: if p then q; not p; therefore not q. The trouble is that this argument form is invalid; to see why, just consider the example above. Surely, it is possible the streets *are* wet—for example, a catch basin overflowed, the street cleaners flushed down the street—despite no rain at all. This argument is invalid because of its form, and we cannot trust any argument of this form. It has a related invalid argument form that is almost equally popular; its name is *affirming the consequent,* and this is its form: if p, then q; q; therefore, p. We leave it to your imagination to see why this form of argument is also invalid.

A large fraction (we cannot be more precise) of our daily reasoning is inductive, and to the few pages in Chapter 3 devoted to this topic we have added seven or eight more pages in this chapter. In the following pages, our aim is to take a couple of examples (involving fatality, or the risk thereof, caused by smoking) as the skeleton on which to hang our discussion of evidence, observation, inference, probability, confirmation, and related concepts essential to inductive reasoning. Brief though our discussion is, we think that at a minimum it should help instructors make these important concepts more accessible and usable by students and thus add to their available tools for diagnosing and constructing arguments.

Finally, we begin the chapter with a discussion of deduction, amplifying what we offered as a bare-bones introduction in Chapter 3. Here we offer another dozen terms (*dilemma, hypothetical syllogism,* and so on) that are standard vocabulary for the discussion of formal deductive reasoning. Some instructors may find it useful to work their way through our discussion with their students in class (perhaps in conjunction with the parallel material found in Chapter 3). Most instructors, we suspect, will find this material of use mainly for occasional reference. All (at least all instructors) can profit to greater or lesser degree merely by (carefully) reading these pages once over.

1. Abortion might be said to be a form of prenatal homicide—the killing of an unborn human being—but not murder, since the human embryo and fetus are months away from being a person. The fallacy is using a term (*murder*) that connotes the death of a person when no person is present in a prenatal homicide.

2. We think that it does matter whether the person in question is dying in any case, and whether he or she is suffering pain, especially pain that cannot be controlled by drugs.

3. The fallacy here is arguing for a general rule on the basis of a sample of one.

4. Invoking a right to listen whenever and to whatever you want is silly; the fallacy here is that there is no such right in the first place.

5. The comment suggests that it's better to be selfish and safe than altruistic at some personal risk. But is it really better? Better according to what standard or criterion? We side with the Good Samaritan, not with his selfish critic.

6. The epigram comes from American history out west in the 1870s. The fallacy here is tacitly recommending a violent course of action when dealing with strangers—or foreign nations—that is, assuming without any evidence that you cannot trust whoever knocks on your door.

7. There really isn't any fallacy here; the three generalizations are often invoked because they sum briefly the truth of the matter.

8. No fallacy here, either.

9. The fallacy here is inferring from dozens of suicide leaps off the bridge that there is no other or better way to prevent such acts than by closing the bridge down.

10. The fallacy here, from a practical point of view, is that there is little in common between the Japanese American claim for reparations and the current claim by African Americans for reparations. The Japanese American community in 1942 was well defined and relatively small in number, and calculating its losses was not an insuperable task. In all three respects, the situation with today's African Americans is different.

11. This is controversial, but we think that the statement is essentially correct. True, trees and stones do not bleed, whereas dogs and cats, as well as wild animals, do, and they also can feel pain. For some, following the lead of the great Jeremy Bentham, these feelings—pleasure and pain—are all that matters. One of us thinks otherwise. Human rights take their origin from the way they connect with distinctive capacities that only humans (so far) are known to have, chief among which is a sense of self. (The other of us has kept as many as four dogs at once. He holds a different view.)

12. The fallacy here is treating a mathematical average carried to one decimal point as though it were a whole number, in this case a number of children. For example, suppose there were 15 children whose ages sum to 45. The average age of the children is 45 divided by 15, or 3—a whole number. But suppose the ages of the 15 children sum to 42. Now the average is 2.8—not the number of children in any family.

13. The fallacy here is the same as the one we met in item 3.

14. It is possible to do as the Red Queen does, verdict first and evidence later. But you couldn't run a criminal justice system following this rule. The fallacy here is treating verdict and evidence as though the order or sequence in which they are carried out doesn't matter to the outcome of the trial, when of course it usually does. This rule violates a fundamental rule of criminal law, namely, that the accused has

a right to see the evidence being used against him, except after the trial is over, at which point giving the defendant access to the evidence against him is largely no longer of interest.

15. What counts as an "adequate reason" to believe that the moon has a back side when no such thing could be seen? Notice that the issue here is not whether the moon is spherical. Eclipses surely suggest that it has a circular (even if not spherical) shape. A spherical back side is surely a possibility. Since the issue is not whether you can rule out any particular shape for a back side, it seems reasonable to assume that the moon has some sort of back side, just as every three-dimensional object does.

16. The fallacy here is thinking of alcoholism as a highly likely outcome from steadily increasing the consumption of alcohol. It all depends on the dosage and the frequency. We can easily imagine cases of this sort; they turn on the volume and strength of the alcohol being imbibed. And because volume and frequency of consumption are relevant to the onset of alcoholism, we can equally imagine cases where no such addiction develops, because the dosage is small and the frequency moderate.

17. The big Indian is the mother of the little Indian.

18. This is the notorious gambler's fallacy, also known as the Monte Carlo fallacy. If you toss a coin fifteen times and each time the coin comes up heads, or comes up tails, or alternates heads and tails, you are probably dealing with some kind of unfair coin. If you toss a fair coin, the odds are 50-50 that it will come up heads. Since the heads-or-tails behavior of a fair coin has no effect on the *next* toss, the a priori probability of a coin coming up heads on the next toss is again 50-50, that is, identical to the a priori probability of the coin coming up tails. The fallacy is to think that the outcome of the current toss of a fair coin has some effect on the outcome of the next toss, and so on indefinitely, when it doesn't.

19. Well, in a lighthearted mood, one might agree; perhaps a bit of exercise each Sunday morning would be good for what ails one. But the reply of the loyal churchgoer will be that we have spiritual needs, too, and they cannot be served by walking or jogging. The fallacy, if there is one, is to think that physical needs are more important than spiritual ones, when a reasonable person might seek ways to satisfy both kinds of needs.

20. The fallacy here is ad hominem, acting as though a person's political affiliations govern all the beliefs and behavior of that person. Perhaps they do, but that is highly unlikely.

21. The fallacy here is post hoc, ergo propter hoc ("after this, therefore because of this"). For all we know, the terrorists have backed off, but not because our defense systems are so good. Perhaps they have run out of large sums of cash to buy weapons and finance attacks. Perhaps the supply of suicidal terrorists has declined. Perhaps they are thinking up new attacks that they will unleash in the next few weeks or months. And so on.

22. Well, just how reliable are press releases from the White House these days? Can we trust whatever they tell us? Surely, caution is advised. Pretty clearly, anyone who argues in this manner is committing the fallacy of appeal to authority, and also is arguing in a circle—offering as evidence the very issue that is to be proved. The statement comes down to this: You can trust them because they are trustworthy.

23. True, the theory of evolution so far cannot explain how life began. But perhaps in time it will, or perhaps some entirely new theory will supersede natural selection in the spirit of Darwin. In any case, it is an empirical question just how much Darwinism can explain. There is no reason to think that the failure, so far, of

natural selection to explain the origin of life is a reason for believing that intelligent design is the best or the only other explanation.

24. We are not devotees of Serrano's career, and we think the title he chose, *Piss Christ*, is in the worst possible taste. But there is no fallacy, certainly not any obvious one, on which to hang such a judgment. Given that the image (it is a photograph) exists (or did exist), we can imagine many who would like to see it if only to make a judgment of its worth for themselves. As for public funding, we are not deeply troubled by using a tiny portion of federal tax revenues to support the project; we do, however, find it difficult to see how Serrano's photograph could win out against any serious competition for public support. But let the panel of judges for such competitions decide on the merits.

25. We think the statement is true—but we would go further. Thomas should have expected more evidence before he believed his eyes. To settle the question in his mind—viz., is this man the resurrected Jesus of Nazareth, the Son of God—more evidence than a few scars on the man's body is required. After all, we are talking about one of the greatest miracle stories of western civilization, and it is difficult to overestimate the evidence it is reasonable to require. The fallacy, if any, lies in Thomas's willingness to believe on the strength of the slender evidence before him.

26. One way to read this narrative is to judge the baseball player guilty of the fallacy of post hoc, ergo propter hoc, which we have seen earlier in item 21.

27. This is an old Yankee saying, but it's not much of a dilemma. If it's a small hole, you could fix it in the rain, provided the rain is not too heavy. Better still, you could fix it on a day of good weather, knowing that it will rain sometime in the future, even if not soon, and that it's better to fix the hole than to leave it, even if doing so interrupts something you'd rather do, like working in the garden or watching the Patriots on their way to another Super Bowl victory. The fallacy here is thinking there is a serious dilemma when there isn't.

28. Because there's a better explanation. What we are witnessing is what sailors call a ship hull down on the horizon. The hull disappears from view as the ship moves steadily away from the pier (or shore) and at right angles to the beach (or shore), and so on with ever taller parts of the ship until the entire ship is lost to view. But no sinking is involved—though of course it might be involved. It's just very unlikely.

29. *Proves* in this familiar saying means "tests" (cf. the related noun, *proof,* when we speak of a photographic *proof* or when we say, "The proof of the pudding is in the eating"). Surely testing a rule by looking for exceptions is an important aspect of scientific reasoning. The fallacy lies in misunderstanding what *proves* means in this context.

30. Herbivores eat fruit and vegetable matter. Herbs such as oregano, thyme, rosemary, sage, and the rest do not form the diet of any herbivores, so far as we know. Perhaps the reason is that herbs tend to grow on small plants, whereas your standard herbivores—elephants, hippopotami—feast on large leaves.

31. First, the text of the ad is ambiguous. Does it mean "More doctors smoke Camels than smoke any other cigarette" or does it mean "More doctors smoke Camels than all the doctors who smoke other cigarettes plus all those who abstain from smoking"? The former version is probably what is meant. In any case, there is an appeal to authority implicit in the caption. Who am I to argue with doctors; if they prefer Camels, I should at least try a pack and see how I like them. Besides, if doctors prefer Camels, then surely these cigarettes must be safe to smoke whether or not others are equally safe. (All nonsense.)

32. Killing five to save one is absurd on its face—unless, of course, the five are hardened criminals and the one is a Nobel Prize–winning scientist. The really

tempting alternative is killing one to save five. This version violates the Kantian principle that one should never use a person as a means to serve the ends of other persons—in this case, the desire of the five to survive. Of course, if the one consents to being used by the five for their survival, that's another matter altogether. Morality respects sacrifice; it does not demand it. We cannot lodge a complaint if no one volunteers to be sacrificed. If the right to life means anything at all, it means that the many have no right to take the life of the one, since to do so violates the right to life of the one. There is, of course, much more to be said. Some of that more can be found in the slender volume by Hugo Bedau, *Making Mortal Choices: Three Exercises in Moral Casuistry* (1997).

Max Shulman

Love Is a Fallacy (p. 383)

There are lots of laughs here, but the piece *does* teach effectively; students are more likely to remember Max Shulman's discussion of fallacies than ours. One can also use the story—especially the first paragraph—to talk about style. Read the first sentence aloud in class ("Cool was I and logical") and ask students what sorts of expectations are set up. Most will see that he *must* be kidding. And so on through the paragraph, to "And—think of it!—I was only eighteen."

We urge you to assign this story.

10
A Psychologist's View:
Rogerian Argument (p. 392)

Carl R. Rogers

Communication: Its Blocking and Its Facilitation (p. 394)

An occasional student has told us that Carl R. Rogers is "merely trying to apply psychology" to outwit his opponent, but we believe this interpretation is mistaken. Rogers was much concerned with reducing tension so that issues could be more easily discussed, not with deceiving the parties involved. Still, it is easy to see how students might think that "psychology" is a weapon to be wielded—something akin to bluffing at poker—in order to win. We are reminded of the advice that an old actor gave to a young one: "The most important thing is sincerity. When you can fake *that*, you can do anything."

It's not hard to find comments about argument that come close to the actor's view. Consider, for instance, Samuel Butler's "It is not he who gains the exact point in dispute who scores most in controversy, but he who has shown the most forbearance and the better temper." Or Lord Chesterfield's advice to his son: "If you would convince others, seem open to conviction yourself." But Butler's concern with scoring most and Chesterfield's use of *seem* (as opposed to *be*) set their comments sharply apart from Rogers's. Similarly, consider Ben Franklin: "Those disputing, contradicting, and confuting people are generally unfortunate in their affairs. They get victory, sometimes, but they never get good will, which be of more use to them." Rogers would probably agree, but he would rightly claim that he is not concerned with gaining goodwill so that it will be of "use" to him; he is concerned with helping the world to achieve peace.

Much closer to Rogers than Butler, Chesterfield, or Franklin is Pascal: "When we wish to correct with advantage, and to show another that he errs, we must notice from what side he views the matter, for on that side it is usually true." Close—but still short of Rogers's view, since Rogers recognizes that the other side not only may be right from its own point of view but may indeed be right enough so that we can come to accept at least part of that point of view. Consider these key statements:

> The whole task of psychotherapy is the task of dealing with a failure in communication. (para. 1)

> If you really understand another person in this way, if you are willing to enter his private world and see the way life appears to him, without any attempt to make evaluative judgments, you run the risk of being changed yourself. You might see it his way, you might find yourself influenced in your attitudes or your personality. (para. 11)

We imagine that most people would agree with Rogers in theory, but some opposing voices have been heard. For us, the most telling objection is that Rogers speaks as a white male—that is, as a member of the group that for centuries has done most of the speaking and has done very little listening. His advice—in effect, "Calm down, listen to me, and see things from my point of view"—is good advice for people like Rogers but is less useful (we have heard it said) for women, gays and lesbians, blacks, Hispanics, and other marginalized people. Some members of these groups say that they have listened long enough, and that it is now their turn to speak out and to speak out forcefully. Let straight white males, they argue, do the listening for a change.

One other point must be made about Rogerian argument. Rogers was talking about *talking*, about people who are actually facing their hearers. But instructors who use our book are for the most part concerned with *writing*, and they may wonder if Rogers's essay is relevant to writers. We offer two short answers: (1) Assign and discuss the essay, and (2) urge students to make use of the checklist in the text (p. 400) when they write their next essays. We think that if students read the essay and pay attention to the checklist, they not only will write better essays but also may become better people.

Edward O. Wilson

Letter to a Southern Baptist Minister (p. 400)

When students read an essay, they are inevitably concerned chiefly with the content of the argument rather than with the essayist's strategies, but here and there in our text we urge students to study an essayist's *ways* of arguing. That is, we urge them to see how the writer is conducting the argument. We give Wilson's essay in this chapter not because we are especially concerned with his views of God or, for that matter, of nature, but because we want students to see how he goes about talking to—well, we can put it bluntly—the opposition. And this will be our concern here.

The opening paragraph in effect offers a warm, hearty handshake. In the very first sentence Wilson says, "I feel I know you well enough to call you friend." In the second sentence he says that "we grew up in the same faith," and in the third he is a bit more specific: "I went under the water." In other words, Wilson, like the pastor whom he addresses, was baptized. (Not all students will understand "I went under the water.") In the fourth sentence he confesses that he no longer is a believer, but in this very sentence he goes on to express confidence that if he and his reader speak of their "deepest beliefs," it will be "in a spirit of mutual respect and good will." After all, he goes on to say, assuring his reader, not only are they both Americans but they are Southerners, people who share a code of "civility and good manners." Wilson has certainly made every effort to ingratiate himself. Only the most churlish reader would refuse to listen to what Wilson has to say.

Paragraph 2: Wilson begins, "I write to you now for your counsel and help." Well, what reader (or listener) would refuse to offer advice and help to this nice man who says he needs our assistance? Wilson then goes on to sketch his reader's central views.

Paragraph 3: Wilson begins, by way of contrast, with a sketch of his own views, which of course differ sharply from his supposed auditor's.

Paragraph 5: Wilson asserts that the "difference in worldview" does not separate the two men in all things, and he goes on to say that both of them value "security, freedom of choice, personal dignity, and a cause to believe in that is larger than ourselves." This last belief is especially important: "A cause . . . that is larger than ourselves" has a vaguely religious sound that is not present in "freedom of choice."

Paragraph 6: The paragraph begins, "Let us see, then, if we can, and you are willing, to meet." Again we hear the earnest expression of a desire to share, to work things out courteously.

Paragraph 7: After "Pastor, we need your help," Wilson says, "The Creation—living Nature—is in deep trouble." Notice—and we think this is very important—that Wilson uses a capital letter for "Creation." We think the use of a capital is important because it is our guess that his auditor might use a capital letter in speaking of "the Creator." That is, Wilson is doing all that he possibly can do to establish common ground, to speak the language of his auditor.

It would be very easy to proceed through the essay in this fashion, but it is unnecessary; so let's jump to paragraph 14, which Wilson begins thus:

> To make the point in good Gospel manner, let me tell the story of a young man newly
> trained for the ministry, and so fixed in his Christian faith that he referred all questions of
> morality to readings from the Bible.

Again, in his reference to "good Gospel manner," Wilson reminds us that he was brought up as a churchgoer—remember, in his first paragraph he said that he "went under the water"—and he then goes on to offer the surprising information that the young man of the story was Charles Darwin, in 1832. The next paragraph quotes from Darwin in 1859, speaking of "grandeur," and of something "breathed into a few forms or into one." We take it that Darwin's "breathed into" evokes Genesis 2:7, "And the Lord God formed man of the dust of the ground, and breathed into his nostrils the breath of life. And man became a living soul." Darwin was doing his best to imply that his vision had its affinities with the Judeo-Christian vision, and that's what Wilson is also doing, for instance, in his seventeenth paragraph, where he speaks of Darwin's "*reverence* (emphasis ours) for life."

The essay concludes with the assertion that Wilson and his Christian reader "have a common purpose," at least concerning the "life-and-death issue" of the future of the planet. It's all very Rogerian.

11
A Rhetorician's View: Rhetorical Analysis of Nontraditional Texts (p. 404)

Unfortunately, today in ordinary speech, the word *rhetoric* is chiefly used with negative connotations, in such phrases as "empty rhetoric," "mere rhetoric," and "rhetoric, not action." On the other hand, criticism of rhetoric is hardly new: In ancient times, Plato criticized the Sophists for pretty much the same reason that some people today criticize "rhetoric," that is, that it allegedly is divorced from truth and is used chiefly for deceptive purposes.

The high view of rhetoric of course is very different: It is (as we several times say in the text) both (1) an *instrument for discovering truth* and then (2) an instrument for propagating the truth by means of persuasive devices, and thus it is an art or a skill that every responsible citizen should possess. As teachers of argumentative writing, we subscribe to this high view.

Here are two quotations affirming the high value of rhetoric:

Histories make men wise; poets, witty; the mathematics, subtle; natural philosophy, deep, moral, grave; logic and rhetoric, able to contend.

Francis Bacon (1561–1626)

The design of Rhetoric is to remove those Prejudices that lie in the way of Truth; to Reduce the Passions to the Government of Reasons; to place our Subject in a Right Light, and excite our Hearers to a due consideration of it.

Mary Astell (1666–1731)

This chapter is especially concerned with providing students with tools that enable them to analyze twenty-first-century forms of argument, for example, electronic communications.

12
A Literary Critic's View:
Arguing about Literature (p. 420)

Classroom discussion usually centers on the meaning of a work, and almost always some-one raises the question, "Do you really think that's what the author intended?" But ever since the publication of W. K. Wimsatt Jr. and Monroe C. Beardsley's "The Intentional Fallacy," *Sewanee Review* 54 (Summer 1946), conveniently reprinted in W. K. Wimsatt Jr.'s *The Verbal Icon* (1954), it has been impossible (we think) to talk easily about the author's intention.

To begin with, most authors have not in any explicit way set forth their inten-tions: We have, for example, *Hamlet,* but not Shakespeare's comment on his intention in the drama. Nevertheless, students may say that if an author has stated what he or she intended, we should interpret the work accordingly. But we might respectfully point out that the stated intention is not always fulfilled in the work. The author doubtless intended to write a great work—but does this intention mean that the work is great? The author intended to write a serious work—but we may find it absurd. Does the author's intention make the work less absurd? Or, conversely, the writer may have intended only to earn money. A famous instance is Dr. Johnson, hurriedly writing *Rasselas* to pay the costs of his mother's funeral but nevertheless producing a masterpiece. Wimsatt and Beardsley have taught us that the work "means" what the work itself says, not what the author says he or she meant it to mean. In the words of Lillian Hellman, "The writer's intention hasn't anything to do with what he achieves." Or in the words of D. H. Lawrence, "Never trust the artist. Trust the tale."

Although "The Intentional Fallacy" remains the classic text, you may want to suggest that students interested in this topic should read Beardsley's later comments on inten-tion in his *Aesthetics: Problems in the Philosophy of Criticism* (1958) and in his *The Possibility of Criticism* (1970).

The proper question to ask, we believe, is not "What did the author mean?" but, rather, "What does the text say?" We can, of course, try to see what the work meant in its own day—that is, in its historical context. For instance, if we are thinking about *The Merchant of Venice* or about *Othello,* we can try to collect information about Elizabethan atti-tudes toward Jews or toward Moors, respectively, but even with such material, we will not be able to say much about Shakespeare's intention. *The Merchant of Venice* contains at least one extended passage (3.1.55–65) in which Shylock is presented far more sympathetically than any Jew in any other Elizabethan text (Did Shakespeare perhaps find Shylock coming to life, and did he give him better lines than he intended?). As for *Othello,* well, no other Elizabethan drama has a tragic hero who is a Moor. The mere fact that Shakespeare alone made a Moor the central figure in a tragedy—a genre that displayed human greatness—suggests that we will not get much insight into Othello by seeing how other dramatists represented Moors or, for that matter, even by seeing how Shakespeare represented Moors in other plays (*Titus Andronicus* and *The Merchant of Venice*). To read *Othello* is to see a Moor who is incontestably different from the Moors in all other Elizabethan plays (including Shakespeare's other plays), and we do great injustice to the heroic Othello if we push him into the mold of "the Elizabethan Moor," which in effect means the Moor as depicted by people who were not Shakespeare.

Let's take a particular passage in T. S. Eliot's "The Love Song of J. Alfred Prufrock" (Chapter 27). After the epigraph from Dante, the poem begins thus: "Let us go then, you and I." Who is the "you"? In this manual we suggest that "Prufrock" is an internal monologue in which the timid self ("I") addresses his own amorous self as "you." (We don't say that *every* "you" in the poem is the amorous self.) It happens that a reader asked Eliot (apparently in the mid-1940s, some thirty years after Eliot wrote the poem) who the "you" is, and Eliot replied:

> As for THE LOVE SONG OF J. ALFRED PRUFROCK anything I say now must be somewhat conjectural, as it was written so long ago that my memory may deceive me; but I am prepared to assert that the "you" in THE LOVE SONG is merely some friend or companion, presumably of the male sex, whom the speaker is at that moment addressing. . . .

> (Kristian Smidt, *Poetry and Belief in the Work of T. S. Eliot,* 85.)

Several points are worth noting: (1) The statement was made long after the poem was written, and Eliot grants that any such late statement "must be somewhat conjectural"; (2) he nevertheless is "prepared to assert" that the "you" is "some friend or companion"; (3) although he is prepared to make this assertion, the assertion itself is rather imprecise (there is a difference between a "friend" and a "companion") and he immediately goes on to reveal (by saying "presumably of the male sex") that he himself no longer has (if he ever did have) a clear idea of who the "you" is. How helpful, then, is his comment? True, if one wants to say that the author is the decisive authority, presumably one can rule out the view that the "you" in the poem is (for the most part) the amorous self, the self urging the timid self to go forward. But, we suggest, the test is to read the poem to see if the suggestion makes sense.

Eliot himself occasionally commented at some length on the topic of intention. For instance, in "The Social Function of Poetry" (1945) after saying that "a great deal more goes to the making of poetry than the conscious purpose of the poet," he went on to add, "And in recent times, a reason why we have become more cautious in accepting a poet's expressed intention as evidence of what he was really doing, is that we have all become more conscious of the role of the unconscious." And in "The Frontiers of Criticism" (1956) he mentions, of a published interpretation of "Prufrock" that he had recently read, "[The author set forth] an attempt to find out what the poem really meant—whether that was what I had meant it to mean or not. And for that I was grateful." Possibly Eliot's expression of gratitude is spoken with tongue in cheek (though we do not think so), but even if one does think Eliot is being ironic, the case for the authority of the author's interpretation is undermined; the author may (or may not) be speaking ironically, so how much weight can we give to his comments? In any case, in the context of the entire essay, it is clear that Eliot really does believe that a work cannot be reduced to what the author "intended."

One last quotation from Eliot, this one from *The Use of Poetry and the Use of Criticism* (1933, 130):

> A poet can try, of course, to give an honest report of the way in which he himself writes: the result may, if he is a good observer, be illuminating. And in one sense, but a very limited one, he knows better what his poems "mean" than can anyone else; he may know the history of their composition, the material which has gone in and come out in an unrecognisable form, and he knows what he was trying to do and what he was meaning to mean. But what a poem means is as much what it means to others as what it means to the author; and indeed, in the course of time a poet may become merely a reader in respect to his own works, forgetting his original meaning.

These sentences make sense, but we also see the force of the commonsense view that a competent author shapes the material so that it embodies his or her meaning. This meaning may change during the process of composition—the writer finds his or her intention shifting and therefore revises the work—but, in this view, the creator of a work does know, at the end, what the meaning of the work is. Notice that we say "a competent author." Obviously an incompetent author may compose a work that is inadvertently incoherent or ludicrous and be unaware of the result. But a competent author, in this view, shapes the work—admittedly modifying the original intention as the work proceeds—and at the end has produced a work in which all of the elements cohere and on whose meaning he or she can comment. This, we say, is a commonsense view; the only trouble, again, is that most writers have not commented on their works (for example, Chaucer, Shakespeare), and those writers who have commented (for example, Eliot) have often made inconclusive remarks. Aside from Eliot, none of the poets, story writers, or dramatists represented in this book have commented on the works we reprint.

Robert Frost

Mending Wall (p. 426)

Some critics applaud the neighbor in Robert Frost's "Mending Wall," valuing his respect for barriers. For an extreme version, see Robert Hunting, "Who Needs Mending?" *Western Humanities Review*, 17 (Winter 1963: 88–89). The gist of this faction is that the neighbor wisely realizes—as the speaker does not—that individual identity depends on respect for boundaries. Such a view sees the poem as a Browningesque dramatic monologue like "My Last Duchess," in which the self-satisfied speaker unknowingly gives himself away.

Richard Poirier, in *Robert Frost* (1977), makes the interesting point that it is not the neighbor (who believes that "good fences make good neighbors") who initiates the ritual of mending the wall; rather, it is the speaker: "I let my neighbor know beyond the hill." Poirier suggests that "if fences do not 'make good neighbors,' the making of fences can," for it makes for talk—even though the neighbor is hopelessly taciturn. For a long, judicious discussion of the poem, see John C. Kemp, *Robert Frost: The Poet as Regionalist* (1979, 13–25).

Andrew Marvell

To His Coy Mistress (p. 435)

First, we touch on our final question, the emendation of "glew" to "dew" in line 34. This emendation has found wide acceptance, but the original reading may be right, not in the ordinary sense of glue, of course, but in a sense that H. Grierson suggested, "a shining gum found on some trees."

Probably most of the discussion in class will concentrate on the structure of the poem and the question of whether the poem is offensively sexist. As for the tripartite structure, which we call attention to in a question in the text, we want to make two points here. First, we do not see it as a Hegelian matter of thesis/antithesis/synthesis, although many readers do see it this way. We see it, as we indicate in the text, as a matter of a supposition, a refutation, and a deduction.

The supposition is somewhat comic, with the lover offering to devote two hundred years to the praise of each breast, and it is even somewhat bawdy in his offer to devote "thirty thousand to the rest": After all, what can "the rest" be, after he has praised her forehead, eyes, and breasts? This apparently leisurely state might, at first thought, seem to be ideal for a lover, but when one thinks about it, one perceives its barrenness: "We would sit down, and think which way / To walk, and pass our long love's day" (lines 3–4). Nothing is fulfilled: "An age at least to every part, / And the last age should show your heart" (lines 17–18), which is to say that after centuries of praising this or that part, the last age—an unimaginably long period—would be devoted to praising the countless good qualities of her heart, for instance her generosity, kindness, piety, and whatever else. It all sounds rather barren.

The second unit begins with lines that are among the most famous in English literature: "But at my back I always hear / Time's wingèd chariot hurrying near" (lines 21–22). These lines seem to introduce swiftness and vitality into the poem; but when one comes to think further about this unit, one notices that, at least so far as the man and the woman are concerned, they don't do much here either. In the "deserts of vast eternity," her beauty will *not* be found; his song will *not* be heard; they will not embrace. The chief actors will be the worms, who will "try" her virginity. If in the first unit the speaker spoofs the woman, showing her as a caricature of the disdainful mistress, in the second unit he savagely attacks her verbally, with talk of graves and worms. And here, too, as we have just said, nothing much happens.

In the third unit, there is plenty of (imagined) action, action that they share, unlike the earlier action of the speaker praising the beloved or of her refusing his offers. This joint action, sexual union, is indicated by "we," "us," and "our." But the imagery and the emotion are not what we might have expected. The savagery persists, notably in the images of "fire" and "birds of prey" (rather than the doves of Venus, which we might expect in a love poem) and in the verbs "devour" and "tear." Instead of time devouring the lovers, they devour time, but now we feel that the speaker's assertions lacerate himself as well as the beloved.

This gets us to our main point: We see the poem not so much as primarily a love poem or even as a poem of seduction (which is what disturbs many students), but as primarily a poem about the desperate condition of human beings, as the speaker sees it. To this extent, what interests a reader (we think) is the emotional states through which the speaker moves, from teasing the beloved (the first unit), to twisting the knife (the second unit), to forcing himself to face the facts that he has been thrusting under her eyes (the third unit).

Kate Chopin

The Story of an Hour (p. 438)

The first sentence of Kate Chopin's story, of course, proves to be essential to the end, though during the middle of the story, the initial care to protect Mrs. Mallard from the "sad message" seems almost comic. Students may assume, too easily, that Mrs. Mallard's "storm of grief" is hypocritical. They may not notice that the renewal after the first shock is stimulated by the renewal of life around her ("the tops of trees . . . were all aquiver with the new spring of life") and that before she achieves a new life, Mrs. Mallard first goes through a sort of death and then tries to resist renewal: Her expression "indicated a suspension of intelligent thought," she felt something "creeping out of the sky," and she tried to "beat it back with her will," but she soon finds herself "drinking in a very elixir of life through that open window," and her thoughts turn to "spring days, and summer days."

Implicit in the story is the idea that her life as a wife—which she had thought was happy—was in fact a life of repression or subjugation, and the awareness comes to her only at this late stage. The story has two surprises: The change from grief to joy proves not to be the whole story, for we get the second surprise, the husband's return and Mrs. Mallard's death. The last line ("the doctors . . . said she had died . . . of joy that kills") is doubly ironic: The doctors wrongly assume that she was overjoyed to find that her husband was alive, but they were not wholly wrong in guessing that her last day of life brought her great joy.

In a sense, moreover, the doctors are right (though not in the sense they mean) in saying that she "died of heart disease." That is, if we take the "heart" in a metaphorical sense to refer to love and marriage, we can say that the loss of her new freedom from her marriage is unbearable. This is not to say (though many students do say it) that her marriage was miserable. The text explicitly says "she had loved him—sometimes." The previous paragraph in the story nicely calls attention to certain aspects of love—a satisfying giving of the self—and yet also to a most unpleasant yielding to force: "There would be no one to live for her during those coming years; she would live for herself. There would be no powerful will bending her in that blind persistence with which men and women believe they have a right to impose a private will upon a fellow creature."

51

A biographical observation: Chopin's husband died in 1882, and her mother died in 1885. In 1894, in an entry in her diary, she connected the two losses with her growth. "If it were possible for my husband and my mother to come back to earth, I feel that I would unhesitatingly give up every thing that has come into my life since they left it and join my existence again with theirs. To do that, I would have to forget the past ten years of my growth—my real growth."

Having said what we have to say about the story, we now offer our own responses to the critical assertions in the text to which we ask students to respond.

1. We don't think the railroad accident is a symbol of the destructiveness of the Industrial Revolution. In our view, something in a text becomes symbolic by virtue of being emphasized, perhaps by being presented at considerable length or perhaps by being repeated at intervals. Nothing in the story connects the train with the Industrial Revolution; it is not, for instance, said to have altered the landscape, changing what was once an agrarian community into an industrial community. On the other hand, we think that in this story the coming of spring is symbolic of new life. Why? For one thing, Chopin explicitly says in the fifth paragraph that the "tops of trees . . . were all aquiver with the new spring life." She goes on to talk of "the delicious breath of rain" and of sparrows twittering. The rain of course is refreshing, and it is a fact that water brings about renewed life. Further, literary tradition (cf. Chaucer's reference to April showers at the start of *The Canterbury Tales*) has given spring showers a symbolic meaning. Sparrows are associated with sexuality (the sparrow is an attribute of Aphrodite), but we don't usually bring this up in class because Chopin mentions the sparrows only briefly and because students are not likely to know of the tradition. (This point seems to us not worth arguing.) A few paragraphs later Chopin tells us that something was coming toward Mrs. Mallard "out of the sky, reaching toward her through the sounds, the scents, the color that filled the air." Surely, therefore, it is reasonable to say that Chopin is emphasizing the season—its sounds, scents, and colors. A few paragraphs later, Chopin tells us that Mrs. Mallard was thinking of "spring days, summer days." In short, *in the story* spring is given an emphasis that the train is not, and so we tend to think that the spring is not just the spring but is something more, something whose implications we should attend to.

2. To say that the story claims that women rejoice in the deaths of their husbands seems to us to be a gross overgeneralization. The story is about one particular woman. True, in reading any work we may find ourselves saying, "Yes, life is sometimes like that," or some such thing. But nothing in the story suggests that it is about "women," and certainly nothing suggests that Mrs. Mallard's response toward the death of her husband is *typical* of "women."

3. The view that her death at the end of the story is a just punishment strikes us as going far beyond the text; we find no evidence that Chopin judges Mrs. Mallard harshly, and we think we can point to contrary evidence—for instance, to the sympathetic way in which her response is set forth.

5. We do not agree that the story is good *because* it has a surprise ending—but we also do not condemn it because of the ending. True, some critics would argue that surprise endings are tricks, that such endings are far less important than plausible characters, and so on. Our own view is that if a story offers virtually nothing but a surprise ending, it is probably a weak story—one can hardly read it a second time with any interest—but a certain amount of surprise surely is desirable. Most, maybe all, realistic prose fiction makes use of foreshadowing; expectations are set up, but they are fulfilled in slightly unexpected ways. We are reminded of a passage in E. M. Forster's *Aspects of the Novel* (1927):

> Shock, followed by the feeling, "Oh, that's all right," is a sign that all is well with plot: characters, to be real, ought to run smoothly, but a plot ought to cause surprise.

Of course one might argue that this view is arbitrary; here is a chance to ask students what values they might establish—what makes them say that a story is good or bad or so-so.

Plato

"The Greater Part of the Stories Current Today We Shall Have to Reject" (p. 443)

This excerpt from Plato's *Republic* is a passage near the end of Book II, in which Socrates undertakes to describe the proper education for that handful of the young intended to become the guardians or rulers of the ideal state. (Throughout the dialogue, we hear nothing about how the rest of the population is to be educated, that presumably being a matter of no interest.) After explaining the importance of "gymnastics," or bodily training, Socrates turns to "music," or training for the soul. To be fair, one must not take Platonic-Socratic admonitions out of context; nevertheless, there is some reason to believe that—unlike Socrates, who relied on the free air of Athens to carry out his ideas about education of the citizenry—Plato, the son of an Athenian nobleman, really did believe that a stricter regimen involving some censorship of the prevailing methods was appropriate.

Plato's argument for discarding the Homeric tales about the gods depends on accepting the principle that whatever is good can be the cause only of good things—hence the gods, being wholly good, cannot cause any of the bad things that the prevailing mythology attributes to them. Plato knows that the gods are wholly good only because that is part of his implicit definition of deity—as though he had said, "I [we?] wouldn't call it divine unless it was (morally) good."

Plato even goes so far as to allege that in his ideal state, it would be "sinful, inexpedient, and inconsistent" to permit the poets to say that "those who were punished were made wretched through god's action." Presumably, he thinks it would be inconsistent to allow this statement (question 3) because it would contradict something that the elder guardian-teachers themselves avow: namely, that (as Plato says at the end of the excerpt) "God is the cause, not of all things, but only of good." Thus when a poet presents a story in which a god is depicted as making a person "wretched" (and we assume that being made wretched is not a "good" thing, but that getting your deserved punishment is), this interpretation contradicts the doctrine above because it makes the god out to be the cause of something not "good."

Some will complain that Plato assumes, on no explicit evidence, that "children cannot distinguish between what is allegory and what isn't," and he shows throughout that he underestimates the capacity of children to distinguish the silly from the serious, the cheap from the dear, and the obscene from the respectful (our question 2). It is, of course, an empirical question—and not an easy one to answer—whether children can make these distinctions. But it is needless to speculate whether they can make them in the abstract or in a wholly nonsocial environment. As we remember our childhood and that of our friends, we testify that we had no great difficulty in making these distinctions and that an unremitting diet of Saturday afternoon B-grade films at the local movie palace or the standard TV fare of the 1950s did not hopelessly muddle our values and our sense of reality. Obviously, we did not feed only on such stuff, any more than children today see nothing except what is on the most violent television shows. Even if we overestimate our own ability as youngsters to sort the wheat from the chaff, we doubt that the best way to develop judgment about what is harmful, tasteless, offensive, and worse is to deny all access to the meretricious, salacious, and blasphemous. Even if this is too serene (or radical) a view to gain favor, one must eventually face the question *quis custodiet custodies,* or "Who shall guard the guardians?" Plato does not need to worry about this problem because he, unlike the rest of us, deals by definition with an ideal state and its appropriately ideal government, one that is incapable of the provinciality of every known board of public censorship.

13
A Debater's View: Individual Oral Presentations and Debate (p. 450)

If you require students to engage in formal debates, you may want to put a few books on reserve in the library. We especially recommend Bill Hill and Richard W. Leeman, *The Art and Practice of Argumentation and Debate* (1997). Also of some use are Jon M. Ericson, James J. Murphy, and Raymond Bud Zeuschner, *The Debater's Guide*, 3rd ed. (2003), and Leslie Phillips, William S. Hicks, and Douglas R. Springer, *Basic Debate*, 4th ed. (1996).

If you don't use formal debates but you do ask students to make oral presentations, we think you may still suggest that students read this chapter, paying special attention to the checklist. And you may want to emphasize these four points:

1. Provide transitions, such as *In the first place, further*, and *finally*.

2. Summarize occasionally, especially as you move from one point to the next.

3. Have a pretty full outline, and don't hesitate to glance at it occasionally while speaking, but do not read your speech.

4. As a listener, be courteous (no eye-rolling).

Part Four

CURRENT ISSUES: OCCASIONS FOR DEBATE

SOME THOUGHTS ABOUT ARGUMENT, ESPECIALLY ABOUT DEBATES AND BINARY THINKING

Anyone who has read the prefaces to a few recent texts on argument will have noticed that most of them disparage the idea that an argument is essentially a conflict, the presentation of a thesis with material that is intended to refute countertheses. These prefaces are quite different from those of an older generation, in which students were taught how to "marshall" evidence, how to "attack" the weak points in an "opponent's" argument, how to "defend" their own position, and, in short, how to "win" an argument. Thus we teachers of composition were given textbooks with militant titles such as *Point Counter-Point* and *Crossfire*. Today it is regularly said—and we ourselves say this in our text and in the classroom—that an argument is an effort to get at the truth, an endeavor in which those who hold other views are our fellow workers, helping us to refine our ideas, with the ultimate goal of arriving at a position that reasonable folks can agree on. This is especially evident in the Toulmin method, where the claim, the grounds, and the warrant all converge on the truth. (It is a sign of the times that the textbook formerly called *Crossfire* has been reissued with a new title, *Dialogues*.) In the preface to our text, and then again later in the text, we quote two passages, one by Edmund Burke and one by John Stuart Mill, that are constantly in our minds, and that we believe ring true to our experience. Here yet again are the passages:

> He that wrestles with us strengthens our nerves, and sharpens our skill. Our antagonist is our helper. (Burke)

> He who knows only his own side of the case knows little. (Mill).

Both of these passages imply, however faintly, that after careful thought, with the help of a worthy antagonist, we can pretty much arrive at a sound conclusion, or at least we can work out something that those with whom we disagree can agree with. In our text, the chapter on Rogerian argument especially emphasizes this point, and we want to say again that we think there is a good deal to it.

And yet honesty compels us to say that our lives—in and out of the classroom—have brought us also to another view, a view that is stated eloquently by Isaiah Berlin in a small collection of essays called *The Crooked Timber of Humanity* (1991). In one essay, "The Pursuit of the Ideal," he mentions that Tolstoy and many of his contemporaries held

> the belief that solutions to the central problems existed, that one could discover them, and, with sufficient selfless effort, realize them on earth. They all believed that the essence of human beings was to be able to choose how to live: societies could be transformed in the light of true ideals believed in with enough fervour and dedication. (3–4)

Berlin goes on, later in the essay, to say that "There are many different ends that men may seek and still be fully rational," and here we must quote him at some length:

> What is clear is that values can clash—that is why civilisations are incompatible. They can be incompatible between cultures, or groups in the same culture, or between you and me. You believe in always telling the truth, no matter what; I do not because I believe that it can sometimes be too painful and too destructive. We can discuss each other's point of view, we can try to reach common ground, but in the end what you pursue may not be reconcilable

with the ends to which I find that I have dedicated my life. Values may easily clash within the breast of a single individual; and it does not follow that, if they do, some must be true and others false. Justice, rigorous justice, is for some people an absolute value, but it is not compatible with what may be no less ultimate values for them—mercy, compassion—as arises in concrete cases. (12)

These words seem wise to us, and indeed they have helped us to get through some faculty meetings in which we briefly thought of murdering our colleagues. They have also helped us to get through some class hours in which we briefly thought of taking up some other line of work. The truth is, on certain polarizing issues there is no middle way: Today, abortion and capital punishment are prime examples. Yes, negotiation takes place—for instance, one can agree that teenagers may not be executed—but the fact is, capital punishment either is lawful or not. Similarly, one can negotiate about whether abortion may or may not be performed in the case of incest and rape, but the issue remains: A fetus either may be aborted or not.

This sort of thinking has emboldened us to include in *Current Issues* not only casebooks, where multiple views are heard, but also a few debates, where we get pairs of strongly opposed voices. In our headnote to these debates, we call attention to the limits of binary thinking, and we caution students that some *either/or* arguments may be reductive, but again, we think it is healthy to recognize that on some issues, persons of intelligence and good faith may ultimately disagree.

Finally, we want to end this self-indulgent meditation by quoting a passage from Kenneth Burke's *The Philosophy of Literary Form* (1941), a passage that, like the passages from Burke and Mill, we also quote in our text because we want students to know them.

> Imagine that you enter a parlor. You come late. When you arrive, others have long preceded you, and they are engaged in a heated discussion, a discussion too heated for them to pause and tell you exactly what it is about. In fact, the discussion had already begun long before any of them got there, so that no one present is qualified to retrace for you all the steps that had gone before. You listen for a while, until you decide that you have caught the tenor of the argument; then you put in your oar. Someone answers; you answer him; another comes to your defense; another aligns himself against you, to either the embarrassment or gratification of your opponent, depending upon the quality of your ally's assistance. However, the discussion is interminable. The hour grows late, you must depart. And you do depart, with the discussion still vigorously in progress. (110–11)

Most of the essays in Part Four (five debates) are fairly short. As we suggested earlier, you may want to use one or more of these pairs when assigning the first five chapters, in discussions of such matters as assumptions, evidence, and tone.

Because these topics have inspired much writing in the last few years, they can be used to introduce students to new ways of finding sources. Each pair of debates can, however, be taken by itself. By the time a student has read both sides of one debate, he or she is in a pretty good position to write an essay on the issue or to analyze one of the arguments.

14
Student Loans: Should Some Indebtedness Be Forgiven? (p. 465)

First, a bit of background gathered from an article in the *New York Times*, September 9, 2012.

At the time of the article,

- About 5.9 million people had fallen at least twelve months behind in making payments.
- One in six borrowers was in default.
- Defaulted loans added up to about $76 billion.
- In 2011, the Department of Education paid $1.4 billion to private collection agencies to find defaulters.
- In 1211, the average default was $17,005.
- Borrowers who attended profit-making colleges—about 11 percent of all students—accounted for nearly half of the defaults. (A loan is declared in default when it is delinquent for 360 days.)
- Although defaulters often try to avoid detection, for instance by changing their telephone number, almost all defaulters are located.
- Only about 1 percent of the debtors are written off, usually because of death or disability.

Barbara Smaller (cartoon)

I'm looking for a career (p. 132)

It is a commonplace today that the job one prepares for will have changed by the time one begins the job. In the last decade even the profession of teaching has changed vastly because of new technology—no laughing matter for oldsters who have difficulty coping even with e-mail and attachments. In fact, one of today's standard arguments on behalf of a more-or-less traditional liberal arts education is that it teaches the student how to *think*, which in a swiftly changing world is more important than teaching a particular subject matter or a particular skill. The idea in this argument (we don't say it is true; we just say it is common) is that subject matter changes, and skills (e.g., how to use a slide rule) become obsolete, but habits of critical thinking, accompanied by a mind well-stocked with the achievements of the past, provide tools for adapting to changing conditions.

Robert Applebaum

Debate on Student Loan Debt Doesn't Go Far Enough (p. 465)

Applebaum's essay certainly is "bold," to use a word that he himself uses in his first paragraph.

It may be a good idea to ask students to search out his assumptions. As we see it, among his assumptions are these:

- Colleges, seeing "free money" (i.e., dollars paid in tuition by poor students who put themselves into debt), outrageously started to overpay administrators, and to build handsome but unnecessary facilities.

- Starting salaries are nowhere near enough to enable students to repay the loans, so students now learn that they bought a product (an education that was supposed to get them a job with a decent salary) at a ridiculously inflated price.

- Forgiveness of debt thus is not a handout but is closer to a refund.

- Students will spend the forgiven debt, thus boosting the economy.

Applebaum explicitly says (para. 3), "The Student Loan Forgiveness Act of 2012 is not a free ride, nor is it a bailout." In his view, he and his fellow borrowers were defrauded. Education "is a public good" (para. 4), and therefore "Education should be a right" (para. 5). It follows, then (at least for Applebaum), that the members of his generation should not be shackled with debt (in para. 6 he speaks of "indentured servitude") in order to get the education that society needs.

Well, one certainly knows where Applebaum stands. In our view, the next essay, by Justin Wolfers, demolishes Applebaum's economic argument, *but* we do think that Applebaum's fourth paragraph makes good sense. We here quote most of the paragraph:

> Every other country in the industrialized world has figured out how to pay for higher edu-cation for its citizens, but here in America, we continue to treat education as a commodity that benefits only the individual obtaining the education, rather than what it truly is: a public good and an investment in our collective future as a country.

Discuss. (We should add that although in this passage he speaks of education as a pub-lic good, and as an investment in the future of the nation, it seems to us that elsewhere in the essay he speaks about a college education as something that is valuable only because of the dollars that it apparently entitles the degree holder to earn.)

Justin Wolfers

Forgive Student Loans? Worst Idea Ever (p. 469)

Wolfers, an economist, looks at Applebaum's essay only as an economist. That is, he is concerned with Applebaum's argument that the economy will thrive if the government forgives each indebted student $50,000. Wolfers does not address the issue of whether or not higher education is (as Applebaum claims) a "right."

We think his response sounds pretty convincing, though we also think that Applebaum raises an issue in his fourth paragraph (we quote most of the paragraph in this manual, in our brief comment on Applebaum's essay) that must be seriously considered. In short, it is our guess that Wolfers is right in saying (in his final sentence) that no economist will agree with Applebaum, but we continue to think that Applebaum's essay raises—admittedly, in an almost incidental way—a significant issue concerning the role of education in a democracy, an issue that goes beyond the question of loan forgiveness.

15
Are Integrated Devices Safer Than Handheld Devices While Driving? (p. 471)

Mitch Bainwol

Pro (p. 471)

Our first question in the text invites students to think about Bainwol's assumptions. His underlying assumption, we think, is that people will insist on using phones in cars, though he does not put it this way. Rather than saying that drivers will talk on phones, he says that "consumers are going to communicate" (para. 6) and that "drivers are going to insist on staying connected behind the wheel" (para. 10). That is, he uses language with positive connotations ("communicate," "insist on staying connected") to describe what an opponent might call yakking or, at best, conversing.

A few other obvious points: In his first paragraph Bainwol admits there is a problem, "distracted driving"—but in this paragraph he also shrewdly sets up boundaries: The question, he says, is "how . . . to ameliorate it in the real world where drivers demand connectivity." That is, by speaking of the real world, and by claiming that drivers "demand connectivity," he in effect tries at the very outset to rule out of bounds (or at least to label as unrealistic) any counterview that in effect says that drivers should be prohibited from using phones while driving. Similarly, his assertion in his second paragraph that "technology has transformed our society forever" implies that we *must* live with the new technology.

In short, before he gets around to offering *evidence*, he has made assertions that—if a reader accepts them—pretty much make it unnecessary for Bainwol to offer any evidence, or to face and rebut counterviews. Thus, in Bainwol's view, to demand that drivers *not* use phones (again, in his words, give up "connectivity" and cease to "communicate") is to "put our heads in the sand and demand a behavioral shift," that is, to act in an utterly foolish manner. (Our second question in the text alludes to Bainwol's allusion [para. 4] to the popular belief that an ostrich, when pursued, buries its head in the sand and thus, because it cannot see its enemy, thinks that it cannot be seen. Not all students are familiar with this image that connotes the folly of thinking that a problem will go away if we pretend it doesn't exist.)

Bainwol's argument, then, is that attempts to banish communication are unrealistic, and fortunately technology has produced "integrated systems" that operate as a "safety filter," a filter that "mitigates accident risk and saves lives" (para. 5). He ends his essay by reaffirming his assumption that drivers insist on "staying connected behind the wheel," and that the real issue, then, is to "construct policy" that requires drivers to use the technology. Just that. (To put one's trust in a policy of banning the use of phones while driving is, he has explained, to behave like an ostrich.)

While we are talking about persons who defend the use of phones in automobiles, we may as well list the commonest arguments that we have heard, even though Bainwol doesn't offer them:

1. Phones are valuable in times of emergencies (e.g., drivers can call to report accidents they see on the road, or a vehicle that is driving erratically).

2. Distractions other than phones (e.g., conversing with a passenger, eating, lighting a cigarette, adjusting a mirror) probably cause a larger number of fatal accidents than talking on a telephone.

3. Police have more important jobs to do than looking for drivers who are using telephones.

4. If we really want to reduce accidents due to the use of phones, we should (a) educate drivers, and (b) urge them to purchase hands-free devices.

There are, of course, pretty good responses to all of these arguments, as you will hear in class if the issues come up.

OMG (Advertisement) (p. 473)

This advertisement, like most ads, uses words and imagery, but it probably is atypical in that the two media—at least at first glance—are equally impressive. Probably most ads use an image to hook the reader with a general message (e.g., a picture of an attractive family loading a car, in effect saying, "You can be like these happy folks"), and then some text for a more specific message to sell the particular brand of car. In the ad we reproduce, however, the text—"OMG" (text-talk for "oh my God")—and the image showing the spider-web pattern of the cracked and blood-stained glass both immediately seize our attention; the additional words, at the bottom, are important but decidedly ancillary.

We say "spider-web," but the image also evokes a target: In effect the image says, "If you text while driving, you are making yourself a deadly target." And the printed words, "Get the message," play on the business of sending messages, but this is no playful message, just as the large OMG is (*un*characteristically) *not* playful. The additional words ("Texting while driving is a deadly distraction") are almost unnecessary: The image and the texter's OMG do most of the work.

Incidentally, though initialism (that's what the specialists call such things as *OMG*, *LOL*, and *WTF*) is now especially associated with texting, it is really nothing new. Early examples: *AM, PM, FYI, PS, ROTC*.

Rob Reynolds

Con (p. 474)

We offer some responses to the questions that we raise in the text:

1. By using "so-called" (in "so-called naturalistic studies") Reynolds of course seeks to discredit the studies, implying that in fact they are not what their name claims them to be. The term "naturalistic studies" is new to us, but in the context, it pretty clearly means artificially constructed studies (i.e., carefully controlled studies) that apparently closely resemble real events.

2. Reynolds's use of "rigged with" (rather than "equipped with") is a nice example of the use of a negatively charged word in order to sway a reader.

3. By comparing those who defend the use of supposedly safer phones to the cigarette makers who defended filtered cigarettes, Reynolds of course seeks to discredit his opponents. Is the comparison fair? Or, to put it in the language associated with argument, is the analogy false? Our own view, as we state in our discussion of analogy, is that *all* analogies are "false," in that (to use the famous words of Bishop Joseph Butler) "Every thing is what it is, and not another thing." Take the famous adage, "Don't change horses in midstream," which usually in effect means (e.g., during a presidential election in a time of war), "Stay with the leader in this moment of crisis." Well, it is an effective line—it ordinarily makes good sense not to try to change one's mount while in the middle of a river—but, gee, choosing a different president to lead the government during a time of crisis is *not* really the

same as changing a mount in difficult circumstances. Again, "Every thing is what it is, and not another thing." Having said this, we want to add that we think the automakers who say, in effect, "Drivers will use these apps anyway; we just want to make it safer" are indeed pretty close to the cigarette makers who pushed filters. Still, there is a difference.

16
The Local Food Movement: Is It a Better Way to Eat? (p. 476)

First, a few words about "local" and "locavore." In speaking of food and farming, Congress has said that *local* (and *regional*) refer to food produced within four hundred miles of the place where it is sold, *or* food produced anywhere within the state in which it is sold. The word *locavore* (= consumer of local food) was coined in 2005.

Most farming is still a matter of planting in acres of dirt, but hydroponic greenhouses, where plants grow not in soil but in mineral-infused water, take up much less space, and they are proliferating. In these greenhouses, any crop can be produced all year round, whereas, for instance, a dirt farm in New England that produces strawberries can grow them for only about six weeks. Still, locally grown food is thought to constitute only about 1 percent of what we eat.

Second, a reminder: In Chapter 8, we print a relevant essay, James McWilliams's "The Locavore Myth."

Stephen Budiansky

Math Lessons for Locavores (p. 476)

Budiansky's opening paragraph seems prolocavore, but anyone with some experience reading arguments will sense that he is setting something up in order to knock it down. And in fact the title—"Math Lessons for Locavores"—implies that Budiansky will be putting down locavores.

We say "putting down," but perhaps those words are too strong. Certainly he lectures to locavores, but we find his tone acceptable—especially when compared with the fury of Kerry Trueman's response, which we reprint immediately after Budiansky's piece. But we will talk about Trueman's tone when we discuss her essay below. As for the present essay, we found it highly informative, and it struck us as forceful but within the bounds of courteous discourse. True, he uses such words as "self-indulgent," "do-gooders," "arbitrary," "thrown around," and "without any clear understanding," but we were not fully aware of this sort of language until we reread the piece. On first reading, we were fully taken by the details, and we pretty much looked *through* rather than *at* the language.

A word about the structure of the essay: Like many, many other writers, Budiansky ends by returning to a motif introduced in his first paragraph. We discuss this strategy in the parent text, when we talk about drafting an argument (p. 228).

Kerry Trueman

The Myth of the Rabid Locavore (p. 479)

From the very beginning—even from the title with "Myth" and "Rabid"—the essay is extremely belligerent: In the first paragraph we get "self-proclaimed," "stuffed together," "flimsy," "boilerplate," "patronizing"—all in one sentence. In the third paragraph things get even rougher, with some scatological humor:

Throw in a bunch of dubious and/or irrelevant statistics that appear to be truly locally sourced—i.e., pulled out of your own behind.

We do not doubt that Trueman makes some good points, but we think that if she toned it down a bit, she might be more convincing, more effective. For one thing, although she is annoyed by what she calls Budianski's patronizing title ("Math Lessons for Locavores"), she probably should have taken his title more seriously. He really is talking largely about math—especially the energy costs of transporting food. Thus, she scolds him for neglecting certain topics, such as "support for more ecological farming practices" and "more humane treatment of livestock." But a reader might reply, "Yes, the issues you name are certainly issues of immense importance, but the author of a very short essay called "Math Lessons for Locavores" ought not to be expected to include discussion of them.

What we are saying adds up to this: We think Trueman makes many good points, but by letting her righteous anger take over, she does a disservice to her argument and thus to her cause. We doubt that readers want to ally themselves with someone who says (para. 15), "Budiansky needs to be taken out to the foodshed and pummeled with his own lousy logic." In our text, when we discuss a writer's persona, we caution students against displays of ill temper that will alienate a reader. Trueman's essay may be a good illustration.

17
The Death Penalty: Is It Ever Justified? (p. 483)

Background

The continuing salience of the death penalty in our society (as well as the popularity of the topic with users of this book) encourages us to retain in this edition two essays (the debate between Edward Koch and David Bruck) and to use a third essay (by Sister Helen Prejean) later in the book, in Chapter 26, What Is the Ideal Society? Indeed, we reprint enough material to permit a modest research paper to be written on the strength of this chapter alone.

As a preface to these essays, here are some basic facts about the death penalty as of 2010, based on information provided by the federal Bureau of Justice Statistics, Amnesty International, the NAACP Legal Defense Fund, and the Death Penalty Information Center: About 3,400 people are currently under sentence of death in thirty-five states (fifteen states have no death penalty); all of these prisoners have been convicted of some form of criminal homicide. About 18,000 persons are homicide victims each year, about 14,000 persons are convicted of these crimes, and about 300 are sentenced to death. The overwhelming majority of persons on death row are male (nearly 99 percent); about half are white, and of the rest, some 1,500—or about 40 percent of the total—are African American. In 80 percent of the executions, the murder victim was white.

In the years since 1976, when the Supreme Court validated the constitutionality of the death penalty, 1,195 persons have been executed. The number of executions annually has ranged from zero in 1978 and 1980 to twenty-five in 1987 and sixty in 2005. The vast majority have occurred in the South; Texas has executed the most, and five states (Colorado, Idaho, New Mexico, Tennessee, and Wyoming) have executed only one; nine of the death-penalty jurisdictions have executed none. Nine states still use the electric chair, five use the gas chamber, three use hanging, one uses the firing squad, and thirty-six use lethal injection; seventeen allow the prisoner to choose between alternatives (for example, hanging or lethal injection).

In recent years, two-thirds of those on death row had a prior felony conviction; 8 percent had a prior conviction of criminal homicide.

The elapsed time between conviction and execution is considerable—ten to fifteen years is not uncommon—owing principally to the appeals taken in state and federal courts. Recently, roughly 40 percent of all death sentences have been reversed on appeal in federal courts. (It is not known how many were reinstituted by state courts after either retrial or resentencing.)

Our excerpts in this chapter do not attempt to present the "human" side of the death penalty—the experiences of the condemned waiting for execution on death row, the frustration inflicted on surviving relatives and friends of the deceased victim by the delays in carrying out the death sentence, the impossible demands made on attorneys on both sides to meet court-imposed deadlines. From among the many books devoted to these aspects of the whole controversy, two deserve mention. One is *Dead Man Walking* (1993), by a Roman Catholic nun, Sister Helen Prejean, focusing on her experiences in Louisiana. (The excerpt from this book that we reprint is focused on a different aspect of the whole subject.) The film of the same title, made from her book, available on videocassette and DVD, has proved to be a remarkable stimulus to classroom discussion. The other book is *Among the Lowest of the Dead* (1995), by a journalist, David Von Drehle, based on his extensive study of Florida's death-row prisoners. Neither book is devoted primarily to the argument pro or con, but each adds immeasurably to a better understanding of the impact of the current death-penalty system on individual lives.

Elsewhere in the world, according to Amnesty International, as of 2009, 95 countries have abolished the death penalty by law and another 122 by practice, including all of western Europe and all the eastern nations that were satellites of the former USSR (except Poland, which has had, since 1988, an unofficial moratorium on executions; Belarus still continues to use the death penalty).

Two essays we've previously included are George Ryan's "Speech Announcing Commutation of All Illinois Prisoners' Death Sentences" and Gary Wills' "The Dramaturgy of Death," both of which would supplement this debate nicely. Former governor Ryan's clemency statement is unique in offering a full-scale critique of capital punishment as it is actually practiced, in contrast to the more abstract discussions by other thinkers presented in this section. What the essay may lack in style, originality, and economy of language, it makes up with its earnest appeal to the sensibility and imagination of the audience.

Did Ryan's use of his clemency powers have much effect on the thinking and practices of other governors with large death-row populations? Not so far as we can tell, though the future may tell a different story. Could it be that Ryan has had few imitators because other governors have not had to face the awful truth that there are unquestionably innocent prisoners on their death rows?

The essay by Wills offers a novel approach to the discussion of the death penalty by taking a passage from Friedrich Nietzsche (written more than a century ago) in which he identifies and evaluates the purposes or functions of punishment generally. Wills then uses this larger framework to develop the special features of the death penalty. A total of fourteen such purposes or functions are identified, with the result that light is shed on the death penalty from each of these directions. Classroom discussion for at least two sessions could profitably be devoted to identifying how many of these topics that Nietzsche and Wills find relevant are found in the death-penalty practices currently used in America, along with an account of their relative importance.

Edward I. Koch

Death and Justice: How Capital Punishment Affirms Life (p. 483)

The controversy over the death penalty is a perennial focus of high school debate, and some students will have encountered the issue there. Extensive discussion of almost every claim advanced or contested by former New York City Mayor Edward I. Koch and by David Bruck (author of the following essay) can be found in the scholarly literature on the subject; for starters, look at *The Death Penalty in America: Current Controversies* (1997), edited by Hugo Bedau. An unusually extensive exchange in a modified debate format, between John Conrad and Ernest van den Haag, is found in their book, *The Death Penalty: A Debate* (1983).

Koch opens with several examples that hold our attention. They allow him to get the ironist's advantage by the end of his second paragraph ("their newfound reverence for life"), and they hint at his combative style, which helped make his autobiographical book, *Mayor* (1984), into a best seller.

Koch's essay is a bit unusual among those in the text because he adopts the strategy of advancing his side of the argument by succinctly stating and then criticizing the arguments of the other side. Because he is in control, of course, the other side has to be content with his selection and emphasis; by allowing the other side no more than a one-sentence statement per argument, he makes it look pretty unconvincing.

Koch's concluding paragraphs (15 and 16) are particularly strong because he manages to show his sensitivity to a major claim by the opposition ("the death of . . . even a convicted killer . . . diminishes us all"), even as he implies that the alternative he favors is nevertheless better than the one he opposes. The important details of his own position (question 5) he leaves unspecified.

David Bruck

The Death Penalty (p. 489)

David Bruck's style of argument can be usefully contrasted to Edward I. Koch's. Bruck begins not as Koch did with an example or two (Bruck offers his first example only at para. 4) but with a brief recap of Koch's central position—that morality requires society to execute the convicted murderer. Then, instead of a patient (tedious?) argument-by-argument examination of Koch's position, Bruck tries to make headway by rubbing our noses in some of the disturbing details about the plight of persons on death row that, he implies, cast a different light on the morality of executions.

He then directly challenges (paras. 7–8) one of Koch's principal factual contentions about the possibility of erroneous executions. While we're at it, we can correct Bruck when he writes that Hugo Bedau's research involved about 400 cases "in which the state eventually *admitted* error." The research showed that the state admitted error in 309 out of 350 cases—and also that no state has ever admitted executing an innocent person, although Bedau reports that his research shows twenty-three such erroneous executions since 1900. Subsequent to the Koch-Bruck debate, this research has been published in the book, *In Spite of Innocence* (1992), by Michael Radelet, Hugo Bedau, and Constance Putnam.

Worry over convicting the innocent in capital cases reached a new degree of intensity during 2000. In Illinois, prompted by the fact that in recent years as many death-row prisoners had been released because of their innocence as had been executed, Governor George Ryan declared a statewide moratorium on executions, to last until he could be assured that effective remedial procedures were in place. Thus Illinois became the first capital punishment jurisdiction to comply with the 1996 recommendation from the House of Delegates of the American Bar Association, urging a nationwide moratorium on the death penalty until procedures were introduced to ensure fairness, due process, and competent counsel for capital defendants. Much of the background to Ryan's decision is discussed in the recent book *Actual Innocence* (2000) by Jim Dwyer, Peter Neufeld, and Barry Scheck. They relate the stories of recent cases (many, but not all, of them involving the use of DNA evidence to exonerate the innocent) that show just how easy it is for the innocent to be convicted and sentenced to death.

In the Koch-Bruck debate, the mayor had the last word, although we didn't reprint it in the text. His objections to Bruck's rebuttal may be found in *The New Republic* (May 20, 1985, p. 21). The main assertion in Koch's response is that "a truly civilized society need not shrink from imposing capital punishment as long as its procedures for determining guilt and passing sentence are constitutional and just." The reader of Koch's original article may well wonder where in it he succeeded in showing that these "procedures" in our society, as actually administered, are "just."

A word about question 4, on the polygraph or "lie detector." The so-called lie detector does not, of course, detect lies. It records physiological phenomena such as abnormal heart beat that are commonly associated with lying. Opponents say it is based on the premise that there is a "Pinocchio effect," a bodily response unique to lying. Opponents of the polygraph argue that the effects recorded, such as an increased heart rate or blood pressure, can have other causes. That is, these changes may reflect personal anxieties apart from lying, and, on the other hand, the symptoms may be suppressed by persons who in fact are lying. Wu-Tai Chin, the CIA employee who spied for China for thirty years, "passed" polygraph tests many times. The American Psychological Association, after a two-year study, concluded flatly that polygraph tests are "unsatisfactory." It is also noteworthy that findings from polygraphs are not admitted as evidence in federal courts.

18
Genetic Modification of Human Beings:
Is It Acceptable? (p. 495)

Ronald M. Green

Building Baby from the Genes Up (p. 495)

The essential body of the argument raised in Green's essay appears in his discussion of the "four major concerns" raised by genetic engineering. He presents them in the following order (Does he regard this order as a reflection of their relative importance?): (1) adverse effects on parenting, (2) a diminution in our freedom of action, (3) aggravating undesirable social class conflicts, and (4) playing God. It is not much of a surprise when we learn that he is not persuaded by any of these arguments, much less all. Neither are we. Our take on this quartet of reasons places the most popular argument, (4), at the bottom of the list. As for the other three, our hunch is that it's a dead heat.

Green asks (Is it a rhetorical question?), "Why should a child struggle with reading difficulties when we could alter the genes responsible for the problem?" (para. 4). Several reasons might lead a thoughtful critic to conclude that we cannot afford such genetic engineering. One of these reasons might be that there is the risk of terrible side effects in erasing the genes relevant to reading difficulties. Even if there were few or no risks of such side effects, there might be a very high economic cost in implementing such genetic interventions. Yet another reason might be the unreliability of the diagnosis. The sum of these costs might be properly regarded as outweighing the benefits. Or so those who oppose such biochemical interventions might argue. Green does not explore this territory as deeply as one might wish.

He loads the dice (in whose favor?) when (in para. 5) he invokes the 1997 science fiction film *Gattaca*. In the world of Gattaca, "its eugenic obsessions have all but extinguished human love and compassion." Since we are dealing entirely with a fictitious society (with unmistakable overtones of Aldous Huxley's *Brave New World* [1932]), why not depict one in which the eugenic designers have figured out ways to increase human love and compassion, a cheerful disposition, happiness, and to foster traits such as honesty, altruism, pacific temperament, and other virtues? Green comes close to this idea in his closing paragraph.

Richard Hayes

Genetically Modified Humans? No Thanks (p. 499)

Hayes offers the reader a full-scale assault on Ronald Green's essay. His sole concession to those who side with Green is the use of genetic engineering to save lives and cure illnesses. He explicitly rejects genetic modifications designed to yield "heritable genetic enhancement" (paras. 7 and 8). He criticizes Green for failing to distinguish these two different uses of genetic modification and he enlists "public opinion" and the laws of "nearly 40 countries" that agree with him.

Hayes gives a beautiful example of invoking the slippery slope argument, worth quoting in full: "Once we begin genetically modifying our children, where do we stop?" (para. 3). Hayes seems not to notice that this objection will arise against even the limited use of the genetic modifications he would allow. Once the genie is out of the bottle—well, you can write the script for the rest of the parade of horrors that Hayes offers us. Hayes also thinks that "Green most fervently wants us to embrace . . . heritable genetic enhancement" (para. 7). This makes Green look like a rabid fanatic, not at all consistent with the style in which he presents himself to the reader. And irresponsible as well, when he says that "Green blithely announces his confidence" (para. 9). We think that a fairer assessment of Green's essay would reveal a cautious exploration of a highly controversial social policy on which we are a long way from having said the last word on either side of the debate.

Part Five

CURRENT ISSUES: CASEBOOKS

19
A College Education: What Is Its Purpose? (p. 505)

Andrew Delbanco

3 Reasons College Still Matters (p. 505)

We begin indirectly, by offering at the outset not a discussion of Delbanco but a famous quotation by William Cory (1823–1892), a schoolmaster at Eton. And, indeed, when he talks about going to a "school," he means a school, not a college or a university. But we think his words apply very well to a college—most obviously to a liberal arts college but, we will briefly argue, also to colleges that emphasize vocational training. Here is Cory's quotation, taken from a letter he wrote.:

> At school you are engaged not so much in acquiring knowledge as in making mental efforts under criticism. A certain amount of knowledge you can indeed with average faculties acquire so as to retain; nor need you regret the hours you spent on much that is forgotten, for the shadow of lost knowledge at least protects you from many illusions. But you go to a great school not so much for knowledge as for arts and habits; for the habit of attention, for the art of expression, for the art of assuming at a moment's notice a new intellectual position, for the art of entering quickly into another person's thoughts, for the habit of submitting to censure and refutation, for the art of indicating assent or dissent in graduated terms, for the habit of regarding minute points of accuracy, for the art of working out what is possible in a given time, for taste, for discrimination, for mental courage, and for mental soberness. Above all, you go to a great school for self-knowledge.

These words pretty much embody our idea of a liberal education—especially, if we had to choose just a phrase or so, the passage about acquiring the habit of "indicating assent or dissent in graduated terms." Cory is speaking about what today is called "critical thinking," a topic we discuss at length in our first three chapters. It is our belief that most liberal arts courses—*and especially introductory courses in composition or argument or rhetoric*—inevitably are largely devoted to this sort of thinking. We grant, however, that some courses are not, for instance, introductory courses in which a student learns a foreign language—although even in the earliest stages of learning a foreign language one begins to see things from an unaccustomed point of view!

What about courses that are designed to prepare a student for a particular career, let's say a course in accounting for a business major or a course in psychology for a nursing major? It is our strong impression that almost all such courses *do* require students to enter "into another person's thoughts," *do* develop "the habit of regarding minute points of accuracy," *do* help a student to master "the art of working out what is possible in a given time," and they *do* help to develop "taste, . . . discrimination, . . . mental courage, and . . . mental soberness." Admittedly, such courses usually do not introduce a student to unfamiliar Great Ideas—they do not immediately present students with challenging new conceptions—but we believe that almost all college courses (in two-year colleges as well as four-year colleges), sometimes almost in spite of themselves, help students to achieve "self-knowledge."

End of sermon on the value of college courses, including those offered by programs with a decided vocational slant.

Delbanco offers three reasons on behalf of acquiring a liberal education: (1) It enables people to live better lives; (2) a democracy requires educated citizens; and (3) a liberal education helps a person to "enjoy life" (para. 16). The last might seem frivolous, but he puts it in the culminating or climactic position. Our seventh question in the text asks students to comment on Delbanco's sequence. We ourselves are entirely satisfied with his arrangement, but of course other arrangement might be equally satisfactory. He might have led off with this relatively personal angle and then moved to the grander social aspects. Indeed, Delbanco risked—with the arrangement that he settled on—descending with a bump, trivializing the issue, but (again) we find his arrangement satisfactory. In our view, this relatively modest reason (allegedly suggested to him by an alumnus) allows him to end in a down-to-earth manner.

We are *not* saying that the sequence of the three points really doesn't matter; rather, we are saying that it *does* matter, and that a different sequence would produce a somewhat different essay. Delbanco is writing for the general public—or, rather, that part of the general public that reads articles and books about the value of a college education. If he had been writing in a journal that is read chiefly by college administrators, we think he might have put this business about pleasure first and then gone on to discuss the grander issues. But given his audience, he chose to end with a down-to-earth reason. Seems good to us.

Patrick Allitt

Should Undergraduates Specialize? (p. 510)

By all means, permit young would-be physicists to pursue physics from the get-go—(our answer to question 2); they ought to be "free" to do so. But let us teachers and course advisers also try to persuade them to broaden their collegiate studies. They might not have another chance until they retire and can take a postgraduate extension course in the Great Books of Western Civilization. A freshman humanities course for all students, whatever their major fields, can go a long way toward providing a minimal exposure to some area of history, literature, philosophy, and fine arts—the Renaissance and Reformation, say—without overburdening the science students' program of studies.

Some students, especially those born abroad or born of parents who were educated abroad, may be familiar with a system of higher education that differs from American higher education. If you have any such students, you may want to ask them to comment on the system and to indicate what they think are its strengths and weaknesses.

A few other points, chiefly about Patrick Allitt's ways of arguing: We think it is worth mentioning that the essay is somewhat unusual in its emphasis on the first person. Allitt draws on his own experience as a student, and also on his experience as the father of a woman who is now in college. In short, we tell students, writers of arguments often cite authorities, and there are some instances in which the writers themselves are authorities. If a student is writing about an issue in which he or she has been significantly involved, there is no reason to hesitate to draw on this firsthand experience.

A second point concerning Allitt's argument is this: The argument is a comparison, and inexperienced writers can learn from Allitt some ways of organizing a comparison. Notice that in his first paragraph he introduces the basic issue—his own education versus his daughter's—and in his second paragraph he indicates that "these two college adventures differ sharply." Readers know exactly what to expect. The next four paragraphs are devoted to talking about his own education, and then, in the seventh paragraph, we get a clear transition: "Frances, by contrast, is entering a decentralized system." And of course we then get several paragraphs devoted to the American system. There is none of that dizzying back-and-forth ping-pong structure of alternating paragraphs with "A is this, B is that," "Thus A, while B," "Again A, whereas B . . . ." We don't say that one should never alternate paragraphs when writing a comparison, but many students have been told in high school that a proper comparison keeps going back and forth. Nonsense. There is nothing wrong with indicating the nature of the comparison at the outset, then setting forth one half, and then setting forth the other half. Of course in setting forth the second half, one must be careful to establish connections with the first half, usually by very briefly reminding the reader of this or that feature. The comparisons that break apart are those that set forth a block and then set forth a second block *and do not connect the second with the first*. Allitt's essay clearly is not guilty of this error.

Finally, we note—and this point is obvious—Allitt ends by focusing on American education. His final paragraph is not "Thus we see that in England A, but in America Y." Rather—because his real point is American education—he devotes all of the final paragraph to American education.

Carlo Rotella

No, It Doesn't Matter What You Majored In (p. 516)

Rotella's eighth (i.e., his-next-to-last) paragraph ends by saying that a college graduate ought to be able to "deliver a sustained reasoned argument. . . . It's a craft, like cabinet making." Obviously there are two points here, one about the college graduate as someone who can reason, and a second about reasoning as a craft, an acquired skill. We are inclined to agree with both points: The author/editors of a textbook on critical thinking (Rotella's "reasoned argument") of course believe that this subject can be taught, which is to say that students can *learn* to "deliver a sustained reasoned argument," and they believe students can learn how to do this because reasoning is (or, better, it *largely* is) a "craft," that is, something with basic principles that reasonably intelligent people can master.

Now, of course there is more to a liberal education than the ability to reason. Briefly, we subscribe also to a statement from Allan Bloom's *The Closing of the American Mind*:

> The liberally educated person is one who is able to resist the easy and preferred answers, not because he is obstinate but because he knows others worthy of consideration.

But this is *not* to say (in our view) that the only "liberal" courses are those evidently devoted to Big Ideas, World Classics, and so on. An introductory course in (say) anthropology might well bring the student into contact with someone from a culture notably different from his or her own, a culture that offers unfamiliar views: A Caucasian student might find herself interviewing a Chinese immigrant, or even a first-generation American Chinese, and might thus come into contact with unfamiliar ideas "worthy of consideration." Indeed the cultures need not be so evidently different: Encountering someone whose religious beliefs are different, or whose economic status is different, can have profound educational effects.

And—here we add a self-congratulatory note—we think that the essays in our text go a long way toward introducing students to unfamiliar ideas that are (in Bloom's words) "worthy of consideration." Students (including those enrolled in programs that essentially are designed to prepare them for careers in business or nursing or police work or engineering or whatever) who are familiar with these readings are learning to think about ideas that are worthy of consideration.

Alina Tugend

Vocation or Exploration: Pondering the Purpose of College (p. 518)

Perhaps foolishly (though of course we don't think so), we have touched on *vocational* education in our comments on the essays by Delbanco and Rotella, so we urge you to glance at those discussions (above) in this manual. The gist of our view is that many courses usually regarded as vocational can in fact contribute to a liberal education.

Mark Edmundson

Education's Hungry Hearts (p. 521)

We think this essay presents no difficulties even to inexperienced readers, and here we will confine ourselves to offering our responses to some of the questions we raise in the text.

1. Our first question concerns the effectiveness of the title and the opening paragraph. If the term "Hungry Hearts" is known to the reader, from Bruce Springsteen's song, it will certainly arouse attention (which of course is what the *exordium* of a speech is supposed to do), but even if it is not known, the phrase itself stirs some interest: The reader wants to know, "Well, who are these 'hungry hearts,' and exactly what about them?" The first paragraph identifies the source of the phrase—and presumably convinces the reader to stay with the essay, since the reader knows who Springtseen is and now wants to know how this term and this popular figure are going to to fit into an essay that appeared in the *New York Times*.

   The first paragraph is engagingly colloquial, with its "Really?" and its "Is that so?" and when he goes on at the end of the first paragraph to say, "At the risk of offending the Boss, I want to register some doubts," presumably the reader is hooked, that is, will stay with the piece in order to learn what the doubts are.

   The second paragraph, still part of the opening—that is, the part of the essay in which the writer (we might almost say the speaker or even the rhetorician) gets the hearers' attention, establishes his or her own bona fides, and sets out the issue—is highly personal. We learn that Edmundson has taught for thirty-five years and has had some four thousand students, so we are presumably willing to grant that he is highly experienced, and he ought to have something interesting to say about students and about education. Of course by the time readers finish the essay they may conclude that they were mistaken in this assumption—that despite the author's experience, he has nothing to say—but, again, we think that a reader on first encountering this paragraph is inclined to assume that the essayist is worth listening to. In rhetorical terms, Edmundson here is concerned with *ethos*, that is, with presenting himself as someone of goodwill.

   And, to put it bluntly, his argument rests almost entirely on this presentation of himself as someone who ought to be listened to on this topic. He offers nothing in the way of statistics, nothing in the way of deductive logic, nothing in the way of authorities. Yes, he does mention such names as Freud, Kafka, Blake, Nietzsche, and Lionel Trilling, but not as authorities on what college has to offer, or what kinds of students are the best students. On these issues, we have to trust Edmundson, whose evidence is the four thousand students who have passed his desk—he offers some generalizations about good and bad students—and some other persons whom he has encountered, for instance, his friend Paul Rizzo, a person utterly unknown to the reader. If we are impressed by this sort of inductive evidence, it is because Edmundson has presented himself as the sort of guy that readers like and can identify themselves with, someone who is not whining, someone who does not have a chip on his shoulder, someone who is not essentially advancing his own agenda but, rather, someone who is concerned with the general welfare. Again (and in short), a matter of persuasion by *ethos*.

2. Our second question following the essay is about Edmundson's concluding paragraph—the paragraph in which he tells us about Paul Rizzo's current life. As we have just said, this is hardly proof if one is thinking of proof as logical argument, but we think the paragraph is at least moderately effective as a piece of persuasive writing. A reader sort of *likes* this Rizzo guy and is impressed with him, even though the reader knows almost nothing about him.

3. Where, if anywhere, does Edmundson explicitly state his thesis? The thesis is implied in paragraphs 4 and 5 and is stated explicitly in his sixth paragraph, just before the middle of this short essay. In a long essay, a reader certainly wants the thesis to be stated earlier than just before the middle, but in an essay of the length of Edmundson's, we think the position is satisfactory; that is the reader learns it within a minute.

4. As we have been saying, Edmundson offers very little in the way of *reasons*—and that is partly why we offer it early in the book. He doesn't give statistics, he doesn't cite relevant authorities, he doesn't offer syllogisms. He offers himself, *ethos*. (We don't use this word until our third chapter, but there is no harm—indeed, there can be much merit—in an instructor introducing it earlier.)

Marty Nemko

America's Most Overrated Product: The Bachelor's Degree (p. 523)

We have not taught this essay, but we imagine that it will produce much discussion in classrooms, both in two-year and in four-year institutions.

Nemko describes himself as a "career counselor," and it may well be that, face-to-face with a given individual, he can give sound advice that will save the person tens of thousands of dollars and will also enable the advisee to have a happy career. Certainly the scenario he establishes in his first paragraph (a student who did poorly in high school tells Nemko that he or she has been attending college for five years, is $80,000 in debt, and still has 45 credits to go) is distressing, which means that it is an effective piece of writing. Nemko's second paragraph is also effective: He offers "the killer statistic" that 40 percent of the people who graduated in the bottom 40 percent of their classes, and whose first institutions are four-year colleges, will not have earned a diploma eight and a half years later. And he follows this assertion with an assertion that pretty clearly implies that many four-year colleges are engaged in a con game: "Yet four-year colleges admit and take money from hundreds of thousands of such students each year!"

So here is our problem with the essay: On the one hand, Nemko's title is catchy and probably has a good deal of truth to it; he seems to know what he is talking about (he cites statistics), and his sympathy is with the underdog, but the suggestion that colleges are engaged in a swindle makes us a bit uneasy, even a bit suspicious. Yes, no doubt admissions officers are aware that there are desks and beds to be filled—in other words, that a certain number of tuition-paying students is needed to keep the place going—but the cynicism implied in "take money from hundreds of thousands of students" unnerves us. Perhaps we are unnerved because we fear the assertion may be true, but we think our uneasiness proceeds from a sense that Nemko thinks of college only in terms of dollars and cents and the higher incomes that college graduates earn. By the way, Nemko's assertion that college graduates of course earn more because "they're bright, more motivated, and have better family connections" (para. 5) seems to us to be only partly true: They do have better family connections, and they probaby are more motivated so far as making money goes, but we are not sure that they are brighter. We have met plenty of very bright carpenters, plumbers, electricians, beauticians, musicians—and indeed gardeners and butchers and farmers. Academic success probably ought not to be equated with brightness. Or, put it this way: People can be smart in different ways. But yes, a college degree probably does tell an employer that the job candidate is fairly intelligent, fairly diligent, fairly socialized. The employer may then believe, "This is the person for me. As for specialized skills needed for this particular job, well, X can learn them here; what I want is someone who is fairly intelligent, fairly diligent, fairly socialized, and the bachelor's degree probably is a sign of these qualities."

In his eighth paragraph Nemko casts a cold eye on the colleges' assertion that "A college education is more about enlightenment than employment," and he brings up the issue of large lecture classes, implying that students are getting short-changed: The small classes are taught mostly (he says) by graduate students. We think there is much to be said for senior professors—or at least those of them who are good with small groups—teaching some small classes, but we also believe that a large lecture course can be highly effective.

We have already mentioned that Nemko uses statistics. In his second paragraph, for instance, he speaks of "a study cited by Clifford Adelman," and in his ninth paragraph he speaks of "the latest annual national survey of freshmen conducted by the Higher Education Research Institute," but he never gets around to giving exact titles and specific page references, and we have the feeling (admittedly merely a feeling) that the studies may be more nuanced than Nemko suggests. For instance, in his ninth paragraph Nemko mentions a study that reports that 44.6 percent of the freshmen surveyed "said they were not satisfied with the quality of instruction they received." But exactly what was the context, what was the exact queston the students were asked? For instance, if the students were indeed talking about their courses as a whole—in other words, their academic experience in college thus far (as we think Nemko implies)—the figure is indeed alarming. But what if the response was given to a question such as "Are you satisfied with the instruction in all of the courses that you have taken?" Or "Were you dissatisfied with the instruction in any course?" Surely, it will not be surprising or distressing to learn that a student taking four courses, some of which are required rather than elected, is unhappy with one or even two. Furthermore, anyone who has served on a tenure committee and has read dozens or even hundreds of students' evaluations of a candidate for tenure knows that the range of responses may be wide: 10 percent of the students say a given course is the best they have had, 80 percent say the course is pretty good, and the remaining 10 percent say they got little or maybe nothing from the course.

What about Nemko's bulleted proposals, for example, that colleges post on their Web sites the results of a "value added" test? Well, we are all in favor of transparency, and it would indeed be interesting to see the statistics that he calls for, though it is hard to imagine that colleges would or could comply. To take a single instance: How likely is it that colleges can gather the "salary data" of graduates (sixth bullet)?

Our final comment: We are inclined to agree with Nemko's last paragraph (it begins, "College is a wise choice for far fewer people than are currently encouraged to consider it"), but we think that his somewhat belligerent tone and his failure to give exact citations for his sources weaken his essay.

Charles Murray

Should the Obama Generation Drop Out? (p. 528)

We are not quite sure what to make of this essay. We imagine that most people—instructors as well as undergraduates—will agree with the last sentence in Murray's opening paragraph, "It's what you can do that should count when you apply for a job, not where you learned to do it." But we don't see how he gets from this position to one of his basic assumptions, stated in his fourth paragraph:

> For most of the nation's youths, making the bachelor's degree a job qualification means demanding a credential that is beyond their reach. It is a truth that politicians and educators cannot bring themselves to say out loud: A large majority of young people do not have the intellectual ability to do genuine college-level work.

Curiously, in his next few paragraphs Murray offers as proof the readers' inability today to succeed in a subject other than their chosen major:

> You think I'm too pessimistic? Too elitist? Readers who graduated with honors in English literature or Renaissance history should ask themselves if they could have gotten a B.S. in physics, no matter how hard they tried. (I wouldn't have survived freshman year.) Except for the freakishly gifted, all of us are too dumb to get through college in many majors.

74

This may well be true—but, at least as we see it, these assertions argue against Murray's basic point that "a large majority of young people do not have the intellectual ability to do genuine college-level work." He seems to be saying that college graduates—such as his readers and Murray himself—could not graduate if they had been forced to major in certain fields, and this is somehow taken to be proof that most of today's youngsters are unfit for college. Unless he is saying—and we do not think this is his point—that his own inability to handle physics shows that he himself does not have "the intellectual ability to do genuine college-level work," the evidence he offers indicates that indeed a person can be weak in one area or another, and yet still do creditable work in several other areas. That is, the evidence Murray offers—the reader's inability to do good work in all academic areas—undercuts his own position, since he assumes that his reader is a college graduate.

Probably most colleges and universities recognize that students have varying competencies, and they offer a variety of courses suited to these differences. For instance, there may be an introductory physics course that is designed for would-be physicists, and quite another physics course—still respectable—designed for the nonspecialist. Or take composition courses: A college may (1) exempt some students from the basic course, and (2) require some other students to take a one-term course, and (3) require yet other students to take a two-term course.

As we understand it, Murray is talking about two topics which are barely related: One topic is

> Unfortunately, a College Education Is Now Regarded as a Pre-Requisite for Most Jobs, Even for Jobs That Should Not Require It.

and a second topic is

> Most Young People Are Not Fit to Go to College.

Our own view is that he is right about the first of these topics and wrong about the second. But our view doesn't matter: What matters is Murray's essay, which is a good example of an essay that lacks focus.

Let's talk only about his proposal that potential employers stop asking for a college degree. He suggests two alternatives: "certification tests" (paras.1–12) and "samples" (or "examples") of the candidate's work. Certainly, samples of work ought to do the trick in some areas (let's say, jewelry making, or—Murray's own example—computer programming), but "certification tests" seem to us to be a bad idea. Is Murray talking about a sort of SAT for this job and that job? Who would make the tests for, say, the job of an editorial assistant at a textbook publisher, a car salesman, or a receptionist at a health center? And who would score them? And how many people would agree that indeed the tests test what they are supposed to test?

Briefly, then, we agree with Murray's proposed battle cry, "It's what you can do that should count when you apply for a job, not where you learned to do it," and we strongly approve of his decision to use this very line again as the last line of his essay. (Here he is following the sound rhetorical strategy of returning, in the final paragraph, to a topic introduced in the opening, a strategy that we suggest in our book, where we talk about concluding paragraphs.) We also agree that the widespread requirement of a degree—even for jobs that do not require anything learned at college—is deplorable. Young persons who want to be carpenters or chefs or gardeners or fishermen or actors or writers, and whose experiences in high school have convinced them that they do not wish to undergo further academic training, should be encouraged to engage in their chosen fields. But of course persons with these same ambitions, if they wish to go first to college, should be encouraged to do so, which means, among other things, that somehow college should be made financially possible for them. They probably will, we think, live better lives as carpenters, chefs, gardeners, fishermen, actors, and writers than if they had not gone to college. But we digress: We will again say (1) we are skeptical of some of Murray's proposed solutions, and (2) we very much doubt his assumption that "A large majority of young people do not have the intellectual ability to do genuine college-level work" (para. 4).

Louis Menand

Re-imagining Liberal Education (p. 534)

Vocationalism (question 3) is a neologism derived from vocation, which in turn comes from the Latin for "calling," now a rather dated expression. Lawyers were once said to be called to the bar; doctors, and especially clerics, were said to have a calling—or to lack one, if they were so unfortunate. Who is to do the calling and how one is to decide whether he or she has been called to medicine, or to teaching, or to some other career or profession is not obvious. In our time, few, if any, teachers would claim that they were called to the profession they practice. It is not entirely clear what Louis Menand means by the term in this context. We wonder whether what the term means for him might better be expressed as indoctrination or training, both of them illiberal academic pursuits. Notice also the slightly negative connotation the term has when he says (para. 2) that permitting early entry into a field of concentration "smacks of vocationalism," as though it were a vulgar or otherwise bad thing to permit such early entry.

In teaching this essay we think we would get things going by quoting from paragraph 6, where Menand says, "The Deweyan answer . . . would be that you cannot teach people a virtue by requiring them to read books about it." Exactly why do we require students to read certain books?

For us, the most important part of Menand's essay is his final paragraph, with his comment about John Dewey and with his observation that teachers play a role far beyond their role as teachers of particular subjects.

20
Hydraulic Fracturing: Is Fracking Worth the Environmental Cost? (p. 538)

Don Carns Jr.

Shale Drilling Is a Disaster Waiting to Happen (p. 538)

The opening paragraph (beginning "I will be direct and to the point") presents the writer as, well, as someone who is direct and to the point. No nonsense here, no elaborate windup, no fancy rhetoric (in the negatives sense of the word), just (so Carns suggests) straight talk, though of course the student of rhetoric understands that this presentation of the self is in fact a rhetorical strategy, the establishment of an engaging *ethos*.

Carns goes on to present some technical material, but he is careful not to use technical terms; nothing here will cause readers to scratch their heads and mumble to themselves, "I don't understand what he is talking about." Of course he may be wrong, wrong, wrong—and that's what the next essay claims, but we do think that to the uninformed viewer, Carns comes across pretty well.

Scott Cline

Unfounded Fears about Shale Gas Obscure Facts (p. 541)

Like Carns—the essayist whom he is rebutting—Cline comes across as a guy who can be counted on to speak clearly and truthfully.

His first sentence accuses Cline of being "long on fiction and short on facts," and in his second paragraph Cline playfully re-creates the alleged fiction, a combination of the Gothic novel and sci-fi: "vast mysterious subterranean cave systems . . . [with] radioactive material in drinking water." He then returns to the present, and to his own voice, "Geez, where do I begin to correct this fictional nonsense?"

Our own impression is that Cline is knowledgeable; certainly he is confident that the facts speak for themselves. For example, he says

> Also, radioactive shale cuttings cannot hurt anyone. The extra radioactivity that people might obtain by standing next to a pile of Marcellus or Utica shale cutting is insignificantly small compared with the dose that we naturally receive from cosmic radiation, our environment, and even the food we eat.

> And radioactivity is not a threat to our drinking water. All water that returns to the surface is reused, injected, or treated so that drinking water maintains the mandated standards.

The writer of this comment on Cline's letter does not have the faintest idea if Cline is correct, but the writer also believes that Cline couldn't be saying these things if they weren't at least more or less true, true in general. And of course Cline *does* grant that there are at least *some* bad side effects of fracking, though he insists these are minor. The strategy here is venerable: Admit some weaknesses, and thus the writer gains the reader's trust that the writer sees both sides and is offering an informed opinion. What does Cline grant?

> In reality shale gas exploration boils down to a temporary traffic nuisance that can be solved by working with local communities to minimize short-term inconveniences and making sure that the water that returns to the surface through the wellbore is properly stored, transported, and either recycled or treated.

This assertion may or may not be true, but we do think it is an effective piece of writing.

Aubrey K. McClendon

Is Hydraulic Fracturing Good for the Economy? Pro (p. 542)

McClendon begins by citing a study done by Pennsylvania Sate University, presumably an impartial work. Obviously, if he had cited a study done by the gas industry, readers would be suspicious and would be unconvinced by findings that claimed fracking would bring great wealth to the area and that it had no downside. In short, McClendon begins effectively, citing an authority that the reader presumably trusts even though the reader has little or no knowledge of Penn State (other than its football team) and has not looked at the report.

Our first question in the text makes the point that McClendon originally delivered the material as a talk, probably with visual aids. In a small way, the bullets in his published essay are a sort of visual persuasion. In the text, we ask about the effect of bullets, especially compared with, say, a numbered list. It is our belief that bullets add a punchiness, a vigor, to the material that a numbered list (or a lettered list) does not have.

Our third question asks about McClendon's final paragraph, which we reproduce here:

> And remind me, what value [have] these shale gas protestors created? What jobs have they created? You know the answer, and so do I, and it's time that we contrast what we do for a living [versus] what they do for a living.

It is hard-hitting, heavily ironic: McClendon does not expect an answer when he asks his question "And remind me, what value [have] these gas protestors created?" And his original audience—presumably businessmen and engineers—must have congratulated themselves when they compared their jobs with those of the protestors. Unfortunately, we have no idea about who the protestors were—maybe students and their do-nothing, idle, highbrow professors. In any case, in its context, these final contemptuous words probably worked very well, but in print, addressed to the solitary reader, they make an impression that must be quite different from what was intended.

Jannette M. Barth

Is Hydraulic Fracturing Good for the Economy? Con (p. 544)

In her first paragraph Barth makes a distinction between capital-intensive industries (e.g., oil and gas industries, industries that require an immense amount of money, for instance for equipment, but that do not require hordes of workers) and labor-intensive industries (she doesn't give an example, but an extreme example would be a major law office, which requires lots of lawyers—people filling jobs—but very little money other than to pay for furnishings and rent).

Barth goes on to argue that the vision of drilling as a sort of money tree that will make everyone rich is a fantasy. There are *costs*, she insists, such as damage to highways, loss of revenue from hunters and tourists, and so on. Incidentally, in paragraph 3, when Barth cites some areas that will be losers, she says:

> Examples of industries likely to be negatively affected include agriculture, tourism, organic farming, wine making, hunting, fishing and river recreation.

Isn't this list a bit padded? Doesn't "agriculture" *include* "organic farming" and maybe "wine making," too, and perhaps "tourism" includes a good deal of "river recreation." Still, we do see Barth's point: One cannot just count the dollars that roll in. Further proof of some of the world's wisest words, "There is no such thing as a free lunch."

21
Drugs: Should Their Sale and Use
Be Legalized? (p. 546)

Background

Next to AIDS, drugs—their use and abuse and the costs of the efforts to control them—may well be the nation's most publicized if not its most pressing social problem. Unlike AIDS, however, drug use leaves few of the users dead; and many of those who do die from drugs do not do so from overdosing or suicide, but from shoot-outs in turf wars and busted deals. The four essays we present take several divergent views of the problem and its solution.

In his inaugural address early in 1989, President George H. W. Bush reassured the nation by declaring "This scourge will end." A few months later, in a special broadcast on the drug problem, he reported that although "23 million Americans were using drugs" regularly in 1985, that number had dropped in 1988 by "almost 9 million." The president credited this gain to his administration's four-point campaign: tougher penalties, more effective enforcement, expanded treatment programs, and education to reach the young who had not yet started to use drugs. An enthusiastic elaboration of the government's efforts is presented in the articles we reprint by William J. Bennett, the nation's first drug czar (a good guy, not to be confused with a "drug kingpin," who is a bad guy), and by James Q. Wilson.

Others are more skeptical. Here are some of the disturbing facts reported in a review article, "What Ever Happened to the 'War on Drugs'?" by Michael Massing in the June 11, 1992, issue of the *New York Review of Books.*

> How many people are using illegal drugs and how frequently? According to a 2008 household survey reported by the National Institute of Drug Abuse, some 20.1 million of us used such drugs within a month prior to the survey.

What about treatment for those who want to shake the drug habit? During President Reagan's first term (again relying on data provided by Michael Massing in his survey), funds for treatment centers (adjusted for inflation) dropped by nearly 40 percent. During Reagan's second term, when crack cocaine reached epidemic proportions in the nation's inner cities, treatment centers were overwhelmed. Both the numbers of those seeking help and the extent of the treatment they needed had grown enormously. With the cocaine-related death of college basketball star Len Bias fresh on everyone's mind, the Bush administration approved a budget of $1.6 billion for treatment centers run by the states, an increase of 50 percent over the funds provided by his predecessor. But even this increase failed to meet the demand for treatment.

Turning from the issues of salience and success in the war on drugs, what is it costing us? In a 1990 article by Ethan Nadelmann, "Should Some Illegal Drugs Be Legalized?" in *Issues in Science and Technology,* we are told that the nation spent $10 billion to enforce our drug laws in 1987, perhaps twice that amount in 1990. Between 40 percent and 50 percent of all felony convictions are for drug offenses. In 1989 alone, "between three-quarters of a million and a million people were arrested . . . on drug charges." To this we must add the indirect costs. International enforcement, interdiction, and domestic enforcement—all essential elements in the government's strategy—have yet to succeed. To put it simply, we need to keep two things in mind. First, we have so far failed to keep drugs from being brought into the country. All the drugs illegal in this country and in wide use nevertheless (opium and heroin, cannabis, coca and cocaine) are native to many foreign countries and are a major cash crop in much of the world. Second, we have not succeeded in drying up demand despite granting substantial resources to law enforcement to do so.

Literature on the drug problem continues to roll off the presses; of the five books in Massing's review survey, we recommend especially *The Search for Rational Drug Control* (1992) by Franklin E. Zimring and Gordon Hawkins, an author team highly regarded for their shelf of books on virtually every problem in criminal justice.

William J. Bennett

Drug Policy and the Intellectuals (p. 546)

William J. Bennett gives a vigorous defense of the national drug policy he was assigned to carry out by the first Bush administration. He attacks intellectuals (the only two he names are the liberal columnist Anthony Lewis and the conservative spokesman William F. Buckley Jr. in para. 8; but he alludes to a host of unnamed "prominent residents" on the campuses of Princeton, Wisconsin, Harvard, and Stanford in para. 18) for their faults in blinding themselves and the nation to the evils of legalizing drug use, a policy supported (he says) by "a series of superficial and even disingenuous ideas" (para. 8).

Here's a quick summary of Bennett's seven-point argument against the legalization of drugs (question 3): (1) Criminalizing drugs provides an incentive to stay out of the business (para. 10); (2) no one has figured out how to carry out a policy of legalization of drugs across the board, from marijuana to PCP (para. 11); (3) if drugs are legalized, their use will "soar" (para. 13), thereby increasing the harm and suffering to the users; (4) the cost to the nation of more drug use would be "intolerably high" (para. 14); (5) drug-related crimes would not decrease at all (para. 15); (6) the terrible problems we have with legalized alcohol are a foretaste of the even graver problems we would have were all drugs legalized (para. 16); (7) apart from all the foregoing, "heavy drug use destroys character," "dignity and autonomy" (para. 17). We have to admit Bennett makes a pretty convincing argument, spiced with barbs at "America's pundits and academic cynics" along the way.

Were someone to accuse Bennett of hypocrisy or inconsistency (question 4), he might well reply in the same manner that he does regarding legalization of alcohol (para. 16): No doubt it would be a futile effort for society now to make tobacco use illegal; yet he would be better off (as he might well admit) if he had never acquired the nicotine habit and if he could get rid of it. But whether he can is his personal medical problem; there is no inconsistency in his urging a policy to the effect that everyone (himself included) avoid harmful illegal drugs, even if he is unable to cease using a harmful legal drug himself. Of course, he might also take another line, that nicotine addiction is not as harmful as addiction to any illegal drug. But that is an empirical claim, and it is far from clear whether it is true.

James Q. Wilson

Against the Legalization of Drugs (p. 553)

This essay following William J. Bennett's reminds us of the "good cop/bad cop" routine in police interrogation. We debated whether to include both these essays, since the argument in each is pretty much the same. But the tone is so different—James Q. Wilson thoughtful and patient, Bennett using words as though they were clubs—that we thought this difference itself is worth some reflection. (Students might well be set the task of reading these two essays as a pair and explaining what, if anything, is different in the two arguments and, that apart, which essay has the more persuasive, effective tone.)

The idea of "victimless crimes" (our question 1) gained prominence in the 1960s, as part of an argument for decriminalizing various drug and sex offenses, as well as gambling. When consenting adults engage in illegal practices that harm no one (or harm only themselves), so the argument went, they have committed a victimless crime. But such acts ought to be decriminalized because the criminal law in such cases is improperly invading privacy, liberty, and autonomy. (John Stuart Mill made this argument famous, although he did not use the term *victimless crimes*.) Wilson seems to object to this argument on two grounds (para. 24). First, he rejects the criterion of state intervention as too narrow: "Society is not and could never be," he says, "a collection of autonomous individuals." So we need the criminal law here and there for admittedly paternalistic purposes. Consequently, even if drug abuse were a victimless crime, Wilson might not approve of its legalization. Second, he rejects the factual minor premise of the victimless crime argument; drug use is harmful not only to the user but also to others who have not or cannot consent (there is "fetal drug syndrome," for example).

Wilson is a skillful, polished arguer, and we draw attention to some of these features of his essay in two of our questions (the second and the fourth). The "economic dilemma" that the drug legalizers face, to which Wilson refers in his paragraph 37 (our fourth question), can be formulated somewhat more briefly than he does, as follows: Tax money from legalized drugs will pay for the cost of regulation and treatment of users, abusers, and addicts, or it will not. If it does, then the tax rate on drugs must be set quite high, but this will lead to tax evasion and crime and a black market in drugs. If tax money from drugs does not fully finance the costs of regulation and treatment, then we will have more addicts and either inadequately financed treatment centers or less tax money for other public needs. But none of these alternatives is acceptable. Therefore, we cannot reasonably legalize drugs in the expectation that taxing them (as alcohol and tobacco are now taxed) will enable society to pay for the costs.

Like any dilemma worthy of the name (see our discussion of the dilemma in the text), this one has a disjunctive tautology as its major premise (that is, the premise states two exhaustive and exclusive alternatives). Such a premise is invulnerable to criticism. Criticism can be directed, however, at each of the two other conditional premises ("if . . . , then . . ."), as they are empirical generalizations and vulnerable on factual grounds. Or criticism can be focused on the premise that expresses how unacceptable the dilemma is. Perhaps one of these alternatives is not so bad after all, especially when compared with the costs of losing the war on drugs. One way to develop that thought would be by constructing a counterdilemma, showing the awkward consequences of *not* legalizing drugs. (Here, we leave that task for another day.)

In his criticism of Nadelmann (paras. 25–26), Wilson accuses him of "a logical fallacy and a factual error." The fallacy is to infer (1) the percentage of occasional cocaine users who become "binge users" when the drug is *legal* from (2) the percentage who become "binge users" when (as at present) the drug is *illegal*. Why does Wilson think this is a fallacy? To be sure, (1) and (2) are quite independent propositions, and it is possible that the percentage of users would grow (rather than stay roughly constant, as Nadelmann infers) as soon as the drug is legalized. But by how much? At what rate? In the face of antidrug education? These unanswered questions apart, what Wilson needs to show us is that in general, or perhaps in some closely parallel case, the number of those who do X when doing X is illegal has no relationship to the number of those who do X when doing X is legal. But Wilson hasn't shown this at all.

As for the "factual error," it looks to us as though Wilson has caught Nadelmann in an error (see para. 27).

Milton Friedman

There's No Justice in the War on Drugs (p. 567)

Milton Friedman was the nation's best-known free-market economist and the author of many books, including *Capitalism and Freedom* (1962). He and his fellow conservatives seem to be divided over the nation's "war on drugs." Some, like William J. Bennett, strongly favor fighting the use of illegal drugs with unrelenting fervor. Others, believing that drug use harms only or principally the user, oppose government interference (either in the form of regulation or outright prohibition) and favor using free-market methods to control its use. Friedman is of the latter persuasion. He hints at reasons of this sort in his paragraph 2, where he quotes himself from 1972. There, in a phrase, his position was this: Persuasion, yes; coercion, no.

What is surprising about Friedman's essay is that he does not rely on free-market reasoning. It's not that he rejects such reasoning; it's rather that he invokes what he describes as "ethical" considerations of several different sorts. They constitute a variety of objections, each of which represents one kind of empirical consequence of the policy of the past four decades but inadequately foreseen when the war on drugs was launched with much fanfare by President Nixon in 1972.

Regarding question 1, here is one way the thesis of his essay might be stated in a sentence: "The unethical consequences of the nation's war on drugs far outweigh whatever advantages have been or might be gained." (This version is inspired by the rhetorical question Friedman asks at the end of his essay, in para. 12.)

As to question 2 (and also question 4), an "expediential" objection to the war on drugs would be any claim that its harmful consequences (for example, in tempting the police into corruption) outweigh its good consequences. A moral (or ethical) objection would be that our drug policies violate some moral norm, standard, or principle (for example, the principle that adults ought to be left free of governmental interference to act as they wish—including using drugs—so long as they do not harm others).

Elliott Currie

Toward a Policy on Drugs (p. 570)

Elliott Currie's position on the drug controversy (our question 4) includes three steps: (1) move toward decriminalizing the drug user (but not necessarily the trafficker), (2) treat marijuana (use as well as dealing?) "differently" from (he means more leniently than) "the harder drugs" (mainly heroin and cocaine, we surmise), and (3) permit medical experimentation with certain drugs (which ones he does not say, but marijuana is the obvious example) (para. 18). These recommendations (all adopted in one way or another, he says, by "some European countries") fall well short of radical decriminalization of drugs, but if Currie is right, to go any further is to cause predictable costs and harms that make radical decriminalization the wrong social policy.

Is Currie convincing that these steps, and these only, are a reasonable compromise between those who want to carry on the "war on drugs" no matter what the costs and those who want all aspects of drug use, sale, and manufacture to be permitted by law? (He presented these views over two decades ago, and we suspect he would say today that precious little progress has been made over this period to bring any of these three recommendations to come to pass.) We do not have a better proposal to offer, and we think at the very least that his middle way between the two extremes deserves careful thought. The prospect of ideas such as his receiving careful thought at the highest levels in our governments, state and federal, are not encouraging.

In our question 2 we mention three possible steps to reduce the role of drugs in our lives, steps Currie does not mention. Why doesn't he? As a guess, we suggest this. He would reject our first suggestion (curbing manufacture of illegal drugs) because either most of the drugs in question are not manufactured in the United States or the one that mainly is (marijuana) he wants largely to decriminalize. Perhaps he would reject our second suggestion (reducing imports of illegal drugs) on the grounds that federal agencies have tried for years to do precisely this but to little effect and that tax dollars to curb heavy drug importing can be more effectively spent elsewhere. As for our third suggestion (aggressive public education), perhaps he could argue it is implicit and is presupposed in much of what he says.

The evident uniqueness of the magnitude of the drug problem in this country troubles us. Currie mentions the issue (para. 21), but he offers no explanation for our unfortunate plight. We mention (question 5) three possible explanations that seem to us unconvincing. We don't have a fourth to offer for contemplation. So long as there is no convincing and generally accepted explanation, it seems likely to us that the drug problem will not abate. Meanwhile, the human cost in our drug policies ought to terrify and infuriate. In New York, for example, drug laws enacted during the Rockefeller administration (as reported by the Fortune Society) mandate a fifteen-years-to-life sentence for the sale of two ounces or the possession of four ounces of an illegal drug. Is there any convincing reason why our society ought to persist in enacting and enforcing such laws? We earnestly doubt it.

22
Junk Food: Should the Government Regulate Our Intake? (p. 581)

Anonymous Editorial

New York Times (p. 582)

Adopting a fairly common argumentative strategy, the opening paragraph speaks well of a proponent of the view that the essay will oppose. And then, having shown its goodwill, the essay turns to attacking the proponent's proposal.

The reversal comes early in the second paragraph, with *however*, the third word in the paragraph. The third and fourth paragraphs make it clear that the editorial is not merely negative and is not merely going to say that the mayor should mind his own business, that government should leave people alone, and so on. Rather, these paragraphs offer suggestions about what the mayor's office *should* be doing. The approach, then, is not at all along libertarian lines. Quite the opposite: The government is encouraged to educate the public "to make sound choices," and thus it should "keep up its tough anti-obesity advertising campaigns" (para. 4).

The final paragraph suggest, in fact, that the trouble with "nannying" is that it might have the reverse effect; that is, it "might well cause people to tune out."

Anonymous

Pictorial Advertisement, The Nanny (p. 584)

The ad was sponsored by the Center for Consumer Freedom, an organization established in 1995 with funds from Philip Morris. In 1995, the center's cause was opposition to attempts to curb smoking in restaurants, but it now engages in a variety of actions on behalf of the fast-food, alcohol, and tobacco industries.

The ad shows a photo-shopped image of Mayor Bloomberg in a purple button-down knit dress, hunched but towering over a toylike New York City skyline. Large letters at the top identify the figure as "The Nanny," and in case we miss the point, smaller letters at the bottom of the image say, "New Yorkers need a Mayor, not a Nanny." And in between, some text tells us that "Nanny Bloomberg has taken his strange obsession with what you eat one step further."

Is the image amusing? Answers will vary. Some viewers may say that this image, showing a man wearing a funny-looking woman's outfit, standing in a funny position with his knees together, ridicules not only Bloomberg but (when you think a moment about it) also ridicules nannies, that is, ridicules women who devote their lives to the strenuous and important task of supervising children. And these viewers, or others, may point out that although the ad speaks of "Nanny Bloomberg's strange obsession" with what we eat, one cannot get through the day without seeing in the newspaper or hearing on radio or TV something about the dire effects of obesity in the United States, notably its connection to heart disease and to Type 2 diabetes. Lots of people (not just the mayor and his subordinates) are talking about lots of illness, lots of death, lots of physical and mental suffering, and lots of money—money spent on unhealthful foods, and money spent on consequent medical treatment. These people are not behaving ridiculously.

Daniel E. Lieberman

Evolution's Sweet Tooth (p. 585)

When the anti-Bloomberg advertisement (text, p. 584) asks, "What's next? Limits on the width of a slice of pizza . . .?" it is introducing the kind of argument that has been called "the slippery slope." (We discuss this kind of thinking—this kind of fallacy— in the text, p. 372.) Lieberman raises the issue in his first paragraph, rightly saying that this libertarian objection deserves attention, and his essential argument turns out to be yes, we *should* go beyond sugary drinks, *should* descend the slope—and we *do* need a nanny; that is, we need authoritative enforcement. Here is how he puts it in his second paragraph:

> Lessons from evolutionary biology support the mayor's plan: when it comes to limiting sugar in our food, some kinds of coercive action are not only necessary but also consistent with how we used to live.

"Coercive action"!!! Why? and How? we may well ask. And Lieberman tells us—first by sketching the biological background that has caused this problem of obesity, and then by sketching possible courses of action—*why* coercion is not only necessary but also consistent. The possible courses of action, he says in paragraphs 7–9, are these:

- Do nothing.
- Rely on education.
- Collectively restore our diets to a more natural state through regulations.

"Regulations" of course mean laws, which gets us back to libertarian objections. Lieberman grants that the Bloomberg proposal is paternalistic (the male version of nannyism). But he insists that it "is not an aberrant form of coercion," and it is (he says in para. 9) "a very small step toward restoring a natural part of our environment." And who, one might ask, can argue against restoring what is "natural"? One might ask, however, is it indeed "a very small step" or is it the first paternalistic step down a slippery slope?

> In paragraphs 10 and 11 Lieberman argues—surely he is correct—that we *are* paternalistic with children:

> Youngsters can't make rational, informed decisions about their bodies, and our society agrees that parents don't have the right to make disastrous decisions on their behalf. Accordingly, we require parents to enroll their children in school, have them immunized, and make them wear seat belts. We . . . don't let children buy alcohol or cigarettes. If these are acceptable forms of coercion, how is restricting unhealthy doses of sugary drinks that slowly contribute to disease any different?

If you read these sentences in class, a lively discussion will follow.

Mark Bittman

Bad Food? Tax It, and Subsidize Vegetables (p. 587)

Bittman begins his argument with a time-tested formula: He calls our attention to a problem. And, to further engage our interest—in effect, to assure us that he is a writer we will enjoy reading—he includes a bit of word play (the business about SAD, at the end of the first paragraph). And, while we are mentioning SAD, we can here call attention to the fact that he *ends* the essay by returning to the Standard American Diet, which is to say that he, like most professional authors, provides a structural model that students might well emulate.

In his fourth paragraph he offers a reason why we cannot count on the food industry to provide healthful food, and so, he says, the federal government should intervene "as an agent of the public good." In the view of the sponsors of the anti-Bloomberg advertisement that we reproduce in the text on page 584, such intervention is nannyism, but as Lieberman points out in his essay, everyone (or almost everyone) agrees that nannyism is sometimes appropriate when we are dealing with youngsters. For instance, we do not let them buy alcohol or tobacco.

The fifth paragraph points out that the government does already meddle in the food industry: It *subsidizes* certain crops—so why (Bittman argues) should we not tax unhealthful crops? The tax would (para. 7) reduce the consumption of unhealthful foods, and the revenue could be used to subsidize (and thus bring down the price of) healthful food, a win/win situation.

In his ninth paragraph Bittman grants that this proposal would of course upset the processed food industry, and it would also upset the consumers of such goods because the prices of such things (e.g., soda and chips) would be increased. But his response is that "public health is the role of the government." (The libertarians may have a different view.)

"The benefits are staggering," he tells us in paragraph 19, and "the need is dire" (para. 20). (Libertarians will not agree.) "Education alone is no match for marketing dollars that push the very foods that are the worst for us" (para. 20). In paragraph 21 he cites $344 billion as the projected health cost of obesity in 2018—a figure that may well urge a reader to think sympathetically about a tax on those who help to generate this cost. In order to support his proposal, he cites "the historic 1998 tobacco settlement" (para. 22), which undoubtedly has resulted in a substantial decrease in smoking and thereby immense medical savings. And in paragraph 25 he again refers to the successful campaign against smoking, the idea being that history supports his proposal.

23

Facebook: How Has Social Networking Changed How We Relate to Others? (p. 594)

Lauren Tarshis

Is Facebook Making You Mean? (p. 594)

We think that almost all of the essays in our book are well-written, and that in some degree they can serve as models for students. That is, instructors can invite students to look at *how* the authors go about their business of developing arguments: What does this opening paragraph *do*, why does the author define this term but not that term, why does the author devote two paragraphs to this point but only one paragraph to that point? When we do this sort of thing in class, we are in effect saying, "See what is going on in these essays, see how writers go about their business. You find this writing effective. Now try to get some of *that* into your own writing."

Tarshis's essay seems to us to lend itself to such an approach. After all, she does not bring to the topic any highly specialized knowledge that the student cannot possibly have. True, she quotes a source or two and occasionally says something like "Experts say," but the meat and potatoes of the essay is in her presentation of material available to all of us. Thus, when she is making the point (para. 14) that online communication deprives us of clues that are available with other forms of communication, she gives some very good examples:

> One of the most important ways in which we communicate with each other is through subtle emotional signals—your best friend's blush when you mention a girl he likes, the flash of anger in your mother's eyes when you say you'll take out the garbage *later*. Over the phone we can hear a change in a person's tone, or the ominous pause that sends a message to back off. Online communication takes all of these signals away.

The basic point—that communication is not just words, but consists also of "subtle emotional signals"—is made clear and memorable by the *details* that Tarshis provides, and these details are not based on esoteric information that students cannot reasonably be supposed to be familiar with.

The end of her essay—two paragraphs, the second of which consists of only two words—also seems to us to be worth discussing in class. Ordinarily of course one would *not* end with a two-word paragraph, but here it is effective—for reasons that students will easily see *if* you ask them to discuss it.

Steven Levy

Facebook Reset (p. 596)

Levy adopts a highly informal tone—notice the contraction in his first sentence ("didn't"), the beginning of the second sentence ("After all"), and the use of "pretty much" in his third sentence. None of these things is surprising, since the piece originally appeared in *Wired*—not, for instance, in a book published by the University of Chicago Press. We find Levy's writing engaging; we do not think he descends into vulgarity, or that he is nudging us in the ribs. A reader never doubts that Levy is a competent writer and is well-informed about his topic. His second paragraph, for instance, begins thus: "The list is the gateway through which people observe our major life events, causal musings, physical peregrinations, and crop yields on FarmVille." Our point? We think it is worth calling attention to Levy's tone: By observing it, students can learn that a writer can be informal and at the same time can convey authority.

We confess that we wrote the preceding paragraph a few hours after one of our colleagues told us that he *never* allows students to use the first-person singular pronoun. We doubt that we want to see it in an undergraduate honors essay on, say, "Orwell's Use of Metaphor as a Persuasive Device" (except in the Preface), but we certainly think it can be used in college writing that is directed at the general reader.

Speaking of metaphor, we want to call attention to Levy's effective metaphor in his third paragraph, where he says that his Facebook collection of friends "resembles the contents of a house occupied by a hoarder." He goes on:

> I make my way past heaps of classmates, overfriendly PR people, and folks whose amusing conversations in hotel bars led to morning-after friend requests. Open a closet and out tumble a Chinese poet, sources from stories I wrote for now-defunct publications, and one of my son's high-school friends with whom he hasn't spoken in years. Trying the front door, I trip over the mashup artist Girl Talk, whom I met once in Pittsburgh. Meanwhile, many of my best friends and closest business contacts aren't even in the house.

In several places in our book, and in this manual, we claim that students can learn to *write* by studying the writing of others. That is, students can learn the importance of an engaging (or at least a clear) title, of an opening paragraph that does not merely repeat the title, of transitions that help the reader to see where the author is going, and so on, but we do confess that some aspects of good writing probably cannot be taught—and one of these is the use of metaphor. Here is Aristotle (in the *Poetics*) on the subject:

> But the greatest thing by far is to have a command of metaphor. This alone cannot be imparted by another; it is the mark of genius, for to make good metaphors implies an eye for resemblances. (1459a4)

Still, even if we cannot teach students how to invent metaphor, we can at least alert them to perceive it in what they read—and to enjoy it. Levy's final paragraph, with its use of "Mulligan" (a second chance to make a move in a game) is, in its smaller way, another use of metaphor that is probably beyond most of us—certainly, it is beyond the inventive power of the writer of this comment—but it is worth calling to the attention of students, with the aim of helping them to see that reading can be fun.

Jenna Wortham

It's Not about You, Facebook, It's about Us (p. 598)

We don't think this essay can cause any readers any difficulties. For us, the chief interest is whether our students will find it true. That is, does this business (see especially para. 7–8) about not knowing how to live *with* Facebook and how to live *without* it correspond to the experience of students? Students may offer plenty of examples confirming Wortham's assertion that there really is an issue—or, on the other hand, maybe they won't.

If you do assign the essay and ask for a written response, we suggest that you caution your students to make certain that their essay has a *point* (a thesis) and an organization, so that it is not simply a string of anecdotes ("This happened, and that happened, and then another thing happened").

The piece was written early in 2012, so it ought to reflect current thinking.

Stephen Marche

Is Facebook Making Us Lonely? (p. 600)

It seems to us that it takes Marche a while to get there, but his final answer to the question he poses in his title is, in effect, "No, it is really doing something worse. It has produced a new kind of isolation. We spend an inordinate amount of time with the Internet and thus we neglect our connection with the real world. [Why the Internet is not part of the real world is unclear to the writer of this comment.] Our alleged obsession with the Internet deprives us of the opportunity to 'forget about ourselves for a while.'"

Our third question asks about Marche's reference (para. 17) to "social capital," a term that we assume will be unfamiliar to most first-year students. *Capital* is wealth—dollars, real money—used for the production of more wealth (e.g., dollars that are invested); *social capital* is another sort of wealth, not dollars that produce more dollars but social connections (*social* is ultimately from the Latin word *socius*, "companion") that produce wealth. Examples: a friend who helps you to get a job or a promotion or who buys a product you are selling. In short, if a person's contacts, connections, network can generate money (presumably because the friends *trust* the individual), that person possesses "social capital." While we are talking about forms of capital, we add, almost irrelevantly, that a college degree can be considered "educational capital."

Marche cites many studies, or, more precisely, he mentions many studies but sometimes he gives little information about how to identify them. For example, in para. 8, he speaks with a maddening lack of specificity about "A 2005 analysis of data from a longitudinal study of Dutch twins." It is our guess that many readers may be skeptical of such studies. Possibly we are reflecting only our own skepticism, our own distrust of sociological surveys, but we think that many readers may believe that their own responses, their own perceptions of loneliness, are better guides than are the statistical surveys of such topics as "family loneliness" (see our fourth question).

Josh Rose

How Social Media Is Having a Positive Impact on Our Culture (p. 612)

This essay—like many essays discussing Facebook—is highly personal. It is hard for us to imagine an essayist of, say, even ten years ago (to say nothing of an essayist of the generation of George Orwell) writing such sentences as (para. 2):

> First, on my way to go sit down and read the newspaper at my coffee shop, I got a message from my 10-year-old son, just saying good morning and letting me know he was going to a birthday party today. I don't get to see him all the time. He's growing up in two houses, as I did.

Of course a decade ago ten-year-olds were not sending messages to their fathers, and even if they were, their fathers would not think such messages were worth talking about to other adults. But today, as the presence of our casebook indicates, messaging is a hot topic. And we have tried to choose notably interesting essays on this topic. Still, we must confess that as we scanned dozens of essays in order to find a few for our casebook, we often felt that (to adapt Rose's fourth paragraph) one man's treasure is another man's TMI.

Our second question in the text invites students to talk—rather, to write—about *how* they use new media. Our hope, we confess, is that they will report, sure, they have fun with it, but they also use it to get access to information and that helps them to become better human beings.

24
Immigration: What Is to Be Done? (p. 615)

Background

Before looking at David Cole's article, we will (1) give some history and (2) survey the chief arguments for and against keeping the gate open.

In 1924, the law provided a national-origins quota system that favored northern and western Europe and severely restricted immigration from everywhere else. This system was replaced in 1965 by a law (with amendments) that said there were three reasons to award visas to immigrants:

1. An immigrant might possess certain job skills, especially skills that this country needs. (Relatively few visas were awarded on this basis.)

2. An immigrant might be a refugee from war or from political persecution and so eligible for "political asylum."

3. An immigrant might be related to an American citizen or to a legal alien (the "family reunification policy").

In 1965, when this policy was formulated, there was little immigration from Latin America, the Caribbean, and Asia. Today, 90 percent of all immigration to the United States comes from those areas. Upward of 80 percent are people of color. Whatever our policy is, it is *not* racist. What about numbers, rather than percentages? The peak decade for immigration was 1901 to 1910, when about 8.7 million immigrants arrived, chiefly from southern and eastern Europe. Some authorities say that 1981 to 1990 matched this, if illegal immigrants are included; but in any case, in 1901 to 1910, the total U.S. population was less than one-third of what it is today. After 1910, immigration declined sharply; in all of the 1930s, only about 500,000 immigrants came to the United States, and in all of the 1940s, there were only about 1 million including refugees from Nazi persecution. The figure now is about 1.5 million annually, plus an unknown number of illegal immigrants (the usual guess is half a million annually). Of illegal immigrants in the United States in 2005, 6 percent came from Canada and Europe, 13 percent from Asia, 56 percent from Mexico, 22 percent from elsewhere in Latin America, and 3 percent from Africa and elsewhere.

What about ethnic identity in the recent past, from 1880 onward? When Nathan Glazer and Daniel Patrick Moynihan wrote *Beyond the Melting Pot* (1963), they found that the ethnic groups that had arrived between 1880 and 1920 retained their identities. Will Herberg, in *Protestant, Catholic, Jew* (rev. ed. 1960), found that at best there was a "triple melting pot"—that is, people married outside their ethnic groups but still within their religious groups. Thus, Italian Americans for the most part married Catholics, but these Catholics might be Irish; similarly, German Jews married Jews, but they might be Russian Jews. From 1980 onward, however, religious identity too was shaken. For instance, half of all Italian Americans born after World War II married non-Catholics; 40 percent of Jews marrying in the 1980s married Gentiles (according to Robert C. Christopher, *Crashing the Gates* [1989]).

In selecting material for our text, we read fairly widely, and we noticed that certain arguments kept recurring. Because instructors may find it useful to have the chief arguments on both sides, we list them. Please understand that we are not endorsing any of these arguments; we are just reporting them.

Arguments in Favor
of a Relatively Open Door

1. *Immigrants provide cheap labor and do not displace native-born workers.* Immigrants work as gardeners, farm laborers, domestic helpers, restaurant employees, and so on. They do not displace American workers, since Americans (white and African American) will not take these jobs at the current wages. True, Americans *would* take the jobs if the pay were higher—a majority of the people who do jobs such as domestic work, agricultural labor, taxi driving, and valet parking are Americans, not immigrants—but the fact is, the pay is low, and *in areas where there are a great many immigrants* the wages are very low and Americans reject the jobs.

    But, again, it is argued that immigrants do not displace American workers. In 1980 the Mariel boatlift brought 125,000 Cubans, increasing Miami's workforce by 7 percent virtually overnight, but it had no effect on the wages of skilled or unskilled labor, black or white. Further, job losses are more than offset by new jobs generated by immigrants; after all, immigrants need housing, food, and so on, and therefore they are a new market.

2. *Immigrants provide high-tech knowledge.* Silicon Valley depends largely on immigrant engineers, microchip designers, and so on.

3. *Immigrants stimulate the economy.* Many immigrants have founded companies, thereby generating thousands of jobs.

4. *Immigrants are assimilating at the usual rate.* Despite assertions that immigrants today are not assimilating, they are in fact assimilating in pretty much the same ways that their predecessors did. Their children marry outside the group (in California, nearly half of the native-born Asians and Latinos marry into other ethnic groups), their grandchildren often do not know the language of the immigrants, and so on. The charge that immigrants do not assimilate is an old one; for instance, it was regularly said of the Irish in the nineteenth century.

5. *Immigrants are not a threat to the peace of the cities.* San Jose, California, is the eleventh-largest city in the United States, with a white population less than 50 percent, but it has the lowest murder and robbery rates of any major city in the United States, and it has virtually no ethnic conflict. El Paso is 70 percent Latino, but it has one of the lowest rates of serious crime or murder; the robbery rate is one-half that of Seattle, an overwhelmingly white city of similar size. Hawaii, too—the state with the lowest percentage of whites in the United States—has a low rate for serious crime and little ethnic conflict.

6. *Immigrants may cost us something in the short run, but in the long run they add to the country.* They are energetic workers, increasing the supply of goods and services with their labor, and increasing the demand for goods and services by spending their wages. Refugees—the immigrant group that gains the most public sympathy—are the immigrants who cost the government the most in welfare and in Medicaid.

7. *Immigrants from developing societies are likely to have strong family structures.* We fret that immigrants from developing nations are likely to be poorer and less well educated than those from Europe, but they come from traditional societies with strong moral codes. The collapse of family values originated not with the arrival of Haitians, but in the white Anglo communities, where, for instance, in 2001, 22.5 percent of the children were born out of wedlock.

8. *We are a nation of immigrants; our strength is derived from our openness to all cultures.* The fear of immigrants is now in large measure a fear of cultures new to the United States, and a fear of persons of color. In some instances, it is rooted in hostility to what one writer calls "anti-progressive Iberian values"—that is, the values of Roman Catholic Latinos.

Arguments in Favor of Shutting the Door, or Keeping It Only Narrowly Ajar

1. *Immigrants cost the United States money.* (a) Since most immigrants are at the low end of the wage scale, and (b) since they have children of school age, they cost local governments more in services (especially education, health services, and welfare) than they pay in sales and income taxes. Moreover, (c) they constitute a disproportionate percentage of prisoners (in California, 20 percent of the prison population).

2. *Today's immigrants are not assimilating at the rate that earlier immigrants assimilated.* In the past, most immigrants came from England, Ireland, or Europe, and they were glad to put their old countries behind them. Many never returned to the countries of their birth, partly because they had no affection for those countries and partly because the trip was long and costly. Today, many Latinos fly back and forth between the United States and Central or South America, thereby keeping up their cultural ties with their countries of origin. And in fact the new emphasis on multiculturalism encourages them to retain their identities rather than to enter into the melting pot. The result is the nation's loss of a common culture, a common language.

   The culture of our country is essentially northern European and Christian. The vast increase in Latinos and Asians brings into question whether we will continue to have a national identity.

3. *Immigrants deprive Americans of jobs.* By working in substandard conditions and for substandard wages, immigrants keep wages low and they deprive citizens of jobs. In California and in Texas it is especially evident that immigrants have displaced unskilled native-born workers.

4. *Immigrants today are less skilled than those of the past.* Because they are less skilled, they are more likely to become a burden to the state.

5. *Immigration is unfair to countries from where the immigrants come.* Among the immigrants from developing nations are some who are politically dissatisfied or who are economically unfulfilled. These are precisely the people who can improve their own countries; this brain drain is unfair to those countries. (The usual reply to this is to say that such people emigrate precisely because they cannot exercise their talent in their native countries because of various obstacles.)

6. *It is nonsense to justify immigration today by saying, "We are a nation of immigrants."* First of all, most nations are nations of immigrants. For instance, England was invaded by the Vikings, by people from Germanic areas, and later by the Norman French. Even the supposedly homogeneous Japanese are believed to have experienced several waves of prehistoric immigration from Korea. Second, that immigration was good for us in the past does not mean it still is good for us. The times have changed. For instance, today the country is heavily populated and the immigrants come from different cultures.

The Two Basic Questions

Finally, it is probably appropriate to say that both sides agree there are two basic questions:

1. Which and how many immigrants ought we to take? (The usual answer to the first part of this question is, "People like me.")

2. How ought we to enforce the law—that is, what measures can reduce illegal immigration? (About 95 percent of the illegal border crossings come from Mexico—but many of these illegal entrants do not stay in this country. Further, many illegal immigrants do *not* enter surreptitiously; they enter legally, but stay beyond the time specified on their visas.)

Current answers to this second question often take the form of responding to a bill that the late Senator Arlen Specter introduced in 2006. The gist: Illegal immigrants who entered before January 7, 2004, could apply for a three-year guest-worker visa, renewable once (for another three years) if the applicant paid a $1,000 fine and cleared a background check. After six years, if the applicant showed competence in English and paid another $1,000 fine and paid back taxes, he or she could apply for citizenship.

What else to do: Today, one often hears—again, usually in response to Specter's proposal—that we should (1) erect a high wall (literal or metaphoric) (i.e., we should expand the Border Patrol), (2) strictly enforce workshop rules (i.e., severely penalize employers of undocumented workers), and (3) widen the gate (i.e., ease the pressure for visas).

The DREAM Act: An acronym for Development, Relief, and Education for Alien Minors. First introduced in the Senate in 2001, it is still much talked about. The gist, as set forth in Wikipedia, is as follows:

- Conditional permanent residency for certain undocumented residents of good moral character who

  - graduate from U.S. high schools.

  - arrived in the U.S. as minors.

  - lived here continuously for at least five years before the bill's enactment.

- If they complete two years of military service or two years at a four-year college or university, they can obtain temporary residency for a six-year period. Within the six years, they may qualify for permanent residency if they have

  "acquired a degree from an institution of higher learning in the UnitedStates, or have completed at least two years in a bachelor's degree program or higher degree program, or have served in the armed forces for at least two years and, if discharged, received an honorable discharge."

The chief arguments against the DREAM Act are that it is, in effect, amnesty, a reward for illegal immigration, and that it invites further illegal immigration.

David Cole

Five Myths about Immigration (p. 615)

David Cole's use of the word *myths* in his title suggests that he subscribes to the old adage, "The best defense is a strong offense." His basic strategy, clearly, is to say that X, Y, and Z are untrue—with the implication that his own views must therefore be true.

In the course of his opening attack he introduces the Know-Nothings (properly called the American Party), the anti-immigrant and anti-Catholic (specifically, anti-Irish) movement in the 1850s. Subgroups of secret societies formed (for example, the Order of the Star-Spangled Banner), but when members were asked awkward questions about their beliefs, they replied with a stock statement, to the effect that they knew nothing, hence the nickname.

In short, Cole begins by introducing the Know-Nothings, a most unpleasant bunch who were associated with hatred of immigrants, and he then announces that the persons he opposes subscribe not to "mistakes" or "errors," but to myths—enduring, attractive-looking falsehoods. All in all, a rhetorically effective beginning. We are surprised, however, that he does not repeat the powerful word *myths*. For instance, he could have said, "Myth No. 1," "Myth No. 2," and so on, and he could have explained why he calls them myths rather than mistakes, errors, falsehoods, or whatever.

In the third paragraph he introduces the point that he is descended from the poor Irish whom the Know-Nothings wanted to keep out, the idea being that he is a decent guy so we can see how wrong these foes of immigrants were. In the next paragraph he clarifies the point; yesterday it was the Irish, but since the Irish—"they"—have now become "us," of course, today's unwanted immigrants go by a different name. The "they" of our times, he says, "are Latin Americans (most recently, Cubans), Haitians and Arab Americans, among others."

We don't need to comment on Cole's "myths," except to say, first, that some of the things in our list of pros and cons at the beginning of this discussion may be useful in evaluating his views, and, second, in his discussion of the myth concerning the costs of immigrants (paras. 10–13), he does in fact grudgingly admit that on the local level, immigrants may cost the community money: "At most, such figures suggest that some redistribution of federal and state monies may be appropriate" (para. 11).

Let's end by returning to Cole's rhetoric. We think his final paragraph is effective. In it, he returns to the "they" versus "us" of his opening (paras. 3–4), and he more or less appeals to the decency of his readers: "I was always taught that we will be judged by how we treat others" (para. 19). The implication is that we should be decent, just, and so on, and that we do not at present treat immigrants fairly or humanely. He hasn't quite proved this—one might, for a start, insist that he could show a little more sympathy for the taxpayers in some communities (Texas and California)—but probably most readers will agree that he comes across as a decent fellow and that he has given us some things to think about.

Barry R. Chiswick

The Worker Next Door (p. 619)

We want to give a bit of background relevant to the specific issue of immigrants versus American citizens in low-paying jobs. In a recent *New York Times* article, according to the Center for Immigration Studies, "immigrants are a majority of workers in only 4 of 473 job classifications: stucco masons, tailors, produce sorters, and beauty salon workers, but even in these four categories native-born workers account for more than 40 percent of the workers." Thus, although virtually all of the grape cutters in the San Joaquin Valley are immigrants, half of all agricultural workers in the United States are native-born. Similarly, although a majority of cab drivers and valet parkers in New York City are immigrants, when viewed nationwide, cab drivers and valet parkers are mostly native-born.

On the front page of the September 22, 2006, *New York Times*, a story ran about fruit rotting in California and Washington because pickers could not be found. Here are the third and fourth paragraphs and the beginning of the fifth:

> Now harvest time has passed and tons of pears have ripened to mush on their branches, while the ground of Mr. Ivicevich's orchard reeks with rotting fruit. He and other growers in Lake county, about 90 miles north of San Francisco, could not find enough pickers.
>
> Stepped-up border enforcement kept many illegal Mexican immigrant workers out of California this year, farmers and labor contractors said, putting new strain on the state's shrinking seasonal farm labor force.
>
> Labor shortages have also been reported by apple growers in Washington and upstate New York.

Are the least-educated Americans at a disadvantage because of immigrant workers? Yes, where they compete with immigrants. But the point seems to be this: It is *not* true that there are jobs Americans will not do. What is true is that some Americans will not do these jobs when the pay is very low.

Let's look briefly at Chiswick's essay, chiefly to see what a student can learn from it about writing an argument. Chiswick begins, "It is often said that . . ." Experienced readers will expect that—pretty soon—they will get a "but." Of course it is conceivable that the writer would go on to say that what is often said is indeed true, but nine times out of ten the writer is setting up a view that he or she will reject, and that is exactly what Chiswick is doing here. The first lesson that inexperienced writers can learn from Chiswick, then, is this: The opening sentence in an essay is, so to speak, the beginning of a dramatic plot that has its twists and turns but that is clearly in the writer's mind. We need hardly add that we are *not* saying that when one first sits down to draft an essay, the entire essay is in one's mind. Not at all; throughout *Current Issues* we argue that the act of writing is a way of getting ideas, of (so to speak) finding out what one thinks about a topic. But when one *revises* a draft, one then thinks seriously about how one will present the material effectively to a reader, and one is concerned with opening sentences, transitions, and so forth.

Chiswick's first paragraph ends by more or less setting forth the implications of the opening sentence: If there are jobs that Americans won't do, and if there are no immigrants to do them, will the lettuce go unpicked, lawns unmowed, plates unwashed? The second paragraph bluntly says that "this assertion seems implausible." We have one minor quarrel with the writing here: The first paragraph does *not* end with an "assertion"; rather, it ends with a series of questions. Still, we understand what Chiswick means, and we think his second paragraph is effective. It pretty clearly compels the reader to agree that the position set forth in the first paragraph is "implausible"—of course the lettuce will get picked, the dishes will get washed, and so on. Further, Chiswick offers a statistic that seems compelling; immigrants are concentrated in six states (we probably didn't know this, but it seems plausible; we have no reason to doubt it), and even within these six states, immigrants "are concentrated in a few metropolitan areas." This all makes sense; Chiswick seems to know what he is talking about, and probably readers feel that they can trust him. Additional statistics in the third paragraph help to convey the idea that Chiswick is knowledgeable. We should add, too, that his statistics do not overwhelm the reader. Chiswick does not sandbag us, does not offer so many statistics that we can't follow him or that we decide this sort of thing is not for us. His piece is reader-friendly.

He begins his sixth paragraph with "True," a transition that tells the readers he is conceding something, but that also tells them that the concession does not undermine his thesis. When we teach, we find that we can't overemphasize the importance of transitions, which is partly to say that when we read students' essays, we regularly encounter interesting points but we are not clear where the author is going. When in a conference we point out that words such as *but, on the other hand,* or *further* are missing, students often express surprise.

Chiswick nicely begins his final paragraph with a transition ("The point is"). Also of interest, in terms of his strategies as a writer, is his upbeat ending and his implicit congratulation of the reader, who is presumably an American citizen rather than an undocumented immigrant. Chiswick speaks of "the genius of the American people"—hey, that's you and me—and of their "ingenuity"—that's *our* ingenuity. How can we disagree with a writer who has such a high opinion of us?

John Tierney

Ángels in America (p. 622)

As we see it, Tierney's fundamental argument is an appeal to fairness. Tierney himself comes across as a nice guy (here we are talking about *ethos*), and he presents Ángel as a nice guy (hardworking family man—though, yes, by illegally entering into the United States "he violated the law," as Tierney admits in para. 6). Incidentally,

Ángel's very name helps to establish him as a good guy, but in any case, whatever his name, he seems to be a pillar of society: He began with a low-paying job, worked his way up to better-paying jobs, is married, owns a home, has a daughter, pays taxes, is striving to improve his English. All that can be said against him, apparently, is that he entered our country illegally, and we can hardly blame an impoverished Mexican for trying to improve his life.

Again, Tierney relies chiefly on the issue of fairness: Is it fair that Tierney's grandfather could come here from Ireland and become a citizen, but Ángel, a man whose career resembles that of Tierney's grandfather, cannot? But we should add that Tierney does offer supporting evidence. He gives us details about Ángel's life—his jobs, his income, the cost of his house, the fact that his daughter speaks English, and so on. He also reports some counterarguments, and then he offers counterarguments to those counterarguments. For example, he says that some people say that Mexicans do not assimilate as well as earlier immigrants because Mexicans are closer to home than most earlier immigrants; he then points out that the children of these Mexican immigrants *do* assimilate for example, they speak English (paras. 7–8).

Still, the strength of Tierney's argument is chiefly in its appeal to our sense of fairness and—we think this is important—its appeal to readers who resemble Tierney, that is, whose grandparents or great-grandparents came to this country when it was easy to enter. Of course such a person might say, "Yes, my grandparents just walked in, and I am immensely grateful that they did, but, well, things have changed, and, er, tough. We now have laws, and that's that. My grandparents were lucky, and therefore I was lucky. Guys like Ángel are out of luck. Too bad, I'm sorry, but it's not my fault. The law is the law, and that's that." One might say something along these lines—but one also might *not* say it, might feel that "Yes, America is a place where hardworking folks like my grandparents were welcomed and we should still welcome such people. Further, we should realize that they are an asset to our country."

Question: Does Tierney go too far in the direction of tugging at our heartstrings when he ends his essay by imagining Ángel saying, "I would like them [Republicans on Capitol Hill] to tell my American daughter why her father can't stay with her"? (Our own answer is that Tierney makes a mistake by ending thus. It's a bit too easy to reply, "You want us to tell her why? OK, we will tell her that her father entered illegally.") In our view, he should have quit a bit earlier in the paragraph, when he raised the question of whether Ángel is "less deserving than [the Republicans'] immigrant ancestors."

Victor Davis Hanson

Our Brave New World of Immigration (p. 624)

First, a word about Victor Davis Hanson's title. The words *brave new world* come originally from Shakespeare's *The Tempest* (5.1.183), where the innocent Miranda utters them when she sees the persons who have been shipwrecked on the island where she has lived since infancy, with only her father (Prospero), the spirit Ariel, and the monster Caliban. The entire speech runs this:

> O wonder!
>
> How many goodly creatures are there here!
> How beauteous mankind is! O brave new world,
> That has such people in't.

Brave means something like "splendid," "excellent," a meaning that survives in *bravo*, a shout expressing approval of excellence. Prospero, who has seen much more of life and has firsthand knowledge of the wicked behavior that characterizes much of life—he and Miranda had been ousted from their kingdom by his villainous brother and set adrift in a rotten boat that took them to the island—wryly comments, "'Tis new to thee."

Brave new world thus has from the start, in Shakespeare, an ironic tone: Miranda is *not* speaking ironically—she means what she says—but her father (and the audience) knows that the world is *not* the splendid thing she takes it to be. The phrase is famous because Aldous Huxley used it as the title of a novel, *Brave New World* (1932), a dystopian novel (a book showing an ironic utopia, an imagined world that conceals its horror) in which people are carefree but only because they are drugged and because many of the things that we value, such as art, literature, and religion, have been eliminated from their lives. In short, although Miranda uses the phrase *un*ironically, because Huxley's book is so widely known, the phrase today is almost always ironic, as it is in Hanson's use. For Hanson, an America filled with immigrants is a utopia on the rocks, a society that no right-thinking American wants to see or live in.

The title of the essay immediately engages those readers who have heard the phrase before and who may have read Huxley's novel. The first paragraph expresses sympathy and perhaps even admiration for "Mexican laborers [who] do the backbreaking work of weeding cotton, thinning tree fruit, and picking strawberries." The second paragraph continues to describe crews of workers, but now a faintly ominous note is introduced: These workers "provide the sort of unmatched labor at the sort of wages that their eager employers insist they cannot find among citizens." So, we are told that (1) these workers work very cheaply and that (2) "eager employers insist" Americans won't accept these wages. At least in retrospect, we can hear alarm bells in *eager* and *insist*—a hint that Hanson will take a different view. And indeed, the very next paragraph begins, "But," and by the end of this one-sentence paragraph, we are told that "there is something terribly wrong with a system predicated on a cynical violation of the law."

The next paragraph, the fourth, narrates a story about a dreadful accident in which a van with migrants hit a pickup truck and exploded, killing three people and injuring eight others. Hanson reports his story cautiously ("Perhaps the van had blown a bald tire. Perhaps the driver was intoxicated"), and he explains that "we will probably never know" because "the driver ran away from the carnage of the accident" (para. 5). He does not express outrage that the driver left the scene of the accident; rather, Hanson merely observes, in a factual way, "That often happens when an illegal alien who survives an accident has no insurance or driver's license."

In short, Hanson is establishing a persona (cautious, thoughtful writer, sympathetic to hardworking immigrants, reporting the sad facts), and at the same time he is showing "the carnage" that immigrants—or at least *these* immigrants—in their vans cause. He goes on (para. 7): "Such mayhem is no longer an uncommon occurrence here," and he gives some examples that he has witnessed. Then he gets a bit more specific, mentioning (para. 8) "young males from Mexico," some "60 percent . . . without a high-school degree," who presumably are the causes of this "carnage" (para. 5) and "mayhem" (para. 7). But there is nothing personal, nothing to suggest animosity toward these Mexicans who "send nearly half of their hard-won checks back to kin in Mexico" (para. 8). Still, a reader must begin to wonder: Gee, isn't this a situation that we *must* do something about? How long can we tolerate Mexicans who cause carnage and mayhem?

In his ninth paragraph Hanson recognizes that "many Americans—perhaps out of understandable and well-meant empathy for the dispossessed who toil so hard for so little—support this present open system of non-borders." Hanson *does* see things from another point of view, but he quickly adds, "I find nothing liberal about it," and presumably his readers are ready to agree with him.

From this point onward, Hanson is outspoken in his hostility. In the final third of the essay, he speaks of "zealots," "cynicism" and "a venal Mexican government" (para. 10), and of "a perpetual class of unassimilated recent illegal arrivals" (para. 12). His final two paragraphs are directed not against immigrants, but against those of us—Americans—who do not require immigrants to accept the "bargain of an American melting pot" and who are "happy" enough when the migrants in their vans keep "out of sight and out of mind." But his last sentence brings us back to his opening paragraph: "Sometimes, though, they tragically do not."

Like so many other skillful essayists, Hanson ends by returning to something he set up at the beginning. We have heard some teachers of writing complain that this structure is a cliché, and they caution their students against using it. We differ.

Cardinal Roger Mahony

Called by God to Help (p. 627)

The idea that refusing to aid a fellow human being in need violates a higher law, "the law of God" (question 3), is not a new idea; it is found in the Bible and has been invoked by saints and martyrs ever since. It is the card that trumps all aces. And it is perfectly appropriate for a cardinal to invoke it where he can. Of course it is not a persuasive argument for others, who must rely either on secular reasoning or religious views that are not Judeo-Christian or Muslim. But does a God-fearing cardinal have no other option than disobedience of the sort Mahony favors? We think not.

First (as to question 4), we hear nothing from Mahony about priests being ready to go to jail for their beliefs, as was essential to the classic doctrine of civil disobedience practiced by Henry David Thoreau, Mohandas Gandhi, and Martin Luther King Jr. One might argue that go-to-jail disobedience is implicit in the cardinal's essay. Even so, it's better to make such inferences explicit and not leave them to guesswork.

Second, Mahony does not discuss the practice of past centuries when Catholic priests recused themselves from compliance with Protestant clerical orders. And so he does not discuss whether he should counsel the priests under his authority to recuse themselves from compliance with the demands of the proposed Border Protection, Antiterrorism, and Illegal Immigration Control bill, if it or something like it were to be enacted.

As to question 1, we are not told by the cardinal whether the proposed law imposes mandatory rather than discretionary punishment for violations. If the law imposes mandatory punishment, the case for disobedience is, we think, stronger than if a judge or jury is given discretion as to the sentencing of a convicted offender who violates the law in order to provide humanitarian assistance. Under a discretionary punishment—but not under a mandatory punishment—the sentencer can take into account the intentions of the violator, which, in cases of this sort, are crucial to understanding the behavior of a priest who obeys the cardinal's orders by violating the law.

As to question 5, we think it highly likely that no sensible prosecutor would proceed against a priest who disobeys the law out of respect for his cardinal's orders, especially when the priest can argue that he is facing a moral dilemma: Either way, he acts in violation of the law, the moral law as interpreted by the cardinal and the statutory law as interpreted by the criminal courts. As to exaggerating the threat, the cardinal might well argue that once this law is enacted, it becomes possible—even if it remains unlikely—for the criminal courts to act against the liberty of the priests. How much this exaggerates the plight of the priests is hard to say for certain, as it involves the decisions of many different officials with the power to inflict or withhold punishment.

One way to look at the difference between providing humanitarian assistance without also supporting illegal immigration is to invoke the doctrine of double effect (most familiar to us in the Catholic understanding of abortion and euthanasia). The cardinal might argue that, whereas the provision of humanitarian aid is an intentional act, the support for illegal immigration—admittedly a consequence of the aid—is not the intention of the donor, even though it is a foreseeable result of the aid.

A Note about this selection: As we note in the headnote and in question 8, in January 2013, Cardinal Mahony was relieved of his clerical and administrative duties due to his involvement in attempting to cover up the Church's sexual abuse of boys by priests. We were torn about whether or not to include this essay, which we have included in previous editions, because of the damage this new information has done to Mahony's credibility. Do Mahony's crimes nullify his point of view on topics unrelated to the sexual abuse scandal, or may his ethos be preserved on certain issues though it is thoroughly discolored on others? This is a question you might want to raise among your students, as we do in the questions that follow the essay. In the end, we decided Mahony's point of view still contributed interesting points to a discussion of immigration, but we would have felt remiss if we had not acknowledged his role in covering up unconscionable acts that occurred under the watch of the Archdiocese of Los Angeles.

25

Service: Should the United States Require Young People to Perform Public Service? (p. 630)

Barack Obama

Commencement Address (p. 630)

President Obama offers in his commencement address not an argument but a story—the story of his life and the role in it for public service that connects it to events in the recent past—to the Peace Corps in particular and the contributions made by the 164 Wesleyan graduates. He sketches some of the progressive ideas—expanding the Foreign Service and the Peace Corps—that he intends to implement in his administration. The result is a mixture of stories and events, episodes, and travels that take the listener on a journey of hope and aspiration.

One theme that runs through Obama's remarks is the theme of public service. He mentions several forms such service can take—as it has taken in his life from community service in Chicago to the White House. He does not give an exhaustive list of such kinds of service—that would be tedious and not appropriate for the occasion. Perhaps the most significant form of public service that he doesn't mention is service in the armed forces. Perhaps he doesn't mention it because he never served in the military.

A second theme runs through Obama's address: the life and career of Senator Ted Kennedy, who at the time (May 2008) was terminally ill (Kennedy died in August 2009). Obama uses his sketch of Kennedy's life to make vivid many of the ideas for public service that he wants to illustrate. Not everybody admires and respects the senator. On the contrary, Kennedy embodied all the things that right-wing politicians abhor. But for liberals, Kennedy was the outstanding example of public service in our time. It is therefore appropriate for President Obama to end his address by recounting the many kinds of examples of such service that Senator Kennedy provided.

Peter Levine

The Case for "Service" (p. 636)

As Peter Levine explains in his third paragraph, public service, as he intends to use that term, involves "a variety of programs funded by the government but often organized by private contractors." That is pretty vague—and abstract as well, as Levine (a philosopher) presumably realizes. So he offers us a more detailed conception of public service that remedies these faults (if that is what they are). This more detailed account is embodied in the Kennedy-Hatch Serve America Act of 2008 (S.3487). Indeed, for all practical purposes, the conception of public service that is the focus of Levine's essay is the conception that underlies this act.

Levine specifies (para. 2) three "social objectives" that this act would address by providing subsidies: reducing the dropout rate in schools and colleges, improving public health, and treating energy as a scarce resource. Thus your work as a volunteer for Habitat for Humanity, however admirable it might be, would not count as public service in the sense of this act, because Habitat is funded entirely by volunteer workers and receives no government funding. What about the private contractor Blackwater International, hired in the public sector to carry out American security operations in Iraq and Afghanistan? That organization won't count either, only this time the reason is the military nature of the services it rendered. Levine wants to know in each case whether "an expanded civilian service initiative with these priorities merits government support" (para. 3). His essay has the purpose of explaining and justifying an affirmative answer, and he does so in cautious, measured tones.

One of the vexing problems that faces anyone eager to expand public service into new arenas is whether participation ought to be *mandatory*. Another is whether participation ought to be *universal*. If it's mandatory, there will be decent and law-abiding citizens, like the Amish, who will be inclined not to participate because they refuse to render any kind of government service that is enforced by law. Levine seems not to have any worries along these lines; perhaps they are not deeply troubling because the numbers of such conscientious objectors would be very small (as has proved to be true with the military draft in all of our wars in this century).

The other problem, whether participation ought to be as wide as possible—indeed, universal—is more significant, and Levine recognizes it as such. His remedy? Out of about 14.5 million citizens eighteen or older who are possible enrollees in such programs, space should be provided for 250,000 participants. Anything with much larger enrollment would burden available resources beyond the manageable. Anything with much smaller enrollment would fail to yield a cohort large enough to make a noticeable impact. These seem to us to be reasonable parameters. Even so, the reader cannot fail to note that reasonable as these numbers are, they are based pretty obviously on estimates that are subject to radical revision in light of facts that could be uncovered only by some form of empirical test or trial run (paras. 16–18).

Throughout his essay, Levine shows he is sensitive to the difference between advocating a certain program, say, for employing teenagers in the good-faith belief that if it is adopted it will reduce teenage crime, and the belief that the program as advocated actually achieves measurable success in that endeavor. A useful exercise would be to make a list of a dozen or so of the programs Levine mentions and then to indicate the extent of our knowledge about the success that these programs have so far achieved. The classic example of a case where this distinction was not clearly made is found in the work of Robert Martinson in the early 1970s, when he exposed the failure of programs for penal reform to reach their putative rehabilitative goals.

Levine next turns to the issue of explaining and remedying the "identity gap" between the citizenry and their local, state, and federal governments. That there is such a gap we must grant. The explanation for the gap that Levine favors is professionalization in the form of a "growing monopoly over education by credentialed, professional experts, especially state and district administrators and test-writers" (para. 20). Whether programs of the sorts that Levine deplores should be shelved in favor of programs he could support is largely a political question. Many such programs are known to be available; what is missing is the funding for them. As for the explanation of the gap, there are alternatives to the one Levine favors, such as this one: For some years, even decades, the growth of two-income families has reduced the time and energy available to the parents of school-age children to take an active interest in the education of their children. To be sure, this is only an empirical hypothesis. But it is a perfect case of what Levine himself notes when he says "it is only a hypothesis that community service is an efficient and effective way to address national problems" (para. 8).

At the end of the day you will want to decide whether Levine has shown why he favors creation of programs and policies that reflect the changes he would like to see adopted, and whether he is right to be reasonably optimistic that some, if not all, such changes are feasible.

Thomas E. Ricks

Let's Draft Our Kids (p. 645)

Probably we can separate two large issues: (1) Ought we to have a draft, so that (in General McChrystal's words, quoted in Ricks's first paragraph) the entire nation "has skin in the game" if there is a war? (2) If it is agreed that there should be a draft, is Ricks's proposal, with its three options, a good one? There is plenty here to discuss, and we are confident that students will have plenty to say, even if they do nothing more than respond to the questions that we append to the essay.

Ricks begins his essay in a fairly traditional way, with a quotation from an authority. What makes the quotation of more than routine interest is that—as Ricks explains in his second paragraph—the point of view expressed is *unusual* for a high-ranking officer, and thus the reader is interested to see what Ricks will do with it.

A word about Ricks's final paragraph (in our fifth question we ask students to discuss the writer's strategies here): Ricks published his essay in July 2012, only seven months after the conflict in Iraq had come to an official end (December 18, 2011); so his claim that a draft of the sort he proposes "might . . . make American think more carefully before going to war" would, of course, have had an immediacy that it cannot have today. Still, we think it is a highly effective ending.

Dave Eggers

Serve or Fail (p. 648)

We think there is some confusion over what Dave Eggers wants. His paragraph 12 clearly speaks of "the unwilling college volunteer"—an oxymoron if ever there was one: If the students are unwilling, then they are not volunteers, and if they are volunteers, then they are not unwilling. But in the same paragraph he speaks of the "transformative" powers of volunteering—something that does not happen, he implies, under a coercive practice.

Here's a student exercise suggested by the confusion cited above. Divide up Eggers's essay into three columns under the following headings: (1) passages in which he seems to want volunteers, (2) passages in which he seems to want full student participation, even if coerced, and (3) passages that are ambiguous. As for which position is the dominant one, we leave that to be decided by carrying out the sorting exercise described above. Our hunch is that category (2) will turn out to be dominant.

Part Six

ENDURING QUESTIONS: ESSAYS, A STORY, POEMS, AND A PLAY

26
What Is the Ideal Society? (p. 655)

We at first thought of having a section titled "Utopia," but as we worked on it, the idea seemed needlessly limited, and "Utopia" gave way to the present chapter. Still, several of the readings we give here are utopian. The utopian element in this section allows us here to introduce a comment by Gertrude Himmelfarb, in *Marriage and Morals among the Victorians* (1986):

> "Utopian" is one of the more ambiguous words in our vocabulary. To some it signifies an ideal that is commendable if not entirely realistic, a goal to aspire to, a vision of excellence that leads us, if not to the best, then at least to the better—a benign and altogether innocent image. To others it suggests exactly the opposite, a dangerous illusion which tempts us, in the name of the best, to reject the better and end up with the worse. The yearning for perfection that makes reality seem irredeemably flawed creates so large a discrepancy between the ideal and the reality that nothing less will suffice than a total transformation of reality—of society, the polity, the economy, above all, of human nature.

Thomas More

From *Utopia* (p. 655)

For a sampling of the amazing variety of interpretations of Thomas More's *Utopia*, one has to look at only the essays reprinted in the Norton Critical Edition of *Utopia* (1975), edited by Robert M. Adams. *Utopia* has been seen, for example, as a book advocating Christianity (in particular, Roman Catholicism), communism, or colonialism. It seems fairly clear to us, however, that More is not advocating any of these things, at least not as an end in itself. Rather, in this humanistic work, he is giving his version of an ideal state based on *reason* alone. But he is a Christian speaking to Christians; presumably his sixteenth-century readers were supposed to say to themselves, "If people without revelation can achieve this degree of decency, surely we, with Christ's help, can achieve more. Our society is far inferior to Utopia; let us strive to equal and then to surpass it."

Perhaps the best short essay on *Utopia* is Edward Surtz's introduction to the Yale paper edition, though Father Surtz sees the book as more Christian than do many other commentators. Among Surtz's points are these:

1. The Utopians are typically Renaissance people, balancing Epicureanism with Christianity, having the best of both worlds. They pursue personal pleasure "until it conflicts with social or religious duties, that is, with the just claims of God or fellow citizens" (p. xiv). The term *pleasure* covers many kinds of actions, from scratching an itch to doing virtuous deeds.

2. Utopian communism "is not an end in itself but the best means to the end: pleasure for all the citizens collectively as well as individually" (p. xiv). "The ultimate Utopian ideal of communism is . . . to be of one mind. . . . Sharing material possessions can succeed only if there is first one heart and soul in all" (p. xv).

3. Modern critics too often emphasize More's political, social, and economic innovations and neglect his opinions on education, ethics, philosophy, and religion.

4. More's Utopians are not saints; some are even criminals. More does *not* believe, as
some moderns do, that people can be conditioned (brainwashed) to think they are
freely cooperating in a society that in fact enslaves them. More's Utopians have
some leeway, as in the choice of an occupation and in the use of leisure. Believing
in the immutability of the soul, they believe that one's final end is not worship of
the state but union with the Absolute.

Most students, when asked for the meaning of *utopian*, will come up with such pejora-
tive words as *unrealistic, impractical, escapist*. They will be surprised, then, to see how realistic
More's view of human nature is. He is fully aware, for instance, of such vices as laziness
and, especially, pride—not only in nonutopian countries but even in Utopia. Indeed, he
seems to feel that most of our ills are due to pride. To restrain pride, almost all Utopians
must engage in manual labor and must wear a simple garment, and, again to restrain
pride, there is no private property. Notice that More does not put the blame for our wicked
actions entirely on private property or on any other economic factors. True, he does say
that Europeans greedily seek to attain superfluities because they fear they may some day
be in want, but it is evident that even Utopia has wrongdoers. That is, even the utopian
system cannot prevent some people from engaging in wicked behavior. More does think,
however, that some systems allow our wicked natures to thrive, and so he devises a political, economic, and social system that keeps down pride (the root of the other deadly sins).

But it is not only pride that is kept in check. Utopia is severely regulated in many
ways. For instance, Utopians are free to do what they wish during their leisure time—
provided that they don't loaf, gamble, or hunt. Similarly, they are free to talk—provided
that they don't talk politics, except at special times. Discussion of state affairs, except at the
appointed times and places, is punishable by death. George Orwell's Big Brother is present
in More's Utopia, but R. W. Chambers is probably right when he argues (in his *Thomas
More* [1935]) that Utopia is founded not on terrorism, but on "religious enthusiasm," in
particular on faith in God and in the immortality of the soul. Still, even "religious enthusiasm" has, for many readers, something unpleasant about it—something too monastic,
too rigid, too disciplined, too cold.

Although one understands and sympathizes with More's condemnation of the pride
that engenders social injustice, one can't help but feel that Utopia, with its rational distribution of labor and its evening lectures on edifying topics, is the poorer for lacking the
messy vitality of life. (In Utopia, everything seems terribly static: The constitution doesn't
change, population is fixed, clothing is uniform, freedom of thought is limited.) On the
other hand, we must remember that in the Europe of More's day (and still in much of
the world), the masses had to toil from sunrise to sunset to live at a subsistence level.
Today's college students (and their professors) find More's Utopia overly restrictive, but
they should remember that (1) it is a society of material prosperity for all citizens and a
society with a good deal of leisure, and (2) it was freer and more tolerant than any of the
European societies of its day.

Additional Topics for Critical Thinking and Writing

1. Can it be said that whatever the merits or weaknesses of More's proposal, he has
astutely diagnosed the problems of society?

2. More's spokesman says that European society "is a conspiracy of the rich to
advance their own interests under the pretext of organizing society" (para. 41).
Can the same be said of our society? Explain.

3. Is More's view of human nature "utopian" in the modern sense of the word; that
is, is it uncharacteristically benign? Explain.

104

Niccolò Machiavelli

From *The Prince* (p. 669)

Harvey Mansfield Jr., in the introduction to his translation of *The Prince* (1985), argues that for Niccolò Machiavelli, the only moral laws are those made by human beings: "The rules or laws that exist are those made by governments or other powers acting under necessity, and they must be obeyed out of the same necessity. Whatever is necessary may be called just or reasonable, but justice is no more reasonable than what a person's prudence tells him he must acquire for himself, or submit to, because men cannot afford justice in any sense that transcends their own preservation" (p. xi).

This reading seems, in a way, much like the work of Karl Marx, who argues that ideology (including ideas of justice) is created by the ruling class, though Marx also seems to believe that because this class achieved power through historical necessity, its ideals—during the period in which it holds power—indeed are true. Witness Marx's praise of the bourgeoisie for redeeming the masses from the "idiocies" of rural life.

Perhaps the heart of the issue is this: Although we may believe that we should be governed by people of honor, Machiavelli (and most utilitarians) would argue that personal goodness and political usefulness are distinct things. A person may be an adulterer, a liar, a sadist, or whatever but may still be an effective guardian of the state. Or, expressed more mildly, a governor may sometimes have to sacrifice personal morality for the safety of the state. Bernard Williams argues, in *Public and Private Morality* (Stuart Hampshire, ed., 1978), that to preserve civilized life, we need politicians who can bring themselves to behave more badly than we ourselves could do. We want them to be as good as possible—and certainly not to be people who act wickedly on a whim or take pleasure in acting wickedly—but to be able to sacrifice personal moral values for political ones. (This idea makes for lively class discussion.)

A related point: If a leader is widely regarded as immoral, he or she loses an important strength: the goodwill of the public. A small example: A senator who is known to have extramarital affairs can probably survive and can be an effective and even an important senator, but a senator who is regarded as a lecher probably cannot.

On the question of whether cruelty may be beneficial to the state: Machiavelli apparently believed that before a state can be justly ruled, there must be a ruler, and to survive, the ruler must be cunning and ruthless. One wonders, of course, if a person with these qualities will also act reasonably, using power for the well-being of the state rather than for purely personal goals. Machiavelli, living in the turmoil of early sixteenth-century Italy, concentrates on the qualities necessary for a leader to survive. Thomas More (see the previous selection in the text), on the other hand, shows us a utopia with almost no political problems, and thus he can concentrate on the morality of the state rather than on the personal characteristics of the governors. Or put it this way: In Machiavelli, it is the ruler against his rivals and his subjects, whereas in More, it is society against the individual's unruly passions.

Additional Topics for Critical Thinking and Writing

1. Imitating Machiavelli's style, notably his use of contrasting historical examples, write an essay of 500 words, presenting an argument on behalf of your own view of some quality necessary in a leader today. You may, for example, want to argue that a leader must be a master of television appearances or must be truthful, compassionate, or versed in history. Your essay will, in a sense, be one chapter in a book called *The Prince Today*.

2. James M. Burns's biography of President Franklin Delano Roosevelt is titled *Roosevelt: The Lion and the Fox* (1956). Judging from your rereading of this selection

from *The Prince,* indicate in a paragraph the characteristics of Roosevelt that the biographer is suggesting by this title. Read Burns's biography and write a thousand-word essay in which you evaluate the aptness of the title, given the facts about Roosevelt's career and Machiavelli's views.

Thomas Jefferson

The Declaration of Independence (p. 678)

In discussing almost any argument (for that matter, in discussing any writing), it is usually helpful to consider the intended or imagined *audience(s)*. With minimal assistance, students can see that the Declaration of Independence has several audiences (question 1). These audiences can perhaps be described thus:

1. The "candid world" (para. 5), addressed out of "a decent respect to the opinions of mankind" (para. 1)

2. The king and his ministers (the grievances are blamed on them)

3. The British people (students who do a research paper on the Declaration will learn that some passages censuring the British people were deleted to maintain good relations)

4. France (the Declaration announces that the "United Colonies" have "full power to levy War, conclude Peace, contract Alliances, establish Commerce, and to do all other Acts and Things which Independent States may of right do." Most historians see in these words a bid for foreign aid—military supplies from France)

5. Those colonists who were not eager for independence

Attention may be given to the *speaker* of the Declaration—that is, to the self-image (question 3) that the colonists present. Jefferson refers to "a decent respect to the opinions of mankind" (para. 1), and he admits that "Governments long established should not be changed for light and transient causes" (para. 4). Notice, too, his assertion that "We Have Petitioned for Redress in the most humble terms" (para. 33). In short, the colonists present themselves not as radicals or firebrands, but as patient, long-suffering people who are willing to put their case before the tribunal of the world. Notice such words as *duty, necessary,* and *necessity.* They are not rebels; rather, they have been "plundered" and "ravaged" and are exerting a right—the right of the people to alter or to abolish a government that fails to fulfill the legitimate purpose of government (para. 4).

Some attention in class can also be profitably given to discussing the *structure* of the work:

1. The first sentence announces the colonists' purpose, explaining "the causes which impel them to the separation."

2. The core of the document is an exposition of the causes, in two sections:

    a. Theoretical and general justification (for example, "self-evident" truths) and

    b. The list of despotic British actions.

3. The Declaration concludes with the response of the colonies (the signers pledge their lives).

Students can also be shown how the explicit assumptions of the Declaration—

1. All men are created equal and are endowed with "unalienable rights,"

2. Governments are instituted to preserve these rights,

3. People have a duty and a right to throw off a despotic government,

— can be cast into this *syllogism:*

1. If a government is despotic, the people have a right to overthrow it and to form a new government.

2. The British government of the American colonies is despotic.

3. Therefore, the people have a right to overthrow it and to form a new government.

The major premise is not argued but is asserted as an "unalienable right." The minor premise is arrived at inductively (instances are cited, and a generalization is drawn from them).

Additional Topics for Critical Thinking and Writing

1. The Declaration is an argument for revolution in a particular society. Investigate conditions in some society (for example, Cuba, China, Iran, El Salvador, Nicaragua), and argue that, on the grounds of the Declaration, people in that society do—or do not—have the right to revolt.

2. Read Chapter 19 of John Locke's *Essay Concerning Civil Government* (first published in 1690) and write a 500-word essay in which you identify all those passages or ideas found in Locke that appear also in the Declaration. Are there any ideas in Locke's chapter that have no parallel in the Declaration but that nevertheless seem to you to be relevant to its purpose and content?

Elizabeth Cady Stanton

Declaration of Sentiments and Resolutions (p. 682)

Elizabeth Cady Stanton's Declaration of 1848 is the historic precursor of the decade-long effort that finally failed in 1982 to enact an Equal Rights Amendment (ERA) to the Constitution. The Fourteenth Amendment, enacted twenty years after the first Woman's Rights Convention at Seneca Falls, New York, did provide that no state "shall . . . deprive any person of life, liberty, or property without due process of law, nor deny any person within its jurisdiction the equal protection of the laws." At face value, that might look like the rejection of gender as a basis for lawful discrimination. Opponents of ERA in the 1970s who professed sympathy with feminist claims for constitutional equality often pointed to the language quoted as if that settled the matter. Not so, however.

The term *male* entered the Constitution in the Fourteenth Amendment itself (see section 2), thereby helping to etch more clearly the implicit and historic male bias of the Constitution and the laws from the beginning and indicating that "due process" and "equal protection" were not to be given a gender-free reading. An Illinois case of 1873 settled this issue for decades. Arguing that she was entitled under the Fourteenth Amendment to be admitted to the bar, Myra Bradwell unsuccessfully fought her case through the state courts to the U.S. Supreme Court. The language of the majority's decision enshrined in constitutional interpretation the worst excesses of male chauvinism (see *Bradwell v. Illinois,* 83 U.S. 130 [1873]). Even the right to vote ("elective franchise") (para. 4) was not incorporated into the Constitution until 1920 (the Nineteenth Amendment). Full equality of the sexes under the laws and the Constitution, whether or not it is a good thing, still does not exist in our society.

Civil death (question 3) is the ultimate extreme to which a person can be reduced: denial by law of all civil rights, privileges, immunities, and liberties. (Not even prisoners on death row, today, suffer civil death.) Stanton elaborates the point (paras. 9–11). It was commonplace among feminists of the nineteenth century to point out that marriage under law was functionally equivalent to civil death.

It was not, however, functionally equivalent to chattel slavery (which was to last another fifteen years after the Seneca Falls Convention; not surprisingly, the women who organized the convention were staunch abolitionists). It might be a useful classroom exercise for students to explore the differences under law in the 1840s between the status of American white women, as the Declaration reports it, and the status of American black slaves. An excellent source for slave law is A. Leon Higginbotham Jr., *In the Matter of Color* (1978).

Martin Luther King Jr.

I Have a Dream (p. 687)

The setting (the steps of the Lincoln Memorial, in Washington, D.C., on the centennial of the Emancipation Proclamation) plays an important part in this speech. By the way, few students know that the Emancipation Proclamation did not in fact free any slaves. In 1862, President Lincoln announced that he would declare free the slaves of any state that did not return to the Union. None of the states that had seceded accepted the invitation to return, and so on January 1, 1863, he announced the Emancipation Proclamation. It did not apply to slaves in states such as Maryland and Kentucky that had chosen to stay in the Union, and of course, it had no force in the Confederacy. Still, the symbolic importance of the Proclamation was and is immense, and it is part of King's speech.

King's association with Lincoln is evident not only in the setting but also in the language. The opening words, "Five score," evoke the "Four score and seven years ago" of the Gettysburg Address, and Lincoln himself was evoking the language of the Bible. King's speech, too, richly evokes the Bible ("dark and desolate valley," "God's children," "cup of bitterness," "trials and tribulations," "storms of persecution," "every hill and mountain shall be made low, the rough places will be made plain and the crooked places will be made straight, and the glory of the Lord shall be revealed, and all flesh shall see it together" — this last from Isaiah 40:4–5).

Another symbol, in addition to Lincoln and to the Bible, is the "American dream" (para. 11, but foreshadowed in the title of the speech), which King, like most other Americans, identifies with the remark in the Declaration of Independence that "All men are created equal." King also identifies his dream (and himself) with "My country, 'tis of thee," and (in the final paragraph) with black spirituals.

The exalted language of the Bible and the Declaration is joined with the humble language of commerce, the "promissory note," the "bad check" of paragraphs 3 and 4, and the whole (because it is a speech) is rich in evocative repetition, especially parallelisms (again a biblical device).

All these devices and allusions are fairly obvious, and that is part of their point. King is emphasizing that speaker and audience share a culture; and though the immediate audience in Washington was predominantly black, King knew that his words would also reach a larger audience of whites—whites who share this culture.

The structure (question 6) is this: The first part gives a historical perspective; the second, an exhortation not to fall into evil; the third, an exposition of the dream, a picture of the better world that the hearers can help to bring about.

Additional Topic for Critical Thinking and Writing

King's speech stresses the twin themes of equality and freedom and does not suggest that the two might be in tension or conflict with each other. Do you agree that there is no tension? Try to state precisely the freedom(s) and equalities for which King pleads. Is our society any closer to achieving these goals today, do you think, than in 1963?

W. H. Auden

The Unknown Citizen (p. 691)

In "The Unknown Citizen," the speaker's voice is obviously not the poet's. The speaker—appropriately unidentified in a poem about a society without individuals—is apparently a bureaucrat. For such a person, a "saint" is not one who is committed to spiritual values but one who causes no trouble.

Additional Topics for Critical Thinking and Writing

1. What is W. H. Auden satirizing in "The Unknown Citizen"? (Students might be cautioned to spend some time thinking about whether Auden is satirizing the speaker, the citizen, conformism, totalitarianism, technology, or what.)

2. Write a prose eulogy of 250 words satirizing contemporary conformity or, if you prefer, contemporary individualism.

3. Was the speaker free? Was he happy? Argue your view.

4. In a paragraph or two, sketch the values of the speaker of the poem, and then sum them up in a sentence or two. Finally, in as much space as you feel you need, judge these values.

Langston Hughes

Let America Be America Again (p. 692)

It is sometimes difficult to remember that poets (or at least some of them) once were regarded as national bards, celebrating the ideals of society. On the whole, today we distrust public oratory, and we are much more comfortable with the idea of the poet as the reporter of private feelings. In short, we prefer the private lyric to such public lyric forms as the ode and the hymn. People who believe that poetry ought to address public themes are likely to complain that poetry has turned inward on itself and has retreated from life. They may point out that although there are all sorts of poetry festivals and public readings, the poetry is likely to be confessional—for instance, the expression of the emotions of an abandoned woman, a gay man, or the child of immigrant Jews or Hispanics. In fact, such poems are deeply rooted in the politics and social practices of our age. (For an example, see Mitsuye Yamada, "To the Lady," p. 771.)

Still, it must be said that poems explicitly about the nation—patriotic poems—are now rare. We can hardly imagine a poet today writing something like "Barbara Frietchie" (the stuff of our school days), "Paul Revere's Ride," or "O Captain, My Captain." Today we seem chiefly to value what Harold Bloom has crankily called "The Poetry of Resentment." Hughes did not by any means write the sort of poetry that Bloom castigates, but the Hughes poems that we value most highly do seem to come directly from the life that he observed closely—for instance, his poems about prostitution and poverty in Harlem. But there is another Hughes, the Hughes who for a while saw himself as an heir to Walt Whitman and especially to Carl Sandburg, and it was in this role that he wrote "Let America Be America Again." Although the influence of Whitman and Sandburg was great, Hughes of course drew also on black sources. In particular, the motif that America has been America (the land of the free) only for some whites was common in black prose, for instance, in the writings of Frederick Douglass. Hughes also drew, very evidently, on radical socialist thought, and doubtless that is why (as we indicate in question 3) *Esquire* published only the first fifty lines. Lines 1–50 offer a strong indictment, but they stop short of preaching revolution. The gist of the idea in these lines is that America today should be true to its original ideals, the ideals of the founding fathers. No one can disapprove of this ideal. But Hughes goes a bit further: Blacks, he says, have not shared in this society ("America never was America to me"), and early in the poem, he links the marginalization of blacks with that of poor whites (line 19) and immigrants (line 45). True enough; almost everyone would grant, "Yes, it's not just that today we have lost some of our ideals; we failed from the start to extend them to all of our people." But beyond line 50 the poem gets more radical, as Hughes specifies additional victims—unemployed people on relief (line 53) and Native Americans (line 65). The suggestion that injustice extended to groups beyond blacks must have sounded menacing enough even to the liberal editors of *Esquire,* but in line 73 we hear (and the editors of *Esquire* must have heard) a still more radical note, a call to revolution: "We must take back our land again" and "We, the people, must redeem / The land, the mines, the plants, the rivers" (lines 82–83). The editors doubtless knew that this talk of the redemptive power of "the people," especially as opposed to the "leeches" of line 72, was the voice of the extreme left wing. Our own view, for what it is worth, is that the shorter poem (lines 1–50, as opposed to 1–86) is the better poem, partly, we confess, because the call to "take back" the land is left unexplained.

Ursula K. Le Guin

The Ones Who Walk Away from Omelas (p. 695)

When Thomas More called his book *Utopia,* he punned on the Greek "good place" (*eu topos*) and on "no place" (*ou topos*). Like all of the rest of us, he knew that the fully happy society is "no place," if only because accidents, disease, and death are part of life. Ursula K. Le Guin's narrator gives us a fairly detailed description of an imagined happy society (para. 1)— Omelas is "bright-towered by the sea," the old celebrants in the festival wear "long stiff robes of mauve and gray," and the boys and girls are "naked in the bright air, with mudstained feet and ankles and long, lithe arms"—but the narrator also is vague about many things that we would dearly like to know. For instance, although the narrator tells us that there is no king and there are no slaves in Omelas, the narrator also makes a confession, "I do not know the rules and laws of their society" (para. 3). The story includes other confessions of ignorance, and at one point, the narrator, aware that the narrative thus far has been unconvincing and fairy-tale-like (for example, those bright towers by the sea), almost gives up and urges the reader to imagine Omelas "as your own fancy bids."

Doubtless Le Guin is vague about important matters because she—like everyone else—cannot depict a convincing utopia that can withstand scrutiny. But she is also vague for a more important reason: She is not earnestly writing a utopian tale like, say, Edward Bellamy's *Looking Backward.* Rather, she is raising a moral problem, or, more exactly, she is amplifying a problem that William James had raised. Omelas need not be a convincing presentation of the perfectly happy life, and indeed the narrator makes Omelas most convincing when he (or she?) prefaces the information about the suffering child with these words: "Do you believe? Do you accept the festival, the city, the joy? No? Then let me describe one more thing" (para. 6). When we learn about the wretched child, Omelas becomes much more believable, for we are all aware that much of our happiness in fact depends on the suffering of others. These others may be the exploited workers whose painful labor allows us to eat and dress well; they may be the sick, whose ills make some physicians prosperous; they may be the aggrieved, whose lawsuits pay the college tuition for the children of lawyers; they may even be the suffering animals whose pain in medical laboratories may help to alleviate our own pain. In short, whoever we are, some of our happiness depends on the misfortunes of other creatures—and at times we are aware of this fact. Le Guin's happy city now becomes easily understandable: It is an image not of an ideal world but of our world.

Where a parable usually evokes a fairly clear moral and leaves us in little doubt about how we ought to act, this story leaves us puzzled. It heightens our awareness of a cruel fact of society, but it does not tell us how we can reform our society. Put another way, where does one go when one walks away from Omelas? Can we really envisage the possibility of a happy life that is not in any way based on suffering and injustice somewhere? Is the story therefore pointless, mere fantasy, mere escapism? Presumably, Le Guin is simply seeking to make us think so that we will learn to act in ways that minimize the suffering of others. It is inconceivable that life will ever be utopian, but it is not inconceivable that injustice and human suffering may be reduced.

Additional Topics for Critical Thinking and Writing

1. How convincing does the narrator think the picture of Omelas is? Why do you suppose that Le Guin does not offer details about the laws of the land? Does Omelas become more convincing when we learn about the child? Support your response with evidence.

2. What is the point of walking away from Omelas? Can the walker go to a better society? If not, is the story pointless? (Put another way, the story is a fantasy, but is it also escapist fiction?)

Helen Prejean

Executions Are Too Costly—Morally (p. 701)

Sister Helen Prejean has proved to be the most influential figure—speaker, lobbyist, film consultant, writer, and spiritual adviser to men on death row—currently opposing the death penalty in the United States. Her humor, warmth, and compassion have been much admired, and she has earned the respect of many whose lives have been ravaged by the murder of a loved one—whether in a crime of homicide or in a legally authorized execution. She has brought to the public debate a down-home human approach noticeably absent from much of the discourse on this subject.

The excerpt we reprint from her popular book *Dead Man Walking* is devoted largely to examining the biblical support for (or opposition to) capital punishment. She neglects to mention what many think is the best single passage in the Bible on this subject, Genesis 4:9–16—God's response to Cain for murdering his brother, Abel. God punishes Cain in three ways: He is exiled, he is cursed, and he is stigmatized (so that others will recognize him for the murderer he is). Perhaps no other passage in the Bible so personalizes God's punishment meted out to a murderer — not perhaps a perfect paradigm for how today's opponents of the death penalty would have murderers punished, but worthy of their thoughtful reflection.

The Judeo-Christian posture on the death penalty is a long story. A small fraction of it is related in paragraphs 11 through 15. Those who seek more must consult the hefty recent monograph by James J. Megivern, *The Death Penalty: An Historical and Theological Survey* (1997). Professor Megivern explains how the Christian church at the time of the First Crusade (1095) abandoned its early commitment to pacifism in favor of Christian triumphalism with sword in hand, led by Pope Gregory VII (1073–1085), his successor Pope Urban II (1042–1099), and St. Bernard of Clairvaux (1090–1153). Their enemies were infidels (read Jews and Muslims) and soon thereafter Christian heretics. According to Megivern, the epitome of this transformation in the Christian ethic of war and peace, of violence and pacifism, appears in the *Chanson d'Antioche*, "the greatest of the vernacular epics of the First Crusade." Christ is portrayed as hanging on the cross and assuring the good thief to his side that "from over the seas will come a new race which will take *revenge* on the death of the father." Thus, as Megivern notes, was brought to pass a "total reversal of the actual teachings of Jesus."

27
How Free Is the Will of the
Individual within Society? (p. 706)

Plato

Crito (p. 708)

The headnote in the text gives a fairly full account of the context of *Crito*, both in Socrates' life and in Plato's dialogues. After decades of relative neglect, this dialogue, with its argument over the citizen's obligation to the state, has recently aroused interest among scholars, and several good books (among them those by A. D. Woozley and Richard Kraut) now are available to guide the interested reader through the intricacies of Plato's text.

The dialogue can be divided into three parts of unequal length and importance. In the brief first part (which ends when Crito says "Your death means a double calamity for me," para. 26), Plato does little more than set the stage. In the longer second part (which ends when Socrates offers the plea of "the Laws and Constitution of Athens," para. 91), Crito makes his feeble attempt to persuade Socrates to escape, and Socrates in rather leisurely fashion examines and rejects Crito's reasons. The final and longest part is also the most important because in it, Socrates advances an early version of the social contract argument for political obligation, later made famous and influential by John Locke and Jean-Jacques Rousseau and revived in recent years in the sophisticated moral philosophy of John Rawls (see his *A Theory of Justice*, 1971). Socrates makes no attempt to rebut this long argument; the reader (along with Crito) is led to think that Socrates must, in all honesty, concede each step and so draw the conclusion the Laws want him to draw.

As for the adequacy of this argument (question 6), the notion of a "just agreement" between the individual citizen and the abstract state looks quite implausible if taken literally, even in the city-state of Athens. But if taken as a metaphor or as a model of an ideal relationship between the individual and the laws, then one has to answer this question: How can a hypothetical or ideal relation impose any actual or real obligation on anyone? The result is a classic dilemma for social-contract theorists, not easily resolved.

The dialogue can be effectively paired with Martin Luther King Jr.'s "Letter from Birmingham Jail" (p. 738). The most obvious difference between the positions of Socrates and King (questions 8 and 9) is that Socrates implies that the laws of Athens are just—though, unfortunately, wrongly applied to Socrates himself by his Athenian judges—whereas King asserts that the laws of Alabama are unjust and implies their application to him is unjust. In particular, Socrates implies that he gave his free and informed consent to the authority of the laws of Athens, whereas King implies that black Americans never gave their free consent to segregation laws.

George Orwell

Shooting an Elephant (p. 721)

George Orwell explicitly tells us that his experience as a police officer in Burma was "perplexing and upsetting" (para. 2). (One might compare this statement with the feelings of Thomas Hardy's soldier in "The Man He Killed," p. 755.) He characterizes himself as "young and ill-educated" at the time (clearly in the past), and he says he was caught between his hatred of imperialism and his rage against the Burmese. The essay's paradoxical opening sentence foreshadows its chief point (that imperialism destroys the freedom of both the oppressor and the oppressed), but Orwell devotes the rest of the first paragraph, with its ugly characterizations of the Burmese, to dramatizing his rage. Students unaware of Orwell's preoccupation with decency may fail to understand that the first two paragraphs do not contradict, but reinforce, each other. The racial slurs in the first paragraph and elsewhere in the essay are deliberate; they show the alienation from normal feelings, the violations of self that were, as Orwell goes on to show, the by-products of his role.

That he was playing a role—but a role that captured the player—is highlighted by the theatrical metaphors that accumulate as he is about to shoot the elephant: He sees himself as a "conjurer" with a "magical rifle," as an "actor," and as "an absurd puppet" (para. 7).

The essay's final paragraph, with its cold tone, its conflicting half-truths and rationalizations, again effectively dramatizes the deadening of feeling and loss of integrity that Orwell experienced and that he believes all who turn tyrant experience.

Walter T. Stace

Is Determinism Inconsistent with Free Will? (p. 728)

The general position taken by Walter T. Stace on the free-will controversy is owed—though Stace doesn't mention it—to the Scots philosopher David Hume. In his *Enquiry Concerning Human Understanding* (1748), Section VIII, "Of Liberty and Necessity," Hume argues that if acting of one's own free will means acting without external coercion or internal compulsion, and if "necessity" (or determinism) means that every event has a cause, then there is no incompatibility between the two. We reprint Stace's version of the solution to the free-will problem (a version of what is now called *compatibilism*) rather than Hume's because it is briefer and much more accessible to the modern reader.

The answer to question 1, stated as a formal deductive argument, goes like this:

1. If one acts without free will, then one cannot be held responsible for what one does.

2. If one cannot be held responsible for one's acts, then moral praise and blame—morality, in short—are impossible.

3. Therefore, if one acts without free will, then morality is impossible.

The argument as stated is surely valid. It has the form: If p, then q; if q, then r; therefore, if p, then r—a case of a hypothetical syllogism and a valid form of reasoning. Most philosophers think it is sound; whether it is, of course, depends on the truth of both premises. Of the two, premise 1 is likely to be the more controversial.

Now consider question 9. Here is a valid argument in the spirit of Stace's views in paragraph 28:

1. A person's acts must be the effects of her beliefs and decisions for her to be morally responsible for those acts.

2. A person's acts must be predetermined for those acts to be the effects of her beliefs and decisions.

3. Therefore, unless determinism is true at least as regards a person's acts, no one is morally responsible for anything.

Here, the more problematic premise is the second one.

Regarding question 2, a classic example of a purely verbal dispute is arguing whether a glass of water is half full or half empty or whether you are taller than I am or I am shorter than you are. Such disputes are absurd, since in truth, neither party can be correct unless the other is also; what is at stake in the dispute is nothing but each disputant's preferred way of stating the facts. There is no dispute about any fact of the matter.

Stace's claim that the free-will controversy is "merely verbal" or is "a semantic problem" (para. 3) is slightly more complicated. The problem arises because the term *free will* has been incorrectly defined ("by learned men, especially philosophers," he says), with the result that nothing counts as action of one's own free will. This, Stace argues, is absurd because in the ordinary sense of the phrase "He did so-and-so of his own free will," it is perfectly clear that such an imputation has plenty of applications. So Stace in effect says the free-will controversy is "merely verbal" because whether we act with a free will turns entirely on how we define *free will*.

As a side note, Stace's strategy in this essay is reminiscent of the linguistic analytic philosophy that flourished in the 1950s and 1960s here and in Great Britain (though a reader of the book from which our excerpt is taken will find no other evidence of sympathy with that style of philosophy). He proposes to defend the compatibility of free will and determinism by relying on "common usage . . . in ordinary conversation" (para. 6)—that is, he will rely on the way ordinary people talk in deciding whether someone did or did not act of his or her own free will. We think his examples of conversation (paras. 9–10, 14) do reflect ordinary usage and show us how we do use the term *free will*. These snippets also show that people believe they can tell whether someone is acting out of a free will; Stace implies this is enough to show they are correct in this belief (and he does not seem to worry about addressing that issue directly).

Not one to have been overawed by professional academic philosophers—prior to a midcareer move into teaching and writing philosophy, Stace had rendered long years in the British foreign service and, like many of his British academic contemporaries in the early twentieth century, never pursued any postgraduate degrees in philosophy—Stace concocts an outrageous imaginary conversation between a philosopher and a jury foreman (para. 12). The philosopher's unforgivable error, Stace claims, is to think that a person can act of his or her own free will if and only if that act is *not* the effect of any causes. But as the earlier hypothetical dialogues showed, not being the effect of any cause has nothing to do with the meaning of *free will* in ordinary discourse.

Stace does not point out that his pompous philosopher talks as if he had made a momentous discovery: "There is no such thing as free will." Compare that to "there is no such thing as a square circle" and "there is no such thing as a unicorn." Both these propositions are true, but only the latter is true as a matter of fact; the former is true by implicit definition of the terms. Has the philosopher who insists there is no such thing as free will made a discovery about any matter of fact? No. Has he drawn a necessary conclusion from the ordinary meaning of the terms being used? Again, no. (By the way, just what real, as opposed to imaginary, philosophers Stace may have in mind here is not clear to us. His discussion is none the worse if in fact no philosophers ever actually argued as in his example.) So the philosopher's rejection of the very possibility of anyone acting of free will can be entirely ignored.

The classic objection to compatibilism of the sort Stace defends is that it fails to guarantee that there are free *acts* because it fails to guarantee that these acts are the effects of a free *will*. The careful reader will note that the explicit definitions that Stace gives (para. 18) of free versus unfree *acts* are silent on the freedom or unfreedom of the *will*. Libertarians (in the metaphysical, not the political, sense of that term) argue, plausibly enough, that unless the will is free, the acts caused by that will cannot be free. And so one might well reject Stace's definition of "acts done freely" as acts where the "immediate causes are psychological states of the agent" because that is far too broad and too silent on the status of the agent's will. It is too broad because it all depends on just what kind of "psychological state" is in question. For surely a person who acts out of inner

114

compulsion, posthypnotic trance, or an addiction would not be said to act freely. It is too silent because we need to know more about what constitutes the psychological states that do result in free acts. We do not have an adequate theory of free will until we have solved these problems.

For further reading in the spirit of the Hume-Stace approach to the problem of free will, we select from a whole library of books one that is unusually original, informative, and even entertaining, the volume titled *Elbow Room* (1984) by our colleague D. C. Dennett.

Martin Luther King Jr.

Letter from Birmingham Jail (p. 738)

Martin Luther King Jr.'s letter was prompted by a letter (printed in the text) by eight Birmingham clergymen. His letter is unusually long ("Never before have I written so long a letter," para. 48) because he was jailed at the time and thus was unable to speak to audiences face-to-face.

King here goes to some length to show that his work is thoroughly in the American (and Judeo-Christian) tradition. That is, although he rebuts the letter of the eight clergymen, he represents himself not as a radical or in any way un-American (and of course not as an opponent of the Judeo-Christian tradition), but as one who shares the culture of his audience. Thus, although he rejects the clergymen's view that he is impatient, he begins by acknowledging their decency. They are, he says, "men of genuine good will"—and in saying this, King thereby implies that he, too, is a man of good will. Moreover, King's real audience is not only the eight clergymen, but all readers of his letter, who are assumed to be decent folk. Notice, too, in his insistence that he is speaking on an issue that involves all Americans, his statement that "injustice anywhere is a threat to justice everywhere" (para. 4). But his chief strategy early in the letter is to identify himself with Paul (para. 3) and thus to guide his mainly Christian audience to see him as carrying on a tradition that they cherish. Notice also the references to Niebuhr, Buber (a Jew), and Jesus.

It is usual, and correct, to say that King is a master of the appeal to emotion. This essay reveals such mastery, as when he quotes a five-year-old boy: "Daddy, why do white people treat colored people so mean?" (para. 14). And because King is really addressing not so much the eight clergymen as a sympathetic audience that probably needs encouragement to persist rather than reasons to change their beliefs, an emotional (inspirational) appeal is appropriate. But the essay is also rich in lucid exposition and careful analysis, as in paragraph 6 (on the four steps of a nonviolent campaign) and paragraphs 15 and 16 (comparing just and unjust laws).

Additional Topics for Critical Thinking and Writing

1. Think of some injustice that you know something about, and jot down the facts as objectively as possible. Arrange them so that they form an outline. Then, using these facts as a framework, write an essay (possibly in the form of a letter to a specific audience) of about five hundred words, presenting your case in a manner somewhat analogous to King's. For example, don't hesitate to make comparisons with biblical, literary, or recent historical material, to use personal experiences, or to use any other persuasive devices you wish, including appeals to the emotions. Hand in the objective list along with the essay.

2. If some example of nonviolent direct action has recently been in the news, such as actions by persons fearful of nuclear power plants, write an essay evaluating the tactics and their effectiveness in dealing with the issue.

3. Read Plato's *Crito,* and also Plato's *Apology* (in your library). Write an essay of five hundred words explaining whether, as King says, "Socrates practiced civil disobedience (para. 10)."

Peter Cave

Man or Sheep? (p. 752)

Cave opens his essay on a light note, or at least on a lighter note than if he hadn't ended his first paragraph with the final two words ("and long"). As things stand, it is difficult to find much to cheer us up in Hobbes's view of the world, a view that has had few dissenters since 1651, when his great book, *Leviathan*, was published. For it is the main feature of that book—and the social contract theory that it explains and defends—that Cave is leaning on throughout this chapter of his book.

Social contract theory—whose leading historical advocates are Hobbes, John Locke, Jean-Jacques Rousseau, Immanuel Kant, and, in our day, John Rawls—and the theory of political obligation it advocates have the greatest challenge from the moral point of view in confronting the questions: Do we have an obligation to obey the law? Are we obligated by the deeds of our predecessors? Social contract theorists give an affirmative answer to both questions. But are they the correct answers? It is easy to see examples where it appears that they are. Institutions of every variety, shape, and scope are already fully functioning when we arrive at birth. We neither create nor sustain them. But we do benefit from them with or without any desire to do so.

The social contract theory gets its name from the way in which society is thought to be held together by a contract. The contract's central feature is that we are bound by tacit and hypothetical consent (as Cave explains) to create and obey the law, not just because it is advantageous to do so (which it is), but because we owe it to each other to comply with the law and the legal and social institutions that constitute it. It is also easy to see ways in which such a contract is at best a model for rational social relationships rather than anything more descriptive. Surely we are not in fact related to each other by means of a free, voluntary agreement to obey all the laws of our society.

Thomas Hardy

The Man He Killed (p. 755)

Almost every student will be able to report the occurrence of some action they took that seems just to have happened, unwilled and inexplicable. Or if they can explain it, the consequences nevertheless seem vastly disproportionate to the action. With such happenings in mind, one finds oneself murmuring that chance governs all or, if one is given to proverbs, "Man proposes, God disposes." Taking a long view of things, they may comment on how little each of us can actually control by our wills. After all, we did not will our own existence or the family that surrounds us, and it takes only a little thought to realize that, had a different person in the admissions office read our application, we might not have been admitted to the college where we now are taking classes and making friends. And yet most students will also report that they certainly *feel* free—that they can decide to come to class or to cut class, to take this course or that course, to major in this subject or that subject, and to enter this field or that field. Samuel Johnson, in a passage that we reprint in the text, sums up this contradictory state: "All theory is against the freedom of the will; all experience for it."

Thomas Hardy's speaker, presumably a fairly simple, ordinary fellow (notice the diction, which includes such words as "'list" [for "enlist"] and "off-hand-like") who enlisted because he was out of work and had no money, found himself (given the date, probably in

South Africa, during the Boer War) face-to-face with another man, who was, he had been told, his "foe," so he did what he was supposed to do: He shot his "foe." The experience has stayed in his mind, and the best *reason* he can offer for his action is to say that war is "quaint and curious." But the fact that he is repeating the story indicates that he himself is not fully satisfied with his own explanation. Presumably he thinks he acted freely, but he is somewhat puzzled by his action. We, with our superior view, can see that he was the victim of economic circumstances (he was unemployed) and the victim of an imperialistic government that used him for its own purposes.

In discussing the poem one may find oneself talking about the irony of fate, whereby a man who joined the army to keep himself alive finds that he has to kill another man who is pretty much like him. Almost surely, students will see that there is a gap between their awareness and the speaker's unawareness, but they may also agree that all of us, no matter how clever we think we are, move in a world that is largely mysterious to us, a world that (in Hamlet's words) "shapes our ends, / Rough-hew them how we will."

T. S. Eliot

The Love Song of J. Alfred Prufrock (p. 756)

Few instructors in introductory courses will encounter students who have much familiarity with poetry, but you may find that some students have read Robert Browning's "My Last Duchess" and have been instructed in the ways of the dramatic monologue, usually defined as a poem with a speaker and a listener. It will be necessary to explain to these students that "Prufrock" is a different sort of monologue, an internal monologue. At least this is the way we take it; the "you" is the speaker's amorous self, addressed by his timorous self. In our view, the speaker does not actually make a visit—or at least may not—and does not speak aloud to anyone; rather, he imagines a visit, with all of its distressing episodes, and we hear an unspoken inner debate. In the words that John Stuart Mill used to characterize lyric poetry, we get "feeling confessing itself to itself."

"Prufrock" gives us a particularly inhibited protagonist, but we assume that all readers can empathize with his sense of paralysis. After all, the epigraph that opens the poem—in medieval Italian, a language that most of us do not know—is in itself almost enough to terrify the reader, to turn all of us into Prufrocks who dare not read another line lest we again reveal our inadequacies. Having said this, we want to assure instructors that the poem *can* be taught effectively, despite all of the footnotes. Students enjoy talking about the speaker's name (a combination of *prude* and *frock*, therefore suggesting what in politically incorrect days was called an *old maid*?), about the people at the cocktail party commenting on Michelangelo, about the comic rhyme of *crisis* and *ices*, about Prufrock momentarily gaining strength by the absurd expedient of thinking about his collar and his stickpin, and so forth. A good way to proceed is to ask a student to read the first stanza and then to invite comments on what the students like (or find especially interesting) about the passage. In our experience, with only a little assistance, they will comment on particularly memorable phrases and images. And so on, stanza by stanza; they may admit, for instance, that Prufrock's terrors (his fear that people will say, "How his arms and legs are thin") are not foreign to their own thoughts. Have they ever feared they would be judged absurd? (We have never gone so far as to ask if they have ever judged themselves absurd.) Do they dare to wear clothing not sanctioned by contemporary fashion?

Susan Glaspell

Trifles (p. 761)

Some students may know Susan Glaspell's other version of this work, a short story titled "A Jury of Her Peers." Class discussion can focus on the interchangeability of the titles.

Trifles could have been called "A Jury of Her Peers," and vice versa. A peer, of course, is an equal, and the suggestion of the story's title is that Mrs. Wright is judged by a jury of her equals—Mrs. Hale and Mrs. Peters. A male jury would not consist of her equals because, at least in the context of the story and the play, males simply don't have the experiences of women and therefore can't judge them fairly.

Murder is the stuff of TV dramas, and this play concerns a murder, of course, but it's worth asking students how the play differs from a whodunnit. Discussion will soon establish that we learn, early in *Trifles,* who performed the murder, and we even know, fairly early, *why* Minnie killed her husband. (The women know what is what because they correctly interpret "trifles," but the men are baffled, since they are looking for obvious signs of anger.) Once we know who performed the murder, the interest shifts to the question of whether the women will cover up for Minnie.

The distinction between what the men and the women look for is paralleled in the distinction between the morality of the men and the women. The men stand for law and order and for dominance (they condescend to the women, and the murdered Wright can almost be taken as a symbol of male dominance), whereas the women stand for mutual support or nurturing. Students might be invited to argue about why the women protect Minnie. Is it because women are nurturing? Or because they feel guilt for their earlier neglect of Minnie? Or because, being women, they know what her sufferings must have been like and feel that she acted justly? All of the above?

Mitsuye Yamada

To the Lady (p. 771)

First, some background: In 1942, the entire Japanese and Japanese American population on the Pacific coast—about 112,000 people—was relocated and incarcerated. More than two-thirds of the people moved were native-born citizens of the United States. (The 158,000 Japanese residents of the Territory of Hawaii were not affected.)

Immediately after the Japanese attack on Pearl Harbor, many journalists, the general public, Secretary of the Army Henry Stimson, and congressional delegations from California, Oregon, and Washington called for the internment. Although Attorney General Francis Biddle opposed it, on February 19, 1942, President Franklin D. Roosevelt signed Executive Order 9066, allowing military authorities "to prescribe military areas . . . from which any or all persons may be excluded." In practice, no persons of German or Italian heritage were disturbed, but the Japanese and Japanese Americans on the Pacific coast were rounded up (they were allowed to take with them "only that which can be carried") and relocated in camps. Congress, without a dissenting vote, passed legislation supporting the evacuation. A few Japanese Americans challenged the constitutionality of the proceeding but with no immediate success. (For two good short accounts, with suggestions for further readings, see the articles titled "Japanese Americans, wartime relocation of," in *Kodansha Encyclopedia of Japan,* 4:17–18, and "War Relocation Authority" in *Kodansha Encyclopedia of Japan,* 8:228. For a readable account of life in a camp, see Jeanne Wakatsuki Houston's *Farewell to Manzanar,* 1973.)

It may be interesting to read Mitsuye Yamada's poem aloud in class, *without* having assigned it for prior reading, and to ask students for their responses at various stages—after lines 4, 21, and 36. Lines 1 to 4 pose a question that perhaps many of us (young and old, and whether of Japanese descent or not) have asked, at least to ourselves. The question, implying a criticism of the victims, shows an insufficient awareness of Japanese or Japanese American culture of the period. It also shows an insufficient awareness of American racism; by implying that protest by the victims *could* have been effective, it reveals ignorance of the terrific hostility of whites toward persons of Japanese descent.

The first part of the response shows one aspect of the absurdity of the lady's question. Japanese and Japanese Americans were brought up not to stand out in any way (certainly not to make a fuss) and to place the harmony of the group (whether the family or society as a whole) above individual expression. Further, there was nothing that these people could effectively do, even if they had shouted as loudly as Kitty Genovese did. For the most part, they were poor, had no political clout, and were hated and despised as Asians. The absurdity of the view that they could have resisted effectively is comically stated in "should've pulled myself up from my / bra straps" (echoing the red-blooded American ideal of pulling oneself up by one's bootstraps), but of course, the comedy is bitter.

Then the speaker turns to "YOU," nominally the "lady" of the title but in effect also the reader, and by ironically saying what we would have done, points out what in fact we did not do. (The references to a march on Washington and letters to Congress are clear enough, but most students will not be aware of the tradition that the King of Denmark said that he would wear a Star of David [line 27] if Danish Jews were compelled by Nazis to wear the star.)

Thus far, the speaker has put the blame entirely on the white community, especially since lines 5 to 21 strongly suggest that the Japanese Americans *couldn't* do anything except submit. Yet the poem ends with a confession that because Japanese Americans docilely subscribed to "law and order"—especially the outrageous Executive Order 9066—they were in fact partly responsible for the outrage committed against them. The last line of the poem, "All are punished," is exactly what Prince Escalus says at the end of *Romeo and Juliet.* Possibly the echo is accidental, though possibly the reader is meant to be reminded of a play, widely regarded as "a tragedy of fate," in which the innocent are victims of prejudice.

This poem can be the starting point for an argumentative research paper concerning the internment (or was it "relocation"?) of Japanese Americans during World War II. Was the internment justifiable, given the circumstances? Was it legal? Is the compensation voted by Congress in 1988 appropriate? (The law promised $20,000 to each of the 75,000 survivors of the camps.)

28
What Is Happiness? (p. 774)

Thoughts about Happiness, Ancient and Modern (p. 774)

We have never taught any of these quotations, but it is our guess that students will enjoy writing about them, perhaps by amplifying one, by opposing one, or by juxtaposing two quotations.

Some of the passages are sternly moral (such as Shaw's "We have no more right to consume happiness without producing it than to consume wealth without producing it"); some seem almost proverbial (Mill's "Ask yourself whether you are happy, and you cease to be so"; Wharton's "If only we'd stop trying to be happy, we could have a pretty good time"; Frost's "Happiness makes up in height for what it lacks in length"); some are so worldly wise that they seem cynical (Graham Greene's "Point me out the happy man and I will point you out either egotism, selfishness, evil—or else an absolute ignorance"); some—but what is the use of classifying these engaging observations? We do think, to repeat, that students will enjoy taking one of them as a text and amplifying it or perhaps offering counterexamples.

Daniel Gilbert

Does Fatherhood Make You Happy? (p. 775)

Reminder: The essay was published a few days before Father's Day, hence the references to the holiday. Note, too, by the way, that Gilbert not only begins by referring to the holiday but also ends by returning to it, which is to say that he employs a writer's age-old strategy for wrapping things up: Return, via an allusion or a verbal echo, to something said in the opening paragraph. (We have met an occasional teacher of composition who dismisses such a strategy, saying, "I don't want my students to write according to a formula." But real writers in the real world *do* use these time-tested formulas—or rhetorical patterns or templates or strategies, or whatever one wants to call them.)

The essay is perhaps the most lighthearted piece in the book, and it must have been recognized as lighthearted by readers of the *New York Times*, but students—such is their earnestness and perhaps their fear when they confront a textbook—sometimes can hardly believe that the essay is meant to be entertaining as well as informative. One hopes, however, that students hear a genial note by the end of the first paragraph, when they read that after receiving gifts of after-shave and neckties, "millions of fathers . . . have precisely the same thought at precisely the same moment: 'My children,' they think in unison, 'make me happy.'"

Under the joking, however, there is a serious point. We are not sure that what Gilbert says about fatherhood is true, but we are fairly certain that he is right when he says that a baseball game that is tedious for eight-and-a-half innings because there was no scoring can become a wonderful game—in memory—when a batter hits a home run in the bottom of the ninth. As Gilbert puts it, "Memories are dominated by their most powerful—and not their most typical—instances" (para. 9). Gilbert is rather prosaically saying pretty much what Robert Frost said more epigrammatically, "Happiness makes up in height what it lacks in length."

Henry David Thoreau

Selections from Walden *(p. 778)*

[As for Clothing]

Given the passages about clothing, this may be a convenient place for us to list all of the chief uses of clothing that we can think of. Probably the three chief functions can be listed as:

1. Protection or comfort;
2. Concealment, and
3. Display.

But we divide Display into

a. Identification, and

b. Ornament or individualization.

And we add yet another relatively unimportant category:

4. Utility.

The categories are not exclusive and coordinated, but we think they are useful anyway.

- **Protection or comfort**: against heat and cold, rain, thorns, weapons, hockey pucks, and so on

- **Concealment**: for protection (e.g., camouflage uniforms), but it can also conceal to serve the needs of modesty.

- **Identification**: to identify the wearer's sex (or at least it used to do this) and status, for example, as a member of the idle rich, a proper business executive, a student, an admiral. The uniforms of athletes—say, football players—protect, and they also identify. Speaking of uniforms, it is worth noting that although a uniform can establish authority (a police officer, a priest, a nurse), a uniform often subordinates (e.g., prisoner, bellhop).

- **Ornament or individualization**: the cut of clothing—to say nothing of the fabric, jewelry, and accessories—can serve to ornament for aesthetic reasons (probably to establish status) or to individualize. If clothing can serve the purposes of modesty by concealing, it can also work the other way, by heightening sexual attractiveness. That is, clothing can reveal as well as conceal, or, to put it a little differently, clothes can emphasize by elaborately hiding. Without our clothing, we look pretty much alike; with clothing, we can make ourselves distinctive. Note that in tropical climates, where little clothing seems to be worn, body painting was common, presumably revealing a desire to enhance the all-too-ordinary body.

- **Utility**: providing pockets and belts, useful for carrying stuff

It happens, by chance, that the preceding comments were written only a day before a young man of our acquaintance, who had been accepted by the undergraduate college of business administration at a midwestern university, received information telling him that an orientation session would be held on such-and-such a day, and that he was expected to wear "business casual" clothing. "Business casual" for men, it seems, means a blazer, a button-down shirt, no tie, and khaki pants. The prospect of wearing these items gave this pre-freshman a good deal of pleasure, especially since he did not own a blazer and therefore he told his parents that he had to buy one, as well some additional shirts with button-down collars. (We refrained from quoting Thoreau: "Beware of all enterprises that require new clothes, and not rather a new wearer of clothes," para. 2.) But is it possible that Thoreau did not see that when one wears new clothes, one may become a new person?

A topic for discussion: Has Thoreau said anything that may lead you to change the way you dress? If so, explain. If not, do you think he has nothing to say, or do you think he does indeed make some good points but you nevertheless will choose to ignore him?

[*We do not ride on the railroad; it rides upon us.*]

Admittedly, Thoreau sometimes can be a bit of a nag, but we think this passage is quite wonderful. Although in our seventh question we suggest that a student may doubt the wisdom of Thoreau's assertion that "Our life is frittered away by detail," we nevertheless do see his point, and we do experience the force of "let your affairs be as two or three, and not a hundred or a thousand . . . and keep your accounts on your thumb nail." And then he really gets going, with the claim (midway in the passage) that the nation "lives too fast." This gets him to the railway—the jetliner of his day—and to an especially wonderful passage about the nation living too fast:

> It lives too fast. Men think that it is essential that the *Nation* have commerce, and export ice, and talk through a telegraph, and ride thirty miles an hour, without a doubt, whether *they* do or not; but whether we should live like baboons or like men, is a little uncertain. If we do not get out sleepers, and forge rails, and devote days and nights to the work, but go to tinkering upon our *lives* to improve *them*, who will build railroads? And if railroads are not built, how shall we get to heaven in season? But if we stay at home and mind our business, who will want railroads? We do not ride on the railroad; it rides upon us. Did you ever think what those sleepers are that underlie the railroad? Each one is a man, an Irishman, or a Yankee man. The rails are laid on them, and they are covered with sand, and the cars run smoothly over them. They are sound sleepers, I assure you. And every few years a new lot is laid down and run over; so that, if some have the pleasure of riding on a rail, others have the misfortune to be ridden upon. And when they run over a man that is walking in his sleep, a supernumerary sleeper in the wrong position, and wake him up, they suddenly stop the cars, and make a hue and cry about it, as if this were an exception. I am glad to know that it takes a gang of men for every five miles to keep the sleepers down and level in their beds as it is, for this is a sign that they may sometime get up again.

Surely there is great power in Thoreau's almost comic reduction of the nation's "commerce" to exporting ice, talking through the telegraph, and riding an astounding thirty miles in an hour. This gets Thoreau to the irony—OK, to the sarcasm (but it's clever)—of "And if railroads are not built, how shall we get to heaven in season?" For us, the most memorable part of the passage is the part beginning "We do not ride on the railroad; it rides upon us." He continues, punning on "sleepers" (railway ties, and persons who are sleeping): The ties are laid down at the cost of human lives, chiefly lives exhausted in the effort, but occasionally a life is quite literally destroyed, accidentally, in the process of constructing the railroad. The passage is worth quoting again:

> Did you ever think what those sleepers are that underlie the railroad? Each one is a man, an Irishman, or a Yankee man. The rails are laid on them, and they are covered with sand, and the cars run smoothly over them. They are sound sleepers, I assure you.

We have sometimes read this passage aloud in class, and it seems to us—though perhaps we are pushing things—that Thoreau is conveying something of the sound of the railroad through repetition, especially through the abundant *m*'s, *n*'s, and *r*'s, indeed through the repetition of "sleepers" and "man." Try saying aloud "Each one is a man, an Irishman, or a Yankee man," and see if you don't agree that Thoreau is somehow evoking the sound of a railroad train.

Darrin M. McMahon

In Pursuit of Unhappiness (p. 783)

In regard to questions 2 and 6, a hedonist is anyone who believes that pleasure is the only or the highest good. The term *hedonism* comes from the Greek *hedone*, "happiness" or "pleasure." In Aristotle, *hedone* is contrasted with *eudaimonia*, "well-being." John Stuart

Mill was a qualitative hedonist; he believed that some pleasures were better than others, by which he did not mean merely that they were more pleasant. Jeremy Bentham was a quantitative hedonist; he believed that, ceteris paribus, the more pleasant some experience is, the better it is.

As to question 8, an argument to the effect that we are happier today than we were three centuries ago might proceed by asserting that a higher percentage of people (say, in the United States) are today able to fulfill their desires than was true in 1700, and successful pursuit of one's desires is (part of) what we mean by being happy. The issue, of course, is an empirical one and is not open to direct verification or falsification. Still, one might hope to find evidence in journals, diaries, and letters for the years 1650 through 1750 that reveal the miseries so many people suffered but no longer do. Take, as just one example, smallpox—a deadly disease at that time, and now virtually wiped out.

The answer to question 3 depends, of course, on how much prior knowledge or conjecture about happiness you have been exposed to. We confess to not (yet) having read McMahon's book, *Happiness: A History* (2006), and we doubt whether many who read this entry will have done so either. So each of us will have to answer this question as we see fit and will have to do so without being exposed to the most recent scholarship on the topic.

Question 5 asks us to think about whether suffering is our natural state. From an evolutionary point of view, it seems highly unlikely. Why would we want to prolong our lives to the point of ability to procreate if we were miserable all or most of the time? McMahon wants to go farther; he thinks we were "meant to be" happy. Are we wrong to think we sense intelligent design lurking in the background? In any case, that may not be McMahon's intention.

Epictetus

From *The Handbook (p. 786)*

Our headnote is longer than usual because we try to provide students with a brief introduction to stoicism. Students who have seen the film *Gladiator* (2000) with Richard Harris as Marcus Aurelius will doubtless be able to supplement our comments. We didn't want to overload the introductory note, so we didn't introduce the stoic idea of *apatheia*. But in classroom discussion of the stoic indifference to everything external (riches or poverty, sickness or health) because such things are neither good nor bad but merely indifferent, you may want to introduce this word. (The Greek word for "lack of feeling" gives us our word *apathy*, though the meanings are somewhat different, since the English word suggests a kind of slackness or inattentiveness rather than a principled dispassionateness.)

Some of the passages that we quote from *The Handbook* are old favorites of ours, from our student days—which is not to say that we claim to have ever lived the stoic life. Indeed, another favorite passage of ours is Jonathan Swift's bitter comment, "The Stoical scheme of supplying our Wants by lopping off our Desires is like cutting off our feet when we want shoes."

We confess that we are a trifle uneasy about including a stoic piece in a section on happiness, since the stoics were not concerned with happiness. They were concerned with duty and virtue: One does one's duty (that is, one acts rationally), and having done one's duty (having behaved virtuously), one then might experience pleasure, but pleasure is not the goal and indeed pleasure is not even a good. It is our impression that with the stoics, we are pretty close to Voltaire's view at the end of *Candide:* "We must cultivate our garden" ([I] faut cultiver notre jardin).

Bertrand Russell

The Happy Life (p. 789)

Some students may be distressed by Bertrand Russell's use of the pronoun *he* ("the moralist . . . he") where we would now say *he or she.* If the issue comes up in class, it is easy to inform students that the use of the masculine pronoun in a generic sense was common when Russell wrote this essay in 1930.

Russell's view of happiness seems to us to be pretty close to the mainline classical view, as found in Aristotle's *Nicomachean Ethics:* Happiness is not a matter of good sensations and certainly not a matter of pleasant sensations rooted in ignorance. (In *A Tale of a Tub*, Jonathan Swift famously defines happiness as "a perpetual possession of being well-deceived" and "felicity" as "the serene peaceful state of being a fool among knaves.") If Americans are asked to quote a line or phrase that has "happiness" in it, they probably will quote the Declaration of Independence, which speaks of "the pursuit of happiness," but Russell, like Aristotle, sees happiness as a by-product, something that comes out of an active relationship with others. For Aristotle, happiness is not something to be pursued, and it certainly is not gained by monitoring one's thoughts by "mindfulness training" (a term we saw on a poster advertising a course in how to be happy). Nor is it a matter of physical sensations (something experienced while drinking cold beer or taking a hot bath). Rather, happiness is a state of equanimity that incidentally arises from living the virtuous life, and the virtuous life is a life lived in society.

For Russell, happiness is not a matter of selfless behavior (the narrow moralistic view). Indeed, according to him, for the active person (we almost said "for the active man"), "the whole antithesis between self and the rest of the world . . . disappears as soon as we have any genuine interest in persons or things outside ourselves" (para. 2).

Russell probably would not have thought that he had much in common with the Dalai Lama, but we think some of our comments below on the essay by the Dalai Lama may also be relevant to Russell's essay.

The Dalai Lama and Howard C. Cutler

Inner Contentment (p. 791)

The Dalai Lama, in many of his writings, returns to a basic theme: Ignorance conditions us to think that we are separate entities, opposed to a hostile universe. The conquest of greed (or avarice), hatred (or aversion), and delusion (or ignorance)—what Buddhists call "the three poisons"—frees us from a condition of suffering or craving ("dis-ease," Sanskrit *dukkha*) and leads us to a twofold condition of *wisdom* (we see through the delusions of self-preoccupation, and we experience bliss) and *compassion* (we express our bliss in a concern for others). That is, in this enlightened condition, we are free from self-concern— from a desire to maintain our sense of ego and from our hatred of anything that opposes our concept of ourself—and in this new state, we express an unselfish concern for others and can achieve happiness.

We want to offer a few additional words about "the self," especially because so many students wish "to find themselves" or "to be true to themselves." (This issue is raised in Danielle Crittenden's essay on page 798.) We sometimes quote Robert Frost's "The Silken Tent," which begins, "She is as in a field a silken tent," and goes on to describe the tent, supported by a central cedar pole, that "is loosely bound / By countless silken ties of love and thought / To everything on earth the compass round." That is, the tent is supported— stands as a tent—because of its ties to the ground. It is what it is, it is a self, because of its connections with others. An episode in Henrik Ibsen's play *Peer Gynt* also comes to mind.

Peer wants to be himself, so he casts off relationship after relationship—friends, business associates, family members—in an effort to be himself. Late in the play Ibsen shows Peer with an onion; he peels off layer after layer, and, of course, he finds no internal hard core, no self within; the self consists of relationships with others.

You may know a good deal more about Buddhism than we do, but in case you have no familiarity with it, we offer some background.

Very briefly, Buddhism was founded in the sixth century B.C.E. by Siddhartha, crown prince of the Shakya kingdom in what is now the India-Nepal border. Rich, married, and a father, he became dissatisfied with his perception of illness, old age, and death, and he abandoned his princely life to learn if there was more to life than the usual course of birth, death, and (in the creed he grew up in) rebirth—an endless merry-go-round of suffering. After living for six years as an ascetic, he abandoned asceticism, took normal food, meditated, and became a Buddha (Enlightened One). Henceforth, he was known as Shakyamuni (the Sage of the Shakya) or the historical Buddha.

The enlightenment he achieved had to do with his perception of reality. We can hardly be expected to explain exactly what this is, but the gist is that unhappiness in life comes from craving—from a desire to satisfy the self, which is conceived of as something opposed to the rest of the universe.

Buddhism, of course, is immensely complicated. It has a long history, it has developed many schools, and there is much argument about terms such as *self,* but we can probably say that the heart of Buddhism is the belief that suffering is omnipresent. The Buddha taught that the way to escape suffering is by awareness of the Four Noble Truths:

1. All existence is characterized by suffering; the human condition (though it includes temporary pleasures) is one of physical and psychological disease.

2. Suffering is caused by attachment, by a thirst for selfish pleasure, and orientation to the transient.

3. Suffering can be eliminated, but only by ceasing to crave.

4. One can cease to crave only by leading a disciplined, moral life, and this is set forth in the Eightfold Path, which takes one from the realm of suffering to Nirvana.

With some hesitation—this is getting complicated—we give one version of the Eightfold Path, which the Buddha taught in his first sermon. These are not eight successive stages but are eight practices that are to be engaged in simultaneously. We are aware that each of the following points needs considerable amplification, and it may be that you will want some students to give reports on some aspects of Buddhism.

1. Right view (understanding reality, which means understanding the Four Noble Truths)

2. Right intention (resolution to renounce desire, and to commit to goodwill and harmlessness)

3. Right speech (avoidance of lying, angry words, and gossip)

4. Right action (avoidance of harming, dishonesty, and sexual misconduct)

5. Right livelihood (avoidance of harmful ways of making a living, including dealing with weapons, living creatures, and intoxicants)

6. Right effort (cultivation of what is wholesome)

7. Right mindfulness (clear consciousness, arrived at by contemplating the body, feeling, and states of mind)

8. Right concentration (a stage in meditation in which mental activity ceases and the mind is united with the object of meditation)

By these practices, it is said, one extinguishes the passions (which produce ignorant actions) and arrives at enlightenment.

Attempts to eliminate passion—to detach oneself from the things of this world—are not, of course, limited to Buddhism. One can easily find Christian texts that urge renunciation:

> But I say unto you, That whosoever looketh on a woman to lust after her hath committed adultery with her already in his heart. / And if thy right eye offend thee, pluck it out, and cast it from thee: for it is profitable for thee that one of thy members should perish, and not that the whole body should be cast into hell. (Matthew 5:28–29)

> He that loveth father or mother more than me is not worthy of me: and he that loveth son or daughter more than me is not worthy of me. (Matthew 10:37)

> And everyone that hath forsaken houses, or brethren, or sisters, or father, or mother, or wife, or children, or lands, for my name's sake, shall receive an hundredfold, and shall inherit everlasting life. (Matthew 19:29)

We are not saying that in the matter of renunciation, Christianity and Buddhism are the same. We daily try (especially when we ask students to write a comparison) to keep in mind a remark by Bishop Joseph Butler: "Everything is what it is, and not another thing." Still, if some students find the Buddhist ideal of renunciation odd, we think it is worth citing some Christian texts that strike many people as no less odd.

C. S. Lewis

We Have No "Right to Happiness" (p. 794)

So C. S. Lewis tells us that we have no "right to happiness." Before complaining too loudly, consider the possible objections he might be raising. Perhaps we have no right to happiness because we have no rights at all. That's what Jeremy Bentham and John Stuart Mill would have said in the 1830s, had they been asked. Perhaps instead Lewis holds that we do have rights, but in the case of happiness we confuse a right to happiness with it being right to seek and preserve such happiness as we can obtain—and it is right to seek and preserve our happiness. There may be other possibilities, too.

The right to happiness has never been very popular with the theorists and manifestos purporting to state what our rights are. It doesn't appear in the French Declaration of the Rights of Man and Citizen (1789), and it is missing from the list of "natural rights" identified and defended by John Locke ("life, liberty, and property" [1690]). Nor was it mentioned in the Universal Declaration of Human Rights (1948). It appears only and famously in the American Declaration of Independence in the memorable phrase "the right to life, liberty and the pursuit of happiness."

These, however, are what we might call some of the political dimensions to an alleged right. Lewis's essay is not concerned with these dimensions at all (though he does discuss them briefly, in paragraphs 12–13). He is concerned with happiness in our private lives and the alleged right to happiness in that setting. He mocks the idea when he draws the parallel between this alleged right and "a right to good luck" (para. 6) or "a right to be six feet tall" (para. 6). Lewis rehearses some general ideas about our rights in paragraph 7, correctly pointing out that some rights are lawfully protected freedoms and other rights are lawful claims to certain benefits or services. The American legal philosopher W. N. Hohfeld added two further kinds of rights: powers, as with Congress's power to raise taxes, and immunities, as with the immunity against self-incrimination specified in the Fifth Amendment to the federal Constitution. This fourfold set of rights has become the standard conception of rights both moral and legal. It seems to play no role in Lewis's understanding of the alleged right to happiness.

Is he correct in mocking the right to happiness by comparing it with the right to good luck or the right to be six feet tall? (See questions 4 and 5.) It can't just be that our luck and our height are not within our control; many things in life are not within our control, but they involve no rights; for example, we have no control over our age, but that is not because we have no right to being the age we happen to be. Perhaps it is because the things to which we have a right are terribly important to our status as rational, autonomous agents, whereas our age or height or luck does not play such a central role. (We might imagine a world in which everyone did have a right to be six feet tall, but that is another story altogether—though it would be a useful exercise to think of the circumstances in which such a right would exist.)

Question 6 takes us into a discussion of legal and moral rights: A legal right is a right created by some form of legal enactment—by statutory, judicial, or constitutional law that gives one a legal claim, such as to a piece of real estate. A moral right is any right created or recognized by moral theory or principle—for example, a moral claim based on a promise, which may or may not also be enforceable by law. One might have a moral and a legal claim to the same thing, just as one might lack both a moral and a legal claim to something.

We do not agree with Lewis (see question 7) that an alleged right to happiness is really an alleged right to sexual happiness. He offers no convincing evidence on the point, and we can think of none. Were he correct, no one would have a right to happiness before about the age of twelve. That seems to us quite unconvincing.

We are not biologists and so our answer to question 8 is little better than an educated guess. We can see how monogamy for women might well be a biological necessity; there seems to us good reason to believe that women in general are hardwired toward monogamy, whereas men in general are hardwired to spread their sperm as broadly as possible. Lewis is like us, not a biologist, and so his pronouncements about women's sexual nature need to be greeted cautiously. We grant that he gives a clear and persuasive argument in paragraph 28 in support of his claim about monogamy.

Danielle Crittenden

About Love (p. 798)

We include this piece for several reasons: We think it is readable; we think it is provocative; we think the point about "being oneself" is immensely important; and we think it will perhaps especially interest older students, especially those who are or who have been married.

In our discussion (in this manual) of the selection by the Dalai Lama, we talk at some length about this business of the "self"—we raise the idea that perhaps there is no "self" apart from the relationships we build with others—so we will not go into the matter here, but we urge you to consider assigning the Dalai Lama's essay along with Danielle Crittenden's. We also urge you to look back at the first selection in this chapter, "Thoughts about Happiness," where you will find several quotations that fit nicely with Crittenden's argument. For instance, the comment by Mary Wollstonecraft Shelley and the second comment by Shaw ("We have no more right to consume happiness without producing it than to consume wealth without producing it") imply that happiness is a product of a virtuous interaction—not of the preservation of one's independence.

We have not taught this essay, but it is our guess that it will provoke lively discussion and interesting written responses.

Judy Brady

I Want a Wife (p. 801)

Incidental passages of satire, employing an ironic voice, appear throughout the book, but Judy Brady's essay, like Jonathan Swift's "A Modest Proposal" in Chapter 5, is satiric from beginning to end. Since our book is chiefly about argument (reasoning) rather than about the broader topic of persuasion, we discuss irony very briefly. And because of our emphasis on engaging the audience's goodwill by presenting oneself as benign, and because of Carl Rogers's point about reducing the sense of threat to the reader (see Chapter 12), we advise students to think twice before they use irony in their arguments. Still, Brady's essay offers an opportunity to talk about the power of verbal irony or satire—in Frank O'Connor's definition, "The intellectual dagger opposing the real dagger."

In talking about this satire, one can point out that in "I Want a Wife," as in much other satire, the persona more or less appears as an innocent eye, a speaker who merely describes, in a simple, objective way, what is going on. (The reader, not the speaker, says, "This is outrageous." The speaker never explicitly states her thesis.) Thus, in the essay Brady is not a creature with a name but merely a member of a class. She is simply "a Wife." We then get the terrifying list of things that a Wife finds thrust on her. These are scarcely described in detail, but the mere enumeration of the chores becomes, by the volume of its unadorned accumulation, comic — and stinging. One is reminded of John Dryden's comment, in *Origin and Progress of Satire* (1692), distinguishing between invective (direct abuse) and verbal irony:

> How easy is it to call "rogue" and "villain," and that wittily. But how hard to make a man appear a fool, a blockhead, or a knave, without using any of those opprobrious terms.

Whether things have changed since 1971, when Brady's essay first appeared in *Ms.* magazine, is a question that might be argued. One might also ask (though of course one doesn't expect a balanced view in satire) if things in 1971 really were the way Brady saw them. Did marriage really offer nothing to a wife? No love, no companionship, no security? Were all husbands childish and selfish, and all wives selfless?

Right from the start, each of us studied, or "read," only one disci-   5
pline; mine was history. Half my friends read in other academic disciplines: physics, biochemistry, English, French, and so on. The other half
read in vocational disciplines like medicine, law, and engineering. Central to the entire system was early specialization. Even the broadest curriculum choice, PPE (Philosophy, Politics, and Economics), consisted of
just three elements.

Learning was organized through the tutorial system. Every week I
and one other student met our tutor. He had assigned a paper the previous week, and we had spent the time reading widely in the relevant
literature. One of us read his paper aloud to begin the tutorial, then the
tutor rubbished it and told us, in blistering detail, what we should have
written, and how we should have interpreted the readings. The tutors
didn't show any delicate concern for our feelings.

Frances, by contrast, is entering a decentralized system. Here the
assumption is that the person who gets the education is going to be its
chief beneficiary and that, accordingly, she should bear the cost. As a
member of the great American middle class, she belongs to a generation whose parents have been fretting about the cost of higher education from the moment they beheld their newborns. Paying your way
through Emory or its sisters in the American college big leagues is
almost certain to cost more than $150,000. It's also a system in which
half or more of her generation of eighteen-year-olds enroll in some kind
of postsecondary institution; she'll be one of literally millions of freshmen this fall.

Criteria for admission are diverse. Doing well in high school is still
a terrific idea, and, bless her heart, Frances has. But ever since seventh
grade her teachers and counselors have nudged her to perform community service, play music and competitive sports, act, publish poems,
edit magazines, do internships in hospitals, and in a dozen other ways be
extracurricular to give her an edge in college applications. Being a legacy
or (as in her case) the child of a professor certainly helps.

She will study the liberal arts. In practice that means a couple of science classes, a bit of math, a language, a social-science-methods course,
a spot of history, some "health" (such as "Principles of Physical Education," which is the Emory meaning of PPE), something in the performing
arts, and then the nine or ten courses of a typical major. None of those
courses will be vocational, but ideally they'll make her a well-rounded
individual—mature, informed, and tolerant.

She will take classes containing from six to one hundred students.   10
Occasionally she'll have to write a paper, but she'll rarely have to read one
aloud to her teacher. She'll be in discussion groups with professors and
teaching assistants, all of whom have been trained in sensitivity and diversity. Counselors, tutors, and an array of considerate "campus life" helpers
will surround her. After four years, she'll probably have to select a graduate
school to pursue her vocation, buckling down there to more years of toil.

How do the two systems compare in the eyes of someone who has seen plenty of each? The great virtue of the British system, particularly the early specialization, was that it enabled us to learn one discipline really well, to become far more deeply engaged with it than was possible for our American counterparts. It gave a marvelous opportunity to students who already knew where they were going to pursue their ambitions without distraction. As an undergraduate, I was already studying historical theory and the philosophy of history, which here is deferred to graduate school.

Its great and equal drawback was that it forced some students to choose too soon, before they were ready. An old girlfriend thought she wanted to be a psychologist but decided after a year that it had been a terrible idea, and had to petition to switch into French, which detained her at college a year longer than the rest of us. The system assumed freshmen were grown-ups who knew their own minds. Anyone familiar with a crowd of seventeen- and eighteen-year-olds knows that assumption is not always dependable.

The great virtue of the American system is its breadth. How impressed I was, as a TA at Berkeley, to have undergraduates in my very first history discussion group mention a relevant insight from Freud that they had picked up in "Psych," or refer to Laffer Curves that they'd studied in "Econ." They made me feel a trifle narrow and parochial.

Then they handed in their papers and wrote their finals, and my feelings of inadequacy disappeared. The great American drawbacks revealed themselves: The students' writing was awful, and their knowledge utterly superficial. Their breadth was the breadth of rivers an inch deep. The experience also drove home to me the truth, verified hundreds of times since, that the study of history is simply far too difficult for most students.

There are pros and cons to both systems. Surely it's possible, now, to combine the merits of each rather than putting up with their weaknesses. I think more American colleges should offer the chance to specialize right from the outset to those students who want it. Bright young physicists who want only to study physics should be free to do so, without laboring through courses in art history that seem to them a waste of valuable time. 15

In the same way, students who already have a clear vocational objective at the age of eighteen should be able to pursue it at top schools. My own experience showed that most law and medical students at Oxford *wanted* to get busy in preparation for the careers they had chosen, and were glad to be able to do so. (Incidentally, it didn't make them philistines; they enjoyed literature and read widely in other disciplines, just as I read plenty of great novels and a little science, even though I didn't take classes in those areas.)

At the same time, the vast American system can maintain the liberal-arts option for those who prefer it and don't yet have a clear sense of direction. Students with the right frame of mind thrive on studying diverse subjects until they're ready, sometimes at age twenty or older, to make a stronger commitment. But let's get rid of the idea that liberal arts is for everyone. America's commitment to equality and to universal education is noble and invigorating. But it shouldn't mean that one size fits all.

TOPICS FOR CRITICAL THINKING AND WRITING

1. In paragraph 6 Allitt says that his tutor "rubbished" his papers and that "the tutors didn't show any delicate concern for our feelings." Was this system barbaric, or can something be said for it? In your response, you may want to draw on your personal experience.

2. Do you agree that in college "bright young physicists who want only to study physics should be free to do so" (para. 15)? Explain.

3. Do you wish you were having a college education like the one that Allitt had at Oxford? Explain why or why not in an essay of 250–500 words.

4. In general, would you prefer a system of narrow specialization in higher education or a system that affords great breadth? Explain in 250–500 words.

5. Do you think that Allitt's attempt to join together the best of the Oxford and the American systems (paras. 15–17) is a good idea, or do you think not? Give your reasons in 250–500 words.

Letters of Response by Carol Geary Schneider and Ellis M. West

To the Editor:

Patrick Allitt is right to question whether common frameworks guiding American undergraduate education have outlived their usefulness ("Should Undergraduates Specialize?" *The Chronicle Review,* June 16). The alternatives he proposes, however—specialization for those who know what they want to study and liberal arts for the less focused—are both decidedly inadequate for today's students.

In a volatile, globally interdependent, and fast-changing world, everyone will need more liberal education, not less. But we need a new approach to the design of undergraduate liberal education, a design that takes full account of the needs of an innovation-fueled economy and an increasingly complex and globally interconnected society.

Today's college students should not be presented with a false choice between either vocational preparation or liberal-arts education defined as nonvocational personal development. It is time to embrace a far more purposeful approach to college that sets clear expectations for all students, cultivates the achievement of a set of essential skills and capacities, and enables every student to place his or her interests—including career aspirations—in the broader context of a complex and fast-changing world.

Students certainly should have every opportunity to pursue their interests in depth, and this pursuit can begin as early as the first year of college. But while doing so, they should also be working to develop strong intellectual and practical skills that can be transferred to new settings when the students or their fields move, as they surely will, in new and unexpected directions. Students should develop the ability to communicate clearly; to think through the ethical, civic, and intercultural issues relevant to their interests; and to locate those interests in a wide-ranging understanding of the world in which they live.

To prepare students well both for productive work and responsible citizenship in a complex world, we need a new vision for liberal education that emphasizes inquiry and integration and transferability of learning, rather than narrow depth or shallow breadth. 5

CAROL GEARY SCHNEIDER
President, Association of American Colleges and Universities
Washington, D.C., August 4, 2006

To the Editor:

Breadth or depth? Patrick Allitt, using the British system as a model, makes a case for allowing some college students—those "who already have a clear vocational objective at the age of eighteen"—to start studying their chosen vocation, like law or medicine, at the beginning of their time in college. They would also be excused from having to take general-education courses such as "art history that seem to them a waste of valuable time." The traditional liberal-arts option—a breadth of courses—would be available to (but presumably not required of) only those students "who prefer it and don't yet have a clear sense of [vocational] direction."

Allitt's case, however, is fundamentally flawed because it is based on a false assumption—that the primary, if not sole, purpose of higher education is to train students in and for a particular vocation. If that were its purpose, then of course early specialization would make sense. . . . Allitt overlooks at least two other purposes of education that in America have been more important than vocational training and that have justified a broad, liberal-arts education.

The first of these purposes is to enable students to get their act together. In other words, a liberal-arts education has traditionally provided students an opportunity to decide what kind of persons they want to be—not just what kind of work they want to do. It forces them to confront the "big questions," as the Teagle Foundation likes to phrase it (see W. Robert Connor's "The Right Time and Place for Big Questions," *The Chronicle Review*, June 9), questions having to do with the purpose or meaning of their lives, including the moral values to which they should adhere.

The second traditional purpose of a liberal-arts education is closely related to the first—to prepare students to be good citizens in a free and democratic society. At a minimum, this means teaching them to be concerned about the public good, to respect the dignity and worth of all persons, and to be informed about our political system and public issues.

Other purposes of a liberal-arts education, such as cultivating a love 5 of beauty, could also be mentioned. In short, as Aristotle argued centuries ago, because humans are spiritual, moral, political, and aesthetic beings, not just producers of goods and services, they should be encouraged, if not required, to study subjects that will help to make them genuinely happy.

Granted, more and more liberal-arts colleges seem to be less and less committed to those goals. Fewer courses are required for a degree; general-education requirements seem to be justified only to give as many departments as possible a piece of the action; and faculty members are concerned mainly with their own disciplines and areas of research and not with the overall education of their students. De facto specialization seems to be the name of the game.

Given this reality, perhaps Allitt can be excused for overlooking the traditional purposes of a higher education. I can only hope that Emory University, where his daughter will be a first-year student in the fall and which is one of my alma maters, has not forsaken these purposes.

Ellis M. West

Professor of Political Science, University of Richmond

Richmond, Va., August 4, 2006

Topics for Critical Thinking and Writing

1. Schneider asserts (para. 4) that while students are pursuing their "interests in depth . . . they should also be working to develop strong intellectual and practical skills that can be transferred to new settings when the students or their fields move. . . . Students should develop the ability to communicate clearly; to think through the ethical, civic, and intercultural issues relevant to their interests; and to locate those interests in a wide-ranging understanding of the world in which they live." Do you think that at least to some degree you are engaged in such a program? If not, why not? Do you perhaps think Schneider's program is overly ambitious? Explain.

2. West says (para. 3) that one purpose of education in America "is to enable students to get their act together. In other words, a liberal-arts education has traditionally provided students an opportunity to decide what kind of persons they want to be." Are you taking courses partly "to get your act together"? Explain.

3. West says (para. 5) that a second purpose of a liberal-arts education is rooted in the fact that we are "spiritual, moral, political, and aesthetic beings." Students should therefore "study subjects that will help to make them genuinely happy." Your view of West's assumptions?

Carlo Rotella

Carlo Rotella, director of the American Studies Program at Boston College, is the author of several books. He also is a regular columnist for the Boston Globe, *which published this essay on December 24, 2011.*

No, It Doesn't Matter What You Majored In

I woke up on Wednesday morning with two routine but pressing jobs to accomplish: I had a column to write, and I had a stack of twenty-page papers to grade. The two duties wouldn't seem to have anything to do with each other. But they do, and what they have in common says something about the value of higher education.

Almost everybody agrees that college costs too much. If a relative handful of relatively rich people want to pay a lot to go to the most exclusive schools, that's up to them; it's a victimless crime. But if a good college education costs too much across the board, that's a major social problem, especially because a college degree has increasingly become a minimum qualification for the kind of job that puts you in the middle class—which is where most Americans, wishfully or not, still imagine themselves to belong. And this all looks worse because the economic crisis has hit many public institutions especially hard.

Some have called this situation a higher-education bubble. Some have begun to investigate what students are really getting out of college for their money. They're asking necessary questions about curriculum and teaching, and about institutions' and students' commitment to academic excellence.

But this vitally important discussion is often hamstrung by a tendency to reduce college to vocational education in the crudest, most unrealistic ways. This kind of reduction often zeroes in on the humanities and parts of the social sciences—together often mislabeled as "the liberal arts" (when, in fact, math and science are also part of the liberal arts)—as the most overvalued, least practical aspect of higher education. If you study engineering you can become an engineer, if you study biology or physics you can be a scientist, and if you're pre-med or pre-law then you can go on to be a doctor or a lawyer. But what kind of job can you get if you study Renaissance art, or Indonesian history, or any kind of literature at all?

It's a fair question, even when asked unfairly. If Deval Patrick[1], an   5 English major, was available, I'd let him answer. But he's busy being governor, so I'll take a shot at it.

---

[1]Deval Patrick was governor of Massachusetts when Rotella's article was published. [Editor's note.]

Let's first defenestrate a mistaken assumption that many students and their parents cling to. Prospective employers frequently don't really care what you majored in. They might look at where you went to school and how you did, and they will definitely consider whether you wrote a decent cover letter, but they don't sit there and think, "Anthropology?! We don't need an anthropologist."

They do care that you're a college graduate. What that means, if you worked hard and did your job properly and your teachers did theirs, is that you have spent four years developing a set of skills that will serve you in good stead in the postindustrial job market. You can assimilate and organize large, complex bodies of information; you can analyze that information to create outcomes that have value to others; and you can express your ideas in clear, purposeful language. Whether you honed these skills in the study of foreign policy or Russian novels is secondary, even trivial. What matters is that you pursued training in the craft of mastering complexity, which you can apply in fields from advertising to zoo management.

The papers on my desk are from a course on the city in literature and film. They're about, among other things, 9/11 stories, inner-city documentaries, and the literary tradition of Washington, D.C. Instead of worrying about whether you can get paid to know about these topics, consider this: You can't fake a twenty-page paper. Either you've done the work this semester and know what you're talking about, or you don't. Either you can deliver a sustained reasoned argument, or you can't. It's a craft, like cabinet making.

I make my living building such figurative cabinets—like this column, a miniature one I assembled using skills I learned first in school and then honed doing various jobs in the private and public sectors: policy analyst, teacher, reporter, writer, very small businessman. Whatever else happens at college, higher education is about learning to drive the postindustrial nails straight.

Topics for Critical Thinking and Writing

1. In a sentence or two, state the author's thesis.

2. In your view, does the author offer adequate *support* for the thesis?

3. Do you think the final paragraph—and in particular the final sentence—makes an effective ending? Why, or why not?

4. What sort of personality does the author convey? If he were teaching at your college, would you consider taking a course with him? Why, or why not?

Alina Tugend

Alina Tugend (born 1959), a journalist, has written on a variety of topics, but her specialty is personal finance. Her columns on this topic received a Best in Business Award in 2011 from the Society of American Business Editors and Writers. This article was first published in the New York Times *on May 4, 2012.*

Vocation or Exploration: Pondering the Purpose of College

Our oldest son is finishing up his junior year in high school, and we're already overwhelmed by what I've been calling the college challenge—trying to figure out what college he can get into and what we can afford.

But there's also a bigger debate raging that hovers over all our concerns. What exactly is a university education for? Is it, narrowly, to ensure a good job after graduation? That's how Rick Scott, the governor of Florida, views it. He has made waves by wanting to shift state financing of public colleges to majors that have the best job prospects. Hello science, technology, engineering, and math; good-bye psychology and anthropology. And Senator Ron Wyden, Democrat of Oregon, has introduced the Student Right to Know Before You Go Act, which would require, among other things, that students have access to data on university graduates' average annual earnings. Or is the point of a university degree to give students a broad and deep humanities education that teaches them how to think and write critically? Or can a college education do both?

A little background: Before 1983, receiving a bachelor of arts degree in just about any subject "opened up lots of jobs," said Anthony P. Carnevale, director of Georgetown University's Center on Education and the Workforce. "You could get a B.A. in history and become an accountant. Then the economy underwent a cultural shift." Why the early 1980s? It was a combination of the deep recession of 1980–82 and the growth of computer-based technology. "We started to see a widening distribution of earnings by majors," said Professor Carnevale, who also served as chairman of the National Commission on Employment Policy under President Bill Clinton. And that trend has continued. "I was raised to think what you needed was a college degree," he said. "That's not the game anymore. It's what you major in."

So does that mean I should urge our son to pursue a degree he doesn't have any interest in because it may provide him with a higher-paying job—or any job, for that matter—after college? No, Professor Carnevale said, because if you don't like what you do, you won't do it well. The point is that "young people now need to have a strategy," he said. "If you major in art, realize you will have to get a master's degree. The economic calculus has changed."

Alex Tabarrok, an associate professor of economics at George Mason   5
University and author of the e-book *Launching the Innovation Renaissance* (TED Books), is not just worried about students finishing four years of college with no jobs, but also that they may never get to the graduation podium at all. "At least 40 percent of students drop out of four-year universities before graduation, and it's even higher out of community colleges," he said. "We have the highest college dropout rate in the industrialized world. Everyone recognizes that something is not quite right." Professor Tabarrok said that we, as a country, needed to look more closely at emulating apprenticeship programs offered in European countries that turn out highly skilled workers.

"We tend to look down on vocational training in the United States, but in Europe, that's where the majority of the kids go," he said. "The U.S. mind-set is that there is only one road to an education and to do anything else admits defeat." There are two main arguments against pushing more students into vocational training. The first is that it pigeonholes them in careers at a young age. "We don't want a system where people are tracked from early on," said Andrew Delbanco, a professor of humanities at Columbia University and author of the new book *College: What It Was, Is, and Should Be* (Princeton University Press). The second is that a good liberal arts degree isn't simply a luxury when economic times are good, but a necessity at all times to create an engaged citizenry, he said. "The university should be a place for reflection for the young to explore areas of the human experience, to be fully aware of history and the arts," Professor Delbanco said. "We don't want to have a population that has technical competence but is not able to think critically about the issues that face us as a society." Professor Tabarrok argued, however, that the way the system was set up now, "We're denying students a hands-on education." A lot of high school students, he said, "would love to be paid to work alongside adults and learn."

Do we have to land on one side or another? Not necessarily. To Anne Colby, a consulting professor at Stanford University and author of *Rethinking Undergraduate Business Education* (Jossey-Bass, 2011), the idea that we have to choose between vocational training and the rich, deep learning we associate with liberal arts is a false dichotomy. She and her colleagues studied undergraduate business programs around the country — which more college students major in than any other field — and discovered that the best programs combined major elements of a liberal arts education and professional training.

One example, she said, is the Pathways program at Santa Clara University in California, in which students in all majors take thematically based sequences of courses that draw together several disciplines. Sustainability, the idea that the current generation can meet its needs without sacrificing future generations', can be studied, for example, from the point of view of business, history, philosophy, and politics. And at Indiana University, the Liberal Arts and Management Program offers interdisciplinary courses like "The History of the Automobile: Economy, Politics, and Culture." This program enables students to learn their specialty in the context of history, literature, and other liberal arts.

"Universities need to be more creative in their thinking," she said. And while internships can help bring a practical piece, faculty members need to oversee what is being learned and connect it back to the rest of the academic learning—something that is not done enough, she said. José Luis Santos, an assistant professor of education at the University of California, Los Angeles, also said it was possible for four-year institutions to offer a solid humanities base along with specialization. "Colleges and universities eventually respond to market needs all the time," he said. One example, he said, was how they stepped in to offer Arabic language training when the demand rose for it after Sept. 11. "That's a very good example of realigning to meet market needs," he said. "Colleges and universities eventually respond. It's just at a slow pace. The critique is that they don't do it in a timely manner."

Although much of this is out of an individual student's control, a 10 student (and his parents) can try to think strategically. That doesn't mean entering a major you have no interest in, but using all the resources your institution offers to help think about a career before graduation rolls around. "Some colleges and universities have pretty creative career placement offices that provide events with people in the field," Professor Colby said. "Take advantage of all the extracurricular activities and speakers. And look for coursework that involves the application of knowledge and real-world themes."

And be a part of the debate. Things are changing, and that's not necessarily bad. As Professor Tabarrok said, "Just because something worked in the past doesn't mean it's going to work in the new world we have now."

Topics for Critical Thinking and Writing

1. Do you think that the course for which you have just read Tugend's essay—probably a course largely devoted to critical thinking/writing/rhetoric—is essentially a "practical" course, chiefly aimed at helping you to develop a skill necessary for a job, or is it a course that offers "a broad and deep humanities education" (paragraph 2)? Or both? Explain.

2. Are the reasons you are in college clear to you? If so, what are they? If the reasons are not clear, how do you account for the lack of clarity?

Mark Edmundson

Mark Edmundson teaches English at the University of Virginia. We reprint an essay that originally appeared in the New York Times, *March 31, 2012.*

Education's Hungry Hearts

"Everybody's got a hungry heart," Bruce Springsteen sings. Really? Is that so? At the risk of offending the Boss, I want to register some doubts.

Granted my human sample is not large—but it's not so small either. I've been teaching now for thirty-five years and in that time have had about 4,000 students pass my desk. I'm willing to testify: Not all students have hungry hearts. Some do, some don't, and having a hungry heart (or not) is what makes all the difference for a young person seeking an education.

There's been a lot of talk lately about who should go to college and who should not. And the terms that have guided this talk have mainly been economic. Is college a good investment? Does it pay for a guy who is probably going to become a car mechanic to spend $20,000 to $30,000 going to a junior college for a couple of years? (I'm including the cost of room and board here.) He's probably going to leave with a pile of debt that will take him years to work off. What's more, the current thinking goes, he didn't need that associate degree to end up with his job in the garage. Something similar is true for the young person who is going to become a flight attendant, a home health care aide, a limo driver or a personal security guard. It's not a good investment, we're told. It's not the right way to spend your dough.

The implication here is that paying for college is like putting money into a set of stocks or a mutual fund. It's an *investment*. If the money spent on college doesn't result in an actual cash advantage, then you've made a mistake. If you end up not needing a college degree to pursue your professional life at all, then school was more than a strategic mistake: it was a complete waste. They saw you coming. You got yourself taken.

All of this may be true, but it's true only for those students who 5 showed up at college without the attribute Bruce Springsteen sings about (and in his way celebrates): a hungry heart. For kids who aren't curious, alive, and hungry to learn, going to college and then moving on to a job they could have had anyway is no doubt ill advised. But that's not everyone. There are plenty of young people out there who will end up in jobs that don't *demand* college degrees: yet college is still right for them.

Thirty-five years of teaching has taught me this: The best students and the ones who get the most out of their educations are the ones who come to school with the most energy to learn. And—here's an important corollary—those students are not always the most intellectually gifted.

They're not always the best prepared or the most cultured. Sometimes they think slowly. Sometimes they don't write terribly well, at least at the start. What distinguishes them is that they take their lives seriously and they want to figure out how to live them better. These are the kids for whom one is bought and sold. These are the ones who make you smile when they walk into your office.

How do they get this way? Why is it that some young people, often young people who have not had remarkable advantages, are so alive? They're an amazing pleasure to teach even if their subject-verb agreement isn't always what it might be and they don't know what iambic pentameter is. I can teach them those things. What's way harder to teach—maybe it's impossible—is the love for learning and the openness to experience that these students bring to the seminar table.

Too many current students conform to the description that Lionel Trilling offered in a famous passage from an essay called "On the Teaching of Modern Literature." Trilling had been teaching his students Kafka and Blake, Nietzsche and Freud. "I asked them to look into the Abyss," Trilling writes, "and, both dutifully and gladly, they have looked into the Abyss, and the Abyss has greeted them with the grave courtesy of all objects of serious study, saying: 'Interesting, am I not? And *exciting*, if you consider how deep I am and what dread beasts lie at my bottom. Have it well in mind that a knowledge of me contributes to your being whole, or well-rounded men.' "

And the hungry ones, what about them? Why are there some people who don't see the Abyss of modern literature as a mere cultural acquisition or the equivalent of a theme park ride? Freud says that vital curiosity in adult life often comes from a very active curiosity about sexual matters during childhood. But this seems too much of a reduction, even for Freud. I sometimes think that what the truly hungry students have in common is pretty simple: Their parents loved them a lot and didn't saddle them with gross expectations, spoken or unspoken. These students aren't adventurous because they're insecure and uncertain. It's very much the opposite. Students willing to risk their beliefs and values in school do so because they have confident beliefs and values to risk.

I had a childhood friend named Paul Rizzo. Paul had a hungry heart. 10 He wanted to see everything, know everything, read everything, go everywhere. He had what you might call an associative mind, and he surely didn't cold-cock his SATs. But he did want to learn. He went to some colleges; he took some courses. But I don't think he ever got the quality of education he deserved. That kind of schooling was too often reserved for kids who aced their boards and charmed their teachers and were elected presidents of the Climbers Club by unanimous acclaim.

Paul is still out there, driving a cab, writing fiction, reading what he can and trying to figure it all out. He sees himself as an Everyman type, but not without aspirations of an intellectual and even spiritual sort. Not long ago he used the phrase "Hamlet with a coffee to go" in a note to me and that describes Paul pretty well. The Boss would probably like him, maybe even enough to slip him into a song. Hungry hearts—smart or slow, rich or poor—still deserve a place in the class.

Topics for Critical Thinking and Writing

1. Evaluate Edmundson's title and opening paragraph in the context of persuasive writing. Are they effective? Why, or why not? What about the second paragraph? Effective, or not? Why?

2. Evaluate Edmundson's final paragraph as a final paragraph of a persuasive essay.

3. What is Edmundson's thesis? Does he state it explicitly? If so, where?

4. What kind of proof—if any—does Edmundson offer to support his thesis? How convincing do you find his argument(s)? Why?

Marty Nemko

Marty Nemko, a career counselor, columnist, and radio host based in Oakland, California, has been an education consultant to numerous college presidents. He is the author of four books, including The All-in-One College Guide: A Consumer Activist's Guide to Choosing a College *(2004). We reprint an essay that originally appeared in the* Chronicle of Higher Education *in 2008.*

America's Most Overrated Product: The Bachelor's Degree

Among my saddest moments as a career counselor is when I hear a story like this: "I wasn't a good student in high school, but I wanted to prove that I can get a college diploma. I'd be the first one in my family to do it. But it's been five years and $80,000, and I still have forty-five credits to go."

I have a hard time telling such people the killer statistic: Among high-school students who graduated in the bottom 40 percent of their classes, and whose first institutions were four-year colleges, two-thirds had not earned diplomas eight and a half years later. That figure is from a study cited by Clifford Adelman, a former research analyst at the U.S. Department of Education and now a senior research associate at the Institute for Higher Education Policy. Yet four-year colleges admit and take money from hundreds of thousands of such students each year!

Even worse, most of those college dropouts leave the campus having learned little of value, and with a mountain of debt and devastated self-esteem from their unsuccessful struggles. Perhaps worst of all, even those who do manage to graduate too rarely end up in careers that require a college education. So it's not surprising that when you hop into a cab or walk into a restaurant, you're likely to meet workers who spent years and their family's life savings on college, only to end up with a job they could have done as a high-school dropout.

Such students are not aberrations. Today, amazingly, a majority of the students whom colleges admit are grossly underprepared. Only 23 percent of the 1.3 million high-school graduates of 2007 who took the ACT examination were ready for college-level work in the core subjects of English, math, reading, and science.

Perhaps more surprising, even those high-school students who are 5 fully qualified to attend college are increasingly unlikely to derive enough benefit to justify the often six-figure cost and four to six years (or more) it takes to graduate. Research suggests that more than 40 percent of freshmen at four-year institutions do not graduate in six years. Colleges trumpet the statistic that, over their lifetimes, college graduates earn more than nongraduates, but that's terribly misleading. You could lock the collegebound in a closet for four years, and they'd still go on to earn more than the pool of non-collegebound—they're brighter, more motivated, and have better family connections.

Also, the past advantage of college graduates in the job market is eroding. Ever more students attend college at the same time as ever more employers are automating and sending offshore ever more professional jobs, and hiring part-time workers. Many college graduates are forced to take some very nonprofessional positions, such as driving a truck or tending bar.

How much do students at four-year institutions actually learn?

Colleges are quick to argue that a college education is more about enlightenment than employment. That may be the biggest deception of all. Often there is a Grand Canyon of difference between the reality and what higher-education institutions, especially research ones, tout in their viewbooks and on their Web sites. Colleges and universities are businesses, and students are a cost item, while research is a profit center. As a result, many institutions tend to educate students in the cheapest way possible: large lecture classes, with necessary small classes staffed by rock-bottom-cost graduate students. At many colleges, only a small percentage of the typical student's classroom hours will have been spent with fewer than thirty students taught by a professor, according to student-questionnaire data I used for my book *How to Get an Ivy League Education at a State University*. When students at 115 institutions were asked what percentage of their class time had been spent in classes of fewer than thirty students, the average response was 28 percent.

That's not to say that professor-taught classes are so worthwhile. The more prestigious the institution, the more likely that faculty members are hired and promoted much more for their research than for their teaching. Professors who bring in big research dollars are almost always rewarded more highly than a fine teacher who doesn't bring in the research bucks. Ernest L. Boyer, the late president of the Carnegie Foundation for the Advancement of Teaching, used to say that winning the campus teaching award was the kiss of death when it came to tenure. So, no surprise, in the latest annual national survey of freshmen conducted by the Higher Education Research Institute at the University of California at Los Angeles, 44.6 percent said they were not satisfied with the quality of instruction they received. Imagine if that many people were dissatisfied with a brand of car: It would quickly go off the market. Colleges should be held to a much higher standard, as a higher education costs so much more, requires years of time, and has so much potential impact on your life. Meanwhile, 43.5 percent of freshmen also reported "frequently" feeling bored in class, the survey found.

College students may be dissatisfied with instruction, but, despite that, do they learn? A 2006 study supported by the Pew Charitable Trusts found that 50 percent of college seniors scored below "proficient" levels on a test that required them to do such basic tasks as understand the arguments of newspaper editorials or compare credit-card offers. Almost 20 percent of seniors had only basic quantitative skills. The students could not estimate if their car had enough gas to get to the gas station. 10

Unbelievably, according to the Spellings Report, which was released in 2006 by a federal commission that examined the future of American higher education, things are getting even worse: "Over the past decade, literacy among college graduates has actually declined. . . . According to the most recent National Assessment of Adult Literacy, for instance, the percentage of college graduates deemed proficient in prose literacy has actually declined from 40 to 31 percent in the past decade. . . . Employers report repeatedly that many new graduates they hire are not prepared to work, lacking the critical thinking, writing, and problem-solving skills needed in today's workplaces."

What must be done to improve undergraduate education?

Colleges should be held at least as accountable as tire companies are. When some Firestone tires were believed to be defective, government investigations, combined with news-media scrutiny, led to higher tire-safety standards. Yet year after year, colleges and universities turn out millions of defective products: students who drop out or graduate with far too little benefit for the time and money spent. Not only do colleges escape punishment, but they are rewarded with taxpayer-financed student grants and loans, which allow them to raise their tuitions even more.

I ask colleges to do no more than tire manufacturers are required to do. To be government-approved, all tires must have—prominently molded into the sidewall—some crucial information, including ratings of tread life, temperature resistance, and traction compared with national benchmarks.

Going significantly beyond the recommendations in the Spellings   15
report, I believe that colleges should be required to prominently report
the following data on their Web sites and in recruitment materials:

- Value added. A national test, which could be developed by the major
  testing companies, should measure skills important for responsible
  citizenship and career success. Some of the test should be in career
  contexts: the ability to draft a persuasive memo, analyze an employer's financial report, or use online research tools to develop
  content for a report.

  Just as the No Child Left Behind Act mandates strict accountability of elementary and secondary schools, all colleges should
  be required to administer the value-added test I propose to all entering freshmen and to students about to graduate, and to report
  the mean value added, broken out by precollege SAT scores, race,
  and gender. That would strongly encourage institutions to improve their undergraduate education and to admit only students
  likely to derive enough benefit to justify the time, tuition, and
  opportunity costs. Societal bonus: Employers could request that
  job applicants submit the test results, leading to more-valid hiring
  decisions.

- The average cash, loan, and work-study financial aid for varying
  levels of family income and assets, broken out by race and gender. And because some colleges use the drug-dealer scam—give
  the first dose cheap and then jack up the price—they should be
  required to provide the average not just for the first year, but for
  each year.

- Retention data: the percentage of students returning for a second
  year, broken out by SAT score, race, and gender.

- Safety data: the percentage of an institution's students who have
  been robbed or assaulted on or near the campus.

- The four-, five-, and six-year graduation rates, broken out by
  SAT score, race, and gender. That would allow institutions to better document such trends as the plummeting percentage of male
  graduates in recent years.

- Employment data for graduates: the percentage of graduates who,
  within six months of graduation, are in graduate school, unemployed, or employed in a job requiring college-level skills, along with
  salary data.

- Results of the most recent student-satisfaction survey, to be conducted by the institutions themselves.

- The most recent accreditation report. The college could include the
  executive summary only in its printed recruitment material, but it
  would have to post the full report on its Web site.

Being required to conspicuously provide this information to prospective students and parents would exert long-overdue pressure on colleges to improve the quality of undergraduate education. What should parents and guardians of prospective students do?

- If your child's high-school grades and test scores are in the bottom half for his class, resist the attempts of four-year colleges to woo him. Colleges make money whether or not a student learns, whether or not she graduates, and whether or not he finds good employment. Let the buyer beware. Consider an associate-degree program at a community college, or such nondegree options as apprenticeship programs (see http://www.khake.com), shorter career-preparation programs at community colleges, the military, and on-the-job training, especially at the elbow of a successful small-business owner.

- If your student is in the top half of her high-school class and is motivated to attend college for reasons other than going to parties and being able to say she went to college, have her apply to perhaps a dozen colleges. Colleges vary less than you might think (at least on factors you can readily discern in the absence of the accountability requirements I advocate above), yet financial-aid awards can vary wildly. It's often wise to choose the college that requires you to pay the least cash and take out the smallest loan. College is among the few products that don't necessarily give you what you pay for—price does not indicate quality.

- If your child is one of the rare breed who knows what he wants to do and isn't unduly attracted to academics or to the *Animal House* environment that characterizes many college-living arrangements, then take solace in the fact that countless other people have successfully taken the noncollege road less traveled. Some examples: Maya Angelou, David Ben-Gurion, Richard Branson, Coco Chanel, Walter Cronkite, Michael Dell, Walt Disney, Thomas Edison, Henry Ford, Bill Gates, Alex Haley, Ernest Hemingway, Wolfgang Puck, John D. Rockefeller Sr., Ted Turner, Frank Lloyd Wright, and nine U.S. presidents, from Washington to Truman.

College is a wise choice for far fewer people than are currently encouraged to consider it. It's crucial that they evenhandedly weigh the pros and cons of college versus the aforementioned alternatives. The quality of their lives may depend on that choice.

TOPICS FOR CRITICAL THINKING AND WRITING

1. According to Nemko, "colleges and universities are businesses" (para. 8). What evidence does he cite to support this claim? What confirming or disconfirming evidence has your experience at college offered?

2. Is it true at your college that (para. 9) the faculty "are hired and promoted much more for their research than for their teaching"? Interview one or two of your current instructors for their view on this issue and summarize what you learn in a paragraph or two.

3. Suppose someone argued that a college education is *not* a business because it is a four-year game of increasing difficulty. How might such an argument be developed? Attacked?

4. What are some of the "opportunity costs" of higher education (first item in para. 15)?

5. Nemko specifies numerous things that ought to be done to improve the quality of a college education (para. 15). How many of these do you agree would result in improvements? Which (if any) of his items would you drop? Can you think of a couple to add?

6. Research Project for Extra Credit: Who are the seven U.S. presidents Nemko does *not* name (last item in his bulleted list) who did not attend college? How successful were they as presidents?

Charles Murray

Born in 1943, Charles Murray is a scholar at the American Enterprise Institute and the author, most recently, of Real Education: Four Simple Truths for Bringing America's Schools Back to Reality *(2008). This essay and the letters of response following it were published in the* New York Times *in 2008.*

Should the Obama Generation Drop Out?

Barack Obama has two attractive ideas for improving postsecondary education—expanding the use of community colleges and tuition tax credits—but he needs to hitch them to a broader platform. As president, Mr. Obama should use his bully pulpit to undermine the bachelor's degree as a job qualification. Here's a suggested battle cry, to be repeated in every speech on the subject: "It's what you can do that should count when you apply for a job, not where you learned to do it."

The residential college leading to a bachelor's degree at the end of four years works fine for the children of parents who have plenty of money. It works fine for top students from all backgrounds who are drawn toward academics. But most eighteen-year-olds are not from families with plenty of money, not top students, and not drawn toward academics. They want to learn how to get a satisfying job that also pays well. That almost always means education beyond high school, but it need not mean four years on a campus, nor cost a small fortune. It need not mean getting a bachelor's degree.

I am not discounting the merits of a liberal education. Students at every level should be encouraged to explore subjects that will not be part of their vocation. It would be even better if more colleges required a rigorous core curriculum for students who seek a traditional bachelor's degree. My beef is not with liberal education, but with the use of the degree as a job qualification.

For most of the nation's youths, making the bachelor's degree a job qualification means demanding a credential that is beyond their reach. It is a truth that politicians and educators cannot bring themselves to say out loud: A large majority of young people do not have the intellectual ability to do genuine college-level work.

If you doubt it, go back and look through your old college textbooks,   5 and then do a little homework on the reading ability of high school seniors. About 10 percent to 20 percent of all eighteen-year-olds can absorb the material in your old liberal arts textbooks. For engineering and the hard sciences, the percentage is probably not as high as 10.

No improvements in primary and secondary education will do more than tweak those percentages. The core disciplines taught at a true college level are tough, requiring high levels of linguistic and logical-mathematical ability. Those abilities are no more malleable than athletic or musical talent.

You think I'm too pessimistic? Too elitist? Readers who graduated with honors in English literature or Renaissance history should ask themselves if they could have gotten a B.S. in physics, no matter how hard they tried. (I wouldn't have survived freshman year.) Except for the freakishly gifted, all of us are too dumb to get through college in many majors.

But I'm not thinking just about students who are not smart enough to deal with college-level material. Many young people who have the intellectual ability to succeed in rigorous liberal arts courses don't want to. For these students, the distribution requirements of the college degree do not open up new horizons. They are bothersome time-wasters.

A century ago, these students would happily have gone to work after high school. Now they know they need to acquire additional skills, but they want to treat college as vocational training, not as a leisurely journey to well-roundedness.

As more and more students who cannot get or don't want a liberal 10 education have appeared on campuses, colleges have adapted by expanding the range of courses and adding vocationally oriented majors. That's appropriate. What's not appropriate is keeping the bachelor's degree as the measure of job preparedness, as the minimal requirement to get your foot in the door for vast numbers of jobs that don't really require a B.A. or B.S.

Discarding the bachelor's degree as a job qualification would not be difficult. The solution is to substitute certification tests, which would provide evidence that the applicant has acquired the skills the employer needs.

Certification tests can take many forms. For some jobs, a multiple-choice test might be appropriate. But there's no reason to limit certifications to academic tests. For centuries, the crafts have used work samples to certify journeymen and master craftsmen. Today, many computer programmers without college degrees get jobs by presenting examples of their work. With a little imagination, almost any corporation can come up with analogous work samples.

The benefits of discarding the bachelor's degree as a job qualification would be huge for both employers and job applicants. Certifications would tell employers far more about their applicants' qualifications than a B.A. does, and hundreds of thousands of young people would be able to get what they want from postsecondary education without having to twist themselves into knots to comply with the rituals of getting a bachelor's degree.

Certification tests would not eliminate the role of innate ability—the most gifted applicants would still have an edge—but they would strip away much of the unwarranted halo effect that goes with a degree from a prestigious university. They would put everyone under the same spotlight.

Discrediting the bachelor's degree is within reach because so many 15 employers already sense that it has become education's Wizard of Oz. All we need is someone willing to yank the curtain aside. Barack Obama is ideally positioned to do it. He just needs to say it over and over: "It's what you can do that should count when you apply for a job, not where you learned to do it."

TOPICS FOR CRITICAL THINKING AND WRITING

1. What does the term "bully pulpit" mean? What does Murray mean by calling President Obama's office a "bully pulpit" (para. 1)?

2. What do you think is the appropriate criterion for deciding whether a job warrants requiring that an applicant has either a B.A. or a B.S. degree?

3. What do you think accounts for the fact that a B.A. or a B.S. degree has become a requirement for so many jobs?

4. Explain Murray's reference to the Wizard of Oz (para. 15).

Letters of Response by Charles Axilbund, Jacques Jimenez, Jeff Adler, Lillian Hoodes, Larry Hoffner, Sandra Sherman, and Michel Dedina

To the Editor:

In "Should the Obama Generation Drop Out?" (Op-Ed, Dec. 28), Charles Murray argues that we should have more vocational schools and stop using a college degree as a requirement for jobs.

These "reforms" would institute a class system in the United States on a par with that of Victorian England.

Under these proposals, bachelor's degrees would be restricted to the rich, regardless of qualifications, and the lucky few among the common people who possessed exceptional intellectual endowments. As for the rest, they would receive sufficient training to fill jobs with limited potential for upward mobility.

Mr. Murray's proposals would actually intensify the importance of a prestigious degree—necessary as it would be for entry into the highest occupational echelons.

This might be acceptable if eligibility for these degrees were based 5 on merit alone. But under Mr. Murray's proposals, the rich would have unlimited access, while those less well off would have to compete for limited, subsidized spots in expensive institutions. If this is not a recipe for a closed, permanent upper class, I do not know what is.

CHARLES AXILBUND
Los Angeles, Dec. 28, 2008

To the Editor:

Charles Murray needs to recognize that the liberal arts degree, at its best, validates its holder as one who has skills needed for some of our biggest jobs.

A good half of the liberal arts curriculum is about thinking analogically. The degree says this person has studied "humane letters" and so knows his or her way around a metaphor: how it opens up vistas, alters viewpoints, both frees and constrains thought, and affects decisions.

No one should try to motivate a work force, lead a corporation, plan military strategies, or run a government who does not know how a metaphor works.

Math and science, the other half of the liberal arts curriculum, develop skills that are scarce, yet needed, in our society. They are all about knowing a fact from a factoid, reasoning from data to underlying patterns and practical implications, all while feeding careful observation through the strainer of valid logic.

The liberal arts degree says, or should say, here's someone who has 5 skills we deeply, powerfully, urgently need.

JACQUES JIMENEZ
Stamford, Conn., Dec. 28, 2008

To the Editor:

Devaluing the bachelor's degree would not help students who earn it or those who don't go to college. A bachelor's degree may indeed serve as a foot in the door for a recent graduate, but that's all it does. That graduate still has to show that he or she can do the job.

The degree tells an employer that an applicant had the ability and perseverance to accomplish something.

Charles Murray suggests that instead of degrees, we use "certification tests, which would provide evidence that the applicant has acquired the skills the employer needs." This would amount to a postcollege SAT, when the precollege SAT has enough problems.

An employer takes a chance on any applicant, even one with a degree. There already are two-year colleges and technical training schools for people who can't or won't earn a four-year degree.

The responsible thing to do is to make sure that all students who 5 have the ability to earn a degree aren't prevented from doing so by the cost.

JEFF ADLER
Livingston, N.J., Dec. 28, 2008

To the Editor:

I recently graduated with a bachelor's degree in history and am now in law school, hoping to earn the degree that will lead to a paycheck. Though this will eventually pay my mortgage, my liberal arts education will be what sustains me emotionally, intellectually, and in my relationships with other human beings.

To say that young Americans are, for the most part, "not smart enough to deal with college-level material" and that we must scratch the bachelor's degree from our list of must-haves is to treat a symptom rather than the cause.

Employers must ask that their employees relate to one another and to the world around them; a broad, liberal education helps students to arrive at the point at which that kind of sympathy is possible.

Make college affordable, make it accessible, make it free, make it a requirement for employment. Don't accept defeat.

LILLIAN HOODES
Chicago, Dec. 28, 2008

To the Editor:

Charles Murray's notion of discarding or de-emphasizing academic degrees as a job qualification in lieu of skills or "What you know" makes perfect sense. But let's not stop with postsecondary education.

A greater emphasis on specific job skills in traditional high school education is needed.

Language and mathematics will remain the pillars of our liberal academic institutions, but we also need carpenters, plumbers, electricians, machinists, and more. Our schools should emphasize job skills for those not suited to traditional academic education.

LARRY HOFFNER
New York, Dec. 28, 2008

The writer is a high school teacher.

To the Editor:

Finally, someone dared to say what every college professor knows in her heart: half the students in her classroom shouldn't be there and don't want to be there.

We have created this B.A.-B.S. grail for millions of students who would be far better educated if they could focus on something that they want to learn.

For twelve years, I was a professor of English at the flagship campus of a big state university. My students were majoring in computers, nursing, landscape design, and kinesiology. They didn't care about "Beowulf" or John Milton. The university wanted them there, however, because more four-year graduates meant more money from the legislature. Now we can no longer tolerate such waste.

We should redesign college curriculums so that students can study something useful, get a job, and help redevelop the economy.

Rather than dumbing down "hard" courses, so that everyone picks 5 up a smattering of knowledge they will never use, universities should offer challenging courses in students' majors. If that major takes three instead of four years to complete, that's fine. The goal is to become productive without wasting time or money.

SANDRA SHERMAN
New York, Dec. 28, 2008

The writer is assistant director of the Intellectual Property Law Institute, Fordham Law School.

To the Editor:

Students who have battled for a bachelor's degree will have learned a valuable skill. It is unlikely that most of them will practice only one trade throughout their career. They will have to learn a range of skills that were unheard of when they were students.

Charles Murray should bless them for having learned how to learn. If they are thus armed, our economy will have a chance.

MICHEL DEDINA
San Francisco, Dec. 28, 2008

TOPICS FOR CRITICAL THINKING AND WRITING

1. Do you think Murray would be troubled by Charles Axilbund's claim that Murray's proposal is "a recipe for a closed, permanent upper class"? Explain.

2. What is the significance of Jimenez's distinction between a "factoid" and a "fact"? What *is* the difference? Compare them and give examples.

3. Take one of the letters that seems to you to be especially wrongheaded, and draft a response to that letter-writer.

Louis Menand

Louis Menand, born in Syracuse, New York, in 1952, and educated at Pomona College and Columbia University, is a professor of English and American literature at Harvard University. The author of numerous books, including The Future of Academic Freedom *(1996), Menand also writes regularly for* The New Yorker. *We reprint a portion of a talk that he originally delivered at a symposium held at Rollins College in Florida and published in* Education and Democracy, *edited by Robert Orrill (1997).*

Re-imagining Liberal Education

. . . It is, in most American colleges, impossible to take a course on the law (apart from an occasional legal history course), because knowledge of the law is the preserve of people who go to law school. Yet a knowledge of the law is one of the keys to understanding the political and economic system in which Americans live. Many college students, similarly, never take a class in business, or even in economics. Most take no classes in architecture, education, or engineering, unless they are in a special, and usually segregated, architecture, education, or engineering program. Few students who do not intend to become specialists take courses in subjects touching on health or technology. These are all matters adults have to deal with throughout life, but people who have attended college generally have no more sophisticated an understanding of them than people who have attended only high school.

The suggestion that an understanding of matters of immense practical importance, such as law, business, technology, and health, should have a more central place in the college curriculum smacks of vocationalism, and it is customary to think that nothing could sound more illiberal than that. But the purpose of education is to empower people, to help them acquire some measure of control over their own lives. Some of this empowerment consists of learning how to think critically, how to communicate clearly, how to pose theoretical questions about practical issues. But some of it also must consist in knowing about the way the world works. Critical theory doesn't empower people. Self-esteem doesn't empower people. Knowledge empowers people. You can't dictate what people will do with it, but you can at least give them access to it. That an exposure to the way the world works can be presented in an appropriately high-level curricular setting can be seen in innovative programs underway at a number of private and public colleges. Bradford College, for example, a private college in Massachusetts, offers what it calls a "practical liberal arts" curriculum, in which students combine general education (nonspecialized study) with a "comprehensive" (that is, cross-disciplinary) major and a "practical" (that is, vocationally oriented) minor. Students do internships (called "practical learning experiences") in their junior year. And they are assessed, in part, through portfolios, rather than through individual papers for individual classes. The Bradford program is not vocational. It offers a general education in areas such as "Wellness" and "The Nature of Work" because it presumes that these are matters all college graduates should know something about.

The Bradford model manages to incorporate into its general education curriculum a good deal of exposure to scientific knowledge and methods. One of the drawbacks of the Core Model is that it either omits science completely, or presents it in the form of "culture," as some of the "classic texts." For Dewey,[1] the scientific method was the type for all learning and inquiry. One need not go quite that distance to concede that science and technology do require formal education for nonspecialists to understand, and that most liberal arts colleges do little or nothing to ensure that students receive it in any programmatic way. The modern research university arose in response to the preeminence of scientific approaches to knowledge. The problem of how to put the humanities in proper institutional relation to the sciences has persisted since the turn of the century. The solution has been for scholarship in the humanities to be practiced on a more or less scientific, or positivistic, model (dissertations that constitute "original contributions to knowledge," peer review, and the like), while undergraduate instruction in literature and philosophy stresses moral issues and "human values." It is a divide, between fact and value, that inheres in both prevailing models of liberal education today; and one merit of imagining a fresh model is that it might make this division less antagonistic, an accomplishment that was the aim of nearly everything Dewey wrote.

Innovations similar to Bradford's—particularly out-of-the-classroom, or "service," experience and cross-disciplinary teaching—are becoming standard elsewhere. Twelve Pennsylvania colleges calling themselves the Commonwealth Partnership now advise new Ph.D.s that they must have interests that extend beyond their disciplines, be able to teach "communication skills," be socially involved, and teach by personal example. Candidates for jobs at Evergreen State College in Washington, a public institution, are required to complete a questionnaire about their views on pedagogy and other matters. Professors today have to be able to teach basic skills courses and a much wider range of much-less-specialized courses than they once did. . . .

Let us suppose that the undergraduate curriculum were transformed 5 in a way that eliminated the proto-professional major and that replaced the "culture"-based core requirements with general courses in law, business, government, the arts, and technology—that did not abandon exposure to literature and philosophy, which everyone should have, but that did abandon the idea that literature and philosophy are the mandatory bases for specialized knowledge. What would happen to liberal

---

[1]**Dewey** John Dewey (1859–1952), philosopher of education. [Editors' note.]

education? How could it be re-imagined in a way that would enable colleges to produce students who were well rounded, who had cultural breadth and moral imagination, and who knew how to think critically? How would it help students develop the capacity to display curiosity, sympathy, a sense of principle, and independence of mind?

The Deweyan answer to questions like these would be that you cannot teach people a virtue by requiring them to read books about it. You can only teach a virtue by calling upon people to exercise it. Virtue is not an innate property of character; it is an attribute of behavior. People learn, Dewey insisted, socially. They learn, as every progressive nursery school director will tell you, by doing. Dewey believed that the classroom was a laboratory in which to experiment with the business of participating in the associated life. American higher education provides almost no formal structure, almost no self-conscious design, for imagining pedagogy in this spirit. But the only way to develop curiosity, sympathy, principle, and independence of mind is to practice being curious, sympathetic, principled, and independent. For those of us who are teachers, it isn't what we teach that instills virtue; it's how we teach. We are the books our students read most closely. The most important influence on their liberalism is our liberalism.

TOPICS FOR CRITICAL THINKING AND WRITING

1. In his second paragraph Menand says, "the purpose of education is to empower people, to help them acquire some measure of control over their own lives." Write your own sentence, beginning, "The purpose of education is. . . ."

2. In paragraph 4 Menand says that "candidates for jobs at Evergreen State College in Washington, a public institution, are required to complete a questionnaire about their views on pedagogy." Suppose two questions were these: "In your view, what is the purpose of teaching?" "What do you hope your students will get out of your course in ———?" Now imagine that you are a candidate for a job at Evergreen, teaching any course you wish. Answer each of the two questions, devoting a paragraph or two to each.

3. What is "vocationalism" (para. 2), and what role do you think it ought to play in higher education? What role, if any, does it play for the students in your college?

4. William Cory, a schoolmaster in nineteenth-century England, wrote:

> You go to a great school not for knowledge so much as for arts and habits; for the habit of attention, for the art of expression, for the art of assuming at a moment's notice a new intellectual posture, for the art of entering quickly into another person's thought, for the habit of submitting to censure and refutation, for the art of indicating assent or dissent

in graduated terms, for the habit of regarding minute points of accuracy, for the habit of working out what is possible in a given time, for taste, for discrimination, for mental courage and mental soberness. Above all, you go to a great school for self-knowledge.

What do you think of this view? In an essay of about 500 words indicate "assent or dissent in graduated terms."

For topical links related to the purpose of a college education, see the companion Web site: **bedfordstmartins.com/barnetbedau**.

Hydraulic Fracturing: Is Fracking Worth the Environmental Cost?

Don Carns Jr.

The following letter by Don Carns Jr., a resident of Beans Cove, Pennsylvania, appeared on January 6, 2012, in the Cumberland Times-News, *a daily newspaper that chiefly serves Maryland and adjacent counties of West Virginia. Because newspapers usually print their material in narrow columns, they often reparagraph contributions so that a paragraph rarely consists of more than a sentence or two or three.*

Shale Drilling Is a Disaster Waiting to Happen

I will be direct and to the point: Marcellus Shale requires drilling. Drilling requires casing and grout, which can fail, especially when subjected to 10,000–15,000 PSI, the pressure required for hydraulic fracking.

Drillers rely on solid bedrock to reinforce the casings for such pressure. But when drilling to the needed depths required to reach the Marcellus Shale, solid rock is not always available. There are areas such as caves, faults, folds, water tables, joints, and fissures.

All these are encountered and the casing doesn't have added bedrock support. Casings are manmade, and not perfect. They leak from age, stress, inferior materials, and premature leaks occur.

Failure results in leaks that contaminate subterranean and surface water. Dimock, Pa., is now without drinking water.

Caves and fissures also carry groundwater. Old mines are voids that 5 can be encountered. One of interest is the Greenbrier Formation, which runs from Pennsylvania, through Maryland, and into West Virginia.

This band of limestone contains Maryland's and West Virginia's largest cave systems. Piney Mountain, west of LaVale and the source of LaVale's wells, had in recent years come under fire concerning Marcellus Shale drilling.

As of now, Maryland has a moratorium on Marcellus Shale drilling. Once the "politics" are in place, that will change. Little Allegheny and Piney Mountains have recently discovered large cave systems within them. Piney also has recently discovered fault lines.

These mountains have a very active and complex underground water system, one which feeds the LaVale wells at Red Hill and many local wells.

If drilling were to occur in these places, disaster could happen at any time. Ruined wells, ecosystems are destroyed, natural gas seepage into the large cave systems, and destroyed land streams.

All wells and water sources in any gas well drilling areas should be 10 tested by an independent water testing firm at the expense of those drilling gas wells.

This would establish a baseline to prove water conditions prior to any gas well drilling.

I live in Beans Cove, Pa., in Clearville, Pa. (thirty miles north of Cumberland), and Marcellus Shale drilling is well on its way.

Methane problems, contaminated wells, and road destruction due to the heavy trucks involved with the drilling operation are some of the many problems being experienced.

The EPA now admits fracking near Pavillion, Wyo., has contaminated their groundwater. Penn State Geologist Terry Engelder thinks precautions will prevent accidents. Well, Mr. Engelder, accidents do happen. Mr. Engelder, does water flow uphill? Yes, when water is under 10,000 to 15,000 PSI and underground or above. Gravity, under those conditions, loses its effect. Water and gas will seek its easiest flow path, and if it is uphill, it will follow.

In closing, consider these facts not mentioned by proponents of Mar- 15 cellus Shale drilling:

Heavy trucks supplying the drill sites travel rural roads which are not designed to handle such loads. Who pays for the damage? The taxpayer.

Will the gas being produced go to America? No, it will go to the highest bidder. That is the way of the oil and gas business. Those businessmen are profiteers, not patriotic.

Earthquakes are generated by fracking as evinced in Ohio on Dec. 21.

Radioactivity is the last subject. Marcellus Shale also contains uranium, yes, uranium, and the radioactive decay of uranium-238 makes it a source rock for radioactive radon gas.

This released radioactive material is brought to the surface and 20 released in drilling fluids. In the event of a casing failure and reclaimed fracking fluid seepage, it is also in your drinking water and surface water.

Definitely not a pleasing thought. And more to come.

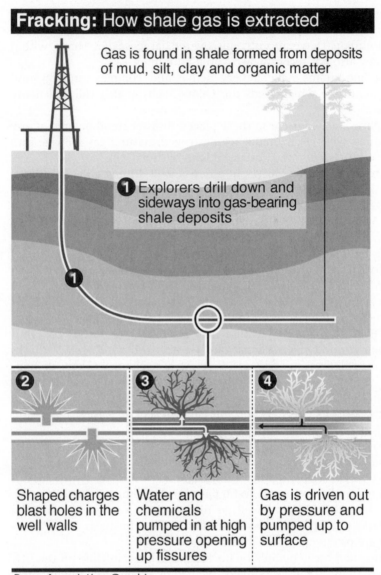

Fracking: How shale gas is extracted

Gas is found in shale formed from deposits of mud, silt, clay and organic matter

1 Explorers drill down and sideways into gas-bearing shale deposits

2 Shaped charges blast holes in the well walls

3 Water and chemicals pumped in at high pressure opening up fissures

4 Gas is driven out by pressure and pumped up to surface

Press Association Graphic

Topics for Critical Thinking and Writing

1. Evaluate Carns's first three or four sentences from a rhetorical point of view—that is, as an opening. Remember: The piece was published in a newspaper, and newspapers usually edit contributions so that a paragraph is not longer than a couple of sentences. Carns may have conceived of his first four sentences as an opening paragraph.

2. What persuasive device(s) does Carns use in paragraphs 16–17?

3. Do you think Carns makes a pretty good case against fracking Marcellus Shale? Explain. (The next reading is a published response to Carns, but you may want to jot down your own response before reading the next selection.)

4. Look at the diagram on p. 540. How does it contribute to your understanding of how fracking works?

Scott Cline

Responding to the letter by Don Carns Jr., Scott Cline published this letter in the Cumberland Times-News, *on January 25, 2012.*

Unfounded Fears about Shale Gas Obscure Facts

The Jan. 6 letter to the *Cumberland Times-News* entitled "Shale Drilling Is a Disaster Waiting to Happen" was long on fiction and short on facts.

Natural gas seepage into vast mysterious subterranean cave systems, casing constructed of inferior materials with no bedrock support, earthquakes, radioactive material in drinking water? Geez, where do I begin to correct this fictional nonsense?

The truth is that the long-term history of gas production and the science behind it shows that very few accidents have occurred and the public has far more to fear from road salting, septic systems, and pharmaceuticals, and household chemicals dumped down drains than it does from any cumulative effect of oil and gas operations.

Neither the shale fracture stimulation itself nor the production of the produced water back to the surface through a properly constructed wellbore poses a risk of fluid migration to sources of drinking water.

The water in rock thousands of feet deep where the fracture stimula-   5 tion occurs is disconnected from our lakes, rivers, and shallow aquifers.

Hydraulic fracturing cannot break through these thousands of feet of rock all the way up to reach shallow aquifers. Hydraulic fracturing is simply the very short-lived few-hour application of hydraulic pressure on the reservoir that creates temporary fractures of a few hundred feet in vertical height over a mile below the surface.

Pressure is then immediately released and the wellbore becomes a pressure sink with any available gas and fluids moving to that pressure sink and up to the surface through the wellbore that has triple or often quadruple redundant layers of steel casing and cement plus tubing that protect the shallow groundwater sources.

Once the well is depleted of energy it is plugged with cement and presents no danger to the groundwater forever.

Also, radioactive shale cuttings cannot hurt anyone. The extra radio-activity that people might obtain by standing next to a pile of Marcellus or Utica shale cutting is insignificantly small compared with the dose that we naturally receive from cosmic radiation, our environment, and even the food we eat.

And radioactivity is not a threat to our drinking water. All water 10 that returns to the surface is reused, injected, or treated so that drinking water maintains the mandated standards.

And contrary to the author's fiction, "fracking" does not cause earthquakes as the energy is less than a hammer dropped to the ground.

Small earthquakes have been suspected in a few isolated instances with industrial waste injection wells but not from hydraulic well fracturing, which is a completely different technology.

In reality shale gas exploration boils down to a temporary traffic nuisance that can be solved by working with local communities to minimize short-term inconveniences and making sure that the water that returns to the surface through the wellbore is properly stored, transported, and either recycled or treated.

The long-term benefits of shale gas development in terms of reduced carbon emissions, economic stimulus, and national security far outweigh these temporary and manageable short-term nuisances.

Topics for Critical Thinking and Writing

1. Evaluate Cline's first two sentences in terms of strategies of persuasive writing.

2. In his third paragraph Cline makes a comparison. How effective is this comparison? Why?

3. Evaluate Cline's last two paragraphs as a conclusion.

4. Let's assume that you have no special knowledge about fracking—that you know nothing beyond what Carns and Cline have told you about it. Which argument do you find the more convincing? Why?

5. If you *do* know something about fracking beyond what Carns and Cline have told you, what do you know, and how might it have been used by one or the other of these writers?

Aubrey K. McClendon

Aubrey K. McClendon, cofounder and CEO of Chesapeake Energy Corporation, delivered the Keynote Address before the Marcellus Shale Insights Conference in Philadelphia on September 7, 2011. We reprint the abridged version, as it was published in CQ Researcher, *December 16, 2011.*

Is Hydraulic Fracturing Good for the Economy? Pro

According to a newly released study of Marcellus natural gas development by Penn State University, the shale-gas revolution is the biggest opportunity to hit Pennsylvania since the steel industry more than 100 years ago. . . .

Consider these numbers:

- Marcellus natural gas development generated $11 billion in value-added regional gross domestic product last year. That number will rise to $13 billion in 2011 and reach $17 billion in 2015. . . .

- Chesapeake [Energy Corp.] has 2.4 million acres under lease in the Marcellus and has already paid almost $2 billion in lease bonus and royalties to farmers, families, and townships across Pennsylvania.

- Direct and indirect employment from this economic boom has already surpassed 140,000 jobs. . . . Chesapeake alone has about 2,100 employees in the Marcellus and about 1,700 of them were hired regionally. According to Penn State, further development of the Marcellus will support 216,000 jobs in 2015. . . .

- If you think this shale discovery and development is like hitting the lottery, you are right, especially if you happen to be the budget director for Pennsylvania. State and local taxes paid will total about $1.2 billion this year and are projected to reach $1.4 billion in 2012. . . .

- Nationally, the numbers only get bigger. Natural gas exploration and development supports about 3.5 million jobs across the country and with continued investment can easily add 500,000 more. By way of example, Chesapeake has added about 3,000 direct employees nationwide in the first eight months of 2011 alone.

But the benefits don't stop there. Chesapeake has one million mineral owners in sixteen states. To put that in perspective, about one in every 300 Americans has an oil and natural gas lease with Chesapeake.

And they have been very well rewarded. We've paid out $9 billion in lease bonuses over the past five years, about $5 billion in royalties over the past four years, and another $2 billion in taxes over the past five years.

And every one of those numbers is going up daily. The lives of 5 millions rest on us getting this issue right and utilizing this American treasure. . . .

And remind me, what value [have] these shale gas protestors created? What jobs have they created? You know the answer, and so do I, and it's time that we contrast what we do for a living [versus] what they do for a living.

Topics for Critical Thinking and Writing

1. McClendon's words were originally delivered as a talk—probably with visual aids—but we of course are reading it. What is the effect of the bullets? Would a *numbered* list be more effective, or less? Why?

2. In a sentence summarize McClendon's argument, his thesis. What argumentative techniques does he use to support his thesis?

3. Evaluate McClendon's final paragraph as a piece of persuasive writing.

Jannette M. Barth

Jannette M. Barth is an economist with the Pepacton Institute and a member of the Catskill Citizens for Safe Energy. On August 23, 2011, she offered testimony at a public hearing of New York State Senator Greg Ball. We give an abridgment, as published in CQ Researcher, *December 16, 2011.*

Is Hydraulic Fracturing Good for the Economy? Con

The gas industry is seriously misleading the public and our politicians. They ignore costs and exaggerate benefits. . . . The oil and gas industry is ten times more capital-intensive than the average industry. Capital-intensive industries, by definition, are not major job creators. It would be far better for our economy, and in particular for job creation, to encourage a more labor-intensive industry.

The studies that claim a positive economic impact from gas drilling tend to be biased, dated, seriously flawed, or inapplicable to our region. It's critical to examine what has been left out of these studies. What costs have not been taken into account? . . .

The studies funded by the gas industry ignore declines in other industries that are likely to result from a combination of pollution, a shift to an industrial landscape, and "crowding out." Examples of industries likely to be negatively affected include agriculture, tourism, organic farming, wine making, hunting, fishing, and river recreation.

The industry-funded studies ignore the fact that there will be damage to infrastructure, especially roads and bridges. In the Fayetteville Shale region, in Arkansas, the state Highway Department reported that the gas industry has caused $455 million worth of damage to highways. Insufficient funds are collected from the industry, and even with a severance tax it appears that the taxpayers of Arkansas will have to pay more than $400 million of the road-repair costs.

The costs of drinking-water contamination and land, stream, and air 5 pollution are ignored in the economic impact studies. The cost of mitigation is ignored and so is the cost in terms of health. . . .

Costs to communities are ignored, including costs due to the increased demand on hospitals, police, fire departments, and emergency health services. . . .

Likely declines in property values are ignored. Supporters of gas drilling say that property values will increase. Rental rates will probably increase due to the influx of transient workers, and hotel occupancy rates may increase. We have seen this happen in Pennsylvania. The value of large tracts of land may increase, but single-family homes and small lots will probably decline in value. . . . Also, some insurance companies are refusing to issue policies on homes with gas wells.

The industry-funded studies take a myopic view. They don't address what happens when the gas is gone, and we may be left with contaminated drinking water, pollution, an industrial landscape, a population with failing health, and vanished employment opportunities.

Topics for Critical Thinking and Writing

1. In the first paragraph what is the meaning of "capital-intensive" and "labor-intensive"?

2. In her third paragraph, arguing against fracking, Barth says the gas industry is likely to negatively affect other industries, including "agriculture, tourism, organic farming, wine making, hunting, fishing, and river recreation." Let's assume her assertion may be true. How valid is it to reply, "Well, so what? Survival of the fittest. That's what the free market and America are all about"?

3. In paragraph 7 Barth asserts that certain kinds of property ("single-family homes and small lots") will "probably decline in value." How strong is this argument?

4. Barth criticizes the industry-funded studies especially for *not* taking this or that into account, but she does not document any falsification. Has she convinced you that the industry-funded studies are untrustworthy? Explain.

21

Drugs: Should Their Sale and Use Be Legalized?

William J. Bennett

William J. Bennett, born in Brooklyn in 1943, was educated at Williams College, the University of Texas, and Harvard Law School. Today he is most widely known as the author of The Book of Virtues: A Treasury of Great Moral Stories *(1993), but he has also been a public servant, Secretary of Education, and a director of the National Drug Control Policy. In 1989, during his tenure as "drug czar," he delivered at Harvard the address that we reprint. Among his recent publications are* The Broken Hearth: Reversing the Moral Collapse of the American Family *(2001),* Why We Fight: Moral Clarity and the War on Terrorism *(2002), and* A Century Turns: New Hopes, New Fears *(2009).*

Drug Policy and the Intellectuals

. . . The issue I want to address is our national drug policy and the intellectuals. Unfortunately, the issue is a little one-sided. There is a very great deal to say about our national drug policy, but much less to say about the intellectuals—except that by and large, they're against it. Why they should be against it is an interesting question, perhaps more a social-psychological question than a properly intellectual one. But whatever the reasons, I'm sorry to say that on properly intellectual grounds the arguments mustered against our current drug policy by America's intellectuals make for very thin gruel indeed.

I should point out, however, that in the fields of medical and scientific research, there is indeed serious and valuable drug-related work going on. But in the great public policy debate over drugs, the academic and intellectual communities have by and large had little to contribute, and little of that has been genuinely useful or for that matter mentally distinguished.

The field of national drug policy is wide open for serious research and serious thinking on both the theoretical and the practical levels; treatment and prevention; education; law enforcement and the criminal-justice system; the proper role of the federal government versus state and local jurisdictions; international diplomacy and foreign intelligence—these are only a few of the areas in which complex questions of policy and politics need to be addressed and resolved if our national drug strategy is to be successful. But apart from a handful of exceptions—including Mark Moore and Mark Kleiman here at the Kennedy School, and Harvard's own, or ex-own, James Q. Wilson—on most of these issues the country's major ideas factories have not just shut down, they've hardly even tooled up.

It's not that most intellectuals are indifferent to the drug issue, though there may be some of that, too. Rather, they seem complacent and incurious. They've made up their minds, and they don't want to be bothered with further information or analysis, further discussion or debate, especially when it comes from Washington. What I read in the opinion columns of my newspaper or in my monthly magazine or what I hear from the resident intellectual on my favorite television talk show is something like a developing intellectual consensus on the drug question. That consensus holds one or both of these propositions to be self-evident: (a) *that the drug problem in America is absurdly simple, and easily solved;* and (b) *that the drug problem in America is a lost cause.*

As it happens, each of these apparently contradictory propositions is 5 false. As it also happens, both are disputed by the *real* experts on drugs in the United States—and there are many such experts, though not the kind the media like to focus on. And both are disbelieved by the American people, whose experience tells them, emphatically, otherwise.

The consensus has a political dimension, which helps account for its seemingly divergent aspect. In some quarters of the far Right there is a tendency to assert that the drug problem is essentially a problem of the inner city, and therefore that what it calls for, essentially, is quarantine. "If those people want to kill themselves off with drugs, let them kill themselves off with drugs," would be a crude but not too inaccurate way of summarizing this position. But this position has relatively few adherents. On the Left, it is something else, something much more prevalent. There we see whole cadres of social scientists, abetted by whole armies of social workers, who seem to take it as catechism that the problem facing us isn't drugs at all, it's poverty, or racism, or some other equally large and intractable social phenomenon. If we want to eliminate the drug problem, these people say, we must first eliminate the "root causes" of drugs, a hopelessly daunting task at which, however, they also happen to make their living. Twenty-five years ago, no one would have suggested that we must first address the root causes of racism before fighting segregation. We fought it, quite correctly, by passing laws against unacceptable conduct. The causes of racism was an interesting question, but the moral imperative was to end it as soon as possible and by all reasonable means: education, prevention, the media, and not least of all, the law. So too with drugs.

What unites these two views of the drug problem from opposite sides of the political spectrum is that the issue, inevitably, is a policy of neglect. To me that is a scandalous position, intellectually as well as morally scandalous. For I believe, along with those I have named as the real experts on drugs, and along with most Americans, that the drug problem is not easy but difficult—very difficult in some respects. But at the same time, and again along with those same experts and with the American people, I believe it is not a lost cause but a solvable one. I will return to this theme, but let me pause here to note one specific issue on which the Left/Right consensus has lately come to rest; a position around which it has been attempting to build national sentiment. That position is legalization.

It is indeed bizarre to see the likes of Anthony Lewis and William F. Buckley lining up on the same side of an issue; but such is the perversity that the so-called legalization debate engenders. To call it a "debate," though, suggests that the arguments in *favor* of drug legalization are rigorous, substantial, and serious. They are not. They are, at bottom, a series of superficial and even disingenuous ideas that more sober minds recognize as a recipe for a public policy disaster. Let me explain.

Most conversations about legalization begin with the notion of "taking the profit out of the drug business." But has anyone bothered to examine carefully how the drug business works? As a recent *New York Times* article vividly described, instances of drug dealers actually earning huge sums of money are relatively rare. There are some who do, of course, but most people in the crack business are the low-level "runners" who do not make much money at all. Many of them work as prostitutes or small-time criminals to supplement their drug earnings. True, a lot of naïve kids are lured into the drug world by visions of a life filled with big money and fast cars. That's what they think the good life holds for them. But the reality is far different. Many dealers, in the long run, wind up smoking more crack than they sell. Their business becomes a form of slavery: long hours, dangerous work, small pay, and, as the *Times* pointed out, no health benefits either. In many cases, steady work at McDonald's over time would in fact be a step *up* the income scale for these kids. What does straighten them out, it seems, is not a higher minimum wage, or less stringent laws, but the dawning realization that dealing drugs invariably leads to murder or to prison. And that's exactly why we have drug laws—to make drug use a wholly unattractive choice.

Legalization, on the other hand, removes that incentive to stay away   10
from a life of drugs. Let's be honest—there are some people who are going to smoke crack whether it is legal or illegal. But by keeping it illegal, we maintain the criminal sanctions that persuade most people that the good life cannot be reached by dealing drugs.

The big lie behind every call for legalization is that making drugs legally available would "solve" the drug problem. But has anyone actually thought about what that kind of legalized regime would look like? Would crack be legal? How about PCP? Or smokable heroin? Or ice? Would they all be stocked at the local convenience store, perhaps just a few blocks from an elementary school? And how much would they cost? If we taxed drugs and made them expensive, we would still have the black market and crime problems that we have today; if we sold them cheap to eliminate the black market cocaine at, say, $10 a gram—then we would succeed in making a daily dose of cocaine well within the allowance budget of most sixth-graders. When pressed, the advocates of legalization like to sound courageous by proposing that we begin by legalizing marijuana. But they have absolutely nothing to say on the tough questions of controlling other, more powerful drugs, and how they would be regulated.

As far as marijuana is concerned, let me say this: I didn't have to become drug czar to be opposed to legalized marijuana. As Secretary of Education I realized that, given the state of American education, the last thing we needed was a policy that made widely available a substance that impairs memory, concentration, and attention span; why in God's name foster the use of a drug that makes you stupid?

Now what would happen if drugs were suddenly made legal? Legalization advocates deny that the amount of drug use would be affected. I would argue that if drugs are easier to obtain, drug use will soar. In fact, we have just undergone a kind of cruel national experiment in which drugs became cheap and widely available: That experiment is called the crack epidemic. When powder cocaine was expensive and hard to get, it was found almost exclusively in the circles of the rich, the famous, or the privileged. Only when cocaine was dumped into the country, and a $3 vial of crack could be bought on street corners did we see cocaine use skyrocket, this time largely among the poor and disadvantaged. The lesson is clear: If you're in favor of drugs being sold in stores like aspirin, you're in favor of boom times for drug users and drug addicts. With legalization, drug use will go up, way up.

When drug use rises, who benefits and who pays? Legalization advocates think that the cost of enforcing drug laws is too great. But the real question—the question they never ask—is what does it cost not to enforce those laws. The price that American society would have to pay for legalized drugs, I submit, would be intolerably high. We would have more drug-related accidents at work, on the highways, and in the airways. We would have even bigger losses in worker productivity. Our hospitals would be filled with drug emergencies. We would have more school kids on dope, and that means more dropouts. More pregnant women would buy legal cocaine, and then deliver tiny, premature infants. I've seen them in hospitals across the country. It's a horrid form of child abuse, and under a legalization scheme, we will have a lot more of it. For those women and those babies, crack has the same effect whether it's legal or not. Now, if you add to that the costs of treatment, social welfare, and insurance, you've got the price of legalization. So I ask you again, who benefits, who pays?

What about crime? To listen to legalization advocates, one might 15 think that street crime would disappear with the repeal of our drug laws. They haven't done their homework. Our best research indicates that most drug criminals were into crime well before they got into drugs. Making drugs legal would just be a way of subsidizing their habit. They would continue to rob and steal to pay for food, for clothes, for entertainment. And they would carry on with their drug trafficking by undercutting the legalized price of drugs and catering to teenagers, who, I assume, would be nominally restricted from buying drugs at the corner store.

All this should be old news to people who understand one clear lesson of prohibition. When we had laws against alcohol, there was less consumption of alcohol, less alcohol-related disease, fewer drunken brawls, and a lot less public drunkenness. And contrary to myth, there is no evidence that Prohibition caused big increases in crime. No one is suggesting that we go back to Prohibition. But at least we should admit that legalized alcohol, which is responsible for some 100,000 deaths a year, is hardly a model for drug policy. As Charles Krauthammer has pointed out, the question is not which is worse, alcohol or drugs. The question is can we accept both legalized alcohol *and* legalized drugs? The answer is no.

So it seems to me that on the merits of their arguments, the legalizers have no case at all. But there is another, crucial point I want to make on this subject, unrelated to costs or benefits. Drug use—especially heavy drug use—destroys human character. It destroys dignity and autonomy, it burns away the sense of responsibility, it subverts productivity, it makes a mockery of virtue. As our Founders would surely recognize, a citizenry that is perpetually in a drug-induced haze doesn't bode well for the future of self-government. Libertarians don't like to hear this, but it is a truth that everyone knows who has seen drug addiction up close. And don't listen to people who say drug users are only hurting themselves: They hurt parents, they destroy families, they ruin friendships. And let me remind this audience, here at a great university, that drugs are a threat to the life of the mind; anyone who values that life should have nothing but contempt for drugs. Learned institutions should regard drugs as the plague.

That's why I find the surrender of many of America's intellectuals to arguments for drug legalization so odd and so scandalous. For the past three months, I have been traveling the country, visiting drug-ridden neighborhoods, seeing treatment and prevention programs in action, talking to teachers, cops, parents, kids. These, it seems, are the real drug experts—they've witnessed the problem firsthand. But unlike some prominent residents of Princeton, Madison, Cambridge, or Palo Alto, they refuse to surrender. They are in the community, reclaiming their neighborhoods, working with police, setting up community activities, getting addicts into treatment, saving their children.

Too many American intellectuals don't know about this and seem not to want to know. Their hostility to the national war on drugs is, I think, partly rooted in a general hostility to law enforcement and criminal justice. That's why they take refuge in pseudosolutions like legalization, which stress only the treatment side of the problem. Whenever discussion turns to the need for more police and stronger penalties, they cry that our constitutional liberties are in jeopardy. Well, yes, they are in jeopardy, but not from drug *policy:* On this score, the guardians of our Constitution can sleep easy. Constitutional liberties are in jeopardy, instead, from drugs themselves, which every day scorch the earth of our common freedom. Yes, sometimes cops go too far, and when they do they should be held accountable. But these excursions from the law are the exception. Meanwhile drug dealers violate our rights every day as a rule, as a norm, as their modus operandi. Why can't our civil libertarians see that?

When we are not being told by critics that law enforcement threat- 20 ens our liberties, we are being told that it won't work. Let me tell you that law enforcement does work and why it must work. Several weeks ago I was in Wichita, Kansas, talking to a teenage boy who was now in his fourth treatment program. Every time he had finished a previous round of treatment, he found himself back on the streets, surrounded by the same cheap dope and tough hustlers who had gotten him started in the first place. He was tempted, he was pressured, and he gave in. Virtually any expert on drug treatment will tell you that, for most people, no therapy in the world can fight temptation on that scale. As long as drugs are found on any street corner, no amount of treatment, no amount of education can finally stand against them. Yes, we need drug treatment and drug education. But drug treatment and drug education need law enforcement. And that's why our strategy calls for a bigger criminal justice system: as a form of drug *prevention*.

To the Americans who are waging the drug war in their own front yards every day, this is nothing new, nothing startling. In the San Jose section of Albuquerque, New Mexico, just two weeks ago, I spoke to Rudy Chavez and Jack Candelarla, and police chief Sam Baca. They had wanted to start a youth center that would keep their kids safe from the depredations of the street. Somehow it never worked—until together they set up a police station right in the heart of drug-dealing territory. Then it worked. Together with the cops, the law-abiding residents cleared the area, and made it safe for them and their children to walk outside their homes. The youth center began to thrive.

Scenes like this are being played out all across the country. I've seen them in Tulsa, Dallas, Tampa, Omaha, Des Moines, Seattle, New York. Americans—many of them poor, black, or Hispanic—have figured out what the armchair critics haven't. Drugs may threaten to destroy their neighborhoods, but *they* refuse to stand by and let it happen. *They* have discovered that it is possible not only to fight back, but to win. In some elite circles, the talk may be only of the sad state of the helpless and the hopeless, but while these circles talk on, the helpless and the hopeless themselves are carrying out a national drug policy. They are fighting back.

When I think of these scenes I'm reminded of what John Jacob, president of the Urban League, said recently: Drugs are destroying more black families than poverty ever did. And I'm thankful that many of these poor families have the courage to fight drugs now, rather than declaring themselves passive victims of root causes.

America's intellectuals—and here I think particularly of liberal intellectuals—have spent much of the last nine years decrying the social programs of two Republican administrations in the name of the defenseless poor. But today, on the one outstanding issue that disproportionately hurts the poor—that is wiping out many of the poor—where are the liberal intellectuals to be found? They are on the editorial and op-ed pages, and in magazines like this month's *Harper's*, telling us with an ignorant sneer that our drug policy won't work. Many universities, too, which have been quick to take on the challenges of sexism, racism, and ethnocentrism, seem content on the drug issue to wag a finger at us, or to point it mindlessly at American society in general. In public policy schools, there is no shortage of arms control scholars. Isn't it time we had more drug control scholars?

The current situation won't do. The failure to get serious about the drug issue is, I think, a failure of civic courage—the kind of courage shown by many who have been among the main victims of the drug scourge. But it betokens as well a betrayal of the self-declared mission of intellectuals as the bearers of society's conscience. There may be reasons for this reluctance, this hostility, this failure. But I would remind you that not all crusades led by the U.S. government, enjoying broad popular support, are brutish, corrupt, and sinister. What is brutish, corrupt, and sinister is the murder and mayhem being committed in our cities' streets. One would think that a little more concern and serious thought would come from those who claim to care so deeply about America's problems.   25

So I stand here this afternoon with a simple message for America's pundits and academic cynics: Get serious about drug policy. We are grappling with complicated, stubborn policy issues, and I encourage you to join us. Tough work lies ahead, and we need serious minds to focus on how we should use the tools that we have in the most effective way.

I came to this job with realistic expectations. I am not promising a drug-free America by next week, or even by next year. But that doesn't mean that success is out of reach. Success will come—I've seen a lot of it already—in slow, careful steps. Its enemies are timidity, petulance, false expectations. But its three greatest foes remain surrender, despair, and neglect. So, for the sake of their fellow citizens, I invite America's deep thinkers to get with the program, or at the very least, to get in the game.

Topics for Critical Thinking and Writing

1. In paragraph 6, Bennett draws a parallel between racism and drug abuse and suggests that society ought to fight the one (drug abuse) as it successfully fought the other (racism). What do you think of this parallel? Explain.

2. Bennett identifies two propositions on the issue of drug abuse that he believes are accepted by "consensus" thinking in America (para. 4). What are these propositions, and what is Bennett's view of them? How does he try to convince the reader to agree with him?

3. What are Bennett's main objections to solving the problem of drug abuse by legalizing drugs?

4. At the time he gave this lecture, Bennett was a cigarette smoker trying to break the habit. Do you see any inconsistency in his opposing legalized marijuana and tolerating (and even using) legalized tobacco?

5. What measures besides stricter law enforcement does Bennett propose for wide-scale adoption to reduce drug abuse? Why does he object to relying only on such measures?

6. Bennett is known to be (or to have been) a heavy gambler, a high roller. On one occasion he said to the press, "It is true that I have gambled large sums of money. . . . I have done too much gambling, and this is not an example I wish to set." Does his admitted heavy gambling weaken his arguments about drugs?

James Q. Wilson

James Q. Wilson (1931–2012) was the first Senior Fellow at Boston College's Clough Center for the Study of Constitutional Democracy and Distinguished Scholar in its Department of Political Science. The author of Thinking about Crime *(1975),* Bureaucracy *(1989), and* Crime: Public Policies for Crime Control *(2002), he was also the coauthor of* Crime and Human Nature *(1985) and the coeditor of* Drugs and Crime *(1990). He wrote widely on culture, government, and politics. The essay that we reprint appeared originally in February 1990 in* Commentary, *a conservative magazine.*

Against the Legalization of Drugs

In 1972, the president appointed me chairman of the National Advisory Council for Drug Abuse Prevention. Created by Congress, the Council was charged with providing guidance on how best to coordinate the national war on drugs. (Yes, we called it a war then, too.) In those days, the drug we were chiefly concerned with was heroin. When I took office, heroin use had been increasing dramatically. Everybody was worried that this increase would continue. Such phrases as "heroin epidemic" were commonplace.

That same year, the eminent economist Milton Friedman published an essay in *Newsweek* in which he called for legalizing heroin. His argument was on two grounds: As a matter of ethics, the government has no right to tell people not to use heroin (or to drink or to commit suicide); as a matter of economics, the prohibition of drug use imposes costs on society that far exceed the benefits. Others, such as the psychoanalyst Thomas Szasz, made the same argument.

We did not take Friedman's advice. (Government commissions rarely do.) I do not recall that we even discussed legalizing heroin, though we did discuss (but did not take action on) legalizing a drug, cocaine, that many people then argued was benign. Our marching orders were to figure out how to win the war on heroin, not to run up the white flag of surrender.

That was 1972. Today, we have the same number of heroin addicts that we had then—half a million, give or take a few thousand. Having that many heroin addicts is no trivial matter; these people deserve our attention. But not having had an increase in that number for over fifteen years is also something that deserves our attention. What happened to the "heroin epidemic" that many people once thought would overwhelm us?

The facts are clear: A more or less stable pool of heroin addicts has 5 been getting older, with relatively few new recruits. In 1976 the average age of heroin users who appeared in hospital emergency rooms was about twenty-seven; ten years later it was thirty-two. More than two-thirds of all heroin users appearing in emergency rooms are now over the age of thirty. Back in the early 1970s, when heroin got onto the national political agenda, the typical heroin addict was much younger, often a teenager. Household surveys show the same thing—the rate of opiate use (which includes heroin) has been flat for the better part of two decades. More fine-grained studies of inner-city neighborhoods confirm this. John Boyle and Ann Brunswick found that the percentage of young blacks in Harlem who use heroin fell from 8 percent in 1970–71 to about 3 percent in 1975–76.

Why did heroin lose its appeal for young people? When the young blacks in Harlem were asked why they stopped, more than half mentioned "trouble with the law" or "high cost" (and high cost is, of course, directly the result of law enforcement). Two-thirds said that heroin hurt their health; nearly all said they had had a bad experience with it. We need not rely, however, simply on what they said. In New York City in 1973–75, the street price of heroin rose dramatically and its purity sharply declined, probably as a result of the heroin shortage caused by the success of the Turkish government in reducing the supply of opium base and of the French government in closing down heroin-processing laboratories located in and around Marseilles. These were short-lived gains for, just as Friedman predicted, alternative sources of supply—mostly in Mexico—quickly emerged. But the three-year heroin shortage interrupted the easy recruitment of new users.

Health and related problems were no doubt part of the reason for the reduced flow of recruits. Over the preceding years, Harlem youth had watched as more and more heroin users died of overdoses, were poisoned by adulterated doses, or acquired hepatitis from dirty needles. The word got around: Heroin can kill you. By 1974 new hepatitis cases and drug-overdose deaths had dropped to a fraction of what they had been in 1970.

Alas, treatment did not seem to explain much of the cessation in drug use. Treatment programs can and do help heroin addicts, but treatment did not explain the drop in the number of *new* users (who by definition had never been in treatment) nor even much of the reduction in the number of experienced users.

No one knows how much of the decline to attribute to personal observation as opposed to high prices or reduced supply. But other evidence suggests strongly that price and supply played a large role. In 1972 the National Advisory Council was especially worried by the prospect that U.S. servicemen returning to this country from Vietnam would bring their heroin habits with them. Fortunately, a brilliant study by Lee Robins of Washington University in St. Louis put that fear to rest. She measured drug use of Vietnam veterans shortly after they had returned home. Though many had used heroin regularly while in Southeast Asia, most gave up the habit when back in the United States. The reason: Here, heroin was less available and sanctions on its use were more pronounced. Of course, if a veteran had been willing to pay enough—which might have meant traveling to another city and would certainly have meant making an illegal contact with a disreputable dealer in a threatening neighborhood in order to acquire a (possibly) dangerous dose—he could have sustained his drug habit. Most veterans were unwilling to pay this price, and so their drug use declined or disappeared.

RELIVING THE PAST

Suppose we had taken Friedman's advice in 1972. What would have 10 happened? We cannot be entirely certain, but at a minimum we would have placed the young heroin addicts (and, above all, the prospective addicts) in a very different position from the one in which they actually found themselves. Heroin would have been legal. Its price would have been reduced by 95 percent (minus whatever we chose to recover in taxes). Now that it could be sold by the same people who make aspirin, its quality would have been assured—no poisons, no adulterants. Sterile hypodermic needles would have been readily available at the neighborhood drugstore, probably at the same counter where the heroin was sold. No need to travel to big cities or unfamiliar neighborhoods—heroin could have been purchased anywhere, perhaps by mail order.

There would no longer have been any financial or medical reason to avoid heroin use. Anybody could have afforded it. We might have tried to prevent children from buying it, but as we have learned from our efforts to prevent minors from buying alcohol and tobacco, young people have a way of penetrating markets theoretically reserved for adults. Returning Vietnam veterans would have discovered that Omaha and Raleigh had been converted into the pharmaceutical equivalent of Saigon.

Under these circumstances, can we doubt for a moment that heroin use would have grown exponentially? Or that a vastly larger supply of new users would have been recruited? Professor Friedman is a Nobel Prize–winning economist whose understanding of market forces is profound. What did he think would happen to consumption under his legalized regime? Here are his words: "Legalizing drugs might increase the number of addicts, but it is not clear that it would. Forbidden fruit is attractive, particularly to the young."

Really? I suppose that we should expect no increase in Porsche sales if we cut the price by 95 percent, no increase in whiskey sales if we cut the price by a comparable amount—because young people only want fast cars and strong liquor when they are "forbidden." Perhaps Friedman's uncharacteristic lapse from the obvious implications of price theory can be explained by a misunderstanding of how drug users are recruited. In his 1972 essay he said that "drug addicts are deliberately made by pushers, who give likely prospects their first few doses free." If drugs were legal it would not pay anybody to produce addicts, because everybody would buy from the cheapest source. But as every drug expert knows, pushers do not produce addicts. Friends or acquaintances do. In fact, pushers are usually reluctant to deal with nonusers because a nonuser could be an undercover cop. Drug use spreads in the same way any fad or fashion spreads: Somebody who is already a user urges his friends to try, or simply shows already-eager friends how to do it.

But we need not rely on speculation, however plausible, that lowered prices and more abundant supplies would have increased heroin usage. Great Britain once followed such a policy and with almost exactly those results. Until the mid-1960s, British physicians were allowed to prescribe heroin to certain classes of addicts. (Possessing these drugs without a doctor's prescription remained a criminal offense.) For many years this policy worked well enough because the addict patients were typically middle-class people who had become dependent on opiate painkillers while undergoing hospital treatment. There was no drug culture. The British system worked for many years, not because it prevented drug abuse but because there was no problem of drug abuse that would test the system.

All that changed in the 1960s. A few unscrupulous doctors began passing out heroin in wholesale amounts. One doctor prescribed almost six hundred thousand heroin tablets—that is, over thirteen pounds—in just one year. A youthful drug culture emerged with a demand for drugs far different from that of the older addicts. As a result, the British government required doctors to refer users to government-run clinics to receive their heroin. 15

But the shift to clinics did not curtail the growth in heroin use. Throughout the 1960s the number of addicts increased—the late John Kaplan of Stanford estimated by fivefold—in part as a result of the diversion of heroin from clinic patients to new users on the streets. An addict would bargain with the clinic doctor over how big a dose he would receive. The patient wanted as much as he could get, the doctor wanted to give as little as was needed. The patient had an advantage in this conflict because the doctor could not be certain how much was really needed. Many patients would use some of their "maintenance" dose and sell the remaining part to friends, thereby recruiting new addicts. As the clinics learned of this, they began to shift their treatment away from heroin and toward methadone, an addictive drug that, when taken orally, does not produce a "high" but will block the withdrawal pains associated with heroin abstinence.

Whether what happened in England in the 1960s was a miniepidemic or an epidemic depends on whether one looks at numbers or at rates of change. Compared to the United States, the numbers were small. In 1960 there were sixty-eight heroin addicts known to the British government; by 1968 there were two thousand in treatment and many more who refused treatment. (They would refuse in part because they did not want to get methadone at a clinic if they could get heroin on the street.) Richard Hartnoll estimates that the actual number of addicts in England is five times the number officially registered. At a minimum, the number of British addicts increased by thirtyfold in ten years; the actual increase may have been much larger.

In the early 1980s the numbers began to rise again, and this time nobody doubted that a real epidemic was at hand. The increase was estimated to be 40 percent a year. By 1982 there were thought to be twenty thousand heroin users in London alone. Geoffrey Pearson reports that many cities—Glasgow, Liverpool, Manchester, and Sheffield among them—were now experiencing a drug problem that once had been largely confined to London. The problem, again, was supply. The country was being flooded with cheap, high-quality heroin, first from Iran and then from Southeast Asia.

The United States began the 1960s with a much larger number of heroin addicts and probably a bigger at-risk population than was the case in Great Britain. Even though it would be foolhardy to suppose that the British system, if installed here, would have worked the same way or with the same results, it would be equally foolhardy to suppose that a combination of heroin available from leaky clinics and from street dealers who faced only minimal law-enforcement risks would not have produced a much greater increase in heroin use than we actually experienced. My guess is that if we had allowed either doctors or clinics to prescribe heroin, we would have had far worse results than were produced in Britain, if for no other reason than the vastly larger number of addicts with which we began. We would have had to find some way to police thousands (not scores) of physicians and hundreds (not dozens) of clinics. If the British civil service found it difficult to keep heroin in the hands of addicts and out of the hands of recruits when it was dealing with a few hundred people, how well would the American civil service have accomplished the same tasks when dealing with tens of thousands of people?

BACK TO THE FUTURE

Now cocaine, especially in its potent form, crack, is the focus of [20] attention. Now as in 1972 the government is trying to reduce its use. Now as then some people are advocating legalization. Is there any more reason to yield to those arguments today than there was almost two decades ago?[1]

I think not. If we had yielded in 1972 we almost certainly would have had today a permanent population of several million, not several hundred thousand, heroin addicts. If we yield now we will have a far more serious problem with cocaine.

Crack is worse than heroin by almost any measure. Heroin produces a pleasant drowsiness and, if hygienically administered, has only the physical side effects of constipation and sexual impotence. Regular heroin use incapacitates many users, especially poor ones, for any productive work or social responsibility. They will sit nodding on a street corner, helpless but at least harmless. By contrast, regular cocaine use leaves the user neither helpless nor harmless. When smoked (as with crack) or injected, cocaine produces instant, intense, and short-lived euphoria. The experience generates a powerful desire to repeat it. If the drug is readily available, repeat use will occur. Those people who progress to "bingeing" on cocaine become devoted to the drug and its effects to the exclusion of almost all other considerations—job, family, children, sleep, food, even sex. Dr. Frank Gawin at Yale and Dr. Everett Ellinwood at Duke report that a substantial percentage of all high-dose, binge users become uninhibited, impulsive, hypersexual, compulsive, irritable, and hyperactive. Their moods vacillate dramatically, leading at times to violence and homicide.

Women are much more likely to use crack than heroin, and if they are pregnant, the effects on their babies are tragic. Douglas Besharov, who has been following the effects of drugs on infants for twenty years, writes that nothing he learned about heroin prepared him for the devastation of cocaine. Cocaine harms the fetus and can lead to physical deformities or neurological damage. Some crack babies have for all

---

[1] I do not here take up the question of marijuana. For a variety of reasons—its widespread use and its lesser tendency to addict—it presents a different problem from cocaine or heroin. For a penetrating analysis, see Mark Kleiman, *Marijuana: Costs of Abuse, Costs of Control* (Greenwood Press, 217 pp.). [Wilson's note.]

practical purposes suffered a disabling stroke while still in the womb. The long-term consequences of this brain damage are lowered cognitive ability and the onset of mood disorders. Besharov estimates that about thirty thousand to fifty thousand such babies are born every year, about seven thousand in New York City alone. There may be ways to treat such infants, but from everything we now know the treatment will be long, difficult, and expensive. Worse, the mothers who are most likely to produce crack babies are precisely the ones who, because of poverty or temperament, are least able and willing to obtain such treatment. In fact, anecdotal evidence suggests the crack mothers are likely to abuse their infants.

The notion that abusing drugs such as cocaine is a "victimless crime" is not only absurd but dangerous. Even ignoring the fetal drug syndrome, crack-dependent people are, like heroin addicts, individuals who regularly victimize their children by neglect, their spouses by improvidence, their employers by lethargy, and their co-workers by carelessness. Society is not and could never be a collection of autonomous individuals. We all have a stake in ensuring that each of us displays a minimal level of dignity, responsibility, and empathy. We cannot, of course, coerce people into goodness, but we can and should insist that some standards must be met if society itself—on which the very existence of the human personality depends—is to persist. Drawing the line that defines those standards is difficult and contentious, but if crack and heroin use do not fall below it, what does?

The advocates of legalization will respond by suggesting that my 25 picture is overdrawn. Ethan Nadelmann of Princeton argues that the risk of legalization is less than most people suppose. Over twenty million Americans between the ages of eighteen and twenty-five have tried cocaine (according to a government survey), but only a quarter million use it daily. From this Nadelmann concludes that at most 3 percent of all young people who try cocaine develop a problem with it. The implication is clear: Make the drug legal and we only have to worry about 3 percent of our youth.

The implication rests on a logical fallacy and a factual error. The fallacy is this: The percentage of occasional cocaine users who become binge users *when the drug is illegal* (and thus expensive and hard to find) tells us nothing about the percentage who will become dependent when the drug is legal (and thus cheap and abundant). Drs. Gawin and Ellinwood report, in common with several other researchers, that controlled or occasional use of cocaine changes to compulsive and frequent use "when access to the drug increases" or when the user switches from snorting to smoking. More cocaine more potently administered alters, perhaps sharply, the proportion of "controlled" users who become heavy users.

The factual error is this: The federal survey Nadelmann quotes was done in 1985, *before* crack had become common. Thus the probability of becoming dependent on cocaine was derived from the responses of users who snorted the drug. The speed and potency of cocaine's action increases dramatically when it is smoked. We do not yet know how greatly the advent of crack increases the risk of dependency, but all the clinical evidence suggests that the increase is likely to be large.

It is possible that some people will not become heavy users even when the drug is readily available in its most potent form. So far there are no scientific grounds for predicting who will and who will not become dependent. Neither socioeconomic background nor personality traits differentiate between casual and intensive users. Thus, the only way to settle the question of who is correct about the effect of easy availability on drug use, Nadelmann or Gawin and Ellinwood, is to try it and see. But the social experiment is so risky as to be no experiment at all, for if cocaine is legalized and if the rate of its abusive use increases dramatically, there is no way to put the genie back in the bottle, and it is not a kindly genie.

HAVE WE LOST?

Many people who agree that there are risks in legalizing cocaine or heroin still favor it because, they think, we have lost the war on drugs. "Nothing we have done has worked" and the current federal policy is just "more of the same." Whatever the costs of greater drug use, surely they would be less than the costs of our present, failed efforts.

That is exactly what I was told in 1972—and heroin is not quite as 30 bad a drug as cocaine. We did not surrender and we did not lose. We did not win, either. What the nation accomplished then was what most efforts to save people from themselves accomplish: The problem was contained and the number of victims minimized, all at a considerable cost in law enforcement and increased crime. Was the cost worth it? I think so, but others may disagree. What are the lives of would-be addicts worth? I recall some people saying to me then, "Let them kill themselves." I was appalled. Happily, such views did not prevail.

Have we lost today? Not at all. High-rate cocaine use is not commonplace. The National Institute of Drug Abuse (NIDA) reports that less than 5 percent of high-school seniors used cocaine within the last thirty days. Of course this survey misses young people who have dropped out of school and miscounts those who lie on the questionnaire, but even if we inflate the NIDA estimate by some plausible percentage, it is still not much above 5 percent. Medical examiners reported in 1987 that about 1,500 died from cocaine use; hospital emergency rooms reported about 30,000 admissions related to cocaine abuse.

These are not small numbers, but neither are they evidence of a nationwide plague that threatens to engulf us all. Moreover, cities vary greatly in the proportion of people who are involved with cocaine. To get city-level data we need to turn to drug tests carried out on arrested persons, who obviously are more likely to be drug users than the average citizen. The National Institute of Justice, through its Drug Use Forecasting (DUF) project, collects urinalysis data on arrestees in twenty-two cities. As we have already seen, opiate (chiefly heroin) use has been flat or declining in most of these cities over the last decade. Cocaine use has gone up sharply, but with great variation among cities. New York, Philadelphia, and Washington, D.C., all report that two-thirds or more of their arrestees tested positive for cocaine, but in Portland, San Antonio, and Indianapolis the percentage was one-third or less.

In some neighborhoods, of course, matters have reached crisis proportions. Gangs control the streets, shootings terrorize residents, and drug dealing occurs in plain view. The police seem barely able to contain matters. But in these neighborhoods—unlike at Palo Alto cocktail parties—the people are not calling for legalization, they are calling for help. And often not much help has come. Many cities are willing to do almost anything about the drug problem except spend more money on it. The federal government cannot change that; only local voters and politicians can. It is not clear that they will.

It took about ten years to contain heroin. We have had experience with crack for only about three or four years. Each year we spend perhaps $11 billion on law enforcement (and some of that goes to deal with marijuana) and perhaps $2 billion on treatment. Large sums, but not sums that should lead anyone to say, "We just can't afford this anymore."

The illegality of drugs increases crime, partly because some users turn 35 to crime to pay for their habits, partly because some users are stimulated by certain drugs (such as crack or PCP) to act more violently or ruthlessly than they otherwise would, and partly because criminal organizations seeking to control drug supplies use force to manage their markets. These also are serious costs, but no one knows how much they would be reduced if drugs were legalized. Addicts would no longer steal to pay black-market prices for drugs, a real gain. But some, perhaps a great deal, of that gain would be offset by the great increase in the number of addicts. These people, nodding on heroin or living in the delusion-ridden high of cocaine, would hardly be ideal employees. Many would steal simply to support themselves, since snatch-and-grab, opportunistic crime can be managed even by people unable to hold a regular job or plan an elaborate crime. Those British addicts who get their supplies from government clinics are not models of law-abiding decency. Most are in crime, and though their per-capita rate of criminality may be lower thanks to the cheapness of their drugs, the total volume of crime they produce may be quite large. Of course, society could decide to support all unemployable addicts on welfare, but that would mean that gains from lowered rates of crime would have to be offset by large increases in welfare budgets.

Proponents of legalization claim that the costs of having more addicts around would be largely if not entirely offset by having more money available with which to treat and care for them. The money would come from taxes levied on the sale of heroin and cocaine.

To obtain this fiscal dividend, however, legalization's supporters must first solve an economic dilemma. If they want to raise a lot of money to pay for welfare and treatment, the tax rate on the drugs will have to be quite high. Even if they themselves do not want a high rate, the politicians' love of "sin taxes" would probably guarantee that it would be high anyway. But the higher the tax, the higher the price of the drug, and the higher the price the greater the likelihood that addicts will turn to crime to find the money for it and that criminal organizations will be formed to sell tax-free drugs at below-market rates. If we managed to keep taxes (and thus prices) low, we would get that much less money to pay for welfare and treatment and more people could afford to become addicts. There may be an optimal tax rate for drugs that maximizes revenue while minimizing crime, bootlegging, and the recruitment of new addicts, but our experience with alcohol does not suggest that we know how to find it.

THE BENEFITS OF ILLEGALITY

The advocates of legalization find nothing to be said in favor of the current system except, possibly, that it keeps the number of addicts smaller than it would otherwise be. In fact, the benefits are more substantial than that.

First, treatment. All the talk about providing "treatment on demand" implies that there is a demand for treatment. That is not quite right. There are some drug-dependent people who genuinely want treatment and will remain in it if offered; they should receive it. But there are far more who want only short-term help after a bad crash; once stabilized and bathed, they are back on the street again, hustling. And even many of the addicts who enroll in a program honestly wanting help drop out after a short while when they discover that help takes time and commitment. Drug-dependent people have very short time horizons and a weak capacity for commitment. These two groups—those looking for a quick fix and those unable to stick with a long-term fix—are not easily helped. Even if we increase the number of treatment slots—as we should—we would have to do something to make treatment more effective.

One thing that can often make it more effective is compulsion. 40 Douglas Anglin of UCLA, in common with many other researchers, has found that the longer one stays in a treatment program, the better the chances of a reduction in drug dependency. But he, again like most other researchers, has found that dropout rates are high. He has also found, however, that patients who enter treatment under legal compulsion stay in the program longer than those not subject to such pressure. His research on the California civil commitment program, for example, found that heroin users involved with its required drug-testing program had over the long term a lower rate of heroin use than similar addicts who were free of such constraints. If for many addicts compulsion is a useful component of treatment, it is not clear how compulsion could be achieved in a society in which purchasing, possessing, and using the drug were legal. It could be managed, I suppose, but I would not want to have to answer the challenge from the American Civil Liberties Union that it is wrong to compel a person to undergo treatment for consuming a legal commodity.

Next, education. We are now investing substantially in drug-education programs in the schools. Though we do not yet know for certain what will work, there are some promising leads. But I wonder how credible such programs would be if they were aimed at dissuading children from doing something perfectly legal. We could, of course, treat drug education like smoking education: Inhaling crack and inhaling tobacco are both legal, but you should not do it because it is bad for you. That tobacco is bad for you is easily shown; the Surgeon General has seen to that. But what do we say about crack? It is pleasurable, but devoting yourself to so much pleasure is not a good idea (though perfectly legal)? Unlike tobacco, cocaine will not give you cancer or emphysema, but it will lead you to neglect your duties to family, job, and neighborhood? Everybody is doing cocaine, but you should not?

Again, it might be possible under a legalized regime to have effective drug-prevention programs, but their effectiveness would depend heavily, I think, on first having decided that cocaine use, like tobacco use, is purely a matter of practical consequences; no fundamental moral significance attaches to either. But if we believe—as I do—that dependency on certain mind-altering drugs *is* a moral issue and that their illegality rests in part on their immorality, then legalizing them undercuts, if it does not eliminate altogether, the moral message.

That message is at the root of the distinction we now make between nicotine and cocaine. Both are highly addictive; both have harmful physical effects. But we treat the two drugs differently, not simply because nicotine is so widely used as to be beyond the reach of effective prohibition, but because its use does not destroy the user's essential humanity. Tobacco shortens one's life, cocaine debases it. Nicotine alters one's habits, cocaine alters one's soul. The heavy use of crack, unlike the heavy use of tobacco, corrodes those natural sentiments of sympathy and duty that constitute our human nature and make possible our social life. To say, as does Nadelmann, that distinguishing morally between tobacco and cocaine is "little more than a transient prejudice" is close to saying that morality itself is but a prejudice.

THE ALCOHOL PROBLEM

Now we have arrived where many arguments about legalizing drugs begin: Is there any reason to treat heroin and cocaine differently from the way we treat alcohol?

There is no easy answer to that question because, as with so many 45 human problems, one cannot decide simply on the basis either of moral principles or of individual consequences; one has to temper any policy by a commonsense judgment of what is possible. Alcohol, like heroin, cocaine, PCP, and marijuana, is a drug—that is, a mood-altering substance—and consumed to excess it certainly has harmful consequences: auto accidents, barroom fights, bedroom shootings. It is also, for some people, addictive. We cannot confidently compare the addictive powers of these drugs, but the best evidence suggests that crack and heroin are much more addictive than alcohol.

Many people, Nadelmann included, argue that since the health and financial costs of alcohol abuse are so much higher than those of cocaine or heroin abuse, it is hypocritical folly to devote our efforts to preventing cocaine or drug use. But as Mark Kleiman of Harvard has pointed out, this comparison is quite misleading. What Nadelmann is doing is showing that a *legalized* drug (alcohol) produces greater social harm than *illegal* ones (cocaine and heroin). But of course. Suppose that in the 1920s we had made heroin and cocaine legal and alcohol illegal. Can anyone doubt that Nadelmann would now be writing that it is folly to continue our ban on alcohol because cocaine and heroin are so much more harmful?

And let there be no doubt about it—widespread heroin and cocaine use are associated with all manner of ills. Thomas Bewley found that the mortality rate of British heroin addicts in 1968 was twenty-eight times as high as the death rate of the same age group of nonaddicts, even though in England at the time an addict could obtain free or low-cost heroin and clean needles from British clinics. Perform the following mental experiment: Suppose we legalized heroin and cocaine in this country. In what proportion of auto fatalities would the state police report that the driver was nodding off on heroin or recklessly driving on a coke high? In what proportion of spouse-assault and child-abuse cases would the local police report that crack was involved? In what proportion of industrial accidents would safety investigators report that the forklift or drill-press operator was in a drug-induced stupor or frenzy? We do not know exactly what the proportion would be, but anyone who asserts that it would not be much higher than it is now would have to believe that these drugs have little appeal except when they are illegal. And that is nonsense.

An advocate of legalization might concede that social harm—perhaps harm equivalent to that already produced by alcohol—would follow from making cocaine and heroin generally available. But at least, he might add, we would have the problem "out in the open" where it could be treated as a matter of "public health." That is well and good, *if* we knew how to treat—that is, cure—heroin and cocaine abuse. But we do not know how to do it for all the people who would need such help. We are having only limited success in coping with chronic alcoholics. Addictive behavior is immensely difficult to change, and the best methods for changing it—living in drug-free therapeutic communities, becoming faithful members of Alcoholics Anonymous or Narcotics

Anonymous—require great personal commitment, a quality that is, alas, in short supply among the very persons—young people, disadvantaged people—who are often most at risk for addiction.

Suppose that today we had, not fifteen million alcohol abusers, but half a million. Suppose that we already knew what we have learned from our long experience with the widespread use of alcohol. Would we make whiskey legal? I do not know, but I suspect there would be a lively debate. The surgeon general would remind us of the risks alcohol poses to pregnant women. The National Highway Traffic Safety Administration would point to the likelihood of more highway fatalities caused by drunk drivers. The Food and Drug Administration might find that there is a nontrivial increase in cancer associated with alcohol consumption. At the same time the police would report great difficulty in keeping illegal whiskey out of our cities, officers being corrupted by bootleggers, and alcohol addicts often resorting to crime to feed their habit. Libertarians, for their part, would argue that every citizen has a right to drink anything he wishes and that drinking is, in any event, a "victimless crime."

However the debate might turn out, the central fact would be that 50 the problem was still, at that point, a small one. The government cannot legislate away the addictive tendencies in all of us, nor can it remove completely even the most dangerous addictive substances. But it can cope with harms when the harms are still manageable.

SCIENCE AND ADDICTION

One advantage of containing a problem while it is still containable is that it buys time for science to learn more about it and perhaps to discover a cure. Almost unnoticed in the current debate over legalizing drugs is that basic science has made rapid strides in identifying the underlying neurological processes involved in some forms of addiction. Stimulants such as cocaine and amphetamines alter the way certain brain cells communicate with one another. That alteration is complex and not entirely understood, but in simplified form it involves modifying the way in which a neurotransmitter called dopamine sends signals from one cell to another.

When dopamine crosses the synapse between two cells, it is in effect carrying a message from the first cell to activate the second one. In certain parts of the brain that message is experienced as pleasure. After the message is delivered, the dopamine returns to the first cell. Cocaine apparently blocks this return, or "reuptake," so that the excited cell and others nearby continue to send pleasure messages. When the exaggerated high produced by cocaine-influenced dopamine finally ends, the brain cells may (in ways that are still a matter of dispute) suffer from an extreme lack of dopamine, thereby making the individual unable to experience any pleasure at all. This would explain why cocaine users often feel so depressed after enjoying the drug. Stimulants may also affect the way in which other neurotransmitters, such as serotonin and noradrenaline, operate.

Whatever the exact mechanism may be, once it is identified it becomes possible to use drugs to block either the effect of cocaine or its tendency to produce dependency. There have already been experiments using desipramine, imipramine, bromocriptine, carbamazepine, and other chemicals. There are some promising results.

Tragically, we spend very little on such research, and the agencies funding it have not in the past occupied very influential or visible posts in the federal bureaucracy. If there is one aspect of the "war on drugs" metaphor that I dislike, it is its tendency to focus attention almost exclusively on the troops in the trenches, whether engaged in enforcement or treatment, and away from the research-and-development efforts back on the home front where the war may ultimately be decided.

I believe that the prospects of scientists in controlling addiction will   55 be strongly influenced by the size and character of the problem they face. If the problem is a few hundred thousand chronic, high-dose users of an illegal product, the chances of making a difference at a reasonable cost will be much greater than if the problem is a few million chronic users of legal substances. Once a drug is legal, not only will its use increase but many of those who then use it will prefer the drug to the treatment: They will want the pleasure, whatever the cost to themselves or their families, and they will resist—probably successfully—any effort to wean them away from experiencing the high that comes from inhaling a legal substance.

IF I AM WRONG . . .

No one can know what our society would be like if we changed the law to make access to cocaine, heroin, and PCP easier. I believe, for reasons given, that the result would be a sharp increase in use, a more widespread degradation of the human personality, and a greater rate of accidents and violence.

I may be wrong. If I am, then we will needlessly have incurred heavy costs in law enforcement and some forms of criminality. But if I am right, and the legalizers prevail anyway, then we will have consigned millions of people, hundreds of thousands of infants, and hundreds of neighborhoods to a life of oblivion and disease. To the lives and families destroyed by alcohol we will have added countless more destroyed by cocaine, heroin, PCP, and whatever else a basement scientist can invent.

Human character is formed by society; indeed, human character is inconceivable without society, and good character is less likely in a bad society. Will we, in the name of an abstract doctrine of radical individualism, and with the false comfort of suspect predictions, decide to take the chance that somehow individual decency can survive amid a more general level of degradation?

I think not. The American people are too wise for that, whatever the academic essayists and cocktail-party pundits may say. But if Americans today are less wise than I suppose, then Americans at some future time will look back on us now and wonder, what kind of people were they that they could have done such a thing?

Topics for Critical Thinking and Writing

1. Wilson objects to the idea that using cocaine is a "victimless crime" (para. 24; see also para. 49). A crime is said to be "victimless" when the offender consents to the act and those who do not consent are not harmed. Why does it matter to Wilson, do you think, whether using illegal drugs is a victimless crime?

2. Wilson accuses Ethan Nadelmann, an advocate of legalization, of committing "a logical fallacy and a factual error" (para. 26). What is the fallacy, and what is the error?

3. Wilson raises the question of whether we "won" or "lost" the war on heroin in the 1970s and whether we will do any better with the current war on cocaine (paras. 30–31). What would you regard as convincing evidence that we are winning the war on drugs? Losing it?

4. In his criticism of those who would legalize drugs, Wilson points to what he regards as an inescapable "economic dilemma" (para. 37). What is this dilemma? Do you see any way around it?

5. Economists tell us that we can control the use of a good or service by controlling the cost (thus probably reducing the demand), by ignoring the cost and controlling the supply, or by doing both. In the war on drugs, which of these three economic strategies does Wilson apparently favor, and why?

Milton Friedman

Milton Friedman (1912–2006), winner of a Nobel Prize in economics, was born in Brooklyn, New York. Educated at Rutgers University, the University of Chicago, and Columbia University, Friedman, a leading conservative economist, had considerable influence on economic thought in America through his academic and popular writings. We reprint a piece that appeared in the New York Times *in 1998.*

There's No Justice in the War on Drugs

Twenty-five years ago, President Richard M. Nixon announced a "War on Drugs." I criticized the action on both moral and expediential grounds in my *Newsweek* column of May 1, 1972, "Prohibition and Drugs":

> On ethical grounds, do we have the right to use the machinery of government to prevent an individual from becoming an alcoholic or a drug

addict? For children, almost everyone would answer at least a qualified yes. But for responsible adults, I, for one, would answer no. Reason with the potential addict, yes. Tell him the consequences, yes. Pray for and with him, yes. But I believe that we have no right to use force, directly or indirectly, to prevent a fellow man from committing suicide, let alone from drinking alcohol or taking drugs.

That basic ethical flaw has inevitably generated specific evils during the past quarter century, just as it did during our earlier attempt at alcohol prohibition.

1. The use of informers. Informers are not needed in crimes like robbery and murder because the victims of those crimes have a strong incentive to report the crime. In the drug trade, the crime consists of a transaction between a willing buyer and willing seller. Neither has any incentive to report a violation of law. On the contrary, it is in the self-interest of both that the crime not be reported. That is why informers are needed. The use of informers and the immense sums of money at stake inevitably generate corruption—as they did during Prohibition. They also lead to violations of the civil rights of innocent people, to the shameful practices of forcible entry and forfeiture of property without due process.

As I wrote in 1972: "Addicts and pushers are not the only ones corrupted. Immense sums are at stake. It is inevitable that some relatively low-paid police and other government officials—and some high-paid ones as well—will succumb to the temptation to pick up easy money."

2. Filling the prisons. In 1970, 200,000 people were in prison. 5 Today, 1.6 million people are. Eight times as many in absolute number, six times as many relative to the increased population. In addition, 2.3 million are on probation and parole. The attempt to prohibit drugs is by far the major source of the horrendous growth in the prison population.

There is no light at the end of that tunnel. How many of our citizens do we want to turn into criminals before we yell "enough"?

3. Disproportionate imprisonment of blacks. Sher Hosonko, at the time Connecticut's director of addiction services, stressed this effect of drug prohibition in a talk given in June 1995:

Today in this country, we incarcerate 3,109 black men for every 100,000 of them in the population. Just to give you an idea of the drama in this number, our closest competitor for incarcerating black men is South Africa. South Africa—and this is pre–Nelson Mandela and under an overt public policy of apartheid—incarcerated 729 black men for every 100,000. Figure this out: In the land of the Bill of Rights, we jail over four times as many black men as the only country in the world that advertised a political policy of apartheid.

4. Destruction of inner cities. Drug prohibition is one of the most important factors that have combined to reduce our inner cities to their present state. The crowded inner cities have a comparative advantage for selling drugs. Though most customers do not live in the inner cities, most sellers do. Young boys and girls view the swaggering, affluent drug dealers as role models. Compared with the returns from a traditional career of study and hard work, returns from dealing drugs are tempting to young and old alike. And many, especially the young, are not dissuaded by the bullets that fly so freely in disputes between competing drug dealers—bullets that fly only because dealing drugs is illegal. Al Capone epitomizes our earlier attempt at Prohibition; the Crips and Bloods epitomize this one.

5. Compounding the harm to users. Prohibition makes drugs exorbitantly expensive and highly uncertain in quality. A user must associate with criminals to get the drugs, and many are driven to become criminals themselves to finance the habit. Needles, which are hard to get, are often shared, with the predictable effect of spreading disease. Finally, an addict who seeks treatment must confess to being a criminal in order to qualify for a treatment program. Alternatively, professionals who treat addicts must become informers or criminals themselves.

6. Undertreatment of chronic pain. The Federal Department of   10
Health and Human Services has issued reports showing that two-thirds of all terminal cancer patients do not receive adequate pain medication, and the numbers are surely higher in nonterminally ill patients. Such serious undertreatment of chronic pain is a direct result of the Drug Enforcement Agency's pressures on physicians who prescribe narcotics.

7. Harming foreign countries. Our drug policy has led to thousands of deaths and enormous loss of wealth in countries like Colombia, Peru, and Mexico, and has undermined the stability of their governments. All because we cannot enforce our laws at home. If we did, there would be no market for imported drugs. There would be no Cali cartel. The foreign countries would not have to suffer the loss of sovereignty involved in letting our "advisers" and troops operate on their soil, search their vessels, and encourage local militaries to shoot down their planes. They could run their own affairs, and we, in turn, could avoid the diversion of military forces from their proper function.

Can any policy, however high-minded, be moral if it leads to widespread corruption, imprisons so many, has so racist an effect, destroys our inner cities, wreaks havoc on misguided and vulnerable individuals, and brings death and destruction to foreign countries?

"Your condition is serious, Mr. Reynolds, but fortunately I recently scored some excellent weed that should alleviate your symptoms."

TOPICS FOR CRITICAL THINKING AND WRITING

1. State in one sentence the thesis of Friedman's essay.

2. Which of the seven reasons Friedman cites in favor of revising our "war on drugs" do you find most convincing? Explain why, in a short essay of 100 words.

3. Friedman distinguishes between "moral and expediential" objections to current drug policy (para. 1). What does he mean by this distinction? Which kind of objection do you think is the most persuasive? Why?

4. If a policy, a practice, or an individual act is unethical or immoral, then it violates some ethical standard or moral norm. What norms or standards does Friedman think that our current drug policy violates?

5. Does Friedman favor a policy on addictive (and currently illegal) drugs that is like our policy on alcohol? Explain in an essay of 250 words how the two policies might differ.

Elliott Currie

Elliott Currie is professor of criminology, law, and society at the University of California, Irvine, and until 2009, vice chair of the Eisenhower Foundation in Washington, D.C., an organization that supports drug-abuse-prevention programs.

We reprint an essay that appeared in the journal Dissent *in 1993; the essay is a slightly revised version of a chapter that first appeared in one of Currie's books,* Reckoning: Drugs, the Cities, and the American Future *(1993).*

Toward a Policy on Drugs

One of the strongest implications of what we now know about the causes of endemic drug abuse is that the criminal-justice system's effect on the drug crisis will inevitably be limited. That shouldn't surprise us in the 1990s; it has, after all, been a central argument of drug research since the 1950s. Today, as the drug problem has worsened, the limits of the law are if anything even clearer. But that does not mean that the justice system has no role to play in a more effective strategy against drugs. Drugs will always be a "law-enforcement problem" in part, and the real job is to define what we want the police and the courts to accomplish.

We will never, for reasons that will shortly become clear, punish our way out of the drug crisis. We can, however, use the criminal-justice system, in small but significant ways, to improve the prospects of drug users who are now caught in an endless loop of court, jail, and street. And we can use law enforcement, in small but significant ways, to help strengthen the ability of drug-ridden communities to defend themselves against violence, fear, and demoralization. Today the criminal-justice system does very little of the first and not enough of the second. But doing these things well will require far-reaching changes in our priorities. Above all, we will have to shift from an approach in which discouraging drug use through punishment and fear takes central place to one that emphasizes three very different principles: the reintegration of drug abusers into productive life, the reduction of harm, and the promotion of community safety.

This is a tall order, but, as we shall see, something similar is being practiced in many countries that suffer far less convulsing drug problems than we do. Their experience suggests that a different and more humane criminal-justice response to drugs is both possible and practical. Today, there is much debate about the role of the justice system in a rational drug policy—but for the most part, the debate is between those who would intensify the effort to control drugs through the courts and prisons and those who want to take drugs out of the orbit of the justice system altogether. I do not think that either approach takes sufficient account of the social realities of drug abuse; and both, consequently, exaggerate the role of regulatory policies in determining the shape and seriousness of the problem. But those are not the only alternatives. In between, there is a range of more promising strategies—what some Europeans call a "third way"—that is more attuned to those realities and more compatible with our democratic values.

One response to the failure of the drug war has been to call for more of what we've already done—even harsher sentences, still more money for jails and prisons—on the grounds that we have simply not provided enough resources to fight the war effectively. That position is shared by the Bush administration and many Democrats in Congress as well. But the strategy of upping the ante cannot work; and even to attempt it on a large scale would dramatically increase the social costs that an overreliance on punishment has already brought. We've seen that the effort to contain the drug problem through force and fear has already distorted our justice system in fundamental ways and caused a rippling of secondary costs throughout the society as a whole. Much more of this would alter the character of American society beyond recognition. And it would not solve the drug problem.

Why wouldn't more of the same do the job?   5

To understand why escalating the war on drugs would be unlikely to make much difference—short of efforts on a scale that would cause unprecedented social damage—we need to consider how the criminal-justice system is, in theory, *supposed* to work to reduce drug abuse and drug-related crime. Criminologists distinguish between two mechanisms by which punishment may decrease illegal behavior. One is "incapacitation," an unlovely term that simply means that locking people up will keep them—as long as they are behind bars—from engaging in the behavior we wish to suppress. The other is "deterrence," by which we mean either that people tempted to engage in the behavior will be persuaded otherwise by the threat of punishment ("general deterrence"), or that individuals, once punished, will be less likely to engage in the behavior again ("specific deterrence"). What makes the drug problem so resistant to even very heavy doses of criminalization is that neither mechanism works effectively for most drug offenders—particularly those most heavily involved in the drug subcultures of the street.

The main reason why incapacitation is unworkable as a strategy against drug offenders is that there are so many of them that a serious attempt to put them all—or even just the "hard core"—behind bars is unrealistic, even in the barest fiscal terms. This is obvious if we pause to recall the sheer number of people who use hard drugs in the United States. Consider the estimates of the number of people who have used drugs during the previous year provided annually by the NIDA (National Institute on Drug Abuse) Household Survey—which substantially *understates* the extent of hard-drug use. Even if we exclude the more than 20 million people who used marijuana in the past year, the number of hard-drug users is enormous: the survey estimates over six million cocaine users in 1991 (including over a million who used crack), about 700,000 heroin users, and 5.7 million users of hallucinogens and inhalants. Even if we abandon the aim of imprisoning less serious hard-drug users, thus allowing the most conservative accounting of the costs of incapacitation, the problem remains staggering: by the lowest estimates, there are no fewer than two million hard-core abusers of cocaine and heroin alone.

If we take as a rough approximation that about 25 percent of America's prisoners are behind bars for drug offenses, that gives us roughly

300,000 drug offenders in prison at any given point—and this after several years of a hugely implemented war mainly directed at lower-level dealers and street drug users. We have seen what this flood of offenders has done to the nation's courts and prisons, but what is utterly sobering is that even this massive effort at repression has barely scratched the surface: according to the most optimistic estimate, we may at any point be incarcerating on drug-related charges about one-eighth of the country's hard-core cocaine and heroin abusers. And where drug addiction is truly endemic, the disparity is greater. By 1989 there were roughly 20,000 drug offenders on any given day in New York State's prisons, but there were an estimated 200,000 to 250,000 *heroin* addicts in New York City alone. To be sure, these figures obscure the fact that many prisoners behind bars for *non*drug offenses are also hard-core drug users; but the figures are skewed in the other direction by the large (if unknown) number of active drug dealers who are not themselves addicted.

Thus, though we cannot quantify these proportions with any precision, the basic point should be clear: the pool of *serious* addicts and active dealers is far, far larger than the numbers we now hold in prison—even in the midst of an unprecedented incarceration binge that has made us far and away the world's leader in imprisonment rates.

What would it mean to expand our prison capacity enough to put 10 the *majority* of hard-core users and dealers behind bars for long terms? To triple the number of users and low-level dealers behind bars, even putting two drug offenders to a cell, would require about 300,000 new cells. At a conservative estimate of about $100,000 per cell, that means a $30 billion investment in construction alone. If we then assume an equally conservative estimate of about $25,000 in yearly operating costs per inmate, we add roughly $15 billion a year to our current costs. Yet this would leave the majority of drug dealers and hard-core addicts still on the streets and, of course, would do nothing to prevent new ones from emerging in otherwise unchanged communities to take the place of those behind bars.

It is not entirely clear, moreover, what that huge expenditure would, in fact, accomplish. For if the goal is to prevent the drug dealing and other crimes that addicts commit, the remedy may literally cost more than the disease. Although drug addicts do commit a great deal of crime, most of them are very minor ones, mainly petty theft and small-time drug dealing. This pattern has been best illuminated in the study of Harlem heroin addicts by Bruce Johnson and his co-workers. Most of the street addicts in this study were "primarily thieves and small-scale drug distributors who avoided serious crimes, like robbery, burglary, assault." The average income per nondrug crime among these addicts was $35. Even among the most criminally active group—what these researchers called "robber-dealers"—the annual income from crime amounted on average to only about $21,000, and for the great majority—about 70 percent—of less active addict-criminals, it ranged from $5,000 to $13,000. At the same time, the researchers estimated that the average cost per day of confining one addict in a New York City jail cell was roughly $100, or $37,000 a year. Putting these numbers together, Johnson and his co-workers came to the startling conclusion that it would cost considerably more to lock up all of Harlem's street addicts than to simply let them continue to "take care of business" on the street.

If we cannot expect much from intensified criminalization, would the legalization of hard drugs solve the drug crisis?

No: it would not. To understand why, we need to consider the claims for legalization's effects in the light of what we know about the roots and meanings of endemic drug abuse. First, however, we need to step back in order to sort out exactly what we *mean* by "legalization"—a frustratingly vague and often confused term that means very different things to different interpreters. Many, indeed, who argue most vehemently one way or the other about the merits of legalization are not really clear just what it is they are arguing *about.*

At one end of the spectrum are those who mean by legalization the total deregulation of the production, sale, and use of all drugs—hard and soft. Advocates of this position run the gamut from right-wing economists to some staunch liberals, united behind the principle that government has no business interfering in individuals' choice to ingest whatever substances they desire. Most who subscribe to that general view would add several qualifiers: for example, that drugs (like alcohol) should not be sold to minors, or that drug advertising should be regulated or prohibited, or (less often) that drugs should be sold only in government-run stores, as alcohol is in some states. But these are seen as necessary, if sometimes grudging, exceptions to the general rule that private drug transactions should not be the province of government intervention. For present purposes, I will call this the "free-market" approach to drug control, and describe its central aim as the "deregulation" of the drug market.

Another approach would not go so far as to deregulate the drug 15 trade, but would opt for the controlled dispensation of drugs to addicts who have been certified by a physician, under strict guidelines as to amounts and conditions of use. Something like this "medical model," in varying forms, guided British policy toward heroin after the 1920s. Under the so-called British system, addicts could receive heroin from physicians or clinics—but the private production and distribution of heroin was always subject to strong penalties, as was the use of the drug except in its medical or "pharmaceutical" form. (A small-scale experiment in cocaine prescription is presently being tried in the city of Liverpool.) Since the seventies, the British have largely abandoned prescribing heroin in favor of methadone—a synthetic opiate that blocks the body's craving for heroin but, among other things, produces less of a pleasurable "high" and lasts considerably longer. The practice of dispensing methadone to heroin addicts came into wide use in the United States in the 1960s and remains a major form of treatment. Methadone prescription, of course, does not "legalize" heroin, and the possession or sale of methadone itself is highly illegal outside of the strictly controlled medical relationship.

Still another meaning sometimes given to legalization is what is more accurately called the "decriminalization" of drug *use*. We may continue to define the production and sale of certain drugs as crimes and subject them to heavy penalties, but not punish those who only *use* the drugs (or have small amounts in their possession), or punish them very lightly—with small fines, for example, rather than jail. Something close to this is the practice in Holland, which is often wrongly perceived as a country that has legalized drugs. Though drug use remains technically illegal, Dutch policy is to focus most law-enforcement resources on sales, especially on larger traffickers, while dealing with users mainly through treatment programs and other social services, rather than the police and courts.

Another aspect of Dutch policy illustrates a further possible meaning of legalization: we may selectively decriminalize *some* drugs, in some amounts, and not others. The Dutch, in practice—though not in law—have tolerated both sale and use of small amounts of marijuana and hashish, but not heroin or cocaine. A German court has recently ruled that possession of small amounts of hashish and marijuana is not a crime, and, indeed, marijuana possession has largely been decriminalized in some American states, though usually as a matter of practical policy rather than legislation.

Let me make my own view clear. I think much would be gained if we followed the example of some European countries and moved toward decriminalization of the drug user. I also think there is a strong argument for treating marijuana differently from the harder drugs, and that there is room for careful experiment with strictly controlled medical prescription for some addicts. For reasons that will become clear, decriminalization is not a panacea; it will not end the drug crisis, but it could substantially decrease the irrationality and inhumanity of our present punitive war on drugs.

The free-market approach, on the other hand, is another matter entirely. Some variant of that approach is more prominent in drug-policy debates in the United States than in other developed societies, probably because it meshes with a strongly individualistic and antigovernment political culture. Indeed, the degree to which the debate over drug policy has been dominated by the clash between fervent drug "warriors" and equally ardent free-market advocates is a peculiarly American phenomenon. Much of that clash is about philosophical principles, and addressing those issues in detail would take more space than we have. My aim here is simply to examine the empirical claims of the free-market perspective in the light of what we know about the social context of drug abuse.

Here the free-market view fails to convince. It greatly exaggerates the benefits of deregulation while simultaneously underestimating the potential costs.

There is no question that the criminalization of drugs produces nega- 20 tive secondary consequences—especially in the unusually punitive form that criminalization has taken in the United States. Nor is there much question that this argues for a root-and-branch rethinking of our current punitive strategy—to which we'll return later in this essay—especially our approach to drug *users.*

But proponents of full-scale deregulation of hard drugs also tend to gloss over the very real primary costs of drug abuse—particularly on the American level—and to exaggerate the degree to which the multiple pathologies surrounding drug use in America are simply an unintended result of a "prohibitionist" regulatory policy. No country now legalizes the sale of hard drugs. Yet no other country has anything resembling the American drug problem. That alone should tell us that more than prohibition is involved in shaping the magnitude and severity of our drug crisis. But there is more technical evidence as well. It confirms that much (though, of course, not all) of the harm caused by endemic drug abuse is intrinsic to the impact of hard drugs themselves (and the street cultures in which drug abuse is embedded) within the context of a glaringly unequal, depriving, and deteriorating society. And it affirms that we will not substantially reduce that harm without attacking the social roots of the extraordinary demand for hard drugs in the United States. Just as we cannot punish our way out of the drug crisis, neither will we escape its grim toll by deregulating the drug market.

The most important argument for a free-market approach has traditionally been that it would reduce or eliminate the crime and violence now inextricably entwined with addiction to drugs and with the drug trade. In this view it is precisely the illegality of drug use that is responsible for drug-related crime—which, in turn, is seen as by far the largest part of the overall problem of urban violence. Criminal sanctions against drugs, as one observer insists, "cause the bulk of murders and property crime in major urban areas." Because criminalization makes drugs far more costly than they would otherwise be, addicts are forced to commit crimes in order to gain enough income to afford their habits. Moreover, they are forced to seek out actively criminal people in order to obtain their drugs, which exposes them to even more destructive criminal influences. At the same time, the fact that the drug trade is illegal means both that it is hugely profitable and that the inevitable conflicts and disputes over "turf" or between dealers and users cannot be resolved or moderated by legal mechanisms, and hence are usually resolved by violence.

For all of these reasons, it is argued, outlawing drugs has the unintended, but inevitable, effect of causing a flood of crime and urban violence that would not exist otherwise and sucking young people, especially, into a bloody drug trade. If we legalize the sale and use of hard drugs, the roots of drug-related violence would be severed, and much of the larger crisis of criminal violence in the cities would disappear.

But the evidence suggests that although this view contains an element of truth, it is far too simplistic—and that it relies on stereotypical assumptions about the relationship between drugs and crime that have been called into serious question since the classic drug research of the 1950s. In particular, the widely held notion that most of the crime committed by addicts can be explained by their need for money to buy illegal drugs does not fit well with the evidence.

In its popular form, the drugs-cause-crime argument is implicitly 25 based on the assumption that addict crime is caused by pharmacological compulsion—as a recent British study puts it, on a kind of "enslavement" model in which the uncontrollable craving for drugs forces an otherwise law-abiding citizen to engage in crime for gain. As we've seen, however, a key finding of most of the research into the meaning of drug use and the growth of drug subcultures since the 1950s has been that the purely pharmacological craving for drugs is by no means the most important motive for drug use. Nor is it clear that those cravings are typically so uncontrollable that addicts are in any meaningful sense "driven" to crime to satisfy them.

On the surface, there is much to suggest a strong link between crime and the imperatives of addiction. The studies of addict crime by John Ball and Douglas Anglin and their colleagues show not only that the most heavily addicted commit huge numbers of crimes, but also that their crime rates seem to increase when their heroin use increases and to fall when it declines. Thus, for example, heroin addicts in Ball's study in Baltimore had an average of 255 "crime days" per year when they were actively addicted, versus about 65 when they were not. In general, the level of property crime appears in these studies to go up simultaneously with increasing intensity of drug use. One explanation, and perhaps the most common one, is that the increased need for money to buy drugs drives addicts into more crime.

But a closer look shows that things are considerably more complicated. To begin with, it is a recurrent finding that most people who both abuse drugs and commit crimes began committing the crimes *before* they began using drugs—meaning that their need for drugs cannot have caused their initial criminal involvement (though it may have accelerated it later). George Vaillant's follow-up study of addicts and alcoholics found, for example, that, unlike alcoholics, heroin addicts had typically been involved in delinquency and crime well before they began their career of substance abuse. While alcoholics seemed to become involved in crime as a *result* of their abuse of alcohol, more than half of the heroin addicts (versus just 5 percent of the alcoholics) "were known to have been delinquent *before* drug abuse." A federal survey of drug use among prison inmates in 1986, similarly, found that three-fifths of those who had ever used a "major drug" regularly—that is, heroin, cocaine, methadone, PCP, or LSD—had not done so until after their first arrest.

Other studies have found that for many addicts, drug use and crime seem to have begun more or less *independently* without one clearly causing the other. This was the finding, for example, in Charles Faupel and Carl Klockars's study of hard-core heroin addicts in Wilmington, Delaware. "All of our respondents," they note, "reported some criminal activity prior to their first use of heroin." Moreover, "perhaps most importantly, virtually all of our respondents reported that they believed that their criminal and drug careers began independently of one another, although both careers became intimately interconnected as each evolved."

More recent research shows that the drugs-crime relationship may be even more complex than this suggests. It is not only that crime may precede drug use, especially heavy or addictive use, or that both may emerge more or less independently; it is also likely that there are several *different* kinds of drugs-crime connections among different types of drug users. David Nurco of the University of Maryland and his colleagues, for example, studying heroin addicts in Baltimore and New York City, found that nine different kinds of addicts could be distinguished by the type and severity of their crimes. Like earlier researchers, they found that most addicts committed large numbers of crimes—mainly drug dealing and small-scale property crime, notably shoplifting, burglary, and fencing. Others were involved in illegal gambling and what the researchers called "deception crimes"—including forgery and con games—and a relatively small percentage had engaged in violent crime. On the whole, addicts heavily involved in one type of crime were not likely to be involved in others; as the researchers put it, they tended to be either "dealers or stealers," but rarely both. About 6 percent of the addicts, moreover, were "uninvolved"—they did not commit crimes either while addicted or before, or during periods of nonaddiction interspersed in the course of their longer addiction careers.

The most troubling group of addicts—what the researchers called 30 "violent generalists"—were only about 7 percent of the total sample, but they were extremely active—and very dangerous; they accounted for over half of all the violent crimes committed by the entire sample. Moreover, revealingly, the violent generalists were very active in serious crime *before* they became addicted to narcotics as well as during periods of nonaddiction thereafter—again demonstrating that the violence was not dependent on their addiction itself. Nurco and his colleagues measured the addicts' criminal activity by what they called "crime days" per year. Addicts were asked how many days they had committed each of several types of crime; since on any given day they might have committed more than one type of crime, the resulting figure could add up to more than the number of days in the year. The violent generalists averaged an astonishing 900 crime days a year over the course of their careers. The rates were highest during periods when they were heavily addicted to drugs. But even *before* they were addicted, they averaged 573 crime days, and 491 after their addiction had ended. Indeed, the most active group of violent generalists engaged in more crime *prior* to addiction than any other group did *while* addicted. And they continued to commit crimes—often violent ones—long after they had ceased to be addicted to narcotics.

None of this is to deny that serious addiction to heroin or other illegal drugs can accelerate the level of crime among participants in the drug culture, or stimulate crime even in some users who are otherwise not criminal. Higher levels of drug use *do* go hand in hand with increased crime, especially property crime. Certainly, many addicts mug, steal, or sell their bodies for drugs. The point is that—as the early drug researchers discovered in the 1950s—both crime and drug abuse tend to be spawned by the same set of unfavorable social circumstances, and they interact with one another in much more complex ways than the simple addiction-leads-to-crime view proposes. Simply providing drugs more easily to people enmeshed in the drug cultures of the cities is not likely to cut the deep social roots of addict crime.

If we take the harms of drug abuse seriously, and I think we must, we cannot avoid being deeply concerned about anything that would significantly increase the availability of hard drugs within the American social context; and no one seriously doubts that legalization would indeed increase availability, and probably lower prices for many drugs. In turn, increased availability—as we know from the experience with alcohol—typically leads to increased consumption, and with it increased social and public-health costs. A growing body of research, for example, shows that most alcohol-related health problems, including deaths from cirrhosis and other diseases, were far lower during Prohibition than afterward, when per capita alcohol consumption rose dramatically (by about 75 percent, for example, between 1950 and 1980). It is difficult to imagine why a similar rise in consumption—and in the associated public-health problems—would not follow the full-scale legalization of cocaine, heroin, methamphetamine, and PCP (not to mention the array of as yet undiscovered "designer" drugs that a legalized corporate drug industry would be certain to develop).

If consumption increased, it would almost certainly increase most among the strata already most vulnerable to hard-drug use—thus exacerbating the social stratification of the drug crisis. It is among the poor and near-poor that offsetting measures like education and drug treatment are least effective and where the countervailing social supports and opportunities are least strong. We would expect, therefore, that a free-market policy applied to hard drugs would produce the same results it has created with the *legal* killer drugs, tobacco and alcohol—namely, a widening disparity in use between the better-off and the disadvantaged. And that disparity is already stunning. According to a recent study by Colin McCord and Howard Freeman of Harlem Hospital, between 1979 and 1981—that is, *before* the crack epidemic of the eighties—Harlem blacks were 283 times as likely to die of drug dependency as whites in the general population. Drug deaths, combined with deaths from cirrhosis, alcoholism, cardiovascular disease, and homicide, helped to give black men in Harlem a shorter life expectancy than men in Bangladesh. This is the social reality that the rather abstract calls for the legalization of hard-drug sales tend to ignore.

Topics for Critical Thinking and Writing

1. Currie claims that "drugs will always be a 'law-enforcement problem'" (para. 1). Why do you think he believes this? Is the evidence he offers adequate to support this troubling judgment?

2. Currie mentions what he regards as "small but significant ways" (para. 2) to reduce the place of drugs in our lives. What are they? Why do you think he doesn't mention (a) curbing the manufacture of illegal addictive drugs, (b) vigorously reducing imports of illegal addictive drugs into the United States, and (c) aggressively educating the public on the harm that illegal addictive drugs cause their users?

3. Why does Currie think that "escalating the war on drugs," with its reliance on "incapacitation" and "deterrence," is doomed to ineffectiveness (para. 6)? Are you persuaded? Explain.

4. Currie eventually states his own views (para. 18). Do you think the essay would have been more effective if he had stated his views in his opening paragraph? Why, or why not?

5. Currie stresses the uniqueness of the drug problem in the United States. What do you think explains "the magnitude and severity of our drug crisis" (para. 21)? Farmers in other countries produce more illegal addictive drugs than ours do. Other countries have graver problems of poverty than we do. Gross manifest disparities between rich and poor are not unique to the United States. So what's the explanation? Does Currie tell us?

6. Why does Currie reject the drugs-cause-crime argument (para. 24)?

> For topical links related to the discussion of the legalization of drugs, see the companion Web site: **bedfordstmartins.com/barnetbedau**.

22

Junk Food: Should the Government Regulate Our Intake?

In the summer of 2012 Mayor Michael R. Bloomberg of New York City made a proposal to severely restrict the sale of certain kinds of drinks. In September 2012 it was approved by the New York City Board of Health and scheduled to go into effect in 2013. Here is the gist of Bloomberg's thinking:

> Sugary drinks—here defined as those with twenty-five or more calories per eight-ounce serving—if consumed in large quantities unquestionably contribute to obesity. It is therefore desirable to discourage the consumption of large amounts of these drinks.
>
> Ban the sale—in delis, fast-food franchises, and street stands—of bottles containing more than sixteen fluid ounces of such drinks.
>
> Larger bottles would be available at grocery stores and convenience stores.
>
> Other kinds of drinks, such as fruit drinks, diet sodas, dairy-based drinks (e.g., milk shakes), and alcoholic beverages would not be restricted.

In short, this proposal was a ban only on selling large containers of certain kinds of drinks in certain kinds of places. And even in the restricted places, consumers could buy any number of the smaller bottles, so the determined consumer could indeed get more than sixteen ounces if he or she wanted to, though at the cost of some inconvenience.

On March 11, 2013, the day before the law was to go into effect, Justice Milton A. Tingling Jr. of the New York State Supreme Court struck down the ban, saying that it was "arbitrary and capricious." Examples of the alleged arbitrariness were (1) the ban did *not* apply to dairy-based sugary drinks such as milk shakes and (2) it would be enforced in restaurants, delicatessens, theaters, and food-carts but not in convenience stores and bodegas. Do these examples strike you as "arbitrary"?

Anonymous Editorial, *New York Times*

This editorial was published on June 1, 2012. We follow it with two letters, both published on June 2, 2012.

A Ban Too Far

Mayor Michael Bloomberg has done a lot to help improve the health of New York City residents. Smoking is outlawed in workplaces, restaurants, and bars. Trans fat is banned in restaurants. Chain restaurants are required to post calorie counts, allowing customers to make informed choices.

Mr. Bloomberg, however, is overreaching with his new plan to ban the sale of sugary drinks larger than sixteen ounces. He argues that prohibiting big drinks at restaurants, movie theaters, stadiums, and other food sellers can help combat obesity. But as he admits, customers can get around the ban by purchasing two drinks.

The administration should be focusing its energies on programs that educate and encourage people to make sound choices. For example, obesity rates have declined slightly among students in elementary and middle schools, with the city's initiatives to make lunches healthier with salad bars, lower-calorie drinks, and water fountains in cafeterias. Requiring students to get more exercise has also helped.

The city should keep up its tough anti-obesity advertising campaigns — one ad shows that it takes walking from Union Square to Brooklyn to burn off the calories from a twenty-ounce soda. The mayor has also started adult exercise programs and expanded the program for more fresh produce vendors around the city.

Promoting healthy lifestyles is important. In the case of sugary 5 drinks, a regular reminder that a sixty-four-ounce cola has 780 calories should help. But too much nannying with a ban might well cause people to tune out.

Letters of Response by Gary Taustine and Brian Elbel

To the Editor:
Mayor Michael R. Bloomberg's effort to promote healthier lifestyles is commendable, but the government has no right whatsoever to go beyond promotion to enforcement. You can't reduce obesity with smaller cups any more than you can reduce gun violence with smaller bullets.

This proposal sets a very bad, very dangerous precedent. Freedom is rarely taken away in supersize amounts; more typically it is slowly siphoned off drop by drop so people don't even notice until they've lost it entirely.

Mayor Bloomberg has spent his eleven years in office stripping away our freedoms one drop at a time. Minorities are stopped and frisked, Muslims are watched, protesters are silenced, and smokers are taxed and harassed beyond reason.

In their apathy, New Yorkers have given the mayor an inch and he has already taken a mile. If we permit him to regulate portion control without a fight, then we don't deserve the few freedoms we have left.

GARY TAUSTINE
New York, June 1, 2012

To the Editor:

Re "A Ban Too Far" (editorial, June 1):

To focus on education when discussing solutions to obesity misunderstands the scientific evidence about what can alter our staggering statistics and what manifestly cannot.

Mayor Michael R. Bloomberg's proposal to restrict the sale of large sugar-sweetened beverages changes the food environment—the places where foods and beverages are bought. The best science affirms that this is exactly the approach that could curb obesity trends. This same science indicates that education-based approaches, which also have their place, will do much less by comparison.

That sugary beverages contribute to obesity is clear. The science also tells us that changing the default beverage choice to something smaller could induce people to consume just that smaller beverage rather than deal with the cost and hassle of buying and carrying two or more.

Time and further research will tell. But the continued focus on simply informing and educating consumers is doomed to failure and diminishes this important policy and the influence it could have on obesity.

BRIAN ELBEL
New York, June 1, 2012

The writer is an assistant professor of population health and health policy at the New York University School of Medicine.

TOPIC FOR CRITICAL THINKING AND WRITING

Draft a letter to the newspaper expressing your support or disapproval—full or in part—of the position taken in the editorial. In your letter you may, if you wish, include a comment about either or both of the published letters of response.

ANALYZING A VISUAL: THE NANNY STATE

Topics for Critical Thinking and Writing

1. Is the ad, showing Mayor Bloomberg as a nanny, funny? Why, or why not? Might anyone, apart perhaps from the mayor, find the ad offensive? Why, or why not?

2. Is the ad truthful in saying that the mayor "wants to make it illegal to serve 'sugary drinks' bigger than 16 oz."?

Daniel E. Lieberman

Daniel E. Lieberman, a professor of human evolutionary biology at Harvard, is the author of The Evolution of the Human Head *(2011). His chief academic interest is why the human body looks the way it does—why, for instance, we have short necks and why we do not have snouts. We reprint an op-ed piece that he published in the* New York Times *on June 6, 2012.*

Evolution's Sweet Tooth

Of all the indignant responses to Mayor Michael R. Bloomberg's plan to ban the sale of giant servings of soft drinks in New York City, libertarian objections seem the most worthy of serious attention. People have certain rights, this argument goes, including the right to drink lots of soda, to eat junk food, to gain weight, and to avoid exercise. If Mr. Bloomberg can ban the sale of sugar-laden soda of more than sixteen ounces, will he next ban triple scoops of ice cream and large portions of French fries and limit sales of Big Macs to one per order? Why not ban obesity itself?

The obesity epidemic has many dimensions, but at heart it's a biological problem. An evolutionary perspective helps explain why two-thirds of American adults are overweight or obese, and what to do about it. Lessons from evolutionary biology support the mayor's plan: when it comes to limiting sugar in our food, some kinds of coercive action are not only necessary but also consistent with how we used to live.

Obesity's fundamental cause is long-term energy imbalance—ingesting more calories than you spend over weeks, months, and years. Of the many contributors to energy imbalance today, plentiful sugar may be the worst.

Since sugar is a basic form of energy in food, a sweet tooth was adaptive in ancient times, when food was limited. However, excessive sugar in the bloodstream is toxic, so our bodies also evolved to rapidly convert digested sugar in the bloodstream into fat. Our hunter-gatherer ancestors needed plenty of fat—more than other primates—to be active during periods of food scarcity and still pay for large, expensive brains and costly reproductive strategies (hunter-gatherer mothers could pump out babies twice as fast as their chimpanzee cousins).

Simply put, humans evolved to crave sugar, store it, and then use it. ₅ For millions of years, our cravings and digestive systems were exquisitely balanced because sugar was rare. Apart from honey, most of the foods our hunter-gatherer ancestors ate were no sweeter than a carrot. The invention of farming made starchy foods more abundant, but it wasn't until very recently that technology made pure sugar bountiful.

The food industry has made a fortune because we retain Stone Age bodies that crave sugar but live in a Space Age world in which sugar is cheap and plentiful. Sip by sip and nibble by nibble, more of us gain weight because we can't control normal, deeply rooted urges for a valuable, tasty, and once limited resource.

What should we do? One option is to do nothing, while hoping that scientists find better cures for obesity-related diseases like heart disease and Type 2 diabetes. I'm not holding my breath for such cures, and the costs of inaction, already staggering, would continue to mushroom.

A more popular option is to enhance public education to help us make better decisions about what to eat and how to be active. This is crucial but has so far yielded only modest improvements.

The final option is to collectively restore our diets to a more natural state through regulations. Until recently, all humans had no choice but to eat a healthy diet with modest portions of food that were low in sugar, saturated fat, and salt, but high in fiber. They also had no choice but to walk and sometimes run an average of five to ten miles a day. Mr. Bloomberg's paternalistic plan is not an aberrant form of coercion but a very small step toward restoring a natural part of our environment.

Though his big-soda ban would apply to all New Yorkers, I think we 10 should focus paternalistic laws on children. Youngsters can't make rational, informed decisions about their bodies, and our society agrees that parents don't have the right to make disastrous decisions on their behalf. Accordingly, we require parents to enroll their children in school, have them immunized, and make them wear seat belts. We require physical education in school, and we don't let children buy alcohol or cigarettes. If these are acceptable forms of coercion, how is restricting unhealthy doses of sugary drinks that slowly contribute to disease any different?

Along these lines, we should ban all unhealthy food in school—soda, pizza, French fries—and insist that schools provide adequate daily physical education, which many fail to do.

Adults need help, too, and we should do more to regulate companies that exploit our deeply rooted appetites for sugar and other unhealthy foods. The mayor was right to ban trans fats, but we should also make the food industry honest about portion sizes. Like cigarettes, mass-marketed junk food should come with prominent health warning labels. It should be illegal to advertise highly fattening food as "fat free." People have the right to be unhealthy, but we should make that choice more onerous and expensive by imposing taxes on soda and junk food.

We humans did not evolve to eat healthily and go to the gym; until recently, we didn't have to make such choices. But we did evolve to cooperate to help one another survive and thrive. Circumstances have changed, but we still need one another's help as much as we ever did.

For this reason, we need government on our side, not on the side of those who wish to make money by stoking our cravings and profiting from them. We have evolved to need coercion.

TOPICS FOR CRITICAL THINKING AND WRITING

1. On May 30, 2012, the *New York Times* quoted Stefan Friedman, a spokesman for the New York City Beverage Association, as saying — with implicit reference to the Bloomberg proposal:

   > The New York City Health Department's unhealthy obsession with attacking soft drinks is again pushing them over the top. . . . It's time for serious health professionals to move on and seek solutions that are going to actually curb obesity. These zealous proposals just distract from the hard work that needs to be done on this front.

   You have just read an essay by a professor of biology. Do you think he would agree with Friedman? Why, or why not?

2. Perhaps the chief argument in favor of limiting the food we can buy and consume, particularly when it harms us, comes down to this: "Your right to harm yourself stops when I have to pay for it." What responses, if any, can you offer to this view?

3. Evaluate Lieberman's opening paragraph. Do you think it is an effective piece of argument? Why or why not?

4. Lieberman's essay ends, "We have evolved to need coercion." Is he in effect saying, "Yes, we need a nanny," i.e., the very view that the political ad on page 584 ridicules?

Mark Bittman

Mark Bittman, a food columnist for the New York Times *and the author of several books about food and cooking, has appeared on numerous TV programs, including a series called* Kitchen Express. *We reprint an essay first published in the* New York Times, *July 24, 2011 — almost a year before the Bloomberg proposal.*

Bad Food? Tax It, and Subsidize Vegetables

What will it take to get Americans to change our eating habits? The need is indisputable, since heart disease, diabetes, and cancer are all in large part caused by the Standard American Diet. (Yes, it's SAD.)

Though experts increasingly recommend a diet high in plants and low in animal products and processed foods, ours is quite the opposite, and there's little disagreement that changing it could improve our health and save tens of millions of lives.

And — not inconsequential during the current struggle over deficits and spending — a sane diet could save tens if not hundreds of billions of dollars in health care costs.

Yet the food industry appears incapable of marketing healthier foods. And whether its leaders are confused or just stalling doesn't matter, because the fixes are not really their problem. Their mission is not public health but profit, so they'll continue to sell the health-damaging food that's most profitable, until the market or another force skews things otherwise. That "other force" should be the federal government, fulfilling its role as an agent of the public good and establishing a bold national fix.

Rather than subsidizing the production of unhealthful foods, we   5 should turn the tables and tax things like soda, French fries, doughnuts, and hyperprocessed snacks. The resulting income should be earmarked for a program that encourages a sound diet for Americans by making healthy food more affordable and widely available.

The average American consumes 44.7 gallons of soft drinks annually. (Although that includes diet sodas, it does not include noncarbonated sweetened beverages, which add up to at least seventeen gallons a person per year.) Sweetened drinks could be taxed at two cents per ounce, so a six-pack of Pepsi would cost $1.44 more than it does now. An equivalent tax on fries might be fifty cents per serving; a quarter extra for a doughnut. (We have experts who can figure out how "bad" a food should be to qualify, and what the rate should be; right now they're busy calculating ethanol subsidies. Diet sodas would not be taxed.)

Simply put: taxes would reduce consumption of unhealthful foods and generate billions of dollars annually. That money could be used to subsidize the purchase of staple foods like seasonal greens, vegetables, whole grains, dried legumes, and fruit.

We could sell those staples cheap—let's say for fifty cents a pound— and almost everywhere: drugstores, street corners, convenience stores, bodegas, supermarkets, liquor stores, even schools, libraries, and other community centers.

This program would, of course, upset the processed food industry. Oh well. It would also bug those who might resent paying more for soda and chips and argue that their right to eat whatever they wanted was being breached. But public health is the role of the government, and our diet is right up there with any other public responsibility you can name, from water treatment to mass transit.

Some advocates for the poor say taxes like these are unfair because   10 low-income people pay a higher percentage of their income for food and would find it more difficult to buy soda or junk. But since poor people suffer disproportionately from the cost of high-quality, fresh foods, subsidizing those foods would be particularly beneficial to them.

Right now it's harder for many people to buy fruit than Froot Loops; chips and Coke are a common breakfast. And since the rate of diabetes continues to soar—one-third of all Americans either have diabetes or are prediabetic, most with Type 2 diabetes, the kind associated with bad eating habits—and because our health care bills are on the verge of becoming truly insurmountable, this is urgent for economic sanity as well as national health.

JUSTIFYING A TAX

At least thirty cities and states have considered taxes on soda or all sugar-sweetened beverages, and they're a logical target: of the 278 additional calories Americans on average consumed per day between 1977 and 2001, more than 40 percent came from soda, "fruit" drinks, mixes like Kool-Aid and Crystal Light, and beverages like Red Bull, Gatorade, and dubious offerings like Vitamin Water, which contains half as much sugar as Coke.

Some states already have taxes on soda—mostly low, ineffective sales taxes paid at the register. The current talk is of excise taxes, levied before purchase.

"Excise taxes have the benefit of being incorporated into the shelf price, and that's where consumers make their purchasing decisions," says Lisa Powell, a senior research scientist at the Institute for Health Research and Policy at the University of Illinois at Chicago. "And, as per-unit taxes, they avoid volume discounts and are ultimately more effective in raising prices, so they have greater impact."

Much of the research on beverage taxes comes from the Rudd Center for Food Policy and Obesity at Yale. Its projections indicate that taxes become significant at the equivalent of about a penny an ounce, a level at which three very good things should begin to happen: the consumption of sugar-sweetened beverages should decrease, as should the incidence of disease and therefore public health costs; and money could be raised for other uses.   15

Even in the current antitax climate, we'll probably see new, significant soda taxes soon, somewhere; Philadelphia, New York (city and state), and San Francisco all considered them last year, and the scenario for such a tax spreading could be similar to that of legalized gambling: once the income stream becomes apparent, it will seem irresistible to cash-strapped governments.

Currently, instead of taxing sodas and other unhealthful food, we subsidize them (with, I might note, tax dollars!). Direct subsidies to farmers for crops like corn (used, for example, to make now-ubiquitous high-fructose corn syrup) and soybeans (vegetable oil) keep the prices of many unhealthful foods and beverages artificially low. There are indirect subsidies as well, because prices of junk foods don't reflect the costs of repairing our health and the environment.

Other countries are considering or have already started programs to tax foods with negative effects on health. Denmark's saturated-fat tax is going into effect Oct. 1, and Romania passed (and then unpassed) something similar; earlier this month, a French minister raised the idea of tripling the value-added tax on soda. Meanwhile, Hungary is proposing a new tax on foods with "too much" sugar, salt, or fat, while increasing taxes on liquor and soft drinks, all to pay for state-financed health care; and Brazil's Fome Zero (Zero Hunger) program features subsidized produce markets and state-sponsored low-cost restaurants.

Putting all of those elements together could create a national program that would make progress on a half-dozen problems at once—disease, budget, health care, environment, food access, and more—while paying for itself. The benefits are staggering, and though it would take a level of political will that's rarely seen, it's hardly a moonshot.

The need is dire: efforts to shift the national diet have failed, because 20 education alone is no match for marketing dollars that push the very foods that are the worst for us. (The fast-food industry alone spent more than $4 billion on marketing in 2009; the Department of Agriculture's Center for Nutrition Policy and Promotion is asking for about a third of a percent of that in 2012: $13 million.) As a result, the percentage of obese adults has more than doubled over the last thirty years; the percentage of obese children has tripled. We eat nearly 10 percent more animal products than we did a generation or two ago, and though there may be value in eating at least some animal products, we could perhaps live with reduced consumption of triple bacon cheeseburgers.

GOVERNMENT AND PUBLIC HEALTH

Health-related obesity costs are projected to reach $344 billion by 2018—with roughly 60 percent of that cost borne by the federal government. For a precedent in attacking this problem, look at the action government took in the case of tobacco.

The historic 1998 tobacco settlement, in which the states settled health-related lawsuits against tobacco companies, and the companies agreed to curtail marketing and finance antismoking efforts, was far from perfect, but consider the results. More than half of all Americans who once smoked have quit and smoking rates are about half of what they were in the 1960s.

It's true that you don't need to smoke and you do need to eat. But you don't need sugary beverages (or the associated fries), which have been linked not only to Type 2 diabetes and increased obesity but also to cardiovascular diseases and decreased intake of valuable nutrients like calcium. It also appears that liquid calories provide less feeling of fullness; in other words, when you drink a soda it's probably in addition to your other calorie intake, not instead of it.

To counter arguments about their nutritional worthlessness, expect to see "fortified" sodas—à la Red Bull, whose vitamins allegedly "support mental and physical performance"—and "improved" junk foods (Less Sugar! Higher Fiber!). Indeed, there may be reasons to make nutritionally worthless foods less so, but it's better to decrease their consumption.

Forcing sales of junk food down through taxes isn't ideal. First off, 25 we'll have to listen to nanny-state arguments, which can be countered by the acceptance of the antitobacco movement as well as a dozen other successful public health measures. Then there are the predictions of job loss at soda distributorships, but the same predictions were made about the tobacco industry, and those were wrong. (For that matter, the same predictions were made around the nickel deposit on bottles, which most shoppers don't even notice.) Ultimately, however, both consumers and government will be more than reimbursed in the form of cheaper healthy staples, lowered health care costs, and better health. And that's a big deal.

THE RESULTING BENEFITS

A study by Y. Claire Wang, an assistant professor at Columbia's Mailman School of Public Health, predicted that a penny tax per ounce on sugar-sweetened beverages in New York State would save $3 billion in health care costs over the course of a decade, prevent something like 37,000 cases of diabetes, and bring in $1 billion annually. Another study shows that a two-cent tax per ounce in Illinois would reduce obesity in youth by 18 percent, save nearly $350 million, and bring in over $800 million in taxes annually.

Scaled nationally, as it should be, the projected benefits are even more impressive; one study suggests that a national penny-per-ounce tax on sugar-sweetened beverages would generate at least $13 billion a year in income while cutting consumption by 24 percent. And those numbers would swell dramatically if the tax were extended to more kinds of junk or doubled to two cents an ounce. (The Rudd Center has a nifty revenue calculator online that lets you play with the numbers yourself.)

A 20 percent increase in the price of sugary drinks nationally could result in about a 20 percent decrease in consumption, which in the next decade could prevent 1.5 million Americans from becoming obese and 400,000 cases of diabetes, saving about $30 billion.

It's fun—inspiring, even—to think about implementing a program like this. First off, though the reduced costs of healthy foods obviously benefit the poor most, lower prices across the board keep things simpler and all of us, especially children whose habits are just developing, could use help in eating differently. The program would also bring much-needed encouragement to farmers, including subsidies, if necessary, to grow staples instead of commodity crops.

Other ideas: We could convert refrigerated soda machines to vending machines that dispense grapes and carrots, as has already been done in Japan and Iowa. We could provide recipes, cooking lessons, even cookware for those who can't afford it. Television public-service announcements could promote healthier eating. (Currently, 86 percent of food ads now seen by children are for foods high in sugar, fat, or sodium.)

Money could be returned to communities for local spending on gyms, pools, jogging, and bike trails; and for other activities at food distribution centers; for Meals on Wheels in those towns with a large elderly population, or for Head Start for those with more children; for supermarkets and farmers' markets where needed. And more.

By profiting as a society from the foods that are making us sick and using those funds to make us healthy, the United States would gain the same kind of prestige that we did by attacking smoking. We could institute a national, comprehensive program that would make us a world leader in preventing chronic or "lifestyle" diseases, which for the first time in history kill more people than communicable ones. By doing so, we'd not only repair some of the damage we have caused by first inventing and then exporting the Standard American Diet, we'd also set a new standard for the rest of the world to follow.

TOPICS FOR CRITICAL THINKING AND WRITING

1. In his first paragraph Bittman makes an assertion that he assumes all readers will accept: "The need [to change our eating habits] is indisputable." He gives a *reason* ("heart disease, diabetes, and cancer are all in large part caused by the Standard American Diet"), but is this reason sufficient for you to agree with his assertion that the need to change diet is "indisputable"? Explain.

2. By the end of the third paragraph has Bittman pretty much won you over—or, on the other hand, has he turned you off by his confidence in his own views? Explain.

3. Bittman states his thesis in his fifth paragraph. Would the essay be equally effective—or perhaps better—if on rereading his draft he had deleted his first four paragraphs? Explain.

4. In paragraphs 9–11 Bittman summarizes possible objections to his position, and then gives reasons for rejecting these objections. Do his reasons—his rebuttals—seem adequate to you? Explain.

5. In paragraph 17 Bittman says that we currently subsidize—i.e., use taxpayer dollars to support—"unhealthful food." As a taxpayer, are you outraged that the government subsidizes corn, soybeans, and other crops? Explain.

6. Are you impressed by the argument (paragraph 18) that some other governments "tax foods with negative effects on health"?

7. Are you impressed—persuaded—by the statistics in paragraphs 20–22 and 26–28? Why, or why not?

8. Bittman's final paragraph—indeed his final sentence—mentions the Standard American Diet. Where does he first mention this diet? In terms of organizing his argument, what is he up to?

Letters of Response by Brown et al.

Another nutri-totalitarian heard from. What's next, a telescreen in every room to make sure we're all eating our broccoli?

It's none of this author's business what my diet is. It's not any bureacrat's business. It's not any politician's business.

If anybody in power pretends to dislike "spending federal dollars" on my health care, fine: stop spending them. Get the government out of the health care industry. Repeal Obamacare and privatize all the rest of it. And if I want to eat a candy bar, I'm happy to eat it at the unsubsidized, untaxed market price.

Why do nutri-totalitarians suppose that only vegetables can be objectively relevant to human survival and the good life, but freedom to make our own choices can't be? We are human beings, not slaves to be remade in the image of their Puritan prejudices.

David M. Brown

I spend hundreds of dollars a month buying healthy food for my family. A variety of fruits, vegetables, organic soy milk, you name it. And yet when we go out with friends, my 20-month-old son will only eat french fries off of someone else's plate. Just tonight he completely shunned fresh broccoli, cucumber, rice, even banana. He is not exposed to junk food advertising and he has every opportunity to eat healthy foods.

Unless you burn off every American's taste buds at birth, you are not going to get people to stop eating junk foods. More big-government taxes and subsidies won't change that.

Tony, Chicago

We can start with restricting the type of food people can buy with food stamps. I get sick just watching the type of food that I see being purchased with food stamps. Then I get sicker when I realize the government is then paying for the health care of the same people they are paying to poison themselves.

Are we nuts?

Sally, Greenwich Village

Topics for Critical Thinking and Writing

1. The first letter, by David M. Brown, asks, "What's next, a telescreen in every room to make sure we're all eating our broccoli?" Is this question an example of the slippery slope fallacy (see page 372), and, if so, can the letter therefore be dismissed?

2. Draft a letter of response either to Tony or to Sally, agreeing or disagreeing, in whole or in part.

23

Facebook: How Has Social Networking Changed How We Relate to Others?

Lauren Tarshis

Lauren Tarshis is the editor of two magazines, Storyworks *and* Scope, *both published by Scholastic. She is also the author of two novels. We reprint an essay from* Scope, *a classroom magazine geared to the middle grades, published September 5, 2011.*

Is Facebook Making You Mean?

Anna* did not think she was being mean. Not really.

She was taking a break from her homework, checking her Facebook page. Maya, a girl she knew from her seventh-grade class, had posted a photo of herself from a recent trip to Disney World. She was standing with Mickey Mouse. Dozens of kids had commented on the picture. The first few comments beneath the photo were sweet.

"Cute!"

"OHHHHHHH!!!!!!!!!"

By the third or fourth comment, the tone had changed.   5

"Nice boyfriend!"

"You're dating?"

"I thought it was kind of funny," Anna remembers. "And so many people had written stuff."

So almost without thinking. Anna typed in a comment of her own: "ummmmm. . . . ew?"

Then she moved on, thinking nothing more about Maya and Mickey.   10

The next day, Anna was called to the assistant principal's office. She stood in shock as the guidance counselor showed her a printout of all the comments on Maya's picture.

*Names and identifying details have been changed.

594

Maya had been so distraught over the comments that she stayed home from school that day. Her mom had called the principal. And now every kid who had posted a joking or sarcastic comment was being called to the office one by one.

Anna was completely confused. "It was just two words," she says.

JOKES THAT GO TOO FAR

Rude comments and insensitive jokes have always been part of the middle school (and adult!) world. But experts say that Facebook and other forms of online communication make the problem worse. One of the most important ways in which we communicate with each other is through subtle emotional signals—your best friend's blush when you mention a girl he likes, the flash of anger in your mother's eyes when you say you'll take out the garbage *later*. Over the phone, we can hear a change in a person's tone, or the ominous pause that sends a message to back off. Online communication takes all of these signals away.

"You don't see the impact of what you write," says Beth Yohe, an   15 associate director for the Anti-Defamation League (ADL), which runs antibullying programs around the country.

This goes not only for jokes and snide comments like Anna's, but also for more hostile behavior. Devon, thirteen, says that not long ago, a friend lashed out at her in a Facebook post. "He said that I had spread rumors about him," Devon explains. "I never did. But he wouldn't stop writing it." The posts, written in all capital letters and punctuated by end-less exclamation points, made it seem like he was screaming in her face.

Devon says the boy is a quiet kid, "always really sweet." She points out that lots of kids act differently on Facebook than they do in person. "I guess because I wasn't right there," she says, "he just let it all out."

REACHING ACROSS WALLS

So does this mean that Facebook is all about hurt feelings and wounded egos?

Not at all. The online world has powerful benefits, especially for kids who find it hard to make friends at school. "These kids can find whole communities online where they feel comfortable," says Yohe.

Online, kids will reach across social boundaries—the invisible walls   20 that often separate one group of friends from another. Aaron, twelve, says that his 459 Facebook friends include kids he doesn't talk to much at school. "We get to know each other better on Facebook," he says.

Studies support the idea that Facebook can help kids build positive connections. Researchers at the University of Virginia found that the majority of kids use Facebook to build solid friendships and to spread positive messages. But what about those "ummmmm . . . ews?" and other comments that are hurtful or embarrassing?

Experts say that just as teens have to learn how to manage more demanding schoolwork and greater responsibilities at home, they also need to learn how to behave more sensitively online. The bottom line: Think before you post. That can be difficult to do, considering that you're probably on Facebook while simultaneously doing homework, watching your little sister, and eyeing the finals of *American Idol*. But the words you post, typed with barely a thought, are out in the world forever.

As schools crack down on all forms of negative online behavior, many are taking steps to help kids learn to avoid problems online. Some, for example, offer in school workshops like the ADL's CyberALLY, which Yohe directs.

In the meantime, some kids, like Anna, are learning through experience. The day she was called to the principal's office, she apologized to Maya.

In person.   25

Topics for Critical Thinking and Writing

1. Do you regard the comments that are quoted in the first few paragraphs as mean — or perhaps merely as acceptable attempts to be amusing? That is, do you think Maya may have overreacted? Explain.

2. Do you think Facebook is making *you* mean? Do you say things that you might not say face to face? If the answer is "Yes," is this always a bad thing? A related question: Is Facebook *making* you mean, or merely allowing your mean nature to express itself?

3. The final paragraph consists of only two words. Is this ending effective? Why, or why not?

Steven Levy

Steven Levy, born in 1951, earned his bachelor's degree at Temple University and a master's degree at Pennsylvania State University. Formerly a senior editor at Newsweek, *he now writes for* Wired, *where in 2011 he published the piece that we reprint. Levy's most recent book is* In the Plex: How Google Thinks, Works, and Shapes Our Lives *(2011).*

Facebook Reset

When Facebook first appeared, the issue of "to friend or not to friend" didn't seem worth sweating over. After all, it wasn't like this college-born networking service was central to your life or anything. Only now, for many of us, it pretty much is. And for too many of its half a billion active users, that carelessly assembled cohort known as the friend list has become a monster.

The list is the gateway through which people observe our major life events, casual musings, physical peregrinations, and crop yields on FarmVille. As Facebook engineers add more features, the friend list becomes ever more critical. But because most of us began assembling it with little sense of its eventual importance, we often accepted requests out of impulse, inertia, or obligation. And sometimes we asked others for Facebook friendship out of idle curiosity or a temporary need to see a photo. Or we just clicked the wrong box.

I propose that Facebook grant us a friend-list do-over. Like most people, I desperately need one: At this point, my collection resembles the contents of a house occupied by a hoarder. I make my way past heaps of classmates, overfriendly PR people, and folks whose amusing conversations in hotel bars led to morning-after friend requests. Open a closet and out tumble a Chinese poet, sources from stories I wrote for now-defunct publications, and one of my son's high-school friends with whom he hasn't spoken in years. Trying to find the front door, I trip over the mashup artist Girl Talk, whom I met once in Pittsburgh. Meanwhile, many of my best friends and closest business contacts aren't even in the house.

Here's how we fix it: On a designated day, everybody's friend list is reset to zero. This goes beyond efforts like National Unfriend Day. I'm suggesting Facebook let us wipe the slate totally clean and start over. Then we can refill the coordinates of our respective social graphs only with appropriate people. Facebook would present us with a list of current contacts, allowing us to reinvite those we want to keep with a single click. We could also import contacts from other services — webmail, calendars, social sites — to round out our modified lists. In return, Facebook would agree to let us export our friend list to other services (thus saving the company from what looks to be an inevitable demand for government regulation if it insists on anticompetitive friend-hoarding).

True, the days following the reset might be stressful; some of our 5 requests might not be reciprocated. But we would also get a whole lot of invites from others, many of whom may well be important people in our lives whom we never thought of as Facebook buddies. A reset would also be a bonanza for Facebook, as any remaining nonmembers would be flooded with invites.

To soften the blow of rejection, everyone would have the chance to post a "statement of friending principles" that would provide a rationale for jilting. Mine would explain that my new standards limit my list to people I actually recognize in person, or at least those with whom I've corresponded. (Exceptions for Girl Talk and other rock stars.) I would also sketch out parameters for requesters: If you beat me up in fifth grade, don't expect a good outcome.

If all went well, our friend lists would much more closely reflect those we want to talk to and be poked by. I propose July 4 for the Great

Facebook Mulligan.[1] It's a perfect day to declare independence from the temporary connections that have become eternal social millstones and to link instead to our true compatriots. Everybody in?

TOPICS FOR CRITICAL THINKING AND WRITING

1. In his first paragraph Levy says Facebook has become "central" to our lives. Is it central to your life? Explain.

2. Do you favor Levy's proposal for a "friend-list do-over" (para. 3), a "reset to zero" (para. 4)? Explain.

Jenna Wortham

Jenna Wortham, a graduate of the University of Virginia, is a technology reporter for the New York Times, *where the following essay appeared in 2012.*

It's Not about You, Facebook. It's about Us.

This month, when Facebook filed to go public, its employees cracked open the Champagne. But I had a flashback—a memory of a two-year-old fight with a good friend.

I was upset over some comments he had posted to my Facebook wall, beneath a status update about a particularly cheesy pop song I was obsessed with at the time. We argued in a flurry of instant messages. He insisted that his remarks were made in good humor, while I was sure that he was making fun of me.

Our bickering became so heated that he furiously typed "I hate Facebook!" and signed off.

We eventually got over it, and the absurdity of the flare-up still embarrasses me. Yet this kind of misunderstanding seems all too common. As our social life migrates to the Web, our emotions move online, too. Simple remarks may seem to be loaded with deeper meanings.

I'm the first one to confess my undying love of the Web's rich cul-   5 ture and community, which is deeply embedded in my life. But that feud with a friend forced me to consider that the lens of the Web might be warping my perspective and damaging some important relationships.

And, lately, Facebook has begun creeping ever deeper into the texture of life, rolling out new features and partnerships that help bind it even more tightly to the fabric that keeps us connected. This has alarmed some people, convincing them that it's time to pull the plug and forgo the service altogether.

---

[1]**Mulligan**, in games, a second chance to perform a move. [Editor's note.]

Many of us are ambivalent about our Facebook relationship. Even though we may occasionally feel that we can't live with Facebook, we also haven't been able to figure out how to live without it.

The degree of this codependency may have no parallel. "I can't think of another piece of passive software that has gotten so embedded in the cultural conversation to this extent before," says Sherry Turkle, a professor at the Massachusetts Institute of Technology and author of *Alone Together*. "This company is reshaping how we think about ourselves and define ourselves and our digital selves."

The symbiotic relationship between Facebook and its users came into sharp focus when the company filed for its initial public offering, revealing just how valuable that codependency is. The intimate details uploaded into the site daily have helped create a company that could be worth as much as $100 billion.

Not everyone was comfortable with that revelation, but beneath the 10 backlash, Professor Turkle said, loomed a larger struggle: users coming to terms with the Web's evolution from a free-wheeling Wild West into a mature marketplace where the currency, personal data, will finance and fuel the next generation of products and services.

"It crystallized a set of issues that we will be defining for the next decade—the notion of self, privacy, how we connect, and the price we're willing to pay for it," she said. "We have to decide what boundaries we're going to establish between ourselves, advertisers, and our personal information."

That quandary is not confined to Facebook. Every social media company, like Twitter and Instagram, a mobile photo-sharing application, and Foursquare, a location-based service, will have to introduce a coherent business model—most likely one that will make use of what it knows about the people who have access to and use its service.

In a way, it's a coming-of-age for the first offspring of the social Web, a generation of companies that are outgrowing their scrappy start-up roots and turning their sites into actual businesses.

Will the relationship between Facebook and its users change after the company goes public? It's not clear that the perception of Google shifted after it went public in 2004. But the Web was very different then.

"There wasn't the same personal connection to Google that there is 15 to Facebook," says Susan Etlinger, a research analyst who advises companies on how to use technology.

Google's original functions were less intimate than Facebook's. "Search," she says, "is more obscure than social networking."

By contrast, those who upload their vacation photos, post updates about their weekends, share the songs they're listening to, and "like" their favorite designers and television shows may have a sense of ownership of these materials that doesn't come into the picture with a simple Web search.

"It's a dynamic that is bred by the very nature of social media because users are the sources of the content," said S. Shyam Sundar, codirector of the Media Effects Research Laboratory at Pennsylvania State University, who studies how people interact with social media. "Users feel like they have a sense of agency, like they are shareholders."

Facebook, and those that come after it, will have the tough task of balancing their users' needs with the demands of shareholders. And, as Facebook evolves into a sustainable business, the trick will be making sure that users don't cool on its tactics. That could be devastating to the company's main source of revenue—showing advertisements to its members based on what it knows about them.

But most are skeptical that it will get to that point.   20

"There's a long way to go before that happens," said Andrew Frank, an analyst at Gartner Research. "The size of their user base and the amount of time people spend on the site is so far off the charts."

Even so, Mr. Frank said Facebook might not be impervious to rivals, or at least to more divided attention from people who shift their time to other parts of the Web where intent is easier to understand and the interactions feel less public.

Facebook's current prominence may not last forever. Today, Mr. Frank said, Facebook seems a permanently dominant player on the Web. But, he adds, "There was a time where people thought that way about AOL, too."

TOPICS FOR CRITICAL THINKING AND WRITING

1. In the first four paragraphs Wortham reports an embarrassing episode in which a friend was for a while estranged. Do you think this sort of thing is especially common on Facebook, or, on the other hand, does this sort of thing happen equally on the telephone or even in face-to-face encounters? Explain.

2. In paragraph 8, Wortham quotes Sherry Turkle about Facebook: "This company is reshaping how we think about ourselves and define ourselves and our digital selves." Your view? Explain.

Stephen Marche

Stephen Marche, born in 1976, has written essays, stories, and a novel. We reprint an essay that was originally published in the Atlantic *in May 2012. You can friend Marche on Facebook or follow him on Twitter.*

Is Facebook Making Us Lonely?

Yvette Vickers, a former *Playboy* playmate and B-movie star, best known for her role in *Attack of the 50 Foot Woman*, would have been eighty-three last August, but nobody knows exactly how old she was when she died. According to the Los Angeles coroner's report, she lay dead for the better part of a year before a neighbor and fellow actress, a woman named Susan Savage, noticed cobwebs and yellowing letters in her mailbox, reached through a broken window to unlock the door, and pushed her way through the piles of junk mail and mounds of clothing that barricaded the house. Upstairs, she found Vickers's body, mummified, near a heater that was still running. Her computer was on too, its glow permeating the empty space.

The *Los Angeles Times* posted a story headlined "Mummified Body of Former Playboy Playmate Yvette Vickers Found in Her Benedict Canyon Home," which quickly went viral. Within two weeks, by Technorati's count, Vickers's lonesome death was already the subject of 16,057 Facebook posts and 881 tweets. She had long been a horror-movie icon, a symbol of Hollywood's capacity to exploit our most basic fears in the silliest ways; now she was an icon of a new and different kind of horror: our growing fear of loneliness. Certainly she received much more attention in death than she did in the final years of her life. With no children, no religious group, and no immediate social circle of any kind, she had begun, as an elderly woman, to look elsewhere for companionship. Savage later told *Los Angeles* magazine that she had searched Vickers's phone bills for clues about the life that led to such an end. In the months before her grotesque death, Vickers had made calls not to friends or family but to distant fans who had found her through fan conventions and Internet sites.

Vickers's web of connections had grown broader but shallower, as has happened for many of us. We are living in an isolation that would have been unimaginable to our ancestors, and yet we have never been more accessible. Over the past three decades, technology has delivered to us a world in which we need not be out of contact for a fraction of a moment. In 2010, at a cost of $300 million, 800 miles of fiber-optic cable was laid between the Chicago Mercantile Exchange and the New York Stock Exchange to shave three milliseconds off trading times. Yet within this world of instant and absolute communication, unbounded by limits of time or space, we suffer from unprecedented alienation. We have never been more detached from one another, or lonelier. In a world consumed by ever more novel modes of socializing, we have less and less actual society. We live in an accelerating contradiction: the more connected we become, the lonelier we are. We were promised a global village; instead we inhabit the drab cul-de-sacs and endless freeways of a vast suburb of information.

At the forefront of all this unexpectedly lonely interactivity is Facebook, with 845 million users and $3.7 billion in revenue last year. The company hopes to raise $5 billion in an initial public offering later this spring, which will make it by far the largest Internet IPO in history. Some recent estimates put the company's potential value at $100 billion, which would make it larger than the global coffee industry—one addiction preparing to surpass the other. Facebook's scale and reach are hard to comprehend: last summer, Facebook became, by some counts, the first Web site to receive 1 trillion page views in a month. In the last three months of 2011, users generated an average of 2.7 billion "likes" and comments every day. On whatever scale you care to judge Facebook—as a company, as a culture, as a country—it is vast beyond imagination.

Despite its immense popularity, or more likely because of it, Facebook has, from the beginning, been under something of a cloud of suspicion. The depiction of Mark Zuckerberg, in *The Social Network,* as a bastard with symptoms of Asperger's syndrome, was nonsense. But it felt true. It felt true to Facebook, if not to Zuckerberg. The film's most indelible scene, the one that may well have earned it an Oscar, was the final, silent shot of an anomic Zuckerberg sending out a friend request to his ex-girlfriend, then waiting and clicking and waiting and clicking—a moment of superconnected loneliness preserved in amber. We have all been in that scene: transfixed by the glare of a screen, hungering for response.

When you sign up for Google+ and set up your Friends circle, the program specifies that you should include only "your real friends, the ones you feel comfortable sharing private details with." That one little phrase, *Your real friends*—so quaint, so charmingly mothering—perfectly encapsulates the anxieties that social media have produced: the fears that Facebook is interfering with our real friendships, distancing us from each other, making us lonelier; and that social networking might be spreading the very isolation it seemed designed to conquer.

Facebook arrived in the middle of a dramatic increase in the quantity and intensity of human loneliness, a rise that initially made the site's promise of greater connection seem deeply attractive. Americans are more solitary than ever before. In 1950, less than 10 percent of American households contained only one person. By 2010, nearly 27 percent of households had just one person. Solitary living does not guarantee a life of unhappiness, of course. In his recent book about the trend toward living alone, Eric Klinenberg, a sociologist at NYU, writes: "Reams of published research show that it's the quality, not the quantity of social interaction, that best predicts loneliness." True. But before we begin the fantasies of happily eccentric singledom, of divorcées dropping by their knitting circles after work for glasses of Drew Barrymore pinot grigio, or recent college graduates with perfectly articulated, Steampunk-themed, 300-square-foot apartments organizing croquet matches with their book clubs, we should recognize that it is not just isolation that is rising sharply. It's loneliness, too. And loneliness makes us miserable.

We know intuitively that loneliness and being alone are not the same thing. Solitude can be lovely. Crowded parties can be agony. We also know, thanks to a growing body of research on the topic, that loneliness is not a matter of external conditions; it is a psychological state.

A 2005 analysis of data from a longitudinal study of Dutch twins showed that the tendency toward loneliness has roughly the same genetic component as other psychological problems such as neuroticism or anxiety.

Still, loneliness is slippery, a difficult state to define or diagnose. The best tool yet developed for measuring the condition is the UCLA Loneliness Scale, a series of twenty questions that all begin with this formulation: "How often do you feel . . .?" As in: "How often do you feel that you are 'in tune' with the people around you?" And: "How often do you feel that you lack companionship?" Measuring the condition in these terms, various studies have shown loneliness rising drastically over a very short period of recent history. A 2010 AARP survey found that 35 percent of adults older than forty-five were chronically lonely, as opposed to 20 percent of a similar group only a decade earlier. According to a major study by a leading scholar of the subject, roughly 20 percent of Americans—about 60 million people—are unhappy with their lives because of loneliness. Across the Western world, physicians and nurses have begun to speak openly of an epidemic of loneliness.

The new studies on loneliness are beginning to yield some surprising preliminary findings about its mechanisms. Almost every factor that one might assume affects loneliness does so only some of the time, and only under certain circumstances. People who are married are less lonely than single people, one journal article suggests, but only if their spouses are confidants. If one's spouse is not a confidant, marriage may not decrease loneliness. A belief in God might help, or it might not, as a 1990 German study comparing levels of religious feeling and levels of loneliness discovered. Active believers who saw God as abstract and helpful rather than as a wrathful, immediate presence were less lonely. "The mere belief in God," the researchers concluded, "was relatively independent of loneliness." 10

But it is clear that social interaction matters. Loneliness and being alone are not the same thing, but both are on the rise. We meet fewer people. We gather less. And when we gather, our bonds are less meaningful and less easy. The decrease in confidants—that is, in quality social connections—has been dramatic over the past twenty-five years. In one survey, the mean size of networks of personal confidants decreased from 2.94 people in 1985 to 2.08 in 2004. Similarly, in 1985, only 10 percent of Americans said they had no one with whom to discuss important matters, and 15 percent said they had only one such good friend. By 2004, 25 percent had nobody to talk to, and 20 percent had only one confidant.

In the face of this social disintegration, we have essentially hired an army of replacement confidants, an entire class of professional carers. As Ronald Dworkin pointed out in a 2010 paper for the Hoover Institution, in the late 1940s, the United States was home to 2,500 clinical psychologists, 30,000 social workers, and fewer than 500 marriage and family therapists. As of 2010, the country had 77,000 clinical psychologists,

192,000 clinical social workers, 400,000 nonclinical social workers, 50,000 marriage and family therapists, 105,000 mental-health counselors, 220,000 substance-abuse counselors, 17,000 nurse psychotherapists, and 30,000 life coaches. The majority of patients in therapy do not warrant a psychiatric diagnosis. This raft of psychic servants is helping us through what used to be called regular problems. We have outsourced the work of everyday caring.

We need professional carers more and more, because the threat of societal breakdown, once principally a matter of nostalgic lament, has morphed into an issue of public health. Being lonely is extremely bad for your health. If you're lonely, you're more likely to be put in a geriatric home at an earlier age than a similar person who isn't lonely. You're less likely to exercise. You're more likely to be obese. You're less likely to survive a serious operation and more likely to have hormonal imbalances. You are at greater risk of inflammation. Your memory may be worse. You are more likely to be depressed, to sleep badly, and to suffer dementia and general cognitive decline. Loneliness may not have killed Yvette Vickers, but it has been linked to a greater probability of having the kind of heart condition that did kill her.

And yet, despite its deleterious effect on health, loneliness is one of the first things ordinary Americans spend their money achieving. With money, you flee the cramped city to a house in the suburbs or, if you can afford it, a McMansion in the exurbs, inevitably spending more time in your car. Loneliness is at the American core, a by-product of a long-standing national appetite for independence: The Pilgrims who left Europe willingly abandoned the bonds and strictures of a society that could not accept their right to be different. They did not seek out loneliness, but they accepted it as the price of their autonomy. The cowboys who set off to explore a seemingly endless frontier likewise traded away personal ties in favor of pride and self-respect. The ultimate American icon is the astronaut: Who is more heroic, or more alone? The price of self-determination and self-reliance has often been loneliness. But Americans have always been willing to pay that price.

Today, the one common feature in American secular culture is its celebration of the self that breaks away from the constrictions of the family and the state, and, in its greatest expressions, from all limits entirely. The great American poem is Whitman's "Song of Myself." The great American essay is Emerson's "Self-Reliance." The great American novel is Melville's *Moby-Dick*, the tale of a man on a quest so lonely that it is incomprehensible to those around him. American culture, high and low, is about self-expression and personal authenticity. Franklin Delano Roosevelt called individualism "the great watchword of American life."

Self-invention is only half of the American story, however. The drive for isolation has always been in tension with the impulse to cluster in communities that cling and suffocate. The Pilgrims, while fomenting spiritual rebellion, also enforced ferocious cohesion. The Salem witch trials, in hindsight, read like attempts to impose solidarity—as do the McCarthy hearings. The history of the United States is like the famous parable of the porcupines in the cold, from Schopenhauer's *Studies in Pessimism*—the ones who huddle together for warmth and shuffle away in pain, always separating and congregating.

We are now in the middle of a long period of shuffling away. In his 2000 book *Bowling Alone*, Robert D. Putnam attributed the dramatic postwar decline of social capital—the strength and value of interpersonal networks—to numerous interconnected trends in American life: suburban sprawl, television's dominance over culture, the self-absorption of the Baby Boomers, the disintegration of the traditional family. The trends he observed continued through the prosperity of the aughts, and have only become more pronounced with time: the rate of union membership declined in 2011, again; screen time rose; the Masons and the Elks continued their slide into irrelevance. We are lonely because we want to be lonely. We have made ourselves lonely.

The question of the future is this: Is Facebook part of the separating or part of the congregating; is it a huddling-together for warmth or a shuffling-away in pain?

Well before Facebook, digital technology was enabling our tendency for isolation, to an unprecedented degree. Back in the 1990s, scholars started calling the contradiction between an increased opportunity to connect and a lack of human contact the "Internet paradox." A prominent 1998 article on the phenomenon by a team of researchers at Carnegie Mellon showed that increased Internet usage was already coinciding with increased loneliness. Critics of the study pointed out that the two groups that participated in the study—high-school journalism students who were heading to university and socially active members of community-development boards—were statistically likely to become lonelier over time. Which brings us to a more fundamental question: Does the Internet make people lonely, or are lonely people more attracted to the Internet?

The question has intensified in the Facebook era. A recent study out 20 of Australia (where close to half the population is active on Facebook), titled "Who Uses Facebook?" found a complex and sometimes confounding relationship between loneliness and social networking. Facebook users had slightly lower levels of "social loneliness"—the sense of not feeling bonded with friends—but "significantly higher levels of family loneliness"—the sense of not feeling bonded with family. It may be that Facebook encourages more contact with people outside of our household, at the expense of our family relationships—or it may be that people who have unhappy family relationships in the first place seek companionship through other means, including Facebook. The researchers also found that lonely people are inclined to spend more time on Facebook: "One of the most noteworthy findings," they wrote, "was the tendency for neurotic and lonely individuals to spend greater amounts of time on Facebook per day than non-lonely individuals." And they found that neurotics are more likely to prefer to use the wall, while extroverts tend to use chat features in addition to the wall.

Moira Burke, until recently a graduate student at the Human-Computer Institute at Carnegie Mellon, used to run a longitudinal study of 1,200 Facebook users. That study, which is ongoing, is one of the first to step outside the realm of self-selected college students and examine the effects of Facebook on a broader population, over time. She concludes that the effect of Facebook depends on what you bring to it. Just as your mother said: you get out only what you put in. If you use Facebook to communicate directly with other individuals—by using the "like" button, commenting on friends' posts, and so on—it can increase your social capital. Personalized messages, or what Burke calls "composed communication," are more satisfying than "one-click communication"—the lazy click of a like. "People who received composed communication became less lonely, while people who received one-click communication experienced no change in loneliness," Burke tells me. So, you should inform your friend in writing how charming her son looks with Harry Potter cake smeared all over his face, and how interesting her sepia-toned photograph of that tree-framed bit of skyline is, and how cool it is that she's at whatever concert she happens to be at. That's what we all want to hear. Even better than sending a private Facebook message is the semi-public conversation, the kind of back-and-forth in which you half ignore the other people who may be listening in. "People whose friends write to them semi-publicly on Facebook experience decreases in loneliness," Burke says.

On the other hand, nonpersonalized use of Facebook—scanning your friends' status updates and updating the world on your own activities via your wall, or what Burke calls "passive consumption" and "broadcasting"—correlates to feelings of disconnectedness. It's a lonely business, wandering the labyrinths of our friends' and pseudo-friends' projected identities, trying to figure out what part of ourselves we ought to project, who will listen, and what they will hear. According to Burke, passive consumption of Facebook also correlates to a marginal increase in depression. "If two women each talk to their friends the same amount of time, but one of them spends more time reading about friends on Facebook as well, the one reading tends to grow slightly more depressed," Burke says. Her conclusion suggests that my sometimes unhappy reactions to Facebook may be more universal than I had realized. When I scroll through page after page of my friends' descriptions of how accidentally eloquent their kids are, and how their husbands are endearingly bumbling, and how they're all about to eat a home-cooked meal prepared with fresh local organic produce bought at the farmers' market and then go for a jog and maybe check in at the office because they're so busy getting ready to hop on a plane for a week of luxury dogsledding in Lapland, I do grow slightly more miserable. A lot of other people doing the same thing feel a little bit worse, too.

Still, Burke's research does not support the assertion that Facebook creates loneliness. The people who experience loneliness on Facebook are lonely away from Facebook, too, she points out; on Facebook, as everywhere else, correlation is not causation. The popular kids are popular, and the lonely skulkers skulk alone. Perhaps it says something about me that I think Facebook is primarily a platform for lonely skulking. I mention to Burke the widely reported study, conducted by a Stanford graduate student, that showed how believing that others have strong social networks can lead to feelings of depression. What does Facebook communicate, if not the impression of social bounty? Everybody else looks so happy on Facebook, with so many friends, that our own social networks feel emptier than ever in comparison. Doesn't that *make* people feel lonely? "If people are reading about lives that are much better than theirs, two things can happen," Burke tells me. "They can feel worse about themselves, or they can feel motivated."

Burke will start working at Facebook as a data scientist this year.

John Cacioppo, the director of the Center for Cognitive and Social   25 Neuroscience at the University of Chicago, is the world's leading expert on loneliness. In his landmark book, *Loneliness*, released in 2008, he revealed just how profoundly the epidemic of loneliness is affecting the basic functions of human physiology. He found higher levels of epinephrine, the stress hormone, in the morning urine of lonely people. Loneliness burrows deep: "When we drew blood from our older adults and analyzed their white cells," he writes, "we found that loneliness somehow penetrated the deepest recesses of the cell to alter the way genes were being expressed." Loneliness affects not only the brain, then, but the basic process of DNA transcription. When you are lonely, your whole body is lonely.

To Cacioppo, Internet communication allows only ersatz intimacy. "Forming connections with pets or online friends or even God is a noble attempt by an obligatorily gregarious creature to satisfy a compelling need," he writes. "But surrogates can never make up completely for the absence of the real thing." The "real thing" being actual people, in the flesh. When I speak to Cacioppo, he is refreshingly clear on what he sees as Facebook's effect on society. Yes, he allows, some research has suggested that the greater the number of Facebook friends a person has, the less lonely she is. But he argues that the impression this creates can be misleading. "For the most part," he says, "people are bringing their old friends, and feelings of loneliness or connectedness, to Facebook." The idea that a Web site could deliver a more friendly, interconnected world is bogus. The depth of one's social network outside Facebook is what determines the depth of one's social network within Facebook, not the other way around. Using social media doesn't create new social networks; it just transfers established networks from one platform to another. For the most part, Facebook doesn't destroy friendships—but it doesn't create them, either.

In one experiment, Cacioppo looked for a connection between the loneliness of subjects and the relative frequency of their interactions via Facebook, chat rooms, online games, dating sites, and face-to-face contact. The results were unequivocal. "The greater the proportion of face-to-face interactions, the less lonely you are," he says. "The greater the proportion of online interactions, the lonelier you are." Surely, I suggest to Cacioppo, this means that Facebook and the like inevitably make people lonelier. He disagrees. Facebook is merely a tool, he says, and like any tool, its effectiveness will depend on its user. "If you use Facebook to increase face-to-face contact," he says, "it increases social capital." So if social media let you organize a game of football among your friends, that's healthy. If you turn to social media instead of playing football, however, that's unhealthy.

"Facebook can be terrific, if we use it properly," Cacioppo continues. "It's like a car. You can drive it to pick up your friends. Or you can drive alone." But hasn't the car increased loneliness? If cars created the suburbs, surely they also created isolation. "That's because of how we use cars," Cacioppo replies. "How we use these technologies can lead to more integration, rather than more isolation."

The problem, then, is that we invite loneliness, even though it makes us miserable. The history of our use of technology is a history of isolation desired and achieved. When the Great Atlantic and Pacific Tea Company opened its A&P stores, giving Americans self-service access to groceries, customers stopped having relationships with their grocers. When the telephone arrived, people stopped knocking on their neighbors' doors. Social media bring this process to a much wider set of relationships. Researchers at the HP Social Computing Lab who studied the nature of people's connections on Twitter came to a depressing, if not surprising, conclusion: "Most of the links declared within Twitter were meaningless from an interaction point of view." I have to wonder: What other point of view is meaningful?

Loneliness is certainly not something that Facebook or Twitter or 30 any of the lesser forms of social media is doing to us. We are doing it to ourselves. Casting technology as some vague, impersonal spirit of history forcing our actions is a weak excuse. We make decisions about how we use our machines, not the other way around. Every time I shop at my local grocery store, I am faced with a choice. I can buy my groceries from a human being or from a machine. I always, without exception, choose the machine. It's faster and more efficient, I tell myself, but the truth is that I prefer not having to wait with the other customers who are lined up alongside the conveyor belt: the hipster mom who disapproves of my high-carbon-footprint pineapple; the lady who tenses to the point of tears while she waits to see if the gods of the credit-card machine will accept or decline; the old man whose clumsy feebleness requires a patience that I don't possess. Much better to bypass the whole circus and just ring up the groceries myself.

Our omnipresent new technologies lure us toward increasingly superficial connections at exactly the same moment that they make avoiding the mess of human interaction easy. The beauty of Facebook, the source of its power, is that it enables us to be social while sparing us the embarrassing reality of society—the accidental revelations we make at parties, the awkward pauses, the farting and the spilled drinks and the general gaucherie of face-to-face contact. Instead, we have the lovely smoothness of a seemingly social machine. Everything's so simple: status updates, pictures, your wall.

But the price of this smooth sociability is a constant compulsion to assert one's own happiness, one's own fulfillment. Not only must we contend with the social bounty of others; we must foster the appearance of our own social bounty. Being happy all the time, pretending to be happy, actually attempting to be happy—it's exhausting. Last year a team of researchers led by Iris Mauss at the University of Denver published a study looking into "the paradoxical effects of valuing happiness." Most goals in life show a direct correlation between valuation and achievement. Studies have found, for example, that students who value good grades tend to have higher grades than those who don't value them. Happiness is an exception. The study came to a disturbing conclusion:

> Valuing happiness is not necessarily linked to greater happiness. In fact, under certain conditions, the opposite is true. Under conditions of low (but not high) life stress, the more people valued happiness, the lower were their hedonic balance, psychological well-being, and life satisfaction, and the higher their depression symptoms.

The more you try to be happy, the less happy you are. Sophocles made roughly the same point.

Facebook, of course, puts the pursuit of happiness front and center in our digital life. Its capacity to redefine our very concepts of identity and personal fulfillment is much more worrisome than the data-mining and privacy practices that have aroused anxieties about the company. Two of the most compelling critics of Facebook—neither of them a Luddite—concentrate on exactly this point. Jaron Lanier, the author of *You Are Not a Gadget*, was one of the inventors of virtual-reality technology. His view of where social media are taking us reads like dystopian science fiction: "I fear that we are beginning to design ourselves to suit digital models of us, and I worry about a leaching of empathy and humanity in that process." Lanier argues that Facebook imprisons us in the business of self-presenting, and this, to his mind, is the site's crucial and fatally unacceptable downside.

Sherry Turkle, a professor of computer culture at MIT who in 1995 published the digital-positive analysis *Life on the Screen*, is much more skeptical about the effects of online society in her 2011 book, *Alone Together*: "These days, insecure in our relationships and anxious about intimacy, we look to technology for ways to be in relationships and protect ourselves from them at the same time." The problem with digital intimacy is that it is ultimately incomplete: "The ties we form through the Internet are not, in the end, the ties that bind. But they are the ties that preoccupy," she writes. "We don't want to intrude on each other, so instead we constantly intrude on each other, but not in 'real time.'"

Lanier and Turkle are right, at least in their diagnoses. Self-presen- 35 tation on Facebook is continuous, intensely mediated, and possessed of a phony nonchalance that eliminates even the potential for spontaneity. ("Look how casually I threw up these three photos from the party at which I took 300 photos!") Curating the exhibition of the self has become a 24/7 occupation. Perhaps not surprisingly, then, the Australian study "Who Uses Facebook?" found a significant correlation between Facebook use and narcissism: "Facebook users have higher levels of total narcissism, exhibitionism, and leadership than Facebook nonusers," the study's authors wrote. "In fact, it could be argued that Facebook specifically gratifies the narcissistic individual's need to engage in self-promoting and superficial behavior."

Rising narcissism isn't so much a trend as the trend behind all other trends. In preparation for the 2013 edition of its diagnostic manual, the psychiatric profession is currently struggling to update its definition of narcissistic personality disorder. Still, generally speaking, practitioners agree that narcissism manifests in patterns of fantastic grandiosity, craving for attention, and lack of empathy. In a 2008 survey, 35,000 American respondents were asked if they had ever had certain symptoms of narcissistic personality disorder. Among people older than sixty-five, 3 percent reported symptoms. Among people in their twenties, the proportion was nearly 10 percent. Across all age groups, one in sixteen Americans has experienced some symptoms of NPD. And loneliness and narcissism are intimately connected: a longitudinal study of Swedish women demonstrated a strong link between levels of narcissism in youth and levels of loneliness in old age. The connection is fundamental. Narcissism is the flip side of loneliness, and either condition is a fighting retreat from the messy reality of other people.

A considerable part of Facebook's appeal stems from its miraculous fusion of distance with intimacy, or the illusion of distance with the illusion of intimacy. Our online communities become engines of self-image, and self-image becomes the engine of community. The real danger with Facebook is not that it allows us to isolate ourselves, but that by mixing our appetite for isolation with our vanity, it threatens to alter the very nature of solitude. The new isolation is not of the kind that Americans once idealized, the lonesomeness of the proudly nonconformist, independent-minded, solitary stoic, or that of the astronaut who blasts into new worlds.

Facebook's isolation is a grind. What's truly staggering about Facebook usage is not its volume—750 million photographs uploaded over a single weekend—but the constancy of the performance it demands. More than half its users—and one of every thirteen people on Earth is a Facebook user—log on every day. Among eighteen-to-thirty-four-year-olds, nearly half check Facebook minutes after waking up, and 28 percent do so before getting out of bed. The relentlessness is what is so new, so potentially transformative. Facebook never takes a break. We never take a break. Human beings have always created elaborate acts of self-presentation. But not all the time, not every morning, before we even pour a cup of coffee. Yvette Vickers's computer was on when she died.

Nostalgia for the good old days of disconnection would not just be pointless, it would be hypocritical and ungrateful. But the very magic of the new machines, the efficiency and elegance with which they serve us, obscures what isn't being served: everything that matters. What Facebook has revealed about human nature—and this is not a minor revelation—is that a connection is not the same thing as a bond, and that instant and total connection is no salvation, no ticket to a happier, better world or a more liberated version of humanity. Solitude used to be good for self-reflection and self-reinvention. But now we are left thinking about who we are all the time, without ever really thinking about who we are. Facebook denies us a pleasure whose profundity we had underestimated: the chance to forget about ourselves for a while, the chance to disconnect.

TOPICS FOR CRITICAL THINKING AND WRITING

1. In his first three paragraphs Marche argues that despite modern technology, "We have never been more detached from one another, or lonelier." What methods does he go on to use, in his effort to persuade? Did his essay convince you? Please explain.

2. In paragraph 6 Marche states that "social networking might be spreading the very isolation it seemed designed to conquer." Does your own experience confirm or refute this assertion? Explain.

3. In paragraph 17 Marche speaks of "social capital." What does this term mean? How do you know?

4. In paragraph 20 Marche discusses the findings of an Australian study of Facebook users. How do you interpret their finding of "significantly higher levels of family loneliness" among Facebook users?

5. Evaluate Marche's final paragraph as a conclusion.

Josh Rose

Josh Rose is the chief creative officer at Weber Shandwick, an internationally recognized public relations firm. We reprint this article that was published on Mashable.com, an online source that reports on digital innovation, on Feb. 23, 2011.

How Social Media Is Having a Positive Impact on Our Culture

Two events today, although worlds apart, seem inextricably tied together. And the bond between them is as human as it is electronic.

First, on my way to go sit down and read the newspaper at my coffee shop, I got a message from my ten-year-old son, just saying good morning and letting me know he was going to a birthday party today. I don't get to see him all the time. He's growing up in two houses, as I did. But recently I handed down my old iPhone 3G to him to use basically as an iPod touch. We both installed an app called Yak, so we could communicate with each other when we're apart.

The amount of calming satisfaction it gives me to be able to communicate with him through technology is undeniably palpable and human. It's the other side of the "I don't care what you ate for breakfast this morning" argument against the mundane broadcasting of social media. In this case, I absolutely care about this. I'd listen to him describe a piece of bacon, and hang on every word. Is it better than a conversation with "real words?" No. But is it better than waiting two more days, when the mundane moment that I long to hear about so much is gone? Yes.

I guess one man's TMI is another man's treasure.

Moments later, I sat down and opened the paper. A headline imme- 5
diately stood out: "In China, microblogs finding abducted kids" with the subhead, "A 6-year-old who was snatched when he was 3 is discovered with a family 800 miles away." Apparently, the occurrence of reclaimed children through the use of China's version of Twitter—and other online forums—has become triumphant news over there. I'm reading about the father's tears, the boy's own confusing set of emotions, the rapt attention of the town and country, and I'm again marveling at the human side of the Internet.

THE PARADOX OF ONLINE CLOSENESS

I recently asked the question to my Facebook friends: "Twitter, Facebook, Foursquare . . . is all this making you feel closer to people or farther away?" It sparked a lot of responses and seemed to touch one of our generation's exposed nerves. What is the effect of the Internet and social media on our humanity?

From the outside view, digital interactions appear to be cold and inhuman. There's no denying that. And without doubt, given the choice between hugging someone and "poking" someone, I think we can all agree which one feels better. The theme of the responses to my Facebook question seemed to be summed up by my friend Jason, who wrote: "Closer to people I'm far away from." Then, a minute later, wrote, "but maybe farther from the people I'm close enough to." And then added, "I just got confused."

It is confusing. We live in this paradox now, where two seemingly conflicting realities exist side-by-side. Social media simultaneously draws us nearer and distances us. But I think very often, we lament what we miss and forget to admire what we've become. And it's human nature to want to reject the machine at the moment we feel it becoming ubiquitous. We've seen it with the printing press, moving pictures, television, video games, and just about any other advanced technology that captures our attention. What romantic rituals of relationship and social interaction will die in the process? Our hearts want to know.

In the *New Yorker* this week [February 14, 2011] Adam Gopnik's article "How the Internet Gets Inside Us," explores this cultural truism in depth. It's a fantastic read and should be mandatory for anyone in an online industry. He breaks down a whole slew of new books on the subject and categorizes it all into three viewpoints: "the Never-Betters, the Better-Nevers, and the Ever-Wasers." In short, those who see the current movement as good, bad, or normal. I think we all know people from each camp. But ultimately, the last group is the one best equipped to handle it all.

FILLING IN THE SPACE WITH CONNECTIONS

Another observation from the coffee shop: In my immediate vicinity,   10
four people are looking at screens and four people are reading something on paper. And I'm doing both. I see Facebook open on two screens, but I'm sure at some point, it's been open on all of them. The dynamic in this coffee shop is quite a bit more revealing than any article or book. Think about the varied juxtapositions of physical and digital going on. People aren't giving up long-form reading, considered thinking, or social interactions. They are just filling all the space between. And even that's not entirely true as I watch the occasional stare out the window or long glance around the room.

The way people engage with the Internet and social media isn't like any kind of interaction we've ever seen before. It's like an intertwining sine wave that touches in and out continuously. And the Internet itself is more complex and interesting than we often give it credit for. Consider peer-to-peer networking as just one example, where the tasks are distributed among the group to form a whole. It's practically a metaphor for the human mind. Or a township. Or a government. Or a family.

The Internet doesn't steal our humanity, it reflects it. The Internet doesn't get inside us, it shows what's inside us. And social media isn't cold, it's just complex and hard to define. I've always thought that you really see something's value when you try to destroy it. As we have now laid witness to in recent news, the Internet has quickly become the atom of cultural media; intertwined with our familial and cultural bonds, and destroyed only at great risk. I think if we search our own souls and consider our own personal way of navigating, we know this is as true personally as it is globally. The machine does not control us. It is a tool. As advanced today as a sharpened stick was a couple million years ago. Looked at through this lens, perhaps we should reframe our discussions about technology from how it is changing us to how we are using it.

Topics for Critical Thinking and Writing

1. In paragraph 8 Rose says, "Social media simultaneously draws us nearer and distances us." If you agree, write a short essay (350–500 words) citing examples that may help to convince a reader of the truth of this assertion.

2. Rose begins his final paragraph with these three sentences:

   > The Internet doesn't steal our humanity, it reflects it. The Internet doesn't get inside us, it shows what's inside us. And social media isn't cold, it's just complex and hard to define.

   Assume for the moment that he is right. Go on to continue his paragraph, offering details that support these sentences.

24

Immigration: What Is to Be Done?

David Cole

David Cole (b. 1958), a professor at Georgetown University Law Center, is a volunteer staff attorney for the Center for Constitutional Rights. This essay originally appeared in The Nation *on October 17, 1994.*

Five Myths about Immigration

For a brief period in the mid-nineteenth century, a new political movement captured the passions of the American public. Fittingly labeled the "Know-Nothings," their unifying theme was nativism. They liked to call themselves "Native Americans," although they had no sympathy for people we call Native Americans today. And they pinned every problem in American society on immigrants. As one Know-Nothing wrote in 1856: "Four-fifths of the beggary and three-fifths of the crime spring from our foreign population; more than half the public charities, more than half the prisons and almshouses, more than half the police and the cost of administering criminal justice are for foreigners."

At the time, the greatest influx of immigrants was from Ireland, where the potato famine had struck, and Germany, which was in political and economic turmoil. Anti-alien and anti-Catholic sentiments were the order of the day, especially in New York and Massachusetts, which received the brunt of the wave of immigrants, many of whom were dirt-poor and uneducated. Politicians were quick to exploit the sentiment: There's nothing like a scapegoat to forge an alliance.

I am especially sensitive to this history: My forebears were among those dirt-poor Irish Catholics who arrived in the 1860s. Fortunately for them, and me, the Know-Nothing movement fizzled within fifteen years. But its pilot light kept burning, and is turned up whenever the American public begins to feel vulnerable and in need of an enemy.

Although they go by different names today, the Know-Nothings have returned. As in the 1850s, the movement is strongest where immigrants are most concentrated: California and Florida. The objects of prejudice are of course no longer Irish Catholics and Germans; 140 years later, "they" have become "us." The new "they"—because it seems "we" must always have a "they"—are Latin Americans (most recently, Cubans), Haitians, and Arab Americans, among others.

But just as in the 1850s, passion, misinformation, and shortsighted 5 fear often substitute for reason, fairness, and human dignity in today's immigration debates. In the interest of advancing beyond know-nothingism, let's look at five current myths that distort public debate and government policy relating to immigrants.

America is being overrun with immigrants. In one sense, of course, this is true, but in that sense it has been true since Christopher Columbus arrived. Except for the real Native Americans, we are a nation of immigrants.

It is not true, however, that the first-generation immigrant share of our population is growing. As of 1990, foreign-born people made up only 8 percent of the population, as compared with a figure of about 15 percent from 1870 to 1920. Between 70 and 80 percent of those who immigrate every year are refugees or immediate relatives of U.S. citizens.

Much of the anti-immigrant fervor is directed against the undocumented, but they make up only 13 percent of all immigrants residing in the United States, and only 1 percent of the American population. Contrary to popular belief, most such aliens do not cross the border illegally but enter legally and remain after their student or visitor visa expires. Thus, building a wall at the border, no matter how high, will not solve the problem.

Immigrants take jobs from U.S. citizens. There is virtually no evidence to support this view, probably the most widespread misunderstanding about immigrants. As documented by a 1994 A.C.L.U. Immigrants' Rights Project report, numerous studies have found that immigrants actually *create* more jobs than they fill. The jobs immigrants take are of course easier to see, but immigrants are often highly productive, run their own businesses, and employ both immigrants and citizens. One study found that Mexican immigration to Los Angeles County between 1970 and 1980 was responsible for 78,000 new jobs. Governor Mario Cuomo reports that immigrants own more than 40,000 companies in New York, which provide thousands of jobs and $3.5 billion to the state's economy every year.

Immigrants are a drain on society's resources. This claim fuels many of 10 the recent efforts to cut off government benefits to immigrants. However, most studies have found that immigrants are a net benefit to the economy because, as a 1994 Urban Institute report concludes, "immigrants generate significantly more in taxes paid than they cost in services received." The Council of Economic Advisers similarly found in 1986 that "immigrants have a favorable effect on the overall standard of living."

Anti-immigrant advocates often cite studies purportedly showing the contrary, but these generally focus only on taxes and services at the local or state level. What they fail to explain is that because most taxes go to the federal government, such studies would also show a net loss when applied to U.S. citizens. At most, such figures suggest that some redistribution of federal and state monies may be appropriate; they say nothing unique about the costs of immigrants.

Some subgroups of immigrants plainly impose a net cost in the short run, principally those who have most recently arrived and have not yet "made it." California, for example, bears substantial costs for its disproportionately large undocumented population, largely because it has on average the poorest and least educated immigrants. But that has been true of every wave of immigrants that has ever reached our shores; it was as true of the Irish in the 1850s, for example, as it is of Salvadorans today. From a long-term perspective, the economic advantages of immigration are undeniable.

Some have suggested that we might save money and diminish incentives to immigrate illegally if we denied undocumented aliens public services. In fact, undocumented immigrants are already ineligible for most social programs, with the exception of education for schoolchildren, which is constitutionally required, and benefits directly related to health and safety, such as emergency medical care and nutritional assistance to poor women, infants, and children. To deny such basic care to people in need, apart from being inhumanly callous, would probably cost us more in the long run by exacerbating health problems that we would eventually have to address.

Aliens refuse to assimilate, and are depriving us of our cultural and political unity. This claim has been made about every new group of immigrants to arrive on U.S. shores. Supreme Court Justice Stephen Field wrote in 1884 that the Chinese "have remained among us a separate people, retaining their original peculiarities of dress, manners, habits, and modes of living, which are as marked as their complexion and language." Five years later, he upheld the racially based exclusion of Chinese immigrants. Similar claims have been made over different periods of our history about Catholics, Jews, Italians, Eastern Europeans, and Latin Americans.

In most instances, such claims are simply not true; "American culture" has been created, defined, and revised by persons who for the most part are descended from immigrants once seen as anti-assimilationist. Descendants of the Irish Catholics, for example, a group once decried as separatist and alien, have become presidents, senators, and representatives (and all of these in one family, in the case of the Kennedys). Our society exerts tremendous pressure to conform, and cultural separatism rarely survives a generation. But more important, even if this claim were true, is this a legitimate rationale for limiting immigration in a society built on the values of pluralism and tolerance? 15

Noncitizen immigrants are not entitled to constitutional rights. Our government has long declined to treat immigrants as full human beings, and nowhere is that more clear than in the realm of constitutional rights. Although the Constitution literally extends the fundamental protections in the Bill of Rights to all people, limiting to citizens only the right to vote and run for federal office, the federal government acts as if this were not the case.

In 1893 the executive branch successfully defended a statute that required Chinese laborers to establish their prior residence here by the testimony of "at least one credible white witness." The Supreme Court ruled that this law was constitutional because it was reasonable for Congress to presume that nonwhite witnesses could not be trusted.

The federal government is not much more enlightened today. In a pending case I'm handling in the Court of Appeals for the Ninth Circuit, the Clinton Administration has argued that permanent resident aliens lawfully living here should be extended no more First Amendment rights than aliens applying for first-time admission from abroad—that is, none. Under this view, students at a public university who are citizens may express themselves freely, but students who are not citizens can be deported for saying exactly what their classmates are constitutionally entitled to say.

Growing up, I was always taught that we will be judged by how we treat others. If we are collectively judged by how we have treated immigrants—those who would appear today to be "other" but will in a generation be "us"—we are not in very good shape.

Topics for Critical Thinking and Writing

1. What are the "five current myths" (para. 5) about immigration that Cole identifies? Why does he describe them as "myths" (rather than errors, mistakes, or falsehoods)?

2. In an encyclopedia or other reference work in your college library, look up the "Know-Nothings" (para. 1). What, if anything, of interest do you learn about this movement that is not mentioned by Cole in his opening paragraphs (1–4)?

3. Cole attempts to show how insignificant the immigrant population really is (in paras. 7 and 13) because it involves such a small fraction (8 percent in 1990) of the total population. Suppose someone said to him, "That's all very well, but 8 percent of the population is still 20 million people—far more than the 15 percent of the population during the years from 1870 to 1920." How might he reply?

4. Suppose Cole is right that most illegal immigration results from over-staying visitor and student visas (para. 8). Why not pass laws prohibiting foreign students from studying here, since so many abuse the privilege? Why not pass other laws forbidding foreign visitors?

5. Cole cites a study (para. 9) showing that "Mexican immigration to Los Angeles County between 1970 and 1980 was responsible for 78,000

new jobs." Suppose it were also true that this immigration was responsible for 78,000 other Mexican immigrants who joined criminal gangs or
were otherwise not legally employed. How might Cole respond?

6. Cole admits (para. 12) that in California, the large population of undocumented immigrants imposes "substantial costs" on taxpayers. Does
   Cole offer any remedy for this problem? Should the federal government
   bear some or all of these extra costs that fall on California?

7. Cole thinks that "cultural separatism" among immigrants "rarely survives a generation" (para. 15). His evidence? Look at the Irish Catholics. But suppose someone argued that this is weak evidence: Because
   today's immigrants are not Europeans, but are Asian and Hispanic, they
   will never assimilate to the degree that European immigrants did—their
   race, culture, religion, and language and the trend toward "multiculturalism" all block the way. How might Cole reply?

8. Do you think that immigrants who are not citizens and not applying for
   citizenship ought to be allowed to vote in state and local elections (the
   Constitution forbids them to vote in federal elections, as Cole points out
   in para. 16)? Why, or why not? How about illegal immigrants?

Barry R. Chiswick

*Barry R. Chiswick holds a Ph.D. in economics from Columbia University. A spe-
cialist in the labor market, Chiswick is head of the economics department at The
George Washington University. We reprint an essay that originally appeared in
the* New York Times *in June 2006.*

The Worker Next Door

It is often said that the American economy needs low-skilled foreign
workers to do the jobs that American workers will not do. These foreign workers might be new immigrants, illegal aliens, or, in the current
debate, temporary or guest workers. But if low-skilled foreign workers
were not here, would lettuce not be picked, groceries not bagged, hotel
sheets not changed, and lawns not mowed? Would restaurants use dis-
posable plates and utensils?

On the face of it, this assertion seems implausible. Immigrants and
low-skilled foreign workers in general are highly concentrated in a few
states. The "big six" are California, Florida, Illinois, New Jersey, New
York, and Texas. Even within those states, immigrants and low-skilled
foreign workers are concentrated in a few metropolitan areas—while
there are many in New York City and Chicago, relatively few are in
upstate New York or downstate Illinois.

Yet even in areas with few immigrants, grass is cut, groceries are
bagged, and hotel sheets are changed. Indeed, a large majority of

low-skilled workers are native to the United States. A look at the 2000 census is instructive: among males age twenty-five to sixty-four years employed that year, of those with less than a high school diploma, 64 percent were born in the United States and 36 percent were foreign born.

Other Americans nominally graduated from high school but did not learn a trade or acquire the literacy, numeracy, or decision-making skills needed for higher earnings. Still others suffer from a physical or emotional ailment that limits their labor productivity. And some low-skilled jobs are performed by high school or college students, housewives, or the retired who wish to work part time. Put simply, there are no low-skilled jobs that American workers would not and do not do.

Over the past two decades the number of low-skilled workers in the   5 United States has increased because of immigration, both legal and illegal. This increase in low-skilled workers has contributed to the stagnation of wages for all such workers. The proposed "earned legalization" (amnesty) and guest worker programs would allow still more low-skilled workers into the country, further lowering their collective wages.

True, the prices of the goods and services that these new immigrants produce are reduced for the rich and poor alike. But the net effect of this dynamic is a decline in the purchasing power of low-skilled families and a rise in the purchasing power of high-income families—a significant factor behind the increase in income inequality that has been of considerable public concern over the past two decades.

In short, the continued increase in the flow of unskilled workers into the United States is the economic and moral equivalent of a regressive tax.

If the number of low-skilled foreign workers were to fall, wages would increase. Low-skilled American workers and their families would benefit, and society as a whole would gain from a reduction in income inequality.

Employers facing higher labor costs for low-skilled workers would raise their prices, and to some extent they would change the way they operate their businesses. A farmer who grows winter iceberg lettuce in Yuma County, Arizona, was asked on the ABC program *Nightline* in April what he would do if it were more difficult to find the low-skilled hand harvesters who work on his farm, many of whom are undocumented workers. He replied that he would mechanize the harvest. Such technology exists, but it is not used because of the abundance of low-wage laborers. In their absence, mechanical harvesters—and the higher-skilled (and higher-wage) workers to operate them—would replace low-skilled, low-wage workers.

But, you might ask, who would mow the lawns in suburbia? The   10 higher wages would attract more lower-skilled American workers (including teenagers) to these jobs. Facing higher costs, some homeowners would switch to grass species that grow more slowly, to alternative ground cover, or to flagstones. Others would simply mow every other week, or every ten days, instead of weekly. And some would combine one or more of these strategies to offset rising labor costs.

"Well, they look pretty undocumented to me."

Few of us change our sheets and towels at home every day. Hotels and motels could reduce the frequency of changing sheets and towels from every day to, say, every third day for continuing guests, perhaps offering a price discount to guests who accept this arrangement.

Less frequent lawn mowing and washing of hotel sheets and towels would reduce air, noise, and water pollution in the bargain.

With the higher cost of low-skilled labor, we would import more of some goods, in particular table-quality fruits and vegetables for home consumption (as distinct from industrial use) and lower-priced off-the-rack clothing. But it makes no sense to import people to produce goods in the United States for which we lack a comparative advantage — that is, goods that other countries can produce more efficiently.

The point is that with a decline in low-skilled foreign workers, life would go on. The genius of the American people is their ingenuity, and the genius of the American economy is its flexibility. And throughout our nation's history, this flexibility, the finding of alternative ways of doing things, has been a prime engine of economic growth and change.

TOPICS FOR CRITICAL THINKING AND WRITING

1. Reread Chiswick's first paragraph, and try to remember the effect it had on you when you first read it. Did you think, "Hey, he is right; of course the lettuce would get picked, the groceries would be bagged, and the hotel sheets would be changed"? Or did you think, "Where is this guy going?" Or what? Evaluate Chiswick's first paragraph as the opening of an argument.

2. What is the program known as "earned legalization" (para. 5)?

3. In paragraph 6 Chiswick says that although cheap labor reduces the price of goods and services for the poor as well as for the rich, "the net effect . . . is a decline in the purchasing power of low-skilled families." Are you convinced? Why, or why not?

4. What is a "regressive tax" (para. 7)?

5. Why does Chiswick think (para. 8) wages would increase if the number of low-skilled foreign workers declined? Are you convinced by his argument? Why, or why not?

6. Suppose someone replied to Chiswick, saying, in effect, "You are right, but the fact is this. We have some 12 million Mexicans living here who entered illegally. America is big enough, and rich enough, and great-spirited enough to welcome them, and in fact America will probably be the gainer." What would you say?

7. Analyze and evaluate Chiswick's essay as an example of persuasive writing. What devices does he use, and how effectively does he use them?

John Tierney

John Tierney, born in 1953, has written for the New York Times *since 1990, where he is now a regular columnist. He is the coauthor of a comic novel,* God Is My Broker *(1998), and the author of* The Best-Case Scenario Handbook *(2002), which tells you how to cope with such unlikely things as an ATM that keeps disgorging money. We reprint one of his columns written for the* New York Times *in April 2006.*

Ángels in America

Ángel Espinoza doesn't understand why Republicans on Capitol Hill are determined to deport Mexicans like him. I don't get it, either. He makes me think of my Irish grandfather.

They both left farms and went to the South Side of Chicago, arriving with relatively little education. My grandfather took a job in the stock-yards and lived in an Irish boarding house nearby. Espinoza started as a dishwasher and lived with his brother in a Mexican neighborhood.

Like my grandfather, who became a streetcar motorman and then a police officer, Espinoza moved on to better-paying jobs and a better home of his own. Like my grandfather, Espinoza married an American-born descendant of immigrants from his native country.

But whereas my grandfather became a citizen, Espinoza couldn't even become a legal resident. Once he married an American, he applied, but was rejected because he'd once been caught at the border and sent home with an order to stay out. Violating that order made him ineligible for a green card and eligible for deportation.

"I had to tell my four-year-old daughter that one day I might not   5
come home," he said. "I work hard and pay taxes and don't want any welfare. Why deport me?"

The official answer, of course, is that he violated the law. My grandfather didn't. But my grandfather didn't have to. There weren't quotas on Europeans or most other immigrants in 1911, even though, relative to the population, there were more immigrants arriving and living here than there are today. If America could absorb my grandfather, why keep out Espinoza?

It's been argued that Mexicans are different from past immigrants because they're closer to home and less likely to assimilate. Compared with other immigrants today, they're less educated, and their children are more likely to get poor grades and drop out of school. Therefore, the argument goes, Mexicans are in danger of becoming an underclass living in linguistically isolated ghettos.

Those concerns sound reasonable in theory. But if you look at studies of immigrants, you find that the typical story is much more like Espinoza's. He dropped out of school at age sixteen in southern Mexico, when his family needed money for medical bills. He paid a coyote to sneak him across the border and went to the Mexican neighborhood of Pilsen in Chicago, a metropolitan area that is now home to the second-largest Mexican population in the nation.

Espinoza started off making less than $4 an hour as a dishwasher in a restaurant that flouted the minimum-wage law. But he became a cook and worked up to $15 an hour. He switched to driving a street-cleaning truck, a job that now pays him $17 an hour, minus taxes and Social Security.

By age twenty-four, he and his wife, Anita, had saved enough to buy   10
a house for about $200,000 in Villa Park, a suburb where most people don't speak Spanish. Now twenty-seven, Espinoza's still working on his English (we spoke in Spanish), but his daughter is already speaking English at her preschool.

There's nothing unusual about his progress. More than half of the Mexican immigrants in Chicago own their own homes, and many are moving to the suburbs. No matter where they live, their children learn English.

You can hear this on the sidewalks and school corridors in Mexican neighborhoods like Pilsen, where most teenagers speak to one another in English. A national survey by the Pew Hispanic Center found that nearly all second-generation Latinos are either bilingual or English-dominant, and by the next generation 80 percent are English-dominant and virtually none speak just Spanish.

Yesterday, the Senate seemed close to a deal letting most immigrants become legal residents. But it fell apart when Republicans fought to add restrictions, including some that could prevent an immigrant with Espinoza's history from qualifying.

Bobby Rush, a Democratic representative from Chicago, is trying to pass protections for the Espinozas and other families in danger of being separated. The issue has galvanized other Chicago public officials and immigrant advocates, who are planning to take the families to Washington to press their case.

I'd like to see Republicans on Capitol Hill explain to Espinoza why   15
he's less deserving than their immigrant ancestors, but that's probably too much to expect. Espinoza has a simpler wish: "I would like them to tell my American daughter why her father can't stay with her."

Topics for Critical Thinking and Writing

1. Evaluate the effectiveness of Tierney's use of Ángel Espinoza in this essay. What does Tierney gain by introducing us to Espinoza?

2. In paragraph 4 Tierney explains why Espinoza is not eligible for a green card. If you could change the system, would you change the provision that makes him ineligible? Why, or why not?

3. Tierney ends his sixth paragraph with a question. What answer would you give to this question?

4. Who or what is a "coyote" (para. 8)?

5. In paragraph 8 Tierney refers to "studies of immigrants," but he does not cite any. Do you assume that there are such studies? Do you also assume, perhaps, that other studies may come to different conclusions? Do you believe that "studies" of this sort are highly relevant to the issue of whether or not immigration laws concerning Mexicans should or should not be revised? Explain.

6. Tierney ends his essay by saying that he would like to hear Republicans on Capitol Hill explain why Espinoza is less deserving than their ancestors. What do you think a Republican on Capitol Hill might say? What would *you* say?

7. Tierney implies that there are only bad reasons for excluding Latino immigrants from citizenship. Do you agree? Explain.

Victor Davis Hanson

Victor Davis Hanson, born in 1953 in Fowler, California, did his undergraduate work at the University of California at Santa Cruz and his Ph.D. work at Stanford University. A specialist in military history, he has taught classics at California State

University at Fresno. A noted conservative, Hanson is a senior fellow at the Hoover Institution. This piece first appeared at realclearpolitics.com on May 25, 2006.

Our Brave New World of Immigration

In the dark of these rural spring mornings, I see full vans of Mexican laborers speeding by my farmhouse on their way to the western side of California's San Joaquin Valley to do the backbreaking work of weeding cotton, thinning tree fruit, and picking strawberries.

In the other direction, even earlier morning crews drive into town—industrious roofers, cement layers, and framers heading to a nearby new housing tract. While most of us are still asleep, thousands of these hardworking young men and women in the American Southwest rise with the sun to provide the sort of unmatched labor at the sort of wages that their eager employers insist they cannot find among citizens.

But just when one thinks that illegal immigration is an efficient win-win way of providing excellent workers to needy businesses, there are also daily warnings that there is something terribly wrong with a system predicated on a cynical violation of the law.

Three days ago, as I watched the daily early-morning caravan go by, I heard a horrendous explosion. Not far from my home, one of these vans had crossed the white line down the middle of the road and hit a pickup truck head-on. Perhaps the van had blown a bald tire. Perhaps the driver was intoxicated. Or perhaps he had no experience driving an overloaded minivan at high speed in the dark of early morning.

We will probably never know—since the driver ran away from 5 the carnage of the accident. That often happens when an illegal alien who survives an accident has no insurance or driver's license. But he did leave in his wake his three dead passengers. Eight more people were injured. Both cars were totaled. Traffic was rerouted around the wreckage for hours.

Ambulances, fire trucks, and patrol cars lined the nearby intersection. That accident alone must have imparted untold suffering for dozens of family members, as well as cost the state thousands of dollars.

Such mayhem is no longer an uncommon occurrence here. I have had four cars slam into our roadside property, with the drivers running off, leaving behind damaged vines and trees, and wrecked cars with phony licenses and no record of insurance. I have been broadsided by an undocumented driver, who ran a stop sign and then tried to run from our collision.

These are the inevitable but usually unmentioned symptoms of illegal immigration. After all, the unexpected can often happen when tens of thousands of young males from Mexico arrive in a strange country, mostly alone, without English or legality—an estimated 60 percent of them without a high-school degree and most obligated to send nearly half of their hard-won checks back to kin in Mexico.

Many Americans—perhaps out of understandable and well-meant empathy for the dispossessed who toil so hard for so little—support this present open system of non-borders. But I find nothing liberal about it.

Zealots may chant *¡Sí, se puede!* all they want. And the libertarian 10 right may dress up the need for cheap labor as a desire to remain globally competitive. But neither can disguise a cynicism about illegal immigration, one that serves to prop up a venal Mexican government, undercut the wages of our own poor, and create a new apartheid of millions of aliens in our shadows.

We have entered a new world of immigration without precedent. This current crisis is unlike the great waves of nineteenth-century immigration that brought thousands of Irish, Eastern Europeans, and Asians to the United States. Most immigrants in the past came legally. Few could return easily across an ocean to home. Arrivals from, say, Ireland or China could not embrace the myth that our borders had crossed them rather than vice versa.

Today, almost a third of all foreign-born persons in the United States are here illegally, making up 3 to 4 percent of the American population. It is estimated that the United States is home to 11 or 12 million illegal aliens, whose constantly refreshed numbers ensure there is always a perpetual class of unassimilated recent illegal arrivals. Indeed almost one-tenth of Mexico's population currently lives here illegally!

But the real problem is that we, the hosts, are also different from our predecessors. Today we ask too little of too many of our immigrants. We apparently don't care whether they come legally or learn English—or how they fare when they're not at work. Nor do we ask all of them to accept the brutal bargain of an American melting pot that rapidly absorbs the culture of an immigrant in exchange for the benefits of citizenship.

Instead, we are happy enough that most labor vans of hardworking helots stay on the road in the early-morning hours, out of sight and out of mind. Sometimes, though, they tragically do not.

TOPICS FOR CRITICAL THINKING AND WRITING

1. Speakers and writers who take care to present themselves as decent, trustworthy people are concerned with what the Greeks called *ethos*, character. What impression do you get of Hanson's character from the first two paragraphs? If you had to guess—basing your guess only on the first two paragraphs—where Hanson stood on immigration, what would you say? Why?

2. What do you make of Hanson's title?

3. The third paragraph begins "But," a clear transition indicating that we will be going in a different direction. What other words in the third paragraph indicate what the writer's position will be?

4. What does Hanson mean in paragraph 3 when he calls the labor market in the San Joaquin Valley "a system predicated on a cynical violation of the law"? Do you agree with that description? Explain.

5. In his eleventh paragraph Hanson speaks of "the myth that our borders had crossed [the immigrants from Mexico]" rather than vice versa. What does he mean by this? Do you agree that it is a myth? Explain.

6. What are the differences between current immigration from Mexico and historic immigration from Europe a century ago (see para. 11)?

7. How does Hanson know that "almost a third of all foreign-born persons in the United States are here illegally" (para. 12)? Could it be that, from a sample of arrested immigrants, 30 percent or so turn out to be illegal? Is such a method of calculation persuasive? Explain.

8. In his next-to-last paragraph Hanson says, "We apparently don't care whether [immigrants] come legally or learn English." Do you agree with this assertion? On what evidence do you base your response?

9. Evaluate Hanson's final paragraph. Given his earlier paragraphs, does the paragraph make an effective ending? Explain.

Cardinal Roger Mahony

Roger Mahony, born in 1936 in Hollywood, California, was ordained a priest in 1962. In 1975 Governor Jerry Brown appointed Mahony as the first chair of the California Agricultural Labor Relations Board, where he worked to resolve disputes between the United Farm Workers and the growers. In 1980 Mahony was appointed bishop, in 1985 archbishop, and in 1991 cardinal. He has made controversial statements, sometimes disturbing liberals and sometimes disturbing conservatives. This following op-ed selection was originally published in the New York Times *in March 2006.*

In 2007 Cardinal Mahoney apologized for sexual abuses of boys by priests, but in 2013 it was revealed that, in fact, he had for years done his best to conceal the criminal activities of such priests and to impede police investigations of such matters. Cardinal Mahoney had retired in 2011, shortly before reaching the mandatory age of retirement, but when the news broke about the cover-ups he was relieved of what few duties he had continued to perform.

Called by God to Help

I've received a lot of criticism for stating last month that I would instruct the priests of my archdiocese to disobey a proposed law that would subject them, as well as other church and humanitarian workers, to criminal penalties. The proposed Border Protection, Antiterrorism, and Illegal Immigration Control bill, which was approved by the House of Representatives in December and is expected to be taken up by the Senate next week, would among other things subject to five years in prison anyone who "assists" an undocumented immigrant "to remain in the United States."

Some supporters of the bill have even accused the church of encouraging illegal immigration and meddling in politics. But I stand by my statement. Part of the mission of the Roman Catholic Church is to help people in need. It is our Gospel mandate, in which Christ instructs us to clothe the naked, feed the poor, and welcome the stranger. Indeed, the Catholic Church, through Catholic Charities agencies around the country, is one of the largest nonprofit providers of social services in the nation, serving both citizens and immigrants.

Providing humanitarian assistance to those in need should not be made a crime, as the House bill decrees. As written, the proposed law is so broad that it would criminalize even minor acts of mercy like offering a meal or administering first aid.

Current law does not require social service agencies to obtain evidence of legal status before rendering aid, nor should it. Denying aid to a fellow human being violates a law with a higher authority than Congress — the law of God.

That does not mean that the Catholic Church encourages or supports illegal immigration. Every day in our parishes, social service programs, hospitals, and schools, we witness the baleful consequences of illegal immigration. Families are separated, workers are exploited, and migrants are left by smugglers to die in the desert. Illegal immigration serves neither the migrant nor the common good.   5

What the church supports is an overhaul of the immigration system so that legal status and legal channels for migration replace illegal status and illegal immigration. Creating legal structures for migration protects not only those who migrate but also our nation, by giving the government the ability to better identify who is in the country as well as to control who enters it.

Only comprehensive reform of the immigration system, embodied in the principles of another proposal in Congress, the Secure America and Orderly Immigration bill, will help solve our current immigration crisis.

Enforcement-only proposals like the Border Protection act take the country in the opposite direction. Increasing penalties, building more detention centers, and erecting walls along our border with Mexico, as the act provides, will not solve the problem.

The legislation will not deter migrants who are desperate to survive and support their families from seeking jobs in the United States. It will only drive them further into the shadows, encourage the creation of more elaborate smuggling networks and cause hardship and suffering. I hope that the Senate will not take the same enforcement-only road as the House.

The unspoken truth of the immigration debate is that at the same time   10 our nation benefits economically from the presence of undocumented workers, we turn a blind eye when they are exploited by employers. They work in industries that are vital to our economy yet they have little legal protection and no opportunity to contribute fully to our nation.

While we gladly accept their taxes and sweat, we do not acknowledge or uphold their basic labor rights. At the same time, we scapegoat them for our social ills and label them as security threats and criminals to justify the passage of anti-immigrant bills.

This situation affects the dignity of millions of our fellow human beings and makes immigration, ultimately, a moral and ethical issue. That is why the church is compelled to take a stand against harmful legislation and to work toward positive change.

It is my hope that our elected officials will understand this and enact immigration reform that respects our common humanity and reflects the values—fairness, compassion, and opportunity—upon which our nation, a nation of immigrants, was built.

TOPICS FOR CRITICAL THINKING AND WRITING

1. Would it matter to Cardinal Mahony's position if the legislation he mentions in paragraph 1 proposed a mandatory rather than a discretionary prison term for violators? Why, or why not?

2. Do you agree with the author that the proposed law is overly broad (para. 3)? How does he argue for such a conclusion? How might you argue for or against it?

3. What's the difference between supporting "humanitarian assistance" to all comers (para. 3) and not "encourag[ing]" or "support[ing] illegal immigration" (para. 5)? Is the distinction an important one? Explain.

4. Does Cardinal Mahony just favor breaking the law (if law it becomes) penalizing those who "assist" undocumented immigrants to remain in the United States? Or does he favor civil disobedience on this issue? What's the difference, in any case?

5. Suppose someone accused the cardinal of exaggerating the threat; no sensible prosecutor or district attorney is going to seek a conviction of someone for "administering first aid" (para. 3) to an illegal immigrant. How might he reply?

6. What are the main features of the Secure America and Orderly Immigration bill (para. 7)? What would it do (if enacted into law) to cure the problem of illegal immigration? Can you think of some other measures that, if enacted into law, might help solve this problem?

7. Do you think it is unfair to tax the earnings of undocumented workers and at the same time refuse to provide them with basic human rights (para. 11)? Explain why or why not in an essay of 250 words.

8. As we say in our biographical headnote, it is now known that Cardinal Mahoney significantly impeded police investigations of the sexual molestation of minors by priests. How does this information affect your evaluation of Mahoney's argument concerning illegal immigrants? No doubt, we can no longer say, "Cardinal Mahoney is known as a highly moral person, so we must take his arguments very seriously" (i.e., the appeal from *ethos*), but can we dismiss his argument on immigration because of his appalling actions concerning sexual predators? Discuss.

For topical links related to the issue of immigration, see the companion Web site: **bedfordstmartins.com/barnetbedau.**

25

Service: Should the United States Require Young People to Perform Public Service?

Barack Obama

President Obama (born in 1961) delivered the commencement address at Wesleyan University in Connecticut in the spring of 2008 while he was a candidate for the presidency. As he explains in the speech, he was substituting for Senator Edward Kennedy, who had recently undergone surgery. Senator Kennedy died in the following year.

Commencement Address

Thank you, President Roth, for that generous introduction, and congratulations on your first year at the helm of Wesleyan. Congratulations also to the class of 2008, and thank you for allowing me to be a part of your graduation.

I have the distinct honor today of pinch-hitting for one of my personal heroes and a hero to this country, Senator Edward Kennedy. Teddy wanted to be here very much, but as you know, he's had a very long week and is taking some much-needed rest. He called me up a few days ago and I said that I'd be happy to be his stand-in, even if there was no way I could fill his shoes.

I did, however, get the chance to glance at the speech he planned on delivering today, and I'd like to start by passing along a message from him: "To all those praying for my return to good health, I offer my heartfelt thanks. And to any who'd rather have a different result, I say, don't get your hopes up just yet!"

So we know that Ted Kennedy's legendary sense of humor is as strong as ever, and I have no doubt that his equally legendary fighting spirit will carry him through this latest challenge. He is our friend, he is our champion, and we hope and pray for his return to good health.

The topic of his speech today was common for a commencement, but one that nobody could discuss with more authority or inspiration than Ted Kennedy. And that is the topic of service to one's country—a cause that is synonymous with his family's name and their legacy.

I was born the year that his brother John called a generation of Americans to ask their country what they could do. And I came of age at a time when they did it. They were the Peace Corps volunteers who won a generation of goodwill toward America at a time when America's ideals were challenged. They were the teenagers and college students, not much older than you, who watched the Civil Rights Movement unfold on their television sets; who saw the dogs and the fire hoses and the footage of marchers beaten within an inch of their lives; who knew it was probably smarter and safer to stay at home, but still decided to take those Freedom Rides down South—who still decided to march. And because they did, they changed the world.

I bring this up because today, you are about to enter a world that makes it easy to get caught up in the notion that there are actually two different stories at work in our lives.

The first is the story of our everyday cares and concerns—the responsibilities we have to our jobs and our families—the bustle and busyness of what happens in our own life. And the second is the story of what happens in the life of our country—of what happens in the wider world. It's the story you see when you catch a glimpse of the day's headlines or turn on the news at night—a story of big challenges like war and recession; hunger and climate change; injustice and inequality. It's a story that can sometimes seem distant and separate from our own—a destiny to be shaped by forces beyond our control.

And yet, the history of this nation tells us this isn't so. It tells us that we are a people whose destiny has never been written for us, but by us—by generations of men and women, young and old, who have always believed that their story and the American story are not separate, but shared. And for more than two centuries, they have served this country in ways that have forever enriched both.

I say this to you as someone who couldn't be standing here today if not for the service of others, and wouldn't be standing here today if not for the purpose that service gave my own life.

You see, I spent much of my childhood adrift. My father left my mother and I when I was two. When my mother remarried, I lived in Indonesia for a time, but was mostly raised in Hawaii by her and my grandparents from Kansas. My teenage years were filled with more than the usual dose of adolescent rebellion, and I'll admit that I didn't always take myself or my studies very seriously. I realize that none of you can probably relate to this, but there were many times when I wasn't sure where I was going, or what I would do.

But during my first two years of college, perhaps because the values my mother had taught me—hard work, honesty, empathy—had resurfaced after a long hibernation; or perhaps because of the example of wonderful teachers and lasting friends, I began to notice a world beyond myself. I became active in the movement to oppose the apartheid regime of South Africa. I began following the debates in this country about poverty and health care. So that by the time I graduated from college, I was possessed with a crazy idea—that I would work at a grassroots level to bring about change.

I wrote letters to every organization in the country I could think of. And one day, a small group of churches on the South Side of Chicago offered me a job to come work as a community organizer in neighborhoods that had been devastated by steel plant closings. My mother and grandparents wanted me to go to law school. My friends were applying to jobs on Wall Street. Meanwhile, this organization offered me $12,000 a year plus $2,000 for an old, beat-up car.

And I said yes.

Now, I didn't know a soul in Chicago, and I wasn't sure what this 15 community organizing business was all about. I had always been inspired by stories of the Civil Rights Movement and JFK's call to service, but when I got to the South Side, there were no marches, and no soaring speeches. In the shadow of an empty steel plant, there were just a lot of folks who were struggling. And we didn't get very far at first.

I still remember one of the very first meetings we put together to discuss gang violence with a group of community leaders. We waited and waited for people to show up, and finally, a group of older people walked into the hall. And they sat down. And a little old lady raised her hand and asked, "Is this where the bingo game is?"

It wasn't easy, but eventually, we made progress. Day by day, block by block, we brought the community together, and registered new voters, and set up after-school programs, and fought for new jobs, and helped people live lives with some measure of dignity.

But I also began to realize that I wasn't just helping other people. Through service, I found a community that embraced me; citizenship that was meaningful; the direction I'd been seeking. Through service, I discovered how my own improbable story fit into the larger story of America.

Each of you will have the chance to make your own discovery in the years to come. And I say "chance" because you won't have to take it. There's no community service requirement in the real world; no one forcing you to care. You can take your diploma, walk off this stage, and chase only after the big house and the nice suits and all the other things that our money culture says you should buy. You can choose to narrow your concerns and live your life in a way that tries to keep your story separate from America's.

But I hope you don't. Not because you have an obligation to those 20 who are less fortunate, though you do have that obligation. Not because you have a debt to all those who helped you get here, though you do have that debt.

It's because you have an obligation to yourself. Because our individual salvation depends on collective salvation. Because thinking only about yourself, fulfilling your immediate wants and needs, betrays a poverty of ambition. Because it's only when you hitch your wagon to something larger than yourself that you realize your true potential and discover the role you'll play in writing the next great chapter in America's story.

There are so many ways to serve and so much need at this defining moment in our history. You don't have to be a community organizer or do something crazy like run for president. Right here at Wesleyan, many of you have already volunteered at local schools, contributed to United Way, and even started a program that brings fresh produce to needy families in the area. One hundred and sixty-four graduates of this school have joined the Peace Corps since 2001, and I'm especially proud that two of you are about to leave for my father's homeland of Kenya to bring alternative sources of energy to impoverished areas.

I ask you to seek these opportunities when you leave here, because the future of this country—your future—depends on it. At a time when our security and moral standing depend on winning hearts and minds in the forgotten corners of this world, we need more of you to serve abroad. As president, I intend to grow the Foreign Service, double the Peace Corps over the next few years, and engage the young people of other nations in similar programs, so that we work side by side to take on the common challenges that confront all humanity.

At a time when our ice caps are melting and our oceans are rising, we need you to help lead a green revolution. We still have time to avoid the catastrophic consequences of climate change if we get serious about investing in renewable sources of energy, and if we get a generation of volunteers to work on renewable energy projects, and teach folks about conservation, and help clean up polluted areas; if we send talented engineers and scientists abroad to help developing countries promote clean energy.

At a time when a child in Boston must compete with children in 25 Beijing and Bangalore, we need an army of you to become teachers and principals in schools that this nation cannot afford to give up on. I will pay our educators what they deserve, and give them more support, but I will also ask more of them to be mentors to other teachers, and serve in high-need schools and high-need subject areas like math and science.

At a time when there are children in the city of New Orleans who still spend each night in a lonely trailer, we need more of you to take a weekend or a week off from work, and head down South, and help rebuild. If you can't get the time, volunteer at the local homeless shelter or soup kitchen in your own community. Find an organization that's fighting poverty, or a candidate who promotes policies you believe in, and find a way to help them.

At a time of war, we need you to work for peace. At a time of inequality, we need you to work for opportunity. At a time of so much cynicism and so much doubt, we need you to make us believe again.

Now understand this—believing that change is possible is not the same as being naïve. Go into service with your eyes wide open, for change will not come easily. On the big issues that our nation faces, difficult choices await. We'll have to face some hard truths, and some sacrifice will be required—not only from you individually, but from the nation as a whole.

There is no magic bullet to our energy problems, for example; no perfect energy source—so all of us will have to use the energy sources we have more wisely. Deep-rooted poverty will not be reversed overnight, and will require both money and reform at a time when our federal and state budgets are strapped and Washington is skeptical that reform is possible. Transforming our education system will require not only bold government action, but a change in attitudes among parents and students. Bringing an end to the slaughter in Darfur will involve navigating extremely difficult realities on the ground, even for those with the best of intentions.

And so, should you take the path of service, should you choose to take up one of these causes as your own, know that you'll experience frustrations and failures. Even your successes will be marked by imperfections and unintended consequences. I guarantee you, there will certainly be times when friends or family urge you to pursue more sensible endeavors with more tangible rewards. And there will be times when you are tempted to take their advice.   30

But I hope you'll remember, during those times of doubt and frustration, that there is nothing naïve about your impulse to change this world. Because all it takes is one act of service—one blow against injustice—to send forth that tiny ripple of hope that Robert Kennedy spoke of.

You know, Ted Kennedy often tells a story about the fifth anniversary celebration of the Peace Corps. He was there, and he asked one of the young Americans why he had chosen to volunteer. And the man replied, "Because it was the first time someone asked me to do something for my country."

I don't know how many of you have been asked that question, but after today, you have no excuses. I am asking you, and if I should have the honor of serving this nation as president, I will be asking again in the coming years. We may disagree on certain issues and positions, but I believe we can be unified in service to a greater good. I intend to make it a cause of my presidency, and I believe with all my heart that this generation is ready, and eager, and up to the challenge.

We will face our share of cynics and doubters. But we always have. I can still remember a conversation I had with an older man all those years ago just before I left for Chicago. He said, "Barack, I'll give you a bit of advice. Forget this community organizing business and do something that's gonna make you some money. You can't change the world, and people won't appreciate you trying. But you've got a nice voice, so you should think about going into television broadcasting. I'm telling you, you've got a future."

Now, he may have been right about the TV thing, but he was wrong 35
about everything else. For that old man has not seen what I have seen.
He has not seen the faces of ordinary people the first time they clear a
vacant lot or build a new playground or force an unresponsive leader
to provide services to their community. He has not seen the face of a
child brighten because of an inspiring teacher or mentor. He has not
seen scores of young people educate their parents on issues like Darfur,
or mobilize the conscience of a nation around the challenge of climate
change. He has not seen lines of men and women that wrap around
schools and churches, that stretch block after block just so they could
make their voices heard, many for the very first time.

And that old man who didn't believe the world could change—who
didn't think one person could make a difference—well he certainly
didn't know much about the life of Joseph Kennedy's youngest son.

It is rare in this country of ours that a person exists who has touched
the lives of nearly every single American without many of us even realizing it. And yet, because of Ted Kennedy, millions of children can see
a doctor when they get sick. Mothers and fathers can leave work to
spend time with their newborns. Working Americans are paid higher
wages, and compensated for overtime, and can keep their health insurance when they change jobs. They are protected from discrimination in
the workplace, and those who are born with disabilities can still get an
education, and health care, and fair treatment on the job. Our schools
are stronger and our colleges are filled with more Americans who can
afford it. And I have a feeling that Ted Kennedy is not done just yet.

But surely, if one man can achieve so much and make such a difference in the lives of so many, then each of us can do our part. Surely, if his
service and his story can forever shape America's story, then our collective
service can shape the destiny of this generation. At the very least, his living example calls each of us to try. That is all I ask of you on this joyous
day of new beginnings; that is what Senator Kennedy asks of you as well,
and that is how we will keep so much needed work going, and the cause
of justice everlasting, and the dream alive for generations to come. Thank
you so much to the class of 2008, and congratulations on your graduation.

TOPICS FOR CRITICAL THINKING AND WRITING

1. What is the central topic of Obama's address (para. 5)? Does he make
   a persuasive case for public service? Are there relevant issues he fails
   to confront? If so, what are they and how do you think they should be
   handled?

2. In paragraph 11 Obama says, "I realize that none of you can probably
   relate to this." Given the immediate context—the sentence that precedes the words we have quoted—do you think most of his hearers
   agreed? Why, or why not?

3. In paragraph 17—a paragraph consisting of two sentences—Obama repeats the word "and" four times. Is the sentence inept, or does Obama have some rhetorical purpose? If so, what is the purpose?

4. In paragraph 20 Obama says that we *do* "have an obligation to those who are less fortunate." Putting aside his specific reason, which he gives in the next sentence, do you agree with this assertion? Why, or why not? Now think about his reason, his assertion that "our individual salvation depends on collective salvation." Does this make sense to you? Explain.

5. The last two paragraphs are a tribute to Ted Kennedy. Do you think they are appropriate and effective? Explain.

6. What sort of persona does Obama project in this speech? Specify certain passages that convey a particular personality, or at least a distinctive tone.

7. Do you know anyone who is a recent immigrant to this country? If so, interview this person and write an essay describing his or her experience adapting to life in the United States.

8. How would you define "green revolution" (para. 24)? Are you and some (all? none?) of your friends or roommates active in this "revolution"? Explain your answer.

9. Conservatives led by former president Ronald Reagan argued that government is the problem, not the solution. Often cited as an exception to this generalization is the case of the G.I. Bill of Rights. Look up its history, and write up your findings in an essay of 350 words. Explain whether or not you agree with Reagan and why.

Peter Levine

Peter Levine (b. 1967) is research director of the Jonathan M. Tisch College of Citizenship and Public Service at Tufts University. Among his publications is a book entitled The Future of Democracy: Developing the Next Generation of American Citizens *(2007). This selection appeared in* Philosophy and Public Policy Quarterly, *Summer/Fall 2008.*

The Case for "Service"

On September 11, 2008, both major presidential candidates traveled to New York City, where some of the nation's most prominent corporations and foundations were sponsoring a forum on civilian community service. September 11 is a solemn day, rich with patriotic meanings, when politicians are expected to demonstrate their commitment to essential American values. But they can choose *which* values to emphasize, from military strength to prosperity to civil rights. This year, Barack Obama and John McCain joined such luminaries as Arnold Schwarzenegger and Hillary Clinton to affirm the value of service. More concretely, they endorsed a bill, the Kennedy-Hatch "Serve America Act of 2008" (S.3487), that would dramatically expand federal support for civilian service programs. Given their support and the leadership of Senators Orrin Hatch and Edward Kennedy, the Serve America Act seems destined for passage—although perhaps not for full funding at a time of economic and fiscal crisis.

The bill has many sections and features, but two of its major objectives are to get at least 250,000 Americans involved in federally supported service every year and to institutionalize "service-learning" (the combination of community service with academic study) in school systems and colleges. Kennedy-Hatch would provide significant new funding to programs that recruit economically disadvantaged Americans to participate in service and service-learning, and it would focus volunteers' work on three social objectives: reducing the dropout rate, improving public health, and conserving energy.

In current legislative parlance, "service" refers to a variety of programs funded by the government but often organized by private contractors. To a philosopher who wants to consider whether government-funded service is a good thing, the heterogeneity of these programs—with their diverse purposes, constituents, and methods—poses a challenge. Nevertheless, "service" constitutes a field of practice, with many overlapping networks of alumni and leaders, similar funding sources, frequent meetings and conferences, a common genealogy, and a shared political agenda—currently focused on the passage of Kennedy-Hatch. We ought to be able to say whether supporting such fields of practice is good public policy, and whether it is wise to *shift* such fields by preferring some of their elements over others. Kennedy-Hatch seeks to alter the field of service through the two proposals mentioned above: investing in lower-income volunteers and focusing on three major social purposes. Does an expanded civilian service initiative with these priorities merit government support?

ADDRESSING NATIONAL CHALLENGES

One major argument for service programs is that federally financed volunteers can effectively address public problems. If Kennedy-Hatch becomes law, it will put Congress on record as saying that "focused national service efforts can effectively tackle pressing national challenges, such as improving education for low-income students, increasing energy conservation, and improving the health, well-being, and economic opportunities of the neediest individuals in the Nation."

It remains to be seen whether this proposition is true. AmeriCorps 5 has sometimes tried to estimate its members' impact on the neighborhoods they serve; a 1995–96 evaluation of Learn & Serve America concluded that each hour volunteered by students was worth about $8.76 to their communities. But such a statistic is not especially helpful in assessing a program's ability to address "pressing national challenges." Perhaps a dollar spent on tax credits would have more impact on energy conservation than a dollar spent to recruit volunteers to weatherize homes.

To take another example, consider YouthBuild, a job training program for disadvantaged youth ages sixteen to twenty-four. YouthBuild members learn construction trades by building houses for people in their communities. An evaluation by the Department of Housing and Urban Development found that the program generated relatively few new housing units. On the other hand, 29 percent of participants who entered without having graduated from high school obtained diplomas while they served, and 12 percent pursued higher education afterwards. These figures suggest that the best rationale for supporting YouthBuild is not that it will address the urban housing crisis, but that, through its impact on participants, it will address the dropout problem.

Certainly the organizers of service programs need to pay *some* attention to their impact on communities. When volunteers contribute tangible public goods, such as affordable homes and clean parks, they offset the programs' costs. Besides, volunteers need to have a positive impact to be satisfied and motivated. If National Civilian Community Corps members never planted any trees, they would become cynical and discouraged.

Nevertheless, it is only a hypothesis that community service is an efficient and effective way to address national problems. I hope the hypothesis is true, but we should also consider other rationales for government support of service programs. As the YouthBuild example suggests, one such rationale emphasizes the value of service not for the recipients, but for the volunteers.

INDIVIDUALS AS PUBLIC ASSETS

Service programs regard individuals as potential public assets, as contributors to the common good. This is philosophically appealing because it reflects a basic principle (which we could call Kantian) of respecting other people's moral agency. Kant insisted that all human beings be treated as responsible, as members of the Kingdom of Ends.

Among the various social groups who tend *not* to be treated that 10 way, disadvantaged youth are a leading example. Many schools and other institutions treat teenagers in low-income communities as bundles of problems or risks. Cumulatively, such treatment sends a debilitating message. An alternative approach is supported by the psychological theory known as "positive youth development." This theory tells us that young people are more likely to avoid pitfalls such as crime, unwanted pregnancy, and academic failure when they are given opportunities to contribute their talents to the community. For low-income youth, the need for such opportunities would seem to be especially great.

Positive youth development is consistent with a Kantian view of human agency, but it is also an empirical theory: It holds that society can enhance individuals' welfare by giving them opportunities to serve. This theory may seem romantic, but it has been vindicated in numerous studies. For example, a randomized experiment showed that it was possible to cut the teen pregnancy rate by offering young women service opportunities. Generalizing from other studies, the Kennedy-Hatch bill notes that "high-quality service-learning programs keep students engaged in school and increase the likelihood that they will graduate."

At present, however, the most expansive and rewarding service programs tend to be provided in affluent schools and communities. In a survey of more than two thousand California students, Joseph Kahne and Ellen Middaugh found that service-learning experiences were less common for African American and Latino youth than for white and Asian youth; less common for students whose parents had low education levels; and much less common for students who had low grade-point averages. To its credit, Kennedy-Hatch addresses such inequalities by giving priority to schools and independent programs that offer service-learning opportunities to disadvantaged students.

SERVICE AND CIVIC ENGAGEMENT

We have seen that service has the potential to benefit those who serve as well as those who are served. One rationale for publicly funded service programs emphasizes its potential to foster the participants' civic identity and improve the relationship between citizens and their government.

Richard Stengel made this case for *universal* service in an August 2007 cover story for *Time* magazine. He began by noting that "while confidence in our democracy and our government is near an all-time low, volunteerism and civic participation since the '70s are near all-time highs." To Stengel, the explanation for this paradox seemed obvious: "People, especially young people, think the government and the public sphere are broken, but they feel they can personally make a difference through community service. . . . People see volunteering not as a form of public service but as an antidote for it."

Stengel argued that universal service, undertaken in a patriotic spirit,   15
would reconnect volunteerism to the ideals of public service and a common civic identity. Devoting a year to national service, he wrote, "should become a countrywide rite of passage, the common expectation and widespread experience of virtually every young American." The program he favored would not be "mandatory or compulsory," he explained. But it would "harness the spirit of volunteerism that already exists and make it a permanent part of American culture." It would also lead, presumably, to greater political participation, in the forms of voting, following the news, and running for public office. In Stengel's view, nothing much

less ambitious than universal national service could achieve the goal of reconnecting millions of Americans to public life.

But the Serve America Act stops far short of creating a universal service program—and I think its relatively small scale is wise. About 4.5 million Americans are eighteen years old. If they were all to participate in service programs, we would need an enormous new infrastructure. As a point of comparison, there are 18 million students enrolled in all the institutions of higher education in the United States. Thus, universal national service programs would have to serve as many young people as one fourth of all our colleges and universities do. To build valuable new learning opportunities for all those participants would cost billions of dollars and require hundreds of thousands of new full-time, permanent positions for corps leaders and administrators.

It is difficult to provide high-quality learning opportunities through service, and we could do damage by calling on young people—especially disadvantaged young people—to fill menial or make-work positions. Michelle Charles has described inner-city Philadelphians doing a deliberately lackluster job on a service project that was designed by outsiders. The project (temporarily removing graffiti from a wall) sounds pointless, and one might argue that the participants' foot-dragging was a form of civic action that achieved a desirable social outcome: ending a misguided program. I am not suggesting that the Philadelphia project is typical. But as Paul Light recently observed, "[T]oo many charitable organizations do not know how to manage volunteers effectively or recruit new employees. Young Americans want the chance to make a difference and learn new skills, not work in the back office stuffing envelopes." Under Kennedy-Hatch, nonprofits applying for federal grants would have an incentive to develop truly educational and meaningful service opportunities. In addition, the bill creates a new commission to investigate how nonprofits use volunteers.

I would support creating as many service positions as we can that do not displace regular employees and that attract applicants because of their social impact and the opportunities they offer for experiential learning. The right number is hard to predict, but 250,000 sounds like a reasonable estimate. (It translates to about 1 in every 18 eighteen-year-olds.) I would want to see AmeriCorps and other federal service programs attracting more applicants than they have places, as evidence that these programs were truly desirable and voluntary. But I hope they would not pick the most academically successful applicants; more important is each candidate's likelihood of benefiting from participation in service.

PUBLIC SERVANTS AND THE REST OF US

The opportunity to engage in the kind of high-quality, rigorously evaluated service envisioned by Kennedy-Hatch has the potential to close what we might think of as an identity gap between citizens and employees of the government. I believe this gap is a major cause of the civic disengagement that Stengel and others bemoan.

Consider the diminishing involvement of parents and other commu- 20 nity members in public education. Belonging to a PTA is about half as common today as it was in 1960, and those parents who are still involved in schools are often asked to provide money or low-skilled labor rather than input on how the schools should be run. In the 1970s, according to the DDB Life Style survey, more than 40 percent of Americans said they worked on community projects, many of which involved education; that percentage is now down to the 20s. There are many explanations for these changes, but surely one reason is the growing monopoly over education by credentialed, professional experts, especially state and district administrators and test-writers.

Elinor Ostrom has shown that in the mid-twentieth century, a substantial proportion of American households had members who served on elected public bodies, such as school boards, at some time in their lives. But consolidation of governments and heavy use of professional managers has reduced such participation to a trivial level. Today, some Americans are in "public service," and the rest are not. Meanwhile, the all-volunteer military, for better *and* for worse, separates civilians from professional warriors in a way that was not true under the draft.

I believe we need to weaken this distinction between public servants and the rest of us—to help people move in and out of public service so that each side learns more about the other. National and community service can be a powerful tool to achieve this goal. It doesn't require universal participation, because the purpose is to generate opportunities for interested individuals to move between the private and public sectors, so that they can learn and contribute in both sectors and create models for others.

Teach for America (TFA) provides a vivid illustration. TFA recruits top graduates from the nation's colleges and universities and places them in public schools—usually low-performing schools—for two years. It differs from federal service programs in that local school authorities employ its teachers directly, but it resembles the Peace Corps and City Year in that it places young people temporarily in full-time public service work. Although many of its recruits have stayed in education (TFA's alumni include many influential school reformers), that was never the program's overriding goal. The idea was that TFA members who left the classroom after two years would become advocates for educational equality. Their experience would motivate them to "continue the struggle" as informed citizens, community activists, school board members, and political leaders.

TFA illustrates another principle as well: The impact of service on volunteers' civic commitments and beliefs is more diverse and unpredictable than the paeans to service typically acknowledge. Many TFA teachers go to work in profoundly dysfunctional school systems—an experience that is hardly likely to strengthen their trust in the public sector. One TFA alumna, Michelle Rhee, has brought controversial corporate efficiency measures to the public schools in Washington, D.C., where she was appointed chancellor in 2007. Traditional liberals, libertarian-leaning conservatives, good-government reformers, efficiency experts, and others will have different *hopes* about what a stint in public service may teach. In my view, we should be willing to learn from the young people who have had that experience.

EXPANDING THE AGENDA

Service has the potential to restore Americans' civic engagement, but   25 it also has limitations. I have already noted the difficulty of providing excellent learning opportunities on a large scale. To make matters worse, federally funded service programs cannot engage in political activities, which narrows the scope of participants' civic action.

The very word "service," moreover, can send a message contrary to the ideal of respecting individual agency that I described above. A recent survey by the National Conference on Citizenship found that, for many people, the word "service" connotes episodic charitable or "helping" behavior. The word can suggest that some people are helpless and therefore need to be served, which is the opposite of the idea that everyone can be a moral agent and a contributor.

We need to find ways to encourage deliberation, problem-solving, the creation of public goods, and other roles for citizens that go beyond service. No one tool will reverse the disengagement of Americans from public life. But several policies, undertaken in a coordinated fashion, could make a substantial difference.

- *Civic education*. There is evidence that teaching young people about civic and political issues increases the odds that they will discuss such issues, join groups, volunteer, and vote later in life. Moreover, the impact of such teaching is enhanced when students engage in community service projects that include research or reflection.

- *Deliberation*. In addition to "serving," citizens should also deliberate, which involves real decision-making. The recent National Conference on Citizenship poll (see graph on page 643) found strong and bipartisan support for a proposal, developed by the nonprofit America*Speaks*, to involve more than one million Americans in a national deliberation on an important public issue. Although it has never been tried, a national deliberation might improve public policy and also provide a valuable model of organized, meaningful public involvement.

- *Influence on local institutions*. A comprehensive reform agenda would include efforts to increase local citizens' influence on everyday public institutions, such as schools, local governments, and police forces. One promising model is the elaborate series of Study Circles that encouraged broad discussion of education in Bridgeport, Conn., and gradually built public support for school reform while raising the level of parental volunteering in the city's schools. In Hampton, Va., youth involvement in boards and committees has improved education and policing in that city.

• *Public service reform.* Finally, a civic engagement agenda would include changing the nature of careers in public service. The imminent

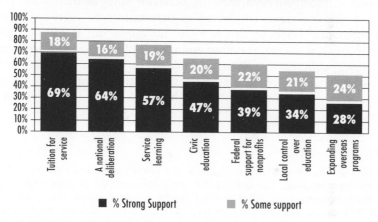

PUBLIC SUPPORT FOR POLICIES TO ENHANCE CIVIC ENGAGEMENT

■ % Strong Support   ■ % Some support

Proposals tested

• Tuition for service: "offering every young person a chance to earn money toward college or advanced training if they complete a full year of national or community service."

• A national deliberation: "involving more than one million Americans in a national discussion of an important public issue and requiring Congress to respond to what the citizens say."

• Service learning: "requiring all high school students to do community service as part of their work for one or more courses."

• Civic education: "requiring high school students to pass a new test on civics or government."

• Federal support for nonprofits: "providing federal money to support nonprofit, faith-based, and civic organizations that use volunteers."

• Local control over education: "changing the law so that local citizens must take the lead in setting standards and choosing tests for students in their local schools."

• Expanding overseas programs: "funding and promoting overseas service as a way of improving our relations with other countries."

Source: National Conference on Citizenship survey ("America's Civic Health Index"), Conducted by CIRCLE (the Center for Information & Research on Civic Learning and Engagement), July 2008.

retirement of roughly one million federal employees offers an opportunity to rethink public service so that jobs in the public sector become more rewarding and creative—to flatten hierarchies and promote collaboration, including partnerships between the government and community groups. Paul Light calls on the next administration to "reverse the federal government's well-deserved reputation as a destination of last resort for young Americans. The government's antiquated personnel system must be modernized to reward performance, not time on the job, and give new recruits the career paths to make a difference faster."

It appears, then, that service is the politically easy part of restoring active citizenship in America. With enough money, we can enroll 250,000 Americans in activities that we call "service," most of which will involve uncontroversial helping behavior such as mentoring children and planting trees, conducted in the volunteers' own communities. On balance, I believe this is a worthy cause. But it will be much harder to use volunteers to define and plan solutions to hard problems, to increase public participation in deliberative decision making, or to redesign the civil service. I support Kennedy-Hatch as an element of the reform agenda. But success on these other fronts will be just as critical to strengthening civic engagement in the United States.

SOURCES

For details on the ServiceNation Summit, see www.bethechangeinc.org/service nation/summit/purpose. The text of the Serve America Act of 2008 is available at www.opencongress.org/bill/110-s3487/show. Other sources: The Center for Human Resources, Brandeis University, *Summary Report, National Evaluation of Learn and Serve America School and Community-Based Programs* (Corporation for National Service, July 1999), p. 24; Maxine V. Mitchell, Davis Jenkins, Dao Nguyen, Alona Lerman, and Marian DeBerry, *Evaluation of the YouthBuild Program* (U.S. Department of Housing and Urban Development, August 2003); Jacquelynne Eccles and Jennifer Appleton Gootman, eds., *Community Programs to Promote Youth Development*, a report of the National Research Council and Institute of Medicine, Board on Children, Youth, and Families, Committee on Community-Level Programs for Youth (National Academies Press, 2002), pp. 181–84; Joseph Kahne and Ellen Middaugh, "Democracy for Some: The Civic Opportunity Gap in High School," CIRCLE Working Paper 59 (February 2008), www.civicyouth. org; Richard Stengel, "A Time to Serve," *Time* (August 7, 2007) (for a link to an online version, see the ServiceNation Web site); Michelle M. Charles, "Giving Back to the Community: African American Inner City Teens and Civic Engagement," CIRCLE Working Paper 38 (August 2005), pp. 15–16, www.civicyouth. org; Paul Light, "Make It Easier to Say Yes to Public Service," *Huffington Post* (Sept. 9, 2008), www.huffingtonpost.com; Robert D. Putnam, *Bowling Alone: The Collapse and Revival of American Community* (Simon & Schuster, 2000), p. 442 (for data on PTA membership); DDB Life Style Survey, www.bowlingalone.com /data.htm (data analyzed by the author); Peter Levine, "Education and the Limits of Technocracy," *Philosophy & Public Policy Quarterly*, vol. 27, no. 3/4 (Summer/ Fall 2007), pp. 17–21; Elinor Ostrom, "A Frequently Overlooked Precondition of Democracy: Citizens Knowledgeable about and Engaged in Collective Action,"

Workshop in Political Theory and Policy Analysis, 2005; America*Speaks, Millions of Voices: A Blueprint for Engaging the American Public in Policymaking* (September 2004), www.americaspeaks.org; Will Friedman, Alison Kadlec, and Lara Birnbeck, *Transforming Public Life: A Decade of Citizen Engagement in Bridgeport, Ct.*, Public Agenda Foundation Center for Advances in Public Engagement, *Case Studies in Public Agenda* (2007), www.publicagenda.org; Carmen Sirianni, "Youth Civic Engagement: Systems and Culture Change in Hampton, Virginia," CIRCLE Working Paper 31 (April 2005), www.civicyouth.org.

TOPICS FOR CRITICAL THINKING AND WRITING

1. How does Levine propose to define "service"? Can you improve on his definition?

2. Summarize in 100 words the main provisions of the Kennedy-Hatch bill, "Serve America Act of 2008." What is its status today?

3. Would you volunteer for some form of public service? What incentives, if any, would be necessary to get you to volunteer for a year or two of public service? What reasons against volunteering would you respect? Explain in an essay of 250 words.

4. What does it mean to say with the philosopher Immanuel Kant that "all human beings [are to] be treated . . . as members of the Kingdom of Ends" (para. 9)? Are you such a member? Why, or why not?

5. Should public service be universal? Mandatory? Evaluate the reasons advanced by Richard Stengel in paragraph 15.

6. What forms of public service would most attract you? Why those and not others as well?

7. Consider the graph on page 643. Imagine you had to explain it to a classmate. What would you stress, and what would you ignore or downplay? Which if any of its findings do you find surprising?

8. Are you impressed with the wealth and variety of sources that Levine relies on in his essay, or are they mainly window dressing? How can you tell which it is?

Thomas E. Ricks

Thomas E. Ricks, a Pulitzer Prize–winning journalist, is a senior fellow at a think-tank called the Center for a New American Security. His most recent book is The Generals: American Military Command from World War II to Today. *We reprint an op-ed piece that appeared in the* New York Times *in 2012.*

Let's Draft Our Kids

In late June, Gen. Stanley A. McChrystal, the former commander of international forces in Afghanistan, called for reinstating the draft.

"I think if a nation goes to war, every town, every city needs to be at risk," he said at the Aspen Ideas Festival. "You make that decision and everybody has skin in the game."

This was the first time in recent years that a high-profile officer has broken ranks to argue that the all-volunteer force is not necessarily good for the country or the military. Unlike Europeans, Americans still seem determined to maintain a serious military force, so we need to think about how to pay for it and staff it by creating a draft that is better and more equitable than the Vietnam-era conscription system.

A revived draft, including both males and females, should include three options for new conscripts coming out of high school. Some could choose eighteen months of military service with low pay but excellent postservice benefits, including free college tuition. These conscripts would not be deployed but could perform tasks currently outsourced at great cost to the Pentagon: paperwork, painting barracks, mowing lawns, driving generals around, and generally doing lower-skills tasks so professional soldiers don't have to. If they want to stay, they could move into the professional force and receive weapons training, higher pay, and better benefits.

Those who don't want to serve in the army could perform civilian national service for a slightly longer period and equally low pay—teaching in low-income areas, cleaning parks, rebuilding crumbling infrastructure, or aiding the elderly. After two years, they would receive similar benefits like tuition aid.

And libertarians who object to a draft could opt out. Those who   5 declined to help Uncle Sam would in return pledge to ask nothing from him—no Medicare, no subsidized college loans, and no mortgage guarantees. Those who want minimal government can have it.

Critics will argue that this is a political non-starter. It may be now. But America has already witnessed far less benign forms of conscription. A new draft that maintains the size and the quality of the current all-volunteer force, saves the government money through civilian national service, and frees professional soldiers from performing menial tasks would appeal to many constituencies.

Others argue that the numbers don't add up. With an average cohort of about 4 million eighteen-year-olds annually, they say, there is simply no place to put all these people. But the government could use this cheap labor in new ways, doing jobs that governments do in other countries but which have been deemed too expensive in this one, like providing universal free day care or delivering meals to elderly shut-ins. And if too many people applied for the eighteen-month military program, then a lottery system could be devised—the opposite of the 1970s-era system where being selected was hardly desirable. The rest could perform nonmilitary national service.

A final objection is the price tag; this program would cost billions of dollars. But it also would save billions, especially if implemented broadly and imaginatively. One reason our relatively small military is hugely expensive is that all of today's volunteer soldiers are paid well; they often have spouses and children who require housing and medical care.

Unmarried conscripts don't need such a safety net. And much of the labor currently contracted out to the private sector could be performed by eighteen-year-olds for much less. And we could raise the retirement age for the professional force from twenty to thirty years of service. There is no reason to kick healthy forty-year-olds out of the military and then give them full retirement pay for forty years. These reforms would greatly reduce both recruiting and pension costs.

Similarly, some of the civilian service programs would help save the government money: Taking food to an elderly shut-in might keep that person from having to move into a nursing home. It would be fairly cheap to house conscript soldiers on closed military bases. Housing civilian service members would be more expensive, but imaginative use of existing assets could save money. For example, V.A. hospitals might have space.

The pool of cheap labor available to the federal government would broadly lower its current personnel costs and its pension obligations — especially if the law told federal managers to use the civilian service as much as possible, and wherever plausible. The government could also make this cheap labor available to states and cities. Imagine how many local parks could be cleaned and how much could be saved if a few hundred New York City school custodians were nineteen, energetic, and making $15,000 plus room and board, instead of fifty, tired, and making $106,329, the top base salary for the city's public school custodians, before overtime.

The savings actually might be a way of bringing around the unions representing federal, state, and municipal workers, because they understand that there is a huge budget crunch that is going to hit the federal government in a few years. Setting up a new noncareer tier of cheap, young labor might be a way of preserving existing jobs for older, more skilled, less mobile union workers.

But most of all, having a draft might, as General McChrystal said, make Americans think more carefully before going to war. Imagine the savings — in blood, tears, and national treasure — if we had thought twice about whether we really wanted to invade Iraq.

TOPICS FOR CRITICAL THINKING AND WRITING

1. From a rhetorical point of view — or, we might say, in terms of argumentative strategy — why does Ricks begin his argument with a quotation by a general?

2. Ricks proposes drafting both females and males — something never yet done in the United States. If a draft is deemed necessary, do you think it should include women as well as men? Explain.

3. Ricks's second option would allow eighteen-year-olds to teach in low-income areas. An implication is that such teaching requires little or no training, no special skill, no talent. Do you agree? Or might a brief period of training—say three weeks—be enough? If the proposal were enacted, what impact might it have on our educational system? Explain.

4. In his fifth paragraph Ricks offers a third option: Libertarians could opt out if they sign a pledge forfeiting, for life, Medicare and all other government assistance. Do you think an eighteen-year-old is sufficiently mature to make this immensely important decision? Explain.

5. Reread Ricks's final paragraph.What strategy or strategies, as a writer, does he employ in an effort to end his argument effectively?

Dave Eggers

Dave Eggers (b. 1970), a cofounder of 826 National, a network of nonprofit learning centers, and the founder and editor of McSweeney's, *an independent publisher, is also an author, most notably of* A Heartbreaking Work of Staggering Genius *(2000),* How We Are Hungry: Stories *(2005), and* What Is the What? The Autobiography of Valentino Achak Deng *(2007). This essay and the letters of response originally appeared in the* New York Times *in 2004.*

Serve or Fail

About now, most recent college graduates, a mere week or two beyond their last final, are giving themselves a nice respite. Maybe they're on a beach, maybe they're on a road trip, maybe they're in their rooms, painting their toenails black with a Q-tip and shoe polish. Does it matter? What's important is that they have some time off.

Do they deserve the time off? Well, yes and no. Yes, because finals week is stressful and sleep-deprived and possibly involves trucker-style stimulants. No, because a good deal of the four years of college is spent playing foosball.

I went to a large state school—the University of Illinois—and during my time there, I became one of the best two or three foosball players in the Land of Lincoln. I learned to pass deftly between my rigid players, to play the corners, to strike the ball like a cobra would strike something a cobra would want to strike. I also mastered the dart game called Cricket, and the billiards contest called Nine-ball. I became expert at whiffle ball, at backyard archery, and at a sport we invented that involved one person tossing roasted chickens from a balcony to a group of us waiting below. We got to eat the parts that didn't land on the patio.

The point is that college is too long—it should be three years—and that even with a full course load and part-time jobs (I had my share) there are many hours in the days and weeks that need killing. And because most of us, as students, saw our hours as in need of killing—as opposed to thinking about giving a few of these hours to our communities in one way or another—colleges should consider instituting a service requirement for graduation.

I volunteered a few times in Urbana-Champaign—at a Y.M.C.A. and   5
at a home for senior citizens—and in both cases it was much too easy to quit. I thought the senior home smelled odd, so I left, and though the Y.M.C.A. was a perfect fit, I could have used nudging to continue—nudging the university might have provided. Just as parents and schools need to foster in young people a "reading habit"—a love of reading that becomes a need, almost an addiction—colleges are best-poised to create in their students a lifelong commitment to volunteering even a few hours a month.

Some colleges, and many high schools, have such a thing in place, and last year Michael R. Veon, a Democratic member of Pennsylvania's House of Representatives, introduced a bill that would require the more than 90,000 students at fourteen state-run universities to perform twenty-five hours of community service annually. That comes out to more than two million volunteer hours a year.

College students are, for the most part, uniquely suited to have time for and to benefit from getting involved and addressing the needs of those around them. Unlike high school students, they're less programmed, less boxed in by family and after-school obligations. They're also more mature, and better able to handle a wide range of tasks. Finally, they're at a stage where exposure to service—and to the people whose lives nonprofit service organizations touch—would have a profound effect on them. Meeting a World War II veteran who needs meals brought to him would be educational for the deliverer of that meal, I would think. A college history major might learn something by tutoring a local middle school class that's studying the Underground Railroad. A connection would be forged; a potential career might be discovered.

A service requirement won't work everywhere. It probably wouldn't be feasible, for example, for community college students, who tend to be transient and who generally have considerable family and work demands. But exempt community colleges and you would still have almost 10 million college students enrolled in four-year colleges in the United States. If you exempted a third of them for various reasons, that would leave more than 6 million able-bodied young people at the ready. Even with a modest ten-hour-a-year requirement (the equivalent of two mornings a year) America would gain 60 million volunteer hours to invigorate the nation's nonprofit organizations, churches, job corps, conservation groups, and college outreach programs.

And with some flexibility, it wouldn't have to be too onerous. Colleges could give credit for service. That is, at the beginning of each year, a student could opt for service, and in return he or she might get credits equal to one class period. Perhaps every twenty-five hours of service could be traded for one class credit, with a maximum of three credits a year. What a student would learn from working in a shelter for the victims of domestic abuse would surely equal or surpass his or her time spent in racquetball class—at my college worth one full unit.

Alternatively, colleges could limit the service requirement to a stu- 10 dent's junior year—a time when the students are settled and have more hours and stability in their schedules. Turning the junior year into a year when volunteering figures prominently could also help colleges bridge the chasm that usually stands between the academic world and the one that lies beyond it.

When Gov. Gray Davis of California proposed a service requirement in 1999, an editorial in the *Daily Californian,* the student newspaper at the University of California at Berkeley, opposed the plan: "Forced philanthropy will be as much an oxymoron in action as it is in terms. Who would want to receive community service from someone who is forced to serve? Is forced community service in California not generally reserved for criminals and delinquents?"

First of all, that's putting forth a pretty dim view of the soul of the average student. What, is the unwilling college volunteer going to *throw food* at visitors to the soup kitchen? Volunteering is by nature transformative—reluctant participants become quick converts every day, once they meet those who need their help.

Second, college is largely about fulfilling requirements, isn't it? Students have to complete this much work in the sciences, that much work in the arts. Incoming freshmen accept a tacit contract, submitting to the wisdom of the college's founders and shapers, who decide which experiences are necessary to create a well-rounded scholar, one ready to make a contribution to the world. But while colleges give their students the intellectual tools for life beyond campus, they largely ignore the part about how they might contribute to the world. That is, until the commencement speech, at which time all the "go forth's" and "be helpful's" happen.

But what if such a sentiment happened on the student's first day? What if graduating seniors already knew full well how to balance jobs, studies, family, and volunteer work in the surrounding community? What if campuses were full of under-served high school students meeting with their college tutors? What if the tired and clogged veins of thousands of towns and cities had the energy of millions of college students coursing through them? What if the student who might have become a foosball power—and I say this knowing how much those skills have enhanced my life and those who had the good fortune to have watched me—became instead a lifelong volunteer? That might be pretty good for everybody.

TOPICS FOR CRITICAL THINKING AND WRITING

1. Eggers argues that colleges should consider instituting a service requirement for graduation. How does he support his argument? What kinds of evidence does he offer?

2. Suppose someone objected to Eggers that he presents a confusing picture of what he desires. Is it "volunteering" (para. 12), or is it service, whether volunteered or not? How should Eggers reply?

3. Let's be a bit cynical. When we were in college, physical ed was a required not-for-credit course. The result? Students became quite skillful in evading it. Why wouldn't the same thing happen with a requirement of public service? Give your reasoned view in 250 words.

4. Does Eggers give us any reason to believe that installing a service participation requirement will have a beneficial effect on the problem of student boredom and mismanagement of spare time — which was the issue with which he opened his essay?

Letters of Response by Dixie Dillon, Sharon S. Epstein, and Patricia R. King

To the Editor:

Dave Eggers has a rather low opinion of college students ("Serve or Fail," Op-Ed, June 13).

As a college senior, I believe that I am a contributing member of the community I live in. Whatever the town-gown troubles may be in Middlebury, the citizens of the town and the students at Middlebury College have helped one another.

I live here. How can Mr. Eggers imagine that I do not work to better my community (though I do not appear in the statistics of structured volunteering, which many students here do)?

By the way, those "intellectual tools" my college experience is providing me do a great deal of good work in our country.

I invite Mr. Eggers to spend a few weeks talking, working, and playing with the students at my college and then to reconsider his plan.   5

DIXIE DILLON
Middlebury, Vt., June 13, 2004

To the Editor:

Dave Eggers's view that colleges should require students to do volunteer work is valuable. But the volunteer work should begin at the elementary school level. The actual volunteer work can be as simple as a group project to make cards for people who are hospitalized or to make food baskets for the poor. In other words, children don't have to be transported to a place to volunteer.

I'd also recommend that parents teach their children volunteering by example. If a parent and a child go together to a place to volunteer, then volunteering becomes a positive and bonding activity learned early in life.

SHARON S. EPSTEIN
Stony Brook, N.Y., June 13, 2004

To the Editor:

Dave Eggers, in proposing a community service requirement for college students, would allow for exemptions. Indeed, I would remind him that like the community college students he mentions, many college students "have considerable family and work demands"; unlike Mr. Eggers, they do not major in social games. All that spare time he talks about does not exist for them.

Many of today's students are not the children of privilege. Believe me, they know how the world works.

PATRICIA R. KING
Tennyson, Ind., June 14, 2004

TOPIC FOR CRITICAL THINKING AND WRITING

Imagine that you are Eggers and that you have seen the three letters of response. Write a letter in which you address all three letter-writers.

ENDURING QUESTIONS: ESSAYS, a STORY, POEMS, and a PLAY

26

What Is the Ideal Society?

Thomas More

The son of a prominent London lawyer, More (1478–1535) served as a page in the household of the Archbishop of Canterbury, went to Oxford University, and then studied law in London. More's charm, brilliance, and gentle manner caused Erasmus, the great Dutch humanist who became his friend during a visit to London, to write to a friend: "Did nature ever create anything kinder, sweeter, or more harmonious than the character of Thomas More?"

More served in Parliament, became a diplomat, and after holding several important positions in the government of Henry VIII, rose to become lord chancellor. But when Henry married Anne Boleyn, broke from the Church of Rome, and established himself as head of the Church of England, More refused to subscribe to the Act of Succession and Supremacy. Condemned to death as a traitor, he was executed in 1535, nominally for treason but really because he would not recognize the king rather than the pope as the head of his church. A moment before the ax fell, More displayed a bit of the whimsy for which he was known: When he put his head on the block, he brushed his beard aside, commenting that his beard had done no offense to the king. In 1886 the Roman Catholic Church beatified More, and in 1935, the four-hundredth anniversary of his death, it canonized him as St. Thomas More.

More wrote Utopia *(1514–15) in Latin, the international language of the day. The book's name, however, is Greek for "no place" (ou topos), with a pun on "good place" (eu topos).* Utopia *owes something to Plato's* Republic *and something to then-popular accounts of voyagers such as Amerigo Vespucci.* Utopia *purports to record an account given by a traveler named Hytholodaeus (Greek for "learned in nonsense"), who allegedly visited Utopia. The work is playful, but it is also serious. In truth, it is hard to know exactly where it is serious and how serious it is. One inevitably wonders, for example, if More the devoted Roman Catholic could really have advocated euthanasia. And could More the persecutor of heretics really have approved of the religious tolerance practiced in Utopia? Is he perhaps in effect saying, "Let's see what reason, unaided by Christian revelation, can tell us about an ideal society"? But if so, is he nevertheless also saying, very strongly, that Christian countries, though blessed with the revelation of Christ's teachings, are far behind these unenlightened pagans?* Utopia *has been widely praised by all sorts of readers—from Roman Catholics to communists—but for all sorts of reasons. The selection presented here is about one-twelfth of the book (in a translation by Paul Turner).*

From *Utopia*

[A DAY IN UTOPIA]

And now for their working conditions. Well, there's one job they all do, irrespective of sex, and that's farming. It's part of every child's education. They learn the principles of agriculture at school, and they're taken for regular outings into the fields near the town, where they not only watch farm work being done, but also do some themselves, as a form of exercise.

Besides farming which, as I say, is everybody's job, each person is taught a special trade of his own. He may be trained to process wool or flax, or he may become a stonemason, a blacksmith, or a carpenter. Those are the only trades that employ any considerable quantity of labor. They have no tailors or dressmakers, since everyone on the island wears the same sort of clothes—except that they vary slightly according to sex and marital status—and the fashion never changes. These clothes are quite pleasant to look at, they allow free movement of the limbs, they're equally suitable for hot and cold weather—and the great thing is, they're all home-made. So everybody learns one of the other trades I mentioned, and by everybody I mean the women as well as the men—though the weaker sex are given the lighter jobs, like spinning and weaving, while the men do the heavier ones.

Most children are brought up to do the same work as their parents, since they tend to have a natural feeling for it. But if a child fancies some other trade, he's adopted into a family that practices it. Of course, great care is taken, not only by the father, but also by the local authorities, to see that the foster father is a decent, respectable type. When you've learned one trade properly, you can, if you like, get permission to learn another—and when you're an expert in both, you can practice whichever you prefer, unless the other one is more essential to the public.

The chief business of the Stywards[1]—in fact, practically their only business—is to see that nobody sits around doing nothing, but that everyone gets on with his job. They don't wear people out, though, by keeping them hard at work from early morning till late at night, like cart horses. That's just slavery—and yet that's what life is like for the working classes nearly everywhere else in the world. In Utopia they have a six-hour working day—three hours in the morning, then lunch—then a two-hour break—then three more hours in the afternoon, followed by supper. They go to bed at 8 P.M., and sleep for eight hours. All the rest of the twenty-four they're free to do what they like—not to waste their

---

[1]**Stywards** In Utopia, each group of thirty households elects a styward; each town has two hundred stywards, who elect the mayor. [All notes are the editors'.]

time in idleness or self-indulgence, but to make good use of it in some
congenial activity. Most people spend these free periods on further education, for there are public lectures first thing every morning. Attendance is quite voluntary, except for those picked out for academic
training, but men and women of all classes go crowding in to hear
them—I mean, different people go to different lectures, just as the
spirit moves them. However, there's nothing to stop you from spending
this extra time on your trade, if you want to. Lots of people do, if they
haven't the capacity for intellectual work, and are much admired for
such public-spirited behavior.

After supper they have an hour's recreation, either in the gardens 5
or in the communal dining-halls, according to the time of year. Some
people practice music, others just talk. They've never heard of anything
so silly and demoralizing as dice, but they have two games rather like
chess. The first is a sort of arithmetical contest, in which certain numbers "take" others. The second is a pitched battle between virtues and
vices, which illustrates most ingeniously how vices tend to conflict with
one another, but to combine against virtues. It also shows which vices
are opposed to which virtues, how much strength vices can muster for a
direct assault, what indirect tactics they employ, what help virtues need
to overcome vices, what are the best methods of evading their attacks,
and what ultimately determines the victory of one side or the other.

But here's a point that requires special attention, or you're liable
to get the wrong idea. Since they only work a six-hour day, you may
think there must be a shortage of essential goods. On the contrary,
those six hours are enough, and more than enough to produce plenty
of everything that's needed for a comfortable life. And you'll understand
why it is, if you reckon up how large a proportion of the population in
other countries is totally unemployed. First you have practically all the
women—that gives you nearly 50 percent for a start. And in countries
where the women *do* work, the men tend to lounge about instead. Then
there are all the priests, and members of so-called religious orders—how
much work do they do? Add all the rich, especially the landowners, popularly known as nobles and gentlemen. Include their domestic staffs—I
mean those gangs of armed ruffians that I mentioned before. Finally,
throw in all the beggars who are perfectly hale and hearty, but pretend
to be ill as an excuse for being lazy. When you've counted them up,
you'll be surprised to find how few people actually produce what the
human race consumes.

And now just think how few of these few people are doing essential
work—for where money is the only standard of value, there are bound
to be dozens of unnecessary trades carried on, which merely supply luxury goods or entertainment. Why, even if the existing labor force were
distributed among the few trades really needed to make life reasonably
comfortable, there'd be so much overproduction that prices would fall
too low for the workers to earn a living. Whereas, if you took all those

engaged in nonessential trades, and all who are too lazy to work—each of whom consumes twice as much of the products of other people's labor as any of the producers themselves—if you put the whole lot of them on to something useful, you'd soon see how few hours' work a day would be amply sufficient to supply all the necessities and comforts of life—to which you might add all real and natural forms of pleasure.

[THE HOUSEHOLD]

But let's get back to their social organization. Each household, as I said, comes under the authority of the oldest male. Wives are subordinate to their husbands, children to their parents, and younger people generally to their elders. Every town is divided into four districts of equal size, each with its own shopping center in the middle of it. There the products of every household are collected in warehouses, and then distributed according to type among various shops. When the head of a household needs anything for himself or his family, he just goes to one of these shops and asks for it. And whatever he asks for, he's allowed to take away without any sort of payment, either in money or in kind. After all, why shouldn't he? There's more than enough of everything to go round, so there's no risk of his asking for more than he needs—for why should anyone want to start hoarding, when he knows he'll never have to go short of anything? No living creature is naturally greedy, except from fear of want—or in the case of human beings, from vanity, the notion that you're better than people if you can display more superfluous property than they can. But there's no scope for that sort of thing in Utopia.

[UTOPIAN BELIEFS]

The Utopians fail to understand why anyone should be so fascinated by the dull gleam of a tiny bit of stone, when he has all the stars in the sky to look at—or how anyone can be silly enough to think himself better than other people, because his clothes are made of finer woollen thread than theirs. After all, those fine clothes were once worn by a sheep, and they never turned it into anything better than a sheep.

Nor can they understand why a totally useless substance like gold should now, all over the world, be considered far more important than human beings, who gave it such value as it has, purely for their own convenience. The result is that a man with about as much mental agility as a lump of lead or a block of wood, a man whose utter stupidity is paralleled only by his immorality, can have lots of good, intelligent people at his beck and call, just because he happens to possess a large pile of gold coins. And if by some freak of fortune or trick of the law—two equally effective methods of turning things upside down—the said coins were suddenly transferred to the most worthless member of his domestic staff, you'd soon see the present owner trotting after his money, like an extra piece of currency, and becoming his own servant's servant. But what puzzles and disgusts the Utopians even more is the idiotic way some people have of practically worshipping a rich man, not because they owe him money or are otherwise in his power, but simply because he's rich—although they know perfectly well that he's far too mean to let a single penny come their way, so long as he's alive to stop it.

They get these ideas partly from being brought up under a social system which is directly opposed to that type of nonsense, and partly from their reading and education. Admittedly, no one's allowed to become a full-time student, except for the very few in each town who appear as children to possess unusual gifts, outstanding intelligence, and a special aptitude for academic research. But every child receives a primary education, and most men and women go on educating themselves all their lives during those free periods that I told you about. . . .

In ethics they discuss the same problems as we do. Having distinguished between three types of "good," psychological, physiological, and environmental, they proceed to ask whether the term is strictly applicable to all of them, or only to the first. They also argue about such things as virtue and pleasure. But their chief subject of dispute is the nature of human happiness—on what factor or factors does it depend? Here they seem rather too much inclined to take a hedonistic view, for according to them human happiness consists largely or wholly in pleasure. Surprisingly enough, they defend this self-indulgent doctrine by arguments drawn from religion—a thing normally associated with a more serious view of life, if not with gloomy asceticism. You see, in all their discussions of happiness they invoke certain religious principles to supplement the operations of reason, which they think otherwise ill-equipped to identify true happiness.

The first principle is that every soul is immortal, and was created by a kind God, Who meant it to be happy. The second is that we shall be rewarded or punished in the next world for our good or bad behavior in this one. Although these are religious principles, the Utopians find rational grounds for accepting them. For suppose you didn't accept them? In that case, they say, any fool could tell you what you ought to do. You should go all out for your own pleasure, irrespective of right and wrong. You'd merely have to make sure that minor pleasures didn't interfere with major ones, and avoid the type of pleasure that has painful aftereffects. For what's the sense of struggling to be virtuous, denying yourself the pleasant things of life, and deliberately making yourself uncomfortable, if there's nothing you hope to gain by it? And what *can* you hope to gain by it, if you receive no compensation after death for a thoroughly unpleasant, that is, a thoroughly miserable life?

Not that they identify happiness with every type of pleasure—only with the higher ones. Nor do they identify it with virtue—unless they belong to a quite different school of thought. According to the normal view, happiness is the *summum bonum*[2] toward which we're naturally impelled by virtue—which in their definition means following one's natural impulses, as God meant us to do. But this includes obeying the instinct to be reasonable in our likes and dislikes. And reason also teaches us, first to love and reverence Almighty God, to Whom we owe our existence and our potentiality for happiness, and secondly to get through life as comfortably and cheerfully as we can, and help all other members of our species to do so too.

The fact is, even the sternest ascetic tends to be slightly inconsistent   15
in his condemnation of pleasure. He may sentence *you* to a life of hard labor, inadequate sleep, and general discomfort, but he'll also tell you to do your best to ease the pains and privations of others. He'll regard all such attempts to improve the human situation as laudable acts of humanity—for obviously nothing could be more humane, or more natural for a human being, than to relieve other people's sufferings, put an end to their miseries, and restore their *joie de vivre,* that is, their capacity for pleasure. So why shouldn't it be equally natural to do the same thing for oneself?

Either it's a bad thing to enjoy life, in other words, to experience pleasure—in which case you shouldn't help anyone to do it, but should try to save the whole human race from such a frightful fate—or else, if it's good for other people, and you're not only allowed, but positively obliged to make it possible for them, why shouldn't charity begin at home? After all, you've a duty to yourself as well as to your neighbor, and, if Nature says you must be kind to others, she can't turn round the next moment and say you must be cruel to yourself. The Utopians therefore regard the enjoyment of life—that is, pleasure—as the natural object of all human efforts, and natural, as they define it, is synonymous with virtuous. However, Nature also wants us to help one another to enjoy life, for the very good reason that no human being has a monopoly of her affections. She's equally anxious for the welfare of every member of the species. So of course she tells us to make quite sure that we don't pursue our own interests at the expense of other people's.

On this principle they think it right to keep one's promises in private life, and also to obey public laws for regulating the distribution of "goods"—by which I mean the raw materials of pleasure—provided such laws have been properly made by a wise ruler, or passed by common consent of a whole population, which has not been subjected to any form of violence or deception. Within these limits they say it's sensible to consult one's own interests, and a moral duty to consult those of the community as well. It's wrong to deprive someone else of a pleasure so that you can enjoy one yourself, but to deprive yourself of a pleasure so that you can add to someone else's enjoyment is an act of humanity

---

[2]*summum bonum* Latin for "the highest good."

by which you always gain more than you lose. For one thing, such benefits are usually repaid in kind. For another, the mere sense of having done somebody a kindness, and so earned his affection and goodwill, produces a spiritual satisfaction which far outweighs the loss of a physical one. And lastly—a belief that comes easily to a religious mind—God will reward us for such small sacrifices of momentary pleasure, by giving us an eternity of perfect joy. Thus they argue that, in the final analysis, pleasure is the ultimate happiness which all human beings have in view, even when they're acting most virtuously.

Pleasure they define as any state or activity, physical or mental, which is naturally enjoyable. The operative word is *naturally.* According to them, we're impelled by reason as well as an instinct to enjoy ourselves in any natural way which doesn't hurt other people, interfere with greater pleasures, or cause unpleasant aftereffects. But human beings have entered into an idiotic conspiracy to call some things enjoyable which are naturally nothing of the kind—as though facts were as easily changed as definitions. Now the Utopians believe that, so far from contributing to happiness, this type of thing makes happiness impossible—because, once you get used to it, you lose all capacity for real pleasure, and are merely obsessed by illusory forms of it. Very often these have nothing pleasant about them at all—in fact, most of them are thoroughly disagreeable. But they appeal so strongly to perverted tastes that they come to be reckoned not only among the major pleasures of life, but even among the chief reasons for living.

In the category of illusory pleasure addicts they include the kind of person I mentioned before, who thinks himself better than other people because he's better dressed than they are. Actually he's just as wrong about his clothes as he is about himself. From a practical point of view, why is it better to be dressed in fine woollen thread than in coarse? But he's got it into his head that fine thread is naturally superior, and that wearing it somehow increases his own value. So he feels entitled to far more respect than he'd ever dare to hope for, if he were less expensively dressed, and is most indignant if he fails to get it.

Talking of respect, isn't it equally idiotic to attach such importance to 20 a lot of empty gestures which do nobody any good? For what real pleasure can you get out of the sight of a bared head or a bent knee? Will it cure the rheumatism in your own knee, or make you any less weak in the head? Of course, the great believers in this type of artificial pleasure are those who pride themselves on their "nobility." Nowadays that merely means that they happen to belong to a family which has been rich for several generations, preferably in landed property. And yet they feel every bit as "noble" even if they've failed to inherit any of the said property, or if they have inherited it and then frittered it all away.

Then there's another type of person I mentioned before, who has a passion for jewels, and feels practically superhuman if he manages to get hold of a rare one, especially if it's a kind that's considered particularly

precious in his country and period—for the value of such things varies according to where and when you live. But he's so terrified of being
taken in by appearances that he refuses to buy any jewel until he's
stripped off all the gold and inspected it in the nude. And even then he
won't buy it without a solemn assurance and a written guarantee from
the jeweler that the stone is genuine. But my dear sir, why shouldn't a
fake give you just as much pleasure, if you can't, with your own eyes,
distinguish it from a real one? It makes no difference to you whether it's
genuine or not—any more than it would to a blind man!

And now, what about those people who accumulate superfluous
wealth, for no better purpose than to enjoy looking at it? Is their pleasure a real one, or merely a form of delusion? The opposite type of psy-
chopath buries his gold, so that he'll never be able to use it, and may
never even see it again. In fact, he deliberately loses it in his anxiety
not to lose it—for what can you call it but lost, when it's put back into
the earth, where it's no good to him, or probably to anyone else? And
yet he's tremendously happy when he's got it stowed away. Now, apparently, he can stop worrying. But suppose the money is stolen, and ten
years later he dies without ever knowing it has gone. Then for a whole
ten years he has managed to survive his loss, and during that period
what difference has it made to him whether the money was there or
not? It was just as little use to him either way.

Among stupid pleasures they include not only gambling—a form of
idiocy that they've heard about but never practiced—but also hunting
and hawking. What on earth is the fun, they ask, of throwing dice onto
a table? Besides, you've done it so often that, even if there was some fun
in it at first, you must surely be sick of it by now. How can you possibly
enjoy listening to anything so disagreeable as the barking and howling of
dogs? And why is it more amusing to watch a dog chasing a hare than
to watch one dog chasing another? In each case the essential activity is
running—if running is what amuses you. But if it's really the thought
of being in at the death, and seeing an animal torn to pieces before your
eyes, wouldn't pity be a more appropriate reaction to the sight of a weak,
timid, harmless little creature like a hare being devoured by something
so much stronger and fiercer?

So the Utopians consider hunting below the dignity of free men,
and leave it entirely to butchers, who are, as I told you, slaves. In their
view hunting is the vilest department of butchery, compared with which
all the others are relatively useful and honorable. An ordinary butcher
slaughters livestock far more sparingly, and only because he has to,
whereas a hunter kills and mutilates poor little creatures purely for his
own amusement. They say you won't find that type of blood lust even
among animals, unless they're particularly savage by nature, or have
become so by constantly being used for this cruel sport.

There are hundreds of things like that, which are generally regarded 25
as pleasures, but everyone in Utopia is quite convinced that they've

got nothing to do with real pleasure, because there's nothing naturally enjoyable about them. Nor is this conviction at all shaken by the argument that most people do actually enjoy them, which would seem to indicate an appreciable pleasure content. They say this is a purely subjective reaction caused by bad habits, which can make a person prefer unpleasant things to pleasant ones, just as pregnant women sometimes lose their sense of taste, and find suet or turpentine more delicious than honey. But however much one's judgment may be impaired by habit or ill health, the nature of pleasure, as of everything else, remains unchanged.

Real pleasures they divide into two categories, mental and physical. Mental pleasures include the satisfaction that one gets from understanding something, or from contemplating truth. They also include the memory of a well-spent life, and the confident expectation of good things to come. Physical pleasures are subdivided into two types. First there are those which fill the whole organism with a conscious sense of enjoyment. This may be the result of replacing physical substances which have been burnt up by the natural heat of the body, as when we eat or drink. Or else it may be caused by the discharge of some excess, as in excretion, sexual intercourse, or any relief of irritation by rubbing or scratching. However, there are also pleasures which satisfy no organic need, and relieve no previous discomfort. They merely act, in a mysterious but quite unmistakable way, directly on our senses, and monopolize their reactions. Such is the pleasure of music.

Their second type of physical pleasure arises from the calm and regular functioning of the body—that is, from a state of health undisturbed by any minor ailments. In the absence of mental discomfort, this gives one a good feeling, even without the help of external pleasures. Of course, it's less ostentatious, and forces itself less violently on one's attention than the cruder delights of eating and drinking, but even so it's often considered the greatest pleasure in life. Practically everyone in Utopia would agree that it's a very important one, because it's the basis of all the others. It's enough by itself to make you enjoy life, and unless you have it, no other pleasure is possible. However, mere freedom from pain, without positive health, they would call not pleasure but anesthesia.

Some thinkers used to maintain that a uniformly tranquil state of health couldn't properly be termed a pleasure since its presence could only be detected by contrast with its opposite—oh yes, they went very thoroughly into the whole question. But that theory was exploded long ago, and nowadays nearly everybody subscribes to the view that health is most definitely a pleasure. The argument goes like this—illness involves pain, which is the direct opposite of pleasure, and illness is the direct opposite of health, therefore health involves pleasure. They don't think it matters whether you say that illness *is* or merely *involves* pain. Either way it comes to the same thing. Similarly, whether health *is* a pleasure, or merely *produces* pleasure as inevitably as fire produces heat, it's equally logical to assume that where you have an uninterrupted state of health you cannot fail to have pleasure.

Besides, they say, when we eat something, what really happens is this. Our failing health starts fighting off the attacks of hunger, using the food as an ally. Gradually it begins to prevail, and, in this very process of winning back its normal strength, experiences the sense of enjoyment which we find so refreshing. Now, if health enjoys the actual battle, why shouldn't it also enjoy the victory? Or are we to suppose that when it has finally managed to regain its former vigor—the one thing that it has been fighting for all this time—it promptly falls into a coma, and fails to notice or take advantage of its success? As for the idea that one isn't conscious of health except through its opposite, they say that's quite untrue. Everyone's perfectly aware of feeling well, unless he's asleep or actually feeling ill. Even the most insensitive and apathetic sort of person will admit that it's delightful to be healthy—and what is delight, but a synonym for pleasure?

They're particularly fond of mental pleasures, which they consider 30 of primary importance, and attribute mostly to good behavior and a clear conscience. Their favorite physical pleasure is health. Of course, they believe in enjoying food, drink, and so forth, but purely in the interests of health, for they don't regard such things as very pleasant in themselves—only as methods of resisting the stealthy onset of disease. A sensible person, they say, prefers keeping well to taking medicine, and would rather feel cheerful than have people trying to comfort him. On the same principle it's better not to need this type of pleasure than to become addicted to it. For, if you think that sort of thing will make you happy, you'll have to admit that your idea of perfect felicity would be a life consisting entirely of hunger, thirst, itching, eating, drinking, rubbing, and scratching—which would obviously be most unpleasant as well as quite disgusting. Undoubtedly these pleasures should come right at the bottom of the list, because they're so impure. For instance, the pleasure of eating is invariably diluted with the pain of hunger, and not in equal proportions either—for the pain is both more intense and more prolonged. It starts before the pleasure, and doesn't stop until the pleasure has stopped too.

So they don't think much of pleasures like that, except insofar as they're necessary. But they enjoy them all the same, and feel most grateful to Mother Nature for encouraging her children to do things that have to be done so often, by making them so attractive. For just think how dreary life would be, if those chronic ailments, hunger and thirst, could only be cured by foul-tasting medicines, like the rarer types of disease!

They attach great value to special natural gifts such as beauty, strength, and agility. They're also keen on the pleasures of sight, hearing, and smell, which are peculiar to human beings—for no other species admires the beauty of the world, enjoys any sort of scent, except as a method of locating food, or can tell the difference between a harmony and a discord. They say these things give a sort of relish to life.

However, in all such matters they observe the rule that minor pleasures mustn't interfere with major ones, and that pleasure mustn't cause pain—which they think is bound to happen, if the pleasure is immoral. But they'd never dream of despising their own beauty, overtaxing their strength, converting their agility into inertia, ruining their physique by going without food, damaging their health, or spurning any other of Nature's gifts, unless they were doing it for the benefit of other people or of society, in the hope of receiving some greater pleasure from God in return. For they think it's quite absurd to torment oneself in the name of an unreal virtue, which does nobody any good, or in order to steel oneself against disasters which may never occur. They say such behavior is merely self-destructive, and shows a most ungrateful attitude toward Nature—as if one refused all her favors, because one couldn't bear the thought of being indebted to her for anything.

Well, that's their ethical theory, and short of some divine revelation, they doubt if the human mind is capable of devising a better one. We've no time to discuss whether it's right or wrong—nor is it really necessary, for all I undertook was to describe their way of life, not to defend it.

[TREATMENT OF THE DYING]

As I told you, when people are ill, they're looked after most sympa- 35 thetically, and given everything in the way of medicine or special food that could possibly assist their recovery. In the case of permanent invalids, the nurses try to make them feel better by sitting and talking to them, and do all they can to relieve their symptoms. But if, besides being incurable, the disease also causes constant excruciating pain, some priests and government officials visit the person concerned, and say something like this:

"Let's face it, you'll never be able to live a normal life. You're just a nuisance to other people and a burden to yourself—in fact you're really leading a sort of posthumous existence. So why go on feeding germs? Since your life's a misery to you, why hesitate to die? You're imprisoned in a torture chamber—why don't you break out and escape to a better world? Or say the word, and we'll arrange for your release. It's only common sense to cut your losses. It's also an act of piety to take the advice of a priest, because he speaks for God."

If the patient finds these arguments convincing, he either starves himself to death, or is given a soporific and put painlessly out of his misery. But this is strictly voluntary, and, if he prefers to stay alive, everyone will go on treating him as kindly as ever.

[THE SUMMING UP]

Well, that's the most accurate account I can give you of the Utopian Republic. To my mind, it's not only the best country in the world, but the only one that has any right to call itself a republic. Elsewhere, people are always talking about the public interest, but all they really care about is private property. In Utopia, where's there's no private property, people take their duty to the public seriously. And both attitudes are perfectly reasonable. In other "republics" practically everyone knows that, if he doesn't look out for himself, he'll starve to death, however prosperous his country may be. He's therefore compelled to give his own interests priority over those of the public; that is, of other people. But in Utopia, where everything's under public ownership, no one has any fear of going short, as long as the public storehouses are full. Everyone gets a fair share, so there are never any poor men or beggars. Nobody owns anything, but everyone is rich—for what greater wealth can there be than cheerfulness, peace of mind, and freedom from anxiety? Instead of being worried about his food supply, upset by the plaintive demands of his wife, afraid of poverty for his son, and baffled by the problem of finding a dowry for his daughter, the Utopian can feel absolutely sure that he, his wife, his children, his grandchildren, his great-grandchildren, his great-great-grandchildren, and as long a line of descendants as the proudest peer could wish to look forward to, will always have enough to eat and enough to make them happy. There's also the further point that those who are too old to work are just as well provided for as those who are still working.

Now, will anyone venture to compare these fair arrangements in Utopia with the so-called justice of other countries?—in which I'm damned if I can see the slightest trace of justice or fairness. For what sort of justice do you call this? People like aristocrats, goldsmiths, or moneylenders, who either do no work at all, or do work that's really not essential, are rewarded for their laziness or their unnecessary activities by a splendid life of luxury. But laborers, coachmen, carpenters, and farmhands, who never stop working like cart horses, at jobs so essential that, if they *did* stop working, they'd bring any country to a standstill within twelve months—what happens to them? They get so little to eat, and have such a wretched time, that they'd be almost better off if they *were* cart horses. Then at least, they wouldn't work quite such long hours, their food wouldn't be very much worse, they'd enjoy it more, and they'd have no fears for the future. As it is, they're not only ground down by unrewarding toil in the present, but also worried to death by the prospect of a poverty-stricken old age—since their daily wages aren't enough to support them for one day, let alone leave anything over to be saved up when they're old.

Can you see any fairness or gratitude in a social system which lav- 40 ishes such great rewards on so-called noblemen, goldsmiths, and people like that, who are either totally unproductive or merely employed in producing luxury goods or entertainment, but makes no such kind provision for farmhands, coal heavers, laborers, carters, or carpenters, without whom society couldn't exist at all? And the climax of ingratitude comes when they're old and ill and completely destitute. Having taken advantage of them throughout the best years of their lives, society now forgets all the sleepless hours they've spent in its service, and repays them for all the vital work they've done, by letting them die in misery. What's more, the wretched earnings of the poor are daily whittled away by the rich, not only through private dishonesty, but through public legislation. As if it weren't unjust enough already that the man who contributes most to society should get the least in return, they make it even worse, and then arrange for injustice to be legally described as justice.

In fact, when I consider any social system that prevails in the modern world, I can't, so help me God, see it as anything but a conspiracy of the rich to advance their own interests under the pretext of organizing society. They think up all sorts of tricks and dodges, first for keeping safe their ill-gotten gains, and then for exploiting the poor by buying their labor as cheaply as possible. Once the rich have decided that these tricks and dodges shall be officially recognized by society—which includes the poor as well as the rich—they acquire the force of law. Thus an unscrupulous minority is led by its insatiable greed to monopolize what would have been enough to supply the needs of the whole population. And yet how much happier even these people would be in Utopia! There, with the simultaneous abolition of money and the passion for money, how many other social problems have been solved, how many crimes eradicated! For obviously the end of money means the end of all those types of criminal behavior which daily punishments are powerless to check: fraud, theft, burglary, brawls, riots, disputes, rebellion, murder, treason, and black magic. And the moment money goes, you can also say goodbye to fear, tension, anxiety, overwork, and sleepless nights. Why, even poverty itself, the one problem that has always seemed to need money for its solution, would promptly disappear if money ceased to exist.

Let me try to make this point clearer. Just think back to one of the years when the harvest was bad, and thousands of people died of starvation. Well, I bet if you'd inspected every rich man's barn at the end of that lean period you'd have found enough corn to have saved all the lives that were lost through malnutrition and disease, and prevented anyone from suffering any ill effects whatever from the meanness of the weather and the soil. Everyone could so easily get enough to eat, if it weren't for that blessed nuisance, money. There you have a brilliant invention which was designed to make food more readily available. Actually it's the only thing that makes it unobtainable.

I'm sure that even the rich are well aware of all this, and realize how much better it would be to have everything one needed, than lots of things one didn't need—to be evacuated altogether from the danger area, than to dig oneself in behind a barricade of enormous wealth. And I've no doubt that either self-interest, or the authority of our Savior Christ—Who was far too wise not to know what was best for us, and far too kind to recommend anything else—would have led the whole world to adopt the Utopian system long ago, if it weren't for that beastly root of all evils, pride. For pride's criterion of prosperity is not what you've got yourself, but what other people haven't got. Pride would refuse to set foot in paradise, if she thought there'd be no underprivileged classes there to gloat over and order about—nobody whose misery could serve as a foil to her own happiness, or whose poverty she could make harder to bear, by flaunting her own riches. Pride, like a hellish serpent gliding through human hearts—or shall we say, like a sucking-fish that clings to the ship of state?—is always dragging us back, and obstructing our progress toward a better way of life.

But as this fault is too deeply ingrained in human nature to be easily eradicated, I'm glad that at least one country has managed to develop a system which I'd like to see universally adopted. The Utopian way of life provides not only the happiest basis for a civilized community, but also one which, in all human probability, will last forever. They've eliminated the root causes of ambition, political conflict, and everything like that. There's therefore no danger of internal dissension, the one thing that has destroyed so many impregnable towns. And as long as there's unity and sound administration at home, no matter how envious neighboring kings may feel, they'll never be able to shake, let alone to shatter, the power of Utopia. They've tried to do so often enough in the past, but have always been beaten back.

TOPICS FOR CRITICAL THINKING AND WRITING

1. More, writing early in the sixteenth century, was living in a primarily agricultural society. Laborers were needed on farms, but might More have had any other reason for insisting (para. 1) that all people should do some farming and that farming should be "part of every child's education"? Do you think everyone should put in some time as a farmer? Why, or why not?

2. More indicates that in the England of his day many people loafed or engaged in unnecessary work (producing luxury goods, for one thing), putting an enormous burden on those who engaged in useful work. Is this condition, or any part of it, true of our society? Explain.

3. The Utopians cannot understand why the people of other nations value gems, gold, and fine clothes. If you value any of these, can you offer an explanation?

4. What arguments can you offer against the Utopians' treatment of persons who are incurably ill and in pain?

5. Take three or four paragraphs to summarize More's report of the Utopians' idea of pleasure.

6. More's Utopians cannot understand why anyone takes pleasure in gambling or in hunting. If either activity gives you pleasure, in an essay of 500 words explain why, and offer an argument on behalf of your view.

7. As More makes clear in the part we entitle "The Summing Up," in Utopia there is no private property. In a sentence or two summarize the reasons he gives for this principle, and then in a paragraph evaluate them.

Niccolò Machiavelli

Niccolò Machiavelli (1469–1527) was born in Florence at a time when Italy was divided into five major states: Venice, Milan, Florence, the Papal States, and Naples. Although these states often had belligerent relations with one another as well as with lesser Italian states, under the Medici family in Florence they achieved a precarious balance of power. In 1494, however, Lorenzo de' Medici, who had ruled from 1469 to 1492, died, and two years later Lorenzo's successor was exiled when the French army arrived in Florence. Italy became a field where Spain, France, and Germany competed for power. From 1498 to 1512 Machiavelli held a high post in the diplomatic service of the Florentine Republic, but when the French army reappeared and the Florentines in desperation recalled the Medici, Machiavelli lost his post, was imprisoned, tortured, and then exiled. Banished from Florence, he nevertheless lived in comfort on a small estate nearby, writing his major works and hoping to obtain an office from the Medici. In later years he was employed in a few minor diplomatic missions, but even after the collapse and expulsion of the Medici in 1527 and the restoration of the republic, he did not regain his old position of importance. He died shortly after the restoration.

Our selection comes from The Prince, *which Machiavelli wrote in 1513 during his banishment, hoping that it would interest the Medici and thus restore him to favor; but the book was not published until 1532, five years after his death. In this book of twenty-six short chapters, Machiavelli begins by examining different kinds of states, but the work's enduring power resides in the discussions (in Chapters 15–18, reprinted here) of qualities necessary to a prince—that is, a head of state. Any such examination obviously is based in part on assumptions about the nature of the citizens of the realm.*

This selection was taken from a translation edited by Peter Bondanella and Mark Musa.

From *The Prince*

ON THOSE THINGS FOR WHICH MEN, AND PARTICULARLY PRINCES, ARE PRAISED OR BLAMED

Now there remains to be examined what should be the methods and procedures of a prince in dealing with his subjects and friends. And because I know that many have written about this, I am afraid that by writing about it again I shall be thought of as presumptuous, since in discussing this material I depart radically from the procedures of others. But since my intention is to write something useful for anyone who understands it, it seemed more suitable to me to search after the effectual truth of the matter rather than its imagined one. And many writers have imagined for themselves republics and principalities that have never been seen nor known to exist in reality; for there is such a gap between how one lives and how one ought to live that anyone who abandons what is done for what ought to be done learns his ruin rather than his preservation: for a man who wishes to make a vocation of being good at all times will come to ruin among so many who are not good. Hence it is necessary for a prince who wishes to maintain his position to learn how not to be good, and to use this knowledge or not to use it according to necessity.

Leaving aside, therefore, the imagined things concerning a prince, and taking into account those that are true, I say that all men, when they are spoken of, and particularly princes, since they are placed on a higher level, are judged by some of these qualities which bring them either blame or praise. And this is why one is considered generous, another miserly (to use a Tuscan word, since "avaricious" in our language is still used to mean one who wishes to acquire by means of theft; we call "miserly" one who excessively avoids using what he has); one is considered a giver, the other rapacious; one cruel, another merciful; one treacherous, another faithful; one effeminate and cowardly, another bold and courageous; one humane, another haughty; one lascivious, another chaste; one trustworthy, another cunning; one harsh, another lenient; one serious, another frivolous; one religious, another unbelieving; and the like. And I know that everyone will admit that it would be a very praiseworthy thing to find in a prince, of the qualities mentioned above, those that are held to be good; but since it is neither possible to have them nor to observe them all completely, because human nature does not permit it, a prince must be prudent enough to know how to escape the bad reputation of those vices that would lose the state for him, and must protect himself from those that will not lose it for him, if this is possible; but if he cannot, he need not concern himself unduly if he ignores these less serious vices. And, moreover, he need not worry about incurring the bad reputation of those vices without which it would be difficult to hold his state; since, carefully taking everything into account, one will discover that something which appears to be a virtue, if pursued, will end in his destruction; while some other thing which seems to be a vice, if pursued, will result in his safety and his well-being.

ON GENEROSITY AND MISERLINESS

Beginning, therefore, with the first of the above-mentioned qualities, I say that it would be good to be considered generous; nevertheless, generosity used in such a manner as to give you a reputation for it will harm you; because if it is employed virtuously and as one should employ it, it will not be recognized and you will not avoid the reproach of its opposite. And so, if a prince wants to maintain his reputation for generosity among men, it is necessary for him not to neglect any possible means of lavish display; in so doing such a prince will always use up all his resources and he will be obliged, eventually, if he wishes to maintain his reputation for generosity, to burden the people with excessive taxes and to do everything possible to raise funds. This will begin to make him hateful to his subjects, and, becoming impoverished, he will not be much esteemed by anyone; so that, as a consequence of his generosity, having offended many and rewarded few, he will feel the effects of any slight unrest and will be ruined at the first sign of danger; recognizing this and wishing to alter his policies, he immediately runs the risk of being reproached as a miser.

A prince, therefore, unable to use this virtue of generosity in a manner which will not harm himself if he is known for it, should, if he is wise, not worry about being called a miser; for with time he will come to be considered more generous once it is evident that, as a result of his parsimony, his income is sufficient, he can defend himself from anyone who makes war against him, and he can undertake enterprises without overburdening his people, so that he comes to be generous with all those from whom he takes nothing, who are countless, and miserly with all those to whom he gives nothing, who are few. In our times we have not seen great deeds accomplished except by those who were considered miserly; all others were done away with. Pope Julius II, although he made use of his reputation for generosity in order to gain the papacy, then decided not to maintain it in order to be able to wage war; the present King of France has waged many wars without imposing extra taxes on his subjects, only because his habitual parsimony has provided for the additional expenditures; the present King of Spain, if he had been considered generous, would not have engaged in nor won so many campaigns.

Therefore, in order not to have to rob his subjects, to be able to 5 defend himself, not to become poor and contemptible, and not to be forced to become rapacious, a prince must consider it of little importance if he incurs the name of miser, for this is one of those vices that permits him to rule. And if someone were to say: Caesar with his generosity came to rule the empire, and many others, because they were generous and known to be so, achieved very high positions; I reply: You are either already a prince or you are on the way to becoming one; in the first instance such generosity is damaging; in the second it is very necessary to be thought generous. And Caesar was one of those who wanted to gain the principality of Rome; but if, after obtaining this, he had lived and had not moderated his expenditures, he would have destroyed that empire. And if someone were to reply: There have existed many princes who have accomplished great deeds with their armies who have been reputed to be generous; I answer you: A prince either spends his own money and that of his subjects or that of others; in the first case he must be economical; in the second he must not restrain any part of his generosity. And for that prince who goes out with his soldiers and lives by looting, sacking, and ransoms, who controls the property of others, such generosity is necessary; otherwise he would not be followed by his troops. And with what does not belong to you or to your subjects you can be a more liberal giver, as were Cyrus, Caesar, and Alexander; for spending the wealth of others does not lessen your reputation but adds to it; only the spending of your own is what harms you. And there is nothing that uses itself up faster than generosity, for as you employ it you lose the means of employing it, and you become either poor or despised or, in order to escape poverty, rapacious and hated. And above all other things a prince must guard himself against being despised and hated; and generosity leads you to both one and the other. So it is wiser to live with the reputation of a miser, which produces reproach without hatred, than to be forced to incur the reputation of rapacity, which produces reproach along with hatred, because you want to be considered as generous.

ON CRUELTY AND MERCY AND WHETHER IT IS BETTER TO BE LOVED THAN TO BE FEARED OR THE CONTRARY

Proceeding to the other qualities mentioned above, I say that every prince must desire to be considered merciful and not cruel; nevertheless, he must take care not to misuse this mercy. Cesare Borgia[1] was considered cruel; nonetheless, his cruelty had brought order to Romagna, united it, restored it to peace and obedience. If we examine this carefully, we shall see that he was more merciful than the Florentine people, who, in order to avoid being considered cruel, allowed the destruction of Pistoia.[2] Therefore, a prince must not worry about the reproach of cruelty when it is a matter of keeping his subjects united and loyal; for with a very few examples of cruelty he will be more compassionate than those who, out of excessive mercy, permit disorders to continue, from which arise murders and plundering; for these usually harm the community at large, while the executions that come from the prince harm one individual in particular. And the new prince, above all other princes,

---

[1]**Cesare Borgia** The son of Pope Alexander VI, Cesare Borgia (1476–1507) was ruthlessly opportunistic. Encouraged by his father, in 1499 and 1500 he subdued the cities of Romagna, the region including Ferrara and Ravenna. [All notes are the editors' unless otherwise specified.]

[2]**Pistoia** A town near Florence; Machiavelli suggests that the Florentines failed to treat dissenting leaders with sufficient severity.

cannot escape the reputation of being called cruel, since new states are full of dangers. And Virgil, through Dido, states: "My difficult condition and the newness of my rule make me act in such a manner, and to set guards over my land on all sides."[3]

Nevertheless, a prince must be cautious in believing and in acting, nor should he be afraid of his own shadow; and he should proceed in such a manner, tempered by prudence and humanity, so that too much trust may not render him imprudent nor too much distrust render him intolerable.

From this arises an argument: whether it is better to be loved than to be feared, or the contrary. I reply that one should like to be both one and the other; but since it is difficult to join them together, it is much safer to be feared than to be loved when one of the two must be lacking. For one can generally say this about men: that they are ungrateful, fickle, simulators and deceivers, avoiders of danger, greedy for gain; and while you work for their good they are completely yours, offering you their blood, their property, their lives, and their sons, as I said earlier, when danger is far away; but when it comes nearer to you they turn away. And that prince who bases his power entirely in their words, finding himself stripped of other preparations, comes to ruin; for friendships that are acquired by a price and not by greatness and nobility of character are purchased but are not owned, and at the proper moment they cannot be spent. And men are less hesitant about harming someone who makes himself loved than one who makes himself feared because love is held together by a chain of obligation which, since men are a sorry lot, is broken on every occasion in which their own self-interest is concerned; but fear is held together by a dread of punishment which will never abandon you.

A prince must nevertheless make himself feared in such a manner that he will avoid hatred, even if he does not acquire love; since to be feared and not to be hated can very well be combined; and this will always be so when he keeps his hands off the property and the women of his citizens and his subjects. And if he must take someone's life, he should do so when there is proper justification and manifest cause; but, above all, he should avoid the property of others; for men forget more quickly the death of their father than the loss of their patrimony. Moreover, the reasons for seizing their property are never lacking; and he who begins to live by stealing always finds a reason for taking what belongs to others; on the contrary, reasons for taking a life are rarer and disappear sooner.

But when the prince is with his armies and has under his command 10
a multitude of troops, then it is absolutely necessary that he not worry about being considered cruel; for without that reputation he will never

---

[3]In *Aeneid* I, 563–64, **Virgil** (70–19 B.C.) puts this line into the mouth of **Dido**, the queen of Carthage.

keep an army united or prepared for any combat. Among the praise-worthy deeds of Hannibal[4] is counted this: that, having a very large army, made up of all kinds of men, which he commanded in foreign lands, there never arose the slightest dissension, neither among themselves nor against their prince, both during his good and his bad fortune. This could not have arisen from anything other than his inhuman cruelty, which, along with his many other abilities, made him always respected and ter-rifying in the eyes of his soldiers; and without that, to attain the same effect, his other abilities would not have sufficed. And the writers of his-tory, having considered this matter very little, on the one hand admire these deeds of his and on the other condemn the main cause of them.

And that it be true that his other abilities would not have been suf-ficient can be seen from the example of Scipio,[5] a most extraordinary man not only in his time but in all recorded history, whose armies in Spain rebelled against him; this came about from nothing other than his excessive compassion, which gave to his soldiers more liberty than military discipline allowed. For this he was censured in the senate by Fabius Maximus, who called him the corruptor of the Roman militia. The Locrians, having been ruined by one of Scipio's officers, were not avenged by him, nor was the arrogance of that officer corrected, all because of his tolerant nature; so that someone in the senate who tried to apologize for him said that there were many men who knew how not to err better than they knew how to correct errors. Such a nature would have, in time, damaged Scipio's fame and glory if he had maintained it during the empire; but, living under the control of the senate, this harm-ful characteristic of his not only concealed itself but brought him fame.

I conclude, therefore, returning to the problem of being feared and loved, that since men love at their own pleasure and fear at the pleasure of the prince, a wise prince should build his foundation upon that which belongs to him, not upon that which belongs to others: He must strive only to avoid hatred, as has been said.

HOW A PRINCE SHOULD KEEP HIS WORD

How praiseworthy it is for a prince to keep his word and to live by integrity and not by deceit everyone knows; nevertheless, one sees from the experience of our times that the princes who have accomplished great deeds are those who have cared little for keeping their promises and who have known how to manipulate the minds of men by shrewd-ness; and in the end they have surpassed those who laid their founda-tions upon honesty.

---

[4]**Hannibal** The Carthaginian general (247–183 B.C.) whose crossing of the Alps with ele-phants and full baggage train is one of the great feats of military history.
[5]**Scipio** Publius Cornelius Scipio Africanus the Elder (235–183 B.C.), the conqueror of Hannibal in the Punic Wars. The mutiny of which Machiavelli speaks took place in 206 B.C.

You must, therefore, know that there are two means of fighting: one according to the laws, the other with force; the first way is proper to man, the second to beasts; but because the first, in many cases, is not sufficient, it becomes necessary to have recourse to the second. Therefore, a prince must know how to use wisely the natures of the beast and the man. This policy was taught to princes allegorically by the ancient writers, who described how Achilles and many other ancient princes were given to Chiron[6] the Centaur to be raised and taught under his discipline. This can only mean that, having a half-beast and half-man as a teacher, a prince must know how to employ the nature of the one and the other; and the one without the other cannot endure.

Since, then, a prince must know how to make good use of the nature 15 of the beast, he should choose from among the beasts the fox and the lion; for the lion cannot defend itself from traps and the fox cannot protect itself from wolves. It is therefore necessary to be a fox in order to recognize the traps and a lion in order to frighten the wolves. Those who play only the part of the lion do not understand matters. A wise ruler, therefore, cannot and should not keep his word when such an observance of faith would be to his disadvantage and when the reasons which made him promise are removed. And if men were all good, this rule would not be good; but since men are a sorry lot and will not keep their promises to you, you likewise need not keep yours to them. A prince never lacks legitimate reasons to break his promises. Of this one could cite an endless number of modern examples to show how many pacts, how many promises have been made null and void because of the infidelity of princes; and he who has known best how to use the fox has come to a better end. But it is necessary to know how to disguise this nature well and to be a great hypocrite and a liar: and men are so simpleminded and so controlled by their present necessities that one who deceives will always find another who will allow himself to be deceived.

I do not wish to remain silent about one of these recent instances. Alexander VI[7] did nothing else, he thought about nothing else, except to deceive men, and he always found the occasion to do this. And there never was a man who had more forcefulness in his oaths, who affirmed a thing with more promises, and who honored his word less; nevertheless, his tricks always succeeded perfectly since he was well acquainted with this aspect of the world.

Therefore, it is not necessary for a prince to have all of the above-mentioned qualities, but it is very necessary for him to appear to have them. Furthermore, I shall be so bold as to assert this; that having them and practicing them at all times is harmful; and appearing to have them

---

[6]**Chiron** (Kī'ron) A centaur (half man, half horse) who was said in classical mythology to have been the teacher not only of Achilles but also of Theseus, Jason, Hercules, and other heroes.

[7]**Alexander VI** Pope from 1492 to 1503; father of Cesare Borgia.

useful; for instance, to seem merciful, faithful, humane, forthright, religious, and to be so; but his mind should be disposed in such a way that should it become necessary not to be so, he will be able and know how to change to the contrary. And it is essential to understand this: that a prince, and especially a new prince, cannot observe all those things by which men are considered good, for in order to maintain the state he is often obliged to act against his promise, against charity, against humanity, and against religion. And therefore, it is necessary that he have a mind ready to turn itself according to the way the winds of Fortune and the changeability of affairs require him; and, as I said above, as long as it is possible, he should not stray from the good, but he should know how to enter into evil when necessity commands.

A prince, therefore, must be very careful never to let anything slip from his lips which is not full of the five qualities mentioned above: He should appear, upon seeing and hearing him, to be all mercy, all faithfulness, all integrity, all kindness, all religion. And there is nothing more necessary than to seem to possess this last quality. And men in general judge more by their eyes than their hands; for everyone can see but few can feel. Everyone sees what you seem to be, few perceive what you are, and those few do not dare to contradict the opinion of the many who have the majesty of the state to defend them; and in the actions of all men, and especially of princes, where there is no impartial arbiter, one must consider the final result.[8] Let a prince therefore act to seize and to maintain the state; his methods will always be judged honorable and will be praised by all; for ordinary people are always deceived by appearances and by the outcome of a thing; and in the world there is nothing but ordinary people; and there is no room for the few, while the many have a place to lean on. A certain prince of the present day, whom I shall refrain from naming, preaches nothing but peace and faith, and to both one and the other he is entirely opposed; and both, if he had put them into practice, would have cost him many times over either his reputation or his state.

Topics for Critical Thinking and Writing

1. In the opening paragraph, Machiavelli claims that a ruler who wishes to keep in power must "learn how not to be good"—that is, must know where and when to ignore the demands of conventional morality. In the rest of the excerpt, does he give any convincing evidence to support this claim? Can you think of any recent political event in which a political leader violated the requirements of morality, as Machiavelli advises?

[8]The Italian original, *si guarda al fine*, has often been mistranslated as "the ends justify the means," something Machiavelli never wrote. [Translators' note.]

2. Machiavelli says in paragraph 1 that "a man who wishes to make a vocation of being good at all times will come to ruin among so many who are not good." (By the way, the passage is ambiguous. "At all times" is, in the original, a squinting modifier. It may look backward to "being good" or forward to "will come to ruin," but Machiavelli probably means, "A man who at all times wishes to make a vocation of being good will come to ruin among so many who are not good.") Is this view realistic or cynical? (What is the difference between these two?) Assume for the moment that the view is realistic. Does it follow that society requires a ruler who must act according to the principles Machiavelli sets forth?

3. In his second paragraph Machiavelli claims that it is impossible for a ruler to exhibit *all* the conventional virtues (trustworthiness, liberality, and so on). Why does he make this claim? Do you agree with it?

4. In paragraph 4 Machiavelli cites as examples Pope Julius II, the king of France, the king of Spain, and other rulers. Is he using these examples to illustrate his generalizations or to provide evidence for them? If you think he is using them to provide evidence, how convincing do you find the evidence? (Consider: Could Machiavelli be arguing from a biased sample?)

5. In paragraphs 6 to 10 Machiavelli argues that it is sometimes necessary for a ruler to be cruel, and so he praises Cesare Borgia and Hannibal. What in human nature, according to Machiavelli, explains this need to have recourse to cruelty? (By the way, how do you think *cruelty* should be defined here?)

6. Machiavelli says that Cesare Borgia's cruelty brought peace to Romagna and that, on the other hand, the Florentines who sought to avoid being cruel in fact brought pain to Pistoia. Can you think of recent episodes supporting the view that cruelty can be beneficial to society? If so, restate Machiavelli's position, using these examples from recent history. Then go on to write two paragraphs, arguing on behalf of your two examples. Or if you believe that Machiavelli's point here is fundamentally wrong, explain why, again using current examples.

7. In *The Prince*, Machiavelli is writing about how to be a successful ruler. He explicitly says he is dealing with things as they are, not things as they should be. Do you think that in fact one can write usefully about statecraft without considering ethics? Explain. Or you may want to think about it in this way: The study of politics is often called *political science*. Machiavelli can be seen as a sort of scientist, objectively analyzing the nature of governing—without offering any moral judgments. In an essay of 500 words, argue for or against the view that the study of politics is rightly called *political science*.

8. In the final paragraph, Machiavelli declares that "one must consider the final result." Taking account of the context, do you think the meaning is that (a) any end, goal, or purpose of anyone justifies using any means to reach it or (b) the end of governing the state, nation, or country justifies using any means to achieve it? Or do you think Machiavelli means both? Something else entirely?

9. In 500 words, argue that an important contemporary political figure does or does not act according to Machiavelli's principles.

10. If you have read the selection from Thomas More's *Utopia*, write an essay of 500 words on one of these two topics: (a) why More's book is or is not wiser than Machiavelli's or (b) why one of the books is more interesting than the other.

11. More and Machiavelli wrote their books at almost exactly the same time. Write a dialogue of two or three double-spaced typed pages in which the two men argue about the nature of the state. (During the argument, they will have to reveal their assumptions about the nature of human beings and the role of government.)

Thomas Jefferson

Thomas Jefferson (1743–1826) was a congressman, the governor of Virginia, the first secretary of state, and the president of the United States, but he said he wished to be remembered for only three things: drafting the Declaration of Independence, writing the Virginia Statute for Religious Freedom, and founding the University of Virginia. All three were efforts to promote freedom.

Jefferson was born in Virginia and educated at William and Mary College in Williamsburg, Virginia. After graduating he studied law, was admitted to the bar, and in 1769 was elected to the Virginia House of Burgesses, his first political office. In 1776 he went to Philadelphia as a delegate to the second Continental Congress, where he was elected to a committee of five to write the Declaration of Independence. Jefferson drafted the document, which was then subjected to some changes by the other members of the committee and by the Congress. Although he was unhappy with the changes (especially with the deletion of a passage against slavery), his claim to have written the Declaration is just.

The Declaration of Independence

When in the course of human events, it becomes necessary for one people to dissolve the political bands which have connected them with another, and to assume among the Powers of the earth, the separate and equal station to which the Laws of Nature and of Nature's God entitle them, a decent respect to the opinions of mankind requires that they should declare the causes which impel them to the separation.

We hold these truths to be self-evident, that all men are created equal, that they are endowed by their Creator with certain unalienable Rights, that among these are Life, Liberty and the pursuit of Happiness.

That to secure these rights, Governments are instituted among Men, deriving their just powers from the consent of the governed.

That whenever any Form of Government becomes destructive of these ends, it is the Right of the People to alter or to abolish it, and to institute a new Government, laying its foundation on such principles and organizing its powers in such form, as to them shall seem most likely to effect their Safety and Happiness. Prudence, indeed, will dictate that Governments long established should not be changed for light and transient causes; and accordingly all experience hath shown that mankind are more disposed to suffer, while evils are sufferable, than to right themselves by abolishing the forms to which they are accustomed. But when a long train of abuses and usurpations pursuing invariably the same Object evinces a design to reduce them under absolute Despotism, it is their right, it is their duty, to throw off such government, and to provide new Guards for their future security.

Such has been the patient sufferance of these Colonies; and such is 5 now the necessity which constrains them to alter their former Systems of Government. The history of the present King of Great Britain is a history of repeated injuries and usurpations, all having in direct object the establishment of an absolute Tyranny over these States. To prove this, let Facts be submitted to a candid world.

He has refused his Assent to Laws, the most wholesome and necessary for the public good.

He has forbidden his Governors to pass Laws of immediate and pressing importance, unless suspended in their operation till his Assent should be obtained; and when so suspended, he has utterly neglected to attend to them.

He has refused to pass over Laws for the accommodation of large districts of people, unless those people would relinquish the right of Representation in the Legislature, a right inestimable to them and formidable to tyrants only.

He has called together legislative bodies at places unusual, uncomfortable, and distant from the depository of their Public Records, for the sole purpose of fatiguing them into compliance with his measures.

He has dissolved Representative Houses repeatedly, for opposing 10 with manly firmness his invasions on the rights of the people.

He has refused for a long time, after such dissolutions, to cause others to be elected; whereby the Legislative Powers, incapable of Annihilation, have returned to the People at large for their exercise; the State remaining in the mean time exposed to all the dangers of invasion from without, and convulsions within.

He has endeavored to prevent the population of these States, for that purpose obstructing the Laws of Naturalization of Foreigners; refusing to pass others to encourage their migration hither, and raising the conditions of new Appropriations of Lands.

He has obstructed the Administration of Justice, by refusing his Assent to Laws for establishing Judiciary Powers.

He has made Judges dependent on his Will alone, for the tenure of their offices, and the amount and payment of their salaries.

He has erected a multitude of New Offices, and sent hither swarms 15 of Officers to harass our People, and eat out their substance.

He has kept among us, in time of peace, Standing Armies without the consent of our Legislature.

He has affected to render the Military independent of and superior to the Civil Power.

He has combined with others to subject us to jurisdictions foreign to our constitution, and unacknowledged by our laws; giving his Assent to their acts of pretended Legislation:

For quartering large bodies of armed troops among us:

For protecting them, by a mock Trial, from Punishment for any Mur- 20 ders which they should commit on the Inhabitants of these States:

For cutting off our Trade with all parts of the world:

For imposing Taxes on us without our Consent:

For depriving us in many cases, of the benefits of Trial by Jury:

For transporting us beyond Seas to be tried for pretended offenses:

For abolishing the free System of English Laws in a Neighbouring 25 Province, establishing therein an Arbitrary government, and enlarging its boundaries so as to render it at once an example and fit instrument for introducing the same absolute rule into these Colonies:

For taking away our Charters, abolishing our most valuable Laws, and altering fundamentally the Forms of our Governments.

For suspending our own Legislatures, and declaring themselves invested with Power to legislate for us in all cases whatsoever.

He has abdicated Government here, by declaring us out of his Protection and waging War against us.

He has plundered our seas, ravaged our Coasts, burnt our towns and destroyed the Lives of our people.

He is at this time transporting large Armies of foreign Mercenaries 30 to compleat the works of death, desolation and tyranny, already begun with circumstances of Cruelty & perfidy scarcely paralleled in the most barbarous ages, and totally unworthy the Head of a civilized nation.

He has constrained our fellow Citizens taken Captive on the high Seas to bear Arms against their Country, to become the executioners of their friends and Brethren, or to fall themselves by their Hands.

He has excited domestic insurrections amongst us, and has endeavored to bring on the inhabitants of our frontiers, the merciless Indian Savages, whose known rule of warfare is an undistinguished destruction of all ages, sexes and conditions.

In every stage of these Oppressions We Have Petitioned for Redress in the most humble terms: Our repeated petitions have been answered only by repeated injury. A Prince, whose character is thus marked by every act which may define a Tyrant, is unfit to be the ruler of a free People.

Nor have We been wanting in attention to our British brethren. We have warned them from time to time of attempts by their legislature to extend an unwarrantable jurisdiction over us. We have reminded them of the circumstances of our emigration and settlement here. We have appealed to their native justice and magnanimity and we have conjured them by the ties of our common kindred to disavow these usurpations, which would inevitably interrupt our connections and correspondence. They too have been deaf to the voice of justice and of consanguinity. We must, therefore, acquiesce in the necessity, which denounces our Separation, and hold them, as we hold the rest of mankind, Enemies in War, in Peace Friends.

We, therefore, the Representatives of the United States of America, 35 in General Congress, Assembled, appealing to the Supreme Judge of the world of the rectitude of our intentions, do, in the Name, and by Authority of the good People of these Colonies, solemnly publish and declare, That these United Colonies are, and of Right ought to be, Free and Independent States; that they are Absolved from all Allegiance to the British Crown, and that all political connection between them and the State of Great Britain, is and ought to be totally dissolved; and that as Free and Independent States, they have full power to levy War, conclude Peace, contract Alliances, establish Commerce, and so all the other Acts and Things which Independent States may of right do. And for the support of this Declaration, with a firm reliance on the protection of Divine Providence, we mutually pledge to each other our lives, our Fortunes and our sacred Honor.

TOPICS FOR CRITICAL THINKING AND WRITING

1. According to the first paragraph, for what audience was the Declaration written? What other audiences do you think the document was (in one way or another) addressed to?

2. The Declaration states that it is intended to "prove" that the acts of the government of George III had as their "direct object the establishment of an absolute Tyranny" in the American colonies (para. 5). Write an essay of 500 to 750 words showing whether the evidence offered in the Declaration "proves" this claim to your satisfaction. (You will, of course, want to define *absolute tyranny*.) If you think further evidence is needed to "prove" the colonists' point, indicate what this evidence might be.

3. Paying special attention to the paragraphs beginning "That whenever any Form of Government" (para. 4), "In every stage" (para. 33), and "Nor have We been wanting" (para. 34), in a sentence or two set forth the image of themselves that the colonists seek to convey.

4. In the Declaration of Independence it is argued that the colonists are entitled to certain things and that under certain conditions they may behave in a certain way. Make explicit the syllogism that Jefferson is arguing.

5. What evidence does Jefferson offer to support his major premise? His minor premise?

6. In paragraph 2 the Declaration cites "certain unalienable Rights" and mentions three: "Life, Liberty and the pursuit of Happiness." What is an unalienable right? If someone has an unalienable (or inalienable) right, does that imply that he or she also has certain duties? If so, what are these duties? John Locke, a century earlier (1690), asserted that all men have a natural right to "life, liberty, and property." Do you think the decision to drop "property" and substitute "pursuit of Happiness" improved Locke's claim? Explain.

7. The Declaration ends thus: "We mutually pledge to each other our lives, our Fortunes and our sacred Honor." Is it surprising that honor is put in the final, climactic position? Is this a better ending than "our Fortunes, our sacred Honor, and our lives," or than "our sacred Honor, our lives, and our Fortunes?" Why?

8. King George III has asked you to reply, on his behalf, to the colonists, in 500 to 750 words. Write his reply. (Caution: A good reply will probably require you to do some reading about the period.)

9. Write a declaration of your own, setting forth in 500 to 750 words why some group is entitled to independence. You may want to argue that adolescents should not be compelled to attend school, that animals should not be confined in zoos, or that persons who use drugs should be able to buy them legally. Begin with a premise, then set forth facts illustrating the unfairness of the present condition, and conclude by stating what the new condition will mean to society.

Elizabeth Cady Stanton

Elizabeth Cady Stanton (1815–1902), a lawyer's daughter and journalist's wife, proposed in 1848 a convention to address the "social, civil, and religious condition and rights of women." Responding to Stanton's call, women and men from all over the Northeast traveled to the Woman's Rights Convention held in the village of Seneca Falls, New York. Her Declaration, adopted by the Convention—but only after vigorous debate and some amendments by others—became the platform for the women's rights movement in this country.

Declaration of Sentiments and Resolutions

When, in the course of human events, it becomes necessary for one portion of the family of man to assume among the people of the earth a position different from that which they have hitherto occupied, but one to which the laws of nature and of nature's God entitle them, a decent respect to the opinions of mankind requires that they should declare the causes that impel them to such a course.

We hold these truths to be self-evident: that all men and women are created equal; that they are endowed by their Creator with certain inalienable rights; that among these are life, liberty and the pursuit of happiness; that to secure these rights governments are instituted, deriving their just powers from the consent of the governed. Whenever any form of government becomes destructive of these ends, it is the right of those who suffer from it to refuse allegiance to it, and to insist upon the institution of a new government, laying its foundation on such principles, and organizing its powers in such form, as to them shall seem most likely to effect their safety and happiness. Prudence, indeed, will dictate that governments long established should not be changed for light and transient causes; and accordingly all experience hath shown that mankind are more disposed to suffer, while evils are sufferable, than to right themselves by abolishing the forms to which they were accustomed. But when a long train of abuses and usurpations, pursuing invariably the same object, evinces a design to reduce them under absolute despotism, it is their duty to throw off such government, and to provide new guards for their future security. Such has been the patient sufferance of the women under this government, and such is now the necessity which constrains them to demand the equal station to which they are entitled.

The history of mankind is a history of repeated injuries and usurpations on the part of man toward woman, having in direct object the establishment of an absolute tyranny over her. To prove this, let facts be submitted to a candid world.

He has never permitted her to exercise her inalienable right to the elective franchise.

He has compelled her to submit to laws, in the formation of which   5
she had no voice.

He has withheld from her rights which are given to the most ignorant and degraded men — both natives and foreigners.

Having deprived her of this first right of a citizen, the elective franchise, thereby leaving her without representation in the halls of legislation, he has oppressed her on all sides.

He has made her, if married, in the eye of the law, civilly dead.

He has taken from her all right in property, even to the wages she earns.

He has made her, morally, an irresponsible being, as she can commit   10
many crimes with impunity, provided they be done in the presence of her husband. In the covenant of marriage, she is compelled to promise obedience to her husband, he becoming to all intents and purposes, her master — the law giving him power to deprive her of her liberty, and to administer chastisement.

He has so framed the laws of divorce, as to what shall be the proper causes, and in case of separation, to whom the guardianship of the children shall be given, as to be wholly regardless of the happiness of women — the law, in all cases, going upon a false supposition of the supremacy of man, and giving all power into his hands.

After depriving her of all rights as a married woman, if single, and the owner of property, he has taxed her to support a government which recognizes her only when her property can be made profitable to it.

He has monopolized nearly all the profitable employments, and from those she is permitted to follow, she receives but a scanty remuneration. He closes against her all the avenues to wealth and distinction which he considers most honorable to himself. As a teacher of theology, medicine, or law, she is not known.

He has denied her the facilities for obtaining a thorough education, all colleges being closed against her.

He allows her in Church, as well as State, but a subordinate position,   15 claiming Apostolic authority for her exclusion from the ministry, and, with some exceptions, from any public participation in the affairs of the Church.

He has created a false public sentiment by giving to the world a different code of morals for men and women, by which moral delinquencies which exclude women from society, are not only tolerated, but deemed of little account in man.

He has usurped the prerogative of Jehovah himself, claiming it as his right to assign for her a sphere of action, when that belongs to her conscience and to her God.

He has endeavored, in every way that he could, to destroy her confidence in her own powers, to lessen her self-respect, and to make her willing to lead a dependent and abject life.

Now, in view of this entire disfranchisement of one-half the people of this country, their social and religious degradation—in view of the unjust laws above mentioned, and because women do feel themselves aggrieved, oppressed, and fraudulently deprived of their most sacred rights, we insist that they have immediate admission to all the rights and privileges which belong to them as citizens of the United States.

In entering upon the great work before us, we anticipate no small   20 amount of misconception, misrepresentation, and ridicule; but we shall use every instrumentality within our power to effect our object. We shall employ agents, circulate tracts, petition the State and National legislatures, and endeavor to enlist the pulpit and the press in our behalf. We hope this Convention will be followed by a series of Conventions embracing every part of the country.

[The following resolutions were discussed by Lucretia Mott, Thomas and Mary Ann McClintock, Amy Post, Catharine A. F. Stebbins, and others, and were adopted:]

Whereas, The great precept of nature is conceded to be, that "man shall pursue his own true and substantial happiness." Blackstone in his Commentaries remarks, that this law of Nature being coeval with mankind, and dictated by God himself, is of course superior in obligation to any other. It is binding over all the globe, in all countries, and at all times; no human laws are of any validity if contrary to this, and such of them as are valid, derive all their force, and all their validity, and all their authority, mediately and immediately, from this original; therefore,

Resolved, That such laws as conflict, in any way, with the true and substantial happiness of woman, are contrary to the great precept of nature and of no validity, for this is "superior in obligation to any other."

Resolved, That all laws which prevent woman from occupying such a station in society as her conscience shall dictate, or which place her in a position inferior to that of man, are contrary to the great precept of nature, and therefore of no force or authority.

Resolved, That woman is man's equal—was intended to be so by the Creator, and the highest good of the race demands that she should be recognized as such.

Resolved, That the women of this country ought to be enlightened in regard to the laws under which they live, that they may no longer publish their degradation by declaring themselves satisfied with their present position, nor their ignorance, by asserting that they have all the rights they want.

Resolved, That inasmuch as man, while claiming for himself intellectual superiority, does accord to woman moral superiority, it is pre-eminently his duty to encourage her to speak and teach, as she has an opportunity, in all religious assemblies.

Resolved, That the same amount of virtue, delicacy, and refinement of behavior that is required of woman in the social state, should also be required of man, and the same transgressions should be visited with equal severity on both man and woman.

Resolved, That the objection of indelicacy and impropriety, which is so often brought against woman when she addresses a public audience, comes with a very ill-grace from those who encourage, by their attendance, her appearance on the stage, in the concert, or in feats of the circus.

Resolved, That woman has too long rested satisfied in the circumscribed limits which corrupt customs and a perverted application of the Scriptures have marked out for her, and that it is time she should move in the enlarged sphere which her great Creator has assigned her.

Resolved, That it is the duty of the women of this country to secure to themselves their sacred right to the elective franchise.

Resolved, That the equality of human rights results necessarily from the fact of the identity of the race in capabilities and responsibilities.

Resolved, therefore, That, being invested by the Creator with the same capabilities, and the same consciousness of responsibility for their exercise, it is demonstrably the right and duty of woman, equally with man, to promote every righteous cause by every righteous means; and especially in regard to the great subjects of morals and religion, it is self-evidently her right to participate with her brother in teaching them, both in private and in public, by writing and by speaking, by any instrumentalities proper to be used, and in any assemblies proper to be held; and this being a self-evident truth growing out of the divinely implanted principles of human nature, any custom or authority adverse to it, whether modern or wearing the hoary sanction of antiquity, is to be regarded as a self-evident falsehood, and at war with mankind.

[At the last session Lucretia Mott offered and spoke to the following resolution:]

Resolved, That the speedy success of our cause depends upon the zealous and untiring efforts of both men and women, for the overthrow of the monopoly of the pulpit, and for the securing to woman an equal participation with men in the various trades, professions, and commerce.

Topics for Critical Thinking and Writing

1. Stanton echoes the Declaration of Independence because she wishes to associate her ideas and the movement she supports with a document and a movement that her readers esteem. And she must have believed that if readers esteem the Declaration of Independence, they must grant the justice of her goals. Does her strategy work, or does it backfire by making her essay seem strained?

2. When Stanton insists that women have an "inalienable right to the elective franchise" (para. 4), what does she mean by "inalienable"?

3. Stanton complains that men have made married women, "in the eye of the law, civilly dead" (para. 8). What does she mean by "civilly dead"? How is it possible for a person to be biologically alive and yet civilly dead?

4. Stanton objects that women are "not known" as teachers of "theology, medicine, or law" (para. 13). Is this still true today? Do some research in your library, and then write three 100-word biographical sketches, one each on well-known woman professors of theology, medicine, and law.

5. How might you go about proving (rather than merely asserting) that, as paragraph 24 says, "woman is man's equal—was intended to be so by the Creator"?

6. The Declaration claims that women have "the same capabilities" as men (para. 32). Yet in 1848 Stanton and the others at Seneca Falls knew, or should have known, that history recorded no example of a woman philosopher comparable to Plato or Kant, a composer comparable to Beethoven or Chopin, a scientist comparable to Galileo or Newton, or a mathematician comparable to Euclid or Descartes. Do these facts contradict the Declaration's claim? If not, why not? How else but by different intellectual capabilities do you think such facts can be explained?

7. Stanton's Declaration is over 165 years old. Have all of the issues she raised been satisfactorily resolved? If not, which ones remain?

8. In our society, children have very few rights. For instance, a child cannot decide to drop out of elementary school or high school, and a child cannot decide to leave his or her parents to reside with some other

family that he or she finds more compatible. Whatever your view of children's rights, compose the best Declaration of the Rights of Children that you can.

Martin Luther King Jr.

Martin Luther King Jr. (1929–1968) was born in Atlanta and educated at More-house College, Crozer Theological Seminary, and Boston University. In 1954 he was called to serve as a Baptist minister in Montgomery, Alabama. During the next two years he achieved national fame when, using a policy of nonviolent resistance, he successfully led the boycott against segregated bus lines in Mont-gomery. He then organized the Southern Christian Leadership Conference, which furthered civil rights, first in the South and then nationwide. In 1964 he was awarded the Nobel Peace Prize. Four years later he was assassinated in Mem-phis, Tennessee, while supporting striking garbage workers.

The speech presented here was delivered from the steps of the Lincoln Memorial, in Washington, D.C., in 1963, the hundredth anniversary of the Emancipation Proclamation. King's immediate audience consisted of more than two hundred thousand people who had come to demonstrate for civil rights.

I Have a Dream

I am happy to join with you today in what will go down in history as the greatest demonstration for freedom in the history of our nation.

Five score years ago, a great American, in whose symbolic shadow we stand today, signed the Emancipation Proclamation. This momentous decree came as a great beacon light of hope to millions of Negro slaves who had been seared in the flames of withering injustice. It came as a joyous daybreak to end the long night of their captivity. But one hundred years later, the Negro still is not free. One hundred years later, the life of the Negro is still sadly crippled by the manacles of segregation and the chains of discrimination. One hundred years later, the Negro lives on a lonely island of poverty in the midst of a vast ocean of material pros-perity. One hundred years later, the Negro is still anguished in the cor-ners of American society and finds himself in exile in his own land. And so we have come here today to dramatize a shameful condition.

In a sense we have come to our nation's capital to cash a check. When the architects of our republic wrote the magnificent words of the Constitution and the Declaration of Independence, they were signing a promissory note to which every American was to fall heir. This note was the promise that all men—yes, black men as well as white men—would be guaranteed the inalienable rights of life, liberty, and the pursuit of happiness.

It is obvious today that America has defaulted on this promissory note insofar as her citizens of color are concerned. Instead of honoring this sacred obligation, America has given the Negro people a bad check, a check which has come back marked "insufficient funds." But we refuse to believe that the bank of justice is bankrupt. We refuse to believe that there are insufficient funds in the great vaults of opportunity of this nation; and so we have come to cash this check, a check that will give us upon demand the riches of freedom and the security of justice.

We have also come to this hallowed spot to remind America of the 5 fierce urgency of *now*. This is no time to engage in the luxury of cooling off or to take the tranquilizing drug of gradualism. *Now* is the time to make real promises of democracy. *Now* is the time to rise from the dark and desolate valley of segregation to the sunlit path of racial justice. *Now* is the time to lift our nation from the quicksands of racial injustice to the solid rock of brotherhood. *Now* is the time to make justice a reality for all of God's children.

It would be fatal for the nation to overlook the urgency of the moment. This sweltering summer of the Negro's legitimate discontent will not pass until there is an invigorating autumn of freedom and equality. Nineteen sixty-three is not an end, but a beginning. And those who hope that the Negro needed to blow off steam and will now be content will have a rude awakening if the nation returns to business as usual. There will be neither rest nor tranquility in America until the Negro is granted his citizenship rights. The whirlwinds of revolt will continue to shake the foundations of our nation until the bright day of justice emerges.

But there is something that I must say to my people who stand on the warm threshold which leads into the palace of justice. In the process of gaining our rightful place, we must not be guilty of wrongful deeds. Let us not seek to satisfy our thirst for freedom by drinking from the cup of bitterness and hatred. We must forever conduct our struggle on the high plane of dignity and discipline. We must not allow our creative protest to degenerate into physical violence. Again and again we must rise to the majestic heights of meeting physical force with soul force. And the marvelous new militancy which has engulfed the Negro community must not lead us to a distrust of all white people; for many of our white brothers, as evidenced by their presence here today, have come to realize that their destiny is tied up with our destiny, and they have come to realize that their freedom is inextricably bound to our freedom.

We cannot walk alone. And as we walk we must make the pledge that we shall always march ahead. We cannot turn back. There are those who are asking the devotees of civil rights, "When will you be satisfied?" We can never be satisfied as long as the Negro is the victim of the unspeakable horrors of police brutality. We can never be satisfied as long as our bodies, heavy with the fatigue of travel, cannot gain lodging in the motels of the highways and the hotels of the cities. We cannot be satisfied as long as the Negro's basic mobility is from a smaller ghetto to a larger one. We can never be satisfied as long as our children are stripped of their selfhood and robbed of their dignity by signs stating "For Whites Only." We cannot be satisfied as long as the Negro in Mississippi cannot vote and a Negro in New York believes he has nothing for which to vote. No, no, we are not satisfied, and we will not be satisfied until justice rolls down like waters and righteousness like a mighty stream.[1]

I am not unmindful that some of you have come here out of great trials and tribulations. Some of you have come fresh from narrow jail cells. Some of you have come from areas where your quest for freedom left you battered by the storms of persecution and staggered by the winds of police brutality. You have been the veterans of creative suffering. Continue to work with the faith that unearned suffering is redemptive.

Go back to Mississippi, and go back to Alabama. Go back to South 10 Carolina. Go back to Georgia. Go back to Louisiana. Go back to the slums and ghettos of our Northern cities, knowing that somehow this situation can and will be changed. Let us not wallow in the valley of despair.

I say to you today, my friends, even though we face the difficulties of today and tomorrow, I still have a dream. It is a dream deeply rooted in the American dream. I have a dream that one day this nation will rise up and live out the true meaning of its creed: "We hold these truths to be self-evident, that all men are created equal." I have a dream that one day, on the red hills of Georgia, sons of former slaves and the sons of former slave owners will be able to sit down together at the table of brotherhood. I have a dream that one day even the state of Mississippi, a state sweltering with the heat of injustice, sweltering with the heat of oppression, will be transformed into an oasis of freedom and justice. I have a dream that my four little children will one day live in a nation where they will not be judged by the color of their skin, but by the content of their character.

I have a dream today. I have a dream that one day down in Alabama—with its vicious racists, with its governor's lips dripping with the words of interposition and nullification—one day right there in Alabama, little black boys and black girls will be able to join hands with little white boys and white girls as sisters and brothers.

I have a dream today. I have a dream that one day every valley shall be exalted and every hill and mountain shall be made low, the rough places will be made plain and the crooked places will be made straight, and the glory of the Lord shall be revealed, and all flesh shall see it together.[2]

This is our hope. This is the faith that I go back to the South with. And with this faith we will be able to hew out of the mountain of despair a stone of hope. With this faith we will be able to transform the jangling discords of our nation into a beautiful symphony of brotherhood. With

---

[1]**justice . . . stream** A quotation from the Hebrew Bible: Amos 5:24. [All notes are the editors'.]

[2]**every valley . . . see it together** Another quotation from the Hebrew Bible: Isaiah 40:4–5.

this faith we will be able to work together, to play together, to struggle together, to go to jail together, to stand up for freedom together, knowing that we will be free one day.

And this will be the day—this will be the day when all of God's chil-   15
dren will be able to sing with new meaning:

> My country, 'tis of thee,
> Sweet land of liberty,
>   Of thee I sing;
> Land where my fathers died,
> Land of the Pilgrim's pride,
> From every mountainside
>   Let freedom ring.

And if America is to be a great nation, this must become true.

And so let freedom ring from the prodigious hilltops of New Hampshire. Let freedom ring from the mighty mountains of New York. Let freedom ring from the heightening Alleghenies of Pennsylvania. Let freedom ring from the snow-capped Rockies of Colorado. Let freedom ring from the curvaceous slopes of California.

But not only that. Let freedom ring from Stone Mountain of Georgia. Let freedom ring from Lookout Mountain of Tennessee. Let freedom ring from every hill and molehill of Mississippi. "From every mountainside let freedom ring."

And when this happens—when we allow freedom to ring, when we let it ring from every village and every hamlet, from every state and every city—we will be able to speed up that day when all of God's children, Black men and white men, Jews and Gentiles, Protestants and Catholics, will be able to join hands and sing in the words of the old Negro spiritual: "Free at last! Free at last! Thank God Almighty. We are free at last!"

TOPICS FOR CRITICAL THINKING AND WRITING

1. Analyze the rhetoric—the oratorical art—of the second paragraph. What, for instance, is gained by saying "five score years ago" instead of "a hundred years ago"? By metaphorically calling the Emancipation Proclamation "a great beacon light of hope"? By saying that "Negro slaves . . . had been seared in the flames of withering injustice"? And what of the metaphors "daybreak" and "the long night of . . . captivity"?

2. Do the first two paragraphs make an effective opening? Why?

3. In the third and fourth paragraphs King uses the metaphor of a bad check. Rewrite the third paragraph *without* using any of King's metaphors, and then in a paragraph evaluate the differences between King's version and yours.

4. King's highly metaphoric speech appeals to emotions. But it also offers *reasons*. What reasons, for instance, does King give to support his belief

that African Americans should not resort to physical violence in their struggle against segregation and discrimination?

5. When King delivered the speech, his audience at the Lincoln Memorial was primarily African American. Do you think that the speech is also addressed to other Americans? Explain.

6. The speech can be divided into three parts: paragraphs 1 through 6; paragraphs 7 ("But there is") through 10; and paragraph 11 ("I say to you today, my friends") to the end. Summarize each of these three parts in a sentence or two so that the basic organization is evident.

7. King says (para. 11) that his dream is "deeply rooted in the American dream." First, what is the American dream, as King seems to understand it? Second, how does King establish his point—that is, what evidence does he use to convince us—that his dream is the American dream? (On this second issue, one might start by pointing out that in the second paragraph King refers to the Emancipation Proclamation. What other relevant documents does he refer to?)

8. King delivered his speech in 1963, more than fifty years ago. In an essay of 500 words, argue that the speech still is—or is not—relevant. Or write an essay of 500 words in which you state what you take to be the "American dream," and argue that it now is or is not readily available to African Americans.

W. H. Auden

Wystan Hugh Auden (1907–1973) was born in York, England, and educated at Oxford University. In the 1930s his witty left-wing poetry earned him wide acclaim as the leading poet of his generation. In 1939 he came to the United States, becoming a citizen in 1946 but returning to England for his last years. Much of Auden's poetry is characterized by a combination of colloquial diction and technical dexterity. The poem reprinted here was originally published in 1940.

The Unknown Citizen

(To JS/07/M/378
This Marble Monument
Is Erected by the State)

He was found by the Bureau of Statistics to be
One against whom there was no official complaint,
And all the reports on his conduct agree
That, in the modern sense of an old-fashioned word, he was a saint,
For in everything he did he served the Greater Community.   5
Except for the War till the day he retired
He worked in a factory and never got fired,
But satisfied his employers, Fudge Motors Inc.
Yet he wasn't a scab or odd in his views,

For his Union reports that he paid his dues,   10
(Our report on his Union shows it was sound)
And our Social Psychology workers found
That he was popular with his mates and liked a drink.
The Press are convinced that he bought a paper every day
And that his reactions to advertisements were normal in every way.   15
Policies taken out in his name prove that he was fully insured,
And his Health-card shows he was once in hospital but left it cured.
Both Producers Research and High-Grade Living declare
He was fully sensible to the advantages of the Installment Plan
And had everything necessary to the Modern Man,   20
A phonograph, radio, a car and a frigidaire.
Our researches into Public Opinion are content
That he held the proper opinions for the time of year;
When there was peace, he was for peace; when there was war, he went.
He was married and added five children to the population,   25
Which our Eugenist says was the right number for a parent of his
    generation,
And our teachers report that he never interfered with their education.
Was he free? Was he happy? The question is absurd:
Had anything been wrong, we should certainly have heard.

Topics for Critical Thinking and Writing

1. Who is the narrator in Auden's poem, and on what sort of occasion is he speaking? How do you know?

2. France, Great Britain, and the United States all have monuments to "The Unknown" (formerly "The Unknown Soldier"). How is Auden's proposed monument like and unlike these war memorials?

3. The poem ends by asking "Was he free? Was he happy?" and the questions are dismissed summarily. Is that because the answers are so obvious? What answers (obvious or subtle) do you think the poem offers to these questions?

4. Evaluate the poem, making clear the reasons behind your evaluation.

5. If you have read the selection from Thomas More's *Utopia*, write an essay of 500 to 750 words—in More's voice—setting forth More's response to Auden's poem.

Langston Hughes

Langston Hughes (1902–1967), an African American writer, was born in Joplin, Missouri, but after his parents divorced, he lived with his grandmother in Lawrence, Kansas, then in Cleveland, and then for fifteen months in Mexico with his father. He returned to the United States in 1921 and spent a year at Columbia University, served as a merchant seaman, and worked in a Paris nightclub, where he showed some of his poems to Dr. Alain Locke, a strong advocate of African American literature. Encouraged by Locke, when Hughes returned to the United States, he studied at the University of Pennsylvania and Lincoln University, where he earned a bachelor's degree. He continued to write, publishing fiction, plays, essays, and biographies; he also founded theaters, gave public readings, and was, in short, a highly visible presence. Esquire *magazine first published an abridged version of "Let America Be America Again" in 1936.*

Let America Be America Again

Let America be America again.
Let it be the dream it used to be.
Let it be the pioneer on the plain
Seeking a home where he himself is free.

(America never was America to me.)   5

Let America be the dream the dreamers dreamed—
Let it be that great strong land of love
Where never kings connive nor tyrants scheme
That any man be crushed by one above.

(It never was America to me.)   10

O, let my land be a land where Liberty
Is crowned with no false patriotic wreath,
But opportunity is real, and life is free,
Equality is in the air we breathe.

(There's never been equality for me,   15
Nor freedom in this "homeland of the free.")

Say, who are you that mumbles in the dark?
And who are you that draws your veil across the stars?

I am the poor white, fooled and pushed apart,
I am the Negro bearing slavery's scars.   20
I am the red man driven from the land,
I am the immigrant clutching the hope I seek—
And finding only the same old stupid plan
Of dog eat dog, of mighty crush the weak.

I am the young man, full of strength and hope,   25
Tangled in that ancient endless chain
Of profit, power, gain, of grab the land!
Of grab the gold! Of grab the ways of satisfying need!
Of work the men! Of take the pay!
Of owning everything for one's own greed!   30

I am the farmer, bondsman to the soil.
I am the worker sold to the machine.

I am the Negro, servant to you all.
I am the people, humble, hungry, mean—
Hungry yet today despite the dream.   35
Beaten yet today—O, Pioneers!
I am the man who never got ahead,
The poorest worker bartered through the years.

Yet I'm the one who dreamt our basic dream
In that Old World while still a serf of kings,   40
Who dreamt a dream so strong, so brave, so true,
That even yet its mighty daring sings
In every brick and stone, in every furrow turned
That's made America the land it has become.
O, I'm the man who sailed those early seas   45
In search of what I meant to be my home—
For I'm the one who left dark Ireland's shore,
And Poland's plain, and England's grassy lea,
And torn from Black Africa's strand I came
To build a "homeland of the free."   50

The free?

Who said the free? Not me?
Surely not me? The millions on relief today?
The millions shot down when we strike?
The millions who have nothing for our pay?   55
For all the dreams we've dreamed
And all the songs we've sung
And all the hopes we've held
And all the flags we've hung,
The millions who have nothing for our pay—   60
Except the dream that's almost dead today.

O, let America be America again—
The land that never has been yet—
And yet must be—the land where *every* man is free.
The land that's mine—the poor man's, Indian's, Negro's, ME—   65
Who made America,
Whose sweat and blood, whose faith and pain,
Whose hand at the foundry, whose plow in the rain,
Must bring back our mighty dream again.

Sure, call me any ugly name you choose—   70
The steel of freedom does not stain.
From those who live like leeches on the people's lives,
We must take back our land again,
America!

O, yes,   75
I say it plain,
America never was America to me,

And yet I swear this oath—
America will be!

Out of the rack and ruin of our gangster death,   80
The rape and rot of graft, and stealth, and lies,
We, the people, must redeem
The land, the mines, the plants, the rivers.
The mountains and the endless plain—
All, all the stretch of these great green states—   85
And make America again!

Topics for Critical Thinking and Writing

1. Hughes says in line 1, "Let America be America again," but do you suppose that America ever was what he seems to assume that it once was?
   For instance, might not his "pioneer" (line 3) have been sexist and racist? Or is it evident that contemporary society is morally inferior to early
   American society?

2. In line 24 Hughes speaks of a system "of dog eat dog," where the
   "mighty crush the weak," and in line 27 he speaks of a system of "profit,
   power, gain, of grab the land." Do you believe that this charge can be
   lodged today against our system of capitalism? Explain.

3. When *Esquire* magazine bought the poem, it bought only the first fifty
   lines. Why do you suppose the magazine declined to publish the remainder? Because the latter part is less good as poetry? Because it is too
   radical? In an essay of 500 words compare the two versions (lines 1–50
   and 1–86), and indicate which version you would publish if you were
   an editor today and why.

Ursula K. Le Guin

*Ursula K. Le Guin was born in 1929 in Berkeley, California, the daughter of a
distinguished mother (Theodora Kroeber, a folklorist) and father (Alfred L. Kroeber, an anthropologist). After graduating from Radcliffe College, she earned a
master's degree at Columbia University; in 1952 she held a Fulbright Fellowship
for study in Paris, where she met and married Charles Le Guin, a historian. She
began writing in earnest while bringing up three children. Although her work is
most widely known to buffs of science fiction, because it usually has larger moral
or political dimensions, it interests many other readers who normally do not care
for sci-fi.*

*Le Guin has said that she was prompted to write the following story by a
remark she encountered in William James's "The Moral Philosopher and the
Moral Life." James suggests there that if millions of people could be "kept permanently happy on the one simple condition that a certain lost soul on the far-off
edge of things should lead a life of lonely torment," our moral sense "would make
us immediately feel" it would be "hideous" to accept such a bargain. This story
first appeared in* New Dimensions 3 *(1973).*

The Ones Who Walk Away from Omelas

With a clamor of bells that set the swallows soaring, the Festival of Summer came to the city Omelas, bright-towered by the sea. The rigging of the boats in harbor sparkled with flags. In the streets between houses with red roofs and painted walls, between old moss-grown gardens and under avenues of trees, past great parks and public buildings, processions moved. Some were decorous: old people in long stiff robes of mauve and gray, grave master workmen, quiet, merry women carrying their babies and chatting as they walked. In other streets the music beat faster, a shimmering of gong and tambourine, and the people went dancing, the procession was a dance. Children dodged in and out, their high calls rising like the swallows' crossing flights over the music and the singing. All the processions wound towards the north side of the city, where on the great water-meadow called the Green Fields boys and girls, naked in the bright air, with mudstained feet and ankles and long, lithe arms, exercised their restive horses before the race. The horses wore no gear at all but a halter without bit. Their manes were braided with streamers of silver, gold, and green. They flared their nostrils and pranced and boasted to one another; they were vastly excited, the horse being the only animal who has adopted our ceremonies as his own. Far off to the north and west the mountains stood up half encircling Omelas on her bay. The air of morning was so clear that the snow still crowning the Eighteen Peaks burned with white-gold fire across the miles of sunlit air, under the dark blue of the sky. There was just enough wind to make the banners that marked the racecourse snap and flutter now and then. In the silence of the broad green meadows one could hear the music winding through the city streets, farther and nearer and ever approaching, a cheerful faint sweetness of the air that from time to time trembled and gathered together and broke out into the great joyous clanging of the bells.

Joyous! How is one to tell about joy? How describe the citizens of Omelas?

They were not simple folk, you see, though they were happy. But we do not say the words of cheer much any more. All smiles have become archaic. Given a description such as this one tends to make certain assumptions. Given a description such as this one tends to look next for the King, mounted on a splendid stallion and surrounded by his noble knights, or perhaps in a golden litter borne by great-muscled slaves. But there was no king. They did not use swords, or keep slaves. They were not barbarians. I do not know the rules and laws of their society, but I suspect that they were singularly few. As they did without monarchy and slavery, so they also got on without the stock exchange, the advertisement, the secret police, and the bomb. Yet I repeat that these were not simple folk, not dulcet shepherds, noble savages, bland utopians. They were not less complex than us. The trouble is that we have a bad habit, encouraged by pedants and sophisticates, of considering happiness as something rather stupid. Only pain is intellectual, only evil interesting. This is the treason of the artist: a refusal to admit the banality of evil and the terrible boredom of pain. If you can't lick 'em, join 'em. If it hurts, repeat it. But to praise despair is to condemn delight, to embrace violence is to lose hold of everything else. We have almost lost hold, we can no longer describe a happy man, nor make any celebration of joy. How can I tell you about the people of Omelas? They were not naïve and happy children—though their children were, in fact, happy. They were mature, intelligent, passionate adults whose lives were not wretched. O miracle! But I wish I could describe it better. I wish I could convince you. Omelas sounds in my words like a city in a fairy tale, long ago and far away, once upon a time. Perhaps it would be best if you imagined it as your own fancy bids, assuming it will rise to the occasion, for certainly I cannot suit you all. For instance, how about technology? I think that there would be no cars or helicopters in and above the streets; this follows from the fact that the people of Omelas are happy people. Happiness is based on a just discrimination of what is necessary, what is neither necessary nor destructive, and what is destructive. In the middle category, however—that of the unnecessary but undestructive, that of comfort, luxury, exuberance, etc.—they could perfectly well have central heating, subway trains, washing machines, and all kinds of marvelous devices not yet invented here, floating light-sources, fuelless power, a cure for the common cold. Or they could have none of that: it doesn't matter. As you like it. I incline to think that people from towns up and down the coast have been coming in to Omelas during the last days before the Festival on very fast little trains and double-decked trams, and that the train station of Omelas is actually the handsomest building in town, though plainer than the magnificent Farmers' Market. But even granted trains, I fear that Omelas so far strikes some of you as goody-goody. Smiles, bells, parades, horses, bleh. If so, please add an orgy. If an orgy would help, don't hesitate. Let us not, however, have temples from which issue beautiful nude priests and priestesses already half in ecstasy and ready to copulate with any man or woman, lover or stranger, who desires union with the deep godhead of the blood, although that was my first idea. But really it would be better not to have any temples in Omelas—at least, not manned temples. Religion yes, clergy no. Surely the beautiful nudes can just wander about, offering themselves like divine soufflés to the hunger of the needy and the rapture of the flesh. Let them join the processions. Let tambourines be struck above the copulations, and the glory of desire be proclaimed upon the gongs, and (a not unimportant point) let the offspring of these delightful rituals be beloved and looked after by all. One thing I know there is none of in Omelas is guilt. But what else should there be? I thought that first there were no drugs, but that is puritanical. For those who like it, the faint insistent sweetness of *drooz* may perfume the ways of the city, *drooz* which first brings a gr at lightness and brilliance to the mind and limbs, and then after some hours a dreamy languor, and wonderful visions at last of the very arcana and inmost secrets of the Universe, as well as exciting the pleasure of sex beyond all belief; and it is not habit-forming. For more modest tastes I think there ought to be beer. What else, what else belongs in the joyous city? The sense of victory, surely, the celebration of courage. But as we did without clergy, let us do without soldiers. The joy built upon successful slaughter is not the right kind of joy; it will not do; it is fearful and it is trivial. A boundless and generous contentment, a magnanimous triumph felt not against some outer enemy but in communion with the finest and fairest in the souls of all men everywhere and the splendor of the world's summer: this is what swells the hearts of the people of Omelas, and the victory they celebrate is that of life. I really don't think many of them need to take *drooz*.

Most of the processions have reached the Green Fields by now. A marvelous smell of cooking goes forth from the red and blue tents of the provisioners. The faces of small children are amiably sticky; in the benign grey beard of a man a couple of crumbs of rich pastry are entangled. The youths and girls have mounted their horses and are beginning to group around the starting line of the course. An old woman, small, fat, and laughing, is passing out flowers from a basket, and tall young men wear her flowers in their shining hair. A child of nine or ten sits at the edge of the crowd, alone, playing on a wooden flute. People pause to listen, and they smile, but they do not speak to him, for he never ceases playing and never sees them, his dark eyes wholly rapt in the sweet, thin magic of the tune.

He finishes, and slowly lowers his hands holding the wooden flute.   5

As if that little private silence were the signal, all at once a trumpet sounds from the pavilion near the starting line: imperious, melancholy, piercing. The horses rear on their slender legs, and some of them neigh in answer. Sober-faced, the young riders stroke the horses' necks and soothe them, whispering, "Quiet, quiet, there my beauty, my hope. . . ." They begin to form in rank along the starting line. The crowds along the racecourse are like a field of grass and flowers in the wind. The Festival of Summer has begun.

Do you believe? Do you accept the festival, the city, the joy? No? Then let me describe one more thing.

In a basement under one of the beautiful public buildings of Omelas, or perhaps in the cellar of one of its spacious private homes, there is a room. It has one locked door, and no window. A little light seeps in dustily between cracks in the boards, secondhand from a cobwebbed window somewhere across the cellar. In one corner of the little room a couple of mops, with stiff, clotted, foul-smelling heads, stand near a rusty bucket. The floor is dirt, a little damp to the touch, as cellar dirt usually is. The room is about three paces long and two wide: a mere broom closet or disused tool room. In the room a child is sitting. It could be a boy or a girl. It looks about six, but actually is nearly ten. It is feeble-minded. Perhaps it was born defective, or perhaps it has become imbecile through fear, malnutrition, and neglect. It picks its nose and occasionally fumbles vaguely with its toes or genitals, as it sits hunched in the corner farthest from the bucket and the two mops. It is afraid of the mops. It finds them horrible. It shuts its eyes, but it knows the mops are still standing there; and the door is locked; and nobody will come. The door is always locked; and nobody ever comes, except that sometimes—the child has no understanding of time or interval—sometimes the door rattles terribly and opens, and a person, or several people, are there. One of them may come in and kick the child to make it stand up. The others never come close, but peer in at it with frightened, disgusted eyes. The food bowl and the water jug are hastily filled, the door is locked, the eyes disappear. The people at the door never say anything, but the child, who has not always lived in the tool room, and can remember sunlight and its mother's voice, sometimes speaks. "I will be good," it says. "Please let me out. I will be good!" They never answer. The child used to scream for help at night, and cry a good deal, but now it only makes a kind of whining, "eh-haa, eh-haa," and it speaks less and less often. It is so thin there are no calves to its legs; its belly protrudes; it lives on a half-bowl of corn meal and grease a day. It is naked. Its buttocks and thighs are a mass of festered sores, as it sits in its own excrement continually.

They all know it is there, all the people of Omelas. Some of them have come to see it, others are content merely to know it is there. They all know that it has to be there. Some of them understand why, and some do not, but they all understand that their happiness, the beauty of their city, the tenderness of their friendships, the health of their children, the wisdom of their scholars, the skill of their makers, even the abundance of their harvest and the kindly weathers of their skies, depend wholly on this child's abominable misery.

This is usually explained to children when they are between eight   10 and twelve, whenever they seem capable of understanding; and most of those who come to see the child are young people, though often enough an adult comes, or comes back, to see the child. No matter how well the matter has been explained to them, these young spectators are always shocked and sickened at the sight. They feel disgust, which they had thought themselves superior to. They feel anger, outrage, impotence, despite all the explanations. They would like to do something for the child. But there is nothing they can do. If the child were brought up into the sunlight out of that vile place, if it were cleaned and fed and comforted, that would be a good thing, indeed; but if it were done, in that day and hour all the prosperity and beauty and delight of Omelas would wither and be destroyed. Those are the terms. To exchange all the goodness and grace of every life in Omelas for that single, small improvement: to throw away the happiness of thousands for the chance of the happiness of one: that would be to let guilt within the walls indeed.

The terms are strict and absolute; there may not even be a kind word spoken to the child.

Often the young people go home in tears, or in a tearless rage, when they have seen the child and faced this terrible paradox. They may brood over it for weeks or years. But as time goes on they begin to realize that even if the child could be released, it would not get much good of its freedom: a little vague pleasure of warmth and food, no doubt, but little more. It is too degraded and imbecile to know any real joy. It has been afraid too long ever to be free of fear. Its habits are too uncouth for it to respond to humane treatment. Indeed, after so long it would probably be wretched without walls about it to protect it, and darkness for its eyes, and its own excrement to sit in. Their tears at the bitter injustice dry when they begin to perceive the terrible justice of reality, and to accept it. Yet it is their tears and anger, the trying of their generosity and the acceptance of their helplessness, which are perhaps the true source of the splendor of their lives. Theirs is no vapid, irresponsible happiness. They know that they, like the child, are not free. They know compassion. It is the existence of the child, and their knowledge of its existence, that makes possible the nobility of their architecture, the poignancy of their music, the profundity of their science. It is because of the child that they are so gentle with children. They know that if the wretched one were not there snivelling in the dark, the other one, the flute-player, could make no joyful music as the young riders line up in their beauty for the race in the sunlight of the first morning of summer.

Now do you believe in them? Are they not more credible? But there is one more thing to tell, and this is quite incredible.

At times one of the adolescent girls or boys who go to see the child does not go home to weep or rage, does not, in fact, go home at all. Sometimes also a man or woman much older falls silent for a day or two, and then leaves home. These people go out into the street, and walk down the street alone. They keep walking, and walk straight out of the city of Omelas, through the beautiful gates. They keep walking across the farmlands of Omelas. Each one goes alone, youth or girl, man or woman. Night falls; the traveler must pass down village streets, between the houses with yellow-lit windows, and on out into the darkness of the fields. Each alone, they go west or north, towards the mountains. They go on. They leave Omelas, they walk ahead into the darkness, and they do not come back. The place they go towards is a place even less imaginable to most of us than the city of happiness. I cannot describe it at all. It is possible that it does not exist. But they seem to know where they are going, the ones who walk away from Omelas.

Topics for Critical Thinking and Writing

1. Summarize the point of the story—not the plot but what the story adds up to, what the author is getting at. Next, set forth what you would probably do (and why) if you were born in Omelas.

2. Consider the narrator's assertion that happiness "is based on a just discrimination of what is necessary" (para. 3).

3. Do you think the story implies a criticism of contemporary American society? Explain.

Helen Prejean

Sister Helen Prejean, born in Baton Rouge in 1939, has been a member of the Order of the Sisters of St. Joseph of Medaille since 1957. In 1993, she achieved international fame with her book Dead Man Walking: An Eyewitness Account of the Death Penalty in the United States, *based on her experiences counseling prisoners on death row in Louisiana prisons. An excerpt is printed here. A film with the same title, starring Susan Sarandon (as Sister Helen) and Sean Penn, was released in 1995. When confronted with the argument that the death penalty is appropriate revenge for society to take on a murderer, Sister Helen said, "I would not want my death avenged—especially by government, which can't be trusted to control its own bureaucrats or collect taxes equitably or fill a pothole, much less decide which of its citizens to kill." The title is the editors'.*

Executions Are Too Costly—Morally

I think of the running debate I engage in with "church" people about the death penalty. "Proof texts" from the Bible usually punctuate these discussions without regard for the cultural context or literary genre of the passages invoked. (Will D. Campbell, a Southern Baptist minister and writer, calls this use of scriptural quotations "biblical quarterbacking.")

It is abundantly clear that the Bible depicts murder as a crime for which death is considered the appropriate punishment, and one is hard-pressed to find a biblical "proof text" in either the Hebrew Testament or the New Testament which unequivocally refutes this. Even Jesus' admonition "Let him without sin cast the first stone," when he was asked the appropriate punishment for an adulteress (John 8:7)—the Mosaic law prescribed death—should be read in its proper context. This passage is an "entrapment" story, which sought to show Jesus' wisdom in besting his adversaries. It is not an ethical pronouncement about capital punishment.

Similarly, the "eye for eye" passage from Exodus, which pro-death penalty advocates are fond of quoting, is rarely cited in its original context, in which it is clearly meant to limit revenge.

The passage, including verse 22, which sets the context reads:

> If, when men come to blows, they hurt a woman who is pregnant and she suffers a miscarriage, though she does not die of it, the man responsible must pay the compensation demanded of him by the woman's master; he shall hand it over after arbitration. But should she die, you shall give life for life, eye for eye, tooth for tooth, hand for hand, foot for foot, burn for burn, wound for wound, stroke for stroke. (Exodus 21:22–25)

In the example given (patently patriarchal: the woman is considered   5
the negotiable property of her male master), it is clear that punishment
is to be measured out according to the seriousness of the offense. If the
child is lost but not the mother, the punishment is less grave than if both
mother and child are lost. *Only* an eye for an eye, *only* a life for a life is
the intent of the passage. Restraint was badly needed. It was not uncommon for an offended family or clan to slaughter entire communities in
retaliation for an offense against one of their members.

Even granting the call for restraint in this passage, it is nonetheless
clear—here and in numerous other instances throughout the Hebrew
Bible—that the punishment for murder was death.

But we must remember that such prescriptions of the Mosaic Law
were promulgated in a seminomadic culture in which the preservation
of a fragile society—without benefit of prisons and other institutions—
demanded quick, effective, harsh punishment of offenders. And we should
note the numerous other crimes for which the Bible prescribes death as
punishment:

contempt of parents (Exodus 21:15, 17; Leviticus 24:17);

trespass upon sacred ground (Exodus 19:12-13; Numbers 1:51; 18:7);

sorcery (Exodus 22:18; Leviticus 20:27);

bestiality (Exodus 22:19; Leviticus 20:15–16);

sacrifice to foreign gods (Exodus 22:20; Deuteronomy 13:1–9);

profaning the sabbath (Exodus 31:14);

adultery (Leviticus 20:10; Deuteronomy 22:22–24);

incest (Leviticus 20:11–13);

homosexuality (Leviticus 20:13);

and prostitution (Leviticus 21:19; Deuteronomy 22:13–21).

And this is by no means a complete list.

But no person with common sense would dream of appropriating
such a moral code today, and it is curious that those who so readily invoke
the "eye for an eye, life for life" passage are quick to shun other biblical
prescriptions which also call for death, arguing that modern societies have
evolved over the three thousand or so years since biblical times and no
longer consider such exaggerated and archaic punishments appropriate.

Such nuances are lost, of course, in "biblical quarterbacking," and   10
more and more I find myself steering away from such futile discussions.
Instead, I try to articulate what I personally believe about Jesus and the
ethical thrust he gave to humankind: an impetus toward compassion,
a preference for disarming enemies without humiliating and destroying
them, and a solidarity with poor and suffering people.

So, what happened to the impetus of love and compassion Jesus set
blazing into history?

The first Christians adhered closely to the way of life Jesus had taught. They died in amphitheaters rather than offer homage to worldly emperors. They refused to fight in emperors' wars. But then a tragic diversion happened, which Elaine Pagels has deftly explored in her book *Adam, Eve, and the Serpent:* in 313 c.e. (Common Era) the Emperor Constantine entered the Christian church.

Pagels says, "Christian bishops, once targets for arrest, torture, and execution, now received tax exemptions, gifts from the imperial treasury, prestige, and even influence at court; the churches gained new wealth, power and prominence."

Unfortunately, the exercise of power practiced by Christians in alliance with the Roman Empire—with its unabashed allegiance to the sword—soon bore no resemblance to the purely moral persuasion that Jesus had taught.

In the fifth century, Pagels points out, Augustine provided the theo-   15
logical rationale the church needed to justify the use of violence by church and state governments. Augustine persuaded church authorities that "original sin" so damaged every person's ability to make moral choices that external control by church and state authorities over people's lives was necessary and justified. The "wicked" might be "coerced by the sword" to "protect the innocent," Augustine taught. And thus was legitimated for Christians the authority of secular government to "control" its subjects by coercive and violent means—even punishment by death.

In the latter part of the twentieth century, however, two flares of hope—Mohandas K. Gandhi and Martin Luther King—have demonstrated that Jesus' counsel to practice compassion and tolerance even toward one's enemies can effect social change. Susan Jacoby, analyzing the moral power that Gandhi and King unleashed in their campaigns for social justice, finds a unique form of aggression:

"'If everyone took an eye for an eye,' Gandhi said, 'the whole world would be blind.' But Gandhi did not want to take anyone's eye; he wanted to force the British out of India. . . ."

Nonviolence and nonaggression are generally regarded as interchangeable concepts—King and Gandhi frequently used them that way—but nonviolence, as employed by Gandhi in India and by King in the American South, might reasonably be viewed as a highly disciplined form of aggression. If one defines aggression in the primary dictionary sense of "attack," nonviolent resistance proved to be the most powerful attack imaginable on the powers King and Gandhi were trying to overturn. The writings of both men are filled with references to love as a powerful force against oppression, and while the two leaders were not using the term "force" in the military sense, they certainly regarded nonviolence as a tactical weapon as well as an expression of high moral principle. The root meaning of Gandhi's concept of *satyagraha* . . . is "holding on to truth" . . . Gandhi also called *satyagraha* the "love force" or "soul force" and explained that he had discovered "in the earliest stages that pursuit of truth did not permit violence being inflicted on one's opponent, but that he must be weaned from error by patience and sympathy. . . . And patience means self-suffering." So the doctrine came to mean vindication of truth, not by the infliction of suffering on the opponent, but on one's self.

King was even more explicit on this point: the purpose of civil disobedience, he explained many times, was to force the defenders of segregation to commit brutal acts in public and thus arouse the conscience of the world on behalf of those wronged by racism. King and Gandhi did not succeed because they changed the hearts and minds of southern sheriffs and British colonial administrators (although they did, in fact, change some minds) but because they *made the price of maintaining control too high for their opponents* [emphasis mine].

That, I believe, is what it's going to take to abolish the death penalty in this country: we must persuade the American people that government killings are too costly for us, not only financially, but—more important—morally.

The death penalty costs too much. Allowing our government to kill citizens compromises the deepest moral values upon which this country was conceived: the inviolable dignity of human persons.

I have no doubt that we will one day abolish the death penalty in   20
America. It will come sooner if people like me who know the truth about executions do our work well and educate the public. It will come slowly if we do not. Because, finally, I know that it is not a question of malice or ill will or meanness of spirit that prompts our citizens to support executions. It is, quite simply, that people don't know the truth of what is going on. That is not by accident. The secrecy surrounding executions makes it possible for executions to continue. I am convinced that if executions were made public, the torture and violence would be unmasked, and we would be shamed into abolishing executions. We would be embarrassed at the brutalization of the crowds that would gather to watch a man or woman be killed. And we would be humiliated to know that visitors from other countries—Japan, Russia, Latin America, Europe—were watching us kill our own citizens—we, who take pride in being the flagship of democracy in the world.

TOPICS FOR CRITICAL THINKING AND WRITING

1. Suppose you interpret the "eye for eye" passage from Exodus (paras. 3–6) not as a "call for restraint" but as support for the death penalty. Does that mean no exceptions whatsoever—that everyone who kills another must be sentenced to death and executed? Would that require abandoning the distinction between murder and manslaughter or between first- and second-degree murder?

2. Prejean lists ten different crimes for which the Bible prescribes death as the punishment (para. 7) and says "no person with common sense

would dream of appropriating [them] today" (para. 9). Do you agree? In an essay of 500 words, defend or criticize the proposition that the death penalty ought to be confined to the crime of first-degree murder.

3. Do you think that someone who endorses the biblical doctrine of "life for life, eye for eye" (para. 4) is also required by consistency to endorse the death penalty for some or all of the ten nonhomicidal crimes Prejean mentions (para. 7)? Explain.

4. In deciding whether to impose the death penalty for serious crimes, what guidance do you think a secular society, such as ours, ought to accept from the Bible? In an essay of 500 words, defend or criticize this thesis: "Biblical teachings ought to play a central role in deciding how we use the death penalty."

5. Prejean does not propose any alternative to the death penalty. Presumably she would favor some form of imprisonment for crimes involving death. She claims that the death penalty is inconsistent with "the inviolable dignity of human persons" (para. 19). Does consistency require her also to reject flogging? Solitary confinement in prison? Life imprisonment without the possibility of parole? Write a 500-word essay on this theme: "Severe Punishment and the Inviolable Dignity of Human Persons."

6. Prejean thinks that if executions were made public, Americans would soon decide to oppose the death penalty (para. 20). Do you agree? Write a 500-word essay for or against the following proposition: "Executions held in public would soon lead to public rejection of the death penalty."

27

How Free Is the Will of the Individual within Society?

THOUGHTS ABOUT FREE WILL

All theory is against the freedom of the will; all experience for it.

—SAMUEL JOHNSON

Free will is doing gladly and freely that which one must do.

—CARL G. JUNG

The will is never free — it is always attached to an object, a purpose. It is simply the engine in the car — it can't steer.

—JOYCE CARY

A man may be a pessimistic determinist before lunch and an optimistic believer in the will's freedom after it.

—ALDOUS HUXLEY

Fatalism, whose solving word in all crises of behavior is all striving is vain, will never reign supreme, for the impulse to take life strivingly is indestructible in the race. Moral creeds which speak to that impulse will be widely successful in spite of inconsistency, vagueness, and shadowy determination of expectancy. Man needs a rule for his will, and will invent one if one be not given him.

—WILLIAM JAMES

Man is a masterpiece of creation if for no other reason than that, all the weight of evidence for determinism notwithstanding, he believes he has free will.

—GEORG C. LICHTENBERG

We human beings do have some genuine freedom of choice and therefore some effective control over our own destinies. I am not a determinist. But I also believe that the decisive choice is seldom the latest choice in the series. More often than not, it will turn out to be some choice made relatively far back in the past.

—ARNOLD TOYNBEE

We are responsible human beings, not blind automatons; persons, not puppets. By endowing us with freedom, God relinquished a measure of his own sovereignty and imposed certain limitations upon himself. If his children are free, they must do his will by a voluntary choice.

—MARTIN LUTHER KING JR.

Life is a card game. You play the hand that is dealt to you.

—PROVERBIAL

We must believe in free will. We have no choice.

—ISAAC BASHEVIS SINGER

TOPICS FOR CRITICAL THINKING AND WRITING

1. If any one of these passages especially appeals to you, make it the thesis of an essay of about 500 words.

2. Take two of these passages—perhaps one that you especially like and one that you think is wrong-headed—and write a dialogue of about 500 words in which the two authors converse. They may each try to convince the other, or they may find that to some degree they share views and they may then work out a statement that both can accept. If you do take the position that one writer is on the correct track but the other is utterly mistaken, try to be fair to the view that you think is mistaken. (As an experiment in critical thinking, imagine that you accept it, and make the best case for it that you possibly can.)

Plato

Plato (427–347 B.C.), an Athenian aristocrat by birth, was the student of one great philosopher (Socrates) and the teacher of another (Aristotle). His legacy of more than two dozen dialogues—imaginary discussions between Socrates and one or more other speakers, usually young Athenians—has been of such influence that the whole of Western philosophy can be characterized, A. N. Whitehead wrote, as "a series of footnotes to Plato." Plato's interests encompassed the full range of topics in philosophy: ethics, politics, logic, metaphysics, epistemology, aesthetics, psychology, and education.

The selection reprinted here, Crito, is the third of four dialogues telling the story of the final days of Socrates (469–399 B.C.). The first in the sequence, Euthyphro, portrays Socrates in his typical role, questioning someone about his beliefs (in this case, the young aristocrat, Euthyphro). The discussion is focused on the nature of piety, but the conversation breaks off before a final answer is reached—perhaps none is possible—because Socrates is on his way to stand trial before the Athenian assembly. He has been charged with "preaching false gods" (heresy) and "corrupting the youth" by causing them to doubt or disregard the wisdom of their elders. (How faithful to any actual event or discussion Euthyphro and Plato's other Socratic dialogues really are, scholars cannot say with assurance.)

In Apology, the second dialogue in the sequence, Plato (who remains entirely in the background, as he does in all the dialogues) recounts Socrates' public reply to the charges against him. During the speech, Socrates explains his life, reminding his fellow citizens that if he is (as the oracle had pronounced) "the wisest of men," then it is only because he knows that he doesn't know what others believe or pretend they do know. The dialogue ends with Socrates being found guilty and duly sentenced to death.

The third in the series is Crito, *but we will postpone comment on it for a moment and glance at the fourth dialogue,* Phaedo, *in which Plato portrays Socrates' final philosophical discussion. The topic, appropriately, is whether the soul is immortal. It ends with Socrates, in the company of his closest friends, bidding them a last farewell and drinking the fatal cup of hemlock.*

Crito, *the whole text of which is reprinted here, is the debate provoked by Crito, an old friend and admirer of Socrates. He visits Socrates in prison and urges him to escape while he still has the chance. After all, Crito argues, the guilty verdict was wrong and unfair, few Athenians really want to have Socrates put to death, his family and friends will be distraught, and so forth. Socrates will not have it. He patiently but firmly examines each of Crito's arguments and explains why it would be wrong to follow his advice.*

Plato's Crito *thus ranks with Sophocles' tragedy* Antigone *as one of the first explorations in Western literature of the perennial theme of our responsibility for obeying laws that challenge our conscientious moral convictions. Antigone concludes that she must disobey the law of Creon, tyrant of Thebes; Socrates concludes that he must obey the law of democratic Athens. In* Crito, *we have not only a superb illustration of Socratic dialogue and argument but also a portrait of a virtuous thinker at the end of a long life, reflecting on its course and on the moral principles that have guided him. We see Socrates living an "examined life," the only life he thought was worth living.*

This translation is by Hugh Tredennick.

Crito

(**SCENE:** *A room in the State prison at Athens in the year 399 B.C. The time is half an hour before dawn, and the room would be almost dark but for the light of a little oil lamp. There is a pallet bed against the back wall. At the head of it a small table supports the lamp; near the foot of it Crito is sitting patiently on a stool. He is an old man, kindly, practical, simple-minded; at present he is suffering from acute emotional strain. On the bed lies Socrates asleep. He stirs, yawns, opens his eyes, and sees Crito.*)

SOCRATES: Here already, Crito? Surely it is still early?

CRITO: Indeed it is.

SOCRATES: About what time?

CRITO: Just before dawn.

SOCRATES: I wonder that the warder paid any attention to you.   5

CRITO: He is used to me now, Socrates, because I come here so often; besides, he is under some small obligation to me.

SOCRATES: Have you only just come, or have you been here for long?

CRITO: Fairly long.

SOCRATES: Then why didn't you wake me at once, instead of sitting by my bed so quietly?

CRITO: I wouldn't dream of such a thing, Socrates. I only wish I were not 10
so sleepless and depressed myself. I have been wondering at you,
because I saw how comfortably you were sleeping; and I deliberately
didn't wake you because I wanted you to go on being as comfortable
as you could. I have often felt before in the course of my life how
fortunate you are in your disposition, but I feel it more than ever
now in your present misfortune when I see how easily and placidly
you put up with it.

SOCRATES: Well, really, Crito, it would be hardly suitable for a man of my
age to resent having to die.

CRITO: Other people just as old as you are get involved in these misfortunes, Socrates, but their age doesn't keep them from resenting it
when they find themselves in your position.

SOCRATES: Quite true. But tell me, why have you come so early?

CRITO: Because I bring bad news, Socrates; not so bad from your point
of view, I suppose, but it will be very hard to bear for me and your
other friends, and I think that I shall find it hardest of all.

SOCRATES: Why, what is this news? Has the boat come in from Delos—the 15
boat which ends my reprieve when it arrives?[1]

CRITO: It hasn't actually come in yet, but I expect that it will be here
today, judging from the report of some people who have just arrived
from Sunium and left it there. It's quite clear from their account that
it will be here today; and so by tomorrow, Socrates, you will have
to—to end your life.

SOCRATES: Well, Crito, I hope that it may be for the best; if the gods will it
so, so be it. All the same, I don't think it will arrive today.

CRITO: What makes you think that?

SOCRATES: I will try to explain. I think I am right in saying that I have to
die on the day after the boat arrives?

CRITO: That's what the authorities say, at any rate.   20

SOCRATES: Then I don't think it will arrive on this day that is just beginning, but on the day after. I am going by a dream that I had in the
night, only a little while ago. It looks as though you were right not
to wake me up.

CRITO: Why, what was the dream about?

SOCRATES: I thought I saw a gloriously beautiful woman dressed in white
robes, who came up to me and addressed me in these words: "Socrates,
to the pleasant land of Phthia on the third day thou shalt come."

CRITO: Your dream makes no sense, Socrates.

SOCRATES: To my mind, Crito, it is perfectly clear.   25

---

[1]**Delos . . . arrives** Ordinarily execution was carried out immediately after sentencing, but
the day before Socrates' trial was the first day of an annual ceremony that involved sending a ship to Delos. When the ship was absent—in this case for about a month—executions could not be performed. As Crito goes on to say, Socrates could easily escape, and
indeed he could have left the country before being tried. [All notes are the editors'.]

CRITO: Too clear, apparently. But look here, Socrates, it is still not too late to take my advice and escape. Your death means a double calamity for me. I shall not only lose a friend whom I can never possibly replace, but besides a great many people who don't know you and me very well will be sure to think that I let you down, because I could have saved you if I had been willing to spend the money; and what could be more contemptible than to get a name for thinking more of money than of your friends? Most people will never believe that it was you who refused to leave this place although we tried our hardest to persuade you.

SOCRATES: But my dear Crito, why should we pay so much attention to what "most people" think? The really reasonable people, who have more claim to be considered, will believe that the facts are exactly as they are.

CRITO: You can see for yourself, Socrates, that one has to think of popular opinion as well. Your present position is quite enough to show that the capacity of ordinary people for causing trouble is not confined to petty annoyances, but has hardly any limits if you once get a bad name with them.

SOCRATES: I only wish that ordinary people *had* unlimited capacity for doing harm; then they might have an unlimited power for doing good; which would be a splendid thing, if it were so. Actually they have neither. They cannot make a man wise or stupid; they simply act at random.

CRITO: Have it that way if you like; but tell me this, Socrates. I hope that 30 you aren't worrying about the possible effects on me and the rest of your friends, and thinking that if you escape we shall have trouble with informers for having helped you to get away, and have to forfeit all our property or pay an enormous fine, or even incur some further punishment? If any idea like that is troubling you, you can dismiss it altogether. We are quite entitled to run that risk in saving you, and even worse, if necessary. Take my advice, and be reasonable.

SOCRATES: All that you say is very much in my mind, Crito, and a great deal more besides.

CRITO: Very well, then, don't let it distress you. I know some people who are willing to rescue you from here and get you out of the country for quite a moderate sum. And then surely you realize how cheap these informers are to buy off; we shan't need much money to settle them; and I think you've got enough of my money for yourself already. And then even supposing that in your anxiety for my safety you feel that you oughtn't to spend my money, there are these foreign gentlemen staying in Athens who are quite willing to spend theirs. One of them, Simmias of Thebes, has actually brought the money with him for this very purpose; and Cebes and a number of others are quite ready to do the same. So as I say, you mustn't let any fears on these grounds make you slacken your efforts to escape;

and you mustn't feel any misgivings about what you said at your trial, that you wouldn't know what to do with yourself if you left this country. Wherever you go, there are plenty of places where you will find a welcome; and if you choose to go to Thessaly, I have friends there who will make much of you and give you complete protection, so that no one in Thessaly can interfere with you.

Besides, Socrates, I don't even feel that it is right for you to try to do what you are doing, throwing away your life when you might save it. You are doing your best to treat yourself in exactly the same way as your enemies would, or rather did, when they wanted to ruin you. What is more, it seems to me that you are letting your sons down too. You have it in your power to finish their bringing up and education, and instead of that you are proposing to go off and desert them, and so far as you are concerned they will have to take their chance. And what sort of chance are they likely to get? The sort of thing that usually happens to orphans when they lose their parents. Either one ought not to have children at all, or one ought to see their upbringing and education through to the end. It strikes me that you are taking the line of least resistance, whereas you ought to make the choice of a good man and a brave one, considering that you profess to have made goodness your object all through life. Really, I am ashamed, both on your account and on ours your friends'; it will look as though we had played something like a coward's part all through this affair of yours. First, there was the way you came into court when it was quite unnecessary—that was the first act; then there was the conduct of the defense—that was the second; and finally, to complete the farce, we get this situation, which makes it appear that we have let you slip out of our hands through some lack of courage and enterprise on our part, because we didn't save you, and you didn't save yourself, when it would have been quite possible and practicable, if we had been any use at all.

There, Socrates; if you aren't careful, besides the suffering there will be all this disgrace for you and us to bear. Come, make up your mind. Really it's too late for that now; you ought to have it made up already. There is no alternative; the whole thing must be carried through during this coming night. If we lose any more time, it can't be done, it will be too late. I appeal to you, Socrates, on every ground; take my advice and please don't be unreasonable!

SOCRATES: My dear Crito, I appreciate your warm feelings very much— 35 that is, assuming that they have some justification; if not, the stronger they are, the harder they will be to deal with. Very well, then; we must consider whether we ought to follow your advice or not. You know that this is not a new idea of mine; it has always been my nature never to accept advice from any of my friends unless reflection shows that it is the best course that reason offers. I cannot abandon the principles which I used to hold in the past simply because this accident has happened to me; they seem to me to be much as they were, and I respect and regard the same principles now as before. So unless we can find better principles on this occasion, you can be quite sure that I shall not agree with you; not even if the power of the people conjures up fresh hordes of bogies to terrify our childish minds, by subjecting us to chains and executions and confiscations of our property.

Well, then, how can we consider the question most reasonably? Suppose that we begin by reverting to this view which you hold about people's opinions. Was it always right to argue that some opinions should be taken seriously but not others? Or was it always wrong? Perhaps it was right before the question of my death arose, but now we can see clearly that it was a mistaken persistence in a point of view which was really irresponsible nonsense. I should like very much to inquire into this problem, Crito, with your help, and to see whether the argument will appear in any different light to me now that I am in this position, or whether it will remain the same; and whether we shall dismiss it or accept it.

Serious thinkers, I believe, have always held some such view as the one which I mentioned just now: that some of the opinions which people entertain should be respected, and others should not. Now I ask you, Crito, don't you think that this is a sound principle?—You are safe from the prospect of dying tomorrow, in all human probability; and you are not likely to have your judgment upset by this impending calamity. Consider, then; don't you think that this is a sound enough principle, that one should not regard all the opinions that people hold, but only some and not others? What do you say? Isn't that a fair statement?

CRITO: Yes, it is.

SOCRATES: In other words, one should regard the good ones and not the bad?

CRITO: Yes.   40

SOCRATES: The opinions of the wise being good, and the opinions of the foolish bad?

CRITO: Naturally.

SOCRATES: To pass on, then: What do you think of the sort of illustration that I used to employ? When a man is in training, and taking it seriously, does he pay attention to all praise and criticism and opinion indiscriminately, or only when it comes from the one qualified person, the actual doctor or trainer?

CRITO: Only when it comes from the one qualified person.

SOCRATES: Then he should be afraid of the criticism and welcome the praise   45 of the one qualified person, but not those of the general public.

CRITO: Obviously.

SOCRATES: So he ought to regulate his actions and exercises and eating and drinking by the judgment of his instructor, who has expert knowledge, rather than by the opinions of the rest of the public.

CRITO: Yes, that is so.

SOCRATES: Very well. Now if he disobeys the one man and disregards his opinion and commendations, and pays attention to the advice of the many who have no expert knowledge, surely he will suffer some bad effect?

CRITO: Certainly. 50

SOCRATES: And what is this bad effect? Where is it produced?—I mean, in what part of the disobedient person?

CRITO: His body, obviously; that is what suffers.

SOCRATES: Very good. Well now, tell me, Crito—we don't want to go through all the examples one by one—does this apply as a general rule, and above all to the sort of actions which we are trying to decide about: just and unjust, honorable and dishonorable, good and bad? Ought we to be guided and intimidated by the opinion of the many or by that of the one—assuming that there is someone with expert knowledge? Is it true that we ought to respect and fear this person more than all the rest put together; and that if we do not follow his guidance we shall spoil and mutilate that part of us which, as we used to say, is improved by right conduct and destroyed by wrong? Or is this all nonsense?

CRITO: No, I think it is true, Socrates.

SOCRATES: Then consider the next step. There is a part of us which is 55 improved by healthy actions and ruined by unhealthy ones. If we spoil it by taking the advice of nonexperts, will life be worth living when this part is once ruined? The part I mean is the body; do you accept this?

CRITO: Yes.

SOCRATES: Well, is life worth living with a body which is worn out and ruined by health?

CRITO: Certainly not.

SOCRATES: What about the part of us which is mutilated by wrong actions and benefited by right ones? Is life worth living with this part ruined? Or do we believe that this part of us, whatever it may be, in which right and wrong operate, is of less importance than the body?

CRITO: Certainly not. 60

SOCRATES: It is really more precious?

CRITO: Much more.

SOCRATES: In that case, my dear fellow, what we ought to consider is not so much what people in general will say about us but how we stand with the expert in right and wrong, the one authority, who represents the actual truth. So in the first place your proposition is not correct when you say that we should consider popular opinion in questions of what is right and honorable and good, or the opposite. Of course one might object "All the same, the people have the power to put us to death."

CRITO: No doubt about that! Quite true, Socrates; it is a possible objection.

SOCRATES: But so far as I can see, my dear fellow, the argument which we   65
have just been through is quite unaffected by it. At the same time
I should like you to consider whether we are still satisfied on this
point: that the really important thing is not to live, but to live well.

CRITO: Why, yes.

SOCRATES: And that to live well means the same thing as to live honorably
or rightly?

CRITO: Yes.

SOCRATES: Then in the light of this agreement we must consider whether
or not it is right for me to try to get away without an official discharge. If it turns out to be right, we must make the attempt; if not,
we must let it drop. As for the considerations you raise about expense and reputation and bringing up children, I am afraid, Crito,
that they represent the reflections of the ordinary public, who put
people to death, and would bring them back to life if they could,
with equal indifference to reason. Our real duty, I fancy, since the
argument leads that way, is to consider one question only, the one
which we raised just now: Shall we be acting rightly in paying
money and showing gratitude to these people who are going to rescue
me, and in escaping or arranging the escape ourselves, or shall we really be acting wrongly in doing all this? If it becomes clear that such
conduct is wrong, I cannot help thinking that the question whether
we are sure to die, or to suffer any other ill effect for that matter, if we
stand our ground and take no action, ought not to weigh with us at all
in comparison with the risk of doing what is wrong.

CRITO: I agree with what you say, Socrates; but I wish you would consider   70
what we ought to *do*.

SOCRATES: Let us look at it together, my dear fellow; and if you can challenge any of my arguments, do so and I will listen to you; but if you
can't, be a good fellow and stop telling me over and over again that I
ought to leave this place without official permission. I am very anxious to obtain your approval before I adopt the course which I have
in mind; I don't want to act against your convictions. Now give your
attention to the starting point of this inquiry—I hope that you will
be satisfied with my way of stating it—and try to answer my questions to the best of your judgment.

CRITO: Well, I will try.

SOCRATES: Do we say that one must never willingly do wrong, or does it
depend upon circumstance? Is it true, as we have often agreed before, that there is no sense in which wrongdoing is good or honorable? Or have we jettisoned all our former convictions in these last
few days? Can you and I at our age, Crito, have spent all these years
in serious discussions without realizing that we were no better than
a pair of children? Surely the truth is just what we have always said.
Whatever the popular view is, and whether the alternative is pleas-
anter than the present one or even harder to bear, the fact remains

that to do wrong is in every sense bad and dishonorable for the person who does it. Is that our view, or not?

CRITO: Yes, it is.

SOCRATES: Then in no circumstances must one do wrong.   75

CRITO: No.

SOCRATES: In that case one must not even do wrong when one is wronged, which most people regard as the natural course.

CRITO: Apparently not.

SOCRATES: Tell me another thing, Crito: Ought one to do injuries or not?

CRITO: Surely not, Socrates.   80

SOCRATES: And tell me: Is it right to do an injury in retaliation, as most people believe, or not?

CRITO: No, never.

SOCRATES: Because, I suppose, there is no difference between injuring people and wronging them.

CRITO: Exactly.

SOCRATES: So one ought not to return a wrong or an injury to any per-   85
son, whatever the provocation is. Now be careful, Crito, that in making these single admissions you do not end by admitting something contrary to your real beliefs. I know that there are and always will be few people who think like this; and consequently between those who do think so and those who do not there can be no agreement on principle; they must always feel contempt when they observe one another's decisions. I want even you to consider very carefully whether you share my views and agree with me, and whether we can proceed with our discussion from the established hypothesis that it is never right to do a wrong or return a wrong or defend one's self against injury by retaliation; or whether you dissociate yourself from any share in this view as a basis for discussion. I have held it for a long time, and still hold it; but if you have formed any other opinion, say so and tell me what it is. If, on the other hand, you stand by what we have said, listen to my next point.

CRITO: Yes, I stand by it and agree with you. Go on.

SOCRATES: Well, here is my next point, or rather question. Ought one to fulfill all one's agreements, provided that they are right, or break them?

CRITO: One ought to fulfill them.

SOCRATES: Then consider the logical consequence. If we leave this place without first persuading the State to let us go, are we or are we not doing an injury, and doing it in a quarter where it is least justifiable? Are we or are we not abiding by our just agreements?

CRITO: I can't answer your question, Socrates; I am not clear in my mind.   90

SOCRATES: Look at it in this way. Suppose that while we were preparing to run away from here (or however one should describe it) the Laws and Constitution of Athens were to come and confront us and ask this question: "Now, Socrates, what are you proposing to do?

Can you deny that by this act which you are contemplating you intend, so far as you have the power, to destroy us, the Laws, and the whole State as well? Do you imagine that a city can continue to exist and not be turned upside down, if the legal judgments which are pronounced in it have no force but are nullified and destroyed by private persons?"—how shall we answer this question, Crito, and others of the same kind? There is much that could be said, especially by a professional advocate, to protest against the invalidation of this law which enacts that judgments once pronounced shall be binding. Shall we say "Yes, I do intend to destroy the laws, because the State wronged me by passing a faulty judgment at my trial"? Is this to be our answer, or what?

CRITO: What you have just said, by all means, Socrates.

SOCRATES: Then what supposing the Laws say, "Was there provision for this in the agreement between you and us, Socrates? Or did you undertake to abide by whatever judgments the State pronounced?" If we expressed surprise at such language, they would probably say: "Never mind our language, Socrates, but answer our questions; after all, you are accustomed to the method of question and answer. Come now, what charge do you bring against us and the State, that you are trying to destroy us? Did we not give you life in the first place? Was it not through us that your father married your mother and begot you? Tell us, have you any complaint against those of us Laws that deal with marriage?" "No, none," I should say. "Well, have you any against the laws which deal with children's upbringing and education, such as you had yourself? Are you not grateful to those of us Laws which were instituted for this end, for requiring your father to give you a cultural and physical education?" "Yes," I should say. "Very good. Then since you have been born and brought up and educated, can you deny, in the first place, that you were our child and servant, both you and your ancestors? And if this is so, do you imagine that what is right for us is equally right for you, and that whatever we try to do to you, you are justified in retaliating? You did not have equality of rights with your father, or your employer (supposing that you had had one), to enable you to retaliate; you were not allowed to answer back when you were scolded or to hit back when you were beaten, or to do a great many other things of the same kind. Do you expect to have such license against your country and its laws that if we try to put you to death in the belief that it is right to do so, you on your part will try your hardest to destroy your country and us its Laws in return? And will you, the true devotee of goodness, claim that you are justified in doing so? Are you so wise as to have forgotten that compared with your mother and father and all the rest of your ancestors your country is something far more precious, more venerable, more sacred, and held in greater honor both among gods and among all reasonable men? Do you not realize that you are even more bound to respect and placate the anger of your country than your father's anger? That if you cannot persuade your country you must do whatever it orders, and patiently submit to any punishment that it imposes, whether it be flogging or imprisonment? And if it leads you out to war, to be wounded or killed, you must comply, and it is right that you should do so; you must not give way or retreat or abandon your position. Both in war and in the law courts and everywhere else you must do whatever your city and your country commands, or else persuade it in accordance with universal justice; but violence is a sin even against your parents, and it is a far greater sin against your country" — What shall we say to this, Crito? — that what the Laws say is true, or not?

CRITO: Yes, I think so.

SOCRATES: "Consider, then, Socrates," the Laws would probably continue, 95 "whether it is also true for us to say that what you are now trying to do to us is not right. Although we have brought you into the world and reared you and educated you, and given you and all your fellow citizens a share in all the good things at our disposal, nevertheless by the very fact of granting our permission we openly proclaim this principle: that any Athenian, on attaining to manhood and seeing for himself the political organization of the State and us its Laws, is permitted, if he is not satisfied with us, to take his property and go away wherever he likes. If any of you chooses to go to one of our colonies, supposing that he should not be satisfied with us and the State, or to emigrate to any other country, not one of us Laws hinders or prevents him from going away wherever he likes, without any loss of property. On the other hand, if any one of you stands his ground when he can see how we administer justice and the rest of our public organization, we hold that by so doing he has in fact undertaken to do anything that we tell him; and we maintain that anyone who disobeys is guilty of doing wrong on three separate counts: first because we are his parents, and secondly because we are his guardians; and thirdly because, after promising obedience, he is neither obeying us nor persuading us to change our decision if we are at fault in any way; and although all our orders are in the form of proposals, not of savage commands, and we give him the choice of either persuading us or doing what we say, he is actually doing neither. These are the charges, Socrates, to which we say that you will be liable if you do what you are contemplating; and you will not be the least culpable of your fellow countrymen, but one of the most guilty." If I said "Why do you say that?" they would no doubt pounce on me with perfect justice and point out that there are very few people in Athens who have entered into this agreement with them as explicitly as I have. They would say "Socrates, we have substantial evidence that you are satisfied with us and with the State. You would not have been so exceptionally reluctant to cross the borders of your country if you had not been exceptionally attached to it. You have never left the city to attend a festival or for any other purpose, except on some military expedition; you have never traveled abroad as other people do, and you have never felt the impulse to acquaint yourself with another country or constitution; you have been content with us and with our city. You have definitely chosen us, and undertaken to observe us in all your activities as a citizen; and as the crowning proof that you are satisfied with our city, you have begotten children in it. Furthermore, even at the time of your trial you could have proposed the penalty of banishment, if you had chosen to do so; that is, you could have done then with the sanction of the State what you are now trying to do without it. But whereas at that time you made a noble show of indifference if you had to die, and in fact preferred death, as you said, to banishment, now you show no respect for your earlier professions, and no regard for us, the Laws, whom you are trying to destroy; you are behaving like the lowest type of menial, trying to run away in spite of the contracts and undertakings by which you agreed to live as a member of our State. Now first answer this question: Are we or are we not speaking the truth when we say that you have undertaken, in deed if not in word, to live your life as a citizen in obedience to us?" What are we to say to that, Crito? Are we not bound to admit it?

CRITO: We cannot help it, Socrates.

SOCRATES: "It is a fact, then," they would say, "that you are breaking covenants and undertakings made with us, although you made them under no compulsion or misunderstanding, and were not compelled to decide in a limited time; you had seventy years in which you could have left the country, if you were not satisfied with us or felt that the agreements were unfair. You did not choose Sparta or Crete—your favorite models of good government—or any other Greek or foreign state; you could not have absented yourself from the city less if you had been lame or blind or decrepit in some other way. It is quite obvious that you stand by yourself above all other Athenians in your affection for this city and for us its Laws;—who would care for a city without laws? And now, after all this, are you not going to stand by your agreement? Yes, you are, Socrates, if you will take our advice; and then you will at least escape being laughed at for leaving the city.

"We invite you to consider what good you will do to yourself or your friends if you commit this breach of faith and stain your conscience. It is fairly obvious that the risk of being banished and either losing their citizenship or having their property confiscated will extend to your friends as well. As for yourself, if you go to one of the neighboring states, such as Thebes or Megara, which are both well governed, you will enter them as an enemy to their constitution[2] and all good patriots will eye you with suspicion as a destroyer of law and order. Incidentally you will confirm the opinion of the jurors who tried you that they gave a correct verdict; a destroyer of laws might very well be supposed to have a destructive influence upon young and foolish human beings. Do you intend, then, to avoid well governed states and the higher forms of human society? And if you do, will life be worth living? Or will you approach these people and have the impudence to converse with them? What arguments will you use, Socrates? The same which you used here, that goodness and integrity, institutions and laws, are the most precious possessions of mankind? Do you not think that Socrates and everything about him will appear in a disreputable light? You certainly ought to think so. But perhaps you will retire from this part of the world and go to Crito's friends in Thessaly? That is the home of indiscipline and laxity, and no doubt they would enjoy hearing the amusing story of how you managed to run away from prison by arraying yourself in some costume or putting on a shepherd's smock or some other conventional runaway's disguise, and altering your personal appearance. And will no one comment on the fact that an old man of your age, probably with only a short time left to live, should dare to cling so greedily to life, at the price of violating the most stringent laws? Perhaps not, if you avoid irritating anyone. Otherwise, Socrates, you will hear a good many humiliating comments. So you will live as the toady and slave of all the populace, literally 'roistering in Thessaly,' as though you had left this country for Thessaly to attend a banquet there; and where will your discussions about goodness and uprightness be then, we should like to know? But of course you want to live for your children's sake, so that you may be able to bring them up and educate them. Indeed! by first taking them off to Thessaly and making foreigners of them, so that they may have that additional enjoyment? Or if that is not your intention, supposing that they are brought up here with you still alive, will they be better cared for and educated without you, because of course your friends will look after them? Will they look after your children if you go away to Thessaly, and not if you go away to the next world? Surely if those who profess to be your friends are worth anything, you must believe that they would care for them.

"No, Socrates; be advised by us your guardians, and do not think more of your children or of your life or of anything else than you think of what is right; so that when you enter the next world you may have all this to plead in your defense before the authorities there. It seems clear that if you do this thing, neither you nor any of your friends will be the better for it or be more upright or

---

[2] **as an enemy to their constitution** As a lawbreaker.

have a cleaner conscience here in this world, nor will it be better for you when you reach the next. As it is, you will leave this place, when you do, as the victim of a wrong done not by us, the Laws, but by your fellow men. But if you leave in that dishonorable way, returning wrong for wrong and evil for evil, breaking your agreements and covenants with us, and injuring those whom you least ought to injure—yourself, your friends, your country, and us—then you will have to face our anger in your lifetime, and in that place beyond when the laws of the other world know that you have tried, so far as you could, to destroy even us their brothers, they will not receive you with a kindly welcome. Do not take Crito's advice, but follow ours."

That, my dear friend Crito, I do assure you, is what I seem to 100 hear them saying, just as a mystic seems to hear the strains of music; and the sound of their arguments rings so loudly in my head that I cannot hear the other side. I warn you that, as my opinion stands at present, it will be useless to urge a different view. However, if you think that you will do any good by it, say what you like.

CRITO: No, Socrates, I have nothing to say.

SOCRATES: Then give it up, Crito, and let us follow this course, since God points out the way.

TOPICS FOR CRITICAL THINKING AND WRITING

1. State as precisely as you can all the arguments Crito uses to try to convince Socrates that he ought to escape. Which of these arguments seems to you to be the best? The worst? Why?

2. Socrates says to Crito, "I cannot abandon the principles which I used to hold in the past simply because this accident [the misfortune of being convicted by the Athenian assembly and then sentenced to death] has happened to me" (para. 35). Does this remark strike you as self-righteous? Stubborn? Smug? Stupid? Explain.

3. Socrates declares that "serious thinkers" have always held the view that "some of the opinions which people entertain should be respected, and others should not" (para. 37). There are two main alternatives to this principle: (a) One should respect *all* the opinions that others hold, and (b) one should respect *none* of the opinions of others. Socrates attacks (a) but he ignores (b). What are his objections to (a)? Do you find them convincing? Can you think of any convincing arguments against (b)?

4. As Socrates shows in his reply to Crito, he seems ready to believe (para. 63) that there are "expert[s] in right and wrong"—that is, persons with expert opinion or even authoritative knowledge on matters of right and wrong conduct—and that their advice should be sought and followed. Do you agree? Consider the thesis that there are no such experts, and write a 500-word essay defending or attacking it.

5. Socrates, as he comments to Crito, believes that "it is never right to do a wrong or return a wrong or defend one's self against injury by retaliation" (para. 85). He does not offer any argument for this thesis in the dialogue (although he does elsewhere). It was a very strange doctrine in his day, and even now it is not generally accepted. Write a 1,000-word essay defending or attacking this thesis.

6. Socrates seems to argue that (a) no one ought to do wrong, (b) it would injure the state for someone in Socrates' position to escape, and (c) this act would break a "just agreement" between the citizen and his state; therefore, (d) no one in Socrates' position should escape. Do you think this argument is valid? If not, what further assumptions would be needed to make it valid? Do you think the argument is sound (that is, both valid and true in all its premises)? If not, explain. If you had to attack premise (b) or (c), which do you think is the more vulnerable, and why?

7. In the imaginary speech by the Laws of Athens to Socrates, especially in paragraph 93, the Laws convey a picture of the supremacy of the state over the individual—and Socrates seems to assent to this picture. Do you? Why, or why not?

8. The Laws (para. 95) claim that if Socrates were to escape, he would be "guilty of doing wrong on three separate counts." What are they? Do you agree with all or any? Why, or why not? Read the essay by Martin Luther King Jr., "Letter from Birmingham Jail" (p. 738), and decide how King would have responded to the judgment of the Laws of Athens.

9. At the end of their peroration (para. 99), the Laws of Athens say to Socrates: Take your punishment as prescribed, and at your death "you will leave this place . . . as the victim of a wrong done not by us, the Laws, but by your fellow men." To what wrong do the Laws allude? Do you agree that it is men and not laws who perpetrated this wrong? If you were in Socrates' position, would it matter to you if you were being wronged not by laws but only by men? Explain.

10. Compose a letter from Socrates to Martin Luther King Jr. in which Socrates responds to King's "Letter from Birmingham Jail" (p. 738).

George Orwell

George Orwell was the pen name adopted by Eric Blair (1903–1950), an Englishman born in India. Orwell was educated at Eton, in England, but in 1921 he went back to the East and served for five years as a police officer in Burma (now Myanmar). Disillusioned with colonial imperialism, he returned to Europe, doing odd jobs while writing novels and stories. In 1936 he fought in the Spanish Civil War on the side of the Republicans, an experience he reported in Homage to Catalonia *(1938). His last years were spent writing in England. His best-known work probably is the satiric allegory* 1984 *(1949), showing a totalitarian state in which the citizens are perpetually under the eye of Big Brother. The following essay is from* Shooting an Elephant and Other Essays *(1950).*

Shooting an Elephant

In Moulmein, in Lower Burma, I was hated by large numbers of people—the only time in my life that I have been important enough for this to happen to me. I was sub-divisional police officer of the town, and in an aimless, petty kind of way anti-European feeling was very bitter. No one had the guts to raise a riot, but if a European woman went through the bazaars alone somebody would probably spit betel juice over her dress. As a police officer I was an obvious target and was baited whenever it seemed safe to do so. When a nimble Burman tripped me up on the football field and the referee (another Burman) looked the other way, the crowd yelled with hideous laughter. This happened more than once. In the end the sneering yellow faces of young men that met me everywhere, the insults hooted after me when I was at a safe distance, got badly on my nerves. The young Buddhist priests were the worst of all. There were several thousands of them in the town and none of them seemed to have anything to do except stand on street corners and jeer at Europeans.

All this was perplexing and upsetting. For at that time I had already made up my mind that imperialism was an evil thing and the sooner I chucked up my job and got out of it the better. Theoretically—and secretly, of course—I was all for the Burmese and all against their oppressors, the British. As for the job I was doing, I hated it more bitterly than I can perhaps make clear. In a job like that you see the dirty work of Empire at close quarters. The wretched prisoners huddling in the stinking cages of the lock-ups, the grey, cowed faces of the long-term convicts, the scarred buttocks of the men who had been flogged with bamboos—all these oppressed me with an intolerable sense of guilt. But I could get nothing into perspective. I was young and ill-educated and I had had to think out my problems in the utter silence that is imposed on every Englishman in the East. I did not even know that the British Empire is dying, still less did I know that it is a great deal better than the younger empires that are going to supplant it. All I knew was that I was stuck between my hatred of the empire I served and my rage against the evil-spirited little beasts who tried to make my job impossible. With one part of my mind I thought of the British Raj[1] as an unbreakable tyranny, as something clamped down, *in saecula saeculorum,*[2] upon the will of prostrate peoples; with another part I thought that the greatest joy in the world would be to drive a bayonet into a Buddhist priest's guts. Feelings like these are the normal by-products of imperialism; ask any Anglo-Indian official, if you can catch him off duty.

One day something happened which in a roundabout way was enlightening. It was a tiny incident in itself, but it gave me a better

---

[1]**British Raj** British imperial government in India and Burma. [All notes are the editors'.]
[2]*in saecula saeculorum* Forever (Latin). A term used in Christian liturgy.

glimpse than I had had before of the real nature of imperialism—the real motives for which despotic governments act. Early one morning the sub-inspector at a police station the other end of the town rang me up on the 'phone and said that an elephant was ravaging the bazaar. Would I please come and do something about it? I did not know what I could do, but I wanted to see what was happening and I got on to a pony and started out. I took my rifle, an old .44 Winchester and much too small to kill an elephant, but I thought the noise might be useful *in terrorem*.[3] Various Burmans stopped me on the way and told me about the elephant's doings. It was not, of course, a wild elephant, but a tame one which had gone "must."[4] It had been chained up, as tame elephants always are when their attack of "must" is due, but on the previous night it had broken its chain and escaped. Its mahout, the only person who could manage it when it was in that state, had set out in pursuit, but had taken the wrong direction and was now twelve hours' journey away, and in the morning the elephant had suddenly reappeared in the town. The Burmese population had no weapons and were quite helpless against it. It had already destroyed somebody's bamboo hut, killed a cow and raided some fruit-stalls and devoured the stock; also it had met the municipal rubbish van and, when the driver jumped out and took to his heels, had turned the van over and inflicted violences upon it.

The Burmese sub-inspector and some Indian constables were waiting for me in the quarter where the elephant had been seen. It was a very poor quarter, a labyrinth of squalid bamboo huts, thatched with palm-leaf, winding all over a steep hillside. I remember that it was a cloudy, stuffy morning at the beginning of the rains. We began questioning the people as to where the elephant had gone and, as usual, failed to get any definite information. That is invariably the case in the East; a story always sounds clear enough at a distance, but the nearer you get to the scene of events the vaguer it becomes. Some of the people said that the elephant had gone in one direction, some said that he had gone in another, some professed not even to have heard of any elephant. I had almost made up my mind that the whole story was a pack of lies, when we heard yells a little distance away. There was a loud, scandalized cry of "Go away, child! Go away this instant!" and an old woman with a switch in her hand came round the corner of a hut, violently shooing away a crowd of naked children. Some more women followed, clicking their tongues and exclaiming; evidently there was something that the children ought not to have seen. I rounded the hut and saw a man's dead body sprawling in the mud. He was an Indian, a black Dravidian coolie, almost naked, and he could not have been dead many minutes. The people said that the elephant had come suddenly upon him round the corner of the hut, caught him with its trunk, put its foot

[3]*in terrorem* As a warning.
[4]*"**must**" Into sexual heat.

on his back and ground him into the earth. This was the rainy season and the ground was soft, and his face had scored a trench a foot deep and a couple of yards long. He was lying on his belly with arms crucified and head sharply twisted to one side. His face was coated with mud, the eyes wide open, the teeth bared and grinning with an expression of unendurable agony. (Never tell me, by the way, that the dead look peaceful. Most of the corpses I have seen looked devilish.) The friction of the great beast's foot had stripped the skin from his back as neatly as one skins a rabbit. As soon as I saw the dead man I sent an orderly to a friend's house nearby to borrow an elephant rifle. I had already sent back the pony, not wanting it to go mad with fright and throw me if it smelt the elephant.

The orderly came back in a few minutes with a rifle and five cartridges, and meanwhile some Burmans had arrived and told us that the elephant was in the paddy fields below, only a few hundred yards away. As I started forward practically the whole population of the quarter flocked out of the houses and followed me. They had seen the rifle and were all shouting excitedly that I was going to shoot the elephant. They had not shown much interest in the elephant when he was merely ravaging their homes, but it was different now that he was going to be shot. It was a bit of fun to them, as it would be to an English crowd; besides they wanted the meat. It made me vaguely uneasy. I had no intention of shooting the elephant—I had merely sent for the rifle to defend myself if necessary—and it is always unnerving to have a crowd following you. I marched down the hill, looking and feeling a fool, with the rifle over my shoulder and an ever-growing army of people jostling at my heels. At the bottom, when you got away from the huts, there was a metalled road and beyond that a miry waste of paddy fields a thousand yards across, not yet ploughed but soggy from the first rains and dotted with coarse grass. The elephant was standing eight yards from the road, his left side towards us. He took not the slightest notice of the crowd's approach. He was tearing up bunches of grass, beating them against his knees to clean them and stuffing them into his mouth.

I had halted on the road. As soon as I saw the elephant I knew with perfect certainty that I ought not to shoot him. It is a serious matter to shoot a working elephant—it is comparable to destroying a huge and costly piece of machinery—and obviously one ought not to do it if it can possibly be avoided. And at that distance, peacefully eating, the elephant looked no more dangerous than a cow. I thought then and I think now that his attack of "must" was already passing off; in which case he would merely wander harmlessly about until the mahout came back and caught him. Moreover, I did not in the least want to shoot him. I decided that I would watch him for a little while to make sure that he did not turn savage again, and then go home.

But at that moment I glanced round at the crowd that had followed me. It was an immense crowd, two thousand at the least and growing every minute. It blocked the road for a long distance on either side. I looked at the sea of yellow faces above the garish clothes—faces all happy and excited over this bit of fun, all certain that the elephant was going to be shot. They were watching me as they would watch a conjurer about to perform a trick. They did not like me, but with the magical rifle in my hands I was momentarily worth watching. And suddenly I realized that I should have to shoot the elephant after all. The people expected it of me and I had got to do it; I could feel their two thousand wills pressing me forward, irresistibly. And it was at this moment, as I stood there with the rifle in my hands, that I first grasped the hollowness, the futility of the white man's dominion in the East. Here was I, the white man with his gun, standing in front of the unarmed native crowd—seemingly the leading actor of the piece; but in reality I was only an absurd puppet pushed to and fro by the will of those yellow faces behind. I perceived in this moment that when the white man turns tyrant it is his own freedom that he destroys. He becomes a sort of hollow, posing dummy, the conventionalized figure of a sahib. For it is the condition of his rule that he shall spend his life in trying to impress the "natives," and so in every crisis he has got to do what the "natives" expect of him. He wears a mask, and his face grows to fit it. I had got to shoot the elephant. I had committed myself to doing it when I sent for the rifle. A sahib has got to act like a sahib; he has got to appear resolute, to know his own mind and do definite things. To come all that way, rifle in hand, with two thousand people marching at my heels, and then to trail feebly away, having done nothing—no, that was impossible. The crowd would laugh at me. And my whole life, every white man's life in the East, was one long struggle not to be laughed at.

But I did not want to shoot the elephant. I watched him beating his bunch of grass against his knees, with that preoccupied grandmotherly air that elephants have. It seemed to me that it would be murder to shoot him. At that age I was not squeamish about killing animals, but I had never shot an elephant and never wanted to. (Somehow it always seems worse to kill a *large* animal.) Besides, there was the beast's owner to be considered. Alive, the elephant was worth at least a hundred pounds; dead, he would only be worth the value of his tusks, five pounds, possibly. But I had got to act quickly. I turned to some experienced-looking Burmans who had been there when we arrived, and asked them how the elephant had been behaving. They all said the same thing; he took no notice of you if you left him alone, but he might charge if you went too close to him.

It was perfectly clear to me what I ought to do. I ought to walk up to within, say, twenty-five yards of the elephant and test his behavior. If he charged, I could shoot; if he took no notice of me, it would be safe to leave him until the mahout came back. But also I knew that I was going to do no such thing. I was a poor shot with a rifle and the ground was soft mud into which one would sink at every step. If the elephant charged and I missed him, I should have about as much chance as a toad under a steam-roller. But even then I was not thinking particularly of my own skin, only of the watchful yellow faces behind. For at that moment, with the crowd watching me, I was not afraid in the ordinary sense, as I would have been if I had been alone. A white man mustn't be frightened in front of "natives"; and so, in general, he isn't frightened. The sole thought in my mind was that if anything went wrong those two thousand Burmans would see me pursued, caught, trampled on and reduced to a grinning corpse like that Indian up the hill. And if that happened it was quite probable that some of them would laugh. That would never do. There was only one alternative. I shoved the cartridges into the magazine and lay down on the road to get a better aim.

The crowd grew very still, and a deep, low, happy sigh, as of people who see the theatre curtain go up at last, breathed from innumerable throats. They were going to have their bit of fun after all. The rifle was a beautiful German thing with cross-hair sights. I did not then know that in shooting an elephant one would shoot to cut an imaginary bar running from ear-hole to ear-hole. I ought, therefore, as the elephant was sideways on, to have aimed straight at his ear-hole; actually I aimed several inches in front of this, thinking the brain would be further forward.

When I pulled the trigger I did not hear the bang or feel the kick—one never does when a shot goes home—but I heard the devilish roar of glee that went up from the crowd. In that instant, in too short a time, one would have thought, even for the bullet to get there, a mysterious, terrible change had come over the elephant. He neither stirred nor fell, but every line of his body had altered. He looked suddenly stricken, shrunken, immensely old, as though the frightful impact of the bullet had paralyzed him without knocking him down. At last, after what seemed a long time—it might have been five seconds, I dare say—he sagged flabbily to his knees. His mouth slobbered. An enormous senility seemed to have settled upon him. One could have imagined him thousands of years old. I fired again into the same spot. At the second shot he did not collapse but climbed with desperate slowness to his feet and stood weakly upright, with legs sagging and head dropping. I fired a third time. That was the shot that did for him. You could see the agony of it jolt his whole body and knock the last remnant of strength from his legs. But in falling he seemed for a moment to rise, for as his hind legs collapsed beneath him he seemed to tower upward like a huge rock toppling, his trunk reaching skywards like a tree. He trumpeted, for the first and only time. And then down he came, his belly towards me, with a crash that seemed to shake the ground even where I lay.

I got up. The Burmans were already racing past me across the mud. It was obvious that the elephant would never rise again, but he was not dead. He was breathing very rhythmically with long rattling gasps, his great mound of a side painfully rising and falling. His mouth was wide open—I could see far down into caverns of pale pink throat. I waited a long time for him to die, but his breathing did not weaken. Finally I fired my two remaining shots into the spot where I thought his heart must be. The thick blood welled out of him like red velvet, but still he did not die. His body did not even jerk when the shots hit him, the tortured breathing continued without a pause. He was dying, very slowly and in great agony, but in some world remote from me where not even a bullet could damage him further. I felt that I had got to put an end to that dreadful noise. It seemed dreadful to see the great beast lying there, powerless to move and yet powerless to die, and not even to be able to finish him. I sent back for my small rifle and poured shot after shot into his heart and down his throat. They seemed to make no impression. The tortured gasps continued as steadily as the ticking of a clock.

In the end I could not stand it any longer and went away. I heard later that it took him half an hour to die. Burmans were bringing dahs[5] and baskets even before I left, and I was told they had stripped his body almost to the bones by the afternoon.

Afterwards, of course, there were endless discussions about the shooting of the elephant. The owner was furious, but he was only an Indian and could do nothing. Besides, legally I had done the right thing, for a mad elephant has to be killed, like a mad dog, if its owner fails to control it. Among the Europeans opinion was divided. The older men said I was right, the younger men said it was a damn shame to shoot an elephant for killing a coolie, because an elephant was worth more than any damn Coringhee coolie. And afterwards I was very glad that the coolie had been killed; it put me legally in the right and it gave me a sufficient pretext for shooting the elephant. I often wondered whether any of the others grasped that I had done it solely to avoid looking a fool.

Topics for Critical Thinking and Writing

1. Did Orwell shoot the elephant of his own free will? Or did he shoot the elephant because he *had* to shoot it? What does he say about this? Do you find his judgment convincing or not? Write a 500-word essay explaining your answer.

2. Was Orwell justified in shooting the elephant? Did he do the right thing in killing it? In the aftermath, did he think he did the right thing? Do you? Write a 500-word essay explaining your answers.

3. Orwell says that "as soon as I saw the elephant I knew with perfect certainty that I ought not to shoot him" (para. 6). How could he claim to "know" this, when moments later he did shoot the elephant?

4. Orwell says in passing, "Somehow it always seems worse to kill a *large* animal" (para. 8). Explain why you think Orwell says this and whether you agree.

[5]**dahs** Large knives.

5. A biographer who did research on Orwell in Burma reported that he could find no supporting documentation, either in the local newspapers or in the files of the police, that this episode ever occurred. Suppose that Orwell made it up. If so, is your response different? Explain.

6. If, pressured by circumstances, you have ever acted against what you might think is your reason or your nature, report the experience, and give your present evaluation of your behavior.

Walter T. Stace

Walter T. Stace (1886–1967), a professor of philosophy at Princeton University for many years, was the author of several books, including Religion and the Modern Mind *(1952), from which this selection is taken. The title is the editors'.*

Is Determinism Inconsistent with Free Will?

The second great problem which the rise of scientific naturalism has created for the modern mind concerns the foundations of morality. The old religious foundations have largely crumbled away, and it may well be thought that the edifice built upon them by generations of men is in danger of collapse. A total collapse of moral behavior is, as I pointed out before, very unlikely. For a society in which this occurred could not survive. Nevertheless the danger to moral standards inherent in the virtual disappearance of their old religious foundations is not illusory.

I shall first discuss the problem of free will, for it is certain that if there is no free will there can be no morality. Morality is concerned with what men ought and ought not to do. But if a man has no freedom to choose what he will do, if whatever he does is done under compulsion, then it does not make sense to tell him that he ought not to have done what he did and that he ought to do something different. All moral precepts would in such case be meaningless. Also if he acts always under compulsion, how can he be held morally responsible for his actions? How can he, for example, be punished for what he could not help doing?

It is to be observed that those learned professors of philosophy or psychology who deny the existence of free will do so only in their professional moments and in their studies and lecture rooms. For when it comes to doing anything practical, even of the most trivial kind, they invariably behave as if they and others were free. They inquire from you at dinner whether you will choose this dish or that dish. They will ask a child why he told a lie, and will punish him for not having chosen the way of truthfulness. All of which is inconsistent with a disbelief in free will. This should cause us to suspect that the problem is not a real one;

and this, I believe, is the case. The dispute is merely verbal, and is due to nothing but a confusion about the meanings of words. It is what is now fashionably called a semantic problem.

How does a verbal dispute arise? Let us consider a case which, although it is absurd in the sense that no one would ever make the mistake which is involved in it, yet illustrates the principle which we shall have to use in the solution of the problem. Suppose that someone believed that the word "man" means a certain sort of five-legged animal; in short that "five-legged animal" is the correct *definition* of man. He might then look around the world, and rightly observing that there are no five-legged animals in it, he might proceed to deny the existence of men. This preposterous conclusion would have been reached because he was using an incorrect definition of "man." All you would have to do to show him his mistake would be to give him the correct definition; or at least to show him that his definition was wrong. Both the problem and its solution would, of course, be entirely verbal. The problem of free will, and its solution, I shall maintain, is verbal in exactly the same way. The problem has been created by the fact that learned men, especially philosophers, have assumed an incorrect definition of free *will*, and then finding that there is nothing in the world which answers to their definition, have denied its existence. As far as logic is concerned, their conclusion is just as absurd as that of the man who denies the existence of men. The only difference is that the mistake in the latter case is obvious and crude, while the mistake which the deniers of free will have made is rather subtle and difficult to detect.

Throughout the modern period, until quite recently, it was assumed, both by the philosophers who denied free will and by those who defended it, that *determinism is inconsistent with free will*. If a man's actions were wholly determined by chains of causes stretching back into the remote past, so that they could be predicted beforehand by a mind which knew all the causes, it was assumed that they could not in that case be free. This implies that a certain definition of actions done from free will was assumed, namely that they are actions *not* wholly determined by causes or predictable beforehand. Let us shorten this by saying that free will was defined as meaning indeterminism. This is the incorrect definition which has led to the denial of free will. As soon as we see what the true definition is we shall find that the question whether the world is deterministic, as Newtonian science implied, or in a measure indeterministic, as current physics teaches, is wholly irrelevant to the problem.

Of course there is a sense in which one can define a word arbitrarily in any way one pleases. But a definition may nevertheless be called correct or incorrect. It is correct if it accords with a *common usage* of the word defined. It is incorrect if it does not. And if you give an incorrect definition, absurd and untrue results are likely to follow. For instance, there is nothing to prevent you from arbitrarily defining a man as a five-legged animal, but this is incorrect in the sense that it does not accord with the ordinary meaning of the word. Also it has the absurd result of leading to a denial of the existence of men. This shows that *common usage is the criterion for deciding whether a definition is correct or not.* And this is the principle which I shall apply to free will. I shall show that indeterminism is not what is meant by the phrase "free will" *as it is commonly used.* And I shall attempt to discover the correct definition by inquiring how the phrase is used in ordinary conversation.

Here are a few samples of how the phrase might be used in ordinary conversation. It will be noticed that they include cases in which the question whether a man acted with free will is asked in order to determine whether he was morally and legally responsible for his acts.

> JONES: I once went without food for a week.
> SMITH: Did you do that of your own free will?
> JONES: No. I did it because I was lost in a desert and could find no food.

But suppose that the man who had fasted was Mahatma Gandhi. The conversation might then have gone:

> GANDHI: I once fasted for a week.
> SMITH: Did you do that of your own free will?
> GANDHI: Yes. I did it because I wanted to compel the British Government to give India its independence.

Take another case. Suppose that I had stolen some bread, but that I was as truthful as George Washington. Then, if I were charged with the crime in court, some exchange of the following sort might take place:

> JUDGE: Did you steal the bread of your own free will?
> STACE: Yes. I stole it because I was hungry.

Or in different circumstances the conversation might run: 10

> JUDGE: Did you steal of your own free will?
> STACE: No. I stole because my employer threatened to beat me if I did not.

At a recent murder trial in Trenton some of the accused had signed confessions, but afterwards asserted that they had done so under police duress. The following exchange might have occurred:

> JUDGE: Did you sign this confession of your own free will?
> PRISONER: No. I signed it because the police beat me up.

Now suppose that a philosopher had been a member of the jury. We could imagine this conversation taking place in the jury room.

FOREMAN OF THE JURY: The prisoner says he signed the confession because he was beaten, and not of his own free will.

PHILOSOPHER: This is quite irrelevant to the case. There is no such thing as free will.

FOREMAN: Do you mean to say that it makes no difference whether he signed because his conscience made him want to tell the truth or because he was beaten?

PHILOSOPHER: None at all. Whether he was caused to sign by a beating or by some desire of his own—the desire to tell the truth, for example—in either case his signing was causally determined, and therefore in neither case did he act of his own free will. Since there is no such thing as free will, the question whether he signed of his own free will ought not to be discussed by us.

The foreman and the rest of the jury would rightly conclude that the philosopher must be making some mistake. What sort of a mistake could it be? There is only one possible answer. The philosopher must be using the phrase "free will" in some peculiar way of his own which is not the way in which men usually use it when they wish to determine a question of moral responsibility. That is, he must be using an incorrect definition of it as implying action not determined by causes.

Suppose a man left his office at noon, and were questioned about it. Then we might hear this:

JONES: Did you go out of your own free will?
SMITH: Yes. I went out to get my lunch.

But we might hear:

JONES: Did you leave your office of your own free will?
SMITH: No. I was forcibly removed by the police.

We have now collected a number of cases of actions which, in the ordinary usage of the English language, would be called cases in which people have acted of their own free will. We should also say in all these cases that they *chose* to act as they did. We should also say that they could have acted otherwise, if they had chosen. For instance, Mahatma Gandhi was not compelled to fast; he chose to do so. He could have eaten if he had wanted to. When Smith went out to get his lunch, he chose to do so. He could have stayed and done some more work, if he had wanted to. We have also collected a number of cases of the opposite kind. They are cases in which men were not able to exercise their free will. They had no choice. They were compelled to do as they did. The man in the desert did not fast of his own free will. He had no choice in the matter. He was compelled to fast because there was nothing for him to eat. And so with the other cases. It ought to be quite easy, by an inspection of these cases, to tell what we ordinarily mean when we say that a man did or did not exercise free will.

15

We ought therefore to be able to extract from them the proper definition of the term. Let us put the cases in a table:

Free Acts	Unfree Acts
Gandhi fasting because he wanted to free India.	The man fasting in the desert because there was no food.
Stealing bread because one is hungry.	Stealing because one's employer threatened to beat one.
Signing a confession because one wanted to tell the truth.	Signing because the police beat one.
Leaving the office because one wanted one's lunch.	Leaving because forcibly removed.

It is obvious that to find the correct definition of free acts we must discover what characteristic is common to all the acts in the left-hand column, and is, at the same time, absent from all the acts in the right-hand column. This characteristic which all free acts have, and which no unfree acts have, will be the defining characteristic of free will.

Is being uncaused, or not being determined by causes, the characteristic of which we are in search? It cannot be, because although it is true that all the acts in the right-hand column have causes, such as the beating by the police or the absence of food in the desert, so also do the acts in the left-hand column. Mr. Gandhi's fasting was caused by his desire to free India, the man leaving his office by his hunger, and so on. Moreover there is no reason to doubt that these causes of the free acts were in turn caused by prior conditions, and that these were again the results of causes, and so on back indefinitely into the past. Any physiologist can tell us the causes of hunger. What caused Mr. Gandhi's tremendously powerful desire to free India is no doubt more difficult to discover. But it must have had causes. Some of them may have lain in peculiarities of his glands or brain, others in his past experiences, others in his heredity, others in his education. Defenders of free will have usually tended to deny such facts. But to do so is plainly a case of special pleading, which is unsupported by any scrap of evidence. The only reasonable view is that all human actions, both those which are freely done and those which are not, are either wholly determined by causes, or at least as much determined as other events in nature. It may be true, as the physicists tell us, that nature is not as deterministic as was once thought. But whatever degree of determinism prevails in the world, human actions appear to be as much determined as anything else. And if this is so, it cannot be the case that what distinguishes actions freely chosen from those which are not free is that the latter are determined by causes while the former are not. Therefore, being uncaused or being undetermined by causes must be an incorrect definition of free will.

What, then, is the difference between acts which are freely done and those which are not? What is the characteristic which is present to all the acts in the left-hand column and absent from all those in the right-hand column? It is not obvious that, although both sets of actions have causes, the causes of those in the left-hand column are *of a different kind* from the causes of those in the right-hand column? The free acts are all caused by desires, or motives, or by some sort of internal psychological states of the agent's mind. The unfree acts, on the other hand, are all caused by physical forces or physical conditions, outside the agent. Police arrest means physical force exerted from the outside; the absence of food in the desert is a physical condition of the outside world. We may therefore frame the following rough definitions. *Acts freely done are those whose immediate causes are psychological states in the agent. Acts not freely done are those whose immediate causes are states of affairs external to the agent.*

It is plain that if we define free will in this way, then free will certainly exists, and the philosopher's denial of its existence is seen to be what it is—nonsense. For it is obvious that all those actions of men which we should ordinarily attribute to the exercise of their free will, or of which we should say that they freely chose to do them, are in fact actions which have been caused by their own desires, wishes, thoughts, emotions, impulses, or other psychological states. 20

In applying our definition we shall find that it usually works well, but that there are some puzzling cases which it does not seem exactly to fit. These puzzles can always be solved by paying careful attention to the ways in which words are used, and remembering that they are not always used consistently. I have space for only one example. Suppose that a thug threatens to shoot you unless you give him your wallet, and suppose that you do so. Do you, in giving him your wallet, do so of your own free will or not? If we apply our definition, we find that you acted freely, since the immediate cause of the action was not an actual outside force but the fear of death, which is a psychological cause. Most people, however, would say that you did not act of your own free will but under compulsion. Does this show that our definition is wrong? I do not think so. Aristotle, who gave a solution of the problem of free will substantially the same as ours (though he did not use the term "free will") admitted that there are what he called "mixed" or borderline cases in which it is difficult to know whether we ought to call the acts free or compelled. In the case under discussion, though no actual force was used, the gun at your forehead so nearly approximated to actual force that we tend to say the case was one of compulsion. It is a borderline case.

Here is what may seem like another kind of puzzle. According to our view an action may be free though it could have been predicted beforehand with certainty. But suppose you told a lie, and it was certain beforehand that you would tell it. How could one then say, "You could have told the truth"? The answer is that it is perfectly true that you could have told the truth *if* you had wanted to. In fact you would have done so, for in that case the causes producing your action, namely your desires, would have been different, and would therefore have produced different effects. It is a delusion that predictability and free will are incompatible.

This agrees with common sense. For if, knowing your character, I predict that you will act honorably, no one would say when you do act honorably, that this shows you did not do so of your own free will.

Since free will is a condition of moral responsibility, we must be sure that our theory of free will gives a sufficient basis for it. To be held morally responsible for one's actions means that one may be justly punished or rewarded, blamed or praised, for them. But it is not just to punish a man for what he cannot help doing. How can it be just to punish him for an action which it was certain beforehand that he would do? We have not attempted to decide whether, as a matter of fact, all events, including human actions, are completely determined. For that question is irrelevant to the problem of free will. But if we assume for the purposes of argument that complete determinism is true, but that we are nevertheless free, it may then be asked whether such a deterministic free will is compatible with moral responsibility. For it may seem unjust to punish a man for an action which it could have been predicted with certainty beforehand that he would do.

But that determinism is incompatible with moral responsibility is as much a delusion as that it is incompatible with free will. You do not excuse a man for doing a wrong act because, knowing his character, you felt certain beforehand that he would do it. Nor do you deprive a man of a reward or prize because, knowing his goodness or his capabilities, you felt certain beforehand that he would win it.

Volumes have been written on the justification of punishment. 25 But so far as it affects the question of free will, the essential principles involved are quite simple. The punishment of a man for doing a wrong act is justified, either on the ground that it will correct his own character, or that it will deter other people from doing similar acts. The instrument of punishment has been in the past, and no doubt still is, often unwisely used; so that it may often have done more harm than good. But that is not relevant to our present problem. Punishment, if and when it is justified, is justified only on one or both of the grounds just mentioned. The question then is how, if we assume determinism, punishment can correct character or deter people from evil actions.

Suppose that your child develops a habit of telling lies. You give him a mild beating. Why? Because you believe that his personality is such that the usual motives for telling the truth do not cause him to do so. You therefore supply the missing cause, or motive, in the shape of pain and the fear of future pain if he repeats his untruthful behavior. And you hope that a few treatments of this kind will condition him to the habit of truth-telling, so that he will come to tell the truth without the infliction of pain. You assume that his actions are determined by causes, but that the usual causes of truth-telling do not in him produce their usual effects. You therefore supply him with an artificially injected motive, pain and fear, which you think will in the future cause him to speak truthfully.

The principle is exactly the same where you hope, by punishing one man, to deter others from wrong actions. You believe that the fear of punishment will cause those who might otherwise do evil to do well.

We act on the same principle with nonhuman, and even with inanimate, things, if they do not behave in the way we think they ought to behave. The rose bushes in the garden produce only small and poor blooms, whereas we want large and rich ones. We supply a cause which will produce large blooms, namely fertilizer. Our automobile does not go properly. We supply a cause which will make it go better, namely oil in the works. The punishment for the man, the fertilizer for the plant, and the oil for the car are all justified by the same principle and in the same way. The only difference is that different kinds of things require different kinds of causes to make them do what they should. Pain may be the appropriate remedy to apply, in certain cases, to human beings, and oil to the machine. It is, of course, of no use to inject motor oil into the boy or to beat the machine.

Thus we see that moral responsibility is not only consistent with determinism, but requires it. The assumption on which punishment is based is that human behavior is causally determined. If pain could not be a cause of truth-telling there would be no justification at all for punishing lies. If human actions and volitions were uncaused, it would be useless either to punish or reward, or indeed to do anything else to correct people's bad behavior. For nothing that you could do would in any way influence them. Thus moral responsibility would entirely disappear. If there were no determinism of human beings at all, their actions would be completely unpredictable and capricious, and therefore irresponsible. And this is in itself a strong argument against the common view of philosophers that free will means being undetermined by causes.

TOPICS FOR CRITICAL THINKING AND WRITING

1. Stace asserts that "if there is no free will there can be no morality" (para. 2). What is his reasoning (see para. 23)? Do you agree?

2. "The dispute is merely verbal," Stace proclaims in paragraph 3. What "dispute"? Why "merely verbal"? What would Stace say to someone who insists that the existence or nonexistence of free will is a question of *fact*?

3. What is *determinism* (para. 5)? Why does Stace seem to think that philosophers are strongly inclined to believe in it?

4. Stace claims that he will show that "indeterminism is not what is meant by . . . 'free will' *as it is commonly used*" (para. 6). What is his argument? What does he think *free will* means as the term is "commonly used"? Are you convinced? Why, or why not? Write a 500-word paper answering these questions.

5. Stace insists that "all human actions . . . are . . . at least as much determined as other events in nature" (para. 18). How might one argue against this?

6. Complete the following definition so that it captures Stace's view: "When Smith did *X*, he acted freely if and only if . . ."

7. Stace mentions some "puzzling cases" (para. 21) that do not quite fit, he admits, his analysis of free will. Give an example of such a case, and explain why it is puzzling.

8. Why does Stace conclude in paragraph 22 that "it is a delusion that predictability and free will are incompatible"? Do you agree? Why, or why not?

9. It seems paradoxical to assert, as Stace does in his last paragraph, that "moral responsibility is not only consistent with determinism, but requires it." Explain Stace's view here in no more than 250 words.

Martin Luther King Jr.

Martin Luther King Jr. (1929–1968) was born in Atlanta and educated at Morehouse College, Crozer Theological Seminary, and Boston University. In 1954 he was called to serve as a Baptist minister in Montgomery, Alabama. During the next two years he achieved national fame when, using a policy of nonviolent resistance, he successfully led the boycott against segregated bus lines in Montgomery. He then organized the Southern Christian Leadership Conference, which furthered civil rights, first in the South and then nationwide. In 1964 he was awarded the Nobel Peace Prize. Four years later he was assassinated in Memphis, Tennessee, while supporting striking garbage workers.

In 1963 King was arrested in Birmingham, Alabama, for participating in a march for which no parade permit had been issued by city officials. In jail he wrote a response to a letter that eight local clergymen had published in a newspaper.

Note: Their letter, titled "A Call for Unity," is printed here, followed by King's response.

A CALL FOR UNITY

April 12, 1963

We the undersigned clergymen are among those who, in January, issued "An Appeal for Law and Order and Common Sense," in dealing with racial problems in Alabama. We expressed understanding that honest convictions in racial matters could properly be pursued in the courts, but urged that decisions of those courts should in the meantime be peacefully obeyed.

Since that time there had been some evidence of increased forebearance and a willingness to face facts. Responsible citizens have undertaken to work on various problems which cause racial friction and unrest. In Birmingham, recent public events have given indication that we all have opportunity for a new constructive and realistic approach to racial problems.

However, we are now confronted by a series of demonstrations by some of our Negro citizens, directed and led in part by outsiders. We recognize the natural impatience of people who feel that their hopes are slow in being realized. But we are convinced that these demonstrations are unwise and untimely.

We agree rather with certain local Negro leadership which has called for honest and open negotiation of racial issues in our area. And we believe this kind of facing of issues can best be accomplished by citizens of our own metropolitan area, white and Negro, meeting with their knowledge and experience of the local situation. All of us need to face that responsibility and find proper channels for its accomplishment.

Just as we formerly pointed out that "hatred and violence have no   5 sanction in our religious and political traditions," we also point out that such actions as incite to hatred and violence, however technically peaceful those actions may be, have not contributed to the resolution of our local problems. We do not believe that these days of new hope are days when extreme measures are justified in Birmingham.

We commend the community as a whole, and the local news media and law enforcement officials in particular, on the calm manner in which these demonstrations have been handled. We urge the public to continue to show restraint should the demonstrations continue, and the law enforcement officials to remain calm and continue to protect our city from violence.

We further strongly urge our own Negro community to withdraw support from these demonstrations, and to unite locally in working peacefully for a better Birmingham. When rights are consistently denied, a cause should be pressed in the courts and in negotiations among local leaders, and not in the streets. We appeal to both our white and Negro citizenry to observe the principles of law and order and common sense.

> C.C.J. Carpenter, D.D., L.L.D., Bishop of Alabama; Joseph A. Durick, D.D., Auxiliary Bishop, Diocese of Mobile-Birmingham; Rabbi Milton L. Grafman, Temple Emanu-El, Birmingham, Alabama; Bishop Paul Hardin, Bishop of the Alabama-West Florida Conference of the Methodist Church; Bishop Nolan B. Harmon, Bishop of the North Alabama Conference of the Methodist Church; George M. Murray, D.D., L.L.D., Bishop Coadjutor, Episcopal Diocese of Alabama; Edward V. Ramage, Moderator, Synod of the Alabama Presbyterian Church in the United States; Earl Stallings, Pastor, First Baptist Church, Birmingham, Alabama.

Letter from Birmingham Jail

April 16, 1963

My Dear Fellow Clergymen:

While confined here in the Birmingham city jail, I came across your recent statement calling my present activities "unwise and untimely."[1] Seldom do I pause to answer criticism of my work and ideas. If I sought to answer all the criticisms that cross my desk, my secretaries would have little time for anything other than such correspondence in the course of the day, and I would have no time for constructive work. But since I feel that you are men of genuine good will and that your criticisms are sincerely set forth, I want to try to answer your statement in what I hope will be patient and reasonable terms.

I think I should indicate why I am here in Birmingham, since you have been influenced by the view which argues against "outsiders coming in." I have the honor of serving as president of the Southern Christian Leadership Conference, an organization operating in every southern state, with headquarters in Atlanta, Georgia. We have some eighty-five affiliated organizations across the South, and one of them is the Alabama Christian Movement for Human Rights. Frequently we share staff, educational, and financial resources with our affiliates. Several months ago the affiliate here in Birmingham asked us to be on call to engage in a nonviolent direct-action program if such were deemed necessary. We readily consented, and when the hour came we lived up to our promise. So I, along with several members of my staff, am here because I was invited here. I am here because I have organizational ties here.

But more basically, I am in Birmingham because injustice is here. Just as the prophets of the eighth century B.C. left their villages and carried their "thus saith the Lord" far beyond the boundaries of their home towns, and just as the Apostle Paul left his village of Tarsus and carried the gospel of Jesus Christ to the far corners of the Greco-Roman world, so am I compelled to carry the gospel of freedom beyond my own home town. Like Paul, I must constantly respond to the Macedonian call for aid.

Moreover, I am cognizant of the interrelatedness of all communities and states. I cannot sit idly by in Atlanta and not be concerned about what happens in Birmingham. Injustice anywhere is a threat to justice

[1]This response to a published statement by eight fellow clergymen from Alabama (Bishop C.C.J. Carpenter, Bishop Joseph A. Durick, Rabbi Milton L. Grafman, Bishop Paul Hardin, Bishop Nolan B. Harmon, the Reverend George M. Murray, the Reverend Edward V. Ramage, and the Reverend Earl Stallings) was composed under somewhat constricting circumstances. Begun on the margins of the newspaper in which the statement appeared while I was in jail, the letter was continued on scraps of writing paper supplied by a friendly Negro trusty, and concluded on a pad my attorneys were eventually permitted to leave me. Although the text remains in substance unaltered, I have indulged in the author's prerogative of polishing it for publication. [King's note.]

everywhere. We are caught in an inescapable network of mutuality; tied in a single garment of destiny. Whatever affects one directly, affects all indirectly. Never again can we afford to live with the narrow, provincial "outside agitator" idea. Anyone who lives inside the United States can never be considered an outsider anywhere within its bounds.

You deplore the demonstrations taking place in Birmingham. But 5 your statement, I am sorry to say, fails to express a similar concern for the conditions that brought about the demonstrations. I am sure that none of you would want to rest content with the superficial kind of social analysis that deals merely with effects and does not grapple with underlying causes. It is unfortunate that demonstrations are taking place in Birmingham, but it is even more unfortunate that the city's white power structure left the Negro community with no alternative.

In any nonviolent campaign there are four basic steps: collection of the facts to determine whether injustices exist; negotiation; self-purification; and direct action. We have gone through all these steps in Birmingham. There can be no gainsaying the fact that racial injustice engulfs this community. Birmingham is probably the most thoroughly segregated city in the United States. Its ugly record of brutality is widely known. Negroes have experienced grossly unjust treatment in the courts. There have been more unsolved bombings of Negro homes and churches in Birmingham than in any other city in the nation. These are the hard, brutal facts of the case. On the basis of these conditions, Negro leaders sought to negotiate with the city fathers. But the latter consistently refused to engage in good-faith negotiation.

Then, last September, came the opportunity to talk with leaders of Birmingham's economic community. In the course of the negotiations, certain promises were made by the merchants—for example, to remove the stores' humiliating racial signs. On the basis of these promises, the Reverend Fred Shuttleworth and the leaders of the Alabama Christian Movement for Human Rights agreed to a moratorium on all demonstrations. As the weeks and months went by, we realized that we were the victims of a broken promise. A few signs, briefly removed, returned; the others remained.

As in so many past experiences, our hopes had been blasted, and the shadow of deep disappointment settled upon us. We had no alternative except to prepare for direct action, whereby we would present our very bodies as a means of laying our case before the conscience of the local and the national community. Mindful of the difficulties involved, we decided to undertake a process of self-purification. We began a series of workshops on nonviolence, and we repeatedly asked ourselves: "Are you able to accept blows without retaliating?" "Are you able to endure the ordeal of jail?" We decided to schedule our direct-action program for the Easter season, realizing that except for Christmas, this is the main shopping period of the year. Knowing that a strong economic-withdrawal program would be the by-product of direct action, we felt that this would be the best time to bring pressure to bear on the merchants for the needed change.

Then it occurred to us that Birmingham's mayoralty election was coming up in March, and we speedily decided to postpone action until after election day. When we discovered that the Commissioner of Public Safety, Eugene "Bull" Connor, had piled up enough votes to be in the run-off, we decided again to postpone action until the day after the run-off so that the demonstrations could not be used to cloud the issues. Like many others, we waited to see Mr. Connor defeated, and to this end we endured postponement after postponement. Having aided in this community need, we felt that our direct-action program could be delayed no longer.

You may well ask: "Why direct action? Why sit-ins, marches, and so 10 forth? Isn't negotiation a better path?" You are quite right in calling for negotiation. Indeed, this is the very purpose of direct action. Nonviolent direct action seeks to create such a crisis and foster such a tension that a community which has constantly refused to negotiate is forced to confront the issue. It seeks so to dramatize the issue that it can no longer be ignored. My citing the creation of tension as part of the work of the nonviolent-resister may sound rather shocking. But I must confess that I am not afraid of the word "tension." I have earnestly opposed violent tension, but there is a type of constructive, nonviolent tension which is necessary for growth. Just as Socrates felt that it was necessary to create a tension in the mind so that individuals could rise from the bondage of myths and half-truths to the unfettered realm of creative analysis and objective appraisal, so must we see the need for nonviolent gadflies to create the kind of tension in society that will help men rise from the dark depths of prejudice and racism to the majestic heights of understanding and brotherhood.

The purpose of our direct-action program is to create a situation so crisis-packed that it will inevitably open the door to negotiation. I therefore concur with you in your call for negotiation. Too long has our beloved Southland been bogged down in a tragic effort to live in monologue rather than dialogue.

One of the basic points in your statement is that the action that I and my associates have taken in Birmingham is untimely. Some have asked: "Why didn't you give the new city administration time to act?" The only answer that I can give to this query is that the new Birmingham administration must be prodded about as much as the outgoing one, before it will act. We are sadly mistaken if we feel that the election of Albert Boutwell as mayor will bring the millennium to Birmingham. While Mr. Boutwell is a much more gentle person than Mr. Connor, they are both segregationists, dedicated to maintenance of the status quo. I have hope that Mr. Boutwell will be reasonable enough to see the futility of massive resistance to desegregation. But he will not see this without pressure from devotees of civil rights. My friends, I must say to you that we have not made a single gain in civil rights without determined legal and nonviolent pressure. Lamentably, it is an historical fact that privileged groups seldom give up their privileges voluntarily. Individuals may see the moral light and voluntarily give up their unjust posture; but as Reinhold Niebuhr[2] has reminded us, groups tend to be more immoral than individuals.

We know through painful experience that freedom is never voluntarily given by the oppressor; it must be demanded by the oppressed. Frankly, I have yet to engage in a direct-action campaign that was "well timed" in the view of those who have not suffered unduly from the disease of segregation. For years now I have heard the word "Wait!" It rings in the ear of every Negro with piercing familiarity. This "Wait" has almost always meant "Never." We must come to see, with one of our distinguished jurists, that "justice too long delayed is justice denied."[3]

We have waited for more than 340 years for our constitutional and God-given rights. The nations of Asia and Africa are moving with jet-like speed toward gaining political independence, but we still creep at horse-and-buggy pace toward gaining a cup of coffee at a lunch counter. Perhaps it is easy for those who have never felt the stinging darts of segregation to say, "Wait." But when you have seen vicious mobs lynch your mothers and fathers at will and drown your sisters and brothers at whim; when you have seen hate-filled policemen curse, kick, and even kill your black brothers and sisters; when you see the vast majority of your twenty million Negro brothers smothering in an airtight cage of poverty in the midst of an affluent society; when you suddenly find your tongue twisted and your speech stammering as you seek to explain to your six-year-old daughter why she can't go to the public amusement park that has just been advertised on television, and see tears welling up in her eyes when she is told that Funtown is closed to colored children, and see ominous clouds of inferiority beginning to form in her little mental sky, and see her beginning to distort her personality by developing an unconscious bitterness toward white people; when you have to concoct an answer for a five-year-old son who is asking: "Daddy, why do white people treat colored people so mean?"; when you take a cross-country drive and find it necessary to sleep night after night in the uncomfortable corners of your automobile because no motel will accept you; when you are humiliated day in and day out by nagging signs reading "white" and "colored"; when your first name becomes "nigger," your middle name becomes "boy" (however old you are) and your last name becomes "John," and your wife and mother are never given the respected

---

[2]**Reinhold Niebuhr** Niebuhr (1892–1971) was a minister, political activist, author, and professor of applied Christianity at Union Theological Seminary. [All notes are the editors' unless otherwise specified.]
[3]**Justice . . . denied** A quotation attributed to William E. Gladstone (1809–1898), British statesman and prime minister.

title "Mrs."; when you are harried by day and haunted by night by the fact that you are a Negro, living constantly at tiptoe stance, never quite knowing what to expect next, and are plagued with inner fears and outer resentments; when you are forever fighting a degenerating sense of "nobodiness"—then you will understand why we find it difficult to wait. There comes a time when the cup of endurance runs over, and men are no longer willing to be plunged into the abyss of despair. I hope, sirs, you can understand our legitimate and unavoidable impatience.

You express a great deal of anxiety over our willingness to break   15 laws. This is certainly a legitimate concern. Since we so diligently urge people to obey the Supreme Court's decision of 1954 outlawing segregation in the public schools, at first glance it may seem rather paradoxical for us consciously to break laws. One may well ask: "How can you advocate breaking some laws and obeying others?" The answer lies in the fact that there are two types of laws: just and unjust. I would be the first to advocate obeying just laws. One has not only a legal but a moral responsibility to obey just laws. Conversely, one has a moral responsibility to disobey unjust laws. I would agree with St. Augustine that "an unjust law is no law at all."

Now, what is the difference between the two? How does one determine whether a law is just or unjust? A just law is a man-made code that squares with the moral law or the law of God. An unjust law is a code that is out of harmony with the moral law. To put it in the terms of St. Thomas Aquinas: An unjust law is a human law that is not rooted in eternal law and natural law. Any law that uplifts human personality is just. Any law that degrades human personality is unjust. All segregation statutes are unjust because segregation distorts the soul and damages the personality. It gives the segregator a false sense of superiority and the segregated a false sense of inferiority. Segregation, to use the terminology of the Jewish philosopher Martin Buber, substitutes an "I-it" relationship for an "I-thou" relationship and ends up relegating persons to the status of things. Hence segregation is not only politically, economically, and sociologically unsound, it is morally wrong and sinful. Paul Tillich[4] has said that sin is separation. Is not segregation an existential expression of man's tragic separation, his awful estrangement, his terrible sinfulness? Thus it is that I can urge men to obey the 1954 decision of the Supreme Court, for it is morally right; and I can urge them to disobey segregation ordinances, for they are morally wrong.

Let us consider a more concrete example of just and unjust laws. An unjust law is a code that a numerical or power majority group compels a minority group to obey but does not make binding on itself. This is *difference*

---

[4]**Paul Tillich** Tillich (1886–1965), born in Germany, taught theology at several German universities, but in 1933 he was dismissed from his post at the University of Frankfurt because of his opposition to the Nazi regime. At the invitation of Reinhold Niebuhr, he came to the United States and taught at Union Theological Seminary.

made legal. By the same token, a just law is a code that a majority compels a minority to follow and that it is willing to follow itself. This is *sameness* made legal.

Let me give another explanation. A law is unjust if it is inflicted on a minority that, as a result of being denied the right to vote, had no part in enacting or devising the law. Who can say that the legislature of Alabama which set up that state's segregation laws was democratically elected? Throughout Alabama all sorts of devious methods are used to prevent Negroes from becoming registered voters, and there are some counties in which, even though Negroes constitute a majority of the population, not a single Negro is registered. Can any law enacted under such circumstances be considered democratically structured?

Sometimes a law is just on its face and unjust in its application. For instance, I have been arrested on a charge of parading without a permit. Now, there is nothing wrong in having an ordinance which requires a permit for a parade. But such an ordinance becomes unjust when it is used to maintain segregation and to deny citizens the First Amendment privilege of peaceful assembly and protest.

I hope you are able to see the distinction I am trying to point out. In 20 no sense do I advocate evading or defying the law, as would the rabid segregationist. That would lead to anarchy. One who breaks an unjust law must do so openly, lovingly, and with a willingness to accept the penalty. I submit that an individual who breaks a law that conscience tells him is unjust, and who willingly accepts the penalty of imprisonment in order to arouse the conscience of the community over its injustice, is in reality expressing the highest respect for law.

Of course, there is nothing new about this kind of civil disobedience. It was evidenced sublimely in the refusal of Shadrach, Meshach, and Abednego to obey the laws of Nebuchadnezzar, on the ground that a higher moral law was at stake. It was practiced superbly by the early Christians, who were willing to face hungry lions and the excruciating pain of chopping blocks rather than submit to certain unjust laws of the Roman Empire. To a degree, academic freedom is a reality today because Socrates practiced civil disobedience. In our own nation, the Boston Tea Party represented a massive act of civil disobedience.

We should never forget that everything Adolf Hitler did in Germany was "legal" and everything the Hungarian freedom fighters did in Hungary was "illegal." It was "illegal" to aid and comfort a Jew in Hitler's Germany. Even so, I am sure that, had I lived in Germany at the time, I would have aided and comforted my Jewish brothers. If today I lived in a Communist country where certain principles dear to the Christian faith are suppressed, I would openly advocate disobeying that country's anti-religious laws.

I must make two honest confessions to you, my Christian and Jewish brothers. First, I must confess that over the past few years I have been gravely disappointed with the white moderate. I have almost reached the regrettable conclusion that the Negro's great stumbling block in his stride toward freedom is not the White Citizen's Counciler or the Ku Klux Klanner, but the white moderate, who is more devoted to "order" than to justice; who prefers a negative peace which is the absence of tension to a positive peace which is the presence of justice; who constantly says: "I agree with you in the goal you seek, but I cannot agree with your methods or direct action"; who paternalistically believes he can set the timetable for another man's freedom; who lives by a mythical concept of time and who constantly advises the Negro to wait for a "more convenient season." Shallow understanding from people of good will is more frustrating than absolute misunderstanding from people of ill will. Lukewarm acceptance is much more bewildering than outright rejection.

I had hoped that the white moderate would understand that law and order exist for the purpose of establishing justice and that when they fail in this purpose they become the dangerously structured dams that block the flow of social progress. I had hoped that the white moderate would understand that the present tension in the South is a necessary phase of the transition from an obnoxious negative peace, in which the Negro passively accepted his unjust plight, to a substantive and positive peace, in which all men will respect the dignity and worth of human personality. Actually, we who engage in nonviolent direct action are not the creators of tension. We merely bring to the surface the hidden tension that is already alive. We bring it out in the open, where it can be seen and dealt with. Like a boil that can never be cured so long as it is covered up but must be opened with all its ugliness to the natural medicines of air and light, injustice must be exposed, with all the tension its exposure creates, to the light of human conscience and the air of national opinion before it can be cured.

In your statement you assert that our actions, even though peace-   25
ful, must be condemned because they precipitate violence. But is this a logical assertion? Isn't this like condemning a robbed man because his possession of money precipitated the evil act of robbery? Isn't this like condemning Socrates because his unswerving commitment to truth and his philosophical inquiries precipitated the act by the misguided populace in which they made him drink hemlock? Isn't this like condemning Jesus because his unique God-consciousness and never-ceasing devotion to God's will precipitated the evil act of crucifixion? We must come to see that, as the federal courts have consistently affirmed, it is wrong to urge an individual to cease his efforts to gain his basic constitutional rights because the quest may precipitate violence. Society must protect the robbed and punish the robber.

I had also hoped that the white moderate would reject the myth concerning time in relation to the struggle for freedom. I have just received a letter from a white brother in Texas. He writes: "All Christians know that the colored people will receive equal rights eventually, but it is possible that you are in too great a religious hurry. It has taken Christianity almost two thousand years to accomplish what it has. The teachings of Christ take time to come to earth." Such an attitude stems from a tragic misconception of time, from the strangely irrational notion that there is something in the very flow of time that will inevitably cure all ills. Actually, time itself is neutral; it can be used either destructively or constructively. More and more I feel that the people of ill will have used time much more effectively than have the people of good will. We will have to repent in this generation not merely for the hateful words and actions of the bad people but for the appalling silence of the good people. Human progress never rolls in on wheels of inevitability; it comes through the tireless efforts of men willing to be co-workers with God, and without this hard work, time itself becomes an ally of the forces of social stagnation. We must use time creatively, in the knowledge that the time is always ripe to do right. Now is the time to make real the promise of democracy and transform our pending national elegy into a creative psalm of brotherhood. Now is the time to lift our national policy from the quicksand of racial injustice to the solid rock of human dignity.

You speak of our activity in Birmingham as extreme. At first I was rather disappointed that fellow clergymen would see my nonviolent efforts as those of an extremist. I began thinking about the fact that I stand in the middle of two opposing forces in the Negro community. One is a force of complacency, made up in part of Negroes who, as a result of long years of oppression, are so drained of self-respect and a sense of "somebodiness" that they have adjusted to segregation; and in part of a few middle-class Negroes who, because of a degree of academic and economic security and because in some ways they profit by segregation, have become insensitive to the problems of the masses. The other force is one of bitterness and hatred, and it comes perilously close to advocating violence. It is expressed in the various black nationalist groups that are springing up across the nation, the largest and best-known being Elijah Muhammad's Muslim movement. Nourished by the Negro's frustration over the continued existence of racial discrimination, this movement is made up of people who have lost faith in America, who have absolutely repudiated Christianity, and who have concluded that the white man is an incorrigible "devil."

I have tried to stand between these two forces, saying that we need emulate neither the "do-nothingism" of the complacent nor the hatred and despair of the black nationalist. For there is the more excellent way of love and nonviolent protest. I am grateful to God that, through the influence of the Negro church, the way of nonviolence became an integral part of our struggle.

If this philosophy had not emerged, by now many streets of the South should, I am convinced, be flowing with blood. And I am further convinced that if our white brothers dismiss as "rabble-rousers" and "outside agitators" those of us who employ nonviolent direct action, and if they refuse to support our nonviolent efforts, millions of Negroes will, out of frustration and despair, seek solace and security in black-nationalist ideologies—a development that would inevitably lead to a frightening racial nightmare.

Oppressed people cannot remain oppressed forever. The yearning 30 for freedom eventually manifests itself, and that is what has happened to the American Negro. Something within has reminded him of his birthright of freedom, and something without has reminded him that it can be gained. Consciously or unconsciously, he has been caught up by the *Zeitgeist*,[5] and with his black brothers of Africa and his brown and yellow brothers of Asia, South America, and the Caribbean, the United States Negro is moving with a sense of great urgency toward the promised land of racial justice. If one recognizes this vital urge that has engulfed the Negro community, one should readily understand why public demonstrations are taking place. The Negro has many pent-up resentments and latent frustrations, and he must release them. So let him march; let him make prayer pilgrimages to the city hall; let him go on freedom rides—and try to understand why he must do so. If his repressed emotions are not released in nonviolent ways, they will seek expression through violence; this is not a threat but a fact of history. So I have not said to my people: "Get rid of your discontent." Rather, I have tried to say that this normal and healthy discontent can be channeled into the creative outlet of nonviolent direct action. And now this approach is being termed extremist.

But though I was initially disappointed at being categorized as an extremist, as I continued to think about the matter I gradually gained a measure of satisfaction from the label. Was not Jesus an extremist for love: "Love your enemies, bless them that curse you, do good to them that hate you, and pray for them which despitefully use you, and persecute you." Was not Amos an extremist for justice: "Let justice roll down like waters and righteousness like an ever-flowing stream." Was not Paul an extremist for the Christian gospel: "I bear in my body the marks of the Lord Jesus." Was not Martin Luther an extremist: "Here I stand; I cannot do otherwise, so help me God." And John Bunyan: "I will stay in jail to the end of my days before I make a butchery of my conscience." And Abraham Lincoln: "This nation cannot survive half slave and half free." And Thomas Jefferson: "We hold these truths to be self-evident, that all men are created equal...." So the question is not whether we will be extremists, but what kind of extremists we will be. Will we be extremists for hate or for love? Will we be extremists for the preservation of injustice or for the extension of justice? In that dramatic scene on Calvary's hill three men were crucified. We must never forget that all three were crucified for the same crime—the crime of extremism. Two were extremists for immorality, and thus fell below their environment.

[5]*Zeitgeist* Spirit of the age (German).

The other, Jesus Christ, was an extremist for love, truth, and goodness, and thereby rose above his environment. Perhaps the South, the nation, and the world are in dire need of creative extremists.

I had hoped that the white moderate would see this need. Perhaps I was too optimistic; perhaps I expected too much. I suppose I should have realized that few members of the oppressor race can understand the deep groans and passionate yearnings of the oppressed race, and still fewer have the vision to see that injustice must be rooted out by strong, persistent, and determined action. I am thankful, however, that some of our white brothers in the South have grasped the meaning of this social revolution and committed themselves to it. They are still all too few in quantity, but they are big in quality. Some—such as Ralph McGill, Lillian Smith, Harry Golden, James McBride Dabbs, Ann Braden, and Sarah Patton Boyle—have written about our struggle in eloquent and prophetic terms. Others have marched with us down nameless streets of the South. They have languished in filthy, roach-infested jails, suffering the abuse and brutality of policemen who view them as "dirty nigger-lovers." Unlike so many of their moderate brothers and sisters, they have recognized the urgency of the moment and sensed the need for powerful "action" antidotes to combat the disease of segregation.

Let me take note of my other major disappointment. I have been so greatly disappointed with the white church and its leadership. Of course, there are some notable exceptions. I am not unmindful of the fact that each of you has taken some significant stands on this issue. I commend you, Reverend Stallings, for your Christian stand on this past Sunday, in welcoming Negroes to your worship service on a nonsegregated basis. I commend the Catholic leaders of this state for integrating Spring Hill College several years ago.

But despite these notable exceptions, I must honestly reiterate that I have been disappointed with the church. I do not say this as one of those negative critics who can always find something wrong with the church. I say this as a minister of the gospel, who loves the church; who was nurtured in its bosom; who has been sustained by its spiritual blessings and who will remain true to it as long as the cord of life shall lengthen.

When I was suddenly catapulted into the leadership of the bus protest in Montgomery, Alabama, a few years ago, I felt we would be supported by the white church. I felt that the white ministers, priests, and rabbis of the South would be among our strongest allies. Instead, some have been outright opponents, refusing to understand the freedom movement and misrepresenting its leaders; all too many others have been more cautious than courageous and have remained silent behind the anesthetizing security of stained-glass windows.

In spite of my shattered dreams, I came to Birmingham with the hope that the white religious leadership of this community would see the justice of our cause and, with deep moral concern, would serve as the channel through which our just grievances could reach the power structure.

I had hoped that each of you would understand. But again I have been disappointed.

I have heard numerous southern religious leaders admonish their worshipers to comply with a desegregation decision because it is the law, but I have longed to hear white ministers declare: "Follow this decree because integration is morally right and because the Negro is your brother." In the midst of blatant injustices inflicted upon the Negro, I have watched white churchmen stand on the sideline and mouth pious irrelevancies and sanctimonious trivialities. In the midst of a mighty struggle to rid our nation of racial and economic injustice, I have heard many ministers say: "Those are social issues, with which the gospel has no real concern." And I have watched many churches commit themselves to a completely otherworldly religion which makes a strange, unbiblical distinction between body and soul, between the sacred and the secular.

I have traveled the length and breadth of Alabama, Mississippi, and all the other southern states. On sweltering summer days and crisp autumn mornings I have looked at the South's beautiful churches with their lofty spires pointing heavenward. I have beheld the impressive outlines of her massive religious-education buildings. Over and over I have found myself saying: "What kind of people worship here? Who is their God? Where were their voices when the lips of Governor Barnett dripped with words of interposition and nullification? Where were they when Governor Wallace gave a clarion call for defiance and hatred? Where were their voices of support when bruised and weary Negro men and women decided to rise from the dark dungeons of complacency to the bright hills of creative protest?"

Yes, these questions are still in my mind. In deep disappointment I have wept over the laxity of the church. But be assured that my tears have been tears of love. There can be no deep disappointment where there is not deep love. Yes, I love the church. How could I do otherwise? I am in the rather unique position of being the son, the grandson, and the great-grandson of preachers. Yes, I see the church as the body of Christ. But, Oh! How we have blemished and scarred that body through social neglect and through fear of being nonconformists.

There was a time when the church was very powerful—in the time 40 when the early Christians rejoiced at being deemed worthy to suffer for what they believed. In those days the church was not merely a thermometer that recorded the ideas and principles of popular opinion; it was a thermostat that transformed the mores of society. Whenever the early Christians entered a town, the people in power became disturbed and immediately sought to convict the Christians for being "disturbers of the peace" and "outside agitators." But the Christians pressed on, in the conviction that they were "a colony of heaven," called to obey God rather than man. Small in number, they were big in commitment. They were too God-intoxicated to be "astronomically intimidated." By their effort and example they brought an end to such ancient evils as infanticide and gladiatorial contests.

Things are different now. So often the contemporary church is a weak, ineffectual voice with an uncertain sound. So often it is an archdefender of the status quo. Far from being disturbed by the presence of the church, the power structure of the average community is consoled by the church's silent—and often even vocal—sanction of things as they are.

But the judgment of God is upon the church as never before. If today's church does not recapture the sacrificial spirit of the early church, it will lose its authenticity, forfeit the loyalty of millions, and be dismissed as an irrelevant social club with no meaning for the twentieth century. Every day I meet young people whose disappointment with the church has turned into outright disgust.

Perhaps I have once again been too optimistic. Is organized religion too inextricably bound to the status quo to save our nation and the world? Perhaps I must turn my faith to the inner spiritual church, the church within the church, as the true *ekklesia*[6] and the hope of the world. But again I am thankful to God that some noble souls from the ranks of organized religion have broken loose from the paralyzing chains of conformity and joined us as active partners in the struggle for freedom. They have left their secure congregations and walked the streets of Albany, Georgia, with us. They have gone down the highways of the South on tortuous rides for freedom. Yes, they have gone to jail with us. Some have been dismissed from their churches, have lost the support of their bishops and fellow ministers. But they have acted in the faith that right defeated is stronger than evil triumphant. Their witness has been the spiritual salt that has preserved the true meaning of the gospel in these troubled times. They have carved a tunnel of hope through the dark mountain of disappointment.

I hope the church as a whole will meet the challenge of this decisive hour. But even if the church does not come to the aid of justice, I have no despair about the future. I have no fear about the outcome of our struggle in Birmingham, even if our motives are at present misunderstood. We will reach the goal of freedom in Birmingham and all over the nation, because the goal of America is freedom. Abused and scorned though we may be, our destiny is tied up with America's destiny. Before the pilgrims landed at Plymouth, we were here. Before the pen of Jefferson etched the majestic words of the Declaration of Independence across the pages of history, we were here. For more than two centuries our forebears labored in this country without wages; they made cotton king; they built the homes of their masters while suffering gross injustice and shameful humiliation—and yet out of a bottomless vitality they continue to thrive and develop. If the inexpressible cruelties of slavery could not stop us, the opposition we

[6]*ekklesia* A gathering or assembly of citizens (Greek).

now face will surely fail. We will win our freedom because the sacred heritage of our nation and the eternal will of God are embodied in our echoing demands.

Before closing I feel impelled to mention one other point in your 45 statement that has troubled me profoundly. You warmly commended the Birmingham police force for keeping "order" and "preventing violence." I doubt that you would have so warmly commended the police force if you had seen its dogs sinking their teeth into unarmed, nonviolent Negroes. I doubt that you would so quickly commend the policemen if you were to observe their ugly and inhumane treatment of Negroes here in the city jail; if you were to watch them push and curse old Negro women and young Negro girls; if you were to see them slap and kick old Negro men and young boys; if you were to observe them, as they did on two occasions, refuse to give us food because we wanted to sing our grace together. I cannot join you in your praise of the Birmingham police department.

It is true that the police have exercised a degree of discipline in handling the demonstrators. In this sense they have conducted themselves rather "nonviolently" in public. But for what purpose? To preserve the evil system of segregation. Over the past few years I have consistently preached that nonviolence demands that the means we use must be as pure as the ends we seek. I have tried to make clear that it is wrong to use immoral means to attain moral ends. But now I must affirm that it is just as wrong, or perhaps even more so, to use moral means to preserve immoral ends. Perhaps Mr. Connor and his policemen have been rather nonviolent in public, as was Chief Pritchett in Albany, Georgia, but they used the moral means of nonviolence to maintain the immoral end of racial injustice. As T. S. Eliot has said: "The last temptation is the greatest treason: To do the right deed for the wrong reason."

I wish you had commended the Negro sit-inners and demonstrators of Birmingham for their sublime courage, their willingness to suffer, and their amazing discipline in the midst of great provocation. One day the South will recognize its real heroes. They will be the James Merediths, with the noble sense of purpose that enables them to face jeering and hostile mobs, and with the agonizing loneliness that characterizes the life of the pioneer. They will be old, oppressed, battered Negro women, symbolized in a seventy-two-year-old woman in Montgomery, Alabama, who rose up with a sense of dignity and with her people decided not to ride segregated buses, and who responded with ungrammatical profundity to one who inquired about her weariness: "My feets is tired, but my soul is at rest." They will be the young high school and college students, the young ministers of the gospel and a host of their elders, courageously and nonviolently sitting in at lunch counters and willingly going to jail for conscience's sake. One day the South will know that when these disinherited children of God sat down at lunch counters, they were in reality standing up for what is best in the American dream and for the most sacred values in our Judaeo-Christian heritage, thereby bringing our nation back to those great wells of democracy which were dug deep by the founding fathers in their formulation of the Constitution and the Declaration of Independence.

Never before have I written so long a letter. I'm afraid it is much too long to take your precious time. I can assure you that it would have been much shorter if I had been writing from a comfortable desk, but what else can one do when he is alone in a narrow jail cell, other than write long letters, think long thoughts, and pray long prayers?

If I have said anything in this letter that overstates the truth and indicates an unreasonable impatience, I beg you to forgive me. If I have said anything that understates the truth and indicates my having a patience that allows me to settle for anything less than brotherhood, I beg God to forgive me.

I hope this letter finds you strong in the faith. I also hope that cir- 50 cumstances will soon make it possible for me to meet each of you, not as an integrationist or a civil-rights leader but as a fellow clergyman and a Christian brother. Let us all hope that the dark clouds of racial preju-dice will soon pass away and the deep fog of misunderstanding will be lifted from our fear-drenched communities, and in some not too distant tomorrow the radiant stars of love and brotherhood will shine over our great nation with all their scintillating beauty.

Yours for the cause of Peace and Brotherhood,
Martin Luther King Jr.

Topics for Critical Thinking and Writing

1. In his first five paragraphs of the "Letter," how does King assure his audience that he is not a meddlesome intruder but a man of goodwill?

2. In paragraph 3 King refers to Hebrew prophets and to the Apostle Paul and later (para. 10) to Socrates. What is the point of these references?

3. In paragraph 11 what does King mean when he says that "our beloved Southland" has long tried to "live in monologue rather than dialogue"?

4. King begins paragraph 23 with "I must make two honest confessions to you, my Christian and Jewish brothers." What would have been gained or lost if he had used this paragraph as his opening?

5. King's last three paragraphs do not advance his argument. What do they do?

6. Why does King advocate breaking unjust laws "openly, lovingly" (para. 20)? What does he mean by these words? What other motives or attitudes do these words rule out?

7. Construct two definitions of *civil disobedience*, and explain whether and to what extent it is easier (or harder) to justify civil disobedience, depending on how you have defined the expression.

8. If you feel that you wish to respond to King's letter on some point, write a letter nominally addressed to King. You may, if you wish, adopt the persona of one of the eight clergymen whom King initially addressed.

9. King writes (para. 46) that "nonviolence demands that the means we use must be as pure as the ends we seek." How do you think King would evaluate the following acts: (a) occupying a college administration building to protest the administration's unsatisfactory response to a racial incident on campus or its failure to hire minority persons as staff and faculty; (b) occupying an abortion clinic to protest abortion? Set down your answer in an essay of 500 words.

10. Compose a letter from King in which he responds to Plato's "Crito" (p. 707).

Peter Cave

Peter Cave teaches philosophy at the Open University and City University of London. He is the author of Can a Robot Be Human? 33 Perplexing Philosophy Puzzles *(2007) and* What's Wrong with Eating People? 33 More Perplexing Philosophy Puzzles *(2008). We reprint an essay from the second book.*

Man or Sheep?

Thomas Hobbes, a key political philosopher of the seventeenth century, wrote that man's life was "solitary, poor, nasty, brutish, and short." The obvious reply is, "It could have been worse, Thomas; it could have been solitary, poor, nasty, brutish—and long."

Hobbes was describing life before the existence of a state, government, and law. Humans are competitive. They lack reason to trust each other, unless there is a powerful authority that sets laws and punishes law-breakers. In a state of nature, individuals would be in constant conflict or, at least, always on their guard, insecure, and ready for battle. The state of nature, of life pre-government, is a state of war. With the state of nature so horrible, human beings would obviously want to get out, into something better. According to Hobbes, they would come together and agree on a sovereign, an absolute authority, to represent and rule over them, giving them security and opportunity to lead reasonable lives.

There are many puzzles, not least why individuals in the state of nature would risk trusting each other to keep to any agreement. Let us, though, not worry about how government arises. Here we are, living within a state. Let us assume we have a government democratically elected. However, whatever the degree of democracy, laws are imposed that restrict what we may do. We may disapprove of some laws because of some moral or religious principles; we may disapprove of other laws simply because they prevent us from getting what we want. The general concern becomes: By what authority does any government rightfully rule over us?

WHY SHOULD WE OBEY
THE STATE AND ITS LAWS?

We may answer in practical terms. We obey the law because we are scared of the consequences of disobedience, not wanting to risk fines and imprisonment. The rational thing to do, given the aim of getting on with our lives as best we can, is to obey. When asked whether man or mouse, some of us tend to squeak and take the cheese. Even more so may most of us squeak, when the tentacles of the law and the long arm of the police take hold. We mice may, indeed, be more akin to sheep, sheepishly following each other in our general obedience. Our puzzle though is what, if anything, makes obeying the law the *right* thing to do—even if we could get away with disobeying.

Many of us benefit because of the state's existence: We are defended 5 from others, receive state education, health services, in return for paying taxes. We are better off with law than without. So, we are obligated, in return, to obey the laws that confer those benefits. One immediate objection is that this justification for lawful obedience fails to work for those who overall do not benefit. A significant number do very badly, sleeping rough, being denied state benefits, and being avoided by those better off. Why should they obey? Also, some at society's top may argue that they contribute more than they receive—probably forgetting that they secured the more because of society's stability and protection of gross inequalities often inherited.

Even when overall we do benefit from the state's existence, it does not follow that we are under any obligation to the benefactor. Did we ever sign up, agreeing that we would accept benefits in return for obeying the law? If someone buys us a drink, without our asking, are we under an obligation to buy one in return?

Reference to "signing up" casts us along another line, a line orientated towards the "social contract." What justifies the state and our obedience is that we consented to the set-up. Some philosophers, John Locke and arguably Hobbes, believed that historically some individuals made contracts to be governed by an authority acting in their interests, leading to our societies. Of course, there is no reason to believe in such historical events; but, even if they occurred, whatever relevance do they have for us today? We were not around hundreds of years ago, engaged in any contractual deals.

The response to that last thought is to spot features of our current lives that may indicate consent. We make use of the state's services; we travel freely on the King's highway, notes Locke—well, today the Queen's highway. This shows that we tacitly consent to the state—or does it? Just because we remain in this country, using its facilities, it does not follow that we consent: After all, what other options are available? Can most people afford to go elsewhere? Would other countries, with acceptable laws, permit entry? It is as if we find ourselves on a ship in the middle of the ocean, with the captain making the point that we are free to leave.

Rationality is often wheeled out, to come to the rescue. True, we were not involved in any original social contract; true, our remaining within our society fails to establish consent. But suppose we were rational, not yet in a society, and needing to create society's laws. Suppose, too, we were ignorant of our sex, race, abilities, and the position we probably would reach in society, be it through chance or talent. In such an original position, behind a veil of ignorance, where everything is fair between us, our thinking, even though we remain as individuals, would not be distorted by a distinctive self-interest differing from the self-interest of others. Rather, our common rationality and interests should lead us to see and accept what would be fair laws, benefits, and rights for all. Behind the veil of ignorance, it would seem rational to consent to a society that permitted basic freedoms, did not discriminate between individuals on irrelevant grounds, and provided welfare benefits for when things go badly. After all, behind the veil of ignorance, we have no idea whether we may end up belonging to minority groups or hitting on hard times. If our current society possesses the features it would be rational to consent to behind the veil, then our obedience today is justified by this hypothetical consent, by what is seen as a hypothetical contract.

The response, by way of jibe, is that hypothetical contracts are not 10 worth the paper they are not written upon. Hypothetical consent is not consent. The jibe, though, misses the point. Justifications can rightly involve hypotheticals. Why did you battle with the man, yanking him from the cliff's path, despite his protests? "Because, had he been sober, he would have consented to the yanking, to save him from risking a fatal fall."

The resort to the veil of ignorance, to rationality, and the hypothetical, though, raises its own puzzles. Quite what does rationality involve behind such a veil? Is it rational, for example, to place liberty higher than greater welfare benefits requiring higher levels of taxation?

Whatever justifications are offered for general obedience to the state, sometimes we morally ought to disobey. Had only many, many consulted their conscience instead of the law, various atrocities, instituted by governments, could have been avoided. Had only many, many been aware of their humanity rather than going along with the mice and the sheep . . .

Mind you, that is so easy for me to say and you to read as, in all likelihood, we sit reasonably well off, looking at this book, not having to stand up and be counted—and also not scraping a living in desperate circumstances. We are cocooned, indeed, from millions of dispossessed in the world for whom life is certainly nasty, brutish, and short.

TOPICS FOR CRITICAL THINKING AND WRITING

1. Name five things or services (e.g., paved sidewalks, the police) that you did not create or establish but from which you benefit (para. 6).

2. Why is the "social contract" so called (paras. 6–8)?

3. Did the voyagers on the *Mayflower* (1620) create a social contract among themselves? How can you tell?

4. Is the following proposition—"We are not morally obligated by the deeds of our predecessors"—true? Why, or why not? Explain your answer.

5. What counts as a free, voluntary compact to obey some laws? What would you have to do to show that you (no longer) consent to be governed by the government under which you live?

Thomas Hardy

Thomas Hardy (1840–1928) was born in Dorset, England, the son of a stonemason. Despite great obstacles, he studied the classics and architecture, and in 1862 he moved to London to study and practice as an architect. Ill health forced him to return to Dorset, where he continued to work as an architect and to write. Best known for his novels, Hardy ceased writing fiction after the hostile reception of Jude the Obscure *in 1896 and turned to writing lyric poetry. We print a poem of 1902.*

The Man He Killed

"Had he and I but met
By some old ancient inn,
We should have sat us down to wet
Right many a nipperkin°!

"But ranged an infantry,   5
And staring face to face,
I shot at him as he at me,
And killed him in his place.

"I shot him dead because—
Because he was my foe,   10
Just so: my foe of course he was;
That's clear enough; although

"He thought he'd 'list, perhaps,
Off-hand like—just as I—
Was out of work—had sold his traps°—   15
No other reason why.

"Yes; quaint and curious war is!
You shoot a fellow down
You'd treat if met where any bar is,
Or help to half-a-crown."   20

---

4 nipperkin Cup.   **15 traps** Personal belongings. [Both notes are the editors'.]

TOPICS FOR CRITICAL THINKING AND WRITING

1. Hardy published this poem in 1902, at the conclusion of the Boer War (1899–1902, also called the South African War), a war between the Boers (Dutch) and the British for possession of part of Africa. The speaker of the poem is an English veteran of the war. Do you think such a poem might just as well have been written by an English (or American) soldier in World War II? Explain.

2. Characterize the speaker. What sort of man does he seem to be? Pay special attention to the punctuation in the third and fourth stanzas—what do the pauses indicated by the dashes, the colons, and the semicolons tell us about him?—and pay special attention to the final stanza, in which he speaks of war as "quaint and curious" (line 17). Do you think that Hardy too would speak of war this way? Why, or why not? Can you imagine an American soldier in the Vietnam War speaking of the war as "quaint and curious"? Explain.

3. Do you think we can reasonably say that the speaker of Hardy's poem possesses free will? Explain your position.

T. S. Eliot

Thomas Stearns Eliot (1888–1965) was born into a New England family that had moved to St. Louis. He attended a preparatory school in Massachusetts, graduated from Harvard University, and then continued his studies in literature in France, Germany, and England. In 1914 he began working for Lloyds Bank in London, and three years later he published his first book of poems, which included "Prufrock." In 1925 he joined a publishing firm, and in 1927 he became a British citizen and a member of the Church of England. In 1948 he received the Nobel Prize for Literature.

The Love Song of J. Alfred Prufrock

S'io credesse che mia risposta fosse
A persona che mai tornasse al mondo,
Questa fiamma staria senza più scosse.
Ma perciocchè giammai di questo fondo
Non torno vivo alcun, s' i' odo il vero,
Senza tema d'infamia ti rispondo.°

S'io ... rispondo The Italian epigraph that begins the poem is a quotation from Dante's *Divine Comedy* (1321). In this passage, a damned soul in hell who had sought absolution before committing a crime addresses Dante, thinking that his words will never reach the earth. He says: "If I thought that my answer were to someone who could ever return to the world, this flame would be still, without further motion. But because no one has ever returned alive from this depth, if what I hear is true, without fear of shame I answer you." [All notes are the editors'.]

Let us go then, you and I,
When the evening is spread out against the sky
Like a patient etherised upon a table;
Let us go, through certain half-deserted streets,
The muttering retreats   5
Of restless nights in one-night cheap hotels
And sawdust restaurants with oyster-shells:
Streets that follow like a tedious argument
Of insidious intent
To lead you to an overwhelming question . . .   10
Oh, do not ask, "What is it?"
Let us go and make our visit.

In the room the women come and go
Talking of Michelangelo.

The yellow fog that rubs its back upon the window-panes,   15
The yellow smoke that rubs its muzzle on the window-panes
Licked its tongue into the corners of the evening,
Lingered upon the pools that stand in drains,
Let fall upon its back the soot that falls from chimneys,
Slipped by the terrace, made a sudden leap,   20
And seeing that it was a soft October night,
Curled once about the house, and fell asleep.

And indeed there will be time
For the yellow smoke that slides along the street,
Rubbing its back upon the window-panes;   25
There will be time, there will be time
To prepare a face to meet the faces that you meet;
There will be time to murder and create,
And time for all the works and days° of hands
That lift and drop a question on your plate;   30
Time for you and time for me,
And time yet for a hundred indecisions,
And for a hundred visions and revisions,
Before the taking of a toast and tea.

In the room the women come and go   35
Talking of Michelangelo
And indeed there will be time
To wonder, "Do I dare?" and, "Do I dare?"
Time to turn back and descend the stair,
With a bald spot in the middle of my hair—   40
[They will say: "How his hair is growing thin!"]
My morning coat, my collar mounting firmly to the chin,
My necktie rich and modest, but asserted by a simple pin—

---

29 works and days The title of a poem on farm life by Hesiod (Greek, eighth century B.C.).

[They will say: "But how his arms and legs are thin!"]
Do I dare   45
Disturb the universe?
In a minute there is time
For decisions and revisions which a minute will reverse.

For I have known them all already, known them all:—
Have known the evenings, mornings, afternoons,   50
I have measured out my life with coffee spoons;
I know the voices dying with a dying fall°
Beneath the music from a farther room.
        So how should I presume?

And I have known the eyes already, known them all—   55
The eyes that fix you in a formulated phrase,
And when I am formulated, sprawling on a pin,
When I am pinned and wriggling on the wall,
Then how should I begin
To spit out all the butt-ends of my days and ways?   60
        And how should I presume?

And I have known the arms already, known them all—
Arms that are braceleted and white and bare
[But in the lamplight, downed with light brown hair!]
Is it perfume from a dress   65
That makes me so digress?
Arms that lie along a table, or wrap about a shawl.
        And should I then presume?
        And how should I begin?
                .....
Shall I say, I have gone at dusk through narrow streets   70
And watched the smoke that rises from the pipes
Of lonely men in shirt-sleeves, leaning out of windows? . . .

I should have been a pair of ragged claws
Scuttling across the floors of silent seas.
                .....
And the afternoon, the evening, sleeps so peacefully!   75
Smoothed by long fingers,
Asleep . . . tired . . . or it malingers,
Stretched on the floor, here beside you and me.
Should I, after tea and cakes and ices,
Have the strength to force the moment to its crisis?   80
But though I have wept and fasted, wept and prayed,
Though I have seen my head [grown slightly bald]
        brought in upon a platter,°

---

52 dying fall Echoes Shakespeare's *Twelfth Night* 1.1.4.   **82 head . . . platter** Alludes to
John the Baptist, whose head was delivered on a platter to Salome.

I am no prophet—and here's no great matter;
I have seen the moment of my greatness flicker,
And I have seen the eternal Footman hold my coat, and
     snicker,   85
And in short, I was afraid.

And would it have been worth it, after all,
After the cups, the marmalade, the tea,
Among the porcelain, among some talk of you and me,
Would it have been worth while,   90
To have bitten off the matter with a smile,
To have squeezed the universe into a ball
To roll° it toward some overwhelming question,
To say: "I am Lazarus,° come from the dead,
Come back to tell you all, I shall tell you all"—   95
If one, settling a pillow by her head,
     Should say: "That is not what I meant at all.
     That is not it, at all."

And would it have been worth it, after all,
Would it have been worth while,   100
After the sunsets and the dooryards and the sprinkled streets,
After the novels, after the teacups, after the skirts
     that trail along the floor—
And this, and so much more?—
It is impossible to say just what I mean!
But as if a magic lantern threw the nerves in patterns
     on a screen: 105
Would it have been worth while
If one, settling a pillow or throwing off a shawl,
And turning toward the window, should say:
     "That is not it at all,
     That is not what I meant, at all."   110
         . . . . .
No! I am not Prince Hamlet,° nor was meant to be;
Am an attendant lord, one that will do
To swell a progress, start a scene or two,
Advise the prince; no doubt, an easy tool,
Deferential, glad to be of use,   115
Politic, cautious, and meticulous;

92–93 ball To roll Echoes Andrew Marvell's "To His Coy Mistress," lines 41–42 (see p. 436).
94 Lazarus Mentioned in the New Testament: John 11; Lazarus rises from the dead at the command of Jesus.
111 Prince Hamlet The next few lines allude to lesser figures in Shakespeare's tragedy, specifically to Polonius, a self-satisfied fatuous courtier.

Full of high sentence,° but a bit obtuse;
At times, indeed, almost ridiculous—
Almost, at times, the Fool.

I grow old . . . I grow old . . .   120
I shall wear the bottoms of my trousers rolled.

Shall I part my hair behind? Do I dare to eat a peach?
I shall wear white flannel trousers, and walk upon the beach.
I have heard the mermaids singing, each to each.
I do not think that they will sing to me.   125

I have seen them riding seaward on the waves
Combing the white hair of the waves blown back
When the wind blows the water white and black.

We have lingered in the chambers of the sea
By sea-girls wreathed with seaweed red and brown   130
Till human voices wake us, and we drown.

Topics for Critical Thinking and Writing

1. One of the most famous images of the poem compares the evening to "a
    patient etherised upon a table" (line 3). Does the image also suggest that
    individuals—for instance, Prufrock—may not be fully conscious and
    therefore are not responsible for their actions or their inactions?

2. Are lines 57 to 60 meant to evoke the reader's pity for the speaker? If
    not, what (if any) response are these lines intended to evoke?

3. The speaker admits he is "At times, indeed, . . . / Almost . . . the Fool" (lines
    118–19). Where, if at all, in the poem do we see him not at all as a fool?

4. Do you take the poem to be a criticism of an individual, a society, nei-
    ther, or both? Why?

5. Evaluate this critical judgment, offering evidence to support your view:
    "The poem is obscure: It begins in Italian, and it includes references that
    most readers can't know. It is not at all uplifting. In fact, in so far as it
    is comprehensible, it is depressing. These are not the characteristics of a
    great poem."

6. The poem is chiefly concerned with the thoughts of a man, J. Alfred
    Prufrock. Do you think it therefore is of more interest to men than to
    women? Explain.

7. The speaker describes the streets he walks as "follow[ing] like a tedious
    argument" (line 8). Is the simile apt? When do you think an argument
    becomes tedious?

---

117 Full of high sentence Full of thoughtful sayings; comes from Chaucer's description
of the Oxford student in *The Canterbury Tales.*

Susan Glaspell

Susan Glaspell (1882–1948) was born in Davenport, Iowa, and educated at Drake University in Des Moines. In 1903 she married George Cram Cook and, with Cook and other writers, actors, and artists, in 1915 founded the Provincetown Players, a group that remained vital until 1929. Glaspell wrote Trifles *(1916) for the Provincetown Players, but she also wrote stories, novels, and a biography of her husband. In 1931 she won the Pulitzer Prize for* Alison's House, *a play about the family of a deceased poet who in some ways resembles Emily Dickinson.*

Trifles

(**SCENE:** *The kitchen in the now abandoned farmhouse of John Wright, a gloomy kitchen, and left without having been put in order—unwashed pans under the sink, a loaf of bread outside the breadbox, a dish towel on the table—other signs of incompleted work. At the rear the outer door opens, and the Sheriff comes in, followed by the County Attorney and Hale. The Sheriff and Hale are men in middle life, the County Attorney is a young man; all are much bundled up and go at once to the stove. They are followed by the two women—the Sheriff's Wife first; she is a slight wiry woman, a thin nervous face. Mrs. Hale is larger and would ordinarily be called more comfortable looking, but she is disturbed now and looks fearfully about as she enters. The women have come in slowly and stand close together near the door.*)

COUNTY ATTORNEY *(rubbing his hands).* This feels good. Come up to the fire, ladies.

MRS. PETERS *(after taking a step forward).* I'm not—cold.

SHERIFF *(unbuttoning his overcoat and stepping away from the stove as if to the beginning of official business).* Now, Mr. Hale, before we move things about, you explain to Mr. Henderson just what you saw when you came here yesterday morning.

COUNTY ATTORNEY. By the way, has anything been moved? Are things just as you left them yesterday?

SHERIFF *(looking about).* It's just the same. When it dropped below zero last 5 night, I thought I'd better send Frank out this morning to make a fire for us—no use getting pneumonia with a big case on; but I told him not to touch anything except the stove—and you know Frank.

COUNTY ATTORNEY. Somebody should have been left here yesterday.

SHERIFF. Oh—yesterday. When I had to send Frank to Morris Center for that man who went crazy—I want you to know I had my hands full yesterday. I knew you could get back from Omaha by today, and as long as I went over everything here myself—

COUNTY ATTORNEY. Well, Mr. Hale, tell just what happened when you came here yesterday morning.

HALE. Harry and I had started to town with a load of potatoes. We came along the road from my place; and as I got here, I said, "I'm going to see if I can't get John Wright to go in with me on a party telephone." I spoke to Wright about it once before, and he put me off, saying folks

talked too much anyway, and all he asked was peace and quiet—I
guess you know about how much he talked himself; but I thought
maybe if I went to the house and talked about it before his wife,
though I said to Harry that I didn't know as what his wife wanted
made much difference to John—

COUNTY ATTORNEY. Let's talk about that later, Mr. Hale. I do want to talk   10
about that, but tell now just what happened when you got to the
house.

HALE. I didn't hear or see anything; I knocked at the door, and still it was
all quiet inside. I knew they must be up, it was past eight o'clock. So
I knocked again, and I thought I heard somebody say, "Come in."
I wasn't sure, I'm not sure yet, but I opened the door—this door
(indicating the door by which the two women are still standing), and there
in that rocker—*(pointing to it)* sat Mrs. Wright. *(They all look at the
rocker.)*

COUNTY ATTORNEY. What—was she doing?

HALE. She was rockin' back and forth. She had her apron in her hand and
was kind of—pleating it.

COUNTY ATTORNEY. And how did she—look?

HALE. Well, she looked queer.   15

COUNTY ATTORNEY. How do you mean—queer?

HALE. Well, as if she didn't know what she was going to do next. And
kind of done up.

COUNTY ATTORNEY. How did she seem to feel about your coming?

HALE. Why, I don't think she minded—one way or other. She didn't pay
much attention. I said, "How do, Mrs. Wright, it's cold, ain't it?"
And she said, "Is it?"—and went on kind of pleating at her apron.
Well, I was surprised; she didn't ask me to come up to the stove,
or to set down, but just sat there, not even looking at me, so I said,
"I want to see John." And then she—laughed. I guess you would
call it a laugh. I thought of Harry and the team outside, so I said
a little sharp: "Can't I see John?" "No," she says, kind o' dull like.
"Ain't he home?" says I. "Yes," says she, "he's home." "Then why
can't I see him?" I asked her, out of patience. "'Cause he's dead,"
says she. *"Dead?"* says I. She just nodded her head, not getting a bit
excited, but rockin' back and forth. "Why—where is he?" says I, not
knowing what to say. She just pointed upstairs—like that *(himself
pointing to the room above)*. I got up, with the idea of going up there.
I walked from there to here—then I says, "Why, what did he die
of?" "He died of a rope around his neck," says she, and just went on
pleatin' at her apron. Well, I went out and called Harry. I thought I
might—need help. We went upstairs, and there he was lyin'—

COUNTY ATTORNEY. I think I'd rather have you go into that upstairs, where   20
you can point it all out. Just go on now with the rest of the story.

HALE. Well, my first thought was to get that rope off. I looked . . . *(Stops, his
face twitches.)* . . . but Harry, he went up to him, and he said, "No, he's

dead all right, and we'd better not touch anything." So we went back downstairs. She was still sitting that same way. "Has anybody been notified?" I asked. "No," says she, unconcerned. "Who did this, Mrs. Wright?" said Harry. He said it businesslike—and she stopped pleatin' of her apron. "I don't know," she says. "You don't *know*?" says Harry. "No," says she. "Weren't you sleepin' in the bed with him?" says Harry. "Yes," says she, "but I was on the inside." "Somebody slipped a rope round his neck and strangled him, and you didn't wake up?" says Harry. "I didn't wake up," she said after him. We must 'a looked as if we didn't see how that could be, for after a minute she said, "I sleep sound." Harry was going to ask her more questions, but I said maybe we ought to let her tell her story first to the coroner, or the sheriff, so Harry went fast as he could to Rivers' place, where there's a telephone.

COUNTY ATTORNEY. And what did Mrs. Wright do when she knew that you had gone for the coroner?

HALE. She moved from that chair to this over here . . . *(Pointing to a small chair in the corner.)* . . . and just sat there with her hands held together and looking down. I got a feeling that I ought to make some conversation, so I said I had come in to see if John wanted to put in a telephone, and at that she started to laugh, and then she stopped and looked at me—scared. *(The County Attorney, who has had his notebook out, makes a note.)* I dunno, maybe it wasn't scared. I wouldn't like to say it was. Soon Harry got back, and then Dr. Lloyd came, and you, Mr. Peters, and so I guess that's all I know that you don't.

COUNTY ATTORNEY *(looking around)*. I guess we'll go upstairs first—and then out to the barn and around there. *(To the Sheriff.)* You're convinced that there was nothing important here—nothing that would point to any motive?

SHERIFF. Nothing here but kitchen things. *(The County Attorney, after again looking around the kitchen, opens the door of a cupboard closet. He gets up on a chair and looks on a shelf. Pulls his hand away, sticky.)*   25

COUNTY ATTORNEY. Here's a nice mess. *(The women draw nearer.)*

MRS. PETERS *(to the other woman)*. Oh, her fruit; it did freeze. *(To the Lawyer.)* She worried about that when it turned so cold. She said the fire'd go out and her jars would break.

SHERIFF. Well, can you beat the woman! Held for murder and worryin' about her preserves.

COUNTY ATTORNEY. I guess before we're through she may have something more serious than preserves to worry about.

HALE. Well, women are used to worrying over trifles. *(The two women move   30 a little closer together.)*

COUNTY ATTORNEY *(with the gallantry of a young politician)*. And yet, for all their worries, what would we do without the ladies? *(The women do not unbend. He goes to the sink, takes a dipperful of water from the pail and, pouring it into a basin, washes his hands. Starts to wipe them on the roller towel, turns it for a cleaner place.)* Dirty towels! *(Kicks his foot against the pans under the sink.)* Not much of a housekeeper, would you say, ladies?

MRS. HALE *(stiffly).* There's a great deal of work to be done on a farm.

COUNTY ATTORNEY. To be sure. And yet . . . *(With a little bow to her.)* . . . I know there are some Dickson county farmhouses which do not have such roller towels. *(He gives it a pull to expose its full length again.)*

MRS. HALE. Those towels get dirty awful quick. Men's hands aren't always as clean as they might be.

COUNTY ATTORNEY. Ah, loyal to your sex. I see. But you and Mrs. Wright 35 were neighbors. I suppose you were friends, too.

MRS. HALE *(shaking her head).* I've not seen much of her of late years. I've not been in this house—it's more than a year.

COUNTY ATTORNEY. And why was that? You didn't like her?

MRS. HALE. I liked her all well enough. Farmers' wives have their hands full, Mr. Henderson. And then—

COUNTY ATTORNEY. Yes—?

MRS. HALE *(looking about).* It never seemed a very cheerful place. 40

COUNTY ATTORNEY. No—it's not cheerful. I shouldn't say she had the home-making instinct.

MRS. HALE. Well, I don't know as Wright had, either.

COUNTY ATTORNEY. You mean they didn't get on very well?

MRS. HALE. No, I don't mean anything. But I don't think a place'd be any cheerfuller for John Wright's being in it.

COUNTY ATTORNEY. I'd like to talk more of that a little later. I want to get the 45 lay of things upstairs now. *(He goes to the left, where three steps lead to a stair door.)*

SHERIFF. I suppose anything Mrs. Peters does'll be all right. She was to take in some clothes for her, you know, and a few little things. We left in such a hurry yesterday.

COUNTY ATTORNEY. Yes, but I would like to see what you take, Mrs. Peters, and keep an eye out for anything that might be of use to us.

MRS. PETERS. Yes, Mr. Henderson. *(The women listen to the men's steps on the stairs, then look about the kitchen.)*

MRS. HALE. I'd hate to have men coming into my kitchen, snooping around and criticizing. *(She arranges the pans under the sink which the Lawyer had shoved out of place.)*

MRS. PETERS. Of course it's no more than their duty. 50

MRS. HALE. Duty's all right, but I guess that deputy sheriff that came out to make the fire might have got a little of this on. *(Gives the roller towel a pull.)* Wish I'd thought of that sooner. Seems mean to talk about her for not having things slicked up when she had to come away in such a hurry.

MRS. PETERS *(who has gone to a small table in the left rear corner of the room, and lifted one end of a towel that covers a pan).* She had bread set. *(Stands still.)*

MRS. HALE *(eyes fixed on a loaf of bread beside the breadbox, which is on a low shelf at the other side of the room. Moves slowly toward it).* She was going to put this in there. (*Picks up loaf, then abruptly drops it. In a manner of returning to familiar things.*) It's a shame about her fruit. I wonder if it's all gone. (*Gets up on the chair and looks.*) I think there's some here that's all right, Mrs. Peters. Yes—here; (*Holding it toward the window.*) this is cherries, too. (*Looking again.*) I declare I believe that's the only one. (*Gets down, bottle in her hand. Goes to the sink and wipes it off on the outside.*) She'll feel awful bad after all her hard work in the hot weather. I remember the afternoon I put up my cherries last summer. (*She puts the bottle on the big kitchen table, center of the room. With a sigh, is about to sit down in the rocking chair. Before she is seated realizes what chair it is; with a slow look at it, steps back. The chair, which she has touched, rocks back and forth.*)

MRS. PETERS. Well, I must get those things from the front room closet. (*She goes to the door at the right, but after looking into the other room steps back.*) You coming with me, Mrs. Hale? You could help me carry them. (*They go into the other room; reappear, Mrs. Peters carrying a dress and skirt, Mrs. Hale following with a pair of shoes.*)

MRS. PETERS. My, it's cold in there. (*She puts the cloth on the big table, and hurries to the stove.*)   55

MRS. HALE (*examining the skirt*). Wright was close. I think maybe that's why she kept so much to herself. She didn't even belong to the Ladies' Aid. I suppose she felt she couldn't do her part, and then you don't enjoy things when you feel shabby. She used to wear pretty clothes and be lively, when she was Minnie Foster, one of the town girls singing in the choir. But that—oh, that was thirty years ago. This all you was to take in?

MRS. PETERS. She said she wanted an apron. Funny thing to want, for there isn't much to get you dirty in jail, goodness knows. But I suppose just to make her feel more natural. She said they was in the top drawer in this cupboard. Yes, here. And then her little shawl that always hung behind the door. (*Opens stair door and looks.*) Yes, here it is. (*Quickly shuts door leading upstairs.*)

MRS. HALE (*abruptly moving toward her*). Mrs. Peters?

MRS. PETERS. Yes, Mrs. Hale?

MRS. HALE. Do you think she did it?   60

MRS. PETERS (*in a frightened voice*). Oh, I don't know.

MRS. HALE. Well, I don't think she did. Asking for an apron and her little shawl. Worrying about her fruit.

MRS. PETERS (*starts to speak, glances up, where footsteps are heard in the room above. In a low voice*). Mr. Peters says it looks bad for her. Mr. Henderson is awful sarcastic in speech, and he'll make fun of her sayin' she didn't wake up.

MRS. HALE. Well, I guess John Wright didn't wake when they was slipping that rope under his neck.

MRS. PETERS. No, it's strange. It must have been done awful crafty and still.   65
They say it was such a—funny way to kill a man, rigging it all up like that.

MRS. HALE. That's just what Mr. Hale said. There was a gun in the house. He says that's what he can't understand.

MRS. PETERS. Mr. Henderson said coming out that what was needed for the case was a motive; something to show anger or—sudden feeling.

MRS. HALE *(who is standing by the table)*. Well, I don't see any signs of anger around here. *(She puts her hand on the dish towel which lies on the table, stands looking down at the table, one half of which is clean, the other half messy.)* It's wiped here. *(Makes a move as if to finish work, then turns and looks at loaf of bread outside the breadbox. Drops towel. In that voice of coming back to familiar things.)* Wonder how they are finding things upstairs? I hope she had it a little more red-up there. You know, it seems kind of *sneaking*. Locking her up in town and then coming out here and trying to get her own house to turn against her!

MRS. PETERS. But, Mrs. Hale, the law is the law.

MRS. HALE. I s'pose 'tis. *(Unbuttoning her coat.)* Better loosen up your things, 70 Mrs. Peters. You won't feel them when you go out. *(Mrs. Peters takes off her fur tippet, goes to hang it on hook at the back of room, stands looking at the under part of the small corner table.)*

MRS. PETERS. She was piecing a quilt. *(She brings the large sewing basket, and they look at the bright pieces.)*

MRS. HALE. It's log cabin pattern. Pretty, isn't it? I wonder if she was goin' to quilt or just knot it? *(Footsteps have been heard coming down the stairs. The Sheriff enters, followed by Hale and the County Attorney.)*

SHERIFF. They wonder if she was going to quilt it or just knot it. *(The men laugh, the women look abashed.)*

COUNTY ATTORNEY *(rubbing his hands over the stove)*. Frank's fire didn't do much up there, did it? Well, let's go out to the barn and get that cleared up. *(The men go outside.)*

MRS. HALE *(resentfully)*. I don't know as there's anything so strange, our 75 takin' up our time with little things while we're waiting for them to get the evidence. *(She sits down at the big table, smoothing out a block with decision.)* I don't see as it's anything to laugh about.

MRS. PETERS *(apologetically)*. Of course they've got awful important things on their minds. *(Pulls up a chair and joins Mrs. Hale at the table.)*

MRS. HALE *(examining another block)*. Mrs. Peters, look at this one. Here, this is the one she was working on, and look at the sewing! All the rest of it has been so nice and even. And look at this! It's all over the place! Why, it looks as if she didn't know what she was about! *(After she has said this, they look at each other, then start to glance back at the door. After an instant Mrs. Hale has pulled at a knot and ripped the sewing.)*

MRS. PETERS. Oh, what are you doing, Mrs. Hale?

MRS. HALE *(mildly)*. Just pulling out a stitch or two that's not sewed very good. *(Threading a needle.)* Bad sewing always made me fidgety.

MRS. PETERS *(nervously)*. I don't think we ought to touch things. 80

MRS. HALE. I'll just finish up this end. *(Suddenly stopping and leaning forward.)* Mrs. Peters?

MRS. PETERS. Yes, Mrs. Hale?

MRS. HALE. What do you suppose she was so nervous about?

MRS. PETERS. Oh—I don't know. I don't know as she was nervous. I sometimes sew awful queer when I'm just tired. *(Mrs. Hale starts to say something, looks at Mrs. Peters, then goes on sewing.)* Well, I must get these things wrapped up. They may be through sooner than we think. *(Putting apron and other things together.)* I wonder where I can find a piece of paper, and string.

MRS. HALE. In that cupboard, maybe. 85

MRS. PETERS *(looking in cupboard).* Why, here's a birdcage. *(Holds it up.)* Did she have a bird, Mrs. Hale?

MRS. HALE. Why, I don't know whether she did or not—I've not been here for so long. There was a man around last year selling canaries cheap, but I don't know as she took one; maybe she did. She used to sing real pretty herself.

MRS. PETERS *(glancing around).* Seems funny to think of a bird here. But she must have had one, or why should she have a cage? I wonder what happened to it?

MRS. HALE. I s'pose maybe the cat got it.

MRS. PETERS. No, she didn't have a cat. She's got that feeling some people 90 have about cats—being afraid of them. My cat got in her room, and she was real upset and asked me to take it out.

MRS. HALE. My sister Bessie was like that. Queer, ain't it?

MRS. PETERS *(examining the cage).* Why, look at this door. It's broke. One hinge is pulled apart.

MRS. HALE *(looking, too).* Looks as if someone must have been rough with it.

MRS. PETERS. Why, yes. *(She brings the cage forward and puts it on the table.)*

MRS. HALE. I wish if they're going to find any evidence they'd be about it. I 95 don't like this place.

MRS. PETERS. But I'm awful glad you came with me, Mrs. Hale. It would be lonesome for me sitting here alone.

MRS. HALE. It would, wouldn't it? *(Dropping her sewing.)* But I tell you what I do wish, Mrs. Peters. I wish I had come over sometimes when *she* was here. I—*(Looking around the room.)*—wish I had.

MRS. PETERS. But of course you were awful busy, Mrs. Hale—your house and your children.

MRS. HALE. I could've come. I stayed away because it weren't cheerful— and that's why I ought to have come. I—I've never liked this place. Maybe because it's down in a hollow, and you don't see the road. I dunno what it is, but it's a lonesome place and always was. I wish I had come over to see Minnie Foster sometimes. I can see now—*(Shakes her head.)*

MRS. PETERS. Well, you mustn't reproach yourself, Mrs. Hale. Somehow we   100
just don't see how it is with other folks until—something comes up.

MRS. HALE. Not having children makes less work—but it makes a quiet
house, and Wright out to work all day, and no company when he
did come in. Did you know John Wright, Mrs. Peters?

MRS. PETERS. Not to know him; I've seen him in town. They say he was a
good man.

MRS. HALE. Yes—good; he didn't drink, and kept his word as well as most,
I guess, and paid his debts. But he was a hard man, Mrs. Peters. Just
to pass the time of day with him. *(Shivers.)* Like a raw wind that gets
to the bone. *(Pauses, her eye falling on the cage.)* I should think she
would 'a' wanted a bird. But what do you suppose went with it?

MRS. PETERS. I don't know, unless it got sick and died. *(She reaches over and
swings the broken door, swings it again; both women watch it.)*

MRS. HALE. You weren't raised around here, were you? *(Mrs. Peters shakes*   105
her head.) You didn't know—her?

MRS. PETERS. Not till they brought her yesterday.

MRS. HALE. She—come to think of it, she was kind of like a bird herself—
real sweet and pretty, but kind of timid and—fluttery. How—she—
did—change. *(Silence; then as if struck by a happy thought and relieved to
get back to everyday things.)* Tell you what, Mrs. Peters, why don't you
take the quilt in with you? It might take up her mind.

MRS. PETERS. Why, I think that's a real nice idea, Mrs. Hale. There couldn't
possible be any objection to it, could there? Now, just what would I
take? I wonder if her patches are in here—and her things. *(They look
in the sewing basket.)*

MRS. HALE. Here's some red. I expect this has got sewing things in it. *(Brings
out a fancy box.)* What a pretty box. Looks like something somebody
would give you. Maybe her scissors are in here. *(Opens box. Suddenly
puts her hand to her nose.)* Why—*(Mrs. Peters bends nearer, then turns her
face away.)* There's something wrapped up in this piece of silk.

MRS. PETERS. Why, this isn't her scissors.   110

MRS. HALE *(lifting the silk).* Oh, Mrs. Peters—it's—*(Mrs. Peters bends closer.)*

MRS. PETERS. It's the bird.

MRS. HALE *(jumping up).* But, Mrs. Peters—look at it. Its neck! Look at its
neck! It's all—other side *to.*

MRS. PETERS. Somebody—wrung—its neck. *(Their eyes meet. A look of growing comprehension of horror. Steps are heard outside. Mrs. Hale slips box
under quilt pieces, and sinks into her chair. Enter Sheriff and County Attorney, Mrs. Peters rises.)*

COUNTY ATTORNEY *(as one turning from serious things to little pleasantries).* Well,   115
ladies, have you decided whether she was going to quilt it or knot it?

MRS. PETERS. We think she was going to—knot it.

COUNTY ATTORNEY. Well, that's interesting, I'm sure. *(Seeing the birdcage.)* Has
the bird flown?

MRS. HALE *(putting more quilt pieces over the box).* We think the—cat got it.

COUNTY ATTORNEY *(preoccupied).* Is there a cat? *(Mrs. Hale glances in a quick covert way at Mrs. Peters.)*

MRS. PETERS. Well, not now. They're superstitious, you know. They leave.   120

COUNTY ATTORNEY *(to Sheriff Peters, continuing an interrupted conversation).* No sign at all of anyone having come from the outside. Their own rope. Now let's go up again and go over it piece by piece. *(They start upstairs.)* It would have to have been someone who knew just the—*(Mrs. Peters sits down. The two women sit there not looking at one another, but as if peering into something and at the same time holding back. When they talk now, it is the manner of feeling their way over strange ground, as if afraid of what they are saying, but as if they cannot help saying it.)*

MRS. HALE. She liked the bird. She was going to bury it in that pretty box.

MRS. PETERS *(in a whisper).* When I was a girl—my kitten—there was a boy took a hatchet, and before my eyes—and before I could get there—*(Covers her face an instant.)* If they hadn't held me back, I would have—*(Catches herself, looks upstairs where steps are heard, falters weakly.)*—hurt him.

MRS. HALE *(with a slow look around her).* I wonder how it would seem never to have had any children around. *(Pause.)* No, Wright wouldn't like the bird—a thing that sang. She used to sing. He killed that, too.

MRS. PETERS *(moving uneasily).* We don't know who killed the bird.   125

MRS. HALE. I knew John Wright.

MRS. PETERS. It was an awful thing was done in this house that night, Mrs. Hale. Killing a man while he slept, slipping a rope around his neck that choked the life out of him.

MRS. HALE. His neck. Choked the life out of him. *(Her hand goes out and rests on the birdcage.)*

MRS. PETERS *(with a rising voice).* We don't know who killed him. We don't know.

MRS. HALE *(her own feeling not interrupted).* If there'd been years and years   130 of nothing, then a bird to sing to you, it would be awful—still, after the bird was still.

MRS. PETERS *(something within her speaking).* I know what stillness is. When we homesteaded in Dakota, and my first baby died—after he was two years old, and me with no other then—

MRS. HALE *(moving).* How soon do you suppose they'll be through, looking for evidence?

MRS. PETERS. I know what stillness is. *(Pulling herself back.)* The law has got to punish crime, Mrs. Hale.

MRS. HALE *(not as if answering that).* I wish you'd seen Minnie Foster when she wore a white dress with blue ribbons and stood up there in the choir and sang. *(A look around the room.)* Oh, I wish I'd come over here once in a while! That was a crime! That was a crime! Who's going to punish that?

MRS. PETERS *(looking upstairs).* We mustn't—take on.   135

MRS. HALE. I might have known she needed help! I know how things can be—for women. I tell you, it's queer, Mrs. Peters. We live close together and we live far apart. We all go through the same things—it's all just a different kind of the same thing. *(Brushes her eyes, noticing the bottle of fruit, reaches out for it.)* If I was you, I wouldn't tell her her fruit was gone. Tell her it *ain't.* Tell her it's all right. Take this in to prove it to her. She—she may never know whether it was broke or not.

MRS. PETERS *(takes the bottle, looks about for something to wrap it in; takes petticoat from the clothes brought from the other room, very nervously begins winding this around the bottle. In a false voice).* My, it's a good thing the men couldn't hear us. Wouldn't they just laugh! Getting all stirred up over a little thing like a—dead canary. As if that could have anything to do with—with—wouldn't they *laugh!* (The men are heard coming downstairs.)*

MRS. HALE *(under her breath).* Maybe they would—maybe they wouldn't.

COUNTY ATTORNEY. No, Peters, it's all perfectly clear except a reason for doing it. But you know juries when it comes to women. If there was some definite thing. Something to show—something to make a story about—a thing that would connect up with this strange way of doing it. *(The women's eyes meet for an instant. Enter Hale from outer door.)*

HALE. Well, I've got the team around. Pretty cold out there.   140

COUNTY ATTORNEY. I'm going to stay here a while by myself. *(To the Sheriff.)* You can send Frank out for me, can't you? I want to go over everything. I'm not satisfied that we can't do better.

SHERIFF. Do you want to see what Mrs. Peters is going to take in? *(The Lawyer goes to the table, picks up the apron, laughs.)*

COUNTY ATTORNEY. Oh, I guess they're not very dangerous things the ladies have picked up. *(Moves a few things about, disturbing the quilt pieces which cover the box. Steps back.)* No, Mrs. Peters doesn't need supervising. For that matter, a sheriff's wife is married to the law. Ever think of it that way, Mrs. Peters?

MRS. PETERS. Not—just that way.

SHERIFF *(chuckling).* Married to the law. *(Moves toward the other room.)* I just   145 want you to come in here a minute, George. We ought to take a look at these windows.

COUNTY ATTORNEY *(scoffingly).* Oh, windows!

SHERIFF. We'll be right out, Mr. Hale. *(Hale goes outside. The Sheriff follows the County Attorney into the other room. Then Mrs. Hale rises, hands tight together, looking intensely at Mrs. Peters, whose eyes take a slow turn, finally meeting Mrs. Hale's. A moment Mrs. Hale holds her, then her own eyes point the way to where the box is concealed. Suddenly Mrs. Peters throws back quilt pieces and tries to put the box in the bag she is carrying. It is too big. She opens box, starts to take the bird out, cannot touch it, goes to pieces, stands there helpless. Sound of a knob turning in the other room. Mrs. Hale snatches*

*the box and puts it in the pocket of her big coat. Enter County Attorney and
Sheriff.)*

COUNTY ATTORNEY *(facetiously).* Well, Henry, at least we found out that she
was not going to quilt it. She was going to—what is it you call it,
ladies?

MRS. HALE *(her hand against her pocket).* We call it—knot it, Mr. Henderson.

TOPICS FOR CRITICAL THINKING AND WRITING

1. The dead canary in the box isn't evidence that Mrs. Wright has killed
   her husband. So what is the point of the dead canary in the play?

2. Do you think the play is immoral? Explain.

3. Assume that Minnie is indicted for murder and that you are asked to
   serve as Minnie's defense lawyer. If you somehow know that the evidence of the canary has been suppressed, would you accept the case?
   Why, or why not? (It is unlawful for *prosecutors* to suppress evidence,
   but it is not unlawful for defense lawyers to withhold incriminating evidence that they are aware of.)

4. Assume that you have accepted Minnie's case. In 500 words set forth
   the defense you will offer for her. (Take any position that you wish.
   You may, for example, argue that she committed justifiable homicide or
   that—on the basis of her behavior as reported by Mr. Hale—she is innocent by reason of insanity.)

5. Assume that Minnie has been found guilty. Compose the speech she
   might give before being sentenced.

6. "*Trifles* is badly dated. It cannot speak to today's audience." In an essay of
   500 words evaluate this view: Offer an argument supporting or rejecting
   it, or take a middle position.

Mitsuye Yamada

*Mitsuye Yamada, the daughter of Japanese immigrants to the United States,
was born in Japan in 1923, during her mother's return visit to her native
land. Yamada was raised in Seattle, but in 1942 she and her family were incarcerated and then relocated to a camp in Idaho, when Executive Order 9066
(signed by President Franklin D. Roosevelt that year) gave military authorities
the right to remove any and all persons from "military areas." In 1954 she became an American citizen. A professor of English at Cypress Junior College in
San Luis Obispo, California, until she retired in 1989, Yamada is the author of
poems and stories.*

*Yamada's poem concerns the compliant response to Executive Order 9066,
which brought about the incarceration and relocation of the entire Japanese and
Japanese American population on the Pacific coast—about 120,000 people. More
than two-thirds of the people moved were native-born citizens of the United States.
(The 158,000 Japanese residents of the Territory of Hawaii were not affected.)
There was virtually no protest at the time, but in recent years the order has been*

widely regarded as an outrageous infringement on liberty, and some younger Japa-nese Americans cannot fathom why their parents and grandparents complied with it. This poem first appeared in Camp Notes and Other Poems *in 1976.*

To the Lady

The one in San Francisco who asked:
Why did the Japanese Americans let
the government put them in
those camps without protest?

Come to think of it I   5
    should've run off to Canada
    should've hijacked a plane to Algeria
    should've pulled myself up from my
    bra straps
    and kicked'm in the groin   10
    should've bombed a bank
    should've tried self-immolation
    should've holed myself up in a
    woodframe house
    and let you watch me   15
    burn up on the six o'clock news
    should've run howling down the street
    naked and assaulted you at breakfast
    by AP wirephoto
    should've screamed bloody murder   20
    like Kitty Genovese°

    Then
YOU would've
    come to my aid in shining armor
    laid yourself across the railroad track   25
    marched on Washington
    tattooed a Star of David on your arm
    written six million enraged
    letters to Congress
    But we didn't draw the line   30
    anywhere
    law and order Executive Order 9066
    social order moral order internal order
    YOU let'm
    I let'm   35
    All are punished.

21 Kitty Genovese In 1964 Kitty Genovese of Kew Gardens, New York, was stabbed to death when she left her car and walked toward her home. Thirty-eight persons heard her screams, but no one came to her assistance. [Editors' note.]

Topics for Critical Thinking and Writing

1. Has the lady's question (lines 2–4) ever crossed your mind? If so, what answers did you think of?

2. What, in effect, is the speaker really saying in lines 5 to 21? And in lines 22 to 29?

3. What possible arguments can you offer for and against the removal of Japanese Americans in 1942?

4. Do you think the survivors of the relocation are entitled to some sort of redress? Why, or why not? If you think they merit compensation, what should the compensation be?

28

What Is Happiness?

THOUGHTS ABOUT HAPPINESS, ANCIENT AND MODERN

Here are some brief comments about happiness, from ancient times to the present. Read them, think about them, and then write on one of the two topics that appear after the last quotation.

> *Happiness is prosperity combined with virtue.*
>
> —ARISTOTLE (384–322 B.C.)

> *Pleasure is the beginning and the end of living happily. . . . It is impossible to live pleasurably without living wisely, well, and justly, and impossible to live wisely, well, and justly without living pleasurably.*
>
> —EPICURUS (341–270 B.C.)

> *Very little is needed to make a happy life.*
>
> —MARCUS AURELIUS (121–180)

> *Society can only be happy and free in proportion as it is virtuous.*
>
> —MARY WOLLSTONECRAFT SHELLEY (1759–1797)

> *The supreme happiness of life is the conviction that we are loved.*
>
> —VICTOR HUGO (1802–1885)

> *Ask yourself whether you are happy, and you cease to be so.*
>
> —JOHN STUART MILL (1806–1873)

> *A lifetime of happiness! No man alive could bear it: it would be hell on earth.*
>
> —GEORGE BERNARD SHAW (1856–1950)

> *We have no more right to consume happiness without producing it than to consume wealth without producing it.*
>
> —GEORGE BERNARD SHAW (1856–1950)

> *If only we'd stop trying to be happy, we could have a pretty good time.*
>
> —EDITH WHARTON (1862–1937)

Happiness makes up in height for what it lacks in length.

—ROBERT FROST (1874–1963)

Point me out the happy man and I will point you out either egotism, selfishness, evil—or else an absolute ignorance.

—GRAHAM GREENE (1904–1991)

Those who are unhappy have no need for anything in this world but people capable of giving them their attention.

—SIMONE WEIL (1909–1943)

Happiness is always a by-product. It is probably a matter of temperament, and for anything I know it may be glandular. But it is not something that can be demanded from life, and if you are not happy you had better stop worrying about it and see what treasures you can pluck from your own brand of unhappiness.

—ROBERTSON DAVIES (1913–1995)

Topics for Critical Thinking and Writing

1. If any one of these passages especially appeals to you, make it the thesis of an essay of about 500 words.

2. Take two of these passages—perhaps one that you especially like and one that you think is wrong-headed—and write a dialogue of about 500 words in which the two authors converse. They may each try to convince the other, or they may find that to some degree they share views and they may then work out a statement that both can accept. If you do take the position that one writer is on the correct track but the other is utterly mistaken, try to be fair to the view that you think is mistaken. (As an experiment in critical thinking, imagine that you accept it, and make the best case for it that you possibly can.)

Daniel Gilbert

Daniel Gilbert (b. 1957) a professor of psychology at Harvard, is the author of Stumbling on Happiness *(2006)—a best seller that won the Royal Society Prize ($20,000) for Science Books. Hearing of the award, Gilbert said, "There are very few countries, including my own, the United States, where a somewhat cheeky book about happiness could win a science prize—but the British invented intellectual humor and have always understood that enlightenment and entertainment are natural friends."*

A high school dropout, Gilbert was nineteen when he visited a community college, intending to take a writing course but enrolling instead in the only course still open—a psychology course.

We reprint here an essay that appeared in Time *a few days before Father's Day in June 2006.*

Does Fatherhood Make You Happy?

Sonora Smart Dodd was listening to a sermon on self-sacrifice when she decided that her father, a widower who had raised six children, deserved his very own national holiday. Almost a century later, people all over the world spend the third Sunday in June honoring their fathers with ritual offerings of aftershave and neckties, which leads millions of fathers to have precisely the same thought at precisely the same moment: "My children," they think in unison, "make me happy."

Could all those dads be wrong?

Studies reveal that most married couples start out happy and then become progressively less satisfied over the course of their lives, becoming especially disconsolate when their children are in diapers and in adolescence, and returning to their initial levels of happiness only after their children have had the decency to grow up and go away. When the popular press invented a malady called "empty-nest syndrome," it failed to mention that its primary symptom is a marked increase in smiling.

Psychologists have measured how people feel as they go about their daily activities, and have found that people are less happy when they are interacting with their children than when they are eating, exercising, shopping, or watching television. Indeed, an act of parenting makes most people about as happy as an act of housework. Economists have modeled the impact of many variables on people's overall happiness and have consistently found that children have only a small impact. A small negative impact.

Those findings are hard to swallow because they fly in the face of our 5 most compelling intuitions. We love our children! We talk about them to anyone who will listen, show their photographs to anyone who will look, and hide our refrigerators behind vast collages of their drawings, notes, pictures, and report cards. We feel confident that we are happy with our kids, about our kids, for our kids, and because of our kids—so why is our personal experience at odds with the scientific data?

Three reasons.

First, when something makes us happy we are willing to pay a lot for it, which is why the worst Belgian chocolate is more expensive than the best Belgian tofu. But that process can work in reverse: When we pay a lot for something, we assume it makes us happy, which is why we swear to the wonders of bottled water and Armani socks. The compulsion to care for our children was long ago written into our DNA, so we toil and sweat, lose sleep and hair, play nurse, housekeeper, chauffeur, and cook, and we do all that because nature just won't have it any other way. Given the high price we pay, it isn't surprising that we rationalize those costs and conclude that our children must be repaying us with happiness.

Second, if the Red Sox and the Yankees were scoreless until Manny Ramirez hit a grand slam in the bottom of the ninth, you can be sure that

Boston fans would remember it as the best game of the season. Memories are dominated by their most powerful—and not their most typical—instances. Just as a glorious game-winning homer can erase our memory of eight and a half dull innings, the sublime moment when our three-year-old looks up from the mess she is making with her mashed potatoes and says, "I wub you, Daddy," can erase eight hours of no, not yet, not now, and stop asking. Children may not make us happy very often, but when they do, that happiness is both transcendent and amnesic.

Third, although most of us think of heroin as a source of human misery, shooting heroin doesn't actually make people feel miserable. It makes them feel really, really good—so good, in fact, that it crowds out every other source of pleasure. Family, friends, work, play, food, sex—none can compete with the narcotic experience; hence all fall by the wayside. The analogy to children is all too clear. Even if their company were an unremitting pleasure, the fact that they require so much company means that other sources of pleasure will all but disappear. Movies, theater, parties, travel—those are just a few of the English nouns that parents of young children quickly forget how to pronounce. We believe our children are our greatest joy, and we're absolutely right. When you have one joy, it's bound to be the greatest.

Our children give us many things, but an increase in our average 10 daily happiness is probably not among them. Rather than deny that fact, we should celebrate it. Our ability to love beyond all measure those who try our patience and weary our bones is at once our most noble and most human quality. The fact that children don't always make us happy—and that we're happy to have them nonetheless—is the fact for which Sonora Smart Dodd was so grateful. She thought we would all do well to remember it, every third Sunday in June.

TOPICS FOR CRITICAL THINKING AND WRITING

1. How would you define the "empty-nest syndrome" (para. 3)?

2. Do you believe the "studies" that Gilbert mentions in his third paragraph? Why, or why not? Similarly, do you believe the "psychologists" of the fourth paragraph? Explain.

3. What does Gilbert mean when he describes the happiness that children cause their parents as "transcendent" (para. 8)? Are there other, non-transcendent, kinds of happiness that parents experience?

4. Let's assume that even if you do not fully accept Gilbert's view about fatherhood and happiness, you are willing to grant that it is just possible that there may be something to what he says. Are you willing to take the next step and say that what he says of fatherhood—he was writing on Father's Day—may also be true of motherhood? Explain.

5. What do you think Gilbert's chief purpose is in this essay? To inform? To persuade? To entertain? Something else? Support your answer with evidence.

6. You may have been told that you should not write paragraphs consisting of only a sentence or two, but Gilbert's essay includes two such paragraphs, 2 and 6. Should Gilbert have revised these paragraphs? Or does their brevity serve a purpose? Explain.

Henry David Thoreau

Henry David Thoreau (1817–1862) was born in Concord, Massachusetts, where he spent most of his life ("I have travelled a good deal in Concord"). He taught and lectured, but chiefly he observed, thought, and wrote. From July 5, 1847, to September 6, 1847, he lived near Concord in a cabin at Walden Pond, an experience recorded in Walden *(1854).*

"As for Clothing" (editors' title) comes from Walden, *Chapter 1. "We do not Ride on the Railroad; It Rides upon Us" (also the editors' title) is from Chapter 2.*

Selections from *Walden*

[AS FOR CLOTHING]

As for Clothing, to come at once to the practical part of the question, perhaps we are led oftener by the love of novelty and a regard for the opinions of men, in procuring it, than by a true utility. Let him who has work to do recollect that the object of clothing is, first, to retain the vital heat, and secondly, in this state of society, to cover nakedness, and he may judge how much of any necessary or important work may be accomplished without adding to his wardrobe. Kings and queens who wear a suit but once, though made by some tailor or dressmaker to their majesties, cannot know the comfort of wearing a suit that fits. They are no better than wooden horses to hang the clean clothes on. Every day our garments become more assimilated to ourselves, receiving the impress of the wearer's character, until we hesitate to lay them aside, without such delay and medical appliances and some such solemnity even as our bodies. No man ever stood the lower in my estimation for having a patch in his clothes; yet I am sure that there is greater anxiety, commonly, to have fashionable, or at least clean and unpatched clothes, than to have a sound conscience. But even if the rent is not mended, perhaps the worst vice betrayed is improvidence. I sometimes try my acquaintances by such tests as these, — Who could wear a patch, or two extra seams only, over the knee? Most have as if they believed that their prospects for life would be ruined if they should do it. It would be easier for them to hobble to town with a broken leg than with a broken pantaloon. Often if an accident happens to a gentleman's legs, they can be mended; but if a similar accident happens to the legs of his pantaloons, there is no help for it; for he considers, not what is truly respectable, but what is respected. We know but few men, a great many coats and breeches. Dress a scarecrow in your last shift, you standing shiftless by, who would not soonest salute the scarecrow? Passing a cornfield the other day, close by a hat and coat on a stake, I recognized the owner of the farm. He was only a little more weather-beaten than when I saw him last. I have heard of a dog that barked at every stranger who approached his master's premises with clothes on, but was easily quieted by a naked thief. It is an interesting question how far men would retain their relative rank if they were divested of their clothes. Could you, in such a case, tell surely of any company of civilized men which belonged to the most respected class? When Madam Pfeiffer,[1] in her adventurous travels round the world, from east to west, had got so near home as Asiatic Russia, she says that she felt the necessity of wearing other than a traveling dress, when she went to meet the authorities, for she "was now in a civilized country, where . . . people are judged of by their clothes." Even in our democratic New England towns the accidental possession of wealth, and its manifestation in dress and equipage alone, obtain for the possessor almost universal respect. But they who yield such respect, numerous as they are, are so far heathen, and need to have a missionary sent to them. Beside, clothes introduced sewing, a kind of work which you may call endless; a woman's dress, at least, is never done.

A man who has at length found something to do will not need to get a new suit to do it in; for him the old will do, that has lain dusty in the garret for an indeterminate period. Old shoes will serve a hero longer than they have served his valet—if a hero even has a valet—bare feet are older than shoes, and he can make them do. Only they who go to soirées and legislative halls must have new coats, coats to change as often as the man changes in them. But if my jacket and trousers, my hat and shoes, are fit to worship God in, they will do; will they not? Who ever saw his old clothes—his old coat, actually worn out, resolved into its primitive elements, so that it was not a deed of charity to bestow it on some poor boy, by him perchance to be bestowed on some poorer still, or shall we say richer, who could do with less? I say, beware of all enterprises that require new clothes, and not rather a new wearer of clothes. If there is not a new man, how can the new clothes be made to fit? If you have any enterprise before you, try it in your old clothes. All men want, not something to *do with*, but something to *do*, or rather something to *be*. Perhaps we should never procure a new suit, however ragged or dirty the old, until we have so conducted, so enterprised or sailed in some way, that we feel like new men in the old, and that to retain it would be like keeping new wine in old bottles. Our moulting season, like that of the fowls must be a crisis in our lives. The loon retires

[1]**Madame Pfeiffer** Ida Pfeiffer (1797–1858), author of travel books. (All notes are the editors'.)

to solitary ponds to spend it. Thus also the snake casts its slough, and the caterpillar its wormy coat, by an internal industry and expansion; for clothes are but our outmost cuticle and mortal coil. Otherwise we shall be found sailing under false colors, and be inevitably cashiered at last by our own opinion, as well as that of mankind.

We don garment after garment, as if we grew like exogenous plants by addition without. Our outside and often thin and fanciful clothes are our epidermis, or false skin, which partakes not of our life, and may be stripped off here and there without fatal injury; our thicker garments, constantly worn, are our cellular integument, or cortex; but our shirts are our liber,[2] or true bark, which cannot be removed without girdling and so destroying the man. I believe that all races at some seasons wear something equivalent to the shirt. It is desirable that a man be clad so simply that he can lay his hands on himself in the dark, and that he live in all respects so compactly and preparedly, that, if an enemy take the town, he can, like the old philosopher, walk out the gate empty-handed without anxiety. While one thick garment is, for most purposes, as good as three thin ones, and cheap clothing can be obtained at prices really to suit customers; while a thick coat can be bought for five dollars, which will last as many years, thick pantaloons for two dollars, cowhide boots for a dollar and a half a pair, a summer hat for a quarter of a dollar, and a winter cap for sixty-two and a half cents, or a better be made at home at a nominal cost, where is he so poor that, clad in such a suit, *of his own earning*, there will not be found wise men to do him reverence?

When I ask for a garment of a particular form, my tailoress tells me gravely, "They do not make them so now," not emphasizing the "They" at all, as if she quoted an authority as impersonal as the Fates, and I find it difficult to get made what I want, simply because she cannot believe that I mean what I say, that I am so rash. When I hear this oracular sentence, I am for a moment absorbed in thought, emphasizing to myself each word separately that I may come at the meaning of it, that I may find out by what degree of consanguinity *They* are related to *me*, and what authority they may have in an affair which affects me so nearly; and finally, I am inclined to answer her with equal mystery, and without any more emphasis of the "they" — "It is true, they did not make them so recently, but they do now." Of what use this measuring of me if she does not measure my character, but only the breadth of my shoulders, as it were a peg to hang the coat on? We worship not the Graces, nor the Parcæ, but Fashion. She spins and weaves and cuts with full authority. The head monkey at Paris puts on a traveller's cap, and all the monkeys in America do the same. I sometimes despair of getting anything quite simple and honest done in this world by the help of men. They would have to be passed through a powerful press first, to squeeze their old notions out of them, so that they would not soon get upon their legs

---

[2]**liber** Inner bark of a tree.

again; and then there would be some one in the company with a maggot in his head, hatched from an egg deposited there nobody knows when, for not even fire kills these things, and you would have lost your labor. Nevertheless, we will not forget that some Egyptian wheat was handed down to us by a mummy.

On the whole, I think that it cannot be maintained that dressing ⁵ has in this or any country risen to the dignity of an art. At present men make shift to wear what they can get. Like shipwrecked sailors, they put on what they can find on the beach, and at a little distance, whether of space or time, laugh at each other's masquerade. Every generation laughs at the old fashions, but follows religiously the new. We are amused at beholding the costume of Henry VIII, or Queen Elizabeth, as much as if it was that of the King and Queen of the Cannibal Islands. All costume off a man is pitiful or grotesque. It is only the serious eye peering from and the sincere life passed within it which restrain laughter and consecrate the costume of any people. Let Harlequin be taken with a fit of the colic and his trappings will have to serve that mood too. When the soldier is hit by a cannon ball rags are as becoming as purple.

The childish and savage taste of men and women for new patterns keeps how many shaking and squinting through kaleidoscopes that they may discover the particular figure which this generation requires today. The manufacturers have learned that this taste is merely whimsical. Of two patterns which differ only by a few threads more or less of a particular color, the one will be sold readily, the other lie on the shelf, though it frequently happens that after the lapse of a season the latter becomes the most fashionable. Comparatively, tattooing is not the hideous custom which it is called. It is not barbarous merely because the printing is skin-deep and unalterable.

I cannot believe that our factory system is the best mode by which men may get clothing. The condition of the operatives is becoming every day more like that of the English; and it cannot be wondered at, since, as far as I have heard or observed, the principal object is, not that mankind may be well and honestly clad, but, unquestionably, that the corporations may be enriched. In the long run men hit only what they aim at. Therefore, though they should fail immediately, they had better aim at something high.

[WE DO NOT RIDE ON THE RAILROAD; IT RIDES UPON US]

Still we live meanly, like ants; though the fable tells us that we were long ago changed into men; like pygmies we fight with cranes; it is error upon error, and clout upon clout, and our best virtue has for its occasion a superfluous and evitable wretchedness. Our life is frittered away by detail. An honest man has hardly need to count more than his ten fingers, or in extreme cases he may add his ten toes, and lump the rest. Simplicity, simplicity, simplicity! I say, let your affairs be as two or three, and not a hundred or a thousand; instead of a million count half a dozen, and keep your accounts on your thumb nail. In the midst of this chopping sea of civilized life, such are the clouds and storms and quicksands and thousand-and-one items to be allowed for, that a man has to live, if he would not founder and go to the bottom and not make his port at all, by dead reckoning, and he must be a great calculator indeed who succeeds. Simplify, simplify. Instead of three meals a day, if it be necessary eat but one; instead of a hundred dishes, five; and reduce other things in proportion. Our life is like a German Confederacy, made up of petty states, with its boundary forever fluctuating, so that even a German cannot tell you how it is bounded at any moment. The nation itself, with all its so-called internal improvements, which, by the way are all external and superficial, is just such an unwieldy and overgrown establishment, cluttered with furniture and tripped up by its own traps, ruined by luxury and heedless expense, by want of calculation and a worthy aim, as the million households in the land; and the only cure for it as for them is in a rigid economy, a stern and more than Spartan simplicity of life and elevation of purpose. It lives too fast. Men think that it is essential that the *Nation* have commerce, and export ice, and talk through a telegraph, and ride thirty miles an hour, without a doubt, whether *they* do or not; but whether we should live like baboons or like men, is a little uncertain. If we do not get out sleepers,[3] and forge rails, and devote days and nights to the work, but go to tinkering upon our *lives* to improve *them*, who will build railroads? And if railroads are not built, how shall we get to heaven in season? But if we stay at home and mind our business, who will want railroads? We do not ride on the railroad; it rides upon us. Did you ever think what those sleepers are that underlie the railroad? Each one is a man, an Irishman, or a Yankee man. The rails are laid on them, and they are covered with sand, and the cars run smoothly over them. They are sound sleepers, I assure you. And every few years a new lot is laid down and run over; so that, if some have the pleasure of riding on a rail, others have the misfortune to be ridden upon. And when they run over a man that is walking in his sleep, a supernumerary sleeper in the wrong position, and wake him up, they suddenly stop the cars, and make a hue and cry about it, as if this were an exception. I am glad to know that it takes a gang of men for every five miles to keep the sleepers down and level in their beds as it is, for this is a sign that they may sometime get up again.

Topics for Critical Thinking and Writing

1. What, according to Thoreau, are the legitimate functions of clothing? What other functions does he reject, or fail to consider?

---

[3]**sleepers** The woody ties beneath railroad rails.

2. Many of Thoreau's sentences mean both what they say literally and something more; often, like proverbs, they express abstract or general truths in concrete, homely language. How might these sentences be interpreted?

   a. We know but few men, a great many coats and breeches.
   b. Dress a scarecrow in your last shift, you standing shiftless by, who would not soonest salute the scarecrow?
   c. If you have any enterprise before you, try it in your old clothes.
   d. Every generation laughs at the old fashions, but follows religiously the new.
   e. When the soldier is hit by a cannon ball rags are as becoming as purple.

3. We have just quoted some of Thoreau's epigrammatic sentences. Is this style effective or not? Explain.

4. Notice that Thoreau writes in long paragraphs. (The first of them runs to more than 450 words—the length of many respectable essays.) Can such long paragraphs do their job effectively? What is the job of a paragraph? Or is there no one such job?

5. Toward the end of paragraph 2 we meet the cliché "new wine in old bottles." Do you think his sentence is effective? Why, or why not? Was this expression a cliché already in Thoreau's day? Complete the following definition: "A word or phrase is a cliché if and only if . . ."

6. In paragraph 7, Thoreau criticizes the factory system. Is the criticism mild or severe? Explain. Point out some of the earlier passages in which he touches on the relation of clothes to a faulty economic system.

7. In paragraph 8, Thoreau asserts that "Our life is frittered away by detail." Is it possible to argue that "Yes, our life is frittered away by detail, but, perhaps oddly, attention to detail—studying for examinations, grading papers, walking the dog—is largely responsible for human happiness"? Explain.

Darrin M. McMahon

Darrin M. McMahon was educated at the University of California, Berkeley, where he received his Ph.D. in 1997. The author of Happiness: A History *(2006), he has taught at Columbia University, Yale University, and New York University. We reprint an essay first published in the* New York Times *on December 29, 2005.*

In Pursuit of Unhappiness

"Happy New Year!" We seldom think of those words as an order. But in some respects that is what they are.

Doesn't every American want to be happy? And don't most Americans yearn, deep down, to be happy all of the time? The right laid out in our nation's Declaration of Independence—to pursue happiness to our hearts' content—is nowhere on better display than in the rites of the holiday season. With glad tidings and good cheer, we seek to bring one year to its natural happy conclusion, while preparing to usher in a happy new year and many happy returns.

Like the cycle of the seasons, our emphasis on mirth may seem timeless, as though human beings have always made merry from beginning to end. But in fact this preoccupation with perpetual happiness is relatively recent. As Thomas Carlyle observed in 1843, "'Happiness our being's end and aim' is at bottom, if we will count well, not yet two centuries old in the world."

Carlyle's arithmetic was essentially sound, for changes in both religious and secular culture since the seventeenth century made "happiness," in the form of pleasure or good feeling, not only morally acceptable but commendable in and of itself. While many discounted religious notions that consigned life in this world to misery and sin, others discovered signs of God's providence in earthly satisfaction. The result was at once to weaken and transpose the ideal of heavenly felicity, in effect bringing it to earth. Suffering was not our natural state. Happy was the way we were meant to be.

That shift was monumental, and its implications far reaching. Among   5 other things, it was behind the transformation of the holiday season from a time of pious remembrance into one of unadulterated bliss. Yet the effects were greater than that. As Carlyle complained, "Every pitifulest whipster that walks within a skin has had his head filled with the notion that he is, shall be, or by all human and divine laws ought to be, 'happy.'"

Carlyle was notoriously cranky, but his central insight—that the new doctrine of happiness tended to raise expectations that could never possibly be fulfilled—remains as relevant today as it was in 1843. Despite enjoying far better living standards and more avenues for pleasure than before, human beings are arguably no happier now than they've ever been.

Sociologists like to point out that the percentage of those describing themselves as "happy" or "very happy" has remained virtually unchanged in Europe and the United States since such surveys were first conducted in the 1950s. And yet, this January, like last year and next, the self-help industry will pour forth books promising to make us happier than we are today. The very demand for such books is a strong indication that they aren't working.

Should that be a cause for concern? Some critics say it is. For example, economists like Lord Richard Layard and Daniel Kahneman have argued that the apparent stagnancy of happiness in modern societies should prompt policymakers to shift their priorities from the creation of wealth to the creation of good feelings, from boosting gross national product to increasing gross national happiness.

But before we take such steps, we might do well to reflect on the darker side of holiday cheer: those mysterious blues that are apt to set in while the streamers stream and the corks pop; the little voice that even in the best of souls is sometimes moved to say, "Bah, humbug." As Carlyle put it, "The prophets preach to us, 'Thou shalt be happy; thou shalt love pleasant things.'" But as he well knew, the very commandment tended to undermine its fulfillment, even to make us sad.

Carlyle's sometime friend and long-time rival, the philosopher John Stuart Mill, came to a similar conclusion. His words are all the more worth heeding in that Mill himself was a determined proponent of the greatest happiness for the greatest number. "Ask yourself whether you are happy, and you cease to be so," Mill concluded after recovering from a serious bout of depression. Rather than resign himself to gloom, however, Mill vowed instead to look for happiness in another way.

"Those only are happy," he came to believe, "who have their minds fixed on some object other than their own happiness; on the happiness of others; on the improvement of mankind, even on some art or pursuit, followed not as a means, but as itself an ideal end. Aiming thus at something else, they find happiness by the way." For our own culture, steeped as it is in the relentless pursuit of personal pleasure and endless cheer, that message is worth heeding.

So in these last days of 2005 I say to you, "Don't have a happy new year!" Have dinner with your family or walk in the park with friends. If you're so inclined, put in some good hours at the office or at your favorite charity, temple, or church. Work on your jump shot or your child's model trains. With luck, you'll find happiness by the by. If not, your time won't be wasted. You may even bring a little joy to the world.

Topics for Critical Thinking and Writing

1. Who or what gives us the "order" to be happy—or is the whole idea silly? (See paragraphs 1 and 9.) Explain.

2. What's the difference between happiness and pleasure, or are these two different ways of saying the same thing? Explain.

3. Has McMahon persuaded you to think of happiness in a fresh way? Explain.

4. McMahon's article was originally published on December 29, so it is not surprising that in his second paragraph he says his readers are preparing "to usher in a happy new year." Try to recall how you spent the most recent New Year's Eve. Was it a happy evening? Or was it tinged with melancholy, perhaps even with sorrow as you remembered sad things and hoped that the next year would be happier? If you can't remember New Year's Eve, think of the last year as a whole: Was it predominantly happy or unhappy? Or can't you judge it in such terms? Explain.

5. McMahon says (para. 4) that since the seventeenth century a shift in thinking has occurred: "Suffering [is] not our natural state. Happy was the way we were meant to be." Assume you are speaking to someone who has not read McMahon's essay. How would you explain this point?

6. John Stuart Mill (para. 10) is often described as a hedonist. What do you have to do or believe to be a hedonist? Are you a hedonist? Explain why or why not in 250 words.

7. Are you likely to take the advice McMahon offers in his final paragraph? Explain.

8. Suppose you believed that we (say, American citizens) are happier today than we were three centuries ago. How would you go about arguing for your belief?

Epictetus

Epictetus (pronounced Epic-TEE-tus) was born in Phrygia (now southwestern Turkey) some sixty years after Jesus and died about 135 c.e. His mother was a slave, and he was brought to Rome as a slave. At an uncertain date he was given his freedom, and he went to Nicopolis in northwestern Greece, where he taught philosophy. One of his students, a Roman named Flavius Arrian, recorded the teachings of Epictetus in two books written in Greek, the Discourses *(or* Lectures*) and the* Handbook *(or* Manual, *often known by its Greek title,* Enchiridion*). Our selection is from a translation by Helena Orozco.*

The doctrine that Epictetus taught is stoicism, which can be briefly characterized thus: The goal of life (as other philosophers of the period would agree) is "happiness" or "a flourishing life" (eudaimonia). The way to achieve this condition is to understand the nature of the good. Such things as health, wealth, and rank are not good because they do not always benefit those who possess them. True, such things are "preferred," and sickness, poverty, and low social status are "not preferred," but all of these are "indifferent" when it comes to being good or evil. The only true good is virtue. Yes, wealth can be useful, but it is not good or bad. What is good or bad is the way in which one makes use of what one has. The life that is happy or fruitful (eudaimôn) is the virtuous life. Of course, some things are beyond our power, but we are able to judge whatever comes to us, to see that what is "not preferred"—for instance poverty—is not bad but is morally indifferent (just as wealth is morally indifferent). And we also have the power to adapt ourselves to whatever comes our way. A slightly later contemporary reported that Epictetus said that if one wanted to be free from wrongdoing and wanted to live a peaceful life, then one should endure *and* abstain.

The stoic doctrine of enduring was put in its most uncompromising way by the Victorian poet William Ernest Henley (1849–1903), in a poem called "Invictus" (that is, "unconquered"). The first stanza runs thus:

> Out of the night that covers me,
> Black as the Pit from pole to pole,
> I thank whatever gods may be
> For my unconquerable soul.

And here is the final stanza:

> It matters not how strait the gate,
> How charged with punishment the scroll,
> I am the captain of my fate;
> I am the master of my soul.

From *The Handbook*

1. Some things are in our control, and some are not. Our opinions are within our control, and our choices, our likes and dislikes. In a word, whatever is our own doing. Beyond our control are our bodies, our possessions, reputation, position; in a word, things not our own doings.

Now, the things that are within our control are by nature free, unhindered, unimpeded, but those beyond our control are weak, slavish, hindered, up to others. Keep in mind, then, that if you think things are free that by nature are slavish, and if you think that things that are up to others are yours, you will be hindered, you will suffer, you will complain, you will blame the gods and your fellows. But, on the other hand, if you take as yours only what in fact is yours, and if you see that what belongs to others belongs to others, nobody will compel you, nobody will restrict you; you will blame nobody, and you will do nothing against your will. No one will harm you, you will have no enemies.

5. People are not disturbed by what happens but by the view they take of what happens. For instance, death is not to be feared; if it were to be feared, Socrates would have feared it. The fear consists in our wrong idea of death, our idea that it is to be feared. When, therefore, we are disturbed or feel grief, we should not blame someone else, but our [false] opinion. An uneducated person blames others for his misfortunes; a person just starting his education blames himself; an educated person blames neither others nor himself.

6. Do not take pride in any excellence that is not your own. If a horse could be proud, it might say, "I am handsome," and such a statement might be acceptable. But when you proudly say, "I have a handsome horse," you should understand that you are taking pride in a horse's good. What has the horse's good to do with you? What is yours? Only your reaction to things. When you behave in accordance with nature, you will take pride only in some good that is your own.

7. As when on a voyage, when the ship is at anchor, if you go ashore to get fresh water, you may amuse yourself by picking up a seashell or a vegetable, but keep the ship in mind. Be attentive to the captain's call, and when you hear the call, give up the trifles, or you will be thrown back into the ship like a bound sheep. So it is in life: If instead of a seashell or a vegetable, you are given a wife or child, fine, but when the captain calls, you must abandon these things without a second thought. And if you are old, keep close to the ship lest you are missing when you are called.

9. Sickness impedes the body but not the ability to make choices, unless you choose so. Lameness impedes the leg, but not the ability to make choices, unless the mind chooses so. Remember this with regard to

everything that happens: Happenings are impediments to something else, but not to you.

15. Remember, behave in life as though you are attending a banquet. Is a dish brought to you? Put out your hand and take a moderate share. Does the dish pass you by? Do not grab for it. Has it not yet reached you? Don't yearn for it, but wait until it reaches you. Do this with regard to children, a spouse, position, wealth, and eventually you will be worthy to banquet with the gods. And if you can forgo even the things that are set before you, you are worthy not only to feast with the gods but to rule with them.

17. Remember: You are an actor in a play that you did not write. If the play is short, then it is short; if long, then it is long. If the author has assigned you the part of a poor man, act it well. Do the same if your part is that of a lame man or a ruler or an ordinary citizen. This is yours to do: Act your part well (but picking the part belongs to someone else).

21. Keep in mind death and exile and all other things that appear terrible—especially death—and you will never harbor a low thought nor too eagerly covet anything.

36. At a feast, to choose the largest portion might satisfy your body but would be detrimental to the social nature of the affair. When you dine with another, then, keep in mind not only the value to the body of the dishes set before you, but the value of your behavior to your host and fellow diners.

43. Everything has two handles, one by which it can be carried and one by which it cannot. If your brother acts unjustly, do not take up the affair by the handle of his injustice, for it cannot be carried that way. Rather, take the other handle: He is your brother, he was brought up with you. Taken this way, it can be carried.

TOPICS FOR CRITICAL THINKING AND WRITING

1. Does Epictetus exaggerate the degree to which events in our lives are under our control? Write a 250-word essay explaining your answer.

2. Epictetus advises us not to fear death. What is his argument?

3. Would you agree with Epictetus that "sickness impedes the body but not the ability to make choices" (excerpt 9)? Is he wrong because there is such a thing as mental illness?

4. Choose one from among the eleven paragraphs by Epictetus that best expresses your own view of life—or are you entirely at odds with what Epictetus believes? Explain.

"If I won the lottery, I would go on living as I always did."

Bertrand Russell

Bertrand Russell (1872–1970), British mathematician and philosopher, was born in Wales and educated at Trinity College, Cambridge, where he later taught. His pacifist opposition to World War I cost him this teaching appointment and earned him a prison sentence of six months. In 1940 an appointment to teach at the College of the City of New York was withdrawn because of his unorthodox moral views. But he was not always treated shabbily. He won numerous prizes, including a Nobel Prize for Literature in 1950. Much of his work is highly technical, but he also wrote frequently for the general public. We reprint a passage from one of his most widely read books, The Conquest of Happiness *(1930).*

The Happy Life

The happy life is to an extraordinary extent the same as the good life. Professional moralists have made too much of self-denial, and in so doing have put the emphasis in the wrong place. Conscious self-denial leaves a man self-absorbed and vividly aware of what he has sacrificed; in consequence it fails often of its immediate object and almost always of its ultimate purpose. What is needed is not self-denial, but that kind of direction of interest outward which will lead spontaneously and naturally to the same acts that a person absorbed in the pursuit of his own virtue could only perform by means of conscious self-denial. I have written in this book as a hedonist, that is to say, as one who regards happiness as the good, but the acts to be recommended from the point of view of the hedonist are on the whole the same as those to be recommended by the sane moralist. The moralist, however, is too apt, though this is not, of course, universally true, to stress the act rather than the state of mind. The effects of an act upon the agent will be widely different, according to his state of mind at the moment. If you see a child drowning and save it as the result of a direct impulse to bring help, you will emerge none the worse morally. If, on the other hand, you say to yourself, "It is the part of virtue to succor the helpless, and I wish to be a virtuous man, therefore I must save this child," you will be an even worse man afterwards than you were before. What applies in this extreme case, applies in many other instances that are less obvious.

There is another difference, somewhat more subtle, between the attitude towards life that I have been recommending and that which is recommended by the traditional moralists. The traditional moralist, for example, will say that love should be unselfish. In a certain sense he is right, that is to say, it should not be selfish beyond a point, but it should undoubtedly be of such a nature that one's own happiness is bound up in its success. If a man were to invite a lady to marry him on the ground that he ardently desired her happiness and at the same time considered that she would afford him ideal opportunities of self-abnegation, I think it may be doubted whether she would be altogether pleased. Undoubtedly we should desire the happiness of those whom we love, but not as an alternative to our own. In fact the whole antithesis between self and the rest of the world, which is implied in the doctrine of self-denial, disappears as soon as we have any genuine interest in persons or things outside ourselves. Through such interests a man comes to feel himself part of the stream of life, not a hard separate entity like a billiard ball, which can have no relation with other such entities except that of collision. All unhappiness depends upon some kind of disintegration or lack of integration; there is disintegration within the self through lack of coördination between the conscious and the unconscious mind; there is lack of integration between the self and society, where the two are not knit together by the force of objective interests and affections. The happy man is the man who does not suffer from either of these failures of unity, whose personality is neither divided against itself nor pitted against the world. Such a man feels himself a citizen of the universe, enjoying freely the spectacle that it offers and the joys that it affords, untroubled by the thought of death because he feels himself not really separate from those who will come after him. It is in such profound instinctive union with the stream of life that the greatest joy is to be found.

TOPICS FOR CRITICAL THINKING AND WRITING

1. In his first paragraph Russell says, "The happy life is to an extraordinary extent the same as the good life." First of all, how do you suppose Russell knows this? How might one confirm or refute the statement? Second, do you agree with Russell? Explain in detail.

2. In his final paragraph Russell says that it is through their interests that people come to feel they are "part of the stream of life, not a hard separate entity like a billiard ball, which can have no relation with other such entities except that of collision." Does this sentence strike you as (a) effective and (b) probably true? Explain.

3. In the final sentence of the final paragraph, Russell says that happy people feel connected to themselves (do not feel internally divided) and connected to society (do not feel pitted against the world). Describe in some detail a person who seems to you connected to the self and to society. Do you think that person is happy? Explain. Describe two people, one of whom seems to you internally divided, and one of whom seems to you separated from society. Now think about yourself. Do you feel connected to yourself and to the world? If so, are you happy?

The Dalai Lama and Howard C. Cutler

The fourteenth Dalai ("ocean-wide") Lama ("superior person"), Tenzin Gyatso, is the spiritual leader of the Tibetan people but has lived in exile in Dharamsala, India, since 1959, when China invaded Tibet. In 1989 he was awarded the Nobel Peace Prize. In 1982 Howard C. Cutler, a psychiatrist who practices in Phoenix, Arizona, met the Dalai Lama while visiting India to study Tibetan medicine. Cutler and the Dalai Lama had frequent conversations, which Cutler later summarized and submitted to the Dalai Lama for approval. The material was then published in a book they entitled The Art of Happiness *(1998). We give one selection.*

Inner Contentment

Crossing the hotel parking lot on my way to meet with the Dalai Lama one afternoon, I stopped to admire a brand-new Toyota Land Cruiser, the type of car I had been wanting for a long time. Still thinking of that car as I began my session, I asked, "Sometimes it seems that our whole culture, Western culture, is based on material acquisition; we're surrounded, bombarded, with ads for the latest things to buy, the latest car and so on. It's difficult not to be influenced by that. There are so many things we want, things we desire. It never seems to stop. Can you speak a bit about desire?"

"I think there are two kinds of desire," the Dalai Lama replied. "Certain desires are positive. A desire for happiness. It's absolutely right. The desire for peace. The desire for a more harmonious world, a friendlier world. Certain desires are very useful.

"But at some point, desires can become unreasonable. That usually leads to trouble. Now, for example, sometimes I visit supermarkets. I really love to see supermarkets, because I can see so many beautiful things. So, when I look at all these different articles, I develop a feeling of desire, and my initial impulse might be, 'Oh, I want this; I want that.' Then, the second thought that arises, I ask myself, 'Oh, do I really need this?' The answer is usually no. If you follow after that first desire, that initial impulse, then very soon your pockets will empty. However, the other level of desire, based on one's essential needs of food, clothing, and shelter, is something more reasonable.

"Sometimes, whether a desire is excessive or negative depends on the circumstances or society in which you live. For example, if you live in a prosperous society where a car is required to help you manage in your daily life, then of course there's nothing wrong in desiring a car. But if you live in a poor village in India where you can manage quite well without a car but you still desire one, even if you have the money to buy it, it can ultimately bring trouble. It can create an uncomfortable feeling among your neighbors and so on. Or, if you're living in a more prosperous society and have a car but keep wanting more expensive cars, that leads to the same kind of problems."

"But," I argued, "I can't see how wanting or buying a more expen-   5 sive car leads to problems for an individual, as long as he or she can afford it. Having a more expensive car than your neighbors might be a problem for them—they might be jealous and so on—but having a new car would give you, yourself, a feeling of satisfaction and enjoyment."

The Dalai Lama shook his head and replied firmly, "No. . . . Self-satisfaction alone cannot determine if a desire or action is positive or negative. A murderer may have a feeling of satisfaction at the time he is committing the murder, but that doesn't justify the act. All the nonvirtuous actions—lying, stealing, sexual misconduct, and so on—are committed by people who may be feeling a sense of satisfaction at the time. The demarcation between a positive and a negative desire or action is not whether it gives you an immediate feeling of satisfaction but whether it ultimately results in positive or negative consequences. For example, in the case of wanting more expensive possessions, if that is based on a mental attitude that just wants more and more, then eventually you'll reach a limit of what you can get; you'll come up against reality. And when you reach that limit, then you'll lose all hope, sink down into depression, and so on. That's one danger inherent in that type of desire.

"So I think that this kind of excessive desire leads to greed—an exaggerated form of desire, based on overexpectation. And when you reflect upon the excesses of greed, you'll find that it leads an individual to a feeling of frustration, disappointment, a lot of confusion, and a lot of problems. When it comes to dealing with greed, one thing that is quite characteristic is that although it arrives by the desire to obtain something, it is not satisfied by obtaining. Therefore, it becomes sort of limitless, sort of bottomless, and that leads to trouble. One interesting thing about greed is that although the underlying motive is to seek satisfaction, the irony is that even after obtaining the object of your desire, you are still not satisfied. *The true antidote of greed is contentment.* If you have a strong sense of contentment, it doesn't matter whether you obtain the object or not; either way, you are still content."

So, how can we achieve inner contentment? There are two methods. One method is to obtain everything that we want and desire—all the money, houses, and cars; the perfect mate; and the perfect body. The Dalai Lama has already pointed out the disadvantage of this approach; if our wants and desires remain unchecked, sooner or later we will run up against something that we want but can't have. The second, and more reliable, method is not to have what we want but rather to want and appreciate what we have.

The other night, I was watching a television interview with Christopher Reeve, the actor who was thrown from a horse in 1994 and suffered a spinal cord injury that left him completely paralyzed from the neck down, requiring a mechanical ventilator even to breathe. When questioned by the interviewer about how he dealt with the depression resulting from his disability, Reeve revealed that he had experienced a brief period of complete despair while in the intensive care unit of the hospital. He went on to say, however, that these feelings of despair passed relatively quickly, and he now sincerely considered himself to be a "lucky guy." He cited the blessings of a loving wife and children but also spoke gratefully about the rapid advances of modern medicine (which he estimates will find a cure for spinal cord injury within the next decade), stating that if he had been hurt just a few years earlier, he probably would have died from his injuries. While describing the process of adjusting to his paralysis, Reeve said that while his feelings of despair resolved rather quickly, at first he was still troubled by intermittent pangs of jealousy that could be triggered by another's innocent passing remark such as, "I'm just gonna run upstairs and get something." In learning to deal with these feelings, he said, "I realized that the only way to go through life is to look at your assets, to see what you can still do; in my case, fortunately I didn't have any brain injury, so I still have a mind I can use." Focusing on his resources in this manner, Reeve has elected to use his mind to increase awareness and educate the public about spinal cord injury, to help others, and has plans to continue speaking as well as to write and direct films.[1]

TOPICS FOR CRITICAL THINKING AND WRITING

1. In the first paragraph, Cutler says that he had long wanted a Toyota Land Cruiser. Exactly why might a person want such a vehicle? Do you

[1]Christopher Reeve died or October 10, 2004. [Editors' note.]

want a Toyota Land Cruiser? Why, or why not? (By the way, a friend of ours—a professor of philosophy—says, "The key to happiness is the key to the ignition." In your opinion, how much truth is there in this philosophic view?)

2. At the end of paragraph 8, Cutler reports that the Dalai Lama suggests that the best way to achieve inner contentment "is not to have what we want but rather to want and appreciate what we have." In the next (final) paragraph, Cutler cites the example of Christopher Reeve. Drawing on your own experiences—which include your experience of persons whom you know or have heard about—can you offer confirming evidence? Explain.

3. Compare the Dalai Lama's views with those of Epictetus (p. 786). Would you say they are virtually the same? Explain.

C. S. Lewis

Clive Staples Lewis (1898–1963) taught medieval and Renaissance literature at Oxford, his alma mater, and later at Cambridge. He wrote about literature; he wrote fiction and poetry. Lewis became an atheist at age thirteen. He held that view until he was about thirty-one years old. He wrote numerous essays and books on Christianity from the point of view of a believer.

We Have No "Right to Happiness"

"After all," said Clare, "they had a right to happiness."

We were discussing something that once happened in our own neighborhood. Mr. A. had deserted Mrs. A. and got his divorce in order to marry Mrs. B., who had likewise got her divorce in order to marry Mr. A. And there was certainly no doubt that Mr. A. and Mrs. B. were very much in love with one another. If they continued to be in love, and if nothing went wrong with their health or their income, they might reasonably expect to be very happy.

It was equally clear that they were not happy with their old partners. Mrs. B. had adored her husband at the outset. But then he got smashed up in the war. It was thought he had lost his virility, and it was known that he had lost his job. Life with him was no longer what Mrs. B. had bargained for. Poor Mrs. A., too. She had lost her looks—and all her liveliness. It might be true, as some said, that she consumed herself by bearing his children and nursing him through the long illness that overshadowed their earlier married life.

You mustn't, by the way, imagine that A. was the sort of man who nonchalantly threw a wife away like the peel of an orange he'd sucked dry. Her suicide was a terrible shock to him. We all knew this, for he told us so himself. "But what could I do?" he said. "A man has a right to happiness. I had to take my one chance when it came."

I went away thinking about the concept of a "right to happiness."   5

At first this sounds to me as odd as a right to good luck. For I believe—whatever one school of moralists may say—that we depend for a very great deal of our happiness or misery on circumstances outside all human control. A right to happiness doesn't, for me, make much more sense than a right to be six feet tall, or to have a millionaire for your father, or to get good weather whenever you want to have a picnic.

I can understand a right as a freedom guaranteed me by the laws of the society I live in. Thus, I have a right to travel along the public roads because society gives me that freedom; that's what we mean by calling the roads "public." I can also understand a right as a claim guaranteed me by the laws, and correlative to an obligation on someone else's part. If I have a right to receive £100 from you, this is another way of saying that you have a duty to pay me £100. If the laws allow Mr. A. to desert his wife and seduce his neighbor's wife, then, by definition, Mr. A. has a legal right to do so, and we need bring in no talk about "happiness."

But of course that was not what Clare meant. She meant that he had not only a legal but a moral right to act as he did. In other words, Clare is—or would be if she thought it out—a classical moralist after the style of Thomas Aquinas, Grotius, Hooker, and Locke. She believes that behind the laws of the state there is a Natural Law.

I agree with her. I hold this conception to be basic to all civilization. Without it, the actual laws of the state become an absolute, as in Hegel. They cannot be criticized because there is no norm against which they should be judged.

The ancestry of Clare's maxim, "They have a right to happiness," is 10 august. In words that are cherished by all civilized men, but especially by Americans, it has been laid down that one of the rights of man is a right to "the pursuit of happiness." And now we get to the real point.

What did the writers of that august declaration mean?

It is quite certain what they did not mean. They did not mean that man was entitled to pursue happiness by any and every means—including, say, murder, rape, robbery, treason, and fraud. No society could be built on such a basis.

They meant "to pursue happiness by all lawful means"; that is, by all means which the Law of Nature eternally sanctions and which the laws of the nation shall sanction.

Admittedly this seems at first to reduce their maxim to the tautology that men (in pursuit of happiness) have a right to do whatever they have a right to do. But tautologies, seen against their proper historical context, are not always barren tautologies. The declaration is primarily a denial of the political principles which long governed Europe: a challenge flung down to the Austrian and Russian empires, to England before the Reform Bills, to Bourbon France. It demands that whatever means of pursuing happiness are lawful for any should be lawful for all; that "man," not men of some particular caste, class, status, or religion, should be free to use them. In a century when this is being unsaid by nation after nation and party after party, let us not call it a barren tautology.

But the question as to what means are "lawful" — what methods of pursuing happiness are either morally permissible by the Law of Nature or should be declared legally permissible by the legislature of a particular nation — remains exactly where it did. And on that question I disagree with Clare. I don't think it is obvious that people have the unlimited "right to happiness" which she suggests. 15

For one thing, I believe that Clare, when she says "happiness," means simply and solely "sexual happiness." Partly because women like Clare never use the word "happiness" in any other sense. But also because I never heard Clare talk about the "right" to any other kind. She was rather leftist in her politics, and would have been scandalized if anyone had defended the actions of a ruthless man-eating tycoon on the ground that his happiness consisted in making money and he was pursuing his happiness. She was also a rabid teetotaler; I never heard her excuse an alcoholic because he was happy when he was drunk.

A good many of Clare's friends, and especially her female friends, often felt — I've heard them say so — that their own happiness would be perceptibly increased by boxing her ears. I very much doubt if this would have brought her theory of a right to happiness into play.

Clare, in fact, is doing what the whole western world seems to me to have been doing for the last forty-odd years. When I was a youngster, all the progressive people were saying, "Why all this prudery? Let us treat sex just as we treat all our other impulses." I was simple-minded enough to believe they meant what they said. I have since discovered that they meant exactly the opposite. They meant that sex was to be treated as no other impulse in our nature has ever been treated by civilized people. All the others, we admit, have to be bridled. Absolute obedience to your instinct for self-preservation is what we call cowardice; to your acquisitive impulse, avarice. Even sleep must be resisted if you're a sentry. But every unkindness and breach of faith seems to be condoned provided that the object aimed at is "four bare legs in a bed."

It is like having a morality in which stealing fruit is considered wrong — unless you steal nectarines.

And if you protest against this view you are usually met with chatter about the legitimacy and beauty and sanctity of "sex" and accused of harboring some Puritan prejudice against it as something disreputable or shameful. I deny the charge. Foam-born Venus . . . golden Aphrodite . . . Our Lady of Cyprus . . . I never breathed a word against you. If I object to boys who steal my nectarines, must I be supposed to disapprove of nectarines in general? Or even of boys in general? It might, you know, be stealing that I disapproved of. 20

The real situation is skillfully concealed by saying that the question of Mr. A.'s "right" to desert his wife is one of "sexual morality." Robbing an orchard is not an offense against some special morality called "fruit morality." It is an offense against honesty. Mr. A.'s action is an offense against good faith (to solemn promises), against gratitude (toward one to whom he was deeply indebted) and against common humanity.

Our sexual impulses are thus being put in a position of preposterous privilege. The sexual motive is taken to condone all sorts of behavior which, if it had any other end in view, would be condemned as merciless, treacherous, and unjust.

Now though I see no good reason for giving sex this privilege, I think I see a strong cause. It is this.

It is part of the nature of a strong erotic passion—as distinct from a transient fit of appetite—that it makes more towering promises than any other emotion. No doubt all our desires make promises, but not so impressively. To be in love involves the almost irresistible conviction that one will go on being in love until one dies, and that possession of the beloved will confer, not merely frequent ecstasies, but settled, fruitful, deep-rooted, lifelong happiness. Hence *all* seems to be at stake. If we miss this chance we shall have lived in vain. At the very thought of such a doom we sink into fathomless depths of self-pity.

Unfortunately these promises are found often to be quite untrue. 25 Every experienced adult knows this to be so as regards all erotic passions (except the one he himself is feeling at the moment). We discount the world-without-end pretensions of our friends' amours easily enough. We know that such things sometimes last—and sometimes don't. And when they do last, this is not because they promised at the outset to do so. When two people achieve lasting happiness, this is not solely because they are great lovers but because they are also—I must put it crudely—good people; controlled, loyal, fairminded, mutually adaptable people.

If we establish a "right to (sexual) happiness" which supersedes all the ordinary rules of behavior, we do so not because of what our passion shows itself to be in experience but because of what it professes to be while we are in the grip of it. Hence, while the bad behavior is real and works miseries and degradations, the happiness which was the object of the behavior turns out again and again to be illusory. Everyone (except Mr. A. and Mrs. B.) knows that Mr. A. in a year or so may have the same reason for deserting his new wife as for deserting his old. He will feel again that all is at stake. He will see himself again as the great lover, and his pity for himself will exclude all pity for the woman.

Two further points remain.

One is this. A society in which conjugal infidelity is tolerated must always be in the long run a society adverse to women. Women, whatever a few male songs and satires may say to the contrary, are more naturally monogamous than men; it is a biological necessity. Where promiscuity prevails, they will therefore always be more often the victims than the culprits. Also, domestic happiness is more necessary to them than to us. And the quality by which they most easily hold a man, their beauty, decreases every year after they have come to maturity, but this does not happen to those qualities of personality—women don't really care twopence about our *looks*—by which we hold women. Thus in the ruthless war of promiscuity women are at a double disadvantage. They play for higher stakes and are also more likely to lose. I have no sympathy with moralists who frown at the increasing crudity of female provocativeness. These signs of desperate competition fill me with pity.

Secondly, though the "right to happiness" is chiefly claimed for the sexual impulse, it seems to me impossible that the matter should stay there. The fatal principle, once allowed in that department, must sooner or later seep through our whole lives. We thus advance toward a state of society in which not only each man but every impulse in each man claims *carte blanche*. And then, though our technological skill may help us survive a little longer, our civilization will have died at heart, and will—one dare not even add "unfortunately"—be swept away.

TOPICS FOR CRITICAL THINKING AND WRITING

1. Having read the entire essay, look back at Lewis's first five paragraphs and point out the ways in which he is not merely recounting an episode but is already conveying his attitude and seeking to persuade his readers.

2. Do you want to argue: If I have a right to happiness, you or someone has a duty to see to it that I'm happy (see para. 7)? Or do you want to argue: No one has a right to happiness because no one has a duty to make anyone happy? Argue one of these positions in 250 words.

3. What's the difference between being happy in a marriage and being content in a marriage? Explain the difference in an essay of 250 words.

4. What is absurd about the idea (para. 6) of having "a right to be six feet tall"? Explain in 100 words or fewer.

5. What, if anything, do the absurd candidates for rights (para. 6) have in common?

6. What's the difference between having a legal right to something and having a moral right to that thing (see paras. 8–9)? Give an example of each.

7. Do you agree with Lewis (paras. 26, 29) that "a right to happiness" really means "a right to sexual happiness"? Why, or why not?

8. Do you agree with Lewis (para. 28) that monogamy is "a biological necessity" for women? Explain, in an essay of 250 words.

Danielle Crittenden

Danielle Crittenden (b. 1963), the founder of The Woman's Quarterly, *has written for numerous publications, including the* New York Times *and the* Wall Street Journal. *We reprint a selection from her book,* What Our Mothers

Didn't Tell Us: Why Happiness Eludes the Modern Woman *(1999). Not all readers agree with her contention that women can be happy only if they will put aside what she sees as misleading feminist ideas.*

About Love

From a feminist view, it would be nice, I suppose—or at the very least handy—if we were able to derive total satisfaction from our solitude, to be entirely self-contained organisms, like earthworms or amoebas, having relations with the opposite sex whenever we felt a need for it but otherwise being entirely contented with our own company. Every woman's apartment could be her Walden Pond. She'd be free of the romantic fuss and interaction that has defined, and given meaning to, human existence since its creation. She could spend her evenings happily ensconced with a book or a rented video, not having to deal with some bozo's desire to watch football or play mindless video games. How children would fit into this vision of autonomy, I'm not sure, but surely they would infringe upon it; perhaps she could simply farm them out. If this seems a rather chilling outcome to the quest for independence, well, it is. If no man is an island, then no woman can be, either. And it's why most human beings fall in love, and continue to take on all the commitments and responsibilities of family life. We *want* the warm body next to us on the sofa in the evenings; we *want* the noise and embrace of family around us; we *want*, at the end of our lives, to look back and see that what we have done amounts to more than a pile of pay stubs, that we have loved and been loved, and brought into this world life that will outlast us.

The quest for autonomy—the need "to be oneself" or, as Wurtzel declares, the intention "to answer only to myself"—is in fact not a brave or noble one; nor is it an indication of strong character. Too often, autonomy is merely the excuse of someone who is so fearful, so weak, that he or she can't bear to take on any of the responsibilities that used to be shouldered by much younger but more robust and mature souls. I'm struck by the number of my single contemporaries—men and women in their early to mid-thirties—who speak of themselves as if they were still twenty years old, just embarking upon their lives and not, as they actually are, already halfway through them. In another era, a thirty-three-year-old man or woman might have already lived through a depression and a world war and had several children. Yet at the suggestion of marriage—or of buying a house or of having a baby—these modern thirtysomethings will exclaim, "But I'm so young!" their crinkled eyes widening at the thought. In the relationships they do have—even "serious" ones—they will take pains to avoid the appearance of anything that smacks of permanent commitment. The strange result is couples who are willing to share *everything* with each other—leases, furniture, cars, weekends, body fluids, holidays with their relatives—just as long as it comes with the right to cancel the relationship *at any moment*.

Unfortunately, postponing marriage and all the responsibilities that go with it does not prolong youth. It only prolongs the illusion of it, and then again only in one's own eyes. The traits that are forgivable in a twenty-year-old—the constant wondering about who you are and what you will be; the readiness to chuck one thing, or person, for another and move on—are less attractive in a thirty-two-year-old. More often what results is a middle-aged person who retains all the irritating self-absorption of an adolescent without gaining any of the redeeming qualities of maturity. Those qualities—wisdom, a sense of duty, the willingness to make sacrifices for others, an acceptance of aging and death—are qualities that spring directly from our relationships and commitments to others.

A woman will not understand what true dependency is until she is cradling her own infant in her arms; nor will she likely achieve the self-confidence she craves until she has withstood, and transcended, the weight of responsibility a family places upon her—a weight that makes all the paperwork and assignments of her in-basket seem feather-light. The same goes for men. We strengthen a muscle by using it, and that is true of the heart and mind, too. By waiting and waiting and waiting to commit to someone, our capacity for love shrinks and withers. This doesn't mean that women or men should marry the first reasonable person to come along, or someone with whom they are not in love. But we should, at a much earlier age than we do now, take a serious attitude toward dating and begin preparing ourselves to settle down. For it's in the act of taking up the roles we've been taught to avoid or postpone—wife, husband, mother, father—that we build our identities, expand our lives, and achieve the fullness of character we desire.

Still, critics may argue that the old way was no better; that the risk of loss women assume by delaying marriage and motherhood overbalances the certain loss we'd suffer by marrying too early. The habit of viewing marriage as a raw deal for women is now so entrenched, even among women who don't call themselves feminists, that I've seen brides who otherwise appear completely happy apologize to their wedding guests for their surrender to convention, as if a part of them still feels there is something embarrassing and weak about an intelligent and ambitious woman consenting to marry. But is this true? Or is it just an alibi we've been handed by the previous generation of women in order to justify the sad, lonely outcomes of so many lives?

What we rarely hear—or perhaps are too fearful to admit—is how *liberating* marriage can actually be. As nerve-racking as making the decision can be, it is also an enormous relief once it is made. The moment we say, "I do," we have answered one of the great, crucial questions of our lives: We now know with whom we'll be spending the rest of our years, who will be the father of our children, who will be our family. That our marriages may not work, that we will have to accommodate ourselves to the habits and personality of someone else—these are, and always have been, the risks of commitment, of love itself. What is important is that our lives have been thrust forward. The negative—that we are no longer able to live entirely for ourselves—is also the positive: *We no longer have to live entirely for ourselves!* We may go on to do any number of interesting things, but we are free of the gnawing wonder of *with whom* we will do them. We have ceased to look down the tunnel, waiting for a train.

The pull between the desire to love and be loved and the desire to be free is an old, fierce one. If the error our grandmothers made was to have surrendered too much of themselves for others, this was perhaps better than not being prepared to surrender anything at all. The fear of losing oneself can, in the end, simply become an excuse for not giving any of oneself away. Generations of women may have had no choice but to commit themselves to marriage early and then to feel imprisoned by their lifelong domesticity. So many of our generation have decided to put it off until it is too late, not foreseeing that lifelong independence can be its own kind of prison, too.

Topics for Critical Thinking and Writing

1. In her second paragraph Crittenden quotes a writer who speaks of "the need 'to be oneself.'" What does "to be oneself" mean? Perhaps begin at the beginning: What is "oneself"? In *Hamlet,* Polonius says to his son,

   > This above all, to thine own self be true,
   > And it must follow, as the night the day,
   > Thou canst not then be false to any man.

   What is the "self" to which one should be true? Notice that in the fourth paragraph Crittenden says that "it's in the act of taking up [certain] roles . . . that we build our identities, expand our lives, and achieve the fullness of character we desire." Does this make sense to you? Explain.

2. In her third paragraph Crittenden talks about "postponing marriage and all the responsibilities that go with it." What responsibilities go with marriage? Might these responsibilities *add* to one's happiness? Explain.

3. In paragraph 6, Crittenden says, "What we rarely hear . . . is how *liberating* marriage can actually be." Consider the married people whom you know best. Does Crittenden's statement apply to some? To most? Does your experience—your familiarity with some married people—tend to offer evidence that confirms or refutes her assertion? Explain.

Judy Brady

Born in San Francisco in 1937, Judy Brady married in 1960 and two years later earned a bachelor's degree in painting at the University of Iowa. Active in the women's movement and in other political causes, she has worked as an author, an editor, and a secretary. The essay reprinted here, written before she and her husband separated, appeared originally in the first issue of Ms. *magazine in 1971.*

I Want a Wife

I belong to that classification of people known as wives. I am A Wife. And, not altogether incidentally, I am a mother.

Not too long ago a male friend of mine appeared on the scene fresh from a recent divorce. He had one child, who is, of course, with his ex-wife. He is looking for another wife. As I thought about him while I was ironing one evening, it suddenly occurred to me that I, too, would like to have a wife. Why do I want a wife?

I would like to go back to school so that I can become economically independent, support myself, and, if need be, support those dependent upon me. I want a wife who will work and send me to school. And while I am going to school I want a wife to take care of my children. I want a wife to keep track of the children's doctor and dentist appointments. And to keep track of mine, too. I want a wife to make sure my children eat properly and are kept clean. I want a wife who will wash the children's clothes and keep them mended. I want a wife who is a good nurturant attendant to my children, who arranges for their schooling, makes sure that they have an adequate social life with their peers, takes them to the park, the zoo, etc. I want a wife who takes care of the children when they are sick, a wife who arranges to be around when the children need special care, because, of course, I cannot miss classes at school. My wife must arrange to lose time at work and not lose the job. It may mean a small cut in my wife's income from time to time, but I guess I can tolerate that. Needless to say, my wife will arrange and pay for the care of the children while my wife is working.

I want a wife who will take care of *my* physical needs. I want a wife who will keep my house clean. A wife who will pick up after my children, a wife who will pick up after me. I want a wife who will keep my clothes clean, ironed, mended, replaced when need be, and who will see to it that my personal things are kept in their proper place so that I can find what I need the minute I need it. I want a wife who cooks the meals, a wife who is a *good* cook. I want a wife who will plan the menus, do the necessary grocery shopping, prepare the meals, serve them pleasantly, and then do the cleaning up while I do my studying. I want a wife who will care for me when I am sick and sympathize with my pain and loss of time from school. I want a wife to go along when our family takes a vacation so that someone can continue to care for me and my children when I need a rest and change of scene.

I want a wife who will not bother me with rambling complaints 5 about a wife's duties. But I want a wife who will listen to me when I feel the need to explain a rather difficult point I have come across in my course of studies. And I want a wife who will type my papers for me when I have written them.

I want a wife who will take care of the details of my social life. When my wife and I are invited out by my friends, I want a wife who will take care of the babysitting arrangements. When I meet people at school that I like and want to entertain, I want a wife who will have the house clean, will prepare a special meal, serve it to me and my friends, and not interrupt when I talk about things that interest me and my friends. I want a wife who will have arranged that the children are fed and ready for bed before my guests arrive so that the children do not bother us. I want a wife who takes care of the needs of my guests so that they feel comfortable, who makes sure that they have an ashtray, that they are passed the hors d'oeuvres, that they are offered a second helping of the food, that their wine glasses are replenished when necessary, that their coffee is served to them as they like it. And I want a wife who knows that sometimes I need a night out by myself.

I want a wife who is sensitive to my sexual needs, a wife who makes love passionately and eagerly when I feel like it, a wife who makes sure that I am satisfied. And, of course, I want a wife who will not demand sexual attention when I am not in the mood for it. I want a wife who assumes the complete responsibility for birth control, because I do not want more children. I want a wife who will remain sexually faithful to me so that I do not have to clutter up my intellectual life with jealousies. And I want a wife who understands that *my* sexual needs may entail more than strict adherence to monogamy. I must, after all, be able to relate to people as fully as possible.

If, by chance, I find another person more suitable as a wife than the wife I already have, I want the liberty to replace my present wife with another one. Naturally, I will expect a fresh, new life; my wife will take the children and be solely responsible for them so that I am left free.

When I am through with school and have a job, I want my wife to quit working and remain at home so that my wife can more fully and completely take care of a wife's duties.

My God, who *wouldn't* want a wife?   10

Topics for Critical Thinking and Writing

1. If one were to summarize Brady's first paragraph, one might say it adds up to "I am a wife and a mother." But analyze it closely. Exactly what does the second sentence add to the first? And what does "not altogether incidentally" add to the third sentence?

2. Brady uses the word *wife* in sentences where one ordinarily would use *she* or *her*. Why? And why does she begin paragraphs 4, 5, 6, and 7 with the same words, "I want a wife"?

3. In her second paragraph Brady says that the child of her divorced male friend "is, of course, with his ex-wife." In the context of the entire essay, what does this sentence mean?

4. Complete the following sentence by offering a definition: "According to Judy Brady, a wife is . . ."

5. Try to state the essential argument of Brady's essay in a simple syllogism. (*Hint:* Start by identifying the thesis or conclusion you think she
is trying to establish, and then try to formulate two premises, based on
what she has written, that would establish the conclusion.)

6. Drawing on your experience as observer of the world around you (and
perhaps as husband, wife, or former spouse), do you think Brady's picture of a wife's role is grossly exaggerated? Or is it (allowing for some
serious playfulness) fairly accurate, even though it was written in 1971?
If grossly exaggerated, is the essay therefore meaningless? If fairly accurate, what attitudes and practices does it encourage you to support?
Explain.

7. Whether or not you agree with Brady's vision of marriage in our society, write an essay (500 words) titled "I Want a Husband," imitating
her style and approach. Write the best possible essay, and then decide
which of the two essays—yours or hers—makes a fairer comment on
current society. Or if you believe Brady is utterly misleading, write an
essay titled "I Want a Wife," seeing the matter in a different light.

8. If you feel that you have been pressed into an unappreciated, unreasonable role—built-in babysitter, listening post, or girl (or boy or man or
woman) Friday—write an essay of 500 words that will help the reader
to see both your plight and the injustice of the system. (*Hint:* A little
humor will help to keep your essay from seeming to be a prolonged
whine.)

Text Credits

e-Pages Credits

Art Credits

Index of Authors and Titles

Index of Terms

Missing something? To access the Bedford Integrated Media that accompanies this text, visit **bedfordstmartins.com/barnetbedau**. Students who do not buy a new book can purchase access to Integrated Media at this site.

Inside the e-Pages for *Current Issues and Enduring Questions*

Additional Readings

Oxfam, The Truth about Women and Chocolate [advertisement]

Aurora Meneghello and Serge Bakalian, Trailer for *Default: The Student Loan Movie* [film trailer]

Josh Harkinson / *Mother Jones*, How Industrial Pot Growers Ravage the Land: A Google Earth Tour [news article and video]

United States Agency for International Development, "How to Feed the Future" and "Mobile Phones Tackling Poverty" [infographics]

Barack Obama, President Obama on the Death of Osama bin Laden [speech]

Casey Neistat, Calorie Detective [investigative report]

The White House, 1 Is 2 Many [public service announcement]

Additional Views on Argument

A Moralist's View: Ways of Thinking Ethically

A Lawyer's View: Steps toward Civic Literacy